THE OXFORD HANDBOOK OF
THE WEIMAR REPUBLIC

THE OXFORD HANDBOOK OF

THE WEIMAR REPUBLIC

Edited by
NADINE ROSSOL
and
BENJAMIN ZIEMANN

Great Clarendon Street, Oxford, OX2 6DP,
United Kingdom

Oxford University Press is a department of the University of Oxford.
It furthers the University's objective of excellence in research, scholarship,
and education by publishing worldwide. Oxford is a registered trade mark of
Oxford University Press in the UK and in certain other countries

© Oxford University Press 2022

The moral rights of the authors have been asserted

First Edition Published in 2022

Impression: 1

All rights reserved. No part of this publication may be reproduced, stored in
a retrieval system, or transmitted, in any form or by any means, without the
prior permission in writing of Oxford University Press, or as expressly permitted
by law, by licence or under terms agreed with the appropriate reprographics
rights organization. Enquiries concerning reproduction outside the scope of the
above should be sent to the Rights Department, Oxford University Press, at the
address above

You must not circulate this work in any other form
and you must impose this same condition on any acquirer

Published in the United States of America by Oxford University Press
198 Madison Avenue, New York, NY 10016, United States of America

British Library Cataloguing in Publication Data

Data available

Library of Congress Control Number: 2021940232

ISBN 978-0-19-884577-5

DOI: 10.1093/oxfordhb/9780198845775.001.0001

Printed and bound by
CPI Group (UK) Ltd, Croydon, CR0 4YY

Links to third party websites are provided by Oxford in good faith and
for information only. Oxford disclaims any responsibility for the materials
contained in any third party website referenced in this work.

Acknowledgements

The *Oxford Handbook of the Weimar Republic* has been three years in the making, and we would like to express our gratitude to the many colleagues who have supported us. Our thanks go to Christina Wipf-Perry, who commissioned the project, and to Stephanie Ireland and Cathryn Steele, who offered support and crucial advice right until the end. Katie Bishop helped us with the technical complexities of editing work, Jane Robson provided superb copy-editing, and Preethi Krishnan steered our book through production.

We are grateful to the contributors, leading experts on Weimar Germany, who have taken time from their other work to offer a concise, interpretive analysis of their respective topic. The chapters in this volume are neither historiographical overviews nor simple textbook glosses. They rather represent an attempt to combine the presentation of structured information with an invitation to reflect on key arguments, continuities, and the complexities of politics, culture, and society in Weimar Germany.

We would also like to thank Christine Brocks, who did the bulk of the translations and compiled the index, and those colleagues who were able to support the translation of their own chapter, or indeed the inclusion of one iconic image. The Department of History at the University of Sheffield and the Department of History at the University of Essex funded the translation of chapters, crucial help that is greatly appreciated. Special thanks go to Moritz Föllmer, who was not only the first to deliver his chapter, but also provided advice, insight, and moral support along the way. We are also grateful to Anthony McElligott, who offered invaluable criticism on our introduction. With great sadness we have to record that Sharon Gillerman, a distinguished scholar of the history of modern German Jewry, passed away shortly after she had submitted her draft chapter. Our thanks go to Paul Lerner and Mark Quigley who helped to finalize her important contribution.

Finally, we would like to thank the German History Society, and here especially Jim Bjork, as well as Takuya Onodera, Akiyoshi Nishiyama, and Jörn Leonhard, who provided at various stages an opportunity to discuss our thinking about the Weimar Republic with equally critical and constructive audiences.

Nadine Rossol and Benjamin Ziemann
March 2021

Contents

List of Maps, Tables, and Illustrations — xi
List of Abbreviations — xiii
List of Contributors — xvii

1. Introduction — 1
   NADINE ROSSOL AND BENJAMIN ZIEMANN

PART I: KEY EVENTS AND POLITICAL DEVELOPMENTS

2. The German Revolution of 1918/19 — 27
   CHRISTOPHER DILLON

3. The Period of Inflation, 1919–1923 — 48
   MARTIN H. GEYER

4. Coalition-Building and Political Fragmentation, 1924–1930 — 72
   MATTHEW STIBBE

5. From Democracy to Dictatorship: The Fall of Weimar and the Nazi Rise to Power, 1930–1933 — 95
   LARRY EUGENE JONES

PART II: POLITY, POLITICS, AND POLICIES

6. The Weimar Constitution — 119
   PETER C. CALDWELL

7. Nationalism and Nationhood — 141
   ERIN R. HOCHMAN

8. Elections, Election Campaigns, and Democracy — 164
   THOMAS MERGEL

9. Federalism, Regionalism, and the Construction of Spaces   193
SIEGFRIED WEICHLEIN

10. The Reichswehr and Armament Policies   218
BENJAMIN ZIEMANN

11. Foreign Policy: The Dilemmas of a Revisionist State   242
JONATHAN WRIGHT

12. Republican Groups, Ideas, and Identities   265
NADINE ROSSOL

13. Social Policy in the Weimar Republic   291
KARL CHRISTIAN FÜHRER

PART III: PARTIES AND THEIR CONSTITUENCIES

14. Liberalism   317
PHILIPP MÜLLER

15. Social Democrats and Communists in Weimar Germany: A Divided Working-Class Movement   340
JOACHIM C. HÄBERLEN

16. The Centre Party, Conservatives, and the Radical Right   363
SHELLEY BARANOWSKI

17. National Socialism   382
DANIEL SIEMENS

18. Antisemitism in the Weimar Republic   404
SUSANNE WEIN AND MARTIN ULMER

PART IV: ECONOMY AND SOCIETY

19. The Overstretched Economy: Industry and Financial Services   429
JAN-OTMAR HESSE AND CHRISTIAN MARX

20. The Middle Classes   454
MORITZ FÖLLMER

21. The Industrial Working Class   475
    PAMELA E. SWETT

22. Agriculture and Rural Society   498
    BENJAMIN ZIEMANN

23. Weimar Bodies: Gender, Sexuality, and Reproduction   521
    UTE PLANERT

24. Transnational Visions of Modernity: America and the Soviet Union   541
    MARY NOLAN

25. German Jews in the Weimar Republic   563
    SHARON GILLERMAN (†)

26. Youth and Youth Movements: Relations, Challenges, Developments   587
    BARBARA STAMBOLIS

PART V: CULTURE

27. Mass Culture   609
    JOCHEN HUNG

28. German Literature 1918–1933   629
    HELMUTH KIESEL

29. Architecture, Town Planning, and Large-Scale Housing
    Estates: Challenges, Visions, and Proposed Solutions   654
    BEATE STÖRTKUHL

30. Religious Cultures and Confessional Politics   680
    TODD H. WEIR AND UDI GREENBERG

31. The Humanities and Social Sciences   702
    LUTZ RAPHAEL

32. Visual Weimar: The Iconography of Social and Political Identities   724
    KERRY WALLACH

33. The Presence of the First World War in Weimar Culture   750
    CLAUDIA SIEBRECHT

Index   775

List of Maps, Tables, and Illustrations

List of Maps

1 The States (*Länder*) in Weimar Germany (1928)	140
2 Germany after the Treaty of Versailles	264

List of Tables

4.1 Coalition governments in Weimar Germany, 1924–1930	76
8.1 Results of elections to the National Assembly and the Reichstag, 1919–1933	178
8.2 The Reich Cabinet 1918–1932 with the most relevant cabinet posts and the governing coalition	182
19.1 World market share of German exports of manufactured goods, 1925–1935 (%)	434
19.2 Indices of export volumes, 1924–1933 (1913=100)	435
30.1 The Confessional identification of Reichstag deputies 1918–1933	685

List of Figures

12.1 Poster design by Hans Scheil, BArch, Plak 002-021-023	275
12.2 Photograph by Georg Pahl, BArch, Bild 102-08216	284
29.1 Photograph by Adolf and Carl Dransfeld. Museum für Kunst und Gewerbe, Hamburg, Inv. Nr. P1998.87	657
29.2 Muzeum Architektury we Wrocławiu, Inv. Nr. MAt-AB-31081	660
29.3 Stadtarchiv Stuttgart, Schenkung Nowak, Nachlass Arthur Ohler, Inv. Nr. 2679-FA 151/1/40	663

29.4	Photograph by Beate Störtkuhl, 2016	664
29.5	William Gaunt, 'A Modern Utopia? Berlin—The New Germany—The New Movement', *The Studio. International Art*, 38 (1929), 859	667
29.6	Photo by Beate Störtkuhl, 2004	668
29.7	Photo by Vladimír Šlapeta, Praha-Brno, 2015	669
29.8	Paul Schmitthenner, *Die Baukunst im neuen Reich* (Munich: Callwey, 1934), figures 12, 13	671
32.1	Photograph by Georg Pahl. BArch, Bild 102-11915	728
32.2	BArch, Bild 183-1990-1015-503	731
32.3	Photograph by Lotte Jacobi. © University of New Hampshire. Used with permission	732
32.4	Photograph by Herbert Hoffmann. BArch, Bild 146-1976-141-25	733
32.5	BArch, Bild 102-01911	737
32.6	BArch, Bild Y 10-KL-8-19882	739
32.7	BArch, Plak 002-042-155	742
33.1	Photograph by Georg Pahl. BArch, Bild 102-00587	757
33.2	Stadtarchiv Kassel, E7.2 no.1271	760

List of Abbreviations

ADGB	Allgemeiner Deutscher Gewerkschaftsbund (General German Trade Union Federation)
AIZ	*Arbeiter Illustrierte Zeitung* (*Worker's Illustrated Journal*)
ALV	Arbeitslosenversicherung (Unemployment Insurance)
Art.	Article
AVAG	Gesetz über Arbeitsvermittlung und Arbeitslosenversicherung (Law on Labour Exchange and Unemployment Insurance)
BdI	Bund der Industriellen (League of Industrialists)
BdL	Bund der Landwirte (League of Farmers)
BIZ	*Berliner Illustrirte Zeitung* (*Berlin Illustrated Journal*)
BNSDJ	Bund Nationalsozialistischer Deutscher Juristen
BVP	Bayerische Volkspartei (Bavarian People's Party)
BPRS	Bund Proletarisch-Revolutionärer Schriftsteller (Association of Proletarian-Revolutionary Authors)
BArch	Bundesarchiv (Federal Archives)
CDI	Centralverband Deutscher Industrieller (Central Association of German Industrialists)
CDU	Christlich Demokratische Union (Christian Democratic Union)
CIAM	Congrès Internationaux d'Architecture Moderne (International Congresses of Modern Architecture)
CNBLP	Christlich-Nationale Bauern- und Landvolk Partei (Christian National Peasants' and Farmers' Party)
CV	Centralverein deutscher Staatsbürger jüdischen Glaubens (Central Association of German Citizens of Jewish Faith)
DAP	Deutsche Arbeiter Partei (German Workers' Party)
DDP	Deutsche Demokratische Partei (German Democratic Party)
DEWOG	Deutsche Wohnungsfürsorge AG (German Housing Company for State Officials and Workers)
DFG	Deutsche Forschungsgemeinschaft (German Research Foundation)

DGSO	Deutsche Gesellschaft zum Studium Osteuropas (German Society for the Study of Eastern Europe)
DINTA	Deutsches Institut für technische Arbeitsschulung (German Institute for Technical Work Schooling)
dj 1.11	deutsche jungenschaft vom 1.11 (German Boyhood of 1.11)
DKG	Deutsche Kolonialgesellschaft (German Colonial Society)
DKP	Deutsch-Konservative Partei (German Conservative Party)
DLV	Deutscher Landarbeiter-Verband (German Association of Agricultural Workers)
DNVP	Deutschnationale Volkspartei (German National People's Party)
DStP	Deutsche Staatspartei (German State Party)
DVFP	Deutschvölkische Freiheitspartei (German-Völkisch Freedom Party)
DVP	Deutsche Volkspartei (German People's Party)
DVSTB	Deutschvölkischer Schutz- und Trutz-Bund (German-Völkisch Protection and Defiance Federation)
FRG	Federal Republic of Germany
GDP	Gross Domestic Product
GDR	German Democratic Republic
ICC	International Chamber of Commerce
IMKK	Interalliierte Militär-Kontrollkommission (Military Inter-Allied Commission of Control)
IRZ	*Illustrierte Reichsbanner Zeitung* (*Illustrated Reichsbanner Journal*)
JAD	Jüdischer Abwehrdienst (Jewish Defence Service)
Jungdo	Jungdeutscher Orden (Young German Order)
KAPD	Kommunistische Arbeiterpartei Deutschlands (German Communist Workers' Party)
KfdK	Kampfbund für deutsche Kultur (Combat League for German Culture)
KPD	Kommunistische Partei Deutschlands (German Communist Party)
KRA	Kriegsrohstoffabteilung (War Raw Materials Department)
M.A.N.	Maschinenfabrik Augsburg-Nürnberg AG
MSPD	Mehrheitssozialdemokratische Partei Deutschlands (Majority Social Democratic Party of Germany)
NCO	Non-Commissioned Officer
NSDAP	Nationalsozialistische Deutsche Arbeiterpartei (National Socialist Workers' Party)
NS-DÄB	Nationalsozialistischer Deutscher Ärztebund (National Socialist League of Physicians)

NSDStB	Nationalsozialistischer Deutscher Studentenbund (National Socialist German Students' League)
NSEP	Nationalsozialistischer Evangelischer Pfarrerbund (National Socialist Pastors' League)
NSFP	Nationalsozialistische Freiheitspartei (National Socialist Freedom Party)
NSLB	Nationalsozialistischer Lehrerbund (National Socialist Teachers' League)
OHL	Oberste Heeresleitung (Army Supreme Command)
PNF	Partito Nationale Fascista (Italian Fascist Party)
POW	Prisoner of War
RDI	Reichsverband der Deutschen Industrie (National Federation of German Industry)
RFB	Roter Frontkämpferbund (Red Front Fighters' League)
RJF	Reichsbund Jüdischer Frontsoldaten (Reich League of Jewish Front Line Soldiers)
RKW	Reichskuratorium für Wirtschaftlichkeit (Reich Productivity Board)
RLB	Reichslandbund (Reich Rural League)
RM	Reichsmark
RSHA	Reichssicherheitshauptamt (Reich Main Security Office)
RVG	Reichsversorgungsgesetz (Reich Pension Law)
SA	Sturmabteilung (Stormtroopers)
SPD	Sozialdemokratische Partei Deutschlands (German Social Democratic Party)
SS	Schutzstaffel
TENO	Technische Nothilfe (Technical Emergency Support)
Ufa	Universum Film A.G.
USPD	Unabhängige Sozialdemokratische Partei Deutschlands (Independent Social Democratic Party of Germany)
VDA	Vereinigung Deutscher Arbeitgeberverbände (Federation of German Employers' Associations)
VOKS	Soviet All-Union Society for Cultural Ties Abroad
WP	Wirtschaftspartei (Business Party)
Wumba	Waffen- und Munitions-Beschaffungsamt (Weapons and Ammunition Procurement Office)
ZAG	Zentralarbeitsgemeinschaft (Central Association of Employers and Employees)

List of Contributors

Shelley Baranowski is Professor of History Emerita at the University of Akron.

Peter C. Caldwell is Samuel G. McCann Professor of History at Rice University.

Christopher Dillon is Senior Lecturer in Modern German History at King's College London.

Moritz Föllmer is Associate Professor of History at the University of Amsterdam.

Karl Christian Führer is Privatdozent at the University of Hamburg.

Martin H. Geyer is Professor of History at Ludwig-Maximilians-University Munich.

Sharon Gillerman (†) was Associate Professor of Modern Jewish History at Hebrew Union College, Los Angeles.

Udi Greenberg is Associate Professor of History at Dartmouth College.

Joachim C. Häberlen is Associate Professor of Modern Continental European History at the University of Warwick.

Jan-Otmar Hesse is Professor of Economic History at the University of Bayreuth.

Erin R. Hochman is Associate Professor of Modern German and European History at Southern Methodist University in Dallas, TX.

Jochen Hung is Assistant Professor of Cultural History at the University of Utrecht.

Larry Eugene Jones is Professor of Modern European History Emeritus at Canisius College.

Helmuth Kiesel is Professor of German Literature Emeritus at the University of Heidelberg.

Christian Marx is Research Fellow at the Institute for Contemporary History in Munich.

Thomas Mergel is Professor of Twentieth Century European History at the Humboldt University in Berlin.

Philipp Müller is Senior Researcher at the Hamburg Institute for Social Research.

Mary Nolan is Professor of History Emerita at New York University.

Ute Planert is Professor of Modern History at the University of Cologne.

Lutz Raphael is Professor of Contemporary History at the University of Trier.

Nadine Rossol is Senior Lecturer in Modern European History at the University of Essex.

Claudia Siebrecht is Senior Lecturer in History at the University of Sussex.

Daniel Siemens is Professor of European History at Newcastle University.

Barbara Stambolis is Professor of Modern History Emerita at the University of Paderborn.

Matthew Stibbe is Professor of Modern European History at Sheffield Hallam University.

Beate Störtkuhl is Senior Researcher at the Federal Institute for Culture and History of the Germans in Eastern Europe in Oldenburg.

Pamela E. Swett is Professor of History at McMaster University.

Martin Ulmer is Teaching Fellow and Director of the Research Group on Jewish Studies at the Ludwig Uhland Institute for Empirical Cultural Studies, University of Tübingen.

Kerry Wallach is Associate Professor of German Studies at Gettysburg College.

Siegfried Weichlein is Professor of Contemporary History at the University of Fribourg.

Susanne Wein is Research Associate at the City Archive of Heilbronn and Associate Fellow at Free University Berlin.

Todd H. Weir is Associate Professor of the History of Christianity and Modern Culture at the University of Groningen.

Jonathan Wright is Emeritus Professor in International Relations and Fellow of Christ Church, University of Oxford.

Benjamin Ziemann is Professor of Modern German History at the University of Sheffield.

CHAPTER 1

INTRODUCTION

NADINE ROSSOL AND BENJAMIN ZIEMANN

The Weimar Republic conjures up any number of colourful and ultimately contradictory images. We see Weimar as a place of innovation across the arts, from the radical theatre of Bertolt Brecht, the modernist architecture of the Bauhaus, to the innovative photomontage of Hannah Höch. We see Weimar as a society in search for new practices of life, including the longing for community in the youth movement and the exploration of different gender roles. Weimar was a place of bold participatory experiments, with the introduction of universal suffrage for both women and men and a constitution that enshrined progressive welfare state policies into law. Yet the Weimar Republic also offers stark reminders about the fragility of modern society and democracy. It was home to rampant antisemitism and the incessant agitation of populists against parliamentary democracy. There was the greatest crisis of the capitalist economy in the twentieth century and the despair it entailed for millions. And then there was the Nazi party, emerging from its humble beginnings in post-war Bavaria to become the largest German party at the ballot box in 1932. After the appointment of Hitler as chancellor on 30 January 1933, Weimar's democracy was quickly dismantled and Germany ushered in the brutal dictatorship of the Third Reich.

The history of the Weimar Republic from 1918 to 1933 is thus a crucial juncture in German and European history. The aim of this *Oxford Handbook* is to provide accessible, up-to-date information on the most relevant aspects of society, culture, and politics in this period, enabling the reader to make sense of the peculiarities and the contradictions of this era. Recent events have garnered renewed interest in the history of the Weimar Republic. The centenary of its founding in 2018 prompted attempts in Germany to see the first republic of the country as a milestone in the development of a democratic culture and thus as a reference point for a positive historical tradition. At the same time, the rise of right-wing populist parties in the Federal Republic, as in many other European countries, has triggered renewed concerns over the stability of democracies. Not only in the German context, the catchphrase 'Weimar circumstances' is a cipher for the dangers produced by the erosion of trust in the parliamentary system, and for the weaknesses of democratic governance vis-à-vis those who despise it and are able to whip up popular resentment against it in times of economic upheaval.[1] We share widespread concerns about the populist tide in recent European politics and are acutely aware of the potential insights that historical comparisons can provide. Yet we also believe that the interest in using Weimar as a historical reference point for the current weaknesses of democracy has to be carefully balanced against one of the main aims of the historian, the attempt to understand the specific context of the past in its own right.[2]

Which picture of the beleaguered republic emerges when historians take the business of historicizing seriously? We will discuss this issue in more detail soon, but want to give some important pointers right away: certainly one that is less dependent on the stark, eye-catching juxtaposition between the 'glitter' of modernist culture and the 'doom' of economic crisis and rise of the Nazis, as each of these polar opposites should be seen in much more complex fashion and many other facets of Weimar Germany come to the fore.[3] To historicize Weimar Germany also means to carefully reconstruct the 'horizon of expectations' of the contemporaries of the 1920s and early 1930s. Hindsight is often a handicap for the historian, and nowhere more so than in regard to the Weimar Republic. While some contemporaries considered 1933 to be the fulfilment of their dreams, it is crucial not to reduce the multi-layered history of Weimar to the mere precursor of the Third Reich.[4] Otherwise we neglect those contemporary expectations that envisaged an entirely different 'present future', possible states of German society and politics that were anticipated in 1925 or 1930 when looking five or ten years into the future.[5] A focus on the outcome in 1933 also limits the attention we pay to the scope for collective agency of Weimar contemporaries, and their ability to shape a future whose outcome they did not know. A thorough intellectual history of Weimar's present futures has revealed a staggering degree of optimism about the future in contemporary thinking. This finding runs against the grain of the conventional argument that the carnage and devastation of the First World War had rung the death knell to the broad current of nineteenth-century optimistic liberal belief in progress.[6] Belief in the ability to change the course of the future was one of the enduring elements of Weimar's intellectual outlook, shared across the political spectrum both by the left and the radical right.

Historicizing Weimar also means considering multiple lines of continuity in German history that feed into different trajectories. Following in the footsteps of émigré historians such as Hans Rosenberg, social historians around Jürgen Kocka and Hans-Ulrich Wehler have developed the notion of a German *Sonderweg* or special path. They emphasize lines of continuity that, roughly defined, lead from the founding of the German nation-state in 1871 to the Nazi seizure of power in 1933. In this view, the preponderance of the military and of popular militarism in Imperial Germany, the lack of parliamentary checks on the power of government, and the grip of the feudal landowners in the Prussian East on the village population were crucial preconditions for 1933. Unlike other Western European nations, the *Sonderweg* argument goes, Germany failed to develop a pluralistic culture of participation that would have allowed it to stave off the fascist onslaught against democracy. In that sense, 1933 was an overdetermined outcome.[7] The notion of the *Sonderweg* has been often criticized as it limits multiple lines of continuity in German history to just one.[8] If we consider 1918/19 as a beginning, through the introduction of female suffrage and the codification of the Weimar Constitution, other lines of continuity come into view. From the vantage point of 1949, when the Federal Republic adopted the Basic Law as its constitution, and even more so from that of 1990, when a reunified Germany reaffirmed the Basic Law, 1919 appears as a foundational moment in the longue durée of German history: for the first time, a German nation-state was at the same time a democratic polity. In this perspective, Weimar is an important part of the prehistory of the current Federal Republic.[9]

In this chapter, we want to introduce our readers to some important strands of historiography that have framed thinking about the Weimar Republic from 1945 to the present. We will look at some of the seminal works by historians in the Federal Republic up till the early 1990s that had a lasting impact on the narratives that were and still are used to write the history of this era. Then we highlight differing agendas and questions that have come to the fore since the 1990s and led to a pluralization of approaches, vistas, and interpretations. Finally, we explain the structure of this volume and our selection of topics.

WEIMAR'S CRISIS: INTERPRETATIONS FROM THE 1950S TO 1990

In post-war Germany, the long shadow of the dying republic lingered over scholarly attempts to write the history of Germany from 1918 to 1933. During the early years of the Federal Republic, resentment against parties and parliamentary rule was still running deep among parts of the West German public. In this difficult political climate, political scientists such as Karl Dietrich Bracher and Kurt Sontheimer were among the first scholars to combine a critical analysis of the Weimar Republic with unequivocal normative support for parliamentary democracy. It was in 1956 that the Swiss journalist Fritz René Allemann coined the reassuring phrase 'Bonn is not Weimar', firmly establishing Weimar as a negative backdrop to the positive achievements of the Bonn Republic.[10] In this political context, from the 1960s to the early 1990s, leading historians in the Federal Republic provided the key narratives that framed most other specialist scholarship and defined the field.[11]

Up until 1990, the overarching imperative of Weimar scholarship was to explain the failure and ultimate dissolution of democratic governance. It is thus no surprise that all but one of the major synthetic monographs in this period prioritize political history and only briefly cover developments in the economy, society, and culture, or use them as a blunt explanatory tool to account for specific political developments. To be sure, approaches to political history can differ vastly, yet most of these accounts adopted a top-down approach that identified agency primarily among the political elites.

First published in 1989 as a summation of his own substantial research, Hans Mommsen's account of the 'squandered freedom' that the republic provided places the moral and political bankruptcy of the liberal bourgeois elites centre stage.[12] To be sure, Mommsen was equally scathing in his critique of the obsolescence and 'ossification' of the social democratic leadership and its affiliated Free Trade Unions, and of the resulting 'immobility' of their politics in defence of the republic.[13] Yet the full weight of Mommsen's ire was clearly reserved for the middle classes, and here in particular for the academically trained members of the educated middle class, the so-called *Bildungsbürgertum*, consisting of physicians, lawyers, Protestant pastors, secondary school teachers, and, crucially, students and their academic teachers. Mommsen identified 'status anxieties' as the key menace that riddled this group during the 1920s and undermined its confidence, if not leading to a wholesale 'dissolution' of the *Bürgertum* altogether. At any rate, the *Bildungsbürger* abandoned their liberal views and turned to an 'antiliberal' political irrationalism. The abandonment of liberal principles by those whose historical task was to defend them played decisively into the hands of the Nazis and their quest for power.[14] For someone who also wrote pioneering articles on the social history of the working class, Mommsen staked a lot on the relevance of the *Bildungsbürgertum*, a social group that comprised less than 1 per cent of the German population in the 1920s.[15]

Another major synthesis of Weimar's history was published in 1993 by Heinrich August Winkler. Like Mommsen, Winkler put politics centre stage. He saw the main problems that explained the demise of democracy in its limited scope for decision-making. Winkler's Weimar is, not unlike Mommsen's, first and foremost an industrial society. Thus, it required a 'class compromise' between organized labour and the corporate interests of the bourgeoisie to facilitate reasonable governance in a context of intense economic pressure. After a promising start, with an agreement between employers and trade unions in late 1918, the so-called Stinnes-Legien agreement, the search for a 'class compromise' wore thin and was abandoned in the late 1920s. When the representatives of heavy industry decided in November 1928 to start a month-long lockout of a quarter of a million workers, they signalled a move to confrontation rather than compromise. This meant that a downward spiral of increasingly bitter conflicts paralysed democracy.[16]

The books by Mommsen and Winkler were the summation of their decades-long research into Weimar politics. With Detlev Peukert's book on Weimar as a 'crisis of classical modernity', first published in 1987, a relative newcomer entered the scene.[17] As his book remains a key reference point for everybody who is interested in Weimar Germany, we want to consider its relevance in some detail. Peukert's account was the first to provide a multi-faceted picture of society and politics from 1918 to 1933, devoting equal attention to mass culture, generational conflicts, and technocratic elements of the welfare state as well as to traditional themes like the impact of hyperinflation and the Treaty of Versailles. Peukert conceived of Weimar as a genuinely modern society, drawing the clear conclusion that the many crises of the era did not result from pre-modern elites or uneven modernization, but from the inherent instability of modernity itself.

It is important to see that Peukert understood modernity not simply as an industrial society in which labour versus capital was the main divide, as Winkler and

Mommsen did. Following ideas that the sociologist Max Weber had developed in his work on the *Protestant Ethic and the Spirit of Capitalism* (1904/5), Peukert identified formal rationalization as the key texture of modernity. According to Weber, formal rationality—essentially, the trend towards optimizing any action that is based on means/ends calculations—was first adopted in the economy, but then became a structural principle of other societal fields and ultimately a central feature of all life orders (*Lebensordnungen*) in modernity.[18] Peukert traced its impact in Weimar society across many different fields. In the industrial economy, he focused on Taylorism: the mechanization of labour processes and the introduction of assembly line production as attempts to increase productivity. In the field of gender and sexuality, he highlighted attempts to promote sexual hygiene and the use of contraceptives. In the field of cultural production, Peukert emphasized the significance of the style of New Objectivity as it tried to create a new realism that incorporated 'objective' ways of seeing into art, informed by media such as film and photography. In the context of welfare policies, massively expanded in the 1920s, he detected traces of a 'social engineering' that not only tried to alleviate hardship, but to tackle exclusion more profoundly by educating lower class people and rationalizing their lifestyle.[19] Welfare policies also provided a crucial example for Peukert's general argument about the ambivalences and inherent contradictions of a rationalized modernity: when the vastly increasing welfare expenditure in the crisis of the late 1920s motivated policymakers to opt for retrenchment, the means/ends calculation of how to best spend the available funds led to a selection between clients who still deserved support and the 'unworthy' who did not. In Peukert's view, a fundamental ambivalence of modernity was laid bare: that progressive policies could prepare the ground for the violently exclusionary policies of the Third Reich.[20] Tracing the ambivalences and self-destructive effects of Weimar's modernity, Peukert thus made a wider point.[21] Weimar has relevance not only because the destruction of parliamentary democracy contains a warning for the present. More generally, it represents a vivid reminder of the dangerous potentials of modernity.

Peukert's short book still represents a benchmark for any complex interpretation of Germany's first republic. This does not mean that all his arguments are conclusive and that his conceptual framework cannot be adapted. It must suffice here to mention two problematic points. First, historians pointed out that a large chunk of welfare state expenditure in Weimar—across the Reich, the Länder, and local government—was not related to inherent problems of 'modernity', but rather to the remnants of total war in the guise of hundreds of thousands disabled veterans, war widows, and orphans who received payments.[22] Historians remain also sceptical whether the eugenicist and exclusionary tendencies of welfare state provision up till 1933 really 'helped to pave the way' for subsequent Nazi policies.[23] Second, Peukert had literally nothing to say about the presence of organized Christianity and practised piety in Weimar cultures. Like many other social historians during the 1980s, Peukert was not attentive to the enduring presence of religious culture and confessional conflict in Weimar Germany. Thus, he clearly overstated rationalization as the key signature of the era and downplayed the significance of life-worlds that did not conform to the imperative of formal rationality.

From Bracher to Peukert and Winkler, West German scholars provided the key synthetic works that framed debate on Weimar from the 1950s to the early 1990s. To be sure, some of the foremost experts on the social and political history of the Weimar Republic were historians in the US and UK, including, to name only three, the late Gerald D. Feldman, Larry Eugene Jones, and Cornelie Usborne. Yet their many path-breaking books and articles, informed by decades of archival research, analysed specific topics and did not provide an overall narrative of German history from 1918 to 1933.[24] This situation only changed after 2000, when several British and US historians published books that offered a synthetic view of Weimar Germany.[25] At this point, however, some established interpretive tropes had already come under scrutiny, and new agendas for research had come to the fore.

Did Weimar Fail? Different Themes and Questions beyond the Crisis Paradigm

From the 1950s to the early 1990s, successive generations of historians came up with different general interpretations of the Weimar Republic. While they identified different causes, they agreed on one point: that the foremost task of any historian of this period was to account for the failure and ultimate destruction of democracy. Historian Michael Stürmer summarized this approach in 1980, stating that Weimar's history had to be seen as a 'Sickness Unto Death', quoting a formulation by the Danish philosopher Søren Kierkegaard.[26] In similar vein, Heinrich August Winkler argued that, in light of 1933 being one of the 'great catastrophes of world history', writing the history of Weimar had to be a form of 'grief work'.[27] This direction of historiography fundamentally changed with a landmark article by the American historian Peter Fritzsche, published in 1996 and provocatively titled 'Did Weimar Fail?' This was a passionate plea to embrace a history that was 'strikingly open-ended' and 'remarkably contingent', to develop new lines of inquiry, employ new conceptual categories, and to see the traditional theme of an embattled democratic system in a new light.[28] Fritzsche's article helped to frame attempts to reconsider Weimar from different angles that were already under way at this point. In the following, we discuss five distinctive, yet also related, themes that have attracted the attention of historians over the past two decades.

There is—first—a revision in our understanding of the notion of a 'crisis' of the Weimar Republic. This term is ubiquitously used in historical writing on Weimar Germany and usually implies a process in which unmitigated problems compounded, leading to the terminal decline of the democratic system. Hans-Ulrich Wehler's usage is telling in this respect: he distinguished a 'crisis of capitalism', a 'crisis of the state', a 'societal crisis', in which the charismatic leader Hitler promised a way out of an 'existential crisis', thus deepening the 'legitimization crisis' of the republic. Amidst this 'bundle of crises', the fate of the republic was sealed.[29] What these and other references to the 'crises' of Weimar have in common is their reification of the term; it is treated as an objective given that has only ever one implication: decline. The critical revision of this historiographical trope has operated at several levels. Historians have pointed out that, rather than being an 'objective' description of a set of circumstances, the notion of 'crisis' has a narrative dimension. While crime rates, population statistics, or unemployment figures appear to be objective data, they only conjure up a crisis when they are embedded in narratives of decline. Empirical studies of crisis narratives in Germany from 1918 to 1933 demonstrate that, while contemporaries often invoked the term 'crisis', not all these narratives were marked by a pessimistic outlook into the future.[30]

This puts the semantics of the concept 'crisis' into sharp relief. In line with the original meaning of the term, it denoted a moment of openness and decision-making about the future course of events. In his analysis of the different meaning of 'crisis' in Weimar discourse, Rüdiger Graf has highlighted the prevalence of optimistic readings of the term and of the expectations for the future that it encapsulated. Thus, Graf turns the narrative of a doomed republic on its head and opens our eyes to something Weimar contemporaries saw all along: that their present could be shaped and changed by individual and collective action, and was characterized by a deep belief in the malleability of society.[31] While the traditional historiography of the Weimar Republic had established the narrative of a fundamental crisis leading to terminal decline so firmly that it hardly needed any further explanation, Graf suggests that 'it is difficult to find any prominent author, politician, intellectual, or journalist in Weimar Germany who publicly used the notion of crisis in a pessimistic or even fatalistic sense'.[32] These revisionist insights into the semantics of 'crisis' in the Weimar Republic stand in a stark contrast to the findings of Richard Overy's magisterial study of public discourse on the future in inter-war Britain. Both diagnostic analyses by social-scientific experts as well as the dissemination of opinions by journalists, writers, and politicians displayed deep-seated anxieties, if not outright paranoia about the future. Public discourse in 1920s and early 1930s Britain was characterized by a thoroughly negative outlook on the future, framed and amplified by the notion of a wholesale crisis of civilization.[33] If any Western European country around 1930 was gripped by an obsession with imminent decline, it was the United Kingdom, not Germany.

A second major field of debate relates to culture. The narrative of the doomed republic dovetailed with the celebration of Weimar's cultural highlights, mainly its metropolitan modernism, which shone more brightly the darker the political history of the young republic became. The catchy (but still false) suggestion that Berlin's population was partying to jazz music and cocaine while the Nazis seized power is rekindled whenever a historical anniversary or a new film production revives the notion of the allegedly wild and golden 1920s. Popular perceptions of this kind were also enshrined in historiography and remained surprisingly unchanged until well into the early 2000s.[34] More recently, however, historians have urged the scholarly community to move beyond the false binary of 'bad' politics and 'good' culture, or, in other words, 'beyond glitter and doom'.[35] What is needed to broaden our view of Weimar culture and to move away from these problematic binaries? The most important ingredient of a renewed history of

Weimar culture is to abandon the focus on a small sample of high-brow artists and their iconic productions, a perspective that Peter Gay inaugurated with his seminal account of the 'outsider as insider', first published in 1968.[36]

Moving away from the highbrow requires attention to previously overlooked areas. We need a more critical and deeply contextualized history of the contemporary audiences for high-brow as well as low-brow culture and its reception. In the literary field, this requires data on the overall output of books, the relevance of specific genres as well as the mechanisms that informed their distribution and reception.[37] In film, a closer look at Fritz Lang's *Metropolis* (1927) reveals that it 'was a box office flop' that almost bankrupted its production company Ufa. While the film, with its images of a futuristic cityscape, has subsequently become 'one of the icons of the 1920s', it was basically ignored by cinema goers at the time of its production.[38] We also need to rethink the proclaimed novelty of certain styles of art. The Bauhaus can serve as a key example here. The modernist design and architecture of its founders and key proponents depended on departures that dated back to the turn of the century, namely the work of the Deutscher Werkbund. Yet after Walter Gropius, Mies van der Rohe, and other leading Bauhaus figures had emigrated to the US, these connections to earlier strands of German modernism got lost, not least due to the clever self-marketing of Gropius. Up until 1933 only one and not even the most successful school of modernist architecture in Germany, the Bauhaus brand emerged as a major international success story only after 1945, and was only then seen as an iconic Weimar production.[39]

As a genre, war literature demonstrates how the focus on specific high-brow texts overlooks what proved successful with mass audiences. With *In Stahlgewittern* (*Storms of Steel*, 1920), Ernst Jünger produced one of the seminal texts in this genre and coined a metaphor that encapsulated the meaning of the front-line experience like none other. The book glorified the war in a way that contradicted the individual experiences of many soldiers, but at the same time offered a sense of collective meaning for suffering. Yet while *In Stahlgewittern* is a key text in Jünger's oeuvre and perhaps the most important German book about the First World War, its circulation prior to 1928/9, when Remarque's *All Quiet on the Western Front* transformed the literary field, was very limited.[40] Among the most widely sold texts about the war, at least before Remarque's book broke all records, were, however, two short pamphlets with no literary pretence—and certainly with no avant-garde qualities—by a school teacher and an anarchist agitator and author, respectively. Yet *Charleville* (1919) by Wilhelm Appens and *Etappe Gent* (*Rear Area Gent*, 1921/1928) by Heinrich Wandt quickly shifted hundreds of thousands of copies because they highlighted, from a left-wing perspective, a scandal that had agitated many German soldiers during the war: the moral corruption and sleaze that German officers in the rear area, at a safe distance from the dangers of the front, had practised.[41]

Ultimately, there was more to Weimar culture than just the avant-garde. A commercialized popular culture, including cinema, spectator sports, and pulp fiction, had emerged since around 1900. With technological innovations such as the introduction of radio broadcasts and sound film, the Weimar era witnessed the proliferation of a media ensemble that comprised and in many ways connected—through reviews, advertisements, and cross-merchandising by media conglomerates—film, radio, popular music, and the daily press. For many educated observers from the *Bildungsbürgertum*, the spectacle of these mass media represented 'bad' culture, commercialized, devoid of higher meaning, and often sexualized, while cultural critics mainly on the left of the political spectrum were concerned about its allegedly depoliticizing effects.[42] Yet the lamentations of these educated critics did not diminish the popular appetite for the different forms of mass culture in the slightest. We need to incorporate low-brow books, films, plays, and other cultural artefacts in our historical imagination of the era and to analyse the media ensemble of mass culture and its audiences. We should also abandon the use of 'dancing on the volcano' as a metaphor that is meant to encapsulate the allegedly carnivalesque and ecstatic feel of Weimar culture.[43] This is a generalization that simply does not ring true.

Reconsideration is—third—required in regard to the scales of Weimar's history, from the local via the national to the global. Historians of Imperial Germany have established that the newly founded nation-state was a key driving force behind the first major wave of globalization from the 1880s onwards. Migration, the high level of economic interconnectedness through exports and imports, German colonies in Africa, East Asia, and the Pacific, and the global reach of German missionary societies are only a few indicators of the extent to which the national and the global were mutually implied in Imperial Germany.[44] Both the First World War and the following peace settlement severely disrupted patterns and pathways of migration, trade, and transnational communication. However, the post-war period cannot simply be described as an era of de-globalization. Even though important export markets were blocked for German industry by the trade measures of the Treaty of Versailles, key branches such as the chemicals industry and machinery construction managed to surpass their pre-war export volume by 1929.[45] Not only in its economy was Weimar Germany substantially shaped by transnational exchanges. Industrialists, trade unionists, and journalists of different political leanings were keen to emulate the blueprints that both the USA and the Soviet Union offered for attempts to rationalize and reform society. Only very few practical models of Americanization were implemented from 1919 to 1933. But the widespread interest in the USA as a beacon of modernity indicates that societal reform was very much a transnational endeavour.[46]

Expert cultures of professionals were another field of intensive transnational exchange, as demonstrated by the many architects and town planners from other European countries who shaped the practice of their German counterparts with their ideas and designs. The new functionalist designs of the 1920s, so typical of the Bauhaus school, were heavily influenced by the Dutch group of artists De Stijl, not least because Theo van Doesburg, one of the founders of De Stijl, taught at the Bauhaus in Weimar 1921/2.[47] Transnationalism was, to give one more example, a key feature of all those activists who campaigned for progressive causes in the peace movement. To be sure, for the pacifists, re-establishing contacts, particularly with their French counterparts, was fraught with problems given the atrocities that the German army had committed in 1914 in Belgium and Northern France. Yet it was possible to rebuilt mutual trust, and in 1927, two leading pacifists, Ludwig Quidde and Ferdinand Buisson, were jointly awarded the Nobel Peace Prize for their contribution to French–German reconciliation and the spirit that had facilitated the 1925 Locarno Treaties.[48]

While Weimar Germany was embedded in significant transnational exchanges in its economy and its networks of experts and activists, it was significantly curtailed in two other important fields of globalization, namely, migration and empire.[49] Imperial Germany had literally been a society 'on the move', with extremely high levels of both internal horizontal mobility, seasonal labour immigration, and emigration. In the third and final great wave of nineteenth-century emigration, 1.8 million Germans had left the country between 1880 and 1893. Post-1918, migration peaked in 1923, when 115,000 Germans went abroad. The overall volume was much lower than prior to 1914, with only 600,000 Germans emigrating from 1919 to 1932, mostly to the Americas.[50] But an even bigger shift occurred in immigration. Imperial Germany, with its booming economy and barely mechanized agricultural sector, had been highly dependent on the import of labour. By 1914, around 1.2 million foreign workers were employed in Germany. The forced deportation of Belgian civilians and the influx of POWs during the Great War increased this number even further. The end of the war in 1918 brought labour immigration to a halt. Most of the POWs and civilian labourers went home, and the republican state was keen to drive both permanent and seasonal migration down to an absolute minimum.[51] By 1924, only 170,000 foreign workers stayed in Germany. Labour policy in the Weimar Republic was geared to secure the primacy of domestic workers over those from abroad, and border controls were much tighter than before 1914. As a result, peak immigration was reached in 1928 with a mere 236,000 foreign workers, and 100,000 of these only had a time-limited permit for seasonal labour.[52] To be sure, about one million Germans who had lived in territories that were ceded to France and Poland under the Treaty of Versailles relocated to Germany.[53] And after the defeat of the Whites in the Russian Civil War in 1920, Germany experienced a large influx of Russian refugees who fled from the Bolsheviks. Nonetheless, most of them moved to other countries, and by 1925 the overall tally stood at a much reduced 150,000.[54] The upshot of all this is clear: during the Weimar Republic, Germany had a much more homogeneous and settled population than prior to 1914, and was less affected by emigration and immigration.

Between 1884 and 1899, Germany had amassed a sizeable colonial empire in Africa, East Asia, and the Pacific Ocean. It came to an end in 1919, when the Treaty of Versailles placed the German colonies under a mandate by the League of Nations. The loss of the colonies outraged many radical nationalists, but only very few of them were ready to join organizations that supported colonial revisionism. The most important of these, the German Colonial Society (Deutsche Kolonialgesellschaft, DKG), saw its membership drop from c.43,000 in 1912 to only 21,420 by 1933. The Women's League of the DKG fared better, increasing membership to 24,000 by 1932.[55] However, compared to the membership figures and widespread local presence of other radical nationalist pressure groups, organized colonial revisionism was small fry. Hence, some historians argue that the real significance of the former colonies in Weimar society did not lie specifically in the political realm, but in the proliferation of 'colonial fantasies', i.e. cultural imaginations and projections that reflected the desire for colonial domination over indigenous people.[56] One medium for the discursive explication of colonial fantasies were 'Africa books', fictional and semi-autobiographical accounts in which the myth of the loyal Askari, black colonial soldiers who were committed to serving their German masters, provided the core narrative. A substantial analysis of this genre estimates that about 100 Africa books were published until the mid-1920s.[57] Some of them became bestsellers. The relevance of these book-length accounts of colonial fantasies has, however, to be set against the backdrop of the overall literary market, with 6,000 books of fiction published in 1925 alone.[58] Whether we look at colonial revisionism or at colonial fantasies: it appears that interest in the former colonies faded quickly, and that the overwhelming majority of Weimar Germans had other issues on their minds.[59]

This brief survey indicates that the global entanglements and transnational connections of Weimar Germany should not be overestimated. Both the nation as an identity space and the nation-state and its capacity to shape the livelihood of millions had a much bigger relevance from 1918 to 1933 than was previously the case in the highly globalized Wilhelmine Germany.[60] As we consider the scales of Weimar's history, we also need to look at the level below the nation-state. The German nation-state, founded in in 1871, was shaped by a long tradition of federalism that reserved powers for the individual states (Länder). Federalism changed its meaning with the shift to a parliamentary democracy, and the Weimar Constitution included some centralizing measures. Yet regional disparity had not only a political dimension, but also a social and cultural one. Regional differences, even within the Länder, were crucial markers of collective identity, shaped by historical traditions, geographical features, and sentimental longings to have a *Heimat*, a place where one belonged.[61] Historicizing Weimar means to situate the German economy, society, and culture in its transnational, national, and subnational contexts and entanglements.

Important shifts have—fourth—occurred in our understanding of the Weimar political system. Conventional accounts of German political history from 1918 to 1933 focused on top-level decision-making in cabinets and party headquarters, which was analysed against the backdrop of the back-door lobbying of economic pressure groups that represented employers and businesses.[62] What was lost in these accounts was not only the relevance of political mobilization at the grassroots level—including that for the Nazi party—and in different public arenas such as the workplace, the streets, and a associational life that revolved, in its bourgeois form, around the *Stammtisch*, a weekly gathering of like-minded members of an association who had reserved a table in a pub. But the traditional political history of the Weimar era was also deficient in conceptual terms as it interpreted the performative side of the political process—the theatrical elements of a politician's speech, the display of flags and other symbols, the visualization of political groups and political scandals in illustrated journals—as a mere sideshow or façade behind which the actual power politics were to be found. More recent approaches to politics diverge from this assumption. They argue that the use of symbolic forms is the very terrain on which the political process and its struggle over power is constituted, and that not only material interests, but also those in recognition, honour, and other values drive collective demands.[63] From the many ramifications of this shift in perspective, only a few aspects can be highlighted here.

The new perspective implies a new look at the polity dimension of the political process, i.e. the written and unwritten rules that frame politics, and the institutions that provide its backbone. In this vein, historians have arrived at a reassessment of the revolution in 1918/19. Rather than being an outright failure, as often stated, the transition starting in November 1918 now appears as a successful project of 'civic revolutionary mobilization' that brought the mighty military machine of the Imperial system to a halt, based on the collective agency of the masses in the army and in many localized uprisings across Germany.[64] Equally important, the revolutionaries decided with overwhelming majority to channel the transformation that they had inaugurated into a National Assembly, based on elections with a free, equal franchise for both men and women. The National Assembly, in turn, devised a constitution that provided a far-reaching framework for progressive reform. At the heart of the new democratic polity were the people, in whose collective will power rested, and the Reichstag, the national parliament, to which they delegated it in elections.[65] A thorough analysis of the cross-party integration of the Reichstag deputies through rituals and different forms of symbolic interaction has not only revealed that inside the parliament a culture of pragmatic compromise mostly prevailed until 1928, but has also led to a positive re-evaluation of the role of parliament in the wider political process.[66]

The focus on symbolic politics has led to a (re)discovery of those groups and forces that supported the republic wholeheartedly. It has often been suggested that Weimar was a 'republic without republicans', a trope that goes back to contemporary journalists and authors on the radical left who castigated the Social Democratic Party (SPD) for its lack of appetite for a more thorough social and economic transformation. Yet former politicians of the German Democratic Party (DDP) and SPD also contributed to the acceptance of this trope. Writing their memoirs in exile or after 1945, they claimed that the lack of a pro-republican narrative and symbols for the representation of the new polity had played a crucial role in its demise.[67] Conveniently, these arguments excused them from any mistakes in political decision-making from 1918 to 1933. Yet recent studies have demonstrated that republican festivities, commemorations, rituals, and symbols were vibrant, colourful, and popular. Efforts to create an engaging set of symbolic republican practices, on a national level organized by the Reich Art Custodian (Reichskunstwart) as part of the Constitution Day, celebrated to commemorate the passage of the Weimar Constitution in the National Assembly on 11 August 1919, reached far beyond the capital and touched the everyday lives of millions. Local conflicts centred on republican symbols—flags, parades, commemorative activities—which were not just political decoration, but stood at the core of local identity formation. The recent understanding that Germany's republicans and their organizations, most prominently the Reichsbanner Black-Red-Gold, were not a quiet minority, but actively, passionately, and visibly participating in the political landscape, has transformed

Weimar's history by adding an important, and often overlooked, dimension to the political arena.[68]

The history of participation, democracy, and politics more generally in Weimar was highly gendered. A key caesura in this respect was the introduction of unrestricted female suffrage in the revolution, first practised in the elections to the National Assembly on 19 January 1919. The enfranchisement of women in Germany was not only progressive, not being limited by specific age restrictions or property qualifications such as for instance those stipulated by the Representation of the People Act in UK in the 1918. It was also transformative in that it provided women with citizenship rights, also enshrined in the Weimar Constitution, and thus allowed and encouraged sustained female involvement in the political sphere in the widest sense, through participation in elections and parties, but also in professional bodies and involvement in everyday political discussions.[69] Yet it would be wrong to read women's citizenship in Weimar through the lens of a progressive narrative of emancipation—a contested term anyway—and left-wing activism. Throughout Weimar elections at Reich and state level, female voters showed a consistent preference for parties that upheld Christian values, namely the German National People's Party (DNVP) and the Catholic Centre Party.[70] When we only count the male vote in the elections for the National Assembly, the socialist parties of the left, the SPD and Independent Social Democratic Party (USPD), jointly achieved an absolute majority. If we only look at younger men born between 1887 and 1898 who had not been able to vote in the last Reichstag elections in 1912, this was most probably a two-thirds majority.[71] Yet Weimar politics was not only gendered via different patterns of participation and (party) mobilization among men and women. Bodies and sexuality also had a political relevance. The struggle against §218 of the penal code, that is, the attempt to decriminalize abortion, was one of the most enduring political struggles of the Weimar era, deeply embedded in the everyday lives of the hundreds of thousands mostly working-class women every year who had an abortion performed.[72] Male bodies were political, too, as the parties of the right, and especially the NSDAP and its paramilitary wing, the Stormtroopers, sought to reorganize a field of masculinity that had been disrupted by the trauma and mutilation many men had experienced during the war.[73] All this does not mean that it is no longer worthwhile to study the politics of interest and party formation; quite the contrary. A detailed reconstruction of the connections between party organization, political realignment at the local level, and the workings of pressure groups remains critical to understanding the reasons why the Nazi party was able to challenge and ultimately supersede the established parties of the German right.[74] Yet all this relentless scheming and lobbying would have been neither plausible nor attractive, had it not been informed by symbolic ideas such as the notion of the people's community and their performative enactment.

Important revisions haven taken place—fifth—in explanations for the rise of the National Socialists. Some older interpretations have lost currency, for instance the notion that the 'victory of violence' that they enacted on the streets catapulted the Nazis to power.[75] Like the suggestion that the republic descended into a civil war in its final years, such arguments seem vastly overstated.[76] Contrary to these assumptions, the use of physical violence peaked at the beginning of Weimar, when it was used to crush revolutionary uprisings by the radical left in 1919/20.[77] Another well-established argument explains the success of the NSDAP by the particularly innovative methods of its propaganda, the power of its slogans, leaflets, posters, and speeches by high-ranking party leaders.[78] Yet the appeal of Nazi propaganda, and especially of the big rallies, has been exaggerated and never effectively proven. A more important factor to win over voters was the intensive organizational effort of the Nazi party at the local level. Hierarchically structured cells, going down to the level of street cells that comprised only a few blocks of houses, offered NSDAP members organizational routines and practices, a sense of belonging and, at points, a warm meal. They helped to anchor the party within the fabric of socially highly diverse local communities and allowed for a quick mobilization when it was needed.[79] Another crucial factor for the increasing acceptance of the Nazi party was the influence of local opinion leaders, especially—but not exclusively—in tightly knit village communities in rural areas. Once Protestant pastors and teachers in villages, or well-respected business owners in small towns, came out as NSDAP supporters, the trust that members of the local population placed into them led many others to follow suit.[80] All these findings corroborate a wider argument, first made regarding the small university town of Marburg: the Nazis were able to gather supporters in highly diverse social settings not so much by persuading and winning them over from the outside, but by converting them from the inside, as they participated in established networks and rituals of sociability like voluntary associations (*Vereine*) or the weekly *Stammtisch* (regulars' table) where ordinary burghers met for a pint.[81]

Another important argument for explaining the success of the Nazi relates to the ideological and symbolic appeal of the vision of a people's community or *Volksgemeinschaft*. The term itself was used by most political parties in the 1920s, including republicans in the SPD and DDP. One major exception remained the KPD, which, apart from brief moments as in 1923, refused to tap into the notion of national solidarity.[82] But of all the parties, it was the NSDAP that ultimately best managed to connect their vision for a renewal of Germany to the longing for a national community that promised to cut across class and other social differences. Their interpretation of the *Volksgemeinschaft*, dovetailing with the focus on a strong leader, appeared to be the most convincing solution to Weimar's perceived problems and was also effective as a mobilizing tool.[83] Closely tied to the emphasis on the solidarity of the national community was the exclusion of the Jews as 'others', outsiders who should and could not belong. Antisemitism in word and deed was widespread in the Weimar Republic, existed in different variations, was supported by many, and tolerated by most. The discursive use of exclusionary language in Weimar Germany shifted the boundaries of what was acceptable to say and write in favour of the radical antisemites.[84] The fight against *völkisch*, racist antisemitism in Weimar Germany did not find enough unambiguous, wholehearted supporters. Ultimately, its ability to draw in socially diverse constituencies was a crucial factor for the success of the Nazi insurrection. This success was neither just the result of cynical manipulation nor of the economic depression. Rather, it depended on a complex process of political realignment that had already started in the mid-1920s and only accelerated during the Great Depression.⁸⁵ The Nazis did not conquer German society from the outside, but rather immersed themselves in the fabric of small-town and rural sociability from the inside.

THE STRUCTURE OF THIS VOLUME

Our handbook provides up-to-date information and authoritative interpretations from an international team of experts. To ensure it is accessible to a wide range of readers, we offer different entry points to Weimar's history depending on prior knowledge and interests. The first section offers a chronological overview with a focus on politics. Moving in four chapters from the German revolution 1918/19 to the dismantling of Weimar democracy in 1933, this section provides a basis for anyone who wants to establish or refresh their knowledge on key events and developments in Weimar Germany's tumultuous history. The four periods delineated in this section (1918/19, 1920–3, 1924–9, and 1930–3) are not fixed entities, not least because they are predominantly defined by political developments, whereas other fields of society (social classes, religion, mass culture) followed a different pattern of periodization or indeed ran through the whole period as a bloc. It is particularly problematic to label the period from 1924 to 1928 as the stable years of the republic, as has been often done in the past. Whether through the proliferation of antisemitic discourse or because a national socialist consensus (in lower case letters) emerged in the nationalist-bourgeois milieu during these years, many of the detrimental forces that ultimately destroyed the republic came to the fore precisely between 1924 and 1928.⁸⁶ The rest of our handbook is structured in thematic blocks, covering the three aspects of the political system (polity/politics/policies) (Part II), parties and their constituencies (Part III), economy and society (Part IV), and culture (Part V). While the chapters relate to each other, each one of them provides enough background information to make their topic accessible without any prior knowledge. Due to the lack of single-volume surveys in the English language that can match the extensive coverage of our handbook, we find it essential that this volume allows anyone who is interested to engage with the extraordinary history of Germany's first democracy.

The structure of our handbook displays a strong focus on the political field in the broadest sense. We consider this justified because the new political framework of the Weimar Republic fundamentally altered how political decisions were reached and thus deeply impacted on the lives of Germany's citizens. The Weimar Constitution brought new rights and freedoms, it promised social improvements, and reshaped the relation between state and citizen. Germans could engage in the political process through individual as well as collective action. Universal suffrage allowed German men and women equally to take part in the political process for the first time as voters and as candidates for political offices. Freedom of assembly and organization meant that collective actions and interests could be put forward through political parties and unions, but also by professional associations and lobby groups, on a much broader basis than prior to 1914.

Politics (domestic and foreign) played an essential role in Weimar Germany, not least because the rules of the political playing field had to be renegotiated. Political affiliation was an important part of both individual and collective identity formation, especially in a society that was so deeply politically divided as Weimar Germany. At the local level, supporters and opponents of the republic faced each other in conflicts over political symbols and material issues. In a time when the political framework had been torn apart and replaced with something radically new for Germany, politics mattered in every aspect of social life.

At this point we can briefly clarify an important aspect of nomenclature that is often misunderstood: the name of the Weimar Republic. When the National Assembly gathered in Weimar in early 1919, the official name for the new polity was one of the debating points. While the deputies for the SPD and USPD voted in favour of 'German Republic', the bourgeois parties, including the left-liberal DDP, agreed that the name Deutsches Reich should be retained. The liberal jurist Hugo Preuß, who had drafted the constitution, agreed on the grounds that the 'name Reich' linked the republic to the tradition of a unified nation-state that had been established in 1871. The republican constitution was thus called the 'Constitution of the German Reich' (Verfassung des Deutschen Reichs), and this official name prompted many pro-republican organizations such as the Reichsbanner Black-Red-Gold to incorporate the term Reich in their name. It is a bitter irony that the moniker 'Weimar Republic' was first used by those who rejected the democratic state on principle: it was none other than Adolf Hitler who, in a newspaper article in March 1929, provided one of the first recorded usages of this name, while continuing to rail against the republican 'system'.[87]

Our handbook includes chapters on topics that are rarely considered in detail, whether in most general histories of the era or in the existing multi-author companions. They include an analysis of regionalized structures and mentalities that shaped political culture. Often overlooked is also the role of religious cultures and of conflicts between the Christian confessions and vis-à-vis their critics in organized secularism. Absent from our historical imaginary of the Weimar Republic are also the peasants and agricultural labourers, even though almost a third of all gainfully employed Germans worked in agriculture.[88] What these three topics have in common is that they force us to consider the regional variety and the spatial depth of society, culture, and political allegiances in Weimar Germany. Too often, the history of the Weimar Republic is seen through the lens of its bustling metropolis Berlin, with its modernist culture, flamboyant night life, and permissive sexuality, encapsulated in the—often exaggerated—notion of the New Woman and other cultural hallmarks of the allegedly 'Golden Twenties'. But Berlin was not the Weimar Republic.[89]

Even a collection as comprehensive as ours is, however, ultimately selective. Given the constraints on the overall length of the volume, we had to omit some topics that are relevant for the history of the Weimar Republic. One of them is schools and education, significant as educational reform was part of the wider progressive, participatory drive of the pro-republican parties, which implemented crucial changes such as extending compulsory schooling from the age of 14 to that 18, and making the co-education of pupils of different confession in a so-called *Simultanschule* the norm (from which exceptions were permitted).[90] Also not included is a separate chapter on a small, but still highly influential social group, the aristocracy, which comprised c.90,000 families or 0.3 per cent of the population. The nobility lost many privileges in the republican polity, including the holding of administrative and policing power in separate manorial districts (*Gutsbezirke*) in Prussia, which were disbanded in 1927. Yet they continued to rely on patterns of social deference in localized contexts, both in East-Elbian agrarian society and in other parts of Germany. Many members of the nobility openly supported the Nazi party, a crucial influence that particularly mattered in the final months of the republic.[91] A final omission is more detailed information on the styles, innovative directors, and key works in Weimar cinema as an emerging mass medium of the republic. Those who cherish Weimar cinema, however, can turn to several helpful companions on this topic.[92]

We think that the main purpose of a handbook like this is to frame and consolidate knowledge, rather than to enter speculative reflections on the meaning of the past in the light of current circumstances. We do not see much value in conjuring up 'the ghosts of Weimar', as an alarmist discourse that interprets the current problems of parliamentary democracy and the rise of right-wing populism in many European countries against the backdrop of Weimar's predicament.[93] The vast differences between then and now—for instance, the substantial presence of the agrarian sector in Weimar (as well as in many other Central-Eastern European countries) and its role in the rise of right-wing populism; the limited capability of state intervention in the economy in the early 1930s; and, considering the Federal Republic, the ways in which politicians, the police, and a wider public were and are painfully aware of the problem of containing right-wing extremism and thus drew important lessons from the past—place firm limits on the value of any comparison between the early 1930s and the present.

It is important to historicize the very notion of democracy and to emphasize its open-ended, permanently experimental nature, rather than measuring the deficiencies of Weimar's parliamentary system against current normative benchmarks. The rise of right-wing populism and the erosion of trust in parliamentary governance were persistent problems that all European countries, including the UK, faced to differing degrees in the late 1920s and 1930s. To be sure, Germany was not the only country in which these problems facilitated the success of a right-wing dictatorship.[94] Ultimately, the Weimar Republic poses questions about lines of continuity and what historian Helmut Walser Smith has called the 'vanishing point' of German history, that is, the focal point which different lines are approaching.[95] Looking from 1918, 1933 was clearly not the only vanishing point of German history. Weimar's democracy opened up different lines of continuity: to the founding of the Christian Democratic Union in 1946, which realized Weimar era attempts to overcome the confessional divide between Protestants and Catholics; to the West German Basic Law of 1949, which built on Weimar's successes and failures by creating a participatory democracy; and to the burgeoning mass culture, then centred around a new addition to the media ensemble, the television set, and the sexual revolution of the 1960s. Despite their focus on 1918 to 1933, several chapters in this handbook draw attention to continuities that extended well beyond 1933. Continuities and ruptures in Weimar history need to be carefully weighted. This holds especially true for the most problematic aspect of German history, the exclusion and persecution of the Jews. As one historian of the Holocaust observes: 'Before 1933, Jews fled to Germany rather than from it.'[96] Historicizing Weimar thus requires us both to acknowledge that the formation of the Nazi dictatorship in 1933 was not a predetermined, but a contingent outcome, with alternatives open right up to the last minute on 30 January 1933, and to account for the developments that led to this outcome.

Notes

1. Andreas Wirsching, Berthold Kohler, and Ulrich Wilhelm (eds), *Weimarer Verhältnisse? Historische Lektionen für unsere Demokratie* (Stuttgart: Reclam, 2018).
2. Jörn Leonhard, 'Die Weimarer Republik als Metapher und geschichtspolitisches Argument', *Aus Politik und Zeitgeschichte*, 68/18–20 (2018), 11–18.
3. Jochen Hung, Godela Weiss-Sussex, and Geoff Wilkes (eds), *Beyond Glitter and Doom: The Contingency of the Weimar Republic* (Munich: Iudicium, 2012).
4. Unfortunately, Richard J. Evans's first volume of his history of the Third Reich presents the Weimar Republic exactly in this way. See his *The Coming of the Third Reich* (London: Penguin, 2003).
5. Niklas Luhmann, 'The Future Cannot Begin: Temporal Structures in Modern Society', *Social Research*, 43 (1976), 130–52, 140. On the 'horizon of expectations' see Reinhart Koselleck, *Futures Past: On the Semantics of Historical Time*, tr. Keith Tribe (New York: Columbia University Press, 2004), 255–75.
6. Rüdiger Graf, *Die Zukunft der Weimarer Republik: Krisen und Zukunftsaneignungen in Deutschland 1918-1933* (Munich: R. Oldenbourg, 2008), 83–133.
7. See Hans-Ulrich Wehler, *Deutsche Gesellschaftsgeschichte 1715–1990*, 5 vols (Munich: C. H. Beck, 1987–2008), here vols 3 and 4; Jürgen Kocka, 'German History Before Hitler: The Debate about the German Sonderweg', *Journal of Contemporary History*, 23 (1988), 1–23.
8. Thomas Nipperdey, '1933 und die Kontinuität der deutschen Geschichte', in Michael Stürmer (ed.), *Die Weimarer Republik*, 2nd ed. (Königstein/Ts.: Athenäum, 1985), 374–92.
9. See the chapter by Peter Caldwell in this volume. See also Horst Dreier and Christian Waldhoff (eds), *Das Wagnis der Demokratie: Eine Anatomie der Weimarer Reichsverfassung* (Munich: C. H. Beck, 2018), esp. Oliver F. R. Haardt and Christopher M. Clark, 'Die Weimarer Reichsverfassung als Moment in der Geschichte', 9–44, here 43.
10. See Sebastian Ullrich, *Der Weimar-Komplex: Das Scheitern der ersten deutschen Demokratie und die politische Kultur der frühen Bundesrepublik* (Göttingen: Wallstein, 2009); Karl Dietrich Bracher, *Die Auflösung der Weimarer Republik: Eine Studie zum Problem des Machtverfalls in der Demokratie* (Stuttgart, Düsseldorf: Ring Verlag, 1955); Kurt Sontheimer, *Antidemokratisches Denken in der Weimarer Republik: Die politischen Ideen des deutschen Nationalismus zwischen 1918 und 1933* (Munich: Nymphenburger, 1962).
11. For a wider take on historiographical trends until the 1990s see Eberhard Kolb, *The Weimar Republic*, 2nd ed. (London: Routledge, 2005), 139–48.

12. Hans Mommsen, *The Rise and Fall of Weimar Democracy*, tr. Larry Eugene Jones (Chapel Hill, NC, London: University of North Carolina Press, 1996; 1st German ed. 1989). *Die verspielte Freiheit* is the German title of the 1st ed. of Mommsen's book.
13. Mommsen, *Rise and Fall*, 309–10 (quotes), 497.
14. Ibid., 302–13, quotes 302, 303. For the 'dissolution' of the bourgeoisie by 1918 see Mommsen, 'Die Auflösung des Bürgertums seit dem späten 19. Jahrhundert', in Jürgen Kocka (ed.), *Bürger und Bürgerlichkeit im 19. Jahrhundert* (Göttingen: Vandenhoeck & Ruprecht, 1987), 288–315. The erroneous nature of this argument is obvious. What dissolved was not the middle-class per se, but Mommsen's idealized notion of a middle class primarily characterized by liberal rationalism and harmonious sociability. See the chapter by Moritz Föllmer in this volume.
15. See Hans-Ulrich Wehler, *Deutsche Gesellschaftsgeschichte*, vol. 4. *1914–1949* (Munich: C. H. Beck, 2003), 294.
16. Heinrich August Winkler, *Weimar, 1918–1933: Die Geschichte der ersten deutschen Demokratie* (Munich: C. H. Beck, 1993), 45–9, 247–9, 305, 341–2, quote 595.
17. Detlev Peukert, *The Weimar Republic: The Crisis of Classical Modernity*, tr. Richard Deveson (New York: Hill & Wang, 1993; 1st German ed. 1987).
18. Detlev J. K. Peukert, *Max Webers Diagnose der Moderne* (Göttingen: Vandenhoeck & Ruprecht, 1989), here 70–91; the best recent reconstruction of Weber's argument is Peter Ghosh, *Max Weber and 'The Protestant Ethic': Twin Histories* (Oxford: Oxford University Press, 2014).
19. Peukert, *Weimar Republic*, 101–4, 112–18, 134–40 (quote), 167–72.
20. Ibid., 145–6. See the chapters by Karl Christian Führer and Ute Planert in this volume.
21. Peukert, *Weimar Republic*, xiv.
22. Ursula Büttner, *Weimar: Die überforderte Republik 1918–1933. Leistung und Versagen in Staat, Gesellschaft, Wirtschaft und Kultur* (Stuttgart: Klett-Cotta, 2008), 132 for a critique of Peukert see also Young-Sun Hong, *Welfare, Modernity, and the Weimar State, 1919–1933* (Princeton: Princeton University Press, 1998).
23. Peukert, *Weimar Republic*, quote 146; see Edward Ross Dickinson, 'Biopolitics, Fascism, Democracy: Some Reflections on our Discourse about "Modernity"', *Central European History*, 37 (2004), 1–48.
24. See only Gerald D. Feldman, *The Great Disorder: Politics, Economics and Society in the German Inflation, 1914–1924* (Oxford: Oxford University Press, 1993); Feldman and Irmgard Steinisch, *Industrie und Gewerkschaften 1918–1924: Die überforderte Zentralarbeitsgemeinschaft* (Stuttgart: DVA, 1985); Larry Eugene Jones, *German Liberalism and the Dissolution of the Weimar Party System, 1918–1933* (Chapel Hill, NC, London: University of North Carolina Press, 1988); Jones, *Hitler versus Hindenburg: The 1932 Presidential Elections and the End of the Weimar Republic* (Cambridge: Cambridge University Press, 2015); Cornelie Usborne, *The Politics of the Body in Weimar Germany. Women's Reproductive Rights and Duties* (Basingstoke: Macmillan, 1992); Usborne, *Cultures of Abortion in Weimar Germany* (New York. Oxford: Berghahn Books, 2007).
25. The best short survey remains Matthew Stibbe, *Germany 1914–1933: Politics, Society and Culture* (Harlow: Longman, 2010); see also Anthony McElligott, *Rethinking the Weimar Republic: Authority and Authoritarianism 1916–1936* (London: Bloomsbury, 2014). The book by Eric D. Weitz, *Weimar Germany: Promise and Tragedy* (Princeton: Princeton University Press, 2007), is geared towards a very selective sample of the modernist high-brow culture in the German capital, an approach that was already problematic at

the time of publication. See the critique by Peter Jelavich, *Central European History*, 42 (2009), 163–5.
26. Michael Stürmer, 'Einleitung', in Stürmer (ed.), *Die Weimarer Republik*, 13–36, here 13.
27. Winkler, *Weimar*, 11.
28. Peter Fritzsche, 'Did Weimar Fail?', *Journal of Modern History*, 68 (1996), 629–56, quotes 632–3.
29. Wehler, *Gesellschaftsgeschichte*, vol. 4, 589–92.
30. Moritz Föllmer and Rüdiger Graf (eds), *Die 'Krise' der Weimarer Republik: Zur Kritik eines Deutungsmusters* (Frankfurt/Main: Campus, 2005). Helmuth Kiesel, *Geschichte der deutschsprachigen Literatur 1918–1933* (Munich: Beck, 2017), 90–1, points out correctly that the discursive construction of 'crisis' should not be turned into an absolute, and that Weimar's crises were to some degree discursively 'invented', but also 'experienced'.
31. Graf, *Die Zukunft der Weimarer Republik*.
32. Rüdiger Graf, 'Either-Or: The Narrative of "Crisis" in Weimar Germany and in Historiography', *Central European History*, 43 (2010), 592–615, here 602.
33. Richard Overy, *The Morbid Age: Britain and the Crisis of Civilization, 1919–1939* (London: Penguin, 2010), quotes 50, 93.
34. See Weitz, *Weimar Germany*.
35. Jochen Hung, '"Bad" Politics and "Good" Culture: New Approaches to the History of the Weimar Republic', *Central European History*, 49 (2016), 441–53; Hung et al., *Beyond Glitter and Doom*.
36. Peter Gay, *Weimar Culture: The Outsider as Insider* (London: Secker & Warburg, 1968).
37. See the chapter by Helmuth Kiesel in this volume.
38. Karl-Christian Führer, 'High Brow and Low Brow Culture', in Anthony McElligott (ed.), *Weimar Germany* (Oxford: Oxford University Press, 2009), 260–81, quote 274.
39. See the chapter by Beate Störtkuhl in this volume, and Paul Betts, 'Die Bauhaus Legende: Amerikanisch-Deutsches "Joint Venture" des Kalten Krieges', in Alf Lüdtke et al. (eds), *Amerikanisierung: Traum und Alptraum im Deutschland des 20. Jahrhunderts* (Stuttgart: Steiner, 1996), 270–90.
40. See the critical edition: Ernst Jünger, *In Stahlgewittern: Historisch-kritische Ausgabe*, 2 vols (Stuttgart: Klett-Cotta 2014), ed. Helmuth Kiesel. See also the chapters by Claudia Siebrecht and Helmuth Kiesel in this volume.
41. Benjamin Ziemann, *Violence and the German Soldier in the Great War: Killing–Dying–Surviving* (London: Bloomsbury Academic, 2017), 203–24.
42. See the chapter by Jochen Hung in this volume.
43. Peter Gay was probably among the first historians to use the metaphor, but it goes back to Joseph Goebbels, who used it in his novel *Michael*, published in 1929. See Gay, *Weimar Culture*, p. xiv; Thomas W. Kniesche and Stephen Brockmann, 'Introduction. Weimar Today', in their *Dancing on the Volcano: Essays on the Culture of the Weimar Republic* (Columbia, SC: Camden House), 1994), 1–18, here 4. For a sustained critique, see Sabina Becker, *Experiment Weimar: Eine Kulturgeschichte Deutschlands 1918–1933* (Darmstadt: wbg Academic, 2018), 521–6.
44. See Sebastian Conrad, *Globalisation and Nation in Imperial Germany* (Cambridge: Cambridge University Press, 2010); Jürgen Osterhammel and Sebastian Conrad (eds), *Das Kaiserreich Transnational* (Göttingen: Vandenhoeck & Ruprecht, 2004).
45. See the chapter by Jan-Otmar Hesse and Christian Marx in this volume.
46. See the chapter by Mary Nolan in this volume.

47. See the chapter by Beate Störtkuhl in this volume.
48. See Karl Holl, *Pazifismus in Deutschland* (Frankfurt/Main: Suhrkamp, 1988), 158–74, and the chapter by Jonathan Wright in this volume.
49. See the themes in Emily S. Rosenberg (ed.), *A World Connecting, 1870–1945* (Cambridge, MA: Belknap Press, 2012).
50. Sebastian Conrad and Philipp Ther, 'On the Move: Mobility, Migration, and Nation 1880–1948', in Helmut Walser Smith (ed.), *The Oxford Handbook of Modern German History* (Oxford: Oxford University Press, 2011), 573–90; for a detailed breakdown see Dietmar Petzina, Werner Abelshauser, and Anselm Faust, *Sozialgeschichtliches Arbeitsbuch III: Materialien zur Statistik des Deutschen Reiches 1914–1945* (Munich: C. H. Beck, 1978), 35.
51. Conrad and Ther, 'On the Move', 579–80.
52. See Ulrich Herbert, *Geschichte der Ausländerbeschäftigung in Deutschland 1880 bis 1980* (Berlin, Bonn: J. H. W. Dietz Nachf., 1986), 114–19; Jochen Oltmer, *Migration und Politik in der Weimarer Republik* (Göttingen: Vandenhoeck & Ruprecht, 2005), 309–423.
53. Annemarie Sammartino, *The Impossible Border: Germany and the East, 1914–1922* (Ithaca, NY: Cornell University Press, 2010), 96–119.
54. Oltmer, *Migration und Politik*, 261–7.
55. Edgar Hartwig, 'Deutsche Kolonialgesellschaft', in Dieter Fricke (ed.), *Lexikon zur Parteiengeschichte: Die bürgerlichen und kleinbürgerlichen Parteien und Verbände in Deutschland (1789–1945)*, vol. 1 (Cologne: Pahl-Rugenstein, 1983), 724–48, here 725; Lora Wildenthal, 'Gender and Colonial Politics After the Versailles Treaty', in: Kathleen Canning, Kerstin Barndt, and Kristin McGuire (eds), *Weimar Publics/Weimar Subjects: Rethinking the Political Culture of Germany in the 1920s* (New York, Oxford: Berghahn, 2010), 339–59, figure 346.
56. Florian Krobb and Elaine Martin, 'Introduction: Coloniality in Post-Imperial Culture', in their *Weimar Colonialism: Discourses and Legacies of Post-Imperialism in Germany After 1918* (Bielefeld: Aisthesis, 2014), 9–44, 9–11.
57. Britta Schilling, *Postcolonial Germany: Memories of Empire in a Decolonized Nation* (Oxford: Oxford University Press, 2014), 13–40, figure 14.
58. Kiesel, *Geschichte*, 153.
59. Jörn Leonhard, *Der überforderte Frieden. Versailles und die Welt 1918–1923* (Munich: C. H. Beck, 2018), 1222.
60. This is not the same as talking about a general 'de-globalization' during the 1920s, which is the point of contention for many of the contributions in Christoph Cornelißen and Dirk van Laak (eds), *Weimar und die Welt: Globale Verflechtungen der ersten deutschen Republik* (Göttingen: Vandenhoeck & Ruprecht, 2020). See for instance Gabriele Lingelbach, 'Globalgeschichtliche Perspektiven auf die Weimarer Republik: Globalisierungs- und Deglobalisierungstendenzen in der Zwischenkriegszeit', 23–49, here 25.
61. See the chapter by Siegfried Weichlein in this volume.
62. Mommsen, *Rise and Fall*, and Winkler, *Weimar*, represent different versions of the same formula.
63. See Thomas Mergel, 'Überlegungen zu einer Kulturgeschichte der Politik', *Geschichte und Gesellschaft*, 28 (2000), 574–606; Wolfgang Hardtwig, 'Performanz und Öffentlichkeit in der krisenhaften Moderne: Visualisierung des Politischen in Deutschland 1900-1936', in Herfried Münkler and Jens Hacke (eds), *Strategien der Visualisierung: Verbildlichung als Mittel der politischen Kommunikation* (Frankfurt/Main, New York: Campus, 2009), 71–92. Important edited collections include: Wolfgang Hardtwig (ed.), *Ordnungen in der*

Krise: Zur politischen Kulturgeschichte Deutschlands 1900–1933 (Munich: R. Oldenbourg, 2007); Ute Daniel et al. (eds), *Politische Kultur und Medienwirklichkeiten in den 1920er Jahren* (Munich: Oldenbourg, 2010). A biography of a key player that successfully draws on this new agenda: Wolfram Pyta, *Hindenburg: Herrschaft zwischen Hohenzollern und Hitler* (Munich: Siedler 2007), see esp. 57–67.

64. See the chapter by Chris Dillon in this volume.
65. See the erroneous remark by Evans, *Coming*, 80, that the Weimar Constitution 'was essentially a modified version' of Imperial Germany's 1871 Constitution.
66. See Thomas Mergel, *Parlamentarische Kultur in der Weimarer Republik. Politische Kommunikation, symbolische Politik und Öffentlichkeit im Reichstag* (Düsseldorf: Droste, 2002), and Wolfram Pyta, 'Die Weimarer Republik als Experimentierfeld demokratischer Kompromisskultur', *Historisches Jahrbuch*, 140 (2020), 22–67.
67. See for instance Ernst Lemmer, *Manches war doch anders: Erinnerungen eines deutschen Demokraten* (Frankfurt/Main: Heinrich Scheffler, 1968), 151; Gustav Radbruch, *Der innere Weg: Aufriß meines Lebens*, 2nd ed. (Göttingen: Vandenhoeck & Ruprecht, 1961), 130.
68. See the chapters by Nadine Rossol and Joachim Häberlen in this volume, and Nadine Rossol, *Performing the Nation in Interwar Germany: Sport, Spectacle and Political Symbolism 1926–1936* (Basingstoke: Palgrave, 2010).
69. See Kathleen Canning, 'Between Crisis and Order. The Imaginary of Citizenship in the Aftermath of War', in Hardtwig (ed.), *Ordnungen in der Krise*, 215–28.
70. A balanced account of women in Weimar politics in Helen Boak, *Women in the Weimar Republic* (Manchester: Manchester University Press, 2013), 63–133.
71. As calculated by Detlef Lehnert, '"Weimars" Chancen und Möglichkeiten, Strukturen und Normen—eine Problemskizze', in Michael Dreyer and Andreas Braune (eds), *Weimar als Herausforderung: Die Weimarer Republik und die Demokratie im 21. Jahrhundert* (Stuttgart: Steiner, 2016), 102–21, 108–9.
72. See the landmark study by Karen Hagemann, *Frauenalltag und Männerpolitik: Alltagsleben und gesellschaftliches Handeln von Arbeiterfrauen in der Weimarer Republik* (Bonn: J. H. W. Dietz, 1990).
73. See the chapter by Ute Planert in this volume.
74. See Larry Eugene Jones, *The German Right, 1918–1930: Political Parties, Organized Interests and Patriotic Associations in the Struggle Against Weimar Democracy* (Cambridge, New York: Cambridge University Press, 2020).
75. Evans, *Coming*, 266–88.
76. Dirk Blasius, *Weimars Ende: Bürgerkrieg und Politik 1930–1933* (Göttingen: Vandenhoeck & Ruprecht, 2005).
77. See Dirk Schumann, *Political Violence in the Weimar Republic 1918–1933: Battles for the Streets and Fears of Civil War* (New York: Berghahn Books, 2009).
78. Evans, *Coming*, 229, 257–9, 263–5.
79. See Anders G. Kjøstvedt, 'The Dynamics of Mobilisation: The Nazi Movement in Weimar Berlin', *Politics, Religion and Ideology*, 14 (2013), 338–54, and the chapter by Daniel Siemens in this volume.
80. See Jürgen W. Falter, *Hitlers Wähler* (Munich: C. H. Beck, 1991), 325–7, 340–8, and the chapter by Benjamin Ziemann in this volume.
81. Rudy Koshar, 'From Stammtisch to Party: Nazi Joiners and the Contradictions of Grass Roots Fascism in Weimar Germany', *Journal of Modern History*, 59 (1987), 1–24.

82. Wolfgang Hardtwig, 'Volksgemeinschaft im Übergang: Von der Demokratie zum rassistischen Führerstaat', in Detlef Lehnert (ed.), *Gemeinschaftsdenken in Europa* (Cologne, Weimar: Böhlau, 2013), 227–54.
83. Thomas Mergel, 'Führer, Volksgemeinschaft und Maschine: Politische Erwartungsstrukturen in der Weimarer Republik und dem Nationalsozialismus 1918–1936', in Wolfgang Hardtwig (ed.), *Politische Kulturgeschichte der Zwischenkriegszeit 1918–1939* (Göttingen: Vandenhoeck & Ruprecht, 2005), 91–127; Peter Fritzsche, *Germans into Nazis* (Cambridge, MA, London: Harvard University Press, 1998).
84. See the chapter by Susanne Wein and Martin Ulmer in this volume.
85. See the chapter by Thomas Mergel in this volume.
86. See, among others, the chapters by Susanne Wein and Martin Ulmer and by Daniel Siemens in this volume. See already Larry Eugene Jones, '"The Dying Middle": Weimar Germany and the Fragmentation of Bourgeois Politics', *Central European History*, 5 (1972), 23–54; Peter Fritzsche, 'The NSDAP 1919–1934: From Fringe Politics to the Seizure of Power', in Jane Caplan (ed.), *Nazi Germany* (Oxford: Oxford University Press, 2008), 48–72, 60, 69 on the 'national socialist consensus'.
87. Sebastian Ullrich, 'Mehr als Schall und Rauch: Der Streit um den Namen der ersten deutschen Demokratie 1918–1949', in Föllmer and Graf, *Die 'Krise' der Weimarer Republik*, 187–207, quotes 190, 199.
88. See the chapters by Siegfried Weichlein, Todd Weir and Udi Greenberg, and Benjamin Ziemann in this volume.
89. See Benjamin Ziemann, 'Weimar was Weimar: Politics, Culture and the Emplotment of the German Republic', *German History*, 28 (2010), 542–71, here 545–6, 566–7.
90. Some elements of education reform are covered in the chapter by Barbara Stambolis. For a thorough coverage of schools and pedagogical reform see the excellent volume by Dieter Langewiesche and Heinz-Elmar Tenorth (eds), *Handbuch der deutschen Bildungsgeschichte*, vol. 5. *1918–1945: Die Weimarer Republik und die nationalsozialistische Diktatur* (Munich: C. H. Beck, 1989).
91. See Heinz Reif (ed.), *Ostelbische Agrargesellschaft im Kaiserreich und in der Weimarer Republik: Agrarkrise—junkerliche Interessenpolitik—Modernisierungsstrategien* (Berlin: Akademie, 1994); Eckart Conze et al. (eds), *Aristokratismus und Moderne: Adel als politisches und kulturelles Konzept 1890–1945* (Cologne: Böhlau, 2013). On the Nazification of the aristocracy see Stephan Malinowski, *Nazis and Nobles: The History of a Misalliance* (Oxford: Oxford University Press, 2020).
92. See Thomas Elsaesser, *Weimar Cinema and After: Germany's Historical Imaginary* (London: Routledge, 2000); Christian Rogowski (ed.), *The Many Faces of Weimar Cinema: Rediscovering Germany's Filmic Legacy* (Rochester, NY: Camden House, 2010). Siegfried Kracauer, *From Caligari to Hitler. A Psychological History of the German Film* (London: Dobson, 1947), seems now dated in its teleological narrative that interprets Weimar cinema mainly as a contributor to the rise of the Nazis.
93. Daniel Bessner, 'The Ghosts of Weimar: The Weimar Analogy in American Thought', *Social Research*, 84 (2017), 831–55.
94. Useful entry points into these debates are Andreas Wirsching (ed.), *Herausforderungen der parlamentarischen Demokratie: Die Weimarer Republik im europäischen Vergleich* (Munich: Oldenbourg, 2007); Thomas Mergel, 'Dictatorship and Democracy, 1918–1939', in Smith (ed.), *Oxford Handbook*, 423–53.

95. Helmut Walser Smith, 'The Vanishing Point of German History', *History and Memory*, 17 (2005), 269–95.
96. Christian Gerlach, *The Extermination of the European Jews* (Cambridge: Cambridge University Press, 2016), 36.

Bibliography

Becker, Sabina, *Experiment Weimar: Eine Kulturgeschichte Deutschlands 1918–1933* (Darmstadt: wbg Academic, 2018).
Bessel, Richard, *Germany After the First World War* (Oxford: Oxford University Press, 1993).
Boak, Helen, *Women in the Weimar Republic* (Manchester: Manchester University Press, 2013).
Canning, Kathleen, Kerstin Barndt, and Kristin McGuire (eds), *Weimar Publics/Weimar Subjects: Rethinking the Political Culture of Germany in the 1920s* (New York: Berghahn, 2010).
Fritzsche, Peter, *Germans into Nazis* (Cambridge, MA, London: Harvard University Press, 1998).
Kolb, Eberhard, *The Weimar Republic*, 2nd ed. (London: Routledge, 2005).
McElligott, Anthony, *Rethinking the Weimar Republic: Authority and Authoritarianism 1916–1936* (London: Bloomsbury, 2014).
Mommsen, Hans, *The Rise and Fall of Weimar Democracy* (Chapel Hill, NC, London: University of North Carolina Press, 1996).
Peukert, Detlev, *The Weimar Republic: The Crisis of Classical Modernity* (New York: Hill & Wang, 1993).
Stibbe, Matthew, *Germany 1914–1933: Politics, Society and Culture* (Harlow: Longman, 2010).

PART I
KEY EVENTS AND POLITICAL DEVELOPMENTS

CHAPTER 2

THE GERMAN REVOLUTION OF 1918/19

CHRISTOPHER DILLON

On Sunday 10 November 1918, the influential liberal newspaper *Berliner Tageblatt* greeted the overthrow of Kaiser Wilhelm II as 'the greatest of all revolutions'.[1] Like the reigning dynasties of the other German states, Prussia's House of Hohenzollern had just been deposed by a popular uprising of soldiers and civilians. Political power was now vested in an all-socialist Council of People's Delegates (Rat der Volksbeauftragten), co-chaired by veterans of the German Social Democratic Party (SPD). Just one week ago, reflected the *Tageblatt* editor, Theodor Wolff, 'there was a military and civilian apparatus so fortified, so enmeshed and so deeply rooted, that its rule seemed assured for many ages'. Now it had been swept away on a single Saturday afternoon, in scenes reminiscent of the great paintings of the French Revolution. 'Never before', rejoiced Wolff, 'was such a solidly built and fortified Bastille taken in one fell swoop'.[2]

Wolff's assessment may appear eccentric in light of subsequent events. The German Revolution of 1918/19 would dash the hopes of its most ardent supporters. It also disappointed generations of German historians, who fixated on its shortcomings and missed opportunities.[3] But historical judgements are becoming more qualified, more inclined to reflect the dramatic changes experienced in 1918/19. The German Revolution delivered an armistice, a republic, parliamentary democracy, and the first-ever socialist government of an advanced industrial economy. In the context of the tumultuous post-war history of central and eastern Europe, it did so comparatively peaceably. As well as recognizing these achievements, this chapter advocates deeper engagement with the synchronicity of the German Revolution as a lived and contingent event. In the first weeks of November 1918, hardly any newspaper or commentator, regardless of political leaning, doubted that a genuine and historic revolution had taken place.[4] The revolution unleashed the political imagination of its supporters and mobilized across class, gender, and generation. It was widely experienced, for better or for worse, as a political, social, and cultural rupture. A reappreciation of the revolution in these terms will register its societal penetration, its destruction of inherited patterns of authority, its generation of new affiliations and antipathies, and its complex and contested legacy for the Weimar Republican project.

A Revolution in Context

At the end of September 1918, the German Army's Supreme Command (OHL) concluded that the military situation on the western and Balkan fronts necessitated an immediate armistice. General Erich Ludendorff, the OHL's Quartermaster General and driving force, called for a new government with democratic credentials to negotiate with the American President Woodrow Wilson. Hitherto scathing in his rejection of domestic political reform, Ludendorff hoped in this way to preserve the German army as a political force and to pass the buck for the peace terms onto civilian politicians.[5] Popular pressure for constitutional reform had been building since the much-vaunted 'civic truce' (*Burgfrieden*) declared on the German home front at the outbreak of war in 1914.[6] The cumulative strains of mobilization for industrialized warfare had exposed and aggravated domestic fractures, as it had in all combatant nations.[7] War bonds, casualty lists, and ration cards gave ordinary Germans a direct personal stake in the state's economic and military decisions. The protracted duration of the war and increasingly desperate material shortages began to undermine the perceived legitimacy of Germany's autocratic political system. The resultant accumulation of popular war-weariness and social grievances by no means amounted to a coherent revolutionary programme, but it did intersect with the critique and political language of increasingly vocal radical and socialist groups on the home front. This intersection was most visible in rising industrial militancy and appeared particularly menacing to the political order when an anti-war faction of the SPD peeled away to form the Independent German Social Democratic Party (USPD) in April 1917.

The most serious such expression of wartime dissent were the great munitions strikes of January 1918. These were characterized by Arthur Rosenberg, the pioneering historian of the Weimar Republic, as a 'dress rehearsal' (*Generalprobe*) for the revolution.[8] A transnational phenomenon, the strikes began in Austria in protest against the Central Powers' implacable stance during the Brest-Litovsk peace treaty negotiations with Bolshevik Russia. The annexationist demands made by the OHL offended socialist sensibilities and also starkly contradicted the *Burgfrieden* narrative that the Central Powers were waging a purely defensive struggle against Russian despotism. More than a million German workers downed tools in industrial centres across the Reich, demanding peace without annexations, the restoration of civil liberties, the end of military discipline in factories, and reform of the Prussian state parliament franchise that gave Prussian conservatives so much power under Bismarck's 1871 Constitution.[9] These demands were relayed via so-called workers' councils (*Arbeiterräte*), factory-based committees first elected during industrial disputes the previous year. The terminology recalled the *soviets* (councils) of Russian revolutionary culture and signified the strikers' repudiation of the traditional institutions of the German labour movement, which they regarded as compromised by participation in the *Burgfrieden*. The courts proceeded in draconian fashion against purported agitators and ringleaders. Around 50,000 strikers were drafted into the army, adding another combustible element to officers' by now wavering authority at the front.

Until the summer of 1918, Ludendorff remained confident that military victory for the Central Powers would shore up Germany's time-honoured political arrangements. But now, on 5 October, the relatively liberal Prince Max von Baden was appointed German Chancellor. Social Democratic ministers also entered the Cabinet for the first time. Most important of all, a constitutional amendment was passed requiring the Chancellor to enjoy the confidence of a majority of legislators in the Reichstag (the German parliament). To thunderous applause from his Reichstag caucus, the Majority Social Democratic Party (MSPD) leader Friedrich Ebert hailed the October 1918 reforms as the 'birth of German democracy'.[10] The October reforms and accompanying armistice request did seemingly address the primary causes of domestic disquiet. The course of the ensuing weeks, however, brings to mind Alexis de Tocqueville's dictum that 'the most critical moment for bad governments is the one which witnesses their first steps towards reform'.[11] The reforms were at once too modest for the discontented and too extravagant for supporters of the Imperial German order. The infelicitous optics of appointing a prince to the position of democratic Chancellor were compounded by von Baden's political ineptitude and unwarranted self-regard.[12] The parliamentarization of German government had been won without a political spectacle to arrest the senses. Military authority remained ubiquitous and food shortages desperate: as Rosenberg put it, 'the man on the street' could not discern the change.[13] In the newly empowered Reichstag, the normally dour USPD leader Hugo Haase demanded greater ambition and expressed the near millenarian horizon of expectation taking shape on the radical left. 'We are convinced', he enthused, 'that out of all this misery there will finally emerge the complete emancipation of humanity'.[14]

On the nationalist right, meanwhile, the mood was darkening. The Pan-German newspaper of record, *Deutsche Zeitung*, decried the October reforms as a 'bloodless coup' orchestrated by sinister Jewish forces.[15] Hot-headed plans for a defiant *levée en masse* (*Volkskrieg*) against the armistice terms were entertained even by milder spirits such as the industrial tycoon and public intellectual Walther Rathenau.[16] At the same time, the naval top brass was developing an ambitious scheme to launch the entire High Seas fleet towards Britain and rekindle domestic enthusiasm for the war through a stirring engagement with the Royal Navy. The orders were issued on 29 October, the day after the constitutional reforms were passed in the Reichstag. Within hours, the operation was abandoned as stokers and sailors in Wilhelmshaven mutinied at what they saw as a suicide mission. The uprising soon spread to the port city of Kiel. On 3 November, after military police fired into a crowd of sailors and civilians, leaving nine dead and twenty-nine wounded, the authorities lost control of the situation. When the MSPD's military spokesman, Gustav Noske, arrived to negotiate with the mutineers, a large crowd serenaded him with bullish, though as yet premature, cries of 'glory to the Republic'.[17]

The sailors' mutiny inspired similar uprisings across the other north German ports—Lübeck, Bremen, Cuxhaven, and, critically, Hamburg, Germany's second largest city.[18] A party of Kiel sailors arrived here by railway and would, in the ensuing days, participate as rail-borne revolutionary evangelists in upheavals throughout the Reich.[19] Accounts of the November revolution frequently speak of its 'spreading' like a 'fire', 'flood', or even, in one case, an 'avalanche', from the Baltic Sea across Germany.[20] But this fatalistic imagery does not capture the localized dynamics of a popular mobilization against war and authoritarianism. In the far south of the Reich, Bavaria's venerable Wittelsbach dynasty was overthrown in Munich on 7 November even as the upheaval in Hamburg was unfurling. Although a contingent of sailors was stranded in the city due to the disruption in Kiel, they were not party to the Bavarian revolutionaries' planning. The USPD propagandist Kurt Eisner, mindful that potentially de-escalating constitutional concessions were due to be introduced in Bavaria the following day, had already resolved to use a scheduled anti-war rally on the Theresienwiese as a springboard for revolution.[21] In Frankfurt am Main, too, the presence of detachments of uniformed sailors was largely ornamental in a localized revolution where Independents and factory activists made the running.[22] In Berlin, a latecomer to the revolution, von Baden's final gambit of sealing off the capital's rail connections failed because the driving force behind events there were local Revolutionary Shop Stewards (*Revolutionäre Obleute*). This network of militant factory activists had formed in opposition to the *Burgfrieden* politics of the trade union movement and played a leading role in the wartime munitions strikes. The defection, on 9 November, of the Berlin-based Naumburg Rifle Battalion, reputedly unmatched in its devotion to the Hohenzollern dynasty, sealed Wilhelm's fate. Without even consulting him, von Baden announced the Kaiser's abdication. Berlin's enterprising press ensured this bombshell news was circulated in print within fifteen minutes.[23]

On the same day, von Baden ceded his office of Reich Chancellor to Ebert as the MSPD leader. A transitional Council of People's Delegates was formed from three members each of the MSPD and USPD, co-chaired by Ebert and Haase. The hope that this symbolized a healing of the wartime schism in the Social Democratic movement was widely shared on the German left. The People's Delegates were endorsed in office by an assembly of representatives from Berlin workers' and soldiers' councils. Ebert's dual role as Chancellor and co-chair of the People's Delegates made him the key figure. But his authority was, in practice, ambiguous. The handover of the Chancellorship violated Article 15 of the Imperial Constitution, according to which only the Kaiser could appoint the Reich Chancellor.[24] The Berlin councils' claim to speak for a national council movement was, at best, tenuous. Their assembly on 9 November, moreover, made demands for the socialization of industrial sectors and for the restoration of diplomatic relations with Bolshevik Russia which strayed beyond Ebert's presumptive caretaker mandate.[25] The most important measures of the revolution were simply inaugurated by proclamation on 12 November. These were the restoration of civil liberties, the abolition of laws that restricted rural workers in their personal freedom and contractual arrangements, and the promise of universal suffrage. On 15 November, the introduction of an eight-hour working day, a long-standing demand of the labour movement, was announced as part of the so-called Stinnes-Legien Pact, following negotiations between German industrialists and trade unions. These were major and enduring achievements. They did not, however, heal the rifts on the German left. Rival declarations of a new republic on 9 November by the MSPD's Philipp Scheidemann, from the Reichstag, and by the radical Karl Liebknecht, from the extra-parliamentary venue of the Royal Palace, augured ill for the harmony of the revolutionary movement. The British Prime Minister David Lloyd George warned his War Cabinet the following day that events were 'taking a similar course in Germany to that which had taken place in Russia'.[26]

REVOLUTIONARY MOBILIZATIONS

'No other popular event in German history', judges one historian, 'had filled the national stage so completely or had enrolled so many participants as had the November Revolution'.[27] The revolution generated a civic energy which astonished observers. To Ben Hecht, the well-connected Germany correspondent for the *Chicago Daily News*, every day 'was like a presidential pre-election eve at home ... All was politics, revolution, antirevolution.'[28] The diarist Victor Klemperer felt similarly. The revolution was 'always there, from morning to evening ... day in and day out', he recorded.[29] Activists like Toni Sender, a female firebrand in Frankfurt, worked around the clock, mortgaging their health to the revolutionary cause.[30] By March 1919, jaded by months of upheaval, the renowned sociologist Max Weber despaired of 'the general vain and bustling inclination to participate in everything'.[31] The crowds on the streets in early November 1918 betokened a period of intense political mobilization and contestation which would echo throughout the history of the new republic. The council movement that had emerged from industrial disputes during the war flourished across Germany, assuming diverse forms and enrolling new social constituencies. Weber himself was, early on, an enthusiastic participant in Heidelberg. Elections called in December 1918 for a constituent National Assembly inspired feverish campaigning across the political spectrum. Beyond the formal institutions of public life, too, social venues and the everyday were politicized. Urban centres teemed with demobilizing soldiers expecting state recognition of their sacrifice in the post-war reconstruction. Horizons of hope and foreboding, expectations raised and dashed, would shape the course of the German revolution in powerful and unpredictable ways.

In early November 1918, power was vested in the streets. The crowds of the revolution were the spearhead of a popular counter-mobilization against militarism and autocracy. These crowds are less storied than the multitudes of August 1914 who greeted the outbreak of war with jubilation in German cities.[32] But their visual record is more impressive. The November 1918 crowds were more diverse and their aesthetic less choreographed by a learned patriotic repertoire. Photographs and newspaper reports register organized radicals, striking workers, sailors and soldiers, women, teenagers, and curious onlookers of all backgrounds.[33] These crowds performed the November revolution as political theatre and spectacle. Their usurpation of public space defied wartime restrictions on freedom of assembly and the relationship between participants and observers was liminal.[34] The near-universal unwillingness of police and military assets to disperse crowds rendered the collapse of state authority unsparingly visible. Never before, in decades of ebullient political rallies, had protestors milled around freely on Berlin's Unter den Linden, the grand stage of Imperial pageantry. All across Germany, town halls, police stations, prisons, barracks, newspaper offices, train and telegraph stations were rallying points for a mass performance of popular sovereignty. Above all, the crowds signified the triumph of a social protest movement rather than a transfer of political power building on the October reforms. This explains why they somewhat unnerved the Council of People's Delegates, the high political beneficiaries of the revolution. Schooled in the SPD's elaborate organizational structures, Ebert and Scheidemann were left feeling queasy and exposed by the unpredictable politics of the pavements. Ebert's very first 'Appeal to German Citizens' on 9 November admonished them to 'clear the streets!'[35] 'Calm and order' (*Ruhe und Ordnung*) were the anointed watchwords of the MSPD's revolution. The new government, nevertheless, drew populist legitimacy from the memory of the November 1918 crowds, and the streets would remain critical sites of political assertion and contestation. The quiescence of urban public space was closely monitored by an excitable news media as a barometer of order and 'anarchy'.[36] Radical spirits on the left, in particular, discerned in this as an opportunity to exert pressure on the Ebert government.

Similar ambivalence attended the relationship between the government and a rival claimant to popular democratic sovereignty, the council movement. The Council of People's Delegates welcomed the endorsement of Berlin's councils on 9 November. But its MSPD contingent, in particular, viewed the council phenomenon with grave misgivings as a Russian import alien to the traditions of the German labour movement.[37] The councils also soured relations between the MSPD and bourgeois political groups for whom they were, at best, a waste of public funds and, at worst, instruments of Leninist class dictatorship. The MSPD was committed to convoking a democratic constituent assembly, which was unlikely to deliver a socialist majority, as soon as the demobilization of the army permitted. From this perspective, the councils seemed likely to be purely a transitional instrument until the National Assembly settled Germany's constitutional arrangements. Much ink has been spilled over the decades by historians debating whether or not this was a missed opportunity for the young republic.[38] The councils, in this reading, might have been deployed strategically to enforce a more thorough democratization of the economy and state administration. These debates have generated invaluable empirical research, but their contours are drawn by counterfactual speculations which diminish the synchronic integrity of the 1918/19 revolution as a lived historical event. In the following, the council movement will be read instead as a form of civic revolutionary mobilization.

By the time the revolution began in Berlin on 9 November, workers' and soldiers' councils had been formed in every west German city and the movement stretched deep into the south.[39] Indeed, the council scene was especially lively in Bavaria, Germany's second largest and southernmost state. Labour movement activists throughout Bavaria responded with enthusiasm to Prime Minister Kurt Eisner's inaugural invitation to 'take part in the construction of a new world!' A far more adventurous spirit than Ebert, Eisner was attentive to revolution's need for spectacle and charismatic example. He enthused to Theodor Wolff on 22 November that the Bavarian revolution was 'a magnificent piece of theatre'.[40] More than any other politician of the era, Eisner grasped the propaganda potential of the council movement as a performance of transformation. He cast the Bavarian councils as pedagogic instruments of a direct, substantive democracy which would complement and ultimately supplant the stale formalism of 'bourgeois parliamentarism'.[41] Within a fortnight of his triumph in Munich, the council movement had reached every town and perhaps a majority of villages in Bavaria.[42] In the provinces, citizens gathered in public space at the invitation of left-wing activists for the constituent meeting of a workers' council. Sometimes this was a festive occasion, accompanied by music. Almost always there were hortatory speeches extolling the historic moment at hand with paeans, so characteristic of the German Revolution, to maintaining 'calm and order'.[43] The councils' members, voted in by acclamation, tended to be veterans of the labour movement with the necessary experience in committee work. It is important to note that, even in Bavaria, this first generation of council activists broadly supported elections for a national constituent assembly as soon as possible.

Throughout Germany, soldiers' councils were formed in quick succession to workers' councils if the local garrisons had not already constituted one of their own accord.[44] In contrast to neighbouring Austria, where the two types of council remained discrete, they usually assumed joint authority as a workers' and soldiers' council. Ensconced comfortably in town halls or district offices adorned with red flags, the workers' representatives busied themselves with social issues such as unemployment assistance and equitable food distribution, while the soldiers' councils were responsible for public order. Majority and Independent Social Democrat council activists continued to disagree vehemently about wartime *Burgfrieden* politics, but generally worked companionably to address the administrative challenges they had inherited.[45] The councils waged a constant struggle against hoarding and the black market by ensuring existing directives were enforced, relishing any ruffled feathers this caused. They compiled registers of landlords with spare rooms to ameliorate a housing crisis that was already severe in towns bloated by wartime manufacturing and that worsened throughout the demobilization. Their deliberations and proclamations were communicated through the local press, where they were accorded prominence by editors. One distinguished historian contends that these quotidian council activities were 'valuable' but 'entirely non-political'.[46] This assessment rests on a very narrow, statist conception of the political. For the German Revolution was made by feverish activity from below as well as high political drama. Weber celebrated the civic spirit he witnessed on the Heidelberg Workers' and Soldiers' Council, which had done 'things splendidly and without any idle talk'.[47] The topos of the aloof Wilhelmine bureaucrat was a guiding anti-type for council members, who held surgeries for those seeking support and were inundated by citizens offering advice.[48] They often dealt brusquely at first with local dignitaries and bureaucracies. Municipal elites throughout the Reich, from elected officials, bureaucrats, and army officers to priests, pastors, and newspaper editors, had, almost without exception, acted as cheerleaders for the war effort and its cult of 'holding out' (*Durchhalten*) in dire material adversity. In this respect, the council movement from below was a perpetuation of the politicized wartime peace movement. The evaporation of monarchical and, as it seemed, military authority exposed local elites to the sobering claims of popular sovereignty. The councils empowered new political actors to challenge a patrician hierarchy previously insulated by restrictive property-based communal franchises. This lent their formation something of the character and dynamics of local insurgencies in a world turning 'upside down'.[49] In Hamburg, for example, despite a strong local labour movement, city governance had been in the hands of wealthy senators elected for life. On 12 November, the new Workers' and Soldiers' Council marched into the Senate and curtly dismissed its members at gun point. 'All bridges between the present and the past are burned', the senators were informed.[50]

In practice, the complexities of addressing Hamburg's troubled public finances soon prompted a retreat from this revolutionary maximalism. The Senate was permitted to reconvene with four council representatives added to its ranks with the power of veto. This strategy of supervising, rather than replacing, municipal institutions became typical across Germany. Although it disappointed the more radical elements of the council movement, the political symbolism of supervision should not be overlooked. In Frankfurt, for example, the youthful Toni Sender sat as a council delegate on the city's fusty and geriatric Board of Aldermen. She was also elected as a USPD delegate to the city council. It is indicative of the civic invigoration brought by the revolution that its public galleries, deserted during the Kaiserreich, were now packed to the rafters.[51] The extent to which council delegates were able to remove recalcitrant officials varied greatly. The Council of People's Delegates and the governments of the German states were anxious not to disrupt public administration and fought to minimize dismissals and resignations. The struggle was particularly unequal in conservative East Prussia, where only 15 of 105 *Landräte* (county administrators) were removed from their posts.[52] It was bleaker still in the areas of the Rhineland occupied by Allied soldiers on 1 December 1918 under the armistice terms. The military occupiers did not recognize Rhineland councils. Despite loudly stated war aims of democratizing the German state, Allied officers worked solely through the Wilhelmine administrative apparatus. The US army explained that this gave them access to 'thoroughly capable officials' rather than 'appointees of Workingmen's Councils whose selections were made during the hysteria of revolution'.[53] The French army, which had already dissolved councils formed in Alsace-Lorraine, took an equally hard line on those in its zone of occupation. The Communist International concluded bitterly that 'the Allies are strangling the revolution in the occupied areas'.[54] The prospect of council radicalism and 'Bolshevism' provoking Allied military intervention on a still broader scale would remain a structural constraint throughout the revolution.

The German council movement also diverged from the Russian precedent in its organizational diversity. While rural Russia was slow to engage with the soviet phenomenon, peasant councils (*Bauernräte*) emerged rapidly in parts of agrarian Germany. There were spontaneous and radical peasant councils in Upper Silesia and Bavaria, regions with traditions of rural populism.[55] More typical of German peasant councils, however, were those sponsored by the old Agrarian League (*Bund der Landwirte*) as a conservative counterweight to urban trade unions and workers' councils. These were characterized by a defensive, anti-democratic outlook.[56] Rather more engaged were the middle-class councils (*Bürgerräte*) formed in towns and cities throughout Germany to broker bourgeois interests in the reshaped political fray. Their political tenor was anti-socialist but not necessarily anti-revolutionary. Indeed, there was an insurgent quality to the middle-class councils' independence from the traditional, patrician institutions of bourgeois political culture.[57] The mobilization of middle-class occupational interests in the *Bürgerräte* was nevertheless distasteful to many activists of the workers' movement, for whom the councils were instruments of emancipation rather than privilege. Addressing an assembly of workers' councils in Berlin on 19 November, the Revolutionary Shop Steward leader Richard Müller declared: 'Comrades, be aware! We already have "landlords' councils." What's next? "Millionaires' councils"? Such councils we don't need.'[58]

One social constituency that was, in contrast, extremely poorly represented by the council movement was women. German women had grown ever more visible in wartime public life as teachers, nurses, postal workers, and tram conductors, as well as in the charity and welfare sectors.[59] Even allowing for the tendency of police and officialdom to linger in their reports over female contributions to domestic unrest, it is clear that women were central to the public articulation of social dissent during the war.[60] Women led the hard-pressed German pacifist movement and were prominent in industrial disputes both as strikers and shop stewards.[61] The enfranchisement of German women, long demanded by the SPD, was arguably the single most transformative measure of the revolution. At a stroke, the nascent German democracy rested on an electorate in which females outnumbered males by some two million. On 17 November 1918, the Women's Suffrage Society and the SPD held a celebratory event in Frankfurt's Paulskirche.[62] The revered site of the National Assembly of the 1848 revolution, it signified the fulfilment of that earlier revolution's emancipatory ideals. The socialist women's magazine *Die Gleichheit* ('Equality') rejoiced that German women were now 'the freest in the world'.[63] The Munich suffragists Lida Gustav Heymann and Anita Augspurg likened the advent of revolution to 'a beautiful dream' and recalled 'winter months full of work, hope, and happiness'.[64] Much of their work focused on the political education of women in preparation for the National Assembly elections. On Eisner's insistence, a Section for Women's Rights was created within the new Bavarian Ministry for Social Welfare. In Braunschweig, Minna Faßhauer became Germany's first-ever female government minister when she was appointed People's Commissar for Education.[65] The socialists Clara Zetkin and Rosa Luxemburg, the outstanding intellectual force on the radical left, were influential advocates of a second, social revolution. On the political right, German women promoted conservative and maternalist values.[66] In most German states, nevertheless, women had been barred from formal politics until 1908 and were often still treated as intruders into a masculine sphere. On 19 November, Heymann brought a packed beer hall in Munich to its feet when she warned that forces were stirring to roll back women's hard-won equality.[67] The scholar and social reformer Dr Rosa Kempf was heckled when she became the first women to address Bavaria's revolutionary Provisional National Council the following month. She reported attending political meetings which routinely descended into violence and feared that a general atmosphere of menace inhibited other women from participating in the revolution.[68] The thirty-seven female legislators returned to the National Assembly in January 1919 also faced a mixed reception from male colleagues.[69] But at 8 per cent of the total deputies, female participation in the Assembly comfortably outshone that of the supposedly radical council movement. At the first Reich Congress of Workers and Soldiers' Councils in December 1918, just two of the 489 delegates were women.

Counter-Revolutionary Mobilizations

This dismal showing was congruent with a broader masculinization of the revolution by the turn of the year. The demobilization of the German army, which began in late November, was decisive. The orderly return of front-line units was celebrated at a lavish homecoming parade in Berlin, whose streets teemed, for the first time since the revolution, with army officers, garlands, and with the old black-white-red flag of Imperial Germany. At the largest of these events, on 10 December, Ebert lauded the troops' 'manful' fortitude and maintained that 'no enemy has overcome you'.[70] The vast majority of soldiers, once they had crossed the Rhine, thought only of getting home to their families. They were not the brutalized, vengeful veterans of later nationalist mythology. By mid-February 1919, almost the entire eight million-strong army had been demobilized.[71] German women bore the economic brunt, losing their jobs to returning veterans in what the feminist journal *Die Frau* characterized as 'an all-out backlash against working women in general'.[72] Irrespective of the subjective outlook of the soldiers themselves, their return to German soil fired the counter-revolutionary imagination. Right-wing forces re-emerged emboldened under the cover of the army. On 6 December, a group of mid-ranking army officers attempted to arrest Richard Müller's Executive Council and to install Ebert as dictator. Ebert politely demurred and the scheme quickly collapsed. But news of the attempted putsch reached a demonstration in north Berlin organized by the Spartacist League, a far-left faction led by Rosa Luxemburg and Karl Liebknecht. A unit of sixty loyalist soldiers was dispatched to intercept the Spartacists near a tram stop. Seemingly in a state of panicked excitement, these troops opened fire on an incoming tram at the cost of sixteen civilian fatalities.[73] The most lethal episode of violence in the revolution to date, it set the scene for six weeks of violent unrest in the capital.

This incident was not the German army's first intervention in revolutionary politics. On 10 November, the very day that Theodor Wolff celebrated the demise of Prussian militarism in the *Berliner Tageblatt*, Ludendorff's successor Wilhelm Groener spoke to Ebert. He assured him of the OHL's support, subject to the preservation of the officer corps and the convocation of a constituent assembly. The significance often attached to these pleasantries as a 'pact' is exaggerated. For one thing, the ability of either party to shape events remained limited. On 16 December 1918, the Congress of Councils convened in the Prussian State Parliament. Although it voted by 400 to 50 votes in favour of January elections for the National Assembly, the Congress also passed, unanimously, the so-called Seven Hamburg Points which demanded the elimination of military rank and abolition of the standing army.[74] It also became clear over Christmas that Groener lacked dependable military resources to support Ebert. For some time, relations had been souring between the government and the People's Naval Division (Volksmarinedivision), a unit created primarily from Kiel sailors after 9 November. On 23 December, the division revolted against the withholding of its pay and kidnapped the Berlin MSPD city commander Otto Wels. Ebert requested the Prussian War Minister to send in troops, who began shelling the division's base on the morning of Christmas Eve. But the assault ended in crushing humiliation for the government and OHL soldiers, who lost fifty-six men to the rebels' eleven.

This debacle, dubbed 'Ebert's Bloody Christmas' by the Spartacists, had two important consequences. The USPD withdrew from the Council of People's Delegates in protest at the use of military violence against sailors whom it honoured as heroes of the revolution. Its left wing, already chafing at the Congress of Councils' vote for a National Assembly, was now in the ascendancy. Second, the government and OHL redoubled their search for robust military assets to protect the state against the far left and to guard the Assembly. At the beginning of January, to ease the demobilization process, the War Ministry announced that soldiers unable to find work could volunteer to remain in the army until they did so. It was largely from this pool of men that the Freikorps, the shock troops of the counter-revolution, were initially recruited.[75] On 4 January, Ebert and Gustav Noske, who had joined the government when the Independents departed, inspected the first of these new formations at Zossen, an army base near Berlin. Impressed by their masculine bearing, Noske reportedly slapped Ebert on the shoulder in delight.[76]

These volunteers did not have to wait long to wage counter-revolution. A few days previously, in an atmosphere of bitter recrimination on the left, the German Communist Party (KPD) had been formed. Its founding delegates voted overwhelmingly against participating in the National Assembly elections.[77] The resolution, which implied a preference for putschist adventure, was passed against the express wishes of Luxemburg and Liebknecht. This dynamic was echoed often in the following months, as the leaderships of the Communists, shop stewards, and USPD either lost control over or deferred to revolutionary impulses within the membership. The best-known instantiation of spontaneous insurrectionism is the January 1919 uprising in Berlin. Its popular descriptor of the 'Spartacist Revolt' is highly misleading, because it was neither planned nor led by Spartacists. The January uprising was provoked by the dismissal of Berlin police chief Emil Eichhorn, a USPD radical and a thorn in the side of the Council of People's Delegates. The KPD, USPD, and shop stewards called for protest demonstrations the following day and were caught completely off guard by a huge turnout running into the hundreds of thousands.[78] Events soon got out of hand when small groups of armed hotheads occupied the premises of the hated MSPD newspaper *Vorwärts* and of liberal publishing houses. Overestimating the appetite for a second, social revolution both inside and outside the capital, Liebknecht and other radicals declared support for the occupations and called for a general strike to overthrow Ebert and prevent the National Assembly elections. In reality, this was a muddled and far-fetched scheme which would likely have petered out of its own accord had it not been for a partisan Berlin media baying for blood.[79] The MSPD, already revelling in a self-righteous posture of protecting order and press freedom, discerned an opportunity to reassert the authority of the state after the humiliation of 'Bloody Christmas' and to cement relations with the bourgeois camp in the future National Assembly. Noske was only too eager to seize the initiative. On 11 January, loyalist soldiers began shelling the *Vorwärts* building and quickly overran the occupiers. Noske now called in his Freikorps to cleanse Berlin's streets of radicals. At least 150 purported Spartacists, many of them simply ordinary strikers, were killed; 400 were arrested, at least nine of whom were murdered in captivity. Now in hiding, Liebknecht wrote that the German Revolution had been 'drowned' by a 'horrendous counter-revolutionary mudslide from backwards elements of the people and the propertied classes'.[80] He was hunted down and soon reported to have been 'shot while attempting to escape', a transparent fiction hotly defended by the MSPD and its collaborators in the media. Luxemburg's corpse was fished out of a canal several months later. Ebert was impressed by the Freikorps' performance. As he remarked to a meeting of the governments of the German states on 31 January, 'if one has sufficient means of force, then governing is easy; it has been very difficult to create a military force; finally, we have succeeded'.[81]

Ebert was as good as his word and the violence in Berlin echoed across the Reich. Socialist or council-based republics were declared at Cuxhaven and Bremen in January 1919, in Mannheim and Brunswick in February, and in Bavaria in April. In every case, the declarations were impetuous and improvised, and in every case exemplary counter-revolutionary terror brought the escapade to a bitter conclusion.[82] One protagonist in this peripatetic campaign of state violence likened it to a 'crusade'.[83] Bremen's council republic, at twenty-five days, lasted the longest. A free port city with a tradition of labour radicalism, its workers' council was controlled by communists and USPD radicals who had refused to recognize the Congress of Councils' call for National Assembly elections. On 10 January, in solidarity with the Berlin uprising, the communists proclaimed an 'Independent Republic of Bremen'. The Bremen Senate was deposed, and local citizens informed that counter-revolutionary activity would be dealt with by firing squad.[84] In practice, the wind was quickly taken from the revolutionaries' sails by the withdrawal of bank credit and by National Assembly elections which revealed little public appetite for radical adventures. Threatened with military intervention by Berlin, the Republic's leadership offered to resign in order to avoid bloodshed. On 4 February, nevertheless, Noske's troops marched in alongside a local Freikorps and deposed the Republic at the cost on both sides of 75 dead and 200 wounded, among them many civilians. A state of siege was declared and surviving council activists rounded up via prepared arrest lists. Some thirty years later, Noske still looked back with pride on the didactic 'example' he had set in Bremen.[85]

These measures against the radical left further shook the MSPD's hold over a labour movement already disenchanted with the returns of the revolution since the decrees of November 1918. The composition of the National Assembly, which returned a non-socialist majority, pointed towards still further compromise with bourgeois forces. The MSPD won 165 of its 423 seats and the UPSD just 22, leaving the notional socialist bloc well short of control. This meant that there was little prospect of the councils securing a meaningful role in the new constitution. The British blockade, which remained in place to ensure German compliance with the future peace treaty, also soured opinion against Entente liberalism. The leadership of the socialist Free Trade Unions, tarnished by its wartime *Burgfrieden* politics, proved unable to contain labour radicalism. Metal workers, in particular, led a spontaneous mass protest movement which repudiated the Stinnes-Legien Pact and championed the immediate socialization of industry.[86] Conceptions of 'socialization' varied extensively. A floating signifier, it could denote the full-fledged nationalization of the commanding heights of industry, the syndicalist takeover of specific enterprises, or simply improved wages and conditions. This polyvalence was an asset. 'The idea of socialization', lamented the Merseburg district President in February 1919, 'has completely turned the heads of the great mass.'[87] Workers' councils moved in a radical direction with the demobilization of the generally moderating soldiers and soldiers' councils. In the Ruhr area, a hotbed of revolutionary activism, early tremors of unrest in late December 1918 developed into a full-blown general strike which ravaged the economy. In central Germany, strikes in chemicals and mining sectors were suspended only after government commitments to introduce workplace councils (*Betriebsräte*) as instruments of economic democracy and to nationalize the coal industry. In Berlin, workers' councils proclaimed a general strike in early March 1919, demanding a formal institutionalization of the council movement and the fulfilment of the Seven Hamburg Points, now updated to include the dissolution of all Freikorps. The government opted for military action in Berlin and the Ruhr. Noske declared a state of siege in the capital and sent in 30,000 Freikorps men kitted out with tanks, howitzers, and military aircraft. On 9 March he issued an infamous, and unlawful, 'Order to Execute' (*Schießbefehl*) under which anyone caught with weapons was to be summarily shot.[88] The carnage lasted until 12 March and resulted in over a thousand lives lost, the majority of them unarmed strikers. Both *Vorwärts* and Wolff's *Berliner Tageblatt* endorsed the conduct of Noske's troops.[89]

This was not the end of the counter-revolutionary 'crusade'. In Bavaria, the political mood had turned against Kurt Eisner with his publication of Foreign Ministry documents highlighting Germany's role in the outbreak of the war. His government's anticlerical school policies were also unpopular and jolted the powerful Catholic establishment out of fatalistic apathy.[90] Yet the advent of a second, council-driven revolution in February still caught most observers off guard. Capital had been fleeing to Bavaria in recent months as a safe haven from the tumult elsewhere in the Reich.[91] The trigger was Eisner's assassination by a right-wing university student on 21 February. The ensuing political chaos crested in the successive declarations of two council republics, the second led by communists. The Munich police were disarmed, and a Red Army of communists, demobilized soldiers, and prisoners of war raised, equipped, and paid for in part through extortion and plundering of the city's wealthier quarters. In poorer districts, posters were put up inviting inhabitants to seize the flats of the well-to-do, while the communist leader Eugen Leviné, a veteran of the 1905 revolution in Russia, pondered starving bourgeois children who otherwise would 'grow into enemies of the proletariat'. A torrent of idealistic decrees socialized mines, banks, universities, and the press. Even the somber mind of the Munich-based novelist Thomas Mann foresaw council socialism spreading triumphantly from Bavaria across Germany to the Entente countries.[92]

In fact, the council regimes' penetration was too shallow for such projects and the whole initiative would doubtless soon have collapsed if left to its own devices. The OHL and MSPD, once again, were not prepared to wait. The deposed Bavarian government of the MSPD Prime Minister Johannes Hoffmann appealed for local Freikorps to crush the 'Russian terror' in Munich. Its haul of 15,000 Bavarian volunteers was complemented by a similar number of troops dispatched south by Berlin.[93] Once again, an Order to Execute was issued to the counter-revolutionary troops. Their thirst for revenge was spurred by the revolutionaries' execution of ten hostages in a Munich school, among them a Bavarian countess. This senseless act became the most notorious atrocity of the entire German Revolution, dominating its public memory in the Weimar and Nazi eras. Yet it was far outmatched by the murderous violence of the Bavarian Freikorps and Noske's troops. Well over 600 people were killed in the military assault on Munich, many, as in Berlin, executed after capture.

The Freikorps campaign of 1919 was a calculated and lethal performance of authority by the German state.[94] It assured the army a prominence in the political life of the future republic out of all proportion to its thinned ranks after the Versailles treaty. The military operations were, however, merely part of a much broader counter-mobilization by pre-revolutionary institutions against the settlement of November 1918. An unreconstructed German judiciary pursued revolutionary activists with unexampled resolve, holding 5,000 trials in Bavaria alone. It stayed notoriously partisan in its counter-revolutionary sympathies long into the republic.[95] German universities remained strongholds of romantic nationalism and of lurid 'stab-in-the-back' conspiracy theories which cast the German Revolution as the cause, rather than consequence, of military defeat.[96] The Christian churches, too, were soon redoubts of an expansive counter-revolutionary milieu. Their traditional role of legitimizing the political order from the pulpit had drawn them deeply into the war effort and the resultant need to account spiritually and theologically for defeat bred an institutional sympathy for stab-in-the-back legends which cast socialists, liberals, and Jews as false prophets.[97] The Protestant churches, nationalist in temper, faced a further crisis of legitimation with the disappearance of the German monarchs, their worldly figureheads and patrons. Article 137 of the Weimar Constitution, which declared 'there is no state church', marked for them a traumatic end to the historic union of throne and altar. Even before the National Assembly met, an anti-revolutionary piety had been fanned by Prussian state decrees banning religious observance in schools.[98] Similar measures by the Eisner regime in Bavaria were denounced as a fresh 'culture war' by Archbishop Michael von Faulhaber, who thundered a few years later that the 1918/19 Revolution had been 'perjury and high treason... forever branded with the mark of Cain'.[99] Neither of the German churches would distinguish itself in articulating democratic values during the republic.

On the anniversary of his ecstatic welcome for the revolution, Theodor Wolff penned a reflective editorial in the *Berliner Tageblatt*. This one was less upbeat. Wolff conceded that 'much of the spirit of the monarchical state' still obtained in republican Germany. Drawn, once again, to comparison with the French Revolution, he bemoaned the German revolutionaries' lack of a 'Beaumarchais to poke fun at the departed' or a 'Marseillaise to lift the spirit'.[100] The prominent socialists Ernst Däumig and Oskar Maria Graf made the same point.[101] The lament was misplaced. The young republic was, after all, hardly lacking in gifted satirists, while the Russian revolutionaries of 1917 had found the *Marseillaise* perfectly serviceable as inspiration.[102] It was paradigmatic of German revolutionaries' self-flagellation for having staged a revolution which was purportedly, in Däumig's words, 'lame in the loins' compared to that of France or Russia.[103] Yet disappointment was baked into the comparison. The social and political order of Germany, an advanced industrialized state, was incongruent with revolutionary programmes devised in agrarian economies. Its institutions were more resilient and deeply woven into the social fabric. As the USPD discovered in the National Assembly elections, there was little public appetite for further revolutionary upheaval. Those elections indicated that even participants in the popular upheavals of November 1918 considered the revolutionary mandate to have been discharged through the armistice, the eviction of the German monarchies, and the convocation of a constituent assembly. They were content to leave the details to be thrashed out between the new democratically elected politicians. The Assembly's record suggests that, on balance, they were vindicated. Although its delegates found only a token role for councils in the new political arrangements, long-standing social democratic goals were fulfilled in the confirmation of universal suffrage, parliamentary democracy, unfettered freedom of association, comprehensive welfare provision, and the separation of church and state. These were clearly achievements of the revolution: as Wolff noted in his 1919 editorial, it was hard to envisage them all being delivered by von Baden under the October reforms, with Ludendorff lurking behind the scenes. By any objective measure, they have a more compelling claim to sit centre stage in accounts of the revolution than the curiously peripheral Spartacists whose fate so captivates the historical imagination. This does not mean that the counter-revolutionary violence of 1919 was peripheral in historical terms, any more than that its many atrocities can be cordoned off from the record of German social democracy as the work of rogue Freikorps reactionaries.[104] This state violence ensured that the German Revolution was brought to an end in 1919, just as the MSPD and OHL intended. To be sure, some chronologies of the revolution extend to 1920, or even 1923, to encompass ongoing labour militancy and attempted insurrections from both right and left. But the German Revolution as a constitutional question reached its conclusion with Ebert's swearing-in as Reich President on 21 August 1919. As Harry Kessler, one of our most astute guides to the era, noted in his diary, the banality of that ceremony belied the historic profundity of the moment.[105] A glance eastwards towards the bloodshed and civil war which ravaged huge swathes of the former Austro-Hungarian, Russian, and Ottoman Empires after 1918 throws the accomplishment into sharp relief.[106] The ensuing struggles of the successor democracies created in central and eastern Europe also alert us to the fundamental vitality of the Weimar Republic as an experiment in popular sovereignty. The German Revolution of 1918/19 delivered a boisterous, disputatious, pluralistic, and sophisticated democracy with all the potentialities attendant upon that government form. It should not be read, ahistorically, through the prism of the republic's eventual demise.

Notes

1. Theodor Wolff, 'Der Erfolg der Revolution', *Berliner Tageblatt*, 10 Nov. 1918.
2. Ibid.
3. Eberhard Kolb, *The Weimar Republic* (London and New York: Routledge, 2005), 149–59.
4. Wolfgang Niess, *Die Revolution von 1918/19 in der deutschen Geschichtsschreibung: Deutungen von der Weimarer Republik bis ins 21. Jahrhundert* (Berlin: De Gruyter, 2013), 18–23.
5. Michael Geyer, 'Insurrectionary Warfare: The German Debate about a Levée en Masse in October 1918', *Journal of Modern History* 73 (2001), 459–527, here 465–73.
6. Benjamin Ziemann, 'Total War as a Catalyst of Change', in Helmut Walser Smith (ed.), *The Oxford Handbook of Modern German History* (Oxford: Oxford University Press, 2015), 378–99.
7. John Horne (ed.), *State, Society, and Mobilization in Europe during the First World War* (Cambridge: Cambridge University Press, 1997).
8. Arthur Rosenberg, *Imperial Germany: The Birth of the German Republic 1871–1918*, tr. Ian F. Morrow (Oxford: Oxford University Press, 1970), 207, 215.
9. Ralf Hoffrogge, *Working Class Politics in the German Revolution: Richard Müller, the Revolutionary Shop Stewards and the Origins of the Council Movement*, tr. Joseph B. Keady (Leiden: Brill, 2014), 49.
10. *Verhandlungen des Reichstags*, vol. 314, 193 Sitzung, 22 Oct. 1918, 6161.
11. Alexis de Tocqueville, *The Old Regime and the Revolution* (New York: Harper & Brothers, 1856), 214.
12. For a withering study, see Lothar Machtan, *Prinz Max von Baden: Der letzte Kanzler des Kaisers. Eine Biographie* (Berlin: Suhrkamp, 2013).
13. Rosenberg, *Imperial Germany*, 255.
14. *Verhandlungen des Reichstags*, vol. 314, 193 session 22 Oct. 1918, 6190.

15. Heinrich August Winkler, *Germany: The Long Road West 1789-1933* (Oxford: Oxford University Press, 2013), 328.
16. Geyer, 'Insurrectionary Warfare', 459-60.
17. Mark Jones, *Founding Weimar: Violence and the German Revolution of 1918/19* (Cambridge: Cambridge University Press, 2016), 38-43.
18. Eberhard Kolb, *Die Arbeiterräte in der deutschen Innenpolitik, 1918-1919* (Frankfurt am Main: Ullstein, 1978), 71-82.
19. Ulrich Kluge, *Soldatenräte und Revolution: Studien zur Militärpolitik in Deutschland, 1918/19* (Göttingen: Vandenhoeck & Ruprecht, 1975), 69-82.
20. 'Avalanche' is used by Francis L. Carsten in *Revolution in Central Europe* (Berkeley and Los Angeles: University of California Press, 1972), 33.
21. Allan Mitchell, *Revolution in Bavaria: The Eisner Regime and the Soviet Republic* (Princeton: Princeton University Press, 1965), 88-94.
22. Kluge, *Soldatenräte*, 75-6; Toni Sender, *The Autobiography of a German Rebel* (London: George Routledge & Sons, 1940), 87-96.
23. Bernhard Fulda, *Press and Politics in the Weimar Republic* (Oxford: Oxford University Press, 2009), 45.
24. Manfred Baldus, 'Die Novemberrevolution und ihre Fragen an das Recht', in Andreas Braune and Michael Dreyer (eds), *Zusammenbruch, Aufbruch, Abbruch? Die Novemberrevolution als Ereignis und Erinnerungsort* (Stuttgart: Franz Steiner Verlag, 2019), 221-32.
25. 'Aufruf der Versammlung der Arbeiter-und Soldatenräte Berlins vom 10 November 1918 mit den Aufgaben für den Rat der Volksbeauftragten', *Dokumente und Materialien zur Geschichte der deutschen Arbeiterbewegung*, vol. 2 (Berlin: Dietz, 1958), 348-9.
26. The National Archives, CAB 23/14, Minutes of the Meeting of the War Cabinet 10 November 1918, 299.
27. Peter Fritzsche, *Germans into Nazis* (Cambridge, MA: Harvard University Press, 1998), 93.
28. Ben Hecht, *A Child of the Century* (New York: Primus, 1985 [1954]), 282.
29. Victor Klemperer, *Munich 1919: Diary of a Revolution* (Cambridge: Polity, 2017), 9-10.
30. Sender, *Autobiography*, 107-13.
31. Marianne Weber, *Max Weber: A Biography* (New Brunswick, NJ: Transaction Books, 1988), 649.
32. Jeffrey Verhey, *The Spirit of 1914: Militarism, Myth and Mobilization in Germany* (Cambridge: Cambridge University Press, 2000), 21-47.
33. For lavish photographic histories of the Revolution in two key loci see Andreas Hallen and Diethart Krebs (eds), *Revolution und Fotografie: Berlin, 1918/19* (Munich: Nishen, 1989); Rudolf Herz and Dirk Halfbrodt (eds), *Revolution und Fotografie: München 1918/19* (Munich: Nishen, 1988).
34. Mark Jones, 'The Crowd in the German November Revolution 1918', in Klaus Weinhauer, Anthony McElligott, and Kirsten Heinsohn (eds), *Germany 1916-1923: A Revolution in Context* (Bielefeld: Transcript, 2015), 37-57.
35. Jones, 'Crowd', 54.
36. Jones, *Founding Weimar*, passim.
37. Kolb, *Arbeiterräte*, 169-82.
38. Kolb, *Weimar Republic*, 149-59; Wolfgang Mommsen, 'The German Revolution, 1918-1920: Political Revolution and Social Protest Movement', in Mommsen, *Imperial Germany: Politics, Culture and Society in an Authoritarian State* (London: Arnold, 1997), 233-54.

39. Kolb, *Arbeiterräte*, 71–113; Kluge, *Soldatenräte*, 48–93; Carsten, *Revolution*, 33–49, 144–209.
40. Theodor Wolff, *Through Two Decades*, tr. E. W. Dicks (London and Toronto: William Heinemann, 1936), 146. Translation corrected.
41. Articulated at length in a speech on 30 Nov. 1918: *Verhandlungen des Provisorischen Nationalrates des Volksstaates Bayern im Jahre 1918/1919. Beilagen-Band, Beilage 2* (Munich, 1919), 13–23.
42. Mitchell, *Revolution*, 145–6; Willy Mattes, *Die Bayerischen Bauernräte: Eine Soziologische und Historische Untersuchung über Bäuerliche Politik* (Stuttgart and Berlin: Cotta, 1921), 96.
43. For a detailed survey of localities, see Carsten, *Revolution*, 144–209.
44. Kluge, *Soldatenräte*; 145–59; Carsten, *Revolution*, 69–77, 144–77.
45. Reinhard Rürup (ed.), *Arbeiter- und Soldatenräte im rheinisch-westfälischen Industriegebiet: Studien zur Geschichte der Revolution 1918/19* (Wuppertal: Hammer, 1975).
46. Carsten, *Revolution*, 194.
47. Weber, *Max Weber*, 633.
48. Moritz Föllmer, 'The Unscripted Revolution: Male Subjectivities in Germany, 1918–1919', *Past and Present*, 240 (2018), 161–92, here 173–5.
49. Martin H. Geyer, *Verkehrte Welt: Revolution, Inflation und Moderne, München 1914–1924* (Göttingen: Vandenhoeck & Ruprecht, 1998).
50. Volker Stalmann (ed.), *Der Hamburger Arbeiter-und Soldatenrat 1918/19* (Düsseldorf: Droste, 2013), 187–9; Carsten, *Revolution*, 144–6.
51. Sender, *Autobiography*, 106–25.
52. Kolb, *Arbeiterräte*, 360, 371–83; Anthony McElligott, *Rethinking the Weimar Republic: Authority and Authoritarianism, 1916–1936* (London: Bloomsbury, 2014), 157–65.
53. *American Military Government of Occupied Germany 1918–1920: Report of the Officer in Charge of Civil Affairs* (Washington, DC, 1943), 268–9.
54. 'Extracts from the Theses on the International Situation and the Policy of the Entente', in Jane Degras (ed.), *The Communist International 1919–1943: Documents*, vol. 1 (Oxford: Oxford University Press, 1956), 33.
55. Mattes, *Bauernräte*; Carsten, *Revolution*, 178–209. On Russia, Orlando Figes, *Peasant Russia, Civil War: The Volga Countryside in Revolution 1917–1921* (Oxford: Phoenix Press, 1989).
56. Heinrich Muth, 'Die Entstehung der Bauern-und Landarbeiterräte im November 1918 und die Politik des Bundes der Landwirte', *Vierteljahrshefte für Zeitgeschichte*, 21 (1973), 1–38.
57. Peter Fritzsche, *Rehearsals for Fascism: Populism and Political Mobilization in Weimar Germany* (Oxford: Oxford University Press, 1990), 21–92.
58. Gabriel Kuhn, *All Power to the Councils! A Documentary History of the German Revolution of 1918–1919* (Pontypool: PM Press, 2012), 64.
59. Helen Boak, *Women in the Weimar Republic* (Manchester: Manchester University Press), 14–25.
60. Kathleen Canning, 'Suffrage and Subjectivity After the First World War', in Kathleen Canning, Kerstin Barndt, and Kristin McGuire (eds), *Weimar Publics/Weimar Subjects: Rethinking the Political Culture of Germany in the 1920s* (New York: Berghahn Books, 2010), 116–37.
61. Hoffrogge, *Working Class Politics*, 29, 49, 65.
62. Helga Grebing, *Frauen in der deutschen Revolution 1918/19* (Heidelberg: Stiftung Reichspräsident-Friedrich Ebert-Gedenkstätte, 1994), 9.

63. Boak, *Women*, 63.
64. Lida Gustava Heymann and Anita Augspurg, *Erlebtes—Erschautes: Deutsche Frauen kämpfen für Freiheit, Recht und Frieden 1850–1940* (Frankfurt am Main: U. Helmer, 1992), 178.
65. Helen Boak, 'Women in the German Revolution', in Gaard Kets and James Muldoon (eds), *The German Revolution and Political Theory* (Cham: Springer International Publishing, 2019), 25–44, here 34.
66. Raffael Scheck, *Mothers of the Nation: Right-Wing Women in Weimar Germany* (Oxford and New York: Bloomsbury, 2004), 23–47.
67. 'Frauenversammlung', *Münchener Post*, 20 Nov. 1918.
68. *Verhandlungen des Provisorischen Nationalrates des Volksstaates Bayern im Jahre 1918/1919*, 5 Sitzung, 18 Dec. 1918 (Munich, 1919), 114.
69. Christopher Dillon, 'Masculinity, Political Culture, and the Rise of Nazism', in Christopher Fletcher et al. (eds), *The Palgrave Handbook of Masculinity and Political Culture in Europe* (London: Palgrave Macmillan, 2018), 379–402, here 381–82.
70. Scott Stephenson, *The Final Battle: Soldiers of the Western Front and the German Revolution of 1918* (Cambridge: Cambridge University Press, 2009), 225–48.
71. Wolfram Wette, 'German Demobilisation 1918–1919', in Chris Wrigley (ed.), *Challenges of Labour: Central and Western Europe 1917–1920* (London: Routledge, 1993), 176–95.
72. Ingrid Sharp, 'The Disappearing Surplus: The Spinster in the Post-War Debate in Weimar Germany', in Ingrid Sharp and Matthew Stibbe (eds), *Aftermaths of War: Women's Movements and Female Activists, 1918–1923* (Leiden and Boston: Brill, 2011), 135–58, here 146.
73. Jones, *Founding Weimar*, 104–10.
74. Printed in Ben Fowkes, *The German Left and the Weimar Republic: A Selection of Documents* (Leiden & Boston: Brill, 2014), 229–30.
75. Wette, 'German Demobilisation', 183–4. On these much-mythologized formations see Hagen Schulze, *Freikorps und Republik, 1918–1920* (Boppard am Rhein: H. Boldt, 1969).
76. Stephenson, *Final Battle*, 311.
77. Ottokar Luban, 'The Role of the Spartacist Group after 9 November 1918 and the Formation of the KPD', in Norman Laporte and Ralf Hoffrogge (eds), *Weimar Communism as Mass Movement: 1918–1933* (Chadwell Heath: Lawrence & Wishart, 2017), 14–65.
78. The best account of the uprising is Jones, *Founding Weimar*, 173–209. A generous assessment of the MSPD's role is offered by Winkler, *Long Road*, 348–50.
79. Jones, *Founding Weimar*, 192–6.
80. Robert Gerwarth, *The Vanquished: Why the First World War Failed to End, 1917–1923* (London: Penguin Books, 2017), 126.
81. Gerald D. Feldman, *The Great Disorder: Politics, Economics and Society in the German Inflation, 1914–1924* (Oxford: Oxford University Press, 1993), 123. For the prehistory see Kluge, *Soldatenräte*, 325–41.
82. Kolb, *Arbeiterräte*, 325–39.
83. Jones, *Founding Weimar*, 246.
84. Karl-Ludwig Sommer, 'Die Bremer Räterepublik, ihre gewaltsame Liquidierung und die Wiederherstellung "geordneter Verhältnisse" in der Freien Hansestadt Bremen', *Niedersächsisches Jahrbuch für Landesgeschichte*, 77 (2005), 1–30.
85. Ibid., 13.
86. Mommsen, 'German Revolution', 241–53; Dick Geary, 'Radicalism and the Worker', in Richard J. Evans (ed.), *Society and Politics in Wilhelmine Germany* (London: Barnes & Noble, 1980), 267–86.

87. Feldman, *Disorder*, 123
88. Jones, *Founding Weimar*, 252–8.
89. Ibid., 270–1.
90. Mitchell, *Revolution*, 188.
91. Martin H. Geyer, 'Munich in Turmoil: Social Protest and the Revolutionary Moment 1918–19', in Wrigley, *Challenges of Labour*, 51–71, here 62.
92. *Thomas Mann Diaries*, tr. Richard and Clara Winston (London: Robin Clark, 1984), 44.
93. Gerwarth, *Vanquished*, 130.
94. Jones, *Founding Weimar*, *passim*.
95. McElligott, *Rethinking*, 99–111.
96. Niess, *Revolution*, 26–59.
97. Ibid., 35–6.
98. Claus Motschmann, *Evangelische Kirche und preussischer Staat in den Anfängen der Weimarer Republik: Möglichkeiten und Grenzen ihrer Zusammenarbeit* (Lübeck & Hamburg: Matthiesen, 1969), 28–31; Dirk Bockermann, '*Wir haben in der Kirche keine Revolution erlebt.*' *Der kirchliche Protestantismus in Rheinland und Westfalen 1918/1919* (Cologne: Rheinland-Verlag, 1998).
99. Derek Hastings, *Catholicism and the Roots of Nazism: Religious Identity and National Socialism* (Oxford: Oxford University Press, 2011), 104.
100. *Berliner Tageblatt*, 10 Nov. 1919.
101. Niess, *Revolution*, 25–6; Oskar Maria Graf, *Prisoners All*, tr. Margaret Green (London: Alfred A Knopff, 1928), 413.
102. Orlando Figes and Boris Kolonitskii, *Interpreting the Russian Revolution: The Language and Symbols of 1917* (New Haven: Yale University Press, 1999), 36, 62.
103. Föllmer, 'Unscripted Revolution', 161.
104. Winkler, *Long Road West*, 349–50; Jones, *Founding Weimar*, 337–8.
105. Count Harry Kessler, *The Diaries of a Cosmopolitan, 1918–1937* (London: Phoenix Press, 2000), 108–9.
106. Gerwarth, *Vanquished*, *passim*.

Bibliography

Carsten, Francis L., *Revolution in Central Europe* (Berkeley and Los Angeles: University of California Press, 1972).

Feldman, Gerald D., *The Great Disorder: Politics, Economics and Society in the German Inflation, 1914–24* (Oxford: Oxford University Press, 1993).

Föllmer, Moritz, 'The Unscripted Revolution: Male Subjectivities in Germany, 1918–1919', *Past and Present*, 240/1 (Aug. 2018), pp. 161–92.

Fritzsche, Peter, *Germans into Nazis* (Cambridge, MA: Harvard University Press, 1998).

Gerwarth, Robert, *The Vanquished: Why the First World War Failed to End, 1917–1923* (London: Penguin Books, 2017).

Hoffrogge, Ralf, *Working Class Politics in the German Revolution: Richard Müller, the Revolutionary Shop Stewards and the Origins of the Council Movement*, tr. Joseph B. Keady (Leiden: Brill, 2014).

Jones, Mark, *Founding Weimar: Violence and the German Revolution of 1918/19* (Cambridge: Cambridge University Press, 2016).

Kuhn, Gabriel, *All Power to the Councils! A Documentary History of the German Revolution of 1918–1919* (Pontypool: PM Press, 2012).

Mitchell, Allan, *Revolution in Bavaria: The Eisner Regime and the Soviet Republic* (Princeton: Princeton University Press, 1965).

Mommsen, Wolfgang, 'The German Revolution, 1918–1920: Political Revolution and Social Protest Movement', in Mommsen, *Imperial Germany: Politics, Culture and Society in an Authoritarian State* (London: Arnold, 1997), 233–54.

Stephenson, Scott, *The Final Battle: Soldiers of the Western Front and the German Revolution of 1918* (Cambridge: Cambridge University Press, 2009).

Weinhauer, Klaus, Anthony McElligott, and Kirsten Heinsohn (eds), *Germany 1916–1923: A Revolution in Context* (Bielefeld: Transcript, 2015).

CHAPTER 3

THE PERIOD OF INFLATION, 1919–1923

MARTIN H. GEYER

In research on the Weimar Republic, it is common to refer to the years from the time after the revolution until the start of hyperinflation and the occupation of the Ruhr in 1923 as a period of inflation. After the revolution, economic issues and the repercussions on politics, society, and culture played an increasingly important role for contemporaries. 'The economy is our fate', as the industrialist Walther Rathenau, who later became foreign minister, stated in 1921.[1] Recent research has emphasized the successes of the republic in the demobilization of the million-strong army, the reinitiation of the peace economy, and the reduction of unemployment.[2] However, political life remained almost permanently in a post-revolutionary crisis mode, with internal and external uncertainties, including reparations and later hyperinflation, playing a major role.

Dubious Stabilization

The Reichstag elections on 6 June 1920 marked a turning point in the history of the young republic and the revolutionary developments from November 1918 onwards. Particularly the MSPD (Majority Social Democratic Party of Germany) and the DDP (German Democratic Party), and to a lesser degree the Catholic Centre Party, suffered electoral defeat. This was a significant watershed as these parties, constituting the Weimar Coalition, had embodied the alliance since the peace resolution in 1917 between the labour movement, political Catholicism, and democratic bourgeoisie. While they had won 76.4 per cent of the vote at the elections to the National Assembly in January 1919, their share now dropped to 43.6 per cent. The winners of the 1920 elections were the conservative bourgeois parties DVP (German People's Party) and DNVP (German National People's Party), on the one hand, and the left wing of the labour movement with

USPD (Independent Social Democratic Party of Germany), on the other, while the KPD (Communist Party of Germany) remained marginal with 2.1 per cent. The subsequent elections were to confirm the decline in popularity of the liberal democratic parties and in 1920 reversed a trend that they had enjoyed since the later years of Imperial Germany.[3] Rather, the Conservatives were on the rise—proven by the 1924 elections—as well as the headline-grabbing and strident antisemitic and anti-republican *völkisch* groups.

The 1920 election result was indicative of the political polarization and change of mood that occurred in summer 1919. One of the fateful constellations of the early Weimar Republic was that the signing of the peace treaty and the adoption and entry into force of the constitution took place at about the same time. Even the majority parties of the Weimar Coalition signed the treaty only reluctantly and under massive international pressure on 28 June 1919, after the cabinet of Philipp Scheidemann (SPD) had resigned in protest shortly before. The new cabinet of Gustav Bauer (SPD) was a temporary solution. A few weeks later, on 31 July, the Reichstag, with an overwhelming majority, voted in favour of the Weimar Constitution, albeit without the votes of USPD, DVP, and DNVP. This did not bode well. The rejection of the constitution subsequently caused severe problems in forming political coalitions with the DVP, and even more so with the radically oppositional DNVP.[4] This was particularly true for Reich politics where reparations played a prominent role, and to a lesser extent for the states. The DNVP, consisting of former Conservatives, Christian Socialists, *Völkische,* and National Liberals, did not oppose parliamentarianism per se, which had been practised before. Rather, they had reservations about new forms of democratic, parliamentary politics based on rules and power relations different to those of Imperial Germany.[5]

For good reason, the Weimar Constitution is considered a victory of liberal democratic powers, as it allowed for many new future prospects. One of them was the promise of a welfare state and the possibility of transferring private businesses to public ownership. The freedom of association gave workers and employees the right to form political and economic associations and 'cooperate, on an equal footing, with employers in the regulation of wages and of the conditions of labour, as well as in the general development of the productive forces' (Art. 165). Political democracy was to be underpinned with economic rights.[6]

While the revolutionary mood of the first half of 1919 gradually died down and the number of political strikes swiftly declined, starting in 1920, the fight for wage increases became fiercer. Social-political reforms were presented as alternatives to socialization, including the Works Councils Act (Betriebsrätegesetz), which had been brought forward as a draft bill in August 1919, granting trade unions much more influence at shop floor level than before. When the DDP sided with the employers, the Bauer government almost collapsed in winter 1919. USPD and left-wing trade union groups called for a protest gathering in front of the Reichstag building on 13 January 1920, against the watering down of the proposed law. The degeneration of this demonstration into a storming of the Reichstag was not part of the plan. An exchange of fire between protesters and security troops, consisting of Reichswehr units and Freikorps fighters, resulted in forty-two deaths and more than a hundred wounded. Based on Article 48 of the Weimar

Constitution, Reich President Friedrich Ebert imposed a state of emergency on large parts of Germany.[7]

These events fuelled deep-seated resentments of the left against the MSPD and the hated armed forces. This applied similarly to the radical political right that blatantly expressed their hatred for the Weimar Republic, risking a showdown in spring 1920. This began with a war of words. In addition to stab-in-the-back accusations linking the military defeat and the revolution, a corruption campaign was launched against Minister of Finance Matthias Erzberger (Centre Party), and other politicians, among them Friedrich Ebert.[8] Erzberger was a target for many reasons: his involvement as co-initiator of the peace resolution of 1917, as signatory of the armistice in November 1918, and as a high-profile democratic politician, but also because of his plans to implement drastic taxes on higher incomes and wealth, including the 'Reichsnotopfer', a onetime and substantial tax to consolidate state finances.[9] The campaign against the prominent Centre Party politician was fought out in the press and in court and damaged him (and, in fact, Philipp Scheidemann) so severely that he finally resigned. But the confrontation went beyond words. While the first assassination attempt on Erzberger in January 1920 failed, the next one on 26 January 1921 eventually cost him his life.

Mid-March 1920 saw the decisive showdown over the so-called Kapp-Lüttwitz putsch, caused by both fundamental and self-serving interests. The much-hated Versailles Treaty required the army size to be reduced to 100,000 men, necessitating the dismissal of hundreds of thousands of soldiers and Freikorps members. With striking hubris, General von Lüttwitz issued an ultimatum, demanding not only that President Ebert stop the reduction of troops but also that he and the government resign, to be followed immediately with a snap election. When Lüttwitz was dismissed shortly afterwards, he and his followers staged a coup on 13 March against the government and appointed Lüttwitz's fellow campaigner Wolfgang Kapp, a high-ranking East Prussian civil servant, as Reich chancellor. All putschists came from circles around the annexationist Fatherland Party of the First World War, including figureheads like Kapp and the World War General Erich Ludendorff. They set their hopes on von Lüttwitz, who was in command of Central German and East Elbian Reichswehr units and large parts of the Freikorps, among them the Freikorps Ehrhardt, known for their helmets emblazoned with swastikas. During the night of 13 March, the revolting troops occupied Berlin. Several members of the Reich government and the President were forced to flee to Stuttgart. However, after only a few days, it became obvious that this poorly planned and executed putsch had failed.[10]

The events were a disaster for all involved. This is particularly true for the putschists, who overestimated the support from the military and the civil service and underestimated the resistance of the labour movement. However, the government under Gustav Bauer (SPD), with the already controversial Minister of Defence, Gustav Noske (SPD), and even President Friedrich Ebert (SPD), were also duped. Prior to the events they had already showed gross negligence in dealing with the ringleaders. This resulted in the fall of the Bauer government. Even the successful nationwide general strike, declared immediately at the beginning of the coup, was an ambivalent victory for the labour movement. It showed the power of the labour movement not only in the cities but also in rural areas. Any resistance was swiftly quelled. Yet at the same time, the general strike also opened a Pandora's box of militarization. In many places, trade unions established workers' self-protection units. The Red Ruhr Army, with about 50,000 workers, was particularly forceful, bringing large parts of the Ruhr area under its control in March 1920. When many of these units did not disband, the new government under Hermann Müller (SPD) deployed the Reichswehr and Freikorps squads, including some that had revolted against the government shortly before. Under the conditions of the declared state of emergency, the government forces and Freikorps units cracked down on the Bolshevists—as they called the protesters—with rampant hatred, committing atrocities such as executions and blatant murders, which were in no way less violent than the events in spring 1919. It was not a surprise that the Brigade Ehrhardt, which had previously supported the putschists, randomly shot at protesting workers, killing twelve people and injuring several dozens, when they marched through the Brandenburg Gate on their orderly retreat from Berlin on 18 March.[11]

These events confirmed existing resentments that the left had against the—in their eyes—reactionary and counter-revolutionary bourgeoisie and the capitalist class. For the supporters of the USPD and the KPD, the MSPD was the party of class treason and repression. They particularly targeted the state government of Carl Severing (SPD) in Prussia that had been established in the course of the Kapp putsch and that took strong action not only against Kapp putschists but also against the left-wing opposition, particularly, but not exclusively, in the context of the events at the Ruhr.[12]

Initially, the mood among Conservatives was gloomy. The republic had prevailed, putsch attempts were clearly nothing to write home about, and foreign political revision receded dimly into the distance. There was a lack of suitable personnel. The Emperor was discredited even though Prussian monarchists did not tire of conjuring up old Imperial splendour.[13] Only in Bavaria was the Kapp putsch successful. Here, the Bavarian 'Ordnungszelle' (Cell of Law and Order) under Minister President Gustav Ritter von Kahr (BVP) became the hope of nationalist reactionary circles, including the military, and would keep German politics in suspense in the years to follow.[14] Despite general discontent and the sympathy harboured for the Kapp putschists among the military, they ultimately failed because the leadership of the Reichswehr neither wanted to shoot their own troops nor supported the putschists. The agreement between the Reich President and the military, forged during the revolution, lasted. The Chief of the Army Command, General Hans von Seeckt, came to the conclusion that a revision of the Versailles Treaty was possible only with, rather than against, the new state.[15]

Despite the surprisingly swift demobilization of the army of millions and the beginning of the transition from war to peace production, the economic situation remained tense until the summer of 1920, which resulted in much discontent. The end of the British naval blockade after the signing of the peace treaty in July 1919 only gradually improved the economic situation. Notwithstanding a huge excess demand for consumer goods, there was a shortage of all kinds of raw materials, particularly coal. Infrastructure was in a dire state. The lack of foreign currency impeded the import of American food products, and the free floating of exchange rates from September 1919 drove inflation up and caused substantial price increases.

Supply shortfalls and inflation ruled everyday life in Weimar. Just like during wartime, national and municipal offices were in charge of allocating food based on ration books and fixed maximum prices. In addition, there were comprehensive price controls of many everyday products. This already inadequate system increasingly fell apart over the course of the revolution. Rationed food alone hardly guaranteed survival, which in turn fuelled the black market. The departure from the state-controlled war economy promised a way out of this situation, but it initially resulted in a further increase in already high prices and, consequently, in even more indignation. In some cases, fields and shops were looted. Antisemitic voices made themselves heard among the protests, insinuating a connection between inflation and shortages and the role of Jews in the economy and state administration.[16]

The departure from the state-controlled, subsidized public food provisions also aimed to limit public debt. The war had been funded predominantly by printing money rather than collecting taxes. This did not change much in the post-war period, as internal burdens resulting from the war mounted. These included expenditures for war invalids and dependants as well as for refugees and expelled persons, who crowded into Germany from areas that were separated from the Reich and who had to be provided for and compensated for their lost assets. The protracted demobilization further required high sums. Strikes and unrest crippled the economy in many places and thus brought about a decline in tax income. Public debt was unambiguous in its implications: in March 1919, at the end of the fiscal year 1918/19, public debt amounted to 156 billion marks, while at the end of the following budget year it was 184 billion marks.[17] That was a significant increase, even considering the currency devaluation that had occurred in the meantime.

In order to consolidate public finances, Reich Minister of Finance Matthias Erzberger took drastic measures.[18] They included a squeeze on the taxpayer and a fundamental reform of the tax system and the finance administration that passed into the hands of the Reich. The problem was that, even under the condition of moderate money devaluation, taxes were often payable in arrears (particularly by affluent taxpayers)—in other words, they were paid with devalued money.

The other side of this consolidation strategy was to limit public spending. Yet this was almost harder than increasing taxes, owing to the growing inflation and the acute social hardship suffered by the poorer sectors of the population. Social protests against spending cuts were greatly feared. Such cuts would have hit officials as well as white- and blue-collar workers of the country's inflated civil service. Like workers and employees of the private sector, these groups were highly unionized, insisted on salary increases, and did not shy away from strikes to fight for their demands.[19] Moreover, public investment, particularly in railway and road construction as well as hydroelectric energy production, was urgently needed, given how badly the infrastructure had been damaged during the war. The state control of the housing market brought the private housebuilding sector to a standstill, so that state and municipalities had to step in. Last but not least, reparations had to be paid. The Versailles Treaty of 1919 postponed the final settlement to a later date. However, substantial payments in kind, including coal and locomotives as well as initial monetary payments, were due on 1 May 1921, and the victorious powers demanded the payment of 20 million in goldmark rather than in (paper) mark. These costs burdened the national budget.

Many other countries also put on their reform agendas the consolidation of public finances and the stabilization of the currency, accompanied by the return to the gold standard. This required drastic steps of budgetary consolidation and credit restrictions of the central banks everywhere, resulting in rising unemployment and a growing number of bankruptcies. In the British Isles, trade unions responded with large-scale general strikes, which prompted government to impose temporary states of emergency. This demanded a strong state, at least a government capable of acting to enforce such a policy against the resistance of its own constituencies. At stake were more than economic issues: the return to the gold standard was accompanied by the commitment to return to the political, social, and economic normality of the pre-war period.[20]

Germany only adopted this austerity policy towards the end of hyperinflation. The historians Gerald D. Feldman and Carl-Ludwig Holtfrerich attributed this decision to economic political reasons, connected with the reparations: first steps towards such a policy of budgetary consolidation in winter 1919–20 did in fact improve the external value of the mark, but in return they bogged down the economy and caused unemployment. A moderate inflation proved to be a 'lubricant' that kept the wheels of the economy moving and ensured full employment. Production in Germany was cheaper than abroad, and the country attracted the interest of the international financial world. Particularly American banks became increasingly involved on a large scale with Germany. Small domestic investors in the United States were lured with the argument that Germany would catch up with the industrial powers and the mark would recover, which sparked hopes for speculative profits.[21]

Did this phase of inflation help 'save German democracy', as Gerald D. Feldman has argued?[22] Revolutionary energies soon died away. A good indicator for this was the first split within the USPD in October 1920 and thus the beginning of the party's collapse, even though this party, more than any other, embodied the political resistance against Imperial Germany and the revolutionary movement on shop floor level. The majority of the party leadership and Reichstag members had switched to the SPD by 1922, leaving the remaining USPD a shadow of its former self. This is particularly striking because the majority of the USPD members still saw themselves as supporters of a Marxist party that refused to cooperate with bourgeois parties. The SPD shifted to the right with its Görlitz programme of September 1921. It no longer referred to the class character of the state or maintained its traditional hostility towards the state, committing to the 'democratic people's state' instead.[23] This would subsequently cause many party internal controversies within the—generally strengthened—SPD. They all referred to the fiercely contested formation of coalitions with bourgeois parties, particularly the DVP, and cutbacks in the social-political achievements of the revolution.

At the same time, former USPD members who switched to the KPD turned this party into a mass membership party for the first time in its history. In 1921, the KPD, under the leadership of Karl Radek and the Comintern, miscalculated its power following this new surge in membership and instigated the so-called March Action in the Central German industrial region, a stronghold of the left since the war and the revolution. It aimed at sparking a broad national uprising, which failed miserably, not least because the Prussian government took rigorous measures to counter it by deploying police units. It is striking that it was not the KPD that made headlines but the charismatic Max Hölz. Hölz was a member of the KAPD, an anarcho-syndicalist group which had split off from the KPD. He became famous for his violent actions such as arson, lootings, bank robberies as well as the bombing of and attacks on trains, committed in a Robin Hood style.[24] In 1921 and again in 1923, the revolutionary mobilization of the masses was a 'revolutionary illusion', as Curt Geyer, who returned to the SPD in 1922 after having switched to the USDP and the KPD, stated in retrospect.[25]

The increasing number of assassinations left an alarmingly bloody trail through the post-war period, highlighted by the murders of Kurt Eisner, Rosa Luxemburg, and Karl Liebknecht. In his book *Vier Jahre politischer Mord* (*Four Years of Political Murder*), published in 1922, the mathematician and publicist Emil Julius Gumbel from the University of Heidelberg listed 376 political murders between 1919 and 1922, of which 354 could be ascribed to the right side and 22 to the left side of the political spectrum.[26] In August 1921, Matthias Erzberger was killed and in June 1922 Foreign Minister Walther Rathenau (DDP). Rather than single perpetrators, radical right-wing gangs of murderers were responsible for these deeds. The assassins could be traced to Bavaria and the Bavarian Ordnungszelle, which held its protecting hand over this culture of radical right-wing and nationalistic movements. Adolf Hitler with his NSDAP was only one of several leading figures and beacons of hope. They all shared the view that the enemy stood on the left, meaning not only the Marxist SPD but also Democrats and other bourgeois politicians.[27] They believed they were fighting a war after the war, whether over issues of rearmament, in border fights such in Upper Silesia in 1921 or in Memel Territory in 1923, or in general against the 'November criminals' and the Versailles Treaty. A highly differentiated media landscape provided a plethora of mouthpieces for these groups.

Contrary to expectations, the murder of Rathenau produced a strong pro-republican mobilization. There was widespread outrage at this political murder, which temporarily overshadowed political differences. The Foreign Minister was granted the first state funeral since Bismarck. Like after the Kapp putsch, the radical right was temporarily paralysed. The republic bared its teeth by enacting the Law for the Protection of the Republic of 21 July 1922. This new legislation allowed bans on political parties, restrictions of the freedom of the press and freedom of opinion, and trials for high treason. On 11 August 1922, the first celebration of the constitution took place in the Reichstag, thus starting a tradition; it was, as Reich Minister of the Interior Adolf Köster (SPD) stated, 'a powerful demonstration of republican Germany'.[28]

If we take the value of the mark as an indicator for stability, it becomes obvious that economic confidence in the republic decreased from summer 1922 onwards. Germany was on the brink of hyperinflation: while in early 1922 a dollar cost 45 mark, it was 75 mark in June, 270 mark in August, and 1,807 mark in December—after that, the German currency was in free fall.[29] This development was closely linked to decisions on reparations and foreign policy.[30] After being postponed in 1919, the issue of reparations increasingly took centre stage at the 1920 conference in the Belgian town of Spa. Both the amount and German economic capability were discussed. The reparation claims that the Allies put on the table in January 1921 were, from the German perspective, still exorbitant, even after they were reduced by half after protests. After heated debates they issued the London Ultimatum on 5 May 1921: 132 billion goldmark with 2 billion annual interest and repayment charges, in addition 26 per cent of the annual export value; all as payments in kind and money. The first billion was due in late August 1921 and issued with an ultimatum: in the event of non-compliance the Allies threatened to occupy the Ruhr area. In order to reinforce their claims their troops occupied Düsseldorf, Duisburg, and Ruhrort as 'sanction cities'. Payment was made promptly.

It is not that the Allied demands, particularly the annual payments, could not have been fulfilled. However, political and diplomatic conflicts caused a high degree of uncertainty, which in turn affected confidence in the German currency. In May 1921, the Fehrenbach government (Centre Party) collapsed because the DVP refused to support its policy towards reparations. The new government under Joseph Wirth, again a minority government of Centre Party, SPD, and DDP, was fragile.[31] Did the reparation claims overstrain Germany's capability? Would the so-called 'policy of fulfilment' ruin the country and fuel currency devaluation? The British economist John Maynard Keynes supported such assumptions of the impossibility to meet the demands.[32] The Wirth government used the defiant slogan of 'policy of fulfilment' in the same vein— which the political opposition then took up, polemically referring to the 'fulfilment politicians'. Subsequently, inflation became, to some extent, a self-fulfilling prophecy: Germany's former war enemies could be blamed for the monetary and economic plight.[33] German filibustering was not without success. In 1922, the first reparation charges in form of cash payments were suspended and replaced by payments in kind in the form of coal, steel, and timber. German wishes for a temporary suspension of reparation payments were unlikely to succeed. If anything, a reduction might have been possible, yet this hope was dashed over the course of 1922. The formation of the cabinet under Raymond Poincaré in February 1922 impeded an agreement with France while, at the same time, the German position hardened: 'First bread, then reparations!' became the slogan of the Wirth government in summer 1922.[34]

Against the backdrop of the reparations, much attention was given to Germany's rapprochement policy with the young and internationally isolated Soviet Union and the Treaty of Rapallo in April 1922, under which both countries renounced all reparations and other claims.[35] The news of the treaty struck like a thunderbolt during the conference in Genoa where the former belligerent countries negotiated the post-war financial and economic system and, in doing so, the future reparations. For outsiders the political machinations of the parties, in which the Reich President was involved to a significant extent, was inscrutable. After much ado, the grand coalition with the DVP in the end did not materialize. Instead, in November 1922 a centre-right government without the SPD under the independent but decisively conservative Wilhelm Cuno was formed.[36] The former manager of the HAPAG shipping company took up the slogan 'First bread, then reparations!' and went even further in filibustering reparations by also refusing to meet payments in kind in the form of coal and timber. This was, as the Reparation Commission decided, a breach of treaty provisions. France and Belgium carried out their threat, responding with the military occupation of the Ruhr area, including adjacent regions, on 11 January 1923 as a productive pledge. An army of 100,000 soldiers were to secure the transport of the pending reparation payments in kind. In return, the German government stopped all reparation payments and called for passive resistance on 13 February 1923, supported by an overwhelming Reichstag majority. Originally intended as a brief demonstration of power, this situation dragged on for months, leading the whole of Germany into the chaos of hyperinflation.

With the so-called 'Ruhr campaign' (*Ruhrkampf*), Germany found itself fighting a 'war after the war'.[37] Small- and large-scale businesses, state offices, civil servants, miners, and, not least, railway workers went on strike. The occupation forces countered with arrests, severe penalties through martial courts and the expelling of 180,000 persons. In some cases, passive resistance turned into violent acts of sabotage: the demolition of bridges, track, and channel systems as well as direct attacks on representatives of the occupation forces and German collaborators. When 29-year-old Albert Leo Schlageter, a former Freikorps soldier and member of the NSDAP, was tried for espionage and bombings and executed in late May 1923, he became a martyr and was put on a pedestal, even by the Communists.[38]

Only to a certain extent did the pledge prove 'productive' for France and Belgium, and the deployment of large numbers of troops turned out to be rather expensive. However, the human and economic costs of the Ruhr occupation were much higher for Germany. Wages and salaries were continued to be paid in the occupied areas, businesses received compensation, and vast amounts of money disappeared into dubious channels of subsidized companies, trade unions, and the bureaucracy. Eventually, Germany was forced to buy coal from abroad with its scarce foreign currency by expanding the budget deficit: money printing machines ran hot. Trust in the German currency waned once and for all, domestically and abroad. The German people got used to handling thousands, from summer onwards millions, and from October even billions of mark in everyday life. Despite a good harvest, famine loomed because inflation halted economic exchange and people stockpiled goods of all kinds.

In the summer of 1923, the Cuno government faced a political and economic disaster. France refused any concessions, the issue of reparations was still unsolved, and economic problems mounted. Passive resistance was no longer broadly supported. The only question remaining was when, how, and under whose leadership the chaos could be stopped. The termination of passive resistance was a bitter admission of defeat with imminent domestic implications, all the more pronounced because the political stand-off over the reparations issue had to be resolved. The first victim was the Cuno cabinet. The grand coalition of DVP, Centre Party, DDP, and SPD under Gustav Stresemann (DVP), formed on 13 August 1923, terminated passive resistance on 26 September, heralding a long struggle over the currency reform.[39] In October 1923, the Deutsche Rentenbank was founded: its reserves were mortgaged against agricultural, manufacturing, and other industrial real estate, that is, material assets that had not suffered from hyperinflation. On 15 November the so-called Rentenmark was introduced on this basis at a rate of 1 Rentenmark to equal 1 trillion Papiermark and an exchange rate of 1 US dollar to equal 4.2 Rentenmark. It is often overlooked that the currency reform was by no means a foregone success and was not concluded until late August 1924, when the Rentenmark was finally replaced by the Reichsmark.

INFLATION: THE SILENT PROPERTY REVOLUTION

While people had talked for years in general about rising prices (*Teuerung*), the term inflation entered everyday language during 1923. Its repercussions were contested right from the beginning. According to the Hamburg-based banker Max Warburg, Germany was 'a country divided into three classes of society: one that suffers and goes under in decency; another that profiteers cynically and spends recklessly; and another that writhes in desperation, and wishes to destroy in blind fury whatever is left of a government and a society that permits such conditions'.[40] Such depictions of publicly exhibited wealth, particularly of the newly rich, on the one hand, and the poverty of the urban population with impoverished middle-class families, war cripples, homeless people, and prostitutes, on the other, were widespread. Even today, they continue to influence our view of this particular year, alongside the depictions of people exchanging paper money with an exceedingly high nominal value that could buy next to nothing. But this was only one side of the coin. Indeed, during the first half of the year 1923, not only industry and trade but also the arts still flourished. Unemployment was low, pubs, cafes, cinemas, and theatres were well attended, and leisure activities such as sports and hiking experienced a heyday due to the eight-hour day. As it was not worth one's while to save money for the future, it was spent quickly and freely.

These conflicting images of the Weimar Republic that are largely due to different perspectives on the phenomenon of inflation can still be found in historiography and literature. Economic historians in particular have taken a critical look at the—traditionally—negative assessment of the repercussions of inflation, recalling the difficult economic point of departure after four years of war. In 1920, industrial production had reached only little more than half and German national income at best two-thirds of pre-war levels.[41] Even without reparations, war-induced burdens were enormous. The currency devaluation kept the economy going and caused a redistribution of wealth.

The state had piled up debt, but the currency devaluation decreased the real value of these debts in goldmark or US dollar terms. At the end of inflation, public budgets were largely free of debt. In other words, the currency devaluation had the same effect as a wealth tax that was paid by a broad audience—albeit not by all to the same extent.

Similarly, many businesses emerged stronger from the inflation period. The ratio of nominal capital in 1913 to nominal capital in 1924 in the iron and steel industry was 100:134, in the mining industry 100:136, and in the chemical industry even 100:227. It was, however, a different picture for trade and banking, where the ratio was 100:30.[42] Thus, industry, trade, and banking were unequally affected; banks and insurance companies had lost an enormous amount of capital. Thousands of small and medium-sized businesses in all sectors went bust in 1924. The transition from war to peace production, the loss of former import and export markets as well as the restrictions of the Versailles Treaty were huge challenges for all businesses. All balance sheets were overshadowed by inflation, which impeded secure accounting and kept many, even defunct, companies alive. Businessmen who had access to the credit market and were open to taking risks—that is, who adopted an inflation mentality—could borrow money at ridiculously low interest rates that could later be repaid at a hugely decreased value. Contemporaries spoke of *Inflationsblüten*: unsound businesses and businessmen who thrived thanks to the inflation and often went bankrupt with the currency reform. The Ruhr industrialist Hugo Stinnes, who had established a highly complex corporation operating in the field of heavy and electrotechnical industry since the war, has long been regarded a prime and scandalous example of using cheap financing options together with the devaluation of debts as an economic strategy. Indeed, there were numerous entrepreneurs, often surprisingly young ones and many of them self-made men, who were Stinnes's equals in pursuing this inflationary economic strategy.[43]

Many blue- and white-collar workers as well as large sections of the bourgeoisie, among them civil servants, doctors, and solicitors, were economically worse off than before the war. Especially in phases of rapid inflation when prices rose dramatically, their incomes lagged behind. One can discern a discrepancy between the fact that hourly wages, especially of workers, remained relatively high but lagged when calculated on a weekly and monthly basis; this has to do with the introduction of the eight-hour-day, which reduced weekly working time. Those organized in trade unions and employed by (large-scale) industrial companies were in a relatively favourable economic situation. A good example of this is the large group of miners who, in 1923, by way of the *Reichsknappschaft*, also received a separate, privileged public health insurance and pension scheme. Even during the hyperinflation, the trade unions were able to negotiate an inflation compensation for their members.[44] This is the reason why historians often speak of an 'inflation consensus'.[45] By this they mean a kind of inflation mentality that was widespread, a way in which individuals, economic groups, and the state came to terms with and adapted to the currency devaluation.

A specific characteristic of inflation was the levelling of income, which had already started during the war and accelerated afterwards. Put simply, this meant, for instance, that the income of higher earners among white-collar workers, civil servants, and skilled workers moved closer to that of lower paid income groups. Across all occupations, it was the higher income groups that suffered the greatest income losses. Strikingly, the general trend in women's income was, in comparison, better across all sectors during the post-war inflation period. White-collar workers and civil servants in particular regarded this levelling of income as a form of social and economic proletarianization and a threat to the *Mittelstand*, which is certainly one reason for the negative assessment of the inflation period. But more than any other group, this levelling process affected owners of capital assets. It goes without saying that inflation destroys monetary assets, including savings, state bonds, insurance, and endowment capital, even without hyperinflation.[46] For those living off their savings the currency devaluation posed a dramatic form of—silent—property expropriation. The so-called *Kapitalkleinrentner*—that is, people who had until then lived off their savings—among them many women, became the contemporary epitome of inflation losers. Yet this group was only the tip of the iceberg. Large parts of the bourgeoisie were affected, not least the educated middle class, including doctors, solicitors, and other members of the free professions. For example, the economist and university professor Werner Sombart, who made a name for himself with his historical analysis of modern capitalism in the pre-war period, lost large parts of his fortune because of several bad financial decisions.[47] This fuelled resentment everywhere. The liberal economist Moritz J. Bonn noted in hindsight that the business world developed 'a capitalist variant of communist expropriation': 'They robbed not their class enemies, but the broad mass of their own supporters.'[48] These and similar remarks were driven by conflicts and battles over the distribution of wealth within a society that was already fragmented into classes, status groups, and political convictions. They also reveal experience and expectations that had changed since the war and were often compared with idealized descriptions of *The World of Yesterday* (Stefan Zweig), that is, with the pre-war time of alleged certainties.[49]

Against the backdrop of hyperinflation, many authors and contemporaries stated that the world had turned upside down as a result of the 'witches' sabbath of devaluation' (Elias Canetti).[50] A prime example is the scholar of Romance literature and diary writer Victor Klemperer, who felt he was being drawn into the maelstrom of inflation and insecurity despite his long-desired appointment as tenured professor at the University of Dresden in 1920. In his diary, he constantly lamented the shortage of money and financial problems, described initially small, later larger speculative transactions in foreign currency and shares, and was obsessed with food and prices, including worst excesses of 'profiteers'. These utterances, which he himself regarded as 'pathetic', stopped promptly after the currency reform and appeared again in 1930. Despite his everyday frustrations over the economic situation, Klemperer also enjoyed some small successes in his speculative transactions that came as a surprise for him and helped him and his wife make ends meet. 'I even feel excitement and pleasure in the dash of Bohemian life-style of our [uncertain] way of living and the uncertainty of the overall situation', he wrote in 1923.[51]

As many other contemporaries, Klemperer was well aware that the old ways no longer held sway: That 'the time is out of joint'[52] was the seemingly trivial expression that can be seen as a metaphor of experiencing modernity with its vanishing values.

One aspect of this modernity was the increasingly worthless paper money that was no longer based on the gold standard, which the much-maligned inflation profiteers with their bad business morality were able to exploit. The so-called 'rentiers', as well as 'many intellectual workers'—the economist Alfred Weber referred to 'rentier-intellectuals'—who lived off their savings seemed to be boldly anachronistic in this modern society.[53] The new social figurehead was the white-collar worker and their specific leisure culture including sport, cinemas, and weekends. New forms of lifestyle spread in all areas. The artistic avant-garde flourished under the conditions of inflation during the early 1920s.[54] Many of them targeted the ubiquitous mediocrity of the everyday world of money. But just like shares, coins, and other valuables, art works were in high demand in the flight to real assets. Artists such as George Grosz threw their portfolios on the market, signed or unsigned, with or without hand-colouring, on cheap or on high-quality paper, suitable for any group of buyers. Klemperer wrote about a university colleague who bought art works and books as 'dividend investment' and spent hundreds of thousands of marks to bind books in the most beautiful fashion, 'all very refined and cultured. Still, a bitter and unconceivable feeling remains over this excessive and industrialized way of earning money.' This was a modernity where it seemed that 'everything solid melts into air'.[55] Many retrospective descriptions of these turbulent times have consolidated this image.

Currency Stabilization, State of Emergency and Dictatorship in Autumn and Winter 1923–4

In late November 1923, the publisher Ludwig Feuchtwanger wrote to his author Carl Schmitt that, in light of recent events, 'every day offers visual and practical instructions on general political science'. He continued that the much-read masters of the past, such as Machiavelli, Bodin, and Hobbes, had now become 'disconcertingly alive'. Schmitt answered dryly that this was particularly true of Hobbes.[56] Contemporaries of the inflation period often referred to the image of the 'war of everyone against everyone', together with the demand for dictators, 'strong men', and a 'strong government'. The winter of 1923–4 was the training ground of the state of emergency. Germany had seen debates on dictatorship since the war and the revolution, but in late autumn 1923, when money increasingly lost its function as a medium of exchange and state authority seemed to be dissolving, these only accelerated. Newspapers reported on lootings and unrest over rising prices throughout Germany, in which the participants were women, youth, unemployed people, but also political activists of the left as well as antisemitic and *völkisch* groups. They looted shops and sold the confiscated goods at 'decent prices'. Pogrom-like riots in the Berlin Scheunenviertel in early November, which started as protests of unemployed people and snowballed into excesses against the Jewish population of this and other Berlin boroughs, were only the tip of the iceberg. Here, a rampant antisemitism came blatantly to light.[57] Even today it is still not known how many people were killed nationwide in these lootings (which, however, were largely not driven by antisemitism)—not least due to the deployment of security forces, including military units. Signs of anarchy could be observed in Prussian Rhineland and Bavarian Palatinate in the west of the country, where German separatists supported by France scaled up their activities, occupied public buildings and proclaimed 'autonomous republics'. This resulted in civil war-like conditions when self-declared separatists faced also violent opposition of broad sections of the population.[58]

Did these events not bode well for a 'German October' (by analogy with the Russian October of the Bolshevists in 1917), as representatives of the KPD and the Communist International such as Karl Radek were suggesting?[59] Moscow also assumed that the chaos of hyperinflation had created a revolutionary situation. Soviet money and military experts helped establish the so-called Proletarian Hundreds (Proletarische Hundertschaften), a paramilitary body, which soon had more than 50,000 members. The KPD accelerated the establishment of (price) control commissions that were to undertake self-help action against usurers, black-marketeers, and unreasonably high prices and to confiscate goods and food products.[60] The aim was to create a broad, united proletarian front. Part of this strategy was that the KPD joined the SPD governments in Saxony and Thuringia during the first half of October.

The political course of the KPD remained contested. As the majority of the delegates of left-wing trade unionists, Communists, and Social Democrats stated at a meeting in Chemnitz on 21 October, the financial hardship caused by hyperinflation did not bode well for a general strike. As a result, the isolated KPD leadership under Heinrich Brandler cancelled the planed actions. A local riot in Hamburg on 23 October ended in bloody clashes. The Communist revolutionary slogans were grist for the mill of those who nursed plans for a 'national dictatorship', and pointed to the looming danger from the left. They brandished the spectre of an imminent civil war, a state of anarchy that could only be resolved by the power of a dictator.

Indeed, 26 September marked the end of passive resistance when Reich President Ebert, in consultation with the Stresemann government, declared a nationwide state of military emergency based on Article 48, Section 2, of the constitution.[61] Fear of riots and protests against the end of passive resistance—a second stab-in-the-back, as some suggested—was only one reason for this step. The key factor was that the Bavarian government had pressed ahead by declaring a state of emergency for Bavaria (based on Article 48, Section 5), pre-empting the Reich government and thus forcing the hand of both Stresemann and Ebert. The appointment of Gustav Ritter von Kahr as Bavarian state commissioner general made clear which way the wind was blowing. Von Kahr, who became Minister-President of Bavaria in March 1920, was the great hope of the conservatives in the Bavarian People's Party. He maintained manifold relations with the Reichswehr and combat leagues, including those around Ludendorff and Hitler, who increasingly became competitors in the political arena. The Bavarian state of emergency, first imposed after the quelling of the council republic in 1919, turned into a trademark of the Bavarian Ordnungszelle under von Kahr. This involved cracking down on left-wing parties (including the SPD) and their members, the excessive use of *Schutzhaft* (protective custody), bans on public meetings, and civil rights restrictions on left-wing party members. At the same time, institutions of a security state, such as the state police, Reichswehr, and combat leagues, were expanded. This was a blatant criticism of the grand coalition with the Social Democrats in Berlin and the Social Democratic Reich Minister of the Interior. In November 1923, von Kahr initiated the internment and expulsion of so-called 'Eastern Jews' from Germany.[62]

With the state of emergency in September 1923, the executive power was given to the Minister of the Reichswehr, Otto Geßler (DDP), who delegated his authorities to the regional military district commanders. As a result, they obtained extensive powers vis-à-vis the state governments and authorities. Even before and particularly after the failed Hamburg uprising, the minister of the Reichswehr and the chancellor put more pressure on the left-wing state government in Saxony under Erich Zeigner (SPD). They issued an ultimatum that demanded the exclusion of the KPD from the Saxon government and threatened with a *Reichsexekution*, that is the takeover of political control by the Reich government and the military occupation of these states (based on Article 48, Section 1 of the constitution). When the left-wing Saxon government did not comply with this order, the Reich execution was put into force on 28 October: authorized by President Ebert, Chancellor Stresemann deposed the members of the Saxon government as well as the leadership of regional and municipal authorities. On the next day, the Reichswehr occupied Saxony and put the police forces under Reichswehr command. The Proletarian Hundreds were banned and disarmed. After 6 November, similar steps were taken against the government in Thuringia. Civil Reich commissioners (*Reichskommissare*), in cooperation with representatives of the Reichswehr, took responsibility for state government affairs. It was thanks to President Ebert that this course of action remained only a brief interlude. As early as 31 October, the Saxon diet elected a newly formed Social Democratic government, and in Thuringia a bourgeois government supported by the *Völkische* was elected by the diet. In 1923, many in Germany, including the military, wished for a general political cleansing, for instance governments without the participation of Social Democrats, including in Prussia. In December, the new Saxon government protested that 'a general who dares to declare all Social Democratic civil servants unreliable and suspend them from office based only on their party-political view defies democracy'.[63]

Resentment ran high among Social Democrats. On 3 November they left the Stresemann government in anger. The SPD was embittered not only by the events in Saxony but also by those in Bavaria, where the Reich government and Reichswehr bought time for opportunistic reasons despite the fact there were enough good reasons to impose a Reich execution here as well. In Bavaria the Reichswehr refused to comply with orders from Berlin and sided with State Commissioner von Kahr. This was a form of high treason. The leadership of the Reichswehr under von Seeckt made it very clear that it would not support a Reich execution against Bavaria.

Following the events in Saxony, Thuringia, and Bavaria, and the SPD leaving government, various plans on setting up a dictatorship and staging a 'national revolution' mushroomed that had been germinating over the weeks and months during the state of military emergency. One such plan was to have a directorate independent of parliament and vested with extraordinary powers (echoing Napoleonic France). The exponents were politically involved industrialists and politicians with connections to the Agrarian League (Bund der Landwirte, BdL) and the Pan-German League (Alldeutscher Verband), whose members were intermeshed with DNVP and DVP. Ebert was aware of these plans, in particular because the initiators assumed that such a directorate could only be formed by using the emergency powers of the Reich President. However, it remained an open question who was deemed suitable to fill the posts in such a directorate. In September, Stinnes already told the US Ambassador to Berlin: 'Such a man must speak the language of the people and be a member of a bourgeois party, and such a man is available right now.'[64] It is fair to assume that he was thinking of von Kahr rather than of Hitler.

From the outset, the chief of the Reichswehr, Hans von Seeckt, played a major role in these dictatorship plans. Many in the military had high hopes for him. The fact that all these plans came to nothing was, to some extent, due to his personality, but in particular to the events in Bavaria. Since the founding of the NSDAP in February 1920, it had become an influential power in this state. Its leader, Adolf Hitler, was known as a 'drummer' of the national cause. Despite a great deal of distrust und suspicion, governmental authorities, police, and Reichswehr regarded the young movement with favour. Since the occupation of the Ruhr and passive resistance, Hitler had become a power in Bavaria that could no longer be ignored. In autumn, von Kahr, Hitler, and his allies in the *völkisch* camp fought for the leadership of the national movement. The events came to a head on the eve of the anniversary of the November revolution on 9 November 1923 at a large meeting in the Munich Bürgerbräukeller. Right in the middle of von Kahr's speech, which was fraught with invectives against Marxism and Berlin, Hitler, armed with a pistol, stormed onto the stage, interrupted von Kahr and declared the dismissal of the Bavarian and the Reich government—to the cheers of the bourgeois audience. He then promised the formation of a 'national government'. Von Kahr and his allies, taken completely by surprise, withdrew their forced commitment to the coup, and within hours the Bavarian police forces quelled the putsch in front of the Feldherrnhalle in Munich by firing a volley of bullets.[65]

Also during the night of the putsch, Friedrich Ebert placed executive powers directly in the hands of von Seeckt (instead of Minister of the Reichswehr Geßler): the general was, as a result, able to 'take all necessary measures for the safety of the Reich', as the first public statement read. By this means, the military was closer to power than ever before.[66] However, hopes of a 'dictatorship Seeckt' were quickly dashed. By transferring the power to von Seeckt on the night of the putsch, the Reich President made the general dependent on him: von Seeckt's first task was to implement law and order in Bavaria. As it turned out, the 'military dictator', ordered by Ebert, acted within the framework of the constitution and under the leadership of the President. Nevertheless, the measures von Seeckt took are of major importance, particularly in the light of the following years. They consisted, among other things, of party and newspaper bans, the repeal of civil rights and increase of penalties, including military protective custody as well as interventions in economic life.[67]

At the core of all these events was the objective of restoring public order and safety. Other occasions when the state of emergency was declared concerned the remedy of economic and fiscal hardship based on Article 48. By these means the President authorized the government to make extensive decisions on economic issues without consulting the Reichstag. Parliament could have vetoed it but did not, even when the SPD had left the government and was in opposition. In the same vein, the Reichstag passed several enabling laws and, in doing so, delegated its legislative powers to the governments (and indirectly to the state bureaucracies)—and prorogued itself. This was intended to enable the government to 'take those measures it regards as necessary and urgent in view of the distress of the people and of the Reich', as the enabling law of 8 December 1923 stipulated.[68] This was in fact nothing else than a 'naked dictatorship law'[69]—in this case issued by the Reichstag.

For half a year, military, state bureaucracy and Reich government governed with Article 48 for the restoration of law and order and with economic emergency decrees and enabling laws. Similar arrangements were made in the individual states. A plethora of decrees and laws were issued that would never have passed the Reichstag without the state of emergency, particularly with such speed. The issue was extremely contested and resulted in some bitterness because important achievements of the revolution such as the eight-hour day were put up for negotiation, which the SPD was reluctant to agree to for a long time.[70] One of these measures was the gradual staff reduction in the public sector by 25 per cent, which was decided on 17 October 1923. As a result, 400,000 civil servants, employees, and workers of the public sector were laid off before 1 April 1924, among them a disproportionately high number of women. Salaries and wages were reduced to 60 per cent of the pre-war level, and the eight-hour day was watered down while taxes and duties increased. Reichsbahn and Reichspost were no longer subsidized.[71] The harshness of this austerity policy was due to efforts to revise some of the social and political gains of the revolution (like the eight-hour day), but even more so because for a long time it remained uncertain whether or not the currency reform would be successful or the country would bounce back into inflation. On 15 February 1924, the last fixed-term enabling law expired, and a few days later the Reichstag convened again. When Social Democrats, Communists, and German Nationals attempted to amend the austerity measures issued by the government, the Reich President, following a request from the government, dissolved the Reichstag on 13 March. Snap elections were scheduled for 4 May, which gave the government some further breathing space.

After the winter of 1923–4, German society was weary. Images of huge amounts of worthless paper money that had been burnt or given to children as play money became deeply entrenched in collective memory, not least thanks to media coverage. The currency reform was experienced in connection with utmost material hardship, numerous bankruptcies, a high unemployment rate, and extremely low incomes. The gloomy economic situation improved only during the second half of 1924 when US credit flowed into Germany in the context of an agreement, known as the Dawes Plan, that was reached with regard to the reparations question.

The DNVP emerged as the winner of the Reichstag elections in May 1924 more clearly than it had four years earlier. As an opposition party that had not participated in any government coalition it could tap into the discontent of bourgeois strata, the rural population, and German National employees, workers, and civil servants. Social protest was, quite literally, German National, accompanied by an underlying rampant antisemitism. It resonated with the public when German Nationals blamed the revolution of 1918–19, the democratic republic, and the reparations for the consequences of inflation that were uniformly regarded as negative. To many it appeared obvious that the new state as well as powerful economic interests had shed their debts at the expense of broad sections of the population.[72] The DNVP became deeply absorbed in the topic of currency revaluation, that is, a tax-funded financial compensation for savers and holders of private and public bonds. The *Kapitalkleinrentner* were the symbol of this moral fight for justice, a fight that dragged on for years. The topic was particularly explosive because judges of the Reich Court in Leipzig reviewed the issue of revaluation and threatened not to recognize the recently adopted laws. In their words, it was a fight of the 'people's sense of justice' against unjust laws. This was an unknown, even revolutionary, assumption of judicial review in the German constitutional tradition. When the DNVP, as a party in government, abandoned its former position on this matter, the protest of the 'sense of justice against the laws' drifted off to the *Völkische*.[73]

From 1924 onwards, contemporaries took stock of the inflation situation, identifying the losers and winners. As we have seen, statistically this was a mixed picture, putting many (self-)assessments into perspective: the *Mittelstand* was not 'destroyed', the system of social inequality based on access to societal and political power and status via education, habitus, and social position was largely marked by continuities, notwithstanding political and social caesuras. Despite the levelling consequences of inflation, Germany was still a class society. In contrast to many expectations, capitalism had prevailed, even though its representatives complained bitterly about high social burdens, taxes, and state interventions. The country was deeply divided, not only politically but also, thanks to inflation, socially: between urban and rural communities, consumers and producers, house owners and tenants, creditors and debtors, as well as workers, farmers, and the bourgeoisie. Even contemporaries saw the reason for the breakdown of social contract relations in the dominance of particular interests. This applied not least to the bourgeois liberal parties that always tried to reconcile and integrate different interest groups of their bourgeois base.[74]

There was, however, a broad consensus regarding the negative assessment of inflation winners and 'inflation blossoms' that were targets of criticism and denounced as the cause of inflation. This became obvious in several political, financial, and economic scandals. Many different topics were negotiated in this context: hardship and waste, the alleged corruption of republican politicians, and not least excesses of speculative capitalism that had actually happened during the inflation period but were now caricatured and attacked as 'Jewish capitalism'. Was this capitalism obliterated? Racist antisemitism and anti-capitalism, which have always gone hand in hand, developed an explosive power with disastrous results after the beginning of the Great Depression. The question was whether the specious prosperity had revealed remaining structural economic problems. Were the—perhaps not sufficiently radical—austerity politics that had started with the currency reform to be continued under the conditions of the Great Depression?[75]

The enthusiasm and spirit of optimism that marked the revolutionary period had faded in 1924, being replaced by soberness and a new sense of reality. Putsches and uprisings had failed, the republic prevailed as political form of rule. It looked like the republicans were in control. Politicians, military, and bureaucracy had practised the state of emergency with many variations, be it to combat social and political unrest, economic and fiscal emergencies, or to protect the republic. This had created significant practical precedents that became important again under the changed political conditions after 1930 and were finally directed against the republic.

It is much harder to determine the medium- and long-term psychological repercussions of the inflation, especially hyperinflation. They include the recurrent fear of inflation in Germany, with repeated references to the year 1923, even today. And then, there is the point raised by the novelist Elias Canetti that 'a crime of such an extent' as experienced during the Nazi period would have been unthinkable without inflation as a 'mass phenomenon' with its severe devaluation processes. 'It would have been hardly possible to push them [the Nazis] that far', Canetti has written, 'if they had not experienced a few years earlier an inflation in which the Mark was worth a billionth of the original value. And it was this inflation as a mass phenomenon they unloaded on the Jews.'[76]
Translated from German by Christine Brocks.

Notes

1. Walther Rathenau, 'Rede auf der Tagung des Reichsverbandes der Deutschen Industrie, gehalten in München am 28. September 1921', in Walther Rathenau (ed.), *Gesammelte Reden* (Berlin: S. Fischer Verlag, 1921), 241–64.
2. Most prominently, Carl-Ludwig Holtfrerich, *The German Inflation 1914–1923* (Berlin and New York: De Gruyter, 1986); Gerald D. Feldman, *The Great Disorder: Politics, Economics, and Society in the German Inflation, 1914–1924* (New York and Oxford: Oxford University Press, 1993; Richard Bessel, *Germany After the First World War* (Oxford: Oxford University Press, 1993); see for an overview Anthony McElligott, *Rethinking the Weimar Republic: Authority and Authoritarianism, 1916–1936* (London: Bloomsbury Academic, 2014); Heinrich August Winkler, *Weimar 1918–1933: Die Geschichte der ersten deutschen Demokratie* (Munich: C. H. Beck, 1993).
3. Jürgen Falter, Thomas Lindenberger, and Siegfried Schumann, *Wahlen und Abstimmungen in der Weimarer Republik: Materialien zum Wahlverhalten 1919–1933* (Munich: C. H. Beck, 1986), 44; Karl Rohe, *Wahlen und Wählertraditionen in Deutschland: Kulturelle Grundlagen deutscher Parteien und Parteisysteme im 19. und 20. Jahrhundert* (Frankfurt/Main: Suhrkamp, 1992), 142.

4. Hans Mommsen, *Die verspielte Freiheit: Der Weg der Republik von Weimar in den Untergang 1918–1933* (Berlin: Ullstein, 1989), 63–140.
5. Daniela Gasteiger, *Kuno von Westarp (1864–1945): Parlamentarismus, Monarchismus und Herrschaftsutopien im deutschen Konservatismus* (Berlin and Boston: De Gruyter Oldenbourg, 2018), 147–201.
6. Stefan Scholl, *Begrenzte Abhängigkeit: 'Wirtschaft' und 'Politik' im 20. Jahrhundert* (Frankfurt/Main: Campus Verlag, 2015), esp. 73–105; Horst Dreier, 'Grundrechtsrepublik Weimar', in Christian Waldorff (ed.), *Das Wagnis der Demokratie: Eine Anatomie der Weimarer Reichsverfassung* (Munich: C. H. Beck, 2018), 175–94.
7. Heinrich August Winkler, *Der Schein der Normalität: Arbeiter und Arbeiterbewegung in der Weimarer Republik 1924 bis 1930* (Berlin and Bonn: J. H. W. Dietz Nachf., 1985), 183–294.
8. Martin H. Geyer, *Kapitalismus und politische Moral, oder: Wer war Julius Barmat?* (Hamburg: Hamburger Edition, 2018), esp. 64–79; Klaus Epstein, *Matthias Erzberger und das Dilemma der deutschen Demokratie* (Berlin: Leber, 1962).
9. Feldman, *Great Disorder*, 162–3, 198–9.
10. Also for the following: Heinz Hürten, *Der Kapp-Putsch als Wende* (Opladen: Westdeutscher Verlag, 1989); Gasteiger, *von Westarp*, 178–85.
11. Winkler, *Weimar 1918–1933*, 131–5; Karin Hartewig, *Das unberechenbare Jahrzehnt: Bergarbeiter und ihre Familien im Ruhrgebiet 1914–1924* (Munich: C. H. Beck, 1993), 485; Martin H. Geyer, 'Grenzüberschreitungen: Vom Belagerungszustand zum Ausnahmezustand', in Nils Werber, Stefan Kaufmann, and Lars Koch (eds), *Erster Weltkrieg: Kulturwissenschaftliches Handbuch* (Stuttgart and Weimar: J. B. Metzler, 2014), 341–84, 363.
12. Thomas Alexander, *Carl Severing. Ein Demokrat und Sozialist in Weimar* (Frankfurt/Main: Lang, 1996), 451–503.
13. On monarchism see Gasteiger, *Von Westarp*, 202–18.
14. Diethard Hennig, *Johannes Hoffmann, Sozialdemokrat und bayerischer Ministerpräsident: Biographie* (Munich: Saur, 1990), 424–44.
15. On the republican military consensus Rüdiger Bergien, *Die bellizistische Republik: Wehrkonsens und 'Wehrhaftmachung' in Deutschland 1918–1933* (Munich: Oldenbourg, 2012), 75–120.
16. Martin H. Geyer, 'Teuerungsprotest, Konsumentenpolitik und soziale Gerechtigkeit während der Inflation: München 1920–23', *Archiv für Sozialgeschichte*, 30 (1990), 181–215.
17. Figures in Ursula Büttner, *Weimar: Die überforderte Republik 1918–1933: Leistung und Versagen in Gesellschaft, Wirtschaft und Kultur* (Stuttgart: Klett-Cotta, 2008), 168.
18. In detail Feldman, *Great Disorder*, 156–65.
19. Johannes Bähr, *Staatliche Schlichtung in der Weimarer Republik: Tarifpolitik, Korporatismus und industrieller Konflikt zwischen Inflation u. Deflation 1919–1932* (Berlin: Colloquium Verlag, 1989).
20. These constellations are emphasized by Holtfrerich, *German Inflation*, 197–220, and Feldman, *Great Disorder*, 165–227; Gerald D. Feldman, 'The Political Economy of Germany's Relative Stabilization during the 1920/21 Depression', in Gerald D. Feldman (ed.), *The German Inflation Reconsidered: A Preliminary Balance* (Berlin and New York: De Gruyter, 1982), 180–206; see also Barry Eichengreen, *Golden Fetters: The Gold Standard and the Great Depression, 1919–1939* (Oxford: Oxford University Press, 1992).
21. Holtfrerich, *German Inflation*, 206–20, 198; Stephen A. Schuker, *American 'Reparations' to Germany, 1919–33: Implications for the Third-World Debt Crisis* (Princeton: International Finance Section, Department of Economics, Princeton University, 1988).

22. Feldman, *Great Disorder*, 854–5; Niall Ferguson, *Paper and Iron: Hamburg Business and German Politics in the Era of Inflation, 1897–1927* (Cambridge, MA: Cambridge University Press, 1996), 269–309.
23. Susanne Miller, Heinrich Potthoff, *Kleine Geschichte der SPD: Darstellung und Dokumentation 1848–1990*, 7th rev. and updated ed. (Bonn: Dietz, 1991), 76–8.
24. Max Hoelz, *Vom 'Weißen Kreuz' zur Roten Fahne: Jugend-, Kampf- und Zuchthauserlebnisse* (Berlin: Malik-Verlag, 1929, reprint 1969); Sigrid Koch-Baumgarten, *Aufstand der Avantgarde: Die Märzaktion* (Frankfurt/Main: Campus, 1986).
25. Curt Geyer, *Die revolutionäre Illusion: Zur Geschichte des linken Flügels der USPD* (Stuttgart: Deutsche Verlags-Anstalt, 1976).
26. Emil Julius Gumbel, *Vier Jahre politischer Mord* (Berlin-Fichtenau: Verlag der Neuen Gesellschaft, 1922), 81.
27. Martin Sabrow, Der Rathenaumord: Rekonstruktion einer Verschwörung gegen die Weimarer Republik (Munich: Oldenbourg, 1994).
28. Gotthard Jasper, *Der Schutz der Republik: Studien zur staatlichen Sicherung der Demokratie in der Weimarer Republik 1922–1930* (Tübingen: Mohr, 1963); Mathias Grünthaler, *Parteiverbote in der Weimarer Republik* (Frankfurt/Main: Lang, 1995), 229 (quote); Manuela Achilles, 'Reforming the Reich: Democratic Symbols and Rituals in the Weimar Republic', in Kathleen Canning, Kerstin Brandt, and Kristin McGuire (eds), *Weimar Publics/Weimar Subjects: Rethinking the Political Culture of Germany in the 1920s* (New York and Oxford: Berghahn Books, 2010), 175–91.
29. For an overview see McElligott, *Rethinking*, 35–51. For the following see Feldman, *Great Disorder*, 309–507; Bruce Kent, *The Spoils of War: The Politics, Economics and Diplomacy of Reparations 1918–1932* (Oxford: Oxford University Press, 1989).
30. Peter Krüger, *Die Außenpolitik der Weimarer Republik*, 2nd ed. (Darmstadt: Wissenschaftliche Buchgesellschaft, 1993).
31. Also for the following see Heinrich Küppers, *Joseph Wirth: Parlamentarier, Minister und Kanzler der Weimarer Republik* (Stuttgart: Franz Steiner Verlag, 1997), 104–22.
32. John Maynard Keynes, *The Economic Consequences of the Peace* (London: Macmillan, 1920).
33. Feldman, *Great Disorder*, 344–84.
34. Küppers, *Joseph Wirth*, 137, 199.
35. Ralf Hoffrogge, 'Der Sommer des Nationalbolschewismus? Die Stellung der KPD-Linken zum Ruhrkampf und ihre Kritik am "Schlageter-Kurs" von 1923', *Sozial.Geschichte Online*, 20 (2017), 99–146.
36. Walter Mühlhausen, *Friedrich Ebert 1871–1925: Reichspräsident der Weimarer Republik* (Bonn: J. H. W. Dietz Nachf., 2006), 552–93.
37. Also for the following: Gerd Krumeich, 'Der "Ruhrkampf" als Krieg: Überlegungen zu einem verdrängten deutsch-französischen Konflikt', in Gerd Krumeich and Joachim Schröder (eds), *Der Schatten des Weltkriegs: Die Ruhrbesetzung 1923* (Essen: Klartext Verlag, 2004), 9–24; Conan Fischer, *The Ruhr-Crisis: 1923–1924* (Oxford: Oxford University Press, 2010); Jonathan Wright, *Gustav Stresemann: Weimar's Greatest Statesman* (Oxford: Oxford University Press, 2002), 157–91.
38. Hoffrogge, 'Der Sommer des Nationalbolschewismus?'
39. Klaus-Dieter Krohn, *Stabilisierung und ökonomische Interessen: Die Finanzpolitik des Deutschen Reiches 1923–1927* (Düsseldorf: Bertelsmann Universitätsverlag, 1974); Winkler, *Revolution zur Stabilisierung*, 608–12; Feldman, *Great Disorder*, 780–802.

40. Ferguson, *Paper and Iron*, 342.
41. Holtfrerich, *German Inflation*, 224, 294.
42. Gerald D. Feldman and Heidrun Homburg, *Industrie und Inflation: Studien und Dokumente zur Politik der deutschen Unternehmer 1916-1923* (Hamburg: Hoffmann & Campe, 1977), 164. It should be noted that for the banks the extremely low valuation of their stocks in the stabilization year of 1924 came into play.
43. Gerald D. Feldman, *Hugo Stinnes: Biographie eines Industriellen 1870-1924* (Munich: C. H. Beck, 1998); Paul Ufermann, *Könige der Inflation* (Berlin: Verlag für Sozialwissenschaft, 1924); see also Christian Pierer, *Die Bayerischen Motoren Werke bis 1933: Eine Unternehmensgründung in Krieg, Inflation und Weltwirtschaftskrise* (Munich: Oldenbourg, 2011); Geyer, *Wer war Julius Barmat?*
44. Werner Abelshauser, 'Verelendung der Handarbeiter? Zur sozialen Lage der deutschen Arbeiter in der großen Inflation der frühen Zwanziger Jahre', in Hans Mommsen and Winfried Schulze (eds), *Vom Elend der Handarbeit: Probleme historischer Unterschichtenforschung* (Stuttgart: Klett-Cotta, 1981), 445-76; Holtfrerich, *German Inflation*, 221-78; Andreas Kunz, *Civil Servants and the Politics of Inflation in Germany, 1914-1924* (Berlin and New York: De Gruyter, 1986); Rudolf Tschirbs, *Tarifpolitik im Ruhrbergbau 1918-1933* (Berlin and New York: De Gruyter, 1986); Geyer, *Verkehrte Welt*, 142-56.
45. The term was coined by Gerhard A. Ritter, see Gerald D. Feldman, 'Der Historiker und die deutsche Inflation', in Feldman, *Vom Weltkrieg zur Weltwirtschaftskrise* (Göttingen: Vandenhoeck & Ruprecht, 1984), 55-66, here 60; Andreas Kunz, 'Verteilungskampf oder Interessenkonsensus? Einkommensentwicklung und Sozialverhalten von Arbeitnehmergruppen in der Inflationszeit 1914 bis 1924', in Gerald D. Feldman (ed.), *The German Inflation: A Preliminary Balance* (Berlin and New York: De Gruyter, 1982), 345-84.
46. Michael Hughes, *Paying for the German Inflation* (Chapel Hill, NC, and London: University of North Carolina Press, 1988); Geyer, *Verkehrte Welt*, 205-22.
47. Friedrich Lenger, *Werner Sombart 1863-1941: Eine Biographie* (Munich: C. H. Beck, 1994), 257-71.
48. Moritz Julius Bonn, *Wandering Scholar* (New York: John Day, 1948), 151.
49. For another description of inflation see Stefan Zweig, *Die Welt von Gestern: Erinnerungen eines Europäers* (Frankfurt/Main: Büchergilde Gutenberg, 1968). Originally published 1944.
50. Elias Canetti, *Masse und Macht* (Düsseldorf: S. Fischer, 1981), 211. Originally published 1960.
51. Victor Klemperer, *Leben sammeln, nicht fragen wozu und warum: Tagebücher 1918-1932*, ed. Walter Nowojski, 2 vols (Berlin: Aufbau Verlag, 1996), vol. 1. *Tagebücher 1918-1924*, 258, 645, 702; the entrepreneur and later finance minister, Hermann Dietrich (DDP), was economically much better off than Klemperer, but made ends meet with similar small-scale businesses, see Desiderius Meyer, *Hermann Dietrich: Bürgertum und Liberalismus in der Weimarer Republik* (Ph.D. LMU Munich, 2018), 177-212.
52. Klemperer, *Leben sammeln*, vol. 1, 697.
53. Alfred Weber, *Die Not der geistigen Arbeiter* (Munich: Duncker & Humblot, 1923).
54. See Harry Graf Kessler, *Das Tagebuch: 1880-1937*, ed. Roland S. Kamzelak and Ulrich Ott, 9 vols. (Stuttgart: Klett-Cotta, 2007), vol. 7.: *1919-1923*; Bernd Widdig, *Culture and Inflation in Weimar Germany* (Berkeley, CA: University of California Press, 2001).

55. Klemperer, *Leben sammeln*, vol. 1, 703; Marshall Berman, *All That is Solid Melts into Air: The Experience of Modernity* (New York: Simon & Schuster, 1982); Geyer, *Verkehrte Welt*, esp. 243–277, 379–388.
56. *Briefwechsel 1918–1935: Carl Schmitt, Ludwig Feuchtwanger*, ed. Rolf Riess, with a preface by Edgar J. Feuchtwanger (Berlin: Duncker & Humblot, 2007), letters from 12 and 24 Nov. 1923, 44, 45.
57. Molly Loberg, *The Struggle for the Streets of Berlin: Politics, Consumption, and Urban Space* (Cambridge: Cambridge University Press, 2018), 90–104.
58. Martin Schlemmer, '*Los von Berlin*': *Die Rheinstaatbestrebungen nach dem Ersten Weltkrieg* (Cologne: Böhlau, 2007).
59. Also for the following see Winkler, *Von der Revolution zur Stabilisierung*, 619–24, 655–64; Mühlhausen, *Friedrich Ebert*, 641–75; see the sources in Bernhard H. Bayerlein, Leonid G. Babičenko, Friderich I Firsov, and Aleksandr Ju. Vatlin, *Deutscher Oktober 1923: Ein Revolutionsplan und sein Scheitern* (Berlin: Aufbau, 2003).
60. Geyer, 'Teuerungsprotest', 210–12.
61. Also for the following Heinz Hürten (ed.), *Das Krisenjahr 1923: Militär und Innenpolitik 1922–1924* (Düsseldorf: Droste, 1980); see Mühlhausen, *Friedrich Ebert*, 628–40, 759–63.
62. Ernst Deuerlein (ed.), *Der Hitler-Putsch: Bayerische Dokumente zum 8./.9.11.1923* (Munich: Deutsche Verlags-Anstalt, 1962). Rainer Pommerin, 'Die Ausweisung von Ostjuden aus Bayern 1923: Ein Beitrag zum Krisenjahr der Weimarer Republik', *Vierteljahrshefte für Zeitgeschichte*, 34 (1986), 311–40.
63. Hürten, *Krisenjahr 1923*, xvi–xvii and document 128, 185 (quote).
64. Feldman, *Stinnes*, 888.
65. Deuerlein, *Hitler-Putsch*.
66. *Akten der Reichskanzlei, Die Regierung Stresemann I und II, 13. August 1923 bis 6. Oktober 1923, 6. Oktober bis 30. November 1923*, 2 vols, ed. Karl-Dietrich Erdmann and Martin Vogt (Boppard: Boldt, 1978), vol. 2, 998–1000.
67. Mühlhausen, *Friedrich Ebert*, 692–6; 'Denkschrift des Reichswehrministers über den Ausnahmezustand, 12. Aug. 1924', in Hürten, *Krisenjahr 1923*, document 207, 348.
68. 'Ermächtigungsgesetz vom 8. Dezember 1923', *RGBl* (1923), 1179; a full list of decrees in *Akten der Reichskanzlei, Die Kabinette Marx I u. II, 3. Nov. 1923 bis 2. Juni 1924, 3. Juni 1924 bis 15. Jan. 1925*, ed. Günter Abramowski, 2 vols (Boppard: Boldt 1973), 369–73.
69. 'Zusammenfassung der vom Truppenamt vorgetragenen Beurteilung der inneren Lage', 7. Dec. 1923, in Hürten, *Krisenjahr 1923*, document 133, 196.
70. Klaus-Dieter Krohn, 'Helfferich contra Hilferding: Konservative Geldpolitik und die sozialen Folgen der deutschen Inflation 1918 bis 1924', *Vierteljahrschrift für Sozial- und Wirtschaftsgeschichte*, 62 (1975), 62–92; Feldman, *Great Disorder*, 736–53.
71. Andreas Kunz, 'Stand versus Klasse: Beamtenschaft und Gewerkschaften im Konflikt um den Personalabbau 1923/24', *Geschichte und Gesellschaft*, 8 (1982), 55–86.
72. Hughes, *Paying for the Inflation*; Larry Eugene Jones, 'Inflation, Revaluation, and the Crisis of the Middle-Class Politics: A Study in the Dissolution of the German Party System, 1922–28', *Central European History*, 12 (1979), 143–68.

73. Martin H. Geyer, 'Recht, Gerechtigkeit und Gesetze: Reichsgerichtsrat Zeiler und die Inflation', *Zeitschrift für Neuere Rechtsgeschichte*, 16 (1994), 349–72; Bernd Rüther, *Entartetes Recht: Rechtslehren und Kronjuristen im Dritten Reich* (Munich: dtv, 1994).
74. Larry Eugene Jones, *German Liberalism and the Dissolution of the Weimar Party System 1918–1933* (Chapel Hill, NC: University of North Carolina Press, 1988).
75. See Geyer, *Wer war Julius Barmat?*
76. Canetti, *Masse und Macht*, 212.

Bibliography

Bessel, Richard, *Germany after the First World War* (Oxford: Clarendon Press, 1993).

Feldman, Gerald D., *The Great Disorder: Politics, Economics, and Society in the German Inflation, 1914–24* (New York. Oxford: Oxford University Press, 1993).

Feldman, Gerald D., *Hugo Stinnes: Biographie eines Industriellen 1870–1924* (Munich: C.H. Beck, 1998).

Fischer, Conan J., *The Ruhr Crisis* (Oxford: Oxford University Press, 2003).

Geyer, Martin H., *Verkehrte Welt. Revolution, Inflation und Moderne: München 1914–1924* (Göttingen: Vandenhoeck & Ruprecht, 1999).

Hartewig, Karin, *Das unberechenbare Jahrzehnt. Bergarbeiter und ihre Familien im Ruhrgebiet 1914–1924* (Munich: C.H. Beck, 1993).

Holtfrerich, Carl-Ludwig, *The German Inflation 1914–1923* (Berlin. New York: De Gruyter, 1986).

Hughes, Michael, *Paying for the German Inflation* (Chapel Hill, NC. London: University of North Carolina Press, 1988).

Loberg, Molly, *The Struggle for the Streets of Berlin. Politics, Consumption, and Urban Space, 1914–1945* (Cambridge: Cambridge University Press, 2018).

Widdig, Bernd, *Culture and Inflation in Weimar Germany* (Berkeley/Cal.: University of California Press, 2001).

CHAPTER 4

COALITION-BUILDING AND POLITICAL FRAGMENTATION, 1924–1930

MATTHEW STIBBE

In the (West) German Federal Republic of the late 1950s and early 1960s, conservative intellectual critics of the Weimar Republic accused it of having failed to reconcile the historically bound idea of the state with the exceptional security requirements of modern, easily endangered, and permanently crisis-prone parliamentary democracies. In their view, the authority of the state, and in particular its governability and freedom to formulate and execute rational policies, took priority over the needs of organized political movements to represent the particular material interests or ideological doctrines of their mass membership.[1] This principle proved impossible to uphold under Weimar, given the sheer number of political parties represented in the Reichstag; their failure to combine to form healthy majorities in defence of the prevailing constitutional order (as opposed to negative majorities attacking it or rendering it unworkable); and their supposed tendency to put the interests of party unity above the imperative to come together in support of the legitimate—and state-affirming—exercise of executive power, particularly at times of severe internal or external challenge.[2]

The humiliating spectacle of a Reich Chancellor—the non-party technocrat Hans Luther—being openly mocked on the floor of the Reichstag when he reminded warring Weimar parliamentarians in January 1926, during one of the periodic crises in his minority cabinet, that Germany 'must somehow be governed' was itself an illustration of how low the authority of the governing class had fallen since the days of Bismarck.[3] Also regarded as unworthy of a constitutional, law-abiding state were the 1928 and 1930 amnesties for politically motivated murders committed before 1924, granted in the name of Reich President Paul von Hindenburg but actually initiated by the Reichstag (rather than the courts) and supported by all parties bar the SPD.[4] In opposition to the alleged chaos and democratic excess of the Weimar era, the framers of the West German constitution or 'Basic Law' in 1948–9 sought to create what they saw as a *Kanzlerdemokratie*, a liberal parliamentary system that nonetheless restored dignity to the office of Chancellor as chief executive of the federal government and incentivized the formation of 'responsible' political parties whose remit was to gain the broadest support possible for themselves *and* the constitutionally settled state rather than representing particular sectional interests.[5]

The central contention of this chapter is that the conservative critique of Weimar democracy is deficient not only because of its old-fashioned, state-bound historism—which is reminiscent of what Fritz K. Ringer calls the 'German mandarin tradition'[6]—but also because of its one-sided take on German political culture itself during the 1920s, not least in the period 1924–30. Certainly, when compared to the Federal Republic in the second half of the twentieth century, cabinets came and went under Weimar with alarming frequency. In total there were twenty-one different Reich administrations between 1919 and 1933, headed by thirteen different Chancellors. To outside observers, there was scant evidence of any 'reorientation' in the attitude of coalition and opposition parties towards the workings of parliamentary government and its role in democratic state-building, even in the republic's politically calmer 'middle years', a verdict subsequently endorsed by critical (West) German scholars like Michael Stürmer.[7] Yet it is also clear that government at Reich and state levels would have been altogether impossible without some desire for compromise and coalition-building on the part of politicians. The assassination of Foreign Minister Walther Rathenau by ex-Freikorps members in 1922, the hyperinflation and Ruhr crises of 1923, followed by a communist uprising in Hamburg, Reich interventions against left-wing governments in Saxony and Thuringia, and the failed Hitler putsch in Munich in the autumn of that year, brought with them a desire to steady and rationalize politics as a necessary counterpart to currency revaluation, and did so in a way that cut across previous 'boundaries between liberal and conservative visions of authority'.[8]

The army was also keen to end the nation-wide military state-of-emergency imposed by Reich President Friedrich Ebert in September 1923, and to bring to a close the extraordinary executive powers granted to Reichswehr Head of Army Command Hans von Seeckt on 8–9 November, preferring, at this stage, to have a more behind-the-scenes role in German politics. The lifting of emergency military rule on 28 February 1924, at the instigation of Seeckt rather than civilian Reich ministers, was an important moment in this respect.[9] It allowed Reichstag elections to take place on 4 May (and again on 7 December) in an atmosphere of relative calm. It also brought with it the repeal of detention without trial, the unbanning of the KPD and various extreme right-wing groups, the return of parliamentary sovereignty over law-making for a period lasting more than six years, and the gradual restoration of constitutional government and separation of powers in Bavaria, Thuringia, and Saxony after a brief interlude in 1923–4 when they were governed by state- or Reich-appointed civilian plenipotentiaries (*Staats-* or *Reichskommissare*).[10]

This chapter will examine how power-sharing between parties was negotiated and communicated in the years 1924–30, and will focus on some notable successes of coalition government, in particular the passing of a new Reich law on unemployment insurance in 1927. It will also broaden the concept of 'coalition-building' to encompass the sphere of direct elections, when German voters were treated—or were asked to treat themselves—as one single constituency representing 'the people' as an indivisible whole. In particular it will look at the two-round contest for the Reich Presidency in 1925, narrowly won by the former commander-in-chief, Hindenburg, and at the referendum campaigns of 1926 and 1929, the first fought by a temporary alliance of the left in support of the dispossession of the former royal households, and the second by a short-term collaboration between nationalist and radical right groupings in opposition to the Young Plan.

None of the governmental or cross-party alliances considered here were stable or uncontested, however, and the third part of the chapter will explore the growing fragmentation of politics as the 1920s came to an end. The splintering of the right, particularly after the poor performance of the conservative-nationalist DNVP in the 1928 Reichstag election, and the collapse in support for the liberal DVP and DDP in face of the rise of more narrow middle-class economic interest parties, has drawn most attention in the scholarly literature.[11] However, there were also signs of fracture on the left, not only in regard to worsening relations between the SPD and KPD, but also the appearance of dissident groups like the KPD-O (Communist Party-Opposition). The chapter will conclude by considering how best to explain and evaluate this fragmentation. Was it mostly down to the conflict between economic restraints and utopian expectations, as Detlev J. K. Peukert argued in a landmark book on Weimar Germany first published in 1987?[12] Or do we need an approach that takes greater account of the communicative, performative, symbolic, and spatial dimensions of political experience? If so, might this apply not only at parliamentary level—as Thomas Mergel has expertly demonstrated in his cultural history of the Reichstag as the Weimar Republic's highest law-making body[13]—but also in relation to the above-mentioned presidential election of 1925 and referendum campaigns of 1926 and 1929, during which alternative, more direct ways of 'represent[ing] the people in its entirety' were put on show?[14] Finally, how is this period of coalition-building and political fragmentation to be seen in relation to the broader issue of continuity and change, or stability and crisis, in Weimar's history?

COALITION-BUILDING IN THE PARLIAMENTARY SPHERE

When Friedrich Ebert ended the military state-of-emergency in February 1924, the first cabinet of the Catholic Centre Party (Zentrum) politician Wilhelm Marx, supported by a shifting combination of parties in the Reichstag and empowered to undertake a step-by-step revaluation of the Mark through the passage of a time-limited Enabling Act on 8 December 1923, had already been in office for several weeks. However, to fit with the time-frame of this chapter, it makes more sense to begin the analysis of coalition-building with the second Marx cabinet, formed after the 4 May elections. This was a minority government with ministers drawn from three 'bourgeois' parties, the Zentrum, the DDP, and the DVP, or having no party affiliation at all. The forces behind the second Marx cabinet had just 138 out of 472 Reichstag seats between them, so the government had to rely on the ad hoc support of the centre-left SPD (with 100 seats), or the conservative-nationalist DNVP and other right-wing parties (with 95 plus seats), to get business through parliament. This was hardly sustainable in the long run. Indeed, the Reichstag elected in May 1924 was finally dissolved on 20 October 1924, having sat for the last time on 30 August, when, as a condition of the Dawes Plan, the new currency, the gold-backed Reichsmark, was approved without a formal vote.[15]

The Reichstag election of 7 December 1924 led, a month later, to the resignation of the second Marx government and the formation of the first *Bürgerblock* or all-inclusive 'bourgeois' cabinet under the non-party former Minister of Finance, Luther, with the backing of four major right-of-centre parties, the DVP, the DNVP, the Zentrum, and the Bavarian People's Party (BVP). This government enjoyed something closer to a parliamentary majority, with (on paper) between 242 and 274 of the 493 seats, depending on whether the left-liberal DDP were in or out. It lasted almost until the end of 1925, when the DNVP withdrew its support in protest at the Locarno Treaties and especially the Rhineland Pact, under which Germany formally recognized its new, post-1919 borders in Western Europe. The Locarno Treaties subsequently passed through the Reichstag with SPD support, but the latter's refusal to compromise with the DVP on domestic policy and defence spending put paid to the idea of a broader 'grand coalition', at least for the time being.[16] Instead, Luther was able to continue as Chancellor under a reconfigured minority 'bourgeois' government until May 1926.

From May 1926 to June 1928 Marx headed two further minority 'bourgeois' cabinets, the first without DNVP backing, and the second, from January 1927, a revived *Bürgerblock* cabinet with several DNVP ministers in tow, including Oskar Hergt as deputy chancellor and Minister of Justice. Whether this meant that, behind the scenes, the still staunchly anti-republican DNVP was on a path to piecemeal or 'silent' parliamentarization in the mid-1920s, until its substantial loss of support among core followers in the May 1928 Reichstag election forced a marked shift to the right under new leader Alfred Hugenberg, is a matter for debate.[17] The other, more mainstream 'bourgeois' parties now fell in behind a 'grand coalition' headed by the SPD, who, having increased their vote share from 26 per cent to just under 30 per cent, could claim to have nominally 'won' the election. With SPD chairman Hermann Müller as Chancellor, this new, five-party administration of the centre-left and centre-right was the last to govern Weimar Germany on a purely parliamentary and constitutional basis. Müller's successor, the conservative Catholic politician Heinrich Brüning, who from March 1930 headed a minority centre-right government without the SPD, used presidential decree to force through those of his policies that were unable to secure majority support in the Reichstag. (Table 4.1 sets out the parliamentary numbers and parties for the period.)

Were there any patterns in how these different coalitions were put together and how they were presented in the media? And to what extent was the experience at Reich level

Table 4.1. Coalition governments in Weimar Germany, 1924–1930

Headed by	Formed on	Resigned on	Parties backing	Notional parliamentary majority
Wilhelm Marx (Zentrum)	3 June 1924	15 Jan. 1925	Zentrum, DDP, DVP	138 out of 472 seats (= −196)
Hans Luther (non-party)	15 Jan. 1925	5 Dec. 1925	Zentrum, DNVP, DVP, BVP, (DDP)	242 (274) out of 493 seats (= −9 (+55))
Hans Luther (non-party)	19 Jan. 1926	12 May 1926	Zentrum, DDP, DVP, BVP	171 out of 493 seats (= −151)
Wilhelm Marx (Zentrum)	16 May 1926	17 Dec. 1926	Zentrum, DDP, DVP, BVP	171 out of 493 seats (= −151)
Wilhelm Marx (Zentrum)	28 Jan. 1927	12 June 1928	Zentrum, DNVP, DVP, BVP	242 out of 493 seats (= −9)
Hermann Müller (SPD)	28 June 1928	27 Mar. 1930	SPD, Zentrum, DDP, DVP, BVP	301 out of 491 seats (= +111)

Source: Wahlen in der Weimarer Republik, http://www.gonschior.de/weimar.

also reflected in coalition-building at state level? In answer to the first question, it is important to distinguish between objective realities and subjective perceptions. In retrospect, the frequent changes of government in Weimar Germany masked considerable underlying continuities both in policy and personnel, and a growing self-understanding of the Reichstag as a 'social space' where deals were made and legislation enacted. Gustav Stresemann, for instance, was able to retain the position of Foreign Minister—and thereby to personify Weimar foreign policy during this period—from 30 November 1923 through to his untimely death on 3 October 1929, when he was replaced by DVP colleague Julius Curtius. In spite of opposition to his pro-western approach from the DNVP and other parties further to the right (and extreme left), he managed to achieve a string of successes: the Dawes Plan in 1924, the Locarno Treaties in 1925, Germany's entry into the League of Nations in 1926, the Young Plan in 1929, and the Allies' withdrawal from their military occupation of the Rhineland between 1927 and 1930, five years ahead of schedule.[18] Otto Gessler of the DDP remained even longer as Defence Minister, from March 1920 to January 1928, and the Catholic politician Heinrich Brauns survived a full eight years as Minister of Labour, from June 1920 to June 1928. Other figures served more or less continuously in office, even if they switched portfolios, including Hans Luther (Minister of Agriculture, December 1922–October 1923; Minister of Finance, October 1923–January 1925; Chancellor, January 1925–May 1926); Julius Curtius (Minister of Economic Affairs, January 1926–October 1929; Foreign Minister, October 1929–October 1931); Karl Stingl (Minister of Post, November 1922–August 1923 and January 1925–December 1926); and Stingl's BVP colleague, Georg Schätzel (Minister of Post, January 1927–May 1932).[19]

Parliamentary life itself was increasingly conducted on a cross-party basis at Reich level, with a common semantics and shared understanding of how to conduct legislative business effectively—barring one or two admittedly prominent exceptions. Historians are especially keen to highlight the so-called flag-incident of May 1926, when a seemingly trivial dispute over which flag(s) should be flown over Germany's overseas trade missions and consulates—a matter of great symbolic importance to republicans and anti-republicans alike—led to a vote of no confidence and the collapse of the second Luther cabinet.[20] For Franklin C. West, and others, the 'crisis over the Flag Decree' was one example, among many, of the core problem with Weimar's multi-party system, namely that 'no party's leadership could or would undertake actions which threatened its own party's unity'.[21] Compromises between the parties were only possible when made 'at a minimum cost to their own principles'.[22] However, this view is in need of revision, or at least nuancing. In particular, it should not blind us to the manner in which—as Benjamin Ziemann puts it—the 'formal rules and informal procedures [of parliamentary life]' had a cultural impact of their own, 'foster[ing] a sense of cohesion among the deputies which was able to transcend the political cleavages'.[23] From January 1925, Paul Löbe of the SPD served as President of the Reichstag, as he had already done between June 1920 and May 1924. This proved critical not only in holding executive power to account, but in enabling its lawful, democratic exercise, especially when getting aspects of Stresemann's foreign policy through parliament. He was supported by Vice-Presidents from the DNVP, DVP, and Zentrum. Thus, even when outside government, the SPD parliamentary group had a critical role in the domestic law-making process, and a vested interest in its smooth running, irrespective of questions of wider party unity; the same can be said for the DNVP, at least until May–June 1928.[24]

One of the most relevant pieces of social legislation enacted during this period was the Law on Labour Exchanges and Unemployment Insurance (Gesetz über Arbeitsvermittlung und Arbeitslosenversicherung, AVAVG), which was passed by the Reichstag on 16 July 1927 and came into force on 1 October 1927. This law established a new financial basis for granting benefits to the short-term, involuntarily unemployed from contributions made by employers, employees, and the Reich, and with the needs of family dependants taken into account. Payments would be for a maximum of twenty-six weeks.[25] It also set up a series of labour exchanges to assist those looking for work. It was much criticized in retrospect because it was based on an assumed average of only 700,000 and maximum of 1.4 million unemployed persons at any one time, and thus proved completely unworkable during the Great Depression after 1929. It was also held up by right-wing economists from at least 1928 onwards as an example of the 'excessive', business-unfriendly ambitions of Weimar social policy.[26] Nonetheless, Rudolf Wissell, the SPD Minister of Labour in the 'grand coalition' government of 1928–30, noted in an article published a month after he left office that the law, for all its problems, 'closed a gap in the existing system of social insurance' and thereby 'fulfilled an old working-class demand'. More importantly, it was supported by the 'overwhelming majority of the Reichstag, from the German Nationalists to the Social Democrats'.[27] Indeed, of

493 eligible deputies, 355 voted for it, and only 47—the entire National Socialist and Communist contingents and a handful of dissident DNVP members—against.[28]

For Wissell, following an economic determinist model, this showed that 'the year 1927 was very favourable for social policy' because 'the economic crisis of 1926 had been overcome and the labour market was in good shape', at least in comparison to the winter of 1928–9.[29] Yet it could also be read in a different way, as an indication that day-to-day parliamentary culture and cross-party coalition-building under Weimar mattered as an independent factor in the production of social policy options, in the creation of spaces for political compromise, and even in progress towards democratic state-building. At stake, in other words, was more than just tactical gains for the 'immovable' economic interest groups that Stürmer (among others) sees as dominating the choices made by government and opposition parties in the years 1924–8.[30]

Parliamentary culture apart, much has been made of the SPD's supposed 'policy of abstention' at Reich level after 1923, as seen in its 'negative' approach to coalition negotiations in October-December 1924, December 1925-January 1926, and even in May–June 1928, when its improved showing in the Reichstag election made its participation in government all but inevitable.[31] The 'grand coalition' is sometimes characterized, negatively, as a time when the Social Democrats obstinately refused to abandon the role of chief opposition party while at the same time holding some of the most important offices of state, namely the Reich Chancellery and the Ministries of Finance, Interior, and Labour. At one point in 1928, the SPD ministers even voted against a defence measure in the Reichstag—the building of 'battle cruiser A' (*Panzerkreuzer A*)—that they had actually approved in cabinet, because the party's parliamentary group instructed them to do so.[32] Wissell, as Minister of Labour, found himself constantly caught between his personal sympathy with the more radical positions on social policy adopted by the Free Trade Unions and left-wing deputies from his own party, and the conservative, pro-business views not only of the 'bourgeois' members of the Müller cabinet, but also of his SPD colleague, the Minister of Finance Rudolf Hilferding.[33]

The 'peculiar negotiating structures of the Reichstag' also contributed to what Mergel refers to as the fundamental 'opaqueness' of parliamentary procedures in Weimar Germany, leading to a cultural disconnect with political movements and trends outside parliament (as opposed to a lack of day-to-day consensus among parliamentarians). For a bill to pass into law, party manifestos and headline-grabbing rhetoric often had to give way to long-drawn-out committee work, the elevation of expert legal and technical advice over partisan media presentation, and the resolution of political disagreements through close attention to detail and forensic analysis. The AVAVG was a classic example. Here the original government bill already contained 175 separate clauses; by the time the amended version was passed on 16 July 1927, this had risen to 275.[34] In July 1928, shortly after Wissell became Minister of Labour, cabinet and parliament agreed changes to the conditions under which unemployment benefits could be claimed—including extensions, under some circumstances, beyond the twenty-six week limit—in spite of the opposition of employers' groups and right-wing parties, and in spite of claims by the Free Trade Unions that the new measures did not go far enough.[35] Given these added complications, it becomes more understandable why the incoming Chancellor, Müller, initially sought to keep the incumbent Minister of Labour, the Catholic priest and Christian trade unionist Brauns, in post in June 1928 in preference to his own party colleague, Wissell. Yet in the end, the attitude of the right wing of the Zentrum, which demanded the recall of Brauns and a reduced commitment to the 'grand coalition', forced Müller's hand.[36]

That the cumbersome process of coalition-building did little to endear elected politicians to the German public is reflected in the declining voter turn-out at elections, from a highpoint of 83.0 per cent in January 1919 to 77.4 per cent in May 1924, 78.7 per cent in December 1924 and 75.6 per cent in May 1928.[37] However, this should not be taken as a sign that 'ordinary' Germans were abandoning the notion that indirect or parliamentary democracy was the best way of representing their interests at national and state level. The non-party-affiliated, but usually conservative local, regional, and supra-regional press encouraged sceptical but not entirely rejectionist attitudes, partly as a means of boosting its own importance as an extra-parliamentary force and partly to underline its claim to represent the allegedly true or directly expressed, authentic voice of the people against the so-called self-serving politicians in Berlin (or, as the Bavarians often complained, in 'Red' Prussia). True, only a handful of influential, but hardly representative, left-liberal national newspapers, such as the *Berliner Tageblatt* and the *Vossische Zeitung*, as well as the supra-regional Catholic organ the *Kölnische Volkszeitung* and the SPD's daily journal *Vorwärts*, could be relied upon to support the republic wholeheartedly. But this did not mean that the remaining papers were all unremittingly hostile to the new constitutional order, even if they often played to the 'nationalism and anti-socialism' of their largely 'bourgeois readership'.[38] The German-Jewish publicist Edgar Stern-Rubarth, editor-in-chief of the Reich's official press agency, Wolffs Telegraphisches Büro, and a leading advocate of Stresemann's foreign policy, including Franco-German reconciliation, summed up the dilemma facing successive republican administrations in 1927: 'In Metternich's time we bought the journalists, in Bismarck's time we appointed them, today we have to win them over'.[39]

How far did this also reflect the experience of coalition-building and political communication at municipal and state, as opposed to Reich, level? Between 1924 and 1930, variations on the *Bürgerblock*-style of coalition government were tried out in several states (Thuringia, Bavaria, Brunswick, Mecklenburg-Schwerin, Mecklenburg-Strelitz, Württemberg, and others). On the other hand, SPD-led 'grand coalitions' ruled for much of the same period in Prussia, Baden, Hamburg, Hesse, Saxony, Anhalt, and elsewhere. The KPD did not have much influence in any state governments after the 'emergency' of 1923–4, just as it was not much of a threat nationally. Even in the once staunchly 'Red' city-state of Hamburg, where the parliamentary arithmetic in the provincial assembly might in principle have allowed an SPD-KPD coalition in 1927–31, or a minority SPD administration 'tolerated' by the KPD, the Social Democrats still preferred to continue in government with the 'bourgeois' DVP and DDP.[40] The radical right—in the form of the NSDAP and fellow-travellers from the ultra-nationalist and ultra-conservative wings of the DNVP—only really became a disruptive force after the state elections in Thuringia in December 1929 and the Reichstag elections in September 1930.[41]

State governments, like Reich governments, had an opportunity and an obligation to get legislation passed, to win over journalists, and to build broader confidence among the population. The largest state, Prussia, had already served as an 'unlikely rock of democracy' in the years 1918–25, principally by means of power-sharing between the pro-Weimar parties (SPD, DDP, Zentrum, and latterly the DVP),[42] but also because SPD Minister of Interior Carl Severing won the admiration of the more conservative republican parties through his willingness to appoint non-SPD members to senior administrative positions, and his readiness, alongside Ebert, Gessler, and Seeckt, to countenance authoritarian measures in the face of communist threats.[43] He continued to play that role following the return of the Weimar coalition of SPD, DDP, and Centre Party to office in Prussia, after an extremely brief interlude of minority 'bourgeois' rule, in April 1925. Indeed, for many observers Severing personified the 'new' Prussia: an empirically oriented, pragmatic, and yet still quasi-authoritarian state that practised dictatorial *and* liberal forms of rule simultaneously. As a British Foreign Office memorandum in March 1927 noted:

> Broadly speaking, Prussia is still a 'Beamtenstaat', a State administered by Prussian civil servants working in conjunction with local officials appointed by the duly elected representatives of the people . . . It is safe to say that the majority of these appointments to-day are in the hands of the Weimar parties, Centre, Democrats and Social Democrats . . . [although] the majority of Prussian officials being civil servants holding permanent appointments, changes can only be effected gradually . . . the Oberregierungspräsident, the Regierungspräsident and the Landrat are all nominated by the Ministry of Interior . . . So far as actual internal administration is concerned, the [November 1918] revolution made little or no change.[44]

On the negative side, the ability of 'Weimar Prussia' to influence Reich policy—for instance in matters of external defence, media, health, education, policing, or all-round governance and use of state-of-emergency legislation—was diminished in view of the fact that the offices of Prussian Minister-President and Reich Chancellor were no longer held by the same person, as they frequently had been under the old Kaiserreich, and the Minister-President no longer sat *ex officio* in the Reich cabinet.[45] Attempts to overcome this, seen, for instance, in hopes that the sitting Minister-President, Otto Braun, might be proposed for the post of Chancellor after the May 1928 Reichstag elections, were thwarted when the SPD executive committee insisted on Müller instead.[46] Bavaria, governed by a clerical-conservative coalition under BVP leader Heinrich Held between 1924 and 1933, would also most likely have vetoed any attempt to 'reunite' the positions of Reich Chancellor and Prussian Minister-President, especially under a popular but ultimately centralizing, bureaucratizing, and rationalizing Social Democrat politician like Braun.[47]

In spite of developing increasing professional expertise in the realm of mass communications, state governments faced even greater challenges in selling a particular message to the voting public than Reich governments. As Matthias Lau has shown, efforts by the *Länder* to steer the regional or provincial media in a particular direction via their own press offices were met with criticisms that such methods were tantamount to an unwarranted politicization of the state's duty to inform its citizens about policy options in an impartial manner, or, worse still, were condemned as a deliberate attempt by 'liberals' to curb free speech.[48] By such means a false equivalence was sometimes constructed between republican and extreme anti-republican forms of political communication, with the conservative, provincial, and clerical right claiming that it was the 'modernizing', 'secular' republicans who had attacked them and destabilized 'their' political order first by introducing 'foreign' or western-style parliamentary-democratic methods without consulting the 'people'.[49]

In Bavaria, the populist BVP Minister-President Held developed his own version of this, supporting the war hero Hindenburg unfailingly while openly opposing Stresemann's 'pro-Allied' foreign policy and regularly pitting South German particularism against the Reich government in Berlin.[50] But there were also countervailing trends and alternative constellations. In post-1923 Hamburg, for example, the governing SPD-DVP-DDP coalition, permanent civil servants, and members of the local press all felt a common interest in representing their city-state's economic importance, and its strategic dependence on free trade and stable international relations, to neighbouring Prussia and the rest of Germany. Here, the asymmetric culture wars waged in the public arena between virulent anti-republicans and the less virulent, but sometimes equally polarized, 'Weimar' parties were largely avoided because of the 'cooperative atmosphere' in which the state's relationship with journalists was negotiated and renewed.[51] Local members of the DNVP also voiced their unease at the open hostility shown by the national party towards the Locarno Treaties in 1925, believing, correctly, that this would hinder their ability to offer middle-class Hamburg voters a credible alternative to the DVP's openness towards power-sharing with the SPD.[52]

COALITION-BUILDING AND DIRECT ELECTIONS

Direct elections—namely referendums and presidential contests—occurred less frequently under Weimar than parliamentary ones, but they were equally important to the twin cultural processes of coalition-building and political fragmentation.[53] The alliances brought together to fight direct elections were indeed very temporary and did nothing to halt the trend towards fragmentation, even if they also reveal a strange consensus between parties and commentators on the importance of symbolic issues in constructing rival visions of the nation. They were often accompanied by real or imagined spikes in street violence and emotion-driven battles over public spaces.[54] And, as Joseph Addison, British *chargé d'affaires* in Berlin, wrote to Conservative Foreign Secretary Sir Austen

Chamberlain on 11 June 1926, they poisoned public discourse by 'rais[ing] every conceivable legal and moral problem[,] ... rous[ing] every shade of political thought [and] monopolis[ing] public attention to the exclusion of all else'.[55]

The disruptive effect of direct elections was further magnified by the fact that they were typically won or lost on the ability of campaigners to mobilize a broad mass of politically indifferent voters, or voters who were less interested in the substance of parliamentary elections than in the symbolism of 'victory'. What mattered was to achieve spatial and representational dominance for one's candidate, 'flag', 'colours', or otherwise overpublicized cause, with 'success' typically measured in terms of the number of rallies and meetings organized, the number of posters plastered across city landscapes, and so on.[56] At the start of the June 1926 referendum on dispossession of the princes, for instance, the KPD reported that it was planning to throw 33 million items of printed material into the campaign, that the SPD was preparing a further 20 million, and that the 'monarchist' side had already distributed 22 million leaflets in Berlin alone.[57] Finally, direct elections tended to reduce complex political issues to a binary and seemingly irreversible 'yes' or 'no' choice. Staying neutral was not a practical option, meaning that direct elections totalized and fractured political communities simultaneously. Furthermore, although there might be a democratic 'result', political conflict could not be reduced *after* a direct election by displacing it into the more opaque and therefore less immediately polarizing fields of parliamentary procedure and the technical sides of framing legislation. In this sense, direct elections laid 'the seeds of the escalation of [political] violence' after 1930, as Dirk Schumann puts it.[58]

The first direct election in the Weimar era, the two-round presidential contest in March–April 1925, won on 26 April by the Reichsblock's candidate, Hindenburg, in fact sidestepped major political questions altogether to focus solely on the 77-year-old former commander-in-chief's 'heroic' personality and 'sacrificial' candidature. The Reichsblock, made up of right and centre-right Protestant parties, had in fact nominated the more divisive Karl Jarres, DVP mayor of Duisburg and Reich Minister of Interior in 1923-4, as its candidate in the first, inconclusive vote on 29 March. Jarres's decision to stand down in favour of Hindenburg was a strategic one, conditional on the simultaneous withdrawal of the BVP's Heinrich Held. It enabled the Reichsblock to expand its support beyond the Protestant-nationalist middle class to include right-wing Catholic voters in Bavaria and elsewhere, and even some nationally minded democrats who were reluctant to support the republican Volksblock's official candidate, Wilhelm Marx, in the second round. Yet it also came at a price, leading to a 'dilution' of the right-wing message and a blurring of political boundaries to the point where Hindenburg's victory could not be claimed as a clear-cut triumph of monarchism over republicanism. Franz Seldte, leader of the radical-nationalist veterans' association, the Stahlhelm, foresaw this, noting in a circular to heads of local branches on 10 April 1925:

> There is no doubt that millions of voters voting for Hindenburg on 26 April will immediately return to their traditional party and interest affiliations after the election. The election result will not be a verdict on the strength of the national movement, but

will only be a sign of how broad and great Hindenburg's veneration is amongst the largest sections of society.[59]

Hindenburg's style of campaigning also added to these concerns. He refused to speak to sympathetic right-wing journalists or to travel around the country addressing core supporters. He stayed at home in Hanover, while his campaign team spent most of their energies targeting his opponents rather than selling 'their' candidate. In particular, they attempted to use KPD leader Ernst Thälmann's attacks on Hindenburg as a 'mass slaughterer' and 'General of Defeat' to cast the entire 'anti-Hindenburg' camp, including the moderate Catholic republican Marx, as 'unpatriotic' and disrespectful towards the memory of the war dead.[60] When he did make public pronouncements, for instance in a special radio broadcast on 24 April, Hindenburg avoided all political content, and instead sought to construct a direct relationship between the German people and himself as their national 'saviour'.[61] This tactic worked in so far as Hindenburg won the election, gaining over four million more supporters than Jarres in the first round and beating Marx by 14.66 million to 13.75 million votes. But it was not an overwhelming victory, and certainly it was not a clear-cut indication that the nationalist camp now had a secure upper hand: indeed, almost as many Germans, 14.46 compared to 14.66 million, voted in favour of the outright dispossession of the German princely households in the left-initiated people's referendum (*Volksentscheid*) of 20 June 1926.[62]

This referendum has to be understood in the context of a broader period of political tension at national level lasting from the collapse of the first Luther government in December 1925 over the Locarno Treaties to the formation of the new *Bürgerblock* government in January 1927. Between those times, minority cabinets led by Luther and Marx had to get each of their policies through parliament on the basis of ad hoc arrangements with opposition parties. One piece of legislation put forward by the DDP and approved by the Luther cabinet was for a Reich-wide law which would unify arrangements for the compensation of the former royal households in Germany in respect of possessions left behind when they abdicated in 1918 and ensure that the interests of the people and state were balanced against the principle of respect for property rights. The DNVP, with its landowner base, was opposed to any legislation that involved confiscation or compulsory purchase of land. At the other extreme, the KPD, backed by the left-wing of the SPD and the German League for Human Rights (Deutsche Liga für Menschenrechte), demanded a solution involving total confiscation without compensation or right to judicial appeal. Reluctantly, and because it was unwilling to adopt the only other option on offer, namely supporting the DDP's bill in the Reichstag, the SPD leadership agreed to co-sponsor a referendum on this issue, believing that, even if the vote were lost, it would have advantages in terms of symbolically (re)establishing the party's left-wing credentials.[63]

In fact, staging a referendum by popular initiative on a contentious issue was not all that easy—indeed, it was largely untried before 1926—and winning one was almost impossible. The first step was to form a coalition of interested parties and pressure groups around a proposed law to be directly initiated in the name of the people, in this case the expropriation of the princes without compensation. However, having agreed the wording of the proposed law, the SPD and KPD failed to persuade centrist 'bourgeois' parties like the DDP or the Zentrum officially to join them, giving the referendum campaign a distinctly sectarian aura from the outset. The next stage was to win an initiating petition (*Volksbegehren*) by collecting the signatures of at least 10 per cent of eligible voters, something which was achieved with surprising ease: overall 12.52 million signatures, more than three times the required number, were collected between 4 and 17 March.[64] However, the final step was to achieve not just 50 per cent of the vote in the actual referendum, but 50 per cent of the votes of *all* eligible voters—a much higher bar. All the opposing side had to do was dissuade people from voting at all, as abstention was the de facto equivalent to 'no'.[65] On the other hand, for the 'yes' side, both the petition stage and the referendum stage depended on winning over voters who were usually politically indifferent or unlikely to have a firm party allegiance. The political emotions that needed to be mobilized to achieve this often involved having to marshal symbolic resentments against the 'system' at local level and raise them to the status of a national or even world-historical cause. The KPD in Berlin's working-class Neukölln district, and its paramilitary organization, the Red Front Fighters' League (Roter Frontkämpferbund, RFB), remarked upon this in an article published in January 1926 in the party newspaper, *Die Rote Fahne*:

> Never before have the Red Front Fighters been received by the population of Neukölln as on last Sunday. They were invited into the houses, given chocolate, beer, cognac, wine, cigars and cigarettes out of joy because the insatiable muzzles of the Hohenzollerns, and their like, were finally going to be stopped. Time and again people emphasized: 'We are certainly not supporters of the Communists, but on this question, we will go along with them completely.'[66]

However, Neukölln was already one of the KPD's principal strongholds and, since the war, the location of many violent clashes between the Prussian police and the revolutionary left over the symbolic 'ownership' of public space in Berlin.[67] Furthermore, the article in *Die Rote Fahne* was written before pressure from its own grassroots supporters had forced the SPD to commit itself to backing the plebiscitary initiative, in other words, before the KPD had any idea that a referendum was a serious possibility. The mobilization of 12.52 million signatures for the petition in March—including 1.6 million in Berlin—together with 14.46 million 'yes' voters on polling day, 20 June 1926, was a much more impressive achievement than the 'conquest' of Neukölln, and required the creation of a much broader political base. The Nazis, it should be noted, achieved just 13.75 million votes at the height of their success in July 1932.[68] Yet in June 1926 14.46 million was only 36.38 per cent of eligible voters, not the requisite 50 per cent. The referendum therefore failed to achieve a concrete outcome, which was arguably a much bigger blow to the SPD than the KPD. The latter had championed the 'people' against the former princes. The former could hardly now go back to the 'lesser evil' of supporting the DDP bill in the Reichstag, which was formally abandoned by the new Marx government in July 1926 anyway.

The failure to find a national solution left the matter in the hands of the individual states, but the general public can only have been further confused when the Prussian government under Otto Braun actually came to an agreement with lawyers representing the House of Hohenzollern, an agreement that was approved, with SPD abstentions, in the Prussian parliament in October 1926.[69] Meanwhile, in the Reichstag, political combinations remained fluid and uncertain, with the SPD continuing to back Stresemann's pro-western foreign policy but failing to prevent a majority of bourgeois parties coming together in December 1926 to pass, by 248 to 158 votes, the so-called 'Law to Protect Youth against Trashy and Smutty Literature'. Liberal and left-wing voices criticized this piece of legislation for reimposing censorship and undermining artistic freedom of expression. However, no attempt was made to repeal it by the SPD-led government after 1928, reflecting a 'cross-party consensus in the Reichstag on the need for the moral protection of youth'.[70]

The events of 1926 had certainly done nothing among left-of-centre voters to enhance the standing of the Reichstag and state parliaments as bastions of republican values against the (presumed) reactionary-monarchist President. On the other hand, some non-socialist politicians had seen in Hindenburg's election a chance for the creation of a moderate conservative consensus, one that combined elements of monarchism and republicanism, authoritarianism and parliamentarism, to create what Luther in January 1926 called a 'government of the centre' (*Regierung der Mitte*).[71] 'Moderate' conservatism was a highly complex and shifting construct, one that at times promised more openness (towards the SPD on the left or the DNVP on the right) and at other times a narrowing of options and a preference for authoritarian modes of government or a 'dictatorship within the bounds of the constitution'.[72] The way in which the June 1926 referendum on dispossession of the former princes split the forces supporting a 'government of the centre', and in particular the Zentrum and the DDP, down the middle, was another sign of the disruptive impact of direct elections.[73] The DDP was forced to defend its bill in the Reichstag, while its youth wing, the Reichsorganisation der demokratischen Jugend, openly sided with the supporters of the referendum, as did a faction of the parliamentary party under Ludwig Bergsträsser and Ernst Lemmer.[74]

The republican paramilitary organization the Reichsbanner, which leaned strongly towards the SPD but also had supporters from the 'centrist' DDP and Zentrum in its ranks and was therefore officially obliged to stay neutral in the referendum, also found itself in a deeply uncomfortable position in 1926, with some left-wing and even moderate branches coming out in defiance for a 'yes' vote.[75] In Leipzig, Saxony, the KPD and RFB even sought to sow discord by issuing a flysheet calling on the local Reichsbanner to abandon its official stance and join them in a 'united front' campaign under the distinctly non-neutral slogan: 'Out with the Princes' Parliament! Out with Hindenburg and Marx!'[76] In Berlin, the referendum was sold by the KPD to Reichsbanner members with the claim that the joint KPD-SPD agitation for the initiating petition had already helped to prise 'a large number of former Hindenburg voters from the Hindenburg-Block'.[77]

In these circumstances, fragmentation of the 'centre' could not be avoided, to the detriment of the new (minority) Reich government under Wilhelm Marx which had to deal with unanswered questions from the referendum. Indeed, its first response was to present a bill in the Reichstag which would have prevented further referendums being called on the initiative of only 10 per cent of voters. However, as this was a constitutional change, it required a two-thirds majority, and extremist parties could easily block it. The Prussian government too felt awkwardly compromised, not least as the House of Hohenzollern had been the main focus of pre- and post-referendum anti-monarchist feeling. The SPD drew the appropriate lesson and did not back any more referendum initiatives during the remaining years of the Weimar Republic (and beyond). Nonetheless, anti-Weimar parties were emboldened to make further attempts to use the referendum option as a means of inflaming public opinion against the Reichstag and the mainstream parties. In October 1928, for instance, the KPD launched an initiating petition against the building of 'battle cruiser A' in a bid to further its 'united front' strategy by exploiting divisions between the four SPD Reich ministers and the party's parliamentary base and rank and file. However, it failed to get the requisite number of signatures to begin an actual referendum campaign, falling well short of the 10 per cent threshold with just 2.94 per cent of eligible voters. The decision of the SPD to distance itself from the petition is the main explanation for its collapse—even though the party's elected deputies continued to oppose *Panzerkreuzer A* in the Reichstag.[78]

Twelve months later, a new extra-parliamentary combination calling itself the National Opposition, and made up of a temporary alliance of the DNVP, the NSDAP, the Stahlhelm, the National Rural League (Reichslandbund), and the Pan-German League, achieved 4.14 million signatures—or 10.02 per cent of eligible voters—in its initiating petition against the Young Plan. The subsequent referendum, on 22 December 1929, was far less successful than the 1926 campaign in electoral terms—just 5.84 million Germans, or 13.81 per cent of all voters, backed the National Opposition's proposal that Reich ministers and elected deputies be banned from ratifying the Young Plan on pain of prosecution for treason.[79] Indeed, the Young Plan did not appear to be an issue around which the conservative and radical right could rally a significant amount of middle-class nationalist discontent with the republic, including among the 14 per cent of voters who had supported splinter economic protest and anti-tax candidates in the 1928 Reichstag elections as opposed to mainstream Weimar parties or the DNVP.[80]

The Young Plan was subsequently placed before the Reichstag, where it was ratified by a clear-cut majority of 265 to 192 in March 1930, and then signed into law by Hindenburg in accordance with his constitutional duties.[81] To a certain extent, the campaign against it had burnished the credentials of the Nazi party as the authentic voice of populist national opposition to the republican 'system', and as more consistent in its approach than the 'moderate' DNVP and Stahlhelm members who had shied away from all-out attacks on Hindenburg as well as the 'grand coalition' government in their campaign literature.[82] This was by no means down to Hitler alone; rather it was the 'collective effort' of the party as a whole, which consciously 'targeted the masses', particularly in places where its main competitor was the DNVP.[83] Even so, the real breakthrough for the Nazis came only in the Reichstag elections of September 1930, and had more to do with opposition to Brüning's deflationary policies and contempt for his decision to seek an early dissolution of parliament after failing to secure majority support for his budget cuts than it did with an emotional rejection of the Young Plan.

Coalition-Building and Political Fragmentation

The inclusion of direct elections alongside parliamentary culture in an analysis of coalition-building and political fragmentation in Weimar Germany is illuminating on several fronts. In particular it shows that open-endedness and opportunity for expression of different visions of the future were possible alongside contemporary (and subsequent) narratives of an *überforderte Republik* or a democracy that had (already) 'overreached' itself and had too many alternative futures to choose from.[84] Direct elections drove a coach and horses through established party allegiances, the existing nexus between 'high' and 'low' politics, and the more settled structures of indirect representation, but they failed to act as an emotionally satisfying vent for political discontent. All they did was confirm that Germany and Germans were deeply fragmented along political lines, with divisions manifesting themselves along a range of overlapping axes. Some of these cleavages were ideological, some party-political, some war-related, some not, some national, some local, some material, and some purely symbolic. But none of them, not even the 'people versus the princes' slogan of the referendum campaigners in 1926, could give a positive definition to the republic and who it represented.

True, Otmar Jung is probably right to argue that, politically, the strong 'yes' vote in 1926 'killed the monarchist cause' in Germany in one bold stroke and thus to some extent reset the symbolic meaning—if not the practical consequences—of Hindenburg's presidential victory in 1925.[85] However, to call it a left-populist, or even more broadly, a socially progressive, republic-affirming campaign would be to ignore the fact that the coalition of Germans who came together in support of 'total confiscation' of princely property was a unique and highly complex one that provided no base for creating a broader political community or set of values. Alongside ardent republicans, it included many centrists and right-wingers upset by the 'confiscation' of 'their' private savings during the currency revaluation of 1923–4, not to mention the usual group of abstainers who, confusingly, could not on this occasion choose to abstain, and thereby display their contempt for *all* Weimar parties, simply by not voting.[86] In other words, the second lesson of this campaign, irrespective of the explanations offered by the left and right at national level, was the more profound for cultural understandings of Weimar politics, namely—as Jung puts it—that it was pointless trying to 'translate the affinities and enmities of the parliamentary sphere into the plebiscitary realm'.[87]

There were of course other 'spaces', beyond the plebiscitary and the parliamentary, where signs of even greater political fragmentation were visible in the late 1920s. The most important of these was the sphere of political violence, which followed its own performative, communicative, spatial, and symbolic rules.[88] The clearest instance of street battles resurging in a more aggressive form after the winter of 1928–9 was the three days of fighting between radical leftists and the Prussian police in the Wedding and Neukölln districts of Berlin on 1–3 May 1929, an event known as 'Bloody May' (*Blutmai*).[89] Law-breaking also came to the countryside in the form of the Landvolkbewegung, a 'self-help' group of disaffected farmers founded in January 1928 in Schleswig-Holstein and spreading from there to other parts of the rural North, which carried out attacks on tax inspectors and occasional bombings of government offices.[90] Both the 'Blutmai' and the Landvolkbewegung were regionally specific developments, but anticipated the more general crisis of 1930–3 when 'transgressing the limits' set by the constitution and the rule of law became the main paradigm of government and the main raison d'être of all, or nearly all, political action.[91] Even before 1930, these transgressions played a part in the growing fragmentation of the DNVP and its rural ally, the Reichslandbund, into 'moderate' and 'extreme' elements, frustrating once and for all hopes that the DNVP might morph into something similar to the Conservative party in Britain.[92] Among anti-fascists, 'breaching the limits' not only cemented the now all-but unhealable KPD-SPD split but aided the formation of dissident communist groups like the KPD-O. The latter was opposed to KPD leader Thälmann's hard-line tactics against the social democrat 'left' and Free Trade Unions, but shared his belief that the coming revolution would only be achieved by means of an 'armed uprising of the proletariat' and a 'fierce, bloody civil war'.[93]

None of this made the state-political impasse of the early 1930s inevitable, or the 'failure' of the Weimar constitution absolute.[94] The poor showing of the 'yes' side in the anti-Young Plan campaign serves as a useful reminder of the limits of extra-parliamentary radical nationalist mobilization, even in the winter of 1929–30. So too does mass republican flag-waving of the type still seen in August 1930 at the time of the public festivities following the final withdrawal of Allied troops from the Rhineland.[95] Support for the extreme left was patchy and confined to particular regions, with most working-class Germans continuing to back the SPD, even after the disappointments of the 'grand coalition' and the party's subsequent 'toleration' of Brüning's austerity measures. As the district leadership of the KPD in Hesse secretly reported in October 1928, left-leaning workers in factories in Frankfurt am Main and Offenbach were disappointed by the SPD ministers' support for the building of battle-cruiser A, but were willing to 'forgive this one error' and could not be won over to the communist cause.[96] Throughout 1929, republican visions of democracy remained strong, while the mood among the middle class in early 1930 was more reminiscent of 1923–4 when there was widespread pragmatic acceptance that the collapse of the currency did not (have to) mean the collapse of the constitution. Until the Nazi electoral breakthrough in September 1930, the chief political alternative to social democracy, as McElligott suggests, was 'stability based on conservative and traditionalist authority',[97] a stability that was desired by many mainstream German voters and politicians in the years 1924–30, even if it was not absolutely achievable.

Conclusion

Do these new insights still allow us to follow Peukert in locating the 'crisis' of Weimar modernity not just in the Great Depression, but in the six-year period that preceded it? The cultural and economic uncertainties of the late 1920s were certainly manifest in the intertwined processes of coalition-building and political fragmentation, and expressed themselves in a bewildering array of material hopes, 'fears of national extinction', and less tangible, but equally real, 'symbolic conflicts'.[98] The terms of domestic economic agreements—including the ambitious unemployment insurance scheme of 1927—afforded concrete, if temporary, meaning to social policy but did not fix new visions of national life in a pedagogical or civic sense.[99] Parliamentary culture followed its own rules and customs, but failed to command the wholehearted understanding and respect of vast swathes of the ordinary population.[100] Direct elections were an independent factor in creating expectations of material resolution and symbolic victory, and proceeded according to a logic beyond the control of any one party, movement, or coalition. Yet, they too were unable to provide a clear, authoritative answer to what the republic was, who it was for, and where its future lay.

However, if the period 1924–30 is seen on its own terms, rather than in relation to other epochs, a different picture emerges. True, the established parties had not yet worked out how to contain political emotions and symbolism within the parliamentary sphere, as opposed to allowing them to spill out into plebiscitary initiatives, street violence, and public spectacle, but they were at least beginning to recognize that this was one of their main challenges—and an important rationale for coalition-building beyond narrow party interest. A certain, qualified loyalty to the Weimar constitution had established itself, albeit one that to varying degrees looked for authoritarian solutions *within* the bounds of the constitution, including limitations on freedom of expression, avoidance of referendums where possible, and use of Article 48 in emergency situations.[101] The decision to dissolve parliament in July 1930 was in this sense the real beginning of the end for Weimar, not only because it represented an unwarranted abuse of presidential power, but because it signalled the abandonment of all pretence at disinterested coalition-building and pitted the naked anti-democratic ambition of Brüning and his minority austerity government against a growing range of parliamentary and extra-parliamentary, law-abiding and law-breaking opponents.

Notes

1. As argued, most recently, by Frank Biess, *Republik der Angst: Eine andere Geschichte der Bundesrepublik* (Reinbek bei Hamburg: Rowohlt Verlag, 2019), esp. 198–205.
2. Such views could also be found among jurists and officials in the Federal Ministry of Interior. See Martin Diebel, *'Die Stunde der Exekutive': Das Bundesinnenministerium und die Notstandsgesetze 1949–1968* (Göttingen: Wallstein Verlag, 2019).

3. Speech made by Luther before the Reichstag, 27 January 1926, reproduced in *Verhandlungen des Reichstags*, vol. 388, 149 Sitzung, III. Wahlperiode 1924/8 (Berlin: Verlag der Reichsdruckerei, 1926), 5170. Cited in Franklin C. West, *A Crisis of the Weimar Republic: The German Referendum of 20 June 1926* (Philadelphia: American Philosophical Society, 1985), 14.
4. George L. Mosse, *Fallen Soldiers: Reshaping the Memory of the World Wars* (Oxford: Oxford University Press, 1990), 171. According to Article 49 of the Weimar Constitution of 1919: 'The Reich President exercises the right of amnesty. Reich amnesties require a Reich law.'
5. See here Sebastian Ullrich, *Der Weimar-Komplex: Das Scheitern der ersten deutschen Demokratie und die politische Kultur der frühen Bundesrepublik, 1945–1959* (Göttingen: Wallstein Verlag, 2009), esp. 269–302.
6. Fritz K. Ringer, *The Decline of the German Mandarins: The German Academic Community, 1890–1933* (Cambridge, MA: Harvard University Press, 1969), 82.
7. See Michael Stürmer, 'Koalitionen und Oppositionen: Bedingungen parlamentarischer Instabilität' (1967), reproduced in Michael Stürmer (ed.), *Die Weimarer Republik: Belagerte Civitas*, 2nd ed. (Königstein-im-Taunus: Athenäum-Verlag, 1985), 237–53, here 250. Also Stürmer's bigger study, *Koalition und Opposition in der Weimarer Republik 1924–1928* (Düsseldorf: Droste, 1967), here esp. 283.
8. Anthony McElligott, *Rethinking the Weimar Republic: Authority and Authoritarianism, 1916–1936* (London: Bloomsbury, 2014), 7.
9. Stürmer, *Koalition und Opposition*, 34–7.
10. Heinrich August Winkler, *Weimar 1918–1933: Die Geschichte der ersten deutschen Demokratie* (Munich: C. H. Beck, 1993), 235, 252–3.
11. Larry Eugene Jones, '"The Dying Middle": Weimar Germany and the Fragmentation of Bourgeois Politics', *Central European History*, 5/1 (1972), 23–54.
12. Detlev J. K. Peukert, *The Weimar Republic: The Crisis of Classical Modernity* (London: Allen Lane, 1991).
13. Thomas Mergel, *Parlamentarische Kultur in der Weimarer Republik: Politische Kommunikation, symbolische Politik und Öffentlichkeit im Reichstag* (Düsseldorf: Droste Verlag, 2002).
14. See also Mergel, 'High Expectations—Deep Disappointment: Structures of the Public Perception of Politics in the Weimar Republic', in Kathleen Canning, Kerstin Barndt, and Kristin McGuire (eds), *Weimar Publics/Weimar Subjects: Rethinking the Political Culture of Germany in the 1920s* (New York and Oxford: Berghahn Books, 2010), 192–210, here 194.
15. Winkler, *Weimar*, 238, 266, 268.
16. Mergel, *Parlamentarische Kultur*, 206; Hans Mommsen, *The Rise and Fall of Weimar Democracy* (Chapel Hill, NC, and London: University of North Carolina Press, 1996), 208.
17. See Benjamin Ziemann, 'Weimar was Weimar: Politics, Culture and the Emplotment of the Weimar Republic', *German History*, 28/4 (2010), 542–71, here 562–3.
18. Jonathan Wright, *Gustav Stresemann: Weimar's Greatest Statesman* (Oxford: Oxford University Press, 2004).
19. A list of the most important ministers in each cabinet can be found in Ursula Büttner, *Weimar: Die überforderte Republik 1918–1933: Leistung und Versagen in Staat, Gesellschaft, Wirtschaft und Kultur* (Stuttgart: Klett-Cotta, 2008), 810–12.
20. On the 'flag incident', see Winkler, *Weimar*, 311–12.
21. West, *A Crisis*, xi, 8.
22. Ibid., 17.

23. Ziemann, 'Weimar was Weimar', 561.
24. Cf. Mergel, *Parlamentarische Kultur*, esp. 323–31.
25. Mommsen, *Rise and Fall*, 227.
26. David E. Barclay, *Rudolf Wissell als Sozialpolitiker 1890–1933* (West Berlin: Colloquium Verlag, 1984), 210; McElligott, *Rethinking*, 79–81.
27. Rudolf Wissell, 'Einundzwanzig Monate Reichsarbeitsminister', *Die Arbeit: Zeitschrift für Gewerkschaftspolitik und Wirtschaftskunde*, 7/4 (Apr. 1930), 217–28. English translations taken from Ben Fowkes (ed.), *The German Left and the Weimar Republic: A Selection of Documents* (Chicago: Haymarket Books, 2014), 40–2, here 40-1.
28. Hans-Walter Schmuhl, *Arbeitsmarktpolitik und Arbeitsverwaltung in Deutschland 1871–2002: Zwischen Fürsorge, Hoheit und Markt* (Nuremberg: Zentralamt der Bundesanstalt für Arbeit, 2003), 142.
29. Wissell, 'Einundzwanzig Monate', 40.
30. Stürmer, 'Koalitionen und Oppositionen', 249.
31. Mommsen, *Rise and Fall*, 190–1, 208, 248.
32. Mergel, *Parlamentarische Kultur*, 415.
33. Barclay, *Rudolf Wissell*, 211.
34. Mergel, *Parlamentarische Kultur*, 221.
35. Barclay, *Rudolf Wissell*, 209–10.
36. Mommsen, *Rise and Fall*, 248–9. See also William L. Patch Jr., *Christian Trade Unions in the Weimar Republic, 1918–1933: The Failure of 'Corporate Pluralism'* (New Haven and London: Yale University Press, 1985), 125–6.
37. See Wahlen in der Weimarer Republik, at http://www.gonschior.de/weimar.
38. Bernhard Fulda, *Press and Politics in the Weimar Republic* (Oxford: Oxford University Press, 2009), 119.
39. Matthias Lau, *Pressepolitik als Chance: Staatliche Öffentlichkeitsarbeit in den Ländern der Weimarer Republik* (Stuttgart: Franz Steiner Verlag, 2003), 26.
40. Richard A. Comfort, *Revolutionary Hamburg: Labor Politics in the Early Weimar Republic* (Stanford, CA: Stanford University Press, 1966), 130.
41. Barry A. Jackisch, *The Pan-German League and Radical Nationalist Politics in Interwar Germany, 1918–39* (Farnham: Ashgate, 2012).
42. Dietrich Orlow, *Weimar Prussia, 1918–1925: The Unlikely Rock of Democracy* (Pittsburgh, PA: University of Pittsburgh Press, 1986).
43. Martin H. Geyer, 'Grenzüberschreitungen: Vom Belagerungszustand zum Ausnahmezustand', in Niels Werber, Stefan Kaufmann, and Lars Koch (eds), *Erster Weltkrieg: Kulturwissenschaftliches Handbuch* (Stuttgart and Weimar: Metzler, 2014), 341–84, here 366, 370; Diebel, *Die Stunde der Exekutive*, 155.
44. British Foreign Office memorandum on the history of the constitutional and political changes which have occurred since the revolution in the eighteen Federal States which now form the German Reich, 30 Mar. 1927, The National Archives, Kew, London (henceforth TNA), FO 425/549.
45. Christopher Clark, *Iron Kingdom: The Rise and Downfall of Prussia, 1600–1947* (London: Allen Lane, 2006), 621–2. For an extensive discussion of Prussia in the years 1925–30, see also Hagen Schulze, *Otto Braun oder Preußens demokratische Sendung: Eine Biographie* (Frankfurt am Main: Propyläen, 1977), 475–625.
46. Mommsen, *Rise and Fall*, 249–50.
47. Schulze, *Otto Braun*, 533, 590, 593.

48. Lau, *Pressepolitik*, 225, 242, 245.
49. Jackisch, *The Pan-German League*, esp. 30–2. See also Geyer, 'Grenzüberschreitungen', 353, 366.
50. See, for instance, British ambassador Viscount d'Abernon's remarks on a speech by Held in a note to Sir Austen Chamberlain, 26 Apr. 1926, in TNA, FO 425/548.
51. Lau, *Pressepolitik*, 51.
52. British Foreign Office memorandum, 30 Mar. 1927 (see note 43). The DNVP's vote share in Reichstag elections in Hamburg fell from 21.61% in December 1924 to 12.84% in May 1928, a considerably larger decline than the national average. On the other hand, Stresemann's party, the DVP, actually increased its vote in Hamburg from 13.15% to 13.82%, making it second place behind the SPD on 36.83%. See Wahlen in der Weimarer Republik, at http://www.gonschior.de/weimar.
53. Otmar Jung, *Direkte Demokratie in der Weimarer Republik: Die Fälle 'Aufwertung', 'Fürstenenteignung', 'Panzerkreuzerverbot' und 'Youngplan'* (Frankfurt am Main and New York: Campus Verlag, 1989).
54. Dirk Schumann, *Political Violence in the Weimar Republic, 1918–1933: Fight for the Streets and Fear of Civil War* (New York and Oxford: Berghahn Books, 2009), 176, 205; Fulda, *Press and Politics*, 125–6.
55. Addison to Chamberlain, 11 June 1926, in TNA, FO 425/548.
56. Benjamin Ziemann, *Contested Commemorations: Republican War Veterans and Weimar Political Culture* (Cambridge: Cambridge University Press, 2013), 112.
57. ZK der KPD an das Sekretariat des EKKI, 4 June 1926, in Bundesarchiv Berlin, Stiftung Archiv der Parteien und Massenorganisationen der ehemaligen DDR (henceforth SAPMO-BArch), RY 5/566, Bl. 17.
58. Schumann, *Political Violence*, 312.
59. Anna von der Goltz, *Hindenburg: Power, Myth, and the Rise of the Nazis* (Oxford: Oxford University Press, 2009), 87.
60. Ibid., 94–5.
61. Ibid., 90–1.
62. See Wahlen in der Weimarer Republik, at http://www.gonschior.de/weimar. Also West, *A Crisis*, 273.
63. Mommsen, *Rise and Fall*, 239–42.
64. Jung, *Direkte Demokratie*, 55.
65. Ibid., 10.
66. West, *A Crisis*, 10.
67. See Axel Weipert, *Das Rote Berlin: Eine Geschichte der Berliner Arbeiterbewegung 1830–1934*, 2nd ed. (Berlin: Berliner Wissenschafts-Verlag, 2019), esp. 137–41.
68. Ibid., 143; Büttner, *Weimar*, 803.
69. Jung, *Direkte Demokratie*, 59; West, *A Crisis*, 12; Schulze, *Otto Braun*, 508–9.
70. McElligott, *Rethinking*, 137.
71. Luther before the Reichstag, 27 Jan. 1926 (as note 3).
72. McElligott, *Rethinking*, 181–8.
73. On the tensions that the 1926 referendum caused inside the Zentrum in particular, see Karsten Ruppert, *Im Dienst am Staat von Weimar: Das Zentrum als regierende Partei in der Weimarer Demokratie 1923–1930* (Düsseldorf: Droste Verlag, 1992), 210–27.
74. Ulrich Schüren, *Der Volksentscheid zur Fürstenenteignung 1926* (Düsseldorf: Droste Verlag, 1978), 162, 224, 226.

75. Ziemann, *Contested Commemorations*, 176–7.
76. *Reichsbanner in Leipzig!* Flysheet from June 1926, issued by the KPD, Bezirksleitung Westsachsen, in association with the RFB. See Sammlung der Bibliothek des Reichsgerichts, housed in the Staatsbibliothek, Berlin.
77. ZK der KPD, Referentenmaterial, 4 June 1926, in SAPMO-BArch, RY 1/1277, Bl. 1–4, here Bl. 4.
78. Jung, *Direkte Demokratie*, 104.
79. Ibid., 126, 140.
80. Peter Fritzsche, *Rehearsals for Fascism: Populism and Political Mobilization in Weimar Germany* (Oxford: Oxford University Press, 1990), 129, 185–6.
81. McElligott, *Rethinking*, 54.
82. Jackisch, *The Pan-German League*, 164, 175.
83. Jung, *Direkte Demokratie*, 130.
84. See Büttner, *Weimar*. Also Rüdiger Graf, *Die Zukunft der Weimarer Republik: Krisen und Zukunftsaneignungen in Deutschland 1918–1933* (Munich: Oldenbourg Verlag, 2008).
85. Jung, *Direkte Demokratie*, 59.
86. Fulda, *Press and Politics*, 124–5.
87. Jung, *Direkte Demokratie*, 92.
88. Schumann, *Political Violence*.
89. Chris Bowlby, 'Blutmai 1929: Police, Parties and Proletarians in a Berlin Confrontation', *Historical Journal*, 29/1 (1986), 137–58; Weipert, *Das rote Berlin*, 144–6.
90. Fritzsche, *Rehearsals for Fascism*, 114–18.
91. Geyer, 'Grenzüberschreitungen', 372–3.
92. Thomas Mergel, 'Das Scheitern des deutschen Tory-Konservatismus: Die Umformung der DNVP zu einer rechtsradikalen Partei 1928-1932', *Historische Zeitschrift*, 276 (2003), 323–68.
93. *Plattform der Kommunistischen Partei Deutschlands (Opposition)* (Berlin: Reichsleitung der KPD-O, 1930), 5–6.
94. For a critical approach to discourses on Weimar's constitutional 'failure', see Dieter Grimm, 'Mißglückt oder glücklos? Die Weimarer Reichsverfassung im Widerstreit der Meinungen', in Heinrich August Winkler (ed.), *Weimar im Widerstreit: Deutungen der ersten deutschen Republik im geteilten Deutschland* (Munich: R. Oldenbourg, 2002), 151–61.
95. Nadine Rossol, *Performing the Nation in Interwar Germany: Sport, Spectacle and Political Symbolism, 1926–1936* (Basingstoke: Palgrave Macmillan, 2010), esp. 80–101.
96. Bezirksleitung Hessen der KPD, Bericht über die Durchführung der Kampagne gegen Panzerkreuzerbau, 22 Oct. 1928, in SAPMO-BArch, RY 1/2850, Bl. 94–9.
97. McElligott, *Rethinking*, 77.
98. Peukert, *The Weimar Republic*, 276–7; Ziemann, *Contested Commemorations*, 112.
99. McElligott, *Rethinking*, 5.
100. Mergel, *Parlamentarische Kultur*.
101. Büttner, *Weimar*, 507.

Bibliography

Fulda, Bernhard, *Press and Politics in the Weimar Republic* (Oxford: Oxford University Press, 2009).

Jackisch, Barry A., *The Pan-German League and Radical Nationalist Politics in Interwar Germany, 1918–39* (Farnham: Ashgate, 2012).

McElligott, Anthony, *Rethinking the Weimar Republic: Authority and Authoritarianism, 1916–1936* (London: Bloomsbury Academic, 2014).

Mergel, Thomas, *Parlamentarische Kultur in der Weimarer Republik: Politische Kommunikation, symbolische Politik und Öffentlichkeit im Reichstag* (Düsseldorf: Droste Verlag, 2002).

Rossol, Nadine, *Performing the Nation in Interwar Germany: Sport, Spectacle and Political Symbolism, 1926–1936* (Basingstoke: Palgrave Macmillan, 2010).

Schumann, Dirk, *Political Violence in the Weimar Republic, 1918–1933: Fight for the Streets and Fear of Civil War*, tr. Thomas Dunlap (New York and Oxford: Berghahn Books, 2009; German original, Klartext, 2001).

von der Goltz, Anna, *Hindenburg: Power, Myth, and the Rise of the Nazis* (Oxford: Oxford University Press, 2009).

West, Franklin C., *A Crisis of the Weimar Republic: The German Referendum of 20 June 1926* (Philadelphia: American Philosophical Society, 1985).

Ziemann, Benjamin, 'Weimar was Weimar. Politics, Culture and the Emplotment of the Weimar Republic', *German History*, 28/4 (2010), 542–71.

Ziemann, Benjamin, *Contested Commemorations: Republican War Veterans and Weimar Political Culture* (Cambridge: Cambridge University Press, 2013).

CHAPTER 5

FROM DEMOCRACY TO DICTATORSHIP

The Fall of Weimar and the Nazi Rise to Power, 1930–1933

LARRY EUGENE JONES

THE challenge confronting the historian who seeks to understand or explain the series of events that culminated in Adolf Hitler's appointment as Chancellor on 30 January 1933 is to situate the role of human agency in the web of structural and cultural factors that were responsible for the collapse of Weimar democracy. To be sure, the paralysis of Weimar democracy at the beginning of the 1930s was the result of interest antagonisms that had been exacerbated by the runaway inflation of the early 1920s, the social cost of stabilization in the second half of the 1920s, and the outbreak of the world economic crisis to the point where it was no longer possible to forge a reliable domestic consensus for the conduct of policy either at home or abroad. But the structural mode of analysis that works so well to explain the collapse of Weimar democracy is not sufficient to explain how and why this crisis ended with Hitler's appointment as Chancellor. As Harold James wrote thirty years ago, the collapse of Weimar democracy and Hitler's appointment as Chancellor represent 'two logically separate processes' that require fundamentally different analytical strategies if the latter is to be properly understood.[1] In other words, the blockage of economic and political interests at the national level created what Karl Dietrich Bracher identified in his classic study on the dissolution of the Weimar Republic as a power vacuum in which the actions of individual historical actors were suddenly invested with much greater causal agency than might otherwise have been the case.[2] A particularly critical development in this respect was the invocation of Article 48 emergency powers in the spring of 1930, a development that effectively transferred ultimate responsibility in the decision-making process from the Reichstag to Reich President Paul von Hindenburg and the camarilla that had assembled itself around him. Although this represented a critical step in the transition from democratic to dictatorial rule, this did not mean that Hitler's accession to power was the only way in which the political crisis that had descended upon Germany in the early 1930s could have been resolved. The situation that existed in Germany from 1930 to 1933 was extremely fluid, and there was no clear way out of the impasse in which Germany's political leaders found themselves at the beginning of the 1930s.[3]

The chapter that follows will examine the period from the onset of the world economic crisis in the late 1920s to Hitler's appointment as Chancellor in January 1933, with specific focus on a series of critical junctures in the history of the late Weimar Republic where the decisions and actions of individual historical actors assumed much greater causal agency than they might otherwise have possessed. It focuses in particular on the strategic calculations that informed the actions of last three chancellorships of the Weimar Republic and how they changed over time, with specific attention to the role that not just individual political priorities but also chance, arbitrariness, and petty animosities played in the demise of Weimar democracy and Hitler's installation as Chancellor. This, in turn, will illuminate the way in which those in positions of influence responded to the structural crisis of Weimar democracy in ways that either sought to mitigate that crisis or that eviscerated Germany's democratic institutions and, in so doing, paved the way for the establishment of the Third Reich. At the same time, it is essential to remember that all of this transpired against the background of a heightened level of political violence that was the legacy of the First World War and the trauma of Weimar's birth and that resurfaced with renewed intensity with the deepening economic crisis of in the early 1930s. This manifested itself primarily in the plethora of paramilitary and patriotic organizations that appeared in Germany in the immediate postwar period and that extolled what they saw as the virtues of service at the front in an unrelenting assault on the Weimar Republic as the symbol of Germany's national humiliation. Their presence on the German political stage had a radicalizing effect on the parties and institutions of the German right and severely restricted their room for manoeuvre as they confronted the diplomatic consequences of Germany's lost war and the economic chaos it had left in its wake.[4]

Heinrich Brüning and Government by Presidential Decree

By the end of 1929 it had become demonstrably clear that Weimar's democratic institutions were no longer capable of producing a reliable parliamentary consensus for the conduct of national affairs. The conflict between the Social Democrats (Sozialdemokratische Partei Deutschlands or SPD) and the German People's Party (Deutsche Volkspartei or DVP) over ways to fund a state unemployment insurance programme that had only begun to feel the effects of the deepening economic crisis had produced a rift within the national government that by the spring of 1930 would prove irreparable. The Müller government had been formed in the summer of 1928 following strong gains by the Social Democrats in the national elections earlier that May. The business interests on the DVP's right wing remained adamantly opposed to an accommodation with the SPD but ultimately relented in face of the strong stand that DVP party chairman and German Foreign Minister took in support of the 'Great Coalition'. But Stresemann's untimely death in September 1929 robbed the Müller cabinet of the lynchpin that was holding it together, and in late March 1930 the SPD Reichstag delegation withdrew its support from the Chancellor and cleared the way for the formation of a new government in which the Social Democrats were no longer represented.[5]

It was against the background of these developments that Reich President Paul von Hindenburg turned to Heinrich Brüning, a prominent Christian labour leader who in December 1928 had been elected chairman of the Reichstag delegation of the German Centre Party (Deutsche Zentrumspartei). Brüning was a man of many contradictions that make it difficult to reduce his politics to a common denominator. Brüning is perhaps best described as a constitutional conservative who was committed to Germany's return to great power status through a systematic revision of the Weimar Constitution, a sharp reduction of spending at all levels of government, and a negotiated end to Germany's reparations burden. At the same time, Brüning remained deeply committed to the parliamentary system of government, despite his criticism of the German party system as it had developed in the Weimar Republic, and was sympathetic to the creation of an interconfessional Christian people's party along the lines of the 'Essen Program' that his colleague Adam Stegerwald had proposed at the 1920 Essen congress of the Christian labour movement.[6] Nowhere was Brüning's commitment to the principles of parliamentary government more apparent than in his efforts to prevent the collapse of the Müller cabinet in the period immediately preceding his own appointment to the chancellorship on 31 March 1930.[7]

As Chancellor, Brüning commanded a government that reached from the left wing of his own party, where the appointment of Joseph Wirth to the Ministry of the Interior was designed to reconcile the Social Democrats to his ascendancy to the chancellorship, to the more moderate elements on the left wing of the German National People's Party (Deutschnationale Volkspartei or DNVP). The appointment of Martin Schiele and G. R. Treviranus to the Ministries of Agriculture and Occupied Territories respectively was carefully calculated to exploit the divisions that had developed within the DNVP and to undercut the influence of Alfred Hugenberg, who had ascended to the DNVP party chairmanship in October 1928. Though implacably opposed to any form of collaboration with the hated Weimar system, Hugenberg acquiesced in the heat of the moment to pressure from the moderates within his own party and reluctantly assented to the DNVP's support of the Brüning cabinet in what was one of the most bitter defeats of his political career.[8] The driving force behind the formation of the Brüning cabinet was the Reichswehr's Kurt von Schleicher, who as the military's key strategist shared Brüning's scepticism about the viability of Germany's parliamentary institutions and favoured a more authoritarian style of government that relied upon the special emergency powers that Article 48 of the Weimar Constitution had vested in the office of the

Reich President.⁹ While Brüning was fully prepared to invoke presidential emergency powers in order to implement the legislation he thought necessary for Germany's fiscal and economic recovery, he remained committed to the basic principles of parliamentary democracy and would abandon them only as a last resort.¹⁰

Hugenberg's decision to allow his party's delegation to the Reichstag to vote for the installation of the Brüning cabinet came under sharp attack from the more militantly anti-republican elements on the DNVP's right wing, with the result that the DNVP party chairman reversed his course once again and instructed his party's Reichstag delegation to vote against the government when Brüning returned to the Reichstag a few days later with the legislation to authorize both a programme of agrarian relief and new taxes to cover the growing deficit in the national budget. This, in turn, triggered a mutiny within the delegation on the part of approximately thirty Nationalist deputies who proceeded to vote for the government's legislative package, thus securing its acceptance with the votes of the various middle parties that supported the Brüning cabinet and the help of twenty-four Social Democratic abstentions.¹¹ This scenario repeated itself in July 1930, though this time the defection of the Social Democrats left Brüning without the parliamentary majority he had used in April to secure the passage of his farm and tax bills, with the result that he had no choice but to invoke presidential emergency powers to enact his legislative agenda. To be sure, the use of Article 48 was not new, having been deployed in 1923–4 by fellow Centrist Wilhelm Marx to enact legislation to stabilize the German currency after the runaway inflation of the early 1920s. The difference here, however, was that Brüning was using Article 48 to enact legislation that had been rejected by a majority in the Reichstag and that remained in force even after Brüning dissolved the Reichstag following its vote to rescind his government's emergency powers. This represented a dramatic exception to the use of Article 48 powers that was unprecedented in the history of the Weimar Republic.¹²

The dissolution of the Reichstag on 18 July 1930 was highlighted, among other things, by the exodus of what remained of the moderate wing of the DNVP. In the campaign for the Reichstag elections that were scheduled to take place later that fall, Brüning and his government hoped that those who had seceded from the DNVP would soon reconstitute themselves as a viable political force with at least sixty seats in the Reichstag.¹³ But much to Brüning's disappointment the secessionists regrouped into three different political parties—the Conservative People's Party (Konservative Volkspartei or KVP), the Christian-Social People's Service (Christlich-sozialer Volksdienst), and the Christian-National Peasants and Farmers' Party (Christlich-nationale Bauern- und Landvolkpartei or CNBLP)—without issuing such much as a joint campaign statement.¹⁴ Moreover, Brüning and his supporters failed to take into account the radicalizing effect that the deteriorating economic situation had begun to have on the electoral behaviour of those who had traditionally supported Germany's non-socialist parties and the impact this would have upon the electoral prospects of the right-wing National Socialist German Workers' Party (Nationalsozialistische Deutsche Arbeiterpartei or NSDAP) under the leadership of Adolf Hitler. With nearly six and a half million votes and 107 seats in the newly elected Reichstag, the NSDAP emerged as the undisputed winner in the

September 1930 Reichstag elections.[15] This, along with the fragmentation of Germany's moderate right, meant that Brüning had no real alternative to the use of Article 48 when it came to combating the fiscal and economic consequences of the Great Depression. Although the institutions of parliamentary government continued to function at the state level in Prussia, Bavaria, and elsewhere, the likelihood of a return to parliamentary democracy at the Reich level was virtually non-existent.[16]

Three weeks after the NSDAP's sensational breakthrough at the polls, Brüning met first with the Social Democrats and then with Hitler to assess his political options. The fact that he conferred with the Social Democrats before meeting with Hitler showed, among other things, that it was to left and not to the right that Brüning looked for support.[17] In the meantime, Brüning and his cabinet struggled to cope with Germany's deepening economic crisis, with another round of Article 48 legislation in December 1930. A fiscal conservative, Brüning sought to address Germany's growing budgetary deficit through a series of far-reaching reductions in the general level of government spending. The burden of Brüning's efforts to address the growing deficit in Germany's national budget fell most heavily upon the shoulders the professional civil service at the national, state, and municipal levels, where cuts in salary and benefits over the course of the Brüning chancellorship would amount to 28 per cent of the nominal income of those in the state civil service.[18] Herein, however, lay a fatal contradiction in Brüning's long-term political strategy in that these cuts would have a demoralizing and in some cases radicalizing effect upon Germany's civil service at the precise moment that Brüning was trying to shift the balance of power from the Reichstag to the executive branch of government with its full complement of professional civil servants. This was a contradiction that Brüning was never able to resolve and that severely undercut the effectiveness of his experiment of government by presidential decree.[19]

In the meantime, the effects of Germany's deepening economic crisis had spread well beyond the professional civil service to other sectors of German society, earning Brüning the epitaph of 'hunger chancellor'. This was particularly true of the agrarian sector, where the emergency farm programme that Brüning and Schiele had introduced with a fanfare in April 1930 had failed to stem the rising tide of rural indebtedness or offset the dramatic collapse of agricultural prices on the world market. Although the crisis affected small farmers and large landowners alike, it was the latter that posed a particular problem for the Brüning cabinet. In the fall of 1930 large landed agriculture from east of the Elbe orchestrated the takeover of Germany's largest and most influential agricultural interest organization, the National Rural League (Reichs-Landbund or RLB), and forced Schiele from its presidency. From this point on, the RLB would become one of Brüning's most obstreperous political opponents, gravitating ever more ominously into the orbit of the NSDAP.[20] Industry, on the other hand, adopted a more tactful approach to Brüning and his cabinet. Although many of Germany's industrial leaders were suspicious of Brüning's ties to the Christian labour movement and criticized his apparent reluctance to address the critical question of wage costs, the National Federation of German Industry (Reichsverband der Deutscher Industrie or RDI)—first under the leadership of Carl Duisberg and then under that of Gustav Krupp von Bohlen und Halbach—assiduously avoided being drawn into domestic political strife and frequently had to rein in those within the organization like Paul Reusch who demanded 'the sharpest possible opposition' to the policies of the national government. Not until September 1931, when the RDI joined eleven of Germany's most influential business associations in releasing a joint manifesto that criticized the government's failure to deliver on issues of vital concern to the German business community, did it abandon its self-restraint in its relationship to the Brüning cabinet and add its voice to the chorus of those who were demanding a change of direction in the conduct of national policy.[21]

None of this was lost upon Schleicher, the architect of the Brüning cabinet. Schleicher was alarmed above all else by the NSDAP's sensational breakthrough in the 1930 Reichstag elections and realized that the deepening economic crisis only played to the advantage of Hitler and his fellow Nazis. Schleicher realized that Hitler could no longer be dismissed out of hand and began to formulate the outlines of a strategy that sought to mitigate the radicalism of the Nazi movement by saddling it with governmental responsibility in the hope that this would deprive the NSDAP of the obvious advantages it enjoyed as an opposition party. Bringing the Nazis into the government would have the further advantage of providing Germany's conservative elites with the mantle of popular legitimacy they needed to undertake a fundamental revision of Germany's constitutional system that would culminate in their restoration to the position of power they had enjoyed before the war.[22] An opportunity to implement this strategy, however, would not come until the outbreak of the German banking crisis in the early summer of 1931, a new round of emergency legislation with all of its concomitant hardship for the German public, and a dramatic erosion of Brüning's popularity as the Chancellor who was guiding Germany through the world economic crisis. It was against the background of these developments that Schleicher and his entourage began to pressure Brüning into exploring the possibility of extending his government to include the more radical parties on the German right.[23] With Hindenburg lending his voice to those who sought the reorganization of the national government and the inclusion of the radical right, Brüning felt that he had no choice but to schedule a meeting with the DNVP's Alfred Hugenberg that took place after some hesitation on 27 August 1931. But when Brüning invited Centre party chairman Ludwig Kaas to the meeting without informing Hugenberg, this turned what the DNVP party chairman had hoped would be a private meeting with Brüning into a meeting between the leaders of their respective parties in a way that dramatically reduced Hugenberg's leverage with the Chancellor. Infuriated by Brüning's ploy, Hugenberg rehearsed his familiar bromides about the government's failure to provide the effective leadership the nation so desperately needed and refused to enter into serious discussion about how the deadlock that currently had the nation in its grip might be broken. Brüning, on the other hand, could breathe a sigh of relief that he had successfully deflected the pressure from Hindenburg and Schleicher for an extension of his government to the right.[24]

Brüning's reprieve was short-lived. On 10 October 1931 Hitler, Hugenberg, and the forces of the radical right met in Harzburg to issue a virtual declaration of war against the Brüning government and to prepare for what they hoped would end in the transfer of power to a united German right. The sense of unity demonstrated at Harzburg, however, proved ephemeral—particularly in light of tensions between the NSDAP and the more traditionally conservative elements of the national front—and Brüning was able to survive a vote of no-confidence on 16 October after having reorganized his cabinet a scant three days earlier.[25] But in many respects, the Harzburg rally and the Chancellor's victory in the Reichstag were only the prelude to what would prove to be the ultimate test of Brüning's ability to navigate the troubled waters of right-wing politics in Weimar Germany: the 1932 presidential elections. Hindenburg's seven-year term as Reich President would expire in the spring of 1932, and the various factions on the German right jostled for position, in an effort to determine the ultimate shape of the new order that would emerge from the ruins of Weimar democracy. Brüning, who believed that Hindenburg's re-election was the only reliable bulwark against the rising tide of Nazism and radical nationalism, not only persuaded Hindenburg to stand for re-election but became the driving force in the Hindenburg campaign as the lynchpin of a loose coalition of parties that stretched from the Social Democrats through the various parties in the middle to the moderate conservatives who had abandoned the DNVP in protest against Hugenberg's leadership of the party.[26] Hitler, on the other hand, seemed to been a bit ambivalent about running against someone of Hindenburg's stature and waited almost to the last minute to declare his candidacy.[27] The wild card in all of this was Theodor Duesterberg, the leader of a right-wing veterans' organization known as the Stahlhelm who became Hugenberg's campaign proxy and whose candidacy ultimately prevented Hindenburg from receiving the absolute majority he needed to win the election on the first ballot.[28]

The Duesterberg candidacy would prove to be one of those serendipitous episodes in the history of the late Weimar Republic that would have a profound effect upon the subsequent course of events. Had Hugenberg and the Stahlhelm not nominated Duesterberg as the putative candidate of the national opposition, Hindenburg would almost certainly have been re-elected as Reich President on the first ballot. As it was, Hindenburg received 49.6 per cent of the votes cast in the first round of voting on 5 April and had to endure a run-off election in which Hitler was able to close the margin between them by nearly two-and-a-half million votes and thus claim that he and not Hindenburg was the real victor in the election.[29] Hindenburg's failure to receive an absolute majority in the first round of voting also allowed the Nazis to sustain the momentum of their propaganda campaign against the parties that supported Hindenburg from the first ballot in March through the state elections in Prussia, Bavaria, and Württemberg in late April, a prospect that Nazi propaganda chief Joseph Goebbels relished. At the same time, the fact that Hindenburg had failed to win re-election outright severely strained his relationship with Brüning and provided Schleicher with the opening he needed to orchestrate Brüning's removal from office at the end of May 1932.[30]

In assessing Brüning's tenure as Chancellor, one is confronted with a mixed record. There can be little doubt that Brüning's fiscal conservatism was unsuited to the crisis that descended upon Germany in the early 1930s and that it greatly intensified the effects the Great Depression had on virtually all sectors of German society. To be sure, this was something of which Brüning himself was aware, although the public works programme he was contemplating would take effect only after he had negotiated an end to Germany's reparations burden. Nor can it be denied that Brüning's reliance upon Article 48 and the authoritarian manner in which he went about implementing his policies severely compromised the legitimacy of Germany's republican institutions and set the stage for their ultimate destruction by his successors in power.[31] But Brüning was no admirer of authoritarianism for its own sake and remained loyal to the basic principles of the Weimar Constitution. In the turmoil that characterized the last year of his chancellorship he instinctively turned to the Social Democrats and not to the anti-republican German right in search of the parliament backing he so desperately needed. At the same time, Brüning envisaged an eventual return to parliamentary government, though with reforms that would render it more capable of responding to the type of economic crisis that Germany experienced at the beginning of the 1930s.[32] Ironically Brüning's crowning achievement as Chancellor was the evacuation of Allied troops from the Rhineland in the summer of 1930, an event that freed Germany's conservative elites from the external restraints that would have kept them from replacing Germany's democratic institutions with an authoritarian system of government more in line with their values and interests.[33]

Franz von Papen and the Assault on Weimar

The appointment of Franz von Papen as Brüning's successor on 1 June 1932 represented a dramatic intensification in the struggle to replace Germany's republican institutions with a more authoritarian system of government. Papen's appointment as Chancellor was another of those events in the last years of the Weimar Republic for which there is no logical explanation. Papen had spent most of his political career as a back-bencher in the Centre Party's delegation to the Prussian state parliament, where he had served as a spokesman for Catholic aristocratic interests in the Rhineland and Westphalia and had accomplished little of note aside from alienating his party's national leaders by supporting Hindenburg and not Marx in the 1925 presidential elections. An outspoken opponent of the Centre's cooperation with the Social Democrats in the Prussian state government, Papen had strived, though without notable success, to lead the Centre into the orbit of the German right.[34] Had it not been for friendships with Hindenburg and Schleicher that dated back to the First World War, it is unlikely that Papen would ever have been considered for the chancellorship. What Schleicher saw in Papen was not just someone who shared his views on the desirability of bringing the Nazis into the government but also someone who, as a member of the Centre, would be useful in securing the party's help in service of his 'taming strategy'. All of this, however, backfired when the Centre reacted to Papen's appointment with a sharply worded statement in which it denounced the intrigues that had led to Brüning's dismissal as Chancellor and rejected the new cabinet as an 'interim solution' that failed to realize the goal of national concentration for which it had presumably been formed. Papen further aggravated the situation by responding with an open letter to Centre party chairman Ludwig Kaas in which he announced his resignation from the party on the pretext that it was impossible to reconcile his ultimate goal of a 'synthesis of all truly national forces' with membership in a political party.[35]

The situation in which the Papen government found itself in the first weeks of June 1932 was further complicated by the failure of the NSDAP to honour the commitments it had made to Schleicher in the weeks preceding the installation of the new cabinet. The formation of the Papen cabinet had been predicated upon the assumption that the new Chancellor would be able to reach an accommodation not only with the Centre but also with the National Socialists, whose leadership indicated that it would be willing, if not to enter his cabinet, then at least to tolerate it if three conditions were met. First, Hitler demanded the immediate dissolution of the Reichstag and the call for new elections that would reflect the NSDAP's growing popularity at the polls. Second, the Nazi party leader demanded that the government lift the ban on Nazi paramilitary forces and specifically the Storm Troopers or SA that Reich Minister of the Interior Wilhelm Groener had implemented in the aftermath of the April 1932 elections. And finally, Hitler demanded the removal of the state government in Prussia since it no longer commanded an absolute majority in the Landtag.[36] Taking Hitler at his word, the Papen government proceeded to schedule new elections at the end of July, lift the ban on the SA, and remove the Prussian state government, including its minister president Otto Braun, from office on 20 July 1932. The last of these moves dealt a staggering blow to one of the pillars of Weimar democracy and left the Social Democratic party leadership uncertain as to how it should proceed. Torn between those in the Reich Banner Black-Red-Gold (Reichsbanner Schwarz-Rot-Gold) and Iron Front (Eiserne Front) who called for action and those in the leadership of the socialist labour movement who doubted that their membership still possessed the will to fight, the leaders of the SPD resigned themselves to the hopelessness of the situation in which they found themselves and ultimately did nothing.[37]

All of the above had been predicated on the assumption that the Nazis would keep their commitments to Schleicher by joining the Papen cabinet or treating it with a measure of good will and decorum. But the Nazis, now in the midst of a full-scale campaign to win a majority in the Reichstag, turned the full force of their propaganda apparatus against Papen and the 'social reactionaries' he had assembled in his cabinet. Capitalizing upon the widespread distress that the ever deepening economic crisis had left in its wake, the Nazis scored a dramatic victory at the polls in which they received almost fourteen million votes and elected a total of 230 deputies to the new Reichstag.[38] The outcome of the Reichstag elections of 31 July 1932 left Schleicher's 'taming strategy' in shambles. An essential prerequisite for the success of this strategy had always been the existence of a large and united bourgeois party sufficiently powerful to contain the Nazi movement and subordinate it to the agenda of Germany's conservative elites. But the magnitude of the Nazi victory and the virtual decimation of the non-Catholic parties between the Social Democrats and the DNVP meant that Schleicher and his associates would not be able to negotiate from a position of strength in their dealings with Hitler and the NSDAP but from one that was decidedly weaker than it had been before the election.

This became immediately apparent in the first week of August when Schleicher met with Hitler and the NSDAP's Gregor Strasser in an attempt to determine the conditions under which the NSDAP might be willing to join the national government. When Hitler announced that under no circumstances would he and his party be satisfied with anything less than the chancellorship for himself and four cabinet posts for other Nazi officials, Schleicher countered—though whether he was serious or simply being facetious was far from clear—that he would present the plan to the Reich President, only to have Hindenburg respond with great indignation that he would never appoint 'that Bohemian corporal' to the post of Chancellor.[39] Not only did the passion of Hindenburg's retort suggest a loss of confidence in Schleicher's political judgement, but it set the stage for a fateful meeting between the Reich President and the Nazi party leader in the presence of the Chancellor on 13 August. Hitler entered the meeting after brief conferences with Schleicher and Papen in which they had failed to disabuse the Nazi party leader of his demands for absolute power. Hindenburg, however, lost no time in dispelling Hitler's hopes that their meeting would result in his appointment as Chancellor by brusquely asking the Nazi party leader under what conditions would his party be willing to join the current government. Furious with Papen for having led him to believe that he would become Chancellor, Hitler responded that under no circumstances would his party enter a government that did not stand under his personal leadership. Anything less would be unworthy of the leader of Germany's largest and most powerful political party. Hitler's tirade continued in the hallway outside Hindenburg's office where Hitler assailed the Chancellor for the humiliation he had just suffered in the presence of the Reich President and reaffirmed his categorical refusal to accept a subordinate position under Papen or anyone else.[40]

The debacle of 13 August effectively defined relations between the NSDAP and the Papen cabinet for the next three months. The Nazis immediately intensified their polemics against Papen and his entourage, and on 12 September they publicly embarrassed the Chancellor when Hermann Göring, acting in his capacity as president of the Reichstag, proceeded to a vote on a Communist motion of no-confidence without so much as allowing Papen to address the Reichstag and read an order to dissolve the Reichstag that had been signed by Hindenburg. Not only was Papen's ineptitude on full display for the entire nation to see, but more importantly Hindenburg's order would have authorized the postponement of new elections beyond the sixty-day period stipulated in Article 24 of the Weimar Constitution. This would then give the social and economic reforms with which the Papen cabinet sought to combat the deepening economic crisis an opportunity to take effect and thus help the government stem the rising tide of political radicalism on the left and right. Göring studiously ignored the Chancellor's frantic efforts to attract his attention and proceeded to a vote on the Communist motion of no-confidence, which passed by an overwhelming 512 to 42 margin. He then announced the removal of the Papen government without ever giving the Chancellor an opportunity to address the Reichstag.[41] This was a fiasco without precedent in the history of German parliamentarism.

The dissolution of the Reichstag on 12 September 1932 set the stage for another round of elections, the fifth since the beginning of the year. In the meantime, Papen sought to embellish his credentials as Chancellor by using Article 48 emergency powers to introduce a series of measures designed to solidify his position with Germany's conservative economic elites. Papen had already used Article 48 at the beginning of July to reduce unemployment insurance benefits by 23 per cent, a move that followed major cuts in emergency assistance and welfare payments that had been enacted the previous month. In a similar move, the government subjected the incomes of all those who were currently employed or who received retirement benefits to a levy, the proceeds of which were to be used to fund public work projects and the Voluntary Labour Service (Freiwilliger Arbeitsdienst). The net effect of this was to force the workers themselves to bear the burden of combating unemployment. At the same time, Papen moved to reassure Germany's industrial leadership by announcing a programme to stimulate economic recovery through job creation and new tax incentives for private business. But the funds allocated for job creation were far from sufficient and in some cases took the form of tax credits as bonuses for firms that hired new workers. At the same time, the fact that these and related programmes were all enacted into law by means of Article 48 represented a direct assault upon the fiscal sovereignty of the individual German states and became an essential component in the creation of what one of Papen's official propagandists, Walther Schotte, called the 'new state'.[42] The driving force behind the government's efforts to replace parliamentary democracy with a more authoritarian system of government that was not subject to the vicissitudes of Weimar party politics was Papen's Minister of the Interior, Baron Wilhelm von Gayl. According to Gayl, this was to be accomplished by strengthening the powers of the Reich President, who alone would appoint the Chancellor and cabinet ministers without requiring parliamentary approval. Similarly, Gayl sought to transform the upper house or Reichsrat into a house of dignitaries with lifetime appointments that would have an absolute veto over the legislative actions of the lower house or Reichstag. Gayl's proposed revision of the Weimar Constitution fell short of calling for a restoration of the monarchy, but in every other respect it represented an attempt to restore the power relationships that had existed in Germany before the First World War.[43]

The proclamation of the 'new state' as the cornerstone of the government's campaign for the November 1932 Reichstag elections only confirmed the essentially reactionary character of Papen's political vision and left him profoundly estranged from the vast majority of the German electorate. But the Nazis too were having difficulties maintaining order and discipline in their own ranks as frustration with Hitler's inability to transform his promises into practice became increasingly manifest. The outcome of the new elections that took place on 6 November would come as a rude shock to Hitler, Goebbels, and other party strategists. For instead of confirming the NSDAP's inexorable march to power, the elections saw the party suffer the loss of over two million votes and its representation in the Reichstag fall from 232 to 196 deputies. The losses stemmed in large part from the migration of rural and middle-class voters to the DNVP and DVP, both of which were able to recoup some of the losses they had suffered to the Nazis in July. The Communists also recorded slight gains, while the Centre, Bavarian People's Party (Bayerische Volkspartei or BVP), and other parties in the middle of the political spectrum sustained small losses of their own. For Hitler and the NSDAP, on the other hand, the election results exposed a curious anomaly that would have a profound effect on the subsequent history of the Weimar Republic, namely, that the party had failed to secure a substantial breakthrough into the two voting blocs that were absolutely essential for a Nazi seizure of power via the ballot box, organized labour and the Catholic electorate. Quite simply, what this meant was that Nazi hopes of gaining power through the ballot box were not feasible.[44] If Hitler and his party were to gain power, then it would only be through an accommodation with Germany's conservative elites that certainly shared the NSDAP's determination to destroy the existing political order but not necessarily the more radical features of the Nazi programme.

By this time, Papen's relationship with Schleicher had grown increasingly strained. Schleicher had orchestrated Papen's appointment to the chancellorship in large part because he hoped that the new Chancellor would be able to reach an accommodation with the Nazis whereby they would either join or tolerate his government. Those hopes collapsed when the Nazis failed to honour the agreement they had struck with Schleicher prior to Papen's ascendancy to the chancellorship and began instead to attack Papen as the embodiment of social and political reaction. Schleicher had hoped that something might be still be salvaged from his overtures to the Nazis by arranging the meeting between Hindenburg and Hitler on 13 August. But this too ended in another bitter setback for the Chancellor, who blamed Schleicher for the fiasco of his meeting with Hitler. The final straw was Papen's performance in the Reichstag on 12 September and the embarrassing defeat he suffered at the hands of Göring. At this point, Schleicher saw no alternative but to go ahead with new elections according to the schedule stipulated in the Weimar Constitution and put on hold plans for declaring a state of emergency that would permit postponing new elections beyond the sixty days specified in the constitution. But when the elections of 6 November and the subsequent negotiations with Hitler, Hugenberg, and Kaas failed to break the political stalemate that had existed since Papen's appointment as Chancellor, Schleicher became increasingly concerned that the Reichswehr might become caught in the middle of a civil war between opponents of the existing political system on the left and right and informed the Reich President that the military could no longer support Papen as Chancellor.[45] Throughout these developments, Hindenburg remained adamantly opposed to Hitler's appointment as Chancellor for fear that this might lead to the establishment of a party dictatorship, and he continued to support the creation of a *Kampfkabinett* under Papen that was based not upon a parliamentary majority in the Reichstag but upon his powers as Reich President. When Schleicher expressed his fears that this might lead to a civil war that the Reichswehr could not contain, a frustrated Hindenburg turned to his Minister of Defence and directed him to assume the responsibilities of the chancellorship.[46] This was not what Schleicher had expected or wanted. But the lack of genuine political options and the direct order he had received from Hindenburg left him with no alternative but to accept the office of Chancellor.

The Schleicher Interlude

Kurt von Schleicher remains a controversial figure in the late history of the Weimar Republic. To some Schleicher epitomizes the so-called Prussian tradition with all of its antidemocratic and authoritarian accoutrements; to others he represents Weimar's last hope of keeping the Nazis from power. The fact of the matter, however, was that the range of options available to Schleicher for dealing with Hitler upon his appointment as Chancellor was extremely limited. Schleicher's own 'taming strategy' had been dealt a severe blow by the outcome of the November Reichstag elections and by the failure of those bourgeois forces that still opposed Nazism to settle their differences and come together in a single political party. This in turn meant that Schleicher would not be negotiating with Hitler from a position of strength but from one of weakness that left him exposed to the machinations of Papen and the presidential entourage. Schleicher had followed Hitler's political career since the early 1920s and had a hard time taking him seriously as the leader of Germany's largest political party. Schleicher had been particularly annoyed by Hitler's antics in the negotiations to avoid the presidential elections in the spring of 1932 by extending Hindenburg's term of office through the adoption of a special resolution in the Reichstag. In private correspondence following the collapse of these negotiations, Schleicher fumed at Hitler and declared him totally unfit for the office of the Reich President.[47] Nor did Hitler's behaviour when he met with Schleicher in early August or at his subsequent meeting with Hindenburg a week later do much to assuage Schleicher's doubts. Schleicher, however, had begun to develop an interest in Gregor Strasser, head of the NSDAP's Reich Organization Leadership (Reichs-Organisations-Leitung der NSDAP), and arguably the second most important figure in the Nazi leadership. Whether it was as the result of the remarkably conciliatory tone of a highly publicized speech that Strasser had delivered in the Reichstag in May 1932 or his demeanour at Schleicher's aforementioned meeting with Hitler, Strasser would come to play an increasingly important role in Schleicher's political calculus once he assumed the chancellorship in early December 1932.[48]

It was against the background of these developments that Schleicher began to toy with the idea of a broad political front—or *Querfront*, as it was frequently called—stretching from the socialist and Christian labour unions through the Centre, BVP, and the remnants of the Protestant middle parties to the left wing of the Nazi Party. Although the extent to which Schleicher remained in contact with Strasser during the Papen chancellorship remains unclear, he mentioned his contacts with Strasser at a dinner with the French ambassador to Germany André François-Poncet just days before he assumed the chancellorship and seemed reasonably optimistic that Strasser might be able to line up support within the NSDAP for a new cabinet should he be asked to form one.[49] At the same time, Schleicher and members of his entourage entered into exploratory talks with the leaders of the General German Trade Union Federation (Allgemeiner Deutscher Gewerkschaftsbund or ADGB), the umbrella organization of the socialist labour movement that was closely allied with the Social Democrats.[50] At the heart of these negotiations was a firm and irrevocable commitment to reducing unemployment through job creation and a massive state-financed public works programme to be implemented under the aegis of Schleicher's newly appointed minister of job creation, Günther Gereke.[51] Just how much faith Schleicher placed in all of this remains a matter of historical conjecture,[52] particularly since the entire project fell apart in the first week of December when Strasser failed to convince Hitler to support the Schleicher cabinet, resigned all of his party offices save his seat in the Reichstag, and left Berlin for a vacation in Italy.[53] By the time that Strasser returned to Berlin in the first week of January 1933 for a round of high-level meetings that included a private conference with the Reich President and an offer of the vice chancery in Schleicher's cabinet and the minister presidency of Prussia,[54] the leaders of the ADGB had backed away from the project, no doubt under heavy pressure from the SPD whose leaders still distrusted Schleicher on account of his role in the dismissal of the Prussian government in July.[55] Strasser, in the meantime, continued to disavow any interest in organizing a secession by the NSDAP's more moderate elements and remained firm in his conviction that the party's future course lay in entering the national government on terms that were commensurate with its strength in the Reichstag.[56]

Schleicher's overtures to the socialist labor movement and speculation about a massive public works programme that would be financed out of state resources aroused concerns among Germany's economic elites. Reusch and the leaders of German heavy industry were particularly outspoken in their criticism of Schleicher's social and economic policies, were distressed by his failure to give the capitalist economic system his unqualified endorsement in his radio address to the nation in the middle of December, and expressed fears that the planned job creation programme would trigger a new inflationary spiral.[57] The Chancellor with whom German industry felt the closest affinity had been Papen, and the National Federation of German Industry and other industrial interest organizations were determined to use all of the resources at their disposal to make certain that Schleicher continued in his footsteps.[58] Organized agriculture had also enjoyed a close relationship with Papen and reacted sharply to Schleicher's refusal to raise tariffs on agricultural imports out of concern for the effect this would have on organized labour and consumers. But it was Schleicher's plans for resettling unemployed German workers on bankrupt estates east of the Elbe River that produced the greatest outrage. The Reich Rural League, the largest and most influential of Germany's agricultural interest organizations, responded to this by issuing what amounted to a virtual declaration of war against the Schleicher government at a meeting of its executive committee in mid-January 1933, a move that set in motion the series of events that would eventually culminate in Schleicher's resignation as Chancellor.[59] In the meantime, Papen had insinuated himself back into the political equation with a much publicized speech at the German Gentlemen's Club (Deutscher Herrenklub) in mid-December 1932 in which he had called once again for the inclusion of the NSDAP in any new governmental constellation. This led to what was supposed to have been a secret meeting between Papen and Hitler in the house of Cologne banker Kurt von Schröder on 4 January 1933.[60] Schleicher learned of the meeting only when a photograph of the participants entering Schröder's house appeared the following day in a Berlin newspaper, but he apparently accepted Papen's reassurances that the former chancellor was only working in the best interests of the government and did not understand Papen's real intent until it was too late.[61] For Hitler, on the other hand, Papen's intervention could not have come at a more fortuitous moment. For although he had succeeded in preventing Strasser's resignation from developing into a major secession of Nazi moderates, party morale remained low and party finances were a disaster. Whether the NSDAP could regain its dynamic momentum remained to be seen.[62]

For reasons that are difficult to explain, Schleicher seems to have been oblivious to the intrigues that Papen was spinning behind his back. In a series of press conferences he held in the middle of January 1933, Schleicher struck an optimistic note about the immediate political future and displayed no sense of urgency with respect to the situation in which he found himself. At the same time, Schleicher dismissed rumours that he was working with Strasser to organize a secession on the part of Nazi moderates and cited the failure of the secession that had taken place on the left wing of the DNVP in 1929–30 as a reason for his disinterest.[63] In the meantime, Papen was busy lining up the alliance of forces that would spell his demise. Not only did Papen meet secretly with Hitler on numerous occasions in the second and third weeks of January, but he reached out to the DNVP's Hugenberg and the Stahlhelm's Franz Seldte. But neither organization was as open to an arrangement with the Nazis as the unflappable Papen. Hugenberg had been repeatedly burned by Hitler, first in the 1929 crusade against the Young Plan, then again at the Harzburg rally in the fall of 1931, and most recently in the presidential elections in the spring of 1932. The DNVP had waged a bitter campaign against the NSDAP in both of the 1932 Reichstag elections, and there was a sizeable contingent within the party led by Ernst Oberfohren and Otto Schmidt-Hannover that was adamantly opposed to any alliance with Hitler.[64] The same was true of the Stahlhelm, where a serious rift had developed between Seldte and Duesterberg, who was still brooding over Hitler's treatment of him in the presidential elections earlier that spring.[65] Undeterred by these developments, Papen efforts to reach an accord with Hitler received strong support from his patrons in German heavy industry, who were desperate for an end to the chaos in Berlin and a return to a modicum of economic normalcy. Presumably this would take place through the formation of a new government that included the Nazis but with Papen at its helm.[66]

By far the most important development in the chain of events that culminated in Hitler's rise to power, however, was that Hindenburg himself was suddenly amenable to the creation of a cabinet with Hitler as its Chancellor and Papen as his Vice Chancellor.

Under the terms of this arrangement, Papen would presumably be vested as the representative of Germany's conservative elites with the authority of the Reich President to hold the Nazi party leader and his followers in check. Whether Hindenburg's change of heart reflected the influence of Papen and other members of the presidential entourage or was simply a matter of the Reich President acting on his own initiative to try and restore the unity of the German nation remains a matter of historical conjecture.[67] In the meantime, Schleicher's position had become increasingly hopeless. The Chancellor would make one last request to the Reich President on 28 January for emergency powers that would have allowed him to dissolve the Reichstag without calling for new elections, but was dismissed with little more than token expressions of gratitude for his service.[68] Two days later Hitler was formally installed as Chancellor of a government of 'national concentration' in which Papen became Vice Chancellor flanked by Hugenberg at the Ministries of Economics and Agriculture and Seldte at the Ministry of Labour. All of this was premised on the assumption that the conservatives in the cabinet—after all, they held ten of the thirteen cabinet posts—would be able to control Hitler and harness the dynamism of the Nazi movement to their own political agenda. This, however, would prove a fatal miscalculation, for over the next three months the Nazis completely outmanoeuvred their conservative allies and forced them to the periphery of the decision-making process. With the passage of the Enabling Act in the fourth week of March 1933, what had begun as a last-ditch effort to contain the Nazis had completely collapsed.[69] The Nazis were in firm control of the state apparatus and only had the more radical forces within their own movement to fear.

Conclusions

None of this was in any way whatsoever inevitable or predetermined. To be sure, there were structural and cultural factors that severely limited the range of options that were available to those in positions of responsibility. At the very least, the economic devastation and subsequent radicalization of the German middle strata meant that the restoration of parliamentary democracy was out of the question. But the situation from the November 1932 Reichstag elections through the end of January 1933 was extremely fluid. Among other things, it was by no means certain that Hitler would be able to master the crisis in the NSDAP that had been created by Strasser's resignation, and it required an extraordinary demonstration of his leadership skills and personal charisma to hold the party together as an instrument of his political will. Second, Papen's meeting with the Nazi party leader on 4 January 1933 was the desperate act of a man whose exaggerated sense of self-importance and desire for revenge left him vulnerable to the machinations of a more skilled and resolute Hitler. Even then, the negotiations were never easy and almost collapsed at the last minute when the DNVP's Hugenberg came within seconds of walking out of the installation ceremonies on the morning of 30 January as a result of Hitler's failure to honour his demand that there be no new Reichstag elections. Only a complete paralysis of will by Hugenberg at the moment the new cabinet officers were being presented to the Reich President kept Hitler's installation as Chancellor on track.[70]

Going back even further, there were other moments in the period from 1930 to 1933 when the actions of individual players carried more causal agency than usual. In the case of Brüning, it was his rigid adherence to a deflationary fiscal policy that greatly aggravated the effects of the deepening economic crisis and that in turn radicalized increasingly large sectors of the German population. Brüning was certainly aware of other and less traumatic strategies for combating the depression but failed to implement them, largely for reasons of foreign policy, until it was too late. The real problem, however, came with Schleicher's intervention in the political process. For while the choice of Brüning as Müller's successor in the spring of 1930 was certainly reasonable in light of other alternatives, the Chancellor's use of Article 48 to enact his social and economic programs was consistent with the long-term strategy of Schleicher and Germany's conservative elites to decouple the exercise of executive authority from the constantly shifting vicissitudes of Weimar party politics. The turn to Article 48 was a particularly ominous moment in the dissolution of the Weimar Republic, for it transferred responsibility in the decision-making process from the Reichstag to the Reich presidency at a point in time when Hindenburg's declining faculties left him vulnerable to manipulation by individuals in the presidential camarilla who suddenly found themselves invested with enormous power to pursue schemes of their own without legislative oversight.

In the meantime, Schleicher's obsession with 'taming' the Nazis by saddling them with the burden of governmental responsibility not only rested on a fundamental misreading of Hitler and the situation within the NSDAP but encouraged delusional fantasies in the presidential entourage about the possibilities of working with Hitler. This included the Reich President himself, who for reasons that remain largely unexplained overcame his aversion to Hitler he had shown in the second half of 1932 and succumbed to the counsel of those in the presidential camarilla who saw Hitler's elevation to the chancellorship as the only possible antidote to the ever deepening political crisis in which Germany found itself. But the most fateful decision of all was Papen's appointment as Chancellor in June 1932, most likely to satisfy a personal whim of the Reich President. Not only was Papen totally unqualified for the position to which he had been appointed, but he proved to be a wild card that not even Schleicher could control once he was in office. And once he had been removed from office, Papen would turn on Schleicher with a malevolence that manifested itself in a total disregard for the realities of the day and led him into his ill-fated courtship of Hitler. By this time, however, the dismissal of Groener, Brüning, and even the supercilious Papen had severely weakened Schleicher's hand with the Reich President and left him powerless to prevent what he foresaw as an unmitigated disaster for the German nation. In the final analysis, Papen's crowning achievement—the formation of the 'government of national concentration' on 30 January 1933—was as much the result of petty animosities, strategic miscalculations, and the willful disregard for consequences as it was the product of the great depression and the paralysis of Weimar democracy.

Notes

1. Harold James, 'Economic Reasons for the Collapse of the Weimar Republic', in Ian Kershaw (ed.), *Weimar: Why did German Democracy Fail?* (New York: St Martin's Press, 1990), 30–57, here 30–1.
2. Karl Dietrich Bracher, 'Demokratie und Machtvakuum: Zum Problem des Parteienstaates in der Auflösung der Weimarer Republik', in Karl Dietrich Erdmann and Hagen Schulz (eds), *Weimar: Selbstpreisgabe einer Demokratie. Eine Bilanz heute* (Düsseldorf: Droste Verlag, 1984), 109–34, as well as Bracher, *Die Auflösung der Weimarer Republik: Eine Studie zum Problem des Machtverfalls in der Demokratie*, 3rd ed. (Villingen-Schwarzwald: Ring Verlag, 1960), 26–7.
3. This has been argued at greater length in Larry Eugene Jones, 'Why Hitler Came to Power: In Defense of a New History of Politics', in Konrad H. Jarausch, Jörn Rüsen, and Hans Schleier (eds), *Geschichtswissenschaft vor 2000: Perspektiven der Historiographiegeschichte, Geschichtstheorie, Sozial- und Kulturgeschichte. Festschrift für Georg G. Iggers zum 65. Geburtstag* (Hagen: Margit Rottmann Medienverlag, 1991), 256–76.
4. Larry Eugene Jones, *The German Right, 1918–1930: Political Parties, Organized Interests, and Patriotic Associations in the Struggle Against Weimar Democracy* (Cambridge: Cambridge University Press, 2020), 161–75. For the broader context, see Robert Gerwarth, 'The Central European Counter-Revolution: Paramilitary Violence in Germany, Austria, and Hungary after the Great War', *Past and Present*, 200 (2008), 175–209. On the specific contours of paramilitary violence in the late Weimar Republic, see Dirk Schumann, *Political Violence in the Weimar Republic, 1918–1933: Fight for the Streets and Fear of Civil War*, tr. Thomas Dunlap (New York and Oxford: Berghahn Books, 2009), 215–315.
5. For further details, see Hans Mommsen, *The Rise and Fall of Weimar Democracy*, tr. Elborg Forster and Larry Eugene Jones (Chapel Hill, NC, and London: University of North Carolina Press, 1986), 281–92. On the role of the Social Democrats, see Donna Harsch, *German Social Democracy and the Rise of Nazism* (Chapel Hill, NC, and London: University of North Carolina Press, 1993), 51–9.
6. In this respect, see Leo Schweringer, 'Stegerwalds und Brünings Vorstellungen über Parteireform und Parteiensystem', in Ferdinand A. Hermens and Theodor Schieder (eds), *Staat, Wirtschaft und Politik in der Weimarer Republik: Festschrift für Heinrich Brüning* (Berlin: Duncker & Humbolt, 1967), 23–40.
7. E.g. see Breitscheid's protocol of a conversation with Brüning, 1 Feb. 1930, reprinted in Rudolf Morsey, 'Neue Quellen zur Vorgeschichte der Reichskanzlerschaft Brünings', in Hermens and Schieder, *Staat, Wirtschaft und Politik*, 207–31, here 210–12. See also William L. Patch, Jr., *Heinrich Brüning and the Dissolution of the Weimar Republic* (Cambridge: Cambridge University Press, 1998), 48–71.
8. On Hugenberg's capitulation, see Jones, *German Right*, 540–2. On Hugenberg's election and policies as DNVP party chairman, see John A. Leopold, *Alfred Hugenberg: The Radical Nationalist Campaign Against the Weimar Republic* (New Haven and London: Yale University Press, 1977), 35–83.
9. Jones, *German Right*, 527–30.
10. Patch, *Brüning*, 73–94.
11. Jones, *German Right*, 542–5.
12. Ibid., 551–3. See also Thomas Wisser, 'Die Diktaturmaßnahmen im Juli 1930: Autoritäre Wandlung der Demokratie?', in Rolf Grawert, Bernhard Schlink, Rainer Wahl, and

Joachim Wieland (eds), *Offene Staatlichkeit: Festschrift für Ernst-Wolfgang Böckenförde zum 65. Geburtstag* (Berlin: Duncker & Humblot, 1995), 415–34.

13. Entry for 14 Sept. 1930 in Hermann Pünder, *Politik in der Reichskanzlei: Aufzeichnungen aus den Jahren 1929–1932*, ed. Thilo Vogelsang (Stuttgart: Deutsche Verlags-Anstalt, 1961), 58–9.
14. For further details, see Jones, *German Right*, 359–60.
15. Mommsen, *Rise and Fall of Weimar Democracy*, 314–17. For a more detailed analysis of the 1930 election results, see Thomas Childers, *The Nazi Voter: The Social Foundations of Fascism in Germany* (Chapel Hill, NC, and London: University of North Carolina Press, 1983), 119–91.
16. For an overview, see Shelley Baranowski, 'The Collapse of the Weimar Parliamentary System', in Shelley Baranowski, Armin Nolzen, and Claus-Christian-Szejnmann (eds), *A Companion to Nazi Germany* (New York: John Wiley & Sons, 2018), 63–76.
17. For the most detailed reconstruction of this meeting, see Patch, *Brüning*, 133–6. See also Heinrich Brüning, *Memoiren 1918–1934* (Stuttgart: Deutsche Verlags-Anstalt, 1970), 192–8.
18. Harold James, *The German Slump: Politics and Economics, 1924–1936* (Oxford: Oxford University Press, 1986), 67–71.
19. Hans Mommsen, 'Staat und Bürokratie in der Ära Brüning', in Gotthard Jasper (ed.), *Tradition und Reform in der deutschen Politik: Gedenkschrift für Waldemar Besson* (Frankfurt am Main: Ullstein, 1976), 81–137.
20. James, *German Slump*, 262–78. See also Stephanie Merkenich, *Grüne Front gegen Weimar: Reichs-Landbund und agrarischer Lobbyismus 1918–1933* (Düsseldorf: Droste Verlag, 1998), 300–52.
21. For further information, see Henry A. Turner, Jr., *German Big Business and the Rise of Hitler* (New York and Oxford: Oxford University Press, 1985), 124–42, 158–71, and Reinhard Neebe, *Grossindustrie, Staat und NSDAP 1930–1933: Paul Silverberg und der Reichsverband der Deutschen Industrie in der Krise der Weimarer Republik* (Göttingen: Vandenhoeck & Ruprecht, 1981), 80–110.
22. For further details, see Larry Eugene Jones, 'Taming the Nazi Beast: Kurt von Schleicher and the End of the Weimar Republic', in Hermann Beck and Larry Eugene Jones (eds), *From Weimar to Hitler: Studies in the Dissolution of the Weimar Republic and the Establishment of the Third Reich, 1932–1934* (New York and Oxford: Berghahn Books, 2019), 23–52, here 24–5.
23. On these overtures, see Astrid von Pufendorf, *Die Plancks: Eine Familie zwischen Patriotismus und Widerstand* (Berlin: Propyläen, 2006), 246–54.
24. This is best documented in [Reinhold Quaatz], *Aus dem Tagebuch von Reinhold Quaatz 1928–1933*, ed. Hermann Weiß and Paul Hoser (Munich: Oldenbourg, 1989), 143–7. See also Brüning, *Memoiren*, 375–8, as well as the recent article by Michael Schellhorn, '"Mit dem Zentrum niemals!" Alfred Hugenberg und die Deutsche Zentrumspartei in der Endphase der Weimarer Republik (1928-1933)', *Historisch-politische Mitteilungen* 26 (2019), 27–64, here 46–7.
25. For further details, see Larry Eugene Jones, *Hitler versus Hindenburg: The 1932 Presidential Elections and the End of the Weimar Republic* (Cambridge: Cambridge University Press, 2016), 108–18.
26. Ibid., 206–9, 298. See also Patch, *Brüning*, 239–41.
27. Larry Eugene Jones, 'Adolf Hitler and the 1932 Presidential Elections: A Study in Nazi Strategy and Politics', in Markus Raasch and Tobias Hirschmüller (eds), *Von Freiheit,*

Solidarität und Subsidiarität—Staat und Gesellschaft der Moderne in Theorie und Praxis. Festschrift für Karsten Ruppert zum 65. Geburtstag (Berlin: Duncker & Humblot, 2013), 550–73, here 558–64.
28. On the Duesterberg candidacy, see Volker R. Berghahn, *Der Stahlhelm—Bund der Frontsoldaten 1918–1935* (Düsseldorf: Droste Verlag, 1966), 195–219.
29. Jones, *Hitler versus Hindenburg*, 274–313.
30. Patch, *Brüning*, 247–71. See also Wolfram Pyta, *Hindenburg: Herrschaft zwischen Hohenzollern und Hitler* (Berlin: Siedler, 2009), 685–98.
31. This is argued most forcefully in Hans Mommsen, 'Die Stellung der Beamtenschaft in Reich, Ländern und Gemeinden in der Ära Brüning', *Vierteljahrshefte für Zeitgeschichte*, 21 (1973), 151–63, esp. 163–5.
32. Patch, *Brüning*, 324–5. See also Werner Conze, 'Die Reichsverfassungsreform als Ziel der Politik Brünings', *Der Staat*, 11 (1972), 209–17.
33. Mommsen, *Rise and Fall of Weimar Democracy*, 298–9.
34. Larry Eugene Jones, 'Franz von Papen, the German Center Party, and the Failure of Catholic Conservatism in the Weimar Republic', *Central European History*, 38 (2005), 191–217, here 196–9.
35. Ibid., 210–11. See also Rudolf Morsey, 'Die Deutsche Zentrumspartei', in Erich Matthias and Rudolf Morsey (eds), *Das Ende der Parteien 1933* (Düsseldorf: Droste Verlag, 1960), 281–453, here 306–14.
36. Heinrich Brüning, 'Ein Brief', *Deutsche Rundschau*, 70 (1947), 1–22, here 11–14.
37. Harsch, *German Social Democracy*, 193–202. See also Klaus Schönhoven, 'Strategie des Nichtstuns? Sozialdemokratischer Legalismus und kommunistischer Attentismus in der Ära des Präsidialkabinette', in Heinrich August Winkler (ed.), *Die deutsche Staatskrise 1930–1933: Handlungsspielräume und Alternativen* (Munich: R. Oldenburg Verlag, 1992), 59–76.
38. Mommsen, *Rise and Fall of Weimar Democracy*, 454–9.
39. Benjamin Carter Hett, *The Death of Democracy: Hitler's Rise to Power and the Downfall of the Weimar Republic* (New York: Henry Holt & Co., 2018), 153.
40. Jones, 'Taming the Nazi Beast', 28–9. See also Pyta, *Hindenburg*, 717–20, and Hett, *Death of Democracy*, 154–6.
41. Hett, *Death of Democracy*, 157–8.
42. Mommsen, *Rise and Fall of Weimar Democracy*, 471–4.
43. Ibid., 478–9.
44. Ibid., 483–4. See also Thomas Childers, 'The Limits of National Socialist Mobilisation: The Elections of 6 November 1932 and the Fragmentation of the Nazi Constituency', in Thomas Childers (ed.), *The Formation of the Nazi Constituency, 1919–1933* (Totowa, NJ: Barnes & Noble, 1986), 232–59.
45. Jones, 'Taming the Nazi Beast', 31–2.
46. Pyta, *Hindenburg*, 759–66.
47. Jones, *Hitler versus Hindenburg*, 139–48, 306–7.
48. On Strasser, see Udo Kissenkoetter, *Gregor Strasser und die NSDAP* (Stuttgart: Deutsche Verlags-Anstalt, 1978), 145–77, and Peter D. Stachura, *Gregor Strasser and the Rise of Nazism* (London: Allen & Unwin, 1983), 103–90.
49. Hett, *Death of Democracy*, 165–6.

50. For the most balanced discussion of these negotiations, see Harsch, *German Social Democracy*, 207–12, 220–4. For further details, see Richard Breitman, 'On German Social Democracy and General Schleicher, 1932–1933', *Central European History*, 9 (1976), 352–78, here 362–9, and Heinrich Muth, 'Schleicher und die Gewerkschaften 1932: Ein Quellenproblem', *Vierteljahrshefte für Zeitgeschichte*, 29 (1981), 189–215, here 209–13.
51. For further details, see Herbert Marcon, *Arbeitsbeschaffungspolitik der Regierungen Papen und Schleicher: Grundsteinlegung für die Beschäftigungspolitik im Dritten Reich* (Bern and Frankfurt am Main: Peter Lang, 1974), 253–75.
52. Henry A. Turner, Jr., 'The Myth of Hitler's *Querfront* Strategy', *Central European History*, 41 (2008), 673–82.
53. Jones. 'Taming the Nazi Beast', 32–5. See also Henry A. Turner, Jr., *Hitler's Thirty Days to Power: January 1933* (Reading, MA: Addison-Wesley, 1996), 24–8.
54. Jones, 'Taming the Nazi Beast', 36.
55. For further details, see Harsch, *German Social Democracy*, 223–4, and Breitman, 'German Social Democracy', 370–5.
56. Turner, *Hitler's Thirty Days*, 84–6.
57. Peter Langer, 'Paul Reusch und die "Machtergreifung"', *Mitteilungsblatt des Instituts für Soziale Bewegungen*, 28 (2003), 157–202, here 187–90.
58. Turner, *German Big Business*, 304–13. See also Joachim Petzold, *Franz von Papen: Ein deutsches Verhängnis* (Munich and Berlin: Buchverlag Union, 1995), 115–18.
59. Bernd Hoppe, 'Von Schleicher zu Hitler: Dokumente zum Konflikt zwischen dem Reichslandbund und der Regierung Schleicher in den letzten Monaten der Weimarer Republik', *Vierteljahrshefte für Zeitgeschichte*, 45 (1997), 629–57, here 645–51.
60. Petzold, *Papen*, 136–7.
61. For further details, see Heinrich Muth, 'Das "Kölner Gespräch" am 4. Januar 1933', *Geschichte in Wissenschaft und Unterricht*, 37 (1986), 463–80, 529–41.
62. Dietrich J. Orlow, *The History of the Nazi Party*, 2 vols (Pittsburgh, PA: University of Pittsburgh Press, 1969–73), vol. 1, 290–7.
63. Jones, 'Taming the Nazi Beast', 36–7.
64. Larry Eugene Jones, '"The Greatest Stupidity of my Life": Alfred Hugenberg and the Formation of the Hitler Cabinet, January 1933', *Journal of Contemporary History*, 27 (1992), 63–87, esp. 75–6. See also Peter Wulf, 'Ernst Oberfohren und die DNVP am Ende der Weimarer Republik', in Erich Hoffmann and Peter Wulf (eds), *Wir bauen das Reich. Aufstieg und Herrschaftsjahre des Nationalsozialismus in Schleswig-Holstein* (Neumünster: Wachholtz, 1983), 165–87.
65. Berghahn, *Stahlhelm*, 245–63.
66. Petzold, *Papen*, 145–8, 160–2.
67. See Pyta, *Hindenburg*, 780–98.
68. Jones, 'Taming the Nazi Beast', 39.
69. Hermann Beck, *The Fateful Alliance: German Conservatives and Nazis in 1933. The Machtergreifung in a New Light* (New York and Oxford: Berghahn Books, 2008), 83–113.
70. Jones, 'Greatest Stupidity', 76. On the ceremonial installation of the Hitler cabinet, see in particular Volker Ullrich, *Hitler: Ascent 1889–1939*, tr. Jefferson Chase (New York: Vintage Books, 2016), 368–70.

Bibliography

Bracher, Karl Dietrich, *Die Auflösung der Weimarer Republik: Eine Studie zum Problem des Machtverfalls in der Demokratie*, 3rd ed. (Villigen/Schwarzwald: Ring-Verlag, 1960).

Harsch, Donna, *German Social Democracy and the Rise of Nazism* (Chapel Hill, NC, and London: University of North Carolina Press, 1993).

Hett, Benjamin Carter, *The Death of Democracy: Hitler's Rise to Power and the Downfall of the Weimar Republic* (New York: Henry Holt & Co., 2018).

Jones, Larry Eugene, *Hitler versus Hindenburg: The 1932 Presidential Elections and the End of the Weimar Republic* (Cambridge: Cambridge University Press, 2016).

Jones, Larry Eugene, *The German Right, 1918–1930: Political Parties, Organized Interests, and Patriotic Associations in the Struggle against Weimar Democracy* (Cambridge: Cambridge University Press, 2020).

Mommsen, Hans, *The Rise and Fall of Weimar Democracy*, tr. Elborg Forster and Larry Eugene Jones (Chapel Hill, NC, and London: University of North Carolina Press, 1986).

Patch, William L., Jr., *Heinrich Brüning and the Dissolution of the Weimar Republic* (Cambridge: Cambridge University Press, 1998).

Pyta, Wolfram, *Hindenburg. Herrschaft zwischen Hohenzollern und Hitler* (Berlin: Siedler, 2009).

Schulz, Gerhard, *Von Brüning zu Hitler: Der Wandel des politischen Systems in Deutschland 1930–1933* (Berlin: de Gruyter, 1992).

Turner, Henry A., Jr., *German Big Business and the Rise of Hitler* (New York and Oxford: Oxford University Press, 1985).

Turner, Henry A., Jr. *Hitler's Thirty Days to Power: January 1933* (Reading, MA: Addison-Wesley, 1996).

PART II
POLITY, POLITICS, AND POLICIES

CHAPTER 6

THE WEIMAR CONSTITUTION

PETER C. CALDWELL

THE story of the Weimar Constitution is about legal rules, processes, and rights. It is also about the nature of the revolution of 1918/19 and of Germany's first democracy, about the perils facing democracy itself, and about how enemies of liberal democracy could use its rules to destroy democracy. Was the constitution the legal embodiment of the spirit of democratic revolution, or was it a means of limiting both democracy and revolution? Did the constitution institutionalize the principles of inclusion and self-determination, opening the way for the German people to decide their own future? Or did the constitution merely open the way to irresponsible party rule while undermining the foundations of German unity?

These questions arose already in the first years of the Republic. Indeed, many already saw the conditions under which the constitution formed as an existential threat to democracy and to Germany itself. Whether the Versailles Treaty really posed such an existential threat to Germany has been revised in recent years,[1] but the challenges to German political order at the time certainly did seem huge: Polish separatism in the East, endorsed by the victors of the First World War; Bavarian and Rhenish dalliance with separatism, which opened the way for French influence and was enhanced by the occupation of the Rhine and Ruhr Valleys; the threat of civil war from the left in 1919, 1920, and 1923, and putsch attempts from the right in 1920 and 1923; not to speak of the challenges of coming to terms with the vast waste of wealth and people associated with the war itself (and conveniently blamed on the Versailles Treaty), to name just a few of the crises the new democracy would have to face. Half a decade after the ratification of the Weimar Constitution, the new constitutional democracy had seen a series of crises—and survived. But not without putting the democratic system under stress, and revealing how little many Germans, especially intellectuals, identified with it.[2] After 1929, the crises returned, and by 1933 the Weimar Constitution was no more.

As most recent commentators agree, the constitution's construction did not force the republic to fail.[3] Half a decade of systematic subversion by conservative forces from within, at the highest level by President Paul von Hindenburg, hollowed it out. The Great Depression created social pressures that undermined moderate parties and also provided an opportunity for conservatives to engineer a constitutional change toward a more authoritarian system. A quasi-legal putsch dismantled the ruling government of Prussia in 1932, one of the last bulwarks of democracy. And, last but not least, over half of German voters abandoned democratic parties after 1930, a crisis that paralysed the state and opened the way for a constitutional break. It is hard to imagine what democratic constitution could have survived these challenges.

The present chapter leaves the political story to other contributors to this volume. It seeks instead to describe the constitution and the debates that took place around it that helped to define the new democracy. The chapter begins with the revolution of 1918/19, which produced a revolutionary constitution—even as parties across the political spectrum tried to forget about the republic's revolutionary origins.[4] After describing the constitution as a revolutionary break with the old system and the foundation of the republic on the principle of popular sovereignty, the chapter next turns to the way the constitution formed democratic institutions. In Dieter Grimm's description, democratic constitutions create state organs rather than organize pre-existing power; in other words, institutions are created by the constitution and therefore stand under it. Such was also the case in Weimar Germany, a democratic system that established a complex system of governance that presupposed inclusion of all social groups and political pluralism.[5] A third section describes the federalist and direct democratic aspects of the new republic, and a fourth the basic rights asserted by the Weimar Constitution, which included both individual and communal aspects. Finally, the chapter ends by identifying the main stress points in the constitution that played a role in the destruction of democracy itself.

A Revolutionary Constitution

The constitution was the product of revolution. The 1918/19 revolution was first and foremost a rejection of the war, which carried with it a rejection of the political structures that had carried out the war. According to the Imperial Constitution of 1871, the governments of the individual states, whether formed by hereditary monarchs or by bourgeois elites elected by restricted suffrage, formed a kind of collective monarch through the Federal Council (Bundesrat), with the Prussian king playing the leading role and acting as emperor (Kaiser). These were supposed to be the leaders of the state. They had instead avoided responsibility, had put military men in charge of society during the war, and had with the agreement of the old Reichstag suspended labour rights and labour protections along with rights of free speech and free assembly. Peace meant not just an end to war, it meant an end to wartime control of society by the state, an end to the attempt of Generals Hindenburg and Erich Ludendorff in the General Staff to militarize labour and mobilize economic resources, channelling both into the war effort. Although the Reichstag limited the extent of direct power over society demanded by the General Staff, military involvement with everyday life became a fact during the war. The soldiers and workers who started the revolution in early November 1918 were most certainly not interested in increasing central, militarized control over society on the lines that Lenin would eventually follow (with admiration for the accomplishments of Hindenburg and Ludendorff).[6] It cannot be surprising, then, that the direct demands of the first soldiers' councils of 1918 involved suspending war-related rules to assert basic civil rights: releasing political prisoners and ensuring freedom of speech and of the press. Nor is it surprising that the Council of People's Deputies, a collective body exercising dictatorial power in the first stage of the revolution, announced on 12 November 1918 its suspension of the state of siege, the end of the Auxiliary Service Law, and the implementation of the eight-hour workday, but not a new, socialist republic.[7] Peace meant a break with the old regime and its wartime practices, not a call for a specific kind of social revolution.

Beyond peace, the revolution was obviously also about inclusion, which meant overcoming the exclusion of some workers and most women from participating in local, state, and national elections. The 1871 Constitution, based as it was on the exclusionary systems in place in individual states, came to an end on 9 November 1918. At the level of the states, the individual monarchs fell, and with them the constitutions that presupposed the existence of those monarchs. The Federal Council, without its state sovereigns, ceased to exist. The Social Democratic leader Friedrich Ebert, who was named (illegally—or rather revolutionarily) German Chancellor and after 10 November de facto leading member of the six-person Council of People's Deputies, dissolved the old Reichstag, elected before 1914 on the basis of laws that systematically reduced the representation of workers and did not permit women to vote.[8] The decision to hold early elections for a national constituent assembly was taken by the Council of People's Deputies, including USPD representatives, and also by the Congress of Councils in its meeting from 16–21 December. This was a decision taken by a revolutionary assembly for inclusion of all citizens, and not just working-class men, in the process of forming a new order, a decision for pluralism and parties. There was, in short, a decision to create 'an open framework for an experiment in democracy' that was radically inclusive.[9]

Well before the National Assembly met to work out the new constitution, the revolution of 1918/19 had made a clear decision for a democratic government that negated the old regime: the states, the monarchs, the place of the military, the unequal systems of representation. The revolution had decided for women's rights and workers' rights and indeed the rights of all other members of the nation, and for the self-determination of the German nation as a whole. Or, as Article 1 of the constitution says: 'All state power originates with the people.' The revolutionary leadership operated with logical consistency, denying to itself the right to create the new legal order in the name of the people, deferring nationalization of basic industry by way of revolutionary decree, and calling for new elections so that the nation could represent itself. The overwhelming majority of Germans, men and women, voted for the parties that supported an inclusive democratic republic and parliamentary democracy: nearly 40 per cent for the Social Democrats, 19.7 per cent for the Catholic Centre Party, and 18.5 per cent for the left-liberal German Democrats, a supermajority of 76.1 per cent. 7.6 per cent went to the far-left Independent Socialists, leaving the traditional right, which might have supported the old regime, with only a bit more than 15 per cent of the vote. These percentages dictated the number of delegates to the National Assembly, which convened in the town of Weimar—renowned as the home of German classicism, but more important far from the ongoing violence in Berlin. For the first time, women could vote. Although women were underrepresented both among the candidates and among the delegates, nevertheless 37 of the 423 members of parliament were women, spread across all the major parties. It was the task of the National Assembly to determine in the constitution how the German people would represent itself politically.[10]

While formally holding that power, however, the National Assembly's members knew that many basic decisions had already been made: for parliamentary democracy, for basic rights, for limited state power, and to retain some decentralization, for example. A minority on the right, including the Nationalists and the People's Party, denied the legitimacy of the revolution and therefore the democracy itself; on the far left the Independent Socialists criticized the revolution for not having gone far enough. Representatives from the so-called Weimar Coalition (Social Democrats, the left liberals of the German Democratic Party (Deutsche Demokratische Partei, DDP), and Centre Party) worked out compromise positions in order to create a document that a majority of delegates would approve. The National Assembly approved the Weimar Constitution by a vote of 262 to 75, an overwhelming majority. Some eighty-four representatives, however, were not present for the vote. The violence of spring 1919, when the transitional government put down the radical councils' movement by force, alienated many on the left.[11] The assembly did not, of course, approve council rule in Germany, but it did make an opening to some form of councils in the political system. It did not eliminate the problem of militarism and state aggression in Germany, but it did state clearly that the military stood under the control of the elected representatives of the people. It did not seek to implement a new social order, but it did open the door to future decisions by the German people as a whole about their social order. It was revolutionary in the sense that it described clearly how the people would govern itself, especially in comparison with the 1871 Constitution, which seemed designed to obscure authority and paralyse popular representation. Its notion of the future also contained a kind of republican pathos, a sense of transience rather than permanence in its decision-making: the people had to give themselves their own future, in ways that the founders could not predict.[12] As Hugo Preuß, the German-Jewish jurist and democrat who steered the entire process of constitution-writing, remarked, 'The Constitution of the German Republic of August 11, 1919, is the legal expression of the Revolution of November 9, 1918.'[13]

Between Parliamentary and Presidential Democracy

Little serious thought had been given in Germany to the idea of constitutional democracy in the years before 1918. The sociologist and liberal nationalist Max Weber certainly provided a biting critique of German politics during the war, calling for a more robust parliament. In the light of the revolution, his proposal looked rather timid. There were also few actual models of democratic republics to draw on. The United States was the oldest, which combined strong presidential authority with a strict separation of powers (and a variety of oddities like the electoral college). The US constitution had failed to hold the republic together just a half century before. The US president could create his own governments and had extensive control over a patronage system of civil servants; although Congress could drastically curtail presidential ambitions, whether through its control of the budget or in other ways, there was a sharp line between Congress and presidential cabinet. The US system was a recipe for unprofessional officials, overly powerful executives, and an irresponsible legislative branch, and not a model that the German founders wanted to emulate. The other important model available came from the French Third Republic, created in the wake of the French defeat against Germany in 1871. This parliamentary system was unstable (at least at the coalition level; many ministers actually stayed in their positions over years), and without a strong executive.[14] The framers of the Weimar Constitution sought an alternative to both models in what has been termed a 'semi-presidential' system that aimed to empower and connect both president and parliament.[15]

The parliament or Reichstag was central to the new democracy, and was indeed the first state organ to be described in detail in the constitution. There was something approaching consensus in the National Assembly about the centrality of the Reichstag; defenders of a councils' republic were more marginal. At the same time, though, distrust of parliament as an institution was widespread, especially on the right. The Reichstag was elected by all men and women over 20 years old, making Weimar Germany more democratic than the United States before the mid-1960s, with its disenfranchisement of poor and African-American voters, than France, which excluded women, and than Great Britain, which excluded many women from the vote even after the Representation of the People Act of 1918. Again, there was broad agreement about universal suffrage, even though there was unease even within the Democratic Party about granting all women the vote.

The constitution also required that representatives be elected according to the 'principle of proportional voting' (Art. 22), in response to the ways the pre-war electoral districts had watered down the urban and in particular the Social Democratic vote. Although many liberals and conservatives had opposed proportional voting, which increased the power of parties, in favour of majority voting, they went along with proportional representation for elections to the National Assembly in 1919 for fear that otherwise a landslide vote for the left would all but eliminate their parties. The National Assembly endorsed this decision for proportional representation and party pluralism. The principle of proportional voting required by the constitution could be guaranteed in many different forms. In the Weimar Republic, it essentially assigned representatives to each party in numbers reflecting the total vote for each party. For example, if a party won sufficient votes for twenty-five candidates, then candidates number 1 through 25 on the party's list would become representatives. The process gave parties extensive power over their individual representatives, since the parties created the lists. The process also ensured many parties in a country that was politically fractured, which meant many different voices in the Reichstag. In sum, the voting system for the Reichstag recognized and reinforced party pluralism—intentionally. But precisely this party pluralism concerned critics.

The Reichstag developed and administered its own rules; it was not under the control of other parts of the political system. Elections to the Reichstag occurred at least every four years. In practice, however, the president's right to dissolve the Reichstag ensured that no parliament served all four years. That said, there was more continuity than might appear at first glance, since individuals like Foreign Minister Gustav Stresemann served under successive governments—in his case from 1923 to 1929.[16] The Reichstag furthermore had the power to require a chancellor or minister to appear before it, and had the power to declare its lack of confidence in either the chancellor or a minister, causing individuals or an entire government to resign (Art. 54). Therefore, unlike in the old constitution, the Reichstag could now exercise political control over the government. Added to these controls was the right of 20 per cent of the members of parliament to open a commission of inquiry into governmental activities, which empowered minority critics to reveal government actions (Art. 34). And last but not least, the Reichstag could charge members of the government and even the president with violating the law, and send a case to be heard before the Staatsgerichtshof (Art. 59), a new constitutional court with limited jurisdiction to decide conflicts between top state organs. From the point of view of the founders, the Weimar Constitution seemed to ensure a strong parliament.

At the same time, though, it established a strong president who would be able to act if the parliament were unable to act or irresponsible. The strong president was a controversial point for many Social Democrats and certainly for Independent Social Democrats. Conservative, liberal, and Catholic parties, however, echoed the arguments of Hugo Preuß and Max Weber that the political parties, formed under the old regime, might be too irresponsible to exercise power in the interest of the whole nation.[17] The constitution required the president to be at least 35 years old; other requirements, such as that he (or she) be a citizen for at least ten years—which would have excluded Hitler—were rejected by the National Assembly. The president was elected by 'the entire German nation' (Art. 41), in a two-stage vote: if the first vote, when many parties put their candidates forward, did not produce an absolute majority, then a second round would take place. The second round would not be a run-off election among the top contenders, but one in which newcomers could enter the race, as Paul von Hindenburg did in 1925 and Adolf Hitler did in 1932. In the second round, a simple majority was required to elect a president. The intention was to produce a single executive representative of the entire nation. But a single president did not produce a politically unified nation. The complex system produced candidates from multiple parties. The presidential vote was therefore not a plebiscite to affirm a single leader. It rather left large numbers of voters in the camp of the losing team and deprived of a representative 'voice' in the presidency for the long, seven-year term (with no term limits). Presidential systems need not lead to greater legitimacy for the government, but may in fact lead to greater distrust and disunity on the part of opponents.[18] The claim of many on the right that the presidency represented the unified nation, in opposition to the way that multiple parties fragmented the nation, did not accord with empirical reality. The political implications of these two different conceptions of democracy—unified nation under a leader or pluralistic interests organized in a parliament—only gradually became apparent over the course of the republic, for example in the debate among lawyers described at the end of this section.[19]

The president possessed broad powers. The president named the chancellor and ministers and had the right to remove them at will, and the constitution did not suggest that parties in the Reichstag should present cabinet proposals to the president, as would happen in a parliamentary system (Art. 53); certainly Art. 54, as already noted, gave the Reichstag the right to withdraw confidence from a minister, but that was a negative, not a positive, act. The power to form a cabinet lay with the president, not the Reichstag. The president also commanded the armed forces directly (Art. 47), on the US model. Article 48 granted the president broad emergency powers: to force the states (renamed *Länder*, to underline their loss of status in the new constitution) to follow national law (par. 1), and to suspend certain constitutional rights as part of re-establishing 'public security and order' (par. 2). These emergency powers would prove indispensable in the first years of the republic, as President Ebert grappled with the threat of civil war from both left and right in 1919 and 1920, the French occupation of the Ruhr district in 1923, and the Beer Hall Putsch in 1923. Ebert used Article 48 extensively to counter rebellions, and in 1923 even to remove a leftist government in Saxony that had begun to violate the constitution. During the economic and social upheavals between 1922 and 1924, he even used Article 48 to pass legislation—in coordination with the Reichstag, to be sure, but nonetheless not following a normal legislative procedure. Ebert dramatically broadened the range of actions covered by Article 48. While Ebert used emergency decrees to protect the republic, Article 48 later provided a tool for the camarilla around President Hindenburg seeking a more authoritarian government after 1929.[20]

But for all the ways Article 48 ultimately contributed to the end of the republic, one should not forget that it was originally designed to fit into a system of checks and balances. The Reichstag, for example, had the right to require the president to suspend emergency decrees (Art. 48, par. 3). A parliament could challenge the government's declaration of a state of emergency, as occurred in 1930 and 1932. Furthermore, the constitution required the Reichstag to develop a clearer set of guidelines on the use of emergency powers (Art. 48, par. 5). Parliamentary attempts after 1925 to define and limit presidential powers in this way were, however, opposed and undermined by conservatives around Hindenburg, who relied on expansive definitions of emergency powers for their plans for a presidential regime.[21] The Reichstag also had the right to remove the president (Art. 43, par. 2). That process, however, was difficult in practice: first the Reichstag had to approve the motion with a two-thirds vote; second, the proposal to remove the president was to be presented as a referendum to the German nation. By comparison, the president's right to dissolve parliament (Art. 25) was simple and direct. He was barred from dissolving parliament twice for the same reason, but in politics every occasion looks somewhat different, so that rule had little practical effect.

Article 48 was not intended to undermine the parliament but to support it in difficult times. And that was certainly how President Ebert, a committed democrat, used the article during the first, difficult years of the republic. His aim was to re-establish order; he did so, however, in cooperation with parliament, aiming to reinforce it. President Hindenburg, by contrast, used Article 48 in the time of crisis to strengthen the power of the president. He aimed to name ministers 'above parties', in other words not bound to individual parties in parliament, echoing the anti-party (and anti-democratic) sentiment of the right. His anti-parliamentary attitudes were amplified by the unwillingness of parties to take responsibility in the difficult years of the republic. Hindenburg's anti-parliamentary intentions became clear in 1930, when a grand coalition broke under the pressure of demands to reduce unemployment insurance as the Great Depression took hold. The Centre Party leader Heinrich Brüning was named chancellor of a 'presidential' cabinet without a parliamentary majority on 29 March 1930. In July 1930, it presented a finance bill to the Reichstag without consultation, which the Reichstag rejected. The government then implemented the same bill by means of Article 48, leading the Reichstag to rescind the decree. Hindenburg thereupon dissolved parliament, reimplemented the decree, and called new elections. The elections on 14 September 1930 gave the Nazi Party 18.3 per cent and the Communist Party 13.1 per cent of the vote; protest voters effectively neutralized parliament. To avoid another even more disastrous vote, the democratic parties of the Reichstag had to tolerate the presidential decree. Hindenburg's use of Article 48 had helped him to engineer a crisis that paralysed parliament—but that also left him without a clear popular base, setting in motion the ultimate collapse of the republic in 1932–3. The writers of the Weimar Constitution did not intend to outfit a representative of the old regime like Hindenburg with such powers, but in fact they did so.[22]

President and parliament in this balancing act represented the nation differently. The president spoke with one voice, seeming to represent the entire nation. The parliament spoke with many voices; indeed the system of voting ensured that parties with different opinions would be represented. Each, in other words, articulated the 'will of the people' differently—with consequences for the way the constitution was imagined. Hugo Preuß's conception of the constitution mirrored in many ways the conceptions of the founders in the United States. For both, the 'people' existed in multiple ways in the political process. They were represented through their plural voices and the plurality of parties in the Reichstag, mirroring social reality. They were also represented by a single person in the president, as a way to counterbalance the pluralism of the Reichstag. In addition, the people could act directly through popular legislative initiatives and referendums (discussed in the next section). The constitution (and Preuß) in other words rejected the notion that the people's will was only expressed through one organ or process, just as the Federalists in the US sought to provide safeguards against usurpation by an office.[23]

Hermann Heller, one of the small number of Social Democrats to become a leading constitutional thinker in the republic, presented a strong theory of this notion of democracy as a process of forming the 'will of the people'. The process itself forced communication of principles and interests, potentially leading to a different outcome than the direct expression of opinion prior to such a process. Heller's approach, like that of Preuß, rejected the idea that the will of the people existed prior to the process, such as both far-right and far-left parties assumed in the Weimar Republic.[24] Heller and Preuß both assumed that a constitution required some kind of underlying national consensus about values, an assumption that other democrats did not necessarily accept. The lawyer Hans Kelsen, himself instrumental in writing Austria's new democratic constitution, thought about democracy in ways similar to Preuß and Heller, but with the crucial distinction that Kelsen questioned the existence of a 'popular will' as being anything other than ideology. For Kelsen, democracy was a process for organizing interests and power, not a reflection of an underlying consensus, which he claimed did not exist in reality. The argument for a democratic system was not that it expressed the will of all the people, since empirically that was simply not the case. The argument was rather that the democratic system better satisfied most people than any other system, and that it left open the possibility for another majority to change the 'will of the people' in the future.[25] Kelsen's approach was without a doubt disturbing to many, including Heller on the left, insofar as it asserted that citizens in a democracy should agree to accept decisions as legal even if they were based on values with which they disagreed. This was the cost of accepting the fact of pluralism and the wager of democratic self-determination, as both Kelsen and other lawyers on the moderate left like Gustav Radbruch argued at the time.[26]

Much of the right still imagined the nation unified in wartime, and viewed parties and parliament as artificially dividing the nation. Some, like the former General Ludendorff, translated their belief in a unified and homogeneous nation into violent action, while others sought to transform the republic into an authoritarian regime based on the plebiscitary decision of the nation. Their arguments, while anti-parliamentary, nonetheless made use of the idea of national or popular self-rule. They were part of a debate about what democracy was, even while advocating authoritarianism.[27]

Other Means of Representing the People: Federalism and Direct Democracy

The key tension in the Weimar constitutional system lay in the relationship between president and parliament—between unitary executive authority and pluralistic party politics or, as the critics of the Reichstag put it, between action and endless debate. Two other organizational aspects of the constitution require discussion as well: federalism and direct democracy. Both emerged out of the revolutionary break of 1918/19. The revolution was in a basic way about federalism. The old regime formed out of a contract among the leaders of the individual German states, most of them hereditary monarchs. An important strand of pre-revolutionary German constitutional theory stressed the original and persisting sovereignty of the states in the empire. German constitutional reality looked different, to be sure, with the de facto centralization of the military command in Prussia even before the war and the growth of centralized administrative structures as well as legislation after 1890. The First World War accelerated these tendencies toward centralization.[28] The logic of the revolution seemed to work against states' claims to sovereignty. And now the German nation claimed to form the new central state. At the very least, Preuß assumed that the revolutionary nation would reorganize the Länder in a more rational way, breaking apart Prussia, for example, which had dominated Imperial Germany through its military, its massive territory, and its population.[29]

The monarchs of the former states were forced to abdicate during the revolution. But after the revolution, the idea of Länder—lower-level, democratically elected entities with their own systems for governance and administration—remained. Preuß did not reckon with the enduring power of their administrative apparatuses, which had not stopped functioning. Nor did he reckon with the distrust felt by citizens of the individual states about plans to give away sections of their territory to other states or to form a new state. And not least he was surprised by the insistence of governments, whether on the radical left or on the authoritarian right (both in the case of Bavaria!), on defending the constitutional rights of the Land. The Länder did not cease to be sites of political identification even after the end of the monarchies. With some minor exceptions, their borders remained the same as they had been in the German Empire.[30]

At the same time, the new constitution dramatically reduced the powers of the Länder.[31] It required that each Land have a democratic constitution based on the principle of proportional voting, like the nation as a whole (Art. 17), ensuring that the Länder states could not continue to exclude certain social groups from voting, maintain a monarchy, or impose a dictatorship. All the Länder adopted a one-chamber system in which the parliament elected the government (i.e. without a separate, elected executive). The constitution rejected the idea of granting special privileges to specific Länder as conditions for their joining, which had been done as part of the 1871 settlement creating a unified Germany. The constitution did not enumerate areas of legislation reserved to the Länder, but listed instead legislative powers at the Reich level and asserted the principle that 'national law takes precedence over the Land law' (Arts 6–13). While the Länder continued both to administer and to adjudicate laws, the constitution clearly granted national institutions the right to intervene, directly administer, and create national courts to unify the German legal system, including a new State Court (Staatsgerichtshof) to rule on conflicts between nation and Land (Arts 14, 103, 107, 108).

This diminished authority of the Länder became apparent in the new National Council (Reichsrat), which replaced the old Bundesrat. The Reichsrat was a kind of assembly of civil servants carrying out the directives of the individual Länder executives.[32] To ensure that Prussia did not dominate the Reichsrat, the constitution required that no single Land name more than 40 per cent of the total delegates, and that half of Prussia's delegates be named by provincial authorities within Prussia (Arts 61, 63). The Reichsrat's political role was limited at best. It was an administrative entity, whose right to exercise a suspensive veto on Reichstag legislation (Art. 74) served more to impede the Reichstag than to contribute to legislation.

Nonetheless, individual Länder retained quite a lot of power, including most of the responsibility for maintaining internal security. Länder governments could issue emergency decrees according to Article 48 paragraph 4, although either Reichstag or president could demand that they be rescinded. This Reich-level oversight was limited, however, by the weakness of the national government, which relied on the administration and police of the Länder to preserve order, while not being able to rely on the national army to defend the republic against right-wing groups if such cases led the president to proclaim an emergency. When in 1922 Bavaria, a major Land with its own administration and police, refused to enforce the laws aimed at the extreme right after the assassination of Walther Rathenau, there was little that the Reich could do, even if it had made use of Article 48 to demand compliance with Reich laws: Bavaria's judges applied the laws and Bavaria's police enforced the laws with a bias against the left and for the right, as the lenient treatment of Adolf Hitler after his coup attempt showed. By contrast, Ebert was able to send the army in to put down the Communist party in the smaller states of Saxony and Thuringia.[33]

Political reality, in other words, gave the larger Länder far more power than might be guessed from the constitution itself. Indeed, this reality made it possible for Prussia to become the guardian of the republic even as voters turned to anti-republican parties and the national government sought to undermine the constitution. But at the same time, the structure of the Reichsrat prevented Prussia from becoming a stronger source of stability in national politics. And looming over it all was the problem that Prussia encompassed over 60 per cent of the territory and the population of Germany, a kind of state within the state. The federalism problem preoccupied reformers throughout the Weimar Republic, in occasionally surprising ways.[34] A convinced democrat like Hans Nawiasky argued for Bavaria that the new constitution was founded on a contract with the former states, a construction that was intended to reinforce the rights of Länder; that argument also accorded with the particularist aims of the conservative Bavarian government. In its extreme reading, it was no doubt wrong, but Nawiasky did grasp a basic part of the Weimar Constitution: the notion that both central state and Land stood under the same constitution. Neither was in a sense 'sovereign', since both were under law. On the other side of the political spectrum, the conservative Carl Schmitt deemed strong Land rights not to be in accord with the national, i.e. unitary, nature of the Weimar Constitution, a position that aligned with the democrat Hugo Preuß's position.[35]

These theoretical positions came into focus in July 1932, when the Papen government used a presidential emergency decree to smash the Prussian caretaker government under the control of a pro-republican coalition. Not only was the government replaced by a commissar named by Hindenburg's new Chancellor, Franz von Papen, but also the Prussian delegates to the Reichsrat were removed, which directly impinged on the Land's national representation. Furthermore, most heads of police forces were replaced, ensuring that the police would better follow the political direction of the central state. The reasons given were specious: President Hindenburg had suspended a ban on the Nazi Stormtroopers, unleashing a wave of violence across Germany, and then blamed the Prussian government for being unable to restrain the violence and for supporting the Communist party, a party that the republican coalition abhorred. The case itself was about the machinations of Papen and Hindenburg, to be sure, but also about deeper issues related to federalism: for and against the right of courts to review executive power, for and against the rights of the Länder, and not least about the relationship between constitution and constituted organs of the central state.[36]

Direct democracy represented another structural principle of the Weimar Constitution. Although in practice of limited political importance, the presence of direct democratic tools helped to give the Weimar Constitution its reputation as the most democratic constitution of its time. Under certain conditions a referendum could be held to decide a controversial matter, such as to approve redrawn borders of a Land (Art. 18); to decide on legislation when the president opted to put a statute approved by the Reichstag before the people (Art. 73, par. 1); to demand a referendum on a law rejected by the Reichstag with at least 30 per cent of Reichstag members in support of it (Art. 73, par. 2); to resolve a dispute between Reichstag and Reichsrat, on order of president (Art. 74, par. 3); to approve a constitutional amendment of the Reichstag when the Reichsrat demanded (Art. 76); and to vote on legislation initiated by the people, if the Reichstag rejected it (Art. 73, par. 3).[37] Notably, with the exception of the final rule, all of these rules required that an organ elected directly or indirectly by the people (president, Reichstag, Reichsrat) initiate the process: these were not really coming directly from 'the people' nor were they automatic, even in the case of constitutional amendments. With the exception of the final rule, furthermore, none were actually used during the Weimar Republic.

In the case of popular referendums on popular initiatives, only two actually came to a vote. The 1926 referendum to expropriate the property of the former ruling houses of Germany raised the question of what should happen to royal property, which was in a sense identical with the state before the revolution and now had become private. Social Democrats and Communists called for the expropriation of the former monarchs without any compensation, and had some support from Centre and Democratic Party politicians. A successful referendum required a positive majority of at least half of all qualified voters, a large quorum that created a large hurdle for popular initiatives. A massive campaign from the right called for a boycott of the vote; even though the voters supported the referendum by more than a ten-to-one margin, only 39.3 per cent of those entitled to vote did, and the referendum failed. A second referendum in 1928, sponsored by the Communist party, sought to block the construction of an armed cruiser, and also to undermine support for the Social Democrats. The Communist party succeeded in alienating all the other parties, and were not even able to gather enough signatures for a vote. A third referendum, the so-called 'Law Against the Enslavement of the German People, came from the Nazis and the Nationalists on the far right in 1929, and called for an end to all reparations payments. The petition barely gathered enough votes to call a referendum, and once more opponents simply did not vote in the referendum itself. About 15 per cent of the voting population actually voted, strongly in support of the measure—but did not deliver enough votes for it to become law.[38]

One final example of direct democracy is important, namely the presidential election. But as noted, the two presidential elections held in the Weimar Republic did not produce a clear, popular mandate for the winner, if anything they generated more disunity. The *vox populi* was either weak or divided.

Transforming Liberal Rights in a Social Era

Basic rights did not play a big role in the initial drafts of the Weimar Constitution. Minimal statements about equality before the law and religious freedom in the first draft of 3 January 1919 were expanded in the second draft of 20 January to include freedom of scholarship, of the press, of assembly, of property, and the principle of personal freedom, all basic liberal rights associated with the democratic revolutions of the late eighteenth century. The inattention of Hugo Preuß to rights was understandable in context. First, the 1871 Constitution, which did have democratic elements, did not enumerate rights, but left them to be articulated through ordinary legislation—as they indeed were. Second and related, the democratic legislator would, in a sense, be the final arbiter over rights through law in any case—a position shared by the Founders of the US republic. Third, there was no tradition of judicial review of legislation for its conformity to basic rights in Germany, and such judicial review only existed to a limited degree in the United States at the time (as shown by the very limited protections afforded to minorities and in particular African Americans against state laws for a full century after the Civil War of 1861-1865). Finally, Preuß thought that the decision to focus on basic rights had undermined the revolution in 1848, and he wanted to avoid a similar outcome now.[39]

Just as the process of writing the constitution transformed the relationship between the state and the Länder, so did it transform the discussion of rights. In early spring 1919, during the Constitutional Committee's meetings, the social reformer Friedrich Naumann introduced a kind of catechism of social values into the discussion of the committee working on the draft constitution. His point was to move beyond liberal individual rights to pull the national community together after the war. Naumann's intervention should be seen in international context. In 1917, the new, revolutionary Mexican constitution went into great detail about social and communal rights that supplemented liberal ones. In 1918, the Soviet Declaration of the Rights of Labouring and Exploited People and the 1918 Russian Constitution sought to replace the principles of liberal constitutionalism entirely, replacing individual rights with rights of the exploited against the exploiters. Social reformers of the late German Empire—like Naumann, but also to his left and to his right—tried to introduce social measures that would preserve social and communal norms within liberal modernity. Even without Naumann's intervention, it seems likely that some form of social and communal rights would have entered the constitution.[40]

The second major section of the constitution, 'Basic Rights and Duties of the Germans', was drafted by the Constitutional Committee over spring 1919. Delegates from multiple parties participated in the drafting process, including from parties on the right that rejected the revolution. The result was a collection of fifty-seven articles, each containing one or more individual rights, organized into five sections: individual rights, communal life (including the family, youth, and the civil service), religious freedom and religious organizations, education and schools, and economic life. By including both rights and duties, the section sought to describe the values and norms that bound Germany together at a time when internal struggles and the challenges of military defeat were putting the nation under pressure. In short, the section was intended to help integrate the nation, in the conservative jurist Rudolf Smend's famous term.[41]

'Integration', or creating an organic, unified nation, could sell rights short, however. The legal tradition against which Smend rebelled stressed how rights protected individuals and minorities. The Democrat Richard Thoma, one of the most distinguished experts on police law, asserted in contrast to Smend the importance even of seemingly weak rights. The right to the inviolability of the home, for example, seemed weak insofar as it permitted the legislature to outline conditions under which the home could be invaded by the state. But such rights limited police action to what was expressly allowed by the legislature. This key principle of the rule of law prohibited the kind of unlimited discretion that executive authorities would enjoy later under National Socialism. Other rights, he noted, seemed toothless, but in fact called upon legislators to create a new legal framework, for example, new labour laws. And the strongest rights could only be limited by constitutional amendment. In some limited cases, rights could even override existing law, as occurred with respect to laws banning women from certain civil service jobs, for example.[42] Rights for Thoma and others were not reducible to the goal of national integration.

'Integration' seemed to suggest a unified set of national values, but the rights and duties outlined in the constitution were anything but, as critics noted. The constitution contained many compromises. It could scarcely be otherwise in a society that was divided in so many ways. The constitution was, as the Catholic lawyer and historian Konrad Beyerle later wrote, a treaty forming a state and aiming at peace and understanding among the different groups in German society.[43] Article 153, for example, both guaranteed private property and described the conditions for its expropriation; Article 119 asserted that the family was the foundation of communal life, while Article 121 required that legislation provide the same conditions for the physical, spiritual, and social development of children born out of marriage as for children born into married families. One of the better known criticisms of the Weimar Constitution, put forward by both right and left, was that its rights system consisted of 'dilatory formal compromises' in Carl Schmitt's phrase, i.e. compromises that evaded a clear decision on basic values or the shape of society. That criticism—which could also come from the left, as Schmitt's student Otto Kirchheimer showed—implied that the constitution was a transitional document, pending a supposedly deeper and more legitimate decision of the people, a 'real' constitution: the real principle of unity or homogeneity of the nation.[44] But were these rights actually contradictory? Property might be guaranteed, for example, as a principle, but at the same time the article left the way open for socialization, according to a procedure that would ensure careful decision-making and help to preclude capricious action. The balancing act of Article 153, in other words, forced lawmakers to consider the costs and benefits of a decision about property. The parties involved in making the constitution could no doubt agree about the importance of the family (apart from a handful of radicals, no political movement in Germany aimed to abolish the family), while also insisting that the state be restrained from harming the development and the future of children born outside of marriage. Guaranteeing social institutions did not preclude recognizing other social realities; compromises were possible, and not merely dilatory or formal.

Lawyers on both left and right could agree that the constitution preserved and protected certain basic institutions such as marriage, family, and property. Even the republican lawyer Gerhard Anschütz, perhaps the most important commentator on Weimar constitutional law and a defender of strict textual interpretation of the laws, agreed with this broader reading of rights as defending a minimum basic content of institutions, including the Reichstag and the Länder.[45] He and other democrats also saw the danger in such readings, however, for this method could divide the constitution into essential and inessential parts, allowing an interpreter to assert that a deeper constitution trumped the 'mere' constitutional text. Perhaps, for example, the family was the real, essential institution protected, and therefore children born out of marriage were secondary and not protected in the same way. Or maybe the (divided) parliament was really an inessential part of the constitution compared to the (unitary) president, or the right of workers to organize labour unions articulated in Article 159 was not an essential right. Konrad Beyerle, who had helped to write the basic rights, warned that setting essential against seemingly inessential rights amounted to an attempt 'to devalue basic rights in the eyes of the nation',[46] and to reject the idea that people with differing opinions could come together to found a polity.

The search for values and institutions in the basic rights therefore could have anti-pluralist and even anti-democratic implications. Conservative judges, for example, could make their own values the basis of judgment in order to limit representative democracy and resist what many called 'parliamentary absolutism', a key term already in 1919. The debate over how to interpret the principle of equality before the law (Art. 109) illustrates the stakes of these debates on rights. The traditional interpretation was in fact of fundamental importance to the idea of the rule of law and of the *Rechtsstaat*: laws formally applied equally to everyone who was subject to them. The formality of the law permitted legislators to discriminate among groups, e.g. between men and women in family law, or between household servants and masters. But according to the traditional interpretations, a statute defining murder, for example, would apply equally to master and servant, or, in a less likely case, a statute defining the duties of a house servant would apply to a millionaire who worked as a house servant. The key principle was that the rule of law excluded distinctions outside of the statute itself. Critics insisted, however, that the principle of equality before the law had a deeper meaning, that it required statutes to be in accord with a higher justice. Inequality of condition required unequal treatment as a principle of justice: justice for men was different from justice for women, for example, and the Aristotelian principle of 'distributive justice', of providing each with appropriate justice ('to each his own') should guide the legislature. This argument became important when, in 1925, the highest court considered overturning legislation that had resolved the hyperinflation crisis because it was not deemed fair to people with pensions; the argument was stated more forcefully in 1925 by the later justice of the West German Federal Constitutional Court Gerhard Leibholz, who justified judicial review of legislative acts to guard against capricious decisions that treated specific groups unjustly. On the one hand, Leibholz was arguing for judges to check the power of the legislature when it threatened to usurp the original power of the people in the constitution; but on the other hand, as critics noted, the argument undermined the power of the elected parliament to make decisions based on values, and handed that power to judges, setting a kind of secular clergy above democratic lawmakers.[47] This episode probably did reveal anti-democratic tendencies among conservatives in the Weimar Republic, but like so many other constitutional debates of the time, it also raised a fundamental issue for any democracy: at what point does democratically created legislation undermine the rules and basic values of democracy itself?

Stress Points and the End of the Republic: To What Extent was the Constitution to Blame?

The key question of the 1940s and 1950s was whether the Weimar Constitution doomed German democracy. The argument that the constitution failed to give the republic the means of its own self-defence, so important for the notion of 'militant democracy' after 1949 in West Germany, does not square with the facts. Article 48 gave the president extraordinary powers, which were used directly and violently against the left in the early republic and were used to hinder Communist and National Socialist militias near the end. The Nazi Stormtroopers regained their freedom to engage in violence not because of a lack of presidential powers, but because Hindenburg suspended measures against them. The legislative process gave the Reichstag the ability to pass laws against enemies of the republic on both right and left, most important the laws to protect the republic after 1922, and the Reichstag made ample use of this power. But these laws and measures could not stop judges from applying lenient sentences, they could not keep enemies of democracy like Hitler from using trials to amplify their message and portray themselves as martyrs—in other words, weapons to protect the republic could also serve opponents as reasons to attack the republic. Most important, the very actions taken by the executive at the end of the republic to undermine and eventually destroy it were presented by its defenders as actions in defence of the republic: militant democracy served as an argument essentially for military dictatorship defending 'national unity' to the exclusion of parties and Länder. Rather than providing a moral fable about how liberal democracies cannot protect themselves, the experience of the Weimar Republic reveals the dilemmas facing all democracies of how to deal with radical challenges to democracy while still respecting democratic values.

The argument that proportional voting and the resulting fracturing of the party system undermined parliamentary politics neglects the facts, first, that Germany already had five or more parties before 1914 (as it does today) and, second, that not small parties but rather large ones destroyed the republic. Majority voting could well have brought the National Socialists to power more quickly and more effectively than did proportional voting, which ensured oppositional voices until the end.[48] Once more, Weimar does not provide a story of error but opens up the underlying problem of how best to organize elections while preserving the ability of citizens to express their preferences: there is no democratic voting system without risk.

The argument that Article 48 destroyed the republic is only half correct. President Ebert's use of Article 48 in the turbulent early years probably saved the republic. It was not Article 48 itself that contributed to the republic's downfall, it was the failure of the system of checks and balances to work. In particular Article 25, permitting the president to dissolve parliament, essentially pulled the rug out from under the Reichstag's power to limit presidential emergency powers, and his ability to name a cabinet without the participation of parliament opened the way to a presidential regime. That said, it was President Hindenburg and his camarilla who decided to use the constitutional system to marginalize the Reichstag and, they hoped, to permanently exclude the Social Democrats from power, and without the SPD there could be no democratic majority. It was Hindenburg who used the paralysis of the Reichstag to advance his own goal of increasing presidential power, protecting his ministers from votes of no-confidence, and gradually replacing legislation with decree. That the policy ultimately undermined the Hindenburg government itself, leaving it paralysed at the end of 1932 in the face of a hostile and no longer tolerant Reichstag, was a predictable response to Hindenburg's actions. The president and government at the end of the Weimar Republic made use of the constitution with the aim of making rules for a new, authoritarian system of governance; they were willing to accept constitutional failure.[49]

The argument that elements of direct democracy in the constitution undermined the republic has become ever less convincing.[50] The direct democratic elements played very little role in policy-making, as noted above, although they certainly played a role in political life: the 1926 referendum about expropriating the former ruling houses, for example, drove a wedge between the Social Democrats on the left and the liberal parties on the right, since the referendum limited property rights. Ernst Fraenkel's argument from the 1950s about the effect of direct democracy appears to blame the masses for Hitler instead of confronting how elites systematically and consciously destroyed democracy.[51]

Democratic constitutions are sets of rules, procedures, and values that seek to organize the many voices in society and to provide a path to legislative, executive, or other kinds of decisions. They balance a closed system of rules with an openness to decision-making, even about the rules themselves. Without that openness, which if taken seriously always involves risk, they are not democratic. Although a democratic constitution can certainly permit laws and measures to protect itself against enemies—as the Weimar Republic did—it cannot require that all people, including elites, accept the rules of the game. Democratic constitutions can function better or worse under specific conditions, but do not cause the end of democracies. They do serve to 'make certain alternatives more attractive to others' for political actors, but they cannot predict all political constellations.[52] Individuals and groups can act to subvert and destroy democracies, and even the best constitution in such a case may do little more than channel those destructive aims.

The Weimar Constitution, in short, did not create the elites seeking to destroy it, and it did not force German citizens to vote for large parties whose aim was the destruction of democracy. To answer these questions, one must move beyond the constitution and into the realm of political culture.[53] One can in retrospect describe some aspects of the Weimar Constitution that could have been better, especially the balance of power between Reichstag and president. But the Weimar Constitution was not to blame for the perfidy of elites and the betrayal of democracy and basic values by so many German citizens.

Notes

1. Sally Marks, 'Mistakes and Myths: The Allies, Germany, and the Versailles Treaty, 1918–1921', *Journal of Modern History*, 85 (2013), 632–59.
2. Ursula Büttner, *Weimar: Die überforderte Republik* (Stuttgart: Klett-Cotta, 2010); Jörg-Detlef Kühne, *Die Entstehung der Weimarer Reichsverfassung* (Düsseldorf: Droste, 2018), 109–18.
3. Udo Di Fabio, *Die Weimarer Verfassung: Aufbau und Scheitern* (Munich: Beck, 2018), 6–8; Christoph Gusy, *Die Weimarer Reichsverfassung* (Tübingen: Mohr Siebeck, 1997), 465–7.
4. Alexander Gallus (ed.), *Die vergessene Revolution von 1918/19* (Göttingen: Vandenhoeck & Ruprecht, 2010).
5. Dieter Grimm, *Souveränität: Herkunft und Zukunft eines Schlüsselbegriffs* (Berlin: Berlin University Press, 2009), esp. 43; Grimm, *Deutsche Verfassungsgeschichte 1776–1866* (Frankfurt am Main: Suhrkamp, 1988), 12.
6. Michael Geyer, 'Zwischen Krieg und Nachkrieg—die deutsche Revolution 1918/19 im Zeichen blockierter Transnationalität', in Gallus (ed.), *Die vergessene Revolution*, 211.
7. Gerhard A. Ritter and Susanne Miller (eds), *Die deutsche Revolution 1918–1919. Dokumente*, 2nd ed. (Hamburg: Hoffmann & Campe, 1975), 47, 89, 103–4.
8. Walter Mühlhausen, *Friedrich Ebert 1871–1925* (Berlin: Dietz Nachf., 2006), 106–14.
9. Detlev Peukert, *The Weimar Republic* (New York: Hill & Wang, 1993), 50; see also Heinrich August Winkler, *Die Sozialdemokratie und die Revolution von 1918/19* (Berlin: Dietz, 1979); Andreas Wirsching, *Die Weimarer Republik: Politik und Gesellschaft* (Munich: Oldenbourg, 2000), 6–9, 51–5.
10. Key primary sources for the National Assembly are to be found in *Die Deutsche Nationalversammlung im Jahre 1919*, ed. Eduard Heilfron (Berlin: Norddeutsche Buchdruckerei und Verlagsanstalt, n.d.); the transcripts of the assembly's Constitutional Committee (Verfassungsausschuss), available digitally at <http://dl.ub.uni-freiburg.de/diglit/nat_vers1919>; and in Heinrich Triepel, *Quellensammlung zum Deutschen Reichsstaatsrecht*, 4th ed. (Tübingen: Mohr Siebeck, 1926). General guide to sources in Kühne, *Entstehung*, and Heiko Bollmeyer, *Der steinige Weg zur Demokratie: Die Weimarer Nationalversammlung zwischen Kaiserreich und Republik* (Frankfurt am Main: Campus, 2007).
11. Gusy, *Die Weimarer Reichsverfassung*, 77.
12. Ulrich K. Preuß, *Constitutional Revolution: The Link between Constitutionalism and Progress*, tr. Deborah Lucas Schneider (Atlantic Heights, NJ: Humanities Press, 1995), 68–71.
13. Hugo Preuß, *Deutschlands Republikanische Reichsverfassung* (1923), in *Politik und Verfassung in der Weimarer Republik, Gesammelte Schriften*, vol. 4, ed. Detlef Lehnert (Tübingen: Mohr Siebeck, 2008), 308; Peter C. Caldwell, 'Hugo Preuss's Concept of the

Volk: Critical Confusion or Sophisticated Conception?', *University of Toronto Law Journal*, 63 (2013), 351–60.

14. Gusy, *Die Weimarer Reichsverfassung*, 98–115; Bollmeyer, *Steiniger Weg*, 223–34; Peter Graf Kielmansegg, 'Der Reichspräsident—ein republikanischer Monarch?', in Horst Dreier and Christian Waldhoff (eds), *Das Wagnis der Demokratie: Eine Anatomie der Weimarer Reichsverfassung* (Munich: Beck, 2018), 219–21; critical: Gertrude Lübbe-Wolff, 'Das Demokratiekonzept der Weimarer Reichsverfassung', *Wagnis der Demokratie*, 116–17; Ernst Fraenkel, 'Die repräsentative und die plebiszitäre Komponente im demokratischen Verfassungsstaat' (1958), in *Gesammelte Schriften*, ed. Alexander von Brünneck et al. (Baden-Baden: Nomos, 1999), vol. 5, 199–205.
15. Maurice Duverger, 'A New Political System Model: Semi-Presidentialism', *European Journal of Political Research*, 8 (1980), 165–87; Cindy Skach, *Borrowing Constitutional Designs: Constitutional Law in Weimar Germany and the French Fifth Republic* (Princeton: Princeton University Press, 2005).
16. Jonathan Wright, *Gustav Stresemann: Weimar's Greatest Statesman* (New York: Oxford University Press, 2002); Juan Linz, 'Presidential or Parliamentary Democracy: Does it Make a Difference?', in Linz and Arturo Valenzuela (eds), *The Failure of Presidential Democracy: Comparative Perspectives* (Baltimore: Johns Hopkins, 1994), vol. 1, 31–2.
17. Ludwig Richter, 'Reichspräsident und Ausnahmegewalt: Die Genese der Artikels 48 in den Beratungen der Weimarer Nationalversammlung', *Der Staat*, 37 (1998), 221–47.
18. Kielmansegg, 'Reichspräsident', 222–3; Di Fabio, *Die Weimarer Verfassung*, 95–105, 71–8, 167–81; Héctor Fix-Fierro and Pedro Salazar-Ugarte, 'Presidentialism', in *Oxford Handbook of Comparative Constitutional Law* (New York: Oxford, 2012), 629–49, with further references to the debates, and Linz, 'Presidential or Parliamentary Democracy', 8–21.
19. Lars Vinx (ed.), *The Guardian of the Constitution: Hans Kelsen and Carl Schmitt on the Limits of Constitutional Law* (New York: Cambridge, 2015).
20. M. Rainer Lepsius, 'From Fragmented Party Democracy to Governance by Emergency Decree and National Socialist Takeover: Germany', in Juan Linz and Alfred Stepan (eds), *The Breakdown of Democratic Regimes* (Baltimore: Johns Hopkins, 1978), vol. 2, 50; Hans Mommsen, *The Rise and Fall of Weimar Democracy* (Chapel Hill, NC: University of North Carolina Press, 1996), 202–3, 219–20, 244–5, 285–8, 430–1; Mühlhausen, *Friedrich Ebert*, 722–74.
21. Kielmansegg, 'Reichspräsident', 234.
22. Wolfram Pyta, *Hindenburg: Herrschaft zwischen Hohenzollern und Hitler* (Munich: Pantheon, 2009); Anna von der Goltz, *Hindenburg, Myth, and the Rise of the Nazis* (New York: Oxford University Press, 2011); Di Fabio, *Die Weimarer Verfassung*, 95–105, 71–8, 167–81; Mommsen, *Rise and Fall*, 57–8; Bollmeyer, *Steiniger Weg*, 287–9; Linz, 'Presidential or Parliamentary Republic'.
23. Caldwell, 'Hugo Preuss's Concept of the Volk', 347–83; see Bollmeyer, *Steiniger Weg*.
24. Heller, *Staatslehre* (Tübingen: Mohr Siebeck, 1983), 259–69; David Dyzenhaus, *Legality and Legitimacy: Carl Schmitt, Hans Kelsen, and Hermann Heller in Weimar* (New York: Cambridge University Press, 1999); Thomas Vesting, 'Staatslehre als Wirklichkeitswissenschaft: Zu Hermann Hellers Idee einer politischen Organisation der Gesellschaft', *Der Staat*, 31 (1992), 161–86.
25. Hans Kelsen, in *Veröffentlichungen der Vereinigung der Deutschen Staatsrechtslehrer*, vol. 3 (Berlin: Walter de Gruyter, 1927), 54–5; Matthias Jenstaedt and Oliver Lepsius (eds),

Verteidigung der Demokratie (Tübingen: Mohr Siebeck, 2006); Lars Vinx, *Hans Kelsen's Pure Theory of Law* (New York: Cambridge University Press, 2015), esp. chs 4–5.
26. See Gustav Radbruch, 'Der Relativismus in der Rechtsphilosophie' (1934), in *Gustav Radbruch Gesamtausgabe*, ed. Arthur Kaufmann (Heidelberg: Müller, 1987), vol. 3, 17–22; Caldwell, *Popular Sovereignty and the Crisis of German Constitutional Law: The Theory and Practice of Weimar Constitutionalism* (Durham, NC: Duke University Press, 1997), 92–6.
27. Christopher Gusy (ed.), *Demokratisches Denken in der Weimarer Republik* (Baden-Baden: Nomos, 2000).
28. Gusy, *Weimarer Reichsverfassung*, 225; Martin Otto, 'Revolutionen auf Raten: Das Ende der Monarchie in den deutschen Kleinstaaten als politischer Prozess', in Stefan Gerber, *Das Ende der Monarchie in den deutschen Kleinstaaten* (Cologne: Böhlau, 2018), 85–108.
29. Anke John, *Der Weimarer Bundesstaat: Perspektiven einer föderalen Ordnung* (Cologne: Böhlau, 2012).
30. Ibid., 172–80.
31. Gusy, *Weimarer Reichsverfassung*, 227–42.
32. Ibid., 251–62; Gerhard Anschütz, *Die Verfassung des Deutschen Reichs vom 11. August 1919*, 14th edn. (Aalen: Scientia, 1987), 336; Bollmeyer, *Steiniger Weg*, 248–9.
33. John, *Weimarer Bundesstaat*, 179–80; Gusy, *Weimarer Reichsverfassung*, 264; Gusy, *Weimar: Die wehrlose Republik? Verfassungsschutzrecht und Verfassungsschutz in der Weimarer Republik* (Tübingen: Mohr Siebeck, 1991), 139–47.
34. John, *Weimarer Bundesstaat*, passim.
35. Hans Nawiasky, *Grundprobleme der Reichsverfassung* (Berlin: Springer, 1928), 64–8; Caldwell, *Popular Sovereignty*, 69–73.
36. Vinx, *Guardian of the Constitution*; Dyzenhaus, *Legality and Legitimacy*, 70–85; Dyzenhaus, 'Legal Theory in the Collapse of Weimar', *American Political Science Review*, 91 (1997), 121–34; John, *Weimarer Bundesstaat*, 217–20.
37. Gusy, *Weimarer Reichsverfassung*, 383.
38. Anschütz, *Verfassung des Deutschen Reichs*, 384–5, 390–1; Gusy, *Weimarer Reichsverfassung*, 96–8; Hanns-Jürgen Wiegand, *Direktdemokratische Elemente in der deutschen Verfassungsgeschichte* (Berlin: BWV, 2006), 71–95.
39. Michael Dreyer, *Hugo Preuß: Biographie eines Demokraten* (Stuttgart: Steiner, 2018), 383–8.
40. Walter Pauly, *Grundrechtslaboratorium Weimar: Zur Entstehung des zweiten Teils der Reichsverfassung vom 14. August 1919* (Tübingen: Mohr Siebeck, 2004); Anschütz, *Verfassung des Deutschen Reichs*, 507–14; Ewald Wiederin, 'Die Weimarer Reichverfassung im internationalen Kontext', in Dreier and Waldhoff, *Wagnis der Demokratie*, 54–7; Michael Stolleis, 'Die soziale Programmatik der Weimarer Reichsverfassung', in *Wagnis der Demokratie*, 195–218.
41. Rudolf Smend, *Verfassung und Verfassungsrecht*, repr. in *Staatsrechtliche Abhandlungen*, 3rd ed. (Berlin: Duncker & Humblot, 1994); Smend (ed.), *Die Verfassung des Deutschen Reiches* (Berlin: Sieben Stäbe, 1929), esp. xxiv–xxv.
42. Dreier, 'Grundrechtsrepublik Weimar', 175–94; Richard Thoma, 'Die juristische Bedeutung der grundrechtlichen Sätze der Reichsverfassung im allgemeinen', in Hans-Carl Nipperdey (ed.), *Die Grundrechte und Grundpflichten der Reichverfassung*, 3 vols (Berlin: Reimar Hobbing, 1929–30); Anschütz, *Verfassung des Deutschen Reichs*, 560, 563–4, 586–7, and Gertrud Bäumer, 'Die Weimarer Verfassung als Grundlage deutschen Frauenlebens', in *Deutsche Einheit, Deutsche Freiheit: Gedenkbuch der Reichsregierung zum 10. Verfassungstag, 11. August 1929* (Berlin: Zentralverlag, 1929), 167–71.
43. Konrad Beyerle, 'Wesen und Entstehung der Grundrechte in der Reichsverfassung von Weimar', in *Deutsche Einheit, Deutsche Freiheit*, 153.

44. Carl Schmitt, *Constitutional Theory*, tr. Jeffrey Seitzer (Durham, NC: Duke University Press, 2008), 84–9; Otto Kirchheimer, 'Zur Staatslehre des Sozialismus und Bolschewismus' (1928), in *Von der Weimarer Republik zum Faschismus* (Frankfurt am Main: Suhrkamp, 1976), 32–7.
45. Anschütz, *Verfassung des Deutschen Reichs*, 516.
46. Beyerle, 'Wesen und Entstehung der Grundrechte', 153.
47. Leibholz, *Die Gleichheit vor dem Gesetz* (Berlin: Liebmann, 1925). Extensive critique by Anschütz in *Verfassung des Deutschen Reichs*, 522–30.
48. Di Fabio, *Weimarer Verfassung*, 131–2, 257.
49. Grimm, 'Weimars Ende und Untergang', in Dreier and Waldhoff, *Wagnis der Demokratie*, 263–87, esp. 279, and Gusy, *Weimar—eine wehrlose Republik?*, 57.
50. Kühne, *Entstehung*, 199–212.
51. Lübbe-Wolff, 'Das Demokratiekonzept der Weimarer Reichsverfassung', in Dreier and Waldhoff, *Wagnis der Demokratie*, 131–4.
52. Lepsius, 'From Fragmented Party Democracy', 50.
53. Christoph Gusy, 'Verfassungsgebung in den Ländern: Politische Kultur zwischen demokratischem Aufbruch und regionalen Traditionen', *Journal der juristischen Zeitgeschichte*, 13 (2019), 47–65; Manuela Achilles, 'With a Passion for Reason: Celebrating the Constitution in Weimar Germany', *Central European History*, 43 (2010), 666–89; Achilles, 'Reforming the Reich: Democratic Symbols and Rituals in the Weimar Republic', in Kathleen Canning, Kerstin Brandt, and Kristin McGuire (eds), *Weimar Publics/Weimar Subjects: Rethinking the Political Culture of German in the 1920s* (New York: Berghahn, 2010), 175–91.

BIBLIOGRAPHY

Anschütz, Gerhard, *Die Verfassung des Deutschen Reichs vom 11. August 1919*, 14th ed. (Aalen: Scientia, 1987; 1st publ. 1933).
Caldwell, Peter C., *Popular Sovereignty and the Crisis of German Constitutional Law: The Theory and Practice of Weimar Constitutionalism* (Durham, NC: Duke University Press, 1997).
Canning, Kathleen, Kerstin Brandt, and Kristin McGuire (eds), *Weimar Publics/Weimar Subjects: Rethinking the Political Culture of German in the 1920s* (New York: Berghahn, 2010).
Dreier, Horst, and Christian Waldhoff (eds), *Das Wagnis der Demokratie: Eine Anatomie der Weimarer Reichsverfassung* (Munich: Beck, 2018).
Dyzenhaus, David, *Legality and Legitimacy: Carl Schmitt, Hans Kelsen, and Hermann Heller in Weimar* (New York: Cambridge University Press, 1999).
Gusy, Christopher, *Die Weimarer Reichsverfassung* (Tübingen: Mohr/Siebeck, 1997).
Gusy, Christopher (ed.), *Demokratisches Denken in der Weimarer Republik* (Baden-Baden: Nomos, 2000).
Jacobson, Arthur, and Bernhard Schlink, *Weimar: A Jurisprudence of Crisis* (Los Angeles: University of California Press, 2002).
Kelsen, Hans, and Carl Schmitt, *Hans Kelsen and Carl Schmitt on the Limits of Constitutional Law*, ed. Lars Vinx (New York: Cambridge, 2015).
Schmitt, Carl, *Constitutional Theory* (Durham, NC: Duke University Press, 2008).
Stolleis, Michael, *A History of Public Law in Germany, 1914–1945* (New York: Oxford University Press, 2004).
Vinx, Lars, *The Guardian of the Constitution: Hans Kelsen and Carl Schmitt on the Limits of Constitutional Law* (New York: Cambridge University Press, 2015).

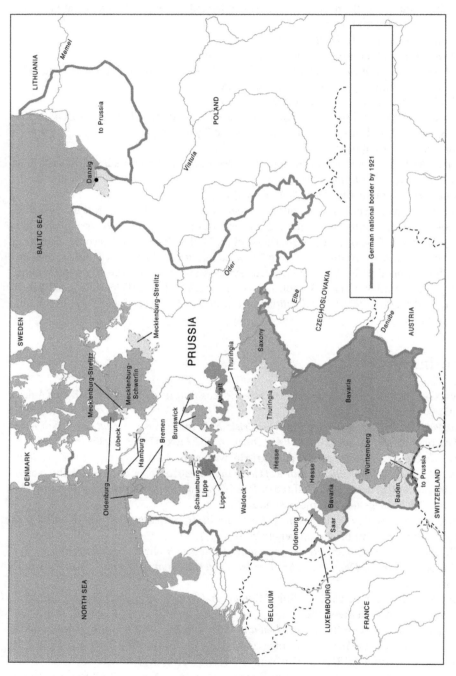

Map 1 The States (*Länder*) in Weimar Germany (1928). By 1929, Waldeck was incorporated into Prussia.

Source: Adapted from: https://en.wikipedia.org/wiki/States_of_the_Weimar_Republic (accessed 15 February 2021)

CHAPTER 7

NATIONALISM AND NATIONHOOD

ERIN R. HOCHMAN

In a 1926 pamphlet, Gustav Radbruch, a member of the Social Democratic Party of Germany (SPD) and a prominent legal theorist, argued that 'the German nation does not end at the German borders. It includes the German minorities in all areas, which our historical fate has separated from the territory of the German Reich. It includes above all our tribal brothers (*Stammesbrüder*) in German-Austria.' He went on to call for an *Anschluss* (the political unification of Germany and Austria), and expressed his desire to achieve 'ein Volk, ein Reich', meaning one nation, one empire.[1]

At first glance, his language is striking, for it would appear to be more representative of right-wing thinking than socialist ideas in the Weimar Republic. After all, radical right groups such as the Nazi Party (NSDAP) were known for their unrelenting determination to expand Germany's boundaries to include all 'ethnic Germans' in a single state. Further suggesting that the author was a Nazi was his use of the phrase 'ein Volk, ein Reich'. This slogan, with 'ein Führer' (one leader) added on the end, became popular during the Nazi annexation of Adolf Hitler's native Austria in 1938, an event which led to the extension of the Nazi dictatorship and brutal violence against the country's Jewish population. Radbruch's rhetoric therefore seemingly embodied an antisemitic, militaristic, and authoritarian nationalism associated with the Nazis, and Germany in general. However, although Radbruch used the same national rhetoric as right-wing groups, he invested these terms with completely different meanings than his adversaries. Unlike the Nazis, who vehemently opposed the Weimar Republic on the grounds that democracy was un-German, Radbruch had penned his tract to celebrate the Weimar Constitution on the occasion of its seventh anniversary. He argued that the German national spirit and love of the fatherland animated the democratic republic. Not only did the political basis of his nationalism differ from that of the Nazis, but so too did his definition of a German nation. In the same passage where he declared 'ein Volk, ein Reich', he explained:

> For us [republicans], the nation is not a community of descent and blood (*Gemeinschaft der Abstammung und des Blutes*), which does not exist in a pure form; rather, it is a community of historical destiny and a living culture. … In the spirit of a constitution that emphatically commemorates the reconciliation of peoples (*Völkerversöhnung*), and even more so racial reconciliation within the German people (*Rassenversöhnung innerhalb des deutschen Volkes*), how should we not be agreed upon the firmly established awareness that Germans of different descent (*Abstammung*) are nonetheless Germans of the same national spirit and worth![2]

To clarify this point, Radbruch recognized that individuals with immigrant, Jewish, and socialist backgrounds were 'national comrades (*Volksgenossen*)', an understanding of national belonging vociferously contested by the political right. This combination of sentiments—admiration for the democratic republic, a belief in German nationalism, desire for an *Anschluss*, and a more inclusive understanding of nationhood—was not unique to Radbruch. His fellow members of the SPD, as well as representatives from the left liberal German Democratic Party (DDP) and the left wing of the Catholic Centre Party, advanced similar ideas. These republicans, the term the supporters of the Weimar Republic used to describe themselves, viewed German nationalism as central to their celebration, legitimization, and defence of Germany's first full-fledged experiment with democracy.

Radbruch's pamphlet is just one of many examples that prompts a reconsideration of German nationalism in the Weimar Republic. Ever since the Nazis unleashed a genocidal war in the name of a German nation, scholars have located the origins of the murderous regime in German nationalism. According to these arguments, German nationalism was antisemitic, racist, and anti-democratic from its very beginnings. It represented a 'bad' nationalism based on ethnic and racial definitions of nationhood, which scholars contrasted with western democracies' 'good' civic nationalism, or patriotism, whereby all citizens of the state were members of the nation.[3] Yet such a distinction ignores the fact that there was never a single form of German nationalism, especially in the Weimar era. It is certainly true that conservatives and right-wing radicals in the Weimar Republic used a racist, antisemitic, authoritarian, and militaristic form of German nationalism to attack democracy, its supporters, and the post-war international order. However, the political right was not the sole voice of German nationalism in the inter-war period. As more recent scholarship has shown, republicans crafted their own form of German nationalism in order to popularize the new form of government.[4] They challenged the political right's claims that democracy and Germany, internationalism and nationalism, and Jews and Germans were mutually exclusive. These republicans created a form of German nationalism that was democratic, peaceful, and more inclusive. As this chapter will therefore illustrate, multiple and contradictory German nationalisms existed in the Weimar Republic.

The contestation of the meaning and purpose of German nationalism was not simply the result of the tumultuous nature of Weimar democracy. In the early nineteenth century, before a state called Germany even existed, a so-called German Question emerged as German speakers scattered across multiple kingdoms, principalities, duchies, and free cities began debating what form a future German nation-state should take. This 'German Question' encompassed disputes related to politics, geography, and population. What form of government was best suited to Germany? Where should the boundaries of a German nation-state be drawn? Who could be members of a German national community? The first serious attempt to tackle these questions occurred during the Revolution of 1848–9, when representatives from across German-speaking Central Europe gathered at the Frankfurt Parliament to create a unified Germany. Delegates argued about whether a future Germany should be *großdeutsch* (greater German), which would include Austrian territories, or *kleindeutsch* (smaller German), which would exclude Austria and be dominated by Prussia. They also debated who should be granted rights and what type of constitutional arrangement the new state should have.[5] Their efforts ultimately came to naught, as the Austrian Habsburg and the Prussian Hohenzollern dynasties crushed the revolution. Instead, many aspects of the 'German Question' would be solved by Otto von Bismarck, a conservative aristocrat who wished to expand Prussian power. Through three wars against Denmark, Austria, and France from 1864 to 1871, Bismarck forged a *kleindeutsch* state with a largely authoritarian basis. Although he created the Reichstag, a parliament elected by universal male suffrage, power resided with the Kaiser (emperor).

While Bismarck had seemingly answered the 'German Question' about borders and politics, there were still extensive debates about who could be members of a German national community following the creation of Germany in 1871. Bismarck tried to consolidate the power of conservatives in the new state by labelling his opponents 'enemies of the Reich'. He claimed that Catholics' loyalty to the Pope and socialists' devotion to an international working class made them unpatriotic. Members of both groups heavily disputed Bismarck's assertions.[6] Additionally, even though many Germans with a Jewish background proclaimed their Germanness, conservatives increasingly embraced pseudoscientific racism to argue that Jews, as well as people of colour, could never be German, due to supposedly unalterable racial differences.[7] Compounding the confusion over membership in a German nation was the notion of a German *Kulturnation*, or cultural nation, which included German speakers beyond the boundaries of the Reich.[8] Thus, although Bismarck 'unified' Germany, internal unity remained elusive as debates persisted about who was German.

Initially, the outbreak of the First World War in 1914 seemed to put an end to the unresolved question about national belonging. At that moment, Kaiser Wilhelm II declared that he no longer recognized parties or confessions. This proclamation raised hopes among the population that the war would bridge the political, religious, and social divisions plaguing Imperial Germany, thereby creating a unified *Volksgemeinschaft* (national community) that included all Germans regardless of their background. As the war dragged on and sacrifices mounted, however, this feeling of unity gave way to disillusionment as divisions re-emerged. The political right embraced radical nationalist goals, including extensive territorial annexations, the expulsion of 'non-Germans' from some conquered areas, and an intensified demonization of alleged 'enemies within'. In contrast, the SPD, Centre Party, and left-liberal precursors of the DDP rejected annexationist war aims and instead called for the *Volk*, which can be translated as both nation and people, to play a greater role in politics. These opposing national aspirations carried into the post-war period as Germans of varying political stripes sought to achieve a true *Volksgemeinschaft*, a concept popularized by the war that these rival groupings continued to understand in contradictory ways after November 1918.[9]

Indeed, the national idea played a pivotal role in the political and cultural struggles that occurred in Germany following the First World War. This was partly due to developments on the world stage. The notion of the right to national self-determination, the creation of supposed nation-states from Europe's fallen empires, and the formation of an organization named the League of Nations cemented the importance of the concept of the nation to both international and domestic politics.[10] Moreover, at home, the aftermath of the war lent new urgency to all aspects of the 'German Question'. Gone were the *kleindeutsch* borders and the monarchical system created by Bismarck. Revolution and the redrawing of boundaries in East Central Europe offered Germans tantalizing possibilities to develop and implement new ideas about which political system, borders, and populations best suited Germany. Each of the following sections will explore how first the opponents of the republic and then its supporters sought to answer these aspects of the 'German Question'.

The Politics of Nationalism

The revolution that spread across Germany in the waning days of the First World War compelled Germans to rethink what type of government was most appropriate for their country. Although the conservative elites fretted about their loss of power with the overthrow of the monarchy, other Germans saw the opportunity to remake the political system. Communists hoped to create a Bolshevik-inspired government, the lower middle classes wanted a corporatist state honouring their work, the radical right proposed a dictatorship based on the ideas of a strong leader and 'racial purity', and republicans worked to establish a parliamentary democracy. In the battle for political legitimacy, all parties and associations, with the exception of the Communists, used German nationalism to contest their opponents' idea of good governance and to support their own particular political vision.

For the political right, the new democratic republic was a national tragedy. Although there was much in-fighting among the conservative German National People's Party (DNVP), the Nazi Party, anti-republican paramilitary groups such as the Freikorps and the Stahlhelm, and radical nationalist associations like the Pan-German League,[11] they were united in their bitterness about Germany's defeat, the Treaty of Versailles, the country's diminished stature, and the state's socialist president. Looking for ways to undermine the republic, the disparate forces on the political right relied on German nationalism. One of the chief ways that the political right attacked democracy and its proponents was to falsely claim that the Weimar Republic had only emerged because Jews, Marxists, and republicans had stabbed the German army in the back, leading to its loss in the First World War. Using this 'stab-in-the-back' myth, conservatives and right-wing radicals alleged that the founders of the infant democracy were national traitors who had brought a foreign form of government to Germany. Alfred Fletcher, a member of the DNVP, asserted that the republic was the result of an 'execrable crime against the nation'.[12] Similarly, Adolf Hitler wrote in *Mein Kampf* that 'today in our Republic the power lies in the hands of the same men who engineered the revolution, and this revolution represents the vilest high treason, nay, the most wretched piece of villainy in all German history'.[13] This 'treason' had paved the way for the Treaty of Versailles, according to the political right, and made it possible for the western Allies to impose democracy on Germany. Such denunciations were prevalent among the manifold conservative and right-wing organizations, appearing in newspapers, books, speeches, campaign posters, political rallies, and celebrations.

According to this logic, democratic and republican values were not authentically German; they represented a break with German history. The political right contrasted the inauspicious conditions that resulted in the republic's founding with the triumphant circumstances that led to the creation of Germany in 1871. Groups from across the political right portrayed republicans as the 'wreckers of Bismarck's creation'.[14] Through the promotion of this 'Bismarck myth', anti-republican groups argued that the essence of the republic did not suit Germany. Parliamentary democracy and the party system it fostered, according to them, created factions that prevented the realization of the *Volksgemeinschaft* and weakened the country's international prestige. Only a forceful and charismatic leader like Bismarck would be able to unite the German *Volk* and restore Germany's global power.[15]

While they were united in maligning democracy, there were disagreements within the political right about the type of government that was most German. Conservatives discussed a possible monarchical restoration. Rejecting the republic, a 1926 article in the conservative *Kreuz-Zeitung* stated, 'We are completely convinced that we can only find the way back to unity and to freedom if we create a state constitution that genuinely speaks to the historical development of the German Reich and the structure of national life. German leadership finds its expression and its symbol in monarchist thought.'[16] Failing a monarchical restoration, conservatives hoped to establish an authoritarian regime that would reinstate their control over the state and recreate the glories of Imperial Germany. Their view of imperial values as synonymous with Germanness was evident in their refusal to embrace the republic's new colours of black-red-gold, which they labelled as 'essentially foreign', to use the words of the Naval League of German Women (Flottenbund Deutscher Frauen).[17] Instead, conservatives continued to use the imperial black-white-red flag.[18] Their support for Paul von Hindenburg in the 1925 presidential election also shows their equation of imperial principles with national ones. As a Prussian aristocrat, the 'victor of Tannenberg', and head of the Third Supreme Command of the military in the First World War, Hindenburg raised his supporters' hopes that the 'national hero' would get rid of the republic and lead to a resumption of the 'good old days'.[19]

Unlike conservatives, the Nazis thought that a return to the previous government was not enough to revitalize Germany. Hitler hoped to create a new type of political system based on the notion of a strong leader (*Führer*) and the concept of race. Although race is a social construct and not a biological fact, pseudoscientific racism had become widely accepted in Germany by the late nineteenth century. This pseudoscience of 'race' became increasingly important to that era's *völkisch* beliefs, which combined Romantic thought with the desire for ethnocultural homogeneity. Such *völkisch* thinkers invented a mythical 'Aryan race' that they then contrasted with an allegedly threatening and rootless 'Jewish/Semitic race', as well as a supposedly inferior 'Negro race' and 'Slavic race' among others. Such ideas greatly influenced Hitler's thinking after the First World War.[20] In *Mein Kampf*, he asserted that the state was 'a means to an end. Its end lies in the preservation and advancement of a community of physically and psychically homogenous creatures. This preservation itself comprises first of all existence as a race ... '[21] Hitler saw the destruction of the democratic republic as the first step in achieving this racist goal. Although their specific political visions differed, both the radical and conservative right used German nationalism to denounce the Weimar Republic.

For right-wing extremists, such rhetoric was a call to action. They staged coups to overthrow a political system that they saw as un-German. The Freikorps, right-wing paramilitary units consisting of veterans who refused to demobilize, attempted a putsch in 1920 and Hitler attempted another in 1923. Such groups also committed political assassinations. For instance, the Organization Consul, an offshoot of the Freikorps, murdered prominent supporters of the republic in order to achieve its stated goals of the 'broadest care of the national idea' and the 'fight against the antinational Weimar constitution'.[22] In 1921, its members assassinated Matthias Erzberger, a member of the left wing of the Centre Party who had the ignominious distinction of signing the Armistice in November 1918. A year later, the right-wing assassins turned their weapons on Walther Rathenau, a German patriot, Jew, industrialist, and foreign minister at the time of his murder. Before their assassinations, both men had been the target of vicious attacks by conservative and right-wing politicians and publications for their alleged betrayal of the German *Volk*.[23] Extremist nationalism thus led to tragic consequences for the republic and its supporters.

On the centre right of the political spectrum was the German People's Party (DVP), which used German nationalism to alternatively oppose and support the republic.[24] Under the leadership of Gustav Stresemann, who as foreign minister from 1923 to 1929 did much to restore Germany's international reputation, the party reluctantly worked to stabilize the republic. Stresemann, who was an avowed monarchist in the immediate post-war years, became a pragmatic supporter of the republic by 1922, a transition he saw 'as a matter of national duty'.[25] However, before his transformation, the party voted against the Weimar Constitution in 1919.[26] As the party moved further to the right following Stresemann's death in 1929, it embraced authoritarian ideas. Its 1931 programme stated, 'Everything in constitutional life that is un-German and alien to our nature, ..., must be overcome'.[27]

Republicans vociferously disputed the political right's claims that they had betrayed the German nation by supporting democracy. As Ludwig Haas, a member of the DDP and a leading figure in the Central Association of German Citizens of Jewish Faith (Centralverein deutscher Staatsbürger jüdischen Glaubens), declared at a republican celebration in 1925, 'the radical right associations have also spread the lie among the people as though they alone possess love of the fatherland and a genuine national feeling. ... We republicans love our fatherland at least as much. For us, love of the fatherland is a matter of the heart; ... We know that a German future is only possible on the basis of the republic. Because we love our fatherland, we are therefore republicans.'[28] For Haas and his fellow republicans, the new government was a direct expression of German national sentiments because in a democracy the *Volk* was the source of the state's power.

To support this argument, republicans developed a distinctive form of German nationalism. At the heart of this endeavour was the *großdeutsch* idea, the historical notion that Germany should include Austria. By making the *großdeutsch* idea the basis of their nationalism, republicans could demonstrate that the German national movement was tied to demands for political freedoms from its early nineteenth-century beginnings.[29] In particular, republicans focused their own version of German history on the Frankfurt Parliament of 1848–9, for it had sought to create a German nation-state with a parliamentary system and had included Austrian representatives. 'This will to unification, to the bringing together of a united body politic, is the fulfillment of the dream that the best of our *Volk* dreamed of a hundred years ago; it is the fulfillment of the desires that moved the [Frankfurt Parliament] in 1848. It has been impeded by the special interests of the different German dynasties. But, in the long run, it cannot be stopped where democracy and the will of the *Volk* prevails,' declared Paul Löbe, the president of the Reichstag for most of the republic and a member of the SPD, at an *Anschluss* rally in Vienna in 1925.[30] By drawing a direct connection between the Frankfurt Parliament and the Weimar Republic, republicans contended that democracy was not a foreign imposition or the result of a wartime stab in the back. Rather, it was a national tradition rooted in German history. Moreover, by blaming the monarchies for the failure of the Frankfurt Parliament and the exclusion of Austria from Germany following the Austro-Prussian War of 1866, Löbe and other republicans could argue that the monarchical form of government prevented the realization of German unity. Only a representative form of government, republicans asserted, could place national interests above particularistic ones to forge a 'greater Germany'.

Given the monarchies' interference in the national movement and Bismarck's creation of a 'smaller Germany', republicans proclaimed that they were better Germans than their political adversaries. As the chairman of the Potsdam branch of the Reichsbanner Schwarz-Rot-Gold, the veterans' and paramilitary group created to defend the republic, argued, 'our nationalism is of a completely different type from that of our opponents'. Their foes' 'conservative nationalism' was nothing more than the 'spiritual heritage of the *Kleindeutschen*', which had excluded '10 million Germans' in Austria from Germany. Republican *großdeutsch* nationalism, on the other hand, was 'older'—dating back to 1848—and 'feels the heartbeat of the entire German *Volk*, not only Prussia's'.[31] By basing their nationalism on the *großdeutsch* idea, republicans created their own form of nationalism to legitimize democracy. This is why Radbruch mentioned his 'tribal brothers' in Austria in the statement that opened this chapter, and why Haas also spoke of his desire to see Austro-German unity in his speech quoted above.

Even though the political right continued to label the republic and its supporters un-German, this republican nationalism did generate an enthusiastic response. To popularize the new form of government, republicans staged numerous festivities and rallies that celebrated democracy and foregrounded their national and *großdeutsch* argument. The Reichsbanner, which had nearly one million members,[32] became the most important coordinator of such events. Together with the Republikanischer Schutzbund, the paramilitary arm of the Social Democratic Party of Austria, it organized cross-border visits for Constitution Days, its own anniversaries, sightseeing trips, as well as sporting and choral events to create what it called a 'powerful demonstration for the republican and *großdeutsch* ideas'.[33] Spectators variously witnessed torchlight parades, seas of black-red-gold flags, bands playing patriotic music, and fireworks. Such occasions drew impressive crowds, with the largest festivity attracting an estimated 800,000 people, including 1,500 Schutzbund members, for the Reichsbanner's tenth anniversary celebrations of the Weimar Constitution in Berlin in 1929. In every one of these cases, observers described the excitement among local populations caused by the presence of Austrians in Germany and Germans in Austria.[34] The republicans' *großdeutsch* nationalism did have an emotional resonance, showing that the Weimar Republic was *not*, as older histories insisted, a 'republic without republicans', a republic with only 'rational republicans', or a democracy lacking symbolism.[35]

THE GEOGRAPHY OF GERMAN NATIONALISM

Although Weimar's political factions advanced competing answers to the question of what form of government best suited the German *Volk*, they agreed that a German nation did not end at the borders of the Reich. This belief was partly due to millions of German speakers who had emigrated overseas, a group referred to as *Auslandsdeutsche* (Germans abroad), in the nineteenth century. Added to these emigrants were German national minorities who lived in the new states created in East Central Europe after the First World War. These *Grenzlanddeutsche* (borderland Germans) included former citizens who were in the territories taken away from Germany by the Treaty of Versailles, as well as former citizens of the Habsburg and Russian Empires. Given this situation, both the enemies and supporters of the Weimar Republic agreed that *Volkszugehörigkeit* (national belonging) became more important than *Staatszugehörigkeit* (state belonging, i.e. citizenship).[36] Yet the similarities ended there. In accordance with their political goals, anti-republicans and republicans proposed different plans for where and how Germany's borders should be redrawn.

According to the political right, the republic had failed to defend the Reich's territorial integrity, thereby threatening the strength and security of the nation. Conservatives and right-wing extremists wrongly insisted that the republic was to blame for the Treaty of Versailles, which had led to the return of Alsace-Lorraine to France, the awarding of Eupen and Malmedy to Belgium, the loss of Posen and much of West Prussia to Poland, League control of the largely German-speaking city of Danzig, and the loss of Germany's overseas colonies. Additionally, the treaty called for plebiscites to occur in the northern areas of Schleswig in early 1920 (part of which were then transferred to Denmark), two districts in East and West Prussia in the summer of 1920 (most of which went to Germany), and Upper Silesia in 1921 (partitioned between Germany and Poland despite a majority vote to rejoin Germany).[37]

Conservatives and right-wing radicals used *völkisch*, anti-republican, and militaristic forms of German nationalism to protest these reduced borders. They participated in nationalist associations devoted to supporting Germans beyond the Reich's borders, ranging from the extremist Pan-German League (Alldeutscher Verband) to the more moderate Association for Germandom Abroad (Verein für das Deutschtum im Ausland).[38] Additionally, they produced propaganda that equated the loss of these territories to a body shorn of its limbs: the 'bleeding borders' caused by the peace settlement put the *Volksgemeinschaft*, conceived of as a national body, at risk.[39] Compounding this discontent among the political right was the Allied occupation of the left bank of the Rhine for fifteen years and League of Nations' rule over the Saar region for fifteen years (with France gaining control of the coal mines for this period). The French and Belgian occupation of the Ruhr, which lasted from 1923 until 1925 in response to Germany falling behind on its reparation payments, only added to the indignation. Although not permanent territorial losses for Germany, these occupations were no less threatening to the German nation in the eyes of conservatives and right-wing agitators.

For the political right, these territorial adjustments and occupations threatened the *Heimat*, meaning homeland. The notion of *Heimat* had become important to German political life following unification in 1871, as it allowed the inhabitants of the various territories that became part of Germany to translate their love of their local *Heimat* into love of the German fatherland. In the Weimar era, both the political right and republicans used the idea of *Heimat* to advance their opposing political agendas. Republicans spoke of their love of *Heimat* in an effort to cultivate democratic citizens. Yet, it was the opponents of democracy who ultimately dominated *Heimat* activism, especially during the Great Depression. With an emphasis on *Heimat*, they highlighted the need for strong states' rights in order to thwart republican control of conservative provincial and local governments. Conservative and right-wing activists also understood *Heimat* in a *völkisch* way, emphasizing the connection between blood and soil: any threat to the *Heimat* by internal or external enemies represented a threat to the wellbeing of the *Volk*. Moreover, the occupied regions became a 'school for political violence' for the Nazis, who claimed that they alone could protect the *Heimat* given the failures of the existing government to do so.[40]

The most threatening aspect of the occupations, according to the political right, was the French use of colonial troops. Racism and white supremacy were central to conservative and right-wing politics. Consequently, the political right mounted a racist propaganda campaign that called the colonial troops 'the black horror on the Rhine' and the 'black pest', as well as falsely accused these soldiers of raping German women. They referred to the children of German women and colonial troops as the 'Rhineland bastards'. With this vitriolic and dehumanizing language, conservatives and the radical right emphasized that whiteness was essential to defining Germanness. They decried the possibilities of 'racial mixing', which they alleged would lead to a degeneration and the consequent downfall of a supposedly Germanic race. In this regard, the political right drew on Social Darwinist theory of the previous century: humans could be divided into 'races', the 'white race' was superior to all others, and these 'races' were locked into a life-or-death struggle to determine which would thrive and which would perish.[41] Although completely false, this concept led groups such as the right-wing German Emergency Association against the Black Shame (Deutscher Notbund gegen die schwarze Schmach) to warn 'that our population will be saturated with mixed-racial offspring, which means it will be … rendered less valuable for generations to come'.[42] Worries about Germany's borders were, for the political right, very much connected to *völkisch* conceptions of Germanness and eugenic concerns about racial hygiene.

Further illustrating the importance of racist thinking to the discussion of borders was the role of antisemitism in the political right's propaganda. The far right blamed Jews for perpetrating the 'black horror on the Rhine'.[43] It also decried the immigration of Eastern European Jews to Germany after the First World War. At rallies and in publications during the early years of the republic, the political right spread antisemitic conspiracy theories that Jews were 'war profiteers' who had benefited at the expense of starving Germans and were responsible for the spread of Bolshevism.[44] The republic had failed to police Germany's borders and protect the nation, according to this view. There was, as historian Annemarie Sammartino has argued, a 'crisis of sovereignty' that the political right used to undermine the legitimacy of the Weimar Republic.[45]

Central to these nationalist campaigns were conservative and right-wing women. These women played a prominent role in promoting specious claims by depicting themselves simultaneously as victims of predatory 'racial others' and as the group best suited to ensure the reproduction and education of a 'German race'. To illustrate these arguments, they made 'pilgrimages to the bleeding border' in the East, joined radical nationalist organizations, and created women's associations devoted to these causes. By portraying themselves as the key actors in guarding 'racial purity', these women could make the case for their important role in national life while simultaneously promoting an anti-feminist agenda that viewed a woman's primary function to be the caretaker of her husband, children, and home.[46]

For many on the political right, the defence of Germany's existing borders and the return of Germany's 'lost territories' were not enough. Hitler, for example, ridiculed a reversion to Germany's pre-war boundaries as a 'political absurdity' because they did not include all 'people of German nationality' in Europe.[47] Yet his demands went beyond simply uniting all Germans in a single state. The Nazis and even the Stahlhelm insisted that Germany needed to take over Eastern Europe to provide *Lebensraum* (living space) to the nation. This 'living space', according to Social Darwinist thinking, was a necessity, for it would provide the land and resources required for a 'Germanic race' to flourish and win the supposed racial struggle.[48] A firm believer in the *Lebensraum* principle by the mid-1920s, Hitler concluded that, if Germany failed to colonize Eastern Europe, 'there will be no Germany'.[49] The political right therefore advanced aggressive and racist forms of nationalism that went beyond simply demanding Germans' right to national self-determination or the restoration of Imperial Germany's borders.

The only way to achieve these territorial goals and restore Germany's strength, according to conservatives and the radical right, was to overturn the entire post-war order: the Weimar 'system', the Treaty of Versailles, and the League of Nations. They consequently opposed Stresemann's policy of fulfillment, in which he concluded agreements with western powers to revise reparation payments, to permit Germany to join the League of Nations, and to end the occupation of the Rhineland early. They saw these various plans as increasing the German *Volk*'s 'enslavement' to foreign powers.[50] In place of the republic, they pushed for strong leadership and the restoration of Germany's military might. As Hugo Stinnes, an industrialist on the right wing of the DVP and an opponent of Stresemann's foreign policy, said, 'only a war can bring us out of our situation'.[51] The nationalisms of the political right therefore were based on Social Darwinism, racism, antisemitism, militarism, aggressive expansionism, and hostility to the republic.

Despite talk about a united and racially pure German *Volk* extending beyond the Reich's borders, conservative and right-wing propaganda did not coincide with the realities of East Central Europe. In stark contrast to the political right's rhetoric, the German minority in Poland was not monolithic. Members of this minority had belonged to three different empires before the war: Germany, Austria-Hungary, and Russia. Reich officials and nationalist associations treated these German populations in Poland differently, offering varied levels of financial and cultural support to former citizens versus those who were not. There was also rivalry among German organizations in Poland, meaning that national unity was elusive.[52] Moreover, although greatly diminished following the collapse of Europe's multinational empires at the end of the First World War, 'national indifference' remained a force in the region. Given that nationality and ethnicity are social constructs and not biological certainties, individuals in places like Czechoslovakia would switch between declaring themselves German or Czech based on their economic and social needs.[53] These rivalries and difficulties in determining who was German in East Central Europe highlight how utterly false the racial ideologies underpinning the political right's expansionary vision were.

Like the political right, the supporters of democracy wished to enlarge Germany's borders. Yet their territorial revisionism, like their nationalism, looked completely different. Consistent with their *großdeutsch* nationalism, they focused their revisionism on accomplishing an *Anschluss*. Indeed, they were at the forefront of the *Anschluss* movement in the Weimar period.[54] They invested their time and energy in the cause, filling top positions in the Austro-German People's League (Österreichisch-Deutscher Volksbund), the most prominent *Anschluss* organization.[55] Additionally, they challenged the occupation of the Rhineland, Ruhr, and Saar, the awarding of South Tyrol to Italy, and the partition of Upper Silesia, all areas which they saw as fitting within their democratic, national framework. They viewed the prohibition on an *Anschluss* as a violation of Austrians' right to self-determination, the occupations as cases of French imperialism, the abuse of Germans' rights in South Tyrol as a crime of Italian Fascism, and the partition of Upper Silesia as a violation of a popular referendum.

In advancing these territorial aims, they qualified their demands. By focusing their revisionism on an *Anschluss*, the supporters of the Weimar Republic underlined that their desire to expand Germany's borders did not threaten neighbouring countries because Austrians were mostly German-speaking and very supportive of union with Germany. Estimates at the time indicate that 90 to 95 percent of Austrians wished to join the Reich.[56] The unification of the two countries was therefore simply a matter of self-determination for a population that overwhelmingly identified as German. While an *Anschluss* would lead to the extension of Germany's eastern border, republicans rejected the colonization of Eastern Europe. They showed concern for German national minorities living there, but emphasized that they did not want to annex these areas. '[T]he *großdeutsch* idea has nothing in common with the pan-German (*alldeutsch*) fantasies' that entailed 'the oppression and subjugation of foreign peoples', Wilhelm Nowack, a Reichsbanner leader and DDP member, explained.[57] Unlike the political right, republicans did not seek to jeopardize the territorial sovereignty of neighbouring states.[58]

Moreover, republicans insisted that not only would they pursue an *Anschluss* through peaceful means, but that an Austro-German union would also help to guarantee peace in Europe. Republicans supported the post-war international order and wanted to achieve an *Anschluss* through the League of Nations. After all, the peace treaties permitted an Austro-German union with approval from the League's Council.[59] A number of republicans also maintained that by creating a larger state in the heart of the continent, an *Anschluss* would be the first building block in creating a 'united states of Europe'.[60] Such an idea followed from some republicans' involvement in pan-European organizations.[61]

In these pleas for an *Anschluss*, republicans highlighted that the political basis of their Greater Germany was distinctive. As Walter Kolb, the head of the Republican Student Cartel (Republikanisches Studentenkartell) and a leader of the Reichsbanner, declared at a 1926 republican rally in Vienna, 'the *Großdeutschland* of the Nazis will never ever be our *Großdeutschland*. We will wage the fiercest fight against whomever wants a Germany that should prove to be a danger to world peace; however, we welcome fighters who want to create a *großdeutsch*, free, and social republic with us.'[62] Similarly, Joseph Wirth, a member of the Centre Party who served as chancellor in 1921–2, envisioned the creation of a 'great German state of social justice, of international peace and of German happiness' that stretched from Cologne to Vienna.[63] Republicans saw the unification of Germany and Austria as a way to strengthen democracy and demonstrate their national convictions. Therefore, not all calls for an *Anschluss* in the Weimar era were a harbinger of Nazi empire, as some scholars have claimed.[64]

Because the concept of *Volkszugehörigkeit* took precedence over that of *Staatszugehörigkeit* after the First World War, the idea of a global German diaspora played a role in the struggle for political legitimacy as well. In this regard, the enemies and champions of Weimar democracy were not debating how Germany's borders should be redrawn; rather, they sought to use the notion of a German diaspora and rally support from Germans overseas in attempts to bolster their particular political and national viewpoints.[65] One of the many ways that Germans at home and abroad endeavoured to accomplish this goal was to create branches of organizations directly connected to Weimar politics. There were Stahlhelm chapters in countries such as South West Africa (today Namibia), the United States, Argentina, China, Portugal, and Italy. The Nazi Party formed the Foreign Organization (Auslands-Organisation) in 1931, and by the following year claimed to have dozens of groups and almost 3,000 members worldwide.[66] Yet Germans abroad were not simply the precursors of Nazi fifth-columnists. The Reichsbanner also created chapters in Portugal, the Netherlands, Bulgaria, Argentina, and the United States. Additionally, it lent support to independent German-republican organizations in places such as Mexico and Brazil. Highlighting the conflicting attempts to speak for a German diaspora was the Reichsbanner's newspaper, which asserted in 1927 that these republican groups abroad 'show that the arguments of the political right's press about the Germans abroad (*Auslandsdeutschen*) standing behind the monarchist idea and black-white-red [the colours of the imperial flag] are nothing more than the deliberate deception of the public opinion in Germany'.[67] As the formation of overseas Reichsbanner, Stahlhelm, and Nazi Party chapters illustrates, the battle over how to answer the 'German Question' was fought on a global scale.

The Boundaries of Nationhood

Although there was widespread agreement across the political spectrum that a German nation spanned the world, there was no analogous consensus about the boundaries of nationhood. Once again, the political right and republicans engaged in heated disputes about nationalism, this time over the question of who was part of a German nation. The political right prescribed strict requirements for membership in a German national community, which stood in contrast to republicans' more inclusive thinking about national belonging.

For conservatives and right-wing radicals, there were multiple reasons—some temporary, others permanent—to exclude a person from the German *Volk*. In the first category were prohibitions based on an individual's political views. While the political right believed that all republicans were traitors to a German nation, socialists (alongside anti-republican communists) became a focal point of the attacks. The political right, picking up on the arguments made by conservatives in Imperial Germany, insisted that the Marxist parties were unpatriotic due to their commitment to an international working class. Encapsulating this antipathy towards socialism was the 1931 party platform of the DVP, which denounced Marxism for 'breeding a sickly international and pacifist romanticism in the place of a resolute will devoted to the fatherland'.[68] Furthermore, the political right argued that the Marxist parties prevented the realization of the *Volksgemeinschaft* by foregrounding class conflict over national bonds. On both accounts, the political right voiced its desire to crush the socialists and communists. As Hitler stated, 'the question of the future of the German nation was the question of destroying Marxism'.[69] However, this form of exclusion was not permanent; if workers gave up their Marxist beliefs, they could become full-fledged Germans.

Such a stance contrasted with the permanent exclusion of so-called racial others from the *Volksgemeinschaft*. As we saw in its campaign against 'racial mixing' in the Rhineland, the political right seized upon the pseudoscientific racism that had become popular in the nineteenth century. Conservatives and right-wing radicals used this concept of race to exclude not only people of colour but also Jews from the national community, falsely arguing that Jews constituted a foreign race as well. Indeed, the German journalist Wilhelm Marr coined the term antisemitism in 1879 to describe this new type of racial hatred of Jews in contrast to older ones based on religious difference and Jews' position in the economy and politics.[70] Adherents of this *völkisch* notion claimed that, given Jews' allegedly distinctive blood, not even conversion to Christianity would enable Jews to become German.

These types of arguments about Jews permeated the thinking of the numerous parties and organizations on the political right. Antisemitism and racism were at the heart of Nazi ideology. As firm believers in *völkisch* and Social Darwinist ideas, Nazi leaders thought that the German *Volk* was locked into a struggle with supposedly inferior 'races' bent on its destruction. Above all, the Nazis believed that 'the Jew' represented the most existential threat to the 'Aryan race', an artificial concept developed in the nineteenth century.[71] They therefore advanced a purely racist understanding of Germanness, in which anyone who allegedly possessed 'Aryan blood' could be a member of the *Volksgemeinschaft*, but 'racial others' were firmly excluded. For conservative groups, there were, as recent scholarship has highlighted, internal disagreements about how prominent antisemitism should be in their platforms and policies.[72] Despite this 'situational antisemitism', in which the emphasis on antisemitism depended upon each organization's needs and the political situation in Germany at a particular moment, conservatives promoted a conception of nationhood that barred Jews.[73] The DNVP, following a split with some of its extreme antisemitic members in 1922, created the *Völkisch* National Committee of the German National People's Party (Völkischer Reichsausschuß der Deutschnationalen Volkspartei) to prevent other radical antisemites from leaving the party. Additionally, the DNVP prohibited membership for Jews and their spouses beginning in 1924.[74] Likewise, the Stahlhelm, and its female counterpart, the Queen Luise League (Bund Königin Luise), introduced 'Aryan paragraphs' in the mid-1920s to their membership clauses, preventing Jews from joining their associations and a German national community more broadly.[75] Regardless of the extent to which organizations on the political right embraced antisemitism, they all used hatred of Jews as another way to attack the legitimacy of the Weimar Republic, often calling it the 'republic of the Jews'.[76] *Völkisch* ideas were thus central to the political right's anti-republican nationalism.

Republicans objected to such a narrow conception of nationhood. Similar to the political right, they spoke of a German *Volk* and *Volksgemeinschaft*, but did so in a significantly more inclusive way. Exemplifying this alternative definition of nationhood was a statement from Heinrich Eduard Jacob, the Vienna correspondent for the left-liberal *Berliner Tageblatt* who hailed from a Jewish background. He accused the political right in Germany and Austria of engaging in 'almost daily acts of class and race hatred, which did not contribute to bringing Germans together, but rather to splintering Germans apart'.[77]

For republicans, a socialist worldview did not preclude national feelings. SPD members explained how their international commitments grew out of their love of the nation. They also served in leading positions in organizations devoted to the German national cause, such as the Austro-German People's League, and staged events with their socialist comrades in Austria where the *Anschluss* idea was a dominant motif.[78] For instance, German socialist politicians and a soccer team attended a 1927 sport festival and election rally held by the Austrian Social Democrats in Vienna, during which the *Anschluss* idea featured prominently. Hermann Müller, the head of the German delegation and twice chancellor of the republic, told a crowd of 35,000, 'The avant-garde of the *Anschluss* is always Social Democracy, which since its founding was *großdeutsch*. We Germans and Austrians together bear witness to the *großdeutsch* republic. Not as a holiday gesture, not as sport, but as a matter of the heart'.[79] Müller's declaration typifies several arguments that the SPD made to counter the political right's attacks on them as unpatriotic. Just as was the case with the general republican historical narratives, socialists contended that their party had always been true to the *großdeutsch* idea. In these party histories, socialist luminaries—ranging from early socialist thinkers such as Karl Marx and Friedrich Engels to the party's founders such as August Bebel and Wilhelm Liebknecht—had been the chief proponents of a *Großdeutschland* in opposition to the *Kleindeutschland* promoted by their conservative opponents.[80] By using the *großdeutsch* idea, socialists, just like the larger republican coalition, could claim they were genuinely committed to German nationalism, just a nationalism that looked different from that of their foes.

Furthermore, republicans rejected the exclusion of Jews from the national community. Those from Jewish backgrounds showed the speciousness of the political right's assertions about them by proclaiming their German national commitments, participating in national festivities organized by republican groups such as the Reichsbanner, and serving in important roles in the Austro-German People's League. Jews could join these organizations due to the fact that republicans from non-Jewish backgrounds rejected an antisemitic understanding of nationhood.[81] Thus, an early advertisement for First World War veterans to join the Reichsbanner decried the 'wild demagogues, who advance the shameless misuse of the concepts of fatherland

and nation, who hide their own guilt and secret aims behind disgraceful Jew-baiting'. Decrying this 'stupid antisemitism', the advertisement recognized that Jews 'had fought and bled shoulder to shoulder' with Protestants and Catholics.[82] Republicans objected to Jews' exclusion from the national community and sought to show that the stab-in-the-back myth was a lie.

The republican inclusion of socialists, Jews, and even foreign-language immigrants and minorities[83] in a German nation was not simply due to a civic form of nationalism in which citizenship and nationality were synonymous. As republicans' support for an *Anschluss* and appeals to Germans abroad indicate, even the republican form of German nationalism incorporated cultural and ethnic concepts. They suggested that a shared culture, language, and commitment to the German *Volk*, regardless of citizenship, were important elements in delineating nationhood. Additionally, the supporters of democracy, both those from Jewish and non-Jewish backgrounds alike, used the concepts of 'blood' and 'tribes (*Stämme*)' to describe a German nation that stretched across state borders. Although scholars have often interpreted such definitions of nationhood as *völkisch*,[84] republicans repeatedly eschewed a *völkisch* understanding of Germanness when discussing a geographically expansive nation. Like Radbruch at the beginning of this chapter, the socialist Konrad Haenisch specified that his desire for a 'greater German national community' had nothing to do with a 'narrow-minded and bigoted racial fanaticism'.[85] In fact, the concept of tribes enabled Jews and linguistic minorities to simultaneously stress their particularities and their membership in a German *Volk*. Such a stance should perhaps not be surprising, as the preamble of the Weimar Constitution pronounced that the German *Volk* was 'united in its tribes'.[86] Republicans therefore used cultural and ethnic ideas in a more inclusive way, and did so in their efforts to foster democratic values.

This, of course, does not mean that republicans entirely omitted unsavoury elements from their nationalism. Although they opposed racial antisemitism, there were republicans who harboured racist views based on the colour of a person's skin. While the SPD, the Centre Party, and the precursor of the DDP had protested attempts to outlaw 'mixed marriages' in Germany's colonies during the imperial era,[87] members of these parties did promote anti-Black racism. Even the SPD had circles that 'instead of international solidarity of the proletariat [promoted] the white racial solidarity against the "Negro"', as the scholar Fatima El-Tayeb has shown.[88] This racism carried over into the Weimar era, with some republicans participating in the 'black horror' campaign alongside the political right.[89] It also explains why the Weimar Coalition parties at times demanded the return of Germany's overseas colonies.[90] There were limits to the inclusiveness of republicans' ideas about nationhood, showing the pervasiveness of anti-Black racism in defining Germanness.

While the vitriol against colonial soldiers among the political right remained high, it was contested within and did diminish among the republican parties.[91] Thus, there were supporters of democracy who promoted racist views based on skin colour; however, the overarching republican version of German nationalism still differed in a number of ways from the nationalisms promoted by the political right. Unlike their opponents, republicans embraced socialists, Jews, and foreign-language minorities and immigrants as members of the national community.

Conclusion

As we have seen, there were conflicting answers to the question of what, where, and who could be considered German after the First World War. Conservatives and the radical right used German nationalism in their persistent attempts to undermine the republic, insisting that democracy was foreign to Germany and only came about due to a national betrayal by republicans, Marxists, and Jews during the First World War. To further discredit the republic, the political right used Social Darwinist ideas to wrongly blame the new government for weakening Germany's borders, which reduced Germany's stature and allowed so-called racial others to allegedly infiltrate and weaken the nation. Anyone who had 'foreign blood' or Marxist views was to be excluded from the national community, according to opponents of the republic.

Republicans forcefully contested these claims. Using the *großdeutsch* idea, they showed how democratic ideals were authentically connected to German nationalism. These democratic principles carried over into their designs for redrawing Germany's borders. They wished to revise Germany's boundaries, but in a way that would promote peaceful international relations and would recognize the national self-determination of other peoples in Europe. While they thought that a German nation extended beyond state borders (and thus beyond a purely civic understanding of nationhood), republicans developed a more inclusive idea of Germanness. There were notable constraints on this inclusivity, as the anti-Black racism of some republicans shows; however, unlike the political right, they argued that Jews, foreign-language immigrants, and socialists were 'national comrades'. Thus, not all ethnic or expansionist statements were predicated on the *völkisch* ideals of 'blood and soil'.

This fierce debate about national values highlights that multiple German nationalisms existed in the Weimar era. Even though the members of the SPD, DDP, and Centre Party were never able to convince the political right that they were loyal Germans, we should not dismiss this republican endeavour. They could never do so precisely because they advanced an understanding of nationalism and nationhood that fundamentally opposed the national beliefs and goals of conservatives and right-wing radicals. Republicans possessed genuine national feelings, which elicited enthusiastic reactions among large numbers of people. This emotional response to republican nationalism highlights that the Weimar Republic was not a 'republic without republicans'. The excitement for republican nationalism only diminished due to a number of situational factors in the early 1930s, such as the manifold effects of the Great Depression and the 1931 decision by the International Court at The Hague to prohibit an economic union between Germany and Austria that could have served as a first step towards an *Anschluss*.[92] The triumph of Nazi ideas about nationalism and politics was therefore not inevitable.

Notes

1. Gustav Radbruch, *Republikanische Pflichtenlehre: Eine Rede zur Verfassungsfeier* (Kiel: Gauvorstand Schleswig-Holstein Reichsbanner Schwarz-Rot-Gold, [1926]), 4–5, in Archiv der sozialen Demokratie, Bonn (AdsD), Nachlass Franz Osterroth, Box 53, Fasz. 140.
2. Radbruch, *Republikanische Pflichtenlehre*.
3. Hans Kohn, *The Idea of Nationalism: A Study in its Origins and Background* (1944; reprint New Brunswick, NJ: Transaction Publishers, 2005); Fritz Stern, *The Politics of Cultural Despair: A Study in the Rise of the Germanic Ideology* (Berkeley, CA: University of California Press, 1961); George Mosse, *The Nationalization of the Masses: Political Symbolism and Mass Movements in Germany from the Napoleonic Wars through the Third Reich* (New York: Howard Fertig, 2001 [1975]); Liah Greenfeld, *Nationalism: Five Roads to Modernity* (Cambridge, MA: Harvard University Press, 1992); Rogers Brubaker, *Citizenship and Nationhood in France and Germany* (Cambridge, MA: Harvard University Press, 1992).
4. Jürgen Heß, *'Das ganze Deutschland soll es sein': Demokratischer Nationalismus in der Weimarer Republik am Beispiel der Deutschen Demokratischen Partei* (Stuttgart: Klett-Cotta, 1978); Bernd Buchner, *Um nationale und republikanische Identität: Die deutsche Sozialdemokratie und der Kampf um die politischen Symbole in der Weimarer Republik* (Bonn: J. H. W. Dietz Nachf., 2001); Robert Gerwarth, 'The Past in Weimar History', *Contemporary European History*, 15 (2006), 1–22; Nadine Rossol, *Performing the Nation in Interwar Germany: Sport, Spectacle and Political Symbolism, 1926–1936* (Houndmills and New York: Palgrave Macmillan, 2010); Manuela Achilles, 'With a Passion for Reason: Celebrating the Constitution in Weimar Germany', *Central European History*, 43 (2010), 666–89; Eric Bryden, 'Heroes and Martyrs of the Republic: Reichsbanner *Geschichtspolitik* in Weimar Germany', *Central European History*, 43 (2010), 639–65; Benjamin Ziemann, *Contested Commemorations: Republican War Veterans and Weimar Political Culture* (Cambridge: Cambridge University Press, 2013); Erin Hochman, *Imagining a Greater Germany: Republican Nationalism and the Idea of Anschluss* (Ithaca, NY: Cornell University Press, 2016).
5. Brian Vick, *Defining Germany: The 1848 Frankfurt Parliamentarians and National Identity* (Cambridge, MA: Harvard University Press, 2002).
6. Geoff Eley, *From Unification to Nazism: Reinterpreting the German Past* (Boston: Unwin Hyman, 1986), 61–84; Helmut Walser Smith, *German Nationalism and Religious Conflict: Culture, Ideology, Politics, 1800–1914* (Princeton: Princeton University Press, 1995); Dieter Groh and Peter Brandt,*'Vaterlandslose Gesellen': Sozialdemokratie und Nation 1860–1990* (Munich: C. H. Beck, 1992).
7. Peter Pulzer, *The Rise of Political Anti-Semitism in Germany and Austria*, rev. ed. (Cambridge, MA: Harvard University Press, 1988); Shulamit Volkov, 'Antisemitism as a Cultural Code: Reflections in the History and Historiography of Antisemitism in Imperial Germany', *Leo Baeck Institute Yearbook*, 23 (1978), 25–46; Fatima El-Tayeb, *Schwarze Deutsche: Der Diskurs um 'Rasse' und nationale Identität, 1890–1933* (Frankfurt: Campus, 2001); Fatima El-Tayeb, '"Blood is a Very Special Juice": Racialized Bodies and Citizenship in Twentieth-Century Germany', *International Review of Social History*, 44 (1999), 149–69; Peter Walkenhorst, *Nation—Volk—Rasse: Radikaler Nationalismus im Deutschen Kaiserreich, 1890–1914* (Göttingen: Vandenhoeck & Ruprecht, 2007).

8. James Sheehan, 'What is German History? Reflections on the Role of the Nation in German History and Historiography', *Journal of Modern History*, 53 (1981), 1–23; David Luft, 'Austria as a Region of German Culture: 1900–1938', *Austrian History Yearbook*, 23 (1992), 135–48.
9. Peter Fritzsche, *Germans into Nazis* (Cambridge, MA: Harvard University Press, 1998); Belinda Davis, *Home Fires Burning: Food, Politics, and Everyday Life in World War I Berlin* (Chapel Hill, NC: University of North Carolina Press, 2000); Steffen Bruendel, *Volksgemeinschaft oder Volksstaat: Die 'Ideen von 1914' und die Neuordnung Deutschlands im Ersten Weltkrieg* (Berlin: Akademie Verlag, 2003); Walkenhorst, *Nation*.
10. Rogers Brubaker, *Nationalism Reframed: Nationhood and the National Question in the New Europe* (Cambridge: Cambridge University Press, 1996); Erez Manela, *The Wilsonian Moment: Self-Determination and the International Origins of Anticolonial Nationalism* (New York: Oxford University Press, 2007).
11. Larry Eugene Jones (ed.), *The German Right in the Weimar Republic: Studies in the History of German Conservatism, Nationalism, and Antisemitism* (New York: Berghahn Books, 2014); Barry Jackisch, *The Pan-German League and Radical Nationalist Politics in Interwar Germany, 1918–39* (London: Routledge, 2012).
12. Alfred Fletcher, 'Der Schwindel der Demokratie, ein Nachwort zur "Verfassungsfeier"', *Ostpreussische Zeitung*, Aug. 1924, in Bundesarchiv Berlin (BArch), R1501/116872, fo. 168.
13. Adolf Hitler, *Mein Kampf*, tr. Ralph Manheim (Boston: Houghton Mifflin, 1971), 542.
14. Quoted in Robert Gerwarth, *The Bismarck Myth: Weimar Germany and the Legacy of the Iron Chancellor* (Oxford: Oxford University Press, 2005), 39.
15. Gerwarth, *Bismarck Myth*.
16. 'Verfassungshymnen und ihr wahrer Gehalt', *Kreuz-Zeitung*, 11 Aug. 1926.
17. Letter from Hauptgeschäftsstelle des Flottenbundes Deutscher Frauen to Reichskanzler Dr. Wirth, 1 Aug. 1921, in BArch, R1501/116485, fo. 1
18. Buchner, *Um nationale und republikanische Identität*, 45–131; Nadine Rossol, 'Flaggenkrieg am Badestrand: Lokale Möglichkeiten repräsentativer Mitgestaltung in der Weimarer Republik', *Zeitschrift für Geschichtswissenschaft*, 56 (2008), 617–37; Hochman, *Imagining a Greater Germany*, 48–67.
19. Anna von der Goltz, *Hindenburg: Power, Myth, and the Rise of the Nazis* (Oxford: Oxford University Press, 2009), 89, 91.
20. George Mosse, *The Crisis of German Ideology: Intellectual Origins of the Third Reich* (New York: Grosset & Dunlap, 1964); Ian Kershaw, *Hitler 1889–1936: Hubris* (New York: W. W. Norton, 1999).
21. Hitler, *Mein Kampf*, 393.
22. Quoted in Martin Sabrow, *Der Rathenaumord: Rekonstruktion einer Verschwörung gegen die Republik von Weimar* (Munich: R. Oldenbourg, 1994), 34.
23. Sabrow, *Der Rathenaumord*.
24. Larry Eugene Jones, *German Liberalism and the Dissolution of the Weimar Party System, 1918–1933* (Chapel Hill, NC: University of North Carolina Press, 1988); Dieter Langewiesche, *Liberalism in Germany*, tr. Christiane Banerji (Princeton, NJ: Princeton University Press, 2000), 250–305.
25. Quoted in Hans Mommsen, *The Rise and Fall of Weimar Democracy*, tr. Elborg Forster and Larry Eugene Jones (Chapel Hill, NC: University of North Carolina Press, 1996), 127.
26. Langewiesche, *Liberalism*, 277.

27. German People's Party (DVP), 'Program', 1931, in Anton Kaes, Martin Jay, and Edward Dimendberg (eds), *The Weimar Republic Sourcebook* (Berkeley, CA: University of California Press, 1994), 115–16, here 116.
28. 'Trommelschlag und Hörnerklang', *Das Reichsbanner*, 2. Beilage, 1 Mar. 1925, 9–12, here 11.
29. Karl Rohe, *Das Reichsbanner Schwarz Rot Gold: Ein Beitrag zur Geschichte und Struktur der politischen Kampfverbände zur Zeit der Weimarer Republik* (Düsseldorf: Droste, 1966), 227–45; Buchner, *Um nationale und republikanische Indentität*, 168–84; Gerwarth, 'The Past in Weimar History'; Bryden, 'Heroes and Martyrs'; Hochman, *Imagining a Greater Germany*, 21–47.
30. 'Massenversammlung und Anschlußkundgebung', *Oesterreich-Deutschland*, Oct. 1925, 5–11, here 6.
31. Ortsgruppe Potsdam des Reichsbanners Schwarz-Rot-Gold (ed.), *Das Reichsbanner und Potsdam* (Berlin, 1924), 15–18, in AdsD, Bestand Reichsbanner, Exponate 30.
32. Ziemann, *Contested Commemorations*, 15.
33. Letter from the Reichsbanner Schwarz-Rot-Gold Bundesvorstand to the Republikanischer Schutzbund, 3 July 1924, in Verein für die Geschichte der Arbeiterbewegung, Vienna, Partei-Archiv vor 1934, Mappe 35/1931.
34. Hochman, *Imagining a Greater Germany*, 131–68. On other republican celebrations, see Achilles, 'With a Passion'; Rossol, *Performing the Nation*; Hochman, *Imagining a Greater Germany*, 88–107.
35. Peter Gay, *Weimar Culture: The Outsider as Insider* (New York: Harper Torchbooks, 1968), 23–45; Mosse, *The Nationalization of the Masses*, 124–5; Detlev Peukert, *The Weimar Republic: The Crisis of Classical Modernity*, tr. Richard Deveson (New York: Hill and Wang, 1993), 5–6, 35; Mommsen, *Rise and Fall*, 71; Pamela Swett, 'Celebrating the Republic without Republicans: The Reichsverfassungstag in Berlin, 1929–1932', in Karin Friedrich (ed.), *Festive Culture in Germany and Europe from the Sixteenth to the Twentieth Century* (Lewiston, NY: Edwin Mellen, 2000), 281–302.
36. Dieter Gosewinkel, *Einbürgern und Ausschließen: Die Nationalisierung der Staatsangehörigkeit vom Deutschen Bund bis zur Bundesrepublik Deutschland* (Göttingen: Vandenhoeck & Ruprecht, 2001), 328–68; Annemarie Sammartino, *The Impossible Border: Germany and the East, 1914–1922* (Ithaca, NY: Cornell University Press, 2010), 96–119, 156–70; Brubaker, *Nationalism Reframed*, part II; Hochman, *Imagining a Greater Germany*.
37. Mommsen, *Rise and Fall*, 89–128.
38. John Hiden, 'The Weimar Republic and the Problem of the Auslandsdeutsche', *Journal of Contemporary History*, 12 (1977), 273–89; Elizabeth Harvey, 'Visions of the *Volk*: German Women and the Far Right from the Kaiserreich to Third Reich', *Journal of Women's History*, 16 (2004), 152–67.
39. Elizabeth Harvey, 'Pilgrimages to the "Bleeding Border": Gender and Rituals of Nationalist Protest in Germany, 1919–1939', *Women's History Review*, 9 (2000), 201–29.
40. Celia Applegate, *A Nation of Provincials: The German Idea of Heimat* (Berkeley, CA: University of California Press, 1990), 149–96; Martina Steber, *Ethnische Gewissheiten: Die Ordnung des Regionalen im bayerischen Schwaben vom Kaiserreich bis zum NS-Regime* (Göttingen: Vandenhoeck & Ruprecht, 2010), 193–320.
41. El-Tayeb, *Schwarze Deutsche*, 142–202; Christian Koller, *'Von Wilden aller Rassen niedergemetzelt': Die Diskussion um die Verwendung von Kolonialtruppen in Europa zwischen Rassismus, Kolonial- und Militärpolitik (1914–1930)* (Stuttgart: Franz Steiner Verlag, 2001), 207–61; Tina Campt, 'Converging Spectres of an Other Within: Race

and Gender in Prewar Afro-German History', *Callaloo*, 26 (2003), 322–41; Julia Roos, 'Women's Rights, Nationalist Anxiety, and the "Moral" Agenda in the Early Weimar Republic: Revisiting the "Black Horror" Campaign against France's African Occupation Troops', *Central European History*, 42 (2009), 473–508; Julia Roos, 'Nationalism, Racism and Propaganda in Early Weimar Germany: Contradictions in the Campaign against the "Black Horror on the Rhine"', *German History*, 30 (2012), 45–74; Iris Wigger, *The 'Black Horror on the Rhine': Intersections of Race, Nation, Gender and Class in 1920s Germany* (London: Palgrave Macmillan, 2017).
42. Quoted in Roos, 'Women's Rights', 488.
43. Wigger, *'Black Horror'*, 228–9; Koller, *'Von Wilden'*, 246–9.
44. Sammartino, *Impossible Border*, 120–37, 171–8; Adam Seipp, '"Scapegoats for a Lost War": Demobilisation, the Kapp Putsch, and the Politics of the Streets of Munich, 1919–1920', *War & Society*, 25 (2006), 35–54.
45. Sammartino, *Impossible Border*, 1–17.
46. Harvey, 'Visions'; Harvey, 'Pilgrimages'; Raffael Scheck, *Mothers of the Nation: Right-Wing Women in Weimar Germany* (Oxford: Berg, 2004); Roos, 'Women's Rights'; Wigger, *'Black Horror'*.
47. Hitler, *Mein Kampf*, 649.
48. Kershaw, *Hitler*; 'Berlin Stahlhelm Manifesto', 1927, in Kaes et al., *The Weimar Republic Sourcebook*, 339–40.
49. Hitler, *Mein Kampf*, 654.
50. Eric Weitz, *Weimar Germany: Promise and Tragedy* (Princeton: Princeton University Press, 2007), 95–6, 143–5; Scheck, *Mothers*, 117–36.
51. Quoted in Weitz, *Weimar Germany*, 145.
52. Winson Chu, *The German Minority in Interwar Poland* (Cambridge: Cambridge University Press, 2012).
53. Jeremy King, *Budweisers into Czechs and Germans: A Local History of Bohemian Politics, 1848–1948* (Princeton: Princeton University Press, 2002), 153–88; Pieter Judson, *Guardians of the Nation: Activists on the Language Frontiers of Imperial Austria* (Cambridge, MA: Harvard University Press, 2006), 233–57; Tara Zahra, *Kidnapped Souls: National Indifference and the Battle for Children in the Bohemian Lands, 1900–1948* (Ithaca, NY: Cornell University Press, 2008), 106–68. Also see T. Hunt Tooley, *National Identity and Weimar Germany: Upper Silesia and the Eastern Border, 1918–1922* (Lincoln, NE: University of Nebraska Press, 1997).
54. Stanley Suval, *The Anschluss Question in the Weimar Era: A Study of Nationalism in Germany and Austria, 1918–1932* (Baltimore: Johns Hopkins University Press, 1974).
55. Hochman, *Imagining a Greater Germany*, 195–236.
56. Erin Hochman, 'The Failed Republic, 1918–1933?', *Contemporary Austrian Studies*, 28 (2019), 45–63, here 51.
57. W. Nowack, 'Kein Preußen und kein Oesterreich', *Das Reichsbanner*, 15 Dec. 1924, 3–4.
58. Heß, *'Das ganze Deutschland'*, 184–251; Hochman, *Imagining a Greater Germany*, 21–47.
59. Heß, *'Das ganze Deutschland'*, 184–251; Hochman, *Imagining a Greater Germany*, 21–47.
60. Wilhelm Heile, 'Der "Anschluss" und der europäische Friede', *Oesterreich-Deutschland*, Oct. 1928, 1–5, here 5.
61. Heß, *'Das ganze Deutschland'*, 252–316; Suval, *Anschluss Question*, 81–2.
62. 'Eine Anschlußkundgebung der republikanischen Studentenschaft', *Arbeiter-Zeitung*, 11 July 1926, 13.

63. 'Trommelschlag und Hörnerklang', *Das Reichsbanner*, 2. Beilage, 1 Mar. 1925, here 10.
64. Julie Thorpe, *Pan-Germanism and the Austrofascist State, 1933–1938* (Manchester: Manchester University Press, 2011), 16–44; Mark Mazower, *Hitler's Empire: How the Nazis Ruled Europe* (New York: Penguin, 2008), 15–30. For refutations, see Winson Chu, Jesse Kauffman, and Michael Meng, 'A Sonderweg through Eastern Europe? The Varieties of German Rule in Poland during the Two World Wars', *German History*, 31 (2013), 318–44; Suval, *Anschluss Question*, 75–111; Heß, 'Das ganze Deutschland'; Hochman, *Imagining a Greater Germany*.
65. Hiden, 'Weimar Republic'; Michael Goebel, 'Decentering the German Spirit: The Weimar Republic's Cultural Relations with Latin America', *Journal of Contemporary History*, 44 (2009), 221–45; H. Glenn Penny, 'German Polycentrism and the Writing of History', *German History*, 30 (2012), 265–82; H. Glenn Penny and Stefan Rinke (eds), 'Rethinking Germans Abroad', Special Issue, *Geschichte und Gesellschaft*, 41 (2015), 173–346.
66. 'Kartei-Abteilung', in BArch, NS9/259, fo. 14; Donald McKale, *The Swastika Outside Germany* (Kent, OH: Kent State University Press, 1977).
67. 'Schwarzrotgold im Ausland', *Das Reichsbanner*, Beilage, 1 Oct. 1927, 155–6, here 156.
68. German People's Party, 'Program', here 115.
69. Hitler, *Mein Kampf*, 155.
70. Pulzer, *The Rise of Political Anti-Semitism*, 47–57; Volkov, 'Antisemitism'.
71. Kershaw, *Hitler*; Mosse, *Crisis*, 294–311.
72. Jones, *The German Right*.
73. Brian Crim, 'Weimar's "Burning Question": Situational Antisemitism and the German Combat Leagues, 1918–1933', in Jones, *The German Right*, 194–219. On their role in transmitting *völkisch* ideology, see Mosse, *Crisis*, 237–53.
74. Larry Eugene Jones, 'Conservative Antisemitism in the Weimar Republic: A Case Study of the German National People's Party', in Jones, *The German Right*, 79–107.
75. Crim, 'Weimar's "Burning Question"', 200–4; Harvey, 'Visions', 158.
76. Weitz, *Weimar Germany*, 333.
77. Reprinted in 'Ein Dolchstoß gegen den Anschluß', *Arbeiter-Zeitung*, 9 May 1929, 3.
78. Hochman, *Imagining a Greater Germany*, 21–47, 131–68, 195–236.
79. 'Das Osterfest des Arbeitersports', *Arbeiter-Zeitung*, 19 Apr. 1927, 1–2, here 2.
80. Alfred Low, *The Anschluss Movement, 1931–1938, and the Great Powers* (Boulder, CO: East European Monographs, 1985), 48–52; Buchner, *Um nationale und republikanische Identität*, 168–84.
81. Hochman, *Imagining a Greater Germany*, 1–20, 38–45, 99–101, 195–227.
82. 'Kriegsteilnehmer, Republikaner!', *Das Reichsbanner*, 15 Apr. 1924, 1.
83. Hochman, *Imagining a Greater Germany*, 42–7.
84. Eric Kurlander, *The Price of Exclusion: Ethnicity, National Identity, and the Decline of German Liberalism, 1898–1933* (New York: Berghahn Books, 2006); Sammartino, *Impossible Border*, 96–119, 156–70; Stefan Vogt, 'Strange Encounters: Social Democracy and Radical Nationalism in Weimar Germany', *Journal of Contemporary History*, 45 (2010), 253–81; Adelheid von Saldern, '*Volk* and *Heimat* Culture in Radio Broadcasting during the Period of Transition from Weimar to Nazi Germany', *Journal of Modern History*, 76 (2004), 312–46.
85. Konrad Haenisch, 'Deutsche Volksgemeinschaft', *Heim ins Reich*, 1 May 1922, 1–2, here 2.
86. Till van Rahden, 'Germans of the Jewish *Stamm*: Visions of Community between Nationalism and Particularism, 1850 to 1933', in Neil Gregor, Nils Roemer, and Mark

Roseman (eds), *German History from the Margins* (Bloomington, IN: Indiana University Press, 2006), 27–48; Gosewinkel, *Einbürgern und Ausschließen*, 353–68; Hochman, *Imagining a Greater Germany*.

87. Jens-Uwe Guettel, 'The Myth of the Pro-Colonialist SPD: German Social Democracy and Imperialism before World War I', *Central European History*, 45 (2012), 452–84.
88. El-Tayeb, *Schwarze Deutsche*, 70.
89. El-Tayeb, *Schwarze Deutsche*, 142–202; Koller, 'Von Wilden', 207–26; Roos, 'Women's Rights'; Sandra Mass, 'Von der "schwarzen Schmach" zur "deutschen Heimat": Die Rheinische Frauenliga im Kampf gegen die Rheinlandbesetzung, 1920–1929', *Werkstatt Geschichte*, 32 (2002), 44–57.
90. Heß, 'Das ganze Deutschland', 241–51; El-Tayeb, *Schwarze Deutsche*, 71; 'Richtlinien der Deutschen Zentrumspartei', 1922, in Wolfgang Treue (ed.), *Deutsche Parteiprogramme seit 1861* (Göttingen: Musterschmidt-Verlag, 1954), here 141.
91. Koller, 'Von Wilden', 227–33; Roos, 'Nationalism'.
92. Suval, *Anschluss Question*, 146–65; Gerwarth, *Bismarck Myth*, 134–9; Hochman, *Imagining a Greater Germany*, 131–68 and 195–236.

Bibliography

Chu, Winson, *The German Minority in Interwar Poland* (Cambridge: Cambridge University Press, 2012).

El-Tayeb, Fatima, *Schwarze Deutsche: Der Diskurs um 'Rasse' und nationale Identität 1890-1933* (Frankfurt: Campus, 2001).

Fritzsche, Peter, *Germans into Nazis* (Cambridge, MA: Harvard University Press, 1998).

Gerwarth, Robert, *The Bismarck Myth: Weimar Germany and the Legacy of the Iron Chancellor* (Oxford: Oxford University Press, 2005).

Hochman, Erin, *Imagining a Greater Germany: Republican Nationalism and the Idea of Anschluss* (Ithaca, NY: Cornell University Press, 2016).

Jones, Larry Eugene (ed.), *The German Right in the Weimar Republic: Studies in the History of German Conservatism, Nationalism, and Antisemitism* (New York: Berghahn Books, 2014).

Kershaw, Ian, *Hitler 1889-1936: Hubris* (New York: W. W. Norton, 1999).

Rossol, Nadine, *Performing the Nation in Interwar Germany: Sport, Spectacle and Political Symbolism, 1926–1936* (Houndmills and New York: Palgrave Macmillan, 2010).

Sammartino, Annemarie, *The Impossible Border: Germany and the East, 1914–1922* (Ithaca, NY: Cornell University Press, 2010).

Scheck, Raffael, *Mothers of the Nation: Right-Wing Women in Weimar Germany* (Oxford: Berg, 2004).

Wigger, Iris, *The 'Black Horror on the Rhine': Intersections of Race, Nation, Gender and Class in 1920s Germany* (London: Palgrave Macmillan, 2017).

CHAPTER 8

ELECTIONS, ELECTION CAMPAIGNS, AND DEMOCRACY

THOMAS MERGEL

'Who remained the victor in this most dreadful of all wars? It is democracy. The only great power among our adversaries that was not a democracy has collapsed, just as we have.'[1] This is how, during the negotiations about the Weimar constitution, the liberal *Frankfurter Zeitung* described the lesson learned from the First World War. Many people believed that this lesson was without alternative because the only other option possible in this situation—the monarchy—was compromised.[2] A positive meaning of the emphatic term 'democracy', however, remained somewhat open, as did the question of how this objective was to be translated into political structures. In all events, one thing was clear: political decision-making had to be based on the legitimacy of a large majority. In practice, this could take various forms. 'Democracy' was not only a new system, but had to be practised and learned by new political players.

The decision in favour of parliamentary democracy had been made shortly after the revolution. The appointment of Max von Baden as Reich Chancellor and the 1918 October Reforms, which implemented the parliamentary form of government, set the course for parliamentary democracy before revolutionary movements even surfaced. Strictly speaking, one option was already set: the parties of the later Weimar Coalition (DDP, SPD, and Centre Party) wanted a republic with a parliamentary and accountable government based on political parties and legitimized by universal suffrage of all adult citizens.

Indeed, the alternative, a council system, which was intensely publicly debated during the winter days of 1918/19, comprised ideas about legitimacy that were different from those of parliamentary representation. The concept of general citizenship and universal suffrage was not part of the council system. Instead, only those who were actively involved in the production process (and, in the event of war, in the military) were to be guaranteed a right to participation. In contrast, those outside the wage labour system, such as housewives or pensioners, were not. Thus, only 'manual and mental workers' had the active right to vote for the councils—other than workers also civil servants and white-collar employees, but not the self-employed and employers. The council system also envisioned the 'room for manoeuvre' of the elected differently, as it stipulated the imperative mandate rather than the freedom of conscience of the deputies. However, soon a broader understanding of the council system emerged that also included peasants', citizens', teachers', and students' councils, which all basically practised self-administration during the confusing revolutionary period.[3] In general, soldiers' councils were by no means dominated by radical groups; besides, many of their members were not workers at all but had a bourgeois background.[4] And yet, apart from a few radical socialist circles, the council system as the new political order was not under consideration, even during the revolutionary period of 1918/19.[5]

Thus, as early as winter 1918/19, parliamentary democracy based on general citizenship rights had no alternative. This proved significant when those who were to represent the citizenry and had to make political decisions were up for selection. Thus, suffrage, elections, and election campaigns in particular were in the eye of observers and commentators (and even more so of historiographical reconstructions after 1945). They were supposed to prove how 'democratic' the Weimar Republic was. In the wake of the debate on continuity between the Weimar and Bonn democracies, there was, first, an underlying normative expectation to assess the level of democracy in Weimar in comparison with the Federal Republic.[6] Second, for a long time research has ignored that the Weimar democracy did not emerge out of nothing but was built on a long tradition. Political orientations and voting decisions after 1918 were determined by mentalities and affiliations that had developed long before the First World War. Political participation being bound by tradition as well as its shifts and changes is possibly at odds with the expectations that many have had in hindsight regarding the political behaviour of the people of Weimar Germany.

This chapter explores political participation, its rules and interpretations, against the backdrop of, first, a concept of democracy that was not informed by the normative example of the Federal Republic and, second, traditions and mentalities that continued. Therefore, this contribution focuses on affiliations rather than political convictions, which are often difficult to prove. Due to the limited amount of space, national elections take centre stage. Departing from (1) a substantial extension of the electorate and (2) a discussion of ideas of political affiliation and 'good politics', the third section examines the conditions for and possibilities of political participation. The fourth focuses on forms of political communication and competition within election campaigns, before finally election results are analysed, centred around the question of which concepts of a good political society they reveal.

New Voters

With the constitutional transition from Imperial Germany to the Weimar Republic, German citizenship, as manifested in the right to vote, was significantly extended.[7] First and foremost, women were allowed to vote as well as men, which more than doubled the electorate due to the surplus of women after the war: in 1919, women accounted for 54 per cent of the voters. From the late nineteenth century onwards, the demand for women's suffrage had increased and was realized in Northern Europe before the First World War. In particular, Social Democrats had supported this claim, not least in the hope of gaining a substantial share of the women's vote.[8] With the revolution, women's suffrage was, without further discussion, back on the table and implemented by the provisional revolutionary government as one of its first actions.[9] This step resulted in a plethora of political educational works that wanted to teach women political engagement and how to vote.[10]

Subsequently, the voting age was reduced from 25 to 20 years, bringing about a substantial rejuvenation of the electorate. As the last election had been back in 1912, approximately 12 million first-time voters, who had been socialized during the war, were called to the ballot; among them were slightly more than 5 million men, many of them war veterans.[11] Added to these two large new groups were hundreds of thousands of migrants and refugees from former German territories in the West and East, as well as refugees of German descent from Russia. Around a million people would immigrate into Germany until the mid-1920s—people who were entitled to German citizenship and thus had the right to vote.[12] This increased the electorate 2.5 times, from 14.4 million at the last Reichstag elections before the war in 1912 to 37.4 million at the election to the National Assembly in January 1919. More than half of them were first-time voters. By 1933, the number of people entitled to vote had grown to 44.2 million.[13] In sheer numbers, the Weimar Republic brought about a revolutionary extension of political participation.

This extension was not politically neutral. However, not all changes took the same direction.[14] It is fair to assume that migrants leant towards the right wing. Among young voters, the overwhelming majority voted left—probably up to 75 per cent among soldiers—and many of them supported the more radical left-wing party USPD (Independent Social Democratic Party). While young voters were initially largely ignored by campaign strategists, women took centre stage in the attention of all parties and were addressed as a group of its own.[15] A noticeable majority of them voted for the conservative parties such as the DNVP (German National People's Party) and the Catholic Centre Party.[16] That was an unsettling experience for the left-leaning parties, particularly for the liberal DDP (German Democratic Party), which considered itself a 'women's party' (although this did not mean that the DDP intended to grant women much influence in its committees).[17] Apparently, socialist class struggle and cultural liberalism were less attractive to women than the promise of preserving tradition, family, and religion. Albeit not consistent across all elections, gender-specific vote counting exists for the years from 1919 onwards.[18] According to Detlef Lehnert's calculations, 20 per cent more men than women voted for SPD and USPD in 1919, meaning that 40 per cent of women, but at least 50 per cent of men voted for left-wing parties.[19] During the 1920s, this gap decreased to between 10 and 15 per cent.[20] Women's new significance as political subjects also had consequences for parliamentary representation. The elections to the National Assembly resulted in almost 10 per cent of deputies being female. This amount was among the highest in international comparison and was only persistently surpassed in Germany after 1980. Over the course of the Weimar Republic, this proportion dropped to 4 per cent in March 1933—the more the republic shifted to the right, the less female its political representatives became.[21]

AFFILIATIONS, POLITICAL MENTALITIES, AND THE LONGING FOR COMMUNITY

An evenly integrated society of citizens who all make rational decisions individually and under the condition of civil equality and, in so doing, creating a common will, is mere fiction. Various inequalities, interests, and different forms of collective affiliation structure every society. Owing to Germany's heterogeneous regional and confessional structure, a complex mix particularly of social inequality, confessional affiliation, and regional origin had emerged from early Imperial Germany. As historians have commonly agreed, these different forms of affiliations together generated a few, distinct major groups with clearly distinguishable basic political convictions which cannot be differentiated based on one sole category of inequality (such as class). The sociologist M. Rainer Lepsius developed an influential model that describes German society from the foundation of the Reich to the end of the Weimar Republic as being dominated by four different 'social-moral milieus', which coexisted separately from one another. These milieus embraced their members 'from the cradle to the grave', offering an encompassing culture of interpretation, a society in a society. Lepsius emphasized the 'coincidence of several structural dimensions such a religion, regional tradition, economic position, cultural orientation'.[22] As Lepsius explained, the socialist working-class, the Catholic, the bourgeois-liberal, and the Protestant-conservative milieus were based on their respective value orientations, daily lives, and collective organizations. Lepsius referred to parties in terms of functioning as 'political committees' of these milieus.

It is particularly significant that this theory did not postulate one 'main antagonism', such as the class antagonism, but attached equal importance to cultural, regional, and, first and foremost, confessional patterns of affiliation, not only focusing on interests in a rational sense but also on traditions and mentalities. While the concept of milieus has been met with some criticism because it exaggerated the lines of difference between milieus and overestimated their internal coherence,[23] it still has great explanatory power. It can explain, on the one hand, the stability of political groups in Germany and, on the other, the novelty of the NSDAP and its, at least partially, cross-milieu power. And this had been Lepsius's main objective.

The political scientist Karl Rohe, on the other hand, has convincingly argued that milieus were not equally distant from one another.[24] Particularly the bourgeois-liberal and the conservative-national milieus were closer to one another than to other milieus. Here, Protestantism, as well as the shared regional roots in northern and eastern

Germany served as a unifying factor. These deliberations point to a political three-camp structure with various transitions *within* the socialist, Catholic, and national camps, rather than *between* them.

It is striking that, despite fundamental political changes, the party system of the Weimar Republic was very similar to that of Imperial Germany. On the left, there was the socialist camp, deeply divided since the war. With the exception of the regional foundation of the BVP (Bavarian People's Party), the Catholic camp with the Centre Party had hardly changed at all. The national camp remained heterogeneous: with the DDP and the DVP (German People's Party), liberals continued to adhere to the traditional divide between left-wing and right-wing liberalism. The DNVP as the successor of the two conservative parties of Imperial Germany established itself on the right of the national camp. By stressing the national aspect and, at the same time, focusing on the new democratic emphasis of a 'people's party', the DNVP claimed to step out of the shadow of the Old Prussian elites, albeit without overcoming the heterogeneity of—and, at times, the deep divide between—liberal and reactionary conservatism.[25]

Despite this stability, several distinctive changes in the political landscape occurred. The first one was the nationalization of party competition. Owing to the first-past-the-post system in Imperial Germany, its milieu parties had been particularly successful in their regional strongholds: the working-class milieu in (larger) cities and industrial areas, the Catholic milieu in Westphalia, Silesia, Bavaria, and the Rhineland, the conservative milieu in Old Prussia, and the liberal-bourgeois milieu in the cities and in South-West Germany. Notwithstanding their claim to be parties of the entire German people, most of them had been regional or stronghold-parties. This changed in the Weimar Republic. With proportional representation, all parties were obliged to run in all places. Thus, the voting system significantly contributed to the national integration of the political system.

The second change was a stark increase of tensions within the political camps, which resulted from the new possibilities of governing. Under the constitutional system of Imperial Germany, all politics had been opposition politics and could therefore focus on fundamental principles. Now, new opportunities of policy-making required pragmatic actions. At the same time, the implementation of democracy increased the expectations of more room for manoeuvre of the parties. The tension between pragmatic and principle-based politics, together with raised expectations, put all camps to the test. In 1918/19, Social Democrats had vigorously seized the opportunity by taking over government, which alienated the revolutionary part of the labour movement. Right-wing parties also struggled, with pragmatic strategies being highly criticized by fundamental adversaries of the republic within their own parties—such as the DVP with Gustav Stresemann's foreign politics and the DNVP with conservative republicans in their ranks. Even the Centre Party saw several Catholic opponents of the republic leaving the party due to its republican course. It also had to put up with the separation of the BVP, which considered the new political course as too progressive and feared Catholicism would be betrayed by democracy. It seems that Karl Rohe's three-camp concept underestimates these inner tensions. The formation of competing parties within a milieu is a strong indication of its internal fragility. In the Weimar Republic, opposition to and agreement with the new political system, radicalism and moderateness coexisted within individual camps and were not easily reconciled.

It is part and parcel of system changes that fundamental questions relating to the system are negotiated over the course of a certain transition time. This is not only characteristic of the Weimar Republic. During the first two decades of the Third French Republic, elections were also plebiscites about the republic as a whole.[26] Opposition was also always opposition to the system, and, thus, everyday issues could easily become questions of principle. Matters that had previously not been considered political issues at all became 'political' questions. Against this backdrop, 'politicization' meant that all kinds of issues were forced into the Procrustean bed of political alliances and 'principles'.[27] This resulted in polarizations that did not necessarily arise from political matters per se but emerged from a narrow basic consensus and, ultimately, reduced the willingness to compromise.

Given the segmented political landscape of the Weimar Republic, with its different milieus, this polarization was of particular acuteness because the milieus' different horizons of meaning were, in principle, mutually exclusive. Compromises and coalitions, necessary in a multi-party system, often put an enormous strain on parties and politicians. Yet, segmentation and politicization came to a halt in light of the collectively targeted subject of the Weimar Republic: the people (*Volk*).[28] This concept implied a communality that was to overarch and overcome partial affiliations and was advocated by all political parties, apart from the radical left. In practice, however, the 'people' was seen as a conglomerate of different interest groups that were competing against one another and themselves became political actors in the process. The understanding of society being structured along occupational and economic interests could result in the idea, frequently ventilated in everyday discourses, that it was different professions, instead of voters, that decided upon the outcome of elections. 'The Chambers of Crafts have delegated a secretary. The merchants are represented by 10 businessmen', stated the right-wing liberal newspaper *Der Tag* as it described the composition of the Reichstag after the spring elections in 1924.[29]

All sides lamented these inner conflicts—different milieus and camps, different economic or class interests, and affiliations to different confessions and regions—as the fundamental ill of the German people, and measured them by the counter model, the concept of a 'people's community' (*Volksgemeinschaft*). This concept evoked a deep, pre-political unity of the people that only suffered the disadvantage of not (yet) being achieved. The concept of the people's community was by no means a preserve of right-wing parties and, thanks to its semantic polyvalence, it could be used in many ways. Its visionary goal was not pluralistic heterogeneity but homogeneous unity, and, as such, it offered hope and expressed suffering from disunity at the same time. This manifested itself in various ways: Social Democratic politicians, when talking about people's community, referred to an agreement between employers and employees and a welfare state characterized by solidarity; Centre Party politicians thought of the recognition of Catholics as fully equal citizens; agrarian politicians meant the balance between cities and countryside. Achieving the 'real' or 'true' people's community was a goal that every politician promised; and every politician who wanted to win elections was well advised to address the people's community. The concept tapped into a suffering from difference, which was, however, produced by its own modus operandi as a fundamentalist term.

Suffrage, Voting Justice, and Democracy

The consequences of these collective self-descriptions were rather democratizing. They brought to the fore that all citizens were equal, which had repercussions for suffrage. Many votes had been lost in Imperial Germany due to the first-past-the-post system, and the design of constituencies had been unfair. This and the coalition attitude of the bourgeois parties were the reasons why the vote share of the SPD—they won 35 per cent in 1912—never translated into the equivalent number of seats. Therefore, 'justice' was a central value when the new voting system of the Weimar Republic was introduced.[30] Every vote was to count and count equally. It was an uncontested fact that this could only be achieved by proportional suffrage; there were hardly any discussions about this in the Weimar National Assembly. Only Friedrich Naumann, a representative of the DDP, was concerned that proportional suffrage would render a transition of power, which he deemed necessary for the parliamentary system, impossible—given the seemingly entrenched support bases of the milieu parties: 'parliamentary system and proportional representation are mutually exclusive.'[31]

Weimar suffrage was aimed at making the Reichstag (as well as the diets of the single states which had a similar suffrage) a mirror of the electorate. Instead of the decision-making role, it was the representational function of parliaments that took centre-stage. For this reason, no one suggested a minimum vote requirement, as is implemented in most of today's proportional voting systems. Proportional representation had repercussions for the form of political representation: rather than candidates, parties dominated the elections. Thirty-five large constituencies—in comparison to 397 in Imperial Germany—and party lists, rather than individual candidates, ran for elections. Party machines gained a decisive role in recruiting the political elite. The thought of a *local* electorate being represented by a candidate, which came into being around 1848, gave way to the idea that *national* communities of conviction had to be represented. This favoured the election of programmes and parties before the election of persons.

The proportional voting system and its underlying idea of representation facilitated a multi-party system. Due to the lack of decisive majorities, coalitions were the only means of government, and it often took weeks after the elections until they were negotiated. Governing was further complicated by the lack of an election threshold. Interest parties and programmatic splinter parties surfaced and gained seats in the Reichstag. These protest parties were rather small, but they boomed around the mid-1920s and gained up to a seventh of the vote, which gave them a potential for interference. The 1928 Reichstag consisted of fifteen parties, including the Reichspartei für Volksrecht und Aufwertung (Reich Party for Civil Rights and Revaluation) and the Sächsische Landvolk (Saxon Peasants) with two seats each, the Landbund (Rural League) and the Deutsch-Hannoversche Partei (German-Hanoverian Party) with three each. Nine out of these fifteen parties had less than 5 per cent of seats.[32]

Even contemporaries described this as a problem of both democratic legitimacy and the decision-making ability of parliamentary institutions.[33] There was a plethora of reform proposals, ranging from an increase in the voting age (because young voters were deemed to lack the required political maturity), to hybrid forms of majority and proportional representation, reducing the size of constituencies, or the implementation of plural votes to open instead of fixed party lists where voters could tick their favourite candidates. It is striking that it was the DDP of all parties that, in 1929, proposed the introduction of a 3 per cent voting threshold—striking because this could potentially harm the party itself.[34] All these proposals were rejected in light of the idea of voting justice, according to which no vote was to be lost and which was shared by all parties, despite practical problems.

In the early Federal Republic, the political scientist Ferdinand Hermens and his students particularly blamed proportional representation for being the crucial reason for the demise of the Weimar Republic.[35] Today, this hypothesis is no longer maintained. It underestimates the deeply rooted social, political, and cultural divides within the electorate, which would have led to a revival of the old structure of regional parties, instead of an idealized two-party system, had the majority voting system been introduced. And it overlooks that, after the experienced injustices during Imperial Germany, proportional representation facilitated the political integration of vast parts of the electorate because it promised that all votes counted. International comparison also casts doubt on the alleged correlation between proportional representation and governability.[36] Despite a proportional voting system, for years Austria had a two-party system, Canada has a multi-party system despite proportional representation, and Israel is governed effectively although currently thirteen parties are represented in parliament (2021).

The hypothesis also fails to see reforms of the Weimar Republic in the contemporary European context.[37] The voting age in Germany was average in comparison. The war, which of course had been fought largely by young men, forced a reduction of the voting age in every country. In many European countries, demands had been voiced in 1918 to introduce proportional representation, and many countries had done so, particularly the newly established states such as Poland (1918), Czechoslovakia (1920), but also Italy (1919) and the Netherlands (as early as 1917). After the left urged for proportional representation, France introduced a hybrid voting system. Germany implemented women's suffrage before other major European countries including the United Kingdom, France, and Italy.[38] Thus, Weimar's voting system was state of the art and consistent with international political trends.

Moreover, in contrast to many other political systems, the Weimar Republic offered a fundamentally new form of political participation: elements of direct democracy.[39] The Reich President, the highest office of the state, was directly elected under universal suffrage and, alongside the Reichstag, constituted the second pillar of democratic legitimacy. This was a substantial novelty in Europe.[40] In 1919, around the election of the Social Democrat Friedrich Ebert for Reich President, which was still executed by the National Assembly, the liberal sociologist Max Weber and other keen observers demanded such a plebiscitary election, because they did not trust parliament with the important and consequential decision of choosing the head of state. According to Weber, addressing major reform projects, such as socializations, required a 'self-elected spokesman of the masses'. In this sense, Weber rather imagined the plebiscitary leader as a socialist. The fact that he used the notion 'dictator' in this context indicates that he understood the Reich President not only as an expansion of political participation but also as the leadership of a single individual based on the masses, who, if push come to shove, could in fact act dictatorially. This was stipulated in Article 48 of the Reich constitution, which granted the Reich President the right to issue emergency decrees. But Weber understood the presidential elections as an expression of democracy and urged the Reichstag to 'recognise ... the direct election of the leader'. 'Let democracy not place this weapon of anti-parliamentary agitation in the hands of its enemies.'[41] Even the liberal Max Weber's choice of words indicates a specific understanding of democracy and a certain scepticism towards parliamentary representation: the latter was not necessarily regarded as more democratic than direct elections through the people—quite the contrary. Weber's words also reflect concerns over the rule of parties and their functionaries, which today we would describe as populist.

In practice, however, the direct election of the leader did not turn out as envisaged by the founders of the republic or Max Weber. Instead, it came to be the expression of a need for a strong leader in the face of a parliament whose ability to govern was rather limited—and indeed even *against* it. The election of Friedrich Ebert crushed the hopes for fundamental revolutionary changes and instead held out the prospect of a cooperation between workers and bourgeoisie. When, after his death in February 1925, new elections were due—now as direct elections—they were already held in a climate of controversy between proponents of the liberal republic and a broad conservative and right-wing opposition, which, however, cannot be dismissed wholesale as anti-republican. While in the first ballot most candidates had been party officials, militant anti-republican and moderate conservatives gathered in the so-called 'Reichsblock' with Paul von Hindenburg as candidate in the second voting round. The fact that the ex-general still enjoyed great prestige as 'the victor of Tannenberg' shows the extent to which the military defeat—in which Hindenburg had, of course, played his part—had already been pushed to the back of collective memory. In contrast to his competitor from the 'Volksblock' (People's Bloc), the former Reich Chancellor Wilhelm Marx (Centre Party), who represented the policies of the Weimar coalition, the non-politician Hindenburg was presented as the leader of the masses 'above the parties'.[42]

And yet, the Weimar electorate did not vote in these elections according to principle. This is shown by the fact that even the BVP—Catholic, albeit at a distance to the Centre Party—did not endorse the Catholic candidate Wilhelm Marx but the Protestant Hindenburg. Initially, the Reichsblock had reservations about Hindenburg, not least because he, to the disappointment of the right-wing opposition, assured the electorate that he would comply with the constitution. Yet the general only narrowly prevailed in the second ballot. Despite inner conflicts within the Reichsblock, Hindenburg represented the right-wing camp as its common candidate, and this arrangement proved sustainable. The 1925 presidential election was an important step for voters on their path to the NSDAP. Many of those who voted for Hindenburg in 1925, in particular former first-time voters, also voted for the NSDAP after 1930.[43]

It may seem paradoxical that, at the next presidential elections in 1932, Hindenburg ran as candidate of the republican camp and that many of his former supporters now endorsed his competitor Adolf Hitler.[44] This indicates the dilemma of the republicans in light of the rise of the NSDAP and its candidate. But it is also evidence that Hindenburg had failed in fulfilling the hopes of the right-wing camp. He had been willing neither to breach the constitution, nor to interfere substantially in daily politics. He was respected far beyond the national camp as a national integration figure and had demonstrated that a conservative could serve the republic. However, it is also indicative of the republicans' agony that they were unable to nominate a renowned candidate from their own ranks who would not be regarded as a party politician. Even Social Democrats saw Hindenburg as an integrative figure, and election campaigns presented him as a guarantor of overcoming the antagonism between the parties. His competitor was Adolf Hitler, who was supported by the radical right and won 30 per cent in the first ballot and 37 per cent in the second. In the eyes of the public, Hitler was certainly more of a party politician than Hindenburg. But he ran the election under the explicit slogan of 'paving the way for the new Germany'[45] and, therefore, represented a vision for the future in contrast to the 84-year-old Hindenburg. Thus, presidential elections always signified an aspect of the representation of the people, which was not limited to parliamentary representation and the president could, in some sense, criticize the latter 'from outside'.

A new element of direct democracy, scarcely tested in other European countries, was the referendum. A national electoral law to this effect was passed in April 1920, in the wake of the Kapp putsch. The referendum was, on the one hand, in accordance with the more plebiscitary orientation of the political system. On the other, the politics of the National Assembly were anything but plebiscitary and sought to curb direct democracy. In particular, the required majority of more than 50 per cent of those eligible to vote made referendums foredoomed to failure as a great majority of voters had to participate. Such a mobilization was effectively impossible to achieve, and the call to stay away from the ballot was enough to undermine any plebiscite.[46] Several single German states also introduced the referendum, the first referendum taking place in Munich as early as December 1919 (on the deselection of the city council).

Only two out of seven nationwide petitions for a referendum reached the necessary amount of voters to be admitted as plebiscites. The first was the referendum on the expropriation of the princes on 20 June 1926—initiated by the KPD and tentatively supported by the SPD—that demanded the expropriation without compensation of the former ruling houses that were deposed in 1918/19. The second, in 1929, was against the final regulation of reparations as stipulated in the Young Plan and launched by a right-wing coalition under the leadership of the DNVP chairman Alfred Hugenberg. Both referendums took place without a chance of success, even though most of the people who went to the ballots voted in favour of them. However, the turnout of the referendum on the expropriation of the princes was 40 per cent, whereas the one against the Young Plan only achieved 13.5 per cent. In both cases, the opponents of the republic were the minority. On the other hand, plebiscites were exploited by the respective anti-republican parties that advertised their anti-republic opposition with a blaze of publicity, though the importance of the campaign against the Young Plan for the Nazis should not be overestimated.[47] Moreover, referendums could potentially lead to severe rifts within the political camps. The campaign for the expropriation of the princes, for instance, led to conflicts between bourgeois elites and Catholic workers within the Centre Party, with the latter being rather open to the former rulers' expropriation without compensation.[48] Thus, plebiscites could drive wedges between dominant parliamentary power groups.

In this sense, the plebiscitary elements of Weimar democracy did not serve the republican cause. However, they certainly did have a democratizing effect as they mobilized citizens, not least habitual non-voters, to make collective decisions. They brought topics into play that were not on the agenda of the political institutions, such as the expropriation of the princes. And finally, they were polarizing—not necessarily in respect to factual issues, but, rather, regarding questions of the political system and persons. In the process, the legitimacy of parties as custodians of the people's will was challenged time and time again.

ELECTION CAMPAIGNS AND POLITICAL COMMUNICATION

The polarizing effect applied to elections in general. The right-wing liberal newspaper *Deutsche Allgemeine Zeitung* voiced a widely shared opinion when, in 1920, it referred to the Reichstag election campaigns as a 'fight' (*Kampf*), namely as a 'fight, not fussy about the means it uses'. It wrote about 'whirling of political discord and political resentment'— that is, elections divided society and turned people into enemies.[49] From the nineteenth century onwards, liberal elites knew a tested method that would counter this: objectivity. They understood elections as part and expression of the political education of the unemancipated masses, and, therefore, election campaigns were an opportunity for political pedagogy. Even in Imperial Germany it had been customary to invite candidates of the opposing parties to party events. This still occurred in the Weimar Republic. Objective debate was intended to prevent commotion. In the meantime, however, the masses were not as unemancipated as before, while the rift between different milieus and camps was widening. The notion that supporters of the German National People's Party would be convinced by arguments of left-liberal DDP competitors at an election rally and subsequently leave the DNVP in order to join the DDP was a bizarre story, one that even claimed news value.[50] It should be noted that election campaigns in the Weimar Republic were still predominantly based on meetings and speeches, and on the concept of the citizen who was politically knowledgeable, interested, and capable of following a line of thought.

International comparison highlights German peculiarities.[51] While in the United Kingdom election campaigns were conducted along the lines of the market model and candidates presented themselves to the, so to speak, highest-bidding 'customer', German campaigns aimed to mobilize and organize followers, who were seen as an internally homogeneous and externally discrete social group. In this sense, election campaigns turned into a political stage where different camps gathered, presented themselves, and mobilized their followers. Elections rallies largely addressed those who were already convinced, rather than those who had yet to be won over. Party-affiliated organizations such as churches, trade unions, but also local associations, helped mobilize their own camp. Even door-to-door canvassing targeted predominantly those who were known as party supporters. A large part of the press saw itself as party-affiliated or even as an extension of a certain party, and by no means as an objectively reporting voice of the political public.[52] Nevertheless, the illusion of rationality was maintained. Election rallies were not carnivalesque shows with a lot of alcohol and brawls, as was traditional in England, but instructions based on speeches and articles and discussions of the candidates involved, less often in the open air than in enclosed venues, often with entrance fees. The same applied to the campaign material of the parties, which presented itself as the continuation of the political communication of Imperial Germany, overladen with dense text. This was produced in great masses, so that city squares and streets were covered in flyers before the elections. The election campaign manuals published by the parties, an invention of Imperial Germany and often consisting of several hundreds of pages, again flourished in the Weimar years. They cost money and comprised the entire line of argument of a party—and were also contributing to political education.

New media also provided novel forms of political communication, which could reach beyond milieu boundaries.[53] This did not apply to the radio, which was largely seen as a public educational institution. Some election speeches were broadcast in 1924, but this practice was discontinued at the instigation of most of the parties and the Minister of the Interior. The cinema was not yet used as a medium of mass communication as it was mainly a localised enterprise. Weimar advertisements did not get beyond the first attempts with moving pictures. New printing and reproduction methods, however, opened up the new possibility of using images in print media. From 1924, particularly from 1928, the SPD presented its candidates in newspapers by including photographs and captions, such as: 'Franz Künstler, machine fitter from Berlin Neukölln. The type of worker, who is ambitious and striving forward by himself. Leader of the Social Democratic Party Greater Berlin and thus manager of the election campaign in the

Berlin constituencies.'[54] Despite proportional representation, the parties sought to present their candidates as individuals. Illustrated journals also included politicians as iconic figures.

More striking than the realistic pictorial depiction of politicians was a political iconography that differed substantially from visual cultures known from advertisement or photography.[55] Large, strongly coloured posters presented political symbols that could be attributed to different parties and competed in conquering the public space. As early as 1920, billboard-tearing squads, deployed by the state administration, attempted to regulate and clean public spaces as well as they could.[56] These new media were mostly used in cities. Their impact in small towns and villages should not be overestimated. Here, election campaigns were still largely meetings with speeches and often discussions, with flyers and, possibly, small processions.

This also applied to the Nazis. For a long time, historians have described their elections campaigns and their 'stirring' and emotionally charged visual propaganda as technologically and aesthetically revolutionary, with startling resemblance to the visual imagery of communist propaganda.[57] Recent research, on the other hand, emphasizes that National Socialism was predominantly a gathering movement that permeated even small towns and villages, infecting association life and notables.[58] These gatherings and meetings, mostly funded by entrance fees, were dominated by spoken language. Thus, despite its effective and staged use of images, marches, and light domes—all of those only occurred after 1933—the Nazis followed the speech-centred tradition of German political communication. By swiftly adopting new technologies of acoustic amplification such as microphones and loudspeakers, the Nazis were able to fill large event venues with sound, virtually silencing dissent.[59]

Though Nazi election rallies were in many ways modelled on common political conventions, they still focused on a personalistic presentation of Adolf Hitler as the 'Führer' and populist tribune of the masses. This strategy was increasingly professionalized and reached out for the countryside from the late 1920s onwards. Hitler was turned into a brand, and this is the reason why the Nazi movement was named as 'Hitler movement' on the ballot paper.[60] Adolf Hitler, who was not a German citizen until 1932 and thus unable to be elected, figured in election campaigns as the symbol of a political longing that wanted to be embodied in an individual. This concept was used extensively in the campaign for the 1932 presidential elections. In April, Hitler embarked on a nationwide campaign trail—by plane. In seven days, he visited twenty-one cities. He flew to a different location three to four times a day, welcomed by cheering and carefully choreographed crowds, gave a speech and disappeared into the air. The filmmaker Leni Riefenstahl accompanied this 'Deutschlandflug'. Her film *Hitler over Germany* was an aesthetically ground-breaking propaganda product. It linked the idea of personal accessibility, which manifested itself in masses of enthusiastic people, particularly young ones, with the image of the flying Hitler 'over' Germany, thus closely connecting the longing for a leader with Adolf Hitler.[61]

This was by no means a matter of course. Longing for a leader was ubiquitous in the Weimar Republic and not limited to the anti-republican right. Expectations did not necessarily focus on a dictatorship, but on an organic unity between the political leadership and the people.[62] Even the left, but more so the bourgeois centre and the right, sought for a leader who, in Max Weber's sense, possessed charisma and legitimacy so that he could speak for everyone and bind together all Germans, making them a united people. A leader was longed for who would defy the political 'machine' of the republic via his charisma and whose authentic personality would reconcile leadership and followers.[63] The representation of Hitler as this leader equally tapped into ideas from the left that this man had to be a member of the people and adopted demands from the right of a man who was a decisive leader, also internationally. These two expectations were combined to a homogeneous and harmonic unity via the notions 'national' and 'social'.

ELECTION RESULTS: A REPUBLIC WITHOUT REPUBLICANS?

The classic narrative of the elections results during the Weimar Republic is based on the hypothesis of the increasing departure from democracy, which was bolstered by the Great Depression and manifested itself in a polarized radicalization. It goes like this: in the elections of the National Assembly, the 'Weimar Coalition' of MSPD, Centre Party, and DDP was able to win 72.4 per cent of the vote with an impressing turnout of 83 per cent, that is almost four-fifths of the mandates of the National Assembly.[64] Despite the competition from the USPD, the SPD could continue its upward trend from Imperial Germany and won almost 38 per cent. The Centre Party was also able to top its former results with 16 per cent. More surprising was the performance of the left-liberal DDP with 18.6 per cent: most historians and contemporaries explained this success as the liberal bourgeoisie wanting a strong DDP in government to prevent the SPD of implementing too far-reaching socialist measures.[65]

This was the majority that the Weimar Republic was built upon, that adopted the new constitution, elected the Reich President, and signed the Versailles Treaty. But this majority swiftly vanished in the Reichstag elections of 1920 after the Kapp putsch. The Weimar Coalition only gained 43.6 per cent and was never able to win a majority again throughout the entire Weimar years.[66] In this 'republic without republicans', changing coalitions governed, often based only on a minority with the pledged support of the SPD and under growing pressure from anti-democratic parties on the left (KPD) and the right (DNVP, NSDAP), which became ever stronger (Table 8.1).

In the wake of the economic crisis, voting behaviour became more radicalized. The NSDAP in particular benefited from this development, winning the 1930 Reichstag elections by a landslide. Including the KPD, which had been on the rise from 1924 onwards and got dangerously close to the SPD in November 1932, there was a 'negative majority' of anti-democrats in July 1932. The DNVP, whose vote share almost halved until 1932, and particularly the liberal parties, first and foremost the DDP that was nearly

Table 8.1. Results of elections to the National Assembly and the Reichstag, 1919–1933

	National Assembly 19 January 1919		1st Reichstag 6 June 1920		2nd Reichstag 4 May 1924		3rd Reichstag 7 December 1924		4th Reichstag 20 May 1928		5th Reichstag 14 September 1930		6th Reichstag 31 July 1932		7th Reichstag 6 November 1932		8th Reichstag 5 March 1933	
Eligible voters (in Millions)	36.766		35.949		38.375		38.987		41.224		42.957		44.226		44.374		44.685	
Votes cast (in Millions)	30.524		28.463		29.709		30.704		31.165		35.225		37.162		35.758		39.654	
Turnout in per cent	83.0		79.2		77.4		78.8		75.6		82.0		84.1		80.6		88.8	
Deputies in total	423		459		472		493		491		577		608		584		647	
DNVP	3.121	10.3%	4.249	15.1%	5.696	19.5%	6.206	20.5%	4.381	14.2%	2.458	7.0%	2.177	5.9%	2.959	8.3%	3.136	8.0%
	44		71		95		103		73		41		37		52		52	
NSDAP (1924 as: NS-Freiheitsbewegung)	–		–		1.918	6.5%	0.907	3.0%	0.810	2.6%	6.409	18.3%	13.745	37.3%	11.737	33.1%	17.277	43.9%
					32		14		12		107		230		196		288	
Business Party/ Bavarian Peasants League (Wirtschaftspartei/ Bayerischer Bauernbund)	0.275	0.9%	0.218	0.8%	0.694	2.4%	1.005	3.3%	1.397	4.5%	1.362	3.9%	0.146	0.4%	0.110	0.3%	–	
	4		4		10		17		23		23		2		1			
German-Hanoverian Party (Deutsch-Hannoversche Partei)	0.077	0.2%	0.319	1.1%	0.320	1.1%	0.263	0.9%	0.195	0.6%	0.144	0.4%	0.047	0.1%	0.064	0.2%	0.048	0.1%
	1		5		5		4		3		3		–		1		–	
Rural League (Landbund)	–		–		0.574	2.0%	0.499	1.6%	0.199	0.6%	0.194	0.65%	0.097	0.3%	0.105	0.3%	0.084	0.2%
					10		8		3		3		2		2		1	
Christian National Peasants' and Rural Peoples Party (Christlich-Nationale Bauern- und Landvolk-Partei	–		–		–		–		0.581	1.9%	1.108	3.2%	0.091	0.2%	0.046	0.1%	–	
									10		19		1		–			

Party	1919	1920	May 1924	Dec 1924	1928	1930	Jul 1932	Nov 1932	Mar 1933
German Peasants' Party (Deutsche Bauernpartei)	—	—	—	—	0.481 / 1.6% / 8	0.339 / 1.0% / 6	0.137 / 0.4% / 2	0.149 / 0.4% / 3	0.114 / 0.4% / 2
Christian Social People's Service (Christlich Sozialer Volksdienst)	—	—	—	—	—	0.870 / 2.5% / 14	0.364 / 1.0% / 3	0.403 / 1.0% / 5	0.383 / 1.2% / 4
DVP	1.345 / 4.4% / 19	3.919 / 13.9% / 65	2.694 / 9.2% / 45	3.049 / 10.1% / 51	2.679 / 8.7% / 45	1.578 / 4.5% / 60	0.436 / 1.2% / 7	0.661 / 1.9% / 11	0.432 / 1.1% / 2
Centre Party	5.980 / 19.7% / 91	3.845 / 13.6% / 64	1.914 / 13.4% / 65	4.119 / 13.6% / 69	3.712 / 12.1% / 62	4.127 / 11.8% / 68	4.589 / 12.5% / 75	4.230 / 11.9% / 70	4.425 / 11.2% / 74
BVP	—	1.238 / 4.4% / 21	0.946 / 3.2% / 16	1.134 / 3.7% / 19	0.945 / 3.1% / 16	1.005 / 3.0% / 19	1.192 / 3.2% / 22	1.095 / 3.2% / 20	1.074 / 2.7% / 18
DDP (from 1930: German State Party)	5.641 / 18.5% / 75	2.333 / 8.3% / 39	1.655 / 5.7% / 28	1.920 / 6.3% / 32	1.505 / 4.9% / 25	1.322 / 3.8% / 20	0.371 / 1.0% / 4	0.336 / 1.0% / 2	0.334 / 0.9% / 5
SPD	11.509 / 37.9% / 165	6.104 / 21.7% / 102	6.009 / 20.5% / 100	7.881 / 26.0% / 131	9.153 / 29.8% / 153	8.577 / 24.5% / 143	7.959 / 21.6% / 133	7.248 / 20.4% / 121	7.181 / 18.3% / 120
USPD	2.317 / 7.6% / 22	5.046 / 17.9% / 84	0.235 / 0.8% / —	0.099 / 0.3% / —	0.021 / 0.1% / —	—	—	—	—
KPD	—	0.589 / 2.1% / 4	3.693 / 12.6% / 62	2.709 / 9.0% / 45	3.264 / 10.6% / 54	4.592 / 13.1% / 89	5.283 / 14.3% / 100	5.980 / 16.9% / 81	4.848 / 12.3% / —
Others	0.131 / 0.5% / 2	0.332 / 1.1% / —	0.930 / 3.1% / 4	0.598 / 2.0% / —	1.445 / 5.5% / 4	0.804 / 2.3% / 1	0.244 / 0.7% / —	0.299 / 0.8% / —	0.005 / — / —

Note: For the individual parties, the left-hand figure gives the votes cast in millions, the second figure the percentage of all votes cast. The figure underneath gives the number of deputies at the beginning of the respective session of parliament.

Source: Adapted from Ursula Büttner, *Weimar: Die überforderte Republik* (Stuttgart: Klett-Cotta, 2008), 802–3.

crushed, were the losers in this development. In 1919, DDP and DVP won together 23 per cent of the vote. In 1930, it was not more than 8.5 per cent and, in 1932, only 2.2 per cent. For many commentators, the 'dying middle' (Larry Eugene Jones) was a sign of the widening gap between the political poles and thus of an existential loss of democratic substance.

The reference point of the hypothesis that assumes a growing hostility towards democracy as briefly outlined above is the elections of the National Assembly. They are deemed to be proof of the initial enthusiasm for the republic, which subsequently quickly faded away. It is, indeed, in need of explanation why in 1919 almost three-quarters of voters were in favour of a political order that many of them, almost with disgust, rejected thirteen years later. Since the 1990s, research has explored more long-term changes in voters' behaviour, orientations, and mentalities. The concept of milieus provides the most important explanations in this respect. In this view, more short-term events such as the global economic crisis and normative questions concerning democratic awareness take a back seat.

Through the lens of the concept of milieus, the 1919 National Assembly elections were rather exceptional. Drawing on Karl Rohe's theory of electoral camps, one can put forward the hypothesis that they were in fact the last elections of Imperial Germany. The long-term trend from the right to the left continued, liberalism could win a fifth or more of the vote and most parties were still, in fact, regional parties. They had not yet been able to establish a structured organization beyond their strongholds, and their radical wings were still rather powerless in organizational terms. The fact that, despite fundamental changes in the electorate, the National Assembly elections showed similar structures to those of the pre-war period, demonstrates the profound power of milieus. The conservative parties benefited from women's suffrage, the SPD from the lowering of the voting age. Even though many from this age cohort did not return from the war, young first-time voting workers voted (initially) just like their fathers or elder brothers (and most female workers did the same).

This changed with the republic. From 1920, shifts *within* these camps, yet rarely *between* them, occurred. In November 1932, the socialist camp still gained 37 per cent (compared with almost 40 per cent in 1920), the Catholic camp 15 per cent (compared with almost 18 per cent in 1920), the national camp 43 per cent (37 per cent in 1920) (see Table 8.1).[67] Rohe argues that the stability of social-moral milieus, which coagulated into political camps, remained unchanged, with a general but limited shift to the right. However, the radicalization process both on the left and on the right *within* the camps, which was directed against the traditional parties, was striking: Social Democracy, Liberals, and Conservatives experienced growing competition from Communists, Nazis, and interest parties. It is difficult to decide whether the political actors saw this process as the departure from democracy or rather as the radicalization of camp-specific expectations. Rohe's explanation for the right is more problematic than for the left, which split as early as during the war. He classes Liberals, Conservatives, and *Völkische* together as one camp, which is less convincing given the heterogeneity of those political orientations. A left-leaning, liberal voter with an urban background was miles away from a small-town Nazi supporter. However, Rohe rightly points out that it was also more difficult for Liberals to finally vote for the socialist or the Catholic camps than for the Nazis.

It is a weakness of both concepts that they understand parties in a rather static fashion. This is, to an extent, unhistorical. Being a supporter of the DNVP in 1928 was different to being one in 1920. The same is true of most of the other parties. All parties had undergone profound changes, which—except for the radicalizing KPD—paved the way into the republic for some parts of them, but also resulted in grave internal conflicts. This particularly applied to the right-wing, bourgeois, and initially openly anti-democratic parties. The DVP under the leadership of Gustav Stresemann evolved from an anti-republican into a right-wing liberal Weimar party, pursuing a foreign political course of reconciliation, which led to Locarno (albeit with a still strong authoritarian wing). In the DNVP Reichstag parliamentary group—which in 1920 had still been largely monarchist—a group of conservative 'Tory democrats' (as they called themselves) planned in 1924 to become a conservative republican party and, in so doing, to make the republic more conservative instead of abolishing it.[68] The 1924 and 1928 election results of these two parties can be read as a silent republicanization of large parts of these parties and their voters. For many voters, everyday political and economic life, which became more and more normal, was a much greater reason for this republicanization than the ideological construct of the 'republic'. After all, the willingness for compromise in 1928 even allowed for a grand coalition—who would have thought so in 1920? (see Table 8.2).

The argument that some anti-republicans were getting used to the republic must, of course, not ignore the limitations of this process—particularly on the grounds of everyday life, rather than for programmatic reasons: the migration of dissatisfied voters to interest parties, which accounted for one-seventh of the electorate in 1928; party infighting within the DNVP, which after 1928 resulted in Hugenberg's seizure of power, in a complete change of leadership, and a profound repositioning in the spirit of nationalistic radicalization. During the grand coalition and under the conditions of the Great Depression, increasing demands were voiced in the SPD to adopt a more distinctive social democratic policy style, which finally led to the end of the grand coalition in 1930. Despicable interest politics and intransigent politics based on principle clashed.

This leads on to the question of the striking election successes of the Nazis from the 1930s onwards. Over the course of only four years, the NSDAP grew from a splinter party with 2.6 per cent in 1928 to the strongest party in the Reichstag with 37.4 per cent in 1932.[69] How stable the voters' verdict in fact was and whether the NSDAP would have been able to attract these voters on a long-term basis must remain open. Volatility was high, and in November 1932 the Nazis lost almost a quarter of those voters that they had added compared to 1930 only a few months earlier. Yet the success of the NSDAP did not come out of nowhere. In state elections, the Nazis had already achieved successes in some smaller north and east German states. In Thuringia, they won 11 per cent in 1929, equalling the vote share of the DDP and DVP together.[70] In this sense, the Great Depression only accentuated political affiliations that had already become visible before.

Table 8.2. The Reich Cabinet 1918–1932 with the Most Relevant Cabinet Posts and the Governing Coalition

Start Date	Coalition	Chancellor	Vice-Chancellor	Foreign Affairs	Interior	Reichswehr	Economy	Finance	Labour
10 November 1918	SPD-USPD (Council of People's Representatives)	Without department: Friedrich Ebert (SPD), Philipp Scheidemann (SPD), Otto Landsberg (SPD), Hugo Haase (USPD), Wilhelm Dittmann (USPD), Emil Barth (USPD)							
29 December 1918	SPD (Council of People's Representatives)	Without department: Friedrich Ebert (SPD), Philipp Scheidemann (SPD), Otto Landsberg (SPD), Rudolf Wissell (SPD), Gustav Noske (SPD)							
13 February 1919	SPD-Centre-DDP (Weimar Coalition)	Philipp Scheidemann (SPD)	Eugen Schiffer (DDP), from 30 April 1919: Bernhard Dernburg	Ulrich von Brockdorff-Rantzau (non-affiliated)	Hugo Preuß (DDP)	Gustav Noske (SPD)	Rudolf Wissell (SPD)	Eugen Schiffer (DDP), from 19 April 1919: Bernhard Dernburg (DDP)	Gustav Bauer (SPD)
21 June 1919	SPD-Centre, from Oct. 1919 on also DDP (Weimar Coalition)	Gustav Bauer (SPD)	Matthias Erzberger (Centre), from 2 October 1919 Eugen Schiffer (DDP)	Hermann Müller (SPD)	Eduard David (SPD), from 5.10.1919 Erich Koch (DDP)	Gustav Noske (SPD)	Rudolf Wissell (SPD)	Matthias Erzberger (Centre)	Alexander Schlicke (SPD)
27 March 1920	SPD-Centre-DDP (Weimar Coalition)	Hermann Müller (SPD)	Erich Koch (DDP)	Adolf Köster (SPD)	Erich Koch (DDP)	Otto Geßler (DDP)	Robert Schmidt (SPD)	Joseph Wirth (Centre)	Alexander Schlicke (SPD)
21 June 1920	Centre-DDP-DVP (bourgeois coalition)	Constantin Fehrenbach (Centre)	Rudolf Heinze (DVP)	Walter Simons (non-affiliated)	Erich Koch (DDP)	Otto Geßler (DDP)	Ernst Scholz (DVP)	Joseph Wirth (Centre)	Heinrich Brauns (Centre)

Start Date	Coalition	Chancellor	Vice-Chancellor	Foreign Affairs	Interior	Reichswehr	Economy	Finance	Labour
10 May 1921	SPD-Centre-DDP (Weimar coalition)	Joseph Wirth (Centre)	Gustav Bauer (SPD)	Friedrich Rosen (non-affiliated)	Georg Gradnauer (SPD)	Otto Geßler (DDP)	Robert Schmidt (SPD)	Joseph Wirth (SPD)	Heinrich Brauns (Centre)
26 October 1921	SPD-Centre-DDP (Weimar coalition)	Joseph Wirth (Centre)	Gustav Bauer (SPD)	Joseph Wirth (Centre), 21 January–24 June 1922: Walther Rathenau (DDP)	Adolf Köster (SPD)	Otto Geßler (DDP)	Robert Schmidt (SPD)	Andreas Hermes (Centre)	Heinrich Brauns (Centre)
22 November 1922	DVP-Centre-DDP (bourgeois party coalition)	Wilhelm Cuno (non-affiliated)	–	Frederic von Rosenberg (non-affiliated)	Rudolf Oeser (DDP)	Otto Geßler (DDP)	Johann Becker (DVP)	Andreas Hermes (Centre)	Heinrich Brauns (Centre)
13 August 1923	SPD-Centre-DDP-DVP (Grand coalition)	Gustav Stresemann (DVP)	Robert Schmidt (SPD)	Gustav Stresemann (DVP)	Wilhelm Sollmann (SPD)	Otto Geßler (DDP)	Hans von Raumer (DVP)	Rudolf Hilferding (SPD)	Heinrich Brauns (Centre)
6 October 1923	SPD (until 3 November 1923) Centre-DDP-DVP (Grand coalition)	Gustav Stresemann (DVP)	–	Gustav Stresemann (DVP)	Wilhelm Sollmann (SPD), from 11 November 1923: Karl Jarres (DVP)	Otto Geßler (DDP)	Joseph Koeth (non-affiliated)	Hans Luther (non-affiliated)	Heinrich Brauns (Centre)
30 November 1923	Centre-BVP-DVP-DDP (bourgeois coalition)	Wilhelm Marx (Centre)	Karl Jarres (DVP)	Gustav Stresemann (DVP)	Karl Jarres (UVP)	Otto Geßler (UDP)	Eduard Hamm (DDP)	Hans Luther (non-affiliated)	Heinrich Brauns (Centre)
3 June 1924	Centre-DDP-DVP (bourgeois coalition)	Wilhelm Marx (Centre)	Karl Jarres (DVP)	Gustav Stresemann (DVP)	Karl Jarres (DVP)	Otto Geßler (DDP)	Eduard Hamm (DDP)	Hans Luther (non-affiliated)	Heinrich Brauns (Centre)

(continued)

Table 8.2. Continued

Start Date	Coalition	Chancellor	Vice-Chancellor	Foreign Affairs	Interior	Reichswehr	Economy	Finance	Labour
15 January 1925	Centre-DDP-DVP-DNVP (bourgeois centre-right coalition, including the DNVP)	Hans Luther (non-affiliated)	-	Gustav Stresemann (DVP)	Martin Schiele (DNVP), from 26 October 1925: Otto Geßler (DDP)	Otto Geßler (DDP)	Albert Neuhaus (DNVP), from 26 October 1925: Rudolf Krohne (DVP)	Otto von Schlieben (DNVP), from 26 October 1925: Hans Luther (non-affiliated)	Heinrich Brauns (Centre)
20 January 1926	Centre-BVP-DVP-DDP (bourgeois coalition)	Hans Luther (non-affiliated)	-	Gustav Stresemann (DVP)	Wilhelm Külz (DDP)	Otto Geßler (DDP)	Julius Curtius (DVP)	Peter Reinhold (DDP)	Heinrich Brauns (Centre)
17 May 1926	Centre-DVP-DDP (bourgeois coalition)	Wilhelm Marx (Centre)	-	Gustav Stresemann (DVP)	Wilhelm Külz (DDP)	Otto Geßler (DDP)	Julius Curtius (DVP)	Peter Reinhold (DDP)	Heinrich Brauns (Centre)
29 January 1927	Centre-BVP-DVP-DNVP (bourgeois centre-right coalition, including the DNVP)	Wilhelm Marx (Centre)	Oskar Hergt (DNVP)	Gustav Stresemann (DDP)	Walter von Keudell (DNVP)	Otto Geßler (DDP), from 19 January 1928: Wilhelm Groener (non-affiliated)	Julius Curtius (DVP)	Heinrich Köhler (Centre)	Heinrich Brauns (Centre)

Start Date	Coalition	Chancellor	Vice-Chancellor	Foreign Affairs	Interior	Reichswehr	Economy	Finance	Labour
29 September 1928	SPD-Centre-BVP-DDP-DVP (Grand coalition)	Hermann Müller (SPD)	–	Gustav Stresemann (DVP), from 4 October 1929: Julius Curtius (DVP)	Carl Severing (SPD)	Wilhelm Groener (non-affiliated)	Julius Curtius (DVP), from 23 December 1929: Robert Schmidt (SPD)	Rudolf Hilferding (SPD), from 23 December 1929: Moldenhauer (DVP)	Rudolf Wissell (SPD)
30 March 1930	Presidential cabinet	Heinrich Brüning (Centre)	Hermann Dietrich (DDP/DStP)	Julius Curtius (DVP)	Joseph Wirth (Centre)	Wilhelm Groener (non-affiliated)	Hermann Dietrich (DDP)	Paul Moldenhauer (DVP), from 28 June 1930: Hermann Dietrich (DDP)	Adam Stegerwald (Centre)
9 October 1931	Presidential cabinet	Heinrich Brüning (Centre)	Hermann Dietrich (DStP)	Heinrich Brüning (Centre)	Wilhelm Groener (non-affiliated)	Wilhelm Groener (non-affiliated)	Hermann Warmbold (non-affiliated)	Hermann Dietrich (DStP)	Adam Stegerwald (Centre)
1 June 1932	Presidential cabinet	Franz von Papen (non-affiliated)	–	Konstantin Freiherr von Neurath (non-affiliated)	Wilhelm Freiherr von Gayl (DNVP)	Kurt von Schleicher (non-affiliated)	Hermann Warmbold (non-affiliated)	Johann Ludwig Graf Schwerin von Krosigk (non-affiliated)	Hugo Schäffer (non-affiliated)
3 December 1932	Presidential cabinet	Kurt von Schleicher (non-affiliated)	–	Konstantin Freiherr von Neurath (non-affiliated)	Franz Bracht (non-affiliated)	Kurt von Schleicher (non-affiliated)	Hermann Warmbold (non-affiliated)	Johann Ludwig Graf Schwerin von Krosigk (non-affiliated)	Friedrich Syrup (non-affiliated)

Source: Ursula Büttner, Weimar. Die überforderte Republik 1918-1933. Leistung und Versagen in Staat, Gesellschaft, Wirtschaft und Kultur (Stuttgart: Klett-Cotta, 2008), 810–12.

It is not least due to the Nazis' success in the countryside that even contemporaries, with the sociologist Theodor Geiger leading the way, explained their election victories with the 'panic of the *Mittelstand*'—the lower middle class—in the wake of the economic crisis.[71] Seymour Lipset has referred to this phenomenon as an 'extremism of the centre'. Particularly Jürgen Falter, based on complex (and sometimes risky) statistical calculations, has shown that this is only half the story.[72] It has long been known that habitual non-voters and voters of interest and regional parties migrated to the NSDAP in their droves and that the Nazis were consistently and early on successful particularly in Protestant rural areas (including in formerly left-liberal dominated regions such as Schleswig-Holstein). But Falter could also show that not only liberal elites but also workers, even, in some regions, dissatisfied Catholic members of the (lower) middle classes, and peasants voted for the Nazi party. According to Falter's calculations, 27 per cent of workers—predominantly from smaller companies and in the countryside rather than industrial workers from the mining industry and major industrial enterprises—gave their vote to the NSDAP in the 1932 July elections, which was when the Nazis gained 37 per cent of the vote share.[73] The NSDAP poached in all camps and was the first party to be able to transcend milieu boundaries. Thus, Falter rightly refers to the NSDAP as a 'people's party of protest'.

The most important aspect of Falter's deliberations is the observation of 'intermediate hosts', as he termed particular interest and protest parties, which initially attracted voters from established parties and lost them to the more radical Nazis. This begs the question of how strong milieu affiliations in fact were. There are good reasons not to overestimate them: there were many people who were workers or Catholics but not anchored in a specific milieu, either because they had difficulties settling in after having recently moved or because an affiliation like these was only one among many others.[74] The theory of milieus addresses the respective core groups; the problems, however, are the people at the margins, who belonged to a certain milieu for social structural reasons, but did not so for reasons of sociability. These deliberations do not primarily refer to the declining cohesion of milieus, instead they focus on the dynamics of Weimar society with its new ways of living and biographical challenges: former soldiers who were forced to find new jobs; young women who started jobs; people from the countryside moving to the cities; small craftsmen and traders who were ruined by the economic crisis; peasants and rural workers whose identity was deeply disturbed by the agrarian crisis. Many others, whose lives did not change substantially at first sight, were driven by the fear that things might get worse soon. Weimar society was highly dynamic, which weakened traditional matters of course.

Having said that, people who were susceptible to the National Socialist message were by no means social outsiders. Early on, local studies have shown that the NSDAP was no party of mavericks and desperados, as its adversaries often tried to suggest, but came from the centre of German society. National Socialism not only drew on nationalism but also on the longing for homogeneity and cohesion, at the same time aggressively cracking down on those whom they stigmatized as not being part of this desired community.[75] The Nazis leaned significantly, but not exclusively, on one single milieu or political camp; they propagated to overcome these boundaries in the spirit of the people's community. In doing so, they answered to the deep disappointment that many voters felt with the political elites. The social and national promise inherent to their message not only attracted those with affiliations to the national camp—albeit they were still the most important voter basis of the Nazis.

Beyond and, in a sense, above traditional milieu affiliations—that is socialist, liberal-bourgeois, Catholic, conservative—the orientation towards the national camp was the most dominant and, which is more important, the most stable one. It is a different kettle of fish whether this entailed the question of 'republic or dictatorship'. Rather than the system of government, issues such as justice, belonging, and a strong need for homogeneity seemed to be of greater importance, particularly in the face of experiences of disunity, for which the parties and their limited capability to cooperate were blamed.

Conclusion

The Great Depression aggravated unease in the republic of parties. This feeling was not so much due to actual achievements or failures of the political system or to an intrinsic democratic awareness. Rather, it measured the existing political mechanisms and conflicts against the social vision of a society of similarities instead of interest political or ideological differences. This society would ultimately overcome political affiliations based on belonging to milieus or camps, establish a tightly run polity instead of a democracy based on negotiations and create unity in the face of foreign adversaries and the deep trauma that the military defeat had caused. Many of these longings tapped into discourses from the First World War, when a myth was built around the concept of community, which was used time and again as a counter image to the republic. And yet, the citizens of the Weimar Republic no longer wanted to be ruled by an old-style authoritarian government—this was a fundamental change compared to the situation before 1918.

Therefore, despite its end, we can still describe the history of the Weimar Republic as one of democratization. This does not only apply to the extent of inclusion, the extension of citizenship, and direct participation of its citizens. Rather than using and projecting back a normative concept of democracy in the sense of today's liberal and parliamentary democracy as a measuring stick, it is more useful to explore the inherent nature of democracy in its traditional sense as the rule of the people, regardless of the political goals that were pursued. The citizens of the Weimar Republic were highly interested in politics, and despite some elections with a decline in turnout (albeit never under 75 per cent: 1928), they diligently went to the ballot, as much and to some extent more often than in many other European states.[76] However, in the final stages they increasingly voted for parties and politicians who were not considered democratic through the lens of western liberalism—and this is not only true of the Nazis. However, these were still elections. They were the result of a longing for leadership and authority, a clear direction and belonging. In this sense, Weimar voters were in line with those of other

European countries. Nationalism and the longing for strong leaders were also common in other states during the inter-war period. In this context, it might be more useful to compare the Weimar Republic with its neighbours in the east and in the south instead of those in the west, which became role models only after 1945.

It was Carl Schmitt's view that 'democracy' was not necessarily only in place when a large number of persons who had the trust of the people (= parliament) took decisions, but also if there was just one person of trust, i.e. a dictator who had been legitimized by acclamation through a plebiscite. The dictator whose legitimacy was based on a popular vote was a people's representative in the same way that parliament was, and hence, according to Schmitt, he could enforce politics against the apparatuses of administration and associations.[77] This interpretation referred to a concept of the people's will that had no real sense of and use for plurality, but focused on a united people of citizens and a coherent *volonté générale*, which resulted from the former. This view was commonly held in Weimar Germany. The fact that in the end someone like Adolf Hitler would appear was unimaginable at the beginning of the republic. It is, however, beyond debate that he was a leader, if not desired, then at least accepted by large parts of the 'people'.

Translated from German by Christine Brocks.

Notes

1. 'Amerikanische Demokratie und ihre Lehren III', *Frankfurter Zeitung*, 250 (3 Apr. 1919).
2. See Lothar Machtan, *Die Abdankung: Wie Deutschlands gekrönte Häupter aus der Geschichte fielen* (Berlin: Propyläen, 2008).
3. Axel Weipert, *Die zweite Revolution: Rätebewegung in Berlin 1919/1920* (Berlin: be.bra Wissenschaft Verlag, 2015), 28–31.
4. Hans-Joachim Bieber, *Bürgertum in der Revolution: Bürgerräte und Bürgerstreiks in Deutschland 1918–1920* (Hamburg: Christians, 1992), 34–7.
5. For the history of the council movement see Eberhard Kolb, *Die Arbeiterräte in der deutschen Innenpolitik* (Düsseldorf: Droste 1962) and Walter Tormin, *Zwischen Rätediktatur und sozialer Demokratie* (Düsseldorf: Droste, 1954).
6. See Sebastian Ullrich, *Der Weimar-Komplex: Das Scheitern der ersten deutschen Demokratie und die politische Kultur der frühen Bundesrepublik* (Göttingen: Wallstein, 2009).
7. See Dieter Gosewinkel, *Einbürgern und Ausschließen: Die Nationalisierung der Staatsangehörigkeit vom Deutschen Bund bis zur Bundesrepublik Deutschland* (Göttingen: Vandenhoeck & Ruprecht, 2001), 345–52.
8. See Ute Rosenbusch, *Der Weg zum Frauenwahlrecht in Deutschland* (Baden-Baden: Nomos, 1998).
9. See Kathleen Canning, 'Das Geschlecht der Revolution—Stimmrecht und Staatsbürgertum 1918/19', in Alexander Gallus (ed.), *Die vergessene Revolution von 1918/19* (Göttingen: Vandenhoeck & Ruprecht, 2010), 84–116.
10. Magnus Hirschfeld and Franziska Mann, *Was jede Frau vom Wahlrecht wissen muss* (Berlin: Pulvermacher 1918); Adele Schreiber, *Revolution und Frauenwahlrecht: Frauen! Lernt wählen!* (Berlin: Arbeitsgemeinschaft für Staatsbürgerliche und Wirtschaftliche Bildung, 1918). See Kathleen Canning, 'Geschlecht', 110–11.

11. This calculation is based on the age pyramid from 1925 printed in Detlev Peukert, *Die Weimarer Republik: Krisenjahre der Klassischen Moderne* (Frankfurt/Main: Suhrkamp, 1987), 93.
12. Klaus J. Bade and Jochen Oltmer, 'Deutschland', in Klaus J. Bade et al. (eds), *Enzyklopädie Migration in Europa: Vom 17. Jahrhundert bis zur Gegenwart* (Paderborn: Schöningh, 2007), 141–70, 153–4.
13. Bernhard Vogel et al., *Wahlen in Deutschland: Theorie—Geschichte—Dokumente 1848–1970* (Berlin: De Gruyter, 1971), 293, 296.
14. See Detlef Lehnert, '"Weimars" Chancen und Möglichkeiten, Strukturen und Normen', in Michael Dreyer and Andreas Braune (eds), *Weimar als Herausforderung: Die Weimarer Republik und die Demokratie im 21. Jahrhundert* (Stuttgart: Steiner, 2016), 103–21, here 108–11; Jürgen Falter, Thomas Lindenberger, and Siegfried Schumann, *Wahlen und Abstimmungen in der Weimarer Republik* (Munich: Beck, 1986), 81–5; Vogel et al., *Wahlen*, 141.
15. Julia Sneeringer, *Winning Women's Votes: Propaganda and Politics in Weimar Germany* (Chapel Hill, NC: University of North Carolina Press, 2002).
16. See Helen Boak, *Women in the Weimar Republic* (Manchester: Manchester University Press, 2013), 78–82.
17. Angelika Schaser, 'Bürgerliche Frauen auf dem Weg in die linksliberalen Parteien 1908–1933', *Historische Zeitschrift*, 263 (1996), 641–80, here 665–6.
18. See Gabriele Bremme, *Die politische Rolle der Frau in Deutschland: Eine Untersuchung über den Einfluß der Frauen bei Wahlen und ihre Teilnahme in Partei und Parlament* (Göttingen: Vandenhoeck & Ruprecht, 1956), 68–77.
19. Lehnert, '"Weimars" Chancen', 108–9.
20. See Vogel et al., *Wahlen*, 141.
21. See Thomas Mergel, *Parlamentarische Kultur in der Weimarer Republik: Politische Kommunikation, symbolische Politik und Öffentlichkeit im Reichstag* (Düsseldorf: Droste, 2012), 104–8; Boak, *Women*, 91–100.
22. Rainer M. Lepsius, 'Parteiensystem und Sozialstruktur: Zum Problem der Demokratisierung der deutschen Gesellschaft', in Lepsius, *Demokratie in Deutschland* (Göttingen: Vandenhoeck & Ruprecht, 1993), 25–50.
23. See e.g. Cornelia Rauh-Kühne, *Katholisches Milieu und Kleinstadtgesellschaft: Ettlingen 1918–1939* (Sigmaringen: Thorbecke, 1991).
24. Karl Rohe, *Wahlen und Wählertraditionen in Deutschland. Kulturelle Grundlagen deutscher Parteien und Parteiensysteme im 19. und 20. Jahrhundert* (Frankfurt/Main: Suhrkamp 1992), 121–63.
25. See Maik Ohnezeit, *Zwischen 'schärfster Opposition' und dem 'Willen zur Macht': Die Deutschnationale Volkspartei in der Weimarer Republik 1918–1928* (Düsseldorf: Droste, 2011).
26. See Jean-Marie Mayeur, *La vie politique sous la troisième république* (Paris: Éd. du Seuil, 1984).
27. See Siegfried Weichlein, 'Teilhabe und Ordnung: Zur Politisierung der Weimarer Gesellschaft', in Karin Groh and Christine Weinbach (eds), *Zur Genealogie des politischen Raums: Politische Strukturen im Wandel* (Wiesbaden: VS Verlag, 2005), 53–76.
28. See Jörn Retterath, *'Was ist das Volk?' Volks- und Gemeinschaftskonzepte der politischen Mitte 1917–1924* (Berlin: De Gruyter Oldenbourg, 2016), 272–372.
29. 'Die Berufsgliederung des neuen Reichstags', *Der Tag* (nightime edition, 17 June 1924).

30. For the election system in the Reich and the German states see Eberhard Schanbacher, *Parlamentarische Wahlen und Wahlsystem in der Weimarer Republik* (Düsseldorf: Droste, 1982).
31. *Verhandlungen der verfassunggebenden Deutschen Nationalversammlung* (Berlin: Julius Sittenfeld 1920), vol. 336, 242.
32. Falter et al., *Wahlen und Abstimmungen*, 44.
33. For a summary of the contemporary arguments and proposals see Ernst Rudolf Huber, *Deutsche Verfassungsgeschichte seit 1789*, vol. 6. *Die Weimarer Reichsverfassung* (Stuttgart: Kohlhammer, 1981), 352–3, Dieter Nohlen, *Wahlrecht und Parteiensystem* (Opladen: Budrich, 2009), 325–6; Johannes Schauff (ed.), *Neues Wahlrecht: Beiträge zur Wahlreform* (Berlin: Stilke, 1929). See Schanbacher, *Wahlen*, 118–49.
34. For the various reform initiatives of the DDP see Werner Schneider, *Die Deutsche Demokratische Partei in der Weimarer Republik 1924–1930* (Munich: Fink, 1978), 146–51.
35. See Ferdinand Hermes, *Demokratie oder Anarchie? Untersuchung über die Verhältniswahl* (Cologne: Westdeutscher Verlag, 1968; 1st ed. 1951); Dankwart A. Rüstow, 'Einige Bemerkungen zur Debatte über das Prinzip der Verhältniswahl', *Zeitschrift für die gesamte Staatswissenschaft*, 106 (1950), 324–48.
36. Matthias Catón, *Wahlsysteme und Parteiensysteme im Kontext: Vergleichende Analyse der Wirkung von Wahlsystemen unter verschiedenen Kontextbedingungen*, Ph.D. thesis, Heidelberg, 2009.
37. Dolf Steinberger and Bernhard Vogel (eds), *Die Wahl der Parlamente und anderer Staatsorgane: Ein Handbuch*, 2 vols (Berlin: De Gruyter, 1969).
38. Nohlen, *Wahlrecht*, 45.
39. Reinhard Schiffers, *Elemente direkter Demokratie im Weimarer Regierungssystem* (Düsseldorf: Droste, 1971).
40. For the constitutional role of the German Reich President see Huber, *Deutsche Verfassungsgeschichte*, 307–23.
41. Max Weber, 'The President of the Reich', in Weber, *Political Writings*, ed. Peter Lassman and Ronald Speirs (Cambridge: Cambridge University Press, 2003), 304–8, here 305, 308.
42. See Wolfram Pyta, *Hindenburg: Herrschaft zwischen Hohenzollern und Hitler* (Munich: Siedler, 2007), 461–76.
43. Jürgen W. Falter, *Hitlers Wähler* (Munich: Beck 1991), 123–6; Hans Mommsen, *Aufstieg und Untergang der Republik von Weimar* (Berlin: Ullstein 1998), 293–6.
44. For the presidential election in 1932 see Larry Eugene Jones, *Hitler versus Hindenburg: The 1932 Presidential Elections and the End of the Weimar Republic* (Cambridge: Cambridge University Press, 2016); Pyta, *Hindenburg*, 645–83.
45. Adolf Hitler in an election speech in Hamburg (1 Mar. 1932) in Institut für Zeitgeschichte (ed.), *Adolf Hitler: Schriften, Reden, Anordnungen*, vol. 4/3 (Munich: Saur, 1997), 153–64, 161.
46. Huber, *Verfassungsgeschichte*, 432–6.
47. Ottmar Jung, 'Plebiszitärer Durchbruch 1929? Zur Bedeutung von Volksbegehren und Volksentscheid gegen den Youngplan für die NSDAP', *Geschichte und Gesellschaft*, 15 (1989), 489–510.
48. For a regional example see Siegfried Weichlein, *Sozialmilieus und politische Kultur in der Weimarer Republik. Lebenswelt, Vereinskultur, Politik in Hessen* (Göttingen: Vandenhoeck & Ruprecht, 1996), 111–15.
49. 'Wahlsabotage', *Deutsche Allgemeine Zeitung* (27 May 1920). See also Margaret L. Anderson, *Practicing Democracy: Elections and Political Culture in Imperial Germany* (Princeton: Princeton University Press, 2000).

50. 'Ein bekehrter Deutschnationaler', *Berliner Tageblatt*, 578 (5 Dec. 1924).
51. See Benjamin Schröder, *Händler und Helden: Wahlen und politische Konfliktkultur in Deutschland und Großbritannien, 1918–35*, Ph.D. thesis, Humboldt University Berlin, 2019.
52. See Bernhard Fulda, *Press and Politics in the Weimar Republic* (Oxford: Oxford University Press, 2009). With a focus on election campaigns Schröder, *Händler*, 245–60.
53. Dirk Lau, *Wahlkämpfe der Weimarer Republik: Propaganda und Programme der politischen Parteien bei den Wahlen zum Deutschen Reichstag von 1924 bis 1930* (Marburg: Tectum Verlag, 2008), 195–255.
54. *Der Abend* (16 Apr. 1928).
55. Thomas Mergel, 'Propaganda in der Kultur des Schauens: Visuelle Politik in der Weimarer Republik', in Wolfgang Hardtwig (ed.), *Ordnungen in der Krise: Zur Politischen Kulturgeschichte Deutschlands 1900–1933* (Munich: Oldenbourg, 2007), 531–59. See also Daniela Janusch, *Die plakative Propaganda der Sozialdemokratischen Partei zu den Reichstagswahlen 1928–1932* (Bochum: Brockmeyer, 1989).
56. Schröder, *Händler*, 70–1.
57. Gerhard Paul, *Aufstand der Bilder: Die NS-Propaganda vor 1933* (Bonn: Dietz, 1990); Corey Ross, *Media and the Making of Modern Germany: Mass Communications, Society, and Politics from the Empire to the Third Reich* (Oxford: Oxford University Press, 2010), 238–42.
58. Randall L. Bytwerk, 'Die nationalsozialistische Versammlungspraxis: Die Anfänge vor 1933', in Gerald Diesener and Rainer Gries (eds), *Propaganda in Deutschland* (Darmstadt: Primus, 1996), 35–50.
59. Schröder, *Händler*, 418–19.
60. Sabine Behrenbeck, '"Der Führer": Die Einführung eines politischen Markenartikels', in Diesener and Gries (eds), *Propaganda in Deutschland*, 51–78.
61. Jones, *Hitler versus Hindenburg*, 293–7. In 1932 Hitler undertook five such flights, but he was not the only one. Hindenburg was meant to travel across Germany on the Zeppelin airship, but the airship was already booked for a journey to South America.
62. Thomas Mergel, 'Führer, Volksgemeinschaft und Maschine: Politische Erwartungsstrukturen in der Weimarer Republik und dem Nationalsozialismus 1918–1936', in Wolfgang Hardtwig (ed.), *Politische Kulturgeschichte der Zwischenkriegszeit 1918–1933* (Göttingen: Vandenhoeck & Ruprecht, 2005), 91–127.
63. Klaus Schreiner, '"Wann kommt der Retter Deutschlands?" Formen und Funktionen von politischem Messianismus in der Weimarer Republik', *Saeculum*, 49 (1998), 107–60.
64. Falter et al., *Wahlen und Abstimmungen*, 39–85.
65. Heinrich August Winkler, *Weimar 1918–1933: Die Geschichte der ersten deutschen Demokratie* (Munich: Beck, 1993), 70.
66. It should be noted that the Weimar Coalition received 49% of the Reichstag seats in 1928.
67. Karl Rohe, *Wahlen und Wählertraditionen in Deutschland. Kulturelle Grundlagen deutscher Parteien und Parteiensysteme im 19. und 20. Jahrhundert* (Frankfurt/Main: Suhrkamp, 1992), 143–9.
68. Thomas Mergel, 'Das Scheitern des deutschen Tory-Konservatismus: Die Umformung der DNVP zu einer rechtsradikalen Partei 1928–1932', *Historische Zeitschrift*, 276 (2003), 323–68.
69. See the chapter by Daniel Siemens in this volume.
70. Falter et al., *Wahlen und Abstimmungen*, 111.
71. Theodor Geiger, 'Panik im Mittelstand', *Die Arbeit*, 7 (1930), 637–54.

72. Falter, *Hitlers Wähler*. See also Thomas Childers, *The Nazi Voter: The Social Foundations of Fascism in Germany, 1919–1933* (Chapel Hill, NC: University of North Carolina Press, 1983). For a focus on the idea of the radicalized middle classes see Jürgen W. Falter, 'Radicalization of the Middle Classes or Mobilization of the Unpolitical? The Theories of Seymour Martin Lipset and Reinhard Bendix on the Electoral Support of the NSDAP in the Light of Recent Research', *Social Science Information*, 2 (1981), 389–430.
73. See the table in Jürgen W. Falter, 'Warum die deutschen Arbeiter während des "Dritten Reiches" zu Hitler standen: Einige Anmerkungen zu Gunther Mais Beitrag über die Unterstützung des nationalsozialistischen Herrschaftssystems durch Arbeiter', *Geschichte und Gesellschaft*, 13 (1987), 217–31, here 229.
74. For a cautious evaluation of the importance of the milieu concept see Adelheid von Saldern, 'Sozialmilieus und der Aufstieg des Nationalsozialismus in Norddeutschland (1930–1933)', in Frank Bajohr (ed.), *Nationalsozialismus in Norddeutschland* (Hamburg: Ergebnisse, 1993), 20–52.
75. William Sheridan Allen, *The Nazi Seizure of Power: The Experience of a Single German Town, 1930–1935* (Chicago: Quadrangle Books, 1984).
76. Participation in political elections differed across Europe after the end of the First World War: 70–80% in Great Britain, 80% in France, 57% in Italy in 1919. Belgium and the Netherlands required their citizens to vote.
77. Carl Schmitt, *Die geistesgeschichtliche Lage des heutigen Parlamentarismus* (Berlin: Duncker & Humblot 1991; 1st ed. 1926), 42.

Bibliography

Boak, Helen, *Women in the Weimar Republic* (Manchester: Manchester University Press, 2013).
Canning, Kathleen, 'Claiming Citizenship: Suffrage and Subjectivity in Germany after First World War', in Kathleen Canning et al. (eds), *Weimar Publics/ Weimar Subjects: Rethinking the Political Culture of Germany in the 1920s* (New York, Oxford: Berghahn, 2010), 116–37.
Childers, Thomas, *The Nazi Voter: The Social Foundations of Fascism in Germany, 1919–1933* (Chapel Hill, NC: University of North Carolina Press, 1983).
Falter, Jürgen W., Thomas Lindenberger, and Siegfried Schumann, *Wahlen und Abstimmungen in der Weimarer Republik* (Munich: Beck, 1986).
Jones, Larry Eugene, *Hitler versus Hindenburg: The 1932 Presidential Elections and the End of the Weimar Republic* (Cambridge: Cambridge University Press, 2015).
Jones, Larry Eugene, and James Retallack (eds), *Elections, Mass Politics and Social Change in Modern Germany* (Cambridge: Cambridge University Press, 1992).
Mergel, Thomas, *Parlamentarische Kultur in der Weimarer Republik: Politische Kommunikation, symbolische Politik und Öffentlichkeit im Reichstag*, 3rd ed. (Düsseldorf: Droste, 2012).
Rohe, Karl (ed.), *Elections, Parties and Political Traditions: Social Foundations of German Parties and Party Systems 1867–1987* (New York: Berg, 1990).
Ross, Corey, *Media and the Making of Modern Germany: Mass Communications, Society, and Politics from the Empire to the Third Reich* (Oxford: Oxford University Press, 2008).
Sneeringer, Julia, *Winning Women's Votes: Propaganda and Politics in Weimar Germany* (Chapel Hill, NC: University of North Carolina Press, 2002).

CHAPTER 9

FEDERALISM, REGIONALISM, AND THE CONSTRUCTION OF SPACES

SIEGFRIED WEICHLEIN

ONE result of the 1918 revolution was the sweeping parliamentarization and democratization of all regional public authorities: the municipalities, counties, provinces, and Länder along with the Reich. Imperial Germany came to an end first in the Länder (for example in states such as Saxony, Bavaria, Lippe, or Anhalt, which constituted the federal nation-state), where some of the monarchies fell before 9 November 1918. Even the left-liberal constitutionalist Hugo Preuß, whose first draft of a constitution envisioned a highly unitary state, recognized this. In 1922 he reflected on the events of November 1918:

> In contrast to the revolutions of firmly established nation-states, here the decisive upheaval did not originate in the center and spread from there; rather it progressed from the periphery to the center. Clearly it was a very decentralized revolution; the traditional list of 25 individual states corresponded to 25 small revolutions, which is precisely what enabled these states to persevere under the new conditions.[1]

The Weimar Republic also recognized Länder, and not merely as administrative units. They had their own elected parliaments and democratically legitimized governments. Although the Weimar National Assembly gave the Reich more power over the Länder than Imperial Germany had done, it did not turn it into a strictly unitary or even centralized government. Instead, Hugo Preuß developed the concept of the 'decentralized unitary state', an idea that other politicians would later endorse. But each party understood the notion differently: leftists and left-wing liberals tended to emphasize the unitarian, unity-oriented aspect and promoted a democratic unitary state for all, while the Catholic Centre Party in the Southern German Länder and in the Rhineland favoured 'decentralization and hoped for the end of Prussia.'[2] But Prussia and the federal state persisted, while the overall emphasis shifted toward unitarianism. As Hugo

Preuß put it, the unity of the Reich was 'the first priority, and the division of the Länder secondary'.[3]

Thus, the Weimar Republic was a multi-level system from the very beginning, dealing with differences and tensions. But the tensions of 1919 were different from those of 1870/71. The founding histories of the Weimar Republic and Imperial Germany, their dynamics and their actors, differed greatly. In 1870/71 the Länder, called *Bundesstaaten*, had created the Reich. It started with the princes granting their approval; only then did the Reichstag deputies, headed by Eduard Simson, offer the crown to Wilhelm I. In the revolution of 9 November 1918 and in the elections to the National Assembly of 19 January 1919, voices of the entire German electorate in the Reich and the Länder—to which women had now been added—rose in resistance to the war, the emperor, and the old 'rotten system'. The Reich finally had been legitimized as a democracy. No longer was it a 'system of circumvented decisions' or a 'delaying formulaic compromise'.[4] Yet even after 1918, the region—both in the Weimar Republic and later in the Federal Republic—had importance: it represented politically authorised territorial rule and was a 'political landscape', as well as a space for production, transport, trade, and for remembering and narrating spatial identities. The region is understood here as 'a flexibly definable structure of the middle level, which enables … the practical definition and delineation of meaningful fields of research between the local (or micro) level and the national (or macro) level'.[5] It presented an argument in public political debates, in local literature and travelogues, and an imagined reference in architecture and painting. Several of these Weimar Republic spatial constructions will be examined here.

The following chapter traces the history of the relationship between the Reich and the Länder, their shifting conceptual frameworks, their consensus patterns, and their conflicts. It examines processes of regionalization in politics, economy, and culture, and focus on both structural processes of regionalization and their cultural interpretation and appropriation. Three areas stand at the centre of the analysis: first, the relationship between Reich and Länder and the dualism between the Reich and Prussia; secondly, the formation of space in the Weimar welfare state and economic decentralization; and thirdly, the Heimat movement.

Federal Politics and the Dualism between Reich and Prussia

From the beginning of the Weimar Republic, the relationship between Reich and Länder was not that of centre to periphery.[6] This was due to the simultaneous revolutions and the democratic representation featured in both. Even if Prussia officially consisted of 'provinces' with a governor (Oberpräsident) heading the administration, these provinces were still not subordinate administrative units: they had voting rights in the National Council (Reichsrat) and had their own provincial state parliaments. On the one hand, the Länder competed with one another, but mostly with Prussia—the biggest and most populous of them. On the other hand, they all competed together with the Reich when it generated initiatives that challenged the federal order or threatened the existence of smaller Länder.

As unitary as the arguments of left-liberals and Social Democrats were after their bad experiences with federalism in Imperial Germany, they could hardly overlook the fact that the Länder had been reorganized in a democratic-parliamentary manner. The fear of Bolshevik centralism further boosted the federal pattern of the Weimar Republic. An overly centralized economy and financial sector would not only invite a Bolshevist revolution; it would increase its chances of success.[7] Many anti-communists believed in 1918/19 that decentralization would thwart a Bolshevist party dictatorship in Germany. On the other hand, the democratic left wing clung to a strongly unitarian concept of democracy. The Paris peace negotiations also made it seem advisable to strengthen the Reich unity against any form of secession or annexation.[8] In general, the war economy and war propaganda had done much to erase federal distinctions and to promote the interests of the Reich. The consequences of war were borne by the Reich alone, and not by the Länder.

Federalism was a constant structure in Weimar politics and society. By 1919, twenty-five Länder remained, although Prussia alone made up two-thirds of the territory and held about 60 per cent of the population. The history of the Weimar Republic is also one of constant attempts to restructure the Reich and the Länder. The 'decentralized unitary state' relied on the unitary state, which was organized in a decentralized manner. The Länder formed little more than self-governing bodies with increased competences. They would be administrative units capable of self-administration, but not of self-legislation and certainly not of self-government. Among the Social Democrats in the Reich, this was met with applause. But it clashed with Länder governments, which they often led and which after 1918 had the same democratic parliamentary legitimacy as the Reich government. Thus it was often the Social Democratic or Independent Social Democratic state presidents who protested against the unitary conceptions of the SPD delegates in the National Assembly in Weimar—especially that of Bavarian Ministerial President Kurt Eisner of the USPD (Independent Social Democratic Party). Not even the decidedly unitarian SPD (Social Democratic Party) could support splitting Prussia and put federalism on a new footing. Rather, the Prussian SPD generally agreed that the Free State of Prussia was the first instalment towards a democratic unitary republic. Democratic Prussia represented the heart of a future unitarian Reich, they argued. This remained the approach of the Prussian government until it was toppled in 1932. The Prussian Minister-President Otto Braun (SPD) said in 1927 that 'Prussia, with its 40 million inhabitants, must remain intact, for it will—and ultimately must—form the core of the future unitary state.'[9] According to Braun, democracy and the republic would not be secured by reorganizing the Reich into Länder of equal size. It would only succeed if the other Länder gradually merged into Prussia, the 'democratic bulwark'.[10]

With regards to its Länder, the Weimar Republic largely kept the territorial order of Imperial Germany. In 1920, the two states of Reuß were merged into the Republic of

Reuß, and Coburg joined Bavaria. In 1922 Pyrmont joined Prussia, followed by Waldeck in 1929. The only major territorial reorganization was the new Free State of Thuringia, under which seven states were joined by a Reichstag law on 30 April 1920: Saxony-Weimar-Eisenach, Saxony-Meiningen, Reuß, Saxony-Altenburg, Saxony-Gotha (not including the region around Coburg), as well as Schwarzburg-Rudolstadt and Schwarzburg-Sondershausen. The city of Weimar, so important for the German cultural nation, also became part of Thuringia.[11] Aside from Prussia and Thuringia, in order of population size, there were the Länder of Bavaria, Saxony, Württemberg, Baden, Hesse, Mecklenburg-Schwerin, Oldenburg, Brunswick, Anhalt, Lippe, Mecklenburg-Strelitz, Waldeck, Schaumburg-Lippe, and the Hanseatic free cities of Hamburg, Bremen, and Lübeck. Thus, the number of Länder dropped from twenty-five to eighteen. According to the Weimar Constitution, all state governments were represented in the National Council roughly according to their size; Prussia represented in the beginning only twenty-five of the sixty-three votes in the National Council, divided in half between the state government and the twelve provinces and Berlin (1919). Of the sixty-six votes in the National Council in 1921, Prussia had twenty-six, Bavaria ten, Saxony seven, Württemberg four, Baden three, Hamburg and Mecklenburg-Schwerin two each, and the other Länder and Hanseatic cities one vote each. The areas in which the Reich held responsibility for legislation grew significantly. The National Council maintained the right to veto, which the Reichstag could then overrule with a two-thirds majority, though this remained an unlikely scenario.

While the Weimar Constitution clearly emphasized unitarianism in financial, economic, social, and transport policy, it did not interfere with the cultural, educational, and law-enforcement sovereignty of the Länder. After 1949, the Federal Republic of Germany adopted the same arrangement, although the Weimar Republic—unlike Imperial Germany—had the legal option to intervene in the states' sovereignty and reorganize them territorially. Nevertheless, the constitutional deliberations did not lead to such territorial reorganizations: 'The political revolution that swept away the old form of government ... was not followed by a "second revolution" that did away with the dynastic-style federal state structure.'[12] While there were many such plans, most of them hit a political brick wall. Some proposed uniting the two Mecklenburgs, or combining the Lippe states and disparate entities such as Oldenburg or Braunschweig. Still, it was remarkable that, from a national perspective, the NSDAP (National Socialist Workers' Party) managed to achieve above-average results after 1929 in precisely those Länder—including Thuringia, Lippe, Hesse, Mecklenburg-Schwerin, and Oldenburg—where territorial reorganization was permanently on the political agenda. In January 1930 Thuringia became the first state to elect a National Socialist minister: Wilhelm Frick.

In the end, there was neither a unitarian reorganization of the Reich nor a strengthening of federalism. Even after 1928, following the Reich reform plans, the order of 1919 remained in place with the exceptions of Thuringia, Pyrmont and then Waldeck. Advocates of the democratic unitary state did not manage to fortify republican democracy and culture against particularist and anti-republican tendencies in the Länder and regions, nor did the few democratic federalists manage to establish the federal state as a constitutive element of democracy. Indeed, both federalists and proponents of a unitary government worked towards ending the republic after 1930: the federalists were eagerly attempting to limit the powers of the republican Reich for conservative and republican-sceptical reasons, while the right-wing centralists were committed to turning the federal order into an authoritarian unitary state.[13]

While the relationship between Reich and Länder was laid out in the constitution with the aim of ensuring peaceful conflict resolution, there was nevertheless a series of violent conflicts between 1919 and 1923 that revolved around the democratic and not the federal order in the Reich. There were four armed interventions by the Reich in the sovereignty of the states, called *Reichsexekutionen* (Reich executions): after the Kapp putsch in 1920 against the Thuringian states and especially against Gotha; in the 1923 Reich crisis against Saxony and indirectly against Thuringia; and finally, in 1932, against Prussia. What looked at first like a defence against left-wing extremists ultimately developed a momentum that was difficult to comprehend, and it was sometimes unclear whether these Reich executions helped to secure democracy. By 1932, when the Reich acted against Prussia, this was certainly no longer the case.[14]

In the autumn of 1923, the option of a Reich execution against Saxony was discussed: the aim was to overthrow the Saxon coalition government of SPD and KPD (Communist Party) under the leadership of Social Democrat Erich Zeigner. Since the Social Democratic Party was part of the grand coalition at Reich level, this amounted to a dispute within the SPD. While the non-Socialist ministers in Berlin considered the mere presence of Communist ministers in the Saxon government to be a breach of the constitution, the SPD ministers would have preferred the Saxon cabinet to resign on its own initiative or under pressure from Reich sanctions. Zeigner rejected that idea, because he believed that only the Saxon state parliament had the right to remove him. Reich Chancellor Gustav Stresemann resorted then to the solution of a Reich execution. With the help of the Reichswehr, he forcibly removed the Saxon state government in Dresden. The appointed civil commissioner, Karl Rudolf Heintze of Stresemann's Deutsche Volkspartei (DVP, German People's Party), acted as Reich Commissioner for Saxony and cleared all Communists and leftist Social Democrats from government and administrative posts. He even banned Social Democratic newspapers. Thuringia had also been governed by the SPD together with the KPD from 16 October 1923. As a consequence, the Reich Cabinet decided on 6 November 1923 to carry out a *Reichsexekution*; in the end a military intervention was not launched, as the two Communist ministers resigned on 12 November, followed by the state government on 12 December. Saxony, the cradle of German social democracy, now saw a dramatic voter shift to the right, accompanied by the fear of civil war; the SPD in particular lost dramatically. As in Thuringia, the political right became strong quite early on.

At the same time, the Reich government did not use the same means to intervene against the right-wing authoritarian regime of Gustav Ritter von Kahr in Bavaria. On 26 September 1923, the Bavarian government named von Kahr General State Commissioner with dictatorial powers, which von Kahr used to form a triumvirate together with the Bavarian Military District Commander General Otto von Lossow and the Head of the Bavarian State Police, Hans von Seißer. This meant that a right-wing dictatorship was within reach in Bavaria—exactly what the coalitions of the Social Democrats with the Communists in Saxony and Thuringia, as well as the 'Proletarian Hundreds', paramilitary groups organized by the KPD, had been trying to thwart. For a while it looked like the Länder governments could be capable of 'checkmating the Reich's power'. That generals like von Lossow could give orders to Länder governments was as much an absurdity in the republic as it was a 'bankruptcy of Reich authority'.[15] But for the Munich triumvirate, it was not about Bavaria seceding from the German Reich; rather, it was about building a national right-wing dictatorship modelled on Italy, where Mussolini had come to power a year earlier with his staged 'March on Rome' on 28 October 1922. The Munich 'March on Berlin', under the leadership of Adolf Hitler, which is so aptly called the 'Beer Hall Putsch', failed on 9 November 1923 under gunfire from the Bavarian State Police. The political lessons were soon drawn: Hitler abandoned the Italian solution—the putsch—and Berlin did not dare to intervene for fear of testing the loyalty of the Reichswehr troops.[16]

The fourth Reich execution contributed to the authoritarian restructuring of the Reich. On 20 July 1932, the Reich government overthrew the SPD-led government of Prussia, under threat of violence. Even the right-wing Bavarian government protested. With the removal of the Social Democrat Otto Braun as Prussian Minister-President, Reich Chancellor Franz von Papen had eliminated the most important obstacle that could have hindered his authoritarian reorganization of the Reich. His pretext for this action was the restoration of public order following the 'Bloody Sunday of Altona', which had cost eighteen lives; but his goal was to completely transform the Reich. Controlling Prussia was the key to achieving this goal.[17]

In fact, the July 1932 Reich execution on Prussia was an anti-democratic and authoritarian answer to a question that others asked as well: how could a federal state exist if one of its member bodies accounted for two-thirds of its territory? A reform of the Reich would have to eradicate the dualism between Prussia and the Reich and replace it with a new territorial order of approximately equal parts. Hugo Preuß had already laid out plans along these lines in early 1919. There were four strands in this long, entangled debate. First, the dualism could remain. Second, Prussian hegemony could return, as in Imperial Germany. Third, it would be possible to divide Prussia into several states. And fourth, Prussia could join with other northern and central German Länder to form an Imperial Territory (Reichsland) under the immediate control of the Reich, as Alsace-Lorraine had been before 1918.[18] This last option was popular in the Prussian government. It was in this spirit that Finance Minister Hermann Höpker-Aschoff of the left-liberal German Democratic Party (DDP) formulated a historical comparison in 1928: 'Just as the Northern Confederation of 1867 was the precursor of the German federal state of 1871, so might a Reichsland of North Germany be the precursor of a unified German state.'[19] Not one of these reform plans was realized, despite numerous commission meetings and much spilled ink. The Reich execution of 20 July 1932 against Prussia provided a political cutoff to this discussion. Nevertheless, the Reich reform plans continued to have an impact beyond 1933 and even 1945.

Germany's political parties were not centralized; instead, they had party districts—regional and local associations that corresponded to the territorial order. Regional political cultures shaped the parties and the party system. On 12 November 1918, the Bayerische Volkspartei (BVP, Bavarian People's Party) separated from the Catholic Centre Party (Zentrumspartei). When it came to coalition politics, the BVP pursued a similar course to that of its sister party, but in the elections for a new Reich president in 1925—being further to the right than the Centre Party—the BVP supported the right-wing candidate Paul von Hindenburg against the Catholic candidate Wilhelm Marx (Centre Party).[20] Political Catholicism continued to represent the confessional map of the Old Reich. The Centre Party strongholds were in the Rhineland, Westphalia, the Danube region, Baden, and in Silesia. While it was a confessional party that crossed class boundaries, it was not a national party and thus remained quite weak in broad swaths of the Reich. In Protestant regions, the liberal DVP (German People's Party) of Gustav Stresemann and the national conservative DNVP (German National People's Party) fulfilled this role. The social milieu of the Social Democrats was concentrated in the areas around Magdeburg, Hanover, and Berlin, as well as in Hesse-Kassel, the Ruhr area, and in Hamburg.[21]

In general, the Weimar party system was highly fragmented and regionalized. National minorities existed in both East and West. For example, both the Polish minority and the much smaller Danish minority voted for their own parties. In rural areas like Schleswig-Holstein, massive protests erupted against Weimar's political order, in the medium term shifting allegiances towards the NSDAP. Rural protest was violent already after the second global agrarian crisis beginning in 1926—thus even before the financial crash of 1929, as contemporary observers like the sociologist Rudolf Heberle pointed out.[22] In his 1931 novel *Bauern, Bonzen und Bomben* (Farmers, Bigwigs and Bombs), author Hans Fallada gave the rural wave of protest in Schleswig-Holstein its literary expression, in sober and matter-of-fact terms.[23] Numerous single lists (*Einheitslisten*), in which several parties banded together for the state parliamentary elections, were now created. Among them were the Anhaltinische Volksgemeinschaft (in 1924), the Braunschweig State Electoral Association (1918–22), the Braunschweig Bürgerliche Einheitsliste (1930), the Bremen Einheitsliste (1927), a series of lists in Lübeck (1921 Bürgerliche Partei Liste, 1924 Wirtschaftsgemeinschaft, 1926/1929 Hanseatischer Volksbund), the Mecklenburg-Strelitzer Economic Association (1920), the Schaumburg Lippische Einheitsliste (1925), the Thüringer Ordnungsbund (1924), and the Thüringer Einheitsliste (1927), in which DNVP, DVP, Centre Party, and Thüringer Landbund allied to form a single list in the 1927 state elections.

These single lists with regional names easily deceived the public about their radical nationalist character. They were not standing up for regional identity, a federal distribution of powers, or federalism. Quite the opposite: as extreme nationalists, the leaders of the single lists saw their enemy in socialism and argued for 'unity', calling for a national community, not a regional one. To avoid giving the impression of pork-barrel politics and to prove their nationalist credentials, many of them used collective terms like 'people', 'economy', or 'unity'. In Mecklenburg-Schwerin, the Mecklenburg

Dorfbund had no success between 1919 and 1921, but in 1929 the 'Single List of National Mecklenburgers' ('Einheitsliste nationaler Mecklenburger') won 44.6 per cent of the vote in the state election. On the whole, the right-wing regional single lists subsequently proved to be less resistant to the Nazi appeal than the established right-wing or left-wing parties.[24]

Still, one cannot speak of the Länder being particularly susceptible to the NSDAP. In the ten Länder that voted from 1932 until Hitler's rise to power in January 1933—not counting Prussia—the NSDAP earned below-average results in Bavaria, Hamburg, Lübeck, Mecklenburg-Strelitz, and Württemberg, but saw above-average results in Hesse, Lippe, Mecklenburg-Schwerin, Oldenburg, and Thuringia. Where the NSDAP was especially successful, it benefited from the single lists, whose intensified polemics drove voters into the party's waiting arms.[25] In the 1932 state elections in Mecklenburg, the 'Single List of National Mecklenburgers' achieved only 2.1 per cent of the vote, while the NSDAP received 49 per cent, an almost complete reversal of the previous state elections results in 1929. Regionalism served as a sort of nationalist combustive agent.[26]

Fiscal Federalism, the Welfare State, and Economic Decentralization

Taxes and federal finance regulations were of decisive importance in the political manoeuvrings between the Reich and the Länder. The Weimar state was also a federal tax state. For the relationship between the Reich and Länder, the 1920 financial reform of Reich Finance Minister Matthias Erzberger (Centre Party) represented a massive push towards centralization. In the financial sense, too, the First World War had dragged the Reich to the brink. War debts were paid not by taxes but by bonds and loans of all kinds. These and the reparations demanded a new approach. This impacted the financial administration, amounts of tax rates and the distribution of the burden. The previous decentralized financial administrations in the Länder was replaced with the Reich Treasury Administration. The Reich now handled most tax-related matters as well, and in return gave the Länder and municipalities a percentage share. Unlike in Imperial Germany, the Länder were now essentially financed by the Reich.[27]

The pre-1918 arrangement was clearly politically motivated. Until 1918, the financial sovereignty of the Länder had ensured that the Reichstag budget law applied to comparatively small sums. Only indirect taxes were under its jurisdiction; all direct taxes, including those affecting assets and income, were the responsibility of the states. Before 1918, the Reichstag could only decide on the use of those taxes that everyone paid indirectly. The unitary intentions of Weimar democracy were soon reflected in the tax constitution. On 3 December 1919, Reich Finance Minister Matthias Erzberger (Centre Party) described the goals of his comprehensive Reich finance reform: 'In the future, the Reich constitution and the tax unit will form the two sturdy brackets that enclose the

German people in a strong unit.... The adage will also apply to the unification of the tax system in Germany: In unity lies power.'[28]

The Reich Finance Reform of 1920 represented a key moment in the financial relations between Reich and Länder, establishing a path dependency for future fiscal federalism after 1949. The proponents of a unitary tax code prevailed over the proponents of fiscal decentralization, much more obviously in the financial constitution than in politics. A unified national fiscal order replaced the twenty-six financial orders of the Länder. While the Reich previously had collected about 5 billion marks, it would now collect 25 billion: 14 billion in direct taxes and 11 billion in indirect taxes that would be shared with the Länder. The sales tax, introduced in 1916, was raised to 7.5 per cent and structured in a highly progressive manner. The income tax, previously handled by the states, was now controlled by the Reich. The Reich income tax of 29 March 1920 replaced the income tax in twenty-five Länder.[29] In Prussia, the income tax had never been higher than 4 per cent. Now, the top tax rate was 60 per cent. A new system of allowances for the minimum subsistence level, children, household, and illness served as a social cushion against these higher taxes; these allowances characterize German tax law to this day.

The Länder received 57 per cent of the income tax. They were financially responsible for justice and science, the arts and religious institutions, as well as for boosting the economy, shared expenses for schools with the municipalities, and paid almost half of the expenses for the police and a quarter of those for the welfare of the unemployed. The municipalities in return retained two-thirds of the expenditures for welfare, housing, and traffic, and three-fifths of all expenditures for internal administration. They shared the costs of schools with the Länder, and covered one-third to one-quarter of the expenses of the police and science, the arts and the churches, and for the care of the unemployed, which would be centralized in the Reich's unemployment insurance system in 1927.[30]

What emerged was a highly competent, centralized Reich financial administration with specially trained civil servants. Until 1932 the Prussian financial administration—which functioned along the same basic principles—still included many Weimar democrats who were united in their opposition to Hitler. Many executives in the federal and Länder governments after 1945 had been in the Prussian financial administration (for example, Hermann Höpker-Aschoff). Twenty-six Länder tax administrations—of which thirteen were in Prussia—and about 1,000 tax offices now levied taxes uniformly in the Reich at the middle and lowest levels. They were no longer responsible for the individual Länder, but created new tax districts of similar size, evenly distributed over the Reich. Later, like the Prussian administrative districts, these new tax districts often became administrative units within the Federal Republic. This spatial division by the Reich fiscal administration embodied the ideal of the unitary minded democrats—a decentralized unitary state—which was even followed by the conservative Johannes Popitz, who headed the Prussian Ministry of Finance as of 1932, and paid for his opposition to Hitler with his life in 1945.

Subsequently, counties and municipalities oriented themselves more towards the Reich than towards the Länder, which had lost parts of their fiscal sovereignty. From

Bavaria came massive protests; the Bavarian People's Party dissolved its partnership with the Centre Party. Throughout the Weimar Republic, the Bavarian government fought against the Reich finance reform and tried to regain an independent fiscal administration as well as its own tax revenues, with the beer tax as its flagship. With tax distribution now staggered according to each state's economic performance and with tax allowances, the new financial order took differences in the financial strength of the Länder and the social imbalances of taxpayers into account. Its political goal was to achieve tax justice on the one hand, and on the other hand to find a third way, beyond socialism and capitalism: the welfare state.[31]

After 1930, the centralist financial federalism gradually wore away the autonomy of the states. During the Great Depression, social spending by local and state governments increased tremendously while their revenues plummeted.[32] Many Länder were facing bankruptcy. As of March 1930, the presidential cabinets at Reich level bundled questions of financial autonomy with the planned Reich reform. In his economic and financial programme that he announced on 29 September 1930, Reich Chancellor Heinrich Brüning claimed the right to influence and control the financial policies of the Länder. The importance of his claim would become clear through four emergency decrees for the 'safeguarding of economy and finance', issued on 1 December 1930, 5 June 1931, 6 October 1931, and 8 December 1931. They intervened radically in the state budgets. On 24 August 1931, the so-called 'Dietramszell Emergency Decree to Secure the Budgets of the Länder and Municipalities' was enacted to restructure the system. It introduced governance by presidential decree into the Länder, analogous to the Reich, empowering the state governments to apply austerity measures without involving the state parliaments and even forcing the municipalities to comply. Thus, the Reich government not only suspended the state constitutions in financial matters, but also changed the tripartite state structure of the Weimar Republic. In his expert reports, Reich Savings Commissioner Friedrich Saemisch also recommended limiting the powers of Länder parliaments. The Länder governments made extensive use of these extraordinary powers, but this did not help their financial situation. Thuringia's Minister of the Interior Wilhelm Frick—the first National Socialist minister—followed Saemisch's recommendations, reforming his state administration accordingly in 1931. Others followed suit, using the mandatory austerity measures to restructure their state governments.[33]

Not only was the financial constitution of the Weimar Republic becoming unitarian and centralized; it was clear soon after 1919 that social policy was moving in the same direction. It was the Reich, and not the Länder, that bore the burden of post-war debts and reparations. The Reich paid for the care of war victims and surviving dependants. The Reich Pension Law of 1920 and several other ad hoc measures resulted from the immediate need for action. Only in the years of relative stability between 1924 and 1930 did a social policy with a systemic approach emerge. The structural decisions of Bismarck's social laws from the 1880s still dominated, as social security schemes were financed not by taxes, but by contributions from workers and employers.[34]

Prosperity and poverty were quite unevenly distributed in German regions after 1918. Between west and east ran an often all too visible prosperity gap. In 1928, the average per capita income in the Prussian province of Silesia was only 84 per cent of the national average; in Pomerania 78 per cent, in Posen-West Prussia 71 per cent, and in East Prussia only 69 per cent. The East-Elbian Prussian provinces were thus the poorest regions in Germany, followed by Bavaria with 88 per cent. In contrast, residents of Berlin and Brandenburg earned about one third more (132 per cent), and Hamburg residents did even better, earning about half again as much as the average German (148 per cent). Also, Saxony could be considered well off, with an income of about 120 per cent of the national average. In central and northwestern Germany, income was above average, at between 104 per cent and 108 per cent of the national average; but in the southern and eastern regions of the Reich income was below average. The numbers for tax revenues showed the same distribution. In the area of the Königsberg Regional Tax Office in Eastern Prussia, per capita revenue from income tax and corporate income tax was between 1925 and 1929 only one third of the national average.[35] In three of Prussia's eastern provinces—Pomerania, Posen-West Prussia, and East Prussia—more than half of all employees were still working in agriculture in 1925. A year later, this region was hit hard by the world agricultural crisis. There was both a west–east and a somewhat less pronounced north–south divide.

Inequality was integral to the social geography of the Weimar Republic. The short phase of structured social policy with a broad societal purpose was unable to mitigate regional and social discrepancies. But the Weimar fiscal and welfare state established new spatial structures that cut beyond the Länder boundaries and formed more or less equal units. New Reich central authorities were created, both in the Reich Treasury and Reich Unemployment Insurance—whose thirteen regional employment offices spanned the borders of the Länder and provinces—and in collective bargaining, with the Ordinance on the Arbitration System of 30 October 1923 and its sixteen large-scale arbitration districts.[36] The Reich Finance Reform of 1920 and the Reich Unemployment Insurance of 1927 created 'regional structures directly linked to the Reich',[37] to which other regional divisions later oriented themselves. Even the telephone system and the route network of Deutsche Lufthansa AG were highly decentralized. While the Telegraphen-Union oriented itself towards Berlin, Wolff's Telegraphisches Bureau (WTB) remained decentralized. From 1923/24, nine radio broadcast districts were on air. Even the Reichstag electoral districts, at first thirty-seven and then—from 1920, reduced to thirty-five—also extended, in part, beyond Länder and provincial borders. Their delineation followed the principles of rationalization and administrative optimization.

The most influential manifestation of this kind of modern, rational, and scientific urban planning came from urban planner Walter Christaller. His theory of 'central spaces', developed in the final years of the republic, was based on the assumption that cities provided infrastructural services for surrounding areas, which gave them a centralizing function: starting with transportation and traffic but increasingly including communications, in the form of telegraphy and telephone. Christaller conceived of the various levels and ranges of services as concentric circles and spoke of upper, middle, and lower centres. His approach also offered the possibility to measure the increase or decrease of centrality functions quantitatively. For the purposes of spatial planning, regions were determined by the intensity and range of cities' centrality. During the Weimar Republic, the urban centres gained new functions that affected the surrounding area profoundly.[38]

Of the industrial regions, the Ruhr area became politically and culturally much more visible during the Weimar period. For a long time it had been the industrial engine of Germany.[39] After 1918/19 the Ruhr area took on its own political contours. In opposition to the 1920 Kapp putsch, a Rote Ruhrarmee (Red Ruhr Army) was formed in the area, mobilizing the region's revolutionary workers. Even if the Red Ruhr Army was soon defeated by right-wing groups and the Reichswehr, it succeeded in turning the region into a stronghold of anarcho-syndicalists (1920–2) and Communists. Another integrating experience was the Ruhr region's 'national resistance' against the French occupation in 1923. It was this occupation that made the Ruhr area a fixed term in the political lexicon of the Weimar Republic. As elsewhere, the Ruhr saw the emergence of a supra-municipal planning authority. The original purpose of the Siedlungsverband Ruhrkohlenbezirk (Settlement Association of the Ruhr Coal Mining District) was to ease the fulfilment of war-reparation payments to the Allies. In addition, it was intended that 600,000 people would move into the Ruhr region, making wages, urban planning, and construction necessary. The Settlement Association was the first to define the Ruhr district on the map. It had long been unclear which municipalities belonged to the Ruhr district and which did not. The syndicate provided spatial data, developed areas, and planned traffic.[40] Local colour as well as local pride was highlighted in popular Ruhr area reports such as Heinrich Hauser's *Schwarzes Revier* (1930), in Ruhr area novels along the lines of Erik Reger's social reportage, *Union der festen Hand* (1931), or in Erich Grisar's photojournalism.[41]

The Weimar experience with the welfare state and democracy influenced postwar West Germany and its substitute national identity: the aim of establishing equal living conditions, as enshrined in Article 72 of the West German Basic Law of 1949. After 1949, many saw the lack of response to economic hardship and the regional disparities after 1930 as the most important cause for Hitler's rise to power. The lesson for the West German society and politics could only be that the establishment of equal living conditions should take the highest priority, taking precedence even over specific regional peculiarities. This connected the development in Germany with that in Austria, but separated it from Switzerland and the United States, where the federal state preceded democracy by several generations and where social inequality was more easily tolerated.[42]

Culture: The Heimat Movement, Regionalism, and Local Milieus

Region and nation no longer represented opposites by the time the Reich was founded in 1871.[43] In trade and transport, the liberal logic of a win-win situation took hold, according to which the cooperation of several Länder and regions benefited everyone in the form of added value. In the cultural sense, too, narratives of national identity at the turn of the century moved closer to home, region, and everyday life. In Germany, as well as other countries, the farmhouse was originally a social place, not a place linked to the nation. This began to change at the end of the nineteenth century. The German terms *Heim* and *Heimat* conjured up the notion of a home as place of settlement, and the idea of a place or region in which social and cultural life is deeply rooted. It included everyday life and its many local variations, and linked them with the nation, a phenomenon that historian Celia Applegate traced in the Bavarian Palatinate.[44] Dutch historian Eric Storm analysed the social dissemination of the national idea in architecture, paintings, and exhibitions in France, Spain, and Germany.[45] The narrative of the region was being rewritten, recoded, and reimagined; the traditional story of the nation's ancient and immemorial origins was embellished with the narrative of the nation as home. The farmhouse became a national symbol, and not only in Germany. Admittedly, it was primarily the stylized farmhouse presented by artists, by world expositions, and their 'pavilions', as the national exhibits in Paris were called beginning in 1867.[46]

The Life Reform movement, in the form of the Deutscher Werkbund and the Garden City movement, was part of the German response to the English Arts and Crafts movement. They shared a yearning to create something real, small-scale, and above all hand-made. It was not only the village and landscape paintings of Worpswede but also the artistic awakening at the root of craftsmanship that were bound closely to the Heimat movement and regionalism. The Life Reform movement sought out locations and spaces outside the city, as did the Wandervogel hiking clubs. Heimat and region valued the anti-modern aspects of nationalism that set the allegedly authentic rural life against urban spaces of inauthenticity. To be sure, region and Heimat cannot be relegated to a backward-looking tradition or even anti-modernism.[47] Still, the anti-Western and anti-modern slant of the Heimat concept was its salient point during the Weimar years. Criticism of cultural and political modernity was firmly anchored in Weimar's regional culture. After the military defeat of Germany in 1918, it was conceivable to view national identity as linked less with territorially expansive ideas than with region and Heimat. The nation itself became regionalized in this way. Historian Hermann Aubin spoke for many when he said on the ninth Westphalia Day in 1928: 'The more the ground of the state swayed, and the looser its central form became, the more stable the surrounding landscape appeared.'[48]

Before 1914, when Leipzig historian Karl Lamprecht wanted to turn Landesgeschichte (regional history) away from its fixation on territory and rule and lead it towards social and cultural aspects, he ran into scepticism in his profession. Yet the First World War did much to change attitudes: even Landesgeschichte interpreted the defeat as a national catastrophe for the German people, not just for the Reich government and the Supreme Army Command. Reconstruction of the nation became the first priority, along with reflection on the vitality of the Heimat.[49] At the same time, references to a nationally defined statehood receded. After the First World War, Lamprecht's Leipzig colleague Richard Kötzschke was applauded when he redefined the relationship between

Landesgeschichte and national history. He considered regional history a contribution toward the overall history of the German people; the region was the 'dwelling place and nourishment of the people, the ground on which they lead their lives and experienced historical events and changes'. The regions and landscapes should be grasped 'in their organic context'. Regional historians had to look at settlement, economy, and culture. For Kötzschke, regional history was essentially settlement research and as such a contribution to *Heimatgefühl*, the feeling of belonging to a home. Historiography covered habitats on both a narrow and broad scale, from local to regional history, from the history of the Reich and the nation to world history. Finally, Landesgeschichte found its place in German universities and was no longer relegated to the circles of dilettantish local-history buffs. Regional history had become an integral part of national history.[50]

Not all regional historians saw the focus on regional history as a contribution to national history, especially not in Bavaria. There, the approach to Landesgeschichte centred on territory, statehood, and political sovereignty. Between 1906 and 1931, Michael Doeberl published his three-volume study on the *Historical Development of Bavaria*. In an unpublished testimony, Doeberl formulated a continuity thesis according to which the state of Bavaria was much older than the German state: 'Bavaria is the oldest German state, one of the oldest in Europe at all . . . . Before there was a German or a French nation, there was a Duchy of Bavaria, whose authority under international law as well as its domestic powers are true reflections of the royal power in the kingdom of the Franks: a real nation.'[51] There was a world of difference between this approach and the regional history carried out by Kötzschke in Leipzig.

An even greater break from the orientation toward territory and rule can be seen in the field of Geschichtliche Landeskunde (historical study of regions) and later in Kulturraumforschung (research into cultural regions), as exemplified by the work of Hermann Aubin. He and his like-minded colleagues replaced 'the artificial dependence on modern administrative borders with the evolved units of popular life'. Their goal was 'to establish the image of historical landscapes as the organic foundation of a history of the German people, across all territorial and modern administrative boundaries'. Only a multidisciplinary approach, including geography, social studies, and cultural studies, could hope to 'capture the depths of German uniqueness, as it has become historicized'.[52] *Volksraum* and cultural space were the keywords of Kulturraumforschung, which aimed at discerning historical regularities or even laws. It also embodied something new, both ideologically and politically. The essence of a people resulted from a sense of a spatial simultaneity of economy, culture, history, and place. In this continuous constellation of several structural dimensions, Kulturraumforschung recognized the iron laws of history.[53] For them, the connection to one's own region was no longer a 'symbolic reference to locality',[54] but a scientifically objectifiable structure, to some extent an algorithm of many structural dimensions that one could pin down if only one had the necessary data. Prominent representatives of the new folkloric reading of regional history were, alongside the aforementioned Richard Kötzschke and Hermann Aubin, Franz Steinbach and Franz Petri, Otto Brunner, Alfons Dopsch, and Oswald Redlich. The institutes of regional history in Bonn and Leipzig, Aubin's Breslau research group, and the Institute for Austrian Historical Research in Vienna were centres for this historical approach. In the Third Reich, they became part of the National Socialist Ostforschung and Westforschung, racist area studies devoted to the *völkisch* essence of regions in the East and the West.[55]

In the case of Weimar Germany's regionalism, one might speak of a thrust reversal of nationalism. After 1890 and again after the First World War, the nationalist mass associations attempted to bring nationalism from the national level to the regional level. In Weimar Germany, political regionalism was gaining strength as a substructure of nationalism. In this respect, German regionalism differed from that of France or Spain, older states where regionalism was compatible with forms of political and cultural decentralization. This was not the case in Germany. This paradox also explained why regions as such are not counted among the German 'sites of memory', to use the concept developed by Pierre Nora.[56] The new regionalism politicized the culture and contributed to the ethnicization and nationalization of the political language. The culture of the Weimar Republic became thoroughly politicized in the civil wars of 1918/19. For example, the nationalistic reaction to the Munich Soviet Republic of May 1919 drove the historical societies in Swabia into a 'tribal ethno-nationalism,' generously spiked with anti-Bavarian regionalism. 'The revolution had politicized the regional and ethnicized the political.'[57] Notions of a *Volksgeist* now referred to the region. What still stood out was the closeness of this Heimat-regionalism to the Life Reform movement and other reform movements in general.

Analogous to 'banal nationalism', regionalism gained a presence in everyday culture.[58] Regions served as reference points in architecture and interior design, spatial planning and tourism, fashion and food, art and culture. The ubiquity of the term 'Heimat' was remarkable: 'Heimat holidays were celebrated, educational Heimat days were held. Heimat folkdance groups were founded and Heimat costume festivals organized, Heimat museums were established or existing museums reorganized according to the Heimat principle, local history was taught in schools, and daily newspapers included Heimat supplements.'[59] Of course, not everyone had the same understanding of the term. There were left, liberal, conservative and new-right versions of the concept. Heimat regionalism was not a uniquely German phenomenon: house construction with a regional character could be found in France, Spain, and England. 'Vernacular houses' and vernacular architecture in supposedly regional style were popping up everywhere.[60]

In a pan-European trend, architecture and urban planning took a local and regional bent. Buildings went up in an often-invented regional style, using local building materials and bearing local characteristics of the building trade. In addition to functional structures—such as those expressed in the Bauhaus style—regional architecture and regional style played an increasingly important role in the Weimar Republic, but also on a European scale. If the cultural critic and architect Adolf Loos considered ornament a crime in 1910,[61] the opposite was true for regional architecture and for the Deutscher Werkbund, where architects such as Hermann Muthesius, Richard Riemerschmid, and Fritz Schumacher radically overhauled the decorative arts. This generation of architects was in close contact with the domestic and foreign reform movements. The Garden

City movement followed the reform ideal, according to which planning and building had to be in harmony with the region and nature. The garden city of Hellerau near Dresden, founded in 1909, embodied the ideals of Life Reform. With its internationally renowned educational institution for rhythmic gymnastics, Hellerau represented the unity of living and working, of culture and education. Other countries had their Basque, Breton, Norman, Cantabrian, and Andalusian styles. As an architectural construction of a region, they generally considered certain distinctive buildings or farm houses to be typical and prescribed them as sources of inspiration. It was national, not regional, protagonists who stylized the region, which is why, for example, the strongest regional movements in Catalonia, the Basque Country, and Brittany distanced themselves from architectural regionalism. Regional movements like the Catalan preferred the modern and cosmopolitan style.[62] Western Europe saw a difference between regional building and regionalism.

But in Imperial Germany as in the Weimar Republic, regionalism had a decidedly national orientation, which is why regional architecture used a nationalistic language. The Werkbund favoured local construction materials like clay, wood, brick, or slate. Paul Schultze-Naumburg, co-founder of the Deutscher Werkbund, strongly favoured the pitched roof over the Bauhaus style and its 'Jewish-Bolshevik flat roof'. *Völkisch* architect Alexander von Senger denigrated the flat roof of the Neues Bauen style as reminiscent of nomads and Arab peasants, 'rootless' people in general. Prompted by a propagandistic photomontage, showing a caravan of camels marching through the newly built *Weißenhofsiedlung* in Stuttgart, the National Socialists called it an 'Arab village'.[63] Paul Schmitthenner and other architects from the 'Stuttgart School' built their Kochenhof housing within sight of Mies van der Rohe's Weißenhofsiedlung. With its gabled roofs, it represented a decidedly traditionalist counter-model.[64]

In the wake of the paroxysms of violence of the First World War, regionalism was attractive because it transcended political and social conflicts. The idea of overcoming all social and political antagonisms in an apolitical homeland far from all political conflict was 'a deeply middle class conception of regionalism'.[65] The Heimat movement's fields of action were also typically middle class: research and instruction. The 'Heimat' association which had been promoting the idea of homeland in Swabia since 1899 with its *Deutsche Gaue* journal, was at the same time anti-socialist, anti-liberal, and radical-national. The popular concept of the association and its chairman, the Catholic clergyman Christian Frank, revolved around the ethnic, the organic, and agrarian romanticism mixed with a dose of criticism of social issues and modernization.[66] In Westphalia's Heimatbund (Heimat League), these characteristics were even more pronounced. As in Swabia, here Heimat appealed to its clientele with a historical search for roots. Heimat activist, researcher, and poet Karl Wagenfeld became its figurehead. In 1915, he had co-founded the Westphalian Heimatbund and worked on its theoretical foundation. Wagenfeld urged Westphalians to return to their roots and restore their personal bonds to folklore, fatherland, homeland, family, and God. Publications and education were charged with strengthening awareness of Westphalian folklore, which would organically combine with other folklore to form an organic German *Volk*. Westphalia saw mass events of the Heimat movement and extensive use of media. Heimat activists were busy on all channels. In addition to annual, large-scale Westphalia Days, they used public lectures, radio broadcasts, and Heimat magazines to convey their message.[67] The 1923 Ruhrkampf and the simultaneous fourth Westphalia Day served to boost the movement and bring it closer to the official agencies of the provincial administration. The Westphalian Heimatbund earned a semi-official character and functioned as the most important 'source of ideas for the development' of municipal, 'state and regional cultural policy'.[68]

In the Catholic district of Eichsfeld, the aspect of religion was added to the Heimat movement. The 'League of the Eichsfelder' saw 'love for the faith of your forefathers' as the core of the love of homeland. Religion, homeland, and nation came together under the motto: 'Loyal to faith, loyal to homeland, and loyal to fatherland.' Eichsfeld Heimat activists, too, used popular publications and media to further their cause. They published two magazines simultaneously: a popular magazine intended for a broad audience and a scientific journal (*Unser Eichsfeld*).[69] The regional associations for Heimatschutz (Protection of Heimat), which had been founded before 1914—the Deutsche Bund Heimatschutz, founded in 1904, the Gesamtverein der Deutschen Geschichts- und Altertumsvereine, and the regional mountain and hiking associations such as the Schwäbische Alpenverein and the Erzgebirgsverein—brought new features to the notion of region and homeland. Their goal was not to base society on territory but rather to build a new society through spatial practices. Even though the territorial aspect of Heimat never completely disappeared, the Heimatschutz movement was less concerned with territory than with the quality and purity of the people. Mixed zones were problematic in this scenario. The concept of purity of the people later secured loyalty to the National Socialists, who pursued the same goal on a racist basis.

A good illustration of this phenomenon is the so-called South Tyrolean question. South Tyrol had been awarded to Italy after the First World War and became the sticking point between Italian fascism and traditional German nationalism on the political right. Particularly the nationalists in the DNVP, but also parts of the NSDAP demanded the return of this territory, among them Joseph Goebbels. But others, most importantly Hitler, showed less interest in South Tyrol because they saw it as a zone of mixed races that was hardly a candidate for expanding the future 'Lebensraum' (living space). As early as 1922, Hitler opined along those lines during a discussion meeting of the Munich NSDAP: 'To this end, Germany must clearly and concisely renounce the Germans in South Tyrol.' But it was only at the Bamberg Leadership Conference in 1926 that Hitler was finally able to assert himself in the party on this issue.[70]

The Heimatschutz movement no longer represented the small-state resentments of either the numerous territories of the Old Empire or the pre-1866 German Confederation that had been deprived of their sovereignty like Hanover or Hesse-Kassel. The Heimat movement used organic terms that showed which way the wind blew: its key words were *Volkskörper* (German body politic), *Volksorganismus* (German organism), *Volksgesundheit* (German public health), *Volkstum* (folklore), and also *Landschaft* (region or landscape), *Natur* (nature), *Kultur* (culture), *Geschichte* (history), and *Raumorganismus* (spatial organism).[71] The Heimatschutz movement was particularly successful in those regions that had had to change their political affiliation in the course of the nineteenth century, like Westphalia; or that were dramatically altered, like Saxony and Thuringia. For them, the notion of Heimat offered continuity beyond all the changes they had endured.

The Heimatschutz associations of Westphalia, Thuringia, and Saxony provided evidence of this encounter between Heimat protectors and National Socialists.[72] Step by step, they ethnicized the concept of Heimat, loaded it with qualities of 'more' and 'less', argued passionately against the Weimar Republic for allegedly being insensitive to the values of Heimat, and finally entered willingly into an alliance with Hitler. For them, Heimat was no longer primarily a place in the geographical sense, but rather a social and emotional entity. The Heimat associations thus finally broke away from the old conservative traditional milieus in the German states, which had been striving for political sovereignty, and became part of the *völkisch* movement.[73] The Heimatschutz associations explicitly delegitimized the territorial cessions of the Versailles Treaty. Their goal was to 'confront the artificial construction principle of the fragmented Reich, including its dynastic and arbitrary federalism, with an alternative concept that would do justice to the supposedly natural, spatially and historically inherited and therefore somatically vital components of Heimat'.[74] The Heimatschutz associations enjoyed the financial support of the Länder and the Reich.

Border regions offered a particularly favourable ambience for the folklore work of Heimat protectors. The political temperature rose noticeably as soon as the focus shifted from regionalization to defence, resistance, and a proclaimed 'struggle for survival'. In these border regions—such as Schleswig-Holstein, Upper Silesia, Gdansk, and the Sudetenland, which folklorists considered a border region—Heimat work developed an explosive power. The term *Grenzland* (borderland) was used to describe these areas. In 1920, plebiscites led to the transfer of Northern Schleswig to Denmark. The Schleswig-Holstein Association, founded in 1919, and its journal *Der Schleswig-Holsteiner* had campaigned in this 'border struggle' on both sides of the border, with the aim of bringing Northern Schleswig back to the Reich. In Northern Schleswig, the work of folklorists to 'preserve native German culture' took centre stage. In addition to folklore publications, instruments of 'borderland work' included adult education centres, the development and expansion of Landeskunde, regional history, and the Low German dialect. Folklore was first and foremost a tool of borderland work. A key figure in the German minority milieu was Johannes Schmidt-Wodder, who represented Northern Schleswig in the Folketing, the Danish Parliament in Copenhagen, and was well connected with European minority organizations.[75] Language affiliation played a central role in this form of borderland work. To achieve border revision, the Schleswig-Holstein Association worked on the 'cultural re-appropriation of space that Germans perceived as threatened'.[76] Hybridity and mixing of populations were obstructive to this goal.

The tendency towards linguistic and political unification of a region met with the greatest resistance in the mixed-ethnic areas, especially in the eastern part of Germany.

Masuria, in southern East Prussia, had been part of Prussia for centuries. Most of its population was Polish-speaking and Protestant. Other ethnically mixed areas included southern Warmia, northeastern East Prussia, Pomerania, Upper and Lower Lusatia, and Upper Silesia. Minorities outside the boundaries of the Reich included the Kashubs, who lived north and west of Danzig, and the Protestant Poles who lived in the southern part of the former province of Posen. These regions formed the core of 'German national and cultural-soil research' (Volks- und Kulturbodenforschung) during the 1920s and 1930s, which worked in various regions with opposite arguments.[77] In the west, it was argued that Alsace-Lorraine should rejoin Germany, since it had long been linked to the Reich as a state. In the east, on the other hand, Polish-speaking Masurians should remain in Germany since they were 'cultural Germans with a non-German vernacular'. Even the German term 'Masuren' (or their degrading term for Uppersilesians: 'Wasserpolen'— water Poles) was an artificial trope that was supposed to distinguish their Polish dialect from high Polish. Accordingly, the Masurians were considered a 'national intermediate layer' or 'embryonic *Volk*'.[78] This talk of being 'between' and 'embryonic' blurred the fact that at no other time and place in European history had an ethnic group identified for so long with a nation that spoke a different language. In the referendum of 11 July 1920, the Masurians chose to remain with East Prussia.

Conclusion

Regions were repositories for temporal structures, experiential spaces, and expectational horizons. Spatial orders of the nineteenth century existed in the 1920s alongside spatial constructions that anticipated the Federal Republic. Between the two was the Weimar Republic. The spaces of administration scarcely corresponded to those of traffic, industry, and trade. Several spatial orders were superimposed on one another. The fact that Hitler preferred to use an airplane in his campaign appearances in 1932 suggests that he could use various spatial structures. This was to his advantage. An interpretative approach to spatial mobility could begin with the spatial experiences of the First World War, which knew both mobility and immobility. The experience of vast spaces and breath-taking mobility in the east was just as memorable as the experience of frontlines that fluctuated by a few kilometers for years in the west and the south. Borders were heavily defended and yet easy to cross. What seemed to have been built to last forever collapsed in a short time.

If one assumes, as this chapter does, that spaces and experiences correspond, one must conclude that the simultaneity of several spatial orders was based on different experiences. These included the attachment to older forms of statehood, high mobility in search for employment, communication over long distances, social security after employment in different locations, and the longing for a meaningful interpretation of the defeat in the First World War. Each of these experiences included notions of space. Labour and industry, social insurance and taxation, always operated within spaces that were at odds with those constructed by the state. Finally, the radio's destruction of distance started in the Weimar Republic as well. In principle, radio made the German people simultaneous before the loudspeaker, a lesson understood by Joseph Goebbels.

Federalism and the federal state, the decentralized unitary state, the Heimat movement, Reich reform plans and the constant attempts at territorial reorganization, the economic regions, and transportation areas can be interpreted as attempts to create political, economic, and cultural orders in space. These structures fell in line with various imperatives: centralization and decentralization, rationalization and optimization, and—increasingly—ethnicization. There was not one single order of space, but rather many orders that were difficult to align with one another. The constitution of 1871 had tried to create a political order on the two levels of the Reich and the Länder, by separating the lawmaking powers of the Reich and the Länder. That also applied in the Weimar Republic, but with many more responsibilities for the Reich. The West German Federal Republic of 1949 was preceded by two mechanisms that were becoming increasingly common after 1919: coordination and cooperation. Even before 1914, the Reich and the Länder cooperated: The former enacted laws and the latter carried them out. The Weimar parties in the governing coalitions had to cooperate and constantly coordinate after 1919. But the will and capacity for cooperation declined. Trade unions and employers cooperated for a while, approving national collective agreements, until the employers abandoned this cooperation in 1923. Ultimately, the Weimar Republic was a laboratory of attempts to order space and territory, some of which pointed to the future. The impact of Weimar's 'decentralized unitary state' would be felt in the Federal Republic, even though the West German 'unitary federal state' (Konrad Hesse) strengthened the Länder and set a more federalism-friendly tone overall.

Translated from German by Toby Axelrod.

Notes

1. Hugo Preuß, *Artikel 18 der Reichsverfassung* (Berlin: C. Heymann, 1922), 3.
2. Jörn Retterath, *'Was ist das Volk?': Volks- und Gemeinschaftskonzepte der politischen Mitte in Deutschland 1917–1924* (Berlin: de Gruyter Oldenbourg, 2016); Manfred Heimers, *Unitarismus und süddeutsches Selbstbewußtsein: Weimarer Koalition und SPD in Baden in der Reichsreformdiskussion 1918–1933* (Düsseldorf: Droste, 1992).
3. Hugo Preuß, 'Deutschlands republikanische Reichsverfassung (1923)', in Detlef Lehnert (ed.), *Politik und Verfassung in der Weimarer Republik* (Tübingen: Mohr Siebeck, 2008), 329–30.
4. Wolfgang J. Mommsen, 'A Delaying Compromise: The Division of Authority in the German Imperial Constitution of 1871', in Mommsen, *Imperial Germany, 1867–1918: Politics, Culture and Society in an Authoritarian State*, tr. Richard Deveson (London: Arnold, 1995), 20–40.
5. Detlef Schmiechen-Ackermann and Thomas Schaarschmidt, 'Regionen als Bezugsgröße in Diktaturen und Demokratien', *Comparativ*, 13 (2003), 7–16, here 9.
6. For a critique of the centre–periphery model see Celia Applegate, 'A Europe of the Regions: Reflections on the Historiography of Sub-National Places in Modern Times', *American Historical Review*, 104 (1999), 1157–82.

7. Anke John, *Der Weimarer Bundesstaat: Perspektiven einer föderalen Ordnung (1918–1933)* (Vienna: Böhlau, 2012), 146–7.
8. Martin Schlemmer, *'Los von Berlin': Die Rheinstaatbestrebungen nach dem Ersten Weltkrieg* (Cologne: Böhlau, 2007).
9. Otto Braun, *Deutscher Einheitsstaat oder Föderativsystem?* (Berlin: C. Heymann, 1927), 32.
10. Hans-Peter Ehni, *Bollwerk Preußen? Preußen-Regierung, Reich-Länder-Problem und Sozialdemokratie 1928–1932* (Bonn: Verlag Neue Gesellschaft, 1975); Hagen Schulze, *Otto Braun oder Preußens demokratische Sendung: Eine Biographie* (Frankfurt/Main: Propyläen, 1977).
11. Jürgen John, 'Die Gründung des Landes Thüringen im Jahr 1920', *Thüringer Heimatbote: Zeitschrift für Geschichte, Kultur und Umwelt*, 3 (1998), 4–9; Timo Leimbach, *Parlamentarischer Alltag im Land Thüringen 1920–1933* (Erfurt: Landeszentrale für politische Bildung, 2017).
12. Jürgen John, '"Unitarischer Bundesstaat," "Reichsreform" und "Reichs-Neugliederung" in der Weimarer Republik', in Jürgen John (ed.), *'Mitteldeutschland': Begriff–Geschichte–Konstrukt* (Rudolstadt: Hain-Verlag, 2001), 314.
13. Ibid., 320–1.
14. Foroud Shirvani, 'Die Bundes- und Reichsexekution in der neueren deutschen Verfassungsgeschichte', *Der Staat*, 50 (2011), 102–21.
15. John, *Bundesstaat*, 181–2.
16. Heinrich August Winkler, *Von der Revolution zur Stabilisierung: Arbeiter und Arbeiterbewegung in der Weimarer Republik 1918 bis 1924* (Bonn: Dietz, 1985), 648–64, 670–2.
17. Heinrich August Winkler, *Der Weg in die Katastrophe: Arbeiter und Arbeiterbewegung in der Weimarer Republik 1930 bis 1933* (Bonn: Dietz, 1987), 654–64.
18. Gerhard A. Ritter, *Föderalismus und Parlamentarismus in Deutschland in Geschichte und Gegenwart* (Munich: Verlag der Bayerischen Akademie der Wissenschaften, 2005), 39–40.
19. Hermann Höpker-Aschoff, *Deutscher Einheitsstaat: Ein Beitrag zur Rationalisierung der Verwaltung* (Berlin: Stilke, 1928), 26–7.
20. Klaus Schönhoven, *Die Bayerische Volkspartei 1924–1932* (Düsseldorf: Droste, 1972).
21. Thomas Mergel, 'Mapping Milieus: On the Spatial Rootedness of Collective Identities in the 19th Century', in Jim Retallack (ed.), *Saxony in German History: Culture, Society and Politics 1830–1933* (Ann Arbor: University of Michigan Press, 2000), 77–95; Siegfried Weichlein, *Sozialmilieus und politische Kultur in der Weimarer Republik: Lebenswelt, Vereinskultur, Politik in Hessen* (Göttingen: Vandenhoeck & Ruprecht, 1995); Karl Rohe, *Wahlen und Wählertraditionen in Deutschland: Kulturelle Grundlagen deutscher Parteien und Parteiensysteme im 19. und 20. Jahrhundert* (Frankfurt/Main: Suhrkamp, 1992).
22. Rudolf Heberle, *From Democracy to Nazism: A Regional Case Study on Political Parties in Germany* (Baton Rouge, LA: Louisiana State University Press, 1945).
23. Hans Fallada, *Bauern, Bonzen und Bomben* (Berlin: Rowohlt, 1931).
24. Detlef Lehnert, 'Weimarer Bundesstaat zwischen Unitarismus und Föderalismus—ein Nachwort', in John, *Bundesstaat*, 469–86, here 484–5.
25. Ibid.
26. Karl Ditt, 'Die deutsche Heimatbewegung 1871–1945', in Will Cremer and Ansgar Klein (eds), *Heimat: Analysen, Themen, Perspektiven* (Bonn: Bundeszentrale für politische Bildung, 1990), 135–54.

27. Hans-Peter Ullmann, *Der deutsche Steuerstaat: Geschichte der öffentlichen Finanzen vom 18. Jahrhundert bis heute* (Munich: Beck, 2005), 114–23; Peter-Christian Witt, 'Finanzen und Politik im Bundesstaat–Deutschland 1871–1933', in Jochen Huhn and Peter-Christian Witt (eds), *Föderalismus in Deutschland: Traditionen und gegenwärtige Probleme* (Baden-Baden: Gesamthochschule Kassel, 1992), 75–99.
28. *Verhandlungen der Verfassunggebenden Deutschen Nationalversammlung. Stenographische Berichte*, 331 (3 Dec. 1919), 3839.
29. Christopher Dowe, 'Ein föderaler Unitarist? Matthias Erzberger und seine Vorstellungen von Reichsreform und Einheitsstaat', *Historisch-Politische Mitteilungen*, 24 (2017), 15–36, here 31.
30. Ullmann, *Steuerstaat*, 118.
31. Alex Möller, *Reichsfinanzminister Matthias Erzberger und sein Reformwerk* (Bonn: Stollfuss, 1971); Dowe, 'Unitarist'.
32. Ullmann, *Steuerstaat*, 131–40.
33. John, 'Unitarischer Bundesstaat', 354–6.
34. Eckart Reidegeld, 'Staatliche Sozialpolitik in der Weimarer Republik (1919–1930)', in Reidegeld (ed.), *Staatliche Sozialpolitik in Deutschland, vol. 2. Sozialpolitik in Demokratie und Diktatur 1919–1945* (Wiesbaden: Verlag für Sozialwissenschaften, 2006), 43–257.
35. Figures in Heinrich A. Winkler, *Der Schein der Normalität: Arbeiter und Arbeiterbewegung in der Weimarer Republik 1924–1930* (Bonn: Dietz, 1985), 42–3.
36. Georg Hartrodt and Ludwig Preller, *Die Organe der Sozialpolitik im Deutschen Reich* (Berlin: Hobbing, 1928).
37. John, 'Gründung', 337.
38. Walter Christaller, *Die zentralen Orte in Süddeutschland: Eine ökonomisch-geographische Untersuchung über die Gesetzmäßigkeit der Verbreitung und Entwicklung der Siedlungen mit städtischen Funktionen* (Jena: Fischer, 1933); Karl R. Kegler, *Deutsche Raumplanung: das Modell der 'zentralen Orte' zwischen NS-Staat und Bundesrepublik* (Paderborn: Ferdinand Schöningh, 2015).
39. Ulrich Borsdorf, Heinrich Theodor Grütter, and Dieter Nellen (eds), *Zukunft war immer: Zur Geschichte der Metropole Ruhr* (Essen: Klartext 2007).
40. Ariane Leendertz, *Ordnung schaffen: Deutsche Raumplanung im 20. Jahrhundert* (Göttingen: Wallstein, 2008), 49–76.
41. Heinrich Hauser, *Schwarzes Revier* (Berlin: Fischer, 1930); Erik Reger, *Union der festen Hand: Roman einer Entwicklung* (Berlin: Rowohlt, 1931); Erich Grisar, *Ruhrgebietsfotografien 1928–1933* (Essen: Klartext, 2016).
42. Francis Geoffrey Castles, Herbert Obinger, and Stephan Leibfried (eds), *Federalism and the Welfare State: New World and European Experiences* (Cambridge: Cambridge University Press, 2005).
43. Siegfried Weichlein, *Nation und Region: Integrationsprozesse im Bismarckreich* (Düsseldorf: Droste, 2006).
44. Celia Applegate, *A Nation of Provincials: The German Idea of Heimat* (Berkeley, CA: University of California Press, 1990).
45. Eric Storm, *The Culture of Regionalism: Art, Architecture and International Exhibitions in France, Germany and Spain, 1890–1939* (Manchester: Manchester University Press, 2010); Storm, 'Nation-Building in the Provinces: The Interplay between Local, Regional and National Identities in Central and Western Europe, 1870–1945', *European History Quarterly*, 42 (2012), 650–63.

46. Bjarne Stoklund, 'How the Peasant House Became a National Symbol', *Ethnologia Europaea*, 29 (1999), 5–18.
47. Applegate, *Nation of Provincials*.
48. Cited in Karl Ditt, 'Regionalbewußtsein und Regionalismus in Westfalen vom Kaiserreich bis zur Bundesrepublik', *Comparativ*, 13 (2003), 17–31, 20.
49. Winfried Speitkamp, 'Geschichtsvereine—Landesgeschichte—Erinnerungskultur', *Mitteilungen des Oberhessischen Geschichtsvereins Gießen*, 88 (2003), 181–204.
50. Rudolf Kötzschke, *Nationalgeschichte und Landesgeschichte* (Halle an der Saale: Gebauer-Schwetschke, 1924), quotes 3; Peter Steinbach, 'Territorial- oder Regionalgeschichte: Wege der modernen Landesgeschichte. Ein Vergleich der "Blätter für deutsche Landesgeschichte" und des "Jahrbuchs für Regionalgeschichte"', *Geschichte und Gesellschaft*, 11 (1985), 528–40; Nina Lohmann, 'Der "Raum" in der deutschen Geschichtswissenschaft', *Acta Universitatis Carolinae Studia Territorialia*, 10 (2010), 47–93, here 53.
51. Michael Doeberl, *Entwicklungsgeschichte Bayerns*, 3 vols (Munich: Oldenbourg, 1906–31); Arno Mohr, 'Politische Identität um jeden Preis? Zur Funktion der Landesgeschichtsschreibung in den Bundesländern', *Neue Politische Literatur*, 35 (1990), 222–74, quote 262.
52. Hermann Aubin, 'Aufgaben und Wege der geschichtlichen Landeskunde (1925)', in Franz Petri (ed.), *Grundlagen und Perspektiven geschichtlicher Kulturraumforschung und Kulturmorphologie* (Bonn: Röhrscheid, 1965), 17–26; Speitkamp, 'Geschichtsvereine', 193.
53. Ditt, 'Heimatbewegung', 146.
54. Heiner Treinen, *Symbolische Ortsbezogenheit: Eine soziologische Untersuchung zum Heimatproblem* (Opladen: Westdeutscher Verlag, 1966).
55. Lohmann, 'Raum', 52–3.
56. Eric Storm, 'Die Ideologie des Regionalismus in Architekturzeitschriften Deutschlands, Frankreichs und Spaniens 1900–1925', in Kai Krauskopf, Hans-Georg Lippert, and Kerstin Zaschke (eds), *Neue Tradition: Vorbilder, Mechanismen und Ideen* (Dresden: Thelem, 2012), 133–51; Friedrich Prinz, 'Der Weißwurstäquator', in Etienne François and Hagen Schulze (eds), *Deutsche Erinnerungsorte*, vol. 1 (Munich: Beck, 2009), 471–83.
57. Winfried Müller and Martina Steber, '"Heimat": Region und Identitätskonstruktionen im 19. und 20. Jahrhundert', in Werner Freitag, Michael Kißener, and Christine Reinle (eds), *Handbuch Landesgeschichte* (Berlin: de Gruyter Oldenbourg 2018), 646–76, here 666.
58. Michael Billig, *Banal nationalism* (London: Sage, 1995); Eric Storm, 'The Nationalisation of the Domestic Sphere', *Nations and Nationalism*, 23 (2017), 173–93.
59. Müller and Steber, 'Heimat', 667.
60. Storm, 'Regionalismus'; Storm, 'Nation-Building'; Storm, 'Culture of Regionalism'.
61. Adolf Loos, *Ornament und Verbrechen: Adolf Loos. Die Schriften zur Architektur und Gestaltung* (Stuttgart: avedition, 2019).
62. Storm, 'Regionalismus'.
63. Justus H. Ulbricht, 'Wo liegt Kaisersaschern? Mitteldeutsche Mythen- und Symbolorte: Eine Spurensuche "deutschen Wesens"', in John, *Mitteldeutschland*, 135–58, 145–6.
64. Manfred Ulmer and Jörg Kurz, *Die Weißenhofsiedlung: Geschichte und Gegenwart* (Stuttgart: Hampp, 2006); Norbert Borrmann, *Paul Schultze-Naumburg: 1869–1949. Maler, Publizist, Architekt. Vom Kulturreformer der Jahrhundertwende zum Kulturpolitiker im Dritten Reich, ein Lebens- und Zeitdokument* (Essen: Bacht, 1989).

65. Martina Steber, *Ethnische Gewissheiten: Die Ordnung des Regionalen im bayerischen Schwaben vom Kaiserreich bis zum NS-Regime* (Göttingen: Vandenhoeck & Ruprecht, 2010), 311.
66. Müller and Steber, 'Heimat', 665.
67. Ditt, 'Regionalbewußtsein', 20–1; Willi Oberkrome, '"Schutzwall" Heimat. Themenschwerpunkte und weltanschauliche Prämissen der Westfalentage 1920–1933', *Westfälische Forschungen*, 52 (2002), 185–202.
68. Oberkrome, 'Schutzwall', 188; Karl Ditt, 'Die Kulturpolitik des Provinzialverbandes Westfalen 1886 bis 1945', in Karl Teppe (ed.), *Selbstverwaltungsprinzip und Herrschaftsordnung: Bilanz und Perspektiven landschaftlicher Selbstverwaltung in Westfalen* (Münster: Aschendorffsche Verlagsbuchhandlung, 1987), 258.
69. Petra Behrens, 'Regionalkultur und Regionalbewusstsein im Eichsfeld 1920 bis 1990', *Comparativ*, 13 (2003), 32–46.
70. Wolfgang Schieder, *Adolf Hitler—Politischer Zauberlehrling Mussolinis* (Berlin: de Gruyter Oldenbourg, 2017), 7–63, here 30.
71. Willi Oberkrome, 'Stamm und Landschaft. Heimatlicher Tribalismus und die Projektionen einer "völkischen Neuordnung" Deutschlands 1920–1950', in Wolfgang Hardtwig (ed.), *Ordnungen in der Krise: Zur politischen Kulturgeschichte Deutschlands 1900–1933* (Munich: Oldenbourg, 2007), 69–94, here 71.
72. Willi Oberkrome, *'Deutsche Heimat': Nationale Konzeption und regionale Praxis von Naturschutz, Landschaftsgestaltung und Kulturpolitik in Westfalen-Lippe und Thüringen (1900–1960)* (Paderborn: Schöningh, 2004).
73. Oberkrome, 'Stamm'; Oberkrome, 'Schutzwall'.
74. Oberkrome, 'Stamm', 76.
75. Jenni Boie, *Volkstumsarbeit und Grenzregion Volkskundliches Wissen als Ressource ethnischer Identitätspolitik in Schleswig-Holstein 1920–1930* (Münster: Waxmann, 2012).
76. Nina Jebsen, 'Verlorener Raum Nordschleswig: Die Bedeutung volkskundlichen Wissens im deutsch-dänischen Grenzraum 1920–1940', *Volkskundlich-Kulturwissenschaftliche Schriften*, 21 (2011), 19–33, here 32.
77. Andreas Kossert, '"Grenzlandpolitik" und Ostforschung an der Peripherie des Reiches: Das ostpreußische Masuren 1919–1945', *Vierteljahrshefte für Zeitgeschichte*, 51 (2003), 117–46.
78. Ibid., 121–2; Andreas Kossert, *Preußen, Deutsche oder Polen? Die Masuren im Spannungsfeld des ethnischen Nationalismus 1870–1956* (Wiesbaden: Harrassowitz, 2001).

Bibliography

Applegate, Celia, *A Nation of Provincials: The German Idea of Heimat* (Berkeley, CA: Berkeley University Press, 1990).
Boie, Jenni, *Volkstumsarbeit und Grenzregion: Volkskundliches Wissen als Ressource ethnischer Identitätspolitik in Schleswig-Holstein 1920–1930* (Münster: Waxmann, 2012).
Confino, Alon, *The Nation as a Local Metaphor: Württemberg, Imperial Germany, and National Memory, 1871–1918* (Chapel Hill, NC: University of North Carolina Press, 1997).
Heberle, Rudolf, *From Democracy to Nazism: A Regional Case Study on Political Parties in Germany* (Baton Rouge, LA: Louisiana State University Press, 1945).

Murdock, Caitlin E., *Changing Places: Society, Culture, and Territory in the Saxon-Bohemian Borderlands 1870–1946* (Ann Arbor: University of Michigan Press, 2010).

Steber, Martina, *Ethnische Gewissheiten: Die Ordnung des Regionalen im bayerischen Schwaben vom Kaiserreich bis zum NS-Regime* (Göttingen: Vandenhoeck & Ruprecht, 2010).

Stoklund, Bjarne, 'How the Peasant House Became a National Symbol', *Ethnologia Europaea*, 29 (1999), 5–18.

Storm, Eric, 'Nation-Building in the Provinces: The Interplay between Local, Regional and National Identities in Central and Western Europe, 1870–1945', *European History Quarterly*, 42 (2012), 650–63.

Storm, Eric, *The Culture of Regionalism: Art, Architecture and International Exhibitions in France, Germany and Spain, 1890–1939* (Manchester: Manchester University Press, 2010).

CHAPTER 10

THE REICHSWEHR AND ARMAMENT POLICIES

BENJAMIN ZIEMANN

The Reichswehr is an important, yet often overlooked part of the history of the Weimar Republic.[1] The armed forces were crucial for any attempt to rebuild the full sovereignty of a defeated nation. Yet this rebuilding did not only occur in the changed social and political context of a democratic republic. It also followed in the wake of the First World War, which had fundamentally altered the parameters in which the military operated. Waging war in the age of machine warfare, which depended on the production and consumption of tools of destruction on an industrial scale, required the mobilization of manpower and resources across society. Hence, the military ceased to be a separate institution and became embedded in a societal effort to mobilize for total war. While this had been clear since 1916 at the very latest, teasing out the consequences for a revised army structure became the subject of intensive inter-war debates in the German military.[2] In addition, the Treaty of Versailles not only drastically restricted the size and equipment of the German military. It also prohibited the reintroduction of general conscription, thus interrupting a tradition of the Prussian-German military that had very much defined its identity—and its relation to civil society—since the anti-Napoleonic war in 1814.[3]

In line with recent historiography, most notably the pioneering work by historian Michael Geyer, this chapter thus emphasizes the rupture between the late Wilhelmine military and the army of the republic. The dangers that the military posed for the republic were neither the result of a feudal hangover, i.e. the continuing presence of aristocratic officers, nor was the Reichswehr a 'state within the state', as an older historiography has posited.[4] Rather, the rebuilding of the military and its secret rearmament posed a toxic problem for the republic precisely because a military led by professionals pursued a revisionist agenda that took note of the requirement to mobilize not only soldiers, but also the industrial economy and society for war, and actively implicated both republican governments and civilian administrators in its endeavours.[5] I will unfold this argument in a mixture of chronological and thematic sections. First, I will chart the improvised transformation of the military and its politics until 1923, when the imperative to maintain the state monopoly of violence led to a series of stopgap measures, the involvement of parts of the military in two coup attempts in 1920 and 1923, and to a prolonged state of exception. I will then discuss structure, armaments, and war planning of the Reichswehr from 1924 to 1933, followed by an analysis of attempts to mobilize society for homeland defence. A brief section on the politics of the Reichswehr in the final years of the republic concludes the chapter.

Defeat and the Spectre of Civil War: Rebuilding the German Military, 1918–1923

On 11 November 1918, Germany was a defeated nation, and with it its two closest allies, the Austrian-Hungarian Empire and the Ottoman Empire. Yet even before the government had been forced to sign the Armistice, the once mighty Imperial German army had dissolved. After the repeated German offensives at the Western front had proven ineffective by August 1918, and the Allied troops started to advance, the cohesion of the German units gradually collapsed. Increasing numbers of soldiers reported sick, while others, sent back to the front after recovery, managed to 'miss' their units and quite deliberately wandered around in the rear area for weeks, if not months. For the majority, the preservation of their own life in the final months of the war was the key imperative. A not entirely marginal group, however, combined this with political motives, mainly a longing for democratization. In sum, the different forms of shirking, malingering, and outright desertion amounted to a 'military strike' that irreparably hollowed out the core structure of the army.[6] When the sailors of the Imperial Navy at the Baltic Sea harbour in Kiel kick-started the revolution with their revolt on 3/4 November 1918, the field army at the Western front had already lost its capacity to defend the German nation and the Wilhelmine state.

The revolutionary government of the Council of People's Representatives, installed on 10 November, immediately assumed the command over the armed forces. Its main imperative was not a democratic transformation of the army, but the need to meet the demands of the Armistice agreement, which stipulated that the troops in the West—at that point more than three million men—would have to clear French and Belgium territory within three weeks. This was the context for the agreement between the Army Supreme Command (OHL) and the revolutionary government, which is often given the misleading moniker Ebert-Groener 'pact'.[7] In reality, it was not a far-reaching political alliance, but just an understanding to cooperate on technical issues, reached in a series of telegrams and one phone call on 10 and 11 November between Wilhelm Groener, the successor of Erich Ludendorff as First Quartermaster-General and—with Paul von Hindenburg—leader of the OHL, and Friedrich Ebert as leading figure of the Council of

People's Representatives. Ebert agreed to leave the OHL in charge of the field army for an assurance of its loyalty and the promise of a speedy return to Germany and an orderly demobilization, while Groener urged the revolutionary government to support the preservation of discipline and the command structure.[8] This arrangement did not preclude the OHL from hedging more far-reaching plans. Already by mid-November, it had started to select nine divisions—all of them Guards units—that seemed sufficiently intact and motivated to march with full equipment into Berlin, to disarm the Soldier's Councils and other elements of the revolutionary left and thus to restore the 'army's monopoly on armed power'. Ebert, faced with the need to restore control of the capital, half-heartedly agreed to the operation under the command of Major General Arnold Lequis. When the first of the divisions arrived in Berlin on 10 December, the nervous tension in the city was palpable, as their deployment had not gone unnoticed among the revolutionary left. Yet what could have ended up as a coup came to naught, as the homecoming troops were not, as expected, an iron-clad instrument in the hands of their commanders, but quickly melted away 'like butter in the sun', as a high-ranking officer bitterly commented.[9] By mid-December it had become clear that the Council of People's Representatives could not rely on the troops under the command of the OHL to regain the monopoly of state power. In a city in which deserters were greeted with 'rapturous applause' when they talked like the 'converted' about their decision to lay down the weapons, maintaining military discipline had become nigh impossible.[10] When regular front-line troops under the command of Lequis lost a battle against the Volksmarinedivision in Berlin on 23/24 December 1918, which occupied the chancellery and arrested government members, the final disintegration of the field army had become apparent.[11]

In this very moment, the revolutionary government decided to employ the services of units other than those under command of the OHL. We will discuss some types of unit later when we analyse homeland defence as a joint societal undertaking, including the Einwohnerwehren (home guards), the Volkswehr (people's militia), and the Zeitfreiwilligen (Temporary Volunteers). Here, the focus is on the Free Corps (Freikorps). The Free Corps have received a lot of attention, not least because their short-lived existence and their violent exploits became the subject of elaborate literary self-representation and myth-making during the 1920s and 1930s.[12] With their aggressive, toxic style of masculinity and their 'male fantasies' in which they conjured up the devious Bolshevik as the representation of evil, the Freikorps veterans appeared to many historians as a key to unlock the mysteries of the fascist mentality.[13] In a more conventional approach, the Free Corps are seen as 'paramilitary bands' in which volunteers gathered around charismatic leadership figures.[14]

The reality, however, was more complicated and in many ways counter-intuitive. The Free Corps acted with state authorization, their members received their pay from the state and accrued state pension entitlements for every day of service, and they represented state authority. It should not be forgotten that sizeable Free Corps such as the Landesjägerkorps Maercker—built up since December 1918 by General Georg Maercker around the core of the 214th Infantry Division, which he commanded—and the Marine Brigade I, were loyal to the republican transition government under

Friedrich Ebert, contradicting the notion that these units were basically counter-revolutionary mercenaries.[15] When we conceive of the state as holding the legitimate monopoly of power, then the Free Corps *were* the German state, at least in the first half of 1919. The first Free Corps emerged in November and December 1918. Most of them crystallized around the core of former units of the field army, which were replenished with volunteers, usually joining not for any explicit ideological reasons, but for the pay that they would receive.[16] Events in the Prussian East prompted a more proactive approach by the Ebert government. Polish insurgents triggered an uprising in the city of Posen on 27 December 1918, managing to bring large parts of the Prussian province of Posen under their control within weeks. The Ebert government—at this point no longer restrained by the presence of USPD members—responded on 7 January 1919 with a call for volunteers to join units in the Grenzschutz (Border Defence) in the East, thus formally licensing the formation of Free Corps. While some of these units were not deployed in Posen province, but rather for a crackdown on the leftist council movement, skirmishes in the Posen province continued until a demarcation line was agreed with the Western Allies on 16 February 1919. One Free Corps unit that was made up mostly of Social Democratic workers of a locomotives factory received extra mention for its disciplined behaviour. Counting the men who served in Free Corps units is difficult, as fluctuation was high. The best estimates put the overall number at between 250,000 and 400,000 in March 1919.[17]

To be sure, the Free Corps left a trail of corpses in their repeated deployment as a mobile formation against insurgents from the radical left from January 1919 onwards in what amounted to a local or regional civil war. Major incidents included their violent crushing of the uprising by leftist workers in January in Berlin 1919—often misleadingly called the Spartacus uprising—, the fighting in Berlin in March 1919, which cost the lives of 1,200 socialist workers, and the participation of about 20,000 Free Corps troops in the brutal crackdown against the Munich Council Republic in May 1919.[18] The interpretation of these events very much depends on the perspective that the historian applies. For those who see a missed opportunity for a deeper political transformation in these uprisings, Gustav Noske, the Social Democratic defence expert who authorized the use of the Freikorps, first as a member of the Council of People's Representatives, from March 1919 as the first Reichswehr Minister, may have thought he was acting on the reasons of state, but was in reality nothing more than a puppet of the military and thus betrayed his own left credentials.[19] For those who identify with the victims of the atrocities that the Freikorps committed—of which there were many, including women and children who were mere bystanders—the events in early 1919 are an omen of the unleashing of state violence from 1933 onwards.[20] Things look yet again different from the perspective of the nation-state, defined as the institution that successfully claims 'the monopoly of legitimate physical violence' in its territory, what historian Charles S. Maier has called 'Leviathan 2.0'.[21] From this vantage point, Germany was still in a state of war with the western Allies—only interrupted by periodically extended armistice agreements—until June 1919, and in an undeclared war with the re-emerging nation-state of Poland, while facing multiple uprisings that were tantamount to a localized civil war. For the nation-state, using the violent force of the Free Corps was a precondition for the survival of the democratic republic. It is also helpful to consider the German case in comparative perspective. Key drivers for the cataclysm of paramilitary violence in countries such as Finland, Hungary, Lithuania, Ukraine, and parts of Western Russia were the collapse of the multinational empires of the Habsburg and Romanov dynasties and the self-assertion of secessionist nation-states.[22] The Free Corps were in comparison not only less paramilitary, but also enacted a more targeted violence with fewer fatalities than in these countries.

Already by January 1919, both the OHL and the Ebert government were considering plans to put the army structure on a more systematic footing. This led to the formation of the Provisional Reichswehr, based on a bill that the National Assembly passed on 6 March 1919 by the so-called Weimar coalition of SPD, Centre Party, and DDP. Its key stipulation was to rebuild the army of the republic in continuity with the existing formations, rather than building up a new army from scratch, as the so-called Hamburg Points had demanded with the support of the National Congress of Councils on 18 December 1918. Yet the Provisional Reichswehr also included elements that marked a break with tradition, most importantly the creation of one unified army structure, which abolished the system of separate contingents for Prussia, Bavaria, Saxony, and Württemberg; the Reich President as a civilian commander-in-chief; and the introduction of *Vertrauensleute* (trusted men), who were appointed by the soldiers to support their own welfare and could feed grievances up the chain of command.[23] The subsequent development of army policy, however, was not so much driven by these legal and administrative stipulations, but by foreign policy constraints. The Paris Peace Conference had opened on 18 January 1919. General Hans von Seeckt—who later served as head of the army command from 1920 to 1926—envisaged in April retaining an army of at least 300,000 men and continuing conscription. Yet when the German delegation arrived in Versailles, it quickly learned that the Allied demands were non-negotiable. When the draft of the treaty was handed to the Germans on 7 May 1919, the consternation was great. In the following weeks, frantic debates between high-ranking officers ensued behind the scenes. Against a fronde of officers who conjured up the idea to refuse signing and waging a war against Poland, Wilhelm Groener insisted that such plans were entirely futile and that Germany had to sign the peace treaty. Otherwise, the break-up of the Reich was looming. Groener repeatedly advised the government along these lines, and the German delegation signed the Treaty of Versailles on 28 June 1919.[24]

The military stipulations of the Treaty of Versailles shocked the German military elite and left a deep imprint on its subsequent thinking. The German army had to be reduced to 100,000 men, including 4,000 officers, and a navy of another 15,000 men. All modern weaponry, including an air force, U-boats, tanks, heavy artillery, were prohibited. The remaining vessels of the High Sea Fleet, interned at the British naval base Scapa Flow, had to be surrendered—and were sunk by their own crews in a gesture of defiance on 21 June 1919. Surplus ammunition and weaponry had to be handed to the Allies, and the export and import of armaments were strictly prohibited. Any planning, let alone preparation for a mobilization, was strictly prohibited.[25]

The most immediate repercussion of the Treaty was the discontent the reduction in personnel size triggered. By 10 April 1920, the army had to be reduced to 200,000 men, three months later to the final strength of 100,000. At its peak in the summer of 1919, the Provisional Reichswehr comprised 400,000 men. The Allies also demanded the disbanding of the Free Corps by March 1920, and the Home Guards one month later. For many officers, the end of their professional career was imminent. Status anxieties were compounded by fundamental opposition to the republic, exemplified by the Navy Brigade Ehrhardt, a Free Corps under the command of Hermann Ehrhardt, a radical right-wing nationalist and antisemite. On 10 March 1920, General Walther von Lüttwitz, head of Reichswehr Group Command I in Berlin and in that capacity also in charge of many of the Free Corps, demanded from Ebert and Noske to maintain the current army strength, resignation of the cabinet, early elections, and the position of Reichswehr commander for himself. Ebert flatly rejected this insubordination and placed Lüttwitz on immediate leave, so the coup began on 13 March with the Navy Brigade Ehrhardt entering the capital. When first Noske and then Ebert summoned high-ranking officers in the capital, only Walther Reinhardt, head of the army command, unreservedly supported the idea to suppress the coup with military counter-force. The majority, including Seeckt, either refused taking any part in such an option or were evasive.[26] The government responded by escaping to the south of Germany, and a general strike quickly extinguished the military insurrection and returned the legitimate government to power. Yet even outside the core of the putschists, their coup had laid bare the lack of support for the republic in the Provisional Reichswehr. The navy placed itself in its entirety at the disposal of Wolfgang Kapp—the civilian face of the coup and wannabe Reich Chancellor—and Lüttwitz. While other commanders adopted a more guarded position and waited for the outcome, and some later claimed to have been notified only belatedly, the overall picture is clear: most Reichswehr units in the north and east supported the putsch, while only a smaller number of units in the south and west stood unequivocally behind the legitimate government.[27]

The officers of the Provisional Reichwehr had betrayed the republic which they had under oath sworn to protect. Yet what followed was not a purge of the supporters of Kapp and Lüttwitz, but rather a purge of the few remaining devoted republicans in the corps. Seeckt, who had refused to support Ebert against the 1920 coup, was installed as head of the Heeresleitung (army command) in its wake. A traditional conservative, Seeckt was willing to serve the republican state, even though he rather resented both democratic parties and the constitution, which he famously described in 1923 as *not* being a 'noli me tangere'—i.e. untouchable—for him, as it ran contrary to his political core beliefs. As head of the army command, Seeckt set out to stabilize the Reichswehr and continue its institutional build-up. The Defence Law of 21 March 1921 provided the legal basis for this process. It adopted the military stipulations of the Treaty of Versailles into German law and described the outlines of a 100,000 men army, divided into seven infantry divisions and three cavalry divisions and entirely relying on professional soldiers who had to enlist for a minimum of twelve years, officers for twenty-five years. The Reich President was designated as commander-in-chief, with the Reichswehr minister—from 1920 to 1928 the liberal democrat Otto Geßler—acting as his deputy who nominally exercised day-to-day control. Yet the tacit agreement was that Seeckt would control the internal operations of the Reichswehr in return for its formal loyalty to the republican institutions.[28]

The economic and political crisis in 1923, in the wake of the French occupation of the Ruhr and hyperinflation, brought the political role of the Reichswehr back into sharp relief. From the late summer, Seeckt became the focal point of attempts, driven by the DNVP and other radical-nationalist groups, to replace democratic governance with a dictatorial three-man directorate that would include Seeckt. The head of the army command harboured political ambitions. In October, he drafted a government programme for his tenure as Reich Chancellor, which included a strict centralization of the Reich, an authoritarian state with a second chamber that represented professions, and abolishing trade unions. Paradoxically, though, a mutiny in the Bavarian Reichswehr thwarted Seeckt's political ambitions at this point. On 26 September 1923, the Bavarian government had declared a state of exception and appointed Gustav von Kahr as General State Commissioner. In immediate response, Reich President Ebert declared a state of emergency for the whole of Germany on 27 September, and transferred executive power, in line with Article 48(2) of the constitution, to Reichswehr minister Otto Geßler, who delegated these powers to the commanding generals of the seven military districts (Wehrkreise). Yet the Bavarian Wehrkreis commander, Otto von Lossow, refused to execute an order by Geßler, effectively staging a mutiny against Berlin. The collusion between parts of the Bavarian Reichswehr and the *völkisch* right set into a motion a sequence of events culminating in the Hitler putsch on 9 November 1923, in which von Lossow, vacillating to the last minute, ultimately did not take part. Responding to the news from Munich, Ebert handed all executive powers to Seeckt on 8/9 November, thus tasking him with safeguarding the republic. The putsch in Munich, however, was not quashed by Reichswehr troops, but by Bavarian police.[29]

By early 1924, leading Reichswehr circles were increasingly weary of the political role that the state of emergency had handed to them. In mid-February, Seeckt took the initiative, suggesting to Ebert to end the executive powers of the military by the end of that month. While the radical right objected, Ebert agreed.[30] The nationwide state of emergency from late September 1923 to February 1924 is usually discussed in terms of the use of Article 48, and is either seen as a temporary expedient or as a means of overturning the foundations of Weimar's republican state.[31] Yet it is also necessary to look at the sharp anti-left bias of the measures taken by the military commanders, which almost exclusively targeted Social Democrats and Communists. Newspapers of both parties were either repeatedly banned or placed under pre-emptive censorship. The overwhelming majority of the 3,515 individuals who were taken into 'protective custody' (*Schutzhaft*)—the euphemism so abundantly employed in the Third Reich was already in use—were Communists. Still, some military district commanders lamented the fact that parliamentary immunity had hindered then from placing KPD Reichstag members into *Schutzhaft*. It was no coincidence that military censorship of the press often responded to coverage that was critical of the Reichswehr itself.[32]

The Dynamics of Revisionism: Armaments and War Planning, 1924–1933

In the heated debates that ensued in December 1918 over the future direction of the German military, Seeckt had always emphasized the importance of the international arena and maintained that only rebuilding the Reichswehr would make Germany available as a potential ally. Soviet Russia was the obvious candidate, as the other outcast of the Versailles settlement. Already in 1920 Seeckt had opined that 'only a firm connection with Greater-Russia could offer Germany the prospect of a recovery of its world power status'.[33] Yet after French and Belgian troops invaded the Ruhr district in January 1923, and the Reichswehr command had quickly established that any military resistance was futile, Seeckt's vision had been exposed as a pipe-dream. Any attempt to overcome the limitations of the Versailles order and to build a military that could have some leverage in the international arena would have to accept Versailles in the first place. This acknowledgement picked up ideas that Groener, among others, had already floated in late 1918: that economy and society had to be reorganized and aligned with the military to make any attempt to revise the post-war order viable. The Reichswehr had to let go of any remnants of the Wilhelmine tradition, transform itself into an army of the future, and to prepare for a future war.[34] These attempts only started in earnest by 1924, after the profound shock of the French invasion had laid bare the limits of Seeckt's approach. Hence, 1924, and not the Kapp putsch in 1920, is the major caesura in the history of Weimar Germany's military.

The most radical proponent of this new approach to preparing for another war was Joachim von Stülpnagel. At this point the head of the operations department in the Troop Office (Truppenamt), he delivered a talk with 'Thoughts on the War of the Future' to like-minded officers in the Reichswehr Ministry in February 1924. Stülpnagel simply expressed military common sense when he urged his audience that someday the German people would remove their 'slave chains' and 'tear up the Versailles Diktat'. Yet he gave this idea a very specific slant when, quoting the philosopher Oswalt Spengler, he mused that every nation would fight in major wars over victory or defeat, yet only Germany would fight over 'victory or extermination (*Vernichtung*)'.[35] Stülpnagel harked back to the days of the anti-Napoleonic insurgency in Prussia 1807–15, but unlike then a future uprising against French hegemony had to be firmly under the control of the military. He briefly sketched out the political preconditions for a future war of national liberation, including the suppression of a 'morbid' parliamentary system, the streamlining and coordination of all civil state institutions in the service of war, educating youth to be 'defence-minded' (*wehrhaft*), the creation of 'hatred' against the foreign enemy, a system of 'compulsory labour', and a state-led crackdown against pacifism.[36]

All this amounted to preparing for total war. It was the core premise of Stülpnagel's vision that the distinction between different types of warrior would be 'extinguished' in a future war, and 'all men and all things' would become a 'material and an instrument of war'.[37] In operational terms, given the current weakness of the German nation and its military, this demanded a strategy of attrition in a campaign that would be initially fought on German soil. Given the vast material inferiority of the Reichswehr—Stülpnagel reckoned in 1924 that current stocks of ammunition would last no longer than an hour—the actual military campaign had to be prepared by a guerrilla war, executed by trained civilians in the border regions. This type of border defence implied destruction both of people—the Troop Office expected up to 75 per cent casualties—and of infrastructure, through the targeted detonation of buildings and the chemical poisoning of terrain. This was a scorched earth tactic, yet it was German soil that had to be scorched! Finally, the guerrilla war by trained civilians and the military operations had to be backed up by an all-out economic preparation for war.[38] There was a conceptual, even philosophical component to Stülpnagel's ideas that should not be missed. In his 1924 talk he emphasized that waging a war against the Versailles system—and France in the first instance—would be nothing but an empty 'heroic gesture', had it not been meticulously prepared over an extended period.[39] This can be interpreted as an implicit rejection of the notion of a 'heroic modernity' that gained substantial currency among German intellectuals in the early 1920s, i.e. a modernity in which individuals would respond to the dissolution of societal order with a heroic posture.[40] Stülpnagel's insistence on a sober acknowledgement of the objective facts that underpinned war planning in some ways resembles the realism of the New Objectivity, and it is perhaps more than coincidence that his talk and the formation of this artistic current happened at roughly the same time.

At any rate, what Stülpnagel's ideas implied were systematic attempts to redirect and refashion the Reichswehr further along the lines of a professional army. With a group of like-minded fellow officers, and partly building on already existing structures, work on this task started in 1924/5. To be sure, Stülpnagel's plans were not unanimously welcomed across the Reichswehr officer corps, especially by the traditionalist Seeckt.[41] Only when Seeckt stepped down as head of the army command in 1926, did the pace of change increase, supported by developments in the international arena in the wake of the 1925 Treaty of Locarno. Turning the Reichswehr into a professional army that could think in earnest of revising the Versailles order was a complex and multi-faceted process. Only a few elements are briefly highlighted here. The first step was the implementation of war games that reflected the new thinking, including exercises that simulated guerrilla warfare and the destruction of physical hardware in evacuated territory. Liaising with the Reichsbahn—the republic had centralized all existing railway franchises in a single state-run company—about plans to destroy railway lines in retreat from the enemy complemented these efforts.[42]

Another crucial element of professionalization was military personnel, and here especially officer recruitment. The aristocracy was still vastly overrepresented in the corps, with a share of roughly 20 per cent of all officers. But it would be wrong to see this as indicative of a continuing feudalization of the corps since the Wilhelmine era. The First World War had marked a deep caesura as the high death toll led to the demise of the old corps. More important than the continuing presence of members of the nobility post-1918 is the fact offspring from the landed aristocracy in the Prussian East, the so-called Junker, only had a marginal presence, whereas more than 50 per cent of the aristocratic officers had an officer as father. Applicants always vastly exceeded vacancies—in 1929, the ratio was 1,600 to 196. Thus, the Reichswehr marked a radical break with tradition as it placed a premium on educated officers, many with university degrees, who adopted professional standards and were less interested in status and distinction.[43] Archaic practices such a duelling over questions of honour were not banned outright, but were at least frowned upon, and the exclusive nature of military sociability was broken up and no longer required to define the collective identity of the corps. The officers of the Reichswehr were a professional group, not a separate caste.[44] In line with these developments, a functionalist, in many ways technocratic, attitude prevailed in the barracks. Military work was preparation for war, not the representation of an estate, a *Stand*, and perpetual training was paramount. One visible element of this functionalism was the retention of the field grey uniforms that had been introduced during the First World War. The most radical proposal in this direction came in 1932 out of the Troop Office. It suggested discarding all uniform insignia that indicated rank, and replacing them with signs indicating function, regardless whether they were worn by an officer or an NCO.[45] To realize the radical break with the Wilhelmine tradition that this entailed, we can follow Helmuth von Moltke the younger, the Head of the Prussian General Staff. In 1905, he confided to his diary his deep frustration with the proliferation of symbolic performances under Wilhelm II: 'It makes me sick when I see this nonsense that makes us completely forget the main thing, which is to prepare ourselves earnestly and with bitter energy for war. And so we deck people with multi-coloured ribbons as insignia, which only get in the way of handling the weapons.'[46]

In a very specific sense, the Reichswehr was the complete opposite to the symbolic inflation of the military in the Wilhelmine era. However, the relentless focus on functionalism and professionalism also had a price: unlike the Prussian military prior to 1914, the Reichswehr had no substantial presence in the social imaginary of German society during the 1920s. Instead, the symbolic place of the military was occupied by the nationalist veterans' associations like the Stahlhelm and the Kyffhäuser League.[47] The far-reaching withdrawal of the Reichswehr from the arena of performative symbolism had yet another consequence: judicial means replaced symbolic competition with critics of the military. Between 1924 and 1927 alone, the army brought around 10,000 charges of treason against social democratic and pacifist critics of the Reichswehr, and secured 1,071 sentences.[48]

The next step towards a professional army that would serve the underlying revisionist aims was rearmament. But this strategy was not without risks. German armaments were strictly limited by the Treaty of Versailles, and the Military Inter-Allied Commission of Control (Interalliierte Militär-Kontrollkommission, IMKK), set up by the Treaty and staffed by British, French, and Belgian officers, had far reaching powers to verify the decommissioning of arms, demolition of fortifications, and to inspect and monitor the training facilities and arms procurement practices of the Reichswehr on sites across

Germany.⁴⁹ The Reichwehr could engage in a game of cat and mouse with the inspection teams, and it did so with some success. But any far-reaching rearmament plans could prompt an Allied, or most likely French intervention—the events in 1923 had made that crystal clear—and thus endanger the very increase of German security that the build-up of a much bigger German army was meant to secure.

The best way to avoid this no-win scenario was to engage foreign policy to create a win-win situation. For these reasons, Reichswehr officials liaised intensively with the German Foreign Office on disarmament proposals, starting in 1924. Interventions along this route intensified once the Locarno Treaties in 1925 had normalized relations with the Western powers and Germany had become a member of the League of Nations in September 1926. The League of Nations kick-started multilateral negotiations on arms control measures with the Preparatory Disarmament Conference, which started in Geneva in 1926 and conducted technical talks that continued—with some interruptions—until the Geneva Disarmament Conference was held in 1932/3. German participation in this process began under favourable auspices. For the first time since 1919, Germany entered the field of multilateral diplomacy not as an outcast, but as a recognized partner. Moreover, it could point out (formal) compliance with the disarmament stipulations of the Versailles Treaty, and hence start to challenge the Allies to take their own steps in this direction. None other than Joachim von Stülpnagel outlined the prospects of this approach in a 1926 memorandum on disarmament issues from the perspective of military 'Realpolitik'. Using the leverage that the collectively stated aim of disarmament provided, Germany could try to secure, step by step, key aims such as Allied withdrawal from the Rhineland, a return of the Polish corridor that separated mainland Germany from East Prussia, and the Anschluss of the Austrian Republic as a springboard to restore great power status.⁵⁰ This strategy, however, was not undisputed, even within the Reichswehr ministry, in which hawks demanded to openly table Germany's rearmament aims. Another impediment was the necessary double-speak that this strategy entailed—proclaiming disarmament in the international arena while promoting revisionist policies at home—which faced harsh criticism from the radical right. At any rate, by 1930 Germany was isolated in the Preparatory Disarmament Conference, even from the other revisionist powers China and Soviet Union, and the strategy of engaging foreign policy to achieve a collective levelling of armaments had reached a dead end.⁵¹

The final, in the end most important, step towards military revisionism was rearmament, which in the context of the Versailles stipulations and the IMKK checks could only mean clandestine rearmament. The first steps in this direction were taken already in 1920 when Reichswehr representatives initiated contacts with the Red Army. Using Soviet Russia as a partner for clandestine arms programmes made perfect sense for Seeckt and other top-brass German military, their virulent anti-Bolshevism notwithstanding. Both countries were outcasts in the international order, and shared both enmity and security concerns regarding the assertive Polish state, which in 1920 had just conducted a successful second offensive in the Polish-Soviet War and managed to move the Polish border 250 kilometres further to the east. In addition, German technological know-how could only benefit the Russians. The German-Russian Rapallo agreement in 1922 provided a political framework for the cooperation. In practice, cooperation initially focused on joint industrial ventures for the manufacturing of airplanes, poison gas, and ammunition. This strategy suffered a setback when first the *Manchester Guardian*, then the Social-Democratic *Vorwärts* newspaper and Philipp Scheidemann, using the forum of the Reichstag, exposed shipments of Soviet shells to the port of Stettin in December 1926.[52] But in spite of this partial exposure, the cooperation continued along lines that had already been established in 1924/5: with a focus on advanced arms that were explicitly banned by the Treaty of Versailles: an aerodrome in Lipetsk trained German officers as pilots; at Kazan, Reichswehr officers were trained in using tanks; at a third facility, German and Soviet military personnel experimented with poison gas. Thus, secret cooperation continued until Hitler cancelled it in 1933. The significance of these endeavours was negligible in quantitative terms: 200 German pilots were trained at Lipetsk, a mere thirty tank specialists at Kazan. Yet as trailblazers who could teach others, their expertise was invaluable: twenty of the Lipetsk graduates had a rapid career from 1933 and became Wehrmacht generals.[53]

Back in Germany, systematic rearmament started only in 1926/7, coinciding with the end of Seeckt's tenure and the ending of the IMKK controls in 1927, which made clandestine arms deployment easier to hide. Seeckt's successor, Wilhelm Heye, gave the Reich cabinet a full briefing on the ongoing secret armament measures, and demanded a coordinated structure to fund these illegal programmes out of the Reich budget. The solution was a secret committee of state secretaries, in which delegates of the relevant ministries, aided by the Reich Audit Office, would agree on military spending that could be hidden in the published budget. This covert cooperation, first practised for the 1928 budget, went hand in hand with a systematic approach to armament, which included multi-annual planning rounds, a close coordination with the arms manufacturers, and strict controlling of both the financial and the technological parameters and their implementation.[54] This was a shift from mere 'procurement politics' to coordinated 'armaments management' and resembled a quantum leap because it created a self-perpetuating system of inherent military necessities, or *Sachzwänge* in German parlance.[55] The medium-term aim of these endeavours was an army of twenty-one divisions, trebling the then seven infantry divisions, and securing sufficient weapons supplies for an army of this size. Practical steps were the First Armament Programme, launched in 1928 for the period 1929 to 1933, and the Second Armament Programme, adopted in 1932 for the years 1933 to 1938. An acceleration of armament measures occurred also in the field of personnel. Around 1930, concerns about the dwindling number of those year groups that had received training during the First World War abounded, prompting plans to substantially increase—under the Treaty of Versailles illegal—militia formations to enhance skilled reserves. Necessary legislation was already drafted by the Reichswehr ministry in the winter of 1932, and the Voluntary Labour Service, founded in 1931 and registering more than 250,000 individuals, shared its data with the Reichswehr.[56] Thus, preparation for the reintroduction of general conscription had already begun before Hitler was appointed as chancellor. The dynamics of both pillars of the Reichswehr rearmament programme, build-up of weaponry and enlistment of personnel, pulled the military beyond the political framework that the republic provided.

Homeland Defence: Mobilizing Society and Military-State Hybrids, 1919–1933

The military strike at the Western front, and the rapid pace of the self-demobilization of the returning troops in the autumn of 1918 created, as we have seen earlier, a fundamental dilemma. On the one hand, the disintegration of the old army was the fundamental precondition for the success of the revolution. On the other, the lack of reliable military formations endangered the attempts of the Council of People's Representatives to stabilize a new, republican order, both internally and externally. One way out of this dilemma was, as discussed, the formation of state-licensed Free Corps. Yet the government was also able to rely on the self-mobilization of social groups, who armed themselves along the lines of different political fault-lines. While some of these units were disbanded once the revolutionary transformation ended and the Allies imposed strict controls on German armament, others were transformed into the myriad networks of homeland defence, a secretive, 'black' Reichswehr that complemented the official army.

Among the various forms of self-mobilization that sprang up in 1918/19 we can distinguish four different types. The first were Volkswehr units or people's militias. A law enacted by the Council of People's Representatives on 6 December 1918 envisaged the people's militias as the nucleus of a new, democratic army that would support the revolutionary transition government and implement progressive principles such as the election and accountability of the officers. But the uptake on this promise was haphazard and uneven. Most people's militias were formed by soldiers' councils in cities with a strong socialist majority, but their consolidation was hampered by the internecine struggles between the radical left—which tried to dominate these units—and the majority Social Democrats. Wherever Free Corps came into play, the people's militias were immediately curtailed, and the remaining formations were wound down from March 1919, with only about 11,000 Volkswehr soldiers integrated into the Provisional Reichswehr.[57]

A much more substantial form of social defence mobilization were the Einwohnerwehren (home guards). Their key driver was the militarization of two major social cleavages, those between industrial workers and the middle class in urban areas, and between agrarian producers and urban consumers in rural areas. In the former context, they defended property and maintained public order, in the latter, they defended property and, more importantly, agricultural produce. These units had emerged since November 1918, and were officially endorsed, coordinated, armed, and funded by state authorities across Germany from March 1919. As a means of arming ordinary citizens—mostly with rifles and light machine guns, stocks of heavier weaponry such as field artillery canon were limited—and suppressing social unrest in a localized environment, the home guards were highly successful. An estimate for October 1919 puts the number of guardsmen in Prussia alone at 630,000. Yet contrary to what many of their organizers had hoped for—most prominently among them Georg Escherich, one of the most prolific organizers of paramilitary groups and head of the home guards in Bavaria—they never evolved into counter-revolutionary shock-troops that could be deployed as mobile units. Both urban and rural militiamen were profoundly tired of fighting, fearful of becoming involved in a potentially escalating civil war, and content to simply pacify their immediate surroundings.[58]

Ultimately, the Allies placed pressure on the German government to disband the home guards, which they did in April 1920, yet only on paper. In practice, they were turned into a private entity, a model Georg Escherich had pioneered in Bavarian with the Orgesch (Organization Escherich) and that was subsequently rolled out across the Reich. Only when the Allies issued their London Ultimatum on 5 May 1921, which demanded disbanding all paramilitary units, did the German government comply, inaugurating what was called fulfilment policy. A third, in quantitative terms rather small, type of mobilization for violence was represented by the Zeitfreiwilligen (Temporary Volunteers). They sprang up when Noske and the Prussian Minister of Culture, Konrad Haenisch, called upon students to sign up for border defence in the East on 13 March 1919, but their most widespread deployment came in the spring of 1920 in the brutal crushing of the leftist workers who had defeated the Kapp putsch and pushed, at the Ruhr and elsewhere, for a more radical social and political transformation. Temporary volunteer units were mostly staffed by students and university teachers, many of whom were either war veterans or former reserve officers. Once mobilized, they were integrated into regular Reichswehr units and fought under their command. Temporary volunteers committed some of the worst atrocities of the whole Weimar era, for instance the massacre of Mechterstädt in Thuringia. On 25 March 1920, about twenty members of the Marburg Student Corps killed fifteen unarmed workers, whom they were meant to escort to the town of Gotha, and left their corpses by the roadside.[59]

The final, and with the home guard most seminal, form of social mobilization for homeland defence was the Grenzschutz Ost (Border Defence East). These were groups of volunteers which were called upon from early 1919 to stave off a Polish insurrection against the Prussian provinces in the East, Posen, West Prussia, and Upper Silesia. Some of these volunteers joined the Free Corps that fought against the Bolsheviki in the newly founded Baltic States, the so-called Baltikumer. Latvia specifically authorized the use of German volunteer units in an agreement with the German authorities on 29 December 1918. Yet the presence of German formations hundreds of miles east of the German border aroused suspicion among the Allies, and by December 1919, the Baltikumer had been forced to return to Germany.[60] The situation at the border to Poland remained tense, especially in Upper Silesia. The Treaty of Versailles had stipulated a plebiscite to settle the national affiliation of the province.

Anxious about the outcome, Polish insurgents staged three separate uprisings, in August 1919, August 1920, and again in May 1921. The Border Defence East units that were quashing these uprisings increasingly slipped into radical right-wing activism, especially as they had to be formally disbanded in the wake of the London Ultimatum and were, like some scattered, localized remnants of the home guards, privatized.[61] The increasingly messy situation at the eastern border prompted attempts by the Prussian Ministry of Interior, led by the Social Democrat Carl Severing, to create a framework that would turn the Border Defence East into a state-controlled force. Talks with the Reichswehr ministry about details commenced in late 1922, and by 1923, a set of regulations and guidelines had been established.[62]

These regulations described what became known as the 'black Reichswehr', a term radical pacifists such as Emil Julius Gumbel and the former Reichswehr officer Carl Mertens coined in a stream of publications in which they tried to scandalize the existence of these formations and the collusion of civil authorities in their maintenance.[63] Yet despite their best efforts, the wider public was not interested in these revelations, and the liberal Reichswehr minister Otto Geßler managed successfully to deflect attention by claiming that the term could only refer to short-lived secretive units within the Reichswehr in 1923 in the context of the Buchrucker putsch, named after the main culprit, Major Bruno Buchrucker.[64] However, from 1922/3 the 'black' Reichswehr consisted of three separate organizations that operated outside of the official army structure: the Border Defence militia (Grenzschutz) which operated in the eastern provinces of Prussia and Bavaria near the Czechoslovakian border; the Landesschutz (Territorial Defence), which operated across the Reich in varying levels of density, including, at least until 1928, the de-militarized zone along the Rhine; and the Feldjägerdienst, units that were meant to support a popular insurrection along the lines Stülpnagel had outlined in 1924, which were disbanded in 1928. As all this was a blatant breach of the Treaty of Versailles (and of the Weimar Constitution), and should remain undetected by the IMKK, the secrecy around these arrangements bordered on paranoia. Civil authorities which were involved were meant to shred every single document on this matter. The Landesschutz employed former Reichswehr personnel on a full-time basis, whereas the bulk of the active members were civilians who were called up for exercises. Secrecy reigned, hence reliable figures are hard to come by. But the Border Defence had lists with between 100,000 and 150,000 available volunteers by the late 1920s, and perhaps 20,000 of them participated on a regular basis in exercises.[65]

The part-time volunteers who staffed the black Reichswehr were prepared for the event of a foreign invasion, and so they were activated when French and Belgian troops invaded the Ruhr district in January 1923. The policy of passive resistance that the government pronounced was secretly accompanied by acts of sabotage through the Feldjägerdienst. This included armed attacks with explosives against railway lines—eighty-six in March 1923 alone—or the escape of 300 paramilitaries, including many social democratic workers, from the occupied zone in a train on Easter Monday that forced its way across the Belgian border patrol. The same tactic was deployed to smuggle semi-finished goods for heavy industry firms into the unoccupied zone.[66] The conflict with France and Belgium in early 1923 marked a moment of tremendous belligerence and popular war enthusiasm on a scale that had never been seen in modern German history, not even in August 1914, when actual effervescence had been limited to nationalist members of the middle class (the myth of the August experience was invented later in the war to paper over the increasing cracks in national unity as class conflicts returned with a vengeance). Popular belligerence in early 1923 was genuine, not a result of propaganda, and it reached beyond the usual suspects such like members of nationalist associations, most importantly deep into the social democratic working-class milieu.[67] The 'no more war'-movement provides a litmus test for this. From 1920 to 1922, this pacifist slogan had mobilized hundreds of thousands of social democratic workers who expressed their 'desire for peace' on 1 August. In 1923, the movement collapsed and did not manage to stage more than a few indoor gatherings.[68]

The Territorial Defence and other units of the black Reichswehr demonstrate the hybrid nature of mobilization for war in Weimar Germany, in which the professional army, civilian state authorities, and self-mobilized civilian actors closely cooperated. Another example was the practice of *Wehrwissenschaften*. The term—which roughly translates as defence sciences—was a neologism, coined in 1926 as an umbrella term for all academic endeavours that supported the *Wehrhaftmachung* of the German nation. Defence sciences was a transdisciplinary field that included historians and geographers as well as political scientists and sport scientists. To support the networking among the experts, which included both university staff members and academics working for Reichswehr institutions, but also reached out to students, a Wehrwissenschaftliche Arbeitsgemeinschaft was founded in 1928. The development of this scientific practice was not driven by Nazi ideology, but was seamlessly continued, albeit at a much higher pace, after 1933 in the service of the aggressive preparation of the Third Reich for another war.[69]

Crucially, the mobilization of society for homeland defence also included efforts to utilize education to make the youth ready for military service and war. This was already mentioned in Stülpnagel's 1924 talk, as we have seen, and was a perennial concern for Reichswehr planners, who feared that the abolition of conscription would lead to a fundamental lack of young men with both training in and affinity to the military. Yet for many years, no coherent action was taken. In 1929, another strategy paper circulated in the Reichswehr ministry which highlighted the aim to introduce physical education of school pupils and those who had left school, shooting practice in both schools and universities, as well as military education in these institutions, taught by former army officers who were employed on a full-time basis. Additional measures such as the screening of films about the army and navy in cinemas should complement the practical side with ideological indoctrination.[70] But it was only in late 1932, when Kurt von Schleicher was Reichswehr minister, that concrete proposals in this direction reached the cabinet table, proving a template for subsequent actions taken by the Hitler government.[71]

Reichswehr and Politics in the Final Years of the Republic

From 1919 to 1930, the mobilization of civil society for homeland defence and the organization of a hybrid civil-military infrastructure for the secret Reichswehr had rested on a broad political defence consensus that included actors and parties from the nationalist right, namely the DNVP, to the moderate left, the SPD. Only the left wing of the USPD—which merged with the Communists in late 1920 anyway—and the Communist Party (KPD) remained outside. Moderate social democrats supported this consensus, most notably Carl Severing, who served as Prussian Minister of the Interior 1920 to 1926 and again from 1930 to 1932, and in this capacity aligned the civil administration in the Prussian East with the Border Defence organization. Joseph Wirth, on the very left wing of the Centre Party, was proud to be called the 'father of the black Reichswehr' for his incessant endeavours to foster secretive armaments.[72] In the 1923 Ruhr crisis, Heinrich Brauns, the Centre Party Reich Labour Minister, was a key liaison for and supporter of armed resistance, as was Eduard Hamm, a liberal democrat who served as State Secretary in the Reich Chancellery.[73] Supporting homeland defence was not only a preserve of the right.

Yet by 1930, this consensus had expired, and a policy shift positioned the Reichswehr in an increasingly aggressive stance against the remaining remnants of parliamentary democracy, and towards an active engagement with the radical insurrection that the Nazi movement embodied. In many ways, security issues dominated German politics in 1930–3, both domestically and in foreign policy, and in each case the Reichswehr adopted an approach that would cut itself loose from the remaining restraints that the parliamentary system put in place. This was most obvious in armaments spending. The First Armament Programme allocated 70 million marks per year, roughly 10 per cent of the overall military budget. But the political repercussions were dramatic, as the spending period coincided with the huge cuts in public expenditure that the economic crisis and the austerity policies of Heinrich Brüning entailed. Against this backdrop of shrinking budgets, the programme committed republican governments to long-term spending, thus effectively cancelling the budget authority of the Reichstag and hollowing out the already fragile power of parliament. In October 1931, Hans Schäffer, secretary of state in the Reich Finance Ministry, complained: 'From the budgetary point of view, we are already living in a military dictatorship.'[74]

A new, hardened approach was also visible in the Reichswehr's application in foreign policy. In February 1932, the Geneva Disarmament Conference opened. It provided the prospect of revising important parts of the military stipulations of the Treaty of Versailles, at least those that were in line with the current state of German rearmament planning. At this point, the traditional Reichswehr approach, to use multilateral international agreements as cover for clandestine armaments, was still unchanged. In this respect, Kurt von Schleicher's brief tenure as Reichswehr Minister, commencing in June 1932, marked a considerable change of tack. From 1926, Schleicher had already exerted considerable political influence, first as head of the armed forces department in the Reichswehr ministry, from 1929 as head of the office of ministerial affairs. As minister, he not only presented his plans for an accelerated pace of rearmament, including an increase in the professional army from 100,000 to 144,000 men by 1938, in uncompromising fashion at the cabinet table, securing approval in November 1932. He also developed a revisionist foreign policy agenda that moved beyond multilateralism and relied on bilateral agreements, or on direct unilateral action against the Versailles order.[75]

The defence consensus from moderate left to nationalist right also disintegrated in the context of the black Reichswehr and homeland defence. Several factors combined to create a new, nationalist-bellicose orientation that did not any longer rely on the integration of the moderate left, but rather reformulated the general aim of Wehrhaftmachung—making the nation defence-ready—in confrontation against the left and the republic, and through the inclusion of the radical right in form of the NSDAP. One factor was that the Prussian government under the Social Democrat Otto Braun became weary of the increasingly brazen infiltration of the Border Defence units by the radical nationalist combat league Stahlhelm. Hence, Braun decided in September 1929 to abolish the Stahlhelm in the Rhine province. This was very much in line with the official Reichswehr policy to avoid anything that could endanger the planned withdrawal of the Allies from the Rhineland in 1930, yet nevertheless soured relations with Wilhelm Groener—who had served as Reichswehr minister since 1928—and Schleicher. In their view, the shift to government by decree with Brüning as chancellor was a necessary step to protect the black Reichswehr against any further incursions from Prussia. The ongoing crisis of the agricultural sector in the Prussian East compounded this shift to the right. Supply of agricultural workers on the landed estates, who had been a crucial resource of personnel for the Border Defence units, dried up, making a more systematic reliance on the paramilitary formation of the Nazi Stormtroopers both convenient and promising. At the local level, links between the SA and the Border Defence units had existed for years. It now turned into a systematic integration of the SA into Border Defence, which was completed by 1931. Not only for Schleicher, this was just the first step towards a wider inclusion of NSDAP members into army personnel expansion.[76]

At this point, parts of the junior officer corps had already developed sympathies for the Nazi movement. This was brought to public attention in the so-called Ulm Reichswehr trial in September/October 1930. The trial took place at the Reich Court in Leipzig, but in the dock were three young officers from the detachment of Artillery Regiment 5 that was stationed in Ulm. Dissatisfied with Groener's military policies, which they perceived as a move towards the left, the trio had met Franz Pfeffer von Salomon and other SA leaders in Munich in late 1929. Encouraged by Salomon, they started wooing their fellow officers in Ulm and other garrisons to support the NSDAP. The Reichswehr command initially tried to contain their activities through internal procedures. As the extent of their treasonous behaviour became clear, a trial was unavoidable. During the court proceedings—which allowed Hitler, who was interrogated as a witness, the opportunity to perform his infamous sworn declaration that he would only seize power by legal means—the widespread discontent within younger members of the corps and the extent of support for the NSDAP became apparent. Perhaps more importantly, many high-ranking officers, including Ludwig Beck, the commander of the regiment and later Chief of the Wehrmacht General Staff, agreed that the three had only acted out of false idealism, and that the trial and its publicity was a disgrace.[77] Yet many junior officers were still rather disgusted by the primitive appearance and rowdy behaviour of the Nazi movement, even though they appreciated its fundamental aim to make Germany *wehrhaft* again.[78]

At any rate, more important than the political preferences of junior officers for the events that drove Germany to the Nazi dictatorship in 1932/3 was the military relevance of the Nazi Stormtroopers. The SA is usually seen as a party army that terrorized its opponents through violent street politics.[79] Yet by 1932, thousands of SA members were also part of the state army: either as members of Border Defence units, or in Reichswehr supported activities to make young men—as future conscripts—physically fit. The deep integration of the SA into homeland defence structures, however, created problems when their treasonous intentions were scandalized. This was the tactic used by Otto Braun in March/April 1932. With the heads of other Länder he pushed for a ban of the SA, ultimately convincing the vacillating Groener to enact such a ban on 13 April. Yet this decision became a key reason for Groener's downfall in May, and Schleicher, newly installed as Reichswehr minister in June 1932, rescinded the ban immediately.[80] Military issues also provided not the rationale, but a crucial context for the forced and unconstitutional removal of the Prussian caretaker government under Otto Braun on 20 July 1932 by the Papen government. The Reich institutions now had a direct grip on the Prussian civil administration, enabling them to enforce compliance with border defence measures. By the end of 1932, a defence state, entirely geared towards homeland defence and rearmament and thus a military dictatorship in all but name, had come into existence.[81]

Conclusion

The history of the German military from 1918 to 1933 includes a cast of equally colourful and problematic characters, from right-wing desperados like Ehrhardt or Lüttwitz, radical protagonists of total war such as Stülpnagel, to a relentless schemer and gravedigger of the republic like Schleicher, with very few slightly more savoury figures such as Reinhardt and Groener in between. Yet it would be wrong to see the Reichswehr as driven by the either base or honourable motivations of its top brass. The republic clearly failed to design a military that was unequivocally committed to democratic values, mostly because those engaged socialists who could have staffed such an army in 1919 were at this point either war weary, or preoccupied by internecine infighting among the left, or both. At any rate, a lack of engaged democrats was not the key problem of the Reichswehr. The fundamental conundrum, yet also the key incentive that defence and rearmaments politics posed, was to prepare Germany's return to great power status under the crippling military conditions of the Versailles Treaty. After the shock of 1923, the Reichswehr adopted structures and policies which, despite many internal conflicts, fundamentally implied that the republican state had to be remodelled in service of these ambitions. This interpretation of German rearmament also has crucial implications for the periodization of military policies. In regard to arms build-up and war preparation 1933 was, as historian Bernhard Kroener has convincingly argued, not a 'fundamental caesura', but rather a 'threshold towards gradual acceleration' in the implementation of plans that already been prepared in the republic.[82]

Notes

1. The military is, for instance, absent from Anthony McElligott, *Rethinking the Weimar Republic: Authority and Authoritarianism, 1916–1936* (London: Bloomsbury, 2014).
2. Michael Geyer, 'German Strategy in the Age of Machine Warfare', in Peter Paret (ed.), *Makers of Modern Strategy: Military Thought from Machiavelli to Hitler* (Princeton: Princeton University Press, 1986), 527–97.
3. Ute Frevert, *A Nation in Barracks: Modern Germany, Military Conscription and Civil Society* (Oxford, New York: Berg, 2004).
4. F. L. Carsten, *The Reichswehr and Politics, 1918 to 1933* (Oxford: Clarendon Press, 1966), 401; Hans-Adolf Jacobsen, 'Militär, Staat und Gesellschaft in der Weimarer Republik', in Karl Dietrich Bracher et al. (eds), *Die Weimarer Republik 1918–1933: Politik, Wirtschaft, Gesellschaft* (Düsseldorf: Droste, 1987), 343–68, 368.
5. As a summary: Michael Geyer, 'Professionals and Junkers: German Rearmament and Politics in the Weimar Republic', in Richard Bessel (ed.), *Social Change and Political Development in Weimar Germany* (London: Croom Helm, 1981), 77–133.
6. Benjamin Ziemann, *Violence and the German Soldier in the Great War: Killing–Dying–Surviving* (London: Bloomsbury Academic, 2017), 135–55.
7. Scott Stephenson, *The Final Battle: Soldiers of the Western Front in the German Revolution of 1918* (Cambridge: Cambridge University Press, 2009), 116–21.
8. Ulrich Kluge, *Soldatenräte und Revolution: Studien zur Militärpolitik in Deutschland 1918/19* (Göttingen: Vandenhoeck & Ruprecht, 1975), 136–44.
9. Stephenson, *Final Battle*, 193–257, quotes 218, 255.
10. Diary entry from 1 Dec. 1918: Käthe Kollwitz, *Die Tagebücher* (Berlin: Siedler, 1989), quote 386.
11. Stephenson, *Final Battle*, 258–98.
12. Matthias Sprenger, *Landsknechte auf dem Weg ins Dritte Reich? Zu Genese und Wandel des Freikorpsmythos* (Paderborn: Schöningh, 2008).
13. See the seminal, yet mostly erroneous book by Klaus Theweleit, *Male Fantasies*, 2 vols (Cambridge: Polity, 1987/1988).
14. Richard J. Evans, *The Coming of the Third Reich* (London: Penguin, 2003), 74 (quote), 229.
15. Rüdiger Bergien, *Die bellizistische Republik: Wehrkonsens und 'Wehrhaftmachung' in Deutschland 1918–1933* (Munich: R. Oldenbourg 2012), 80–3.

16. Details in Hagen Schulze, *Freikorps und Republik 1918–1920* (Boppard: Boldt, 1969), 22–47; Peter Keller, *'Die Wehrmacht der Deutschen Republik ist die Reichswehr': Die deutsche Armee 1918–1921* (Paderborn: Schöningh, 2014), 48–81.
17. Boris Barth, *Dolchstoßlegenden und politische Desintegration: Das Trauma der deutschen Niederlage im Ersten Weltkrieg 1914–1933* (Düsseldorf: Droste, 2003), 232–8, figure 237.
18. See Barth, *Dolchstoßlegenden*, 241–6.
19. Wolfram Wette, *Gustav Noske: Eine politische Biographie* (Düsseldorf: Droste, 1987), esp. 417–18, 427.
20. Mark Jones, *Founding Weimar: Violence and the German Revolution of 1918–1919* (Cambridge: Cambridge University Press, 2016).
21. Max Weber, *Wirtschaft und Gesellschaft: Grundriss der Verstehenden Soziologie* (Cologne, Berlin: Kiepenheuer & Witsch, 1964), vol. 2, 1043; see Charles S. Maier, *Leviathan 2.0: Inventing Modern Statehood* (Cambridge, MA: Belknap Press, 2012).
22. John Horne and Robert Gerwarth, 'Vectors of Violence: Paramilitarism in Europe after the Great War, 1917–1923', *Journal of Modern History*, 83 (2011), 489–512.
23. Keller, *Wehrmacht*, 146–89; Harold J. Gordon, jun., *The Reichswehr and the German Republic 1919–1926* (Princeton: Princeton University Press, 1957), 53–89, 147–8.
24. Carsten, *Reichswehr*, 37–48; Gordon, *Reichswehr*, 37.
25. Carsten, *Reichswehr*, 50–2.
26. William Mulligan, *The Creation of the Modern German Army: General Walther Reinhardt and the Weimar Republic, 1914–1930* (New York: Berghahn, 2005), 138–68; Gordon, *Reichswehr*, 90–129.
27. Carsten, *Reichswehr*, 78–88; Heinz Hürten, *Der Kapp-Putsch als Wende: Über Rahmenbedingungen der Weimarer Republik seit dem Frühjahr 1920* (Opladen: Westdeutscher Verlag, 1989), 21–3, on lack of information. Entirely baseless is the claim by Sönke Neitzel, *Deutsche Krieger: Vom Kaiserreich zur Berliner Republik—eine Militärgeschichte* (Berlin: Propyläen, 2020), 85, that three-quarters of the Reichswehr units would have supported the legitimate government, had they been ordered to crack down on Lüttwitz and his troops.
28. Carsten, *Reichswehr*, 103–35, quote 117; for details see Gordon, *Reichswehr*, 161–6, 169–216, 223–9.
29. Carsten, *Reichswehr*, 153–95.
30. Ibid., 196–8.
31. McElligott, *Rethinking*, 186–8.
32. See the documents in Heinz Hürten (ed.), *Das Krisenjahr 1923: Militär und Innenpolitik 1922–1924* (Düsseldorf: Droste, 1980), 75–80, 318–62, figure 348.
33. Cited in Michael Geyer, *Aufrüstung oder Sicherheit: Die Reichswehr in der Krise der Machtpolitik 1924–1936* (Wiesbaden: Steiner, 1980), 35.
34. Geyer, 'Professionals', 96–100.
35. See the excerpt: Lieutenant Colonel Joachim von Stülpnagel, 'Gedanken über den Krieg der Zukunft', Feb. 1924, in Hürten (ed.), *Krisenjahr 1923*, 266–272, quotes 268.
36. Ibid., 270.
37. Quoted in Geyer, *Aufrüstung*, 85.
38. See ibid., 85–9; additional details in Wilhelm Deist, 'Die Reichswehr und der Krieg der Zukunft', *Militärgeschichtliche Mitteilungen*, 45 (1989), 81–92, here 85–7.
39. Quoted in Deist, 'Reichswehr', 87.

40. See Helmuth Kiesel, *Geschichte der deutschsprachigen Literatur 1918–1933* (Munich: Beck, 2017), 91–2.
41. Jacobsen, 'Militär', 354.
42. Geyer, *Aufrüstung*, 100–4.
43. Marcus Funck, 'Schock und Chance: Der preußische Militäradel in der Weimarer Republik zwischen Stand und Profession', in Heinz Reif (ed.), *Adel und Bürgertum in Deutschland: Entwicklungslinien und Wendepunkte im 20. Jahrhundert*, vol. 2 (Berlin: Akademie Verlag, 2001), 127–71, figures 160, 163.
44. Geyer, 'Professionals', 80–2.
45. Ibid., 81, 89.
46. Cited in Isabel V. Hull, *The Entourage of Kaiser Wilhelm II 1888–1918* (Cambridge: Cambridge University Press, 1982), 41; see Jakob Vogel, 'Military, Folklore, Eigensinn: Folkloric Militarism in Germany and France, 1871–1914', *Central European History*, 33 (2000), 487–504.
47. Geyer, 'Professionals', 90.
48. Benjamin Ziemann, *Contested Commemorations: Republican War Veterans and Weimar Political Culture* (Cambridge: Cambridge University Press, 2013), 58.
49. See Jürgen Heideking, 'Vom Versailler Vertrag zur Genfer Abrüstungskonferenz: Das Scheitern der alliierten Militärkontrollpolitik gegenüber Deutschland nach dem Ersten Weltkrieg', *Militärgeschichtliche Mitteilungen*, 28 (1980), 45–68.
50. Geyer, *Aufrüstung*, 119–36, quote 126.
51. Ibid., 136–48.
52. Ibid., 149–60; Manfred Zeidler, *Reichswehr und Rote Armee 1920–1933: Wege und Stationen einer ungewöhnlichen Zusammenarbeit* (Munich: Oldenbourg, 1993), 29–107, 143–7.
53. Zeidler, *Reichswehr*, 107–28, 171–208, figures 302–3.
54. Wilhelm Deist, 'The Rearmament of the Wehrmacht', in Militärgeschichtliches Forschungsamt (ed.), *Germany and the Second World War*. vol. 1. *The Build-up of German Aggression*, trans. P. S. Falla et al. (Oxford: Clarendon Press, 1990), 373–540, here 381–4.
55. Michael Geyer, 'Das Zweite Rüstungsprogramm (1930–1934)', *Militärgeschichtliche Mitteilungen*, 17 (1975), 125–72, quote 125. See Geyer, *Aufrüstung*, 293, 297.
56. Geyer, *Aufrüstung*, 294–7; Bernhard Kroener, 'Mobilmachungsplanungen gegen Recht und Verfassung: Kriegsvorbereitungen in Reichsheer und Wehrmacht 1918 bis 1939', in Bruno Thoß and Hans-Erich Volkmann (eds), *Erster Weltkrieg—Zweiter Weltkrieg: Ein Vergleich. Krieg, Kriegserlebnis, Kriegserfahrung in Deutschland* (Paderborn: Schöningh, 2002), 57–78, here 70–1.
57. Kluge, *Soldatenräte*, 247–50, 325–50.
58. Benjamin Ziemann, *War Experiences in Rural Germany 1914–1923* (Oxford: Berg, 2007), 230–40; Dirk Schumann, *Political Violence in the Weimar Republic, 1918-1933: Fight for the Streets and Fear of Civil War*, trans. Thomas Dunlap (New York, Oxford: Berghahn, 2009), 16–25; Erwin Könnemann, 'Einwohnerwehren', in Dieter Fricke (ed.), *Lexikon zur Parteiengeschichte*, vol. 2 (Cologne: Pahl-Rugenstein, 1984), 569–79, figure 569. The argument by Bergien, *Republik*, 94–107, 391, that the entry of socialist workers into the home guards could have been used for their development into a pro-republican defence force, is based on thin evidence.
59. James J. Weingartner, 'Massacre at Mechterstädt: The Case of the Marburger Studentencorps, 1920', *The Historian*, 37 (1975), 598–618.
60. Schulze, *Freikorps*, 101–201.

61. Bergien, *Republik*, 114–15; see T. Hunt Tooley, 'German Political Violence and the Border Plebiscite in Upper Silesia, 1919–1921', *Central European History*, 21 (1988), 56–98.
62. Bergien, *Republik*, 214–20.
63. Helmut Donat, 'Rüstungsexperte und Pazifist: Der ehemalige Reichswehroffizier Carl Mertens (1902–1932)', in Wolfram Wette (ed.), *Weiße Raben: Pazifistische Offiziere in Deutschland vor 1933* (Bremen: Donat, 2020), 268–301.
64. Carsten *Reichswehr*, 168–9.
65. Bergien, *Republik*, 229–49, 303–51, figures 232.
66. Bergien, *Republik*, 121–5; Gerd Krüger, '"Ein Fanal des Widerstandes im Ruhrgebiet": Das "Unternehmen Wesel" in der Osternacht des Jahres 1923. Hintergründe eines angeblichen "Husarenstreichs"', *Mitteilungsblatt des Instituts für Soziale Bewegungen*, 24 (2000), 95–140, figure 109. Conan Fischer, *The Ruhr Crisis, 1923–1924* (Oxford: Oxford University Press, 2003), 165–81, seems to downplay the significance of violent resistance.
67. Krüger, *Fanal*, 111; Wolfgang Hardtwig, *Freiheitliches Bürgertum in Deutschland: Der Weimarer Demokrat Eduard Hamm zwischen Kaiserreich und Widerstand* (Stuttgart: Steiner, 2018), 99–100. On the mythology of August 1914 see Jeffrey Verhey, *The Spirit of 1914: Militarism, Myth and Mobilization in Germany* (Cambridge: Cambridge University Press, 2000).
68. Ziemann, *Contested Commemorations*, 39.
69. Frank Reichherzer, *'Alles ist Front': Wehrwissenschaften in Deutschland und die Bellifizierung der Gesellschaft vom Ersten Weltkrieg bis in den Kalten Krieg* (Paderborn: Schöningh, 2012).
70. Bernd Ulrich and Benjamin Ziemann (eds), *Krieg im Frieden: Die umkämpfte Erinnerung an den Ersten Weltkrieg* (Frankfurt/Main: Fischer, 1997), 184–5.
71. Kurt von Schleicher to Franz von Papen, 17 Oct. 1932: <https://www.bundesarchiv.de/aktenreichskanzlei/1919-1933/01a/vpa/vpa2p/kap1_1/kap2_44/index.html> (accessed Feb. 2021).
72. Bergien, *Republik*, 59–71, 121–67, quote 115.
73. Krüger, *Fanal*, 98; Hardtwig, *Bürgertum*, 105–7.
74. Deist, 'Rearmament', 382–5. The quote in Hans Mommsen, *The Rise and Fall of Weimar Democracy*, trans. Larry Eugene Jones (Chapel Hill, NC, London: University of North Carolina Press, 1996), 396.
75. Geyer, *Aufrüstung*, 255–97; Deist, 'Rearmament', 392–400.
76. Bergien, *Republik*, 169–90.
77. Klaus-Jürgen Müller, *Generaloberst Ludwig Beck: Eine Biographie* (Paderborn: Schöningh, 2008), 80–8; see Carsten, *Reichswehr*, 308–25.
78. Hans Meier-Welcker, 'Aus dem Briefwechsel zweier junger Offizier des Reichsheeres 1930–1938', *Militärgeschichtliche Mitteilungen*, 14 (1973), 57–100, here 64–6, 71, 74.
79. See, however, the pioneering analysis of SA–Reichswehr relations by Richard Bessel, *Political Violence and the Rise of Fascism: The Storm Troopers in Eastern Germany 1925–1934* (New Haven, London: Yale University Press, 1984), 67–74.
80. The best account of the events in 1932 from a military perspective is Johannes Hürter, *Wilhelm Groener: Reichswehrminister am Ende der Weimarer Republik (1928–1932)* (Munich: Oldenbourg, 1993), 307–54; see Bergien, *Republik*, 366–85.
81. Bergien, *Republik*, 357–66; Geyer, 'Professionals', 110, 112.
82. Kroener, 'Mobilmachungsplanungen', 71.

Bibliography

Bennett, Edward W., *German Rearmament and the West, 1932–1933* (Princeton: Princeton University Press, 1979).

Bergien, Rüdiger, *Die bellizistische Republik: Wehrkonsens und 'Wehrhaftmachung' in Deutschland 1918–1933* (Munich: Oldenbourg 2012).

Carsten, F. L., *The Reichswehr and Politics, 1918 to 1933* (Oxford: Clarendon Press, 1966).

Deist, Wilhelm, 'The Rearmament of the Wehrmacht', in Militärgeschichtliches Forschungsamt (ed.), *Germany and the Second World War*, vol. 1. *The Build-up of German Aggression*, trans. P. S. Falla et al. (Oxford: Clarendon Press, 1990), 373–540.

Geyer, Michael, *Aufrüstung oder Sicherheit: Die Reichswehr in der Krise der Machtpolitik 1924–1936* (Wiesbaden: Steiner, 1980).

Geyer, Michael, 'Professionals and Junkers: German Rearmament and Politics in the Weimar Republic', in Richard Bessel (ed.), *Social Change and Political Development in Weimar Germany* (London: Croom Helm, 1981), 77–133.

Mulligan, William, *The Creation of the Modern German Army: General Walther Reinhardt and the Weimar Republic, 1914–1930* (New York: Berghahn, 2005).

Stephenson, Scott, *The Final Battle: Soldiers of the Western Front in the German Revolution of 1918* (Cambridge: Cambridge University Press, 2009).

Ziemann, Benjamin, *Violence and the German Soldier in the Great War: Killing–Dying–Surviving* (London: Bloomsbury Academic, 2017).

CHAPTER 11

FOREIGN POLICY: THE DILEMMAS OF A REVISIONIST STATE

JONATHAN WRIGHT

Introduction

EMERGING as it did from the First World War, defeat, and revolution, the Weimar Republic was inevitably divided over foreign policy.[1] The divisions over war aims between right and left, between those demanding annexation of parts of France, Belgium, and Russia, and those advocating a compromise peace, became divisions over the responsibility for defeat and revolution and these were carried over into divisions as to what German policy should be in the post-war world. Were the 'warmongers' to blame for having continued the war in a vain attempt to achieve a German empire on the European continent and at the same time resist constitutional reform at home? Or were the parties that later formed the first republican government to blame, the Social Democrats, Catholic Centre Party, and Democrats (Left-Liberals), for having undermined the unity of the home front with their calls for peace and in some cases involvement with strikes? Had the German army, undefeated in the field, been 'stabbed in the back'?

These divisions were exacerbated when the peace terms became known. There was an almost unanimous rejection of them from republican and anti-republican parties alike. Republicans rejected the peace because their hopes that the terms would correspond with President Wilson's wartime declarations in favour of self-determination, free trade, and a League of Nations proved illusory. As a condition of agreeing to an armistice in October 1918, Wilson had demanded the end of 'monarchical autocracy'. The peace terms, however, showed no recognition of Germany's new democratic credentials. It was even treated as, for the time being, unfit to join the League of Nations. Anti-republicans were of course equally opposed to the terms, but they were now also able to attack the republican parties for having trusted in Wilson's principles. This was an effective weapon. The republican parties had won a convincing victory in the elections to the National Constituent Assembly in January 1919 but they lost the absolute majority in the next national elections to the Reichstag in June 1920.

Foreign policy from the beginning involved fundamental questions about the nature of international politics in the post-war world. Should the Versailles Treaty be rejected as it rested in Article 231 on German acceptance of 'the responsibility ... for causing all the loss and damage to which the Allied and Associated Governments and their nationals have been subjected as a consequence of the war imposed upon them by the aggression of Germany and her Allies', an allegation of so-called 'war guilt' which again divided right and left and threatened to provoke a military revolt?[2] Should the treaty also be rejected because its economic clauses, at least, were regarded as impossible to fulfil? Or should Weimar governments bow to superior force and risk the consequences of foreign occupation, possibly including the breaking up of the nation-state which, despite its deep divisions, had survived the strains of war?

Posed in these terms, the Versailles Treaty raised issues far beyond the normal range of party politics. Could any trust be put in a new era of international relations based on liberal principles and international law or did the rhetoric of the League of Nations mask power politics as usual? How could Germany regain its place as a great power among other great powers? Should Germany work to be accepted as a partner in the new system? Or should it wait until the facts of Germany's economic potential and demographic size brought another shift in the international power structure in Germany's favour? The sense of rupture from the rest of Europe and the United States applied not only to governments and political parties but also trade unions, churches, universities, and, in some measure, society as a whole. The Versailles Treaty was seen as a national disaster. Foreign policy in turn came to be seen as a matter of national survival and, consequently, at least for those on the right, a test of whether the republic could and should survive.[3]

Who Made Foreign Policy?

Given the nature of Weimar politics and the centrality of foreign policy, a wide variety of groups was involved. Formally the Foreign Minister was responsible under the authority of the Chancellor. For some periods the Chancellor became his own Foreign Minister—Joseph Wirth (in 1921–2), Gustav Stresemann (August to November 1923), Heinrich Brüning (1931–2). On some occasions, the Reich President took part—under the Weimar Constitution, he concluded treaties on behalf of the republic. The Foreign Ministry (Auswärtiges Amt) moved across largely unreconstructed from empire to republic. Leading officials and senior ambassadors were part of a privileged elite, usually well-connected though not in all cases aristocratic. Sections were reorganized partly onto a regional, geographical basis and greater emphasis given to economic and trade matters. An attempt was also made to widen the basis of recruitment, but this was soon halted and control remained with the most senior officials, the secretaries of state.[4] These individuals, Adolf Georg von Maltzan 1922–4, Carl von Schubert 1924–30, Bernhard von Bülow 1930–6, carried with them the attitudes they had formed during the empire. They became in Count Kessler's words 'must-be republicans'.[5] They had to adjust to a world where other government departments, political parties, the Reichstag foreign affairs committee, the governments of the individual German states (Länder), regions under military occupation in the Rhineland, and German minorities in areas seceded under the Versailles Treaty, lobbies of all kinds, the press, and public opinion expected to influence foreign policy. The secretaries of state advised their political masters, and occasionally represented them in cabinet, press conferences, or even at international meetings, for instance during Stresemann's periods of ill-health. They also sought to protect the primacy of the Foreign Ministry in the making of foreign policy while cooperating with, or resisting, the influence of other departments—defence, economics, and finance. There were also numerous experts who had first been assembled—more than a hundred of them—as part of preparations for the German delegation to the Paris peace conference.[6] These included the historian, Hans Delbrück, and the sociologist, Max Weber, who endorsed Germany's case against the accusation that it bore sole responsibility for the war, the beginning of a long campaign by the Foreign Ministry against 'the war guilt lie'.[7] These groups and individuals overlapped with political parties, and in a multi-party system with weak governments, foreign policy was a major factor in their formation and collapse. The international context was also unstable. Would France be able to enforce the Versailles Treaty? What help would Britain and the United States provide as a counterweight? Should Germany look towards the other excluded potential great power from the Paris peace, the Soviet Union? With so many different groups involved and so much uncertainty, it was not surprising that one of the principal problems for foreign policy was to achieve coherence.

THE THREE PHASES OF WEIMAR FOREIGN POLICY

The first of three distinct phases, from 1919 to 1923, was confused with governments caught between rejection of the Versailles Treaty and attempts to resist its enforcement, on the one hand, and efforts to find compromise solutions on the other, either by cultivating American and British support, or by direct agreement with France. The period also saw the first move towards an independent policy in the Treaty of Rapallo made with the Soviet Union in 1922. The second phase from 1923 to 1929 was marked by a sustained attempt to recover a stable future for Germany as a great power in partnership with the other great powers, finding negotiated solutions to the most pressing problems—reparations, frontiers, and foreign occupation—and joining the League of

Nations. This period was made possible paradoxically by the dramatic crisis produced by the French occupation of the Ruhr in January 1923, in reaction to which not only the German government but also, under British and American influence, a new political majority in France was prepared to adopt a different approach. The third phase lasted from the evacuation of French troops from the Rhineland in June 1930 to Hitler's appointment as Chancellor in January 1933. It saw an upsurge of nationalism in Germany, and, as the depression worsened, a determined effort by the Brüning government to secure the abolition of reparations and the recognition of Germany's right to rearm. A shift from the previous policy of seeking negotiated solutions with the western Allies towards taking unilateral decisions became evident. The proposed Austro-German customs union reflected a return to the pre-war idea of economic empire in central Europe, as the depression and the growth of protectionism weakened the commitment to international trade.

The First Phase, 1919–1923: Defiance and Accommodation

The emotional reaction to the Versailles Treaty made rational foreign policy difficult. The German delegation, led by the Foreign Minister and professional diplomat, Ulrich von Brockdorff-Rantzau (who had been allowed by the government to conduct the negotiations independently) unanimously recommended its rejection. The cabinet was unable to reach agreement and the Democratic Party (DDP), united for rejection, resigned. One minister, Matthias Erzberger from the Centre Party, argued energetically for acceptance to avoid a worse fate. A new government was formed which was willing to accept the treaty without the articles on war guilt and the trial of war criminals—the so-called 'honour clauses'.[8] When the Allies insisted on unconditional acceptance, the government was authorized to sign by the National Assembly on 23 June 1919, a few hours before the ultimatum expired, and a resolution was passed acknowledging that it acted from patriotic motives. The decision referred to 'yielding to overpowering might' and described the terms as representing 'injustice without example'.[9]

The treaty was certainly harsh and its imposition humiliating. At least two members of the German delegation, Brockdorff-Rantzau, who subsequently became ambassador to the Soviet Union, and Bülow, who became secretary of state in 1930, never recovered from the experience.[10] Germany was to be disarmed and the Rhineland occupied for fifteen years. There were also territorial losses, including Alsace-Lorraine and the Saar, the latter put under League of Nations administration with French control of the coal mines subject to a plebiscite after fifteen years. Most controversially, parts of Prussia in the east were transferred to Poland to allow that country a 'corridor' to the sea, cutting East Prussia off from the rest of Germany and putting the German port of Danzig under Polish control with a League of Nations commissioner. Although, in general, ethnic Poles were in the majority in the lost areas, some two million Germans came under Polish rule. Germany also faced severe economic restrictions—indeterminate reparations, transfers of coal to France, restrictions on foreign trade, the surrender of the merchant marine, and confiscation of colonies. In addition, the union of Austria and Germany, which had been voted for by both national parliaments, was prohibited unless the League of Nations should decide otherwise, a clear breach of the principle of self-determination and one which deprived the republic of a badly needed success to restore its nationalist credentials and link it to the revolutionary tradition of 1848.

Yet Germany was not broken up or destroyed. Crucially, France failed to get one of its main aims, the separation of the Rhineland into a buffer state. Its attempt to wrest control of the German economy also failed. German heavy industry proved more dynamic than its French counterpart and by 1925 the balance of power between them again favoured Germany.[11] In the east plebiscites were held in disputed frontier areas, although the way the result was interpreted in Upper Silesia (by a League decision in 1921)—giving Germany the major share of territory but Poland most of the coalfields and industrial areas—caused further unrest.

Despite their objections, the first republican government committed to carrying out the treaty, while pursuing a purely peaceful policy to revise it. The Weimar Constitution also specifically recognized that the rules of international law were binding on Germany.[12] The problem was how to achieve revision in cooperation with the Allies in the immediate post-war years. French governments, having failed to gain the separation of the Rhineland, also lost the Anglo-American guarantee, which had been offered as an alternative form of security, but which lapsed when the United States Senate refused to ratify the Versailles Treaty on 19 March 1920. They saw no option but to maintain the treaty and to impose sanctions to enforce it. The British government under Lloyd George, while wanting to find a compromise on reparations and opposed to the policy of sanctions, was unwilling to break with France, or even to see a direct agreement between France and Germany which might be at the expense of the British share of reparations. American administrations were not willing to recognize a connection between German reparations and the war debts owed by France and Britain to the United States. Yet without receiving reparations, it was not clear how France and Britain could repay the debts. In these circumstances, there was little prospect of Germany securing revision.

German governments faced difficult problems in simply carrying out the treaty. An immediate example was how to meet Allied demands to cut its troop strength to 100,000 men. The German government argued that it needed 200,000 simply to maintain order. It depended on the army and volunteer units (Freikorps) in 1919 to suppress uprisings in Berlin and a soviet republic in Munich, and also to prevent Polish forces occupying land on the eastern frontier. An attempt to disband one of the Freikorps units triggered a military putsch in Berlin in March 1920. Once the putsch had failed, the government used the army to suppress a communist uprising in the Ruhr. This action violated the Versailles Treaty since the area concerned was part of the demilitarized zone. That promptly triggered French sanctions in the occupation of the Frankfurt region, until the German troops withdrew. It was a perfect illustration of how limited the room for manoeuvre of the German government was.[13]

The most difficult issue was reparations. German governments had no incentive to pay more than was necessary to avoid French sanctions. Policy became to demonstrate that Germany could not pay. The war had been financed by inflation and post-war governments adopted the same tactic to finance the republic's new commitments to welfare and to sustain employment, both necessary to prevent labour unrest. The resulting budget deficits were used as evidence that reparations could not be paid. Inflation also had the advantage of making exports cheap, which suited the German argument that the only way to finance reparations would be at the expense of Allied producers. Keynes's influential polemic against the Versailles Treaty, *The Economic Consequences of the Peace* (1919), increased German confidence that it would have damaging consequences for all. In addition, after the republican parties lost their overall majority in the elections of June 1920, the party representing Ruhr industry, the German People's Party (DVP), joined the government, reducing its scope for compromise. The result was deadlock leading to the occupation of three Ruhr cities in March 1921. Further negotiations followed and eventually a new government in May 1921 under Chancellor Wirth, with the SPD replacing the DVP, accepted a reparations schedule but only under the threat of occupation of the whole Ruhr region if it refused. This, however provided only temporary relief and the decision in October 1921 to divide Upper Silesia was a further setback for a policy attacked as 'fulfilment' of the treaty by its critics. By the autumn, it was clear that the government would not be able to make the payment due in January 1922—inflation was now accelerating and undermining its ability to raise credit—and would have to request a moratorium.

On both sides, creative ideas were proposed. The most promising was that Germany provide reparations in kind and labour to help rebuild the parts of France devastated by the war, an idea put forward by Jacques Seydoux, a senior official in the French government and taken up by Walther Rathenau, then Germany's Minister of Reconstruction, and Louis Loucheur, the French Minister for the Liberated Territories. That would avoid the problem of having to pay reparations in foreign currency, which could be earned only from exports or by attracting foreign investment. Rathenau and Loucheur reached an agreement in October 1921 but it failed because of opposition from both French and German industrialists.[14]

Historians have debated whether Germany could have paid the reparations.[15] The sums demanded were not beyond the capacity of an economy the size of Germany's and, in fact, over the whole life of the republic, Germany received considerably more in foreign investment than it paid in reparations. Had German governments had the strength and the will to bring inflation under control and restrict other spending commitments, there is no reason why they could not have paid. However, they had neither the support necessary to impose cuts at the expense of labour nor to dictate to the mining industry. And they lacked the will to give reparations priority, continuing to see them as unjust and an obstacle to economic recovery. There was also growing pessimism within Germany about French intentions. Was the French motive in fact to find justification to occupy the Ruhr in order to pursue its original aim of a separate Rhineland? As Stresemann put it in January 1923, 'France does not want the Rhinegold, France wants the Rhine.'[16] If France was determined to occupy the Ruhr in any case, there was no point in seeking agreement or making payments in advance. These fears were exaggerated but reparations were a matter of security for French governments, indeed the transfer of economic power from Germany to France was the foundation of French security with or without a separate Rhineland state. That made it difficult for each side to compromise.

German foreign policy moved uncertainly looking for support. Under Walter Simons as Foreign Minister 1920–1, and more positively with Walther Rathenau (Foreign Minister from February to June 1922), Germany tried to work with Lloyd George to facilitate his attempts to put pressure on France to find a compromise. Simons also hoped that the United States, which finally signed a peace treaty with Germany in August 1921, could be brought to mediate. In neither case, however, were German governments able to make sufficiently attractive offers for Britain or the United States to respond. With no other option, the idea of agreement with the Soviet Union gained support.

The policy had certain attractions. A direct threat from the Soviet Union was no longer feared after Poland had driven back the Soviet army and annexed Russian territory in the east at the Treaty of Riga in March 1921. This also created a common interest between Germany and the Soviet Union in revision of the Polish frontiers. There were hopes of expansion of German–Soviet trade, initially regulated by an agreement in May 1921, and the military under General Seeckt looked to cooperation with the Soviet Union to evade some of the disarmament provisions of the Versailles Treaty (in tank warfare and training pilots) and as a potential ally. Germany also had an interest in securing from the Russians the renunciation of their right to reparations under the Versailles Treaty. Wirth and Maltzan, then the head of the eastern department in the Foreign Ministry, were persuaded by the advantages of an agreement, though Rathenau (and also President Friedrich Ebert) feared the effect it would have on France and Britain.

The opportunity came in 1922 at an international conference in Genoa called by Lloyd George to reopen European trade with Russia. The Soviet leaders were interested in a separate agreement with Germany to divide the capitalist powers. Lloyd George's tactics of negotiating first with the Russians backfired. Nervous that an agreement would be reached without them, Rathenau gave way and the treaty was signed at Rapallo on 16 April.[17] Its terms were unremarkable, establishing full diplomatic relations, agreeing to renounce claims against each other (reparations and pre-war debts), and establishing trade on a most-favoured-nation basis. However, it caused a sensation, disrupting Lloyd George's ambitions for a general European settlement and strengthening French determination, now with Raymond Poincaré as prime minister, to maintain the Versailles Treaty, if necessary unilaterally.

After the failure of the conference, any prospect of reaching agreement on reparations faded. Fearing a new ultimatum, Germany accepted the conditions for a moratorium imposed by the Allied reparations commission. However, this depended on Germany receiving an international loan, which in turn depended on the report of a bankers' committee set up by the commission. It reported in June that a loan was impossible without a reduction of reparations to a sustainable level to allow the resumption of normal trade and currency stabilization. The refusal of the loan set off a new round of inflation, as German capital sought safety abroad. A major political crisis followed, when Rathenau was assassinated, a target of right-wing fanatics as a Jew and a Foreign Minister associated with 'fulfilment'. When Germany asked for a further moratorium in July, Poincaré demanded 'productive guarantees' for reparations payments, in other words German assets such as state-owned mines and forests. Britain, suspicious of Poincaré's motives, refused to endorse that policy but was unable to offer a satisfactory alternative. In December, a new German government appealed to the United States to intervene and offered a thirty-year guarantee pact for the Rhineland. The American Secretary of State, Charles Evans Hughes, proposed a committee of experts to consider Germany's capacity to pay and a new reparations settlement on 29 December, but that had no attraction for Poincaré. Under pressure from France's own financial difficulties and without a viable alternative, he authorized the occupation of the Ruhr together with Belgium, beginning on 11 January 1923.[18]

The Second Phase, 1923–1929: Realism, its Potential, and Limits

The second phase is the most interesting. Previously, different policies had been tried, sometimes sequentially, sometimes together. There were eight different Foreign Ministers alone between January 1919 and August 1923. In the second phase, German governments, with a single Foreign Minister, Gustav Stresemann, had the opportunity and found the will to pursue a policy which aimed to recover the status of a great power in partnership with the other European great powers and the United States. That was not a radical break but the opportunity now existed to find solutions which met the interests of all the powers. How that opportunity was explored in a period of relative stability shows clearly the nature of foreign policy, its motives, achievements, and limits, in Weimar's parliamentary system.

The severity of the crisis caused by the Ruhr occupation soon became apparent.[19] The German government reacted with a policy of 'passive resistance', a strike by civil servants, miners, and railway workers, financed by the government. This was successful, to the surprise of the French and Belgian occupiers, but financially crippling. When Stresemann became Chancellor in August 1923, it was obvious that it would have to be given up as the currency lost all value and a new currency could not be stabilized if the support continued. Passive resistance was accordingly abandoned on 25 September. That, however, meant that the occupied area—the heart of German industry—had to be left to make its own terms with the French authorities. In effect the German government no longer controlled the Rhine–Ruhr region and, although separatists were in a minority, the danger existed that some form of separation might be imposed. The decision to abandon passive resistance set off further crises. A conservative monarchist regime in Bavaria defied the authority of the Reich government and in neighbouring Saxony and Thuringia, socialist governments with communist participation armed proletarian defence organizations. In October, Stresemann warned the cabinet that they faced 'civil war and therefore the collapse of the Reich'.[20] He authorized military intervention in Saxony and Thuringia, although this led to the resignation of the SPD, depriving his government of its majority. The army command refused to take parallel action against

Bavaria. Instead, General Seeckt tried to make Stresemann resign to allow a 'directorate' of his choosing to take over and rule by emergency decree. That alone, he claimed, would make it possible to end the Bavarian rebellion peacefully. Paradoxically, the fiasco of the Hitler putsch in November saved the situation but it showed how near constitutional government had come to breakdown.

Now, only a change in the international climate could bring relief. Fortunately for the Weimar Republic, the French government also faced serious problems. Although it secured control of the mines and railways, its regime lacked legitimacy. It was not clear how it could sustain its rule over ten million Germans against their will. In addition, it faced growing international isolation. Britain declared the occupation illegal in August. The franc came under strain, and support for Poincaré in France began to weaken. In October he accepted an international committee to investigate Germany's capacity to pay reparations. This proved a crucial concession leading to the appointment of the Dawes committee, whose report in 1924 and its adoption at the London Conference, transformed the situation.[21]

Stresemann's government fell at the end of November 1923 but he was invited by the Centre Party chairman, Wilhelm Marx, to stay as Foreign Minister. He was to remain in that position until his death in October 1929. During these years he acquired a reputation as the exponent of a consistent foreign policy and also as a stabilizing element in the republic. This was in many ways surprising. In his pre-war career he had worked to revive the National Liberal Party by campaigning for imperial expansion. During the war he had sided with the Army Supreme Command in favour of annexation of foreign territory both west and east, though he also advocated constitutional reform. Immediately after the war, when he was discredited because of his wartime stance, he fought back on an antirepublican platform and succeeded in the 1920 elections in regaining the National Liberal share of the vote for his new party, the DVP. He now worked to bring it into government though he faced constant opposition from its right wing. In the period 1920–3, he gradually came to accept the republic as the only form of state with which Germany could recover. In the same years he also developed the argument that France and Germany shared 'a common destiny' and that in the interests of the international economy there must be 'international understanding'. The core of his politics both at home and abroad was realism. He accepted the republic as a 'republican from reason' (*Vernunftrepublikaner*), though in time he identified himself ever more closely with it. He accepted the international situation similarly as rooted in power politics. He defined the aim of German foreign policy, as early as 1919, as to become 'a worthwhile ally (*bündnisfähig*) again'. In that concept too, however, there lay the possibility of development, in this case to partnership as an equal with the other European powers in a common future.[22]

The first step was to secure the adoption of the Dawes Plan. Its advantages were obvious. It offered Germany the return of economic control of the Ruhr, a partial moratorium on reparations payments for four years (as well as in practice a reduction of the final total), and a foreign loan of 800 million gold marks. In return, Germany would accept international supervision of its budget and the new central bank, and also the railways, which would pass from Reich ownership and be used as part security for the payment of reparations. Stresemann was in no doubt that the plan should be accepted. In meetings of the cabinet, with the state (Länder) governments, the DVP, in the Reichstag, in public speeches and newspaper articles, he took the lead in mobilizing support. His arguments were thoroughly pragmatic: the plan offered the chance to enlist the power of American and British capital against 'French imperialism'. If the plan were rejected, the whole world would unite against them with the loss of the occupied zone. There was no alternative: the idea of recovering power by secret rearmament was 'total nonsense'. This did not rule out change in the future. When Germany was strong again, it could 'throw away the crutches'. He even accepted that 'ultimately' Europe's problems would be solved 'by the sword'. He argued only that Germany would not have that power for a long time and would first have to lay the foundations for it. In his own words, his policy was one of 'sober realpolitik'.[23]

These arguments should be understood in their domestic political context. Stresemann was under attack both within his own party (DVP) and from the main right-wing opposition party, the German National People's Party (DNVP), for his move from an anti-republican, nationalist position to acceptance of the republic and a foreign policy suspiciously like 'fulfilment'. In elections in May 1924, the DVP lost a third of its vote and the DNVP (with its ally the Reich Agrarian League, Reichslandbund) became the single largest party. The Dawes Plan required a two-thirds majority in the Reichstag for ratification, as the transfer of the railways required a constitutional amendment. This meant that the DNVP was vital to its passage, and in any case Stresemann favoured bringing the DNVP into government to make it share responsibility. The DNVP's foreign policy spokesman, Karl Helfferich, attacked the Dawes Plan as a 'second Versailles', but the agricultural and industrial lobbies associated with the party were desperate for the foreign loans which it offered. An opportunity therefore existed to divide the DNVP between its interest groups and its nationalist ideologues. That in turn would help to stabilize the republic and ensure a majority for Stresemann's foreign policy.

In the short term he was successful. Poincaré lost his majority in elections in May 1924 and was replaced by a centre-left government. After an initial meeting of the Allies, Germany was invited to join the London Conference in August 1924, being treated for the first time as an equal. The Dawes Plan was agreed, though Stresemann had to accept that the military occupation of the Ruhr would continue for a year. In the ratification debates that followed, the DNVP split down the middle in the final vote on the railway bill, allowing the legislation to pass. Stresemann then pressed for the DNVP to be brought into government. Negotiations broke down, however, as the demands of the DNVP—which had reunited after the Dawes split—were unacceptable to the Centre Party and the DDP. New elections were held in December, in which Stresemann campaigned for unity behind a foreign policy of 'national realpolitik', but they failed to break the deadlock. Eventually, a new 'above party' government was formed in which the DDP, Centre, DVP, and DNVP were represented without being formally bound to support it. Stresemann had succeeded in bringing the DNVP into government. Its industrial and agricultural lobbies were keen to influence the new tariffs which would become possible in January 1925, when Germany was no longer bound under the Versailles Treaty to grant most favoured nation status to the Allies. Nevertheless, the DNVP remained an unreliable partner, with its nationalist wing keen to bring Stresemann down. This was not the consolidation for which he had hoped.

Stresemann carried the main political responsibility but the making of foreign policy depended on the senior officials in the Foreign Ministry and the principal ambassadors. Of these, Carl von Schubert, who became Stresemann's secretary of state in December 1924, was the outstanding personality.[24] He came from a privileged background, a nephew of one of the last Foreign Ministers of the empire and, through his mother, connected to a leading industrial firm in the Saar. He had previously been the director of the British and American department and had established good relations with the British ambassador, Lord D'Abernon. He had been frustrated by the lack of consistency of German foreign policy before Stresemann and soon established a close working relationship with him. Schubert understood the crucial role which Britain could play through its influence with both the United States and France in reshaping the international situation to Germany's advantage. But for that it was essential that Germany should play its part. The key was the problem of French security. Schubert, and the chief legal expert in the Foreign Ministry, Friedrich Gaus, had already worked out proposals for a Rhineland pact in April 1923.[25] When D'Abernon suggested in December 1924 that Germany should revive the idea, Schubert and Stresemann were ready to act.

The German proposals were drawn up in great secrecy, with only the new Chancellor Luther being informed, and communicated to the British and French governments in January and February 1925. In the negotiations that led to the Locarno pact in October, Germany committed itself with France and Belgium and, as external powers Britain and Italy, to a guarantee of the Rhineland frontier, as established by the Versailles Treaty. That meant accepting the loss of Alsace-Lorraine and the demilitarization of the Rhineland but gaining protection against any future French attempt to separate the Rhineland. Germany refused to give a similar guarantee of its eastern frontiers. It signed arbitration treaties with Poland and Czechoslovakia, like those it signed with France and Belgium, but these did not include binding arbitration on frontier issues, only a conciliation procedure. Germany also resisted French attempts to act as a guarantor of these arbitration treaties, though ultimately it acquiesced in France concluding separate agreements with its eastern allies. The Locarno treaties were bound up with the arbitration procedures of the League of Nations and Germany became a member in 1926 with a permanent seat, with the other great powers, on the League council. It also succeeded in gaining an interpretation of Article 16 of the League covenant, the sanctions clause, in view of its disarmed status. Under this interpretation, a state was required to engage in sanctions only 'to an extent which is compatible with its military situation and takes its geographical position into account'. Behind this wording (which was also the way Britain interpreted the clause) lay the German desire to maintain its links with the Soviet Union, which feared that Germany might become involved with the other capitalist powers in action against the Soviet Union.

The Locarno treaties, like the Dawes Plan, were accepted by Germany's leaders out of self-interest. Germany became part of a security system on its western frontiers, preventing a renewal of French sanctions or an Anglo-French alliance. That also enabled it to campaign for an early end to the military occupation of the Rhineland as inconsistent with Locarno, and also for bringing forward the plebiscite in the Saar. In addition, the settlement helped to ensure the continued flow of American loans. Germany joined the League of Nations, giving it symbolic equality with the other great powers, and a position from which it could act as protector of German minorities in areas lost by the Versailles Treaty or, like Danzig and the Saar, which were under the authority of the League. In the east, it kept open its claim to revision of the Polish frontiers, thus creating a crucial political distinction between them and the western frontiers. As Stresemann put it to Maltzan, now ambassador in Washington, 'Our policy over the security pact offer was undoubtedly right, secures the Rhineland from the consequences of a French policy of persecution, has burst the entente apart and opens new possibilities for the East.'[26]

The Locarno treaties, like the Dawes Plan, also represented a choice, to give priority to a western policy over alliance with the Soviet Union. Germany's ambassador, Brockdorff-Rantzau, had been negotiating for such an alliance with the Soviet Foreign Minister, Chicherin, with the goal of 'driving Poland back to its ethnographic frontiers', an aim endorsed by Maltzan and Schubert in December 1924. This was clearly inconsistent with German membership of the League, though Stresemann tried to persuade Brockdorff-Rantzau that, since Germany was not strong enough to take military action, in any case, that did not affect the real position. Brockdorff-Rantzau did not himself favour military action but he resented the priority now given to a western policy and resigned in protest against the Locarno pact, though he was persuaded to remain in post, with the right of reporting direct to President Hindenburg, who was also critical of the League.[27] In fact, Germany was able to renew the Rapallo Treaty with the Soviet Union by the Treaty of Berlin in April 1926. Each side agreed to remain neutral if the other was attacked by a third party, Germany squaring this with its obligations under the League covenant by the addition of the words 'despite peaceful behaviour'.[28] Germany also agreed to a further clause that neither would be involved in an economic boycott of the other, organized by a coalition of third powers. This was sufficient to satisfy the Soviet Union and lay just within the interpretation of Article 16 which Germany had gained from its Locarno partners. Germany had succeeded in retaining its links with the Soviet Union while its relationship with the western powers assumed much greater importance.

As with the Dawes Plan, the main task of defending the Locarno policy fell to Stresemann. The government was a minority coalition of Centre, DVP, and DDP. He also enjoyed the crucial support of the SPD (from outside the government) to provide a majority. The main opposition came from the DNVP, including those who tried to win over President Hindenburg, and General Seeckt. They resented what they saw as the voluntary acceptance of parts of the Versailles Treaty and the weakening of the claim to revision of the eastern frontiers. They were opposed to entry into the League and looked to alliance with the Soviet Union to reverse the Versailles Treaty in the future. In cabinet, which he was attending as an expert, Seeckt argued that revision could come about only 'by armed force'. Stresemann replied that Germany could play that role only 'when we were materially and militarily a power. This would not be the case for a long time ahead.'[29] The DNVP ministers tried to divide the Chancellor, Luther, from Stresemann and, when that failed, and the new tariff law in line with their interests had been passed in August, they had less reason to remain in the government. In October, once the terms of the Locarno treaties were known, the party's provincial organizations reacted overwhelmingly against them and the leadership, fearing another split as over the Dawes Plan, forced the resignation of their ministers. Stresemann's hope of creating a broad national front behind his foreign policy had failed.

In his attempts to win over conservative, nationalist audiences, Stresemann adopted a tone and line of reasoning which implied that his Locarno policy was only a tactic until Germany was strong enough to use other methods. These have led to doubt about his real aims. In a letter to the Crown Prince, on 7 September 1925, he referred to 'the most important thing' as getting 'the strangler from our neck', that is the end of the French occupation of the Rhineland. To achieve that they would have to 'finesse (*finassieren*)' and avoid 'fundamental decisions', that is between opting either for the western powers or the Soviet Union. To another audience, an association representing frontier regions which had been lost or divided by the Versailles Treaty, he gave a cynical account of the arbitration treaty with Poland, claiming that in practice it did not limit Germany's freedom to take military action, though he immediately added 'I am not thinking of war in relation to the eastern question'.[30] These remarks and others like them were clearly part of a campaign to win over natural opponents. Stresemann could adopt these arguments the more easily because he came from a nationalist background and could instinctively play on the feelings of his audience. The question remains whether he was simply making the most effective case for a policy of peaceful revision or whether that policy was itself merely a temporary expedient.[31]

Despite his language on these and other occasions, there is much to suggest that Stresemann saw real opportunities in a policy of peaceful revision and, increasingly, none in war. If Germany could win the cooperation of the western powers, then it would be in a position to pursue revision, in particular, of the Polish frontier 'whose impossible nature is today recognized on all sides'. Stresemann was also impressed by the potential for 'economic understanding between the great industrial nations of Europe' and 'something like the structure of a European community' compared to the present which resembled 'the old Germany with its dozens of states and customs barriers'. Schubert too regularly warned of the danger of an impending collapse of the European economy, if it failed to unite.[32] Stresemann did not feel the same way towards the Soviet Union. He distrusted communist ideology, warning the Crown Prince against 'the utopia of flirting with Bolshevism'. But he hoped it would be possible for Germany, 'the natural great mediator and bridge between east and west', to maintain its influence with the Soviet Union, and even to draw it into the League, so that in the event of an opportunity for revision of the Polish frontiers, Germany would have the support of both the western powers and the Soviet Union.[33]

It soon became clear that such hopes were unrealistic. Britain and France had no serious interest in redrawing the frontiers so recently established and neither Germany nor the Soviet Union was in a position to make Poland agree to frontier revision. Instead German policy became defensive, to maintain the position of the German minorities by secret subsidies and publicizing their grievances at the League, and to resist any attempt to extend the Locarno guarantees to the east. By 1927, Stresemann had concluded that in relation to Poland they would have to be content to wait 'for years ahead' for peaceful revision to work.[34] The same held true for other German aims with lower priority, union with Austria or the return of colonies.

There were some hopeful developments. Germany succeeded in negotiating a series of trade treaties including with Britain (1924), France (1927), and even Poland, after a protracted battle with the German agricultural lobby, in 1930 (though it was never ratified).[35] The steel industries of France, Germany, Belgium, and Luxembourg agreed to form an international cartel in 1926 though the Germans, finding their quota too restrictive, withdrew in 1929 and the cartel collapsed in 1931.[36] In September 1929, the French Foreign Minister, Aristide Briand, launched a plan for a European federation at the League. Stresemann welcomed its economic potential but was reserved about the political consequences, anticipating that they would help to stabilize Poland's frontiers.[37] Each of these examples could be regarded as a promising beginning, but none achieved the progress necessary to outlast the depression.

Even in relation to removing the remaining sanctions of the Versailles Treaty, there was no quick breakthrough. The plan for Rhineland evacuation and return of the Saar in return for an advance payment on reparations by the sale of Dawes bonds, discussed by Stresemann and Briand, at a meeting in the village of Thoiry immediately after Germany joined the League of Nations in 1926, failed to materialize. Briand, encountering opposition at home, distanced himself and the American and British governments also opposed privileging reparations payments to France. In July 1928 Stresemann decided to press the issue of the occupation of the Rhineland, which Poincaré regarded as a guarantee for the payment of reparations. At The Hague Conference in 1929–30 agreement was eventually reached for a final reparations settlement (the Young Plan), again giving Germany a reduction in annual payments (compared to the Dawes Plan) but with, at least in theory, payments continuing to 1988. At the same time, France agreed to withdraw its troops from the Rhineland by June 1930, five years ahead of the date set by the Versailles Treaty, and also to start negotiations on the Saar.[38]

Despite this mixed record, and increasing criticism even from within the government parties, Stresemann did not waver in his commitment to peace.[39] He had defended Locarno in 1925 as a means to the goal of 'a peaceful Germany at the centre of a peaceful Europe'. In the years that followed he argued that a new war would be a disaster for Europe and particularly for Germany, which would form the natural battleground in any major European conflict. Germany, as well as Europe, he said, needed time to heal the wounds of the last war. He appealed to a university audience in Heidelberg in May 1928 to recognize that 'The preservation of peace and the attempts to secure it are not weakness, are not timidity, they are the realistic (*realpolitische*) recognition of our own national interest.'[40] This was not simply rhetoric. In September 1927, Stresemann announced at the League Germany's acceptance, as the first of the great powers, of the 'optional' clause of the statute of the international court. This involved a general commitment to arbitration on the model of the Locarno treaties. In January 1928, Germany made a more far-reaching proposal, which would have required it to accept arbitration even on its eastern frontiers, though the proposal was not adopted by the League's security committee. In April 1928, Germany accepted the American proposal for a treaty renouncing war (the

Kellogg-Briand pact), the first power to do so. Although Germany had tactical reasons for each of these decisions, they all aimed to further the cause of peaceful revision.[41] Germany's growing international reputation was recognized by the award of the Nobel peace prize to Stresemann and his French and British counterparts at Locarno, Briand, and Austen Chamberlain, in December 1926.

When Stresemann died in October 1929, there was still no obvious threat to his policy. The campaign against the Young Plan, which brought together the DNVP leader, Hugenberg, and Hitler, achieved less than 14 per cent of the vote in a plebiscite.[42] But the real problem lay deeper, in the continuing unresolved tension between German expectations of further concessions and French fears of Germany becoming once again the stronger power.[43] The failure of the League to make progress towards the goal of general disarmament (as set out in Article 8 of the covenant) had already led German officials to discuss whether they should press for an equal right to rearm.[44] Stresemann and Briand had established a rapport which eased the tension. And, as yet in Germany, there was no majority for an alternative policy to peaceful revision—neither one of war nor one of renunciation of revision—but the limits of what peaceful revision could achieve were becoming clear. The reaction which followed showed that it lacked a firm basis in public support. The policy was underpinned neither by a successful economy, committed to European integration, nor by strong cultural links to other countries. The commitment to peace, which had never been accepted by conservative elites, was itself increasingly questioned. The persistent campaign against acknowledging war guilt and wartime atrocities, the organization of a volunteer defence force on the eastern frontier, the decision in 1928 to start naval construction, the parades of the nationalist veterans' association (Stahlhelm) and increasingly the Nazi stormtroopers (Sturmabteilung, SA), all helped to keep alive the idea that war was justifiable and might again be necessary.[45]

The Third Phase, 1930–1933: New Directions

The final phase saw a turn away from the policy of seeking common interests with the western powers to one of unilateral action. This change was driven by three factors. There was first a new sense of independence following the French evacuation of the Rhineland in June 1930, which was celebrated as national liberation rather than as a victory for Franco-German understanding.[46] Second, the breakdown of the SPD-led majority government in March 1930 required emergency legislation to correct the budget deficit to be passed by presidential decree. This made government dependent on Hindenburg and his advisers, who promoted a conservative, nationalist agenda and rearmament. Third, and most important, was the onset of the depression with rapidly rising unemployment, increasingly desperate measures to balance the budget, shortage of capital and banking failure leading to a crisis of unprecedented severity and the spectacular rise of the Nazi party.

The shift to the right was soon reflected in foreign policy. The new Foreign Minister, Julius Curtius, saw himself as Stresemann's heir. But when the Briand plan for European federation was presented in May 1930, it was quickly rejected. Bülow, a critic of

Stresemann's policy, replaced Schubert as secretary of state in July. He saw the proposals as intended 'to impose new chains upon us' while the new Centre party Chancellor, Brüning (leading a minority coalition of the bourgeois parties) argued that Germany needed 'sufficient natural living space', which meant that even an economic union of Europe would be unacceptable. Responding to this mood, Curtius promised to give the plan 'a first class funeral'. He and Bülow instead pushed forward their alternative project, a customs union with Austria.[47]

This was not a new idea but previously it had been regarded as impractical because it would be a step towards union with Austria (*Anschluss*). That would be a direct challenge to the Versailles Treaty and the Allies, especially France, and Italy because of its frontier with Austria (and the German population on its side of the frontier), would be bound to oppose it. It was a sign of how much had changed in the Foreign Ministry that Curtius, anxious to establish his reputation as Foreign Minister, and Bülow, who imagined extending the customs union to Czechoslovakia and Hungary and then putting Poland under pressure to concede frontier revision, were not deterred by the prospect of such opposition.[48] The plan was agreed with Austria in January 1931 and made public in March. It caused the predictable outcry and was eventually judged illegal by the international court (albeit by a majority of one). The Austrian government, desperate for international loans to manage the banking crisis, had already withdrawn from the scheme. The whole idea proved an abject failure. Curtius resigned in October and Brüning became his own Foreign Minister.

The customs union scheme was also damaging to another, and potentially more promising, opportunity. This was, surprisingly, to revive the idea of Franco-German partnership. Despite the political and psychological obstacles, and the first major breakthrough of the Nazi party in the elections of September 1930, there remained common interests in overcoming the difficulties. The greatest of these was Germany's need for credit and the availability of capital in France. Leopold von Hoesch, Germany's longstanding ambassador in France, and a staunch supporter of Franco-German reconciliation, worked with the senior official in the French Foreign Ministry, Philippe Berthelot, to bridge the gap between the German need for loans and the French desire to attach political conditions. By March 1931, the difference had been narrowed to the French government asking only for a general commitment to Franco-German cooperation rather than specific political conditions. But as soon as the proposed Austro-German customs union became public, the repercussions in France (among other things, undermining Briand's candidacy to be elected President) killed any chance the scheme may have had.[49]

By the spring of 1931 the German government faced a frightening economic and political crisis. A year before, Brüning and his Finance Minister Hermann Dietrich, thought that the economic downturn would be succeeded by natural recovery as their orthodox deflationary measures took effect. By May 1931 with unemployment rising sharply and falling revenues, a banking system in crisis, and the prospect of further political polarization towards the Nazis and Communists, they no longer had confidence that deflation would work but could see no alternative. At this point they turned to getting relief from reparations both to provide help with the budget and, equally important, a popular target to blame for the crisis. Brüning took control of the policy, telling the cabinet that they would soon have to be prepared 'to pull the emergency cord of reparations' as the political and economic situation would become unsustainable in 1932 and the existence of the government might be in danger from the right. At the same time, they should not admit abroad that they were being driven to raise the reparations issue 'for domestic political reasons'.[50]

Immediately, in June 1931, a new drastic emergency decree, further cutting salaries of public servants and benefits to the unemployed, was combined with a public appeal that the limit of what could be tolerated had now been reached and Germany required relief from its 'unbearable reparations obligations'.[51] The result was another flight of capital, reducing the reserves of the Reich Bank close to the legal minimum and increasing the likelihood of German default on its debt. On 20 June, President Hoover responded to what had become a major international crisis by calling for a one-year moratorium on both war debts and reparations.[52] A complicated series of negotiations followed in which the United States and Britain supported Germany in the cancellation of reparations. Instead, France tried to secure a temporary solution through long-term credit (after which reparations would resume) and political conditions against further revision of the Versailles Treaty. Brüning successfully resisted both. Finding itself isolated, France was forced to give way and reparations were in practice cancelled in July 1932 at a conference in Lausanne.[53] In effect, Germany became the beneficiary of the scale of the depression. The political consequences, however, were disastrous. Brüning had been forced to resign by Hindenburg, who wanted a more right-wing government, on 30 May. In the elections called by his successor, Franz von Papen, in July, the Nazis became easily the largest single party with 37 per cent, making them serious contenders for power (although they still lacked a majority).[54]

In a parallel development to that of reparations, Brüning attended the world disarmament conference in Geneva in February 1932.[55] The German tactic was to argue for general disarmament and at the same time to press for Germany's right to equality (though there were divisions between the Foreign Ministry and the military about the best approach). In 1928, the cabinet (under an SPD Chancellor) had authorized a re-armament programme, which would exceed the Versailles Treaty limits, but its aim was simply to secure frontier defence against Poland. In 1930, however, the army leaders started planning for a larger force which would constitute a credible military threat and this received cabinet authorization in July 1932 under Papen. Papen's first initiative was to offer France a military alliance against the Soviet Union, a bizarre manoeuvre which France immediately communicated to Britain and the Soviet Union.[56] Germany, now with Baron von Neurath as Foreign Minister, then claimed the right to the arms necessary for its national security and on 12 September let it be known that it would no longer take part in the conference. The tactic was effective and in December 1932 Germany was granted 'equality of rights in a system that would provide security for all nations'. Germany rejoined the conference when it resumed on 31 January 1933, the day after Hitler was appointed Chancellor.

The foreign policy of the years 1930–3 did not follow a coherent strategy. Policy was improvised to respond to the perceived failure of Stresemann's peaceful revision and the depression. Germany now looked for an economic sphere of interest in central Europe rather than the expansion of international trade and closer ties with western Europe.

The other major policies were to undermine two remaining pillars of the Versailles Treaty, reparations and disarmament. German aims were not new but the method became one of presenting demands in the form of ultimatums and sticking to them. This was successful as, with British and American support, France was isolated.

The period acted as a bridge from the Weimar Republic to the Third Reich. Brüning was no Nazi but, driven by the depression, his definition of German interests became one of independence not partnership. Others more clearly belonged to both worlds. The conservative nationalist goal of restoring Germany as an authoritarian state, rearmament and remilitarizing the Rhineland, redrawing the Polish frontier, union with Austria, establishing an economic empire in central and south-eastern Europe and regaining colonies, overlapped with Hitler's ideas. His further goal of conquering a vast racial empire in the Soviet Union could be, for the present, discounted. Bülow remained in office until his death in 1936, though he considered resigning in 1933. Neurath remained as Foreign Minister to 1938. Papen was a more extreme example, sharing the idea of conquest in the east. Only two senior diplomats resigned or retired in 1933 out of political conviction.[57] Of course, it was possible to hope that Hitler (if he lasted) would avoid war and be guided by the Foreign Ministry. Initially, as in his speech to the Reichstag on 17 May, Hitler declared his commitment to peace and asked only for equal rights for Germany, though he added that a nation of sixty-five million could not be kept down for ever. It is striking that this speech gained him the unanimous support of the Reichstag, including its SPD members, despite all they had already suffered from the Nazis.[58] That too marked a continuity from the Weimar Republic, showing the strength of feeling behind the demand for equal rights.

Conclusion

As with any power seeking to revise an international system, the foreign policy of the Weimar Republic can be interpreted in different ways. Was the priority to overthrow the system or was there a willingness to become part of it? All Weimar governments aimed to restore Germany as a great power. The dividing line was whether they aimed at Germany's recovery as a partner in the new international system, which inevitably set limits to what could be achieved, or independently of it. Were they committed to peaceful methods or did their calculations include war or, at least, a willingness to take the risk of war? Despite a broad consensus, historians still differ over the degree of Germany's commitment to peaceful revision in the period 1924–9. Krüger, Baechler, and Wright argue that there was such a commitment. Pohl and, before him, Gatzke and Thimme, remain sceptical.[59] These differences show both the inherent ambiguity of the politics of a revisionist power, and also the difficulty of assessing the future prospects of a policy that did not survive the depression.

Another perspective is offered by the experience of the Federal Republic of Germany (FRG) after 1949. It too was a revisionist power operating within a new system of international relations. Chancellor Adenauer, like the leaders of the Weimar Republic, resisted Allied sanctions, for instance the dismantling of German industry which he feared would become a symbol like Versailles. He too looked to regain sovereignty by insisting on equality in principle, when the FRG joined the new European institutions and NATO. He too faced French opposition to German rearmament, and the loss of the Saar to French control. Adenauer also encountered strong opposition to his policy of western integration and proclaimed the goal of reunification, a challenge not only to the German Democratic Republic (GDR) but also to Poland. Only with Willy Brandt's Ostpolitik was a form of recognition granted, first using the Locarno concept of mutual renunciation of force, and then declaring existing frontiers 'inviolable'. Formal recognition of the Polish frontier followed only on 14 November 1990. By that time the most dramatic success for peaceful revision had already been achieved with the collapse of the GDR and German unification.

Despite these similarities, there are greater differences. The American commitment to the defence of Western Europe in the cold war worked also to contain German power and thus to contain French (and British) fears of the FRG. The unconditional surrender of Nazi Germany and occupation by the four powers led to an acceptance of defeat to a degree which did not happen in the Weimar Republic. The success of the FRG's economy and political system gave it the stability and the confidence of others which the Weimar Republic lacked. With all these favourable conditions, the FRG also had time to adjust, and for generational change to occur, forty years compared to Weimar's fourteen. That allowed acceptance of what could not be revised, the Polish frontier, and even the existence of the GDR (before it unexpectedly collapsed). These differences underline the difficulties faced by a revisionist power and the conditions necessary for success. That the foreign policy of the Weimar Republic failed for both domestic reasons and because of the unstable international distribution of power after the First World War is not surprising. In its middle years, at least, it was an interesting failure with the potential for a different outcome.

Notes

1. I would like to thank Professor Gottfried Niedhart for his helpful comments on this chapter.
2. The text of the treaty may be found online from the Library of Congress at: https://www.loc.gov/law/help/us-treaties/bevans/m-ust000002-0043.pdf.
3. For the argument that the consensus against the Versailles Treaty prevented an alternative understanding of Germany's defeat, which could have contributed to a democratic culture, Ulrich Heinemann, *Die verdrängte Niederlage: Politische Öffentlichkeit und Kriegsschuldfrage in der Weimarer Republik* (Göttingen: Vandenhoeck & Ruprecht, 1985). However, divisions between right and left over the experience of war remained. On the importance of republican veterans' (and pacifist) groups in the Weimar Republic and their critique of the Wilhelmine empire, Benjamin Ziemann, *Violence and the German Soldier in the Great War: Killing, Dying, Surviving*, Eng. ed. (London: Bloomsbury, 2017), 159–76.
4. Peter Krüger, *Die Außenpolitik der Republik von Weimar* (Darmstadt: Wissenschaftliche Buchgesellschaft, 1985, 1993), 27–30; Eckart Conze, *Das Auswärtige Amt: Vom Kaiserreich bis zur Gegenwart* (Munich: C. H. Beck, 2013), 41–61.

5. Quoted in Peter Krüger (ed.), *Carl von Schubert (1882-1947): Sein Beitrag zur internationalen Politik in der Ära der Weimarer Republik: Ausgewählte Dokumente* (Berlin: Duncker & Humblot, 2017), 12.
6. Alma Luckau, *The German Delegation at the Paris Peace Conference* (New York: Howard Fertig, 1971), 58.
7. Heinemann, *Die verdrängte Niederlage*, 45.
8. On the German army's resistance to the charge of war crimes, John Horne and Alan Kramer, *German Atrocities, 1914: A History of Denial* (New Haven: Yale University Press, 2001).
9. Luckau, *German Delegation*, 112.
10. Christiane Scheidemann, *Ulrich Graf Brockdorff-Rantzau (1869-1928): Eine politische Biographie* (Frankfurt am Main: Peter Lang, 1998), 11; Hermann Graml, *Bernhard von Bülow und die deutsche Außenpolitik* (Munich: Oldenbourg, 2012), 31.
11. Jacques Bariéty, *Les relations franco-allemandes après la première guerre mondiale, 10 novembre 1918-10 janvier 1925, de l'exécution à la negotiation* (Paris: Editions Pedone, 1977).
12. Krüger, *Außenpolitik*, 89.
13. Ibid., 101-3.
14. Christian Schölzel, *Walther Rathenau: Eine Biographie* (Paderborn: Schöningh, 2006), 306-24.
15. A useful summary in Zara Steiner, *The Lights that Failed: European International History 1919-1933* (Oxford: Oxford University Press, 2005), 198-200.
16. Jonathan Wright, *Gustav Stresemann, Weimar's Greatest Statesman* (Oxford: Oxford University Press, 2002), 205.
17. Krüger, *Außenpolitik*, 147-83; Schölzel, *Rathenau*, 356-60; Gottfried Niedhart, *Die Außenpolitik der Weimarer Republik*, 3rd ed. (Munich: Oldenbourg, 2013), 95-6.
18. Stanislas Jeannesson, *Poincaré, la France et la Ruhr (1922-1924)* (Strasbourg: Presses Universitaires de Strasbourg, 1998).
19. Conan Fischer, *The Ruhr Crisis 1923-1924* (Oxford: Oxford University Press, 2003).
20. Wright, *Stresemann*, 235.
21. Stephen A. Schuker, *The End of French Predominance in Europe: The Financial Crisis of 1924 and the Adoption of the Dawes Plan* (Chapel Hill, NC: University of North Carolina Press, 1976); Patrick O. Cohrs, *The Unfinished Peace after World War I: America, Britain and the Stabilisation of Europe 1919-1932* (Cambridge: Cambridge University Press, 2006), 77-184.
22. Wright, *Stresemann*; Christian Baechler, *Gustave Stresemann (1878-1929): De l'impérialisme à la sécurité collective* (Strasbourg: Presses Universitaires de Strasbourg, 1996). For a different interpretation of Stresemann's personality and politics, Karl Heinrich Pohl, *Gustav Stresemann. The Crossover Artist*, Eng. ed. (New York: Berghahn Books, 2019).
23. Wright, *Stresemann*, 284-5.
24. Peter Krüger, *Carl von Schubert: Außenpolitiker aus Leidenschaft* (Berlin: Duncker & Humblot, 2017). Also the edition of Schubert's papers, Krüger (ed.), *Schubert*. Professor Krüger died before completing his study, which extends only to the end of 1925. The edition, however, covers the whole career with an introduction by Martin Kröger.
25. On Gaus's contribution, Gerhard Stuby, *Vom 'Kronjuristen' zum 'Kronzeugen': Friedrich Wilhelm Gaus. Ein Leben im Auswärtigen Amt der Wilhelmstraße* (Hamburg: VSA, 2008), 228-31.
26. Wright, *Stresemann*, 306.
27. Scheidemann, *Brockdorff-Rantzau*, 651-85. Hindenburg reluctantly accepted the Locarno policy, and disappointed those who hoped he would stand out against it, but he remained concerned and critical; Harald Zaun, *Paul von Hindenburg und die deutsche Außenpolitik 1925-1934* (Cologne: Böhlau, 1999), 392-434.

28. Krüger, *Außenpolitik*, 316–17.
29. Wright, *Stresemann*, 316–17.
30. Ibid., 326–8, 343–6.
31. For the argument that it was simply a temporary expedient, Pohl, *Stresemann*, 208–56.
32. 'Zwischen London und Comersee. Deutschlands Paktpolitik', *Hamburger Fremdenblatt*, 255, 14 Sept. 1925; Wright, *Stresemann*, 325–6; Krüger (ed.), *Schubert*, 436–7.
33. Wright, *Stresemann*, 327, 312, and 357 (broadcast on the Treaty of Berlin, 1 May 1926).
34. Ibid., 403.
35. Krüger, *Außenpolitik*, 254–8, 368–72, 501–2.
36. Clemens August Wurm, 'Internationale Kartelle und die deutsch-französischen Beziehungen 1924–30: Politik, Wirtschaft, Sicherheit', in Stephen A. Schuker (ed.), *Deutschland und Frankreich: Vom Konflikt zur Aussöhnung* (Munich: Oldenbourg, 2000), 97–115. Pohl argues that German heavy industry saw the cartel as simply a stepping stone to regaining 'freedom' and, given the support of the Foreign Ministry for these developments, that casts doubt on Stresemann's commitment to peace. Pohl, *Stresemann*, 216–28. On the ambivalence of such agreements in terms of national interests versus international cooperation, Niedhart, *Außenpolitik*, 67–8.
37. Wright, *Stresemann*, 484–5.
38. Franz Knipping, *Deutschland, Frankreich und das Ende der Locarno-Ära 1928–1931* (Munich: Oldenbourg, 1987), 58–84.
39. In Feb. 1928, the DDP leader Koch-Weser noted in his diary that the Reichstag foreign affairs committee (including SPD members) felt that Stresemann was becoming too full of the common endeavours for peace at the League Council and they would rather hear of successes for Germany. In Nov. 1928, the leading Centre party politician, Ludwig Kaas, referred in the Reichstag to 'the undeniable failures and the undeniable stagnation of German foreign policy'. Wright, *Stresemann*, 411, 435.
40. Ibid., 342, 399–400, 417.
41. Krüger, *Außenpolitik*, 386–96, 409–10.
42. Alfred Milatz, *Wähler und Wahlen in der Weimarer Republik* (Bonn: Bundeszentrale für politische Bildung, 1965), 124–5.
43. Knipping, *Ende der Locarno-Ära*, 215–27; Ralph Blessing, *Der mögliche Frieden: Die Modernisierung der Außenpolitik und die deutsch-französischen Beziehungen 1923–1929* (Munich: Oldenbourg, 2008), 447–66.
44. Krüger, *Außenpolitik*, 473–5.
45. To take one example, the Protestant Church observed the tenth anniversary of the Versailles Treaty on 28 June 1929 as a day of mourning, protesting that it had branded the German people as war criminals; Johannes Hosemann (ed.), *Der Deutsche Evangelische Kirchenbund in seinen Gesetzen, Verordnungen und Kundgebungen* (Berlin: Warneck, 1932), 171–2. On the ways in which radical nationalist representations of war displaced republican remembrance from the end of the 1920s, Benjamin Ziemann, *Contested Commemorations: Republican War Veterans and Weimar Political Culture* (Cambridge: Cambridge University Press, 2013), 268–78.
46. Knipping, *Ende der Locarno-Ära*, 143–8.
47. Andreas Rödder, *Stresemanns Erbe: Julius Curtius und die deutsche Außenpolitik 1929–1931* (Paderborn: Schöningh, 1996), 113–19; Graml, *Bülow*, 86–7; Krüger, *Außenpolitik*, 529.
48. Hermann Graml, *Zwischen Stresemann und Hitler: Die Außenpolitik der Präsidialkabinette Brüning, Papen und Schleicher* (Munich: Oldenbourg, 2001), 89–111.
49. Ibid., 81–8. For a different emphasis, which downplays the crisis, and argues for the continuity of attempts on both sides for Franco-German cooperation, Conan Fischer, *A Vision*

of Europe: Franco-German Relations during the Great Depression, 1929–1932 (Oxford: Oxford University Press, 2017), 85–122.
50. Cabinet minutes, 7 May 1931; *Akten der Reichskanzlei: Die Kabinette Brüning*, 1053–4; quoted by Desiderius Meier, *Hermann Dietrich: Ein liberaler Bürger in der Weimarer Republik*, Diss.Phil., Munich, 2018, 461–2; William L. Patch, *Heinrich Brüning and the Dissolution of the Weimar Republic* (Cambridge: Cambridge University Press, 1998), 150–2.
51. Patch, *Brüning*, 159–60.
52. Patricia Clavin, *The Great Depression in Europe, 1929–1939* (Basingstoke: Macmillan, 2000), 127–8.
53. Ibid., 150–2.
54. Hans Mommsen, *The Rise and Fall of Weimar Democracy*, Eng. ed. (Chapel Hill, NC: University of North Carolina Press, 1996), 457–68.
55. On rearmament policy, Michael Geyer, *Aufrüstung oder Sicherheit: Die Reichswehr in der Krise der Machtpolitik 1924–1936* (Wiesbaden: Franz Steiner, 1980), 243–306.
56. Graml, *Zwischen Stresemann und Hitler*, 208–9.
57. Conze, *Das Auswärtige Amt*, 68–71.
58. Max Domarus, *Hitler: Speeches and Proclamations 1932–1945*, Eng. ed. (London: I. B. Tauris, 1990), vol. 1, 324–34.
59. Hans W. Gatzke, *Stresemann and the Rearmament of Germany* (Baltimore: Johns Hopkins University Press, 1954), Annelise Thimme, *Gustav Stresemann* (Frankfurt am Main: Goedel, 1957).

Bibliography

Bariéty, Jacques, *Les relations franco-allemandes après la première guerre mondiale, 10 novembre 1918–10 janvier 1925, de l'exécution à la negotiation* (Paris: Editions Pedone, 1977).
Cohrs, Patrick, *The Unfinished Peace After World War I: America, Britain and the Stabilisation of Europe 1919–1932* (Cambridge: Cambridge University Press, 2006).
Conze, Eckart, *Das Auswärtige Amt: Vom Kaiserreich bis zur Gegenwart* (Munich: C. H. Beck, 2013).
Fischer, Conan, *A Vision of Europe: Franco-German Relations during the Great Depression, 1929–1932* (Oxford: Oxford University Press, 2017).
Graml, Hermann, *Zwischen Stresemann und Hitler: Die Außenpolitik der Präsidialkabinette Brüning, Papen und Schleicher* (Munich: Oldenbourg, 2001).
Horne, John, and Alan Kramer, *German Atrocities, 1914: A History of Denial* (New Haven: Yale University Press, 2001).
Krüger, Peter, *Die Außenpolitik der Republik von Weimar* (Darmstadt: Wissenschaftliche Buchgesellschaft, 1985, 1993).
Niedhart, Gottfried, *Die Außenpolitik der Weimarer Republik*, 3rd ed. (Munich: Oldenbourg, 2013).
Patch, William L., *Heinrich Brüning and the Dissolution of the Weimar Republic* (Cambridge: Cambridge University Press, 1998).
Pohl, Karl Heinrich, *Gustav Stresemann: The Crossover Artist*, Eng. ed. (New York: Berghahn Books, 2019).
Schuker, Stephen A., *The End of French Predominance in Europe: The Financial Crisis of 1924 and the Adoption of the Dawes Plan* (Chapel Hill, NC: University of North Carolina Press, 1976).
Wright, Jonathan, *Gustav Stresemann, Weimar's Greatest Statesman* (Oxford: Oxford University Press, 2002).

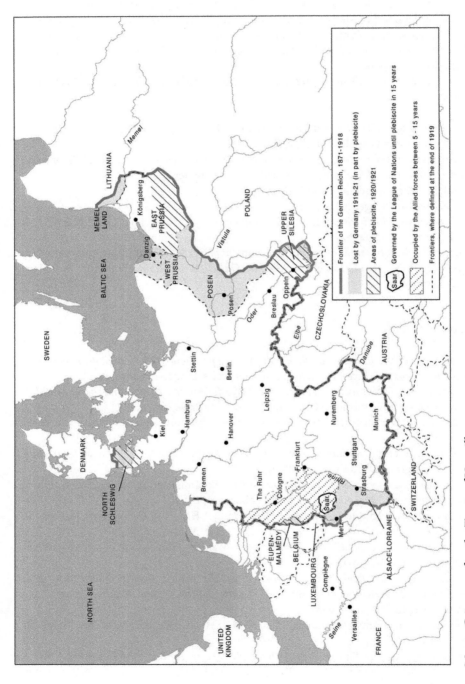

Map 2 Germany after the Treaty of Versailles

Source: Richard J. Evans, *The Coming of the Third Reich* (London: Allen Lane, 2003), 64.

CHAPTER 12

REPUBLICAN GROUPS, IDEAS, AND IDENTITIES

NADINE ROSSOL

Less than two weeks after the German revolution had toppled the monarchy in November 1918, Willy Küster, a citizen from Pomerania, wrote to the new Social Democratic chancellor, and future Reich President, Friedrich Ebert. Küster expressed his delight about the radically changed political reality: 'With joy I greet the new government Ebert … I wish and hope that your government will bring our people what we have all already long carried in our hearts. Hail the republic!! Hail the new government!'[1] Eight years later, in 1926, the social democratic worker-poet Karl Bröger expressed what he considered the essence and the strength of the republic. He published his poem to celebrate the annual festivities commemorating the signing of the Weimar Constitution:

> Constitution Day!
> Let's walk orderly in rank and file
> Proudly flying our flags
> Join us, if you are committed
> Constitution Day!
> We are the people, the republic,
> We create our own destiny
> Million hearts and one beat,
> Constitution Day![2]

Bröger counted among the over one million members of the Reichsbanner black-red-gold, an organization explicitly founded to protect the republic. Given these passionate voices, the fact that the scale of support for the Weimar Republic is still absent from many books seems odd. But, until recently, Weimar's republicans, those who wholeheartedly supported the republic, did not have a good reputation. First, they were blamed for not having been numerous enough to prevent the onslaught of the Nazis and, secondly, for having ignored the importance of appealing symbols, performative politics, and mass mobilizations to generate wide public support for the republic, which, in turn, would have again prevented the rise of the Nazis. Both suggestions are incorrect, and both hark back to the 1920s and 1930s. The trope of a 'republic without republicans' is as old as Weimar itself. In 1919, the Protestant theologian Ernst Troeltsch had already heard many people making this point.[3] Radical left-wing intellectuals, including the journalists Carl von Ossietzky and Kurt Tucholsky, agreed. The longer the Weimar Republic existed, the more its left- and right-wing intellectuals 'paradoxically claimed a weak revolution, that was not really a proper one, had created a republic, that did not want to be one'.[4] In older historiography this fitted well the view of the Weimar Republic as a beleaguered and highly deficient democracy.[5]

The accusation that republicans underestimated the importance of performative politics and, therefore failed to reach the hearts and minds of the German public was also first formulated by contemporaries.[6] Historians shared this evaluation and added a lack of emotionally appealing republican symbols and a deficit in performative politics to the long list of Weimar's shortcomings.[7] Implicitly the propaganda efforts of the Weimar Republic were here negatively compared to Hitler's dictatorship, with surprisingly little reflection on the fundamental differences in the scope for policy-making between a liberal democracy and a totalitarian dictatorship.

Recently the shift to a cultural history of politics inspired historians to approach Weimar's advocates of democracy differently. Moving the focus away from top-level political circles towards grass-roots organizations meant that historians found that republicans were numerous and engaged in performative politics, mass mobilization, and the creation of republican narratives.[8] Conflicts over political symbols demonstrate that these were not superfluous or just a decoration of 'real' political issues, but captured the horizon of experience of many German citizens. Political symbols anchored the republic nationally and locally—they were an essential part of politics.[9] Throughout this chapter we will rediscover Weimar Germany's republicans as an important force in the political landscape. We will explore their organizations and alliances as much as their expectations and hopes for the future of the Weimar Republic. We will see that Germany's republicans energetically gathered mass support for the new state and found appropriate means and symbols to do so. However, putting republicans back into the republic does not mean turning Weimar into a success story. Ambivalences and differences within the republican camp remained. In the end, the republican narrative was not strong enough to bridge the gap between reality and rhetoric.

Supporting the Republic: Republican Groups and Alliances

Weimar contemporaries already differentiated degrees of republican support by distinguishing between *Herzensrepublikaner* (passionate republicans), *Vernunftrepublikaner* (republicans of reason), and *Mußrepublikaner* (forced republicans). *Vernunftrepublikaner* included those who supported the republic out of reason as well as those who accepted the republic for the time being due to a lack of alternatives. The term *Mußrepublikaner* was directed at national conservative politicians who were part of government coalitions when it seemed convenient, but did not disguise their dislike for the republic.[10] When historians examine republican commitment, they often focus on republicans of reason within academic, intellectual, and political circles. The renowned author Thomas Mann and the foreign minister Gustav Stresemann were examples of a slow integration into the republic, while others remained hesitant.[11] *Herzensrepublikaner* were differently motivated and expressed their support for the republic more actively. The suggestion that a genuine republican milieu never properly existed—in contrast to long established and clearly defined social democratic or Catholic ones—addresses a moot point.[12] Republican convictions were articulated in the framework of liberal, social democratic, and Catholic beliefs rather than existing separately. Republicanism was an umbrella term in Weimar Germany that combined a shared set of principles with different political opinions.

The so-called Weimar coalition consisted of the SPD, the left-liberal DDP, and the Catholic Centre Party (Zentrumspartei). These three political parties were the backbone of the Weimar Republic. The Social Democrats were among the most loyal advocates of Weimar—the republic was their project by which they wanted to improve the present and shape the future. There was much in the republican offer that mattered dearly to the SPD including the democratic constitution and new forms of political participation, a commitment to the welfare system and educational reforms, the promises of adequate housing and more rights in the workplace, to name but a few areas.[13] Social Democrats supported the republic as national, regional, and municipal office-holders—among them the first Reich President, Friedrich Ebert, four Reich chancellors, nineteen Reich ministers, thirty-nine heads of German states (Länder), altogether 213 members of national or Länder governments, and numerous local mayors.[14] Furthermore, the SPD had an established and tightly knit net of associations that ranged from organized leisure and educational activities to professional training and, of course, the social democratic trade unions. Mobilizing for the republic in these circles was relatively easy. For example, the social democratic Reichsbund der Kriegsbeschädigten, Kriegsteilnehmer und Kriegerhinterbliebenen (Reich League of Disabled War Veterans, Ex-Servicemen and War Dependants), with its peak membership in 1922 at 830,000, lobbied on behalf of its members, but also contributed to a republican view on the First World War.[15] The prefix 'Reich' in the name here, as well as in other organizations throughout this chapter, indicated that its mobilization and spread was national rather than regional. It had no political connotations.

The left-liberal DDP did not possess a similar network of organizations, even though one of Germany's biggest teacher associations (Deutscher Lehrerverein) was led by DDP members. Thus, the support for the republic came from its politicians. The parliamentary republic with its democratic constitution, drafted by the legal expert and DDP politician Hugo Preuß, encapsulated what the party believed in. While liberal success at the ballot box declined sharply throughout the Weimar years, the contribution of its politicians to the republican project remained immense. The DDP took part in fifteen—of twenty—national governments and occupied key position in the Ministry of Interior (Erich Koch, Rudolf Oeser, Wilhelm Külz) and the Ministry of Defence (Otto Geßler). Walther Rathenau (foreign minister), Theodor Heuss—from 1949 to 1959 the first President of the Federal Republic—Ludwig Haas, and the mayors of Berlin (Gustav Böß), Nuremberg (Hermann Luppe), and Mannheim (Ludwig Landmann) represent just some of the prominent advocates for the republic. The German Democratic Party was also supported by a small circle of republican intellectuals who were prolific and widely heard voices in public discourse. This included for example Theodor Wolff (*Berliner Tageblatt*), Otto Nuschke (*Berliner Volks-Zeitung*), and Georg Bernhard (*Vossische Zeitung*), the editors of Germany's most important republican newspapers, as well as the author Count Harry Kessler.[16]

The Centre Party, the third party of Weimar's republican coalition, served as a bridge between different political camps. Only the Centre Party was part of every national government from February 1919 to May 1932. What might seem opportunistic was in reality a flexibility essential for a party that had to keep its members and voters bound together solely on the basis of the shared Catholic faith and of loyalty to the state. Historian Ursula Büttner asserts that the approach of the Centre Party contributed to more political stability in Weimar as it allowed for coalition building across the political spectrum on national and regional level.[17] However, it was the progressive Social Christian wing— around figures as the finance minister Matthias Erzberger, the head of the Catholic Workers' Associations Joseph Joos, the Reich Chancellors Constantin Fehrenbach, Joseph Wirth, and Wilhelm Marx—that represented the Centre Party's republican credentials. Particularly Joseph Wirth stood for efforts to create republican cooperation with the SPD and the DDP. After the assassination of foreign minister Walther Rathenau in June 1922, the then Reich Chancellor Wirth proclaimed powerfully in the German parliament that the enemies of the republic stood on the political right. Wirth's words cemented his reputation as convinced republican well beyond his own party. In 1926, he founded the Republican Union (Republikanische Union) to bring dedicated republicans together, and published the journal *Deutsche Republik* with Paul Löbe (SPD) and Ludwig Haas (DDP). The Centre Party's support for the republican project differed across Germany. It was stronger in the Rhineland, the Ruhr area, the Rhenish Palatinate, Upper Silesia, and in Baden, often benefiting from the commitment of the Christian unions in these areas.[18]

Weimar's quickly changing governments with different political preferences did sometimes mask long political continuities on another level. For example, the Reich Ministry of the Interior remained a republican stronghold, frequently headed by liberals or Social Democrats (Erich Koch, Adolf Köster, Wilhelm Sollmann, Rudolf Oeser, Wilhelm Külz, Carl Severing). Even when the national-conservative Karl Jarres, followed by the like-minded Martin Schiele, took charge of this ministry from November 1923 to October 1925, other levels of the ministry did not follow this shift. A case in point for a long-serving democratic civil servant was the Reichskunstwart (Reich Art Custodian). As part of the Ministry of the Interior, this small office was headed by the art historian Dr Edwin Redslob. Working from 1920 to 1933, the office coordinated and shaped republican state representation. Redslob was engaged in the creation of new republican state symbols (as much as abolishing old ones), the staging of state festivities and official pageantry, the erection of monuments and the redesign of stamps, seals, coins, and bank notes. His office was small: he needed to organize support and had to fight against financial cuts. But despite these problems, it is important to underline the novelty of Redslob's task. The fact that the young republic possessed a state office that championed symbolic politics by 1920 shows the importance allocated to this field. Furthermore, it was run by a man who wanted to develop a modern republican style of state self-representation and to present democracy as an attraction.[19]

The democrat Arnold Brecht, a top ministerial civil servant, stressed that the republican circle in the Reich Ministry of the Interior was strongly helped by the republicans in key Prussian ministries including the Prussian Ministry for Culture, the Police Department, and the general leadership of its Minister President, the Social Democrat Otto Braun.[20] While the coalition of SPD, DDP, and Centre Party only lasted a few years at the national level, it governed Prussia, Germany's biggest and most populous state, for a majority of the Weimar period —at times including the national conservative DVP (German People's Party). To the surprise of many republicans, Prussia became and remained a bedrock of Weimar democracy. This only ended with the so-called Prussian coup in July 1932 when the national government acted against the Prussian government and replaced its democratic politicians.[21] The Prussian government was often quicker and more forceful in implementing regulations holding its civil servants to account for anti-republican behaviour.[22] To be sure, Prussia consisted of big urban centres as well as sparsely populated rural areas and levels of republican commitment depended heavily on local circumstances. However, support for the republic was the guiding principle for the ministerial leadership. While this did not always trickle down to local communities—or was sometimes deliberately circumvented—the top-level commitment set the tone. Prussia was not the only German state with a government supporting the republic throughout the Weimar years—so were, for example, Baden, Hesse, and Anhalt.[23]

From the very beginning, Weimar was also an educational project. In early December 1918, shortly before the January 1919 National Assembly elections, the Prussian state planned civic education courses for primary school teachers who, in turn, should spread key messages in their local communities. A focus on promoting the social and political achievements of the new state was at the heart of the initiative.[24] The Weimar Constitution stated explicitly that civic education was to be implemented in schools. This brought teachers, who should educate the next generation of republican citizens, into a leading position. Social Democratic teacher associations, often organizing primary school teachers, supported the republic.[25] The teaching profession and its associations helped with a clear move towards republican civic education from 1922 onwards—but the systematic implementation in schools remained uneven.[26]

So far, the focus has largely been on the republican commitment of political parties, ministries, government offices, and regional authorities. From its very beginning, the Weimar Republic also saw the development of republican associations and organizations. In addition to local republican defence leagues, often heavily drawing on Social Democrats and created to safeguard political meetings and members from right-wing attacks, there were two republican organizations that spanned across the country: the Republikanischer Führerbund 1919–22 (Republican Leader's League) and the Republikanischer Reichsbund 1921–33 (Republican Reich League). Documentation is patchy for both organizations, particularly regarding membership figures. Estimates for the peak membership of the Führerbund range from 3,000 to 18,000. Confronted with the violent uprisings in early 1919 and the reliance of the republic on nationalist forces, the Führerbund wanted to 'republicanize' the army and the police to create loyal and committed armed forces for a secure republican state.[27] The army never became a pillar of republican support, although there was more progress in the police. In fact, the so-called 'Schrader association', named after its long-serving head, the Social Democrat Ernst Schrader, organized rank-and-file Prussian policemen and clearly expressed its commitment to the republic. With 78,000 members at its peak in 1932, it was Weimar Germany's biggest police association.[28] The Republikanischer Reichsbund wanted to gather all republicans. Its manifesto, dated 6 March 1921, was signed by sixty-nine prominent politicians, academics, and journalists across the republican spectrum, from the pacifist left to the moderate wings of the SPD and DDP. It called all republicans, men and women, to unite and to participate in building the republic.[29] Explicitly inviting women to be part of the republican project was rather unusual. Republican commitment was often considered as male. Its membership numbers are difficult to establish, with estimates ranging between 20,000 and 100,000. The Republikanischer Reichsbund organized republican festivities, mobilized for republican parties in election campaign, and engaged in educational activities.[30]

In February 1924, the Reichsbanner black-red-gold was founded in Magdeburg. Its name literally referred to the national flag of the Weimar Republic. It was the most important republican organization, and developed out of the work of previous republican unions, including Führerbund and Republikanischer Reichsbund. The Reichsbanner combined the focus of active defence with the aim of creating a republican civic culture. Protecting the republic, gathering republicans, and mobilizing support were among its key aims. As the *Reichsbanner* journal put it: 'The Reichsbanner has to protect the republic and conquer the people for the republic.'[31] With the creation of the Reichsbanner, republicans reacted to attacks by the extreme right that had culminated in the assassinations of republican politicians in the early 1920s, the Hitler putsch in 1923, and aggressive propaganda of the nationalist war veteran associations. The Reichsbanner was non-partisan, uniting all committed male republicans. This claim to stand above party politics was important, but only partially true.[32] Prominent politicians from the SPD, DDP, and Centre Party made up the national governing body of the organization, while the rank-and-file members were overwhelmingly Social Democrats, with some regional exceptions.[33] The Reichsbanner asked republican war veterans to join, stating that those who had already fought for the fatherland were now needed again to protect the republic. But it never confined its membership to war veterans and remained open to all male republicans.[34] Membership numbers rose impressively quickly and peaked at around one million in 1925/26. As quickly as the Reichsbanner grew, it established regional and local branches across Germany, slightly weaker in the South of Germany (apart from Baden) and in the Prussian province of Eastern Prussia (apart from Königsberg).[35] Rural communities remained difficult to win over for the republican organization.

The activities of the Reichsbanner included festivities celebrating the foundation of the Weimar Republic, commemorating the war dead, and remembering republican martyrs as well as organizing social gatherings, local parades, and marches, mobilizing support for the republican parties in national and local elections, protecting party rallies from political enemies, and protesting against policies that were considered anti-republican. The Reichsbanner was essential for the republican cause, even though it mattered less in defending the republic against potential uprisings. Carl Severing, Social Democratic Minister of the Interior in Prussia and responsible for the Prussian police, insisted that there would not be an unofficial auxiliary police force or a Reichsbanner militia.[36] The achievements of the Reichsbanner lay in other areas. The organization visibly mobilized support on regional and local levels and anchored the republic there. Republicans now possessed a strong organization which loudly claimed public and political spaces for its demands. The Reichsbanner turned support for the republic into a local experience, in which citizens could actively take part by joining the local Reichsbanner group or by showing republican support with black-red-gold colours. It was no coincidence that the black-red-gold flag was the symbol of the Reichsbanner and of the German republic.[37]

Support for the republic also came from sections of the press, first, from the Social Democratic side (203 newspapers), covering 5 per cent of the market, including its flagship paper *Vorwärts* and the press of the trade unions.[38] The Catholic press, linked to the Centre Party, held around 13 per cent of the market, but not all Catholic newspapers were keen advocates of the republic, which mirrored the split into national conservative and social-liberal factions of the party. The difficulties of the liberal parties over the course of the Weimar years were reflected in their declining share of the newspaper market.[39] This trend also included the most important left-liberal dailies that remained outspoken advocates of the republic: the *Berliner Volks-Zeitung*, the *Berliner Tageblatt*, the *Vossische Zeitung,* and the *Frankfurter Zeitung*.

Republican publications that targeted very specific readerships included the journals of the Reichsbanner, *Das Reichsbanner* and *Illustrierte Reichsbanner-Zeitung* (*Illustrated Reichsbanner Journal, IRZ*), both of which combined political coverage with organizational news for its members. The small weekly journal *Deutsche Republik*, deliberately rooted in the Weimar coalition, reflected the party affiliation of its three editors, Wirth, Haas, and Löbe, and formulated the need for a united republican front.[40] The pacifist and radical-left journals *Die Weltbühne* and *Das Tage-Buch* aimed at intellectual circles. Particularly *Die Weltbühne* reminded its readers continuously that the republic needed to act more forcefully against its enemies. This included scathing criticism of the SPD for not doing enough in this respect.[41] Even when journals initially only reached a small readership, they could still bring attention to important themes. Local conflicts were often bumped from the bottom up, with republicans first raising their concerns with local newspapers. By the mid-1920s, republicans tried to mobilize their fellow citizens to strongly support the republican press.[42]

Republicans did not stop there. The Republikanische Beschwerdestelle (Republican Complaint Agency), founded in 1924, encouraged citizens to report when local authorities breached regulations on symbolic practices, for example, the lack of republican flags in municipal offices, anti-republican speeches by school directors, or the continuing presence of monarchical symbols at universities. The privately run organization anonymized the letters from the public, forwarded them to the responsible authorities, and demanded swift reactions.[43] In most cases, if not all, the reported incidents were breaches of official regulations. While critics called the Beschwerdestelle petty and denunciatory, its supporters pointed out that the organization only insisted on the implementation of existing regulations.[44] The Beschwerdestelle's function as a republican watchdog demonstrates the active engagement of local citizens. Difficulties of the organization included its accusatory tone, which even irritated democratic officials, and its self-proclaimed role as a critical watchdog of national and local authorities.

Much older than the Beschwerdestelle, the CV (Centralverein deutscher Staatsbürger jüdischen Glaubens, Central Association of German Citizens of the Jewish Faith) was another pillar of republican support. Founded in 1893 to defend Jewish citizens against antisemitic attacks, the CV collected reports on antisemitic incidents and offered legal support for taking these to the courts. Not all antisemitic cases included explicit anti-republican sentiments, but often they went hand in hand. The assassination of Walther Rathenau in June 1922 combined antisemitic and anti-republican notions in the most toxic form.[45] In fact, the Reichsbanner recognized from the very beginning that these two topics were connected and included in its strongly worded commitment to defend the republic an equally forceful statement against antisemitism.[46]

The difficulties of the CV with the way legal cases regarding antisemitic incidents were often dealt with in the courts mirrored the problems regarding anti-republican ones. As a reaction to the murder of Rathenau, which many Weimar politicians interpreted as an attack on the republic itself, the so-called 'Law for the Protection of the Republic' was passed. It could now be considered as high treason when representatives of the republic as well as its symbols were insulted or attacked. This allowed for more severe punishments. The difficulties of the new law came with its practical implementation. Many judges interpreted anti-republican and antisemitic slander as personal insults rather than as a general attack on the republican state form. In this way, courts deliberately undermined the law by repeatedly adjudicating that insults such as 'Jewish republic' were minor offences.[47] Even though the legal outcomes of antisemitic and anti-republican incidents often did not match what the CV and other organizations lobbied for, the cases did not remain unnoticed. Republican newspapers framed them exactly in the political narrative that courts deliberately ignored, as a fight for the soul of the republic that needed to be fought and won at local level.

By the mid-1920s, republicans agreed that greater efforts to strengthen the republic were needed. They were less united in how to achieve this. In hindsight, the democrat Arnold Brecht wrote that 'aggressive propaganda for the democratic-republican idea' could be more easily carried out by political parties and their affiliated organizations. He felt that governments and ministries also had to engage those who were less convinced.[48] Brecht reflected on a political reality in which governments needed to negotiate compromises, but he also generally favoured an inclusive way of integrating all into the republic. The Reichskunstwart Redslob agreed. He relied on an organic process in which eventually 'every citizen wanted to be part of the republic'.[49] Leftist republicans found this unacceptable, as Kurt Tucholsky explained: 'There is only one kind of propaganda for the new republic and that is political action. Everything else is a waste of time.'[50]

Republican Ideas and Their Ambivalences: Past, Present, and Future

Ambivalences within the republican camp were not only obvious when the appropriate tools for republican engagement were debated, but also when republicans thought about the past, present, and future of the new state. Promoting slow and evolutionary progress was considered as appropriate by some, but disappointed others who identified a gap between expectations and reality. We will also see that the republican camp failed to find a prominent place for women within its narrative. The focus on male-connoted activism, centred on 'fighting' for the republic, considerably reduced the areas in which women could demonstrate their republican commitment.

References to 1848 were omnipresent in the Weimar Republic and it is not difficult to understand why. The revolution in March 1848 and the assembly of the parliament in Frankfurt's Paulskirche in May 1848 helped to integrate the new republic into a historical development towards democracy that started in 1848 and, according to republicans, found its fulfilment in Weimar in 1919. Turning the black-red-gold colours into Weimar's national flag already created a powerful symbolic link between the new German republic and the liberal democratic movement of the nineteenth century. The poems of the so-called 'freedom poets' of 1848 were part and parcel of republican ceremonies. The revolutionary poem 'Black-Red-Gold', written by Ferdinand Freiligrath in March 1848, became a staple of Reichsbanner festivities, with its beginning linking beautifully to the Reichsbanner's founding story. It read: 'In grievance and darkness / we had to recover the colours ... Powder is black / Blood is red / and golden shines the flame.'[51] The poster for the Reichsbanner's celebration of the Constitution Day in Frankfurt in 1928, featuring a black-red-gold flag and the Paulskirche, made the link between the Weimar Republic and the national parliament in 1848 most obvious (Figure 12.1).

However, the DDP and the SPD did not always mean the same when they referred to 1848. The SPD honoured the revolutionary legacy of the event, while the DDP focused on the liberal demands of democratization and constitutional rights. In March 1923, the DDP and the SPD held separate commemorative ceremonies to remember the seventy-fifth anniversary of 1848. While both ceremonies included Freiligrath's poetry, the SPD ended with the singing of the International, whereas the DDP sang the national anthem.[52] Yet even though the SPD and the DDP looked at the events of 1848 from different angles, their interpretations were not exclusive, but indicated a shift in focus. The anniversary celebration in Frankfurt in May 1923, organized by the city of Frankfurt together with the Reichskunstwart Redslob, managed to strike a balance of a revolutionary and reformist legacy that equally engaged the Social Democrats and the liberal democrats.[53] In fact, one key demand rooting back to 1848 was shared by the republican camp—the wish for territorial unity between Germany and Austria, a demand the Treaty of Versailles had outlawed. Foregrounding this particular aspect was not without problems as it caught the republic in a defensive role having to explain why these issues had not been resolved yet and with no power to enforce change.[54] However, the benefits of creating a sense of republican nationalism that stressed the unity with republicans in Austria (as the Reichsbanner did with its Austrian counterpart, the republican Schutzbund) outweighed its drawbacks, because it counteracted the persistent right-wing claim that republicans were unpatriotic Germans. It also offered a positive future vision of two newly founded republican states (Germany and Austria) working together towards achieving a nineteenth-century liberal idea.[55]

Linked to the most recent past for Weimar contemporaries was the impact of the First World War, one of the most dominant discursive topics in the 1920s and 1930s. The nationalist right placed the defeat at the doorstep of the republic while glorifying the war experience. Republicans created a fundamentally different framework for narratives about the war by placing its horror at the core and portraying the victimization of the ordinary soldiers as a result of the mismanagement and class hierarchies of the old regime. In this narrative, the Weimar Republic was the only legitimate outcome of the war because it stopped the injustice of the morally bankrupt imperial system and its army.[56] The Reichsbanner and the Reichsbund of Disabled War Veterans, Ex-Servicemen, and War Dependants were at the forefront of these efforts. Both created space for republican, often working-class, veterans to share their war memories. Both organizations also publicly confronted the activities of nationalist veteran associations who claimed the legacy of the war for the political right. Time and time again the Reichsbanner and Reichsbund of Disabled War Veterans, Ex-Servicemen and War Dependants stressed the massive sacrifices for the war among their members and took pains to demonstrate this publicly. Female voices were largely excluded by the Reichsbanner, while war widows had a more prominent role in the Reichsbund.[57]

Presenting republican democracy as the only positive outcome of the war was one avenue republicans took. The other was to negatively link the war to the former

FIGURE 12.1 Constitution Day Celebration of the Reichsbanner in Frankfurt/Main, 11–12 August 1928. The caption reads: 'The 1848 pre-parliament and the national assembly met at Frankfurt's Paulskirche.'

monarchy. Fritz Einert, a Social Democrat and member of the local Reichsbanner group in Schmalkalden, did so in 1926 when he jotted down his recollections of front-line service in the war. Einert refuted the nationalist claim that soldiers had passionately joined under the imperial colours of black-white-red. Instead, he contended that 'the black-white-red ruler's flag' stood for war and would not have been chosen by the soldiers if they had had any choice.[58] The journal of the Reichsbanner made this point about agency even more explicit when it used the vicinity of the outbreak of the war (4 August 1914) and the signing of the Weimar Constitution (11 August 1919) to create a connection between these two events in early August. In late July 1926, its title-page featured a drawing that reminded of the brutality of the war by showing three mutilated corpses caught in barbed wire on a battlefield with the faces of three young soldiers above this scene. A week later, the *Reichsbanner* journal reminded its readers of Weimar's democratic constitution that guaranteed everyone a say in future decisions on war and peace.[59]

The legal scholar and Social Democratic politician Gustav Radbruch claimed in his speech at the Constitution Day festivities in August 1928 the war as a prehistory for the republic: 'The people's army—and a people's army was back then, fighting or suffering, the entire German people, women and men … created the German people's state. We cannot commemorate the constitution of the renewed Germany without remembering the years 1914 to 1918.'[60] In essence, this was a message about democratic citizenship as reward for wartime sacrifices. Unlike the dominant discourse in the Reichsbanner, Radbruch explicitly included women and the home front in his speech, thus broadening the social basis of republicanism to match Weimar's electorate.

Despite Radbruch's inclusion of women, they were often neglected as important carriers of the republican idea. This was a missed opportunity, especially as the introduction of female suffrage, as part of the revolutionary changes in late 1918, allowed women to fully participate in political decision-making processes. For the first time, women, aged 20 and over, could vote and stand to be elected. This democratization of political participation did not only apply to women, but they in particular could now think of themselves as politically active citizens.[61] Yet even within republican circles this key achievement was not used to link women more closely to the republic. This reflected the attitude of the republican parties who were keen to gather the female vote but often unwilling to give serious support to female politicians, especially when this could cause competition with men. Political parties found that women-only meetings, focusing strongly on female-connoted themes, were appropriate and effective ways to engage women.[62] The Reichsbanner's focus on defending the republic and its nature as war veterans' organization defined republican commitment largely as male activism, inevitably limiting the space for women. A Reichsbanner booklet, celebrating the constitution in 1925, captured an attitude to women organisation never fundamentally abandoned. Women were depicted in a drawing, 'decorating the banner of the republic'. Yet no female author penned any of the many articles in the booklet.[63] The Reichsbanner journal *IRZ*, aimed at the republican family, presented women as mothers, sisters, or girlfriends supporting those defending the republic.[64] Other republican organizations equally struggled to find roles for women that went beyond more traditional fields such as the family and education. In line with conventional notions regarding the roles of women in politics, republican organizations and republican parties did not find a conceptual framework that adequately reflected the opportunities and the progressive optimism that the republican state had rekindled with its bold introduction of equal political rights.

Weimar's republicans also thought about the present and the future. The term people's community (*Volksgemeinschaft*) has often been wrongly associated with National Socialism and the extreme right. It was used by all political parties in the Weimar Republic and stood in its more inclusive, progressive reading for a future promise.[65] The republican camp envisioned a community of equals surpassing class differences and articulated this idea particularly in public speeches at festive occasions. This notion did not always convince working-class republicans, who often located their ideas between *Volksgemeinschaft* and class struggle. By contrast, the notion of the people's state (*Volksstaat*) had a long tradition within the SPD, strongly directed against the imperial regime and its restrictions of political participation. For Social Democrats, the Weimar Constitution was the ultimate break with the monarchy and finally guaranteed equal rights of the working class. Similar to the point Fritz Einert made in his recollections, it mattered that the people's state had now replaced the ruler's state.[66] On 10 August 1919, when the constitution was agreed and Reich President Friedrich Ebert was about to sign it, the Social Democratic newspaper *Vorwärts* found that 'the new times' could start now.[67] The SPD believed it could achieve socialism through its work in the republic. Wilhelm Sollmann, Social Democratic politician and Reichsbanner member, wrote in 1924 'that the class struggle in a democratic republic will be politically carried out through reforms ... good reforms will bring us closer to the revolutionary goal of socialism than noisy activities'.[68] Democratic socialism was meant to be the eventual future outcome, achieved through evolution rather than revolution.

While not everybody shared the goal of democratic socialism and its inherent class struggle narrative, many republican intellectuals, journalists, and politicians agreed with the sense of a progressive and evolutionary development of the republic's future. These interpretations were also inspired by the dislike of further revolutionary uprisings, which meant that stressing the slow but continuously progressive outlook and the hard work that still needed to be put into building the republic became even more important.[69] Joseph Wirth, the republican Centre Party politician, reminded in an article in 1928 that the new state had already achieved much, but that there still was a difficult path ahead.[70] The Centre Party understood its position as party of the political centre ground and wanted to avoid further divisions or radicalization. Even its circle of decidedly republican politicians did not link a future vision to the republic.[71]

Not all republicans agreed with this evolutionary approach and to some it seemed particularly misplaced when faced with the growing strength of the Nazi movement in the later years of the Weimar Republic. In March 1930, looking back at the 1920 Kapp putsch, the radical left journalist Carl von Ossietzky lamented the deficiency of German republicanism, compared to France: 'Only in March 1920 [Kapp putsch] and in June 1922 [assassination of Rathenau] the Germans saw the republic like the French had always done, that is as combative, as the daughter of liberty … At that time, the German republic could have gained substance, an idea for itself.' Rational pragmatism, Ossietzky implied, was not enough.[72] In the same month the great coalition, led by the SPD, fell apart and was replaced with a presidential minority government. Two of the three republican parties, the DDP and the Centre Party, moved away from the republican project. Ossietzky was right, the big occasions that mobilized mass support reaching those who were not organized in republican associations had passed by 1930. Yet he still underestimated the importance of evolutionary republican commitment beyond these events.

The Reichsbanner stood with its vision for the future of the republic—at least rhetorically—between the pragmatic republicans and Ossietzky's demands. Karl Bröger had created the Reichsbanner's 'Republican Hymn' in which he combined the classic promise of a bright future with calls to actions. Its last stanza reads: 'Brothers, let us arm in arm / Bravely walk towards the future / Leaving darker times behind / In front of us the bright horizon / Yield those who disrespect our freedom / People beware, brother be on guard! / German republic we swear / Our last drop of blood belongs to you.'[73] Some of the early activism of the Reichsbanner during its founding years had turned into more conventional activities and an increasing focus on sociability. This changed with the growing success of the Nazi party, which revitalized the Reichsbanner's activities but also demonstrated the limits of republican mobilization. From 1929 onwards, the Reichsbanner considered the National Socialists as its main enemy, exemplified in numerous articles, sometimes long explanatory pieces sometimes caricatures, on the topic in its organizational publications. In 1931, the Reichsbanner publicly called upon the national government to do more to defend the republic, but with limited success. The republican organization did not only demand stronger action from the government against the Nazis, it also wanted national and local governments to take up the offer it had made at the very beginning of its founding, namely using Reichsbanner units as protection forces.[74] As before, this was not taken up by the national government, nor by the Prussian one. In December 1931, the Reichsbanner, the SPD, the unions, and the umbrella organization for workers' sports associations joined forces and created the so-called 'Iron Front'. This was a reaction to the foundation of the 'Harzburg Front' two months earlier, which included the nationalist right and the Nazi party. Given the make-up of the Iron Front, it becomes clear that organized defence of the republic was now left largely to the SPD and its organizations. Throughout 1932 the Iron Front mobilized against the National Socialists with mass assemblies, as well as smaller, more targeted, activities in local areas. The cover of the illustrated Reichsbanner journal took up a familiar theme when it tried to mobilize members to donate to the Iron Front as the organization had to raise its own funds. The March 1932 issue showed the photo of a war injured veteran who donated to the Iron Front with the caption 'The republic's poorest son is its most loyal one.' This variation of a quote from a popular war poem by Karl Bröger, which originally referred to the fatherland rather than the republic, underlined the key message: those who had made sacrifices for the fatherland in 1914, did so again in 1932.[75]

Staging the Republic: Performative Democracy and Republican Symbols

Political symbols, narratives and festivities were (and still are) essential for political identity formation and collective mobilization. They create a shared sense of community and purpose by focusing on unifying themes, and did so for Weimar's republicans, too. However, it is important to remember that the republicans' focus on performative politics went beyond considering this as simply festive decoration or political spin. For organizers and participants alike, shaping and staging the republic in a number of different ways expressed something fundamental about the nature of this new state, its sense of community, and its scope for participation. Performative politics and symbolic conflicts mattered so profoundly in Weimar because they captured how citizens engaged with politics.

New political systems abolish and replace previous political symbols to manifest change and to express power. The Weimar Republic was no exception, but a republican repertoire of symbols and narratives was not immediately available after the collapse of the monarchy in November 1918. Red flags on city halls, railways stations, and police headquarters signalled a revolutionary change, but the situation remained confusing regarding political symbols when returning German soldiers were greeted with black-white-red colours of the Kaiserreich and revolutionary red flags. Left-wing artist Käthe Kollwitz placed a 'German black-white-red flag' with 'red republican bunting' and a green fir wreath as a signifier of greeting and respect to those who came home in the window of her Berlin flat. She was not a monarchist but felt this was the most appropriate way to honour those who had fought in the war. At the same time, Kollwitz strongly approved of the political changes occurring in Germany.[76] This curious colour combination was short-lived as black-white-red flags quickly turned into the symbol of those who actively fought against the republic. The red flag lost its initial republican connotation and returned to being the partisan symbol of the SPD as well as that of the newly founded German Communist Party (KPD). Still sparse in the winter of 1918/19 was the display of black-red-gold colours—the most recognizable symbol of the Weimar Republic. Half a year later, in July 1919, the National Assembly debated the political symbols of the new democratic state and ultimately agreed on black-red-gold as national colours. The Social Democratic delegate Hermann Molkenbuhr found this choice perfectly fitting to the republic: 'For Germany the black-red-gold colours are the colours for which democrats have always fought … now at a time in which the democratic demands are put into practice it is time to publicly express this by displaying the black-red-gold symbol.'[77]

Despite the pathos expressed here, the decision for black-red gold was based on a compromise. Black-white-red was still the main colour in several Weimar flags for specific purposes, for instance for the merchant navy and the Reichswehr, which only displayed black-red-gold in the canton, the top inner corner.[78] Some republicans, including the

DDP politician and 'father of the Weimar Constitution' Hugo Preuß, found this compromise went too far. Others considered it as the only possibly solution given the political constellation in the National Assembly.[79] When the delegates debated Germany's new flag in 1919, three colour combinations were on the table: the Communists and the Independent Socialists suggested red, the national conservatives wanted to keep black-white-red, and the Social Democrats, the Centre Party, and the DDP favoured black-red-gold. Only the SPD fully backed black-red-gold, arguing that the country needed to unite around a flag that did not stand for a political party. For the Social Democrats supporting black-red-gold, rather than their own red flag, already stood for a union between the organized working class and the liberal democratic movement. The Centre Party and the DDP were more hesitant and supported black-red-gold as national flag with the already mentioned black-white-red compromise. It was this willingness of the republican parties to find a majority for black-red-gold that created a key political symbol of Weimar democracy.[80] But even in the republican camp there were limits. Six months after the collapse of the monarchy, the black-red-gold flag could only be agreed upon with black-white-red for the merchant navy. The colours black-red-gold were useful for the republicans as they represented a clear break with the monarchy, did not stand for a single party, and helped to link the young republic to the ideas of 1848 and Germany's parliament in the Paulskirche.

The early years of the republic showed that some supporters of black-white-red had more in mind than just reminiscing about the glory of the Hohenzollern monarchy. The Kapp putsch, right-wing attacks, and the assassinations of the politicians Matthias Erzberger and Walther Rathenau demonstrated the murderous intent of those on the nationalist right. These attacks triggered a change in the republican camp towards a strong focus on protecting the republic, as the founding of the Reichsbanner already illustrated. By the mid-1920s, the black-red-gold colours were strongly supported by the SPD, the Centre Party, and the DDP alike as they now stood for defending the current republican state. In May 1926, Reich Chancellor Hans Luther's inept handling of a new flag decree lost him his office. Luther's regulation, signed by Reich President Hindenburg, suggested that embassies and consulates outside of Europe and at ports could fly the merchant navy flag (with black-white-red in the centre) next to the republican colours. What sounds like a technical point created a public outrage. The republican press and the republican parties—with the Centre Party and the DDP as part of Luther's coalition government—deeply disagreed with the chancellor. The Reichsbanner organized mass rallies against Luther's flag regulation.[81] Looking back after 1945, the Social Democrat Otto Braun remained irritated that 'flag issues continued to have far greater significant in the political life of the republic, and outweighed many topics that were materially more important'.[82]

The emotional response in the 1926 flag controversy needs to be placed in a wider context. The years 1925–6 saw the resurfacing of personalities that hardened republicans in their defensive attitude and saw the success of republican mobilization. It started with a republican defeat in 1925: the election of Paul von Hindenburg as Reich President. Now a monarchist held the highest office of the German republic.

A year later, in the summer of 1926, Germany's citizens voted in a referendum on the expropriation of properties of the German princes. The mobilization needed for the referendum (first a people's vote had to be won to proceed with a referendum) went well beyond strict political party lines and can be considered as an impressive commitment to the republic. The Reichsbanner, stressing its non-partisan character, was instrumental in these mobilizing efforts pitching the republican flag against the imperial colours.[83] Hindenburg's election, Luther's flag decree, and the referendum on the princes' properties reminded the republican camp of a widely shared emotional core commitment—the passionate dislike of the Hohenzollern monarchy, other ruling houses, and their representatives.

From the mid-1920s until 1933, local conflicts over political symbols played an important role and strongly engaged citizens. The Reichsbanner staged its activities under the black-red-gold flag, including for example its parades, republican festivals, the founding of new Reichsbanner groups, supporting republican parties in election campaigns, or commemorating republican martyrs. The flag was now loaded with symbolic meanings, represented a republican narrative that linked 1848 to Weimar democracy, centred on defending the present republic and remembering republican sacrifices which ranged from the war dead, over the deceased politicians Matthias Erzberger (Centre Party), Walther Rathenau (DDP), Friedrich Ebert (SPD), to the fatalities of Reichsbanner members. The different layers of significance linked to the black-red-gold colours turned the republican flag into a deeply emotional political symbol, which helps to explain the intensity of symbolic conflicts that were triggered by seemingly trivial events.

A case in point was the so-called 'flag war on the beaches' which occupied the national press in the summers of 1927 and 1928. Republican holidaymakers decorated their sandcastles, wicker beach chairs, or beach huts with black-red-gold flags—a usual practice at German seaside resorts in the 1920s. Republicans brought to the attention of the press as well as to local police authorities that their flags were frequently stolen or vandalized. This prompted the illustrated Reichsbanner journal to remind its readers to take several flags with them on holidays. In the summer of 1927, a holidaymaker on the North Sea island of Sylt asked the local mayor for help as many of his flags had gone missing, including 'the big black-red-gold flag and the 10 small ones dotted around the sandcastle as well as the two republican flags fixed to the wicker beach chair'.[84] Citizens and the republican press reported these incidents. Eventually, the Prussian Minister of the Interior, the Social Democrat Albert Grzesinski, sent more police to protect black-red-gold flags. This episode provides insight into the emotions linked to political symbols at local level, but also demonstrates how republicans managed to escalate an initially small-scale event to communicate a bigger point about the protection of the republican state symbol. Grzesinski was probably not interested in flags on sandcastles, but he recognized the importance of the message he was sending on behalf of the Prussian state—the black-red-gold flag deserved protection because it embodied and signified the republic.[85] Grzesinski's behaviour was in line with the more proactive republican stance of the Prussian state in general.

The Reichsbanner and republican parties mobilized around the black-red-gold colours and called upon the local population to display them on important occasions. They even suggested that republicans should make their consumer choices based on the political convictions of the shop or restaurant owner. 'Republicans only buy at republicans' was a slogan that went hand in hand with boycotting those who had refused to display black-red-gold flags on Constitution Day. The Reichsbanner also promoted small merchandising items including flags, pictures of Reich President Friedrich Ebert, black-red-gold garlands, and coffee mugs, as well as Reichsbanner cigarettes.[86]

Showing support for the republic was not difficult in the mid-1920s and republican as well as anti-republican newspapers counted the display of black-red-gold flags to measure the level of support for the republic.[87] But we need to keep in mind that there was a quantitative engagement with the symbols of the republic that went beyond the counting of flags. Even small signs of republican commitment were heavily invested with emotions and meaning, as the flag conflicts on beaches demonstrated. These incidents often created tensions and occupied local authorities, the police, sometimes the courts and the press. Republican flags did not just disappear from beaches but also from back gardens, front doors, or balconies. Police and court files provide details on these cases as republicans involved the local authorities or the local press. The Republikanische Beschwerdestelle engaged with symbolic conflicts at the local level, for instance by demanding that local authorities displayed republican flags in offices or that the local school removed an imperial symbol. Conflicts were thus not confined to the new republican symbols; they sometimes centred on the abolition of imperial ones. By March 1922, the Weimar Republic had clear regulations on how to deal with the symbols of the former monarchy, including the abolition of pictures or statues of Wilhelm II. The practical implementation, however, was often less straightforward, and the Beschwerdestelle reminded local leaders of the importance of following government guidelines.[88]

Political symbols and narratives work particularly well when they are included in the wider choreography of festivities. The republican state organized different ceremonial events throughout the Weimar years. These included the state funerals of Walther Rathenau (1922), Friedrich Ebert (1925), and Gustav Stresemann (1929) which struck a solemn tone but also served as moments of collective national unity.[89] The political occasion that encapsulated performative politics best in the Weimar Republic was the annual Constitution Day celebration on 11 August, commemorating the day when Friedrich Ebert had signed off the Constitution on this date in 1919. These festivities provide insight into the national staging of the republic, its local repercussions, the agents involved, and the political messages promoted. Constitution Day festivities were celebrated annually from 1921 to 1932 by each government of the Weimar Republic. Even though the national government honoured the day, it never turned into a public holiday due to the lack of a parliamentary majority for this idea. Not even the republican camp was united in its support for the Constitution Day. The left wing of the SPD as well as radical pacifists found that the wrong date had been chosen and that a republican holiday should have been 9 November to commemorate the German revolution in 1918. Another current in the SPD favoured 1 May, Labour Day, a traditional mobilizing event in the socialist labour movement. As there was no agreement at the national level, some German states created their own official or semi-official holidays, demanding that local authorities and schools had to celebrate the constitution on 11 August.[90] How differently the republicans and anti-republicans interpreted the importance of the day is demonstrated by a debate in parliament in the summer of 1929. The tenth anniversary of the republic should be, according to the SPD politician Wilhelm Sollmann, 'a republican offensive'. And he added 'we should not forget where this republic comes from. This state, this republic has been founded and created by the poor, by the poorest peoples' comrades (*Volksgenossen*).' The DNVP delegate Emil Berndt responded that 'the republican demonstration' would stand in contrast to the sentiment of many and was a mere Potemkin village, a façade without proper content.[91]

National ceremonies on Constitution Day followed a traditional pattern of festive speeches and classical music in front of a selected audience in the German Reichstag. Republican officials in charge of organizing these festivities, among them the Reichskunstwart Redslob, were keen to expand the reach and to create more popular events. They aimed at communicating the political nature of the republic and the expression of the people's position within it. The illustrated Reichsbanner journal captured this notion on its cover in August 1925, juxtaposing two photographs under the heading 'Once and Now'. A military parade devoid of ordinary citizens from 1913 was compared to Constitution Day festivities in 1925 in which a large crowd of citizens was celebrating together. The republican festivities, so the message, were not just civilian and more fun, but also a community of equals.[92] Constitution Day celebrations in Berlin expanded over the Weimar years to include popular components like sports, parades, and popular performances, always keen to create popular festivities. The Reichsbanner participated strongly in these national celebrations, but also organized its own to stress the strength of its organization.

In the mid-1920s, a festive parade was added to the events in Berlin which slowly increased in size and scope from 12,000 participants in 1927 to 75,000 in 1929. The republicans, including many Reichsbanner members, marched through the political centre of the capital and publicly occupied one of the most important routes through Berlin in a way that would have been impossible in Imperial Germany. The liberal *Berliner Tageblatt* interpreted the parade in August 1928 as mirroring what the republic stood for when it claimed that it included 'couples, children, young lads with their girls, women and men of all professions'. 'Whoever has seen this, has not only seen an organised torch lit march, but the celebration of the people and the confession of the people.'[93] On the tenth anniversary of the republic, in August 1929, the festivities had expanded even further and included sports events, parades, and, for the first time, the performance of a mass play in Berlin's sport stadium. The Reichsbanner contributed greatly to the Berlin festivities. In addition to being part of the parade, the republican organization had constructed a temporary memorial close to the Brandenburg Gate, consisting of three wooden pillars, 17 metres high, that commemorated 'all the dead of the World War', 'those who sacrificed their lives for the republic and for work', and 'the dead of the Reichsbanner' (Figure 12.2).[94]

FIGURE 12.2 Temporary memorial by the Reichsbanner for the Constitution Day in Berlin, 11 August 1929.

Photo by Georg Pahl.

The Reichskunstwart Redslob oversaw the newly introduced mass event in the sport stadium which involved 11,000 school children and 500 workers in front of 50,000 spectators. The workers entered the stadium and tried to connect ten poles to build a symbolic bridge but needed to call in the youth to help. Dressed in black-red-gold, young people joined, connected the poles, and formed a republican flag on the stadium ground. The play concluded with the raising of the republican flag, the singing of the national anthem, and the youth swearing an oath to the fatherland. The journal *Deutsche Republik* praised the play for symbolically bringing the joyfulness of the youth to the republican state. The political message was obvious. Republican colours framed the community of workers and young people who represented the foundation, as Wilhelm Sollmann had already pointed out, and the future of the republican 'people's state'.[95] Some voices in the republican camp cautioned that the staging of big celebrations still did not mean people were committed republicans and that the republic should first do its homework in ensuring that the constitution was implemented everywhere before it was celebrated with 'a republican parade day'.[96] Their critique failed to recognize that the performative aspect of republican politics was attractive to many and that it helped to carve out a space for the republicans within the political landscape of the time. Some historians have followed contemporary critics such Carl von Ossietzky and have emphasized the militaristic nature of the uniformed Reichsbanner parades that resembled or even imitated the conventional style of other veterans' associations such as the Kyffhäuser League. In this view, the Reichsbanner failed to create a civic republican culture.[97] Other contemporaries disagreed. Carl Misch wrote that the Reichsbanner managed to function 'without parade marches, goose-stepping or standing to attention'.[98] Furthermore, it is not helpful to impose on the past our ideas on what a democratic political culture should look like. The Reichsbanner was less militaristic than other war veterans' associations and most of its members had experienced a different level of militarization as soldiers. Ultimately, the Reichsbanner followed patterns of organizing political activities that originated in the socialist labour movement.

Conclusion

Ambivalences within the republican camp existed from the very beginning due to its nature as an alliance that included different expectations and ideas about the republic. Some republicans felt that the republic had, possibly inevitably, disappointed some of their hopes for the future and not all democrats believed in the same future vision. Historian Thomas Mergel suggests a general sense of disappointment with parliamentary democracy within the public by the end of the Weimar Republic due to overstated expectations.[99] Republican pluralism was a difficult message to communicate. The democratic narrative, which varied considerably between slow integration into the republican project and actively defending it against anyone who was not yet convinced, had difficulties in keeping the republican front together. Radical activism clashed with evolutionary notions of republican progress, and these two strands also formulated different reference points in the past and different ideas for the republic's future. More problematic still, neither faction within the republican spectrum found a comfortable place for women in its rhetoric, performative politics, or symbolic rituals. Women remained confined to passive rather than active roles and to the few traditional fields of engagement (children's education, festive representation) they had already occupied before. Similarly, large sections of the rural population never felt at home in the republic.

But we should not shift the responsibility for the collapse of Germany's first parliamentary democracy to those who supported it. The republic had passionate republicans who actively mobilized for their new state around the black-red-gold flag. It was a republic with many republicans whose activism focused on the notion of equal political participation and the proud understanding that political decisions could not be taken any more without the majority support of the people. The emotions stirred by symbolic conflicts and expressed through public performances encapsulated the strong disdain for the past regime of Imperial Germany and the recognition of Weimar's achievements as the beginning of a better present and a more hopeful future. Therefore, Weimar's republicans, despite their differences and ambivalences, remind us of the strong appeal the republican idea possessed for them.

Notes

1. Bundesarchiv Berlin (BArch), R 43/2501, fo. 189, 21 Nov. 1918.
2. *Das Reichsbanner*, 16, 15 August 1926.
3. Cited in Dirk Schumann, 'Berlin ist nicht Weimar: Die Weimarer Republik und ihre politische Kultur', *Jahrbuch der Akademie der Wissenschaften zu Göttingen* (2016), 102–21, here 112.
4. Helmuth Kiesel, 'Die literarische Verarbeitung der Novemberrevolution in der Weimarer Republik', in Andreas Braune and Michael Dreyer (eds), *Zusammenbruch, Aufbruch, Abbruch? Die Novemberrevolution als Ereignis und Erinnerungsort* (Stuttgart: Steiner, 2019), 265–6. Riccardo Bavaj reminds us of the stance against Weimar on the extreme left: Riccardo Bavaj, *Von links gegen Weimar: Linkes antiparlamentarisches Denken in der Weimarer Republik* (Bonn: J. H. W. Dietz Nachf., 2005).
5. See the introduction to this volume.
6. See Ernst Lemmer, *Manches war doch anders: Erinnerungen eines deutschen Demokraten* (Frankfurt/Main: Heinrich Scheffler, 1968), 151; Gustav Radbruch, *Der innere Weg: Aufriss meines Lebens*, 2nd ed. (Göttingen: Vandenhoeck & Ruprecht, 1961), 130; Otto Braun, *Von Weimar zu Hitler* (Hamburg: Hammonia, 1949), 181.
7. Hagen Schulze, *Weimar 1917–1933* (Berlin: Siedler, 1994), 123; Ute Daniel, 'Die Politik der Propaganda: Zur Praxis gouvernmentaler Selbstrepräsentation vom Kaiserreich zur Bundesrepublik', in Ute Daniel and Wolfram Siemann (eds), *Propaganda: Meinungskampf, Verführung und politische Sinnstiftung 1789–1989* (Frankfurt/Main: Fischer, 1994), 59; Detlef Lehnert and Klaus Megerle, 'Einleitung', in Lehnert and Megerle (eds), *Politische Identität und nationale Gedenktage* (Opladen: Westdeutscher Verlag, 1989), 13; Gerhard Paul, *Aufstand der Bilder: Die NS Propaganda vor 1933* (Bonn: J. H. W. Dietz Nachf., 1990), 54.
8. Bernd Buchner, *Um nationale und republikanische Identität: Die deutsche Sozialdemokratie und der Kampf um die politischen Symbole der Weimarer Republik* (Bonn: J. H. W. Dietz Nachf., 2001); Nadine Rossol, *Performing the Nation in Interwar Germany: Sports, Spectacle and Political Symbolism, 1926–36* (Basingstoke: Palgrave, 2010); Christian Welzbacher (ed.), *Der Reichskunstwart: Kulturpolitik und Staatsinszenierung in der Weimarer Republik 1918–1933* (Weimar: wtv Verlag, 2010); Benjamin Ziemann, *Contested Commemorations: Republican War Veterans and Weimar Political Culture* (Cambridge: Cambridge University Press, 2013), Sebastian Elsbach, *Das Reichsbanner Schwarz-Rot-Gold. Republikschutz und politische Gewalt in der Weimarer Republik* (Stuttgart: Steiner, 2019).
9. See Thomas Mergel, 'Überlegungen zu einer Kulturgeschichte der Politik', *Geschichte und Gesellschaft*, 28 (2000), 574–606; Nadine Rossol, 'Flaggenkrieg am Badestrand: Lokale Möglichkeiten repräsentativer Mitgestaltung in der Weimarer Republik', *Zeitschrift für Geschichtswissenschaft*, 56 (2008), 617–37.
10. For a contemporary account of the three terms see BArch, R 43 I/ 571, fos. 168–9, Gießen 13 Aug. 1927, speech at the Constitution Day festivities 1927. The author Count Harry Kessler coined the term *Mussrepublikaner*: Ute Daniel, *Beziehungsgeschichten: Politik und Medien im 20. Jahrhundert* (Hamburg: Hamburger Edition, 2018), 134–5.
11. See Andreas Wirsching and Jürgen Eder (eds), *Vernunftrepublikanismus in der Weimarer Republik: Politik Literatur, Wissenschaft* (Stuttgart: Steiner, 2008).
12. Schumann, 'Berlin ist nicht Weimar'.
13. See the chapter by Joachim C. Häberlen in this volume.

14. Wilhelm Heinz Schröder, 'Sozialdemokraten in den Reichs- und Länderregierungen der Weimarer Republik 1918/19–1933: Eine Kollektivbiographie', *Historical Social Research*, 23 (2011), 392–446, here 394, 411.
15. Ziemann, *Contested Commemorations*, 15.
16. Marcel Böhles, *Im Gleichschritt für die Republik: Das Reichsbanner Schwarz-Rot-Gold im Südwesten, 1923 bis 1933* (Essen: Klartext, 2016), 217; Ursula Büttner, *Weimar: Die überforderte Republik* (Stuttgart: Klett-Cotta, 2008), 90.
17. Büttner, *Weimar*, 85.
18. Böhles, *Gleichschritt*, 201–2; Benjamin Ziemann, *Die Zukunft der Republik? Das Reichsbanner schwarz-rot-gold* (Bonn: Friedrich Ebert Stiftung, 2011), 20.
19. See Welzbacher (ed.), *Reichskunstwart*; Christian Welzbacher, *Edwin Redslob: Biografie eines unverbesserlichen Idealisten* (Berlin: Matthes & Seitz, 2009); Annegret Heffen, *Der Reichskunstwart: Zu den Bemühungen um eine offizielle Reichskunstpolitik in der Weimarer Republik* (Essen: Blaue Eule, 1986); Rossol, *Performing*.
20. Arnold Brecht, *Aus nächster Nähe: Lebenserinnerungen 1885–1927* (Stuttgart: DVA, 1966), 462–3.
21. See Siegfried Weichlein's chapter in this volume.
22. For an overview see Hagen Schulze, 'Democratic Prussia in Weimar Germany 1919–1933', in Philip G. Dwyer (ed.), *Modern Prussian History 1830–1947* (London: Routledge, 2001), 211–29.
23. Schröder, 'Sozialdemokraten', 394; Böhles, *Gleichschritt*, 26–8.
24. Geheimes Staatsarchiv Preußischer Kulturbesitz, Berlin (GStA PK), I. HA Rep. 90 A, no. 3731, fos. 3–6, 15.
25. Majorie Lamberti, *The Politics of Education: Teachers and School Reform in Weimar Germany* (New York: Berghahn, 2002).
26. Matthias Busch, *Staatsbürgerkunde in der Weimarer Republik: Genese einer demokratischen Fachdidaktik* (Bad Heilbrunn: Julius Klinkhardt, 2016).
27. Elsbach, *Reichsbanner*, 67–74.
28. Manfred Reuter, *'In Treue fest': Eine Studie über ausgewählte Polizeigewerkschaften und Polizeigewerkschafter in der Weimarer Republik* (Frankfurt: Verlag für Polizeiwissenschaft, 2012), 42–58.
29. Elsbach, *Reichsbanner*, 82.
30. Ibid., 81–8.
31. 'Wir haben es gewagt!', *Das Reichsbanner*, 1, 1 Jan. 1925.
32. For general studies on the Reichsbanner see Karl Rohe, *Das Reichsbanner Schwarz-Rot-Gold: Ein Beitrag zur Geschichte und Struktur der politischen Kampfverbände zur Zeit der Weimarer Republik* (Düsseldorf: Droste, 1966); Ziemann, *Die Zukunft*; Elsbach, *Reichsbanner*.
33. Ziemann, *Contested Commemorations*, 69–72. Böhles, *Gleichschritt*.
34. Ziemann, *Contested Commemorations*.
35. Elsbach, *Reichsbanner*, 116–20.
36. Ibid., 110–13.
37. Rossol, *Performing*.
38. Büttner, *Weimar*, 321–2; Detlef Lehnert, 'Weimars Chancen und Möglichkeiten, Strukturen und Normen–Eine Problemskizze', in Michael Dreyer and Andreas Braune (eds), *Weimar als Herausforderung: Die Weimarer Republik und die Demokratie im 21. Jahrhundert* (Stuttgart: Steiner, 2016), 118.

39. Lehnert, 'Weimars Chancen', 118.
40. Joseph Wirth (Centre Party), Ludwig Haas (DDP), and Paul Löbe (SPD) titled their first article in the first edition of the journal 'The Time is Ripe'.
41. Benjamin Ziemann, 'German Pacifism in the Nineteenth and Twentieth Centuries', *Neue Politische Literatur*, 60 (2015), 422.
42. *Das Reichsbanner*, 1 Feb. 1927. See also 'Lest demokratische Zeitungen, ihr stützt Verfassung und Republik!', *Illustrierte Reichsbanner Zeitung*, 20 Feb. 1926; 'Unterstützt die republikanische Presse: Empfehlenswerte republikanische Zeitungen', *Deutsche Republik*, 5 July 1930.
43. Otmar Jung, 'Verfassungsschutz privat: Die Republikanische Beschwerdestelle e.V.', *Vierteljahrshefte für Zeitgeschichte*, 35 (1987), 65–93.
44. Rossol, 'Flaggenkrieg', 633–6.
45. See Avraham Barkai, *'Wehr Dich!' Der Centralverein deutscher Staatsbürger jüdischen Glaubens (C.V.) 1893–1938* (Munich: C. H. Beck, 2002).
46. 'Kriegsteilnehmer, Republikaner!', *Das Reichsbanner*, 1, 15 Apr. 1924.
47. Rossol, 'Flaggenkrieg', 622.
48. Brecht, *Aus nächster Nähe*, 360.
49. Rossol, *Performing*, 60.
50. *Vossische Zeitung*, 12 Apr. 1925, printed in Welzbacher, *Reichskunstwart*, 80.
51. Daniel Bussenius, 'Eine ungeliebte Tradition: Die Weimarer Linke und die 48er Revolution 1918–1925', in Heinrich August Winkler (ed.), *Griff nach der Deutungsmacht: Zur Geschichte der Geschichtspolitik in Deutschland* (Göttingen: Wallstein, 2004), 103–12.
52. Buchner, *Identität*, 177.
53. Ibid., 177–82. For details see Dieter Rebentisch, *Friedrich Ebert und die Paulskirche: Die Weimarer Demokratie und die 75-Jahrfeier der 1848er Revolution* (Heidelberg: Stiftung Reichspräsident-Friedrich-Ebert Gedenkstätte, 1998).
54. Bussenius, 'Eine ungeliebte Tradition', 110–12.
55. Erin Hochmann, *Imagining a Greater Germany: Republican Nationalism and the Idea of Anschluss* (Ithaca, NY: Cornell University Press, 2016).
56. See the chapter by Claudia Siebrecht in this volume.
57. Ziemann, *Contested Commemorations*.
58. Ibid., 114.
59. Cited in Nadine Rossol, 'Weltkrieg und Verfassung als Gründungserzählungen der Republik', *Aus Politik und Zeitgeschichte*, 50–1 (2008), 13–18, here 17.
60. Cited ibid., 16.
61. For the notion of female citizenship in Weimar see Kathleen Canning, 'Claiming Citizenship: Suffrage and Subjectivity in Germany After the First World War', in Kathleen Canning, Kerstin Barndt, and Kristin McGuire (eds), *Weimar Publics/Weimar Subjects: Rethinking the Political Culture of Germany in the 1920s* (New York: Berghahn, 2010), 116–37.
62. Helen Boak, *Women in the Weimar Republic* (Manchester: Manchester University Press, 2013), 69, 86–9, 108–9.
63. *Festschrift zur Verfassungsfeier 1925*: Reichsbanner Schwarz-Rot-Gold Berlin Brandenburg (Berlin: Warenvertrieb des Reichsbanners, 1925), 25.
64. Rossol, *Performing*, 32–3.

65. Thomas Mergel, 'Führer, Volksgemeinschaft und Maschine', in Wolfgang Hardtwig (ed.), *Politische Kulturgeschichte der Zwischenkriegszeit 1918–1933* (Göttingen: Vandenhoeck & Ruprecht, 2005), 98–9.
66. Siegfried Weichlein, '"Die alte Schönheit ist nicht mehr wahr, und die neue Wahrheit ist noch nicht schön": Epochenwahrnehmungen und Zukunftsvorstellungen der republikanischen Kräfte in der Weimarer Republik', in Karsten Fischer (ed.), *Neustart des Weltlaufs? Fiktion und Faszination der Zeitwende* (Frankfurt: Suhrkamp, 1999), 148–9.
67. Weichlein, 'Die alte Schönheit', 147.
68. Wilhelm Sollmann, 'Volkswohl im Volksstaat', in *Das Reichsbanner Schwarz-Rot-Gold* (Magdeburg: Einkaufszentrale des Reichsbanners, 1924), 14.
69. Rüdiger Graf, *Die Zukunft der Weimarer Republik. Krisen und Zukunftsaneignungen in Deutschland 1918–1933* (Munich: Oldenbourg, 2008) 148–53.
70. Joseph Wirth, 'Zum 11 August', *Deutsche Republik*, 45, 10 Aug. 1928, 1434.
71. Weichlein, 'Die alte Schönheit', 160–1.
72. Carl von Ossietzky, 'Von Kapp bis … ?', *Die Weltbühne*, 11, 11 Mar. 1930, 376–7.
73. Cited in Reichszentrale für Heimatdienst (ed.), *Zum Verfassungstag: Eine Materialsammlung* (Berlin: Reichszentrale für Heimatdienst, 1928), 38.
74. Elsbach, *Reichsbanner*, 384–401.
75. Cited in Rossol, 'Weltkrieg und Verfassung', 18.
76. Käthe Kollwitz, *Die Tagebücher* (Berlin: Siedler, 1989), 386.
77. *Verhandlungen der Verfassunggebenden Deutschen Nationalversammlung: Stenographische Berichte*, 327, session 44, 2 July 1919, 1234.
78. See the different options that were agreed by 1921 at <https://de.wikipedia.org/wiki/Liste_der_Flaggen_der_Weimarer_Republik> (accessed 9 Dec. 2020).
79. Buchner, *Identität*, 81–2.
80. Ibid., 45–52.
81. Ibid., 112.
82. Braun, *Von Weimar zu Hitler*, 97.
83. Elsbach, *Reichsbanner*, 163–8.
84. Rossol, 'Flaggenkrieg', 620.
85. Ibid., 619–25.
86. Ibid., 628–30. For images of republican board games, Reichsbanner coffee mugs, and Reichsbanner cigarettes see *Für Freiheit und Republik! Das Reichsbanner Schwarz-Rot-Gold 1924 bis 1933. Begleitband zur Ausstellung der Gedenkstätte Deutscher Widerstand* (Berlin: Gedenkstätte Deutscher Widerstand, 2018), 76–9.
87. For a dispute on the number of republican flags see 'Berlin unter schwarz rot gold. Flagge neben Flagge', *Vorwärts*, 377, 11 Aug. 1927; 'Zahlen beweisen', *Der Tag*, 231, 3 Sept. 1927.
88. See Rossol, 'Flaggenkrieg'.
89. Nadine Rossol, 'Visualizing the Republic: State Representation and Public Ritual in Weimar Germany', in John A. Williams (ed.), *Weimar Culture Revisited* (Basingstoke: Palgrave, 2011), 145–50. On Walther Rathenau's funeral see Manuela Achilles, 'Reforming the Reich: Democratic Symbols and Rituals in the Weimar Republic', in Canning et al., *Weimar Publics*, 175–91.
90. Fritz Schellack, *Nationalfeiertage in Deutschland von 1871 bis 1945* (Frankfurt/Main: Peter Lang, 1990).

91. *Verhandlungen des Reichstags: Stenographische Berichte*, 425, 7 June 1929, 2169–70.
92. Rossol, *Performing*, 61–3.
93. Ibid., 20–1.
94. Ibid., 70; Ziemann, *Contested Commemorations*, 188–91.
95. Rossol, *Performing*, 66–79.
96. Ibid., 60.
97. See Carl von Ossietzky, 'Defending the Republic: The Great Fashion' (1924), in Anton Kaes, Martin Jay and Edward Dimendberg (eds), *The Weimar Republic Sourcebook* (Berkeley, CA: University of California Press, 1994), 110–12. For a similar critique see Hans Mommsen, *Aufstieg und Untergang der Republik von Weimar* (Berlin: Ullstein, 1998), 289; Elsbach, *Reichsbanner*.
98. Carl Misch, 'Mit der Windjacke', *Die Weltbühne*, 49, 25 Sept. 1928, 478–9.
99. Thomas Mergel, 'High Expectations—Deep Disappointments: Structures of the Public Perceptions of Politics in the Weimar Republic', in Canning et al., *Weimar Publics*, 192–210.

Bibliography

Achilles, Manuela, 'Performing the Reich: Democratic Symbols and Rituals in the Weimar Republic', in Kathleen Canning, Kerstin Barndt, and Kristin McGuire (eds), *Weimar Publics/Weimar Subjects: Rethinking the Political Culture of Germany in the 1920s* (New York: Berghahn, 2010), 175–91.

Buchner, Bernd, *Um nationale und republikanische Identität: Die deutsche Sozialdemokratie und der Kampf um die politischen Symbole in der Weimarer Republik* (Bonn: J. H. W Dietz Nachf., 2001).

Elsbach, Sebastian, *Das Reichsbanner Schwarz-Rot-Gold: Republikschutz und politische Gewalt in der Weimarer Republik* (Stuttgart: Steiner, 2019).

Graf, Rüdiger, *Die Zukunft der Weimarer Republik: Krisen und Zukunftsaneignungen in Deutschland 1918–1933* (Munich: Oldenbourg, 2008).

Hochman, Erin, *Imagining a Greater Germany: Republican Nationalism and the Idea of Anschluss* (Ithaca, NY: Cornell University Press, 2016).

Mergel, Thomas, *Parlamentarische Kultur in der Weimarer Republik* (Düsseldorf: Droste, 2002).

Rossol, Nadine, *Performing the Nation in Interwar Germany: Sport, Spectacle and Political Symbolism 1926–36* (Basingstoke: Palgrave, 2010).

Welzbacher, Christian (ed.), *Der Reichskunstwart: Kulturpolitik und Staatsinszenierung in der Weimarer Republik 1918–1933* (Weimar: wtv Campus, 2010).

Ziemann, Benjamin, *Contested Commemorations: Republican War Veterans and Weimar Political Culture* (Cambridge: Cambridge University Press, 2013).

CHAPTER 13

SOCIAL POLICY IN THE WEIMAR REPUBLIC

KARL CHRISTIAN FÜHRER

The Weimar Republic defined itself as a welfare state. The constitution, adopted in August 1919, promised that the new state would shape economic life according to the 'principles of justice to the end that all may be guaranteed a decent standard of living' (Art. 151). Its preamble, moreover, bound the republic to 'further social progress'. In comparison to Imperial Germany, these were new goals and proclamations. The monarchical state did also pursue social policies—the system of statutory social insurance schemes, implemented from 1883 onwards and covering health insurance, workplace accident insurance and a pension scheme, was unique in Europe at this time. However, there was no obligation for the Imperial German state to aim at the well-being of every single citizen.[1] This changed after the revolution of November 1918. The promise of the Weimar Constitution did not only apply to poor people, who were unable to provide for themselves and guarantee a 'decent standard of living' by their own efforts. According to an almost generally accepted understanding, state social politics protected the entire population. For example, Rudolf Wissell, one of the most important trade union leaders of the republic, Social Democrat, and Reich Labour Minister from 1928 to 1930, stated that the nature of the republic as a 'people's state' was manifested in its social policy.[2] In 1924, Heinrich Hirtsiefer, Prussian Minister of Welfare and member of the Catholic Centre Party, even postulated: 'The primary goal of all state organizations is the welfare of its people'.[3]

Indeed, social policy was an important pillar of the Weimar Republic. After 1918, the state claimed a significantly larger share of Germany's gross national product through taxes and other fees than before 1914. Most of this money was spent by the Reich, the states (Länder), and the municipalities for social purposes. Public expenditures for citizens' social security amounted to 11 per cent of the entire national income in 1929, a figure four times higher than before 1914.[4] Historical research literature largely presents sceptical or even negative views on the social policy of the Weimar Republic. Several gaps in the system and harsh criticism of benefit recipients have resulted in the characterization of the 'overburdened Weimar welfare state'.[5] Moreover, controls and criteria to define those who were 'not eligible for benefits' were seen as repressive and a form of social disciplining according to bourgeois standards.[6] Even more importantly, it has been argued that the republic's social policy paved the way for the eugenically selective social policy of the Nazis because it used ideologically charged concepts such as 'people' (*Volk*), 'people's welfare' (*Volkswohl*), and 'people's health' (*Volksgesundheit*) rather than referring to the individual and their rights and hardships.[7]

There are good reasons for these assessments. However, it would be unfair to exclusively focus on shortcomings, negative effects, and ambivalences when assessing the social policy of the Weimar Republic. We can also point to fundamental innovations and significant reforms that furthered the system of social security in Germany. This is the remarkable record of a state that faced the legacy of military defeat and enormous social political challenges. The following chapter takes both sides into account. It is chronologically structured in three parts because the tasks and the scope of action of state social policy heavily depended on the economic situation at the time, which changed often and profoundly between 1918 and 1933.[8]

Social Policy during the First Years of the Weimar Republic

As early as during the revolutionary upheaval of its foundation phase in winter 1918–19, the first German democracy faced a mountain of social problems. More than six million soldiers had to be reintegrated into civilian life, who had been torn away from it by the war. Clearly, the future of these men would determine the future of the republic. Reliable political stability, at least to a certain degree, which was necessary to place the new state order on a firm foundation, could not be achieved by demobilizing masses of soldiers into unemployment and thus social inequality. To avert this danger, the Council of People's Deputies, which acted as provisional interim government from 9 November 1918, adopted several regulations. According to these rules, for example, employers were forced to offer returning veterans who had previously worked at their company their former jobs. The working time was reduced to eight hours a day (with six working days per week) to create as many jobs as possible. Everyone who had previously worked more hours (and this applied to almost the entire workforce) received the same wages, which meant the government decreed a general increase in hourly rates.[9]

Those who could not find work received state benefits: for the first time, all German municipalities were obliged to financially support unemployed workers. This new unemployment welfare regime applied to both men and women. In the given situation, this was a social political imperative because during the war women had taken over jobs in factories and workshops that became vacant when the men left for military service. With the demobilization regulations and the need to re-employ men, many women were threatened with being made redundant and often did not receive benefits. Only those unemployed workers who were regarded as 'being in need' qualified for state benefits, which were intended to avert social hardship through unemployment. If a claimant had their own savings or family members who could support them, the state did not pay any benefits. This means-tested assessment particularly disadvantaged married women: they were almost always regarded as not being in need and expected to rely on support from their husbands. The implementation of unemployment welfare was nonetheless a significant social political step as prior to 1914, unemployed workers did not receive any state benefits. This had changed in several municipalities during the First World War, yet consistent regulations throughout Germany were not issued. Only the young Weimar Republic took care of the 'needy' unemployed. Fifty per cent of the emerging costs were paid out of the Reich budget, the rest came from states and municipalities.[10]

In November 1918 it was still completely unclear how the economic situation of the militarily defeated country would develop. Against this backdrop, the implementation of unemployment welfare by the socialist-led Council of People's Deputies was a bold decision. The number of people who received benefits illustrates how necessary the new welfare system was. In spring 1919, it amounted to about 1.1 million, and in late 1919 500,000 remained unemployed. Benefits were rather modest, contributing towards livelihood rather than securing it. Nonetheless, the fact that both the demobilization of former soldiers, as well as the transition of industrial enterprises from wartime to peacetime production in 1918–9, ran relatively smoothly, resulted to a large degree from interventionist regulations issued by the Council of People's Deputies and the new unemployment welfare regime.[11]

Alongside these regulations, which directly helped many people—particularly the returning soldiers—but also simultaneously created new inequalities, another aspect must be mentioned when assessing the social political situation of the revolutionary phase in Germany in the winter of 1918. On 23 December 1918, the governing Social Democrats issued the Collective Agreement Ordinance that implemented collective bargaining autonomy. It was an important pillar of the new state order and a significant element of the societal structure after the demise of Imperial Germany. The Ordinance largely handed over the determination of wages and working conditions of employees to trade unions and employers' associations. Free negotiations between these organizations were meant to result in collectively accepted contracts, which the state legally guaranteed. Under certain conditions, the Reich Labour Ministry could even declare such a collective agreement as generally binding. In this case, it also applied to those businesses whose owners were not part of an employers' association—otherwise these employers were not bound by the collective agreement.[12]

The fact that the regulation could potentially render collective agreements generally binding points to the social role of the governmentally guaranteed collective bargaining autonomy of trade unions and employers' associations. Collective contracts were meant to reduce workers' and employees' dependency on their respective employers. Together, they were stronger than they were individually. Furthermore, the general application of collective agreements could put a stop to individual employers' attempts to reduce costs by paying and treating their staff poorly. Declaring general application reduced the competition among employers and stabilized the protective impact of collective agreements for employees. This social security through collective agreements set binding minimum standards. Better arrangements for employees could be agreed on both individually and at shop floor level. If a contract had been signed, both parties were obliged to maintain industrial 'peace' for its duration (usually a year): trade unions were not allowed to demand better working conditions or higher general pay; employers had to at least fulfil the provisions stipulated in the contract. If one side were to breach the agreement, the other side could go to court.[13]

In December 1918, the adoption of this regulation was largely politically uncontested. On 15 November 1918 representatives of larger trade unions and the most important employers' associations had already signed an agreement on their own initiative that not only pre-empted key elements of the demobilization regulation such as the eight-hour working day and the obligation to re-employ former soldiers, but also already included main aspects of the regulation on collective bargaining agreements. This was the so-called Stinnes-Legien Agreement, named after Hugo Stinnes, the owner of a major steel and iron corporation, and Carl Legien, the head of the General Commission of the German Trade Unions, the umbrella organization of the Social Democratic-leaning Free Trade Unions. This agreement, however, had not yet created legally binding regulations. Ironically, collective bargaining autonomy required state regulations to function reliably. The Council of People's Deputies adopted these regulations, though in doing so it gave up much of its power to intervene in regulating industrial relations: working conditions of wage earners could no longer be agreed on without employers' associations and trade unions having their say.[14]

Policy-makers limited their own scope of intervention in this field because the system of collective bargaining autonomy was intended to enable an economic fine-tuning that the state was not able to provide. Carefully balanced regulations for individual sectors—which could be agreed on at Reich level or only for certain regions—promised to secure employees' interests without economically overburdening employers. This balance of interests through autonomous negotiations was put into practice on a large scale as early as 1919. By the end of the year, employers' associations and trade unions had signed more than 11,000 different collective agreements for approximately six million employees in more than 270,000 businesses. In 1921, collective bargaining agreements regulated the wages and salaries as well as the working life of thirteen million employees—which accounted for two-thirds of the entire workforce in dependant employment.[15]

Unemployment welfare and collective bargaining agreements were clearly crucial elements of change for the society of the Weimar Republic in contrast to Imperial Germany. At first glance, both regulations seem unrelated, however, in social political terms they belonged together. By implementing them, the state reduced social risks of employees caused by the unpredictability of the economy and the labour market. Another regulation that served the same purpose was issued in February 1919. It obligated all businesses to report vacancies immediately to public employment offices. Thus, job seekers and employers were meant to find each other more easily. Until 1922, a nationwide system of public job placements evolved from this regulation, with trade unions and employers' associations equally participating in its administration. It was free of charge for job seekers and jobs were only placed there when collectively agreed wages were paid.[16] In Imperial Germany the state had barely intervened in the labour market, thus leaving employers in a strong position. Only the republic put the interest groups of employees on an equal footing with employers' associations and guaranteed legally binding collective bargaining agreements. This gave autonomy to the system of collective bargaining, as a social self-governing instrument based on balance and compromise.

Having said that, collective bargaining negotiations can only be successfully concluded if employers' associations and trade unions respect both each other and the system as a whole. This respect existed in the initial phase of the Weimar Republic. All trade unions (including the socialist ones) accepted the system of collective bargaining agreements and the Stinnes-Legien Agreement because state and employers, their traditional opponents, finally officially recognized them. More surprising was the favourable attitude of the employers. During Imperial Germany employers' associations of various economically important sectors had stubbornly refused to accept trade unions. Particularly employers in the mining and the iron and steel industries had refused any contact with trade unions because they wanted to maintain unlimited power at shop floor level. This opposition ended in 1918. Significantly, it was the iron and steel industry that initiated negotiations in the context of the Stinnes-Legien Agreement. The reason for this is clear: in late 1918, the demobilization of soldiers and the transition of the German economy away from the massive war production were inevitable. In this situation trade unions were the only force for stability and thus suddenly highly welcome even to the most conservative employers. In addition, they feared that the revolution—similar to the situation in Russia in 1917—might develop into a socialist seizure of power, threatening free enterprise and the entire capitalist economic system.[17]

Indeed, some employers in the construction, chemical, and electronic industries not only supported the idea of a collective bargaining partnership for pragmatic reasons but because they believed that collective bargaining agreements were the best means of securing internal peace at shop floor level. Furthermore, business owners and managers in these sectors appreciated the security that these agreements brought for operating with labour costs that remained stable on a long-term basis. This, however, did not apply to everyone. Many conservative industrialists mourned their loss of power over their employees.[18] In this sense, it was from the outset obvious that the system of collective bargaining autonomy might come under pressure from this side if economic and political conditions changed.

The Weimar state also strove to strengthen the situation of workers and employees towards their employers at shop floor level. In February 1920, the Reichstag adopted a bill that put businesses with more than twenty employees under the obligation to implement a so-called works council through free and secret ballot. The rights of these new representative bodies remained rather modest—not least because trade unions regarded them as a threat to their own role rather than as a chance to represent employees' rights even more effectively.[19] However, the establishment of works councils significantly changed the atmosphere in companies because owners and managers could not avoid discussions with them. For this reason, the Works Councils Act from 1920 was important. With it, the Weimar Republic once again refuted the idea of the employer as the 'master in the house' who could decide single-handedly over his employees. This was in the interest of the employees and—not surprisingly—irritated conservative employers.[20]

During the early years of the Weimar Republic, the process of currency devaluation accelerated. This process had started as early as autumn 1914 because Imperial Germany had financed the war largely based on loans. At first glance it might seem surprising that inflation caused by the war gained even more momentum when peace returned. Indeed, the continuation of inflation (or rather: the decision not to take measures to stop currency devaluation through a firm austerity programme and cuts of public spending) was part of the social and political compromises that successfully curbed the revolutionary impulse of November 1918. Inflation created an economic pseudo-prosperity and enabled the swift and relatively smooth transition from wartime to peacetime economy. It kept industry, crafts, and commerce going, secured a high employment rate, and thus benefited (at least in the short term) businesses and employees.[21]

However, the continuation of inflation also caused social problems—which became more severe the quicker inflation progressed and the bigger the devaluation of the mark became, compared to pre-war years. Inflation in Germany ended only in autumn 1923 when the mark had almost completely lost its internal and external value. This almost five-year long escalation of currency devaluation, leading up to hyperinflation in 1922–3, drove millions of Germans into destitution. The republic provided only late and insufficient support. This failure certainly weighs heavy when looking at the negative side of the social political balance sheet of the Weimar Republic. People who particularly depended on social benefits became victims of inflation, namely, the approximately 1.5 million elderly people on state pensions. The majority of Germans were proud of the system of social insurance schemes. It provided support for sickness, work-related injuries, permanent invalidity, granted a pension (from the age of 65 from 1917 onwards), and supported widows and orphans. Almost all people in regular employment were subject to these compulsory insurances; employers had to contribute 50 per cent of the insurance payments. Whoever wanted to present Germany as a socially modern state and global role model would refer to this extensive system of social insurances for support in crisis situations. Provided that certain requirements such as the duration of contribution payments were met, there was a legal entitlement to receive benefits.[22]

On the other side of the coin, the system of social insurances had some problematic aspects. Its provisions were stipulated in law at a time when rapid inflation was not known. Once approved, a pension was fixed to the pfennig and there were no adjustments to rising living costs. However, compared to autumn 1914, in early 1918 prices of the most important foodstuffs had more than doubled. This dilemma—fixed pensions on the one hand and massively rising prices on the other—had already put pensioners into dire straits during the war. When inflation accelerated from 1919 onwards, hardship increased. In January 1919, for the first time, an additional allowance was implemented for every pensioner, but it did not fully compensate for the inflation losses that had already kicked in. Subsequent price rises soon devalued the increase in the pension. Further additional payments that were only agreed on after protracted debates between the government, Reichstag, and insurance carriers fizzled out for the same reason.[23] It was not a novel experience for pensioners to live a modest life. Even before the war pensions had not been enough to live on because additional help from children and other relatives was taken for granted. Yet the continuous devaluation of pensions, including all additional allowances, created a new situation in early years of the Weimar Republic. A report, published in 1920, described the living situation of pensioners as follows: 'According to the view of physicians, these people gradually starve to death .... These people become artists in limiting their food intake, they become fragile and prone to sickness and waste away.'[24]

To be fair, destitute pensioners could apply for public support at municipal welfare offices. This was the last resort of Germany's social security network for all who needed help. Historically, it was the oldest institution of social help. Until 1918, it was known in almost all cities as 'poor relief'. This older term illustrates why most elderly, starving, and sick people hesitated or even entirely refrained from turning to welfare offices for help. Regardless of the name of 'municipal support', whoever applied for it had to deal with civil servants who assessed their neediness and personally monitored the benefit recipients and their circumstances. In order to deter 'indolent' and 'immoral' people, welfare was not supposed to be welcoming—this was not only true of Imperial Germany but also of the Weimar Republic. Despite sharp controls, receiving welfare support was still a stigma, and having to go to the welfare office was anything but trivial.[25]

Numerous protest letters written by pensioners to the Reich Labour Ministry during the inflation years movingly show their outrage and indignation in response to the ministerial advice to ask for welfare benefits. Many referred to the spirit of the German social insurance system according to which someone who had paid contributions became legally entitled to receive benefits in later life. Many remembered very well that this system was implemented not least to spare destitute people—particularly the elderly who had worked very hard for decades—the degrading contact with poor relief.[26] A great number of them could not understand the process of money devaluation that made their pensions increasingly worthless. Their protest letters show their lack of knowledge and understanding. Maybe that was the main reason why they adamantly demanded that the state restore the value of their pensions. Despite several additional pension allowances and the implementation of specific welfare benefits, the Weimar Republic failed to meet these demands during the inflation years. At the same time, not one politician tried to explain to the German public that inflation was caused by the unsecured war loans of Imperial Germany. As a result, elderly people and their relatives who were affected by the devaluation of pensions believed that it was the new republic that was to blame for the hardship and despair of pensioners. Even in historical hindsight and without the emotions that affected contemporaries, this can be interpreted as a grave social political failure. During the years of inflation, the Weimar Republic did not adequately address the often life-threatening pauperization of old and invalid people.[27]

The Weimar Republic left a very specific iconography and is thus heavily remembered through images. This includes pictures of war veterans with amputated legs in ragged and torn uniforms on crutches or sitting on the ground begging. Famous painters of the Weimar years such as Otto Dix or George Grosz, who considered themselves as critical chroniclers of their time, left many pictures of such 'war cripples'. All these paintings convey the impression of hardship, misery, and neglect. Indeed, many men had been heavily injured during the war: 1.5 million veterans were disabled through war wounds to such an extent that they were deemed unfit for work. However, it is a moot point whether or not the paintings by Dix and others realistically portrayed the everyday life experiences of war veterans. To be sure, life was difficult for many veterans and throughout the entire Weimar Republic they felt that the 'reward of the fatherland' for their war service had failed to materialize.[28] Yet their discontent was different to what the image of the 'war cripple' suggests. The new state did make strong efforts to help the victims of the First World War. However, it was precisely these efforts that caused a bitter controversy with the veterans.

The conflicts started with the adoption of the Reich Pension Law (Reichsersorgungsgesetz, RVG) in April 1920. It regulated care and support for permanently disabled war veterans and war widows in a new manner. From a historical perspective, it was a very modern law. The RVG can be considered as one of the first examples of an actively intervening and thus simultaneously supportive and punitive public social policy measure. The key goal of the law was the reintegration of war veterans into working life. It created a sophisticated system of benefits, incitements, and penalties to get as many veterans as possible into paid work, including extensive health and curative treatments, artificial limbs, and other aids, as well as publicly funded occupational retraining programmes. Veterans who failed or refused to attend these programmes were punished by reductions or even the entire withdrawal of their pensions. These pensions were graded according to the extent of the disability of individual veterans; the former military rank, however, played no role.[29]

In order to determine the exact amount of support and pension for the individual, the disabled men were examined intensively. Medical experts assessed their injuries to calculate the limitations of their work ability and how it could be restored. Most war veterans experienced these examinations as being mentally stressful —particularly because they were often carried out by long-serving military doctors who, during the war, had enthusiastically sent patients back to the frontlines as swiftly as possible. The elaborated economization of body parts and body functions developed by the RVG ignored the victims' trauma and pain. The loss of a thumb, for instance, was assessed more heavily than that of any other finger because someone who could not clench his hand into a fist was more severely disabled in the workplace. How this corresponded to the experiences of the affected individual was not a matter of concern. Men who had become permanently scarred victims of the war could hardly bear the categorizing by doctors and administrative employees. Thus, the ambitiously designed, modern RVG often caused discontent: the relationship between disabled war veterans and those who were supposed to help them was largely characterized by mistrust.[30]

The fact that the Weimar Republic had, for financial reasons, pursued the strategy to limit support for war veterans to severe cases created even greater indignation. According to the laws of Imperial Germany (that remained in force until April 1920), all war veterans whose fitness for work was permanently reduced by at least 10 per cent received a pension. The RVG drew the line differently: only those whose disability accounted for 20 per cent of their capacity were entitled to a pension. At a single blow, 316,000 men lost their war victim pension that they had received previously. Even though this decision was made to pay other veterans more money (for instance, by taking into account—at least to a certain extent—their professional training when calculating their pensions) the outrage among those affected was massive. In July 1923, at the peak of inflation, the then Reich government of only bourgeois parties acted even more rigidly: 489,000 veterans lost their pension because from now on the disability had to reduce their fitness for work by 30 per cent.[31]

In respect to war victims, politicians and social political experts of the Weimar Republic failed to take into account the great significance that even modest pensions had for individual veterans. Regularly paid benefits were the only appreciation for their suffering, the only evidence that their personal sacrifice for the nation was not in vain. For this reason, veterans fought bitterly for their pensions, even if they did not make a huge difference for them financially. Civil servants responsible for the administration of war victim pensions, however, interpreted this attitude as 'pension psychosis', that is, as a pathological mental disorder, which they intended to combat with all means possible.[32] This was another reason why Weimar's social policy was so negatively regarded by war veterans even though the new state did more for them than for other pensioners.[33] The suggestive artistic depiction of miserable 'war cripples' in paintings of the 1920s does not reflect this difference, which is important for a historically balanced assessment.

A brief overview of the fate of war widows must suffice here. Their number was significant: approximately two million soldiers who were killed during the war left around 600,000 wives and 1,192,000 children. Almost all of these children were very young, the majority of war widows were also young, often under 30. Despite this, many of them did not remarry. According to the RVG, they were entitled to a war widow's pension, which 372,000 widowed women still received in 1924.[34] War orphans received a state pension until they reached the age of 14. War widow and war orphan pensions were very modest and certainly not sufficient to live on. Without the help of parents and other relatives, war widows were forced to work.[35] Particularly women of the bourgeoisie experienced the war death of their husbands not only as emotional loss but also as a drastic biographical rupture. Many of them did not have professional training and could only take on unskilled and accordingly poorly paid jobs. The case of an officer's widow is documented, who before 1914 with her husband belonged to the upper middle class. As a war widow, she worked as address writer of advertisement letters, as packager, lace embroiderer, and finally as cook to contribute to her meagre pension.[36]

The years between 1922 and 1924 belong to a period of the Weimar Republic when social hardship was the everyday reality for a depressingly large proportion of the German population. In 1922–3, inflation accelerated to such an extent that normal everyday life became increasingly impossible. The necessity to live from hand to mouth—before 1914 this was only a reality for working-class families—also became a common feature for bourgeois households, and malnourishment and diseases caused by undernutrition became a mass phenomenon. Additional state aid was only granted to a small group of elderly people, the so-called 'small capital pensioners' (*Kleinkapitalrentner*), of whom there were an estimated 300,000. All of them had been part of the bourgeoisie before 1914 and planned to live off their own capital in old age. Typical 'small capital pensioners' were self-employed artisans and merchants or unmarried daughters without a profession from bourgeois families—that is, people who had never made any contributions to the statutory social security system and thus did not receive any benefits. Furthermore, this was a group of people who had never expected needing to rely on state welfare. Inflation, which devalued financial assets, interest, and rental incomes, equally left those 'small capital pensioners' with nothing, at least from 1922 onwards. Being forced to ask for welfare aid caused them even more psychological problems than pensioners who received disability or old-age benefits. Thus, in February 1923, after protracted political debates, the government implemented special benefits for 'small capital pensioners', funded by the Reich.[37]

State support for people in need always has a dual purpose: it is intended to alleviate individual hardship and to have a socially and politically stabilizing impact. On the other hand, public aid can prove ineffective, for instance if it is granted after such a long time of suffering that the recipients do not overcome their resentment, if it is massively insufficient, or if it causes new injustices. All this applies to the 'small capital pensioners' welfare. It was paid only when inflation had already climaxed; the by this time exponentially increasing money devaluation rapidly made its payments worthless; it was unfair towards those who received local benefits because 'small capital pensioners' were less rigidly monitored. Their welfare is thus an example of a social political measure that failed to achieve any of its objectives.[38]

In early 1924, the hardship of hyperinflation was followed by the hardship of currency stabilization, with unemployment rising up to 3.5 million.[39] At the same time, Reich, states, and municipalities pursued austerity politics to stabilize trust in the value of the newly created currency, the Reichsmark. The repercussions for all those who depended on state benefits were dramatic. Unemployed people received benefits that were 'unbearably low', according to the assessment of trade unions.[40] Now as before, benefits were only paid to recipients who were seen as being in need—even though, from October 1923 onwards, unemployment welfare was funded by contributions of all wage-earning employees (excluding civil servants) and their employers. This type of financing was similar to that of social insurances. Yet, in contrast to insurance, it did not grant contributors any rights. The Reich government that issued an emergency decree to swiftly enforce this reform had good reasons for doing so. The planned currency reform would only be successful if the government was able to eliminate the budgetary deficit.

Those 80 per cent of unemployment benefits that had previously been paid by the Reich were now passed on to those who were in work as well as their employers. The contribution, which initially amounted to 2 per cent, and later to 3 per cent, of the wage, had to be paid in equal shares by employees and employers.[41]

This new wage deduction, and, from the employers' perspective, novel increase in incidental wage costs, might seem marginal. In the severe economic and social crisis following the currency stabilization, the contemporaries applied a different yardstick. Trade unions, for example, claimed that the contribution for unemployment welfare was a heavy burden, particularly for low earners and given decreasing real wages. Employers warned that they would not be able to employ as many people as before with rising incidental wage costs due to the new social welfare contribution. Thus, public benefits for the unemployed as implemented in 1923–4 caused discontent on all sides.[42] The same is true of benefits for the elderly. After the currency reform, social insurances only paid out a very small basic pension, eliminating the connection between individually paid contributions and benefits. Before the inflation period and the currency reform, this connection had been the characteristic feature of the social security system. Again, invalids and elderly people had reason to be disappointed—particularly those who had worked and paid contributions for decades. Furthermore, according to social political experts, the new basic pension was 'in no way sufficient' to secure 'a livelihood'.[43]

Moreover, the contribution for the invalidity and retirement pension, newly fixed at 4 per cent in Reichsmark to be deducted from employees' wages, was more than double the amount of the years before 1914. The full picture of the reasons behind the rise was probably not widely known among contemporaries: money devaluation and the currency reform forced the invalidity and retirement insurance providers to restructure their financing. They had previously operated just like private insurance companies: every person insured built up the foundation for a later pension by paying in contributions (with the help of employers who paid their share). Earnings from investing this money were added to this. After the implementation of the Reichsmark, former assets of the insurance providers had ceased to exist so that, technically, they would have been forced into administration by the winter of 1923–4 at the latest. The Reich government wanted to avoid this radical outcome under any circumstances, although it could have used this situation to reorganize and improve the efficiency of the entire complicated German social insurance system. The new contributions paid in Reichsmark had to serve a different purpose than those of the old retirement insurance: they mainly covered the running costs, that is the already approved pensions for invalids and elderly people. Building up reserves to fund future benefits was only the secondary purpose. For this reason, contributions had to be higher than before 1914.[44]

At first glance this change could be regarded as a mere actuarial formality. In reality it was in social political terms highly significant. The Reich government reinterpreted the spirit of solidarity, on which statutory insurances are based in general: the generation of employed persons paid (again with the help of the employers' share) for the benefits of the elderly people and those unfit for work. Such an 'intergenerational contract' (*Generationenvertrag*)—as it was called later in the Federal Republic of Germany—was a novelty. It is striking that Weimar politicians made no sustained effort to explain the new structure of the retirement insurance to the contributors. Thus, they chose the path of least resistance.[45] It is fair to assume that both employees and employers would have voiced objections to the implementation of the newly fixed contributions if they had fully known about their effect of redistributing funds to elderly people and those who were unfit for work. Thus, there was widespread discontent on both sides about the massive rise in insurance contributions. Indeed, employers had complained about Weimar social policy being too expensive before. This criticism intensified considerably after 1924.[46] It is a matter of debate whether the new contributions in fact overburdened the employers. However, there can be no disagreement on the fact that incidental wage costs were higher than before—due to the newly implemented contributions to the unemployment insurance and the rise of contributions to retirement insurance—and that the payment of these costs had to be covered.

Reconstruction and Rebuilding of the Weimar Republic: Social Policy in the Years of Prosperity

From 1925 onwards, the Weimar Republic experienced some years of relative economic prosperity and—closely connected with this—a period of political stability. During this time, the German social security system gradually overcame the profound crisis of 1923–4. Benefits such as retirement pensions and other financial aid continually increased. In 1926, unemployment benefits, for example, reached a level that civil servants of the Reich Labour Ministry regarded as dangerously high because it allegedly undermined the work ethic of the unskilled workforce.[47] Around the same time, retirement and invalidity pensions also reached a level equivalent to the purchasing power of the pre-war period. In 1925, the previously established basic pension was abolished. Instead, benefits were newly calculated according to the duration of a pensioner's contribution payments. However, elderly and invalid people could still hardly survive on their pension. Only single men who had worked for a very long time managed to do so. All others, and particularly elderly women, who were no longer fit for work, depended on their families, charity organizations, or municipal welfare.[48]

In the mid-1920s, municipal welfare, this last resort of the German social network, was more modern than ever before. A Reich decree, issued in early 1924, standardized for the first time municipal regulations on welfare entitlements. The discriminatory nature of public welfare was reduced; for the first time recipients were, to some extent, granted a say in how welfare offices worked. Financial benefits that had been extremely low in 1924 increased due to the improved financial situation of municipalities. Nonetheless, many people still feared the social stigma that was associated with receiving welfare benefits.[49] Welfare for 'small capital pensioners', which was continued as a separate branch of social welfare, with the cities bearing its costs from 1924 onwards instead of the Reich, also increased. However, the Weimar state got little thanks for this. 'Small capital pensioners' who had lost almost all their former assets through the currency reform were a strikingly effective lobby, advocating their own interests and drumming up support for the full compensation of their financial losses. This stirred up a permanent debate on the revaluation of former 'Goldmark' accounts, which already strained the political climate in Germany in the seemingly calm middle years of the republic—not least because antidemocratic parties such as the DNVP (German National People's Party) and the NSDAP (National Socialist German Workers' Party), which was still relatively small at that time, unscrupulously championed the demands of 'small capital pensioners' with no ifs and buts.[50]

The practices of youth welfare most probably contributed to the continuing bad image of public welfare in the Weimar Republic despite the 1924-reform. Youth welfare was a relatively new branch of municipal social politics that was massively expanded and professionalized during the Weimar years. The Reich Youth Welfare Law from 1922— which only came into force in 1924—standardized the regulations of this special care for children and young people up to 21 years of age. It stipulated a general 'right to education' and resulted in the establishment of municipal youth welfare offices. They were not only responsible for the guardianship of all illegitimate children but also for the care of young people who had come into conflict with the law or were deemed as morally 'vulnerable' for other reasons.[51]

This segment of public social politics was in urgent need of a consistent professionalization across all levels. Like no other authority, youth welfare workers had the right to massively intervene in personal rights of those people they were supposed to help. Their most repressive option was to refer children or teenagers to prisonlike houses of correction, against the will of their parents, without the right to be heard and for an indefinite period. However, for political reasons the law of 1924 only went halfway: the republic shied away from conflicts with both Christian churches that had operated several such houses from the late nineteenth century onwards and were not inclined to refrain from this part of 'youth work'. As a result, new state-run houses of correction were established, with some of them pursuing ambitious progressive educational programmes. They existed alongside church institutions where pupils were still treated like prisoners without any rights. Numerous scandals in church youth centres were revealed when young people started violent protests, which attracted great public attention in the late 1920s.[52]

Although these incidents triggered an intensive debate on a reform of youth welfare, no consensus was reached. On the contrary, during the years of the Great Depression, many youth welfare workers were increasingly inclined to distinguish between 'improvable' and 'inferior' young people, treating both groups differently. This seems to anticipate the selective social policy of the Nazis. Contemporaries were well aware of the repressive measures that municipal youth welfare offices could adopt. The threat of committing a pig-headed teenager to a house of correction was still part of the educational repertoire of parents in the Weimar Republic.[53]

The Weimar Republic achieved a clear social political success with the implementation of unemployment insurance. In July 1927, the Reichstag, by a large majority, passed a bill that established compulsory unemployment insurance and, closely connected with this, the implementation of a restructured and centralized network of public employment offices. This was intended to ensure continuous information on vacancies for unemployed workers. For this reason, they had to come into an employment office every day at a certain time. For checking purposes, cards containing the unemployed individual's personal data were stamped; therefore the German term 'Stempeln gehen' (literally, 'go and get a stamp', equivalent to 'be on the dole') soon became synonymous for being unemployed. Central aspects of the law were modelled closely along the other German social insurances: employees who paid contributions acquired a general entitlement to benefits in the event of unemployment; the employers always paid 50 per cent of their employees' contributions; trade unions and employers' associations were equally represented at important administrative bodies that operated as insurance providers. The unemployment insurance (ALV) is undisputedly the greatest social political achievement of the Weimar Republic. Its implementation gave the complex system of the other compulsory insurances a stable foundation because unemployed individuals without compensation ran the risk of not paying contributions for other social insurances which excluded them from or reduced their future benefits. In contrast to previously granted unemployment welfare—which was abolished with the new law coming into effect—the ALV was no longer exclusively paid to needy people. This particularly benefited unemployed women, who previously had to rely on the support of their relatives.[54]

From 1923, it was politically widely accepted that the country needed unemployment insurance. The former implementation of contributions for unemployment welfare, which did not involve any rights or entitlements for the contributors, had already set the course in this direction. Yet the details of the new insurance were heavily contested. Who was supposed to belong to the group of compulsorily insured persons? For how long should unemployment benefits be paid? What was its upper limit and its minimum? How was the contribution rate to be calculated and who decided on its amendments? There were no simple and uncontested answers to these questions. For these reasons, the passing of the law was delayed.[55] Inevitably, the ALV law was the result of complex negotiations and compromises between very different interest groups. Against the backdrop of the insurance crisis, which started as early as 1929, the following aspects are important to keep in mind. The AVL could support up to 600,000 unemployed individuals at the same time. Deficits in the event of higher unemployment figures were to be balanced by Reich subsidies, which were paid as loans. The Reichstag decided on changes of the contribution rate (3 per cent of the wages in 1927, the same as for unemployment welfare).[56] This was the same as with the other social insurances. All these regulations were based on the expectation that the economic upswing Germany experienced from 1925 would continue in the long term. This optimism proved illusionary and the funding of the ALV and the question of the amount of benefits for unemployed people became central issues of German domestic politics.

Drawn into the Maelstrom: Social Policy during the Great Depression from 1929

As early as winter 1929–30, the economic downturn that had just started in the USA reached Europe. Germany was one of the countries deeply affected by the Great Depression. We can only estimate the number of people who were made redundant in Germany and searched for work in vain due to the global recession, because the official statistics by no means include all of them. In late 1932, their number probably amounted to around 7.6 million Germans (the authorities counted six million). Only 11.4 million Germans were in paid work—in 1928 it had been 18.2 million.[57] Never before had public support been more important than during this period. Yet financial means were limited. Deflationary policy pursued by all Reich governments aggravated this problem. Thus, it was inevitable that the Weimar Republic disappointed expectations of its citizens in need.

Unemployment insurance is a prime example of this irresolvable dilemma. Before the start of the Great Depression, it already faced major financial problems because, as early as winter 1927–8, the German economy slowed down. In the following winter, the deficit of the ALV—which the Reich was forced to balance by loans—increased massively. In late March 1930, the last parliamentary cabinet (the grand coalition led by the Social Democratic Reich Chancellor Hermann Müller) of the Weimar Republic collapsed over the political struggle on how to reduce the financial burden on the Reich budget and the taxpayer. Indeed, all government parties approved an increase in contributions to the ALV by 0.5 per cent; the bourgeois parties of the coalition, however, also demanded a reduction in benefits. The SPD firmly rejected these cost-cutting measures in the midst of a serious crisis for social reasons and the government collapsed over this issue in March 1930.[58] Since unemployment figures continued to rise, the presidential cabinets that followed also had to address the deficits of the ALV. They reduced the unemployment insurance that had been implemented with such great hopes to a shadow of what had been originally planned. In 1932 it offered minimal benefits for exorbitantly high contributions that increased from originally 3 per cent of the wages to 6.5 per cent. At the same time, the benefit duration was reduced from twenty-six to only six weeks. Benefit cuts (by 10 to 12 per cent in June 1931 and further 23 per cent in June 1932) were added. On top of that, the presidential cabinets, in the interest of securing ALV finances and the Reich budget, made women and young people up to the age of 21 second-class employees. Their entitlement to benefits was withdrawn despite them having paid insurance contributions for years before their unemployment. They only received payments in the event of neediness, that is if they could prove that they were not supported by relatives.[59]

For all these reasons, the ALV lost its significance in supporting the unemployed. For them, municipal welfare became the most important social security institution instead, even though its payments were also cut. In general, welfare was still only paid in the event of 'being in need'. Moreover, the support was a loan that had to be paid back as soon as the recipient was able to do so. In 1932, approximately 40 per cent of officially registered unemployed were supported by welfare.[60] About 1.2 million of these six million people received no public support. The same is true of the even bigger group of unemployed people who were not officially registered. They were shadowy figures because they had fallen through the cracks of the social security system or rather never had access to it in the first place. This applied, for instance, to young people who did not find an apprenticeship or a job as unskilled worker after leaving school.[61]

Whoever wanted to witness social misery did not have to go far in Germany during these years. There were probably tens of thousands of homeless young people who eked out a living, either on their own or in small groups, because their impoverished parents had thrown them out or because mental pressure due to the crisis had destroyed their families. An even stronger signal of crisis were the so-called 'wild settlements' that emerged in the vicinity of many big cities from 1930. Unemployed people who could no longer afford the rent occupied fallow sites and patched up shelters for themselves and their relatives. These 'slums', reluctantly tolerated by the authorities, were a novelty in Germany.[62]

The government also used emergency decrees to cut other social insurance benefits. For example, preventive measures for co-insured wives and children, previously offered by the health insurance, were abolished, and pensions paid by the invalidity and retirement insurance were cut to a similar degree as those of the ALV.[63] This might lead to the conclusion that Weimar social policy was radically slashed and profoundly changed after 1929. Yet the contrary is true. The percentage of public expenditure spent on social aid was even larger during the years of the Great Depression than before.[64] The enormous extent of misery, however, overburdened the social security system that had hardly worked effectively before. Under the difficult circumstances this result was almost inevitable. Only a socially much fairer tax system and a broad public consensus about a profound financial redistribution from the top down would have helped the victims of the Great Depression. Yet both projects lacked the necessary political support. For this reason, the very fact that various segments of the social security system were continued throughout the years of severe economic crisis must be considered a success. There was even public funding for the construction of rented flats but due to the economic difficulties the Reich Labour Ministry ordered that from 1930 onwards only very small and modestly equipped flats were to be subsidized.[65]

This chapter on the social political achievements and problems of the Weimar Republic would be incomplete without revisiting the system of collective bargaining agreements that the new state regulated and guaranteed in 1918–9. It comes as no surprise that negotiations between the social partners became increasingly difficult during the economic crisis after 1929. Employers demanded enormous wage reductions; trade unions opposed this, but as they lost a great number of members due to rising unemployment their negotiation power sharply decreased. In many cases, trade unions and employers' associations reached no agreement because their interests were too far apart. A situation without any collective bargaining agreements, as had been typical of employment circumstances in Imperial Germany, was imminent. This would also have affected the competition between employers that was still regulated and limited by binding minimum standards of wages and working conditions. Thus, there were grave concerns and objections among employers and their associations in light of the labour market threatening to slide back into a pre-war situation.[66]

Against this backdrop, one instrument gained importance that the Weimar Republic had implemented in autumn 1923. With an eye to the forthcoming currency reform and anticipated fierce confrontations between employers and employees, the Reich government created the possibility to stipulate a collective bargaining agreement by decree rather than through negotiations between social partners, for which an arbitrator officially commissioned by the state was responsible.[67] Historical research has deemed the invention of this 'binding arbitration' as a grave political mistake. According to this view, the republic took the pressure off trade unions and employers to reach an agreement. This allegedly led to an unwillingness to compromise, fierce controversies, and the politicization of wage formation eventually resulted in increased hostility between the state and the employers.[68]

Indeed, there were industrialists, particularly from heavy industry, who generally opposed the rules of collective bargaining autonomy. However, this uncompromising opposition was by no means typical of all German employers. Binding arbitration did not change that.[69] Historical criticism of this political instrument of collective bargaining is also inaccurate in another respect: it overestimates the significance of binding arbitration and ignores the complexity of the arbitration process. It was always initiated upon request of at least one social partner, was carried out in several phases, provided the possibility to reach an agreement via negotiations, and left the decision over the content of the binding contract largely to impartial experts. Thus, it was at best an indirect instrument of political wage formation.[70]

Moreover, the Reich Labour Ministry, even at the height of the crisis in 1932, only put twenty collective bargaining agreements into effect by decree. Regional mid-level authorities of the arbitration process confirmed 120 binding arbitration contracts; 310 arbitrator's awards were not officially confirmed, which means that in these cases the situation was not regulated by collective agreements. At the same time, almost 10,000 collective bargaining agreements still existed. Indeed, mainly major and economically important industries with many employees were regulated by arbitrated agreements. But collective bargaining autonomy was still functioning at that time, in that not only trade unions but also most employers avoided the abolition of collective arrangements without any replacement.[71] On this basis, both sides would have been able to start over as soon as the economy recovered.

Conclusion

To evaluate the historical significance of the described achievements, problems, and crises of the German social security system between 1918 and 1933, we should first look at the political history of the Weimar Republic. Clearly, the new state did not win the loyalty of its citizens through its social policy. At best, the residents of the attractive, publicly subsidized newly built housing might have taken a different view. Other than that, even those who received public benefits were disgruntled and critical towards Weimar social politics. Employers who had to pay 50 per cent of social security contributions without any apparent advantage to themselves grew increasingly furious about the rapid rise in these contributions. This was particularly true of the years of economic crisis after 1929 when the ALV gradually became more and more expensive.

Is there a connection between growing discontent and the seizure of power by the NSDAP in January 1933? There is no clear answer to that question. Unemployed people more often voted for the Communist party than for the Nazis. On the other end of the scale, only a few employers declared their support for the NSDAP prior to Hitler's rise, although all of them considered the republic's social policy as too expensive. We do not know enough about the voting behaviours of war victims, recipients of social security benefits, and 'small capital pensioners' to reliably assess if they contributed to the success of the Nazis in the last years of the Weimar Republic. We should therefore refrain from assuming that they turned into followers of the NSDAP because of their dashed hopes.

Second, we must ask what significance Weimar social policy had for the subsequent history of this type of state support. There are clear lines of continuity between the republic and the Nazi period, in particular the selective approach towards those in the care of welfare authorities which was widely accepted in the practices of youth welfare offices and the discourses among experts.[72] At the same time, the Nazis negated several social political reforms of the Weimar Republic. They completely abolished the system of collective bargaining agreements and autonomy, suppressed SPD-leaning Free Trade Unions as well as the Christian trade unions, disempowered works councils, and gave the Nazi state the right to decide on wages and work conditions.[73] Employees' rights, which the Weimar state had regarded with such high esteem, fell back to their basic minimum. Moreover, self-administration with equal representation, an essential element of the social security system that the Reichstag strongly confirmed and strengthened with the 1927 Unemployment Law, was completely eliminated.[74] The Nazis also restructured the financing of the invalidity and retirement pension: as before 1924, the insurance accumulated assets that were allegedly intended to fund future pension payments and make them crisis-proof. In reality, they were directed into the armament programme of the Nazi regime.[75] In comparison, the positive aspects of social policy between 1918 and 1933, which are easily overlooked when exclusively focusing on misery and discontent of many inadequately supported people, come clearly to the fore. The highly ambitious goal of the Weimar Republic to provide a 'decent standard of living' was evidently not achieved for many. The new state did, however, 'further social progress'—as promised in its constitution.

Translated from German by Christine Brocks.

Notes

1. Gerhard A. Ritter, *Sozialversicherung in Deutschland und England. Entstehung und Grundzüge im Vergleich* (Munich: C. H. Beck, 1983).
2. Richard Wissell, 'Einleitung', in *Deutsche Sozialpolitik 1918–1928: Erinnerungsschrift des Reichsarbeitsministeriums* (Berlin: E. S. Mittler & Sohn, 1929), iii.
3. Heinrich Hirtsiefer, *Die staatliche Wohlfahrtspflege in Preußen 1919–1923* (Berlin: C. Heymann, 1924), iii.
4. Gabriele Metzler, *Der deutsche Sozialstaat: Vom bismarckschen Erfolgsmodell zum Pflegefall* (Stuttgart and Munich: DVA, 2003), 69.
5. Jürgen von Kruedener, 'Die Überforderung der Weimarer Republik als Sozialstaat', *Geschichte und Gesellschaft*, 11 (1985), 358–76.
6. Detlev J. K. Peukert, *Grenzen der Sozialdisziplinierung: Aufstieg und Krise der deutschen Jugendfürsorge von 1878 bis 1932* (Cologne: Bund, 1986). For a critical overview see Young-Sun Hong, *Welfare, Modernity, and the Weimar State, 1919–1933* (Princeton: Princeton University Press, 1998), 5–9.
7. Metzler, *Sozialstaat*, 82–3.
8. As an overview on all aspects of Weimar social policy compare still Ludwig Preller, *Sozialpolitik in der Weimarer Republik* (Kronberg/Ts.: Droste, 1978; first publ. 1949); Eckart Reidegeld, 'Staatliche Sozialpolitik in der Weimarer Republik (1919–1930)', in Reidegeld, *Staatliche Sozialpolitik in Deutschland*, vol. 2. *Sozialpolitik in Demokratie und Diktatur 1919–1945* (Wiesbaden: VS Verlag, 2006), 43–257.
9. Gunther Mai, 'Arbeitsmarktregulierung oder Sozialpolitik? Die personelle Demobilmachung in Deutschland 1918 bis 1920/24', in Gerald D. Feldman (ed.), *Die Anpassung an die Inflation* (Berlin and New York: De Gruyter, 1986), 202–36.
10. Karl Christian Führer, *Arbeitslosigkeit und die Entstehung der Arbeitslosenversicherung in Deutschland 1902–1927* (Berlin: Colloquium Verlag, 1990), 131–43; Petra Weber, *Gescheiterte Sozialpartnerschaft—Gefährdete Republik? Industrielle Beziehungen, Arbeitskämpfe und der Sozialstaat. Deutschland und Frankreich im Vergleich 1918–1933/39* (Munich: Oldenbourg 2010), 179–90.
11. See figures in Führer, *Arbeitslosigkeit*, 147.
12. Preller, *Sozialpolitik*, 231, 255–61; Johannes Bähr, *Staatliche Schlichtung in der Weimarer Republik: Tarifpolitik, Korporatismus und industrieller Konflikt zwischen Inflation und Deflation 1919–1932* (Berlin: Colloquium Verlag, 1989), 13–35.
13. Michael Ruck, 'Institutionelle Bedingungen gewerkschaftlichen Handelns und Konfliktverhaltens nach der Novemberrevolution; Von der autonomen Regelung der Arbeitsbeziehungen zur Schlichtungsverordnung vom Oktober 1923', in Karl Christian Führer, Jürgen Mittag, Axel Schildt, and Klaus Tenfelde (eds), *Revolution und Arbeiterbewegung in Deutschland 1918–1920* (Essen: Klartext, 2013), 237–55, 239–43, with references to different assessments of trade unions in individual industries.
14. Gerald D. Feldman and Irmgard Steinisch, *Industrie und Gewerkschaften 1918–1924: Die überforderte Zentralarbeitsgemeinschaft* (Stuttgart: DVA, 1985); Karl Christian Führer, *Carl Legien 1861–1925: Ein Gewerkschafter im Kampf um ein 'möglichst gutes Leben' für alle Arbeiter* (Essen: Klartext, 2009), 209–30.
15. *Deutsche Sozialpolitik 1918–1928*, 47.
16. Führer, *Arbeitslosigkeit*, 228–51.
17. Weber, *Gescheiterte Sozialpartnerschaft*, 121–31, 191–4.

18. Ibid., 195–200.
19. Werner Plumpe, *Betriebliche Mitbestimmung in der Weimarer Republik: Fallstudien zum Ruhrbergbau und zur chemischen Industrie* (Munich: Oldenbourg, 1999), 37–66; Rudolf Tschirbs, 'Arbeiterausschüsse, Betriebsräte und Gewerkschaften 1916–1922: Versuch einer Neubewertung', in Führer et al., *Revolution und Arbeiterbewegung*, 257-84, esp. 271–84.
20. Werner Milert and Rudolf Tschirbs, *Die andere Demokratie: Betriebliche Interessenvertretung in Deutschland 1848 bis 2008* (Essen: Klartext, 2012), 155–67. For a rather sceptical assessment see Plumpe, *Betriebliche Mitbestimmung*, 407–40.
21. See the chapter by Martin H. Geyer in this volume.
22. Gerhard A. Ritter and Klaus Tenfelde, *Arbeiter im Deutschen Kaiserreich 1871 bis 1914* (Bonn: J. H. W. Dietz, 1992), 691–716, esp. 715.
23. See in detail Karl Christian Führer, 'Für das Wirtschaftsleben "mehr oder weniger wertlose Personen": Die Lage von Invaliden- und Kleinrentnern in den Inflationsjahren 1918–1924', *Archiv für Sozialgeschichte*, 30 (1990), 145–80.
24. H. Heymann, 'Hilfe für die versinkenden Volksschichten', *Zeitschrift für Kommunalwirtschaft*, 10 (1920), 94–5.
25. Wilfried Rudloff, *Die Wohlfahrtsstadt: Kommunale Ernährungs-, Fürsorge- und Wohnungspolitik am Beispiel Münchens 1910–1933*, 2 vols (Göttingen: Vandenhoeck & Ruprecht, 1998), 95–170, 330–56, 601–21, 843–51.
26. Führer, 'Für das Wirtschaftsleben', 152–3.
27. Greg Eghigian, 'The Politics of Victimization: Social Pensioners and the German Social State in the Inflation, 1914–1924', *Central European History*, 26 (1993), 375–403.
28. Sabine Kienitz, *Beschädigte Helden: Kriegsinvalidität und Körperteile 1914–1923* (Paderborn: Schöningh, 2008), 65–109; Iris Groschek, 'Wo bleibt der Dank des Vaterlandes? Zur Situation der Schwerkriegsbeschädigten des Ersten Weltkrieges unter besonderer Berücksichtigung Hamburgs', *Zeitschrift des Vereins für hamburgische Geschichte*, 88 (2002), 147–77.
29. Robert W. Whalen, *Bitter Wounds: German Victims of the Great War, 1914–1939* (Ithaca, NY, and London: Cornell University Press, 1984), 131–40; Michael Geyer, 'Ein Vorbote des Wohlfahrtsstaates: Die Kriegsopferversorgung in Frankreich, Deutschland und Großbritannien nach dem Ersten Weltkrieg', *Geschichte und Gesellschaft*, 9 (1983), 230–77.
30. Whalen, *Bitter Wounds*, 141–66; Kienitz, *Beschädigte Helden*, 151–286.
31. Whalen, *Bitter Wounds*, 136, 146, 156.
32. Greg Eghigian, 'Die Bürokratie und das Entstehen von Krankheit: Die Politik und die "Rentenneurosen" 1890–1926', in Jürgen Reulecke and Adelheid Gräfin zu Castell Rüdenhausen (eds), *Stadt und Gesundheit: Zum Wandel von 'Volksgesundheit' und kommunaler Gesundheitspolitik im 19. und frühen 20. Jahrhundert* (Stuttgart: Steiner, 1991), 203–23.
33. For a comparison with Great Britain see Deborah Cohen, *The War Come Home: Disabled Veterans in Britain and Germany 1914–1939* (Berkeley, CA: University of California Press, 2001).
34. Figures in Richard Bessel, *Germany After the First World War* (Oxford: Clarendon Press, 1993), 225, 227.
35. Karin Hausen, 'Die Sorge der Nation für ihre "Kriegsopfer": Ein Bereich der Gesclechterpolitik während der Weimarer Republik', in Jürgen Kocka, Hans-Jürgen Puhle, and Klaus Tenfelde (eds), *Von der Arbeiterbewegung zum modernen Sozialstaat: Festschrift*

für Gerhard A. Ritter zum 65. Geburtstag (Munich: Saur, 1994), 719–39; Whalen, *Bitter Wounds*, 69–81.
36. Helene Hurwitz-Stranz (ed.), *Kriegerwitwen gestalten ihr Schicksal: Lebenskämpfe deutscher Kriegerwitwen nach eigenen Darstellungen* (Berlin: C. Heymann, 1931), 34.
37. Führer, 'Für das Wirtschaftsleben'; Robert Scholz, '"Heraus aus der unwürdigen Fürsorge": Zur sozialen Lage und politischen Orientierung der Kleinrentner in der Weimarer Republik', in Christoph Conrad (ed.), *Gerontologie und Sozialgeschichte: Wege zu einer historischen Betrachtung des Alters* (Berlin: Deutsches Zentrum für Altersfragen, 1983), 319–50.
38. Führer, 'Für das Wirtschaftsleben'; David F. Crew, *Germans on Welfare: From Weimar to Hitler* (New York and Oxford: Oxford University Press, 1998), 89–115.
39. Führer, *Arbeitslosigkeit*, 148.
40. Cited ibid., 464.
41. Preller, *Sozialpolitik*, 363–5; Führer, *Arbeitslosigkeit*, 295–8.
42. Führer, *Arbeitslosigkeit*, 463–6.
43. Cited in Führer, 'Für das Wirtschaftsleben', 167.
44. Karl Christian Führer, 'Untergang und Neuanfang: Die Rentenversicherungen für Arbeiter und für Angestellte im Jahrzehnt der "Großen Inflation" 1914–1924: Ein Vergleich', in Stefan Fisch and Ulrike Haerendel (eds), *Geschichte und Gegenwart der Rentenversicherung in Deutschland: Beiträge zur Entstehung, Entwicklung und vergleichenden Einordnung der Alterssicherung im Sozialstaat* (Berlin: Duncker & Humblot, 2000), 247–69; Martin H. Geyer, 'Soziale Rechte im Sozialstaat: Wiederaufbau, Krise und konservative Stabilisierung der deutschen Rentenversicherung 1924–1937', in Klaus Tenfelde (ed.), *Arbeiter im 20. Jahrhundert* (Stuttgart: Klett-Cotta, 1991), 406–34.
45. On this complex problem see Philip Manow, 'Kapitaldeckung oder Umlage: Zur Geschichte einer anhaltenden Debatte', in Fisch and Haerendel, *Geschichte und Gegenwart*, 154–8.
46. Führer, *Arbeitslosigkeit*, 202–9.
47. Führer, *Arbeitslosigkeit*, 468–9.
48. Führer, 'Für das Wirtschaftsleben', 168.
49. See also Crew, *Germans on Welfare*; Rudloff, *Die Wohlfahrtsstadt*, 569–99.
50. Führer, 'Für das Wirtschaftsleben', 179.
51. Marcus Gräser, *Der blockierte Wohlfahrtsstaat: Unterschichtjugend und Jugendfürsorge in der Weimarer Republik* (Göttingen: Vandenhoeck & Ruprecht, 1995), 37–68; Elizabeth Harvey, *Youth and the Welfare State in Weimar Germany* (Oxford: Oxford University Press, 1993), 152–85.
52. Gräser, *Der blockierte Wohlfahrtsstaat*, 81–131; Edward Ross Dickinson, '"Until the Stubborn Will is Broken". Crisis and Reform in Prussian Reformatory Education, 1900–34', *European History Quarterly*, 32 (2002), 186.
53. Detlev J. K. Peukert, 'The Lost Generation: Youth Unemployment at the End of the Weimar Republic', in Richard J. Evans and Dick Geary (eds), *The German Unemployed* (London: Croom Helm, 1987), 172–93; Gräser, *Der blockierte Wohlfahrtsstaat*, 148–66.
54. Christian Berringer, *Sozialpolitik in der Weltwirtschaftskrise: Die Arbeitslosenversicherungspolitik in Deutschland und Großbritannien im Vergleich 1928–1934* (Berlin: Duncker & Humblot, 1999), 74–122.
55. Führer, *Arbeitslosigkeit*, 170–227; Peter Lewek, *Arbeitslosigkeit und Arbeitslosenversicherung in der Weimarer Republik 1918–1927* (Stuttgart: Steiner, 1992), 153–286.

56. Preller, *Sozialpolitik*, 363–76; Hans-Walter Schmuhl, *Arbeitsmarktpolitik und Arbeitsverwaltung in Deutschland 1871–2002: Zwischen Fürsorge, Hoheit und Markt* (Nuremberg: Bundesanstalt für Arbeit, 2003), 143–55; Lewek, *Arbeitslosigkeit*, 328–68.
57. Berringer, *Sozialpolitik*, 174, 184.
58. Bernd Weisbrod, 'Die Krise der Arbeitslosenversicherung und der Bruch der Großen Koalition (1924–1929)', in Wolfgang J. Mommsen (ed.), *Die Entstehung des Wohlfahrtsstaates in Großbritannien und Deutschland 1850–1950* (Stuttgart: Klett-Cotta, 1982), 196–212; Schmuhl, *Arbeitsmarktpolitik*, 171–8; Berringer, *Sozialpolitik*, 390–408, 439–60.
59. Heinrich August Winkler, *Der Weg in die Katastrophe: Arbeiter und Arbeiterbewegung in der Weimarer Republik 1930 bis 1933*, 2nd ed. (Bonn: J. H. W. Dietz, 1990), 22–32; Preller, *Sozialpolitik*, 431–50.
60. Heidrun Homburg, 'Vom Arbeitslosen zum Zwangsarbeiter: Arbeitslosigkeit und Fraktionierung der Arbeiterschaft in Deutschland 1930–1933 am Beispiel der Wohlfahrtserwerbslosen und der kommunalen Wohlfahrtshilfe', *Archiv für Sozialgeschichte*, 25 (1985), 251–98; as a case study see Rudloff, *Die Wohlfahrtsstadt*, 885–949.
61. Peukert, 'Lost Generation'.
62. Winkler, *Der Weg in die Katastrophe*, 35–41; Eve Rosenhaft, 'The Unemployed in the Neighbourhood: Social Dislocation and Political Mobilisation in Germany 1929–33', in Evans and Geary, *The German Unemployed*, 194–227.
63. Preller, *Sozialpolitik*, 459–73.
64. Volker Hentschel, *Geschichte der deutschen Sozialpolitik 1880–1980* (Frankfurt/Main: Suhrkamp, 1983), 130–5.
65. Preller, *Sozialpolitik*, 483–95, esp. 488.
66. Karl Christian Führer, 'Von der Selbstbestimmung der Tarifparteien zur staatlichen Verantwortung für die Lohnbildung: Das tarifliche Schlichtungswesen des Baugewerbes in der Weimarer Republik 1924–1932', in Führer (ed.), *Tarifbeziehungen und Tarifpolitik in Deutschland im historischen Wandel* (Bonn: J. H. W. Dietz, 2004), 107–9.
67. Bähr, *Staatliche Schlichtung*, 63–104.
68. Metzler, *Sozialstaat*, 78–9.
69. For more details see Weber, *Gescheiterte Sozialpartnerschaft*, 764–83.
70. Bähr, *Staatliche Schlichtung*, 234–95.
71. Figures in *Statistisches Jahrbuch für das Deutsche Reich 1933* (Berlin: Reimar Hobbing, 1933), 316–17.
72. Peukert, *Grenzen der Sozialdisziplinierung*, 263–304; for a different focus see Hong, *Welfare* 239–76.
73. Winkler, *Der Weg in die Katastrophe*, 907–49.
74. Schmuhl, *Arbeitsmarktpolitik*, 223–31.
75. Manow, 'Kapitaldeckung', 158.

Bibliography

Cohen, Deborah, *The War Come Home: Disabled Veterans in Britain and Germany 1914–1939* (Berkeley, CA: University of California Press, 2001).

Crew, David F., *Germans on Welfare: From Weimar to Hitler* (New York and Oxford: Oxford University Press 1998).
Führer, Karl Christian, *Arbeitslosigkeit und die Entstehung der Arbeitslosenversicherung in Deutschland 1902–1927* (Berlin: Colloquium Verlag, 1990).
Harvey, Elizabeth, *Youth and the Welfare State in Weimar Germany* (Oxford: Oxford University Press, 1993).
Hong, Young-Sun, *Welfare, Modernity, and the Weimar State, 1919–1933* (Princeton: Princeton University Press, 1998).
Peukert, Detlev J. K., *Grenzen der Sozialdisziplinierung: Aufstieg und Krise der deutschen Jugendfürsorge von 1878 bis 1932* (Cologne: Bund, 1986).
Weber, Petra, *Gescheiterte Sozialpartnerschaft—Gefährdete Republik? Industrielle Beziehungen, Arbeitskämpfe und der Sozialstaat. Deutschland und Frankreich im Vergleich (1918–1933/39)* (Munich: Oldenbourg, 2010).
Whalen, Robert W., *Bitter Wounds. German Victims of the Great War, 1914–1939* (Ithaca, NY, and London: Cornell University Press, 1984).

PART III

PARTIES AND THEIR CONSTITUENCIES

CHAPTER 14

LIBERALISM

PHILIPP MÜLLER

CAMPAIGNING for the national elections in March 1933, the Reichstag representative of the liberal German People's Party (Deutsche Volkspartei) and well-known industrialist Richard Merton (1881–1960) argued that liberals were necessary allies of Adolf Hitler's new government. Merton had come to believe that 'party politics' was responsible for the political and economic crisis in Germany in the early 1930s and hoped that the success of National Socialism meant the end of the party system of the Weimar Republic. In its place, Merton suggested, liberals should help to establish an authoritarian government serving the common good of the German nation. His campaign motto read: 'Hail Hitler, but vote for "List 7" [The German People's Party].'[1]

Merton, who had a Jewish background and could only be convinced to leave Germany for England in 1938 after having spent several weeks in the concentration camp Buchenwald, was not an exception among Weimar liberals.[2] Rather, once the Weimar Republic was established, liberals of all colours looked askance at parliamentary democracy and political parties. Some of those advocating the new democratic state characterized themselves as *Vernunftrepublikaner* (republican by reason) in order to express that their support was not wholehearted.[3] The lack of resistance shown by liberal delegates when the Reichstag effectively abolished itself after the elections in 1933 with the Enabling Act of 28 March 1933, and the fact that prominent liberals like Gertrud Bäumer (1873–1954), Theodor Heuss (1884–1963), and Richard Merton initially hoped to cooperate with the Nazi regime, has in the past prompted observers to detect long-term deficits within German liberalism. In this reading, the burden of the authoritarian creation of the German nation-state between 1866 and 1871, the cartelization of German heavy industry after the Great Depression of 1873, and an arrangement between German entrepreneurs and the military in the naval arms race with Great Britain from the end of the nineteenth century had an enduring influence on political liberalism in Germany: It stopped its representatives from developing a position in which they could wield political influence and from forcing the traditional elites to accept a bourgeois regime. Above all, this interpretation claims, German liberals faltered in their loyalty to liberal principles and preferred to support programmes of national unification instead of democracy.[4]

Yet this description of Weimar liberals bearing the mark of nineteenth-century 'illiberalism' (Fritz Stern) has come under attack for several reasons. First, the argument rests on normative assumptions that neglect the fact that liberalism has developed in a variety of contrasting formations. Specifically, it fails to take into consideration that an important strand of liberalism in different national contexts was convinced that individual freedom could only be preserved if political and economic liberties were tamed by the strong hand of public institutions. Among other possibilities, liberal arguments could be used to defend a powerful state that was able to enforce public welfare policies or promote imperialist strategies to the advantage of the national economy. Supporting liberal values and pronounced forms of nationalism was far from a contradiction in terms.[5] Second, assuming that advocates of liberalism in Germany did not need to adapt and change their views when confronted with the consequences of the First World War and a hitherto unknown form of democracy turns the argument of long-term structural deficits into a straitjacket that disregards history. The hypothesis of a dominating illiberal heritage within German liberalism cannot account for the fact that the political, social, and economic changes contemporaries had to face after 1918 presented profound challenges to established political mindsets. They forced liberals to question and transform their views and ideas. The notion of 'crisis' in the sense of a situation of uncertainty, openness, and malleability, which has been stressed in accounts of Weimar society in general, indicates an understanding of Weimar liberalism that was more than the result of a nineteenth-century legacy.[6]

Thus, historians have stopped tracking liberalism as a single phenomenon through time. Rather, they understand it as a changing set of concepts that produced various liberalisms in different historical settings.[7] Following this line of reasoning, Weimar liberalism cannot be reduced to the history of its self-abandonment in 1933, but should rather be understood from its efforts to deal with the interconnection of political and economic difficulties post-1918, and via the various suggestions for possible responses. Weimar liberals defended and disputed traditional outlooks and explored adaptations that led into several directions. These discussions did not have a stabilizing effect on Weimar's liberal political parties and provoked the disillusionment of many former adherents. Yet, they also triggered a renewal of liberalism in various fields.[8] I will first discuss the structural causes and strategic choices that led to the difficulties of Weimar's liberal parties. Then, key controversies on the possible adaptation of political and economic liberalism to the contemporary circumstances are presented. In the third section I concentrate on the opposition liberalism faced after the First World War in many European countries, and draw attention to the international dimension of liberalism during the inter-war period.

Political Liberalism

Taking a liberal stance in Germany after the Great War was particularly challenging because the ideological confrontations between 1914 and 1918 had spread the assumption that liberalism was a Western outlook, irreconcilable with the allegedly specific German tradition of freedom. The acceptance of the Treaty of Versailles by the German delegation in June 1919 was generally perceived as a submission to the demands of the Western Allies and nourished the impression that the ratification of the new democratic constitution a few weeks later was untrue to the 'German spirit'. Subsequently, particularly conservative forces branded supporters of the republic as agents of a Western political system that was imposed on the German people.

Against this backdrop, the acceptance of the republican constitution revived the split between left-wing and right-wing German liberals that had already emerged from the conflicts surrounding the founding of the Kaiserreich in the late 1860s. The former National Liberal Party now became the liberal-conservative German People's Party (Deutsche Volkspartei, DVP) while supporters of the former left-liberal Progressive People's Party founded the German Democratic Party (Deutsche Demokratische Partei, DDP).[9] The continuing rivalry between the two liberal parties proved to be a fatal burden under the new circumstances of the republic.

Faced with the new situation of democratic competition, the DDP and the DVP soon faced a process of continuous decline. Together, the two liberal parties attracted almost 23 per cent of the vote in the elections to the National Assembly in January 1919. From then on, with a short breather in the second 1924 election, the electoral results went downhill. In both Reichstag elections of 1932, neither of the liberal parties was able to attract 2 per cent of the electorate. The only often-overlooked exception in this development was communal liberalism, which was able to maintain a strong, albeit waning, influence in the large cities. Although the municipal three-class franchise—which had given liberal candidates in the Kaiserreich clear advantages—was abolished after 1918, liberals succeeded in filling the post of mayor in Leipzig, Frankfurt at the Main, Hamburg, and other major cities during almost the entire period of the Weimar Republic. It seems difficult to give a general explanation for this resilience against the overall trend, since local conditions were apparently often decisive. Politically questionable manoeuvres such as new elections before the abolishment of the three-class franchise, the formation of a coalition of all groups that saw themselves as bourgeois, or the consistent willingness to cooperate with the Social Democrats seem to have played important roles according to the specific context.[10]

An argument that is frequently invoked to explain the decline of the two liberal parties at the national level holds that the Weimar Republic witnessed a process of dissolution of the German middle classes, who represented the traditional voting pool of the liberal parties.[11] According to this view, the economic hardships of the Weimar era exacerbated a fragmentation of the *Bürgertum*, which in turn hampered the organizational efforts to establish support for liberals that could face the competition of the umbrella associations of the Social Democrats and the National Socialists. Implicitly, this reading relies on an input model of political legitimacy where political parties express the interests and convictions of their constituency. It uses the modern mass party as a yardstick to explain the failure of political liberalism of the inter-war period, assuming that the success of political parties depends on their ability to establish and maintain bonds between the party leadership and a large social milieu whose interests the party represents and whose commitment ensures electoral success and party funding.

Even though this interpretation offers an alternative to the thesis of an illiberal heritage within German liberalism, its two main assumptions need to be questioned. First, the mass party was not a universal endpoint of history, but a specific type that proved successful only under certain conditions and succumbed to the catch-all party of the second half of the twentieth century. Unlike the supposedly outdated liberal model, the catch-all party was able to mobilize electoral support without addressing the interests of a particular social milieu or forming a well-tied web of supporting associations.[12] Second, in view of this fact, the input model of political legitimacy needs to be supplemented with an output model that emphasizes the function of parties to shape the convictions of supporters. If the catch-all party shows that the backing of political parties by a specific social constituency is not necessarily decisive for electoral success, the difficulties of both liberal parties during the Weimar period in creating successful political strategies have to be scrutinized more closely. Once the focus is shifted to the output model of political legitimacy, it becomes clear that a main reason for the failure of Weimar's political liberalism was the inability of the party leaderships to carve out a coherent liberal position that could convince voters. The difficulties of creating a consistent language of liberalism did not arise from an alleged dissolution of the middle classes but rather from a set of changes and predicaments, starting with the impairment of the traditional relationship between political liberalism and the state during the Weimar period.

Due to the restricted access to suffrage and education the ties between political liberalism and the state were still particularly strong before the First World War. Although liberals of different orientations and the monarchy in Germany did not necessarily share the same political outlook, they still, to a large extent, converged with public servants of the state administration by ties of social background and interest. Consequently, support for their demands on the state did not depend on the pressure of external societal organizations. In addition, to the extent that social democracy gained weight in political elections, liberals increasingly perceived state bureaucracy as an effective and independent means of social reform.[13] These conditions kept the liberal party leadership from abandoning an older conception of politics that assumed there to be only one coherent national interest a government had to implement and liberalism had to be in pursuit of.[14] To be sure, increasing conflicts within both liberal parties showed that this model had reached its breaking point on the eve of the First World War, but the overall focus on the nation-state remained the guiding principle of political liberalism and became even more important after 1914.[15]

The First World War and the Weimar Republic placed new strains on these forms of political practice. The size of the state bureaucracy had increased enormously since the late nineteenth century, and during the war, the number of state institutions and employees expanded even further. Since public service became a less restricted field, the state was increasingly perceived as a less reliable resource for social elites to further their careers and exert political influence. As a consequence, liberal attitudes towards the state became more ambivalent. This ambivalence was reinforced by the widespread image of the new republican state being an imposition from the West and by the previously unthinkable role of the Social Democrats as one of the leading parties in government; the latter were now blamed for filling civil service jobs according to party preferences.[16] These changes particularly deepened the rift between more conservative liberal currents and the Weimar state. They increased the appeal of the nation and the *Volk* as ideological orientations, and did nothing to endear the liberals to the republic.[17]

Under these conditions, three main areas of difficulty arose when the leaderships of both liberal parties had to make decisions on the strategic line their parties should pursue in the political power struggle. A first set of problems emerged from the reinforced stress on the nation as the key value of political orientation. On the one hand, this orientation created an ideological flexibility that allowed the leadership of the two liberal parties to join, either on their own, but often also in tandem, and become partners in all but two of the twenty coalition governments from 1919 to 1932. Highlighting the importance of the nation and the *Volksgemeinschaft* was flexible enough to allow an alliance with various coalition partners. This ensured an influence on governance in stark contrast to and despite the declining support for both parties at the polls. On the other hand, joining various coalition governments by claiming to serve the common good of the nation did not create a loyal pool of supporters. Rather, the wavering strategy and the stress on broader national issues detached the liberal parties from specific social interests and prompted divisions within the liberal camp.[18] When, for example, the DVP chose to focus its campaign for the Reichstag election of 1928 on the national merits of its foreign policy, it did not respond to the economic concerns of pensioners, war veterans, small businessmen, and artisans. The defeat at the polls provoked controversial discussions within the party on its future role in forming coalition governments.[19]

Secondly, developing a consistent liberal position was also impeded by the dependence of both parties on financial support from the business sector. For the DDP and the DVP, being in government was crucial to secure their funding. As they could not draw on the dues of a large party membership, both parties relied on different forms of partnership with vested interests who were attracted by the influence the liberal parties had through the executive branch. Since business federations could only offer the financial means for campaigns to convince voters, not the voters themselves, liberals had the possibility to negotiate with their donors. Pursuing the immediate interests of industrialists, liberals argued, would alienate important groups of supporters like white-collar employees, civil servants, family farmers, and non-socialist workers and thus diminish the liberal influence on government policies.[20] Still, on more than one occasion both DVP and DDP either had to compromise and face the dissatisfaction of voters or decline financial support and accept the emergence of splinter parties who represented the interests of specific economic groups in a more straightforward way. For example, starting in 1927 leading industrialists from the Ruhr set up a fund for the candidates of all bourgeois parties. The lion's share went to the DVP and helped to finance its subsequent local and national election campaigns. However, in return for this financial support, the DVP had to accept the nomination of candidates close to industry and, as a consequence, lost its credibility for many groups of voters.[21]

Thirdly, defining the party line according to contingent circumstances like changing coalition partners and donors could only be achieved if the party leadership was able to make its decisions in a more or less autonomous way. Accordingly, both liberal parties consisted of rather weak local associations that faced a small circle of national party spokesmen whose dependence on the overall support of the party membership was mitigated in various ways. Whereas the political strategy made a top down leadership necessary, it prevented a representation of specific social and local interests and rather confirmed the traditional conception of forming the interests of the liberal cause from the top.[22] For example, the party leadership of the DDP continuously ignored the objections of fellow party members from Hamburg who were unhappy with the national party's support of conservative motions like the law to protect youth from allegedly morally questionable writings in 1926 or the construction of armoured cruisers (Panzerkreuzer A) in 1928. The local party branch still received more than 10 per cent of the vote in the election for the city parliament in 1932, while the left-liberal results in Hamburg in Reichstag elections increasingly reflected the general national decline.[23]

Summing up, these factors produced a situation that made it difficult for both liberal parties to offer a perspective that could have attracted a large, persistent group of supporters. Rather than a growing fragmentation of the German middle classes—who might have never formed a cohesive social group—the decline of the liberal parties was to a large extent produced by political liberalism itself. The party protagonists were caught in a strategic dilemma that pushed them to opt for programmatic pragmatism, changing coalitions, and an autonomous party leadership rather than for a coherent ideological orientation and the formation of ties with a potential constituency. Whereas this strategy helped them to maintain their funding and, at least for some time, a position of political influence at the national level, it impeded the establishing of a clear language of liberalism that could have formed the basis for broader support.[24] Cardinal moments of the history of Weimar party liberalism illustrate how these factors were interconnected in a process that eventually made the liberal parties politically insignificant.

An early important turning point was the failure to create a single unified party after the monarchy had been abolished in the wake of the revolution in November 1918. Negotiations between leaders of the two traditional liberal parties of the Kaiserreich and a new group of left-liberal intellectuals (the journalist Theodor Wolff and the sociologist Alfred Weber, among others) were not successful because each group hoped to become the dominating liberal force in the future.[25] After the liberal leaders abandoned the project of a unified party in late 1918, the long-lasting split between left-wing and right-wing German liberalism was reproduced. Throughout the Weimar years, the German Democratic Party and the German People's Party made great efforts to establish themselves as an alternative to each other.

Whereas the left-liberal German Democratic Party supported the republican state, the German People's Party initially advocated a return to a form of monarchy and voted against the Weimar Constitution in July 1919. Although their political demands were not far removed from each other on many other political questions, the effects of their competing claims to represent the true interests of the nation became particularly visible when the acceptance of the Versailles Treaty split the National Assembly at Weimar in the early summer of 1919. The German People's Party unanimously condemned an acceptance as a betrayal of national interests and thereby intensified the controversy within the left-liberal German Democratic Party concerning whether anything but a refusal of the Allied peace terms corresponded with their goal to coin a new national identity. In late June 1919, the profound disagreement among DDP-parliamentary delegates provoked their withdrawal from the governing coalition with the Majority Socialists and the Catholic Centre Party. Only three months later, in October 1919, the leaders of the German Democratic Party decided to re-enter the government in order to soften the influence of works councils (*Betriebsräte*) on managerial decision-making in businesses. These manoeuvres left the left liberals exposed to allegations that they lacked conviction and danced to the tune of the Majority Socialists. They contributed to significant losses in the elections for the first national parliament in 1920, to the benefit of the German People's Party.[26]

While this development demonstrated the divisions competing positions could produce within the left-liberal camp, the policy measures to end the hyperinflation in 1923 had devastating consequences for both liberal parties. Although many members of the middle classes faced the loss of their fortunes due to the monetary devaluation, others, like debtors and big business, also benefited.[27] More important for the fate of political liberalism than an often invoked eclipse of the middle classes was the perception of the counter-inflationary measures and the effects the inflation had on the liberal party organizations.

After the assassination of the left-liberal Foreign Secretary Walther Rathenau in 1922, the German People's Party gave up its principled opposition to the republic and joined the government. When the party chairman Gustav Stresemann became head of a coalition government in 1923, his administration managed to end inflation by introducing a currency reform senior officials and ministers of both liberal parties had co-designed. In order to stabilize the financial situation, the government acted to reduce posts in public administration, cut the public sector wage bill and the availability of loans, and this was especially felt by small and medium-sized firms and farmers. These measures contributed to the success of the new currency, but they alienated traditionally important groups of supporters from the liberal parties. At the same time, reducing the circulation of money also created a difficult situation in the following years for the reconstruction of the local liberal party branches who had to let most of their employees go during the crisis. Now, business held on to its financial resources and showed a general hesitation to resume donations to the liberal parties. In the parliamentary elections in May 1924, the German Democratic Party and the German People's Party lost about a third of their former seats and a new competitor gained ground, the Business Party (Wirtschaftspartei), claiming to better represent small businessmen and homeowners. Hopes of both liberal parties to reverse the negative trend in the subsequent Landtag elections were more than once disappointed, also due to the relative success of other liberal splinter parties like the People's Justice Party (Volksrechtspartei, VRP) in Saxony in 1926.[28]

After the beginning of the Great Depression a new minority government, under the leadership of Heinrich Brüning from the Catholic Centre Party, tried to steer through the crisis by bypassing parliament with emergency decrees. When the Reichstag vetoed the decrees for the national budget and was subsequently dissolved in the summer of 1930, left- and right-wing liberals started new negotiations to forge a block of the political centre. Although both sides claimed to put the interests of the nation before party needs, their leaders were unable to find an agreement and thereby increased the divisions within their own organizations. Subsequently, the German Democratic Party temporarily formed an alliance with the political arm of the Young German Order—an organization that fused elements of the bourgeois youth movement with the ideology of a militarist and antisemitic combat league—and changed its name to German State Party (Deutsche Staatspartei, DStP). Whereas the party leadership hoped this strategy would lead to new support from the younger generation and moderate conservatives, the antisemitic and nationalist rhetoric of the Young German Order were met with strong disapproval from their own left wing.[29] Within the German People's Party, the decision of the party executives to stop negotiations with the left liberals caused the disaffection of local party organizations who had vehemently demanded a fusion of all liberal forces. This conflict added to the dispute within the German People's Party between a faction that advocated a reduction of the tax burden for business, a faction that wanted to avoid a reduction of the salaries of civil servants, and a faction that opposed further cuts in the welfare system. In the elections held in September 1930, DStP and DVP lost significantly and were reduced to 3.8 and 4.5 per cent of the vote, respectively.[30]

The development of female activists within the liberal parties offers an interesting parallel to the general decline of Weimar political liberalism. Women obtained the right to vote in late 1918 and were granted equal civil rights by the constitution of 1919. Women outnumbered male voters and became a much-courted group of supporters for all parties. During the campaign for the National Assembly elections in 1919, the left liberals were confident that they would be able to benefit from women's suffrage because most of the prominent leaders of the bourgeois women's movement had joined their ranks and prepared appeals to attract female votes. Gertrud Bäumer, a leading representative of the women's movement, became one of three party vice-chairpersons in 1919, while other women were members of the executive council of the DDP. But the efforts of the mobilizing organization under the direction of Helene Lange, Alice Salomon, Marie Baum, and others did not return the expected success. Despite a comparably high number of female candidates on the left-liberal slate and the fairly high turnout of female voters in 1919 and 1920, the majority of women preferred to vote for the Catholic Centre and the right-wing German National People's Party (Deutschnationale Volkspartei, DNVP).[31] The DVP fared slightly better than its left-liberal competitor and received more votes from women than men in the 1920 elections. In its campaign, the party avoided a strong emphasis on equal rights and stressed the role of women in a common endeavour to rebuild the nation. As the left-liberal campaign claimed to represent the 'party of women', leading women of the DVP like Clara Mende and Marie Bernays accused their competitor of playing into the hands of particular interests instead of supporting the greater needs of the German *Volk*.[32]

Subsequently, the failure to win the women's votes contributed to significantly weakening the influence of women in the DDP and intensified discussions on the proper way to address political issues among liberal women in general. Whereas some focused on gender equality, others found that women should serve the nation in accordance with their specific female nature. Both sides argued that women should assume a function in public life, but whereas the former group demanded equal social and political rights, the latter declared that female characteristics were especially suited to reinforcing the spiritual and community side of the German nation. During the course of the 1920s, the latter position gained in importance. When the left liberals decided to merge with the Young German Order in 1930, Gertrud Bäumer endorsed the greater emphasis on the *Volksgemeinschaft*, claiming that women were specifically capable of ending the 'sickness' of current party politics and buttressing the common national spirit. Others, like Marie-Elisabeth Lüders and Agnes von Zahn-Harnack, strongly opposed the shift to the right that went along with the new party line.[33] Neither faction of the liberal women's movement accepted the picture of women as housewives and mothers in the Nazi regime after 1933, nor did they trust the Nazi leadership. But some like Bäumer—who lost her high-ranking position in the Ministry of the Interior in 1933—thought that the *Volksgemeinschaft* offered the opportunity to acknowledge the role of women in fostering the spiritual values of the nation. Lüders hoped that the compulsory service discussed in the wake of the preparation for war would include women alongside men and thereby promote the female cause.[34]

An important background for the idea among liberals to co-opt elements of National Socialism and their hope to influence Nazi policies were the controversies during the years of the Weimar Republic on the changes of liberal values and goals that were suitable for responding to the contemporary challenges. I examine these controversies in the following section.

LIBERALISM IN THE MAZE

When the DDP was re-established as the German State Party in 1930, the member of the party executive and subsequent President of the Federal Republic, Theodor Heuss, explained that each party had to submit itself to the 'law of change ... because people's minds start to move, because individuals and classes detached themselves from tradition'.[35] Many liberals departed from former convictions in the Weimar Republic, arguing that the economic and political conditions made an adaption of liberal thinking necessary. Efforts to renew liberalism were older than the Weimar Republic and received an important impetus at the turn of the century through political associations like the

Nationalsozialer Verein (1896) and the Gesellschaft für Soziale Reform (1901). A widely received publication by the influential reform advocate Friedrich Naumann (1860–1919) was titled 'The Renewal of Liberalism' (1906).[36] But the German monarchical system and the economic globalization around 1900 placed these discussions in a specific pre-war context that fundamentally changed when the question of liberal principles was addressed under the conditions of democracy and the post-war economy after 1918. Unlike in Imperial Germany, parliament gained in importance once the government depended on its majority, and this new significance drove liberal observers to a more critical perspective on parliamentarism and political parties. Bearing the experience of the war economy in mind, neither entrepreneurs nor economists were advocating a prolongation of economic regulation by the state. But faced with a situation of lost markets, the rise of large corporate enterprises, and new overseas competitors, entrepreneurial freedom seemed to involve as many risks as chances and this impression changed the evaluation of free entrepreneurship and state–business relations.

From a historical perspective, the often assumed kinship between liberalism and democracy is a contingent relationship because liberals in Germany and elsewhere did not see democratization as a goal in itself. Rather, it was conceived as one possible instrument to promote opportunities for the personal development of the individual. In this way, a cardinal feature of democracy contained lights and shadows. On the one hand, the selection of political leaders through elections could prove to be more effective in ending or preventing the closure of a governing elite whose unlimited claim to power endangered the freedom of others. On the other hand, this selective mechanism bore the risk of establishing a government that would seek to realize particular social goals rather than promoting the opportunities of the individual citizen, because democracy provided the majority with the possibility to impose its views on others.[37]

In the early years of the republic, some of its liberal supporters held that competitive elections were the best guarantee to find political representatives that were qualified to lead the nation. In contrast to an aristocracy by birth, they claimed, democracy would select an aristocracy of capability and endow its members with the authority to work efficiently. In turn, these political representatives were supposed to have an educational effect on voters and thereby help to create a society of democratic citizens.[38] Other liberals, however, remained unconvinced by these arguments and favoured a political authority 'above politics', independent from the influence of democracy. In this spirit, under the supervision of liberal constitutional lawyers like Hugo Preuß (1860–1925), the Weimar Constitution equipped the government with the possibility to bypass parliament in order to circumvent political debates in times of emergency. During the crisis in 1923 and 1924, enabling laws helped to support the counter-inflationary measures of the liberal cabinet of Gustav Stresemann. In 1923, the liberal army minister Otto Geßler urged Reich President Friedrich Ebert to use his executive power (*Reichsexekution*) to suspend the radical leftist state governments of Saxony and Thuringia, claiming that the integrity of the Reich was in danger. Left- and right-wing liberals believed these steps to be justified, and accepted or even endorsed the fact that they temporarily suspended the government's accountability to parliament. In March 1933, the legal measures to counteract the financial and economic crisis in 1923 were used as a precedent to end parliamentary control altogether by the Nazi government through the Enabling Law. Initially, even left-liberal delegates like Theodor Heuss—who in 1933 voted in favour of the law—did not understand this development as a final defeat of liberalism, but rather as a restoration of political authority. This judgement has to be seen against the backdrop of the experience of government instability throughout the 1920s and the escalation of political turmoil in the early 1930s.[39]

When by 1930 political liberalism had dissolved into a group of splinter parties, liberal critics of parliamentary democracy gained in importance. A rising number of liberals blamed Weimar's parliamentary democracy for producing a form of party politics that failed in producing the right leadership. The selection of party candidates, they complained, followed the logic of particular networks and personal interests and increased the divisions within German society. As a consequence, adherents of both left-wing and right-wing liberalism started to advocate a new form of politics that would push back the influence of political parties and allow for a new relationship between the *Volk* and its leaders.[40] Which form of governance would be able to achieve this became the object of a controversial debate in the late 1920s and early 1930s. Whereas some believed that the abolition of the party-list voting system, proportional representation, and the party whip would lead to a new political class of independent delegates who could deliberate the common good, others held that a more decisive reform of parliamentary politics was necessary. Some liberals suggested supplementing the political parliament with a legislative body of delegates, chosen by the economic professions. This Second Chamber was supposed to restrict the scope of parliamentary legislation— an idea that liberals in many other European countries shared.[41] Still others argued that liberals should join political movements that avoided any resemblance to party organizations in order to represent the true spirit of the German *Volk* more directly.[42]

Interpreting these reflections as a renunciation of liberalism does not answer the question of why important liberal figures could see National Socialism—which presented itself as an anti-party movement of the *Volk*—as an ally. A first step towards an analysis that avoids normative assumptions about a timeless core of liberalism is to consider the erroneous conviction of many contemporary liberals at this stage that they would be able to influence the course of a Nazi government. This belief was encouraged by the widespread perception that the political disintegration of the Weimar Republic paved the way to a German society disrupted by the material interests of particular social groups. After forming a government on the basis of parliamentary majorities had become impossible in 1930, both liberal parties aimed to strengthen the executive branch in relation to parliament. Especially the younger generation of liberals hoped for a new authoritative leadership through National Socialism that was able to re-establish a common national spirit. For liberals like Gertrud Bäumer, this spirit represented the precondition of liberal reforms she had been advocating throughout her political life.[43]

The necessity to adapt liberalism to new challenges was also felt by entrepreneurs and economists. However, both groups did not necessarily endorse the same prescriptions. The practice of economic liberalism has always differed from textbook economics.

Businessmen never fully adopted the liberal principle of free trade, but rather focused on making profits with as little risk as possible.[44] In Germany, protectionism through tariff barriers became de facto an accepted instrument not only among agricultural and industrial pressure groups, but also among important sections of political and academic liberalism from the late 1870s. Still, it would be a mistake to see rational choice as the driving force that motivated German company owners and managers. The discussions on economic liberalism provided German business with an influential guideline to direct and express their interests and demands.

The main inspiration for entrepreneurs who discussed liberal economic principles was not academic theory in economics, but suggestions by business associations and their spokesmen.[45] In their perspective, the war and the Treaty of Versailles had produced an economic environment that made individual entrepreneurial efforts pointless. The war economy, spokesmen of business federations explained, had accelerated methods of mass production that needed capital investments which exceeded the financial resources of company owners. Rather than relying on private assets, businesses increasingly tended to finance their investments through corporate financial arrangements. The strategy of mass production, a second argument held, needed large sales markets in order to be profitable, whereas the post-war peace settlement had multiplied the borders within Europe by creating new states. Individual actors did not have the possibility to negotiate ways to overcome the tariff barriers these states used to shore up their own industries, whereas collective efforts had a different kind of leverage. Moreover, a third strand of argument emphasized, the post-war situation created difficult conditions for economic individualism because companies in the United States were able to flood the European markets with goods while being protected by high tariffs. On the contrary, German manufacturers had to cope with the transition to peacetime economy, reparations, and the ensuing turbulences of the German currency—which, according to reform advocates, was a situation that made it difficult for individual entrepreneurs to survive.[46]

Based on this assessment, economic liberalism had to be adapted. Rather than relying on a free competitive market, reformers argued, business federations should help to establish collective agreements that organized the production and exchange of goods. In a certain sense, this was not a departure from former practices: businessmen had always been aware of the fact that markets relied on infrastructural prerequisites that needed to be established in advance—i.e. monetary conventions, common shipping volumes, the standardization of semi-processed and processed products. But in the post-war period the establishment of new national and international business associations (like the Reich Association of German Industry, Reichsverband der Deutschen Industrie) and the perceived economic difficulties encouraged spokesmen to push their demands further. The economic individual, they held, would only be able to persist if freedom of action was preserved by collective strategies like shared research and developments costs, joint distribution and procurement channels, or protective alliances against market disturbances. Without collective measures in support of the corporate landscape, this strand of argument warned, economic activities would soon be controlled by large state-run combines. In contrast, self-administered organization could help to rationalize German companies and facilitate their return to their pre-war economic success. Leaders of the Reich Association of German Industry and other business associations especially presented cartels as an adequate response to the changed economic situation of their time. In contrast to former positions, entrepreneurial coordination in general, and cartels in particular, were now not conceived as measures against temporary crises, but as a reaction to a new stage of capitalism. Businessmen and many liberal economists were increasingly convinced that the future of economic liberalism lay in these and other efforts of self-coordination.[47]

A different suggestion to adapt former liberal convictions to the changes of contemporary capitalism was developed in the wake of the Great Depression by a group of German economists led, among others, by Walter Eucken, Alexander Rüstow, and Wilhelm Röpke. After the Second World War, their position was labelled as *Ordoliberalismus* or ordo-liberalism, drawing on the Latin term 'ordo', which described an order or overarching framework. These reform proposals also highlighted the increasing difficulties of individual economic actors in opposing overpowering forces. But from this perspective, it was the concentration of economic interests in trusts and business federations and their dominance over the state that lay at the root of the problem.[48] Although the nascent ordo-liberals only developed full-blown accounts in the second half of the 1930s, they had already complained before 1933 that the competitive energies of society had been paralysed by the seizure of the state through economic forces.[49] A first step to counteract these developments, Walter Eucken and Wilhelm Röpke argued, was to free the state from the influence of 'mass democracy'. In their eyes, only a restriction of parliamentarism would allow the establishment of a state above vested interests. In a second step, the state would provide a space for economic transactions between independent market participants and enforce the principles of a free market economy. This could be achieved if the state, acting from a position above particular interests, would ensure economic freedom by crushing monopolies of economic power that stopped competition from functioning. In contrast to the reform advocates in German business federations, but also deviating from laissez-faire liberalism, this conception relied on a strong state that intervened in the economy. For the ordo-liberals, the traditional liberal concept of the self-regulating market governed by an 'invisible hand' had lost its appeal.[50]

In 1933, Wilhelm Röpke and Alexander Rüstow went into exile and were part of the discussions at the Colloque Walter Lippmann, a conference of economists, intellectuals, and businessmen in Paris in 1938 that has been characterized as the cradle of neo-liberalism of the second half of the twentieth century. The participants of the Paris meeting did not agree on a common diagnosis of contemporary difficulties, and each side claimed to make the more crucial propositions for a renewal of liberalism.[51] Like the controversy of liberals on democracy, this discussion represents the struggle of the 1920s and 1930s over the form liberalism should take in view of the contemporary political and economic challenges.

Domestic Liberalism Contested— Liberal Internationalism Explored

Due to political and economic circumstances, liberalism was confronted with specific difficulties in Germany. In some respects, however, it suffered the same fate as liberalism in many other national contexts. During the inter-war period, liberals were widely contested in European societies and experienced a fragmentation and decline in their supporters. This process had already started before the First World War, but intensified after 1918. For the historian Eric Hobsbawm, the decrease of liberal democracies in Europe and elsewhere was equivalent to a universal 'Fall of Liberalism'.[52] In the United Kingdom, the fate of British political liberalism was sealed in the early 1920s, when it turned into a second-tier party and split between a left-wing and a right-wing faction. The division within liberalism had been exacerbated by the war and was further fuelled after 1918 by the question whether the liberal doctrine could still provide answers in view of the vastly expanded role of the state in society and economy. Leaving office in 1922, Lloyd George was the last liberal Prime Minister in British history to date. After the general elections of 1923, the Liberal Party collapsed and never came close to its former importance in the House of Commons.[53] In France, liberals were unable to overcome a cleavage between progressive and more orthodox positions that had already contributed to the end of liberal dominance in parliament at the turn of the century. During the 1920s, the differences within the liberal camp provoked recurrent secessions of subgroups and new alliances with different political partners. They also thwarted liberal reform projects, above all suggestions for a new system of proportional representation in the Chamber of Deputies that would have improved chances of liberals vis-à-vis their political competitors. Under these circumstances, curtailing parliamentary rights and strengthening the executive power of the state became prominent liberal demands.[54] In 1936, Auguste Detœuf, a public intellectual and vice-president of the French company Alsthom, declared: 'The liberalism of the 19th century is dead. It is pointless to try and revive it. We have to adapt to the new circumstances.'[55]

While liberals in Germany and throughout Europe struggled in their different domestic contexts, they were also protagonists of efforts to establish a new liberal internationalism after 1918. This period of internationalism was short-lived, but liberals perceived it as a possible counterweight to the difficulties they faced at home. New public and private institutions like the League of Nations, the Permanent Court of International Justice, and the International Chamber of Commerce were established to promote the restoration of a liberal order. European Liberals were convinced that a return to the global economic liberalism of the pre-war period was not only possible but necessary, and tried to create a political framework that would ensure the re-establishment of economic policies like the Gold Standard, balanced budgets, and a removal of trade restrictions. At the same time, the creation of new nation-states through the Versailles settlement turned the issues of minority rights and state sovereignty into urgent questions and led to the idea of a supranational judicial body that could monitor the treatment of ethnic minorities within the new states.[56] While many believed that democratically elected parliaments were a difficult or even unreliable partner in realizing these efforts, the international setting seemed to offer the chance to work on a new liberal order more freely.[57]

German liberals were at the forefront of the national delegations to the League of Nations, the World Economic Conference, the International Chamber of Commerce (ICC), and the Permanent Court of International Justice. When Germany was admitted as a new member of the ICC in 1925 and the League of Nations in 1926, the state secretary of the Ministry of Economic Affairs Ernst Trendelenburg (1882–1945), the president of the German Association of Chambers of Commerce and Industry, Franz von Mendelssohn (1865–1935), and the former Minister of Economics Eduard Hamm (1879–1944) became active figures of liberal internationalism (among many others). They served as members of the Economic Consultative Committee of the League of Nations, as members of the executive committee and the council of the ICC, and as participants and advisers of the first World Economic Conference in Geneva in 1927. Walther Schücking (1875–1935), professor for international law at the University of Marburg and founding member of the DDP, became the first German judge at the Permanent Court in The Hague.[58]

These endeavours were encouraged by Gustav Stresemann, who was the German foreign minister from 1923 until his death in 1929. For him, integrating Germany into the networks of international politics and connecting German companies to European partners was the only promising way to break free from the conditions of the Treaty of Versailles and the post-war international isolation of Germany. He saw the possibility of economic, political, and legal cooperation under the supervision of international organizations like the League of Nations as an important step in the process of promoting German interests. Stresemann's foreign policy and the strategies of other liberal German representatives within the new international organizations of the interwar period were to a large extent characterized by combining a support for liberal internationalism and the nationalist motive of peaceful revisionism of the Versailles order.[59] Even then, combining liberal internationalism with nationalist ideas was not a German prerogative. Historian Mark Mazower has described the efforts of British nationalists to use the League of Nations as a means of defending imperial claims against the mounting critics of imperialism.[60]

The German commitment to minority rights was not driven by idealist notions, but by the effort to promote the cause of ethnic Germans who had become citizens of Eastern European countries like Poland and Czechoslovakia in 1919. At the same time, accepting the authority of international courts when the protection of minorities was at stake meant abandoning the former adherence to the principle of state sovereignty which had hampered the success of former international legal agreements. Interwar German liberals were ready to join other Western countries in their support for international legal institutions and to expose the appeal to sovereign rights of semi-peripheral democracies as backward.[61]

With respect to the restoration of an economic liberal order, American and British officials encouraged the reintegration of Germany into the international community and were able to push France into the same direction in 1924 through promises for financial aid if France would end its occupation of the German industrial heartland, the Ruhr.[62] Reinforcing trade relations with German companies promised a network of commercial relations that was supposed to act as a safeguard against a repetition of the economic slump many European countries experienced in the early 1920s. At the same time, establishing close economic ties could also be understood as a safety measure against future German military aggression. Still, the possibilities to return to economic liberalism in the post-war situation became the subject of controversial debates. The World Economic Conference in Geneva in 1927 illustrated a conflict pattern that characterized numerous meetings of the Council of the ICC and the Economic Consultative Committee of the League of Nations.[63] The British delegates supported a reduction of tariff rates by a return to the most-favoured-nation treatment, a reciprocal bilateral regulation that accorded for both sides the trade advantages of the most favoured nation within their trade relations. By contrast, the French delegation and especially the former Minister of Finance and leading member of the French liberal party Democratic Alliance (Alliance démocratique), Louis Loucheur argued for supplementary measures by private business arrangements.[64]

Neither side was able to implement its views and after the beginning of the world economic crisis in late 1929 most European states followed policies that made the projects of liberal internationalism look unrealistic. The Nazi government left the League of Nations in October 1933 after a public referendum that supported the decision with 95 per cent of the vote. Still, liberals like Walther Schücking, despite official German efforts to withdraw him, stayed at the Permanent Court of International Justice in The Hague and the German delegation to the ICC continued to attend its meetings and conferences throughout the 1930s and early 1940s. The German contribution to liberal internationalism in the Weimar years was too short-lived and discordant to make a lasting impact, but many of its supporters did not disappear when National Socialism came into power. Rather, in ways that still need to be further assessed, they continued to seek possibilities to realize their goals, and the international level remained a preferred field of action.[65]

Conclusion

When Richard Merton attempted to present liberalism as an indispensable partner of a government under the leadership of National Socialism in March 1933, he failed miserably. Compared to the elections in November 1932, the DVP lost about half of its votes in Merton's home town Frankfurt, a former liberal stronghold, and Merton lost his Reichstag seat. His efforts to promote liberalism in this way not only demonstrate a distorted view of the political reality of the early 1930s but also the effects of contemporary developments that pushed liberals to question and revise their ideological repertoire. Merton's contributions to the contemporary discussions and his ambivalence towards the Nazi regime illustrate the difficulties faced by liberalism to find an adequate response to the political and economic challenges of the Weimar Republic.

These difficulties were increased by the steady decline of the liberal parties in the 1920s and early 1930s. Liberals failed to overcome a cluster of interrelated dilemmas. Joining various coalition governments secured political influence and funding opportunities, but did not lead to a coherent programme that could have attracted a steady group of supporters. In addition, reacting to changing political circumstances of different governments and donors reinforced a top down party structure that prevented strong ties with a network of local liberal associations. This strategy encouraged divisions within the liberal camp, as the decision of the party leaderships against a formation of a common liberal block in 1930 illustrated, and ultimately contributed to the political insignificance of the liberal parties.

Controversial debates on the adaptation of liberal values to contemporary circumstances accompanied this process. Many liberals increasingly believed that an authoritative form of decision-making was the only thing that could rescue the freedom of the individual—against a dominant majority that could use parliamentary democracy to impose its views and against a contemporary capitalism that made individual economic action impossible. But the resulting discussions on a renewal of liberalism were far from unanimous and exacerbated the divisions between different factions. Eventually, they made adherents of liberal reform look for alternative possibilities to exert influence and, in some cases, drove them to support a partnership with right-wing movements.

While democracy became the touchstone of political liberalism in Germany, the international arena offered advantages to liberal endeavours because delegates to committees of the League of Nations were not nominated through democratic elections. In this context, neither the need to answer to elected parliaments nor to party organizations interfered with the traditional liberal self-conception of serving the common good of the nation. After 1945, Richard Merton preferred this perspective over his previous commitment to parliamentary politics. He did not resume his party-political activity, but quickly returned to Germany from his British exile to help the international reintegration of German business as an economic adviser to the West German government.

Notes

1. Hessisches Wirtschaftsarchiv, Darmstadt, Nachlass Richard Merton 2000/319: Richard Merton, An meine Wähler und Nichtwähler! 6 Mar. 1933.
2. Richard Merton, *Erinnernswertes aus meinem Leben, das über das Persönliche hinausgeht* (Frankfurt/Main: Knapp, 1955), here 132–5; on German liberals after 1933 see Eric Kurlander, *Living with Hitler. Liberal Democrats in the Third Reich* (New Haven and London: Yale University Press, 2009).
3. See the contributions to Andreas Wirsching and Jürgen Eder (eds), *Vernunftrepublikanismus in der Weimarer Republik: Politik, Literatur, Wissenschaft* (Stuttgart: Franz Steiner, 2008).

4. Hans-Ulrich Wehler, *Deutsche Gesellschaftsgeschichte*, vol. 4. *Vom Beginn des Ersten Weltkriegs bis zur Gründung der beiden deutschen Staaten 1914–1949* (Munich: C. H. Beck, 2003), 547–50; Jürgen Kocka, 'Bürgertum und Bürgerlichkeit als Probleme der deutschen Geschichte vom späten 18. zum frühen 20. Jahrhundert', in Kocka (ed.), *Bürger und Bürgerlichkeit im 19. Jahrhundert* (Göttingen: Vandenhoeck & Ruprecht, 1987), 21–63, esp. 52–3; Fritz Stern, *The Failure of Illiberalism: Essays on the Political Culture of Modern Germany* (New York: Knopf 1972), esp. xiv–xl.
5. Michael Freeden and Marc Stears, 'Liberalism', in Michael Freeden, Lyman Tower Sargent, and Marc Stears (eds), *The Oxford Handbook of Political Ideologies* (Oxford: Oxford University Press, 2013), 329–47; Catherine Audard, *Qu'est-ce que le libéralisme? Ethique, politique, société* (Paris: Folio, 2009), 21–4. For a well-known case in the German context see Wolfgang Hardtwig, 'Friedrich Naumann in der deutschen Geschichte', in Hardtwig, *Deutsche Geschichtskultur im 19. und 20. Jahrhundert* (Munich: Oldenbourg, 2013), 289–311.
6. Peter Fritzsche, 'Landscape of Design: Crisis and Modernism in Weimar Germany', in Thomas W. Kniesche and Stephen Brockman (eds), *Dancing on the Volcano: Essays on the Culture of the Weimar Republic* (Columbia, SC: Camden House 1994), 29–46; Moritz Föllmer, Rüdiger Graf, and Per Leo, 'Die Kultur der Krise in der Weimarer Republik', in Moritz Föllmer and Rüdiger Graf (eds), *Die 'Krise' der Weimarer Republik: Zur Kritik eines Deutungsmusters* (Frankfurt/Main and New York: Campus, 2005), 9–44; Moritz Föllmer, 'Which Crisis? Which Modernity? New Perspectives on Weimar Germany', in Jochen Hung, Godela Weiss-Sussex, and Geoff Wilkes (eds), *Beyond Glitter and Doom. The Contingency of the Weimar Republic* (Munich: Iudicium Verlag, 2012), 19–30.
7. Duncan Bell, 'What is Liberalism?', *Political Theory*, 42 (2014), 682–715; Michael Freeden, 'European Liberalisms: An Essay in Comparative Political Thought', *European Journal of Political Theory*, 7 (2008), 9–30; Jörn Leonhard, 'From European Liberalism to Languages of Liberalisms: The Semantics of Liberalism in European Comparison', *Rediscriptions*, 8 (2004), 17–51.
8. Peter Fritzsche, 'Did Weimar Fail?', *Journal of Modern History*, 68 (1996), 629–56; Tim B. Müller, 'Die Geburt des Sozial-Liberalismus aus dem Geist der Verwaltung: Zur Erfindung der modernen Wirtschaftspolitik in der Weimarer Republik', in Anselm Doering-Manteuffel and Jörn Leonhard (eds), *Liberalismus im 20. Jahrhundert* (Stuttgart: Franz Steiner, 2015), 127–56; Philipp Müller, 'Kapitalismus der Vermittlung: Neo-Liberalismus in Deutschland und Frankreich nach dem Ersten Weltkrieg', ibid., 97–126; Jens Hacke, *Existenzkrise der Demokratie: Zur politischen Theorie des Liberalismus in der Zwischenkriegszeit* (Berlin: Suhrkamp, 2018).
9. Marcus Llanque, 'The First World War and the Invention of "Western Democracy"', in Riccardo Bavaj and Martina Steeber (eds), *Germany and the 'West': The History of a Modern Concept* (New York and Oxford: Berghahn, 2015), 69–80; Dieter Langewiesche, *Liberalism in Germany*, tr. Christiane Banerji (Basingstoke: Macmillan, 2000), 250–1.
10. Michael Schäfer, *Bürgertum in der Krise: Städtische Mittelklassen in Edinburgh und Leipzig 1890–1930* (Göttingen: Vandenhoeck & Ruprecht, 2003), 254–67; Ursula Büttner, 'Vereinigte Liberale und Deutsche Demokraten in Hamburg 1906–1930', in Ursula Büttner, *Hamburg zur Zeit der Weimarer Republik: Sechs Abhandlungen* (Hamburg: Landeszentrale für politische Bildung, 1996), 43–66; Andreas Wirsching, 'Zwischen Leistungsexpansion und Finanzkrise. Kommunale Selbstverwaltung in der Weimarer Republik', in Adolf M. Birke and Magnus Brechtken (eds), *Kommunale Selbstverwaltung: Local Self-Government. Geschichte und Gegenwart im deutsch-britischen Vergleich* (Munich: K. G.

Saur, 1996), 37–64; Dieter Langewiesche, 'Kommunaler Liberalismus im Kaiserreich: Bürgerdemokratie hinter den illiberalen Mauern der Daseinsvorsorge-Stadt', in Detlef Lehnert (ed.), *Kommunaler Liberalismus in Europa: Großstadtprofile um 1900* (Cologne: Böhlau, 2014), 39–71.

11. Hans Mommsen, 'The Decline of the Bürgertum in Late Nineteenth- and Early Twentieth-Century Germany', in Mommsen, *From Weimar to Auschwitz: Essays in German History*, tr. Philip O'Connor (Cambridge: Polity Press, 1991), 11–27; Konrad H. Jarausch, 'Die Krise des deutschen Bildungsbürgertums im ersten Drittel des 20. Jahrhunderts', in Jürgen Kocka (ed.), *Bildungsbürgertum im 19. Jahrhundert*, vol. 4. *Politischer Einfluss und gesellschaftliche Formation* (Stuttgart: Klett Cotta, 1989), 180–205.
12. Richard S. Katz and Peter Mair, 'Changing Models of Party Organization and Party Democracy', *Party Politics*, 1 (1995), 5–28.
13. Wolfgang Hardtwig, 'Grossstadt und Bürgerlichkeit in der politischen Ordnung des Kaiserreichs', in Hardtwig, *Politische Kultur in der Moderne: Ausgewählte Aufsätze* (Göttingen: Vandenhoeck & Ruprecht, 2011), 105–33.
14. For the historical tradition of this concept in Germany see Paul Nolte. 'Bürgerideal, Gemeinde und Republik: Klassischer Republikanismus im frühen deutschen Liberalismus', *Historische Zeitschrift*, 254 (1992), 609–56.
15. James J. Sheehan, *German Liberalism in the Nineteenth Century* (Chicago University of Chicago Press, 1978), 258–70; Ludwig Richter, 'Auseinanderstrebendes Zusammenhalten. Bassermann, Stresemann und die Nationalliberale Partei im letzten Jahrzehnt des Kaiserreichs', in Wolfram Pyta and Ludwig Richter (eds), *Gestaltungskraft des Politischen: Festschrift für Eberhard Kolb* (Berlin: Duncker & Humblot, 1998), 55–85.
16. Michael Schäfer, *Geschichte des Bürgertums: Eine Einführung* (Cologne: Böhlau, 2009), 195–6.
17. Moritz Föllmer, *Die Verteidigung der bürgerlichen Nation: Industrielle und hohe Beamte in Deutschland und Frankreich 1900–1930* (Göttingen: Vandenhoeck & Ruprecht 2002), 254–65; Wolfgang Hardtwig, 'Volksgemeinschaft im Übergang: Von der Demokratie zum rassistischen Führerstaat', in Detlef Lehnert (ed.), *Gemeinschaftsdenken in Europa: Das Gesellschaftskonzept Volksheim im Vergleich* (Cologne: Böhlau, 2013), 313–55.
18. Langewiesche, *Liberalism*, 291–5.
19. Larry Eugene Jones, *German Liberalism and the Dissolution of the Weimar Party System, 1918–1933* (Chapel Hill, NC: University of North Carolina Press, 1988), 314–15.
20. Ludwig Richter, *Die Deutsche Volkspartei 1918–1933* (Düsseldorf: Droste, 2002), 201–13.
21. Jones, *German Liberalism*, 301–2.
22. Eberhard Kolb and Ludwig Richter, 'Einleitung', in Kolb and Richter (eds), *Nationalliberalismus in der Weimarer Republik: Die Führungsgremien der Deutschen Volkspartei 1918–1933* (Düsseldorf: Droste Verlag, 1998), 30–42; Lothar Albertin, 'Einleitung: Deutsche Demokratie Partei/Deutsche Staatspartei', in Albertin (ed.), *Linksliberalismus in der Weimarer Republik: Die Führungsgremien der Deutschen Demokratischen Partei und der Deutschen Staatspartei 1918–1933* (Düsseldorf: Droste, 1980), xx–xliv.
23. Büttner, 'Deutsche Demokraten in Hamburg', 19–21.
24. Thomas Childers, 'Languages of Liberalism: Liberal Political Discourse in the Weimar Republic', in Konrad H. Jarausch and Larry Eugene Jones (eds), *In Search of Liberal Germany: Studies in the History of German Liberalism from 1789 to the Present* (New York: Berg, 1990), 323–59.

25. Jonathan Wright, *Gustav Stresemann: Weimar's Greatest Statesman* (Oxford: Oxford University Press, 2002), 171–6; Jones, *German Liberalism*, 15–43, 476–7.
26. Jones, *German Liberalism*, 55–7.
27. Gerald D. Feldman, *The Great Disorder: Politics, Economics, and Society in the German Inflation (1914–1924)* (New York and Oxford: Oxford University Press, 1997), 837–58.
28. Jones, *German Liberalism*, 208–22, 268; Richter, *Die Deutsche Volkspartei*, 323–33.
29. Werner Schneider, *Die Deutsche Demokratische Partei in der Weimarer Republik 1924–1930* (Munich: Wilhelm Fink, 1978), 253–60.
30. Richter, *Die Deutsche Volkspartei*, 662–91.
31. Julia Sneeringer, *Winning Women's Votes: Propaganda and Politics in Weimar Germany* (Chapel Hill, NC: University of North Carolina Press, 2002), 4–6, 23–30; Raffael Scheck, 'German Conservatism and Female Political Activism in the Early Weimar Republic', *German History*, 15 (1997), 34–55; Gabriele Bremme, *Die politische Rolle der Frau in Deutschland: Eine Untersuchung über den Einfluß der Frauen bei Wahlen und ihre Teilnahme in Partei und Parlament* (Göttingen: Vandenhoeck & Ruprecht, 1956), 34–5, 76.
32. Sneeringer, *Winning Women's Votes*, 30–7.
33. Angelika Schaser, 'Bürgerliche Frauen auf dem Weg in die linksliberalen Parteien (1918–1933)', *Historische Zeitschrift*, 263 (1996), 641–80.
34. Eric Kurlander, 'Liberal Women and National Socialism: (Dis)continuities in Conceptions of Race, Space, and Social Policy, 1930–1939', in Elke Seefried, Ernst Wolfgang Becker, Frank Bajohr, and Johannes Hürter (eds), *Liberalismus und Nationalsozialismus: Eine Beziehungsgeschichte* (Stuttgart: Franz Steiner, 2020), 133–57; Angelika Schaser, *Helene Lange und Gertrud Bäumer: Eine politische Lebensgemeinschaft*, 2nd ed. (Cologne: Böhlau, 2010), 286–300.
35. Theodor Heuss, 'Abschied und Aufbruch: Ansprache am Gründungsparteitag der Deutschen Staatspartei in Hannover', in Martin Voigt (ed.), *Theodor Heuss, Politiker und Publizist: Aufsätze und Reden* (Tübingen: Wunderlich, 1984), 204–5.
36. Langewiesche, *Liberalismus*, 216–22.
37. Claude Lefort, *Democracy and Political Theory* (Cambridge: Polity Press, 1988), 9–20; Jan Werner Müller, *Contesting Democracy: Political Ideas in Twentieth Century Europe* (New Haven: Yale University Press, 2011), 49–90.
38. Thomas Hertfelder, 'Meteor aus einer anderen Welt: Die Weimarer Republik in der Diskussion des Hilfe-Kreises', in Wirsching and Eder, *Vernunftrepublikanismus*, 29–55.
39. Anthony McElligott, *Rethinking the Weimar Republic: Authority and Authoritarianism 1916–1936* (London: Bloomsbury, 2014), 185–6; Thomas Raithel, *Das schwierige Spiel des Parlamentarismus: Deutscher Reichstag und französische Chambre des Députés in den Inflationskrisen der 1920er Jahre* (Munich: Oldenbourg, 2005), 289–97. Experts in the history of constitutional law discuss controversially to what extent the Enabling Law of 24 Mar. 1933 can be seen in continuity to the enabling laws in the early years of the republic, including that of 13 Oct. 1923. See among others: Christoph Gusy, *Die Weimarer Reichsverfassung* (Tübingen: Mohr Siebeck, 1997), 158–61; Michael Frehse, *Ermächtigungsgesetzgebung im Deutschen Reich 1914–1933* (Pfaffenweiler: Centaurus, 1985), 161–8. Yet, to understand the liberal approval of the 24 Mar. 1933 law, more important than a legal assessment from today's perspective is the fact that liberals did not perceive the law as a break in principle with the earlier use of enabling laws and the Constitution. See Wolfgang Becker, 'Linksliberalismus und Ermächtigungsgesetzgebung in der Weimarer Republik', *Jahrbuch zur Liberalismus-Forschung*, 28 (2016), 91–118.

40. Stefan Grüner, 'Zwischen Einheitssehnsucht und pluralistischer Massendemokratie. Zum Parteien- und Demokratieverständnis im deutschen und französischen Liberalismus der Zwischenkriegszeit', in Horst Möller and Manfred Kittel (eds), *Demokratie in Deutschland und Frankreich 1918–1933/40* (Berlin: De Gruyter, 2002), 219–49.
41. See the contributions of Jeppe Nevers, Elisabeth Dieterman, and Johann Rainio-Niemi in Tim B. Müller and Adam Tooze (eds), *Normalität und Fragilität: Demokratie nach dem Ersten Weltkrieg* (Hamburg: Hamburger Edition, 2015).
42. Grüner, 'Einheitssehnsucht', 232–3; Thomas Mergel, *Parlamentarische Kultur in der Weimarer Republik: Politische Kommunikation, symbolische Politik und Öffentlichkeit im Reichstag*, 3rd ed. (Düsseldorf: Droste, 2012), 466–9.
43. Eric Kurlander, 'Liberalism between Retreat and Accommodation', in Norbert Frei (ed.), *Wie bürgerlich war der Nationalsozialismus?* (Göttingen: Wallstein, 2018), 63–77; Schaser, *Helene Lange und Gertrud Bäumer*, 279–82.
44. See Wolfgang Streeck and Lane Kenworthy, 'Theories and Practices of Neocorporatism', in Thomas Janoski, Robert R. Alford, and Alexander M. Hicks (eds), *The Handbook of Political Sociology: States, Civil Society, and Globalization* (Cambridge, MA: Cambridge University Press, 2005), 441–60.
45. On the marginal position of contemporary economics see Roman Köster, *Die Wissenschaft der Außenseiter: Die Krise der Nationalökonomie in der Weimarer Republik* (Göttingen: Vandenhoeck & Ruprecht, 2011). On the discussion within business federations Philipp Müller, *Zeit der Unterhändler: Koordinierter Kapitalismus in Deutschland und Frankreich 1920–1950* (Hamburg: Hamburger Edition, 2019), 37–89.
46. Hermann Bücher, 'Betrachtungen über die neuen industriellen Organisationen der Wirtschaft', *Die Mitteldeutsche Industrie: Mitteilungsblatt des Verbandes Mitteldeutscher Industrieller*, 15 Apr. 1927; Paul Silverberg, 'Das industrielle Unternehmertum Deutschlands in der Nachkriegszeit', in Silverberg, *Reden und Schriften*, ed. Franz Mariaux (Cologne: Kölner Universitätsverlag, 1951), 49–73.
47. Roman Köster, 'Die Kartell- und Monopoldebatte der Nationalökonomie während der Weimarer Republik', in Peter Collin (ed.), *Treffräume juristischer und ökonomischer Regulierungsrationalitäten* (Frankfurt/Main: Vittorio Klostermann, 2014), 211–33.
48. Ralf Ptak, *Vom Ordoliberalismus zur Sozialen Marktwirtschaft: Stationen des Neoliberalismus in Deutschland* (Opladen: Leske + Budrich, 2004), 33–44.
49. Walter Eucken, 'Staatliche Strukturwandlungen und die Krisis des Kapitalismus', *Weltwirtschaftliches Archiv*, 36 (1932), 297–321; Alexander Rüstow, 'Interessenpolitik oder Staatspolitik?', *Der Deutsche Volkswirt*, 7 (1932), 169–72.
50. Kathrin Meier-Rust, *Alexander Rüstow: Geschichtsdeutung und liberales Engagement* (Stuttgart: Klett-Cotta, 1993), 49–50; Ptak, *Ordoliberalismus*, 41–2.
51. Serge Audier, *Le Colloque Walter Lippmann: Aux origines du 'néo-libéralisme'* (Lormont: Le bord de l'eau, 2012).
52. Eric Hobsbawm, *The Age of Extremes: The Short Twentieth Century 1914–1991* (London: Abacus, 1994), 109–41; for an analysis of different anti-liberal arguments in general see Stephen Holmes, *The Anatomy of Antiliberalism* (Cambridge, MA, and London: Harvard University Press, 1993).
53. Michael Bentley, 'The Liberal Party, 1900–1939: Summit and Descent', in Chris Wrigley (ed.), *A Companion to Early Twentieth-Century Britain* (Malden, MA: Blackwell 2003), 23–37; Michael Freeden, *Liberalism Divided: A Study in British Political Thought 1914–1939* (Oxford: Clarendon Press, 1986).

54. Nicolas Rousselier, 'Le Monde d'après-guerre: La Démocratie libérale triomphante ou dépassée?', in Serge Berstein (ed.), *La Démocratie libérale* (Paris: Presses universitaires de France, 2000), 527–90; Klaus-Peter Sick, 'Vom Opportunisme zum Liberalisme autoritaire: Die Krise des französischen Liberalismus im demokratisierten Parlamentarismus 1885–1940', *Geschichte und Gesellschaft*, 29 (2003), 66–104.
55. Auguste Detoeuf, 'La Fin du libéralisme, Conférence 1er mai 1936', in *De la recurrence des crises économique: Son cinquantenaire 1931–1981* (Paris: Economica, 1982), 71–87, here 71.
56. Mark Mazower, *Dark Continent: Europe's Twentieth Century* (London and New York: Allen Lane, 1998), 51–63.
57. Quinn Slobodian, *Globalists: The End of Empire and the Birth of Neoliberalism* (Cambridge, MA: Harvard University Press, 2018), 27–54; Robert Boyce, *The Great Interwar Crisis and the Collapse of Globalization* (Basingstoke and New York: Palgrave Macmillan, 2009), 17–22.
58. Wolfgang Hardtwig, *Freiheitliches Bürgertum in Deutschland: Der Weimarer Demokrat Eduard Hamm zwischen Kaiserreich und Widerstand* (Stuttgart: Franz Steiner, 2018), 238–41; Martti Koskenniemi, *The Gentle Civilizer of Nations: The Rise and Fall of International Law 1870–1960* (Cambridge: Cambridge University Press, 2001), 221–2.
59. Wright, *Stresemann*, 378–80.
60. Mark Mazower, *No Enchanted Palace: The End of Empire and the Ideological Origins of the United Nations* (Princeton: Princeton University Press, 2009), 28–65.
61. Mazower, *Dark Continent*, 55; Arnulf Becker Lorca, *Mestizo International Law: A Global Intellectual History 1842–1933* (Cambridge: Cambridge University Press, 2014), 182, 197–9.
62. Adam Tooze, *The Deluge: The Great War and the Remaking of Global Order* (London and New York: Penguin, 2014), 458–9.
63. See the report of the industrialist and member of the liberal German Democratic Party Friedrich von Siemens to the Ministry of Foreign Affairs in 'Aufzeichnung des Ministerialrats Feßler (Reichskanzlei) vom 3. Juni 1927', in *Akten zur Deutschen Auswärtigen Politik 1918–1945. Serie B: 1925–1933*, vol. 5, ed. Hans Rothfels (Göttingen: Vandenhoeck & Ruprecht, 1972), 451.
64. Louis Loucheur, 'La conférence économique de Genève', *Revue économique internationale*, 19 (1927), 36–43; Dominique Barjot, 'Les cartels, une voie vers l'intégration européenne? Le rôle de Louis Loucheur (1872–1931)', *Revue Economique*, 64 (2013), 1043–66; Wolfram Kaiser, 'Gesellschaftliche Akteure und Experten in internationalen Organisationen: Die Kartell-Debatte im Völkerbund 1925–1931', in Michaela Bachem-Rehm, Claudia Hiepel, and Henning Türk (eds), *Teilungen überwinden: Europäische und internationale Geschichte im 19. und 20. Jahrhundert* (Munich: Oldenbourg, 2014), 317–28.
65. Madeleine Herren, 'Fascist Internationalism', in Glenda Sluga and Patricia Clavin (eds), *Internationalisms: A Twentieth-Century History* (Cambridge: Cambridge University Press, 2017), 191–212; Philipp Müller, 'Transformation des Liberalismus: Die Internationale Handelskammer im NS-Regime während der 1930er Jahre', in Elke Seefried and Ernst Wolfgang Becker (eds), *Liberalismus und Nationalsozialismus* (Stuttgart: Franz Steiner, 2020), 253–78.

Bibliography

Boyce, Robert, *The Great Interwar Crisis and the Collapse of Globalization* (Basingstoke und New York: Palgrave Macmillan, 2009).

Childers, Thomas, 'Languages of Liberalism: Liberal Political Discourse in the Weimar Republic', in Konrad H. Jarausch and Larry Eugene Jones (eds), *In Search of Liberal Germany: Studies in the History of German Liberalism from 1789 to the Present* (New York: Berg, 1990), 323–59.

Freeden, Michael, and Marc Stears, 'Liberalism', in Michael Freeden, Lyman Tower Sargent and Marc Stears (eds), *The Oxford Handbook of Political Ideologies* (Oxford: Oxford University Press, 2013), 329–47.

Jones, Larry Eugene, *German Liberalism and the Dissolution of the Weimar Party System, 1918–1933* (Chapel Hill, NC, and London: University of North Carolina Press, 1988).

Kurlander, Eric, *Living with Hitler: Liberal Democrats in the Third Reich* (New Haven and London: Yale University Press, 2009).

Langewiesche, Dieter, *Liberalism in Germany*, tr. Christiane Banerji (Basingstoke: Macmillan, 2000).

Ptak, Ralf, *Vom Ordoliberalismus zur Sozialen Marktwirtschaft: Stationen des Neoliberalismus in Deutschland* (Opladen: Leske + Budrich, 2004).

Richter, Ludwig, *Die Deutsche Volkspartei 1918–1933* (Düsseldorf: Droste, 2002).

Sneeringer, Julia, *Winning Women's Votes: Propaganda and Politics in Weimar Germany* (Chapel Hill, NC, and London: University of North Carolina Press, 2002).

Wright, Jonathan, *Gustav Stresemann: Weimar's Greatest Statesman* (Oxford: Oxford University Press, 2002).

CHAPTER 15

SOCIAL DEMOCRATS AND COMMUNISTS IN WEIMAR GERMANY

A Divided Working-Class Movement

JOACHIM C. HÄBERLEN

THE Weimar Republic was the working-class movement's biggest accomplishment; and yet it was also an immense disappointment for many in the working-class movement. When the revolutionary wave spread throughout Germany in November 1918, leading Social Democrats, deeply worried about the prospect of a Bolshevik-style revolution in Germany, tried to put themselves ahead of the revolutionary movement, leading and containing it at the same time. The outcome of the revolution, the republic with its democratic, parliamentary system, equal voting rights for men and women, and the social welfare state, was in many ways a realization of old social democratic demands. Weimar was *their* political project, *their* state. Indeed, Social Democrats were the most committed defenders of the republic. They sought to establish an administration and police force dedicated to the republic, shaped local welfare administrations, worked hard to create a republican culture that would help instil a genuine sense of republicanism beyond merely strategic support, and vigorously fought enemies of the republic both left and right. From the very beginning to the very end, the history of Weimar is thus inextricably tied to the history of the working-class movement.

Yet the working-class movement was more than Social Democracy, and not everyone within the working-class movement, nor even within the Social Democratic Party (Sozialdemokratische Partei Deutschlands, SPD), was happy with the outcome of the revolution. For radical workers, left-leaning Social Democrats, and Communists alike, the revolution had not gone far enough. They had demanded a stronger role for the workers' and soldiers' councils, a more thorough disempowerment of the old elites (e.g. land reforms), and a socialization at least of key industries such as mining. As this did not happen, they felt that Social Democrats had betrayed the revolution. The lasting result was a deeply divided working-class movement that turned into a permanent source of conflict during the Weimar Republic. When the dust of the revolutionary upheaval settled, the Communist Party (Kommunistische Partei Deutschlands, KPD) had emerged as a competitor of Social Democracy on the left that appealed to a significant part of the working classes. For Communists, the republic was nothing but a bourgeois, capitalist state that had to be overthrown in a revolutionary upheaval, and Social Democracy turned out to be one of the main enemies in this revolutionary struggle, as it had betrayed the revolutionary ambitions of the working-class movement. The history of the working-class movement in Weimar thus has to discuss the two major factions, SPD and KPD, and the conflicts between them.

The Working-Class Movement and the Foundation of Weimar

Since its foundation, the call for unity had been a central pillar of the socialist working-class movement. Whatever internal differences existed, only by speaking with one voice and acting unanimously could the movement prevail in its struggles. At the outbreak of the First World War, the party debated whether to support the war and to approve war credits.[1] Arguing that Germany was fighting a defensive war against Tsarist autocracy, the majority was in favour of supporting the war. Adhering to the ideal of unity, even those who disagreed then voted to approve the credits. Yet as the war dragged on, critical voices within the SPD, such as those of Karl Liebknecht and Rosa Luxemburg, became louder. By 1917, the minority within the SPD who disagreed with party's support of the war split away and formed the Independent Social Democratic Party (USPD, Unabhängige Sozialdemokratische Partei Deutschlands). The new party quickly gained ground. After only a few months, it had 120,000 members, compared to 243,000 of the old 'Majority' SPD. In some districts such as Leipzig, the heartland of old Social Democracy, and Greater Berlin, a majority of party members defected to the Independents.[2] On the shop-floor level, workers dissatisfied with the mainstream trade unions and their support of the war found a movement known as Revolutionary Shop Stewards (Revolutionäre Obleute), a tiny though highly effective group that organized strikes with explicitly political demands, calling for peace without annexations. Many of these workers sympathized with the Independent Social Democrats.

While Social Democracy split over the question of war credits, a second cause for division appeared on the horizon that proved even more lasting: the Russian Revolution. Social Democrats initially welcomed the February Revolution that brought an end to the Tsar's autocratic reign. Yet, when the Bolsheviks took over and the country descended into a bloody civil war, moderate Social Democrats were horrified. Avoiding a similar chaos and bloodshed became their central objective.[3] For more radical socialists, however, the Bolshevik revolution was a promise. It proved that a radical break with capitalism was possible, and that an entirely new society could be built.

These internal fractures meant that, when the revolution began to spread from Kiel in early November 1918, the working-class movement was deeply divided.[4] The 'old' SPD could still rely on a dense organizational web, including loyal party newspapers, but they faced an increasingly radicalizing opposition. What course the revolution would take, how radically Germany would be transformed both politically and economically, thus became an open and deeply contested question during the revolution. While the Russian Revolution loomed as a threatening or promising example on the horizon, two more specific issues were at the heart of debate: politically, the role that councils should play, and, economically, if there should be any socializations of key industries.

For the leadership of both social democratic parties, the revolution came as a surprise.[5] They had not organized it, and they were certainly not in control of the revolutionary wave that rapidly spread throughout Germany in early November 1918. Inspired by the Russian example, workers and soldiers formed councils across the country. While the council movement seemed to exemplify the revolutionary spirit of the German working-class movement, the reality was that, in many places, councils not only challenged old authorities, but also collaborated with them, especially on an administrative level, to ensure that food provision would not collapse.[6] The immediate challenge for the social democratic party leadership was to gain control of this movement and the emerging revolutionary authorities. And rather quickly, social democrats succeeded with this task. Though on paper they often shared power with Independent Social Democrats, Majority Social Democrats under the leadership of Friedrich Ebert quickly gained control over the developments. At crucial moments, representatives of the Majority Social Democrats could win votes, they could rely on an organizational web that was still functioning, and they could build on the relationships with old authorities, not least in the military, that had developed during the war. Social Democracy, that is, had not started the revolutionary train, but soon enough it was in charge of it. The question was, then, what would happen to the councils in the new German state.

Drawing on the demands of pre-war social democracy, party leaders such as Ebert were above all interested in electoral reforms that would make Germany, and particularly the state of Prussia, a genuinely democratic country, though not necessarily a republic. Ebert was not even keen on putting an end to the monarchy itself. Yet, when Ebert's colleague Philipp Scheidemann announced the end of the monarchy and the foundation of a republic on 9 November 1918, much to Ebert's dismay, it was clear that a return to a monarchical order was out of question.[7]

Social Democrats thus called for a constitutional assembly—called National Assembly—based on equal voting rights for all German men and women above the age of 20, to debate a new constitution. Their ultimate aim was a form of parliamentary democracy. Councils, by contrast, had played no role in pre-war debates within Social Democracy, and thus were not part of the picture they had in mind.[8] They might have played an important role in the revolution itself, but once the revolution was over, they had basically fulfilled their purposes and their power had to be limited. If at all, factory councils (*Betriebsräte*, not to be confused with the workers' councils radicals had in mind) might play some role in representing workers' interests vis-à-vis employers and defending their rights on the shop floor, but they should not have any political authority. Independent Social Democrats and other radicals, by contrast, argued for the continuing existence of councils formed by workers on a factory basis. Councils should form a pillar of authority in the new state that would provide the working-class movement with an uncontested power base to ensure Germany's transformation into a socialist state. In the end, the outcome of the election for the National Assembly on 19 January 1919, where Majority Social Democrats held 165 seats (of 423), opposed to only 22 Independent Social Democrats, meant that councils did not play any significant role in the new constitution.[9]

A second major issue concerned the socialization of heavy industries such as mining, an old demand by social democracy and something that was, of course, just happening in the Soviet Union. When the revolution spread in early November 1918, capital owners were terrified that they might lose their property. Surprisingly quickly, the leadership of business organizations entered negotiations with trade unions. By mid-November, they had reached an agreement to collaborate in a Zentralarbeitsgemeinschaft (Central Association of Employers and Employees), popularly known as the Stinnes-Legien-Pact, named after the leading industrialist Hugo Stinnes and trade unionist Carl Legien.[10] The agreement granted trade unions rights they had demanded for a long time. Employers accepted unions as collective bargaining partners and agreed to the eight-hour-working day, a long-time demand of the working-class movement, even though a secret chapter of the agreement made this conditional on other industrial nations similarly introducing the eight-hour-working day to prevent Germany from becoming uncompetitive. For both employers and unions, such an agreement was a means to prevent a radicalization of the revolution akin to what has happening in Russia. Unions celebrated the agreement as a 'victory of rare greatness', or, as Legien put it, a 'Magna Charta of German workers'.[11] The left, however, felt disappointed and betrayed. Independent Social Democrat Robert Dißmann, a leading voice of the opposition within trade unions, declared: 'The German working-class cannot sell its right of first birth (*Erstgeburtsrecht*) for the lentil dish (*Linsengericht*) of a capitalist working committee.'[12] Victory or defeat, the agreement was a first indication that large-scale expropriations would not take place.

Yet the question of socialization was far from settled. Independent Social Democrats demanded that coalmines and the steel industry be taken out of the hands of big industrialists. From the perspective of radical socialists, the socialization of key industries was not only a step towards building a socialist economic order, but also politically important as a way to curb the influence of the mostly right-wing industrialists. Yet again, such plans for more radical changes led nowhere. Radical workers not only faced the resistance of old elites, which was to be expected, but also that of trade unions and majority Social Democrats. They worried that potentially chaotic economic experiments would result in a further reduction of coal production, which was already running comparatively low due to sheer physical exhaustion during the war. The German economy and households, they argued, desperately needed coal. Any work stoppages, strikes, or reductions of the working day, as miners demanded, would thus put other workers in jeopardy. Furthermore, if mines were nationalized and no longer privately owned, the Allies might consider them public assets that could be confiscated as part of reparations. Keeping them in private hands was thus a means of shielding mines against Allied claims. On this front, too, radicals lost the argument. No mines and factories were nationalized or put into the hands of workers.[13]

Moderate social democrats and trade unionists could thus claim significant accomplishments: the democratization of German politics, the recognition of unions, and the acceptance of the eight-hour-working day. Under such conditions, Germany might gradually be transformed into a socialist society. For radicals who had longed for a more thorough transformation of both German state and society, however, these outcomes were deeply disappointing. Realizing that hopes for a fundamental revolution that would sweep away the old order were about to be disappointed, radicals took action. In January 1919, the newly founded Communist Party that had emerged out of a group known as Spartacists, led by Liebknecht and Luxemburg, used a protest against the dismissal of Berlin's police chief Emil Eichhorn, a member of the USPD, that had turned violent to call for a general strike to overthrow the moderate government. Making use of right-wing Freikorps, the government put a bloody end to the ill-fated attempted rebellion. Shortly thereafter, Luxemburg and Liebknecht were murdered in Berlin.

Yet, it was not the young KPD that benefited most from disappointed hopes amongst social democrats, but the USPD, whose membership swell to 300,000 by mid-1919, and to 750,000 by the end of the year.[14] When the elections for the National Assembly were held on 19 January 1919, Majority Social Democrats won nearly 38 per cent of the national vote, which made them by far the strongest party, whereas Independent Social Democrats received only 7.6 per cent of the vote. The party leadership around Ebert, these numbers indicate, still enjoyed the support of broad parts of the working-class movement. On 6 June 1920, when the first regular national elections were held, this had changed dramatically. Majority Social Democrats' share of the vote dropped nearly by half to 21.6 per cent, while Independent Social Democrats scored 17.9 per cent (and the nascent Communists 2.1 per cent), a result testifying to the disappointment with social democracy amongst many left-leaning workers. In the heartlands of German industry, such as Berlin (43 per cent), Thuringia (31 per cent), and Saxony (25 per cent), Independent Social Democrats were even stronger than Majority Social Democrats.[15] However, the USPD, a party that had formed around opposition to the war, was also internally divided. Whereas some favoured supporting the emerging republican order, others argued for a proletarian dictatorship and joining the Communist International. By mid-1920, the majority of its cadres opted for the latter option and united with the KPD. Independent Social Democracy, it turned out, did not offer a third way between the moderate reformism of the SPD and the Bolshevism of the KPD.[16] Having become a mass party, the KPD engaged in more armed uprisings, for example in central Germany in March 1921 and in Hamburg in October 1923, that were all put down with force.[17]

Communists were not the only ones disappointed about the moderate course the revolution was taking. Indeed, limiting the perspective to organized political parties would underestimate the complexity of the working-class movement during the tumultuous early years of Weimar. Particularly in the Ruhr area, where traditional trade unions were weak, workers turned to direct action to push for their demands. These workers were more concerned with immediate improvements of their situation, with higher wages and shorter working hours, than with political changes. During numerous strikes, these radicalized workers not only occupied management offices and mines, but also plundered potato storages or the villas of company directors, searching for ham, bacon, and wine cellars. Workers also revolted against workplace hierarchies, on the shop floor as much as in mines.[18] They prevented management and foremen from entering the premises of factories and 'socialized' production sites without any official plan. Usually, the social democratic government reacted by sending troops that put a violent end to many of these uprisings.

As the period of revolutionary uprisings came to an end at the beginning of 1924, the working-class movement was and remained deeply divided, even though the ideal of a unified working-class movement lived on. While the USPD had disbanded, the KPD had established itself as a serious competitor for Social Democracy on the left. Communists blamed Social Democrats for having betrayed the revolution, not least by making use of the much hated and strictly anti-republican Freikorps to put down various armed uprisings by Communists and other leftists. Social Democrats, on the other hand, were terrified by the prospects of a Bolshevik-style revolution in Germany and the chaos and violence this would mean.

BUILDING A SOCIAL REPUBLIC: SOCIAL DEMOCRACY IN WEIMAR GERMANY

'Social Democracy, in the old state an oppositional party, a party of opposition against the state and thus lacking a warm relationship with the idea of the state as such, had to be transformed into a state party after the war, into a responsible pillar of the state which is its [i.e. Social Democracy's] state', wrote Social Democrat and former minister of justice Gustav Radbruch in an obituary for Friedrich Ebert in 1925.[19] Radbruch's observation highlights the deep, and not always easy, transformation Social Democracy underwent in becoming a central pillar for the republic. Legal thinking within the SPD exemplifies this transformation. Scholars such as Hermann Heller, Eduard Bernstein, and later Ernst Fraenkel developed an increasingly 'pluralistic theory of the state and democracy' that combined 'liberal and socialist traditions'.[20] Social Democrats were committed to the new state, and tried to foster a sense of loyalty towards it amongst the population. They worked for and within the state to strengthen it, and to shape it in a social democratic way that would improve the situation of the working class. In very practical ways, Social Democrats made Weimar their state. It offered them a framework in which they could pursue their goals.[21]

Given their fundamentally positive attitude towards the democratic state, Social Democrats—in contrast to Communists—concentrated on winning elections and thus being able to take responsibility in government. After the end of the revolutionary period, the party's results stabilized around 22 per cent and gradually increased to 29.8 per cent in the May 1928 election, only to drop again during the Great Depression to 24.5 per cent in September 1930 and finally 20.4 per cent in the last genuinely free election of November 1932. But despite these losses, Social Democracy continued to be the strongest party in Weimar until the July 1932 elections, when National Socialists overtook them by a large margin (37.4 per cent for the NSDAP, 21.6 per cent for the SPD).[22]

After the first electoral defeat in 1920, Social Democrats, who had been in charge of government immediately after the revolution, withdrew from government—only to return as part of a coalition less than a year later (without a new election having taken place). Until October 1923, Social Democrats participated in various governments, then formed the major opposition party during the years of stability (1924–8). The success in the May 1928 elections allowed Social Democrats to form a government under Chancellor Hermann Müller that lasted until 1930—the longest in the history of Weimar. When Social Democrats lost in the elections of 1930, their time in government had ended.[23]

To gain a sense of Social Democrats' strength, a look below the national level is useful. In Saxony, heartland of German Social Democracy, results fell only in 1920 below 30 per cent, to rise to nearly 42 per cent two years later and then remain stable around 33 per cent. In Prussia, by far the largest of the German states, Social Democrats were consistently the strongest party until the April 1932 elections that saw National Socialists surpass them.[24] Here, Social Democrats controlled, in various coalitions, the government, in particular through their long-term Minister President Otto Braun and his Interior Minister Carl Severing (1920–6, 1930–2; replaced by his comrade Albert Grzesinski from 1926 to 1930). Severing in particular sought to use his powers to build a viable republic capable of defending itself.[25] In the wake of the 1920 Kapp putsch for example, Severing had anti-republican senior civil servants replaced by pro-republicans.[26] Similarly, the Prussian police forces saw a change of leadership to ensure their loyalty to the republic. By 1928, fifteen out of Prussia's thirty police presidents were card-carrying Social Democrats. The rank and file of the police forces, however, remained more hostile to the republic, despite efforts to instil a sense of republicanism amongst them by political education and celebrating the republic.[27]

Social Democrats' positive attitude towards the republican order put the party in a difficult place vis-à-vis its socialist traditions. For some party members, democracy was not enough; they insisted that socialism had to be the final goal. Programmatically, the party tried to become attractive to voters beyond its traditional working-class base. The Görlitz party programme of 1921 described the SPD as the 'party of the labouring people in town and countryside'. Four years later, however, the Heidelberg programme confirmed the party's commitment to Marxist ideology. Returning to a rhetoric of class struggle and overcoming capitalism, the programme described the SPD solely as the party of the working class, and had little to say about clerical workers or farmers. The programmatic attempt to broaden the appeal of Social Democracy to the middle classes had ended. Yet such rhetoric does not mean that Social Democrats turned against the republican order.[28]

Indeed, Social Democracy's social basis broadened beyond its working-class constituency. While it remained predominantly a working-class party, it attracted an increasing number of white-collar workers, civil servants, and the self-employed. In 1930, about 19 per cent of the party's members belonged to these groups (and another 22 per cent were housewives or jobless, though they might well have been part of a proletarian milieu). In particular, in large cities such as Berlin and Hamburg, numerous civil servants were SPD members. This might well have been the result of the party's conscious efforts to democratize the civil service by promoting Social Democrats. The large number of such employees in the SPD in turn might reflect that children of skilled workers, who were the core base of the old SPD, climbed the social ladder by becoming office workers, yet remained attached to the values of their parents' generation.[29] The SPD's voter base was even more socially diverse. While the SPD remained the party of the Protestant urban proletariat, some estimates suggest that by 1930, up to 40 per cent of SPD voters had a middle-class background.[30] In the July 1932 elections, for example, only 22 per cent of eligible blue-collar workers actually voted for the SPD (compared to 23 per cent who voted for the KPD), but 24 per cent of white-collar workers (and 6 per cent for the KPD).[31] Some historians have taken these developments as evidence for the SPD becoming a genuine 'people's party', or *Volkspartei*, that moved beyond its working-class character.[32] Yet neither the support for the republic nor the appeal to a broader constituency meant that the SPD was no longer a party of the working-class movement. It remained tied to the organizations of that movement, notably the trade unions and various socialist associations, and it continued to employ the symbolic language and political iconography, such as red flags, of the old working-class movement.

Politically, Social Democrats' primary concern remained the plight of the working classes. In practical terms, Social Democrats' 'socialism' meant that they tried to curb the detrimental impact of capitalist markets by expanding the welfare state. Social Democrats took an active and crucial role in shaping this welfare state, not least at the municipal level. Before the war, private and religious charity organizations had mostly been in control of local social welfare. As Social Democrats took power in German cities, they tried, often successfully, to develop local welfare programmes under the umbrella of the state. On all levels, Social Democrats were active. In the city of Hamburg, for example, Social Democrats were in charge of the local Welfare Department (Paul Hoffmann, 1919–25, Paul Neumann, 1925–33). Working for the social welfare state also offered rank-and-file Social Democrats opportunities to participate in the state. In Hamburg, for example, 1,463 out of the 2,221 volunteers who effectively ran the welfare administration on the lowest level were members of the social democratic welfare organization Arbeiterwohlfahrt.[33] In Leipzig, to give another example, the parties represented in the municipal council had the right to nominate welfare caseworkers (*Wohlfahrtspfleger*) in accordance with their relative strength. This allowed Social Democrats to nominate roughly 1,000 (out of a total of 2,252) volunteers. Tellingly,

Social Democrats had no problem finding enough volunteers for the job, whereas conservative parties struggled.[34] Indeed, the Communist Party faced similar difficulties, much to the dismay of the party leadership, as many Communists considered such dull bureaucratic tasks a waste of their time.[35] The effect of this participation in local welfare administration was that the republic not only enjoyed the political support of Social Democracy, but that rank-and-file party members took an active role in it. It was here, within the framework of the state, where Social Democrats could do something to practically support workers.

As important as working within the state was for Social Democrats, they also realized the need to foster a sense of republican dedication amongst the populace. Leading Social Democrats embraced the symbolic culture of the republic, its flag, and its national anthem, and thus placed themselves into the traditions of democratic struggles in Germany. The most important organization in this regard was the Reichsbanner Schwarz Rot Gold.[36] At its foundation in spring 1924, the Reichsbanner was formed as a cross-party organization that would unite First World War veterans in support of the republic, including Social Democrats, liberals of the German Democratic Party, and the Catholic Centre Party. In practice, however, it turned out to be a predominantly social democratic organization. And it proved to be a highly successful in organizing veterans. Though the Reichsbanner never published reliable membership numbers, estimates suggest that it could muster nearly a million members by 1928, surpassing the membership of right-wing veterans' organizations by a significant margin.[37]

Yet, as much as the Reichsbanner was an organizational success story, it also provides an example for the limitations of Social Democrats' efforts to build a republican identity that affected not only the Reichsbanner, but the party as a whole. The first issue concerns the role of women in the Reichsbanner and social democracy at large. Like all other fighting leagues, the Reichsbanner was an exclusively male organization. Women played only a marginal role, which made it effectively difficult for women to participate in the organization's pro-republican culture.[38] Women, of course, played a role in the party. Yet, Social Democrats mostly relegated them to the reproductive sphere and related political issues such as social policies, population and health politics, or youth and welfare issues. Other political fields, not least the struggle for the republican order, by contrast, remained a male domain.[39]

Second, the Reichsbanner never was the cross-party organization it claimed to be. In particular towards the end of the republic, the Reichsbanner played an increasing role in supporting Social Democratic election campaigns. Despite efforts to separate party and Reichsbanner, members were keen to link their activism for both organizations.[40] While being firmly integrated into the political fabric in Weimar Germany, not least through various coalitions, the social democratic milieu remained largely separated from liberal supporters of the republic. Socialist milieu organizations contributed further to this separation. To avoid persecution under the Anti-Socialist Laws of Imperial Germany, Social Democrats had formed a great variety of leisure-time organizations in which workers could socialize around seemingly apolitical issues. Singing or practising gymnastics together, workers would learn the practical values of solidarity. During Weimar, these milieu organizations expanded. Not only could social democratic workers do sports in one of the many clubs associated with the Arbeiter Turn- und Sportbund (Workers' Gymnastics and Sports League), but they could also shop in social democratic consumer co-operatives, their children would join socialist youth organizations, and they could have a socialist funeral if they had left the Church. Yet, while these organizations helped integrate workers into a social democratic milieu, they also kept this milieu separate from middle-class associational life, thus contributing to the social fragmentation of Weimar society. Finally, the emphasis on sociability sometimes had depoliticizing effects, as workers cared more about their associational life than about political struggles.[41]

Social Democracy, to sum up, became a key pillar of the republican state, both in terms of governing this state and its ideological support. For social democrats, building a democratic political system and a welfare state had been a tremendous achievement that they sought to defend against attacks from all sides: politically, against threats from both the radical left and the radical left, socially against big business that sought to dismantle the welfare state. At the same time, the political and social system of the republic allowed social democrats to work for both their long-term goal, a vaguely defined socialism that would gradually emerge, and their more immediate goals of improving workers' lives. In that sense, Weimar was a great opportunity for social democrats.

A REVOLUTIONARY PARTY IN NON-REVOLUTIONARY TIMES: COMMUNISM IN WEIMAR GERMANY

Whereas Social Democracy supported the republic, its main competitor on the left, the Communist Party, remained hostile to the new state. Communists had hoped that Germany would follow the example of the Russian Revolution, and blamed Social Democrats as traitors of the working class when this did not happen.[42] As it became clear by 1924 that a revolution was not imminent, Communists faced a difficult situation: they were a party dedicated to revolution in non-revolutionary times. In this situation, Communists pursued a two-sided and contradictory strategy. On the one hand, they tried to build an avant-garde party of disciplined cadres, ready to act when the moment of revolution would arrive. On the other hand, they appealed to the masses and tried to take root in local working-class milieus. Not least, this meant participating in elections and hence in the political system of Weimar they so deeply despised.

In contrast to Social Democrats, for whom winning elections was crucial as a way of gaining power within the state, Communists did not believe in the institutions of parliamentary democracy. From their perspective, election results had a mostly symbolic meaning. They provided the party with a sense of its strength and appeal amongst the populace. Indeed, they had refused to participate in the January 1919 election for the National Assembly altogether. When they decided to participate in the first national election of 1920, they scored only 2.1 per cent. While this might be read as impressive evidence for a lack of radicalism amongst German workers, this would ignore those radicalized workers voting for Independent Social Democrats. Indeed, the KPD only became a significant force after it united with the larger part of the USPD. In May 1924, in the midst of the inflationary crisis, the united party received 12.6 per cent of the vote, though this fell to 9.0 per cent in December that same year after the inflation crisis had come to an end. In the years that followed, the party's share continuously increased, reaching 16.9 per cent in the November 1932 elections. Communists could claim to be on the road to success.

Not surprisingly, major industrial centres were the party's strongholds. In the Prussian state elections, their share increased from 7.4 per cent in February 1921, at a moment when they were still competing with Independent Social Democrats, to 12.8 per cent in April 1932 (and, stunningly, even better, 13.2 per cent, in March 1933 after the Nazis' seizure of power). In Saxony, another industrial heartland of Germany, their share increased from 5.7 per cent in November 1920 to 13.6 per cent in June 1930, with a peak of 14.5 per cent in 1926 (and 16.5 per cent in March 1933). In local elections in Berlin, the KPD even came close to the SPD in the November 1929 election (the last before the Nazis' takeover), accomplishing 24.6 per cent as opposed to 28.4 per cent for the SPD. Unlike Social Democrats, Communists almost never participated in any government, with the notable exception of a short-lived coalition with left-leaning Social Democrats in Saxony in 1923. Yet, this brief experiment of working-class unity was soon ended by an intervention of the national government under Social Democrat Friedrich Ebert.[43]

For a long time, the Communist Party had the reputation of attracting particularly low-skilled, unemployed, and young workers who were not brought up in the traditions of socialism.[44] Even Communists themselves nourished this picture, at times describing the split of the working-class movement in family terms: whereas the father remained faithful to Social Democracy, the young and radical son turned to the KPD.[45] Yet, such images were part of a propaganda that depicted the Communist Party as more youthful, more radical, and more willing to break with the past than the SPD which was blamed for representing the 'aristocracy' of workers. In reality, the composition of the KPD was much more complex and fluid. After a majority of Independent Social Democrats had made the KPD a mass party, the stabilization of the political and economic situation resulted in a drop in membership: by April 1924, the party had only 121,394 members. The figure remained roughly the same until the second half of 1929, when the party counted 124,511 members. Only then, during the Great Depression, did the KPD see a massive influx of new members, so that it counted, by the end of 1932, 360,000 enrolled members, amongst them 252,000 dues paying. Yet, such numbers conceal a massive fluctuation: particularly during the final years of crisis, many people joined the KPD only briefly, and quickly left after their initial enthusiasm ebbed. This fluidity not withstanding, there was a stable core of party activists, some of whom had previously been SPD members.[46]

On average, the KPD was indeed younger and socially more homogeneously proletarian than the SPD. According to data from 1927, nearly 80 per cent of the party's membership were workers, and close to 70 per cent industrial workers, the majority of them skilled workers. Unlike the SPD, whose membership included a significant minority of civil servants, clerical workers, and self-employed professionals, these groups did not play a major role in the KPD. Nevertheless, in absolute terms, the SPD organized three times as many workers as the total KPD membership. While it is true that the share of unskilled workers was higher in the KPD than in the SPD, claiming that the political division of the working-class movement mirrored a social division would overestimate the difference. It would be equally misleading to present the KPD as a party of the unemployed, and the SPD as a party of employed workers. Only during the Great Depression, when employers used the situation to lay off communist workers, did the party membership become predominantly unemployed. By the end of 1932, only 33,000 of its due-paying members were employed in factories. Yet, given the massive unemployment in Germany in those years, such numbers are not surprising. Indeed, Social Democrats faced a similar problem.[47]

The same is true with regards to age. The KPD's membership was, on average, slightly younger than the SPD's, something that had, in fact, already distinguished the USPD from Majority Social Democracy. In both parties, the group of young (age 18–25) members was smaller than those of 50 years or older (by a small margin in the KPD: 12.3 per cent young, 13.6 per cent old; by a larger margin in the SPD 7.7 per cent young, 26.9 per cent old), and in both parties, members between the age of 30 and 40 predominated (KPD: 32.7 per cent, SPD: 25.2 per cent). Finally, the KPD was a predominantly male party, even though it made the most radical claims with regards to women's emancipation. By August 1929, 16.5 per cent of the party members were women—some two-thirds of those the wives of communist husbands, which speaks to the milieu structures that evolved around the Communist Party.[48]

In the absence of a revolutionary situation, Communists prepared for such a moment to arrive. Above all, this meant forming a party of disciplined cadres dutifully working for the final goal of communism. According to Communists, it had been the organizational weakness of the Second Socialist International that had resulted in its failure to prevent the First World War.[49] Hence, the new Communist International, founded in 1919, headquartered in Moscow and de facto under the control of the Soviet Bolsheviks, required all national communist parties to subordinate themselves to the policies devised and the decisions made in Moscow. In theory at least, the decisions would be made the top of the organization, and the regional and local party cells would simply implement these decisions. In that sense, historians have described the Communist Party as a mere foreign policy instrument for Moscow.[50]

Appealing to the masses through propaganda was a second element in the KPD's strategy to prepare for revolution. In times of economic instability, the Soviet Union and its allegedly rationally planned economy seemed to provide an alternative to the chaotic forces of the market in capitalist economies. Not surprisingly then, the communist tabloid *Arbeiter Illustrierte Zeitung* as well as local newspapers published numerous reports and photos celebrating the accomplishments of the Soviet Union.[51] To liberate itself from the chains of capitalism, the proletariat had only to recognize its own strength. Time and again, communist propaganda posters thus portrayed the working class as a strong and masculine giant, opening the factory gates or tearing apart the chains holding back the proletariat. In particular, Communists attacked Social Democrats, usually called 'Social Fascists', for effectively supporting a capitalist system. Yet, Communists also had to compete with National Socialists, who equally promised to liberate the—albeit exclusively German—working class from the yoke of (according to the Nazis, international and Jewish) capitalism. Both Communists and Nazis thus tried to present themselves as vigorous, masculine, and willing to take radical and if necessary violent action to leap into a better future that the republic could not deliver.[52]

The constant emphasis on discipline within the party, however, conceals a much less disciplined reality. Oftentimes, local leaders and rank-and-file members simply ignored the instructions they received from the party leadership. Learning about the central committee's decision to support a right-wing campaign to overthrow the social democratic government of Prussia in July 1931, a Hamburg-based communist leader simply burned the instructions, saying: 'I like my arse too much to use the paper for wiping it.'[53] While the party leadership could easily call for vigorously attacking Social Democrats, party members had to live and work with their Social Democratic colleagues, and what might seem plausible in general did not make sense in 'their' factory or neighbourhood, where attacking popular Social Democrats would have made Communists immensely unpopular. Not least, Communists were typically people keen to oppose authorities, teachers, foremen, or police officers; they would hardly change that behaviour facing party authorities. The party tried hard to enforce discipline, at times even searching members' private apartments, but to no avail.[54] Ultimately, members could simply leave the party and still remain part of the communist milieu. Despite all proclamations to the contrary, the KPD was not run like a small army working for Moscow.

Nevertheless, internationalist propaganda had its appeal. For Communists, the Soviet Union was a promised land worth fighting for, even if they ignored orders given by the party leadership. Ordinary members eagerly bought Lenin and Stalin busts, and named their children after famous Bolsheviks—'Lenin-Adolf', in one particular stunning example—or simply 'Iwan', in admiration for Russia.[55] Personal testimonies by Communists provide a sense of this emotional attachment to the cause. One female Communist for example noted on the back of a photograph of the recently deceased Lenin she had bought at a commemoration ceremony in 1924: 'Rarely had I felt so deeply moved. I had a sad and raw feeling.' While the Soviet Union was a role model for dedicated Communists, it was also a source of guilt. After all, the failure of the German revolution, they felt, had left Lenin and comrades fighting alone and ending up in 'such a horrible situation'.[56] Indeed, as much as communist internationalism focused on the Soviet Union, it was not limited to it. Communists were equally active in anti-imperialist organizations and campaigned for solidarity with victims of racism in the United States.[57] This testifies to the appeal that a distinctly internationalist ideology had in Weimar.

Measured against the ambitions of the party leadership, the KPD was a failure. It never turned into the disciplined party organization they hoped for, attempts to build a strong basis on the shop floor through factory cells spectacularly failed, and the reformist SPD always outnumbered the KPD both in terms of members and in elections. Yet, on the ground, Communist Party activists formed an organization deeply rooted in the local proletarian milieu. The party gave space for radical hopes as much as for pragmatic activism. It was just never as revolutionary and as disciplined as its leaders hoped for.

THE WORKING-CLASS MOVEMENT AND THE FINAL YEARS OF CRISIS

The Great Depression of the early 1930s and the concurrent rise of National Socialism posed new and dramatic challenges for the working-class movement, but also seemed to provide opportunities. How would Social Democrats and Communists respond to mass unemployment and the political violence that became a common occurrence in the streets of German cities? For Social Democrats, the situation was threatening. The rise of political extremism undermined the foundations of the republic, just as the economic crisis put the social welfare state into jeopardy.[58] Not least, it was threatening in a personal way, as Social Democrats became the target of Nazi (and occasionally Communist) violence.[59] Communists, of course, faced similar physical threats. Though far from being mere victims (which was mostly the case for Social Democrats), they were eager to violently assault National Socialists. But Communists also considered the crisis an opportunity. They hoped that steeply rising unemployment numbers would disillusion workers about Social Democracy and the republic in general, and that these workers, in particular if they had been laid off, would be receptive to Communists' calls for radical action. Indeed, the KPD frequently organized demonstrations by unemployed workers that resulted in bloody clashes with the forces of order, much to Social Democrats' dismay who blamed Communists for shedding innocent blood with no purpose.[60] And election results seemed to confirm Communist hopes: in contrast to both National Socialists and Social Democrats who lost in the last free election of November 1932, Communists could improve their results.

As both the economic and the political situation worsened in the early 1930s, Social Democrats found themselves in an increasingly desperate situation with limited options. Fritz Tarnow, leader of the wood workers union, described Social Democrats' dilemma in drastic terms at the last party convention in Leipzig, lasting from 31 May to 5 June 1931. Capitalism, he explained, was deadly sick, and socialists still hoping to overcome the capitalist system might look forward for its quick demise. Yet, Social Democracy also found itself in the awkward role of being the doctor trying to cure capitalism. 'For we are, it seems to me, condemned to being both doctor seriously trying to heal, while still maintaining the feeling that we are heirs who would rather today than tomorrow receive the entire inheritance of the capitalist system.' If capitalism was sick, it meant that the masses suffered, and thus Social Democracy was obliged to do anything it could to help the patient, forgetting for the moment that they wanted to be capitalism's heir.[61] In practical terms, this meant 'tolerating' Chancellor Heinrich Brüning's deflationary policies that entailed cuts for wage earners and welfare recipients despite harsh criticism from both leftist Social Democrats and Communists. Politically, Social Democrats faced a similar dilemma during the presidential elections of 1932, when they decided to support Paul von Hindenburg, infamous Field Marshal during the First World War, to prevent Adolf Hitler from taking office.[62] For Social Democrats, these were certainly bitter choices, but they were in line with their policy of doing everything they could to avoid civil war.

What loomed on the horizon for Social Democrats was above all chaos, which both the Nazis and Communists were spreading. According to Social Democrats, these 'Siamese twins' were both mere youthful rioters, not interested in serious politics that could solve the country's problems.[63] Trusting in rational arguments and civil debate that would take place in parliament, Social Democrats simply abhorred street politics.[64] Only very late and hesitantly did they participate in the symbolic struggles that characterized the final years of Weimar by employing the Three Arrows, a symbol that became associated with Social Democracy and the Reichsbanner, to cross out swastikas painted on walls.[65] Rather, Social Democrats hoped to rely on the forces of order to curb political violence in the streets and to ensure an orderly working of the state.

While Social Democrats tried to maintain public order and hoped for an economic recovery, Communists saw chances for radicalizing workers and engaged in activism, out in the streets violently combating the Nazis.[66] Employing images of 'red' neighbourhoods that had to be defended against a 'brown' invasion, Communists regularly assaulted National Socialist demonstrations and gatherings, but also individual Nazis marked by their insignia in public. For Communists (as well as for Nazis), such violent encounters were opportunities to demonstrate their virility and their willingness to take radical action. In contrast to dull debates in parliament or the endless paperwork that characterized Communist Party activities, street confrontations were actual moments of action that created a sense of purpose and participation for young, unemployed men. Radical action was not limited to fighting Nazis. Conflicts with welfare officials gave Communists opportunities to campaign against the welfare state that could not ameliorate workers' plight, forced evictions of unemployed workers allowed them to mobilize neighbourhoods in acts of practical solidarity.[67] Finally, Communists used wage cuts and redundancies to call for strike action, often defying the advice of moderate trade unions. Such strike actions, they hoped, might spread, turn into a general strike, and ultimately a revolutionary situation. Famously, Communists even collaborated with the Nazis in a strike at the Berlin public transport corporation in October 1932, just before the Reichstag election of 6 November.[68] Yet, such strike movements, including the Berlin strike, failed and resulted in communist activists losing their jobs.

In light of the ultimate defeat of the working-class movement in these struggles, contemporary observers and historians alike have wondered why Social Democrats and

Communists, who faced a common and deadly enemy, the Nazis—who did not much distinguish between both kinds of 'Marxists'—did not join ranks against this enemy, as did their French comrades in 1934 with the Popular Front.[69] Of course, there was no sense of amity between both parties. Not only did party newspapers polemically attack their rivals, but this hostility permeated the rank and file of local working-class milieus as well. As members of both parties lived in the same neighbourhoods and worked in the same factories, Communists had multiple opportunities to attack Social Democrats, sometimes even physically with deadly violence.[70] Furthermore, communist tactics of infiltrating social democratic organizations or posing as 'oppositional' Social Democrats had created massive distrust within the ranks of Social Democrats. Not least, both parties had fundamentally different understandings of how to combat the common enemy. Whereas Communists believed in the importance of fighting the Nazis in the streets, Social Democrats looked down on such violence as apolitical, youthful rowdiness. This deep division of the working-class movement, in theory and practice committed to fighting fascism, made joint action hardly imaginable.

When Hitler became Chancellor in January 1933, the working-class movement indeed offered little resistance.[71] Social Democracy had already lost control of its stronghold Prussia in the so-called Papen Coup of July 1932, when the Reich government under Franz von Papen disposed of the Social Democratic government of Prussia under the pretext of maintaining law and order.[72] Social Democrats fought the decision in court, but did not consider taking extra-parliamentary or extra-legal action, such as calling for a general strike. It is open to debate whether Social Democrats could realistically have done anything, but the message was clear: the reformist working-class movement was not in a position to offer meaningful resistance against any coup. As it turned out on 30 January 1933, Communists were equally incapable of resisting. That very evening, the party had called for a general strike. Yet, apart from the small Swabian village of Mössingen, where the KPD had a strong position in the local working-class milieu, the strike did not materialize.[73] With surprising ease, the Nazi Stormtroopers succeeded, in collaboration with local police forces, in subduing their political opponents. For the working-class movement that had made the struggle against fascism one of its major slogans, it was a resounding defeat.

Conclusion: The Working-Class Movement in Weimar

The working-class movement played a central role in the history of the Weimar Republic. With its democratic constitution and the social welfare state, Weimar was a realization of what the working-class movement had struggled for a long time. Social democracy, which had played a leading role in the revolution, thus became one of the most important sources of support for the republic, even though Social Democrats were, apart from the initial years and a brief period between 1928 and 1930, not at the head of the national government. Social Democrats helped instil a sense of republican loyalty, built republican institutions, and shaped the welfare state. For Social Democrats, the political constitution of the republic provided the framework to accomplish gradual social change by means of disciplined and serious work in the republic's institutions. The republic, that is, at least initially empowered Social Democrats.

But given the revolutionary rhetoric of the pre-war working-class movement and the visions for a socialist future, Weimar was also a disappointment. For radical workers, parliamentary democracy and a social welfare state were not enough, as class society did not perish. Communists represented this perspective. They kept radical traditions alive and looked at the Soviet Union as an example that a radical break with capitalism was indeed possible. It would be easy to blame them for pointless uprisings and bloodshed, for their harsh attacks against Social Democracy, and thus undermining German democracy. While this might be true, it would be a rather limited understanding of Communism in Weimar. It may serve as a reminder that, from the very beginning, different visions for a political and social future competed with each other in Germany, including within the working-class movement. National Socialists, of course, offered their own vision of a future that claimed to be socialist as well, but in contrast to the tradition of working-class internationalism, their socialism was tied to the nation and the German *Volk*. The Communist Party was thus not only a fundamental part of the deeply divided working-class movement, always a thorn for Social Democrats who had to justify themselves vis-à-vis their leftist competitor, but also of Weimar society and politics in general.

Notes

1. On Social Democracy during the First World War, see still Susanne Miller, *Burgfrieden und Klassenkampf: Die deutsche Sozialdemokratie im Ersten Weltkrieg* (Düsseldorf: Droste Verlag, 1974).
2. On the USPD, see Robert F. Wheeler, *USPD und Internationale: Sozialistischer Internationalismus in der Zeit der Revolution*, tr. Agnes Blänsdorf (Frankfurt am Main: Ullstein, 1975); David W. Morgan, *The Socialist Left and the German Revolution: A History of the German Independent Social Democratic Party, 1917–1922* (Ithaca, NY, and London: Cornell University Press, 1975); Werner Bramke and Silvio Reisinger, *Leipzig in der Revolution von 1918/1919* (Leipzig: Leipziger Universitätsverlag, 2009), 50; Dieter Engelmann and Horst Naumann, *Zwischen Spaltung und Vereinigung: Die Unabhängige Sozialdemokratische Partei Deutschlands in den Jahren 1917–1922* (Berlin: Edition Neue Wege, 1993), 31–2. On strikes and protests during the First World War, see also Belinda Davis, *Home Fires Burning: Politics, Identity and Food in World War I Berlin* (Chapel Hill, NC: University of North Carolina Press, 1992); Ottokar Luban, 'Die politischen Massenstreiks in den letzten Weltkriegsjahren und die Haltung der Freien Gewerkschaften', in Karl Christian Führer et al. (eds), *Revolution und Arbeiterbewegung in Deutschland, 1918–1920* (Essen: Klartext, 2013), 121–34.

3. For this argument see Heinrich August Winkler, 'Die Vermeidung des Bürgerkriegs: Zur Kontinuität sozialdemokratischer Politik in der Weimarer Republik', in Manfred Hettling and Paul Nolte (eds), *Nation und Gesellschaft in Deutschland. Historische Essays (Hans-Ulrich Wehler zum 65. Geburtstag)* (Munich: C. H. Beck, 1996), 282–304.
4. On the revolution and the working-class movement, see the contributions in Führer et al., *Revolution und Arbeiterbewegung*.
5. On social democratic politics during the revolutionary period, see Susanne Miller, *Die Bürde der Macht: Die deutsche Sozialdemokratie, 1918–1920* (Düsseldorf: Droste, 1978); Heinrich August Winkler, *Von der Revolution zur Stabilisierung: Arbeiter und Arbeiterbewegung in der Weimarer Republik, 1918 bis 1924* (Berlin: J. H. W. Dietz, 1984).
6. On the council movement and more general radical workers in the revolution, see still Eberhard Kolb, *Die Arbeiterräte in der deutschen Innenpolitik 1918–1919* (Düsseldorf: Droste, 1962); Hans Manfred Bock, *Syndikalismus und Linkskommunismus von 1918–1923: Zur Geschichte und Soziologie der Freien Arbeiter-Union Deutschlands (Syndikalisten), der Allgemeinen Arbeiter-Union Deutschlands und der Kommunistischen Arbeiter-Partei Deutschlands* (Meisenheim am Glan: Hain, 1969); Erhard Lucas, *Zwei Formen von Radikalismus in der deutschen Arbeiterbewegung* (Frankfurt am Main: Roter Stern, 1976).
7. This account draws on Winkler, *Revolution*, 34–58.
8. See Miller, *Bürde der Macht*, 123–4.
9. See the accounts in Winkler, *Revolution*, 198–205, Miller, *Bürde der Macht*, 119–40, 452 (for election results).
10. On the agreement, see Klaus Schönhoven, 'Wegbereiter der sozialen Demokratie? Zur Bedeutung des Stinnes-Legien-Abkommens vom 15. November 1918', in Führer et al., *Revolution und Arbeiterbewegung*, 61–80; Petra Weber, *Gescheiterte Sozialpartnerschaft—Gefährdete Republik? Industrielle Beziehungen, Arbeitskämpfe und der Sozialstaat. Deutschland und Frankreich im Vergleich (1918–1933/39)* (Munich: R. Oldenbourg Verlag, 2010), 191–200.
11. Quoted in Schönhoven, 'Wegbereiter', 69.
12. Quoted in Weber, *Sozialpartnerschaft*, 198.
13. On debates about socialization, see Winkler, *Revolution*, 191–8; Jürgen Mittag, 'Versäumte Chancen oder realitätsnaher Pragmatismus? Die Arbeiterbewegung im Ruhrgebiet zwischen Sozialisierungsdebatten und Proteststreiks 1918–1920', in Führer et al. (eds), *Revolution und Arbeiterbewegung*, 19–44; Miller, *Bürde der Macht*, 141–63. On syndicalists in the Ruhr area demanding socialization, see Jürgen Jenko, 'Eine andere Form von Arbeiterradikalismus: Der Anarcho-Syndikalismus im Ruhrgebiet 1918-1922', in Führer et al. (eds), *Revolution und Arbeiterbewegung*, 175–94; Weber, *Sozialpartnerschaft*, 200–38.
14. Mike Schmeitzner, 'Ambivalenzen des Fortschritts: Zur Faszination der proletarischen Diktatur in der demokratischen Revolution 1918–1920', *Archiv für Sozialgeschichte*, 53 (2013), 113–45, 138.
15. Ibid., 143.
16. Ibid., 144.
17. On violence during the revolution, see most recently Mark Jones, *Founding Weimar: Violence and the German Revolution of 1918–1919* (Cambridge: Cambridge University Press, 2016). On the Mar. 1921 uprising, see Sigrid Koch-Baumgarten, *Aufstand der Avantgarde: Die Märzaktion der KPD 1921* (Frankfurt am Main: Campus Verlag, 1986).

18. For such examples of such radical practices, see Weber, *Sozialpartnerschaft*, 200–38; Moritz Föllmer, 'The Unscripted Revolution: Make Subjectivities in Germany, 1918–1919', *Past and Present*, 240 (2018), 161–92.
19. Gustav Radbruch, 'Friedrich Ebert, der Staatsmann', in *Schleswig-Holsteinsche Volkszeitung*, 3 Mar. 1925, here quoted after Bernd Buchner, *Um nationale und republikanische Identität: Die deutsche Sozialdemokratie und der Kampf um die politischen Symbole in der Weimarer Republik* (Bonn: Dietz, 2001), 11.
20. Hubertus Buchstein, 'Von Max Adler zu Ernst Fraenkel: Demokratie und pluralistische Gesellschaft in der sozialistischen Demokratietheorie der Weimarer Republik', in Christoph Gusy (ed.), *Demokratisches Denken in der Weimarer Republik* (Baden-Baden: Nomos, 2000), 534–606, 561, 567.
21. On Social Democracy during the years of stability, see the detailed account by Heinrich August Winkler, *Der Schein der Normalität: Arbeiter und Arbeiterbewegung in der Weimarer Republik, 1924 bis 1930* (Berlin: J. H. W. Dietz, 1985).
22. A summary of voting results in Weimar can be found online at <http://www.wahlen-in-deutschland.de/aweimralg.htm> (last accessed 17 September 2019). See also Jürgen W. Falter, Thomas Lindenberger, and Siegfried Schumann, *Wahlen und Abstimmungen in der Weimarer Republik: Materialien zum Wahlverhalten, 1919–1933* (Munich: Beck, 1986).
23. For an account of social democratic policies in government, see Winkler, *Schein*.
24. On the SPD in Prussia, see also Hans-Peter Ehni, *Bollwerk Preußen? Preußen-Regierung, Reich-Länder-Problem und Sozialdemokratie 1928–1932* (Bonn: Neue Gesellschaft, 1975).
25. On Severing, see Thomas Alexander, *Carl Severing—ein Demokrat und Sozialist in Weimar* (Frankfurt am Main: Peter Lang, 1996). On Grzesinski, see Thomas Albrecht, *Für eine wehrhafte Demokratie: Albert Grzesinski und die preußische Politik in der Weimarer Republik* (Bonn: J. H. W. Dietz, 1999).
26. Peter Leßmann, *Die preußische Schutzpolizei in der Weimarer Republik: Streifendienst und Straßenkampf* (Düsseldorf: Droste, 1989), 83–8.
27. Hagen Schulze, 'Democratic Prussia in Weimar Germany', in Philip G. Dwyer (ed.), *Modern Prussian History, 1830–1945* (London: Longman, 2001), 211–29, 215–18, numbers n. 10; Hsi-huey Liang, *Die Berliner Polizei in der Weimarer Republik* (Berlin, New York: de Gruyter, 1977), 85–93.
28. This argument follows Klaus Schönhoven, *Der Heidelberger Programmparteitag von 1925: Sozialdemokratische Standortbestimmung in der Weimarer Republik* (Heidelberg: Stiftung Reichspräsident-Friedrich-Ebert-Gedenkstätte, 1995), quote 22. For a detailed discussion of both programmes see also Heinrich August Winkler, 'Klassenbewegung oder Volkspartei? Zur Programmdiskussion in der Weimarer Sozialdemokratie 1920–1925', *Geschichte und Gesellschaft*, 8 (1982), 9–54. Winkler is more critical of Social Democracy for not appealing to the middle classes.
29. Peter Lösche and Franz Walter, 'Auf dem Weg zur Volkspartei? Die Weimarer Sozialdemokratie', *Archiv für Sozialgeschichte*, 15 (1989), 75–136, 86–8.
30. See, with reference to the Sept. 1930 elections, Karl Rohe, *Wahlen und Wählertraditionen in Deutschland: Kulturelle Grundlagen deutscher Parteien und Parteiensystem im 19. und 20. Jahrhundert* (Frankfurt am Main: Suhrkamp, 1992). See also Jürgen W. Falter, 'The Social Bases of Political Cleavages in the Weimar Republic, 1919–1933', *Historical Social Research, Supplement*, 25 (1992), 194–216, 212; Lösche and Walter, 'Auf dem Weg?', 90.
31. Falter, 'Social Bases', 210.
32. See the discussion in Lösche and Walter, 'Auf dem Weg?'

33. See David F. Crew, *Germans on Welfare: From Weimar to Hitler* (New York: Oxford University Press, 1998), 22–9, on Hamburg 27.
34. Paul Brandmann, *Leipzig zwischen Klassenkampf und Sozialreform: Kommunale Wohlfahrtspolitik zwischen 1890 und 1929* (Cologne: Böhlau, 1998), 276–9.
35. Joachim C. Häberlen, *Politik und Vertrauen im Alltag: Die Arbeiterbewegung in Leipzig und Lyon im Moment der Krise, 1929–1933/38* (Göttingen: Vandenhoeck & Ruprecht, 2013), 128.
36. On the Reichsbanner, see Karl Rohe, *Das Reichsbanner Schwarz Rot Gold: Ein Beitrag zur Geschichte und Struktur der politischen Kampfverbände zur Zeit der Weimarer Republik* (Düsseldorf: Droste, 1966); Carsten Voigt, *Kampfbünde der Arbeiterbewegung: das Reichsbanner Schwarz-Rot-Gold und der Rote Frontkämpferbund in Sachsen 1924–1933* (Cologne: Böhlau, 2009); Benjamin Ziemann, *Contested Commemorations: Republican War Veterans and Weimar Political Culture* (Cambridge: Cambridge University Press, 2013).
37. On membership numbers, see Ziemann, *Contested Commemorations*, 65–6
38. Ziemann, *Contested Commemorations*, 78–9.
39. See, with reference to Hamburg, Karen Hagemann, *Frauenalltag und Männerpolitik: Alltagsleben und gesellschaftliches Handeln von Arbeiterfrauen in der Weimarer Republik* (Berlin: J. H. W. Dietz, 1990), 532, 561–6.
40. Ziemann, *Contested Commemorations*, 69–72.
41. On the milieu, see Peter Lösche and Franz Walter, 'Zur Organisationskultur der sozialdemokratischen Arbeiterbewegung in der Weimarer Republik: Niedergang der Klassenstruktur oder solidargemeinschaftlicher Höhepunkt?', *Geschichte und Gesellschaft*, 15 (1989), 511–36. For local case studies also beyond the working-class milieu, see Thomas Adam, *Arbeitermilieu und Arbeiterbewegung in Leipzig 1871–1933* (Cologne: Böhlau, 1999); Siegfried Weichlein, *Sozialmilieus und politische Kultur in der Weimarer Republik: Lebenswelt, Vereinskultur, Politik in Hessen* (Göttingen: Vandenhoeck & Ruprecht, 1996).
42. For the KPD, see above all the seminal study by Klaus-Michael Mallmann, *Kommunisten in der Weimarer Republik: Sozialgeschichte einer revolutionären Bewegung* (Darmstadt: Wissenschaftliche Buchgesellschaft, 1996). A similar perspective takes Ulrich Eumann, *Eigenwillige Kohorten der Revolution: Zur regionalen Sozialgeschichte des Kommunismus in der Weimarer Republik* (Frankfurt am Main: Peter Lang, 2007). For an English-language account, see Eric D. Weitz, 'State Power, Class Fragmentation, and the Shaping of the German Communist Politics, 1890–1933', *Journal of Modern History*, 62 (1990), 253–90; Weitz, *Creating German Communism, 1890–1990: From Popular Protests to Socialist State* (Princeton: Princeton University Press, 1997).
43. See Voigt, *Kampfbünde*, 47–82.
44. On this misleading interpretation, see critical Mallmann, *Kommunisten*, 84–6.
45. See e.g. the communist propaganda novel by Walter Schönstedt, *Kämpfende Jugend: Roman der arbeitenden Jugend* (Berlin: Internationaler Arbeiter-Verlag, 1932).
46. See Mallmann, *Kommunisten*, 87–93.
47. Ibid., 96–7, 103.
48. Ibid., 106, 131–2.
49. For a perspective on the KPD emphasizing its 'stalinization', see Hermann Weber, *Die Wandlung des deutschen Kommunismus: Die Stalinisierung der KPD in der Weimarer Republik* (Frankfurt am Main: Europäische Verlagsanstalt, 1969); Andreas Wirsching, 'The Impact of "Bolshevization" and "Stalinization" on French and German Communism: A Comparative View', in Norman LaPorte, Kevin Morgan, and Matthey Worley

(eds), *Bolshevism, Stalinism, and the Comintern. Perspectives on Stalinization, 1917-53* (Basingstoke: Palgrave Macmillan, 2008), 89-104.
50. See my discussion of communist parties more generally in Joachim C. Häberlen, 'Between Global Aspirations and Local Realities: The Global Dimensions of Interwar Communism', *Journal of Global History*, 7 (2012), 415-37.
51. See e.g. the biography of Willi Münzenberg, editor of the *Arbeiter Illustrierte Zeitung*, by Sean McMeekin, *The Red Millionare: A Political Biography of Willi Münzenberg, Moscow's Secret Propaganda Tsar in the West* (New Haven: Yale University Press, 2003).
52. See Timothy S. Brown, *Weimar Radicals: Nazis and Communists between Authenticity and Performance* (New York: Berghahn Books, 2009).
53. Quoted in Mallmann, *Kommunisten*, 163.
54. Häberlen, *Politik und Vertrauen*, 167; Pamela E. Swett, *Neighbors and Enemies: The Culture of Radicalism in Berlin, 1929-1933* (Cambridge: Cambridge University Press, 2004), 226-7.
55. Mallmann, *Kommunisten*, 232.
56. All quotes from Ulrich Eumann, '"Kameraden vom roten Tuch": Die Weimarer KPD aus der Perspektive ehemaliger Mitglieder', *Archiv für Geschichte des Widerstands und der Arbeit*, 16 (2001), 97-164, here 125-6.
57. See e.g. James A. Miller, Susan D. Pennybacker, and Eve Rosenhaft, 'Mother Ada Wright and the International Campaign to Free the Scottsboro Boys, 1931-1934', *American Historical Review*, 106 (2001), 387-430; John D. Hargreaves, 'The Comintern and Anti-Colonialism: New Research Opportunities', *African Affairs*, 92 (1993), 255-61.
58. This argument is made by Weber, *Sozialpartnerschaft*, 839-52.
59. On Social Democracy at the end of Weimar, see Heinrich August Winkler, *Der Weg in die Katastrophe: Arbeiter und Arbeiterbewegung in der Weimarer Republik 1930 bis 1933* (Berlin: J. H. W. Dietz, 1987); Donna Harsch, *German Social Democracy and the Rise of Nazism* (Chapel Hill, NC: University of North Carolina Press, 1993); Wolfram Pyta, *Gegen Hitler und für die Republik: Die Auseinandersetzung der deutschen Sozialdemokratie mit der NSDAP in der Weimarer Republik* (Düsseldorf: Droste, 1989).
60. On the KPD at the end of Weimar and their attempts to mobilize the unemployed, see Siegfried Bahne, *Die KPD und das Ende von Weimar: Das Scheitern einer Politik 1932-1935* (Frankfurt am Main: Campus-Verlag, 1976); Mallmann, *Kommunisten*, 365-80; Anthony McElligott, 'Mobilising the Unemployed: The KPD and the Unemployed Workers' Movement in Hamburg-Altona during the Weimar Republic', in Richard J. Evans and Dick Geary (eds), *The German Unemployed: Experiences and Consequences of Mass Unemployment from the Weimar Republic to the Third Reich* (New York: St Martin's Press, 1987), 228-60.
61. *Sozialdemokratischer Parteitag in Leipzig 1931 vom 31. Mai bis 5. Juni im Volkshaus* (Berlin, n.d.), 45, quoted in Winkler, *Der Weg in die Katastrophe*, 324-5. I would like to thank Moritz Föllmer for drawing my attention to the speech. 'Wir sind nämlich, wie mit scheint, dazu verdammt, sowohl Arzt zu sein, der ernsthaft heilen will, und dennoch das Gefühl aufrechtzuerhalten, dass wir Erben sind, die lieber heute als morgen die ganze Hinterlassenschaft des kapitalistischen Systems in Empfang nehmen wollen.'
62. Winkler, *Der Weg in die Katastrophe*, 338-58, 511-32.
63. The term 'Siamese Twins' is from an article in the social democratic *Leipziger Volkszeitung*, 17 Sept. 1931, quoted in Häberlen, *Politik und Vertrauen*, 90.
64. For an elaboration of the following argument, see Joachim C. Häberlen, 'Scope for Agency and Political Options: The German Working-Class Movement and the Rise of Nazism', *Politics, Religion and Ideology*, 14 (2013), 377-94.

65. See Richard Albrecht, 'Symbolkampf in Deutschland 1932: Sergej Tschachotin und der "Symbolkrieg" der Drei Pfeile gegen den Nationalsozialismus als Episode im Abwehrkampf der Arbeiterbewegung gegen den Faschismus in Deutschland', *Internationale Wissenschaftliche Korrespondenz zur Geschichte der Arbeiterbewegung*, 22 (1986), 498–533.
66. On violence at the end of Weimar, see Eve Rosenhaft, *Beating the Fascists? The German Communists and Political Violence, 1929–1933* (Cambridge: Cambridge University Press, 1983); Eve Rosenhaft, 'Links gleich rechts? Militante Straßengewalt um 1930', in Thomas Lindenberger and Alf Lüdtke (eds), *Physische Gewalt: Studien zur Geschichte der Neuzeit* (Frankfurt am Main: Surhkamp, 1995), 238–75; Swett, *Neighbors and Enemies*; Brown, *Weimar Radicals*; Dirk Schumann, *Politische Gewalt in der Weimarer Republik 1918–1933: Kampf um die Straße und Furcht vor dem Bürgerkrieg* (Essen: Klartext, 2001).
67. See examples in Häberlen, *Politik und Vertrauen*, 69–72, 159–61.
68. Klaus Rainer Röhl, *Nähe zum Gegner: Kommunisten und Nationalsozialisten im Berliner BVG-Streik von 1932* (Frankfurt am Main: Campus Verlag, 1994).
69. On the French Popular Front, see only Julian Jackson, *The Popular Front in France: Defending Democracy, 1934–38* (Cambridge: Cambridge University Press, 1988).
70. For an elaboration of this argument based on case studies of Leipzig and Lyon, see Häberlen, *Politik und Vertrauen*.
71. See Alf Lüdtke, 'Wo blieb die "rote Glut"? Arbeitererfahrungen und deutscher Faschismus', in Lüdtke (ed.), *Alltagsgeschichte: Zur Rekonstruktion historischer Erfahrungen und Lebensweisen* (Frankfurt am Main: Campus Verlag, 1989), 224–82; Manfred Scharrer (ed.), *Kampflose Kapitulation: Arbeiterbewegung 1933* (Reinbek bei Hamburg: Rowohlt, 1984).
72. See Winkler, *Der Weg in die Katastrophe*, 646–80.
73. Hans-Joachim Althaus et al., *Da ist nirgends nichts gewesen außer hier: Das 'rote Mössingen' im Generalstreik gegen Hitler. Geschichte eines schwäbischen Arbeiterdorfes* (Berlin: Rotbuch Verlag, 1982).

Bibliography

Brown, Timothy S., *Weimar Radicals: Nazis and Communists between Authenticity and Performance* (New York: Berghahn Books, 2009).
Crew, David F., *Germans on Welfare: From Weimar to Hitler* (New York: Oxford University Press, 1998).
Häberlen, Joachim C., 'Scope for Agency and Political Options: The German Working-Class Movement and the Rise of Nazism', *Politics, Religion and Ideology*, 14 (2013), 377–94.
Harsch, Donna, *German Social Democracy and the Rise of Nazism* (Chapel Hill, NC: University of North Carolina Press, 1993).
Mallmann, Klaus-Michael, *Kommunisten in der Weimarer Republik: Sozialgeschichte einer revolutionären Bewegung* (Darmstadt: Wissenschaftliche Buchgesellschaft, 1996).
McElligott, Anthony, *Contested City: Municipal Politics and the Rise of Nazism in Altona, 1917–1937* (Ann Arbor: University of Michigan Press, 1998).
Morgan, David W., *The Socialist Left and the German Revolution: A History of the German Independent Social Democratic Party, 1917–1922* (Ithaca, NY, and London: Cornell University Press, 1975).
Rosenhaft, Eve, *Beating the Fascists? The German Communists and Political Violence, 1929–1933* (Cambridge: Cambridge University Press, 1983).

Swett, Pamela E., *Neighbors and Enemies: The Culture of Radicalism in Berlin, 1929–1933* (Cambridge: Cambridge University Press, 2004).

Weitz, Eric D., *Creating German Communism, 1890–1990: From Popular Protests to Socialist State* (Princeton: Princeton University Press, 1997).

Winkler, Heinrich August, 'Die Vermeidung des Bürgerkriegs: Zur Kontinuität sozialdemokratischer Politik in der Weimarer Republik', in Manfred Hettling and Paul Nolte (eds), *Nation und Gesellschaft in Deutschland: Historische Essays (Hans-Ulrich Wehler zum 65. Geburtstag)* (Munich: C. H. Beck, 1996), 282–304.

CHAPTER 16

THE CENTRE PARTY, CONSERVATIVES, AND THE RADICAL RIGHT

SHELLEY BARANOWSKI

ONE of the most important and durable debates in the scholarship on Weimar Germany has dealt with the role of German landowning, business, military, academic, and civil service elites in the rise of Nazism and the destruction of the Weimar Republic. An older master narrative described the conservative–Nazi relationship as an 'alliance' between the old right and the new that derived from the continuity of elite influence from the Second Empire to the Third Reich. Now a different interpretation compellingly emphasizes the disunity within the right and among elites, which undermined the political effectiveness of both. Unable to satisfy the material needs of their base or respond to deep post-war yearning for a united 'national community' (*Volksgemeinschaft*), the right's electoral support declined well before National Socialism became a major political force.[1]

This chapter focuses on two major Weimar parties with conservative and radical right constituencies, the German National People's Party (Deutschnationale Volkspartei or DNVP) and the Catholic Centre Party (Zentrum), which at first glance appear to have little in common apart from their social diversity. The DNVP emerged from the Protestant conservative milieu originally anchored in the Prussian east and incorporated three additional conservative parties in the process. In the aftermath of the revolution of 1918, it strove to broaden its base to become a national conservative party with sufficient influence to undermine the legitimacy of the Weimar Republic. Throughout its existence, the DNVP consistently opposed what it described derisively as the Weimar 'system', joining governments only when necessary to advance the material interests of its supporters. The Centre on the other hand represented the common confessional interests of the German Catholic milieu since its founding in 1870. Unlike the DNVP, the Centre participated in every national government from 1919 until mid-1932, having accepted the republic's legitimacy. Although the position of the Centre's majority differed from that of the DNVP, the party did not lack for powerful conservative and radical nationalist voices that challenged the party from the right. The DNVP was most consistent in its anti-republican nationalism, which became hegemonic after the migration of much of its electorate to splinter parties and the election of the radical nationalist Pan-German Alfred Hugenberg as party chairman in 1928. Yet if the Centre functioned as a 'state party' within the boundaries of the Weimar Constitution, maintained a relatively stable electorate, and prevented Catholic radical nationalists from displacing the party, the last two Catholic Chancellors, Heinrich Brüning and especially Franz von Papen, accelerated Weimar's demise. The policies of both conformed to the priorities of many conservative elites, who despite the disintegration of the parties they had supported, retained enough power to exploit the one avenue left available to them, access to the highest levels of the state.

The DNVP: Fragmentation and Radicalization

In the aftermath of military defeat, the abdication of the Kaiser, and a leftist revolution, the formation of the German National People's Party reflected a determined and perhaps desperate attempt to mobilize conservatives across the nation to protect their interests. To assure a coherent platform and greater impact, the new movement merged four pre-war conservative parties, the German Conservatives (Deutschkonservative Partei, DKP), the Free Conservatives (Freikonservative Partei), the Christian-Socials (Christlich-Soziale Partei), and the *völkisch* racists of the Deutschvölkische Partei. It also attracted others who had joined the radical-nationalist Fatherland Party (Deutsche Vaterlandspartei) formed in 1917 in opposition to the Reichstag's call for a negotiated peace. The inclusion of 'peoples' and 'national' in the new party's name was meant to project a 'social conscience' that cut across class, regional, and confessional boundaries and mitigate the Prusso-centric, aristocratic, and agrarian elitism that defined the DKP, the oldest of the pre-war conservative parties. The DNVP's leadership under its first party chairman, Oskar Hergt, a former member of the Free Conservative Party, included no representatives from the East Elbian aristocracy.[2]

Initially the new party muted its hostility to the Weimar Republic in its brief platform prepared in advance of the January 1919 elections to the National Assembly, which was to elect a new government and compose a new constitution. In addition to defending free enterprise, private property, the monarchy, and a strong unitary ethnonational state inspired by a Christian and social spirit, the platform expressed the DNVP's willingness to cooperate with any form of government that guaranteed law and order.[3] Nevertheless that qualified moderation did not last. The harsh terms of the Versailles Treaty, which cost Germany its colonies and one-seventh of its pre-war territory (the status of Upper Silesia and the Saar to be determined later by popular referendums), sharply reduced the size of its military, and assigned it the sole responsibility for the outbreak of war, encouraging many conservatives, especially old-style Prussian conservatives, to support the Kapp-Lüttwitz putsch, the first attempt to overthrow the republic in March 1920.[4] Moreover the Versailles Treaty prompted a new and unambiguously anti-republican party platform in response to the new centre-left government's acceptance of the peace terms under duress. Moderates, such as the one-time Free Conservative industrialist Siegfried von Kardorff, who condemned the support of the Kapp putsch and embraced constitutionalism, were either sidelined or abandoned the party altogether.[5] Much discussion has arisen in recent years as to whether the DNVP could have evolved into an equivalent of British Tory conservatism. Could it have become a pragmatic state-supporting party willing to accept the Weimar Constitution and the legitimacy of a parliamentary democracy? The DNVP's decision to enter government in 1925 and again in 1927, an indication of the willingness of its leaders to further the material interests of their constituents, hinted as much. Yet military defeat, a punitive peace settlement that included a huge reparations bill, and chronic economic crises, undermined what potential existed for a conservatism consistent with Weimar constitutionalism.[6]

The DNVP's ambition to achieve a diverse national constituency initially succeeded. It drew conservatively minded Germans across the nation, and on the face of it its social and geographic diversity was impressive.[7] Its local party organizations multiplied across the Reich to include Saxony, Württemberg, Thuringia, and Bavaria, extending well beyond the regional boundaries of the pre-war Conservative Party. In addition to drawing the expected support from estate owners and conservative industrialists, especially those in heavy industry, it established affiliations with peasant organizations, sought out small business proprietors and artisans of the 'old' middle class, and appealed to staunchly conservative white-collar employees and workers belonging to the organizations that composed the Christian labour movement. It also attracted supporters of the Pan-German League, a radical nationalist carryover from the Second Empire, and from the numerous paramilitary and patriotic associations that proliferated after 1918, such as the Young German Order (Jungdeutscher Orden), the United Patriotic Associations of Germany (Vereinigte Vaterländische Verbände), and the Stahlhelm, the umbrella organization for nationalist war veterans. The affiliation of many from the patriotic and paramilitary organizations collectively embodied the first of two major fault lines in the DNVP, the conflict between a militarized and increasingly vehement anti-republican nationalism on the one hand and on the other the advocacy of diverse and often conflicting economic interests.

The DNVP also endeavoured to cross the boundaries of confession and gender. It incorporated Catholics disenchanted with the Centre's leftward tilt in the last years of the war and its participation in the Weimar Coalition with the Social Democratic (Sozialdemokratische Partei Deutschland or SPD) and left-liberal Democratic (Deutsche Demokratische Partei or DDP) parties. Its Reich Catholic Committee founded in 1920 drew conservative and reactionary Catholic landowning aristocrats, intellectuals, and members of the educated middle class, who despised revolution, socialism, materialism, and the alleged 'Judaization' of German society. They advocated confessional reconciliation as essential to the restoration of a Christian corporatist nation ruled either by a hereditary monarchy or by a charismatic leader.[8] The Nationalists were less enthusiastic about mobilizing women, fearing that their enfranchisement would only benefit the left, and it opposed the Weimar Constitution's clause that established equal voting rights for all citizens. Yet conservative women had been well organized before 1914, and they contributed significantly to the war effort, both of which underscored women's potential for expanding the DNVP's electorate. Thus, in December 1918 the party formed its National Women's Committee to prepare for the upcoming elections, which yielded the desired outcome. Conservative women voters boosted the DNVP's turnout in the 1919 national elections and subsequent campaigns. Women's share of the DNVP's electorate ranged from 50 to 60 per cent, second only to the combined female electorates of the Centre and its sister party the Bavarian People's Party. The Christian orientation of both parties and their commitment to defending women's 'natural' role in the home, family, and church proved attractive and reassuring.[9]

The tension between elitism and populism and the particular interests embedded in both composed the second fault line within the DNVP. From the outset, conservative elites survived the revolution's initial threats to the dominant classes. Although by no means indicative of a straightforward carryover of influence from the Second Empire to the Weimar Republic as was once argued, the ability of elites to recover in the face of political and social upheaval spoke for their flexibility and resourcefulness.[10] Industrialists pioneered the practice of strategic compromise by recognizing trade unions and agreeing to collective bargaining and the eight-hour workday. It helped that the Majority Socialists, fearful of a repeat of the Bolshevik revolution in Russia, suppressed the radical Spartacists and the Workers and Soldiers Councils, content to establish a parliamentary democracy and accept the gradual evolution of a socialized economy.[11] Business and industrial leaders divided their support among the bourgeois parties, especially the heir to the pre-war National Liberal Party, the German People's Party (Deutsche Volkspartei or DVP), but those who sided with the DNVP became a critical and indispensable source of financial support. Likewise Prussian agrarian elites persisted, pressured by rural protests against government price controls on agricultural commodities and the socialist campaign to unionize farm workers.[12] Having formed the Central Association of German Conservatives to secure their interests, large estate owners retained their pre-eminence in the newly founded National Rural League (Reichslandbund), the successor to the pre-war Agrarian League (Bund der Landwirte).[13] The Rural League's suppression of the socialist unionization campaign enhanced its stature as did its relentless and ultimately successful campaign to eliminate price controls. Neither agrarian nor business elites could be ignored, not least because the party's patchily integrated regional party organizations depended upon interest group financial contributions to fund the DNVP's electoral campaigns. Elites also occupied prominent positions in the party. The occupations of the DNVP's four party chairmen, Oskar Hergt, Johann Friedrich Winckler, Kuno von Westarp, and Alfred Hugenberg, included a judge and senior official in the Prussian bureaucracy, a long-serving district governor and Protestant layman who served as president of the Saxon and Prussian synods, a titled Prussian civil servant, and a newspaper and media magnate. After two national elections in May and December 1924, in which the DNVP increased its share of the electorate to 19.5 per cent and 20.5 per cent respectively, its Reichstag delegations included thirteen and then fifteen titled aristocrats, not including the substantial numbers of non-noble large landowners.[14]

Nevertheless, the DNVP's diversity imposed limitations. Its labour wing, for example, was not without influence of its own, to which its lobbying for unemployment compensation and the restoration of the eight-hour day would later testify. By the mid-1920s, the Rural League's leadership had become less stridently anti-republican and less elitist, spawned by the need to represent all agriculturalists as evidence of its national influence.[15] Moreover the ineffectiveness of Nationalist elites—that is, the inability to deliver what the DNVP's multiple interest groups wanted—weakened confidence in them, as the DNVP's eventual participation in government would demonstrate. Indeed, from the beginning, signs of disenchantment emerged that underscored DNVP's inability to represent interest groups equally and resolve the conflict between ideological purity and pragmatism. In 1920, the newly formed and explicitly middle-class Business Party (Wirtschaftspartei or WP) lured away the DNVP's small proprietors and artisans, becoming the first of many splinter parties to capitalize on middle-class dissatisfaction. In 1922, the DNVP's racist, *völkisch* wing seceded, having objected to the party's refusal to expel its Jewish members or allow it to maintain its organizational autonomy. Antisemitism was a persistent and ugly feature of DNVP rhetoric especially when merged with other ills, a prime example being the campaign flyers addressed to women, which lumped together Jews, socialists, and French colonial troops who occupied the Rhineland as an existential threat to the home, family, and Christianity. Yet the leadership feared that emphasizing antisemitism in the party platform would undermine the DNVP's ability to influence government policy down the road by alienating the bourgeois liberal parties.[16]

By late 1923 the collapse of the Nazi-initiated Munich putsch, the curtailment of hyperinflation and the stabilization of the German mark and the withdrawal of the French and Belgian troops from the Ruhr suppressed the right-wing violence that had unsettled the republic since its beginnings. The evidence that Weimar would survive prompted the Nationalists to consider entering government to advocate for its constituents. Nevertheless, internal conflicts emerged.[17] Germany's acceptance of the Dawes Plan, concluded by the government of the Centrist Wilhelm Marx and the DVP's Foreign Minister Gustav Stresemann, infuriated DNVP militants for having ensured Germany's 'enslavement' to the international commission charged with monitoring Germany's adherence to the agreement. Yet the terms of the Dawes Plan, which staggered reparations payments and withdrew Allied troops from the Ruhr, offered incentives that won the support of the powerful interests. The prospect of foreign loans was attractive to the National Federation of German Industry (Reichsverband der Deutschen Industrie, or RDI) for it promised access to international capital markets. It appealed to the Christian labour movement and white-collar workers because the infusion of foreign capital could be invested in reducing unemployment. For the National Rural League, the prospect of restoring agricultural protectionism when Germany regained its tariff autonomy depended on the DNVP's acceptance of the Dawes Plan and then securing its place in government. The clash between organized interests, which had something to gain from the agreement, and the militant right, especially that associated with the patriotic leagues. split the DNVP Reichstag delegation. Although the majority voted against the plan, the minority's support enabled passage, leaving a legacy of division and bitterness.[18]

The DNVP's success in the two national elections of 1924 strengthened the party's case for participating in government. Thus in the following year it joined the cabinet of the former Minister of Finance, Hans Luther, and was now in a position to influence policy.[19] Yet the difficult juggling of interest groups and the inevitable need to compromise in coalition governments disappointed even the Nationalists' beneficiaries. The first problem arose from the draconian budget cuts introduced in late 1923 to stabilize the currency, which disproportionately affected the middle and working classes. They included the revaluation of mortgages, investments, and savings that fell well short of the paper value of such instruments, the elimination of civil service positions and cuts in pensions, the imposition of a panoply of taxes on consumption, and compulsory mortgages imposed on agricultural property. The most that the DNVP could achieve, legislation that raised the revaluation from 15 per cent of paper value to 25 per cent fell well short of the demands of embittered small investors. The second problem, addressing the agrarian depression—weakness in the face of foreign competition, mounting indebtedness, and foreclosures—satisfied neither large or small holders.[20] The Rural League did win tariff protection against foreign imports, but the bill's limitations convinced suspicious estate-owning grain producers that the party's industrialists blocked a more generous package that would compromise their access to international capital markets. Then there were the festering wounds of the post-war peace settlement. Capitalizing on the Dawes Plan's long-term goal of restoring German sovereignty over the Ruhr and Rhine basin and the evacuation of Allied troops from east of the Rhine, Gustav Stresemann opened negotiations on a Rhineland security pact with France and Belgium to end the occupation, fix Germany's post-war boundaries, and admit Germany to the League of Nations. The nationalist associations announced in response that unless the DNVP rejected admission to the League of Nations and received the guarantee of a formal repudiation of the 'war guilt' clause of the Versailles Treaty, they would not support the party's continuation in government. Unable to persuade its coalition partners to accept what the patriotic right demanded, the DNVP gave with one hand but took away with the other. It accepted the Locarno Treaty, but to forestall another intra-party schism, the Nationalists resigned from the cabinet.[21]

In 1927, the Nationalists once again joined the government, the fourth cabinet of Wilhelm Marx, at the behest of interest groups and their new chairman, Kuno von Westarp. Yet the divisions that arose and dissatisfaction with the cabinet's inability to deliver, differed little from the DNVP's experience two years earlier. The DNVP's labour wing pushed for the passage of unemployment insurance and the restoration of the eight-hour day to compensate workers, who suffered from the costs of stabilization and the post-stabilization recession, infuriating business leaders, who demanded tax relief and sharp reductions in government spending. Only a laboriously negotiated compromise prevented the latter from withdrawing their financial contributions to the party. The inability of Martin Schiele, the DNVP Minister of Agriculture, to win support from the cabinet for his comprehensive programme to increase tariff protection over the 1925 level and reduce rural indebtedness, alienated the Rural League's membership, who struggled to survive in a catastrophic rural economy. The DNVP's reluctant support for the renewal of the Law for the Protection of the Republic, passed in 1922 in the aftermath of the assassinations of Matthias Erzberger and the Foreign Minister Walther Rathenau, once more enraged the anti-republican patriotic right, especially because it included a paragraph that prevented the return of the Kaiser and his family.[22] Taken together internecine conflict and the lack of intra-party consensus discredited parliamentary politics and opened the door to a radical nationalist alternative embodied in the Pan-German newspaper and film magnate, Alfred Hugenberg. For Hugenberg, the DNVP's interest articulation undermined the party's founding premise, a national conservative movement opposed to the alleged Weimar 'system'. He proposed instead to create a broadly based right-wing 'national opposition', which informed by a coherent anti-republican and anti-Versailles worldview (*Weltanschauung*), would eliminate all parties between the new movement and the Marxist left.[23]

To make matters worse for the Nationalists, clear and ominous signs of middle-class disaffection overlapped with the party's two participations in government. In the two national elections of 1924, the DVNP's gains at the polls indicated that splinter parties had not yet threatened its support. Yet the results of intervening regional elections two years later indicated that the party's struggle with the irreconcilable claims of its diverse interest groups was failing. In the fall of 1926, the regional elections in Saxony testified to the increased attraction to the middle class of splinter parties, among them the Reich Party of the German Middle Class, formerly known as the Business Party, and the Reich Party for People's Justice and Revaluation. Their gains came at the expense of the Protestant bourgeois parties, the DDP, the DVP, and the DNVP. In early 1928, as Germany approached another national election, yet another new party emerged, the Christian National Peasants and Farmers Party (Christlich-Nationale Bauern- und Landvolkpartei or CNBLP), which siphoned support from the Rural League's regional affiliates. Even though the Rural League's leadership had become less elitist and more inclusive, the government's insufficient support for agriculture and the League's decentralized structure encouraged peasants and small farmers to vote with their feet. The results of the 1928 elections confirmed the degree to which the special interest parties had profited at the expense of the liberal parties and the DNVP. In 1919 and 1920, small parties accounted for only 3 per cent of the vote. In 1924 they increased their combined total to 8.3 per cent. By 1928 their combined electorate reached 14 per cent.[24]

The 1928 Reichstag elections testified to the failure of the governmentalist pragmatism that Kuno von Westarp had come to personify. The DNVP lost one-third of its electorate, plunging from 20.5 per cent in December 1924 to 14.2 per cent. The performance of the liberal parties, the DVP and the DDP, was even worse.[25] Even more disturbing were the gains of the Social Democrats, who would now head a 'grand coalition', which extended from the SPD to the Centre. In the wake of the DNVP's shellacking and the resurgence of the left, Hugenberg assumed the party chairmanship from Westarp, already weakened by the withdrawal of support from the powerful Prussian-based Central Association of German Conservatives, which he had helped to found.[26] Seeking to transform the party into an instrument of the radical right, Hugenberg assaulted Stresemann's negotiations toward a final settlement of German reparations payments in return for the withdrawal of Allied forces from the Rhineland. Launching a referendum campaign in the summer of 1929 against what would become known as the Young Plan, the projected 'Law against the Enslavement of the German People', included a provision to try and imprison the signatories of this latest evolution of Stresemann's policy of 'fulfillment'. Hugenberg strove to incorporate all nationalist organizations, including the National Socialists, whose electoral support was at that point modest. For its part the DNVP was reluctant to associate with the Hitler movement because of the party's 'socialism', but for Hugenberg the inclusion of NSDAP in the 'national opposition' was a risk worth taking. In the end, the 'Freedom Law' failed in large part because of objections within the 'national opposition' to the 'imprisonment' clause. Yet that defeat hardly discouraged Hugenberg from further campaigns to solidify a radical nationalist assault against the republic, even at the cost of his own party's viability.[27]

Hugenberg's first decision as chairman, to centralize the DNVP's structure to enforce party discipline and assure a united front, was in itself ironic. He understood the consequences of the party's decentralization, which encouraged fragmentation and made it easier for the Nationalists' middle-class electorate to desert the party. Yet Hugenberg failed to appreciate the disillusion and especially the independence of one-time supporters, who had fuelled the DNVP's disintegration. Furthermore his dictatorial leadership caused further secessions that resulted in new parties, the Christian Social People's Service (Christlich-sozialer Volksdienst) which represented the party's labour wing, and the Conservative People's Party (Konservative Volkspartei). Having witnessed the defections of its local chapters to the CNBLP, Nationalist backers in the Rural League had little choice but to follow suit. Hugenberg placed his hopes in a broad 'national opposition', which would reconstitute the right from below under his leadership, unwilling to appreciate the assertiveness of other elements in the coalition, most notably the National Socialists. Yet he would also undertake another option, lobbying within the state. For conservative elites accustomed to exercising power, the pursuit of their own interests, material or radical nationalist, would only and could only occur at the highest levels of government. The liberal and conservative parties, who once represented them, no longer sufficed as reliable or effective conduits.

The Centre Party and the Catholic Right: Conflict and Cohesion in the Catholic Milieu

Formed in 1870, the Centre sought to protect and represent Catholic interests against a hostile Protestant majority in Prussia. That struggle intensified after German unification with Bismarck's 'cultural struggle' (*Kulturkampf*), which aimed to destroy the political influence of the Catholic clergy and the sedition of what Bismarck believed was the Catholic 'enemy within'.[28] The Centre Party remained true to its *raison d'être* until its dissolution in June 1933. Bound together as much by the Catholic faith and Catholic social teaching as by the Protestant stigmatization of the Catholic minority, the Centre electorate remained relatively stable under the Weimar Republic unlike the Protestant bourgeois parties—this despite the migration of Catholics away from the Centre that began before the First World War and despite worrisome fluctuations in voter support afterwards. The territorial losses stipulated by the Versailles Treaty, which included the loss of Upper Silesia in the former Prussian east, reduced the Centre's constituency. Yet the extension of the franchise to women in 1919 made up for it. Defending the Christian foundations of home, family, and Church bound Catholic women to the party.[29] Nevertheless the Centre's social diversity, composed of workers in the mining and textile industries, peasants, middle-class professionals, industrialists, and titled nobility, contributed to tensions that periodically threatened the party's cohesion, especially in the last two years of the war and after the 1918 revolution. Under the Second Empire, the Centre customarily allied with the Conservative Party because it feared the secularism and anti-Catholicism of the liberal parties and the Social Democrats. Yet the strains of wartime drove the party's Reichstag delegation to move in a different direction. Pushed by Centre's labour movement and the leader of its Reichstag delegation, Matthias Erzberger, the party joined with the Progressives and Majority Socialists to pass the 'Peace Resolution' in July 1917 to demand a negotiated end to the war and the renunciation of forced territorial acquisitions. The elections to the National Assembly in January 1919 continued the alliance inasmuch as the Centre joined with the Majority Socialists and the Democratic Party, the successor to the Progressives, in the 'Weimar Coalition'.[30] This did not mean that the Centre had abandoned its anti-liberalism and anti-socialism, for cultural issues at odds with liberals and the left served to unify Catholics. Nowhere was this clearer than in the Centre's and the Catholic and Protestant churches' opposition to socialists' efforts to curtail the influence of religion in the schools. It was equally evident in the Centre's appeals to women voters, which condemned socialist 'materialism', the socialists' suppression of the public role of Christianity, and the refusal of the left to acknowledge gender difference or women's traditional role as central to the moral fabric of society. Yet, remarkably, a common commitment to the establishment of a liberal democracy brought the parties together.[31]

The reaction to the Centre's leftward tack opened deep internal divisions, prompting the secession of Bavarian Catholics, who in 1919 established the Bavarian People's Party (BVP). Although it subsequently agreed to collaborate with the Centre legislatively, the BVP acted on its own initiative. Following the death of the Social Democratic President Friedrich Ebert in 1925, the BVP endorsed the war hero and icon of national unity, Paul von Hindenburg, rather than supporting Wilhelm Marx, the republican candidate and Centre Party member, whom many Catholics rejected for his association with the anticlerical and anti-monarchist Social Democrats.[32] Yet the main threat to the Centre's survival came from Catholic conservative elites; high-ranking civil servants, and especially landowning aristocrats from the Catholic heartlands of Bavaria, the Rhineland, and Westphalia, who proved as adept as the National Rural League in blocking socialist attempts to organize farm labourers. Contemptuous of popular sovereignty and unsettled by the Catholic labour movement's support for the republic, Catholic conservatives sought a corporatist society as opposed to one divided by class and the restoration of the monarchy, or at least the creation of a divinely sanctioned authoritarian state. Influenced by the *Ur*-catastrophe of the French Revolution, which unleashed liberalism, socialism, freemasonry, and unrestrained materialistic capitalism, they demanded the exclusion of Jews from public life.[33] Among Catholic conservatives, the Rhenish-Westphalian aristocracy stood out in its anti-republican radicalism to the extent that a number of Catholic nobles gravitated to the National Socialists after its electoral breakthrough in September 1930.

The Reichstag elections of 1920 resulted in the defeat of the Weimar Coalition and a drop in the Centre's electorate from 19.7 per cent the previous year to 13.6 per cent.[34] The results emboldened Catholic conservatives to consider political alternatives in light of the evidence of the Centre's vulnerability. For Bavarian conservatives, the secessionist BVP was their party of choice. Others chose among four options.[35] The first championed by the Westphalian nobleman, Franz von Papen, whose tenure as Reich Chancellor in 1932 would become notorious, was to remain in the Centre and aggressively push it to the right. Or alternatively one could simply choose to remain in the party if only to avoid alienating the Catholic clergy and losing the support of the peasantry, which was critical to defending the agrarian interests. The second option, reflected in the decision of Ferdinand von Lüninck, who would become governor of Westphalia during the Third Reich, was to pursue conservative political ends by joining the Stahlhelm. The third, pursued by Ferdinand's brother, Hermann, was a new conservative monarchist party, the Christian People's Party (Christliche Volkspartei), which although envisioned as an alternative to the Centre would cooperate with it on the vital interests of religion and the Church. The final option was the conservative interconfessional solution. One could join the DNVP in an effort to eliminate the historical antagonism between Protestants and Catholics and seek Germany's revitalization as a broadly Christian nation. Prominent Rhenish and Westphalian aristocrats led by Baron Alfred von Landsberg-Steinfurt and his brother Englebert von Landsberg-Velen took the initiative in bringing the DNVP's Reich Catholic Committee into existence. Yet the committee's membership appealed to elites beyond the aristocracy, including one of its most prominent 'young conservative' intellectuals, Martin Spahn.

Of the alternatives to the Centre, the third, the Christian People's Party, did not survive for long. Although modestly successful in Rhineland Catholic districts in the 1920 Reichstag elections, it failed to appeal to peasants who remained staunchly loyal to the Centre. The DNVP's National Catholic Committee was more successful, expanding rapidly after its founding in 1920. In the two national elections in 1924, the DNVP placed Catholic members on both tickets. Yet despite the promise of an inter-confessional conservative partnership, DNVP Protestants and especially the Protestant churches were chronically wary of losing their influence.[36] Those fears culminated in 1929 when a proposed concordat between the Holy See and the Prussian government caused the Lutheran Church to insist that the party demand a comparable agreement. The government's refusal to do so and the party's refusal in return to allow Catholic deputies to vote with their conscience led to the resignation of the Catholic Committee's leadership, except for Martin Spahn, who allied himself with Hugenberg. The Committee's opposition came not just from Protestants but also from the Catholic clergy, who feared an inter-confessional alternative that would water down the substance of the faith and tack too close to the anti-republican right. Nevertheless, whatever the tensions between Catholics and Protestants over DNVP's cultural and religious positions, DNVP Catholics did not abandon their efforts to expand their influence in staunchly Catholic regions, especially among Catholic peasant associations.[37]

Despite the opposition of Catholic conservatives, the Centre was crucial to the formation of republican governments. Unlike the Nationalists for whom the prospect of entering the government sparked bitter internal debate, the Centre's tenure in national cabinets, as well as in the Prussian regional government where the 'Weimar Coalition' survived, remained unbroken until 1932 where it occupied a mediating position comparable to its role in coalitions under the Second Empire. Despite the fluctuations among the Centre's electorate, from 13.2 per cent in 1920, dropping to 11.3 per cent in 1928, and rebounding to 13.5 per cent in 1932,[38] its relative cohesion as a 'worldview party' (*Weltanschauungspartei*) anchored in Catholicism and its flexibility as a coalition partner made it indispensable. Even more remarkable was that its leaders occupied a position that Centrists had not assumed in Imperial Germany, that of Chancellor. During the Weimar era, the Centre produced four, Joseph Wirth, Constantin Fehrenbach, Wilhelm Marx—who led four cabinets—and Heinrich Brüning. A fifth, Franz von Papen, a Centrist of long standing who briefly served as Chancellor in 1932, severed his relationship with the party when he assumed office. Nevertheless, the social diversity of the Centre's electorate all but guaranteed that the party was not immune to division, especially that which re-emerged near the end of the 1920s.

Indeed the disappointing results of the Reichstag elections of 1928, in which the Centre's electorate dropped to 12 per cent from 13.5 per cent in December 1924, renewed fears that the defection of workers, middle-class voters, and peasants signified the erosion of the Catholic milieu.[39] In turn, intra-party conflict escalated, and the party chairman, Wilhelm Marx, was forced to resign. Marx's expected successor, the chair of the Reichstag delegation and leader of the Centre's trade union wing Adam Stegerwald, could not surmount the hostility of civil servants infuriated by Stegerwald's opposition to increasing their salaries. The solution was a dark horse, Ludwig Kaas, a monsignor and canon lawyer with close ties to Cardinal Eugenio Pacelli, the papal nuncio to Germany. In addition to satisfying the Centre's middle-class constituencies, Kaas embodied the party's transcending confessional principles that defined the Catholic milieu, which had been critical in the past to containing factional conflict. By subsequently appointing Stegerwald as chairman of the Centre's Reichstag delegation, Kaas ensured the party's continued cohesion.[40]

Until recently, historians considered Kaas to have been an uncomplicated conservative, an unambiguous and even ominous indication of the Centre's shift to the right.[41] Though this is generally true, Kaas' political views were more nuanced. He accepted the republic's legitimacy and that of its constitution, not least because the Catholic experience as a minority had historically required legal and constitutional protection. Given the Centre's social diversity, Kaas also accepted the party's responsibility to reconcile all interests. To address the deepening inter- and intra-party conflicts that characterized Weimar especially after 1928, Kaas promoted a policy of 'gathering' (*Sammlung*), which would unite all well-meaning politicians from the DNVP to the Social Democrats that would strive for consensus. That such hopes had little likelihood of success in a polarized political climate was the first of Kaas's problems. The second was his weakness as party leader, the result of his political inexperience, his ongoing health problems, and his commitment to his other position as intermediary between the papal nuncio and the German bishops.[42] The third was the ongoing threat of the Catholic right. In addition to having made inroads into Catholic associations loyal to the Centre, DNVP Catholics remained politically active locally, increasing their support from voters, especially academics and students attracted to their radical nationalism and racial antisemitism. The migration of many Westphalian aristocrats to Hugenberg's 'national opposition' and their growing support of the Nazi movement despite the disapproval of the Catholic episcopacy was even more worrisome. By 1931, Catholic support for the Stahlhelm referendum, which aimed to dissolve the Prussian Landtag dominated by the 'Weimar Coalition', gave further indication that the attraction to Nazism was no fluke.[43] Yet the emergence of Kaas as the Centre's unifier promised its continuation as the only intact 'state' party to the right of the Social Democrats, and as a result the Centre held the potential for anchoring a coalition that might have addressed the economic crisis and political gridlock were it not for the disillusion with parliamentary politics among conservative elites and the encroaching authoritarianism at the top.

Conservative Elites and the Authoritarian Solution

In 1930, the collapse of the Grand Coalition, which extended from the Social Democrats to the DVP, ended the last Weimar government that could command a parliamentary majority. Conflicts over public spending and unemployment compensation grew especially acrimonious after the onset of the Great Depression and the sudden death of Gustav Stresemann during the previous year.[44] In response, Reich President Hindenburg and the chief of the military's Office of Ministerial Affairs, Kurt von Schleicher, moved to construct a government of the right, which would rule by presidential authority rather than by parliamentary majority. Unable to persuade the DNVP's former chairman Kuno von Westarp to form a government against the wishes of Alfred Hugenberg,

Schleicher and Hindenberg settled on the leader of the Centre Reichstag delegation, Heinrich Brüning, who had succeeded Stegerwald in 1929. Although appointing two members of the Catholic labour movement, Stegerwald and Joseph Wirth, to cabinet positions that would reassure the Social Democrats, and seeking a broadly based coalition that included the moderate right, Brüning was a dyed-in-the-wool conservative, fiscal and otherwise. He wanted to strengthen the power of the presidency, balance the state budget, and cut spending at all levels of government, all of which converged in his goal of liquidating Germany's obligation to pay reparations to the Allies.

The debate over Brüning's commitment to parliamentary democracy (or the lack of it), continues unabated. Recent scholarship, drawing on the perception of contemporaries, has questioned teleological approaches that see Brüning as having launched Weimar's irreversible collapse.[45] To be sure, Brüning's repeated use of Article 48 of the Weimar Constitution to implement his deflationary policies, which allowed the President to issue emergency decrees without the Reichstag's consent, set a precedent that could not be reversed. Nevertheless the abrupt end to Bruning's tenure in 1932 indicated that for the Chancellor's opposition he was not authoritarian enough. Indeed, Brüning's long career in the Centre, which began serving as Adam Stegerwald's deputy in the Christian labour movement, translated into strong support from the Catholic milieu and the party leader Kaas. In addition, the Centre remained a republican party opposed to the anti-constitutional right. Nowhere was this clearer than in the overwhelming support that Catholics lent to Hindenburg's re-election as President in 1932 in order to block the candidacies of Adolf Hitler and the Stahlhelm leader, Theodor Duesterberg. Catholic bishops, who prohibited priests from joining the paramilitaries and condemned Catholic aristocrats for their increasing support of the Nazi movement, remained loyal to the Centre. The April 1932 state parliamentary elections in Prussia where the 'Weimar Coalition' still prevailed gave further indication of the Centre's durability. Its defence of Catholic cultural and religious values, its continued willingness to cooperate with the Social Democrats, and its strong condemnation of racist nationalism beat back the Catholic right.[46] Yet Brüning's history as a party man and his decision to include organized labour because of it contributed to his undoing.

After 1930, the state—the president's office and the ministerial bureaucracy—was clearly the focal point of political decisions rather than the Reichstag, an avenue that conservative elites appropriated to advance their interests much to Brüning's disadvantage. Dispensing with party politics meant not having to deal with conflicts among dissatisfied interest groups that promised a better chance of success. The demands of large landowners for a sweeping agrarian relief package mediated through President Hindenburg gave the Chancellor and his Minister of Agriculture Martin Schiele little choice but to produce one. That the package ultimately failed to alleviate the agrarian crisis made estate owners more determined to seek Brüning's removal. Industrial elites, especially those in heavy industry who sought the wholesale elimination of compulsory arbitration and the reduction of wages, insisted that Brüning be fired because he refused to abandon the Stegerwald wing of the Christian labour movement and relied on the toleration of the Social Democrats in the Reichstag. Brüning sympathized with the desire of business to cut costs, to which the stunning range of his austerity measures testified. They included wage, salary, and pension cuts in the public sector, cuts in social services, retirement benefits, and public assistance for veterans. They reduced Reich funding for the states, and an emergency income tax on the self-employed and white-collar workers in public service jobs.[47] Yet Brüning did not produce what industrialists most wanted, the political castration of organized labour, Christian and Social Democratic. Moreover, Brüning's belated proposal, which the Centre's labour contingent advocated, to settle bankrupt agrarian estates with unemployed workers infuriated the agrarian elite. Ultimately Brüning lost Hindenburg's confidence. Having sought to govern sharply to the right to strengthen the powers of the presidency, Hindenburg resented that his re-election had resulted from the votes of Social Democrats, Centrists, and Democrats while his two rivals, the Stahlhelm leader Theodor Duesterberg and Adolf Hitler, captured voters who had supported him in 1925.[48] There is no doubt that the fragmentation of the German right and the divisions among elites destroyed the bourgeois parties and contributed to the devastating outcome of 30 January 1933. Yet because conservative elites, now freed from the constraints of party politics, could pursue their interests with fewer complications, their role in the rise of the Third Reich was indispensable.

Despite the Centre's cohesion and its success in keeping the Catholic right at bay, the penultimate pre-Hitler Chancellor, the arch-conservative and long-time Centrist Franz von Papen gave the latter influence at the top. For General Schleicher, who recommended Papen for the position, the Westphalian aristocrat had the right qualifications. He could be counted on to deploy his extensive connections to estate agriculture and industry to back conservative elites who objected to Brüning. Moreover, Papen served in the army as a major during the war, which testified to his suitability to a key component of the conservative establishment. Whereas the Centre supported Brüning, Papen did not, having objected to the Brüning's refusal to reconstruct his government by incorporating what remained of the DNVP and the second largest party in the Reichstag, the National Socialists. Once Papen replaced Brüning, his radical agenda alienated Kaas and ruptured his relationship with the Centre. In addition to attacking the failures of his predecessor's government, Papen lifted the ban on the Nazi Stormtroopers, orchestrated a coup against the Prussian state government, and presided over a 'cabinet of barons', composed of three former DNVP members and six aristocrats who possessed not a scintilla of popular legitimacy. Committed to saving private enterprise and weakening organized labour, Papen's austerity measures were at least as draconian as Brüning's, having issued emergency decrees that imposed a means test for unemployment compensation and gave employers the right to reduce wages below levels set by collective bargaining agreements.[49]

Papen's influence should have evaporated given that his tenure as Chancellor lasted less than six months. Yet his close ties to Hindenburg guaranteed his survival as a political operative, which began with undermining General Schleicher, his former benefactor and successor as Chancellor. Schleicher's efforts to form a coalition that extended from the Social Democratic trade unions to the Centre and to the 'left' wing of the Nazis, made it easy for Papen to do so. Schleicher's proposed public works projects to curtail urban unemployment and the resurrection of Brüning's plan to resettle unemployed workers on bankrupt estates raised the ire of industrialists and agrarians, who demanded Schleicher's ouster. That allowed Papen to pursue a new government that would realize Hindenburg's dream of a united *Volksgemeinschaft*—an anti-Marxist and anti-parliamentarian cabinet dominated by elites but including the National Socialists.[50] A series of meetings with Hitler which Papen initiated, starting with the conference at the home of the Cologne banker, Kurt von Schroeder, in early January 1933 resulted at the end of the month in a conservative-Nazi government of 'national concentration' with Hitler as Chancellor.[51]

Conclusion: Converging Radicalisms

If Franz von Papen undermined the Centre by circumventing it from above, Alfred Hugenberg's contribution to the destruction of Weimar was no less significant. Having organized the 'national opposition' against the Young Plan in 1929, Hugenberg was arguably the first conservative political leader to reach out to the National Socialists. To be sure, Hugenberg soon found that dealing with Adolf Hitler was a challenge, a prime example being the re-emergence of the 'national opposition' at an anti-Brüning rally at Bad Harzburg in October 1931. Unwilling to subordinate himself to 'reactionaries', Hitler went out of his way to assert his party's independence by arriving late to the meeting and ignoring the demonstrations of other right-wing organizations.[52] Nevertheless Hitler's independence did not dissuade Hugenberg from attacking Brüning for having failed to bring the Nazis into his government. Nor for that matter did it deter Hugenberg from lacerating Schleicher, Brüning's successor, for his 'reparliamentarization', his attempt to form a government that included the Centre as well as the Nazis.[53] Nor too did it prevent Hugenberg from asserting his own ambition to oversee economic policy in a conservative-Nazi government of 'national concentration'. Unable to jettison his belief that National Socialist populism could be managed, Hugenberg betrayed the deep-seated assumptions of a media magnate accustomed to exercising power. In so doing, he adhered to what Schleicher called the 'taming strategy', the belief that including Nazis in a government of the right, even if that meant a Hitler chancellorship, would force the Hitler movement to share the burden of responsibility.

Ultimately the execution of the 'taming strategy' emerged from the intersection of two developments, the first of which was the erosion of parliamentary government and the sidelining of the Centre. The second was the authoritarian alternative that began with Brüning, developed further under Papen's 'cabinet of barons', and came to fruition in the government of 'national concentration'. Ironically it was the right-wing Catholic renegade, Franz von Papen, who realized the goals of Hugenberg and other conservative elites disenchanted with parliamentary democracy. Although a thorn in the side of the Centre, the Catholic right was never able to dominate the party. Yet once the office of the Reich President sidestepped parliament as the route to securing conservative interests, it became possible for a single Catholic arch-conservative with the requisite elitist connections and Hindenburg's consent to subvert the republic once and for all. With Hindenburg's support, Papen brought the conservative-Nazi government into existence to protect and advance conservative priorities, eliminate Weimar parliamentarism, and discipline the National Socialists' populist radicalism. That the authoritarian system turned into fascist one was not what conservatives sought. Yet that outcome occurred because conservative elites gambled that the Hitler movement could be contained.

Notes

1. Hermann Beck and Larry Eugene Jones (eds), *From Weimar to Hitler: Studies in the Dissolution of the Weimar Republic and the Establishment of the Third Reich, 1932–1934* (New York/Oxford: Berghahn, 2018), 2–3; Larry Eugene Jones (ed.), *The German Right in the Weimar Republic: Studies in the History of German Conservatism, Nationalism, and Antisemitism* (New York/Oxford: Berghahn, 2013), 1–3. On the development of populist nationalism, see Peter Fritzsche, *Germans into Nazis* (Cambridge, MA, and London: Harvard University Press, 1998).
2. Larry Eugene Jones, *The German Right, 1918–1930: Political Parties, Organized Interests, and Patriotic Associations in the Struggle Against Weimar Democracy* (Cambridge: Cambridge University Press, 2020), 24–32.
3. Jones, *German Right*, 34–5.
4. Eric D. Weitz, *Weimar Germany: Promise and Tragedy* (Princeton and Oxford: Princeton University Press, 2007), 35.
5. Jones, *German Right*, 95–103.
6. This is the suggestion of Thomas Mergel. See his 'Das Scheitern des deutschen Tory-Konservatismus: Die Umformung der DNVP zu einer rechtsradikalen Partei 1928–1932', *Historische Zeitschrift*, 276 (2003), 323–68. See also Mergel's *Parlamentarische Kultur in der Weimarer Republik: Politische Kommunikation, symbolische Politik und Öffentlichkeit im Reichstag* (Düsseldorf: Droste, 2012, 3rd edn.), esp. 323–31.
7. For extensive profiles of the DNVP's target constituencies, see Jones, *German Right*, 28–32, 38–41, 48–76, 113–43, and 145–51.
8. Ulrike Ehret, *Church, Nation and Race: Catholics and Antisemitism in Germany and England, 1918–45* (Manchester; Manchester University Press, 2012), 120–7.
9. On the party affiliations of conservative women, see Raffael Scheck, *Mothers of the Nation: Right-Wing Women in Weimar Germany* (Oxford/New York; Berg, 2004), 4–5, and 23–47, and Julia Sneeringer, *Winning Women's Votes: Propaganda and Politics in Weimar Germany* (Chapel Hill, NC, and London: University of North Carolina Press, 2002), 42–51.
10. For examples, see Fritz Fischer, *Bündnis der Eliten: Zur Kontinuität der Machtstrukturen in Deutschland 1875–1945* (Düsseldorf: Droste, 1979); Hans-Ulrich Wehler, *The German Empire 1871–1918* (Leamington Spa: Berg, 1985), esp. the concluding chapter, and Hans-Jürgen Puhle, *Agrarische Interessenpolitik und preußische Konservatismus im Wilhelminischen Reich (1893–1914): Ein Beitrag zur Analyse der Nationalismus in Deutschland am Beispiel des Bundes der Landwirte und der Deutsch-Konservativen Partei* (Bonn: Verlag Neue Gesellschaft, 1967).

11. Weitz, *Weimar Germany*, 27–8; Hans Mommsen, *The Rise and Fall of Weimar Democracy*, tr. Elborg Forster and Larry Eugene Jones (Chapel Hill, NC, and London: University of North Carolina Press, 1996), 41–4. See also Gerald Feldman, 'German Business between War and Revolution: The Origins of the Stinnes-Legien Agreement', in Gerhard A. Ritter (ed.), *Entstehung und Wandel der modernen Gesellschaft: Festschrift für Hans Rosenberg zum 65. Geburtstag* (Berlin: de Gruyter, 1970), 312–41.
12. On rural unrest during wartime and after, see Jens-Flemming, *Landwirtschaftliche Interessen und Demokratie: Ländliche Gesellschaft, Agrarverbände und Staat, 1890-1925* (Bonn: Verlag Neue Gesellschaft, 1978), 161–251, and Robert G. Moeller, *German Peasants and Agrarian Politics 1914-1924: The Rhineland and Westphalia* (Chapel Hill, NC, and London: University of North Carolina Press, 1986), 68–115.
13. Jones, *German Right*, 55–63. On the resurrection of large landed agriculture, see Dieter Gessner, *Agrarverbände in der Weimar Republik: Wirtschaftliche und soziale Voraussetzungen agrarkonservativer Politik von 1933* (Düsseldorf: Droste Verlag, 1976), 28–65, and Shelley Baranowski, *The Sanctity of Rural Life: Nobility, Protestantism and Nazism in Weimar Prussia* (New York and Oxford: Oxford University Press, 1995), 35–51.
14. Jones, *German Right*, 311–12. For the DNVP's election results, see Thomas Childers, *The Nazi Voter: The Social Foundations of Fascism in Germany, 1919-1933* (Chapel Hill, NC, and London: University of North Carolina Press, 1983), 57–8, 61.
15. Jones, *German Right*, 267–9.
16. Larry Eugene Jones, 'Conservative Antisemitism in the Weimar Republic: A Case Study of the German National People's Party', in Jones, *German Right* , 79–107; Sneeringer, *Winning Women's Votes*, 42–51.
17. On the politics of inflation and stabilization, see Gerald D. Feldman, *The Great Disorder: Politics, Economics, and Society in the German Inflation 1914-1924* (New York/Oxford: Oxford University Press, 1997), 698–835.
18. Jones, *German Right*, 231–40.
19. For a detailed analysis of the 1924 elections, see Childers, *Nazi Voter*, 50–118.
20. On the multiple difficulties of German agriculture, see Harold James, *The German Slump: Politics and Economics 1924-1936* (Oxford: Clarendon Press, 1986), 247–82.
21. Jones, *German Right*, 311–29.
22. Ibid., 331–62.
23. Larry Eugene Jones, '"The Greatest Stupidity of my Life": Alfred Hugenberg and the Formation of the Hitler Cabinet, January 1933', *Journal of Contemporary History*, 27 (1992), 65.
24. Jones, *German Right*, 352–57; For a concise overview, see Attila Chanady, 'The Disintegration of the German National People's Party, 1924-1930', *Journal of Modern History*, 39 (1967), 65–80. See also Childers, *Nazi Voter*, 125–6.
25. Karl Rohe, *Wahlen und Wählertraditionen in Deutschland* (Frankfurt am Main: Suhrkamp, 1992), 145.
26. Daniela Gasteiger, 'From Friends to Foes: Count Kuno von Westarp and the Transformation of the German Right', in Jones, *German Right*, 48–78.
27. Jones, *German Right*, 470–92; John A. Leopold, *Alfred Hugenberg: The Radical Nationalist Campaign Against the Weimar Republic* (New Haven and London: Yale University Press, 1977), 55–83.
28. David Blackbourn, *Apparitions of the Virgin Mary in Nineteenth-Century Germany* (New York: Alfred A. Knopf, 1994), 85–91.

29. Rohe, *Wahlen und Wählertraditionen*, 159. Jürgen Falter, *Hitlers Wähler* (Munich: C. H. Beck, 1991), 171–2; Ehret, *Church, Nation and Race*, 20; Childers, *Nazi Voter*, 42; Sneeringer, *Winning Women's Votes*, 37–42.
30. Roger Chickering, *Imperial Germany and the Great War, 1914–1918* (Cambridge: Cambridge University Press, 2004), 161; Rudolf Morsey, *Die Deutsche Zentrumspartei 1917–1923* (Düsseldorf: Droste, 1966); Klaus Epstein, *Matthias Erzberger and the Dilemma of German Democracy* (Princeton: Princeton University Press, 1959).
31. Sneeringer, *Winning Women's Votes*, 37–42.
32. Ehret, *Church, Nation and Race*, 20; Anna von der Goltz, *Hindenburg: Power, Myth and the Rise of the Nazis* (Oxford: Oxford University Press, 2009), 96–7.
33. Ulrike Ehret, 'Antisemitism and the Jewish Question in the Political Worldview of the Catholic Right', in Jones, *German Right*, 222–33. On the Rhenish-Westphalian aristocracy, see Larry Eugene Jones, 'Catholic Conservatives in the Weimar Republic: The Politics of the Rhenish-Westphalian Aristocracy, 1918–1933', *German History*, 18/1 (2000), 60–85; and Stephan Malinowski, *Vom König zum Führer: Deutscher Adel und Nationalsozialismus* (Frankfurt am Main: Fischer, 2004), 385–94.
34. Eberhard Kolb and Dirk Schumann, *Die Weimarer Republik*, 8th ed. (Munich: Oldenbourg, 2013), 344.
35. On the alternatives, see Jones, 'Catholic Conservatives', 65–75; Moeller, *German Peasants and Agrarian Politics*, 118–35; Ulrike Ehret, 'Antisemitism and the Jewish Question', 220–43.
36. On the founding of the DNVP's Catholic committee, see Christoph Hübner, *Die Rechtskatholiken, die Zentrumspartei um die katholische Kirche in Deutschland bis zum Reichskonkordat von 1933* (Berlin: LIT, 2014), 235–64. See also Jones, *German Right*, 248-9.
37. See Hübner, *Rechtskatholiken*, 265–342, and the effort to make inroads into the peasants' associations, 496–501.
38. Rohe, *Wahlen und Wählertraditionen*, 143.
39. Mergel, *Parlamentarische Kultur*, 418.
40. Jones, *German Right*, 437-44.
41. Kolb and Schumann, *Weimarer Republik*, 79.
42. For a new assessment of Kaas, see Martin Menke, 'Ludwig Kaas and the End of the German Center Party', in Beck and Jones, *Weimar to Hitler*, 79–110.
43. Ehret, *Church, Nation and Race*, 136–7; Hübner, *Rechtskatholiken*, 643-669; Malinowski, *Vom König zum Führer*, 389–94.
44. Mommsen, *Rise and Fall*, 281–2.
45. See Anthony McElligott, *Rethinking the Weimar Republic: Authority and Authoritarianism 1916–1936* (London: Bloomsbury, 2014), 190–1; Tim B. Müller, 'The Opportunities and Challenges of Democracy: Weimar and Beyond', *Bulletin of the German Historical Institute*, 65 (2019), 118–19. See also Larry Eugene Jones's assessment in his *Hitler versus Hindenburg: The 1932 Presidential Elections and the End of the Weimar Republic* (Cambridge: Cambridge University Press, 2016), 68–9. For an alternative interpretation of Brüning, see William L. Patch, Jr, *Heinrich Brüning and the Dissolution of the Weimar Republic* (Cambridge: Cambridge University Press, 1998), 73–89.
46. Jones, *Hitler versus Hindenburg*, 209–12, 325–6.
47. Jones, *Hitler versus Hindenburg*, 77–80. See also Thomas Childers, *The Third Reich: A History of Nazi Germany* (New York and London: Simon & Schuster, 2017), 130.

48. On the presidential election, see Jones, *Hitler versus Hindenburg*, 275–313, 342–3; Wolfram Pyta, *Hindenburg: Herrschaft zwischen Hohenzollern und Hitler* (Munich: Pantheon, 2009), 672–83; and von der Goltz, *Hindenburg*, 142–66.
49. Childers, *Third Reich*, 204.
50. For Hindenburg's objectives, see Pyta, *Hindenburg*, 769–88, and von der Goltz, *Hindenburg*, 167–70.
51. Jones, *Hitler versus Hindenburg*, 346–61; Hübner, *Rechtskatholiken*, 688–99; Larry Eugene Jones, 'Franz von Papen, the German Center Party, and the Failure of Catholic Conservatism in the Weimar Republic', *Central European History*, 38 (2009), 206–17; Pyta, *Hindenburg*, 701–6.
52. Larry Eugene Jones, 'Nationalists, Nazis, and the Assault Against Weimar: Revisiting the Harzburg Rally of October 1931', *German Studies Review*, 29 (2006), 483–94.
53. Jones, 'Greatest Stupidity', 69–70.

Bibliography

Ehret, Ulrike, *Church, Nation and Race: Catholics and Antisemitism in Germany and England, 1918–45* (Manchester: Manchester University Press, 2012).

Hübner, Christoph, *Die Rechtskatholiken, die Zentrumspartei und die katholische Kirche in Deutschland bis zum Reichskonkordat von 1933: Ein Beitrag zur Geschichte des Scheiterns der Weimarer Republik* (Munster: LIT Verlag, 2014).

Jones, Larry Eugene, 'Catholic Conservatives in the Weimar Republic. The Politics of the Rhenish-Westphalian Aristocracy, 1918–1933', *German History*, 18/1 (2000), 60–85.

Jones, Larry Eugene, 'Franz von Papen, the German Center Party, and the Failure of Catholic Conservatism in the Weimar Republic', *Central European History*, 38/2 (2009), 191–217.

Jones, Larry Eugene, *The German Right, 1918–1930: Political Parties, Organized Interests, and Patriotic Associations in the Struggle Against Weimar Democracy* (Cambridge: Cambridge University Press, 2020).

Jones, Larry Eugene, *Hitler versus Hindenburg: The 1932 Presidential Elections and the End of the Weimar Republic* (Cambridge: Cambridge University Press, 2015).

Malinowski, Stephan, *Nazis and Nobles. The History of a Misalliance* (Oxford: Oxford University Press, 2020).

Menke, Martin, 'Ludwig Kaas and the End of the German Center Party', in Hermann Beck and Larry Eugene Jones (eds), *From Weimar to Hitler: Studies in the Dissolution of the Weimar Republic and the Establishment of the Third Reich, 1932–1934* (New York and Oxford: Berghahn, 2018), 79–110.

Mergel, Thomas, 'Das Scheitern des deutschen Tory-Konservatismus: Die Umformung der DNVP zu einer rechtsradikalen Partei 1928–1932', *Historische Zeitschrift*, 276 (2003), 323–68.

Moeller, Robert G., *German Peasants and Agrarian Politics 1914–1924: The Rhineland and Westphalia* (Chapel Hill, NC, and London: University of North Carolina Press, 1986).

Morsey, Rudolf, *Die Deutsche Zentrumspartei 1915–1923* (Düsseldorf: Droste, 1966).

Pyta, Wolfram, *Hindenburg: Herrschaft zwischen Hohenzollern und Hitler* (Munich: Pantheon Verlag, 2009).

CHAPTER 17

NATIONAL SOCIALISM

DANIEL SIEMENS

An analysis of National Socialism cannot be separated from the question of whether or not there existed a specific fascist modernity in inter-war Europe, and, if so, which mobilization forces helped to develop it. This question goes beyond a comparison of German National Socialism with Italian Fascism. While historical research has long understood both movements predominantly as a response to social and political crisis phenomena, recent studies placed a political practice based on a shared 'fascist minimum' centre stage, that is a positive core of fascist ideological positions.[1] In Germany, this political practice was exercised within the political framework of a democratic state until the early 1930s. Thus, the history of early National Socialism is partially an aspect of an increasingly transnational history of democracy.[2]

The following chapter takes this shift in perspective into account. It analyses the history of National Socialism in Germany from the early beginnings of the party in the post-war turmoil in Munich, to setbacks during its rise and finally to the early 1930s when the NSDAP became the most successful party at the ballot box. National Socialism is examined as a modern political and social movement that tapped into the nationalist ideas and traditions of Wilhelmine Imperial Germany, which were exploited, in a new form, for the sake of mass politics during the Weimar Republic.[3] In the same vein as other European fascist movements, the Nazis propagated a new political style that focused on comprehensively mobilizing the members of their national community, where belonging to such a national community was imagined as being predetermined by fate. According to their utopian promise, everyone would, in return, find their place in this community. The precondition for a successful national revival was to permanently overcome liberal democracy.[4] The future beckoned to a new pan-fascist order in continental Europe, one that would have global significance.[5]

These aspects are important in understanding the Nazis' ideological programme and their organization, the reasons for their success in mobilizing people of both sexes as well as their symbolic practices.[6] How did the Nazis manage to present themselves as an alternative to voters who did not belong to the rather circumscribed milieu of *völkisch* nationalistic groups in the Weimar Republic? In the light of new doubts about the long-term persistence of Western-style liberal democracies, this question is not only of historical interest. The history of National Socialism in the Weimar Republic as a paradigmatic example of the erosion and finally abolition of democracy has, during recent years, gained new attention. The question whether the historical experiences in the decade after the First World War can help to explain the different constellations of the twenty-first century will continue to be the subject of controversial debate.[7]

NATIONAL SOCIALISM AS A PARTY AND A PROGRAMME

The National Socialist German Workers' Party (Nationalsozialistische Deutsche Arbeiterpartei, NSDAP) was founded during the immediate post-war period.[8] It emerged from the German Workers' Party (DAP), which was founded in Munich on 5 January 1919, a *völkisch* and antisemitic splinter party that, initially, only had a few dozen members. The later party leader, Adolf Hitler, visited one of the party meetings in autumn 1919 on behalf of the local Reichswehr Group Command No. 4 and joined shortly afterwards as propaganda chief (*Werbeobmann*).[9] On 24 February 1920, the DAP was renamed NSDAP and Hitler proclaimed the 'twenty-five-point programme' that was declared unalterable one year later.[10] Apart from its equally consistent and extremely aggressive anti-Bolshevism and antisemitism, the NSDAP did not distinguish itself by way of elaborate ideological convictions. The twenty-five-point programme was a mixture of old and new goals. It consisted of the popular demand to revise the post-war order as stipulated in the Treaties of Paris (Art. 2), an immigration ban for foreign nationals (Art. 8), and the claim to colonies 'to feed our people and to settle our surplus population' (Art. 3). The then 500,000 German Jews were to be deprived of their German citizenship without exception (Art. 4). In addition, there were populist slogans including the demand for 'profit-sharing in large industrial enterprises' (Art. 14) and 'breaking of the slavery of interest' (Art. 11), which was not elaborated upon, as well as advocating the standpoint of a 'positive Christianity' (Art. 24), a much-discussed issue among church members in subsequent years.[11] Finally, the programme demanded the 'formation of a people's army' (Art. 22), an issue that would regain importance when the leadership of the Reichswehr clashed with the chief-of-staff of the paramilitary stormtroopers (Sturmabteilung, SA), Ernst Röhm, starting in the autumn of 1933.[12] This programme remained the reference point of the party's and its members' ideological identity—except for Article 17, which demanded a 'law for the free expropriation of land for communal purposes'. In a statement from 13 April 1928, Hitler dismissed this extensive demand in order to gain support from peasants and bourgeois groups.

However, the party remained silent about how to implement the twenty-five points. They represented a *völkisch* utopian vision rather than a concrete manifesto that suggested avenues to achieve these goals. No new aims were to be added after they had realized those mentioned in the programme, as this would only have the end 'to increase, artificially, the discontent of the masses and to ensure the continued existence of the Party'.[13] Apparently, the underlying assumption of this position was that parties commonly justified their existence by establishing unrealistic objectives in order to mobilize the support of their followers to overcome the discrepancy between a deficient present and the future ideal. The Nazis, in a way, practised fundamental opposition, presenting themselves as a party of limited duration and dreaming of absolute rule. Italian fascism, after its successful 'March on Rome', was the undisputed role model. Under the leadership of the 'Duce' Benito Mussolini, followers of the Italian National Fascist Party who were partly organized in paramilitary units successfully seized power in October 1922 by occupying decentralized administrative and police buildings. Yet the military occupation of the capital, threatened by the Fascists, failed to materialize because the Italian King, Viktor Emanuel III, refused to let the legitimate government under Luigi Facta declare a state of emergency and, instead, directly appointed Mussolini as the new head of government on 30 October 1922.[14]

The Nazis' path to the levers of power in Germany was neither probable nor inevitable. Indeed, up until the 1923 November putsch—a hasty National Socialist attempt at revolution in Bavaria under the leadership of Hitler and Erich Ludendorff with a planned subsequent 'March on Berlin' to overthrow the Reich government—the NSDAP was, with its radical rhetoric, only successful in attracting some attention at a regional level. It failed to establish more than some scattered cells in most parts of Germany outside of its heartland in southern Bavaria (Altbayern, in German parlance), and neighbouring Franconia, Württemberg, and Thuringia. In many places, the party was seen as an antisemitic rowdy group and an unavoidable nuisance that had to be put up with. Even the *völkisch* camp initially did not attach lasting importance to it. In 1922, there were eighty individual *völkisch* organizations alongside the NSDAP in the German-speaking territories, with the German Völkisch Protection and Defiance Federation (Deutschvölkischer Schutz- und Trutzbund, DVSTB) and its 180,000 members the most influential one. In many places, the DVSTB, and not the NSDAP, was deemed the 'main pillar of the radical right-wing movement', as a police report from Remscheid in 1921 stated.[15] After the murder of Reich Foreign Minister Walther Rathenau on 24 June 1922, which the DVSTB not only condoned but was actively involved in, it was banned in most German states. At that time, the NSDAP had a mere 6,000 members. In December 1920 the NSDAP launched its own mouthpiece, the *Völkischer Beobachter*, however, it was not until February 1923 that this newspaper appeared daily. Initially, the splinter party refrained from participating in elections because, as Hitler argued in 1923, this was futile as long as the party did not command a powerful press outlet and had several convincing public speakers in its own ranks. Both, he concluded, were not the case in 1923.[16] Until November of that year, the NSDAP was entirely focused on a violent counter-revolution that was to overthrow the democratic state in a coup and help establish an authoritarian dictatorship.

Its initially limited number of members should not obscure the fact that the NSDAP was an admittedly small but very determined group that was repeatedly successful in winning over the most radical members of other *völkisch* groups. For instance, after the ban of the DVSTB several of its former members joined the Nazis, among them Reinhard Heydrich, the later head of the Reich Main Security Office (Reichssicherheitshauptamt, RSHA) and Deputy Reich Protector of Bohemia and Moravia, his close colleague, SS Obergruppenführer Werner Best, as well as the subsequent party *Gau* leaders Fritz Sauckel (Thuringia), Julius Streicher (Franconia), Karl Kauffmann (Rhineland-North, later Hamburg), and Hinrich Lohse (Schleswig-Holstein).[17] During the Weimar Republic, more than every second NSDAP member was younger than 30 years old. Most of them were single and thus willing to take on personal risks without being forced to neglect family duties. These self-proclaimed 'old fighters' dedicated themselves to the party and its goals at a very early stage. After 1933, almost all leading Nazis were recruited from this group. Thus, during the Weimar Republic the NSDAP was characterized by a high level of personnel continuity within its leadership ranks and, at the same time, a large fluctuation among its members and sympathizers.[18] Hitler remained party leader up until the last days of the regime in spring 1945; Heinrich Himmler, the recent university graduate and later Reich Leader SS, was directly involved in the 1923 November putsch as a member of the Wehrverband Reichsflagge, headed by the former Captain Ernst Röhm;[19] the later Reichsleiter Alfred Rosenberg became editor-in-chief of the *Völkischer Beobachter* in March 1923; and the later Reich Minister of the Interior and Prussian Minister President, Hermann Göring, assumed command of the Sturmabteilung (SA) of the party in Munich in the same year.

After the failed putsch, whose sixteen victims were immediately declared martyrs of the NSDAP and annually commemorated during the 'Third Reich', the party and its paramilitary organization were banned.[20] The Bavarian judiciary sentenced Hitler to fortress confinement, the mildest form of jail sentence. The Munich high treason trial in the spring of 1924, however, contributed to his prominence across the whole of Germany. Hitler used the extensive press coverage as a forum to spread his political ideas and present himself as a political leader.[21] One of those who, thanks to the trial, became aware of the Nazis was the later Reich Minister of Propaganda, Joseph Goebbels. He noted in his diary on 13 March 1924: 'I am busying myself with Hitler and the National Socialist movement, und will indeed have to do this much more. Socialism and Christ. An ethical foundation. Away from ossified materialism. Back to dedication and to God!'[22]

While the rise of the NSDAP remained slow during almost the entirety of the 1920s, in the middle of the decade a National Socialist consensus emerged in parts of German society. It can be described as a mixture of dashed hopes about the new beginnings of the democratic state, the social consequences of hyperinflation and war loans that had been rendered worthless, as well as resentments against Jews and foreigners that had already surfaced in Imperial Germany and been aggravated in light of the social situation and the high expectations of national solidarity and welfare state provision. This mixture proved highly attractive early on, shown by the success of the short-lived National Socialist Freedom Party (Nationalsozialistische Freiheitspartei, NSFP), a merger of members of the banned NSDAP and the DVFP, which won a remarkable 6.6 per cent of the vote at the Reichstag elections in May 1924. The middle phase of the republic (1924–9) can therefore be rightly described as a period of 'deceptive stability'.[23] During these years, the fundamental opponents of democracy formed and regrouped, initially without this translating into election results. The steadily growing mass movement adopted several ideological core positions of German nationalism and was even seen by some as the Christian response to the challenges of modern, liberal-capitalist society.

Traditional parties such as the right-wing liberal German People's Party (Deutsche Volkspartei, DVP) and the firmly conservative, right-wing nationalist German National People's Party (Deutschnationale Volkspartei, DNVP) were unable to tap into this development. Their elitism increasingly proved out of date and out of touch. In contrast, the NSDAP, which was perceived as youthful and dynamic, reached new groups of voters after its refounding in February 1925. It was not before 1928 that membership figures hit and exceeded the level from before the party ban in November 1923 (approximately 55,000). And yet, an increasing number of people were attracted by the party's promise to overcome functional problems of parliamentarianism and capitalism by means of a nationalist policy that transcended classes. The vagueness of the party manifesto allowed people to interpret and specify the views of the Nazis as they saw fit.[24] In this vein, the NSDAP grew from a Bavarian-located regional party into a milieu party with strongholds in the largely Protestant and agrarian northern and eastern parts of the country and, finally, into a mass movement hitherto unprecedented in Germany. It found support among the nobility, the bourgeoisie, the petty bourgeoisie, and even the working class.[25]

This is why historical research has referred to the NSDAP as the first mass party that reached out across milieu boundaries, or even as a 'fascist people's party'.[26] This approach is building upon older, in some cases contemporary interpretations, which can, however, only explain this phenomenon to a certain degree. Still relevant is, for instance, the '*Mittelstand* theory', coined by the sociologist Theodor Geiger. It explained the rise of the Nazis by a 'panic in the *Mittelstand*' (the lower middle class), or, in another formulation, as an uprising of the 'economically proletarianized and ideologically homeless middle classes' (Siegfried Kracauer).[27] The theory of political confessionalism suggests that the Nazis' success predominantly relied on the support of the (national) Protestant milieu. Both approaches are generally confirmed and differentiated in detail by new studies on the followers of the NSDAP.[28]

We now have empirically valid knowledge confirming that the party got their best election results in Protestant regions, while underperforming in predominantly Catholic areas and bigger cities up until the 1933 Reichstag elections. By presenting itself as the representative of German farmers and the economically squeezed middle classes, the NSDAP initially took root in the rural North and East and could win over many local notables such as pastors, teachers, and estate owners early on, before augmenting its base in the big cities following the Great Depression.[29] Here, the leftist, 'anti-capitalist' wing of the party was rather successful in poaching dissatisfied workers from SPD and KPD. In the cities, the NSDAP presented itself as the national alternative to the socialist workers' parties, with demands such as the socialization of big banks or drastic measures against 'profiteers' showing striking similarities to those of the KPD. Around 1930, between 30 and 40 per cent of newly joined NSDAP members had a working-class background, the self-employed accounted for 29 per cent, and civil servants and employees for 21 per cent. Young people between the age of 18 and 25, who were disproportionally affected by the Great Depression due to their precarious occupational status, supported the party in high numbers and were particularly committed.[30] However, during this time the NSDAP membership was anything but stable. Two-thirds of those who joined between 1925 and 1929 later left the party.[31]

As long as democracy was functioning and achieving visible results—such as the temporary stabilization of the economy in the mid-1920s and the gradual recovery of international reputation—most voters were not ready to support radical anti-parliamentary parties such as the NSDAP. At the Reichstag elections on 20 May 1928, the Nazis received only 2.6 per cent of votes cast. This changed with the political campaign against the reparation scheme stipulated by the Young Plan in 1929, where the Nazis in particular voiced their opposition, and the collapse of the grand coalition under the Social Democrat Hermann Müller in March 1930. His successor, Reich Chancellor Heinrich Brüning (Centre Party), began governing against parliament by employing emergency decrees based on Article 48 of the Weimar Constitution. Only half a year later, at the Reichstag elections on 14 September 1930, the NSDAP increased its vote more than sixfold (18.3 per cent) and became the second strongest party in parliament after the Social Democrats (24.5 per cent). While in 1928 800,000 people voted for the NSDAP, only two years later this number had increased to 6.4 million.[32]

On the morning after the election, the headline of the Berlin-based left-liberal *Vossische Zeitung* read 'Victory of radicalism'. The newspaper commented that the high increase of the 'National Social torrent' was entirely unexpected, despite previous election successes of the NSDAP in Thuringia (where from 1930 the NSDAP was in a coalition government) and Saxony, as well as at the Berlin city council assembly. It continued that the Reichstag elections had shown large parts of the population were alienated from parliament, reasons for this being mass unemployment with simultaneous tax rises, continuous government crises, and the attitude of parts of heavy industry and the finance industry, which had supported the Nazis in the hope they would 'quash Social Democrats and Communists'. While left-wing parties had kept their share (with a vote shift in favour of the Communists), the centre was 'smashed'.[33] For the following two and a half years, this analysis proved to be by and large correct. Of all the parties, the Social Democrats and—to a lesser extent—the Centre Party, as a Catholic milieu party, remained the only relevant political forces committed to the democratic constitutional state. However, the SPD, despite the strong position it had in Prussia until 1932, was not able to translate its claim to leadership into concrete politics on a national level. It is still disputed among historians whether there was a genuine alternative to Brüning's policy of 'authoritarian democracy' in the early 1930s.[34] His political motives and scope of action aside, his policy proved fatal not only regarding social politics but for Weimar democracy in general, because it weakened trust in the capability of parliament to govern, particularly in light of the enormous economic and social political problems of the early 1930s.

This development seemed to confirm all those who, like the right-wing intellectual Edgar Julius Jung, had heralded already in the years before the beginning of a new era, when the 'indifferent ballot carrier, weak in conviction, ... the last remains of the formal democratic era', would be replaced by the 'active, venturous man willing to make sacrifices'.[35] Such views that, depending on the perspective, demanded either the evolution or even complete 'overcoming' of formal democracy in favour of a 'national community' (*Volksgemeinschaft*), based on individual commitment, were, around 1930, met with approval even from young Social Democrats. Their pioneers suggested the Nazis had the wrong answers but were asking the right questions and were critical of capitalism. 'Mere interest organization' had to give way to the creation of 'leadership skills' among the young generation and a 'rejuvenation of politics', also in the left-wing camp. This internal critique, which was voiced in public, played into the hands of the SPD's adversaries, particularly because the young Social Democratic rebels were hardly heard in their own party.[36]

Thus, it was not without reason that in September 1930 the NSDAP was confident they would achieve victory, despite internal quarrels, a new rebellion of discontented SA units under the SA leader in eastern Germany, Walther Stennes, in March 1931, and continuous financial problems. Over more than a decade a glaring discrepancy had existed between the ambitious desire of the party for leadership and their actual election results. Now, the approval ratings suggested the possibility of a government under National Socialist leadership. In addition, leading representatives of National Socialism cultivated an attitude of viewing the present from an 'imagined point in the future'. In doing so, problems of the present appeared as necessary and inevitable transitional phases on the path toward realizing the utopian National Socialist future.[37] At the same time, as a new party of the Weimar Republic, the NSDAP did not share any political responsibilities and could thus not be caught up by its own blame game.[38] National Socialist promises for the future adopted many thoughts of the largely *völkisch* national- and nationalist-leaning *bündische* youth movement of the Weimar Republic, which were impossible to refute with rational arguments. Irrespective of its implausibility, the optimism and confidence in victory were highly attractive.[39]

NATIONAL SOCIALISM AS PRACTICE AND SOCIAL MOVEMENT

After its refounding in February 1925, the NSDAP lost its previous character of a political sect and turned into a centrally controlled mass party that, at the same time, relied heavily on the mobilization of its followers. As a fascist-style party based on the leader principle, it was organized along strictly hierarchical lines with numerous horizontally structured special or party-affiliated organizations, which covered a large part of the German population. Aside from the Hitler Youth, these included the National Socialist Association of Legal Professionals (Bund Nationalsozialistischer Deutscher Juristen, BNSDJ), the National Socialist Teachers' League (Nationalsozialistischer Lehrerbund, NSLB), the National Socialist German Doctors' League (Nationalsozialistischer Deutscher Ärztebund, NS-DÄB), the National Socialist Pastors' League (Nationalsozialistischer Evangelischer Pfarrerbund, NSEP), and the National Socialist German Students' League (Nationalsozialistischer Deutscher Studentenbund, NSDStB).[40]

The significance of these party-affiliated organizations for the rise of the NSDAP from the late 1920s onwards can be illustrated by the examples of the NSLB and NSDStB. The National Socialist Teachers' League formed in 1926 but was only officially founded on 21 April 1929 under the leadership of the primary school teacher Hans Schemm, who was also member of the Bavarian Diet and Gau leader of Upper Franconia. Initially, it had only a few hundred members. In 1931, membership numbers started to increase exponentially, reaching 9,000 in November 1932.[41] Pedagogically, the NSLB aimed at producing 'healthy, strong people of good character', thus counteracting the consequences of 'technical, capitalist culture' that were perceived as problematic. Such a programme was particularly compatible because it emphasized the ideal of German idealism that was to be lived up to—albeit in an allegedly modern and specifically National Socialist fashion. It intended to bring out and foster the supposedly buried skills or suppressed racial qualities of the German people; alleged alien influences such as those of 'Judaism' were to be prevented. Before 1933, the programme of the NSLB remained vague and inconsistent in many details. The League demanded, on the one hand, to overcome 'all class contradictions through the consciousness of shared blood' for all children up to 14 years. On the other, regarding older students it championed 'strictest intellectual selection'.[42] Racial equality and educational elitism were not incompatible for National Social teachers.

The National Socialist German Students' League argued even more stringently. It targeted young men for the future social elite of the Nazi movement and was founded in 1926. Headed by Baldur von Schirach, it grew, from 1928 onwards, into one of the most influential organizations at German universities, benefiting from already widely spread *völkisch* and antisemitic views among German students and professors.[43] Similar to representatives of the *bündisch* youth movement where the NSDStB successfully recruited new members, students of the NSDAP-affiliated organization saw themselves as 'National Socialist avant-garde'.[44] They felt called to free universities from the alleged harmful Jewish influence and imagined themselves setting an example by their 'socialism of action'. Even before 1933, National Socialist students disrupted the lectures of professors considered undesirable and created an atmosphere of fear when they came to university, wearing the brown shirts of the SA and intimidating Jewish and left-wing students. University management usually responded half-heartedly. In light of the rapidly deteriorating career chances of university graduates from the late 1920s, the NSDStB became particularly attractive. At many universities, National Socialist student groups won the absolute majority in student committee elections, such as in Erlangen

(1929) and a year later in Göttingen, Breslau, and Greifswald.[45] As early as July 1931, the NSDStB took over the leadership of the German Student Union, the merger of the General Student Committees of German universities.[46]

With the help of these party-affiliated organizations, the NSDAP had already permeated relevant parts of German society before 1933. Teachers, as multipliers of special knowledge and political opinions, as well as students, the future social elite, were important groups that were particularly suited to both the political mobilization of young Germans and the dissemination of Nazi ideology. From the perspective of the NSDAP, seeking reliable experts in case of a participation in government or even seizure of power, the party could then recruit members from the NS-DÄB and the BNSDJ.

The Nazis only reluctantly referred to themselves as a party; instead they saw themselves as a 'movement'. Even semantically, they wanted to distinguish themselves from other parties of the democratic order—disparagingly dubbed 'the system'—as a fundamental alternative. They insinuated that their political opponents stood for stagnation, idleness, and dependency on foreign powers and financially strong economic interests. It was the NSDAP's strategy to vilify its political opponents and stage-manage itself as an activist movement that was in touch with the common people. For tactical reasons, the party ostensibly abandoned its previous fundamental opposition to Weimar parliamentarianism. Nevertheless, it remained a 'canvassing organization' tailored to its leader Hitler, without dependable institutional channels to balance internal interests.[47] When the violent Italian-style attempt to overthrow the democratic order—as the Nazis saw their attempted putsch in November 1923—failed, they decided to seize political power legally, by participating in elections.

A precondition for this strategy to be successful was the establishment of an effective party organization and propaganda that was visually and acoustically attention-grabbing, which, during the second half of the 1920s, gave the NSDAP the appearance of being a party with significance throughout the whole of Germany.[48] The centre of the party's rebuilding was, again, Munich; from here the Nazis intended to first 'conquer' Bavaria and subsequently the Reich. For this purpose, the party structured the German territory into thirty-three Gaue, each with a 'Gauleiter' (Gau leader), who was in many places initially elected by the NSDAP local groups, but in subsequent years appointed by the party leadership in Munich.[49] The local NSDAP groups continued to play a key role in mobilizing followers. Even in the late 1920s, the party was, at a local level, not much more than a network of like-minded people, who came together sociably once a week and sometimes organized promotional events with speakers trained in the party's so-called Reich leader schools.[50] Such courses took up to three weeks and included 'ideological, intellectual and practical training', trips to the surrounding area, parades, and sports activities.[51] The self-produced histories of local party groups show that grassroots work was often painstaking. Even in the early 1930s, the party was still not evenly spread throughout Germany. During that period, the NSDAP had to cancel several planned talks in Munich for lack of participation; many big events were also not well attended.[52]

From 1927–8, the Gaue, and thus the regional leadership, gained increasing importance within the NSDAP. They were allocated a small share of membership fees, allowing for a financial basis of their own. From now on, Gau leaderships became independent from local groups and could realize their own ideas, even against the will of party grassroots. The centralization process also applied to party-affiliated organizations, particularly the SA.[53] This did not significantly change the slow rise in membership numbers of the NSDAP until 1929–30, but it created the organizational precondition to channel the rapid rise of the Hitler movement in the early 1930s. This was also true of municipal politics. From the late 1920s onwards, the NSDAP organized regular training events at Gau level for its representatives in municipal councils. Thus, the leadership ensured administrative action was brought in line with the goals of the party as a whole. At the same time, this resulted in a revaluation and 'professionalization' of National Socialist municipal work on the ground, which very much increased the visibility of the party. This particularly happened in small and medium-sized cities and earned it a certain degree of appreciation, all the more so because many voters presumably attached more importance to local than to Reich politics. The NSDAP in Saxony was, even before 1933, able to win over approximately 10 per cent of all state officials as party members.[54] The establishment of National Socialist Factory Cell Organizations served a similar purpose. Indeed, setting up such groups in large-scale industrial enterprises provoked protests and resistance from existing workers' representatives. However, among white-collar workers, the Nazi Factory Cells were quite successful in gaining followers.[55] Even political opponents of the Nazis conceded that it required courage to enter the established political territory of SPD and KPD and publicly position oneself with diverging views. In the early 1930s, the left-wing parties made great efforts to convince 'renegades' of the justness of their cause. Rejecting National Socialism as an ideology and political movement did not necessarily result in generally dismissing their representatives on the ground.[56]

Thus, it was by no means only, or even primarily, the confrontational propaganda of the Berlin Gauleiter Joseph Goebbels and his deliberate violation of boundaries or Hitler's 'charisma', a notion which is highly contested among historians, that paved the way for the NSDAP to seize power.[57] The agitation of top National Socialist politicians could only take root because, from the second half of the 1920s onwards, voters saw NSDAP representatives taking care of political issues at the local and regional level and experienced them as grounded and approachable.[58] The fact that they often acted loudly, directly, and ruthlessly carried less weight during the 1920s than in previous decades, when a minimum of respectability was necessary in order to be taken seriously as a political party. Indeed, in the Weimar Republic the deliberate violation of standards of behaviour could contribute to a party's attraction. For a long time, historians of ideas have pointed out that the Nazis could tap into a current critical of modernity and culture that emerged during the Weimar Republic, increasingly gaining political visibility. It merged dashed hopes of the immediate post-war years with ideological dispositions of the time before 1914 that considered culture and civilization as polar opposites and incompatible. According to this view, culture, tradition, and authority were positive values, while civilization, rationality, and democracy carried negative connotations.[59] 'Organization was the watchword, stridency the spirit of the times', as the historian Peter Fritzsche aptly summarized this mentality.[60] Radical commitment, even violent fighting, be it for one's own personal purposes or for the imagined national community, was not only highly accepted but even regarded as positive behaviour in the Weimar Republic.

Early National Socialism must be seen against this backdrop. It was its activism that gained the Nazi movement a growing number of followers, in some cases even regardless of or despite ideological positions. Later, when the Nazis had become a visible political power in the streets throughout Germany, thanks to their activism the political world could no longer ignore them. In this sense, the Nazis were indeed children of the world war and the November revolution. They merged mass mobilization during the post-war period with the symbolic world of Imperial Germany into a new form of populist politics, which they promoted as being both based on tradition and future-oriented.

Even though from 1925 the NSDAP continuously claimed to have renounced violent putsch attempts and be following a legal course to achieve its goals, violence by word and deed remained constitutive elements of its policy. The SA stormtroopers, reorganized in the mid-1920s, were of crucial importance for the success of the party. Originally deployed as a troop of stewards and the de facto private army of regional Nazi politicians, its leaders, former officer Franz Pfeffer von Salomon and his successor Ernst Röhm turned the SA into a nationwide and tightly organized civil war army that had almost 450,000 members in the summer of 1932. Far from the claim that it was only intended to keep the 'spirit of military preparedness' alive in the German people and serve as 'specialist training of the party youth', under their leadership the SA grew into a much-feared terror organization. It provoked its political opponents (Reichsbanner Black-Red-Gold, Steel Helmet, Red Front Fighters' League), which initially outnumbered the SA by far, and was largely responsible for several acts of violence in the early 1930s and thus the 'brutalization' of the domestic climate in the late Weimar Republic.[61]

Equally as important as intimidating and fighting the political opponent was the sensational appeal and advertising effect of the SA's appearance for the Nazis.[62] The sporadic but visually impressive presence of the SA and motorized SA units often made a crucial difference on the ground. Particularly before elections, SA troops tirelessly toured through rural Germany. Rather than presenting their social revolutionary demands, their appearances evoked traditional feelings of national honour. Despite the party's disciplinary and regulatory measures, the individual party activists regarded themselves as being part of a collective National Socialist movement of their own volition and, in doing so, standing out from the masses of the people.[63] Nazi violence took two directions. It was, first, a suitable means to create internal solidarity—that is to foster a bond between Nazi activists through shared experiences and events. Second, it gave the external impression of a powerful and determined troop. It helped the NSDAP that parts of the functional elite within the judiciary and the police force regarded Nazi radicalism and their propensity to use violence as a sort of self-defence, that is, a justified response to the alleged treason of the 'November criminals' and logical consequence of the supposed collapse of society.[64] In a similar vein, the violent behaviour of the SA and the aggressive rhetoric of the NSDAP no longer prevented large parts of the electorate from casting their vote for the Nazi party, at least from the end of the 1920s onward. The strong presence of the National Socialists in rural areas and small towns with less than 10,000 inhabitants, where the majority of the German population lived, was crucial for this shift.

The demeanour of the Nazis, who flew the flag of their party even in the smallest towns and presented themselves as good German patriots, sang popular songs, and wanted to bring back the allegedly 'good old times' in a new and improved national fashion, went down well with many voters during the late 1920s. Despite the fact that women accounted only for 5 to 7 per cent of all NSDAP members during the Weimar Republic and despite the fact it presented itself as decisively 'masculine', many women also voted for the National Socialists. Between 1930 and 1933, the percentage of female voters rose even more sharply than that of male voters.[65] Historical gender research has shown that it was by no means just Hitler's supposed charisma that made the party attractive for many women. The famous triad of 'children, kitchen, church' was not much more than a reactionary stereotype. Rather, the attraction of the NSDAP for women was the combination of reactionary and progressive views, which allowed the female follower of the party to feel appreciated as a woman with specific female qualities without fundamentally questioning the allegedly natural gender inequality that the party propagated.[66] The watchword was equivalency, rather than similarity. The journalist and former politician of the liberal German Democratic Party (Deutsche Demokratische Partei, DDP), Jella Lepman, was among the first to emphasize this aspect. During the early 1940s, while she was living in British exile, Lepman, under the pseudonym Katherine Thomas, described a National Socialist election campaign event with Hitler in October 1932 that she attended as a journalist. The room was filled to its maximum capacity, despite the tickets being relatively expensive. 'Housewives from the petty bourgeoisie' proudly cheered when Hitler Youth and SA marched into the hall. They were extremely receptive to Hitler's promises to address the economic hardships of 'ordinary women of the *Mittelstand*' that he praised as being the backbone of the nation. The marked manly and military character of the entire event enthused both women and men equally.[67] Lepman's bitter insight was that the majority of people present could imagine being part of the prospected people's community, regardless of their sex.

The determined and violent behaviour of the Nazis was one of the main reasons for their rapid rise during a time when the democratic parties ran out of options to form governments due to the lack of parliamentary majorities. Against this backdrop, the NSDAP increasingly appeared to be electable, even to those voters who previously had flatly rejected them. However, it would be simplistic to explain this development by merely pointing to the rampant desperation that followed rapidly growing unemployment figures and, associated with this, the rise of previously latent and rarely openly voiced resentments. Jürgen W. Falter's studies clearly demonstrate that unemployed workers predominantly voted for the KPD and less than averagely for the NSDAP. Contextual effects on the voting behaviour of those who were threatened by unemployment or indirectly affected, such as innkeepers and publicans, can be ruled out.[68] All this was aggravated by the fact that parliamentarianism under Brüning, as already mentioned, was damaged and, therefore, the democratic principle of discussing societal conflicts and proposals for solution in parliament had become fundamentally questionable. There were multiple reasons for the breakthrough of the NSDAP as a mass movement in 1929–30, and only some of them were of an economic nature. Hitler was not the 'last hope' of all those starving and distraught, as the famous election poster by graphic designer Hans Herbert Schweitzer (Mjölnir) from 1932 suggested. In the final years of the Weimar Republic, his party not only became the refuge of disappointed workers and people from the lower middle classes, but also of the national bourgeois right. Leading representatives of the German economy also began to support the NSDAP, sometimes out of conviction, but more often out of opportunism. For them, siding with the Nazis was a means to cultivating a powerful counterweight to the social political demands of the socialist workers' parties. At the same time, only few believed that the Nazis would once and for all put an end to all socialist—and that included for them social political—'experiments'.[69] Social revolutionary demands from the 'left' wing of the NSDAP gave reason for caution. Right up to the end of the Weimar Republic, it was unforeseeable how pro-business this party would act if it came into government.

National Socialism as a Racial Utopia and Promise to Advancement

National Socialism was not only a party-political movement, but also a messianic one. Drawing on social Darwinist principles, its leaders offered a *völkisch* vision to be realized by means of 'social engineering' and radical violence. Like a 'political religion', National Socialism promised its followers salvation in the world they were living in. In contrast to communist utopian concepts, which propagated the creation of a new man and, in doing so, justified the comprehensive reorganization of the political, economic, and social order,[70] the National Socialist vision of the future was a much easier goal for its followers to accomplish. Nazi propaganda claimed that 'the German man' already bore all positive traits, which, however, were often prevented from fully developing. The blame for this almost always rested with the Jews, who the Nazis held responsible for various phenomena that they opposed, as they kept repeating: Jewish black-marketeers supposedly aggravated the suffering of the civilian population during the war, the Jewish press of the Weimar years propagated foreign cultural domination, *Finanzjuden*, meaning Jewish bankers, in the US were working towards selling out the German economy while Jewish 'fulfilment politicians' in Germany surrendered the nation to alien political and economic interests. Finally, Jewish perverts threatened the purity of morally superior German women and girls.[71]

This pronounced antisemitism defined the Jews as a 'race' with a certain set of unchangeable characteristics, which was made the sole criteria of exclusion, regardless of the actual diversity of Jewish life in Europe. As a result, the Nazi dictatorship has, in past decades, often been referred to as a 'racial state'.[72] Recent research, however, has significantly differentiated this paradigm, for instance by emphasizing that 'race' cannot be understood as the final goal of a constantly radicalizing development. Precisely because Nazi racial policy appears to be the implementation of radical demands of eugenicists and 'racial hygienists' who operated not only in early twentieth-century Germany, but also in other European countries and in the USA, simplifying causal attributions are problematic.[73] Mark Roseman has argued that the Nazi's racial policy aimed at creating national unity and healing the 'people's body' rather than establishing a society with race as a defining criterion of permanent, rigidifying inequality.[74]

When examining National Socialism before 1933, it must be highlighted that the programmatic racist statements of the party were made against the backdrop of—and should be analysed in this perspective—the discourse on degeneration, which was widespread and radicalized due to the First World War. The biological improvement of the German race (*Aufzüchtung*) was significantly influenced by the social Darwinist battle for living space and was intended to serve colonial ambitions. While remaining rather vague in the 1920 manifesto, in subsequent years these ambitions increasingly focused on Eastern Europe. This territory became the living and expansion space in which the Nazis wanted the German people to 'renew'. For this purpose they could tap into plans of scientific 'border studies' and their representatives, who from the First World War onwards had advocated 'de-miscegenation' of different ethnic groups and the expansion of German influence in Eastern Europe ('Germanization').[75]

During the Weimar years, these considerations had initially only limited practical significance. The early National Socialists stood in the tradition of the pre-war *völkisch* movement, seeking to put this initially exclusively political concept into a racial context. For want of foreign policy possibilities, the question of a suitable or legitimate living space for the nation had not (yet) arisen. Initially, they were driven by the issue of the physical composition, that is the 'people's body and its supposed "healing"'.[76] The assumption of the early National Socialists that it was possible to substantially improve the racial quality of the German people in a relatively short period of time by means of 'social engineering' reveals an underlying utopian element that was characteristic of their ideology. In this respect, the party targeted not only Jews but also criminals and so-called anti-social elements (*Asoziale*), whose behaviour was attributed to their supposed genetic inferiority by a number of scientists, particularly criminal biologists.[77]

In addition to these rather traditional arguments, a specific mixture of radical antisemitism and individual chances of development must be highlighted as characteristics of early National Socialism. Indeed, antisemitism, often combined with a staunch anti-Bolshevism, was part and parcel of numerous European nationalist movements. However, German National Socialists proved particularly radical in putting their antisemitic views into political practice.[78] This not only applied to the time after 1933, but also to the previous decade. Particularly the experiences of 1923, the year of crisis, fostered 'egoism, ruthlessness and violence' rather than collective self-help, and thus, as some recent research argues, made National Socialist acts of violence appear less extreme.[79] The extent to which Nazi antisemitism was motivated by racial biology during this early phase is, however, still disputed among experts.[80] In any case, Jewish organizations such as the Central Association of German Citizens of Jewish Faith

(Centralverein deutscher Staatsbürger jüdischen Glaubens, CV), the most influential and largest Jewish association of late Imperial Germany and the Weimar Republic, with more than 72,000 members in 1924, reacted swiftly. They began to centrally record incidents that happened throughout Germany, intensified education for combating antisemitism, and made great efforts to build understanding and support among non-Jewish Germans in their fight against antisemitism. Their success was, however, rather marginal.[81]

Around 1930, the Nazi rhetoric of the people's community, with its clear-cut differentiation between in- and outsiders, resonated well with a growing number of Germans, particularly because it built upon fundamental experiences of post-war upheaval and at the same time promised to overcome it. In contrast to the assumptions of older historical research, National Socialism was by no means exclusively collectivist but allowed for a high degree of individualism—at least as long as this was in line with the goals of the 'people's community'.[82] According to historian Moritz Föllmer, 'the Third Reich's techniques of rule included offers to develop freely, without the hindrance of the Weimar "system", to exceed through performance and to realize one's own desires and interests within a racial and imperial context'.[83] The appeal of the National Socialist project was not least fuelled by an 'imaginary openness of social roles', which allowed individuals to fully regard themselves as part and realizers of the 'people's community' without having to abandon their existing social milieus and networks.[84] The 'encouragement and pursuit of individual claims as such ... had a structure-building impact' regarding the exclusion and persecution of the German Jews. National Socialist individuality was negatively defined as distinction and breaking free from supposed or actual shackles. By implication, the Nazi movement offered opportunities and rewarded personal initiative.[85]

In other words, there was a specific National Socialist performance ethic that could unfold in antisemitic action and was based on the contrast between the Aryan individual and the supposedly 'unauthentic', 'rootless', and cosmopolitan Jews.[86] This is a convincing explanation of Nazi radical antisemitism because it is consistent without falling back on the notion of racial hygiene which, as has been argued above, was not (yet) among the most important and promotionally effective ideological positions during the Weimar Republic. Before 1933, being an antisemite was a form of 'self-empowerment' for National Socialists, a chance to take life into one's own hands and demonstrate agency.[87] The majority of National Socialist Germans, however, had only limited chances of achieving such a self-determined lifestyle, not least for economic reasons. The repercussions of the Great Depression aggravated the discrepancy between self-image and real agency—and, in doing so and largely irrespective of racial hygiene, contributed to the Nazis radicalizing their antisemitic agitation.

Conclusion

During the Weimar Republic, the National Socialists were more than a political group that became the strongest party in the Reichstag in 1932 and was able to form the government in late January 1933. They eliminated parliamentary democracy within only one and a half years by replacing it with a dictatorship that was tailored towards Hitler as a leader. This chapter has argued that a perspective with hindsight, from the 'Third Reich' to the rise of the Nazis in the 1920s, must be complemented by an approach that understands National Socialist politics as a version of European fascism and examines its mobilizing power against this backdrop before 1933. With this in mind, the chapter has, first, outlined the development of the NSDAP in Germany, second, analysed National Socialism as a practice and social movement, and, third, examined the racist foundations of its promise to deliver. In contrast to the dominant tendency in previous research, the ideological continuity with earlier decades and the 'organic modernity' of National Socialism have been emphasized. This modernity was supposed to overcome the negative excesses of capitalist societies in the high modern age and prepare German society for the allegedly inevitable struggle for survival.[88]

This chapter has taken a dual approach in discussing these issues. First, it has argued that the Nazis tapped into several ideological positions that were already widespread in Imperial Germany and developed them further into a new populist and nationalist policy. Second, it has shown that the Nazis did not just combat the key aspects of Weimar's political culture, instead they transformed and utilized them for the sake of their own policy. They combined continuity and change in a seemingly egalitarian fashion, announcing the national overcoming, rather than the aggravation, of class society.[89] In particular, the National Socialist promise to promote and reward individual willingness to achieve, as long as it served the alleged 'people as a whole', resonated with a growing number of Germans over the course of the Weimar Republic. They had seen their individual agency diminished due to increasing economic difficulties and, at the same time, gave up hope on being able to reverse this process by their own efforts. For this reason, liberalism as a political force had become insignificant around 1930. It was no longer the association of economically independent and free individuals that seemed to be able to further the country and its citizens, but, on the contrary, the imagined collective—that is, for the National Socialists the 'people's community'—was supposed to offer protection and the chance to develop to the individual. Such an approach allows us to understand early National Socialism as a genuine element of the Weimar Republic and to embed the period from the military defeat and the revolution in 1918–19 to the establishment of Nazi dictatorship in 1933–4 into German history during the first half of the twentieth century. By no means does this perspective ignore the democratic potential of the Weimar Republic, nor does it intend any form of 'normalization' of the subsequent Nazi dictatorship.

Translated from German by Christine Brocks.

Notes

1. Geoff Eley, *Nazism as Fascism: Violence, Ideology, and the Ground of Consent in Germany 1930–1945* (London and New York: Routledge, 2013), 207–8; Sven Reichardt, 'Neue Wege

der vergleichenden Faschismusforschung', *Mittelweg*, 36/16 (2007), 11–12; see the seminal work by Roger Griffin, *The Nature of Fascism* (London: Pinter, 1991). I am grateful to Moritz Föllmer and the two editors of this volume for their valuable comments on a first draft of this chapter.
2. Tim B. Müller and Hedwig Richter, 'Einführung: Demokratiegeschichten. Deutschland (1800–1933) in transnationaler Perspektive', *Geschichte und Gesellschaft*, 44 (2018), 325–35.
3. Benjamin Ziemann, 'The First World War and National Socialism', in Shelley Baranowski, Armin Nolzen, and Claus-Christian W. Szejnmann (eds), *A Companion to Nazi Germany* (New York: Wiley Blackwell, 2018), 47–61.
4. In a transnational perspective: Arnd Bauerkämper and Grzegorz Rossoliński-Liebe (eds), *Fascism without Borders: Transnational Connections and Cooperation between Movements and Regimes in Europe from 1918 to 1945* (New York: Berghahn, 2017); David D. Roberts, 'Fascism and the Framework for Interactive Political Innovation during the Era of the Two World Wars', in António Costa Pinto and Aristotle Kallis (eds), *Rethinking Fascism and Dictatorship in Europe* (Basingstoke: Palgrave Macmillan, 2014), 42–66.
5. Benjamin G. Martin, *The Nazi-Fascist New Order for European Culture* (Cambridge, MA: Harvard University Press, 2016); Werner Daitz, *Lebensraum und gerechte Weltordnung: Grundlagen einer Anti-Atlantikcharta. Ausgewählte Aufsätze von Werner Daitz* (Amsterdam: De Amsterdamsche Keurkamer, 1943).
6. For a recent overview of early National Socialism from a gender historical perspective see the contributions in Gabriele Metzler and Dirk Schumann (eds), *Geschlechter(un)ordnung und Politik in der Weimarer Republik* (Bonn: Dietz, 2016).
7. Among others: Gavriel D. Rosenfeld, 'An American Führer? Nazi Analogies and the Struggle to Explain Donald Trump', *Central European History*, 52 (2019), 554–87.
8. On the history of NSDAP before 1933 see Armin Nolzen, 'The NSDAP's Operational Codes After 1933', in Martina Steber und Bernhard Gotto (eds), *Visions of Community in Nazi Germany: Social Engineering and Private Lives* (Oxford: Oxford University Press, 2014), 87–100; Sven Felix Kellerhoff, *Die NSDAP: Eine Partei und ihre Mitglieder* (Stuttgart: Klett Cotta, 2017).
9. On Hitler's initial years as the leader of the NSDAP see Volker Ullrich, *Adolf Hitler*, vol. 1. *Die Jahre des Aufstiegs 1889–1939* (Frankfurt/Main: Fischer, 2018), 90–152; Hans-Ulrich Thamer, *Adolf Hitler: Biographie eines Diktators* (Munich: Beck 2018), 67–96.
10. Wolfgang Benz, 'Die NSDAP und ihre Mitglieder', in Benz (ed.), *Wie wurde man Parteigenosse? Die NSDAP und ihre Mitglieder* (Frankfurt/Main: Fischer, 2009), 8–9.
11. Manfred Gailus, *Protestantismus und Nationalsozialismus: Studien zur nationalsozialistischen Durchdringung des protestantischen Sozialmilieus in Berlin* (Cologne: Böhlau, 2001); Richard Steigmann-Gall, *The Holy Reich: Nazi Conceptions of Christianity, 1919–1945* (Cambridge: Cambridge University Press, 2003).
12. Daniel Siemens, *Stormtroopers: A New History of Hitler's Brownshirts* (New Haven and London: Yale University Press 2017), 225–32, with further references.
13. Preamble of the twenty-five-point programme of the DAP/NSDAP from 24 Feb. 1920, quoted from: <http://germanhistorydocs.ghi-dc.org/docpage.cfm?docpage_id=4810&language=english> [accessed 5 Nov. 2020].
14. On Italian fascism as a role model see Wolfgang Schieder, 'Das italienische Experiment: Der Faschismus als Vorbild in der Krise der Weimarer Republik', *Historische Zeitschrift*, 262 (1996), 73–125.

15. Walter Jung, *Ideologische Voraussetzungen, Inhalte und Ziele außenpolitischer Programmatik und Propaganda in der deutschvölkischen Bewegung der Anfangsjahre der Weimarer Republik: Das Beispiel Deutschvölkischer Schutz- und Trutzbund* (PhD Diss. Göttingen, 2000), 11, 15; Walter Jung, 'Deutschvölkischer Schutz- und Trutzbund (DVSTB), 1919–1924/35', in Historisches Lexikon Bayerns, <https://www.historisches-lexikon-bayerns.de/Lexikon/Deutschvölkischer_Schutz-_und_Trutzbund_(DVSTB),_1919-1924/35> (accessed 21 Jan. 2020).
16. Siemens, *Stormtroopers*, 17.
17. Jung, *Ideologische Voraussetzungen*, 21; exemplary case study: Ulrich Best Herbert, *Biographische Studien über Radikalismus, Weltanschauung und Vernunft, 1903–1989* (Bonn: Dietz, 1996).
18. On the membership profile of the NSDAP before 1933 see recently Jürgen W. Falter, *Hitlers Parteigenossen: Die Mitglieder der NSDAP 1919–1945* (Frankfurt/Main: Campus, 2020).
19. Peter Longerich, *Heinrich Himmler: Biographie* (Munich: Siedler, 2008), 73–6.
20. On the Nazi martyr cult see Sabine Behrenbeck, *Der Kult um die toten Helden: Nationalsozialistische Mythen, Riten und Symbole* (Vierow bei Greifswald: SH-Verlag, 1996); Daniel Siemens, *The Making of a Nazi Hero: The Murder and Myth of Horst Wessel* (London: I. B. Tauris, 2013); Sarah Thieme, *Nationalsozialistischer Märtyrerkult: Sakralisierte Politik und Christentum im westfälischen Ruhrgebiet (1929–1939)* (Frankfurt/Main: Campus, 2017).
21. The Hitler trial is documented in Otto Gritschneder, Lothar Gruchmann, and Reinhard Weber (eds), *Der Hitler-Prozess 1924*, 4 vols. (Munich: K. G. Saur, 2000).
22. Quoted in Toby Thacker, *Joseph Goebbels: Life and Death* (Basingstoke: Palgrave Macmillan, 2009), 33.
23. Detlev J. K. Peukert, *The Weimar Republic: The Crisis of Classical Modernity*, tr. Richard Deveson (New York: Hill & Wang, 1993), 191–246.
24. Timothy Brown, *Weimar Radicals: Nazis and Communists between Authenticity and Performance* (New York and Oxford: Berghahn, 2009).
25. See the groundbreaking study by Peter Fritzsche, *Rehearsals for Fascism: Populism and Political Mobilisation in Weimar Germany* (New York and Oxford: Oxford University Press, 1991) and Wolfgang Schieder, 'Die NSDAP vor 1933: Profil einer faschistischen Partei', *Geschichte und Gesellschaft*, 19 (1993), 141–54, here 150; Geoff Eley, 'How do we Explain the Rise of Nazism? Theory and Historiography', in Baranowski et al., *Companion to Nazi Germany*, 24–5. On the nobility see Stephan Malinowski, *Nazis and Nobles: The History of a Misalliance* (Oxford: Oxford University Press, 2020).
26. Schieder, 'Die NSDAP vor 1933', 153.
27. Theodor Geiger, *Die soziale Schichtung des deutschen Volkes: Soziographischer Versuch auf statistischer Grundlage* (Stuttgart: Enke, 1932); Siegfried Kracauer, 'Aufruf der Mittelschichten: Eine Auseinandersetzung mit dem "Tat"-Kreis', in Kracauer, *Werke*, 5/3. *Essays, Feuilletons, Rezensionen, 1928–1931*, ed. Inka Mülder-Bach (Berlin: Suhrkamp, 2011), 716–38, quote 731.
28. See Jürgen Falter, *Hitlers Wähler: Die Anhänger der NSDAP 1924–1933* (Frankfurt/Main: Campus, 2020); Olaf Blaschke, *Die Kirchen und der Nationalsozialismus* (Stuttgart: Reclam, 2014); Dirk Hänisch, *Die österreichischen NSDAP-Wähler: Eine empirische Analyse ihrer politischen Herkunft und ihres Sozialprofils* (Vienna: Böhlau, 1998).
29. Alexander Otto-Morris, *Rebellion in the Province: The Landvolkbewegung and the Rise of National Socialism in Schleswig-Holstein* (Frankfurt/Main: Lang, 2013); Wolfram Pyta,

Dorfgemeinschaft und Parteipolitik 1918–1933: Die Verschränkung von Milieu und Parteien in den protestantischen Landgebieten Deutschlands in der Weimarer Republik (Düsseldorf: Droste, 1996).

30. Ingo Haar, 'Zur Sozialstruktur und Mitgliederentwicklung der NSDAP', in Wolfgang Benz (ed.), *Wie wurde man Parteigenosse?*, 60–73; Jürgen W. Falter, 'Spezifische Erklärungsmodelle und Motive der NSDAP-Mitgliedschaft', 'Was wissen wir über die NSDAP-Mitglieder? Ein Blick auf den Forschungsstand', and 'Alte Gewissheiten—neue Erkenntnisse: Ein Resümee', all in Falter (ed.), *Junge Kämpfer, alte Opportunisten: Die Mitglieder der NSDAP 1919–1945* (Frankfurt/Main: Campus, 2016), 65–87, 102–8, 463–75.
31. Falter, 'Alte Gewissheiten', 470.
32. Jürgen W. Falter, Thomas Lindenberger, and Siegfried Schumann, *Wahlen und Abstimmungen in der Weimarer Republik: Materialien zum Wahlverhalten 1919–1933* (Munich: Beck, 1986), 41.
33. 'Sieg des Radikalismus', *Vossische Zeitung*, 435, 15 Sept. 1930, 1.
34. For a partial reassessment of Brüning see William L. Patch, *Heinrich Brüning and the Dissolution of the Weimar Republic* (New York and Cambridge: Cambridge University Press, 1998).
35. Edgar Julius Jung, *Die Herrschaft der Minderwertigen, ihr Zerfall und ihre Ablösung durch ein Neues Reich*, 2nd ed. (Berlin: Verlag Deutsche Rundschau, 1930), 673.
36. Carlo Mierendorff, 'Wahlreform. Die Losung der jungen Generation', *Neue Blätter für den Sozialismus*, 1 (1930), 342–9. See more generally Stefan Vogt, *Nationaler Sozialismus und Soziale Demokratie: Die sozialdemokratische Junge Rechte 1918–1945* (Bonn: Dietz, 2006).
37. Rüdiger Graf, *Die Zukunft der Weimarer Republik: Krisen und Zukunftsaneignungen in Deutschland 1918–1933* (Munich: Oldenbourg, 2008), 130–1.
38. Thomas Mergel, *Parlamentarische Kultur in der Weimarer Republik: Politische Kommunikation, symbolische Politik und Öffentlichkeit im Reichstag* (Düsseldorf: Droste, 2005), 454.
39. Rüdiger Ahrens, *Bündische Jugend: Eine neue Geschichte 1918–1933* (Göttingen: Wallstein, 2015); Graf, *Die Zukunft der Weimarer Republik*, 130–1.
40. Schieder, 'Die NSDAP vor 1933', 153; Benz, 'Die NSDAP und ihre Mitglieder', 10.
41. Uwe Schmidt, *Lehrer im Gleichschritt: Die Nationalsozialistische Lehrerbund Hamburg* (Hamburg: Hamburg University Press, 2006); Fritz Schäffer, *Nationalsozialistischer Lehrerbund (NSLB), 1929–1943*, in *Historisches Lexikon Bayern*, <https://www.historisches-lexikon-bayerns.de/Lexikon/Nationalsozialistischer_Lehrerbund_(NSLB),_1929-1943>; Willi Feiten, *Der Nationalsozialistische Lehrerbund: Entwicklung und Organisation. Ein Beitrag zum Aufbau und zur Organisationsstruktur des nationalsozialistischen Herrschaftssystems* (Beltz: Weinheim, 1981).
42. Schmidt, *Lehrer im Gleichschritt*, 12, 16.
43. Kerstin Thieler, 'Radikale Studenten, herausgeforderte Professoren', in Norbert Frei (ed.), *Wie bürgerlich war der Nationalsozialismus?* (Göttingen: Wallstein, 2018), 41–2, 45.
44. Michael Grüttner, *Studenten im Dritten Reich* (Paderborn: Schöningh, 1995), 19. On the relationship between NSDStB and bündische youth see Ahrens, *Bündische Jugend*; as a case study Siemens, *Making of a Nazi Hero*.
45. Numbers in Grüttner, *Studenten im Dritten Reich*, 496.
46. Ibid., 19–61; Michael H. Kater, *Studentenschaft und Rechtsradikalismus in Deutschland 1918–1933: Eine sozialgeschichtliche Studie zur Bildungskrise in der Weimarer Republik* (Hamburg: Hoffmann & Campe, 1975).

47. Mario Wenzel, 'Die NSDAP, ihre Gliederungen und angeschlossenen Verbände', in Benz, *Wie wurde man Parteigenosse?*, 19.
48. Gerhard Paul, *Aufstand der Bilder: Die NS-Propaganda vor 1933* (Bonn: Dietz, 1990).
49. Mathias Rösch, *Die Münchner NSDAP 1925–1933: Eine Untersuchung zur inneren Struktur der NSDAP in der Weimarer Republik* (Munich: Oldenbourg, 2002) 85–91; Andreas Wagner, *'Machtergreifung' in Sachsen: NSDAP und staatliche Verwaltung 1930–1935* (Cologne: Böhlau, 2004), 55–9.
50. Rudy Koshar, 'From Stammtisch to Party: Nazi Joiners and the Contradictions of Grass Roots Fascism in Weimar Germany', *Journal of Modern History*, 59 (1987), 1–24.
51. Rösch, *Die Münchner NSDAP*, 245.
52. Max Hiemisch, *Der nationalsozialistische Kampf um Bielefeld: Die Geschichte der NSDAP Bielefeld* (Bielefeld: Holtmann, 1933); Rösch, *Die Münchner NSDAP*, 427.
53. Wagner, *'Machtergreifung' in Sachsen*, 57–8.
54. Ibid., 94–104.
55. Oliver Reschke, *Der Kampf der Nationalsozialisten um den roten Friedrichshain 1925–1933* (Berlin: Trafo, 2004), 67–9; Rösch, *Die Münchner NSDAP*, 266–70.
56. This is also shown by the novels of socialist authors from the years 1933–4, in which singular 'good' national socialists are portrayed as misled idealists, such as in Walter Schönstedt, *Auf der Flucht erschossen: Ein SA-Roman* (Paris: Éd. du Carrefour, 1934).
57. On Hitler as a charismatic leader and the limitations of this concept see Ludolf Herbst, *Hitlers Charisma: Die Erfindung eines deutschen Messias* (Frankfurt/Main: Fischer, 2010); Hans-Ulrich Wehler, *Deutsche Gesellschaftsgeschichte*, vol. 4. *Vom Beginn des Ersten Weltkriegs bis zur Gründung der beiden deutschen Staaten 1914–1949* (Munich: Beck, 2003).
58. Koshar, 'From Stammtisch to Party', 21.
59. See the classic study by Fritz Stern, *The Politics of Cultural Despair: A Study in the Rise of the Germanic Ideology* (Berkeley, CA.: University of California Press, 1961).
60. Peter Fritzsche, *Germans into Nazis*, 6th ed. (Cambridge, MA: Harvard University Press, 2003), 97.
61. See Siemens, *Stormtroopers*; Sven Reichardt, *Faschistische Kampfbünde. Gewalt und Gemeinschaft im italienischen Squadrismus und in der deutschen SA*, 2nd ed. (Cologne: Böhlau, 2009).
62. On the 'show effect' of violent action see Randall Collins, *Violence: A Micro-Sociological Theory* (Princeton and Oxford: Princeton University Press, 2008), 281.
63. Siemens, *Stormtroopers*, 62–9.
64. Ibid., 12–13.
65. Falter, 'Alte Gewissheiten', 470; Marit A. Berntson and Brian Ault, 'Gender and Nazism: Women Joiners of the Pre-1933 Nazi Party', *The American Behavioral Scientist*, 49 (1998), 1194.
66. Bernston and Ault, 'Gender and Nazism', 1198, 1208–9; Gudrun Brockhaus, *Schauder und Idylle: Faschismus als Erlebnisangebot* (Munich: Kunstmann, 1997), 168–74.
67. Katherine Thomas (i.e. Jella Lepman), *Women in Nazi Germany* (London: Victor Gollancz, 1943), 23–8.
68. Jürgen W. Falter, *Hitlers Wähler* (Munich: C. H. Beck, 1991), 292–314.
69. On the support for the NSDAP by business leaders see Peter Hayes, 'German Big Business and the National Revolution, 1933–1934', in Hermann Beck and Larry Eugene Jones (eds), *From Weimar to Hitler: Studies in the Dissolution of the Weimar Republic and the*

Establishment of the Third Reich, 1932–1934 (New York and Oxford: Berghahn, 2019), 141–62.
70. Boris Groys and Michael Hagemeister (eds), *Die Neue Menschheit: Biopolitische Utopien in Russland zu Beginn des 20. Jahrhunderts* (Frankfurt/Main: Suhrkamp, 2005).
71. See Daniel Roos, *Julius Streicher und 'Der Stürmer' 1923–1945* (Paderborn: Schöningh, 2014); Alexandra Przyrembel, *'Rassenschande': Reinheitsmythos und Vernichtungslegitimation im Nationalsozialismus* (Göttingen: Vandenhoeck & Ruprecht, 2003).
72. Michael Burleigh and Wolfgang Wippermann, *The Racial State: Germany 1933–1945* (Cambridge: Cambridge University Press, 1991).
73. Peter Becker and Richard F. Wetzell (eds), *Criminals and their Scientists: The History of Criminology in International Perspective* (Cambridge: Cambridge University Press, 2006); Stefan Kühl, *Die Internationale der Rassisten: Aufstieg und Niedergang der internationalen Bewegung für Eugenik und Rassenhygiene im 20. Jahrhundert* (Frankfurt/Main: Campus, 1997).
74. Mark Roseman, 'Racial Discourse, Nazi Violence, and the Limits of the Racial State Model', in Devin O. Pendas, Mark Roseman, and Richard Wetzell (eds), *Beyond the Racial State: Rethinking Nazi Germany* (Cambridge and New York: Cambridge University Press, 2017), 32.
75. Ulrich Prehn, *Max Hildebert Boehm: Radikales Ordnungsdenken vom Ersten Weltkrieg bis in die Bundesrepublik* (Göttingen: Wallstein, 2013).
76. Christian Geulen, 'Ideology's Logic: The Evolution of Racial Thought in Germany from the Völkisch Movement to the Third Reich', in Pendas et al., *Beyond the Racial State*, 200–1.
77. Thomas Kailer, *Vermessung des Verbrechers: Die Kriminalbiologische Untersuchung in Bayern 1923–1945* (Bielefeld: transcript, 2011).
78. Schieder, 'Die NSDAP vor 1933', 144.
79. Michael Wildt, *Volksgemeinschaft als Selbstermächtigung: Gewalt gegen Juden in der deutschen Provinz 1919 bis 1939* (Hamburg: Hamburger Edition, 2007), 63.
80. Hans-Walter Schmuhl, 'Eugenik und Rassenanthropologie', in Robert Jütte (ed.), *Medizin und Nationalsozialismus: Bilanz und Perspektiven der Forschung* (Göttingen: Wallstein, 2011), 24–38.
81. Thomas Reuss, 'Der "Abwehrkampf" des Centralvereins deutscher Staatsbürger jüdischen Glaubens im oberschlesischen Beuthen während der ersten Jahre des Dritten Reiches', in Regina Grundmann et al. (eds), *'Was soll aus uns werden?' Beiträge zur Geschichte des Centralvereins deutscher Staatsbürger jüdischen Glaubens im nationalsozialistischen Deutschland* (Berlin: Metropol, 2020); Anna Ullrich, *Von 'jüdischem Optimismus' und 'unausbleiblicher Enttäuschung': Erwartungsmanagement deutsch-jüdischer Vereine und gesellschaftlicher Antisemitismus 1914–1938* (Berlin: de Gruyter Oldenbourg, 2019).
82. Moritz Föllmer, 'Wie kollektivistisch war der Nationalsozialismus? Zur Geschichte der Individualität zwischen Weimarer Republik und Nachkriegszeit', in Birthe Kundrus and Sybille Steinbacher (eds), *Kontinuitäten und Diskontinuitäten: Der Nationalsozialismus in der Geschichte des 20. Jahrhunderts* (Göttingen: Wallstein, 2013), 30–52; Dietmar Süß, 'Arbeit, Leistung, Bürgertum', in Norbert Frei (ed.), *Wie bürgerlich war der Nationalsozialismus?* (Göttingen: Wallstein, 2018), 100–15.
83. Föllmer, 'Wie kollektivistisch war der Nationalsozialismus?', 33; Martin Broszat, 'Soziale Motivation und Führer-Bindung des Nationalsozialismus', *Vierteljahrshefte für Zeitgeschichte*, 18 (1970), 392–409.

84. Süß, 'Arbeit, Leistung, Bürgertum', 102.
85. Föllmer, 'Wie kollektivistisch war der Nationalsozialismus?', 33, 36.
86. Cathy S. Gelbin and Sander L. Gilman, *Cosmopolitanism and the Jews* (Ann Arbor: University of Michigan Press, 2017); Föllmer, 'Wie kollektivistisch war der Nationalsozialismus?', 40–1.
87. Wildt, *Volksgemeinschaft als Selbstermächtigung*.
88. On the definition and concept of 'organic modernity' see Konrad H. Jarausch, 'Organic Modernity: National Socialism as Alternative Modernism', in Baranowski et al., *Companion to Nazi Germany*, 43–4.
89. Broszat, 'Soziale Motivation', 393–7.

Bibliography

Baranowski, Shelley, Armin Nolzen, and Claus-Christian Szejnmann (eds), *A Companion to Nazi Germany* (New York: Wiley, 2018).

Beck, Hermann, and Larry Eugene Jones (eds), *From Weimar to Hitler: Studies in the Dissolution of the Weimar Republic and the Establishment of the Third Reich 1932–1934* (New York: Berghahn, 2018).

Brown, Timothy, *Weimar Radicals. Nazis and Communists between Authenticity and Performance* (New York and Oxford: Berghahn, 2009).

Eley, Geoff, *Nazism as Fascism: Violence, Ideology, and the Ground of Consent in Germany 1930–1945* (London and New York: Routledge, 2013).

Fritzsche, Peter, *Germans into Nazis* (Cambridge, MA: Harvard University Press, 1998).

Kühne, Thomas, *Belonging and Genocide: Hitler's Community, 1918–1945* (New Haven and London: Yale University Press, 2010).

Pendas, Devin O., Mark Roseman, and Richard F. Wetzell (eds), *Beyond the Racial State: Rethinking Nazi Germany* (Cambridge: Cambridge University Press, 2017).

Siemens, Daniel, *Stormtroopers: A New History of Hitler's Brownshirts* (New Haven and London: Yale University Press, 2017).

Steber, Martina, and Bernhard Gotto (eds), *Visions of Community in Nazi Germany: Social Engineering and Private Lives* (Oxford: Oxford University Press, 2014).

Wildt, Michael, *Hitler's Volksgemeinschaft and the Dynamics of Racial Exclusion: Violence Against Jews in Provincial Germany, 1919–1939* (New York: Berghahn, 2014).

CHAPTER 18

ANTISEMITISM IN THE WEIMAR REPUBLIC

SUSANNE WEIN AND MARTIN ULMER

ANTISEMITISM refers to stigmatizing attitudes, expressed in rhetorical or physical manifestations, that are directed towards Jews as a group. Thus, this broad definition understands antisemitism as an ideological way of thinking, with an inherent claim to explain the world. Historian Robert S. Wistrich describes it as 'the longest hatred', a phenomenon that is not invariable and unchanging.[1] Starting in 1879, the *völkisch* movement in Imperial Germany popularized the notion 'antisemitism' as a combat term, using the neologism coined by the journalist Wilhelm Marr. For some time now, the term antisemitism has become commonly used among scholars and social scientists for all forms of hostility towards Jews. These forms may have changed from pre-modern to modern to racial and finally to so-called secondary antisemitism, which denies and trivializes the Holocaust. The structures themselves, however, have largely remained the same. Antisemites bear resentments and biased stereotypes, even hatred, against Jews—only because they are Jews.[2] They use the expression of 'the Jew' in the collective singular, creating a socio-cultural and ideological construct that by no means corresponds with reality.[3]

The historian Shulamit Volkov has developed the concept of 'antisemitism as a cultural code' for Imperial Germany, which is considered a milestone of historical antisemitism research.[4] A process of cultural polarization that occurred during the last third of the nineteenth century resulted in the emergence of two cultures of interpretation that can, on the one hand, be described as 'antisemitism' and 'emancipation' on the other. The anti-emancipatory camp developed an anti-Jewish language and made antisemitism a matter of course for their culture and a 'cultural code'. German nationalism that construed and imagined the German nation in contrast to the Jews and racial antisemitism, which emerged in the mid-nineteenth century, were the preconditions for this.[5] The assumption of a total difference between Jews and Germans became a key programmatic feature of the nationalist *völkisch* movement in Imperial

Germany.[6] Indeed, antisemitic parties lost their significance around the turn of the century. But the antisemitic worldview that demanded the revocation of Jewish emancipation, penetrated into associations such as the influential League of Farmers (Bund der Landwirte, BdL), the German National Association of Commercial Employees (Deutschnationaler Handlungsgehilfenverband), and student fraternities.[7] The Burgfrieden policy (the cessation of party conflict) of the First World War became fragile as early as 1915. Antisemites spread rumours that Jews shirked from frontline duties, culminating in the slanderous 'Jewish census' in the German army in autumn 1916, initiated by the Pan-German League.[8]

Immediately after the end of the war in 1918, hostilities towards Jews became more radical throughout the German public. The defeat of the German military and the brutalizing experiences at the frontline contributed to this. The end of a restrictive censorship imposed during the war also played a role because it enabled the rise of antisemitic agitation in the public space that developed into a mass phenomenon. *Völkisch* associations gained importance due to their growing numbers and membership as well as their increasing militancy, significantly influencing the political culture. Antisemitism emanated from the anti-republican camp that fought parliamentary democracy after the revolution of 1918–19 tooth and nail. It extended the assertion that the anti-war stance of the political left had caused the German defeat (stab-in-the-back legend) to an alleged Jewish 'stab-in-the-back'. The new government representatives were derogatorily referred to as 'Jewish Marxists' and 'November criminals'.[9] At the latest by the time the Versailles Treaty was signed and the Weimar Constitution, which had been drafted by the 'Jew' Hugo Preuß, was adopted, the anti-democratic camp found a term to sum up the stigmatization of the republic: the 'Jew republic'.

Ideological radicalization was based on another determining element of modern antisemitism: the conspiracy myth of Jewish world domination. Over the course of the Enlightenment and the period of nation-state building, the older stereotype of the 'Jewish conspirer' was subject to a significant shift. 'The Jew' was considered, on the one hand, as the ruler of banks, stock exchanges, and capitalism as a whole with its inscrutable mechanisms, but on the other, and at the same time, as its counterpart, as the inventor of revolutionary Marxism. The German *völkisch* discourse turned the Jews into a 'counter race', a negative principle per se.[10] The paradoxical assertion that 'the Jew' was behind conflicting world systems cannot sufficiently be explained with racism. Thus, when analysing antisemitism, sociological research on prejudice and stereotypes must be complemented by social psychological categories and cultural history.

The most influential antisemitic conspiracy myth is the text of the 'Protocols of the Elders of Zion'. This fabrication, invented by Russian antisemites around 1900, supposedly documents a meeting of Jewish leaders who planned to conquer the world. Despite being debunked as fake early on, from 1920 onwards the 'Protocols' spread, also enjoying high print runs in Germany.[11] Failing efforts to refute this myth reveal the most extreme excesses of a delusional and ideological way of thinking that Saul Friedländer has described as 'redemptive antisemitism'. According to this deeply rooted paranoid ideological trope, spread by Adolf Hitler and many Nazis as the mission of an apocalyptic final fight of the 'Aryan race' against the abstract principle of evil, the salvation of Germany and the world relied on the radical termination of the 'Jewish mortal enemy'.[12]

During the Weimar Republic, the determining elements of antisemitism intensified in the stereotyping of the alien 'Eastern Jew'[13] from the ghetto, on the one hand, and, on the other, the personification of the fantasy image of the 'international Jew' as the puppet master of capitalism and Marxism. Both stereotypes reveal a deep-seated fear of the revolution and 'Jewish Bolshevists' from the East. For many, including the left-wing politicians Rosa Luxemburg and Kurt Eisner, this highly charged atmosphere cost them their lives.[14] At the same time, it was insinuated that left-wing and liberal Germans of Jewish descent ruled the country. In some cases, a Jewish background was construed through the stigmatization of surnames.[15] There was, furthermore, the stereotype of the 'racketeer and usurer' and 'war profiteer'. According to these constructs, the Jew, regardless of whether immigrated from Eastern Europe or born in Germany, wangled a fortune out of the war corporations that had organized the procurement and distribution of raw materials between 1914 and 1918. This stereotyping exceeds xenophobic racism. At the same time, the conspiracy allegation construed the 'inferior race' of the Jews as omnipotent. The paranoid threat scenario of the right-wing agitation aimed at an imaginary 'Weltjudentum', a global network of influential Jews, that had provoked the war and was behind Germany's high reparation claims or intended to propel the nation into a socialist revolution.

This chapter is not only concerned with the violent antisemitism of the streets and hatred against Jews on a practical level, which manifested itself in various forms of exclusion. It also analyses discursive strategies of antisemitic actors of the Weimar Republic. Taking into account the tactics of antisemitic actors, the third section of the chapter explores the reaction of other socio-political milieus.

Exclusion and Violence

In February 1919, the Pan-German League founded the German Völkisch Protection and Defiance Federation (Deutschvölkischer Schutz- und Trutzbund, DVSTB), the largest *völkisch* mass and combat organization before the rise of the Nazis.[16] In its heyday, the DVSTB consisted of 600 active local groups and approximately 200,000 members, predominantly with bourgeois and academic backgrounds, including many students. Until its ban in 1922, it flooded cities and the countryside with radical antisemitic pamphlets and propaganda events and with roistering and heckling.[17] Through the agitation and instigation of violence in cooperation with other *völkisch* groups and paramilitary units (Free Corps, student battalions, Navy Brigade Ehrhardt, the secret Organization Consul), the DVSTB stoked a pogrom mood in the initial years of the republic. Violent incidents and political murders against representatives of the republic became more frequent. The murderers of the Catholic Minister of Finance Matthias Erzberger (1921) and Foreign Minister Walther Rathenau (1922) of Jewish descent came from these ranks.[18] Both ministers were demonized as 'fulfilment politicians' of the allegedly Jewish controlled Allies. The DVSTB used street agitation and means of mass communication such as flyers, leaflets, and stickers as a new strategy.[19] In the first half of 1920 alone, its local groups distributed more than two million flyers, 2.4 million leaflets, and 4.4 million stickers nationwide—not least in the context of the campaign for the Reichstag elections in June 1920. Overall, in 1920 almost eight million flyers were handed out in the streets, at railway stations, in front of barracks and factories, at political meetings, and put into private letterboxes. The range of anti-Jewish topics deliberately addressed different groups of society, including civil servants, craftsmen, soldiers, students, women, workers, and farmers, who were told some allegedly eye-opening facts about the 'Jew Republic' and the 'enslavement of the German people'. This militant street agitation gave the impression of a mighty antisemitic wave, as its manifestations were ubiquitous in public spaces. Alongside the antisemitic press, popular antisemitic literature, and propaganda speeches, *völkisch* antisemitism was a mass phenomenon. Compared to the period before 1914, both its total public presence and its conspiracy ideological content reached a new dimension. The early National Socialist movement modelled its propaganda activities on those of the DVSTB.[20]

Antisemitic violence in the Weimar Republic often had a performative, stage-like quality.[21] Violence or the threat of violence, stage-managed for propagandistic purposes, was part of the strategy to seize power pursued by both the *völkisch* camp and later the NSDAP (National Socialist German Workers' Party). Right-wing rowdies disrupted and heckled events with Jewish speakers, instigated brawls, and deliberately committed assaults and wilful property damage. This practice of violence was multifaceted: it was a manifestation of a new antisemitism of action that stood in contrast to antisemitic publications in Imperial Germany. A high ideological disposition and brutal determination gave these actions the potential to evolve into pogroms. The largest Jewish organization, the Central Association of German Citizens of Jewish Faith (Centralverein deutscher Staatsbürger jüdischen Glaubens, CV), founded in 1893 to combat rising antisemitism, recognized this trend very clearly.[22] For grass-root members of the *völkisch* and antisemitic camp, the radical hatred towards Jews was an important social psychological playground for a range of different practices that blended into one another: from disruption and rowdyism, to property damage, to physical violence against Jews or allegedly Jewish-looking people. The asymmetric violence intimidated the Jewish minority because it created dangerous zones within the public space. According to historian Michael Wildt, the patterns of exclusion of militant anti-Jewish actions contributed to the formation of a National Socialist 'people's community' as early as the 1920s.[23] Unarmed Jews were often abruptly, unexpectedly, and heavily assaulted, however, most perpetrators (at this point) refrained from the use of weapons.

While antisemitic incidents up until 1922 were related to the DVSTB, in 1923 the leadership of *völkisch* violence passed to the Nazis and their Stormtroopers (Sturmabteilung,

SA), individual members of the Reichswehr, and *völkisch* student fraternities. During the crisis year of 1923, the *völkisch* movement worked towards a putsch against the republic and its 'Jewish puppet masters'. To that end, they aimed to inflame the public mood beforehand to forcefully seize power through pogroms, military and civil war actions. Throughout the whole country, antisemitic assaults and abuse against individual Jewish citizens were committed, for example by students in university towns such as Tübingen.[24] In the Scheunenviertel, a neighbourhood in Berlin with a large population of Jews from Eastern Europe, violent acts committed on 5 November 1923 escalated into riots and lootings, with the police intervening when it was too late. Antisemitic agitators had incited several unemployed persons. The results were damage and lootings of 200 shops (among them several shops with non-Jewish owners), dozens of injured, and two dead.[25] During the Hitler putsch on 9 November 1923 in Munich, right-wing radicals took twenty Jews hostage; only the swift crushing of the putsch prevented something even worse occurring. Even before 1923, pogrom lists surfaced in several cities containing the names of wealthy Jews who were planned to be assaulted and looted. With the end of hyperinflation and the putsch atmosphere from the left and the right easing off, manifestations of antisemitism changed. Alongside assaults on Jewish citizens in the countryside and smaller towns and villages, acts of cemetery and synagogue desecration mushroomed across the whole of Germany—200 occurred until 1932. Many of the perpetrators were young Nazis. These forms of staged violence against Jewish symbols aimed to intimidate the Jewish population and provoke reactions in the wider public on the 'Jewish question'. Through a major counter-campaign, the CV was able to reach the wider public, even including conservative circles, and largely curbed the wave of desecrations until 1929.[26]

Many radical antisemites developed a sense of how to disparage, humiliate, and hurt Jews. Alongside assaults on their religion (and suggestions of Jewish kosher slaughter being cruel to animals), this included the mockery of Jewish names (i.e. disparaging a Jewish-sounding name), and the assertion that Jewish Germans did not serve at the frontline during the war. Boycotts against department stores and shops with Jewish owners had a long tradition dating back to Imperial Germany that escalated in the Weimar Republic. Again, the DVSTB was at the forefront. From the mid-1920s, the Nazis continued in the same vein and adopted the agitation line of the 'money grabbing Jew' ('raffende Jude').[27] The political economic boycott intended to gain new voters, particularly female ones. However, Jewish organizations and affected merchants successfully lodged appeals.[28] For this reason, local Nazi activists sometimes fell back on indirect discrimination and advocated to buy only from 'German' or 'Christian' shops. In 1932, the Nazis expanded the boycott actions across the country.[29]

On their way to the seizure of power, the Nazis focused in 1929–30 on the cultural sphere in order to win over new followers from the bourgeoisie that generally opposed cultural innovations. Nazi activists instigated antisemitic uproar against various theatre performances. The turmoil against the play *Shadows over Harlem* (*Schatten über Harlem*) by the Eastern Jewish author Ossip Dymow, dubbed as 'cultural Bolshevist', resulted in the removal of the play from the repertoire of the Stuttgart State Theatre.[30]

With riots and antisemitic and nationalistic campaigns, NSDAP and SA made a nationwide stand against the film adaptation of Erich Maria Remarque's anti-war novel *All Quiet on the Western Front* by the Jewish producer Carl Laemmle from Hollywood. After only a few screenings the film was banned in German cinemas for half a year.[31] Thus, Nazi attacks were often successful, which impressed many Germans who themselves indulged in nationalistic and antisemitic attitudes.

The pointed exclusion of the Jews from the German 'people's community' found specific expression during the internationally much noted so-called 'Kurfüstendammkrawall' on 12 September 1931.[32] The posh Berlin neighbourhood around the Kurfüstendamm, one of the city's main boulevards, was considered a symbolic Jewish space. Around 500 SA men, prepared to use violence, purposefully attacked 'Jewish-looking' people and bawled the Nazi combat watchword 'Germany awake, Juda drop dead'. Only a large police detachment and forty arrests could prevent a violent excess. In summary proceedings the perpetrators were sentenced to prison for breach of the peace. Despite these efforts to curb antisemitic violence and a temporary ban of the SA, organized street violence as well as aggressive propaganda in the print media and at meetings, which often ended with antisemitic assaults, caused noticeable feelings of insecurity and an awareness of crisis in the affected Jewish population.[33]

Alongside violent antisemitic practice, a silent and slow segregation process through state, political, and social institutions, organizations, and their actors began. Jews were gradually ousted from their posts in politics and associations and their claims for equal participation were increasingly ignored.[34] This everyday life antisemitism aimed, more or less deliberately, to achieve a homogeneous 'people's community' free of Jews, violating the equality principle guaranteed by the Weimar Constitution. In the state and municipal contexts, this manifested itself in a rather discreet practice of exclusion. When applying for posts in the civil service or as municipal administrative employees, Jewish Germans, even with better qualifications, were often disregarded. Some universities such as the one in Tübingen no longer appointed Jewish professors and lecturers and almost all student fraternities in Germany systematically excluded Jews. Representatives of Jewish communities were frequently not invited to state or public remembrance ceremonies for the fallen. In Stuttgart, the Israelite Welfare Office had to fight for ten years for a seat at the municipal Youth Commission.[35] Even democratic parties chose fewer candidates of Jewish descent for elections or withdrew them, concerned that they might be attacked.[36]

Growing social antisemitism was clearly noticeable in schools, at holiday destinations, and in the wider public. Several memoirs written by German Jews who later fled into exile describe brawls, verbal abuse, and contempt by teachers and fellow students. Often, the perpetrators came from a German national milieu. The same change appeared in associations and societies. For example, liberal bourgeois associations in Stuttgart had no Jewish members from 1925 onwards, in contrast to Imperial Germany.[37] These findings confirm a general process of exclusion in the Weimar Republic. A certain form of bullying and the withdrawal of many Jews were characteristic of this. A particularly visible form of social stigmatizing was antisemitism in spa towns and seaside resorts.[38]

While from 1900 onwards a latent and sometimes militant hostility towards Jews had not been unheard of in spa towns at the North and the Baltic Sea, it became more widespread in the 1920s. The Jewish Central Association (CV) kept lists documenting antisemitic incidents and supported legal proceedings. It recorded a sudden rise in the number of holiday destinations with anti-Jewish hotels and guesthouses from twenty-four in 1920 to 109 in 1928 and 165 in 1931.[39] Among these destinations were not only spa and seaside towns, but also destinations in the Central German Uplands and the Alps. Often, national *völkisch* guests and like-minded hotel owners enforced 'Jew-free' holiday destinations through antisemitic posters and sing-alongs, swastikas and pennants, as well as threats, abuse, and brawls against Jewish guests. From the end of the 1920s, the Nazis mobilized holiday resorts to expel Jews. Local authorities and the right-wing judiciary readily gave way to this pressure.

Insults and abuse were deeply rooted experiences of many Jews, however, they increased distinctly from 1919 onwards.[40] This often manifested itself in personal conflicts with ordinary fellow citizens who were not known as organized antisemites. In addition, people known as staunch antisemites deliberately provoked quarrels, often in inns, shops, or at work where many people were around. Many affected Jews responded with complaints to the police and lawsuits. The CV established a whole department in support of these cases.[41] Very often, the invective 'Jew republic' ended up in court. The young democracy suffered from the lack of renewal of the military, the civil service, and the judiciary. However, after the murder of Foreign Minister Rathenau, the republic displayed the ability to defend itself by enacting the 'Law for the Protection of the Republic' and extending the State Court at Leipzig to the Constitutional Court for the Protection of the Republic. But even this special court did not take sufficient action against offences directed at the republic and its organizations, nor did it punish antisemitic insults of the new political order.[42] As documented by the CV, many district and regional courts frequently acquitted persons of the charge of insulting and defaming the republic by using remarks such as 'We do not want a Jewish republic' and 'Jews out'.[43] Several courts did not regard these expressions as attacks against the republican order—which would have been punished much harsher—but only as a verbal insult against individual Jews. This points at a dilemma that occurred during the 1920s: despite all efforts, the CV was not able to enshrine in law antisemitic remarks as collective defamation. Antisemitic offences could only be prosecuted as individual cases of insult or religious insult under §166 of the criminal code (Strafgesetzbuch, RStGB) and §130 (incitement to class hatred). Often, libel suits were stayed or the court decided that the Jews were partially at fault. The CV found it particularly alarming that judges often followed the arguments of extreme right-wing defendants in defining the Jews as a race. The courts often deemed the fact that defendants disliked Jews as a race out of conviction as mitigating circumstances. Furthermore, these verdicts confirmed the assumption that race theories were scientifically tenable concepts. This overturned both the offence of religious insult as well as using the word 'Jew' as an insult because facts could not be defamations.

Political Culture and Discursive Strategies

Right-wing conservative and extremist political actors used virtually every event of the Weimar Republic to charge it with their antisemitic agenda. Some examples can illustrate the structure of the antisemitic line of argument, how it impacted society, and how it shifted the boundaries of what could be said. This is particularly relevant because the boundaries of what can be said determine the legitimacy of certain ways of speaking—or how they can be criticized at all. The following three examples are from Reichstag debates. At this place of political discussion, the clashing of expressions of different political camps can, to a large extent, be reconstructed. The press, divided along partisan lines, provided a comprehensive documentation of parliamentary debates that impacted society, while the members of parliament attempted to reflect the views of their party followers. Thus, the debates can serve as an indicator of political culture of the Weimar public.

The brutal assassination on Foreign Minister Walther Rathenau on 24 June 1922 shocked the nation across party lines. This political murder was the escalation of a series of attacks and resulted in a broad republican defence.[44] When the news of the crime arrived at the Reichstag, the leading national conservative politician Karl Helfferich had to hide from outraged left-wing Reichstag members. The day before, he had denounced the Foreign Minister as a 'fulfilment politician'.[45] Numerous leaflets, brochures, and speeches had agitated against Rathenau, not least the battle cry of the Free Corps that openly called for Rathenau's murder: 'Kill Walther Rathenau, the Goddamned Jewish pig'.[46] On 25 June, Reich Chancellor Joseph Wirth, a convinced republican, gave his famous speech, aimed at the DNVP (German National People's Party): 'There is the enemy—and there is no doubt about it: the enemy is on the right!'[47] In the Reichstag, the 'incitement' of the right-wing camp was criticized. However, most speakers did not directly touch upon antisemitism. The fierce criticism of a speech by the Jewish member of parliament Julius Moses (USPD, Independent Social Democratic Party) was an exception. Citing a DNVP publication he showed 'how spiteful' its authors were towards 'the representatives of the German government'. He argued, moreover, that DNVP meetings were 'orgies of anti-Jewish agitation. In secondary schools, students were brought up to hate Jews, and Jewish fellow students were systematically boycotted. In doing so, they plant into the child's soul the very spirit that consequently leads from the barbarization of the imagination to these crimes that we today witness.'[48] Between 1919 and 1933, Moses was the most outspoken politician in Reichstag about the link between antisemitism and criminal deeds. According to an analysis of the daily newspapers, after Rathenau's assassination there was a widespread awareness among large parts of the democratic and left-leaning public about the link between the hostility towards the republic and that towards the Jews.[49]

The so-called 'Eastern Jewish question' was increasingly placed centre stage during the post-war years, which, when immigration from Eastern Europe temporarily grew, many people in Germany perceived as a crisis. Though it was not only Jews who moved to Germany, the *völkisch* antisemitic agitation focused on the alleged mass immigration of 'Eastern Jews' by publishing overinflated or false figures.[50] Furthermore, the right attempted to project the image of 'the Eastern Jew' onto all Jews in Germany. In early August 1920, a large majority of the Reichstag voted in favour of a resolution that requested the government to take appropriate action against the 'mass immigration of alien elements, in particular from the eastern border'. These immigrants were to be brought back after being detained 'in case they prove troublesome'.[51] The wording of the resolution originated from a request of the DNVP, which was also the opinion leader of this topic in the public. Building upon verbal rowdy antisemitism,[52] the party—from which the German Völkisch Freedom Party (Deutschvölkische Freiheitspartei, DvFP) broke away in 1922—referred to Eastern Jews as 'cancer damage' and 'locusts'.[53] Despite this, the bourgeois parliamentary parties supported the resolution, confirming the general xenophobic mood with their own initiatives. In the National Assembly in November 1919, the Catholic Centre Party regarded the immigration of 'thousands', 'particularly from the eastern countries', as the cause of the current housing shortage.[54] The DDP (German Democratic Party) and the DVP (German People's Party) also blamed the influx of 'elements alien to our people' for the introduction of diseases, housing shortages, and the emigration of skilled workers to Western countries.[55] The discourse on the 'Eastern Jewish question' reveals the above-mentioned stereotyping that spread to the bourgeois centre parties. Only the political left opposed antisemitic racial xenophobia.[56] However, the KPD (Communist Party) did use antisemitic stereotypes against a capitalist of Jewish descent during the Barmat Scandal.

It is fair to assume that the Barmat Scandal—a business and corruption affair involving a medium-size corporation in 1925—could only tear the very fabric of the state because the corporation owner Julius Barmat and his brothers were of Eastern Jewish descent.[57] After the First World War, Julius Barmat had used his contacts in the SPD (Social Democratic Party) and to individual Centre Party politicians—both parties represented the allegedly corrupt republic according to its political opponents—to support the establishment of his company. To sum up the facts of the Barmat Scandal: the company conglomerate was no longer able to repay loans granted by the Prussian State Bank, thus it had misappropriated public money, which auditors noticed by chance in late 1924. Proceedings against the Barmat brothers started in 1926 and ended in March 1928 with a lenient sentence. SPD and Centre Party politicians who had been heavily attacked were not even charged.

The starting pistol was fired when a spectacularly large police detachment arrested Julius Barmat in late 1924. The scandal was grist to the mill of antisemitic antirepublicans. Accordingly, the tabloids, particularly the ones of the Alfred Hugenberg's nationalist-conservative publishing conglomerate, and the party press of the political right went head over heels in painting the image of the parvenu nature of 'the eastern Jew' ('from onion merchant to millionaire'[58]). Within a few days, the name Barmat had become the cipher of the inflation profiteer par excellence who had lived an extravagant life at the expense of starving Germans. The right-wing camp considered him a pars pro toto, fuelling their propaganda that 'half a dozen eastern Jews' were pulling the strings and rule in the 'new Germany'.[59] Both the Reichstag and the Prussian State Diet set up parliamentary inquiry committees. Given the media circus around the Barmat affair in early 1925, the formation of a government including the SPD—the winner of the Reichstag elections on 4 December 1924—was out of the question.[60] For over a year numerous metaphors, such as the 'Barmat swamp' and other newly coined terms, circulated in the media and other publications.[61] The press of the workers' party KPD played a particularly dubious role in this respect. As early as during the election campaign of December 1924, it attempted to brand the contacts between Barmat and the SPD as a scandal. In the process, it used racist and antisemitic attributions and nationalist expressions. The Communist daily newspaper *Rote Fahne* personified its enemy, the international capitalist, as a 'ruthless grubber'; moreover, the Barmat family, coming from 'Galicia', did not, the paper alleged, 'defend ... a fatherland'.[62]

The right-wing parties, on the other hand, still agitated against the *Fürstenenteignung* (expropriation of the princes) in 1926, which was to be decided in a referendum, using the slogan: 'Expropriate the princes! Barmat needs money!'[63] The significance of the Barmat affair as a discursive event for the Weimar Republic can hardly be overestimated. The relatively small financial loss was completely disproportioned to the political damage for the republic. Other political affairs came at a much higher price for the taxpayer without creating a public stir. The sum misappropriated in the Barmat affair amounted to 14 million marks. In comparison, the state granted the iron-producing industry at the Ruhr financial support for its losses, due to passive resistance against French and Belgian occupation in 1923, amounting to more than 700 million marks.[64] In 1929, public outrage resurfaced with the news on the Berlin corruption affair of the Eastern Jewish brothers Sklarek.[65] This suggests only norm violations that involved alleged or actual Jews developed into large-scale political scandals. Moreover, anti-republican actors continued to milk such scandals in the mass media. In doing so, their persistent antisemitic interpretations contributed to further destabilizing the republic.[66]

A third example of the discursive strategies of the political right that aggravated antisemitic prejudice are the debates on reparations. From May 1924, the National Socialists, on a joint list with the German Völkisch Freedom Party, were represented in the German parliament. Their speakers focused on filibustering and obstruction, transgressing the unwritten boundaries of what could be said in respect to antisemitism. Their blatant antisemitic attacks were the rule rather than the exception. They also initiated a coding of certain key terms in parliamentary debates. The reparation claims of the Entente to Germany were a dominant topic in the Weimar Republic. To strengthen the damaged national self-confidence, all parties favoured a cross-party consensus, standing shoulder to shoulder and portraying the German people as victims. In this situation it was easy for the right-wing camp to find acceptance for their Manichaean worldview that deemed their own, the 'national', as good and the 'international', the foreign powers, as hostile and evil. What could be more obvious than to vilify this external enemy as Jewish? German Völkisch delegates and National Socialists markedly and continuously suggested that 'Jewish international capital' was behind the Dawes Plan, named after the American chief negotiator Charles G. Dawes, and that *Alljuda* ('All Jewry', borrowed from the term *Alldeutsch* or Pan-German) pulled the strings in Wall Street. They also blamed 'Jewish high finance' for the war.[67] In so doing, the extreme right 'concealed'[68] and fused key terms from the world of finance and capitalism with the adjective 'Jewish', turning them into a negative superlative. Against the backdrop of just having overcome hyperinflation, this constant agitation in the press, parliamentary debates, and, in 1924, December elections campaigns did not fail to have an impact. After years of blatantly antisemitic propaganda, the German Völkisch Freedom Party could even omit the lexeme (basic unit of meaning in a language) 'Jew' or 'Jewish' and still convey its antisemitic meaning. In the 1929–30 Reichstag debates on the reparation plan, developed under the lead of the American Owen Young, National Socialists only used coded antisemitic phrases such as 'international high finance'. The DNVP followed suit. They unanimously incited hostility and created panic. According to their propaganda, the German people would be enslaved by foreign powers up until to the next generation and forced to pay 'tribute' to 'financial capital' or a 'big international bank' (*Großbankhaus der Völkerinternationale*).[69]

In the Reichstag of 1924, the socialist parties largely responded with irony and polemics to the blatantly antisemitic ramblings about 'the Jew' who allegedly ruled over America and the stock exchange. However, in light of growing coded antisemitic phrases these reactions as well as public condemnations of antisemitic rhetoric became less frequent. Most left-wing politicians were probably well aware of the antisemitic nature of this concealed language. Yet they fatally miscalculated the impact of the mere twelve NSDAP members of parliament, assuming they would remain a small group with a crude conspiracy ideology during the fourth legislative term from 1928 to 1930. But it turned out that not only the size of a group was decisive, but ultimately its discursive hegemony, that is, who ultimately determined the rules of what could be said. Continuous antisemitic propaganda gradually normalized these specific speech acts.

Parties and Social Milieus

So far we have analysed the violent practice of antisemites and their discursive strategies of exclusion. This section describes the views of different party-political camps towards antisemitism. Did they support antisemitism, did they remain indifferent, or did they combat it? The statements of the German *völkisch* milieu and the NSDAP left no doubt about their hatred towards the Jews, their hostility against the political left and the parliamentary system.[70] After the failed putsch attempts during the period up to 1923 and the temporary ban of the NSDAP, the party, from 1924 onwards, focused on the legal seizure of power through elections. The combined list of the radical right immediately gained 6.5 per cent in May 1924.[71] However, the Nazis and their antisemitic watchwords were hardly innovative. Demands to abolish the emancipation of Jews in Germany, after their exclusion and expulsion, had their roots in the *völkisch* movement in Wilhelmine Germany since around 1900.[72] The Nazi movement, however, pushed for action. The marching SA formations in uniform supported Adolf Hitler's inflammatory speeches. His maniac obsession with 'the Jew' as the archenemy of the 'Aryan' German people has been analysed by many historians.[73] Here, a perspective informed by cultural history will broaden our understanding: when the NSDAP was re-established in 1925, Hitler was banned from holding public events across the whole of Germany. Yet in August 1925, the state government of Württemberg, a coalition between the Württembergische Bürgerpartei (a regional affiliate of the DNVP) and the Centre Party, allowed him to host a large-scale event in Stuttgart, regardless of this ban.[74] As with all NSDAP events, Jews were not allowed to take part. The keynote speaker appeared in plain clothes, yet his remarks were verbally explosive.[75] The paranoid antisemitism directed against the 'Jew republic' and the idea of an apocalyptic war between different races took centre stage: either an Aryan empire was forged against the Jewish race or the end was nigh. This public appearance by Hitler in front of more than 3,000 people shows, particularly during the more stable phase of the republic, that no follower of the NSDAP could ignore the fact that antisemitism was a key element of the Nazi party. Even later, the 'antisemitic ticket' was not withdrawn.[76] The manifesto for the 1928 Reichstag elections carried the thumbprint of Joseph Goebbels. It contains concealed key terms that implied the Jews alongside blatantly rowdy antisemitic statements.[77] The party continued to use manifest and coded antisemitism in its election campaigns at all propaganda levels.[78] Only for mere tactical reasons did Hitler refrain from anti-Jewish speeches in the final years of the republic, and, based on the division of labour within the NSDAP, left the radical antisemitic agitation to his propaganda specialists Gregor Strasser and Goebbels as well as regional functionaries.[79]

From its foundation in late 1918 onwards, the national conservative DNVP was a melting pot of *völkisch*, right-wing conservative, and anti-republican circles.[80] A large part of nationalist Protestants found their political home here. The grassroots of the party ranged from civil servants to aristocratic *Junker* in East-Elbian Prussia to entrepreneurs of heavy industry. Everything 'Jewish' was deemed as non-Christian and alien, seeming even more dangerous because it would try to gain supremacy in Germany.[81] In parliaments, meetings, and the conservative press empire of the later DNVP leader, Alfred Hugenberg, antisemitism was present from the outset, sometimes more openly, sometimes more coded.[82] The DNVP knew about the force of radical antisemitism in mobilizing followers and increased the dose in the final phase of election campaigns.[83] The discursive concealment of anti-Jewish language was supported by the German nationalist milieu. In their campaign against the Young Plan, DNVP members used expressions such as 'enslavement' to 'financial capital' without having to explicitly mention the image of the 'international Jew'. At the same time, the DNVP was also using manifest and coded antisemitism.[84]

The DVP refrained from openly antisemitic statements in official party statements and formally advocated the freedom of religion. In everyday politics until 1924, however, it stirred up resentments against Eastern Jews. According to its Principles from 1919, the party intended to combat the 'subversive attempts' of 'cosmopolitanism' against the 'German national character', which was in danger due to the democratic order.[85] The DVP deemed Marxism as a much greater danger than antisemitism. After the death of the party leader, Gustav Stresemann (1929), the party shifted to the right and became openly antisemitic.[86] The DVP always favoured forming a coalition with the anti-Jewish DNVP over one with the SPD.

The large minority of Catholics experienced an increase in appreciation and gained influence during the Weimar Republic.[87] Thus, its majority mostly sided with the proponents of the republic. Nevertheless, the Catholic milieu was traditionally anti-Jewish. Christian anti-Judaism, based on the idea that the Jews crucified the saviour, shaped the Catholic mindset well into the twentieth century.[88] The Centre Party—and to a certain extent its Bavarian sister party, the Bavarian People's Party (Bayerische Volkspartei, BVP)—developed into silent advocates of the Weimar Republic. Both parties often participated in coalition governments and pursued pragmatic politics. In its publications, the Centre Party firmly rejected the racial theory of German Christianity and Germanic ideologies like those propagated by Alfred Rosenberg, because they were anti-Catholic and anti-Rome. However, the Centre Party and most Catholics did not reflect on the fact that the Jews had become the target of *völkisch* racial thinking. When Catholics denounced antisemitism they did so in remembrance of the so-called 'culture struggle' (*Kulturkampf*) during the 1870s in Imperial Germany, fearing to be discriminated against as a minority again just as the Jews were now.[89] In 1930, both the BVP and the Centre Party were willing to form coalition governments with the openly antisemitic German national spectrum at Reich and state level and, in 1932, even with the NSDAP.

The left-liberal DDP firmly opposed antisemitism—provided the party recognized it as such, which it failed to do in the case of Eastern Jews. Many Jews were politically progressive and got actively involved in the DDP. The 'ABC of the DDP' from December 1927 read: 'Antisemitism . . is an unethical movement because it appeals to the lowest instincts, deeming a certain strata of equal citizens as inferior only because of their descent.'[90] Due to the demise of liberalism, the DDP faced a declining voter support in all Reichstag elections other than in December 1924. The defamation of the DDP as a 'party of Jews' might have contributed to this. In a failed attempt to prevent slipping into oblivion, the party forged an alliance with the anti-Jewish Young German Order (Jungdeutscher Orden) and was renamed German State Party (Deutsche Staatspartei) in July 1930. However, this resulted in a loss of credibility with many Jewish voters.[91] The non-Jewish bourgeois milieu often remained indifferent towards manifest verbal antisemitism and even violent antisemitic incidents. Many bourgeois liberals only opposed rowdy antisemitic street violence because it fuelled fears of attacks from the right and the left on the public order and of its collapse.

Already the late nineteenth-century socialist labour movement had rejected racial antisemitism. At the same time, it tended not to notice everyday hostility against Jews. Following Karl Marx's problematic 1844 essay 'On the Jewish Question', some socialists portrayed 'the Jew' as being linked to the financial sphere of capitalism.[92] However, during the Weimar Republic, the SPD and USPD were largely attentive and consistent critics of right-wing antisemitism. In the Reichstag several representatives of the USPD took a stance against the agitation against Eastern Jews. From the 1923 pogrom in the Berlin Scheunenviertel to the desecration of Jewish cemeteries, the SPD newspaper *Vorwärts* and other party outlets firmly denounced rowdy antisemitic excesses.[93] Many leading party members of the SPD were of Jewish descent. Until 1922, the SPD repeatedly criticized the use of antisemitism 'as a national weapon' within the DNVP.[94] And yet, social democratic criticisms of *völkisch* conservatives and extreme right-wingers increasingly waned in commitment. Only in passing did Social Democrats address Nazi racial antisemitism, underestimating the particular threat that ideological antisemitism posed to the Jews. Most of them considered racial antisemitism either as a distraction presented by the right or as a lunatic's whim that they ridiculed.[95] In some isolated cases, Social Democratic politicians displayed antisemitic resentment, which can be interpreted as a repercussion of the antisemitic 'cultural code' (Volkov) that was effective across German society as a whole.

The KPD was not interested in forming a decisive position on the so-called 'Jewish Question', because religion was meant to become insignificant under socialism. However, right-wing racial thinking was programmatically rejected, as well as the openly held conspiracy antisemitism. Quite a few leading Communists were of Jewish descent. Yet KPD representatives rarely advocated for the racially persecuted minority of Eastern Jews, not least because they often embraced their religion. The dichotomous contrast between the 'good' proletariat and 'evil' capitalists resulted time and time again in antisemitic personifications of the latter. The analysis of the communist press, propaganda, and meetings shows that some KPD followers strongly believed in the existence of a 'Jewish big capital' and in the Jews dominating the co-called 'financial capital'.[96] As in the Barmat Scandal, the party repeatedly used open and coded antisemitic expressions. However, this latent structural antisemitism within the KPD did not become a manifest antisemitic ideology within the party, which was opposed to the political system, because it never adopted the trope of the 'Jew republic'.[97] Nevertheless, the accusations of the SPD and the DDP that Communist watchwords were barely distinguishable from those of the NSDAP were, to some extent, justified.

Thus, the views and attitudes of the socio-political milieus of Weimar society towards antisemitism were widely divergent: while the *völkisch* and Protestant conservative camps openly propagated antisemitic resentments virtually all the time, SPD, left-liberal parties, and the Centre Party firmly opposed aggressive antisemitic propaganda and racial antisemitism. However, within the milieus of these parties as well as in that of the KPD, indifference, a lack of condemnation or even acceptance of rampant antisemitic positions of the right, and the use of structurally antisemitic language can be found. This mindset was partially based on a deeply rooted cultural code that vaguely associated 'the

Jews' with capitalism. The result was a lack of understanding of the novel potential threat to the German Jews. For this reason, the efforts of the not straightforwardly antisemitic party milieus in defending the Jewish population against *völkisch* propaganda were rather limited.

Conclusion

Antisemitism maintained a strong political and societal presence throughout the Weimar Republic. There were various and diverse manifestations of antisemitism, which by no means can be reduced to a socio-economic crisis phenomenon. During the Weimar Republic, traditional antisemitic patterns became more radicalized on various levels. First, the militant propaganda actions of the ideological antisemites conquered the public space, increasing the risk of pogroms. Their attacks on parliamentary democracy aimed at eliminating the allegedly 'Judaized' republic. The antisemitically charged mood escalated in attacks against Eastern Jews in the Berlin Scheunenviertel during November 1923. Alongside physical antisemitic violence, which, after 1923, found expression in a latent pogrom climate and isolated assaults, there was a tendency to socially exclude Jews through a widespread everyday antisemitism.

Second, antisemitism manifested itself in the public discourse through radical and ideologically grounded content as well as the demand for a strict separation between 'Jewish' and 'German'. It increasingly exposed the features of a delusional conspiracy ideology, suggesting that 'the Jew' ruled Germany, the victorious countries, or global capital markets. The largest lobby group for the Jewish minority, the CV, urged vigilance and did its utmost to ward off all forms of antisemitism. The rather small 'Christian Liberal Association for the Defence against Antisemitism' (Verein zur Abwehr von Antisemitismus), founded in 1890 and striving for education, offered support. Furthermore, a cooperation was established between the CV and the republican Reichsbanner black red gold (Reichsbanner Schwarz-Rot-Gold), which remained conspiratorial for the benefit of both sides. Otherwise the Jewish organization was on its own.[98]

Third, the cultural code of antisemitism changed: according to the principle 'constant dripping wears away a stone' right-wing extremists and, to some extent, German national agitators interpreted most political events within the framework of an antisemitic discourse. As a result, antisemitic patterns of explanation and interpretation spread beyond the traditionally antisemitic right-wing bourgeois milieu. Over the course of several years, the fusion of the lexeme 'Jewish' with certain key terms, constantly propagated by right-wing actors, gained acceptance. Tailored to specific electoral groups, right-wing parties used this as well as coded watchwords in their election campaigns. The voters were generally well aware of the antisemitic meaning of these watchwords. At the same time, condemnation of antisemitism throughout society noticeably waned, shifting the boundaries of what could and could not be said. An antisemitic statement that would have provoked unanimous outrage in 1919, was considered rather normal in 1930. For example, boycotts against and exclusions of Jews from associations or at holiday destinations were increasingly accepted.

The tradition and continuity of hostility towards Jews and antisemitism within the ideology and political practice throughout the history of Germany are evident.[99] However, while the *völkisch* antisemitic movement in Imperial Germany was inherent to the system, this changed radically after 1918. Antisemitic forces, shaped by war experiences, aimed to overthrow the 'Jew republic', which was blamed for the disgrace of the military defeat. The election success of anti-republican parties in June 1920, when the Weimar coalition was voted out of office, was indicative of the future. In the election campaigns, candidates of the USPD, SPD, and DDP had been antisemitically denigrated in text and image.

Although anti-Jewish resentments and exclusionary structures were European and global phenomena, only Germany experienced the rise of a party that always openly proclaimed antisemitism and the exclusion of the Jews as the key goal of its politics. During the rise of the Nazi movement, from 1929 onwards National Socialist antisemitism increasingly gained faithful followers. However, this does not mean that the path to the mass killings of the hated Jews and to the Holocaust was predetermined. Even after 1933, a variety of factors were necessary to enable the gradual break down of moral human norms and, ultimately, the rupture of civilization, the mass murder of the European Jews. One of these factors was the brutal suppression of political opponents from the labour movement after the transfer of power to Hitler and the NSDAP. This was one precondition for the NSDAP to enforce antisemitism as a state policy, without meeting significant resistance. The creation of an '"Aryan" people's community as self-empowerment' (Michael Wildt) between 1933 and 1939 was, as this chapter has shown, only possible through right-wing extremist politics during the 1920s. Still, it must be noted: the Weimar Republic was a democratic constitutional state based on the rule of law with the right of freedom of expression. In general, the state enforced its monopoly on legitimate use of force, and the police, at least to a certain degree, took action against publicly committed antisemitic acts of violence. CV and Jewish victims could press charges over defamation and discrimination, with some of them being successful despite a judicial system that was hardly pro-republican.

However, there was a gradual change in forms of antisemitism within the political culture, which non-Jewish republican forces and the socialist parties failed to recognize and take seriously. No longer was it the traditional verbal aggression from Imperial Germany; the new, ideologized antisemitism pushed for action at all costs and on all levels. Even in the late 1920s the German Jewish minority occasionally failed to see the difference to the long-known phenomenon of antisemitic resentment from the 1890s that one had learned how to deal with.[100] The invective of the 'Jew republic' was the expression of a linked fate: in the German republic, German Jews enjoyed for the first time full equal rights. And after the demise of the democratic order in 1933, they gradually lost their social rights, then their civil rights, then their human rights, and finally their lives.

Translated from German by Christine Brocks.

Notes

1. Robert S. Wistrich, *Antisemitism: The Longest Hatred* (New York: Pantheon Books, 1991). See Max Horkheimer and Theodor W. Adorno, *Dialektik der Aufklärung: Philosophische Fragmente* (Frankfurt/Main: Fischer Taschenbuch Verlag, 1988; first publ. 1947), 177–217.
2. Compare the working definition of antisemitism of the International Holocaust Remembrance Alliance (IHRA) <https://www.holocaustremembrance.com/working-definition-antisemitism> (accessed 4 October 2020).
3. Wolfram Meyer zu Uptrup, *Kampf gegen die 'jüdische Weltverschwörung': Propaganda und Antisemitismus der Nationalsozialisten 1919 bis 1945* (Berlin: Metropol, 2003), 21–3; Martin Ulmer, *Antisemitismus in Stuttgart 1871–1933. Studien zum öffentlichen Diskurs und Alltag* (Berlin: Metropol, 2011), 24–5.
4. Also in the following see Shulamit Volkov, 'Antisemitism as a Cultural Code: Reflections on the History and Historiography of Antisemitism in Imperial Germany', *Yearbook of the Leo Baeck Institute*, 23 (1978), 25–45.
5. Peter Alter, Claus-Ekkehard Bärsch, and Peter Berghoff (eds), *Die Konstruktion der Nation gegen die Juden* (Munich: Fink, 1999); Lutz Hoffmann, 'Der Antisemitismus als Baugerüst der deutschen Nation', in Arbeitskreis Kritik des deutschen Antisemitismus (ed.), *Antisemitismus—die deutsche Normalität* (Freiburg: Breisgau, 2001), 43–58; Klaus Holz, *Nationaler Antisemitismus. Wissenssoziologie einer Weltanschauung* (Hamburg: Hamburger Edition, 2001).
6. Uwe Puschner, *Die völkische Bewegung im wilhelminischen Kaiserreich. Sprache—Rasse—Religion* (Darmstadt: Wissenschaftliche Buchgesellschaft, 2001).
7. Helmut Berding, *Moderner Antisemitismus in Deutschland* (Frankfurt/Main: Suhrkamp, 1988), 110.
8. Ursula Büttner, *Weimar: Die überforderte Republik 1918–1933. Leistung und Versagen in Staat, Gesellschaft, Wirtschaft und Kultur* (Stuttgart: Klett-Cotta, 2008), 287; Werner Jochmann, *Gesellschaftskrise und Judenfeindschaft in Deutschland 1870–1945* (Hamburg: Christians, 1988), 110–17; Ulmer, *Antisemitismus*, 181–2.
9. Martin Ulmer, 'Flugblätter des Deutschvölkischen Schutz- und Trutz-Bundes (1919–1922)', in Wolfgang Benz (ed.), *Handbuch des Antisemitismus*, vol. 6 (Berlin and New York: De Gruyter Saur, 2013), 202–7.
10. See Horkheimer and Adorno, *Dialektik der Aufklärung*, 177, Thomas Haury, *Antisemitismus von links: Kommunistische Ideologie, Nationalismus und Antizionismus in der frühen DDR* (Hamburg: Hamburger Edition, 2002), 28–30; Clemens Heni, 'Ahasver, Moloch und Mammon: Der "ewige Jude" und die deutsche Spezifik in antisemitischen Bildern seit dem 19. Jahrhundert', in Andrea Hoffmann, Utz Jeggle, and Martin Ulmer (eds), *Die kulturelle Seite des Antisemitismus zwischen Aufklärung und Shoah* (Tübingen: Tübinger Vereinigung für Volkskunde, 2006), 51–79; Lars Rensmann, *Demokratie und Judenbild: Antisemitismus in der politischen Kultur der Bundesrepublik Deutschland* (Wiesbaden: VS Verlag, 2004), 96–102, Susanne Wein, *Antisemitismus im Reichstag: Judenfeindliche Sprache in Politik und Gesellschaft der Weimarer Republik* (Frankfurt/Main: Peter Lang, 2014), 33–5.
11. Gottfried zur Beek [Ludwig Müller von Hausen], *Die Geheimnisse der Weisen von Zion: Charlottenburg* (Berlin: Verlag Auf Vorposten, 1920); Wolfgang Benz, *Die Protokolle der Weisen von Zion: Die Legende von der jüdischen Weltverschwörung* (Munich: C. H. Beck, 2007); Wein, *Antisemitismus im Reichstag*, 38–9, 226–8.

12. Saul Friedländer, *Das Dritte Reich und die Juden: Die Jahre der Verfolgung 1933–1939* (Munich: C. H. Beck, 1998), 13–5, 87–128.
13. Trude Maurer, *Ostjuden in Deutschland 1918–1933* (Hamburg: Christians, 1988), 11–16.
14. Büttner, *Weimar*, 292–3; Friedländer, *Das Dritte Reich*, 106–9.
15. Individuals such as Oscar Cohn and Paul Levi were defamed as puppet masters, while many wrongly assumed that Karl Liebknecht and Friedrich Engels were of Jewish origin. See Dietz Bering, *Der Name als Stigma: Antisemitismus im deutschen Alltag 1812–1933* (Stuttgart: Klett-Cotta, 1987); Wein, *Antisemitismus im Reichstag*, 41, 143.
16. Uwe Lohalm, *Völkischer Radikalismus: Die Geschichte des Deutschvölkischen Schutz- und Trutz-Bundes 1919–1923* (Hamburg: Leibniz-Verlag, 1970), 332–3.
17. In Württemberg and Bayern, no ban was imposed: Ulmer, *Antisemitismus in Stuttgart*, 352.
18. Martin Sabrow, *Die verdrängte Verschwörung: Der Rathenau-Mord und die deutsche Gegenrevolution* (Frankfurt/Main: Fischer Taschenbuch Verlag, 1999).
19. For the following: Ulmer, 'Flugblätter', 202–7.
20. Uwe Lohalm and Martin Ulmer, 'Alfred Roth und der Deutschvölkische Schutz- und Trutz-Bund: "Schrittmacher für das Dritte Reich"', in Daniel Schmidt, Michael Sturm, and Massimiliano Livi (eds), *Wegbereiter des Nationalsozialismus: Personen, Organisationen und Netzwerke der extremen Rechten zwischen 1918 und 1933* (Essen: Klartext, 2015), 27.
21. Dirk Walter, *Antisemitische Kriminalität und Gewalt: Judenfeindschaft in der Weimarer Republik* (Bonn: Dietz, 1999), 254.
22. Avraham Barkai, *'Wehr Dich!' Der Centralverein deutscher Staatsbürger jüdischen Glaubens 1893–1938* (Munich: C. H. Beck, 2002), 100–3.
23. Michael Wildt, *Hitler's Volksgemeinschaft and the Dynamics of Racial Exclusion: Violence Against Jews in Provincial Germany, 1919–1939*, tr. Bernard Heise (New York: Berghahn, 2011), 69.
24. Cornelia Hecht, *Deutsche Juden und Antisemitismus in der Weimarer Republik* (Bonn: Dietz, 2003), 169–86; Ulmer, *Antisemitismus in Stuttgart*, 346.
25. See Walter, *Antisemitische Kriminalität und Gewalt*, 153; Hecht, *Deutsche Juden*, 163–8, 177–83; Ulmer, *Antisemitismus in Stuttgart*, 346–7; Wildt, *Hitler's Volksgemeinschaft*, 53–4.
26. Walter, *Antisemitische Kriminalität und Gewalt*, 251; Barkai, *'Wehr Dich!'*, 191.
27. Hannah Ahlheim, *'Deutsche, kauft nicht bei Juden!' Antisemitismus und politischer Boykott in Deutschland 1924 bis 1935* (Göttingen: Wallstein, 2011), 90–105.
28. Sibylle Morgenthaler, 'Countering the Pre-1933 Nazi Boycott Against the Jews', *Leo Baeck Institute Yearbook*, 36 (1991), 127–49, here 147. Cyril Levitt is more critical about the success: Cyril Levitt, 'The Prosecution of Antisemites by Courts in Weimar Republic: Was Justice Served?', *Leo Baeck Institute Yearbook*, 36 (1991), 151–67.
29. Ahlheim, *'Deutsche, kauft nicht bei Juden!'*, 229–37.
30. Ulmer, *Antisemitismus in Stuttgart*, 378–82.
31. For an overview see Erich Maria Remarque-Friedenszentrum: <https://www.remarque.uni-osnabrueck.de/iwnnfilm.htm> (accessed 4 Oct. 2020).
32. For the following: Barkai, *'Wehr Dich!'*, 258–60; Irmtraud Ubbens, 'Zur Presseberichterstattung über die Nazi-Krawalle auf dem Kurfürstendamm am jüdischen Neujahrstag 1931 und die nachfolgenden Gerichtsprozesse', in Michael Nagel and Moshe Zimmermann (eds), *Judenfeindschaft und Antisemitismus in der deutschen Presse über fünf Jahrhunderte: Erscheinungsformen, Rezeption, Debatte und Gegenwehr*, vol. 2 (Bremen: Edition Lumière, 2013), 645–70; Walter, *Antisemitische Kriminalität und Gewalt*, 211–21.

33. Hecht, *Deutsche Juden*, 368–76; Martin Liepach, 'Das Krisenbewußtsein des jüdischen Bürgertums in den Goldenen Zwanzigern', in Andreas Gotzmann, Rainer Liedtke, and Till van Rhaden (eds), *Juden, Bürger, Deutsche: Zur Geschichte von Vielfalt und Differenz 1800–1933* (Tübingen: Mohr Siebeck, 2001), 395–417.
34. For the following see Walter, *Antisemitische Kriminalität und Gewalt*, 97–110; Hecht, *Deutsche Juden*, 274–88, 402–3.
35. Ulmer, *Antisemitismus in Stuttgart*, 331–3, 337–8.
36. Hermann Greive, *Geschichte des modernen Antisemitismus in Deutschland* (Darmstadt: Wissenschaftliche Buchgesellschaft, 1988), 115–16.
37. Ulmer, *Antisemitismus in Stuttgart*, 343–4.
38. Frank Bajohr, *'Unser Hotel ist judenfrei': Bäder-Antisemitismus im 19. und 20. Jahrhundert* (Frankfurt/Main: Fischer Taschenbuch Verlag, 2003); Jacob Borut, 'Antisemitism in Tourist Facilities in Weimar Germany', *Yad Vashem Studies*, 28 (2000), 7–50, here 25–9; Michael Wildt, '"Der muß hinaus! Der muß hinaus!" Antisemitismus in den deutschen Nord- und Ostseebädern 1920–1935', *Mittelweg*, 36, 10/4 (2001), 2–25.
39. Borut, 'Antisemitism in Tourist Facilities', 25–9.
40. Hecht, *Deutsche Juden*; for Württemberg: Ulmer, *Antisemitismus in Stuttgart*, 349–51.
41. Barkai, *'Wehr Dich!'*, 171–9.
42. Büttner, *Weimar: Die überforderte Republik*, 189–93, 253–70. For the following: Barkai, *'Wehr Dich!'*, 163–4, 179–81; Levitt, 'Prosecution of Antisemites', 151–67; Walter, *Antisemitische Kriminalität und Gewalt*, 89–96; Wein, *Antisemitismus im Reichstag*, 96–8.
43. Ludwig Foerder, 'Die "Judenrepublik" in der Rechtsprechung', *Die Justiz*, 1/5 (1925/26), 519–32.
44. Büttner, *Weimar: Die überforderte Republik*, 183–93; Sabrow, *Die verdrängte Verschwörung*; compare Burkhard Asmuss, *Republik ohne Chance? Akzeptanz und Legitimation der Weimarer Republik in der deutschen Tagespresse zwischen 1918 und 1923* (Berlin: De Gruyter, 1994), 415–50.
45. *Verhandlungen des deutschen Reichstags: Stenographische Berichte*, 355, 233 session (23 June 1922), 7988–8001. For the following Susanne Wein, 'Abgeordnete jüdischer Herkunft und Antisemitismus im Weimarer Reichstag', *E-Newsletter für die deutschsprachigen Länder der International School of Holocaust Studies (Yad Vashem)* (Sept. 2012), <https://www.yadvashem.org/de/education/newsletter/7.html> (accessed 4 Oct. 2020); Wein, *Antisemitismus im Reichstag*, 104–5, 345–7.
46. Martin Ulmer, 'Rathenau-Hetze (1922–1925)', in Benz (ed.), *Handbuch des Antisemitismus*, vol. 6, 572.
47. Joseph Wirth, in *Verhandlungen des deutschen Reichstags*, 356, 236 session (25 June 1922), 8058A; Karl Helfferich, in *Verhandlungen des deutschen Reichstags*, 355, 233 session (23 June 1922), 7989–90.
48. Julius Moses, in *Verhandlungen des deutschen Reichstags*, 356, 245 session (6 July 1922), 8329A.
49. Asmuss, *Republik ohne Chance?*, 415–45.
50. See Büttner, *Weimar: Die überforderte Republik*, 286; Maurer, *Ostjuden in Deutschland*, 80–98; Ulmer, 'Flugblätter', 202–7; Walter, *Antisemitische Kriminalität und Gewalt*, 70–9; Wein, *Antisemitismus im Reichstag*, 148–52.
51. *Verhandlungen des deutschen Reichstags*, 344, 17 session (3 Aug. 1920), 625C.
52. On the concept of a 'language of Jew hatred' see Wein, *Antisemitismus im Reichstag*, 433–43.

53. The quotes are from Wilhelm Bruhn (DNVP) in *Verhandlungen des deutschen Reichstags*, 358, 306 session (23 Feb. 1923), 9861B, and Reinhold Wulle (DNVP, later DvFP), who said that you can find 'thousands of Eastern Jews' in 'magnificent apartments ... and as soon as they have filled themselves like grasshoppers' they would migrate to Paris: *Verhandlungen des deutschen Reichstags*, 360, 361 session (9 June 1923), 11258C.
54. *Verhandlungen der deutschen Nationalversammlung*, 340, Anlage no. 1620 (27 Nov. 1919), 1622.
55. Adolf Korell (DDP), in *Verhandlungen des deutschen Reichstags*, 344, 17 session (3 Aug. 1920), S. 629–30, and an interpellation by the DVP in *Verhandlungen des deutschen Reichstags*, 364, Anlage no. 769 (29 Oct. 1920), 549–50.
56. Kurt Rosenfeld (USPD), in *Verhandlungen des deutschen Reichstags*, 344, 17. session (3 Aug. 1920), 626C; for further examples by Wilhelm Sollmann (SPD) and Wilhelm Bartz (KPD) see Wein, *Antisemitismus im Reichstag*, 174–8.
57. See Wein, *Antisemitismus im* Reichstag, 181–224; on the Barmat Affair see Frank Bösch and Norbert Frei (eds), *Medialisierung und Demokratie im 20. Jahrhundert* (Göttingen: Wallstein, 2006); Bernhard Fulda, *Press and Politics in the Weimar Republic* (Oxford and New York: Oxford University Press, 2009); Martin H. Geyer, 'Der Barmat-Kutisker-Skandal und die "Gleichzeitigkeit des Ungleichzeitigen" in der politischen Kultur der Weimarer Republik', in Ute Daniel, Inge Marszolek, Wolfram Pyta, and Thomas Welskopp (eds), *Politische Kultur und Medienwirklichkeiten in den 1920er Jahren* (Munich: Oldenbourg, 2010), 47–80; Martin H. Geyer, *Kapitalismus und politische Moral in der Zwischenkriegszeit. Oder: Wer war Julius Barmat?* (Hamburg: Hamburger Edition, 2018); Stefan Malinowski, 'Skandal als Zerrspiegel der Demokratie: Die Fälle Barmat und Sklarek im Kalkül der Weimarer Rechten', *Jahrbuch für Antisemitismusforschung*, 5 (1996), 46–65, Susanne Wein, 'Von der Person zum Symbol: Der antisemitische Pressediskurs über Julius Barmat und Georg Bernhard in der Weimarer Republik', in Nagel and Zimmermann (eds), *Judenfeindschaft und Antisemitismus*, vol. 2, 555–77.
58. 'Die Machtstellung der Barmats', *Kreuz-Zeitung*, 10, 7 Jan. 1925.
59. Franz Behrens (DNVP), in *Verhandlungen des deutschen Reichstags*, 384, 11 session (22 Jan. 1925), 186C.
60. Büttner, *Weimar: Die überforderte Republik*, 340.
61. 'Chamaden der Barmatiaden', *Bremer Arbeiterzeitung*, 4 Apr. 1925; Hermann Remmele (KPD) spoke of 'Barmatismus' in the Reichstag: *Verhandlungen des deutschen Reichstags*, 384, 32 session (9 Mar. 1925), 940C; see Geyer, *Kapitalismus*, 233–67; Wein, *Antisemitismus im Reichstag*, 188.
62. 'Der Großschieber Barmat und die SPD', *Die Rote Fahne*, 175, 6 Dec. 1924. See Haury, *Antisemitismus von links*, 253–82; Olaf Kistenmacher, *Arbeit und 'jüdisches Kapital': Antisemitische Aussagen in der KPD-Tageszeitung* Die Rote Fahne *während der Weimarer Republik* (Bremen: Edition Lumière, 2016), 117–24.
63. Quoted in Wein, *Antisemitismus im Reichstag*, 188.
64. Wein, *Antisemitismus im Reichstag*, 186, 223–4; Geyer, *Kapitalismus*, 15.
65. Malinowski, 'Skandal als Zerrspiegel', 46–65.
66. 'Finanzskandale—nur "jüdische"?', in Centralverein deutscher Staatsbürger jüdischen Glaubens (ed.), *Anti-anti: Tatsachen zur Judenfrage* (Berlin: Philo, 1932), 17; Bösch and Frei, *Medialisierung und Demokratie*; Fulda, *Press and Politics*; Wein, *Antisemitismus im Reichstag*, 189–91.

67. The quotes are from Reichstag speeches by Reinhold Wulle (DvFP), in *Verhandlungen des deutschen Reichstags*, 360, 361 session (9 June 1923), 11259B and by Albrecht von Graefe (DvFP), in *Verhandlungen des deutschen Reichstags*, 381, 8 session (5 June 1924), 140B. Further examples in Wein, *Antisemitismus im Reichstag*, 234–51.
68. For an explanation of this operation of 'concealing' or 'laminating' antisemitic content see Wein, *Antisemitismus im Reichstag*, 44, 293.
69. Ernst Oberfohren (DNVP) in *Verhandlungen des deutschen Reichstags*, 426, 104 session (29 Nov. 1929), 3297B; further examples in Wein, *Antisemitismus im Reichstag*, 274–87.
70. Compare the election call of the extreme right electoral alliance in *Reichstagshandbuch II. Wahlperiode 1924* (Berlin: Reichsdruckerei, 1924), 318–22.
71. Büttner, *Weimar: Die überforderte Republik*, 802–3.
72. Puschner, *Die völkische Bewegung*, 15–7, 102–15; Ulmer, *Antisemitismus in Stuttgart*, 160–80.
73. Friedländer, *Das Dritte Reich*; Berding, *Moderner Antisemitismus*, 191–8; Holz, *Nationaler Antisemitismus*, 359–430.
74. 'Adolf Hitler in Stuttgart', *Süddeutsche Zeitung*, 17 Aug. 1925, Mittagsausgabe; Ulmer, *Antisemitismus in Stuttgart*, 376–7.
75. Clemens Vollnhals (ed.), *Adolf Hitler: Reden, Schriften, Anordnungen*, vol. 1. *Die Wiedergründung der NSDAP, Februar 1925–Juni 1926* (Munich: Saur, 1992), 144–5.
76. Horkheimer and Adorno, *Dialektik der Aufklärung*, 209–17.
77. Election call of the NSDAP, in *Reichstagshandbuch. IV. Wahlperiode 1928* (Berlin: Reichsdruckerei, 1928), 187–8.
78. See Ulmer, *Antisemitismus in Stuttgart*, 383–404; Anthony Kauders, *German Politics and the Jews: Düsseldorf and Nuremberg 1910–1933* (Oxford: Clarendon Press, 1996), 153–81, 185; Nicola Wenge, *Integration und Ausgrenzung in der städtischen Gesellschaft: Eine jüdisch-nichtjüdische Beziehungsgeschichte Kölns 1918–1933* (Mainz: Phillip von Zabern, 2005), 429–36; Andreas Wirsching, *Vom Weltkrieg zum Bürgerkrieg? Politischer Extremismus in Deutschland und Frankreich 1918–1933/39. Berlin und Paris im Vergleich* (Munich: Oldenbourg, 1999), 461–7.
79. On antisemitism in the DNVP see Larry Eugene Jones, 'Conservative Antisemitism in the Weimar Republic: A Case Study of the German National People's Party', in Jones (ed.), *The German Right in the Weimar Republic* (New York: Berghahn, 2014), 80–107.
80. See Berding, *Moderner Antisemitismus*, 214; Hans Dieter Bernd, *Die Beseitigung der Weimarer Republik auf 'legalem' Weg: Die Funktion des Antisemitismus in der Agitation der Führungsschicht der DNVP* (Hagen, 2004), online <http://deposit.fernuni-hagen.de/33/> (accessed 4 Oct. 2020); Wein, *Antisemitismus im Reichstag*, 102–7.
81. See the party principles from 1920 in Wilhelm Mommsen (ed.), *Deutsche Parteiprogramme* (Munich: Olzog, 1960), 538.
82. On antisemitism in the DNVP see also Jones, 'Conservative Antisemitism', 80–107. Jones argues that, under Hugenberg, the DNVP prioritized anti-Marxism for propaganda purposes, yet we believe that this also had an encoded antisemitic meaning.
83. Ulmer, *Antisemitismus in Stuttgart*, 212–13, 323.
84. The election propaganda parade of the DNVP in Berlin-Neukölln in 1930 had an illustrated poster with the inscription 'We fight the handing over of Germany to the international Jewish capital', see Wein, *Antisemitismus im Reichstag*, 286.
85. Party principles from 1919 in Mommsen, *Deutsche Parteiprogramme*, 522.
86. Berding, *Moderner Antisemitismus*, 214–215. The same applies for the Wirtschaftspartei (Business Party). Soon after 1930, other small, conservative parties that represented the

Landvolk lost their support to the party that had presented their themes in the first place, the NSDAP. See Büttner, *Weimar: Die überforderte Republik*, 221.
87. Büttner, *Weimar: Die überforderte Republik*, 276–82.
88. Olaf Blaschke, *Katholizismus und Antisemitismus im deutschen Kaiserreich* (Göttingen: Vandenhoeck & Ruprecht, 1997).
89. Barkai, 'Wehr Dich!', 292–3; Berding, *Moderner Antisemitismus*, 216–18; Wein, *Antisemitismus im Reichstag*, 116–23.
90. Quoted in Wein, *Antisemitismus im Reichstag*, 125.
91. Berding, *Moderner Antisemitismus*, 215–16.
92. Haury, *Antisemitismus von links*, 166–95; Wein, *Antisemitismus im Reichstag*, 129–32.
93. Asmuss, *Republik ohne Chance?*, 432–8, 531–4.
94. *Handbuch für sozialdemokratische Wähler 1920* (Berlin: Vorwärts, 1920), 133.
95. Wein, *Antisemitismus im Reichstag*, 134–7, 307–10, 428–9, 442–3; Berding, *Moderner Antisemitismus*, 218–19; Ulmer, *Antisemitismus in Stuttgart*, 361–3.
96. Greive, *Geschichte*, 114–15; Haury, *Antisemitismus von links*, 253, 459–60; Kistenmacher, *Arbeit und 'jüdisches Kapital'*; Wein, *Antisemitismus im Reichstag*, 137–44.
97. On the structures of the antisemitic worldview see Haury, *Antisemitismus von links*, 105–14, 456–9; Wein, *Antisemitismus im Reichstag*, 365–9; Kistenmacher, *Arbeit und 'jüdisches Kapital'*, 73–7, 195–201.
98. Barkai, 'Wehr Dich!', 191–204, 213, 258–62.
99. Friedländer, *Das Dritte Reich*; Helmuth W. Smith, *The Continuities of German History: Nation, Religion, and Race across the Long Nineteenth Century* (Cambridge: Cambridge University Press, 2008), 211–34. Smith (217) attaches little importance to antisemitism in the decision to vote for the NSDAP prior 1933, which, according to our research, is not correct.
100. Volkov, 'Antisemitism as a Cultural Code', 45.

Bibliography

Ahlheim, Hannah, 'Establishing Antisemitic Stereotypes: Social and Economic Segregation of Jews by Means of Political Boycott in Germany', *Leo Baeck Institute Year Book*, 55 (2010), 149–73.

Borut, Jacob, 'Antisemitism in Tourist Facilities in Weimar Germany', *Yad Vashem Studies*, 28 (2000), 7–50.

Hecht, Cornelia, *Deutsche Juden und Antisemitismus in der Weimarer Republik* (Bonn: J. H. W. Dietz, 2003).

Jones, Larry Eugene, 'Conservative Antisemitism in the Weimar Republic. A Case Study of the German National People's Party', in Jones (ed.), *The German Right in the Weimar Republic:. Studies in the history of German conservatism, nationalism, and antisemitism* (New York: Berghahn, 2014), 79–107.

Kauders, Anthony, *German Politics and the Jews: Düsseldorf and Nuremberg 1910–1933* (Oxford: Oxford University Press, 1996).

Ulmer, Martin, *Antisemitismus in Stuttgart 1871–1933. Studien zum öffentlichen Diskurs und Alltag* (Berlin: Metropol, 2011).

Volkov, Shulamit, *Germans, Jews, and Antisemites: Trials in Emancipation* (Cambridge: Cambridge University Press, 2006).
Walter, Dirk, *Antisemitische Kriminalität und Gewalt. Judenfeindschaft in der Weimarer Republik* (Bonn: J. H. W. Dietz, 1999).
Wein, Susanne, *Antisemitismus im Reichstag: Judenfeindliche Sprache in Politik und Gesellschaft der Weimarer Republik* (Frankfurt/Main: Peter Lang, 2014).
Wildt, Michael, *Hitler's Volksgemeinschaft and the Dynamics of Racial Exclusion: Violence Against Jews in Provincial Germany, 1919–1939* (New York: Berghahn, 2011).
Wistrich, Robert S., *Antisemitism: The Longest Hatred* (New York: Pantheon Books, 1991).

PART IV

ECONOMY AND SOCIETY

CHAPTER 19

THE OVERSTRETCHED ECONOMY

Industry and Financial Services

JAN-OTMAR HESSE AND CHRISTIAN MARX

Aʟʟ too often, the history of the Weimar Republic is considered teleologically, being explained in relation to its known end. From this perspective, the Weimar economy appears weak and prone to crisis, making its fall during the Great Depression appear almost predestined. This reading leaves promising trends of German economical re-orientation after the shock of the First World War largely neglected and considers them instead as the last gasp of a structurally 'sick economy'.[1] Harking back to the 'Borchardt controversy' over the room for political manoeuvre during the Great Depression, this interpretation has also had lasting influence on the scholarship of the Weimar economy.[2]

In contrast, this chapter will, to a greater degree, emphasize the economic achievements of the 1920s without uncritically adapting the idea of the 'Golden Twenties' or of specious prosperity during the inflation period. Rather, we point out that the Weimar economy and German entrepreneurs did record successes under extremely difficult global circumstances during the inter-war period. The performance of the German economy on the eve of the Great Depression was considerable. Yet, at the same time, demands on the Weimar economy had grown, which appears to have had a lasting effect on both contemporary observers and economic historians. The Weimar economy was expected to generate surpluses that would pay for reparations and national debts, achieve greater prosperity for the masses of employees, and create financial leeway in redistributing wealth. Not least, it should facilitate the expansion of the welfare state, bring about social and technological progress, and build on global successes of pre-war German engineering skills and science. Some contemporary observers seem to have replaced former political and military world power fantasies with economic great power ambitions. In this vein, the industrialist and politician Walther Rathenau stated in a speech to the Reich Association of German Industry (Reichsverband der Deutschen Industrie, RDI): 'The economy is destiny'.[3] Against the backdrop of a fundamentally changed global economy and domestic structural economic problems, these were excessive demands on the German economy. Not only did these demands distinctly mark the contemporary debate but they were often also uncritically adapted by historians.[4] The economic achievements of the pre-war era should not have served as a benchmark for the assessment of the Weimar economy at the time, and should not do so today either.

Consequences of the War and World Market Integration

The First World War profoundly influenced Germany's economic development. At a systematic level, we should distinguish two quite different forms of impact. First, the events of the war immediately and directly impacted the economies of Germany and many other countries, particularly in Europe. Secondly, and in marked difference to this, there were the economic repercussions of the peace treaty of Versailles.

One direct consequence of the war was a structural change of global exchange with long-lasting effects that can be described as a 'decentralization of the global economy'.[5] Trade relations and value chains that used to be focused on Europe as the productive heart of the global economy were torn apart and to some extent shifted towards Pacific and Latin American regions.[6] This dynamic had already begun in the late nineteenth century and was merely accelerated under the conditions of the First World War. It must be stressed that this structural change of the global economy occurred independently of the Versailles Treaty. A second direct consequence of the war was the food crisis that affected Germany in particular. To be sure, the narrative of the Allied 'hunger blockade' has been sufficiently repudiated—unlike, for instance, Austria, Germany did not starve.[7] Yet the war caused a drastic loss of agricultural production and a profound decrease in imports, at the same time as a disastrous mismanagement of domestic food supplies. In comparison with the rather comfortable situation that preceded the First World War, the Weimar Republic began with a food shortage. Thirdly, the war caused a large expansion of state economic control that had previously been limited to influential public-sector companies (including postal services and railways, by far the largest employers in Imperial Germany) and to the special structure of public supply infrastructure in the context of 'municipal socialism'.[8] Municipal socialism refers to efforts of local administrations to control infrastructure companies for reasons of public interest from the second half of the nineteenth century onwards. The First World War, however, saw a fusion of economic administration and economy. Shortly after the war had started, Walther Rathenau was involved in establishing the war raw materials department (Kriegsrohstoffabteilung, KRA). In the context of the 'Hindenburg Programme' of 1916, a comprehensive armaments and economic programme with utopian objectives drawn up by the Army Supreme Command (Oberste Heeresleitung, OHL), the so-called Weapons and Ammunition Procurement Office

(Waffen- und Munitions-Beschaffungsamt) was implemented. This central control office coordinated prices and quantities between state and economy, and incorporated the rudimentary beginnings of a 'state socialist' economic order, which had a lasting impact on the Weimar economy.[9] No other war economy saw a similarly high public expenditure quota of 60 per cent of GDP at the height of the third war year of 1916.[10] Finally, the particular form of war financing chosen by the government in 1914 led to a long-term burden on the Weimar economy: Germany (as well as some other belligerent countries) funded its war expenses through national debt as opposed to taxes. Yet while other nations were able to place war bonds at international capital markets, Germany relied solely on the domestic capital market. After the end of the war, these debts could no longer be serviced. In order to do so, either foreign loans or tax increases would have been necessary, however, both required stable political majorities, which did not exist. Therefore, war expenditures were financed by inflation, which was deliberately accepted, and, in so doing, the savings of the middle classes were indirectly confiscated.[11]

The economic burdens of the Versailles Treaty added further to the grave and long-lasting consequences of the First World War. International research no longer disputes the fact that these were not the reparation payments as such. As Albrecht Ritschl has shown, the largest part of the reparation claims in the amount of 132 billion 'gold marks'[12] that would have represented almost 300 per cent of the national income of 1913, were, according to the 1921 'London ultimatum', 'C bonds'. In contrast to the A and B bonds of the London Schedule of Payments that had to be paid immediately, repayment of and interest on C bonds were shunted to a later time. They were considered a pledge to enforce the recovering of realistic debt claims from other bonds. The real claim—according to the 1924 Dawes Plan around 2 billion RM annually that were even liable to a transfer protection clause—would have been affordable to the German economy.[13] The transfer protection clause of the Dawes Plan stipulated that reparation payments only had to be paid in full if Germany's balance of trade was even. Reparations posed a problem not because of their amount but because they could only be paid via a positive trade balance. Therefore, the Weimar economy had to produce profits abroad and generate foreign currency so that the German state could service their reparation debts. This was precisely the reason why the British economist John Maynard Keynes had criticized the Versailles Treaty. Keynes did not a priori advocate abandoning reparation claims but rather wanted to draw attention to the fact that other stipulations of the treaty rendered it impossible for Weimar Germany to repay her debts.[14] In this sense, the Versailles Treaty was a burden on the Weimar economy, albeit one that was hard to quantify.

The loss of colonies did not hit the Weimar economy particularly badly because hopes of inexhaustible riches had already proved to be an illusion before the war. The cession of territory, particularly the loss of 25 per cent of coal deposits and 75 per cent of iron ore reserves in Upper Silesia and Alsace-Lorraine, carried much more weight. However, this was less painful for some iron and steel companies than previously assumed because they were eligible for state compensation payments for lost investments under the Versailles Treaty.[15] Reparations in kind that, according to the treaty, had to be raised by the German industry, such as coal to France or chemical products, were compensated by the state. In some cases this had the favourable side-effect that German producers could serve foreign markets, which was otherwise forbidden under the Allied foreign-trade regime.[16] These reparations in kind also included the entire German merchant fleet and parts of the new production of German shipyards from the post-war period. Ship owners received state compensation, although this did not recompense the significant loss of importance of German shipping companies, which had advanced to global leaders in passenger transportation across the North Atlantic before the First World War.[17] Where compensation payments could be invested in progressive new buildings before hyperinflation hit, shipyards and shipping companies started the Weimar period from a strong position.

Apart from Germany's loss of trade policy autonomy, which will be discussed in detail below, the loss of all patent and trademark rights was in fact a great burden for the Weimar economy. This was particularly true of sectors such as the chemical and electrical industries, where foreign countries and especially the USA had emerged as important sales markets. As early as the beginning of the war, all foreign possessions of German companies in Great Britain and her Allies were placed under state control. When in 1917 the USA joined the Allied coalition, it issued the Trading with the Enemy Act and established the Office of Alien Property Custodian, which took over control of all American possessions and properties of German parent companies. With 6,000 patents, the chemical industry was the worst affected. It is true that the Versailles Treaty also included regulations concerning the restitution or compensation of wartime confiscations. But because the USA never ratified the Versailles Treaty, this fell into a legal grey area. The Alien Property Custodian increasingly developed into a government office to eliminate German competition in the US market. Foreign properties as well as patent and trademark rights were passed on to US companies. Only in very few cases was compensation granted. It is quite remarkable that some German companies swiftly regained a foothold in the American market even under these circumstances. However, the Weimar economy never achieved the global market-dominating position that some segments had established before 1914—in any case an impossible objective.[18]

Thus, to sum up, rather than the burden of reparations and ceding of territory hampering Germany's economic recovery process, it was changes in the global economic structure that pushed the German economy to the limit and demanded significant adjustments. This included a readjustment of the relationship between state and economy—not least due to the employees' strengthened position in the wake of the Stinnes-Legien Agreement—and, at the same time, a fundamental reformation of global markets. It also led, thirdly, to a restructuring of the entire German economic model. While some strong export sectors, profitable foreign capital investments, and the export of services (such as shipyards, insurance companies, infrastructure building, and plant construction) had previously offset a chronically negative trade balance, the export industry now had to bear this burden on its own, regardless of the aggravated domestic supply situation and intensified international competition.

Apart from stipulations on foreign property, reparations and payments in kind, the Versailles Treaty contained several trade policy restrictions. Germany had to grant unilateral most-favoured-nation status to all signing states—that is, it was forced to concede the most favourable terms without receiving those in return. Therefore, many foreign markets, even though not formally restricted, were not accessible to German companies. In 1925, Germany regained trade policy autonomy and the German government immediately issued a new tariff. With a trade-weighted average tariff rate—which adjusts for the relative share of goods in total imports—of 15 per cent, it was, however, only marginally higher than that of the pre-war period and even lower than the Bülow tariff of 1902.[19] The clear trend towards protectionism, that can be seen in the USA immediately after the First World War, did not start in the Weimar Republic before the end of the 1920s.

In the face of these dilemmas, the Weimar economy relied on its reintegration into the global economy as swiftly and straightforwardly as possible. German governments recognized this at an early stage. To promote and support export and foreign trade industries, they established a broad range of state institutions, from the Foreign Trade Bureau at the Foreign Office to the credit export insurance company 'Hermes' to the Express Service of the Foreign Office 'Eildienst', which was supposed to favourably influence foreign news coverage of German products and companies.[20] The economic significance of these institutions should not be underestimated. Some of them were set up with the direct help of leading industrialists of the Weimar Republic, such as Alfred Hugenberg who was involved in the establishment of the 'Eildienst'. The actual reintegration into the global economy, however, was realized through German companies themselves. Behind the scenes they returned to European markets and the US market and aggressively rushed into ones that were more easily accessible for them: in Latin America, Eastern Europe, and Asia.

One of the secretive strategies of German companies in Europe was to take stakes in foreign companies or set up enterprises through a front man. Not least owing to German 'flight capital', Amsterdam and Zurich became important international banking centres during the inflation period where all (but not only) German high street banks operated, sometimes well-hidden and secretively.[21] Industrial companies such as Carl Zeiss, the Gutehoffnungshütte, or M.A.N. bought or founded enterprises abroad through foreign representatives through which they sold their products.[22] After the First World War, the Beiersdorf company, which produced globally successful toiletries including Nivea, toothpaste, and plasters, set up a non-transparent network of holding companies in Switzerland, the Netherlands, and the USA so as to be able to operate in the world market.[23] During the period of hyperinflation in 1922–23, rather than exporting their products made in Germany, many German enterprises had them either manufactured through subsidiary companies abroad or organized sales through foreign partners. Neither practice was reflected in external trade statistics, which was of course the purpose of the exercise.

At the same time, German companies increased their efforts to be more present in putatively 'free' markets. This was particularly true of Eastern Europe and the Soviet Union, which had already been an important trading partner of Germany before the First World War but gained even more significance in the post-war period, pushing the UK into third place.[24] Trade relations with other eastern and south-eastern European countries that had become dormant during the First World War saw a revival, particularly through activities of the private sector of the economy (Table 19.1).[25]

Table 19.1. World market share of German exports of manufactured goods, 1925–1935, in comparison (%)

Year	Germany	UK	France	USA
1913	22.9	26.7	11.3	10.8
1925	14.8	25.3	13.0	15.1
1926	16.3	23.3	11.6	16.4
1927	16.5	22.7	11.4	16.4
1928	17.3	21.8	10.5	17.2
1929	18.6	20.6	9.8	18.3
1930	19.8	19.4	10.2	15.4
1931	22.5	17.1	10.5	13.3
1932	21.6	19.4	10.6	11.1
1933	20.2	20.8	10.8	10.3
1934	17.7	20.5	10.3	11.8
1935	18.5	20.9	8.5	13.2

Source: Verena Schröter, Die deutsche Industrie auf dem Weltmarkt 1929 bis 1933. Außenwirtschaftliche Strategien unter dem Druck der Weltwirtschaftskrise (Frankfurt/Main: Lang, 1984), 519. Figures are based on Enqueteausschuss 'Ausschuss zur Untersuchung der Erzeugungs- und Absatzbedingungen der deutschen Wirtschaft', which was published under 'Der Außenhandel' by the Institute for World Economy in 1932, complemented with figures from the 1936 Reichsstatistik.

The result of these efforts is remarkable. While the UK, which had dominated the world economy before the First World War, lost global market shares, the Weimar economy could win back its share in some world markets at least until the eve of the Great Depression. Concerning the export of manufactured products Germany held a lead of about 20 per cent over the UK, which had been able to record a market share of 26.7 in 1913.[26] In the late 1920s, top companies such as IG Farbenindustrie made more than half of their revenues through exports, despite the loss of some important patents such as for Bayer's Aspirin.[27] The Gutehoffnungshütte achieved a share in foreign sales of total revenue of 37 per cent (1929–30), Bosch 43 per cent (1929), and Beiersdorf 36 per cent (1930).[28] The iron and steel industry, engineering, and the chemical industry were the strongest exporters. In the late 1920s, each of them accounted for around a tenth of all German exports with an export rate of roughly 30 per cent (Table 19.2).[29]

Of course, the export strength of some industrial sectors cannot obscure the fact that other branches were not able to match pre-war successes. Particularly food exports that had been pivotal for some regions before the First World War hardly achieved more than half of their export volume during the Weimar Republic, mostly due to excess supply and price erosion in the world market.[30] The commodities and heavy industry sectors were also under pressure from foreign competition, which fuelled monopolization and

Table 19.2. Indices of export volumes, 1924–1933 (1913=100)

Year	Food products	Raw materials	Intermediate products	of which: iron and semi-finished products	Manufactured goods	of which: machinery	chemical products
1924	36.2	26.6	35.1	24.0	62.8	60.5	45.1
1925	42.0	63.9	59.6	51.4	74.1	78.4	68.7
1926	42.2	80.6	83.1	80.9	79.2	86.4	79.2
1927	31.0	76.0	77.5	66.1	86.4	91.2	86.8
1928	45.2	79.6	88.1	74.2	94.1	110.1	97.4
1929	55.6	90.3	101.2	86.2	106.7	129.6	108.9
1930	52.0	86.0	86.7	68.1	103.1	134.4	95.9
1931	45.7	79.6	75.5	61.3	92.5	117.7	86.8
1932	25.7	58.9	52.3	36.0	61.2	77.4	67.3
1933	24.7	58.8	47.4	32.7	55.2	59.6	61.2

Source: The indices of the export volumes were calculated by the research group of Walter G. Hoffmann in 1965 by dividing export values by export prices. This calculation is problematic: (1) the territory is not adjusted compared with the pre-war period; (2) foreign trade values of 1928 are based on expert estimates without being further specified. Walther G. Hoffmann, *Das Wachstum der deutschen Wirtschaft seit der Mitte des 19. Jahrhunderts* (Berlin: Springer, 1965), table 129, p. 531, and table 130, p. 534, see also explanations, 532 and 535.

cartelization tendencies that will be discussed in detail below. The foreign economic integration of the Weimar economy was ambivalent: on the one hand, some leading sectors such as machinery and plant engineering as well as the chemical industry showed significant successes in the global market. These sectors were certainly not marked by a so-called 'de-globalization' of the economy, protectionism, and an emerging trend towards autarky. On the other hand, increasing competition in the global market caused a crisis for other parts of the Weimar economy, which led them to advocate protectionism as the sole solution and use intensive political lobbying.

Consumption Prospects and Power of Industry

Political economists of the inter-war period only gradually discovered the distribution effects connected with different foreign trade regimes in the context of the Heckscher-Ohlin model: because countries that are transitioning towards free trade focus on manufacturing products by using abundant factors of production, the owners of these production factors (for instance capital owners)—in theory—benefit more from free trade than the owners of other production factors (workers).[31] It is reasonable to assume that these effects also occurred in the Weimar economy. Yet they were entirely overshadowed by a fundamental redistribution of social wealth during the revolution and the transition to democracy. The Weimar Republic was by no means an egalitarian society, and distribution of income and wealth was still marked by a huge gap. However, in comparison to pre-war levels, there had been a profound levelling of income and wealth. In Imperial Germany, almost one-fifth of the nation's taxable income was accounted for by 1 per cent of earners. Owing to the trade unions' wage policy, several democratization measures for distributing company profits, and, in particular, the losses of assets arising from hyperinflation and resulting income losses, this figure dropped to 11 per cent, which approximately corresponds to the distribution structure of the late twentieth century. The top 10 per cent of income earners, accounting for almost half of the nation's income in 1913, received only 33 per cent of all income in the late 1920s.[32]

The Weimar Republic achieved a profound redistribution of income and wealth within a few years, which was a radical change of the distribution structure in Germany that occurred in no other country to the same extent. After the 1933 seizure of power, the Nazis needed little time to completely reverse this development. In the Weimar Republic, the significantly more egalitarian distribution of income raised the living standards of lower and medium income groups while the lifestyle of upper income groups completely vanished. The number of bourgeois people with private incomes (*Rentiers*), that is, families living on small and medium assets usually invested in the capital market, decreased due to hyperinflation. They and their children swarmed into the labour market, the latter often providing for the family through paid work with which their parents were unfamiliar. The economic historian Knut Borchardt has therefore discussed the by no means implausible assumption that the very negative evaluation of the Weimar economy was in part due to the social background of the critics, since many intellectuals came from this very milieu.[33]

However, the levelling of income differences did not bring the social and financial rise of the majority of the population, which can be illustrated by comparison with other countries. In the 1930s, German families were still lagging behind international levels of consumption, achieving approximately only 63 per cent of US per capita income. Owing to rising food prices, and since urban living spaces were of poor quality and overpriced, they still had higher expenses.[34] Not before the end of the 1920s most working people achieved real incomes that amounted to the level of 1913. If we consider the standard of living to include medical care, life expectancy, and access to education, a slow but clear improvement becomes apparent during the years of the Weimar Republic. However, even these indices lagged behind neighbouring European countries.[35]

In light of this supply situation for large parts of the German people, the Weimar Republic cannot be seen as a full consumer society. For most families, the share of disposable household income was extremely small, rendering free consumption choices almost impossible. Their consumption decisions resembled a roller-coaster ride: in the years marked by high wage increases, the possibilities of a consumer society appeared on the horizon, but immediately vanished in the crisis years of hyperinflation and Great Depression.[36] It was the prospects of the consumer society rather than actual consumption that guided decisions of households and companies, which nonetheless resulted in relevant impulses for the Weimar economy.

Cars were affordable only by the upper strata of the Weimar society. The annual costs of the initial purchase and maintenance, the amount of approximately 1,500 RM, exceeded half of a worker's average annual income. Only 3 per cent of households were potentially able to afford a car in the late 1920s, compared with 25 per cent of British households. In 1930, the Reich statistics recorded 500,000 passenger cars, which amounted to half of those registered in the United Kingdom, a country with more than 20 million fewer inhabitants. As cars were unaffordable for the large majority of families in the Weimar Republic, the country saw mass motorization through motor-bikes, which were much more common than in the United Kingdom. These different forms of motorization were reflected in the structure of Germany's domestic industry, which consisted of numerous small crafts manufacturers. Ford and General Motors's market entries on the eve of the Great Depression signalled a shift in production structures towards mass production within this sector. This gained momentum within the production of civilian goods not before the end of the Second World War.[37]

The compact camera is another consumer product that can provide important insights into the structural changes of the Weimar economy. In 1920, Ernst Leitz introduced the 'Leica' onto the market and witnessed soaring sales. Over a few years, photography developed into a popular hobby of many Germans, spawning a profitable industry. Competing against each other, the new industrial sites in Wetzlar (Leitz) and Brunswick (Rollei, Voigtländer) were forced to be innovative and, at the same time, helped the photochemical industry (Agfa) tap into new markets for private customers.[38] Since German municipalities had pushed ahead with electrification from before the First World War and almost half of households with an annual income of under 3,000 RM were connected to gas and electricity, more than half of all households in Germany owned an electric iron and a quarter a vacuum cleaner.[39] Gramophones, and later radio sets, were also early and very popular consumer goods. Initially radios were sold as assembly kits, which made them less expensive and created an entire do-it-yourself culture with its own distribution structures.[40]

As explained above, the majority of German households could afford durables that were paramount for the breakthrough of consumer society only at a very basic level. Changes in food choices, replacing cheaper plant-based foodstuffs with higher end ones and meat products, proved more important. Industrially processed food such as tinned food and meat extract also boosted their respective industries. The substantial increase in spending on 'education and entertainment' or 'travels and relaxation', as the surveys conducted by the Reich Office for Statistics referred to it, arguably had the greatest societal impact. To be sure, in most households these expenditures rarely accounted for more than 4 to 7 per cent. But they became highly visible to the public, particularly in cities, and contributed to the memories of the Weimar Republic as a culturally flourishing society. Cinema and theatre performances, dance revues, fun fairs, all kinds of exoticism (for instance, at the pleasure palace 'Haus Vaterland' in Berlin) and not least the advent of advertisement with its large-scale, electrically illuminated billboards, played key roles in creating the perception of transitioning towards a consumer society. It was first and foremost the idea rather than the reality of consumption that shaped this phenomenon and—fuelled further by the value loss of money throughout the inflation years—created consumers' expectations that helped establish a consumer society beyond the Weimar period.

Companies had to accommodate these new demands and expectations, which they were successful in doing. The production of consumer goods gained importance. More shops were opened, not only in big cities but also in medium-sized towns, paying more attention to distribution than previously. C&A Brenninkmeijer became the most important clothing chain during this period.[41] Brand names and logos that had been the exception in Imperial Germany's market communication (such as Ludwig Roselius Kaffee HAG) started to dominate the street scene and expanding magazine market. Companies' advertising departments expanded as swiftly as planning and organization departments, the number of sales representatives, and accounting departments. Together with the numerous shop assistants, the 'little shop girls' (*kleine Ladenmädchen*),[42] as the film critic and social theorist Siegfried Kracauer called them, a new and rapidly growing social group emerged that not only shared some new social characteristics but also appeared as consumers. They differed from working-class and civil servants' households in that they had fewer children and spent more money on education and entertainment, travel and relaxation. In the predominantly urban white-collar milieu a kind of avant-garde of the modern consumer society emerged, with behaviours of spending and consuming and a corresponding lifestyle—albeit in the narrow confines of a comparatively modest income.[43] These structural changes in the Weimar economy provide convincing historical proof for the assumption that capitalism not only generates mass production but also the necessary mass consumption.[44]

While the majority of Germans could only gradually improve their living standards and consumption chances, German industry regained its previous strength rather swiftly in comparison. The Weimar economy was marked by an increasing concentration of power at several levels. This is first true of the form and extent of organization. The foundation of the Reich Association of German Industry (Reichsverband der Deutschen Industrie, RDI) in 1919, the first general industrial association in Germany, gave lasting impetus. Second, many sectors saw a tendency to form large corporations and extensive company agglomerations. Against the backdrop of US trust formations, ideas of large-scale horizontal business mergers circulated in Germany from the turn of century onwards, but became fully effective only after the First World War. Third, prominent industrialists tried to influence public opinion by taking over newspaper and media corporations. For instance, Alfred Hugenberg, mining industrialist and media proprietor, clearly contributed to the political polarization of the Weimar Republic by disseminating nationalist views. As former chairman of the Krupp

Managing Board, chairman of the Mining Society (Bergbauverein) and the Mining Association (Zechenverband) from 1912 to 1925, and from 1919 member of the RDI Board of Directors, Hugenberg, at the same time, embodied the concentration of power in a few individuals and the intertwined network of relations between the three areas. Interactions between the concentration of power in associations, businesses, and the media had a huge impact on the relationship between state and economy in the Weimar Republic.[45]

With the Central Association of German Industrialists (Centralverband Deutscher Industrieller, CDI), founded in 1876, and the League of Industrialists (Bund der Industriellen, BdI), established in 1895, German industry had already achieved a high level of organization in Imperial Germany. While the CDI was regionally represented, enjoyed excellent relations with the ministerial bureaucracy, and advocated protective tariffs, the pro-free trade and anti-trust BdI had fewer resources and personalities. With the foundation of the RDI, these differences in interests could be partly overcome. To be sure, many BdI members feared domination by heavy industry, and indeed, this sector was highly influential within the RDI. However, heavy industry alone was not able to determine the fate of the association during the Weimar Republic. Clashes between electrical, chemical, and mining industries and other (medium-sized) businesses created ever new and different constellations, requiring a continuous balancing of interests. The leadership of the RDI, however, consisted of representatives of the major industrial associations and powerful corporations. The RDI's huge influence during the Weimar Republic was predicated on the economic significance of its members and their contacts to the executive and ministerial bureaucracy. All of its executive board members were former high-ranking Reich civil servants.[46]

As early as 1913, the Central Administration of German Employers' Associations (Hauptstelle Deutscher Arbeitgeberverbände), which was affiliated with the CDI, and the Union of German Employers' Associations (Verein Deutscher Arbeitgeberverbände) merged and formed the Federation of German Employers' Associations (Vereinigung Deutscher Arbeitgeberverbände, VDA). Henceforth, economic political issues fell within the scope of the economic associations, social political ones were discussed in the VDA or rather the Central Association of Employers and Employees (Zentralarbeitsgemeinschaft, ZAG). With the ZAG, founded in late 1918, employers recognized trade unions as legitimate representatives of employees. However, many viewed the ZAG as outdated as soon as the leading associations of German industry had met in February 1919 to found the RDI. The ZAG is nonetheless considered the pioneer organization of the German model of social partnership, paving the way for establishing a corporative market economy in Germany. The economic model of social partnership granted associations and trade unions a high level of autonomy in all economic and social political matters, which was intended to help resolve their conflicting interests. Yet the alliance between industrialists and trade unions, which had been a pillar of stability in Imperial Germany during the late stages of the war, swiftly lost its significance. Many employers felt they had, under the pressure of the revolutionary events, agreed to too many and too far-reaching concessions. Instead of settling social conflicts institutionally within the ZAG, industrial action became more frequent during the 1920s. This culminated in the Ruhr Iron Dispute (Ruhreisenstreit) in 1928, the biggest industrial dispute during the entire Weimar Republic, with more than 200,000 workers of the iron and steel industry being locked out.[47]

Contemporary criticism of the RDI—dubbed the 'Reich Association of the German Heavy Industry' ('Reichsverband der deutschen Schwerindustrie')—did not correspond with the actual power balance within the RDI. The electrical and chemical industries had gained much significance in comparison with their position in Imperial Germany.[48] Still, the cession of the Upper Silesian industrial regions and the loss of the Saar area resulted in increased importance of the mining companies at the Ruhr. From 1924, the alliance between the Langnam Association (Langnamverein) and the North Western Group was the most important lobbyist group representing the interests of the heavy industry, both headed by Paul Reusch as chairman and Max Schlenker as manager.[49]

The programme for the 'reconstruction of the German economy' drafted by the industrialist Paul Silverberg already demanded the withdrawal of the state from economic life and—directed against the regulations agreed to by the ZAG—a flexibilization of working hours in late 1922.[50] Although most entrepreneurs did recognize the Weimar constitution as the legitimate foundation of the new state—as Silverberg confirmed in his famous Dresden speech in 1926—many industrialists advocated a roll-back strategy to undo the trade union achievements of the immediate post-war period.[51] Figures such as the industrialist Robert Bosch, who showed a greater understanding of the workers' warranted expectations, remained the exception.[52]

Apart from the foundation of central employers' associations to coordinate industrial interests, the formation of cartels and corporations is a further indication of the concentration of power within the German economy during the 1920s. The extent and the function of the cartels varied according to sector and demand, ranging from the regulations of logistics and turnover to price fixing to production limitations. The revival of the Rhenish-Westphalian Coal Syndicate (Rheinisch-Westfälisches Kohlen-Syndikat, 1893) and new foundations of the German Potash Syndicate (Deutsches Kalisyndikat, 1919) and the German Nitrogen Syndicate (Deutsches Stickstoff-Syndikat, 1919) were reactions to the dire economic situation after the First World War. They can also be seen as a response to increasing calls for socialization during the revolutionary period in 1918–19. The cartel movement was characterized by a tremendous momentum: at the turn of the century, about 300 cartels existed in Imperial Germany; this figure rose to 1,000 in 1920 and to 2,500 in the mid-1920s. This high level of cartelization during the Weimar Republic was reflected in its reputation as the 'country of cartels'. While cartels create predictability and reliability for their members during economically instable and turbulent times, their impact on prices for customers is debated.[53] Company managers intended to limit market uncertainty and often simultaneously pursued a business strategy geared towards fusions, as the major corporations IG Farbenindustrie or Vereinigte Stahlwerke demonstrate.

As early as the mid-nineteenth century, iron and steel companies used fusions and company acquisitions in order to incorporate upstream or downstream companies.

However, it was only around the turn of the century that this form of vertical integration became widely significant. Horizontal fusions such as the Vereinigte Stahlwerke, founded in 1926, were the exception before the First World War. The new steel giant produced about a third of the German steel production and was deemed to be the biggest European steel corporation, at times with more than 200,000 employees.[54] The IG Farbenindustrie that was formed by company fusions at the beginning of the twentieth century and during the First World War was about the same size and enjoyed the same market position. The new chemical colossus accounted for about 30 per cent of the total turnover of the German chemical industry and 22 per cent of all employees of the chemical industry in 1925, rising to 28 per cent in 1929. Even more important was the IG Farbenindustrie in terms of chemical exports: during the second half of the 1920s, its share of all German chemical exports was 57.7 per cent.[55]

Despite the loss of patents and assets held abroad, German chemical companies remained the main competitors of British and US chemical corporations. Not least as a reaction to the foundation of the IG Farbenindustrie in late 1926, four leading British chemical companies merged to form the impressive major corporation Imperial Chemical Industries (ICI). Thus, the concentration process was not limited to the German chemical industry, which was the reason for only very marginal changes in international proportions during the Weimar Republic.[56] The IG Farbenindustrie produced almost all colorants made in Germany and two-thirds of synthetic nitrogen fertilizer. In addition, it was one of the biggest pharmaceutical manufacturers and, just like the Darmstadt-based company Merck, contributed to the export successes of the German pharmaceutical industry that lasted until 1929.[57]

By establishing cartel, corporation, and association structures to protect against growing pressure from international competition, employers continued trends from Imperial Germany. At the same time, they reacted to the new challenge of parliamentary democracy and its public with increasing media propaganda. In particular, Alfred Hugenberg played a pivotal role in this respect. After acquiring several smaller news offices in 1913, he gained control over an entire network of press outlets and extended them into a media corporation. The acquisitions he made in late Imperial Germany can be seen as a response to the strong position of media companies Ullstein and Mosse. However, the takeovers of several regional newspapers, as well as the expansion of the publishing house Scherl-Verlag and the news agency Telegraphen-Union that were subsumed into a media conglomerate consisting of holdings in newspapers, publishing houses, news agencies, and advertising agencies, aimed at attacking the foundations of the Weimar Republic from a right-wing nationalist position.[58]

Yet the employers experienced tensions within their own camp. Owing to economic-political differences, Paul Reusch, the chairman of Gutehoffnungshütte, particularly did not want Hugenberg to have complete control over pro-industrial lobbying and influencing the press. Together with the Haniel family, the owners of Gutehoffnungshütte, Reusch gained control of the publishing houses Süddeutsche Verlagsgesellschaft and Knorr & Hirth, which owned the Munich newspaper *Münchener Neueste Nachrichten*. With their right-wing nationalist press outlets, entrepreneurs such as Hugenberg and Reusch clearly contributed to political polarization and conflict aggravation. In so doing, newspapers and publishing houses controlled by industrialists not only stood in contrast with the working-class press, but more and more conflicts emerged with media outlets under the control of the NSDAP. This played out particularly between the conservative, pro-Bavarian, and pro-federalist *Münchener Neueste Nachrichten* and the National Socialist *Völkischer Beobachter*, printed by the publishing house Franz-Eher-Verlag. Even a meeting between Reusch and Hitler in 1932 could not resolve this conflict.[59]

Although media outlets controlled by the industry did not always act in concert and suffered shrinking income from advertising contracts in the late 1920s, which resulted in financial difficulties, publishing houses and newspapers were an effective instrument for entrepreneurs to circulate their political views. In contrast to many big bankers who were often blamed for being 'nationally unreliable', industrialists were much more successful (albeit not always[60]) in translating their rights of disposal over assets or management positions in companies or associations into rights of political participation. This became abundantly clear at the end of the Weimar Republic.

The exploitation of politics through the economy, as shown for instance in the Gelsenberg affair or in Brüning's Eastern Aid programme (Ostpreußenhilfe) to subsidize the farming sector, was in a way a consequence of particular power relations within the Weimar economy. The 'Green Front', a diversified lobby group for several farmers' associations, successfully criticized the already passed Eastern Aid schemes from 1929. This led to the extension of subsequent agrarian aid programmes for their benefit.[61] The Gelsenberg affair came about when the coal and steel industrialist, Friedrich Flick, sold an overpriced block of shares of the Gelsenkirchener Bergwerks-AG (and by this means the blocking minority in the Vereinigte Stahlwerke) to the German state in 1932, right in the middle of the Great Depression. This example illustrates how entrepreneurs could transform political goals of the German government into economically exploitable potentials.[62] Clearly, Flick had particular skills to use political processes for his own economic interests. But these agreements also show that the government was willing to make major concessions to entrepreneurs and lobbyists while large parts of the population faced unemployment.

Up to the end of the Weimar Republic, neither economic associations nor most entrepreneurs supported the NSDAP financially. In the party-political landscape, business's natural partners were the German People's Party (Deutsche Volkspartei, DVP) and the German National People's Party (Deutschnationale Volkspartei, DNVP). Fritz Thyssen and his donations to the Nazis remained the exception. On the other hand, businesses and associations did little to protect the democratic principles of the Weimar Republic. When their policy of 'gathering' right-wing bourgeois parties was rendered unsuccessful and Franz von Papen, celebrated by parts of the heavy industry, was no longer well received due to his political views, entrepreneurs and economic associations were left with few options. Against this backdrop, the majority of businessmen favoured a long-lasting presidential government. Their weakened position in the wake of the Great Depression was one reason why they did not firmly oppose the rise of the Nazis.

More importantly, however, they misjudged the Nazis' claim to power and their own opportunities to influence.[63]

To be sure, the economy, particularly heavy industry, regained, and in some cases even massively exceeded, its former power through the formation of associations and cartels as well as through holdings in media companies—in a way inversely proportional to the loss of power of the Weimar parliament. But first and foremost, businesses used their regained power to push back demands of the labour movement, negotiate economic advantages for themselves, or limit the state's sphere of influence, rather than prevent the rise of the Nazis by the means available to them. This was helped by the fact that they also shared some foreign and social political views with the Hitler party.

Precarious Financial Sector and the Way into the Great Depression

Political and social conditions were not the only things that changed substantially after the First World War; financial and currency politics also experienced a radical transformation. By financing the war via war bonds and unsecured national debts, the German state held large debts domestically, which triggered a rapid price increase. Prices had already tripled in 1918 in comparison with pre-war levels, and thus the external value of the German currency dropped. Both developments were exacerbated during the subsequent five years under the conditions of Allied reparation claims, although the Versailles Treaty, which Germany signed only reluctantly, initially left open the amount of reparations. As the German government in 1914 had set maximum prices on certain products, the price increases were to begin with rather moderate. But as soon as the first Weimar government suspended the price cap, the repressed inflation took its full effect.[64]

Despite these burdens, the currency situation seemed to calm down at the beginning of the 1920s. After the failed Kapp putsch in mid-March 1920, inflation and the decline in the external value of the mark temporarily stopped. But when at the London Schedule of Payments in March 1921 the Allies established the reparation figure at 132 billion gold marks, the cautious confidence in Germany's political and economic stability was losing ground. In March 1921, Allied troops occupied the German cities Düsseldorf, Duisburg, and Ruhrort, after the German government had rejected the Allies' suggestions about the total amount of reparations.[65] When in December 1922 the Reparations Commission declared that Germany was in default of reparation deliveries and later suggested the Weimar Republic would deliberately withhold consignments, the international conflict escalated. French and Belgian troops invaded the Ruhr area in January 1923.[66] Again, the external value of the mark plummeted while domestic prices increased sharply. Together with negative future expectations, the inflation process accelerated as a self-fulfilling prophecy, resulting in the traumatic hyperinflation of the year 1923.[67]

Government and Reichsbank blamed the Allies' reparation demands for the high inflation rates. They claimed the unilateral 'most-favoured nation' clause that was in effect until 1925 had it rendered impossible for Germany to achieve the trade surplus which was a requirement to settle reparations. Instead, as they suggested, the government was forced to buy gold, or rather gold exchange, in the currency market, driving the price of the mark down. This explanation suited political decision-makers. In reality, however, rapid currency devaluation started before the reparation claims were announced; an increasing part of the reparations had, after all, been paid in kind. Hyperinflation was first and foremost due to the fact that the German government kept inflation running in order to decrease sovereign debt. A policy heavily geared towards monetary value that would have been necessary for a return to a stable currency was politically unenforceable, if only because it would have required major tax increases. Moreover, it would also have stifled the economy. Since from summer 1923 the mark no longer served its actual monetary function, the government, with the support of the designated president of the Reichsbank, Hjalmar Schacht, founded the Deutsche Rentenbank in October 1923. In November 1923, the newly established institution issued a new currency (Rentenmark) backed by real goods, which stopped inflation. At the same time, the Reichsbank adopted a restrictive lending policy, creating trust in the new currency. With the Dawes Plan that had been signed in August 1924 which placed German reparation payments on a new footing, the Rentenmark was replaced by the Reichsmark as the new legal tender, equal in value. Like in pre-war times, the Reichsmark was put on the gold standard. This was made possible by the Allies allowing Germany to borrow 800 million gold marks from the capital market abroad. In so doing, the financial consequences of the war were overcome domestically. Internationally, however, problems did not go away that easily and would shape the subsequent years of the Weimar Republic.[68]

All these financial distortions had direct repercussions on the banking sector, financing opportunities for businesses and investment prospects of foreign investors. When the Dawes Plan came into effect, more foreign capital flowed into Germany from late summer 1924, and the economy picked up again. Yet given the strict lending policy of the Reichsbank and the low equity capital ratio of many banks, businesses had little room for manoeuvre. The German capital market had dried up after overcoming inflation; in line with the lack of capital, the investment ratio was very low.[69] To be sure, the German economy was able to build, to some extent, on export successes from the pre-war period, but the loss of overseas branches, patents, and markets limited business opportunities considerably. Thus, businesses' return on equity decreased. The German economy responded by extensive import of capital. Particularly, major corporations such as Krupp, Gutehoffnungshütte, Thyssen, Deutsch-Lux, and Vereinigte Stahlwerke funded themselves by using their international reputation to take out foreign loans, in particular from the USA.[70]

The boom of the allegedly 'Golden Twenties' was entirely built on foreign capital trickling down the German economy. Apart from the foreign debt of German banks and businesses, several foreign investors found their way into the German industry. In August 1925, the US carmaker Ford founded a subsidiary in Berlin; in 1929, the US corporation General Motors bought the German carmaker Opel, and in the same year, the Dutch synthetic fibres company N. V. Nederlandse Kunstzijdefabriek (Enka) acquired the majority of shares of the Wuppertal-based Glanzstoff corporation.[71] The Weimar economy's high dependency on foreign capital made it extremely vulnerable to global financial crises. This is why it came under so much pressure after 1929.

From the very beginning, the banking sector of the Weimar Republic struggled with profound economic and monetary distortions, suffering from its very low equity ratio from the inflation period onwards. According to the gold mark opening balance from 1924, the share capital of all German joint-stock credit banks accounted for 30 per cent and balance sheet total to 21 per cent of that of the pre-war time.[72] As a result, the banking sector also experienced a concentration process.[73] In the view of many critics, transforming formerly small, regional joint-stock banks into branches of major joint-stock banks diminished the availability of credit for small and medium-sized businesses. This was because head offices in Berlin focused on big businesses, since fewer and bigger loans were easier to control than higher numbers of smaller ones. In the light of economic uncertainties, lenders counted on putatively secure investments and thus favoured old industries and government-guaranteed bonds with their investments.[74]

Due to increasing self-financing activities by industry, the role banks played in financing the industrial sector had already been decreasing before 1914. Between 1914 and 1923, the influence of German banks reached a low point.[75] Yet the problem of the German banking sector was by no means owed to the banks' reluctance to grant credits. If anything, German banks were still too heavily involved in the accommodation of loans, instead of withdrawing from industrial financing as would have been economically advisable. Rather, they granted short-term (foreign) loans for long-term investments. When from 1929 onwards foreign investors withdrew a significant part of their capital from Germany, the banking system collapsed in July 1931.[76]

Capital withdrawals starting in 1929 in particular arose from discussions on the Young Plan and its revision of German reparations.[77] The new programme was to abolish the transfer protection clause of the Dawes Plan and replace it with a regulation that prioritized public creditors over those from the private sector, which drastically increased the contingency risk of foreign investors overnight. The collapse of the American stock market in autumn 1929 and political instability in Germany owing to the Nazi election success in September 1930 aggravated the difficulties of the German capital balance. Large amounts of money were withdrawn from Germany, resulting in the Reichsbank's foreign exchange reserves shrinking as rapidly as cash holdings of German banks did. The Reichsbank had hardly enough sufficient gold reserves to meet payments to foreign capital owners. Problems of the banking system resulted in the German currency coming under pressure—a 'twin crisis'.[78] When in May 1931 the Credit-Anstalt für Handel und Gewerbe, the biggest Austrian credit bank, collapsed, the flight of capital accelerated. Only a few months later, in July 1931, the Darmstädter- und Nationalbank crumbled due to their unreasonable support of Norddeutsche Wollkämmerei ('Nordwolle'). All this showed that German big banks, given their heavy loss of liquidity, were unable to consolidate and restructure the banking system.[79]

Following this were socializations and several big bank mergers, the commercial risk thus passing to the state and the concentration process of the banking sector once again accelerating. The German government reached a standstill agreement with the US and the British governments for short-term German foreign debt. It also implemented strict foreign exchange controls to stop capital flight from Germany. In so doing, all domestic financial transactions were largely isolated from international financial markets.[80]

This resulted in an undersupply of capital for the German economy, causing further insolvencies that only worsened the economic crisis. The government hoped its deflationary politics—that is, a policy geared towards depressing prices—would improve the chances of Germany's export industry in the global market. It was expected that putting a stop to capital imports would give the German economy a chance to earn the money necessary to pay reparations and interests. Ultimately, the Brüning government wanted to prove to the world that it was impossible to procure the claimed sum. Therefore, the negotiations of the 1932 Lausanne Conference that resulted in the agreement to suspend reparations were, in a sense, a success for the Reich Chancellor. But this political victory came at a high economic and, in particular, social cost. Since world market prices of many products dropped much more rapidly than German export prices, the anticipated export boom failed to materialize. Instead, the export-oriented crisis management of the German government deepened the crisis, leading to six million people being unemployed.

Conclusion

Due to global distortions caused by the First World War, the Weimar economy faced difficult conditions. This, however, is similarly true of other European countries. Unemployment was hardly worse than in the UK, the importance of agriculture not significantly higher than in France, and inflation caused similar problems in Austria and Hungary. Striking, on the other hand, are the relatively low living standards and a low domestic saving rate. So what are the specific achievements and failures of the Weimar economy? Why is it collectively remembered in such a negative way? Why are the numerous social political achievements, the clear reduction of income and wealth inequality, and the continuous export strength of some leading sectors not highlighted as successes?

There is, of course, first, the unprecedented collapse of the Weimar economy during the Great Depression, which did not in fact cause the rise of National Socialism but certainly facilitated it. This, together with some industrialists' direct support of the Nazis, clearly devalues the achievement of the Weimar economy. The fact that contemporaries, and even some economic historians, misleadingly benchmarked the Weimar economy with pre-war standards has only added to this. As shown, it was simply impossible for the Weimar economy to live up to pre-war successes under the changed circumstances. Europe was no longer the centre of the global economy as was the case before the war.

The USA and Japan had made great progress in many sectors, pushing European competition out of the market. Indeed, Great Britain suffered even more from this development than Germany.

After a brief economic flash-in-the-pan during the immediate post-war period, the United Kingdom was frozen in recession. Unemployment remained high, world market shares declined continuously, and the country was running a chronic trade deficit with imports remaining at pre-war levels and exports declining. The country was desperate to go back to the pre-war situation, both in political and economic terms. This included a return to the gold standard and pre-war parity, which both occurred in 1925, artificially pushing up foreign prices of British goods. When the Great Depression developed, British exports declined even further and unemployment rose from 10 per cent (before depression) to almost 21 per cent.[81] By abandoning the gold standard in September 1931, Britain chose a path Germany could not go down due to international law. This was an advantage for Britain's relatively quick and more socially acceptable crisis resolution, particularly combined with a shift towards protectionism in the context of the Commonwealth in 1932.[82] However, even the British economy of the inter-war period was unable to live up to pre-war standards.

Compared to Germany and the UK, the French economy of the 1920s enjoyed a relatively positive development. The areas devastated by positional warfare could be rebuilt and economic relations, severed due to the war, were reactivated astonishingly quickly. A weak currency caused an investment boom in some sectors. After the currency stabilization in 1926 and 1928, the French National Bank accumulated massive gold reserves, which strengthened the country's position as a haven for foreign investments. In this sense, French economic history after 1918 enjoyed a relatively positive development: low unemployment and a high growth rate of industrial production were in many respects a counter-image of the British and the Weimar economy.[83] Having said that, the French economy was in a much weaker position than the UK and Germany before the First World War. Besides, the achievements of the 1920s were bought dearly with excessive national debt. For this reason, contemporaries by no means praised the economic policies of the rapidly changing governments. Observers at the time, and later economic historical research, saw adhering to the gold standard as the cause of the perpetuation of a permanent crisis after 1931.[84]

By comparing the development of the Weimar economy to the development of European trading partners and competitors that faced similar global structural problems rather than to the pre-war period, its performance and achievements come to the fore much more clearly. A common characteristic of the three national economies was their effort to return to pre-war conditions and to their former world market position. But the USA exceeded them by far in certain sectors. In the markets of Latin America and in Asia, all three national economies were equally in the defensive. These framework conditions caused similar phenomena in all European countries: industrial concentration processes, cartelization and the emergence of trusts, as well as increasing interference with politics. Weak and temporarily unstable governments as well as increasing political polarization were a common characteristic of all European nations, not least due to the economy influencing politics. In order to assess the failures and achievements of the Weimar economy more appropriately against this backdrop, this chapter has suggested the notion of an 'overstretched economy'. New consumer desires, new social political standards, and a higher living standard; re-establishing the position as world market leader and political support; financial political room for manoeuvre and the rebuttal of reparation claims were the demands that employees, industrialists, and the state imposed on 'the economy'. Under these circumstances there was little room for a realistic assessment of the chances the Weimar economy actually had.

Translated from German by Christine Brocks.

Notes

1. Knut Borchardt, 'Zwangslagen und Handlungsspielräume in der großen Weltwirtschaftskrise der frühen dreißiger Jahre: Zur Revision des überlieferten Geschichtsbildes', in Knut Borchardt, *Wachstum, Krisen und Handlungsspielräume der Wirtschaftspolitik: Studien zur Wirtschaftsgeschichte des 19. und 20. Jahrhunderts* (Göttingen: Vandenhoeck & Ruprecht, 1982), 165–82, here 179.
2. Borchardt, 'Zwangslagen'. For a summary of this discussion see Albrecht Ritschl, 'Knut Borchardts Interpretation der Weimarer Wirtschaft: Zur Geschichte und Wirkung einer wirtschaftsgeschichtlichen Kontroverse', in Jürgen Elvert and Susanne Krauß (eds), *Historische Debatten und Kontroversen im 19. und 20. Jahrhundert* (Stuttgart: Steiner, 2002b), 234–44; see recently Roman Köster, 'Keine Zwangslagen? Anmerkungen zu einer neuen Debatte über die deutsche Wirtschaftspolitik in der Großen Depression', *Vierteljahrshefte für Zeitgeschichte*, 63 (2015), 241–57.
3. Walter Rathenau, *Gesammelte Reden* (Berlin: Fischer, 1924), 264.
4. Referring to the notion of an 'overstretched economy' we are following Ursula Büttner. Cf. Ursula Büttner, *Weimar: Die überforderte Republik 1918–1933: Leistung und Versagen in Staat, Gesellschaft, Wirtschaft und Kultur* (Stuttgart: Klett-Cotta, 2008).
5. Gerd Hardach, *Der Erste Weltkrieg 1914–1918* (Munich: dtv, 1973).
6. Ronald Findlay and Kevin H. O'Rourke, *Power and Plenty: Trade, War, and the World Economy in the Second Millennium* (Princeton: Princeton University Press, 2009).
7. Avner Offer, *The First World War, an Agrarian Interpretation* (Oxford/New York: Clarendon Press, 1989).
8. Gerold Ambrosius, *Der Staat als Unternehmer: Öffentliche Wirtschaft und Kapitalismus seit dem 19. Jahrhundert* (Göttingen: Vandenhoeck & Ruprecht, 1984).
9. Friedrich Zunkel, *Industrie und Staatssozialismus: Der Kampf um die Wirtschaftsordnung in Deutschland 1914–1918* (Düsseldorf: Droste, 1974).
10. Albrecht Ritschl, 'The Pity of Peace: Germany's Economy at War, 1914–1918 and beyond', in Stephen Broadberry and Mark Harrison (eds), *The Economics of World War I* (Cambridge: Cambridge University Press, 2005), 41–76.
11. Gerald D. Feldman, *The Great Disorder: Politics, Economics and Society in the German Inflation, 1914–1924* (New York: Oxford University Press, 1993).
12. The term 'gold mark', which is frequently used in the literature, refers to the fact that the reparation debt was calculated based on the gold parity of the mark, the legal tender of Imperial Germany, in order to protect foreign creditors from a collapse of the mark.

13. Albrecht Ritschl, *Deutschlands Krise und Konjunktur 1924–1934: Binnenkonjunktur, Auslandsverschuldung und Reparationsproblem zwischen Dawes-Plan und Transfersperre* (Berlin: Akademie-Verlag, 2002).
14. John Maynard Keynes, *The Economic Consequences of the Peace* (London: Macmillan, 1919).
15. Christian Marx, *Paul Reusch und die Gutehoffnungshütte: Leitung eines deutschen Großunternehmens* (Göttingen: Wallstein, 2013), 193–5.
16. Werner Plumpe, *Carl Duisberg 1861–1935. Anatomie eines Industriellen* (Munich: Beck, 2016), 603.
17. Hartmut Rübner, *Konzentration und Krise der deutschen Schiffahrt: Maritime Wirtschaft und Politik im Kaiserreich, in der Weimarer Republik und im Nationalsozialismus* (Bremen: H. M. Hauschild, 2005).
18. Geoffrey Jones and Christina Lubinski, 'Managing Political Risk in Global Business: Beiersdorf 1914–1990', *Enterprise and Society*, 13 (2012), 85–119, here 92; Mira Wilkins, 'German Chemical Firms in the United States from the Late Nineteenth Century to the Post-World War II Period', in John E. Lesch (ed.), *The German Chemical Industry in the Twentieth Century* (Dordrecht: Kluwer, 2000), 285–321.
19. Douglas A. Irwin, 'The GATT's Contribution to Economic Recovery in Post-War Western Europe', in Barry Eichengreen (ed.), *Europe's Post-war Recovery* (Cambridge: Cambridge University Press, 1995), 127–50.
20. Heidi J. S. Tworek, *News from Germany: The Competition to Control World Communications, 1900–1945* (Cambridge, MA: Harvard University Press, 2019), 100–2.
21. Youssef Cassis, *Metropolen des Kapitals: Die Geschichte der internationalen Finanzzentren 1780–2005* (Hamburg: Murmann, 2007), 258–65; Christoph Kreutzmüller, *Händler und Handlungsgehilfen: Der Finanzplatz Amsterdam und die deutschen Großbanken (1918–1945)* (Stuttgart: Steiner, 2005).
22. Johannes Bähr, 'Selbstbehauptung, Anpassung und Wandel: Die Carl-Zeiss-Stiftung und die Stiftungsbetriebe im "Dritten Reich"', in Werner Plumpe (ed.), *Eine Vision, zwei Unternehmen: 125 Jahre Carl-Zeiss-Stiftung* (Munich: Beck, 2014), 147–93, here 168; Marx, *Leitung*, 172–7, 232–45.
23. Jones and Lubinski, 'Political Risk'; Alfred Reckendrees, *Beiersdorf: Die Geschichte des Unternehmens hinter den Marken NIVEA, tesa, Hansaplast & Co.* (Munich: Beck, 2018), 86–92.
24. Jan-Otmar Hesse, 'Die globale Verflechtung der Weimarer Wirtschaft: De-Globalisierung oder Formwandel?', in Christoph Cornelißen and Dirk van Laak (eds), *Weimar und die Welt: Globale Verflechtungen der ersten deutschen Republik* (Göttingen: Vandenhoeck & Ruprecht, 2020), 347–77.
25. Stephen G. Gross, *Export Empire: German Soft Power in Southeastern Europe, 1890–1945* (Cambridge: Cambridge University Press, 2015).
26. Schröter, *Industrie*, 519.
27. Patrick Kleedehn, *Die Rückkehr auf den Weltmarkt: Die Internationalisierung der Bayer AG Leverkusen nach dem Zweiten Weltkrieg bis zum Jahre 1961* (Stuttgart: Steiner, 2007), 61.
28. Johannes Bähr and Paul Erker, *Bosch: Geschichte eines Weltunternehmens* (Munich: Beck, 2013), 665; Marx, *Leitung*, 238; Reckendrees, *Beiersdorf*, 87.
29. Gottfried Plumpe, *Die I.G. Farbenindustrie AG. Wirtschaft, Technik und Politik 1904–1945* (Berlin: Duncker & Humblot, 1990), 499.
30. Hoffmann, *Wachstum*, 531–4.

31. Robert C. Feenstra and Alan M. Taylor, *International Economics*, 4th ed. (New York: Worth Publishers, 2017), 89–126.
32. Charlotte Bartels, 'Top Incomes in Germany, 1871–2014', *Journal of Economic History*, 79 (2019), 669–707.
33. Knut Borchardt, 'Die Erfahrung mit Inflationen in Deutschland', in Knut Borchardt, *Wachstum, Krisen, Handlungsspielräume*, 151–61.
34. J. Adam Tooze, *The Wages of Destruction. The Making and Breaking of the Nazi Economy* (London: Allen Lane, 2006), 138–47.
35. Andrea Wagner, *Die Entwicklung des Lebensstandards in Deutschland zwischen 1920 und 1960* (Berlin: Akademie-Verlag, 2008).
36. Claudius Torp, *Konsum und Politik in der Weimarer Republik* (Göttingen: Vandenhoeck & Ruprecht, 2011), 49.
37. Karl Ditt, 'Vom Luxus zum Standard? Die Verbreitung von Konsumgütern der Zweiten Industriellen Revolution in England und Deutschland im frühen 20. Jahrhundert', in Michael Prinz (ed.), *Die vielen Gesichter des Konsums: Westfalen, Deutschland und die USA 1850–2000* (Paderborn: Ferdinand Schöningh, 2016), 81–118, here 85–9; Heidrun Edelmann, *Vom Luxusgut zum Gebrauchsgegenstand: Die Geschichte der Verbreitung des Personenkraftwagens in Deutschland* (Frankfurt/Main: Verband der Automobilindustrie, 1989).
38. Silke Fengler, *Entwickelt und fixiert: Zur Unternehmens- und Technikgeschichte der deutschen Fotoindustrie, dargestellt am Beispiel der Agfa AG Leverkusen und des VEB Filmfabrik Wolfen (1945–1995)* (Essen: Klartext, 2009), 33–63.
39. Ditt, 'Luxus', 95.
40. Kilian J. L. Steiner, *Ortsempfänger, Volksfernseher und Optaphon: Die Entwicklung der deutschen Radio- und Fernsehindustrie und das Unternehmen Loewe, 1923–1962* (Essen: Klartext, 2005).
41. Mark Spoerer, *C&A: Ein Familienunternehmen in Deutschland, den Niederlanden und Großbritannien 1911–1961* (Munich: Beck, 2016).
42. Siegfried Kracauer, 'Die kleinen Ladenmädchen gehen ins Kino (1927)', in Kracauer, *Das Ornament der Masse: Essays* (Frankfurt/Main: Suhrkamp, 1977), 279–94.
43. See for a discussion of this thesis by Sarah Coyner: Torp, *Konsum*, 50–1.
44. Werner Plumpe, *Das kalte Herz. Kapitalismus: Die Geschichte einer andauernden Revolution* (Berlin: Rowohlt, 2019).
45. Heidrun Holzbach, *Das 'System Hugenberg': Die Organisation bürgerlicher Sammlungspolitik vor dem Aufstieg der NSDAP* (Stuttgart: Deutsche Verlagsanstalt, 1981); Tworek, *News*, 141–69.
46. Johannes Bähr and Christopher Kopper, *Industrie, Politik, Gesellschaft: Der BDI und seine Vorgänger 1919–1990* (Göttingen: Wallstein, 2019), 19–49.
47. Gerald D. Feldman and Irmgard Steinisch, *Industrie und Gewerkschaften 1918–1924: Die überforderte Zentralarbeitsgemeinschaft* (Stuttgart: Deutsche Verlagsanstalt, 1985), 37; Stephanie Wolff-Rohé, *Der Reichsverband der Deutschen Industrie 1919–1924/25* (Frankfurt/Main: Lang, 2001), 38–73.
48. Bähr/Kopper, *Industrie*, 36–101.
49. Gerald D. Feldman and Ulrich Nocken, 'Industrieverbände und Wirtschaftsmacht: Zur Entwicklung der Interessenverbände in der deutschen Eisen-, Stahl- und

Maschinenbauindustrie 1900–1933', in Gerald D. Feldman, *Vom Weltkrieg zur Weltwirtschaftskrise. Studien zur deutschen Wirtschafts- und Sozialgeschichte 1914–1932* (Göttingen: Vandenhoeck & Ruprecht, 1984), 131–60, here 147–8; Bernd Weisbrod, *Schwerindustrie in der Weimarer Republik: Interessenpolitik zwischen Stabilisierung und Krise* (Wuppertal: Hammer, 1978), 181–93.

50. Gerald D. Feldman, *Iron and Steel in the German Inflation, 1916–1923* (Princeton: Princeton University Press, 1977), 326–37; Boris Gehlen, *Paul Silverberg (1876–1959): Ein Unternehmer* (Stuttgart: Steiner, 2007), 239–43.

51. Feldman/Steinisch, *Industrie*, 32–4; Gehlen, *Silverberg*; Dirk Stegmann, 'Die Silverberg-Kontroverse 1926: Unternehmerpolitik zwischen Reform und Restauration', in Hans-Ulrich Wehler (ed.), *Sozialgeschichte Heute. Festschrift für Hans Rosenberg zum 70. Geburtstag* (Göttingen: Vandenhoeck & Ruprecht, 1974), 594–610.

52. Bähr/Erker, *Bosch*, esp. 61–8, 102–10.

53. Eva-Maria Roelevink, *Organisierte Intransparenz: Das Kohlensyndikat und der niederländische Markt 1915–1932* (Munich: Beck, 2015); Harm G. Schröter, 'Kartellierung und Dekartellierung 1890–1990', *Vierteljahrschrift für Sozial- und Wirtschaftsgeschichte*, 81 (1994), 457–93.

54. Alfred Reckendrees, *Das 'Stahltrust'-Projekt: Die Gründung der Vereinigte Stahlwerke AG und ihre Unternehmensentwicklung 1926–1933/34* (Munich: Beck, 2000), esp. 59–121.

55. Plumpe, *I.G. Farbenindustrie*, especially 176–78, 456–64; Raymond G. Stokes, 'Von der I.G. Farben bis zur Neugründung (1925–1952)', in Werner Abelshauser (ed.), *Die BASF: Eine Unternehmensgeschichte*, 3rd ed. (Munich: Beck, 2007), 221–358.

56. Plumpe, *I.G. Farbenindustrie*, 178–97.

57. Plumpe, *I.G. Farbenindustrie*, 176–8; Joachim Scholtyseck, 'Im Zeitalter der Weltkriege (1914–1948)', in Carsten Burhop et al. (eds), *Merck 1668–2018: Von der Apotheke zum Weltkonzern*, 2nd ed. (Munich: Beck, 2018), 219–348, here 258–9.

58. Friedrich-Wilhelm Henning, 'Hugenberg als politischer Medienunternehmer', in Günther Schulz (ed.), *Geschäft mit Wort und Meinung: Medienunternehmer seit dem 18. Jahrhundert* (Munich: Oldenbourg, 1999), 101–27, here 111–15, 119–22; Holzbach, *Hugenberg*, 89–98, 259–303.

59. Kurt Koszyk, 'Paul Reusch und die "Münchner Neuesten Nachrichten": Zum Problem Industrie und Presse in der Endphase der Weimarer Republik', *Vierteljahrshefte für Zeitgeschichte*, 20 (1972), 75–103; Peter Langer, 'Paul Reusch und die Gleichschaltung der *Münchener Neuesten Nachrichten* 1933', *Vierteljahrshefte für Zeitgeschichte*, 53 (2005), 203–40.

60. Plumpe, *I.G. Farbenindustrie*, 498–532.

61. Volker Köhler, *Genossen—Freunde—Junker: Die Mikropolitik personaler Beziehungen im politischen Handeln der Weimarer Republik* (Göttingen: Wallstein, 2018), 193–270; Stephanie Merkenich, *Grüne Front gegen Weimar. Reichs-Landbund und agrarischer Lobbyismus 1918–1933* (Düsseldorf: Droste, 1998).

62. Alfred Reckendrees and Kim Christian Priemel, 'Politik als produktive Kraft? Die "Gelsenberg-Affäre" und die Krise des Flick-Konzerns (1931/32)', *Jahrbuch für Wirtschaftsgeschichte*, 2 (2006), 63–93.

63. Bähr/Kopper, *Industrie*, 102–13; Dirk Stegmann, 'Zum Verhältnis von Großindustrie und Nationalsozialismus 1930–1933: Ein Beitrag zur Geschichte der sog. Machtergreifung', *Archiv für Sozialgeschichte*, 13 (1973), 399–482; Henry Ashby Turner, Jr., *Die Großunternehmer und der Aufstieg Hitlers* (Berlin: Siedler, 1985).

64. Carl-Ludwig Holtfrerich, *Die deutsche Inflation 1914–1923: Ursachen und Folgen in internationaler Perspektive* (Berlin: De Gruyter, 1980).
65. Hans Mommsen, *Aufstieg und Untergang der Republik von Weimar 1918–1933*, 2nd ed. (Berlin: Ullstein, 2004), 148.
66. Mommsen, *Aufstieg*, 169–70.
67. Theo Balderston, *Economics and Politics in the Weimar Republic* (Cambridge: Cambridge University Press, 2002), 34–60; Holtfrerich, *Inflation*.
68. Ritschl, *Deutschlands Krise*, esp. 99–100.
69. Karl Erich Born, 'Vom Beginn des Ersten Weltkrieges bis zum Ende der Weimarer Republik (1914–1933)', in Gunther Aschhoff et al. (eds), *Deutsche Bankengeschichte*, vol. 3 (Frankfurt/Main: 1983), 17–146, here 75–7; Gerd Hardach, 'Zwischen Markt und Macht: Die deutschen Banken 1908–1934', in Wilfried Feldenkirchen, Frauke Schönert-Röhlk, and Günther Schulz (eds), *Wirtschaft, Gesellschaft, Unternehmen: Festschrift für Hans Pohl zum 60. Geburtstag*, vol. 2 (Stuttgart: Steiner, 1995), 914–38; Harald Wixforth and Dieter Ziegler, '"Bankenmacht". Universal Banking and German Industry in Historical Perspective', in Youssef Cassis, Gerald D. Feldman, and Ulf Olsson (eds), *The Evolution of Financial Institutions and Markets in Twentieth-Century Europe* (Aldershot: Scolar Press, 1995), 249–72.
70. Marx, *Leitung*, 303–5; Reckendrees, *'Stahltrust'-Projekt*, 139–41; Harald Wixforth, 'Industriekredit und Kapitalmarktfinanzierung zwischen Reichsgründung und Weltwirtschaftskrise', in Thorsten Beckers (ed.), *Bankkredit oder Kapitalmarkt: Alternativen der Industriefinanzierung in Deutschland* (Stuttgart: Steiner, 2002), 15–38.
71. Henry Ashby Turner, Jr., *General Motors and the Nazis: The Struggle for Control of Opel, Europe's Biggest Carmaker* (New Haven: Yale University Press, 2005), 1–5; Ben Wubs, 'Tensions within the Lower Rhine Economy: AKU versus VGF, 1929-1969', in Marten Boon, Hein A. M. Klemann, and Ben Wubs (eds), *Transnational Regions in Historical Perspective* (London/New York: Routledge, 2020), 103–20.
72. Gerd Hardach, 'Banking in Germany, 1918–1939', in Charles H. Feinstein (ed.), *Banking, Currency and Finance in Europe between the Wars* (Oxford: Clarendon Press, 1995), 269–95, here 274–6; Carl-Ludwig Holtfrerich, 'Auswirkungen der Inflation auf die Struktur des deutschen Kreditgewerbes', in Gerald D. Feldman (ed.), *Die Nachwirkungen der Inflation auf die deutsche Geschichte* (Munich: Oldenbourg, 1985), 187–209; Harold James, 'Banks and Bankers in the German Interwar Depression', in Youssef Cassis (ed.), *Finance and Financiers in the European History* (Cambridge: Cambridge University Press, 1992), 263–81, here 267–8.
73. Theo Balderston, 'German Banking between the Wars: The Crisis of the Credit Banks', *Business History Review*, 65 (1991), 554–605, here 554–81; Hardach, 'Banking', 278–80.
74. Gerald D. Feldman, 'Banks and the Problem of Capital Shortage in Germany, 1918–1923', in Harold James, Håkan Lindgren, and Alice Teichova (eds), *The Role of Banks in the Interwar Economy* (Cambridge: Cambridge University Press, 1991), 49–79, here 53–4.
75. Feldman, 'Capital Shortage', here 51–3; Harold James, *The German Slump: Politics and Economics, 1924–1936* (Oxford: Clarendon Press, 1986).
76. Balderston, 'German Banking', here 581–5; Karl Erich Born, *Die deutsche Bankenkrise 1931: Finanzen und Politik* (Munich: Piper, 1967); Harold James, 'The Causes of the German Banking Crisis of 1931', *Economic History Review*, 37 (1984), 68–87.
77. Ritschl, *Deutschlands Krise*, esp. 107–41.

78. Isabel Schnabel, 'The German Twin Crisis of 1931', *Journal of Economic History*, 64 (2004), 822–71; Adam Tooze, *The Deluge: The Great War and the Remaking of the Global Order, 1916–1931* (London: Allen Lane, 2014), 487–507.
79. Hardach, 'Markt'; Ritschl, *Deutschlands Krise*.
80. Dieter Ziegler, 'Die Bankenkrise von 1931', in Johannes Bähr (ed.), *Die Dresdner Bank in der Wirtschaft des Dritten Reichs* (Munich: Oldenbourg, 2006), 43–51.
81. Sidney Pollard, *The Development of the British Economy 1914–1990*, 4th ed. (London: Edward Arnold, 1992), 37–154; Alexander John Youngson, 'Great Britain 1920-1970', in Carlo M. Cipolla (ed.), *The Fontana Economic History of Europe. Contemporary Economies. Part One* (Glasgow: Fontana Books, 1976), 128–79.
82. Barry Eichengreen and Douglas A. Irwin, 'The Slide to Protectionism in the Great Depression: Who Succumbed and Why?', *Journal of Economic History*, 70 (2010), 871–97; Jan-Otmar Hesse, Roman Köster, and Werner Plumpe, *Die Große Depression: Die Weltwirtschaftskrise 1929–1939* (Frankfurt/Main: Campus, 2014), 79–97.
83. Claude Fohlen, 'France 1920-1970', in Cipolla (ed.), *The Fontana Economic History of Europe*, 72–127.
84. Hesse et al., *Große Depression*, 130–42.

Bibliography

Balderston, Theo, *Economics and Politics in the Weimar Republic* (Cambridge: Cambridge University Press, 2002).

Feldman, Gerald D., *The Great Disorder: Politics, Economics and Society in the German Inflation, 1914–24* (Oxford: Oxford University Press, 1993).

Hesse, Jan-Otmar, Köster, Roman, and Plumpe, Werner, *Die Große Depression: Die Weltwirtschaftskrise 1929–1939* (Frankfurt/Main: Campus, 2014).

James, Harold, *The German Slump: Politics and Economics, 1924–1936* (Oxford: Clarendon Press, 1986).

Ritschl, Albrecht, *Deutschlands Krise und Konjunktur 1924–1934: Binnenkonjunktur, Auslandsverschuldung und Reparationsproblem zwischen Dawes-Plan und Transfersperre* (Berlin: Akademie-Verlag, 2002).

Tooze, Adam, *The Deluge: The Great War, America, and the Remaking of the Global Order* (London: Allen Lane, 2014).

Torp, Claudius, *Konsum und Politik in der Weimarer Republik* (Göttingen: Vandenhoeck & Ruprecht, 2011).

CHAPTER 20

THE MIDDLE CLASSES

MORITZ FÖLLMER

In the autumn of 1930, Theodor Geiger published a seminal article on the lower middle class in Germany. His analysis of the *Mittelstand*, as this lower middle class is commonly called, highlighted its fragile position between overbearing businessmen and revolutionary workers. It also stressed its internal divisions, especially between older occupations such as artisans and shopkeepers and newer groups such as salespeople, clerical employees, and low-level civil servants. Geiger granted that artisans had secured a place in the capitalist economy, more so than shopkeepers faced with the competition of large-scale retail enterprises. But what puzzled him was the *Mittelstand*'s stubborn refusal either to form a united front that would override the respective interests of its constituent groups or to adapt its subjective attitudes to its objective situation. Clerical employees might identify as proletarians and the artisans accept their subordinate role within industrial capitalism. In Geiger's view, lower middle-class Germans were clinging on to values that stemmed from an older society of orders or estates (*Stände* in German parlance) and had, in a near-complete class society, become outdated. This defensive stance made them panic in the face of current developments—and consequently vote for the Nazis, not despite but because of the party's confused ideas and unclear proposals. Still, he anticipated that lower middle-class Germans would be 'pushed ever more firmly towards positioning themselves in the class struggle' by developments too powerful to be negated in the long term.[1]

Theodor Geiger was a pioneering sociologist, yet his observations reflected more than his academic preoccupation with issues of social stratification. Published in a trade union journal, they betrayed the typical irritation of a card-carrying Social Democrat that his party's predictions about Germany's path to progress had not quite come true. Appearing shortly after the parliamentary election of 14 September 1930, they also attest to an understandable dismay about the National Socialists' breakthrough as a nationwide political force as well as an equally understandable hope that this success rested on a mere protest vote that would soon shift elsewhere. Finally, they reveal more than a little disdain. Like the cultural critic Siegfried Kracauer, Geiger took a dim view of white-collar employees' interest in the cinema, the jazz club, or the dance hall. To him, these leisurely pursuits exemplified an 'ideology alien to their position', a distraction from the alignment with the working class they should really be opting for. Geiger, the son of a grammar-school teacher, blamed this on a wider decline of *bürgerliche Bildung*, the much-vaunted culture of the educated middle class.[2]

In its explicit analysis as well as in its implicit assumptions, Geiger's article throws up issues that have been at the centre of the historiography on the middle classes in Weimar Germany. How were these sectors of society affected by the various political shifts and economic crises since 1918? How did their occupational experiences and living standards relate to their self-definitions and ideological attitudes? To what extent did middle-class Germans think and act differently than before the First World War, i.e. how do continuities and ruptures need to be weighed against each other? And, most pressingly, how can their disproportionate vote for Hitler and the Nazis be accounted for? These crucial questions have motivated important historical studies from the 1970s to the 1990s and continue to attract scholarly attention. They warrant careful discussion in the following sections, of which the second focuses on economic interest and the third foregrounds associational life. Yet, it is also worth exploring less directly political aspects, by asking how the middle classes experienced, shaped, and perceived the contemporary trend towards a diverse leisure society. Historians of culture and consumption have moved far beyond the dismissiveness of Geiger or Kracauer so that their work can underpin the fourth section. But before we turn to the Weimar years, the history of the middle classes in Imperial Germany requires introduction.

FROM THE LATE NINETEENTH CENTURY TO THE END OF THE FIRST WORLD WAR

Was there, before the First World War, a single middle class, or were there middle classes in the plural?[3] The noun *Bürgertum* suggests the former. It is close in meaning yet not equivalent to the English 'upper middle class' or the French (and Marxist) *bourgeoisie*. The difference is that it is less centred around its members' economic position, even though they needed the means to enjoy a *bürgerliche* lifestyle free of manual labour. Industrialists and bankers clearly belonged to the *Bürgertum*, and so did lawyers and medical doctors. While these groups were, as a rule, affluent and often wealthy, the same did not necessarily go for university professors, grammar-school teachers, senior civil servants, and Protestant pastors, most of whom could afford a maid but needed to exercise budgetary restraint. These belonged to the *Bürgertum* by virtue of their higher education and culturedness, the *Bildung* that, to this day, remains a central notion in Germany. *Bildung* was a powerful norm, promoted by a state that garnered international admiration for the quality of its schools and universities, as well as by a wide array of relevant associations. The emphasis on it was shared by lawyers and medical doctors, many of whom took pride in reading widely or practising music, as well as by many industrialists and bankers, who felt compelled at least to pay it lip service even when having less spare time and cultural inclination.

Together, these different groups are estimated to constitute, at most, 5 per cent of the population before and after 1918, but their social, political, and cultural influence made for a dominant position of the *Bürgertum* within German society. What, besides *Bildung*, might have united them? Political liberalism, with its emphasis on private property, rule of law, and freedom of opinion represented some of the *Bürgertum*'s core values, although this does not mean that it commanded its universal support. Protestantism, closely related in its emphasis on individual self-formation, was an important cohesive force, so that many German Jews were said to secure an entry ticket to the *Bürgertum* by converting. It was intertwined with another unifying force, namely, nationalism. Imperial Germany, the Kaiserreich, had only been founded in 1871 and continued to be celebrated as the fulfilment of God's providence. Nationalism lived off middle-class supporters and spokesmen (the number and role of spokeswomen being rather limited). Not restricted to commemorating the past and cherishing the present, it also looked towards the future. It fuelled wider ambitions—abroad, with respect to colonial acquisitions, and domestically, in the sense of unifying and regenerating an increasingly complex society.

Both Protestantism and nationalism were, however, at least as divisive as they were cohesive, even within the *Bürgertum* itself. The former led to an open or tacit discrimination against those middle-class Jews who did not wish to convert to Christianity. In conjunction with liberal anticlericalism, it also excluded Catholics, who constituted around a third of the German population and comprised lawyers, doctors, and academics alongside farmers, artisans, and industrial workers.[4] Nationalism entailed moderate versions, but it exacerbated domestic conflicts owing to a tendency to measure a complicated political system against the utopian yardstick of perfect unity, view ideological opponents as traitors, and demarcate putatively authentic Germans from social and racial outsiders. Even *Bildung* itself was not solely cohesive. Many middle-class Germans felt undermined by the advent of modernist art and music, whereas others were more open to these cultural developments; the quasi-religious value of *Bildung* rendered it difficult to accept such a coexistence of different tastes. If one adds the increasing differences in economic status, one needs to conclude that the *Bürgertum* was marked by both cohesion and division; the future relationship between both remained unclear.

What of the lower middle class, around another 10 per cent of the German population? Labelled *Kleinbürgertum* (petty bourgeoisie), this was no less heterogeneous. The lower middle class contained groups that dated back to medieval and early modern times, such as bakers, locksmiths, or shoemakers. Besides such master artisans, there were shopkeepers, small businessmen who often felt threatened by new developments while also proving capable of innovation. In addition to this 'old *Mittelstand*', further groups emerged and expanded through the growth of bureaucracy and consumption: low-level civil servants, clerical employees (including typists, an increasingly important occupation for unmarried women), and salespeople in larger shops and department stores. Like with the *Bürgertum*, nationalism was often central to the lower middle class's self-definition. It served to demarcate it from the predominantly internationalist working class while entailing a promise of moral equality with the upper middle class. And, equally similar albeit with a lesser emphasis on *Bildung*, lower middle-class Germans came together in associations. In general, the middle classes possessed national horizons, but their everyday experience and social life was strongly local, bolstering the civic identity of Germany's bigger and smaller cities as well as its numerous towns.

How was this middle-class landscape affected by the First World War?[5] The outbreak of the conflict greatly reinforced an already widespread nationalism. Doctors and senior civil servants encouraged their sons to join the armed forces and enthusiastically contributed to the patriotic effort. The same goes for professors and pastors, whose lectures, pamphlets, and sermons provided ideological justification and purpose. Even those who were initially lukewarm about the war and mostly pursued their own interests, as was the case for many industrialists, presented themselves in an emphatically German light. And those rebel sons of the *Bürgertum* who had become Social Democrats were especially keen for their party to support the war, in a sense rejoining their milieu of origin.[6] As members of associations, *Bürger* (and their wives and daughters, the *Bürgerinnen*) pulled their weight to collect and donate various goods and help to secure food and medical provision. Many tied their economic fortunes to an eventual victory, by signing up for war bonds that offered both a symbolic benefit and a handsome profit, before the decline of these bonds' value through inflation became increasingly evident.

For all the drive toward unity that its outbreak motivated, the war exacerbated pre-existing tensions the longer it went on. Wealthy Germans profited as the owners or shareholders of armament-related companies; if not, they could at least shield themselves from the impoverishment it caused. By contrast, small businesses came under severe strain or even collapsed, unless they could adapt to the exigences of military production. Many *Bildungsbürger* and *Kleinbürger*, ever fearful of sinking to a proletarian existence, suffered from material deprivation. They joined other social groups in blaming 'war profiteers' for a scarcity which, in reality, resulted from Germany's structural disadvantages. Differences between extreme and moderate nationalists, between advocates of military dictatorship and supporters of parliamentary rule, and between antisemites and Jews, were exacerbated from 1916 onwards. Although they were soon to be overshadowed by new developments, these economic and political divisions formed an important backdrop to the history of the middle classes during the Weimar Republic.

OCCUPATIONAL INTERESTS, ECONOMIC DIVISIONS, AND THE SPECTRE OF DECLINE

What did the end of the war, the demise of the monarchies, and the Revolution of 1918/19 mean for the German middle classes? Imperial Germany had provided them with a protective and supportive framework. It had expanded universities while limiting access to them, had maintained social order while guaranteeing liberal freedoms, had enabled political participation while securing the *Bürgertum*'s influence through a plutocratic suffrage system at the municipal and state levels. That this framework had abruptly disbanded, symbolically underlined by Kaiser Wilhelm II's sudden departure to Dutch exile, amounted to a drastic loss of orientation. Staunch nationalists were, moreover, dismayed that their hopes for a European and African empire had turned into a defeat whose full extent transpired in June 1919, when the Treaty of Versailles was signed. More moderate nationalists, too, experienced the conditions imposed by the Allies as a shock, especially the shrinkage of the armed forces and the massive territorial losses to the new country of Poland.

Yet, the political rupture could also be seen as a moment of opportunity. Left liberals and middle-class Catholics were open to work with the moderate Social Democrats for a new constitution and political system. Clerical employees, who had been disadvantaged by unequal suffrage and selective access to higher education, perceived full democratization as progress. Middle-class feminists applauded the introduction of female suffrage, which they saw as a just reward for their patriotic efforts during the war. Professions such as engineering, law, or teaching could hope for a freer development given that the restrictions imposed by the wartime state were now abolished. Their more disadvantaged practitioners, such as solicitors at lower courts or elementary school pedagogues, saw promise in the republican commitment to equality.[7]

Would the balance shift towards ideological rejection of the Weimar Republic or constructive engagement with it? And would the middle classes regain some cohesion or become ever more divided?[8] On an economic level, which was inextricably linked to cultural attitudes, several factors militated against constructive engagement and middle-class cohesion. The (ultimately short-lived) cooperation between industry and labour gave rise to fears that other occupational groups would be squeezed in the middle; it also exacerbated the latent distrust that many *Bürger* harboured against big business with its massive fortunes and complex dealings. Both groups felt disadvantaged by the republic. Major industrialists doubted whether their interests could ever be duly represented in a democratic polity that, as they viewed it, favoured working-class interests over economic rationality and was responsible for a peace with excruciating reparation payments.[9] Senior civil servants and judges, professors and grammar-school teachers, saw their salaries reduced in real terms and blamed the Republic's anti-elitist thrust for undermining their cherished *Bildung*.[10] Furthermore, artisans and shopkeepers demanded, but failed to secure, legal safeguards against the competition of department stores and consumer co-operatives in the name of the *Mittelstand* as the backbone of social stability.[11]

What transpires from these various complaints is a rather paradoxical attitude towards the state. On the one hand, it was accused of overreach, from the eight-hour day to an expansion of universities that appeared to devalue academic degrees, from rent controls that interfered in the relationship between landlords and tenants to an expansion of compulsory medical insurance that threatened to turn independent practitioners into mere employees. On the other hand, the state was frequently called upon to intervene in the respective sector's favour, a dynamic that led to numerous public subsidies for private businesses.[12] In conjunction, both attitudes produced disappointment, although it is important to emphasize that the economic situation of the middle classes was by no means uniformly worse than before the war. Many lawyers and medical doctors enjoyed good professional opportunities. The expansion of large-scale companies created further white-collar jobs, while the growth of the welfare state expanded public-sector employment.

These resentments and divisions might have lessened under different circumstances, but they were exacerbated by the inflation of the post-war years, which culminated in the hyperinflation of 1922 and 1923.[13] The prudently managed inheritances or savings on which so many middle-class Germans had relied first eroded and then evaporated. Aside from the financial disaster, this amounted to a devaluation of virtues such as individual thrift and beliefs in solid economic government. Not only did the state fail to secure stability between private parties; it also ridded itself of debts arising from war and other government bonds. Private creditors incurred massive losses as their outstanding loans could be repaid at a fraction of their former value. Under conditions of rampant inflation, the customary time lag between issuing a bill and receiving payment plagued medical doctors and lawyers. Real salaries fluctuated at best and went into free fall in 1923 as they could not keep up with rapidly rising prices. Civil servants, including grammar-school teachers and professors, employees, and pensioners had been used to a stable if modest financial situation. The unprecedented insecurity ushered in by hyperinflation was disturbing and brought them perilously close to the dreaded proletarian existence.[14]

Having said this, there were also groups that benefited. The republican governments of the post-war years tolerated inflation in order to avoid crashlanding the economy during a difficult transition. This fuelled a boom, short-lived though it was, in some sectors such as banking, construction, or textiles. That mortgages or loans could be liquidated for a fraction of their former value came as good news to those who owed money. Younger middle-class Germans often found it easier than their parents to adapt to an economic situation in which it was more rational to spend money than to save it and buying and selling stocks, businesses, artworks, or real estate trumped investment in solid bonds. All this resulted in new conflicts, not just between the middle classes and farmers or industrial workers but also *within* the former. Inflation pitted creditors against debtors, the young against the old, consumers against shopowners. Bitter accusations abounded, so that the organizations of industry, banking, and retail had to defend their members against the charge of immoral profiteering.

The political effects of inflation were worsened by the fact that, after the stabilization of the currency in the autumn of 1923, compensation for the losses incurred by creditors was not forthcoming. Vivid demands, couched in a rhetoric of the hardworking and thrifty *Mittelstand*, could not change the fact that the conflict between creditors and debtors ran right through the middle classes. Debtors, particularly the representatives of big business, successfully cited the fragility of economic recovery as a reason against the revaluation of individual debts.[15] As a result of this division, support for the two liberal parties, which traditionally laid the strongest claim to the representation of middle-class interests, shrank. Their politicians received precious little recognition for participating in various cabinets after the autumn of 1923, even though the economic and international situation clearly improved under their watch. The conservative German Nationalist People's Party (Deutschnationale Volkspartei, DNVP) and the Catholic Centre Party (Zentrumspartei), albeit less ailing than the liberal parties, also struggled to keep their middle-class voters satisfied and sell the compromises they had to make while in government. They were accused, respectively, of defending big business above all and of favouring the Catholic labour movement. Resulting from this broad discontent, splinter parties emerged that clustered around specific economic or regional interests while increasingly criticizing the entire system of parliamentary democracy. In the federal election of 1928, they collectively gained 14 per cent of the votes, thus overtaking the rapidly shrinking liberal parties and eating away at the conservative electorate.[16]

Notwithstanding its staunch defence of shopkeeper, master artisan, and homeowner interests, the Business Party (Wirtschaftspartei), soon renamed Reich Party of the German *Mittelstand* (Reichspartei des deutschen Mittelstandes) characteristically purported to be a movement with a national mission. It attacked the 'formation of the government by the parties', which resulted from 'this cursed parliamentarism'. The Party for Revaluation and Reconstruction (Aufwertungs- und Wiederaufbaupartei) diagnosed, in 1924, that 'the whole German party system simply reveals its fractitiousness and incompetence'.[17] From such critique of parliamentarism and desire for nationalist unity it would not be a big step to the Nazi rhetoric of the early 1930s. To be sure, not all middle-class Germans were similarly embittered, as lawyers, engineers, and physicians could benefit from improved economic prospects during the second half of the 1920s. But for them, too, stabilization and recovery were ambivalent, given that they occurred against a backdrop of inflation losses, rationalization, and increasing competition (of which the growing number of female university graduates was particularly noticed). Teachers were, moreover, affected by public-sector cuts that led to redundancies and high workloads. While a cautiously pragmatic attitude towards the republic predominated among these professions, they were faced with further contraction and overcrowding once the economic depression made itself felt. As a result, some of their practitioners became receptive to the Nazis' incessant scapegoating and vague but powerfully conveyed 'solutions'. Even industrialists, whose interests were rather favourably considered by the governments of the mid-1920s and early 1930s, were increasingly turning away from the republic.

This multi-faceted middle-class shift to the right owed much to the ways in which occupational interests and economic interests were intertwined with a rhetoric of the *Bürgertum*'s 'crisis'. Hyperbolic as this rhetoric was, its wide use constituted a factor in its own right. As we have seen, it was adopted even by otherwise sober observers such as Theodor Geiger alongside many others who either deplored or applauded that core middle-class values such as *Bildung* were losing their previous importance. Hans

Mommsen, one of the most influential historians of Weimar Germany in the 1970s and 1980s, has stressed the 'decline' or 'dissolution' of the *Bürgertum*, which for him already began in the late nineteenth century and culminated in 1933.[18] In addition to the deepening of economic divisions and the diminished importance of *Bildung*, he points out that transparent, broadly accessible, and politically liberal associations increasingly gave way to secretive, elitist, and anti-liberal 'clubs', 'circles', and 'leagues'. But does Mommsen's thesis stand up to empirical scrutiny, and are dissolution and decline the only plausible angle for writing the history of the middle classes in Weimar Germany? To answer these questions, we need to look beyond occupational and economic concerns, and examine the local level rather than just the national arena.

ANTI-SOCIALIST COHESION, ASSOCIATIONAL LIFE, AND THE RISE OF THE EXTREME RIGHT

How did the middle classes in Germany's cities and towns experience the transition from Imperial Germany to the republic? Again, the picture is mixed, as the demise of the old regime was by no means universally deplored. Many middle-class citizens even perceived the revolution as an opportunity for greater political participation and joined the councils that mushroomed across the country.[19] The lower middle class had been disadvantaged by plutocratic suffrage systems at the municipal and state levels, which is why many *Kleinbürger* were now glad to see them abolished. Democratization was not restricted to equal suffrage and involvement in the council movement but chimed with a widespread desire for a greater say in associational life. Choral, sharpshooting, and gymnastics societies expanded alongside many others; their leading positions were increasingly assumed by younger members and by master artisans, shopkeepers, and clerical employees rather than being monopolized by older lawyers, doctors, and professors.[20]

Conscious that universal suffrage required broader alliances and in the spirit of democratic renewal, many middle-class Germans opened up to collaboration with moderate Social Democrats. As a result, the German Democratic Party (Deutsche Demokratische Partei, DDP) achieved a remarkable 18.5 per cent in the January 1919 elections to the constitutional assembly. This success of left liberalism, however, proved temporary, owing not least to violent confrontations with the radical left. The socialist council republics that sprang up in a number of cities in 1919, the strikes and rebellions in the aftermath of the Kapp putsch (a right-wing attempt to seize power in Berlin), and the brawls or uprisings initiated by local communists were frightening to the middle classes. In hindsight, all these endeavours may appear ill-fated and fraught with contradictions, but this is not how local shopkeepers, industrialists, or lawyers tended to view them. Some organized for self-protection, while others gladly let more combative Freikorps or student fraternities crack down on the radical left. Either way, the upshot was greater middle-class cohesion through demarcation from the socialist working class, from the electoral arena down to cycling or swimming clubs.[21]

Could this defensive cohesion be converted into a more positive dynamic? The middle-class longing for congenial political representation remained diffuse and open-ended. The centre-right German People's Party (Deutsche Volkspartei, DVP) and the conservative DNVP were able to benefit, for a while, from the decline of their left-liberal competitor. However, they were facing the risk of being seen as too stale for the new populist spirit, too wedded to big business to sustain the allegiance of the middle classes, and too compromised by their participation in government. This affected the German People's Party more than the German Nationalist People's Party. In any case, the *Bürgertum* did not see its own electoral volatility as a change in conviction and behaviour. Conservatism in Central or Eastern Germany was not controlled by politicians but promoted in gymnastics or choral societies; in associations devoted to the cultivation of local identity, the commemoration of the war, or (crucial for female participation) charitable causes; in local party chapters that organized both political lectures and social events.[22] In South-western Germany, where liberalism had deeper roots than elsewhere, similar associations upheld traditions of local self-government, anticlericalism, and opposition to Prussian predominance. The difference to the pre-1914 decades was that these initially liberal traditions were now complemented by anti-socialism and marshalled against the Weimar Republic with its centralizing ambitions and Catholic representation in government.[23]

The *Bürgertum's* political loyalties and divisions differed per town or region; the overarching tendency was a yearning for unity and a preference for flexible associations over centralized parties.[24] These associations combined leisurely priorities with a rhetoric of common purpose; the *Volksgemeinschaft*, the national community that constituted such a buzzword of political discourse in the 1920s, was invoked at many a gathering of the local firefighting or sharpshooting society. Associational life was open to non-socialist workers and, either in auxiliary roles or in their own societies, women. It linked to established institutions, such as the Protestant Church,[25] while also overlapping with new organizations, especially nationalist leagues. The Young German Order (Jungdeutscher Orden, often abbreviated as Jungdo) thus enjoyed significant popularity owing to its readiness for anti-communist violence, constant self-mobilization, and quasi-religious idealism. The same goes for the Steel Helmet (Stahlhelm), a right-wing combat league that gathered its members for daytrips with their families alongside paramilitary marches into hostile working-class territory.[26] To such organizational overlaps corresponded commonalities between different generations. Notwithstanding a widespread rhetoric of conflict between 'the young' and 'the old', both often converged when it came to attacking the republic. At the universities, for instance, the difference between increasingly conservative professors and the numerous *völkisch* radicals among their students lay more in political style than in ideological conviction.[27]

In theory, this rightward shift could have been reversed once the uprisings of the radical left ceased and confrontation with France and other former enemy countries over reparation payments gave way to a more conciliatory approach. A reliably moderate middle-class electorate was certainly the hope of the centrist politicians who dominated the cabinets of the mid- and late 1920s, most prominently Foreign Minister Gustav Stresemann. Stresemann was, however, acutely aware of the difficult balancing act between pandering to radicalized middle-class Germans and drawing them into the orbit of parliamentary democracy. The compromises that participation in government and inevitably entailed were increasingly difficult for him and his German People's Party to defend. And after the conservative German National People's Party had turned to the radical right following an electoral defeat in May 1928, Stresemann recognized the temptation for its functionaries to 'ally themselves with the Stahlhelm', 'let the "national idea" shine before the people', and deliver 'threatening speeches' to enthusiastic audiences.[28]

Skilful though he was as a politician, Gustav Stresemann increasingly struggled to satisfy the rising nationalist mood. Before his untimely death in the autumn of 1929, he began to realize that this was no matter of a backward-looking minority. Rightwing enemies of the Weimar Republic were as often young or middle-aged as they were old. Most were not longing for a restoration of the monarchy but anticipating a highly attractive yet vaguely defined future. What they despised was a *System* that they saw as morally dubious. Republican governments and the fragile parliamentary majorities underpinning them enjoyed limited room for manoeuvre and still had substantial achievements to their credit, but that was not the message provincial *Bürger* and *Kleinbürger* received from their preferred newspaper.[29] Parliaments, parties, and bureaucracies moreover appeared rigid and stale from the vantage point of populist rhetoric and associational activism. Official attempts to contain anti-republican activity compounded the problem as they were seen as illegitimate interferences into local political culture. Against this backdrop, middle-class demand for a new and radical movement rose further during Weimar's superficially stable middle years.

How does the rise of the Nazis fit into this picture?[30] This is a pressing question, given that Hitler's party, while also appealing to working-class and upper-class voters, disproportionately relied on the Protestant middle-class electorate alongside the peasantry. It did so by bridging the gap between political extremism and *bürgerliche* normality. The Nazis benefited from an associational life that remained remarkably vibrant, notwithstanding the economic depression and the ensuing financial difficulties. In some places, their functionaries immersed themselves in local clubs or societies, if they had not been respected members in the first place. In others, they were too young, new in town, or professionally marginal thus to gain influence. Either way, they received a lot of credit for their relentless energy and putative idealism, even more so in university towns where they recruited successfully among student fraternities. The Nazis also borrowed some of the forms and rituals of associational life: they held all sorts of celebrations, commemorated the war or the Empire, and catered to local, regional, or Protestant identities. Where it originated, in Munich, the party even created a wholesale social world for its members. It organized a range of leisurely, cultural, and charitable activities, the latter with strong female involvement.[31]

The Nazis thus tapped into a culture of nationalist activism that had increasingly built up in the 1920s. They emerged from the local middle classes rather than infiltrating them from the outside, and provided them with the long-awaited nation-wide organization and anti-socialist force. Concerns about stormtrooper violence and dictatorial ambitions remained, but these were often downplayed in rather benevolent newspaper coverage. The Nazis' rhetoric might have been more extreme than that of the existing parties, interest groups, and associations. But by the time they appeared on the electoral scene, the narrative of the *Volk* arising from an existential predicament had already become rooted among *Bürger* and *Kleinbürger*. For them, it was not a huge step to support a movement with a credible promise to regenerate the *Volkskörper* ('national body'), transcend *Kapitalismus* while safeguarding private property, and generally take Germany out of its *Krise* through bold action.[32]

Seen from the vantage point of associational life, the rise of the Nazis had far more to do with the renewal and cohesion of the middle classes than with their decline or dissolution, contrary to what Hans Mommsen and others have suggested.[33] *Bürger* and *Kleinbürger* felt threatened to be sure. Yet, they were not in 'panic', as claimed by contemporary sociologist Theodor Geiger—quite the opposite. They increasingly demonstrated confidence and assertiveness, in a way that blurred the boundaries to the extreme right. Only by recognizing this can Hitler's electoral breakthrough on 14 September 1930 and the successes of his subsequent campaigns be fully understood. This insight also has broader implications for our understanding of civil society. Political scientist Sheri Berman has pointed out that what is usually considered an asset for democracy, namely, the practice of citizenship in clubs and societies, ended up undermining the Weimar Republic.[34] Civil society can have different political outcomes, ultimately depending on the values that associations and their members endorse. Now that we have established this argument, we can shift our focus from occupational interests and associational life to consumption and culture. Middle-class existence was too diverse to warrant an exclusive focus on 1933; yet, it will also emerge that precisely this diversity created an uneasiness which the extreme right skilfully exploited.

Consumer Choice, Cultural Diversity, and Political Contestation

Weimar 'mass culture' has received much attention from contemporary observers and subsequent scholars. The concept implies widespread adoption across all sectors of society and increasingly homogeneous preferences. This, however, needs to be qualified; on closer inspection, the supposed mass culture predominantly amounted to a middle-class culture. At the time, visiting the cinema on a regular basis was expensive; so was owning a radio and affording the licence fee. In that regard, Germany lagged behind Britain, to say nothing of the United States. In rural areas, radios and cinemas were few and far between. The latter were, to be sure, present in urban working-class neighbourhoods, but the spatial settings and audiences of proletarian *Kintopps* starkly differed from those of plush city centre theatres. Such financial limitations and social barriers affected the content of broadcasts and films. Radio listeners, about two-thirds of whom stemmed from the middle classes, were treated to an evening diet of classical music, opera, and academic lectures. *Bürgerliche* cinemagoers tended to watch German films with artistic ambitions or nationalist messages, a preference that became even more marked with the advent of talkies in 1929.[35]

Having said this, media consumption by the German middle classes was more diverse than appears at first glance. Radio channels also covered sports and broadcasted lighter music or domestic advice during the day, when housewives could listen in.[36] Alongside more ambitious films, middle-class cinemagoers saw American blockbusters, including those by Charlie Chaplin. The same people could combine different preferences, as two of twentieth-century Germany's keenest diarists exemplify. Victor Klemperer, known mostly for his insights into the Third Reich, was as cultured as one would expect from a professor of Romance languages and literatures. But in the cinema, he and his wife sometimes saw high-brow and at other times more popular fare, occasionally feeling ashamed about his choices. When Klemperer bumped into an acquaintance in a cinema in Dresden in 1921, both owned up to their guilty pleasure after an awkward moment and shared their annoyance with *bürgerliche* hypocrisy.[37] The diary of Franz Göll, a clerical employee in Berlin, echoed contemporary fears of degeneration, informed by his wide reading and sense of personal immaturity. Yet, in stark contrast to this declinist and self-effacing narrative, his household account books present him as a confident consumer who made ample use of Berlin's cinemas, theatres, and concert halls.[38]

It was precisely such diversity *within* the middle classes that made new cultural trends so controversial. Thus, live jazz was mainly consumed by affluent city-dwellers in hotels, bars, or dance salons; even less pricy performance venues such as cabarets or music halls did not tend to be frequented by workers. At the same time, other *Bürger* aggressively defended their rigid notion of German culture against the implantation of an Afro-American musical genre.[39] Much the same tension was in evidence on the literary market, which commentators mostly perceived in terms of a 'book crisis'. In actual fact, more literature than before 1914 was sold in kiosks, department stores, and at railway stations or lent from public as well as commercial libraries. What irked the critics was not weak sales but the popular outlook of most books and magazines, their conversion into commodities that eluded elite control. Ironically, the trend towards greater popularity was fostered not least by many middle-class readers with their desires for entertainment and disposable incomes.[40]

A similar blend between diversity and contestation marked the development of high culture, which was overwhelmingly consumed by the middle classes despite the Social Democratic commitment to it. Germany's cities and towns boasted numerous theatres, concert halls, and museums, owing to the fact that these were generously subsidized until the economic depression. Conservative programming along the lines of the late nineteenth-century canon and light entertainment predominated without going unchallenged. The university town of Göttingen dedicated a festival to the eighteenth-century composer Georg Friedrich Händel that initially featured Expressionist productions of his operas before shifting to traditionalist interpretations in the late 1920s.[41] The example shows that the modernism of 'Weimar culture' should not be overstated but was by no means marginal either. The art of Expressionism and *Neue Sachlichkeit* ('new objectivity'), contemporary plays, operas, and symphonies, progressive reinterpretations of older works—none of these would have flourished without sizeable public subsidies and middle-class support. Even in rather conservative Göttingen, the novel stagings of Händel's operas were, for a while, favourably received. Audiences in liberal cities such as Berlin or Frankfurt proved especially open to modernist artworks or productions, thus bolstering an atmosphere of cultural reform.[42]

Taken together, these aspects attest to the German middle classes' intense preoccupation with modernity. Few voices considered a return to pre-1914 times desirable or even possible, but which aspects to endorse, accept, or reject was a matter of controversial debate and experiential uncertainty. Undeniably, large sectors of the middle classes were searching for collective orientation, but without necessarily being in agreement with the Protestant nationalists discussed in the previous section. Some turned to the moderate or radical left, as was the case for the aforementioned sociologist Theodor Geiger, the architectural and cultural critic Siegfried Kracauer, and the anti-fascist lawyer Hans Litten among many others.[43] Others, for instance Gustav Stresemann as one of the republic's most prominent politicians, upheld pre-1914 *Bürgerlichkeit* while edging towards a greater acknowledgement of social and political complexity.[44] Among educated Catholics, nationalism enjoyed significant popularity, but there were other ways of reconciling religious values with the requirements of modernity. A case in point for the latter is Konrad Adenauer, the future chancellor of the Federal Republic, who as mayor of Cologne was responsible for the installation of a green belt, the foundation and subsequent expansion of a new university, and the inauguration of a trade fair.[45] Jews debated Zionism and Orthodoxy alongside German nationalism and socialist internationalism. Notwithstanding a widespread interest in Jewish culture and religion, most remained attached to middle-class values and liberal views.[46]

Some voices even endorsed a society based on personal choice between cultural offerings, consumer goods, and biographical models. That is how Berlin's liberal tabloid press integrated the growth of car ownership, the completion of the first apartment buildings, and the increase in holiday or weekend trips into a broader political vision.[47] This individualism chimed with the priorities of those middle-class women who neither let themselves be defined by motherhood nor got involved in nationalist activism. For all the gendered constraints they were facing, these women increasingly carved out their own spaces. In tension with powerful norms of female sacrifice, they acted as customers demanding painkillers at childbirth.[48] They influenced the book market as avid readers and the development of sports as practitioners or fans of tennis, track and field, and even boxing.[49] An increasing number attended university and entered the graduate labour market, albeit at a time of persistent prejudice and substantial unemployment.[50] In Weimar Germany, many middle-class women were searching for a life of their own, with all the complexity and uncertainty that such a search entailed.[51]

All this might simply have coexisted in a spirit of mutual indifference. In reality, however, the extreme right politicized the cultural divisions within the middle classes.[52] Its own *völkisch* visions remained a minority interest, while its commitment to the nineteenth-century canon hardly made it original. But modernism was a highly effective target, given that it was sufficiently present to provoke outrage yet insufficiently implanted to be widely accepted. By agitating against jazz, the 'New Woman', or the Bauhaus, extreme-right movements secured much agreement from culturally conservative *Bürger*. The Nazis tapped into this potential, with particular resonance when the work in question could be identified with a left-wing or pacifist stance. As soon as Lewis Milestone's *All Quiet on the Western Front*, based on Erich Maria Remarque's bestselling novel, reached the cinemas in 1930, the Nazis disrupted screenings and organized daily demonstrations. In violently defending a heroic image of the First World War, they made important steps in their quest to enter the mainstream. After the film had been intermittently banned, one Göttingen newspaper acclaimed such censorship as 'Goebbels's Victory'.[53]

Foregrounding culture and consumption results in a picture of the middle classes that is marked neither by dissolution nor by cohesion but, first and foremost, by diversity. This diversity is what accounts for 'Weimar culture's' fascination for present-day audiences as well as many observers and participants at the time. Other observers, however, found precisely this diversity problematic or outright contemptible. Why was this so? The fact that so much cultural activity was publicly funded made it prone to political contestation,[54] and even when it was not, the persistence of censorship meant that a government ban could be demanded. Furthermore, the fact that highly charged notions of *Bildung* and *Kultur* retained their prominence rendered it difficult to accept that culture might simply be a matter of consumer preference and transfer across national borders. As we have seen above, the ideal of *Bildung* brought even a Social Democrat such as Theodor Geiger to interpret cultural change in terms of decline. Historians, many of whom hail from the educated middle classes themselves, have tended to echo this contemporary interpretation. They have thus defined the *Bildungsbürgertum* in a way that, come the twentieth century, only allows for a picture of social dissolution and moral failure. Moreover, these historians have overlooked that the discourse on decline reflected a loss more of exclusivity than of actual influence.[55] Seen from a distance, what stands out is the middle classes' social and cultural diversification. However, that this trend was at odds with conservative understandings of *Bildung* had severe political repercussions in the context of the Weimar Republic, for it greatly helped extreme-right movements to root themselves in the *Bürgertum*.[56]

Conclusion

What's the matter with the German middle classes?[57] This was, in a nutshell, the question that already preoccupied some important contemporary observers, who were shocked by the electoral breakthrough of the Nazis and frustrated with white-collar employees' stubborn refusal to align themselves with the working class. The spokesmen of the *Mittelstand* insisted that there was nothing wrong with them but everything with a parliamentary system that privileged both labour and business interests to the detriment of their clientele. In a similar vein, conservative defenders of *Bildung* blamed an overly permissive, government-backed climate for the erosion of Germany's cultural unity. Such perceptions have subsequently, in the 1970s and 1980s, informed historical accounts of the Weimar-era middle classes that stress decline and dissolution. This interpretation is, to be sure, based on pertinent evidence, especially regarding the exacerbation of political, economic, and cultural divisions in times of rupture—although it is important not to overstate the unity of the *Bürgertum* before 1914.

Without denying that important differences and tensions ran through the middle classes, studies of associational life and local politics have arrived at a different picture. From their perspective, the *Bürger* appear increasingly confident rather than panicky, cohesive instead of disintegrated, more on the rise than on the decline. The problem was that this did not stabilize the republic but undermined it. From clubs and societies emerged an urgent quest for *bürgerliche* unity through a right-wing movement on which the Nazis were able to capitalize. The matter with the German middle classes was that their civic involvement did not bolster democracy, despite promising beginnings after 1918, but ultimately paved the road for 1933. Since this was firmly established in the 1990s, relevant historical research has diversified, bringing out a wider range of political options, consumption patterns, and cultural preferences. Importantly, this latest scholarly shift has by no means downplayed the rise of the extreme right in the later years of the republic. On the contrary, it shows how much this rise owed to attacks on cultural diversity in the name of *Kultur*. Middle-class Germans differed from each other in many respects, but the matter with many of them was that they came to see Nazism as compatible with, or even supportive of, their own values.

Consumption and its critique; democratization, progress for women, cultural innovation on the one hand and staunch resistance to these trends and currents on the other; liberalism, conservatism, and political Catholicism—all this harked back to the Kaiserreich and remained crucial to middle-class life during the Federal Republic; furthermore, none of it was specific to Germany.[58] What seems to have been peculiar, however, was the intensity of the preoccupation with crisis as well as the longing for unity. Both made it difficult to accept a diversity and complexity that was also more marked than in other countries.[59] For these reasons, historians will likely debate the role of the German middle classes before and after 1933 for some time to come.[60]

Notes

1. Theodor Geiger, 'Panik im Mittelstand', *Die Arbeit*, 7 (1930), 637–54, 638.
2. Ibid., 647.

3. The following overview is consistent with the otherwise differing accounts in Hans-Ulrich Wehler, *Deutsche Gesellschaftsgeschichte*, vol. 3. *Von der 'Deutschen Doppelrevolution' bis zum Beginn des Ersten Weltkrieges 1849–1914* (Munich: C. H. Beck, 1995), 712–72; Thomas Nipperdey, *Deutsche Geschichte 1866–1918*, vol. 1. *Arbeitswelt und Bürgergeist* (Munich: C. H. Beck, 1990), ch. 9; David Blackbourn, *The Long Nineteenth Century: A History of Germany, 1780–1918* (New York: University Press, 1998), ch. 8.
4. See Thomas Mergel, 'Ultramontanism, Liberalism, Moderation: Political Mentalities and Political Behavior of the German Catholic *Bürgertum*, 1848–1914', *Central European History*, 29 (1997), 151–74.
5. The following two paragraphs draw on Roger Chickering, *Imperial Germany and the Great War, 1914–1918* (Cambridge: Cambridge University Press, 1998), esp. ch. 4.
6. See Wolfgang Kruse, *Krieg und nationale Integration: Eine Neuinterpretation des sozialdemokratischen Burgfriedensschlusses 1914/15* (Essen: Klartext, 1993), 98–106.
7. See, here and elsewhere in this section, Konrad H. Jarausch, *The Unfree Professions: German Lawyers, Teachers, and Engineers, 1900–1950* (New York: Oxford University Press, 1990), part I.
8. The following remarks draw, among others, on Hans-Ulrich Wehler, *Deutsche Gesellschaftsgeschichte*, vol. 4. *Vom Beginn des Ersten Weltkriegs bis zur Gründung der beiden deutschen Staaten 1914–1949* (Munich: C. H. Beck, 2003), 289–309.
9. See the concise summary by Gerald D. Feldman, 'Politische Kultur und Wirtschaft in der Weimarer Zeit: Unternehmer auf dem Weg in die Katastrophe', *Zeitschrift für Unternehmensgeschichte*, 43 (1998), 3–18.
10. See also Christian Jansen, *Professoren und Politik: Politisches Denken und Handeln der Heidelberger Hochschullehrer* (Göttingen: Vandenhoeck & Ruprecht, 1992), 27–31.
11. See Heinrich August Winkler, *Mittelstand, Demokratie und Nationalsozialismus: Die politische Entwicklung von Handwerk und Kleinhandel in der Weimarer Republik* (Cologne: Kiepenheuer und Witsch, 1972) and Larry Eugene Jones, '"The Dying Middle": Weimar Germany and the Fragmentation of Bourgeois Politics', *Central European History*, 5 (1972), 23–54.
12. See Fritz Blaich, '"Garantierter Kapitalismus": Subventionspolitik und Wirtschaftsordnung in Deutschland zwischen 1925 und 1932', *Zeitschrift für Unternehmensgeschichte*, 22 (1977), 50–70.
13. The following two paragraphs draw on Gerald D. Feldman, *The Great Disorder: Politics, Economics, and Society in the German Inflation 1914–1924* (New York: Oxford University Press, 1993), ch. 12; Martin H. Geyer, *Verkehrte Welt: Revolution, Inflation und Moderne: München 1914–1924* (Göttingen: Vandenhoeck & Ruprecht, 1998), chs 4–8.
14. See the documents in Fritz K. Ringer (ed.), *The German Inflation of 1923* (New York: Oxford University Press, 1969), ch. 3.
15. Michael L. Hughes, 'Economic Interest, Social Attitudes, and Creditor Ideology: Popular Responses to Inflation', in Gerald D. Feldman et al. (eds), *Die Deutsche Inflation: Eine Zwischenbilanz* (Berlin: De Gruyter, 1982), 385–408, here 392–6.
16. See Larry Eugene Jones, 'Inflation, Revaluation, and the Crisis of Middle-Class Politics: A Study in the Dissolution of the German Party System, 1923-28', *Central European History*, 12 (1979), 143–68.
17. Quoted in Thomas Childers, 'Interest and Ideology: Anti-System Politics in the Era of Stabilization 1924–1928', in Gerald D. Feldman (ed.), *Die Nachwirkungen der Inflation auf die deutsche Geschichte 1924–1933* (Munich: Oldenbourg, 1985), 1–20, 12–13. On the ways

in which political rhetoric appealed simultaneously to occupational interests and middle-class unity see Childers, 'The Social Language of Politics in Germany: The Sociology of Political Discourse in the Weimar Republic', *American Historical Review*, 95 (1990), 331–57.

18. Hans Mommsen, 'The Decline of the Bürgertum in Late Nineteenth- and Early Twentieth-Century Germany', in *From Weimar to Auschwitz: Essays in German History*, tr. Philip O'Connor (Cambridge: Polity Press, 1991), 11–27. The original German title of Mommsen's essay speaks of *Auflösung*, which translates as dissolution rather than decline.
19. See Hans-Joachim Bieber, *Bürgertum in der Revolution: Bürgerräte und Bürgerstreiks in Deutschland 1918–1920* (Hamburg: Christians, 1992).
20. This key insight has been provided by the pioneering work of Rudy Koshar, *Social Life, Local Politics, and Nazism: Marburg, 1880–1935* (Chapel Hill, NC: University of North Carolina Press, 1986), ch. 4, and Peter Fritzsche, *Rehearsals for Fascism: Populism and Political Mobilization in Weimar Germany* (New York: Oxford University Press, 1990), chs 3 and 4.
21. See Fritzsche, *Rehearsals*, 78–80; Claus-Christian W. Szejnmann, *Nazism in Central Germany: The Brownshirts in 'Red' Saxony* (New York: Berghahn, 1999), 143–8; Alex Burkhardt, *Democrats into Nazis: Middle-Class Radicalisation in a Single German Town* (Newcastle: Cambridge Scholars, 2019).
22. See Frank Bösch, *Das konservative Milieu: Vereinskultur und lokale Sammlungspolitik* (Göttingen: Wallstein, 2002), ch. 4; Helge Matthiesen, *Greifswald in Vorpommern: Konservatives Milieu im Kaiserreich, in Demokratie und Diktatur 1900–1990* (Dusseldorf: Droste, 2000), 111–21, 159–73; Raffael Scheck, *Mothers of the Nation: Right-Wing Women in Weimar Germany* (Oxford: Berg, 2004), ch. 8.
23. Oded Heilbronner, '"Long Live Liberty, Equality, Fraternity, and Dynamite": The German Bourgeoisie and the Constructing of Popular Liberal and National-Socialist Subcultures in Marginal Germany', *Journal of Social History*, 39 (2005), 181–220, here 198–202.
24. See Fritzsche, *Rehearsals*, ch. 7. On the crucial moment of General Field Marshal and nationalist icon Paul von Hindenburg's election to the presidency of the Republic see Fritzsche, 'Presidential Victory and Popular Festivity in Weimar Germany: Hindenburg's 1925 Election', *Central European History*, 23 (1990), 205–24.
25. See Bösch, *Das konservative Milieu*, 93–100; Matthiesen, *Greifswald*, 107, 181–8.
26. See Helge Matthiesen, *Bürgertum und Nationalsozialismus in Thüringen: Das bürgerliche Gotha von 1918 bis 1930* (Jena: Gustav Fischer, 1994), 109–37, 144–6; Fritzsche, *Rehearsals*, ch. 8; Dirk Schumann, *Political Violence in the Weimar Republic, 1918–1933: Fight for the Streets and Fear of Civil War*, tr. Thomas Dunlap (New York: Berghahn, 2009), 159–64, 188–9, 309–10.
27. See Jansen, *Professoren und Politik*, chs 5 and 6; Sonja Levsen, *Elite, Männlichkeit und Krieg: Tübinger und Cambridger Studenten 1900–1929* (Göttingen: Vandenhoeck & Ruprecht, 2006), ch. 6; Ulrich Herbert, '"Generation der Sachlichkeit": Die völkische Studentenbewegung der frühen 20er Jahre in Deutschland', in Herbert, *Arbeit, Volkstum, Weltanschauung: Über Deutsche und Fremde im 20. Jahrhundert* (Frankfurt: Fischer, 1995), 31–58.
28. Letter to Wilhelm Kahl, 3 Mar. 1929, quoted in Ludwig Richter, '"Das ausgleichende Moment des zu bildenden Kompromisses": Überlegungen zum politischen Weg Gustav Stresemanns und der Deutschen Volkspartei in der Weimarer Republik', in Karl Heinrich Pohl (ed.), *Politiker und Bürger: Gustav Stresemann und seine Zeit* (Göttingen: Vandenhoeck & Ruprecht, 2002), 143–61, 143.

29. See Thomas Mergel, *Parlamentarische Kultur in der Weimarer Republik: Politische Kommunikation, symbolische Politik und Öffentlichkeit im Reichstag* (Dusseldorf: Droste, 2002), 362–410; Bernhard Fulda, *Press and Politics in the Weimar Republic* (Oxford: Oxford University Press, 2009), ch. 4.
30. The following passages are based on Koshar, *Social Life*, ch. 5; Bösch, *Das konservative Milieu*, ch. 6; Szejnmann, *Nazism in Central Germany*, ch. 4. Peter Fritzsche expertly summarizes his own and other scholars' research in his *Germans into Nazis* (Cambridge, MA: Harvard University Press, 1998), here ch. 3.
31. See Mathias Rösch, *Die Münchner NSDAP 1925–1933: Eine Untersuchung zur inneren Struktur der NSDAP in der Weimarer Republik* (Munich: Oldenbourg, 2002), 291–305.
32. On these discursive overlaps, see Moritz Föllmer, 'Der "kranke Volkskörper": Industrielle, hohe Beamte und der Diskurs der nationalen Regeneration in der Weimarer Republik', *Geschichte und Gesellschaft*, 27 (2001), 41–67; Föllmer, 'Capitalism and Agency in Interwar Germany', in Föllmer and Pamela E. Swett (eds), *Reshaping Capitalism in Weimar and Nazi Germany* (Cambridge: Cambridge University Press, 2022), 28–54; Rüdiger Graf, 'Either-Or: The Narrative of "Crisis" in Weimar Germany and in Historiography', *Central European History*, 43 (2010), 592–615.
33. Among the scholars of associational life in Weimar Germany since the 1980s, only Oded Heilbronner maintains a narrative of dissolution, for instance in 'German Bourgeoisie', 202; 'The German Bourgeois Club as a Political and Social Structure in the Late Nineteenth and Early Twentieth Centuries', *Continuity and Change*, 13 (1998), 443–73, here 462–3. This has much do to with his small and specific regional sample as well as with problems of evidence and interpretation, see the critical remarks by Matthiesen, *Bürgertum und Nationalsozialismus*, 223; Bösch, *Das konservative Milieu*, 117 n. 15. Szejnmann, *Nazism in Central Germany*, 151, states that 'traditional clubs' were 'disintegrating' in the early 1930s while actually offering a more differentiated picture.
34. Sheri Berman, 'Civil Society and the Collapse of the Weimar Republic', *World Politics*, 49 (1997), 401–29.
35. See Karl Christian Führer, 'A Medium of Modernity? Broadcasting in Weimar Germany, 1923–1932', *Journal of Modern History*, 69 (1997), 722–53; Corey Ross, 'Mass Culture and Divided Audiences: Cinema and Social Change in Inter-War Germany', *Past and Present*, 193 (Nov. 2006), 157–95.
36. See Carsten Lenk, *Die Erscheinung des Rundfunks: Einführung und Nutzung eines neuen Mediums 1923–1932* (Opladen: Westdeutscher Verlag, 1997), chs 3 and 4; Kate Lacey, *Feminine Frequencies: Gender, German Radio, and the Public Sphere, 1923–1945* (Ann Arbor: University of Michigan Press, 1996), ch. 3.
37. Victor Klemperer, *Leben sammeln, nicht fragen wozu und warum: Tagebücher 1918–1924* (Berlin: Aufbau, 1996), 442 (8 May 1921).
38. Peter Fritzsche, *The Turbulent World of Franz Göll: An Ordinary Berliner Writes the Twentieth Century* (Cambridge, MA: Harvard University Press, 2013), 32–59.
39. See Michael J. Schmidt, 'Visual Music: Jazz, Synaesthesia, and the History of the Senses in the Weimar Republic', *German History*, 32 (2014), 201–23, here 204–6; Michael H. Kater, 'The Jazz Experience in Weimar Germany', *German History*, 6 (1988), 145–58.
40. See Gideon Reuveni, *Reading Germany: Literature and Consumer Culture in Germany before 1933*, tr. Ruth Morris (New York: Berghahn, 2006).
41. See Karl Christian Führer, 'High Brow and Low Brow Culture', in Anthony McElligott (ed.), *Weimar Germany* (Oxford: Oxford University Press, 2009), 260–81; David Imhoof,

Becoming a Nazi Town: Culture and Politics in Göttingen between the World Wars (Ann Arbor: University of Michigan Press, 2013), chs 3 and 4.

42. Studies that link the emergence of cultural modernism to the social history of audiences are rare, but see Hansjakob Ziemer, *Die Moderne hören: Das Konzert als urbanes Forum 1890–1940* (Frankfurt: Campus, 2008), chs 4 and 5.
43. On the latter two, see Jörg Später, *Siegfried Kracauer*, tr. Daniel Steuer (Cambridge: Polity, 2020); Benjamin Carter Hett, *Crossing Hitler: The Man Who Put the Nazis on the Witness Stand* (Oxford: Oxford University Press, 2008), esp. part I.
44. See the recent biography by Karl Heinrich Pohl, *Gustav Stresemann: The Crossover Artist*, tr. Christine Brocks (New York: Berghahn, 2019), which places much emphasis on its protagonist's *Bürgerlichkeit* before as well as after the First World War. A similar interpretation of a leading liberal politician is offered in Wolfgang Hardtwig, *Freiheitliches Bürgertum in Deutschland: Der Weimarer Demokrat Eduard Hamm zwischen Kaiserreich und Widerstand* (Stuttgart: Franz Steiner, 2018).
45. See Henning Köhler, *Adenauer: Eine politische Biographie* (Frankfurt: Propyläen, 1994), chs 4 and 6. On the relationship between educated Catholics and modernity, see Richard van Dülmen, 'Katholischer Konservatismus oder die "soziologische" Neuorientierung: Das "Hochland" in der Weimarer Zeit', *Zeitschrift für bayerische Landesgeschichte*, 36 (1973), 254–303.
46. Compare Michael Brenner, *The Renaissance of Jewish Culture in Weimar Germany* (New Haven: Yale University Press, 1998) to Donald L. Niewyk, *The Jews in Weimar Germany* (Manchester: Manchester University Press, 1980).
47. See Moritz Föllmer, *Individuality and Modernity in Berlin: Self and Society from Weimar to the Wall* (Cambridge: Cambridge University Press, 2013), ch. 2. Christine Keitz, *Reisen als Leitbild: Die Entstehung des modernen Massentourismus in Deutschland* (Munich: dtv, 1997), 41–53, demonstrates that in Weimar Germany tourism expanded to involve white-collar employees and better earning workers.
48. See Patricia R. Stokes, 'Purchasing Comfort: Patent Remedies and the Alleviation of Labor Pain in Germany between 1914 and 1933', in Paul Betts and Greg Eghigian (eds), *Pain and Prosperity: Reconsidering Twentieth-Century German History* (Stanford, CA: Stanford University Press, 2003), 61–87.
49. See Kerstin Barndt, *Sentiment und Sachlichkeit: Der Roman der Neuen Frau in der Weimarer Republik* (Cologne: Böhlau, 2003); Erik Jensen, *Body by Weimar: Athletes, Gender, and German Modernity* (New York: Oxford University Press, 2010).
50. See Claudia Huerkamp, *Bildungsbürgerinnen: Frauen im Studium und in akademischen Berufen 1900–1945* (Göttingen: Vandenhoeck & Ruprecht, 1996).
51. Moritz Föllmer, 'Auf der Suche nach dem eigenen Leben: Junge Frauen und Individualität in der Weimarer Republik', in Föllmer and Rüdiger Graf (eds), *Die 'Krise' der Weimarer Republik: Zur Kritik eines Deutungsmusters* (Frankfurt: Campus, 2005), 287–317.
52. The following passage draws on Moritz Föllmer, *Culture in the Third Reich*, tr. Leslie Sharpe and Jeremy Noakes (Oxford: Oxford University Press, 2020), ch. 1.
53. Quoted in Imhoof, *Becoming a Nazi Town*, 160–1; see also Peter Jelavich, *Berlin Alexanderplatz: Radio, Film, and the Death of Weimar Culture* (Berkeley, CA: University of California Press, 2006), ch. 6.
54. This point is made in Führer, 'High Brow and Low Brow Culture', 269.

55. See the critical remarks by Dieter Langewiesche, 'Bildungsbürgertum: Zum Forschungsprojekt des Arbeitskreises für moderne Sozialgeschichte', in Manfred Hettling and Richard Pohle (eds), *Bürgertum: Bilanzen, Perspektiven, Begriffe* (Göttingen: Vandenhoeck & Ruprecht, 2019), 37–57, here 55–6; Klaus Tenfelde, 'Stadt und Bürgertum im 20. Jahrhundert', in Tenfelde and Hans-Ulrich Wehler (eds), *Wege zur Geschichte des Bürgertums* (Göttingen: Vandenhoeck & Ruprecht, 1994), 317–53, here 319–20, 333.
56. See the assessment in Georg Bollenbeck, *Bildung und Kultur: Glanz und Elend eines deutschen Deutungsmusters* (Frankfurt: Suhrkamp, 1996) and Bollenbeck, 'German *Kultur*, the *Bildungsbürgertum*, and its Susceptibility to National Socialism', *German Quarterly*, 73 (2000), 67–83.
57. Compare Thomas Frank, *What's the Matter with Kansas? How Conservatives Won the Heart of America* (New York: Henry Holt, 2004).
58. See the reflections by Thomas Nipperdey, '1933 and the Continuity of German History', in H. W. Koch (ed.), *Aspects of the Third Reich* (Basingstoke: Macmillan, 1985), 489–508.
59. See Moritz Föllmer, 'Which Crisis? Which Modernity? New Perspectives on Weimar Germany', in Jochen Hung, Godela Weiss-Sussex, and Geoff Wilkes (eds), *Beyond Glitter and Doom: The Contingency of the Weimar Republic* (Munich: Iudicium, 2012), 19–30; Dirk Schumann, 'Einheitssehnsucht und Gewaltakzeptanz: Politische Grundpositionen des deutschen Bürgertums nach 1918 (mit vergleichenden Überlegungen zu den britischen Middle Classes)', in Hans Mommsen (ed.), *Der Erste Weltkrieg und die europäische Nachkriegsordnung: Sozialer Wandel und Formveränderung der Politik* (Cologne: Böhlau, 2000), 83–105.
60. Compare the divergent assessments in Hermann Beck, 'The Antibourgeois Character of National Socialism', *Journal of Modern History*, 88 (2016), 572–609, and Norbert Frei (ed.), *Wie bürgerlich war der Nationalsozialismus?* (Göttingen: Wallstein, 2018).

Bibliography

Föllmer, Moritz, *Individuality and Modernity in Berlin: Self and Society from Weimar to the Wall* (Cambridge: Cambridge University Press, 2013).

Fritzsche, Peter, *Rehearsals for Fascism: Populism and Political Mobilization in Weimar Germany* (New York: Oxford University Press, 1990).

Huerkamp, Claudia, *Bildungsbürgerinnen: Frauen im Studium und in akademischen Berufen 1900–1945* (Göttingen: Vandenhoeck & Ruprecht, 1996).

Imhoof, David, *Becoming a Nazi Town: Culture and Politics in Göttingen between the World Wars* (Ann Arbor: University of Michigan Press, 2013).

Jarausch, Konrad H., *The Unfree Professions: German Lawyers, Teachers, and Engineers, 1900–1950* (New York: Oxford University Press, 1990).

Jensen, Erik N., *Body by Weimar: Athletes, Gender, and German Modernity* (New York: Oxford University Press, 2010).

Jones, Larry Eugene, *German Liberalism and the Dissolution of the Weimar Party System 1918–1933* (Chapel Hill, NC: University of North Carolina Press, 1989).

Koshar, Rudy, *Social Life, Local Politics, and Nazism: Marburg, 1880–1935* (Chapel Hill, NC: University of North Carolina Press, 1986).

Matthiesen, Helge, *Bürgertum und Nationalsozialismus in Thüringen: Das bürgerliche Gotha von 1918 bis 1930* (Jena: Gustav Fischer, 1994).

Niewyk, Donald L., *The Jews in Weimar Germany* (Manchester: Manchester University Press, 1980).

Reuveni, Gideon, *Reading Germany: Literature and Consumer Culture in Germany Before 1933* (New York: Berghahn, 2006).

Speier, Hans, *German White-Collar Workers and the Rise of Hitler* (New Haven: Yale University Press, 1986).

CHAPTER 21

THE INDUSTRIAL WORKING CLASS

PAMELA E. SWETT[*]

THE Weimar Republic is closely associated with the industrial working class. After decades in which a working-class identity had strengthened in response to industrialization, urbanization, and the development of Marxist activism through the Social Democratic Party (SPD), working-class soldiers and sailors toppled the monarchy, and their political representatives were at the forefront of the new republic that emerged in 1919. In the years that followed, supported by universal suffrage and the strength of the country's trade unions, German workers stayed front and centre as both participants in and objects of political and economic debate in the Weimar Republic. It is not only because of workers' participation in the fundamental political change of the 1920s that we associate workers with the republic. It is also because of the pronounced interest in working-class daily life in the era's popular culture and vibrant arts scene that we still identify workers and a working-class identity with the Weimar Republic.

In this chapter, the focus is on the social profile of the republic's industrial workers as a group, and not on their political allegiances or on the social policies that supported them. Where did they live and how did they structure their lives? When did they find the term 'worker' or 'working-class' a badge of honour, and in what contexts did such monikers fail to create identity or consensus? The chapter will be divided into three major sections. In the first, workers will be discussed as an occupational group. Who counted as a worker? What sorts of work did they perform? In the second section, workers in their urban environments will be examined, including the daily rhythms and conditions at work and at home. In the final section, the focus will turn to the social and cultural associations that organized workers' leisure time and the novel forms of mass entertainment that were gaining in popularity. Across all three sections the aim will be to show the diversity of experiences that shaped life within the industrial working class. A second aim will be to remind readers that amid this diversity any sense of unity among German workers, vis-à-vis other sectors of society, was also fraught with internal difference, competition, and sometimes discord.

The question of unity or disunity among members of the industrial working class in this volatile period has drawn the attention of scholars since the Weimar Republic itself. Some of the fault lines existed well before 1919—regional and religious differences are key examples, as is gender. Marxism was never fully able to overcome these segmentations and the belief systems that entrenched these differences. Other long-term trends seemed also to be loosening the ties among industrial workers in the first decades of the twentieth century, such as the growing disparity between skilled and unskilled workers and urban and rural environments. The growth of mass culture, which weakened allegiance to worker-specific artistic and leisure activities, and the political discord that divided workers between parties also had important destabilizing effects on working-class identity. Finally, the era's economic turbulence, highlighted by hyperinflation, rationalization, and eventually the Great Depression, further undermined the strength of the industrial working class, as many entered the ranks of the long-term unemployed. All in all, Germany's workers took centre stage in the Weimar Republic like they never had before, and yet they were met with an equally formidable set of provocations. The goal here is to examine the complexity of the category 'industrial worker' to better understand how male and female workers seized these opportunities and faced the era's challenges.

Industrial Worker as an Occupational Category

The founding of the Social Democratic Party in 1875 along with the industrialization of the economy that intensified following the unification of the German nation in 1871 were the main factors in the development of a working-class identity before 1900. Marxism, however, had done more for German workers than simply offering them a framework for understanding the past, analysing present struggles, and imagining political change. It also challenged the churches' authority in the lives of those who were attracted to the political ideology. As we will see later, enough workers would leave the main Christian churches by 1919 that a pronounced secularism coloured many aspects of working-class life by 1933. Another factor that predated the Weimar era, but is central to this story, was the urbanization that accompanied industrialization and shifts in agriculture. In 1871 over 76 per cent of the German population lived in towns and villages with fewer than 5,000 inhabitants, with the vast majority (about 64 per cent) of those living in villages of under 2,000 residents. By 1910 a major demographic shift was under way, which meant that only half of all Germans now lived in communities of less than 5,000 people, and the number living in villages had dropped to 40 per cent.[1] Although the high point for internal migration had been reached around 1910, the trend continued after the First

World War with many young demobilized soldiers choosing to forgo a return to their rural homesteads in favour of new opportunities in the cities, particularly along the Rhine and in the Ruhr valley in the western half of the country.[2]

What other impacts did the First World War have on workers' identity and culture after 1918? Not only had the conflict allowed many men and (a smaller number of) women to see more of the world, making it less attractive to return to village life after 1918. Total war had also made it clear to everyone how important industry was to the nation's future. Industry represented opportunity. The war also led to the politicization of many who felt betrayed by Emperor Wilhelm II and his military leadership, leaving them more suspicious than ever before of nationalism and imperialism, and more deeply aligned with the parties of the left by 1918.[3] The conditions of the defeat also meant that millions of men would leave the military and return to the civilian workforce, which had transformed during the conflict, becoming more productive and more concentrated into large enterprises. The nature of industrial labour had changed during the war, and, given the revolution that arrived on the heels of defeat, there was good reason to believe that working conditions and wages would improve going forward. What's more, many believed the new state owed workers and soldiers, alongside the war widows and orphans, for their service and sacrifice on the battlefield and in the factories.

Let us begin with an overview of those who most likely counted themselves as workers during the Weimar Republic. The 1925 census data show that this social stratum made up about 45 per cent of all men and women in gainful employment. Adding these workers' dependants, the total working class comprised about half of the entire population, or about 32 million in 1925. Only a quarter of these workers and their family members lived in cities. Roughly two-thirds of all workers were employed in industry, with the remaining one-third labouring in agriculture, trade, and commerce.[4] Over four million were organized as members of the powerful ADGB (Confederation of German Trade Unions) in 1930, though this number had declined from a high of over eight million in 1919. Between twelve and fourteen million cast their ballots in support of the two major parties that defined themselves as representing workers' interests: the SPD and the Communist Party (KPD), which together consistently returned 30–40 per cent of all votes in national elections.[5]

To outsiders, the industrial working class appears so homogeneous because of the consistency in terms of the physical labour involved, the social status of manual labourers, and of their presumed political allegiance to the Free Trade Unions and political parties of the left. There were, however, significant differences among workers in terms of lived experience and worldview. For one there was substantial range in terms of the sizes of the factories that employed workers. In 1925, there were still more workers employed in firms with one to five employees (2,837,327) than there were those who worked in firms with more than 1,000 employees (2,109,005). That said, compared to 1907 the percentage of workers in these smallest businesses had declined (from 28.4 down to 22.4 per cent), while those working in the largest factories and mines had increased from 11.9 to 16.6 per cent.[6] These largest employers were clumped in six sectors: mining, machinery, iron and steel, electro-technologies, textiles, and chemical industries.

We also see important variations in the levels of class consciousness, by which we mean the level of awareness by an individual that he or she was part of a working class locked in political struggle against those who held political and economic power. In addition to those who were simply indifferent to the political messaging they encountered, there were also Catholic workers in the Christian Trade Unions and agricultural labourers who remained loyal to the Centre Party or Bavarian People's Party throughout the republican period.[7] A small number of workers organized within the liberal, Hirsch-Duncker unions. A tiny proportion of Protestant blue-collar workers also voted for nationalist parties and were organized within the pro-business 'yellow' trade unions. It is also worth noting that, while voting SPD or KPD was by far the most common political choice among those who considered themselves industrial workers, not everyone who cast their ballots for those parties held a Marxist worldview. Those who did lived almost uniformly in cities over 20,000 residents, worked in a large industrial setting, and had cut ties to Christianity. As historian Heinrich August Winkler once put it, 'in this sense, the majority of workers was class conscious, but only a minority of German society'.[8]

While women's participation as wage labourers was uneven, it was more important than ever. As a result of the immense casualties of the war, there were roughly two million more women than men throughout the republican period, and women made up about three-quarters of the 1.03 million single-person households.[9] Women had always participated heavily on family farms, but this sector was declining. Taking this decline into consideration, women were still entering the workforce at a rate faster than men between the 1907 and 1925 censuses.[10] These gains, however, are largely accounted for by the entrance of women into white-collar work in sales and the growing private- and public-sector bureaucracies. This work was attractive to most women: it was less demanding physically, working conditions were cleaner, and in general these positions were paid slightly better and carried more status. For these reasons, the young women and men who held these positions sometimes came to identify more closely with the middle classes.[11] In the industrial sector, however, women's participation rates had only advanced by 1.9 per cent since 1907, so that by 1925 they made up 20 per cent of the blue-collar labour force. Within this sector, there was great variation: women made up just under 59 per cent of all labourers in the textile industry, but less than 1 per cent in construction. Paper and electrical products manufacturing were also welcoming to female workers, while mining, steel and iron production, and machinery manufacturing remained almost exclusively male domains throughout the Weimar era.[12] Across the manufacturing sector, however, female workers (both skilled and unskilled) earned only about two-thirds of the wages earned by their male counterparts.[13]

Despite the increase in the number of workers employed in larger industrial enterprises, one-third of all Weimar-era workers were employed in non-industrial labour. The largest cohort, the *Landarbeiter*, are discussed elsewhere in this volume. Another substantial sector, Germany's 1.3 million domestic servants, was comprised almost entirely of women, 99 per cent in 1925. The overall numbers of live-in servants had declined sharply since the 1907 census, particularly in terms of the employment of more expensive male servants, a clear result of inflation-period losses among the middle classes. Among those who worked as domestic servants, about two-thirds were between the ages of 18 and 30, and 90 per cent were employed in urban locations. Nannies came in at the bottom of the pay scale; a talented cook earned the most. About 60 per cent of all female servants fell in a middle pay group, earning between 25 and 40 marks per week, which left them well below what women could earn in industrial labour, never mind white-collar salaries. On the one hand, living conditions could be better for this group of workers, depending on the employer. For example, about 95 per cent of female servants had their own bedrooms provided by their employers and living expenses were low. On the other hand, physical and sexual abuse were perennial problems. In addition to women who worked as in-house servants, there were also about 300,000 who served as cleaners or child minders, but lived separately from their employers.[14]

Another distinct group of non-industrial labourers was the *Heimarbeiter* (homeworkers), of whom there were about 406,000 in 1925, up 3.3 per cent from 1907. Traditionally, these were some of Germany's lowest paid workers and their situation did not improve markedly in the republican era. While men were employed in this way, *Heimarbeit* was particularly prevalent among women in cities and rural communities, because they could do the work at home while tending young children. Indeed, as children grew, they were often put to work alongside their parents, and family size in communities that depended on such labour did not decline as fast as elsewhere. In the big cities, like Berlin, finishing work on mass-produced goods was often handled this way, such as sewing appliques on to textiles. In the countryside, there were whole regions known for *Heimarbeit*, the most famous being Thuringia's toy-making communities. The land here was not as fertile as elsewhere, and there were no major markets nearby or efficient transportation corridors, and so residents had long sought income supplements to farming. And given the poverty and isolation of these workers, no care was taken to provide healthy working conditions. In many cases, whole families were thus exposed to harmful chemicals and dust, as the investigative reports of Alexander Graf Stenbock-Fermor and others famously showed in this period.[15]

Beyond these categories of wage labour, sex work was also an option for women looking to make ends meet. And while some prostitutes declared sex work as their chief form of employment, when questioned by police or reformers, most called themselves workers, and referenced other recent or concurrent employment. In one well-known study of prostitution in Leipzig from 1932, of the 3,600 prostitutes' police files examined, 1,025 described themselves as workers and 428 listed 'domestic worker' when filling out the questionnaire. Further evidence that many women moved in and out of the sex trade, depending on the stability of other work, is the fact that the author of the Leipzig study saw seasonal changes in the arrest records of some of the women. For example, women who also worked as domestic servants were rarely questioned by police in December, when holiday preparations and events kept them in demand, but in April the numbers of arrests of female servants for prostitution offences more than doubled.[16]

Finally, it is important to say a few words about the close to one million industrial and craftwork apprentices who toiled in Germany in 1925. About half of them, reports Heinrich August Winkler, would go on to become skilled labourers in the metal, textiles, and wood crafts industries and develop a sense of belonging as members of the industrial working class. The rest would go on to become journeymen in the 1.3 million independent craft firms that existed in the middle part of the decade—in the hope of eventually reaching master status and becoming self-employed. Most of these men would see themselves as part of the old middle class that also included shopkeepers, self-employed craftsmen, and civil servants.[17]

WORK-LIFE AND HOME-LIFE

The early days of the republic were optimistic ones for workers. One of the first dramatic results of the post-war period was the Stinnes-Legien agreement between the major employers' associations and trade unions on 15 November 1918. Among its twelve points were the recognition of the trade unions as the elected representatives of the employees, the codification of the eight-hour day, the election of works councils (*Betriebsräte*) in all factories employing at least fifty workers to monitor working conditions, and the creation of arbitration boards to negotiate collective agreements with equal representation between workers and employers.[18] The SPD seemed to be following through in its effort to stabilize the political situation, and industrial production reflected this optimism—up 45 per cent between 1920 and 1921, followed by a further climb the following year. Despite the demobilization of millions of soldiers, and the promise to welcome them back into their previous positions, in the spring of 1922 the unemployment rate for trade union members stood at a record low of 0.9 per cent.[19]

However, these signs that appeared to forecast a healthy economy moving forward were in fact simply evidence of the inflation that was brewing. While the inflation would soon reach cataclysmic proportions, striking hardest among the middle classes, particularly those living on fixed incomes and those whose savings were liquid rather than propertied, workers also suffered.[20] On average workers had less real income in the early post-war years than they had in 1913, and purchasing power evaporated.[21] Unemployment also increased rapidly. Reaching an annual average of 10 per cent among trade union members in 1922, jumping to about 25 per cent by fall 1923, with another 15 per cent of union members working shortened hours.[22] Real income also declined through 1923 for those who still enjoyed employment. By the autumn of 1923 workers were taking home on average 70 per cent of 1913's real wages.[23]

Violence broke out periodically in response to the crisis, including vandalism and looting of shops, as well as raids on farmers' fields.[24] The inflation also meant the end of the coalition government that included the SPD, and the emergency measures taken by the government included a weakening of the eight-hour day, so critical to workers as a symbol of what the republic had achieved for them. The hyperinflation also had real health outcomes, with cases of tuberculosis and rickets skyrocketing as a result of declining living conditions and diet.[25] This last point is captured well by looking at slaughter house data across the inflation crisis. In the first post-war years (1919–21), the numbers of processed cattle, pigs, and sheep remained consistently below 1913 levels. Only the butchering of horse meat surpassed pre-war levels, far outpacing the data for 1913 in 1922. The reliance on horse meat fell back in 1923, but not because conditions were improving. Instead, the slaughtering of dogs became far more common, with more than double the number of animals reported slaughtered in 1923, compared to the last year before the war.[26] Luckily for workers, who still devoted a larger percentage of their monthly earnings to rent and food, the state had kept the war-era price controls on basic foodstuffs in place as well as the strict rent controls. Without these safeguards, the consequences for workers in terms of health outcomes would have been catastrophic.

Historians have also argued that the chaos of the hyperinflation had important psychological consequences for all Germans, including workers. It meant that all Germans felt their positions in society were under threat and greatly curtailed their ability to plan for the future (even in the short term).[27] In the immediate aftermath of the stabilization of the currency in 1924, workers saw improvement regarding their employment. Unemployment among trade union members declined from 12.4 per cent in July to 7.3 per cent in November of 1924.[28] The introduction of the Dawes Plan also had immediate positive effects on workers' wages, which stabilized at 12 percent below pre-war levels by 1925.[29] Nonetheless, it would be 1928 before workers' average real wages would surpass 1913 levels. This success, however, was short-lived, as real wages dropped below the last pre-war year once again by 1932 in response to the global Depression. In the years following the inflation, workers did not have much success regaining the eight-hour workday and the bilateral cooperation at the heart of the Stinnes-Legien agreement never rematerialized. In May 1924, the ADGB reported that almost 55 per cent of its members worked more than forty-eight hours per week, including 13 per cent who clocked on average more than fifty-four hours per week.[30] It would take cutbacks in production during the Depression before workers generally returned to an average of around forty-eight hours of paid work per week.[31]

The big question remains, however. To what extent did workers' wages keep up with living costs? In other words, did Germany's workers benefit materially from the republican order in the years before the Depression? The Statistical Reich Office reported an increase in national income of 8 per cent by 1929 over 1913. Heinrich August Winkler cautioned, however, that three considerations must be factored into our assessment of this figure. The overall population had grown. Per person the increase only amounts to about 1 per cent. Second, the age distribution had also altered in significant ways. The losses of the war and the declining birthrate in the 1920s meant that the population was older overall with fewer dependants. Third, the loss of capital through reparations must also be factored in. The resulting calculation reveals that the purchasing power per person in 1928 was actually about 8 per cent below the 1913 level.[32]

Beyond these macro-economic developments, there were other changes to industrial labour practices that influenced how workers measured satisfaction and opportunity. One important development was the steps taken to rationalize the factory floor in the second half of the 1920s. Textiles and electrical products manufacturing were two of the more frequently rationalized industries. Automated production lines and other forms of mechanization became common in both sectors by the end of the decade. To some extent these reforms were welcomed by workers, who associated them with opportunities for cleaner and safer working conditions. There was also hope that greater productivity would translate into higher wages. The results, however, were mixed at best, as the sociologist Erich Fromm established in a 1929 survey of industrial workers.[33] Workers did find that some of the more dangerous work in the steel and chemical industries, for example, was alleviated through the use of mechanized lifts and conveyor belts. Better lighting also surely made for safer workspaces.[34] On the other hand, Wolfgang Zollitsch finds that such reforms challenged workers, some of whom struggled under new conditions that included greater outputs and faster paced work.[35] As one respondent to the Fromm survey of workers put it: 'One has to hurry all the time. People become very nervous, bad-tempered and develop resistance to their work.'[36] The rationalization process, where it was implemented, also meant fewer opportunities for upward mobility for those entering the workforce. Given the new time-structured processes, many firms moved to piece-rate wage plans, which workers generally found did not translate into significant increases over their former hourly wages. More importantly, perhaps, those who found themselves laid off because they could not keep up with the new production rates tended to be the older, highly skilled, and best paid workers.[37] The downsizing of the workforce that accompanied many rationalization efforts meant that unemployment averaged around 10 per cent even in the best years of the republic, 1924–9.[38] Overall the wage gap between skilled and unskilled widened slightly as a result of the rationalization of industry in the latter 1920s.[39] For workers in smaller factories and workshops, however, the rationalization of tasks and time was far less noticeable.

Alongside the widening wage gap—some skilled workers took home three times as much as some unskilled industrial labourers, who in turn earned more than domestic servants or *Heimarbeiter*—the level of independence experienced by workers also varied greatly. Large sectors of the labouring population, including most agricultural labourers, apprentices and journeymen, servants, and *Heimarbeiter* still relied heavily on the fairness of their employers, despite laws that had meant to overturn centuries of oppression. This is not to say that industrial workers in Germany's cities were fully secure or free, despite the protections afforded by trade union membership. As has been noted, rationalization and the unstable economic landscape left many workers feeling vulnerable, even highly skilled workers. Female labourers, in particular, in all sectors also still faced severe limitations to their advancement, combined with wage inequality, and other forms of gender-based workplace harassment. While this section has maintained that great variation existed in workplace conditions, at times weakening solidarity, its remaining paragraphs demonstrate that there may have been more that united members of the industrial working class in the domestic sphere.

At the start of the republican era, the Reich Statistics Office estimated that the country lacked as many as 1.5 million residential dwellings.[40] It is not surprising that overcrowding was characteristic of most workers' neighbourhoods. The size and quality of workers' flats were also problematic. Of the 4.5 million apartments in the country's forty-six cities with more than 100,000 inhabitants in 1927, only 320,000 were built after the First World War. And just over half of all apartments in these same urban centres were small, between one and three rooms.⁴¹ About 20 per cent of all households included additional family members or subtenants, both single persons and whole families, beyond the tenant and his/her dependants.⁴² As might be expected, the most crowded were the smallest apartments. One-room apartments had an average occupancy rate close to two people per room. While there was significant regional variation, one study of vocational school students in Essen reported that 108 of 142 students surveyed shared a bed.⁴³ On average a five-member working German family in 1925 had to make do with 1.4 rooms, a far tighter situation than similar sized families would have faced in either France or England at the time.⁴⁴ But it was not just the size of the pre-war apartments that caused distress, it was also the shortage of basic amenities. Only half of all pre-1914 built apartments had their own toilets, and 40 per cent of households had to make use of communal toilets somewhere within the building. The remaining 10 per cent only had access to facilities located in the tenement courtyards. Rent control on pre-war dwellings had been introduced during the high inflationary year of 1922, and additional legislation followed in 1923 to limit landlords' abilities to evict tenants.⁴⁵ As Richard Bessel has commented, 'the major challenge was gaining access to a dwelling, not paying for it'.⁴⁶ These legal measures helped Germans of lower means stay in their homes, but they also served as a disincentive to build new units or improve existing ones.

While the vast majority of new apartments included toilets, as well as other amenities, these residences were still too few in number and in most cases were beyond the means of working-class families. Unskilled workers regularly spent about 10 per cent of family income on rent, but they would need to devote up to 45 per cent of their annual income to cover rent and taxes for a home in one of the new buildings.⁴⁷ Even some skilled workers were priced out of the new dwellings, including the large housing blocks by progressive architects like Bruno Taut. Richard Bessel's dictum does not always apply, therefore, when it comes to the small number of new dwellings erected in these years. Despite the democratic changes that came to Germany after 1919, industrial paternalism continued as a way to counter the strength of the trade unions and bind workers to their employers. Company-owned or subsidized housing was highly sought after, even though such rental contracts still frequently contained clauses that prohibited 'immoral' or 'radical' behaviour.⁴⁸ Other benefits sometimes accrued with time and evidence of good service, like paid holidays after five years of employment.

Food was the largest single expenditure, eating up almost half of working households' incomes, around 2,500 marks annually. Even workers in higher income brackets spent over 40 per cent of income on food. Within this category, the average working household spent the most on meat products, followed by bread and other baked goods, milk, non-butter fats, butter, and potatoes. But that does not mean meat was eaten daily. It was rather saved for the Sunday meal, and all told the average working-class family ate only about one pound of meat products per week, compared to 9 kg of potatoes per week. These data illustrate 'the difference between the everyday diet and the Sunday dinner'.⁴⁹ About 10 per cent of the food budget went to *Genußmittel*, or stimulants in this context. Expenditures on alcohol made up about 60 per cent of this category, though that total may be too low because beer and spirits were purchased for the home but also consumed at local pubs and clubs. Tobacco use was also part of almost all working-class household budgets, representing over a third of expenditures in the *Genußmittel* category.[50]

Finally, it is worth noting that, just as we saw purchasing power lagging behind pre-war rates, food consumption too fell off, particularly through the first half of the 1920s. For example, meat consumption per person did not reach 1912 levels until 1925. Beer consumption dropped a whopping 44 per cent between 1900 and 1925, though this decline was not solely owing to affordability.[51] For one, the quality of beer had declined precipitously, owing to shortages in ingredients during the war that lingered after 1918. In addition, teetotalist and life reform movements advocated against alcohol consumption, with some impact on workers' behaviour.[52] It is worth emphasizing that hunger remained a common experience for many in the inter-war years. Working-class budgets were simply not elastic enough to handle emergency expenditures and life was full of them. Sporadic hunger and in worse cases pervasive hunger remained a regular strain on families and individual health, particularly after the start of the Great Depression in 1929.[53]

Some general trends in household budgeting and planning become visible as incomes increase. Workers in the highest income bracket, those earning about 4,000 marks per year, spent a smaller share on food and rent, the two most basic necessities. This freed them up to spend more on the following categories: clothing, education, household decoration, and miscellaneous items.[54] One factor that significantly altered a household's budget was the number of people who contributed to it. Many of the poorest families were held back by the fact that small children needed to be cared for, limiting the mother's ability to take much paid work. Even then, some mending or washing for others was often included in the mother's daily tasks. As the children got older, it was more likely that the mother could take on waged labour for longer periods outside the home, and older children could eventually earn for the family as well.[55] Over time in this fashion most families could increase substantially the total wages coming into the household. When unemployment, illness, or injury struck, many families turned to subtenants to help recoup lost wages.

As was true across German society, workers were starting to limit the size of their families in these years, particularly in the cities. While urban dwellers with more resources may have sought to invest in the education and cultural experiences of a smaller number of children, for poorer workers crowded housing conditions, pressures on food supply, and the need for mothers to return to work were all disincentives to establishing large families.[56] Family planning and the use of contraception across all classes was increasing in the 1920s, and the annual abortion rate, despite illegality, was estimated to have reached one million by 1930.[57] The consequences of these trends were clear: by the 1933 census two-thirds of all married women had fewer than three children.[58] Reforms to education benefited workers' families, including mandatory primary schooling for all children, which led to further innovation particularly in Social Democratic states that put more attention on active learning, moving away from the strict discipline, religiosity, and rigid rote learning of the past.[59] The percentage of workers' marriages that produced no children also rose from 6.7 per cent for marriages begun in 1904 to as much as 25.9 per cent of marriages that took place between 1925 and 1929.[60]

The biggest blow to living standards often followed the loss of work. Rates of unemployment increased steadily in the latter part of the 1920s, in part due to efforts to cut labour costs through rationalization. This trend began well before the US stock market crash of 1929, German banking crisis of 1931, or worldwide Depression that accompanied those events. Before the onset of the Depression, therefore, there was already a sense that workers were being divided not just by skill, but between 'the steadily employed and the chronically and casually unemployed'.[61] The largest Depression-era tally of registered unemployed in Germany was 6,128,000, as reported in February 1932, though observers noted that at least another million should be added to this sum—men and women who no longer bothered to register as unemployed.[62]

German workers had been promised that the republic would build a public welfare safety net to take care of their needs in crisis. The unemployment insurance that was the central pillar of this system was introduced in 1927, but the scale of the economic crisis that washed over Germany after 1929 made it impossible to maintain. Unemployment affected as much as 40 per cent of the labour force at its highest point, and many men and women exhausted the available unemployment insurance and the supplemental emergency relief available from their local communities. Facing months and even years of further unemployment, many experienced steadily declining living conditions. In other words, the long-term unemployed were cumulatively worse off than those who had recently lost their job and could still draw from public support, personal savings and support from kin. As one contemporary report indicated, the consequences of long-term unemployment were made bare in data demonstrating shifting consumption habits. In the winter of 1932/33, unemployed Germans consumed about half of the meat that the same group had eaten in 1927/28, and three times as much potatoes as five years earlier. Butter and fruit had disappeared entirely from their diets.[63] The despair engendered by the crisis affected all aspects of life, leaving many of the long-term unemployed with little hope or motivation. The famous sociological study of life in the depressed Austrian town of Marienthal, for example, found that at the workers' library 'the number of loans dropped from 1929 to 1931 by 49 per cent', even though the fees for checking out books had been eliminated.[64]

Housing too became a challenge for the long-term unemployed. Conditions were exacerbated by the pre-existing housing shortage, and policies under the Brüning administration to deregulate the market, which led to higher rental prices and large numbers of evictions. The situation was compounded further by the drying up of new investment once the financial crisis struck. Families moved in with relatives or friends, which often meant overcrowding that compromised hygiene and increased the chances of disease. When such arrangements were no longer possible, the unemployed became homeless. There was limited emergency housing run by municipalities, but others found shelter in squats, tent cities, and in tiny buildings on urban garden plots. In 1931, 30,000 homeless Germans were estimated to be living in tent camps in Berlin alone, as depicted in the famous film from that year, *Kuhle Wampe*.[65] The remaining alternatives, which some young men chose, were to hit the road in search of work and to while away the time or take up a free cot in one of the radical political parties' local offices, meeting spaces, or 'barracks'. Both the Communist Party and Nazi Party gained new supporters in the last years of the Weimar Republic by providing material and social support to local unemployed men.[66] Beyond those options, religious charities still helped care for the needy.

The fact that long-term unemployment, and the deprivation that followed, disproportionately affected male workers of 18 to 30 years of age, should not be underestimated.[67] Many seeking apprenticeships in the 1920s would never secure them. In 1930, for example, 793,000 school-leavers were competing for only 290,000 apprenticeships.[68] And even among the lucky few who secured and completed an apprenticeship in the latter part of the decade, many would never make their way into their chosen trades. Their inability to establish financial independence also meant that more remained in their parents' households and delayed starting families of their own. The hopelessness generated among Germany's young men in this situation ultimately can be linked to the growth of radical political movements, namely the Communist and Nazi Party, and the violence that plagued Germany's cities in the last years of the republic.[69]

Workers' Culture

Workers' culture is a multifaceted concept—it involves more than just the formal organizations and associations that sought to reflect the needs and interests of a highly politicized working class. It encompasses older traditions that in some cases predate industrialization and ran counter to the socialist standards of belief and behaviour, such as the initiation rites that journeymen in many crafts still performed. It also includes the particular quotidian rhythms of everyday life. For example, the repertoires of the comedic and musical groups who performed for residents in the cities' tenement courtyards would have been unfamiliar to members of the middle classes, but such well-trodden routines based on insider-knowledge of life in those very tenements helped build and sustain working-class communities. As should be clear by now, workers were a diverse group. Thus, they identified with different elements of workers' culture to differing degrees, depending on individual preferences and changing circumstances. Regional differences, available resources, age, and gender, among other defining characteristics, all played a part in how an individual responded to and shaped his or her own lifeworld.

In Detlev Peukert's classic study of youth in Weimar Germany, we get a glimpse of the diversity of industrial working families' lifestyles. Through a variety of primary source materials, Peukert illustrates the existence of a range of relationships within urban industrial families not so different from those we would find today.[70] Meagre incomes, tight living quarters, and in some cases fathers missing either as a consequence of war or because their days were filled by long hours at the workbench or evenings at the pub, were routine experiences for many in Germany's industrial working class in this period. But such challenges did not always mean families were 'broken' or radicalized. Rather, Peukert emphasized the diversity of attitudes and behaviours. Some families were extraordinarily close, with members of all ages contributing to survival via waged work, housework, or child minding. Other young people showed fatalistic resolve about fallen fathers and respect for their mothers who kept households running. Some families with greater resources had more options to consider when it came to education, leisure pursuits, such as theatre and musical concerts, and even health and nutrition, but these advantages did not always protect a family unit from discord owing to authoritarian—and sometimes violent—fathers, illness or injury, or tensions occasioned by young adults straining for more independence from parental control. Nonetheless, most families found time for activities beyond work. When possible, free time was found in the evenings and on Sunday afternoons for trips to the allotment, hikes, visits to relatives and friends, or strolls around fairgrounds and amusement parks. On their own, many workers read, played instruments, and engaged in craft projects.[71]

Women, whether they had full-time paid labour, casual employment, or no paid work, faced the biggest challenge finding fully free time. Sundays offered the best chance for relaxation, but even then preparing meals, minding the children, and other household chores were likely to occupy much of the day.[72] One entrant in a 1928 writing contest, which asked female textile workers to describe their workdays and weekends, questioned the whole premise of the task, asking 'Is there a weekend for the harried textile worker?' Saturdays are filled with 'washing, sewing, etc', and Sunday mornings are similarly 'filled with work', she explained. Only on Sunday afternoons was this single woman able to find a few hours of 'well-earned rest', though she insisted that married colleagues with children 'know no weekend'.[73] For many men, the local pub continued to play an important role in daily life. Alcohol consumption had declined compared to the pre-1914 period, but regular visits to the pub remained a mark of male privilege in workers' communities. Alcohol undoubtedly was used to combat the drudgery of long, exhausting days of labour, but the pub was equally important as a largely homo-social space in which men could relax, play cards, share information, and for those so inclined, mobilize politically. One characteristic of the local pub was that men from a range of workers' occupations might meet, introducing some diversity into conversation.[74] By the early 1930s, however, as the political landscape became more polarized, some pubs chose to align with a specific political party. In such cases, these pubs came to serve as meeting spaces for party business, and even as launching pads for attacks on political rivals.[75]

Many of the formal workers' social and cultural organizations and associations of the 1920s had their roots in the pre-1914 era, developing in the years after the anti-socialist laws were lifted in 1890. At that time the SPD worked tirelessly to organize members, as a way to differentiate and foster a separate, secular, and Marxist culture. By the start of the twentieth century, 'Social Democracy was rightly seen as akin to a full-dress alternative society'.[76] In the republican years, 'association mania ... shaped virtually all aspects of life' across German society.[77] The biggest workers' associations were connected to sport.

In 1928 over 1.2 million men and women belonged to one of the eleven affiliated branches of the Zentralkommission für Arbeitersport und Körperpflege (Central Commission for Workers' Sport and Hygiene). While the movement had no formal connection to the SPD, it had emerged specifically as a counter to the middle-class gymnastics clubs that had expelled social democrats and other insufficiently patriotic workers in the nineteenth century. The purge encouraged other socialists to leave on their own—and together they saw themselves as representing an alternative community.[78] The physical presence of the organization was felt through the extensive facilities that it managed in working-class districts: 249 gyms, 1,265 sport fields with adjoining locker rooms and meeting spaces, about 100 sites for swimming, and over 200 homes and huts in the countryside to welcome hikers seeking a respite, or even overnight lodging.[79] Despite having no formal party affiliation, about 75 per cent of members were supporters of the SPD and even more (88 per cent) were trade union members.[80] In general, the association was comprised of men and women in skilled labour positions. Participation in these SPD-friendly workers' athletic clubs, however, did not always translate into class consciousness. In one example from Hamburg, several talented football players, including Erwin, the father of the legendary Uwe Seeler, left their workers' club to play for a more competitive 'bourgeois' club in 1932, only to be labelled 'class traitors' in the local SPD newspaper.[81] This anecdote reminds us that individual workers were motivated by many factors, not only a sense of their class belonging. That these skilled players would be accepted on to a bourgeois team indicates further that a commitment to hard class boundaries was fading in some segments of the middle class as well.

As the 1920s wore on, however, the irreconcilable differences that had erupted between the SPD and KPD meant that rivalry was no longer directed solely at the bourgeoisie, but also existed within the ranks of the workers' associations and clubs. Both parties claimed to more accurately and authentically represent workers' needs and desires, both socially and politically. In 1929 the umbrella group Kampfgemeinschaft für Rote Sporteinheit (Association for Fighting for Red Sporting Unity), was established and Communist athletes, particularly in the Ruhr and other cities with strong KPD representation, like Berlin and Hamburg, began switching their clubs and teams over to the new network. Officially as many as 100,000 joined the Red Sport association, but the percentage of young and unemployed members was high in the early 1930s, which limited their participation and ability to pay dues. Similar divisions happened in other workers' cultural organizations as well, so where there had once been a Workers' Choral Club, there now existed an SPD-aligned Workers' Choral Club and a rival Communist-aligned Revolutionary Workers' Choral Club. This division not only weakened the opportunities for political rapprochement, it also meant greater social isolation. And as the smaller Communist-aligned groups tended to attract a younger membership and a less skilled one, cross-generational community building and potential mentorship opportunities were lost.

Catholic workers' associations, trade unions, and political allegiance to the Centre Party and BVP also dated back to the nineteenth century, and not unlike the socialist milieu grew under Bismarck's oppression. In the Weimar era, however, the very close identification with local parishes and their priests weakened, particularly among Catholic industrial workers, and Catholic bishops told local priests that they could withhold the sacraments from workers who supported Social Democracy.[82] Church attendance declined, owing to the general secularization of society and the particular anti-religious attitude of the Marxist parties and trade unions, but many Catholic workers continued to socialize in a Catholic milieu and participate in Catholic social clubs.[83] Nationally, support for the Centre party remained relatively stable during the 1920s, particularly among female adherents.[84] However, among industrial workers Centre Party support was largely confined to the cities of the Ruhr and Rhineland, where large numbers of Polish workers in these communities created Catholic enclaves with their own networks and associations. Elsewhere Catholic workers organized in the Christian Trade Unions and Catholic workers' associations were increasingly drawn to the SPD.

There were also Protestant workers, particularly in central and northern Germany, who did not leave their churches, even though for many Christian beliefs and rituals had lost their relevance. Some of the more consciously agnostic or atheistic workers also joined the Free Thinkers movement.[85] The hope was to build a moral community-minded set of rituals outside of a Christian framework. Ostensibly humanist in intent with little connection to politics, by the end of the decade some Communists sought to politicize the movement's activities. Other organizations and lifestyle trends under the umbrella of life reform were also popular among workers who sought to improve their physical health, strengthen their mental resolve, and find fulfilling leisure pursuits through nudism, dance and exercise, vegetarianism, and teetotalism.

Studies of reading habits indicate that workers mirrored the rest of society in devoting a steady, if small, proportion of their income to the purchase of books and newspapers, and that the overall outlay on reading materials grew in the 1920s. Books remained an expensive purchase for most workers, which limited their acquisition, but magazines and newspapers had become part of every household's weekly budget.[86] As Weimar's crises became more pronounced, newspapers also grew to reflect the divide within workers' neighbourhoods, with major dailies and local newspapers most often representing the party line of either the KPD or SPD. But it also appears that most German workers had access to more than one paper and so diversity of opinion was still transmitted this way. The Communist Willi Münzenberg was successful, for example, in publishing the *Arbeiter-Illustrierte-Zeitung (AIZ)*, which workers across the party divide read, as well as managing a series of smaller newspapers, presses, and movie theatres. The *AIZ* was first released in 1924, but reached over 300,000 copies by the end of the decade. It claimed in 1929 that '42% of its readership was skilled workers, 33 per cent were unskilled and 10 percent were white-collar workers'. The remaining 15 per cent were made up of youngsters, housewives, and other self-employed and middle-class readers.[87] Independent local newspapers also continued to be printed throughout the 1920s, and some workers additionally read the national papers, like the *Vossische Zeitung*, that represented middle-class liberal or even conservative viewpoints. The Communist Party also sought to attract new voters with cultural offerings that entertained as much as they taught about revolution. 'Red revues' as well as agitprop theatre, and films like *Mutter Krausens Fahrt ins Glück* (Mother Krause's trip to happiness, 1929), encouraged a sense of solidarity among workers while also serving as popular leisure time activities.[88]

Beyond and, indeed, at times in contrast to the workers' associations and clubs that grew out of the political divides in Imperial Germany, the 1920s also offered new forms of mass culture that challenged the boundaries between workers and some of the middle classes. The most significant entrants into the popular culture landscape in the 1920s were film and radio. Film was as affordable as it was exciting—and young Berlin workers surveyed in 1929 were similar across industrial sectors, skill levels, and gender in choosing a visit to the local *Kino* more consistently than any other outing as a way to spend their scarce free time and entertainment budgets.[89] Going for a walk was the second most likely option, and a trip to a dance hall followed in third among female workers, though men were less inclined to spend their time this way.[90] While the workers' parties did support film production with political messages in this era, the most popular films tended to be those with cross-class appeal, often originating from Hollywood. The comedies of Buster Keaton and Charlie Chaplin, for example, were universal favourites.[91]

Dance halls too were becoming more of a mass culture experience, with new styles of popular music and trendy dances to match, which began to push the boundaries of class division as well as gender norms. Jazz, for example, had its supporters—and detractors—across class identities; it was age that most clearly determined acceptance or rejection. Young Germans were the most ready to embrace new sounds.[92] Radio took a little longer to get integrated into workers' households—the radio sets and subscription fees were beyond the budgets of many workers throughout the decade. In 1927 a survey of subscribers found that 22.5 per cent were industrial workers, though more would have had access to radio programming in workplace canteens, neighbourhood pubs, and other communal spaces.[93] The Workers' Radio Association aimed to encourage radio listening while maintaining a sense of working-class identity in radio programming.[94] Radio broadcasts filled the airwaves for about ten hours a day. Listening time increased to eighteen hours on Sundays—a sign that radio had become an important part of Sunday's leisure practices. One typical schedule was comprised of about 50 per cent music with the other half of airtime devoted to lectures, news, and advertisements. Of the musical programming about one-third of content was considered 'light entertainment', while the rest was devoted to more 'demanding' artistic content.[95] Historian Corey Ross speculates that the slow pace at which popular music and other 'light entertainment' took the place of more educational listening may have been a further reason why German workers were slow to purchase sets for their homes.[96]

Spectator sport became a mass commodity in the inter-war era, which male workers consumed alongside the men of the middle classes. Boxing and football were particularly popular as spectator sports, as was car racing. Large-scale events like the Workers' Olympics staged in Frankfurt in 1925 offered both a mass spectacle and venue for recognizing workers' athletic achievements.[97] Fans of all sports could follow the ups and downs of their favourite teams and competitors in the daily press, illustrated weeklies, and in sport-specific magazines. In this way reading complemented the growth of other mass leisure pursuits across all classes.[98] And, finally, while men were the greatest consumers of sport, it was in the Weimar era that women, including working-class women, became more closely identified as consumers. The illustrated press and other forms of advertising sought the attention of working-class wives and mothers, and younger women as well, with a whole host of exciting products that promised to create happiness and good health. While many new products were beyond the means of working women, particularly the new durable goods like labour-saving household appliances, there was a large assortment of inexpensive items available that invited women to participate in society as consumers, rather than workers, and to identify in this way, which had the potential to blur class boundaries.[99]

Conclusion

The revolutionary spirit of 1918 and the new republican constitution ratified the following year appeared to open the door for further democratization, economic reform, and the blossoming of new forms of art and culture in Germany. In many ways, legal reforms and shifting attitudes in the post-war years did benefit the country's industrial workers. Politically, they had more rights than ever before. There was greater attention paid to popular forms of cultural expression, and a new respect for the struggles of daily life shaped public discourse. But other struggles were real and on close inspection it is also evident that, despite political reform and the social and cultural openness of the era, the gains made by workers were limited. Instability with regard to wages and employment was a drag on confidence. Parliamentary victories were short-lived. Beyond such obvious structural challenges, however, the material presented in this chapter has also made the case that 'industrial workers' never comprised a fully unified social class with identical needs or desires. Some were beginning to aspire to the middle class. Others held on to Christian values and associations. Rivalries existed between coworkers over skills and status. Women and men lived very different lives. The main workers' political parties, the SPD and KPD, remained deadlocked on fundamental issues. And rural workers had little in common with those in the tenements of the metropolises. On top of all of these long-standing differences, the coming of new forms of mass culture also pulled on the loyalties of workers to any singular identity. In all its early manifestations mass culture began to tap into commonalities within German society across class divides; it also began to offer a language of personal consumption and pleasure that reached across national borders.

Amid these changing circumstances, workers in Germany charted many paths. One road they did not take in large numbers was the one that led to participation in the early waves of support for National Socialism. That said, historic allegiance to the parties and associations of the political left did not leave all workers immune to Nazism. Just as we have seen here through other examples, responses by workers to National Socialism also covered the full spectrum of belief and experience. The economic instability during the republican era, and its intensification after 1929 compounded the forces already weakening working-class unity. Considering both these long-standing differences and contemporary challenges, it was never likely that Germany's workers would pose a unified front to National Socialism. We should not be surprised, therefore, that by 1933 some workers were willing to forgo the gains made in terms of political rights and freedoms for the stability the new ruling party promised. Others put their heads down and continued to struggle to make ends meet and live their lives, indifferent to or in spite of the emerging Third Reich. And others remained resistant and willing to face the brutal consequences of such a stance under Hitler's dictatorship. This range of responses makes sense only when we recognize the diversity of experience that represented life within the industrial working class during the Weimar Republic.

Notes

* Many thanks to Ryan Heyden for his help compiling materials for this chapter and to the two co-editors, Nadine Rossol and Benjamin Ziemann, for their superb advice throughout the writing process.
1. Volker R. Berghahn, *Modern Germany: Economy, Society and Politics in the Twentieth Century* (Cambridge: Cambridge University Press, 1982), statistical appendix, table 2, 271.
2. Steve Hochstadt, 'Migration and Industrialization in Germany, 1815–1977', *Social Science History*, 5 (1981), 445–68, see in particular figure 2, 452.
3. Wolfgang Kruse, 'Krieg und Klassenheer: Zur Revolutionierung der deutschen Armee im Ersten Weltkrieg', *Geschichte und Gesellschaft*, 22 (1996), 530–61; Richard Bessel, *Germany after the First World War* (Oxford: Clarendon Press, 1993) and Belinda Davis, *Home Fires Burning: Food, Politics, and Daily Life in World War One Berlin* (Chapel Hill, NC: UNC Press, 2000).
4. Heinrich August Winkler, *Der Schein der Normalität: Arbeiter und Arbeiterbewegung in der Weimarer Republik 1924 bis 1930* (Berlin: J. H. W. Dietz, 1985), 19; and Hans-Ulrich Wehler, *Deutsche Gesellschaftsgeschichte, 1914–1949*, 2nd ed. (Munich: C. H. Beck, 2003), 310.
5. Gunther Mai, *Die Weimarer Republik* (Munich: C. H. Beck, 2018), 74. While Mai offers the ADBG membership of 4.7 million this includes white-collar workers, or *Angestellten*, in the AfA. If we exclude that sector, about 4.1 million ADGB members are left. See table 2 in Gerard Braunthal, *Der allgemeine deutsche Gewerkschaftsbund* (Cologne: Bund Verlag, 1981), 135.
6. Winkler, *Schein*, 23.
7. On the cooperation and rivalry between the Christian and Free Trade unions in the 1920s see William L. Patch, *Christian Democratic Workers and the Forging of German Democracy, 1920–1980* (Cambridge: Cambridge University Press, 2018), ch. 2.
8. Heinrich August Winkler, *Weimar 1918–1933: Die Geschichte der ersten deutschen Demokratie* (Munich: C. H. Beck, 1993), 290. For more on the social composition of the largest workers' party, the SPD, and its electorate, see Donna Harsch, *German Social Democracy and the Rise of Nazism* (Chapel Hill, NC: UNC Press, 1993), 28–32.

9. Tim Mason, 'Women in Germany, 1925–1940: Family, Welfare and Work', in Tim Mason and Jane Caplan (eds), *Nazism, Fascism and the Working Class* (Cambridge: Cambridge University Press, 1995), 131–211, here 135. See also Karen Hagemann, *Frauenalltag und Männerpolitik: Alltagsleben und gesellschaftliches Handeln von Arbeiterfrauen in der Weimarer Republik* (Bonn: J. H. W. Dietz, 1990).
10. Winkler, *Schein*. Winkler reports that the number of wage labourers had increased by 27.2% over 1907, while accounting for a 13.5% rise in the overall population. When we break down the new workers by gender, women had seen a jump of 35.5%, while the rate of increase for men was only 23.2%. *Schein*, 17.
11. See the chapter in this volume by Moritz Föllmer.
12. Winkler, *Schein*, 14–19.
13. Ibid., 51.
14. Ibid., 109.
15. Ibid., 105–6.
16. Victoria Harris, *Selling Sex in the Reich: Prostitutes in Germany Society, 1914–1945* (New York: Oxford University Press, 2010), 53–5.
17. Winkler, *Schein*, 110. See also the chapter by Moritz Föllmer in this volume.
18. German History in Documents and Images, German Historical Institute, 'Stinnes-Legien Agreement' at http://ghdi.ghi-dc.org/sub_document.cfm?document_id=4015 (accessed 15 June 2020).
19. Winkler, *Weimar*, 143.
20. The perceived 'leveling' of society that accompanied the hyperinflation was a particularly bitter pill for the middle classes to swallow. For a taste see Eric Weitz, *Weimar Germany: Promise and Tragedy* (Princeton: Princeton University Press, 2007), 136–8.
21. Winkler, *Weimar*, 145.
22. Jürgen Freiherr von Kruedener, 'Die Entstehung des Inflationstraumas', in Gerald Feldman et al. (eds), *Konsequenzen der Inflation* (Berlin: Colloquium Verlag, 1989), 213–86, here 225.
23. Winkler, *Weimar*, 245.
24. Frederick Taylor, *The Downfall of Money* (London: Bloomsbury, 2013), 321–2. Molly Loberg, 'A Society Safe for Capitalism: Violent Crowds, Tumult Laws, and the Costs of Doing Business in Germany, 1918–1945', in Moritz Föllmer and Pamela E. Swett (eds), *Reshaping Capitalism in Weimar and Nazi Germany* (Cambridge: Cambridge University Press, 2022), 271–300. On looting in the countryside, see Benjamin Ziemann, *War Experiences in Rural Germany, 1914–23* (London: Bloomsbury, 2007), 198.
25. Berghahn, *Modern Germany*, 69.
26. See von Kruedener, 'Entstehung', 242.
27. Von Kruedener, 'Entstehung', 213–86.
28. Winkler, *Schein*, 47.
29. John A. Moses, 'German Social Policy (Sozialpolitik) in the Weimar Republic, 1919–1933', *Labour History*, 42 (1982), 83–93, here 89.
30. Winkler, *Weimar*, 268.
31. Winkler, *Schein*, 47, and also Karl Christian Führer, 'Arbeitsbeziehungen—Achtstundentag—Arbeitslosenversicherung', in Klaus Schönhoven and Walter Mühlhausen (eds), *Der deutsche Sozialstaat im 20. Jahrhundert* (Bonn: Dietz, 2012), 77–81.
32. Winkler, *Schein*, 50–1.

33. Erich Fromm, a member of the Frankfurt School, included the topic in his important survey of 584 urban workers in 1929 and found a wide range of opinions. One surprising result was the number of SPD members who had a negative view of the changes, despite their party's continued support of rationalization. See Erich Fromm, *The Working Class in Weimar Germany: A Psychological and Sociological Study*, tr. Barbara Weinberger (Cambridge: Harvard University Press, 1984), 98–104.
34. Wolfgang Zollitsch, *Arbeiter zwischen Weltwirtschaftskrise und Nationalsozialismus* (Göttingen: Vandenhoeck & Ruprecht, 1990), 40.
35. Zollitsch, *Arbeiter*, 37.
36. Fromm, *Working Class*, 103–4.
37. Eric D. Weitz, *Creating German Communism, 1890–1990: From Popular Protest to Socialist State* (Princeton: Princeton University Press, 1997), 120.
38. Claudius Torp, *Konsum und Politik in der Weimarer Republik* (Göttingen: Vandenhoeck & Ruprecht, 2011), 33.
39. Weitz, *German Communism*, 118.
40. Bessel, *Germany*, 187.
41. Winkler, *Schein*, 78.
42. Ibid., 78.
43. Detlev Peukert, *Jugend zwischen Krieg und Krise: Lebenswelten von Arbeiterjungen in der Weimarer Republik* (Cologne: Bund-Verlag, 1987), 66.
44. Winkler, *Schein*, 79.
45. Dan Silverman, 'A Pledge Unredeemed: The Housing Crisis in Weimar Germany', *Central European History*, 3 (1970), 112–39, here 118.
46. Bessel, *Germany*, 182.
47. Winkler, *Schein*, 81.
48. Michael Honhart, 'Company Housing as Urban Planning in Germany, 1870–1940', *Central European History*, 23 (1990), 3–21; Weitz, *German Communism*, 112.
49. Torp, *Konsum*, 66.
50. Winkler, *Schein*, 84.
51. Torp, *Konsum*, 67.
52. Sina Fabian, 'Between Criticism and Innovation: Beer and Public Relations in the Weimar Republic', in Föllmer and Swett, *Reshaping Capitalism*, 212–41.
53. Alf Lüdtke, 'Hunger in der Großen Depression: Hungererfahrungen und Hungerpolitik am Ende der Weimarer Republik', *Archiv für Sozialgeschichte*, 27 (1987), 145–76.
54. Winkler, *Schein*, 82.
55. Ibid., 86–7.
56. Ibid., 96–7.
57. Cornelie Usborne, *The Politics of the Body in Weimar Germany* (Basingstoke: Macmillan, 1992), 182.
58. Mason, 'Women in Germany', 144.
59. Marjorie Lamberti, *The Politics of Education: Teachers and School Reform in Weimar Germany* (New York: Berghahn, 2002), 136–7.
60. Merith Niehuss, 'Lebensweise und Familie in der Inflationszeit', in Gerald Feldman, Carl-Ludwig Holtfrerich, and Gerhard A. Ritter (eds), *Die Anpassung an die Inflation* (Berlin: De Gruyter, 1986), 240.
61. Weitz, *German Communism*, 120.

62. Pamela E. Swett, *Neighbors and Enemies: The Culture of Radicalism in Berlin, 1929–1933* (Cambridge: Cambridge University Press, 2004), 138.
63. Torp, *Konsum*, 73.
64. Marie Jahoda, Paul Lazarsfeld, and Hans Zeisel, *Marienthal: The Sociography of an Unemployed Community*, tr. J. Reignall and T. Elsaesser (Chicago: Aldine-Atherton, 1971), 38–9.
65. David F. Crew, *Germans on Welfare: From Weimar to Hitler* (Cambridge: Cambridge University Press, 1998), 177–85, here 184.
66. For examples of how the SA raised funds which were then used to support its members, such as the SA-Insurance scheme, see Conan Fischer, *Stormtroopers: A Social, Economic and Ideological Analysis, 1929–1935* (London: Routledge, 1983), 115.
67. Detlev Peukert, *The Weimar Republic: The Crisis of Classical Modernity* (New York: Hill & Wang, 1993), 253.
68. Peter Stachura, 'The Social and Welfare Implications of Youth Unemployment in the Weimar Germany, 1929–1933', in Stachura (ed.), *Unemployment and the Depression in Weimar Germany* (Houndmills: Macmillan, 1986), 121–47, here 125.
69. Swett, *Neighbors and Enemies*.
70. Peukert, *Jugend*, 66–76.
71. Ibid., 198–201.
72. On the extent of household chores faced by working-class women, see Karen Hagemann, 'Of "Old" and "New" Housewives: Everyday Housework and the Limits of Household Rationalization in the Urban Working-Class Milieu of the Weimar Republic', *International Review of Social History*, 41 (1996), 305–30.
73. Alf Lüdtke (ed.), *'Mein Arbeitstag – mein Wochenende. Arbeiterinnen berichten von ihrem Arbeitsalltag 1928* (Hamburg: Ergebnisse Verlag, 1991), 63–4.
74. Guttsman, *Workers' Culture*, 126–7.
75. Swett, *Neighbors and Enemies*, and Dirk Schumann, *Political Violence in the Weimar Republic: Fight for the Streets and Fear of Civil War*, tr. Thomas Dunlop (New York and Oxford: Berghahn, 2009), 180.
76. Peukert, *Weimar Republic*, 150.
77. David Imhoof, *Becoming a Nazi Town: Culture and Politics in Göttingen between the World Wars* (Ann Arbor, MI: University of Michigan Press, 2013), 37.
78. Guttsman, *Workers' Culture*, 135.
79. Ibid., 137.
80. Ibid., 147.
81. Projektgruppe Arbeiterkultur Hamburg, *Vorwärts und nicht vergessen. Arbeiterkultur in Hamburg um 1930* (Berlin, 1982), 190–1, cited in Josef Mooser, *Arbeiterleben in Deutschland, 1900–1970: Klassenlagen, Kultur und Politik* (Frankfurt a. M.: Suhrkamp, 1984), 194–5.
82. Raymond C. Sun, 'Hammer Blows: Work, the Workplace, and the Culture of Masculinity among Catholic Workers in the Weimar Republic', *Central European History*, 37 (2004), 245–72, here 251.
83. Sun, 'Hammer Blows', 247–8.
84. Peukert, *Weimar*, 155.
85. See the chapter by Udi Greenberg and Todd Weir in this volume.
86. Gideon Reuveni, *Reading Germany: Literature and Consumer Culture in Germany before 1933* (New York: Berghahn, 2006), 87.

87. Maud Lavin, *Cut with the Kitchen Knife: The Weimar Photomontages of Hannah Höch* (New Haven: Yale University Press, 1993), 55.
88. Moritz Föllmer, *Individuality and Modernity in Berlin: Self and Society from Weimar to the Wall* (Cambridge: Cambridge University Press, 2013), 86–7.
89. In the latter part of the 1920s, unskilled workers were able to put aside roughly 1 RM per month for entertainment. As wages increased so too did the money devoted to entertainment – up to 6 RM per month among the most highly skilled and best paid industrial workers. Karl Christian Führer, 'Auf dem Weg zur "Massenkultur"? Kino und Rundfunk in der Weimarer Republik', *Historische Zeitschrift*, 262 (1996), 739–81, here 752; and Corey Ross, 'Mass Culture and Divided Audiences: Cinema and Social Change in Inter-War Germany', *Past and Present*, 193 (2006), 164.
90. Peukert, *Jugend*, 208.
91. For a discussion of Hollywood's success in Weimar, see Thomas J. Saunders, *Hollywood in Berlin: American Cinema and Weimar Germany* (Berkeley, CA: University of California Press, 1994) and Sabine Hake, 'Chaplin Reception in Weimar Germany', *New German Critique*, 51 (1990), 87–111.
92. Fromm, *Working Class*, 148–50.
93. Peter Jelavich, *Berlin Alexanderplatz: Radio, Film and the Death of Weimar Culture* (Berkeley, CA: University of California Press, 2006), 64.
94. Peukert, *Weimar Republic*, 152.
95. Corey Ross, *Media and the Making of Modern Germany: Mass Communications, Society and Politics from the Empire to the Third Reich* (Oxford and New York: Oxford University Press, 2008), 151.
96. Ross, *Media*, 156.
97. Nadine Rossol, *Performing the Nation in Interwar Germany: Sport, Spectacle and Political Symbolism, 1926–1936* (Basingstoke: Palgrave, 2010), 35–41.
98. Reuveni, *Reading Germany*, 91.
99. Weitz, *Weimar Germany*, 146–8.

Bibliography

Braunthal, Gerard, *Socialist Labor and Politics in Weimar Germany: The General Federation of German Trade Unions* (Hamden: Archon, 1978).

Crew, David F., *Germans on Welfare: From Weimar to Hitler* (Cambridge: Cambridge University Press, 1998).

Fromm, Erich. *The Working Class in Weimar Germany: A Psychological and Sociological Study*, tr. Barbara Weinberger (Cambridge, MA: Harvard University Press, 1984).

Guttsmann, W. L. *Workers' Culture in Weimar Germany: Between Tradition and Commitment* (New York: Berg, 1990).

Hagemann, Karen, *Frauenalltag und Männerpolitik: Alltagsleben und gesellschaftliches Handeln von Arbeiterfrauen in der Weimarer Republik* (Bonn: J. H. W. Dietz 1990).

Harsch, Donna, *German Social Democracy and the Rise of Nazism* (Chapel Hill, NC: UNC Press, 1993).

Peukert, Detlev, *Jugend zwischen Krieg und Krise. Lebenswelten von Arbeiterjungen in der Weimarer Republik* (Cologne: Bund-Verlag, 1987).

Swett, Pamela E., *Neighbors and Enemies: The Culture of Radicalism in Berlin, 1929–1933* (Cambridge: Cambridge University Press, 2004).

Usborne, Cornelie, *The Politics of the Body in Weimar Germany: Women's Reproductive Rights and Duties* (Basingstoke: Macmillan, 1992).

Weitz, Eric D., *Creating German Communism, 1890–1990: From Popular Protest to Socialist State* (Princeton: Princeton University Press, 1997).

Winkler, Heinrich August, *Der Schein der Normalität: Arbeiter und Arbeiterbewegung in der Weimarer Republik, 1924 bis 1930* (Bonn: J. H. W. Dietz, 1984).

CHAPTER 22

AGRICULTURE AND RURAL SOCIETY

BENJAMIN ZIEMANN

WRITING in July 1917, the wife of a peasant from Guttentag—a small community in the Prussian province of Upper Silesia, situated 120 kilometres south-east of Breslau, the capital of the province—was clearly upset. Her husband was in captivity as a POW, leaving her to toil on the small farm alone, with only a cow to hitch up as power for the plough and other tillage instruments. But it was not only the daily long hours of hard labour that agitated this woman. She recorded her observations of urban dwellers who came to the farm looking for food:

> One has to work alone but eating we are not meant to do on our own. Because there are munchers who do not work but munching they have to do anyway. Now the stinky cow peasants are meant to shit all over the gentlemen. Dear husband you should be at home right now, you would laugh when you see how the beautiful ladies can beg when they enter our hall, then they pray and fall on their knees crawling through the hall to get a crumb of bread or some potatoes, now the cow peasants are sweet.[1]

This outburst of resentment was clearly situated in the specific economic conditions of the war, which resulted in a severe lack of manpower on farms due to conscription as well as shortages of fertilizer and other raw materials. Yet these hardships were embedded in a wider framework, highlighting the huge gap between town and village in terms of civilization, between the bigoted yet elegant ladies and the 'stinking' peasants. The letter also hints at a knowledge of the power that the peasant wielded as the producer of an often scarce and vital resource: food. Thus, this letter serves as a helpful reminder that the economic activity of peasants was not only governed by the formal rationality of a market economy. Peasants were not individualized market participants: their economic decision-making was embedded in the structures of the family as an economic unit, in the wider framework of the village community, and ultimately in the larger social cleavage between urban consumers and agrarian producers. At each level, social customs and cultural perceptions influenced economic decisions and transactions.

Historians of the Weimar Republic have often entirely overlooked or marginalized peasants and agricultural labourers. This is a mistake, given the quantitative and qualitative significance of agriculture for Germany's economy and society in this period. While the overall size of the primary sector had been rapidly shrinking since the late nineteenth century, according to the 1925 census 30.5 per cent of all gainfully employed persons still worked in agriculture and forestry. By 1933, that figure had decreased only slightly to 28.9 per cent.[2] This is already an indication that, in times of unprecedented economic turmoil, agriculture, with its promise of food subsistence, gained a renewed attraction. Agriculture did not only have an economic dimension, but also a social one—it structured the patterns of village life. In 1925, 35.5 per cent of all Germans lived in rural communities with less than 2,000 inhabitants.[3] To be sure, villagers consisted not only of peasants and agricultural workers, but included artisans, shopkeepers, teachers, the local pastor, and often also industrial workers who commuted to nearby towns. However, up until 1933 and beyond, the ownership of arable land fundamentally shaped the social structures of village life.[4] Of crucial importance for the Weimar Republic was ultimately the political agency of peasants and agricultural workers. While from 1924 waves of social protest had already flared up in various rural regions, from 1928 the deep economic crisis of agriculture triggered a profound crisis of political representation in the countryside that ultimately benefited the Nazis. In this chapter, I will discuss the economic, social, and political patterns of agriculture and rural society.

THE AGRARIAN ECONOMY

The first thing to note about German agriculture is that there was not one uniform rural society, but three distinct types, shaped by historical traditions, patterns of inheritance, and, most importantly, farm size. East of the river Elbe, the peasant clearances in the sixteenth century had led to estate ownership. In Weimar Germany, these estates were no longer the domain of the aristocrats, as by the late 1880s more of the then almost 18,000 estates of more than 100 hectares in the Prussian East were owned by members of the bourgeoisie than by the nobility.[5] But the estates had retained their key economic characteristics: high dependency on wage labourers, specialization in less intensively cultivated produce such as wheat, rye, and potatoes, and an above average mechanization—including tractors, crop-cutting machines, and electricity-powered stationary threshers. Each of these estates cultivated more than 100 hectares of land, a category that represented a mere 0.4 per cent of all German farms. Large estates were predominantly situated in the Prussian provinces of Brandenburg, Pomerania, Eastern Prussia and Silesia, and in the two Mecklenburgs, Mecklenburg-Strelitz and Mecklenburg-Schwerin. In the Prussian provinces East of the Elbe, estates had a share of 40.2 per cent of all land under the plough, which meant that, even there, peasant farms still worked the majority of the land. Thus, we can find the highest overall numbers of agricultural employment in some of these regions, for instance with 60.9 per cent in Posen-West Prussia and 59.7 per cent in Pomerania in 1925.[6]

The second type of rural society was predominant in the north of Germany, in the Prussian provinces of Hanover, Schleswig-Holstein, and Westphalia, in Oldenburg, but also in the Southern Bavarian districts of Upper Bavaria and Bavarian Swabia. It was characterized by farms whose owners were working full-time, cultivating between 5 and 100 hectares of land. In this larger category, those with more than 20 hectares made up only 3.9 per cent of all farms, while those in the middling category of between 5 and 20 hectares represented 18.8 per cent of the total.[7] The latter group was the backbone of regional peasant societies in north-west Germany. In addition to the farmer himself, on average 2.6 of his family members and 0.9 workers—almost exclusively servants (*Gesinde*), unmarried young men and women who lived with the family under the same roof and received board and lodge as part of their remuneration—worked on these farms. Family farms in this category produced both cereals and more labour-intensive root crops such as sugar beet and fodder beet. More importantly, they also raised livestock such as pigs and cattle, on average 4.27 of the former and 6.62 of the latter. Tillage was conducted with horse-drawn tools: on average, each farm in this category owned 1.22 horses.[8]

A third type of farming structure existed mainly in the south-west, in Hesse, Baden, and Württemberg. Here, land was divided upon inheritance between the male heirs. This pattern of partible inheritance had created a patchwork of smaller farms. Smallholders who cultivated less than 2 hectares—59.5 per cent of all German farms—or between 2 and 5 hectares—17.5 per cent of the total—dominated these regions. Livestock farming was an important part of the business in the latter group, but for tillage, these *Kuhbauern* ('cow farmers') had to rely on cows as opposed to horses. The large majority of the farms with under 5 hectares of arable land relied entirely on family labour. Yet, as the marketable output was not large enough to sustain the family, the father of the house had to seek additional industrial work—commuting by bicycle or train—and only farmed over the weekend or upon his return from the factory. He was, in fact, an *Arbeiterbauer* who combined the two roles of factory worker and peasant. Kiebingen near Tübingen in Swabia, Körle in Hesse, and Rödinghausen in East Westphalia—where the manufacturing of cigars and furniture provided opportunity for wage labour in nearby towns—are well-researched examples of villages with many *Arbeiterbauern*. Each of these studies has confirmed that the social structure in these villages continued to depend on the size of land under the plough. Across the Weimar period, *Arbeiterbauern* valued their plot of land as the core marker of their collective identity and as a fall-back mechanism that provided food and employment, hence a 'minimum of security' as well as 'self-determination and self-respect'. In comparison, they associated urban workers with a lifestyle marred by 'insecurity'.[9]

In the decades prior to 1914, agriculture as an economic sector had been able to increase average yields in both crops and livestock farming, the productivity of labour, and its contribution to the aggregate value added, i.e. the value—expressed in monetary terms—of agriculture in the overall economic output. Yet while German pre-war agriculture modernized successfully compared to other European nations—most notably Russia, traditionally a grain exporter—it could not compete with the productivity of the large grain exporting nations such as USA, Canada, Australia, and Argentina. Once steam-powered freight vessels dramatically cut transport costs in the 1870s, German farmers became vulnerable to the fluctuating world market prices of key produce such as wheat, rye, and (tinned) meat. Since Bismarck decided to introduce tariffs on agrarian imports in 1879, German agriculture was shielding behind an increasing wall of tariffs against foreign competition, last updated with the Bülow tariff in 1902. However, the relative prosperity of the agricultural sector prior to 1914 had masked its high dependency on imports: of fodder, of labour, and last but not least of artificial fertilizer, including nitrogen fertilizer and raw phosphate.[10] The August 1914 mobilization for war and the Allied blockade, which interrupted the flow of all three production factors into Germany, contributed significantly to the rapid decline of agricultural output during the First World War. By 1918, the annual production of grain had decreased by 36 per cent, potatoes by 35 per cent, and livestock by 40 per cent, all compared to 1913.[11]

Depleted soil, exhausted farmworkers, reduced numbers of livestock—which provided crucial natural fertilizer in small and medium-sized farms—and a stock of machines and buildings that had not been renewed or replaced for half a decade were all important factors that, from 1919, marked the beginning of a painfully slow recovery of the German agrarian economy. When we look at yield per hectare, the production of wheat, rye, and sugar beets, none, during the fifteen years of the republic, ever reached pre-war levels. Only potato harvests exceeded those in 1913 by 1927. If we look at overall output, taking into account shifts in the size of land that was cultivated with different crops, at least the production of wheat surpassed pre-war levels by the late 1920s. The production of meat also exceeded pre-war amounts by 1928, both for pigs and for beef.[12] Key factors for the somewhat delayed recovery of productivity included the increasing use of artificial fertilizer, although the economic depression had, since the late 1920s, reversed some of the gains that had been achieved up to that point. The main driver behind productivity gains in this period was mechanization. This refers to two different things. First, the replacement of manual labour with horse-drawn machines, for instance through the introduction of simple hay-turning machines, potato diggers, or the sheaf-binding harvester, a crucial piece of technological innovation that was introduced in the early 1920s and could also retrieve corn stalks that were not standing upright. Second, the replacement of human and animal power with machines. Diesel engine powered tractors proved increasingly popular once the company Lanz introduced its 'Bulldog' type to the market in 1921. From the early 1920s to 1933, the number of tractors jumped from 7,000 to 18,000. Yet even then, tractors were only accessible for the large estates in the Prussian East or larger farms of more than 20 hectares in other regions. Much more widespread was the electric motor, which was also affordable for smaller farms with less than 5 hectares land. Mostly used when stationary, they powered threshing machines and mechanized the processing of fodder, but were also used to drive mechanical milkers, 12,000 of which were installed between 1924 and 1930 alone.[13] In all these uses, electrical motors supported tasks that were usually performed by women, thus reducing the extremely large overall workload of the female farm labour force.[14] While mechanization brought productivity gains and lessened the physical burden for some farm workers, it was not sufficient to carry forward the agrarian economy. Compared to industry and the booming services sector, net value added in the agrarian sector—calculated in marks per worker—had fallen further behind by 1925, and increased on its pre-war level by only 9 per cent by 1938.[15]

When we turn our attention to business cycles across the whole period from 1918 to 1933, three distinctive phases are discernible. The years up to 1923 were dominated by inflation, culminating with the period of hyperinflation 1922/23. According to conventional wisdom, peasants and estate owners were among the winners of the inflationary period, as it allowed them to pay off mortgages and other debt with depreciated currency. While this is correct, historians have recently emphasized that agricultural producers had important reasons to count themselves among the losers of inflation. One line of argument highlights the continuity of the controlled economy from 1914 to 1923. Immediately after the war began, the German state imposed a complex and increasingly fine-meshed web of compulsory measures on the market for agrarian produce. A system of ceiling prices and delivery quotas for all major products effectively hindered peasants from realizing the full market price of their goods. They responded by shifting to the black market, only to trigger increasingly intrusive farmyard controls by the police to detect any unaccounted stocks of produce. Even after the war, food provision remained problematic, as the Allied blockade of Germany limited imports until July 1919. The republican government thus continued key elements of the controlled economy. To be sure, controls on potatoes, meat, and milk were lifted from summer 1920 to spring 1921. But the market for grain continued to be partially suspended until the summer of 1923. Up to this point, a grain levy, introduced in 1921, forced all farmers who produced grain on more than 2 hectares of their land to deliver one part of it—determined by the state—for a fixed rate below the market price, which was on average two to three times higher. In the name of urban consumers, the republican state thus suspended the market for agrarian products, to the detriment of their producers.[16] Yet again, it is not sufficient to interpret peasants as being wholly driven by the rationality of markets. Another line of argument thus emphasizes the disruptive effects of the inflationary period on the collective morality of peasant society. Particularly in Catholic regions such as Upper Bavaria, many peasants refrained from engaging in black market transactions for reasons of religious morality. Others, however, were not shy about exploiting the 'inversion of values' that the 'dog-eat-dog inflationary society' brought, as it rewarded not thrift, but speculation. These farmers were happy to extract as much revenue as possible on the black market, and were not ashamed to use the proceeds for the conspicuous consumption of items, serving to underpin their status as producers of scarce goods. In 1922/23, many pianos, motorbikes, and pieces of upmarket furniture were purchased by peasants in Bavaria and other regions, and it is obvious that they were not 'rational' investments that contributed to the economic modernization of the farms. Those who purchased these items were unconcerned that, at that time, during the height of hyperinflation, many urban dwellers were struggling to buy even essential grocery items.[17]

Currency stabilization in 1924 brought new problems. While the inflation had wiped existing debt off the balance sheets, the need for investment quickly created a demand for new mortgages and other forms of credit, which had to be serviced at higher interest rates than prior to 1914. An additional factor was taxation. Immediately after the stabilization, tax collection kicked in with often dramatic results, as many peasants could only make the payments by taking out new mortgages. A new tax on revenue from land was introduced in Prussia in 1924. Estimates vary, but the overall tax burden for most peasants was at least four to five times higher during the republic than prior to 1914. It is no coincidence that the first wave of public protests and demonstrations by peasants in the summer of 1924, mainly in the Prussian province of Brandenburg, was triggered by tax bills and targeted inland revenue offices.[18] Thus, the overall debt of German agricultural producers, which in 1924 stood at only 2 billion marks, had by 1928 quickly tripled to more than 6.8 billion marks.[19] Prior to 1914, German agriculture was partially shielded from foreign competition by a wall of tariffs. The Treaty of Versailles included a most-favoured-nation clause that ruled out tariffs, but at any rate during hyperinflation the cost in foreign currency provided an effective barrier against imports. When the clause expired in 1925, agrarian pressure groups quickly succeeded in their demand to reintroduce tariffs. While the initial 1925 customs law reintroduced the moderate Bülow tariff of 1902 for most products, a series of quick raises followed. By 1931, the tariffs for key products such as rye and wheat exceeded those of 1902 by 300 or even 400 per cent.[20] From 1925 to 1928, agrarian producers could benefit from increasing prices. However, this blossoming was short-lived. Ever since the First World War had reordered international trade routes, grain exporting nations such as Argentina, Canada, and the USA had seized the opportunity and increased their exports, effectively doubling their export of wheat to Europe from 1913 to 1926. From 1928, this led to a quickly accelerating decrease in wholesale prices for all agrarian products in Germany. By 1933, prices for wheat had dropped to 75 per cent, those for potatoes to 64 per cent, and for pork to 51 per cent of their 1925 value.[21] A margin squeeze compounded these problems, as the prices for raw materials and equipment had risen faster prior to the crisis than those for agrarian produce.[22] While agrarian regions across Germany were affected to differing degrees and with slight variations in chronology, the overall outcome was clear: from 1928, the agrarian economy was in the grip of a deep depression. Across the board, agrarian producers were no longer able to achieve a return on their investment. Instead, the accumulated amounts of debt led to a rapidly increasing number of foreclosure sales of heavily indebted farms. While in 1928 a compulsory sale was initiated for 4,890 agricultural properties across Germany, this number had risen to almost 20,00 by 1931, and for 5,800 of them, the foreclosure was executed. Between 1924 and 1932, around 800,000 hectares of farm land were the subject of a compulsory auction, roughly the equivalent of all farmed land in Thuringia.[23]

The Rural Working Class

Rural society was marked by a high degree of social inequality, primarily regulated via the possession (or lack) of arable land. At the bottom of the social ladder were agricultural labourers. Their overall number decreased in our period. Yet the 2.6 million farm workers counted by the 1925 census were still the single largest occupational group in Weimar Germany, much more numerous than, for instance, the 785,000 colliery workers, a group that has received far more attention from historians. Farm workers, however, were divided by large differences in terms of employment structure, family situation, and contractual details. Almost 40 per cent of all farm workers in 1925 belonged to the *Gesinde*. They were servants, working on yearly contracts, mostly on farms with between 10 and 50 hectares of land. The large majority of these servants were female, and for most of them domestic service on a farm was a transitionary phase in their life, often starting at the age of 14 when they left elementary school, and ending at some point in their mid to late twenties when they either decided to seek employment in a town or managed to marry the owner of a small farm. Board and lodging with the family of the farmer was the main remuneration of the servants, and as they lived and toiled together with the unpaid family workers, their close embeddedness in the family structure was a key element of their livelihood.[24] Working as a farm maid was a life lived in the strict confines of a tightly knit, hierarchical, and patriarchal structure, with very little space for personal freedom or the pursuit of individuality. Prior to 1900, domestic service had been a formative part of the life-cycle of many young women, a transitionary phase that shaped their socialization even after they had left the villages.[25] The continuing, substantial presence of this institution during the years from 1918 is a helpful reminder that the significance of the emancipation process often associated with the metropolitan 'New Woman' should not be exaggerated.

To be sure, young female farmhands in Weimar Germany could abandon work in agriculture for the shorter hours of factory work, and some of them did, particularly in highly urbanized regions such as Saxony. But it seems that in traditional farming regions such as Bavaria, many young women who worked as *Gesinde* looked down on factory workers, whom they mocked as 'starvelings' (*Hungerleider*). Particularly from 1929, during the Great Depression and its rampant unemployment, farm work did not seem to be such a bad option after all.[26] If we look at the bigger picture, then it appears that the Weimar Republic saw a partial reversal of the main trend in the agricultural labour market before 1914, which had been a flight from the land (and concomitant complaints about a dangerous lack of labourers). Yet while the overall number of waged agricultural labourers shrank in Weimar, the number of unpaid family workers substantially increased by almost a million, from 3.89 million in 1907 to 4.79 million by 1925, only slightly decreasing to 4.51 million by 1933. In 1925, these family members provided almost half (49.1 per cent) of the overall agricultural workforce.[27] Several factors were at play here. One of them was the lack of conscription in Weimar Germany. Many young men who, at the age of 18, had been drafted into the army for two years prior to 1914 were now available to work on the farm of their parents.[28] But the more important issue was surely the relative stability and food security that the subsistence of a family farm provided, both during the immediate post-war and inflation crisis, and yet again during the Great Depression, when malnutrition and even hunger was a serious problem for urban workers and many unemployed urban dwellers roamed the countryside in search for a sack of potatoes or a hot soup.[29]

Day labourers (*Tagelöhner*, other names were *Drescher* or *Inste*) were the second large group of wage labourers in agriculture, comprising 27.5 per cent of all non-family workers by 1925. They were the biggest source of labour on large estates, which had more than 100 hectares of land. Contrary to what their name suggests, day labourers had a year-long contract, and as the share of seasonal workers dwindled, their numbers increased compared to those of late Imperial Germany. Two core characteristics of their employment structure distinguished the *Tagelöhner* from the *Gesinde*. Their work was, first, a family affair. Not only were the day labourers married, but making their family available as additional labour during peak times such as the harvest was often one of their obligations. In some East-Elbian provinces, the feudal institution of the *Hofgänger* persisted into the Weimar Republic, in which the *Inste* had to provide either one of his older children or a third person, whom he had hired himself, for a specified amount of labour on the estate. The second characteristic of these types of workers was the significance of payment in kind, the *Deputat*. This could comprise a small hut as accommodation, but more importantly a fixed amount of agricultural produce—usually grain or potatoes—and the right to farm a small plot of land that belonged to the estate owner. Thus, more than a third of all *Tagelöhner* were able to run their own miniature farm alongside their daily work, usually slightly less than an acre in size. In the late 1920s, between 70 and 83 per cent of the day labourers' wage consisted of the payment in kind.[30]

The third large group of wage labourers was made up of seasonal workers, comprising 30 per cent of the overall waged workforce. Many of them were employed in medium-size farms that cultivated root crops, in the cultivation of vegetables for markets, or in vineyards. About 430,000 of these seasonal farmhands were migrant workers, the 'pariahs of rural society, despised, exploited, isolated'.[31] As the Weimar Republic imposed a strict immigration policy, no more than a quarter of the migrant workers came from abroad (usually Poland), with their numbers dwindling further in the late 1920s. This was a marked contrast to late Imperial Germany, which had heavily relied on imported labour.

For all categories of agricultural workers, the revolution in 1918 acted as a deep caesura. One of the first decrees of the revolutionary Council of People's Representatives declared the abolition of the Servants' Laws on 12 November 1918. These Servants' Laws—the Prussian one dated back to 1854—and related legislation had effectively kept agricultural workers in a feudal servitude, punishing breach of contract as a criminal offence, prohibiting strikes, and in some cases even legitimizing corporal punishment of the *Gesinde*. These laws had also effectively curbed attempts to unionize rural workers. The social democratic trade union Deutscher Landarbeiter-Verband (DLV), founded in 1909, had managed to gain a mere 12,275 members by 1914. Yet by early 1919, day labourers in the East-Elbian provinces, politicized through the war experience, were liberated by the revolution and ready to pursue their collective interests. The seizure of power by the two parties of the socialist left had clearly put the estate owners on the defensive. By the end of 1919, membership of the DLV had exploded to 624,935. Many strikes by agricultural workers erupted in Pomerania and other East-Elbian provinces in the summer of 1919, and this wave of strikes only subsided in 1921. Hyperinflation in 1923 provided a difficult context for trade union work, leading to a substantial drop in DLV membership. When the stabilization period commenced in 1924, it became quickly apparent that the collective bargaining power of the socialist labour movement in rural East-Elbian Prussia had been broken. Membership of the DLV never recovered to its strength in the immediate post-war period, languishing at a mere 141,778 in 1926. At the same time, the Reichslandarbeiterbund, an employer-friendly sham trade union that had its origins in Pomerania in 1919/20 and was set up and orchestrated by the pressure groups of the estate owners, the Landbünde—to be discussed shortly—mustered 83,720 members.[32]

From 1919 to 1921, the countryside in the Prussian East had seen one of the greatest waves of collective labour protest in the history of the Weimar Republic. Yet by the mid-1920s, all this was a faded memory. The reasons for this swift and decisive pacification of the estate labourers are complex. One of them was direct, brutal repression. Even after the revolution, estate owners could rely on the support of local military commanders. In the summer of 1919, the Reichswehr regional command in Stettin declared a state of emergency for parts of the province of Pomerania to suppress planned strikes by day labourers. On other occasions in 1919, estate owners employed Freikorps members, both to work as strike breakers and to brutalize unionized workers, a practice that the writer Joseph Roth referenced in his novel *The Spider's Web* (1923). The most effective means for the repression of strikes on the estates was the Technische Nothilfe (TENO), which organized urban volunteers for emergency works and was supervised by the Reich Ministry of the Interior. Between 1919 and 1925, it delivered two million hours of work in lieu of workers on strike, three-quarters of it in agriculture. From 1919 to 1921, almost half of all TENO assignments took place in Pomerania.[33]

The second important reason for the pacification of labour protests in the Prussian East was that estate owners swiftly regrouped and recovered their collective leverage. Crucial in this regard was the founding of an Employees' Group by the Rural League (Landbund), the regional pressure group of estate owners in Pomerania in 1919. Under the pretence of a shared corporatist interest of estate owners and workers in the well-being of the agricultural sector, and with a heavy dose of a romanticized ideology of the rural community that united all village folk, the Employees' Group claimed to represent the interests of the day labourers and to conclude collective wage agreements on their behalf. While both the DLV and the Reich Labour Ministry disputed the right of this sham trade union to negotiate for its members, this tactic ultimately proved successful, feeding into the sustained success of the Reichslandarbeiterbund across the whole period up to 1933.[34]

Yet the most important reason for the silencing of the voice of rural labourers in the Prussian East was neither repression nor the leverage of the estate owners, but their own economic self-interest and the failure of the socialist labour movement to acknowledge and represent it properly. A key element of the subsistence of day labourers was the grain they received as payment in kind, the *Deputat*. Prior to 1914, labourers had increasingly used it to fatten pigs, leading to a large increase in the number of pigs in Pomerania. These pigs were consumed by the worker's family, but partly also sold on markets, providing crucial cash revenue that they used to buy clothes and other consumer items. The day labourers' wives looked after the pigs, a task that was much more lucrative than any income that these women could earn by working on the estates. As small agrarian producers, the labourers were affected by the controlled economy during the war, which imposed limits on the size of the payment in kind. When the socialist Reich government extended these restrictions with only slightly improved terms in 1919, it was none other than the Employees' Group of the Rural League that campaigned most vigorously for their complete abolition. In a stark contrast, the socialist DLV failed to support the claims of the rural workers unequivocally, and favoured the interests of the core constituency of the Social Democratic Party (SPD), urban industrial workers who were, by definition, consumers of grain and meat. Not only in 1919, when securing food provision seemed a paramount goal, but also in subsequent years the SPD considered rural workers to be nothing more than an 'auxiliary force' (*Hilfstruppe*).[35] They thus followed their line, developed in the election campaigns from 1900, of interpreting workers' interests primarily as those of urban consumers of bread.[36]

These problems of political representation were compounded by the failure of the Weimar Republic to provide agricultural labourers with a legal framework that protected their interests properly. The Provisional Agricultural Labour Act (Vorläufige Landarbeitsordnung) of 24 January 1919 regulated minimum working conditions, including the right to conclude collective wage agreements, and protected farm workers against dismissal for political or trade union activism. Yet it also stipulated that the length of the working day was eleven hours during the four summer months, ten hours in another four months, and eight hours only during the remainder of the year.[37] For the day labourers in the Prussian East, this was a major point of contention, given that the revolution had brought about the eight-hour working day for industrial workers. But the real problem was that these regulations existed only on paper. The blacklisting of unionized workers and other forms of repression continued throughout the republic, and farmhands were often forced to work beyond the stipulated eleven hours during the summer.[38] There are thus many reasons to disagree with historian Heinrich August Winkler, who has argued that the Weimar Republic was 'a period of social progress' for agricultural workers.[39] There was one exception, though, the *Heuerlinge*, a group of labourers found in Westphalia and other parts of north-west Germany. Their livelihood was based on the leasehold of a plot of land of up to 5 hectares, for which they had to work on the farm of the peasant who owned the land (hence their name, which translates as hirelings). Revenue from cottage industries topped up their income. The *Heuerlinge* were a small but well organized group. In 1919, freshly politicized by the war, they founded the social-democratic North-West German Association of Hirelings (Nordwestdeutsche Heuerleute-Verband) to represent their interests. Their lobbying resonated with the SPD and the Centre Party, and so the Reichstag passed a law in June 1920 that prohibited the sudden cancellation of leaseholds and stipulated a minimum term of two years for them, which protected the *Heuerlinge*. While the peasant associations continued to oppose this legislation—which was repealed in 1933 by the Nazis—the *Heuerlinge* remained stalwart supporters of the Weimar Republic.[40]

THE POPULIST CHALLENGE: AGRARIAN POLITICS AND RURAL PROTEST

The representation of agrarian interests was split along the confessional divide. From the onset of the first agrarian crisis in the 1880s, estate owners and peasants in the Protestant regions of Prussian East adopted the Bund der Landwirte (BdL, League of Farmers) as its main pressure group. Founded in 1893, the BdL was closely affiliated with the German Conservative Party and managed to maximize its leverage by forcing the Reichstag deputies of this party to support its agenda, in return for propaganda support during election campaigns. Centrally organized and dominated by representatives of the landed aristocracy, the BdL stirred up and exploited antisemitic sentiments to further its conservative agenda.[41] Family farmers in the Catholic regions in south and west Germany (Westphalia, Rhineland, Bavaria, Baden, and parts of Hesse) supported the Catholic peasant associations (*Bauernvereine*), organized in regional federations, but from 1900 were coordinated by the Federation of the Christian German Peasants' Associations, which had around 450,000 individual members in 1920. In their regional strongholds, these associations exerted considerable political influence. Georg Heim, who had founded and led the Bavarian Catholic Peasant's Association (and remained its honorary leader until 1933), retained crucial influence on the political scene of the state during the republic, based on the mass constituency of this agrarian pressure group.[42]

By early 1919, the conservative demagoguery of the League of Farmers was in disarray. The lack of success in the fight against the controlled economy had made its claim for effective lobbying unconvincing. For many peasants, the exclusively aristocratic frontbench of the league made the pretence to represent all agricultural producers hollow. In addition, the revolutionary transformation and subsequent rise of the SPD to governing party in the Reich and in Prussia, combined with heavy losses for the Conservatives in the 1919 elections, had drastically reduced the power of agrarian interests more generally. Whereas the last imperial Reichstag elections in 1912 had returned 22 per cent deputies with an agrarian background across all parties, this was reduced to 8 per cent in the National Assembly. In Prussia, where the revolution abolished the antiquated and highly unequal three-class franchise, the effects were even stronger. The Prussian Diet of 1913 had comprised a full quarter of deputies who were estate owners. In the republican Prussian parliament, elected in January 1919, a mere 1.8 per cent were left. These developments and the rapid unionization of the day labourers motivated regional initiatives to regroup agrarian politics through Landbünde (Rural Leagues) who operated at the district and provincial level, independent of the BdL. While the initiatives and circles behind these ventures were diverse, they all combined a much stronger representation of peasants—as opposed to aristocratic estate owners—with an emphasis on the protection of their interests as employers, vis-à-vis the DLV. The Landbünde quickly organized in their own separate umbrella body, and it took the BdL-leadership almost two years of intensive negotiations—and the fiasco of the failed Kapp putsch in March 1920, which both groups had supported—before a merger of the two organizations was agreed upon. The Reich Rural League (Reichslandbund, RLB), established in early 1921, was much less centralized than the BdL before 1914, as the regional Landbünde retained some of their independence.[43]

With about 800,000 members, the RLB remained the most powerful agrarian pressure group in the Weimar Republic. Employing antisemitic ideology and the notion of agricultural producers as a separate professional estate (*Berufsstand*), the RLB rallied peasants and estate owners in the name of a joint cause, lobbied for agrarian interests, and offered tailored tax advice and other services to the peasants who were its members.[44] In terms of party orientation, the RLB was split between a larger current that supported the radical-nationalist German National People's Party (DNVP), and a smaller group affiliated with the right-liberal German People's Party (DVP). Even among the DNVP supporters, a more moderate stance that saw governmental participation as the best way to protect agrarian interests initially prevailed. Only when Alfred Hugenberg seized control of the DNVP in 1928 did those DNVP-members who had consistently advocated a strategy of fundamentalist opposition to the republic gain the upper hand in the RLB.[45] While the RLB and its provincial Landbund organizations were able to orchestrate public protests in East-Elbian Prussia, a key hallmark of agrarian protest across the Weimar Republic was its fragmented nature, including the emergence of grassroots protests and peasants' organizations. Furthermore, peasants took to the streets and publicly voiced their demands well before the onset of the deep crisis of the agrarian economy in 1928.

One good example of both trends is the Free Peasantry. Founded in the Rhineland in early 1919, it quickly spread to parts of Hesse and the Saar, to Lower Franconia and to the Rhenish Palatinate, a region west of the Rhine that belonged to Bavaria and quickly became the stronghold of the new organization. Here, some members were involved in separatist attempts to declare an independent Palatinate at the height of the Ruhr crisis in late 1923. In programmatic terms, the Free Peasantry combined an anti-socialist stance with a bi-confessional Christian agenda. Yet more important than words were deeds, for instance the threat of a delivery strike: withholding delivery of milk, potatoes, and grain to the cities, a tactic that clearly emulated both the rhetoric and practice of the organized labour movement. In the Palatinate, Free Peasantry activists organized several short-lived delivery strikes from 1920 to 1923, and in Lower Bavaria, where delivery strikes were part of a campaign against the grain levy in 1922, several members of the league were indicted, and one of them sentenced to a short prison term. Stabilization in 1924 led to the rapid decline of the Free Peasantry, yet for several years it had managed to mobilize almost 90,000 peasants across south-west Germany.[46] The first agricultural producers to protest in the wake of the currency stabilization were the vintners in the region around the river Moselle, near the border to Luxembourg. In February 1926, hundreds of vintners besieged the tax revenue office in Bernkastel, while some of them stormed the building, chased the tax officers out, dumped files on the streets, and set them ablaze. When fourteen protesters were detained by the police, 700 vintners demanded their release in another round of protests the next day. The state prosecutor duly obliged. In a subsequent trial for breach of the peace, all twenty-nine indicted vintners were acquitted. An expansion of the area under cultivation and cheap imports had squeezed their margins, and the vintners demanded the removal of a tax on wine. A Reichstag committee investigated and, only weeks later, commencing 1 April, the tax was dropped.[47]

Not all peasant protests were as spectacular and effective as this 'vintner's storm'. Yet they were part of a pattern that established itself well before the dramatic drop in grain prices and the subsequent agrarian crisis in 1928. Some of the demonstrations—such as those in Bernkastel—were the result of discontent at the grassroots level. Others, for instance a wave of protests in the Prussian province of Brandenburg in 1926, were orchestrated by the regional Landbund or other pressure groups. When the economic crisis commenced, it had two immediate effects. First, peasant protests took place across all German states and Prussian provinces. Second, they dramatically gained in urgency and, at least partly, also militancy, leading to an overall politicization of agrarian producers.[48] In this wider context, three different regional types of peasant protest emerged. In East-Elbian Germany, where protests were usually organized by the regional representatives of the RLB, a political radicalization of agrarian protests only emerged between 1930 and 1933, when the RLB was influenced by the staunch antirepublican DNVP and later by the NSDAP. A second type existed in the predominantly Catholic regions in the West and South of Germany, where agrarian interests were represented by the Christian peasants' associations. While they made robust claims for a defence of their economic interests, their Catholic ideology and affiliation with the Centre Party ensured that these protests stopped short of an outright rejection of the republican system. Two exceptions prove this rule: the Rhenish and the Westphalian peasant associations under their leaders Clemens Freiherr von Loë and Ferdinand von Lüninck who were both positioned on the radical right wing of the Centre Party. Thus, by 1926, the Rhenish organization withdrew from the Federation of the Christian German Peasants' Associations, which it deemed too accommodated to the republic. Both the Rhenish and the Westphalian association immediately and aggressively attacked Brüning's policies as chancellor. And unlike their counterparts in other regions of Germany, these two Catholic peasant associations did not frame their grievances in predominantly economic terms, asking for tailored support of the agrarian sector, but interpreting them in the context of a wider, radical nationalist attack against the Treaty of Versailles and the burden of the reparations payments.[49]

A third type of agrarian protest emerged where the existing agrarian pressure groups were too disjointed and ineffective to represent the discontent of the farmers. Here, grassroots movements dominated and radicalized almost immediately with the onset of the agrarian economic crisis.[50] The prime example of this type was the Landvolk movement in Schleswig-Holstein. In this Prussian province, many peasants had voted for the left-liberal German Democratic Party (DDP) in the early years of the republic, even though a shift to the right had already been apparent since the mid-1920s. The economic crisis first affected the cattle-raising larger farms in the western marshlands of the province, but even more the somewhat smaller farms in the Geest. Here, a network of peasants around Otto Johannsen organized the first outing of the Landvolk (Rural People's) movement, a series of mass demonstrations with a total of 140,000 participants across the province on 28 January 1928. As the movement quickly gained momentum, it radicalized its action repertoire, organizing tax strikes and committing its members to boycott any compulsory auction of farms that had to declare bankruptcy. The two charismatic leaders of the Landvolk, Claus Heim and Wilhelm Hamkens, advocated even more spectacular action, and in the summer and autumn of 1929, a series of arson and bomb attacks against tax office buildings rattled the province. In October 1930, Heim was sentenced to a lengthy term in prison. At this point, the energies of the Landvolk as a grassroots movement in Schleswig-Holstein were exhausted.[51] It had inspired similar protests on a much smaller scale in many other parts of Germany, though, including the Prussian province of Hanover and Oldenburg.[52]

The Landvolk lacked a more elaborate set of political ideas and objectives that went beyond the defence of their economic interests and the notion of a people's community (*Volksgemeinschaft*), allowing metropolitan *völkisch* writers to swoop in and use the movement as a platform for their own ideas. Bruno von Salomon edited the Landvolk journal and opened its pages to his brother Ernst, who participated in the assassination of Walther Rathenau in 1922, but was released from prison in 1927.[53] The only consistent orientation of the Landvolk movement was its anti-system ideology, a fundamental rejection of the Weimar Republic. It thus effectively worked as a door opener for the Nazis. As the Landvolk movement lost its momentum in 1929/30, the NSDAP exploited the ensuing political vacuum in Schleswig-Holstein. Their success in winning over the rural population in this region depended neither on policy details nor on any elaborate ideology. Rather, it was driven by the grassroots politicization of the peasants and their outright rejection of the system of parliamentary governance. As a police report noted in April 1929:

> In Albersdorf, ordinary, old peasants' wives wore swastikas on their blue work aprons. Talking to those old mothers made you immediately feel that they had no idea at all about the aims and purposes of the National Socialist Party. But they are convinced that all honest people in Germany are exploited nowadays, that the government is incompetent and that the authorities squander way too much tax money. They are further convinced that only the National Socialists can be the saviours out of this supposed misery. These opinions one does not only hear from women, but also

from peasants and other recently converted members of the NSDAP. ... The rural population has been noticed to be engaging in politics vividly ... at every occasion, in the pubs, in the trains etc. All their talks revolve around Germany's liberation, the grand project of the National Socialists.[54]

The momentum for the Nazification of the countryside was provided by the populist nature of the Nazi appeal, which pitted ordinary people against the corrupt elites of the Weimar 'system'. But long-established mechanisms of social pressure and coercion within the village community added weight to the political appeal. The quoted police report stated that 'farmers in the pubs also agreed to employ in future only those labourers and servants (*Dienstboten*) who are members of the National Socialist Party'.[55] Also in early 1929, officials in the village of Sevesten in Oldenburg impounded a boar used for breeding from a farmer called Vorwerk, who was in tax payment arrears. Landvolk members in Sevesten and a neighbouring village had agreed not to bid for the boar. Yet a civil servant bought it anyway and managed to bring it to the small farm of his father. Using a traditional form of village rebuke, the Landvolk activists smashed the farm's door and windows, 'liberated' the boar, and paraded it in public to another nearby village. It quickly transpired that Vorwerk's refusal to pay tax had been a ruse, allowing him and other Landvolk activists to use the impounded boar to terrorize the village community. The traditional village elites, local elders with larger farms, did not dare to challenge the younger Landvolk protesters, who thus scored an easy victory.[56]

While the chronology and the type of agrarian protest from 1928 differed, the outcome was, at least in Protestant regions, always the same: peasants and agricultural labourers changed their political allegiance and voted for the NSDAP. Schleswig-Holstein is a case in point: in the 1919 National Assembly elections, it had returned 27.2 per cent for the left-liberal DDP. Yet in September 1930, the NSDAP scored 27 per cent, and in the July 1932 elections 51 per cent, in both cases the highest return across thirty-five statistical voting districts across Germany. The successor of the DDP, the Deutsche Staatspartei, was down to a mere 1.4 per cent in July 1932.[57] Initially, the NSDAP had not given much thought to the possibility of appealing to agrarian voters, despite some isolated regional efforts from 1925. Only in 1928 did the party leadership issue an official corrective to point 17 of its 1920 party programme, which demanded a law for the 'gratuitous expropriation of soil' for the common good, a clause that was now seen as a deterrent to potential peasant voters. This stipulation, the party explained, would only apply to Jewish property speculation. From early 1930, the party changed direction and devoted an increasing share of its attention and resources to winning over agricultural producers. From August 1930, R. Walther Darré worked as chief adviser on agriculture for the NSDAP-leadership, tasked with building up an 'agrarian policy apparatus'. In a two-pronged strategy, Darré rolled out a network of party members who were trained as agricultural 'expert advisers'. Operating both at the regional and at the county level, jointly with speakers with a peasant background, they were tasked to display the party's interest in and competence around agrarian economic issues. The second leg of this approach was the infiltration of existing agrarian pressure groups, including the chambers of agriculture (Landwirtschaftskammern), which were bodies under public law whose task was to promote technical innovation and professional education in agriculture. Darré had pretty much accomplished this part of his mission when his deputy Werner Willikens was elected as the fourth president of the RLB, a position explicitly created for him, in December 1931.[58]

Darré's party machinery, with its network of advisers at the local and county level, provided the Nazis with something that all other parties throughout the Weimar period lacked: a persistent presence in the depth of the German countryside and thus a position which allowed its members to gain the trust of both peasants and agricultural workers and to blend into the many different regional variations of the Protestant agrarian milieu.[59] The astonishing success of the Nazi party among agrarian voters in the Reichstag elections from 1930 to 1933 was mainly driven by the discontent of both peasants and agricultural workers (including the unpaid family workers) with their economic outlook in a situation in which other modes of political representation—including the Landvolk movement—were inefficient. Yet there were important factors within the village community that supported and sustained the Nazi appeal. Crucial for the formation of political opinions in the countryside was the example of local opinion leaders—the manor lord or *Gutsherr*, peasants with a large farm, the village parson, and the elementary school teacher—and the authority that they wielded in the village context. A school teacher who was a card-carrying SPD member and devoted supporter of the republic could, for instance, try to shift local opinion according to his political preferences. But he would usually face stiff resistance not only from the Protestant pastor, but also from the estate owner or from those who owned large farms. An important prerequisite of Nazi success among agrarian producers was their ability to convince many individuals among all four types of local opinion leader that the party had a legitimate claim to represent the interests of the village community.[60]

Painstaking research by Jürgen W. Falter has established the quantitative dimension of the agrarian support for the Nazis at the ballot box. Confession was the overall most important factor that explains the propensity for the Nazi vote. Thus, the rise of the Nazis among rural constituencies took place in Protestant regions of Germany. As we have seen, the chronology of agrarian protest differed, with Schleswig-Holstein being an early trailblazer for the turn to the Nazis. Thus, by the September 1930 elections, the impact of the agrarian vote was still limited. Yet by the July 1932 elections, a substantial gap had opened up across the whole of Germany, between those predominantly Protestant voting districts with an above average employment in agriculture, and those where a below average number of people worked in agriculture. At this point, the difference was 10 per cent, a 41 per cent share of the Nazi voter in the former districts, compared to 31 per cent in the latter. In the March 1933 elections, the last at least nominally free elections of the Weimar era, the difference increased to twelve points (37 per cent compared to 49 per cent in districts with above average agricultural employment). In other words: across the predominantly agricultural regions of Protestant Germany, every second voter cast his and her ballot for the NSDAP on 5 March 1933. Other factors, for instance the prevalence of family farms compared to large estates, had only limited positive influence. The only other factor that substantially increased the statistical likelihood of agrarian voters to support the Nazis was their level of debt: the higher the debt, the more inclined Protestant peasants were to vote NSDAP.[61] Hence, there is a lot of sense in Eric Hobsbawm's dictum that 'the rise of the Nazi party in Germany between 1928 and 1933 was the last genuine mass movement of peasants at least in the Protestant parts of Germany'.[62] This assertion does not invalidate the general point made by Jürgen Falter, based on his extensive reassessment of the Nazi vote, that the NSDAP was in the first instance a catch-all party of protest that managed to gain voters from all social strata of the (Protestant) electorate. Like other groups in the 'old' *Mittelstand* (for instance artisans), peasants were to some extent an exception to this rule.[63] The key point here is the enormous speed and depth of the Nazification of the agrarian vote. In regions with an already strong conservative tradition prior to 1914—for instance Pomerania—the DNVP held up marginally better. Where many peasants had voted for the left-liberal DDP in the early years of the republic—examples are Schleswig-Holstein and East Prussia—the turn to the Nazis occurred earlier, usually already in September 1930—and was more pronounced.[64] However, it should not be overlooked that in the March 1933 elections, even across Catholic regions, those with a lot of gainful employment in farming displayed a substantially higher NSDAP-voting preference than their urban counterparts.[65]

Living in exile in France, Hellmut von Gerlach, son of an aristocratic landowner who moved to the left in 1918/19, published his memoirs in 1937. Among the greatest 'sins of omission' of the revolution, von Gerlach counted the reluctance to dispossess the Prussian estate owners and distribute their land to small peasants and agricultural workers. Such a move, he implied, would have put the embattled republic on a much firmer footing.[66] However, the absence of any land reform was not a 'sin of omission', but a deliberate decision by the social democrat Otto Braun, who served as the Prussian minister for agriculture in 1918/19. As the Allied blockade of Germany continued until the summer of 1919 and malnutrition was endemic, Braun prioritized secure food provision. A programme to cultivate wasteland and settle urban unemployed on it was the only socialization measure he implemented.[67] Braun's decision in 1918/19 reflects the wider priorities of the SPD towards a consumer-oriented policy, which is one crucial reason why the party failed to win over the millions of agricultural workers who could finally unionize and pursue their collective interests in the republic.

The policies of the SPD reflect the enduring persistence of the urban–rural divide in Weimar Germany. While the economic productivity of the agrarian sector was lagging behind and its profitability basically wiped out by the agrarian crisis since 1927/28, farm work continued to provide subsistence and a sense of status in times of deep economic uncertainty, even for farm workers like the day labourers. Thus, compared to Wilhelmine Germany, the speed of rural flight slowed down from 1918 to 1933 among agricultural workers. For family workers, the trend was reversed. Yet as the quote at the beginning of this chapter reminds us, the status that access to and ownership of land provided was clouded by the tremendous demands of physical labour. A survey of small farms in Württemberg in the late 1920s found that the male peasant had an annual workload of 3,554 hours, and his wife even as much as 3,933 hours, which is equivalent to a working day of twelve to thirteen hours. The wage agreements for agricultural workers in most regions stipulated an annual workload of between 2,700 and 2,900 hours.[68] The working day of industrial workers was considerably shorter. Overall, with the continuation of the controlled economy, the republic failed to endear itself to both peasants and agricultural workers. Peasants were engaged in widespread protests against the apparent neglect of their grievances even before the agrarian crisis commenced in 1927/28. Once the crisis kicked in, the Nazis converted this discontent into support at the ballot box. Their electoral success in Protestant agrarian regions—the single biggest cause of the demise of the republic—was neither based on the blood and soil ideology that *völkisch* propagandists in the party peddled, nor on the allure of romanticized notions of a harmonious village community.[69] Peasants and agrarian labourers voted for the NSDAP because they responded to agrarian discontent with a populist attack against the Weimar system, and because opinion leaders in the village communities supported their cause.

Notes

1. Letter by a farmer's wife from Guttentag to a POW, 1 July 1917: Bavarian State Library Munich, Handschriftenabteilung, Schinnereriana.
2. Dietmar Petzina, Werner Abelshauser, and Anselm Faust, *Sozialgeschichtliches Arbeitsbuch III. Materialien zur Statistik des Deutschen Reiches 1914–1945* (Munich: C. H. Beck, 1978), 55.
3. Ibid., 37.
4. Wolfgang Kaschuba and Carola Lipp, *Dörfliches Überleben: Zur Geschichte materieller und sozialer Reproduktion ländlicher Gesellschaft im 19. und frühen 20. Jahrhundert* (Tübingen: Tübinger Vereinigung für Volkskunde, 1982).
5. Francis L. Carsten, *Geschichte der preußischen Junker* (Frankfurt/Main: Suhrkamp, 1988), 132.
6. The figures in Heinrich Becker, *Handlungsspielräume der Agrarpolitik in der Weimarer Republik zwischen 1923 und 1929* (Stuttgart: Friedrich Steiner, 1990), 18, 54, 58. See Shelley Baranowski, *The Sanctity of Rural Life: Nobility, Protestantism and Nazism in Weimar Germany* (New York: Oxford University Press, 1995).
7. Becker, *Handlungsspielräume*, 54.
8. Rudolf Berthold et al., *Produktivkräfte in Deutschland 1917/18 bis 1945* (Berlin: Akademie Verlag, 1988), figures 264, 267; Burkhard Theine, *Westfälische Landwirtschaft in der Weimarer Republik: Ökonomische Lage, Produktionsformen und Interessenpolitik* (Paderborn: Ferdinand Schöningh, 1991), 220–355.
9. Gerhard Wilke, 'The Sins of the Fathers. Village Life and Social Control in the Weimar Republic', in R. J. Evans and W. R. Lee (eds), *The German Peasantry. Conflict and Community in Rural Society from the Eighteenth to the Twentieth Centuries* (London and Sydney: Croom Helm, 1986), 174–204, quote 175; Becker, *Handlungsspielräume*, figures 54; Kaschuba and Lipp, *Dörfliches Überleben*, 169–77; Kurt Wagner, *Leben auf dem Lande im Wandel der Industrialisierung: 'Das Dorf war früher auch keine heile Welt.' Die Veränderung der dörflichen Lebensweise und der politischen Kultur vor dem Hintergrund der Industrialisierung—am Beispiel des nordhessischen Dorfes Körle* (Frankfurt/Main:

Insel, 1986); Peter Exner, *Ländliche Gesellschaft und Landwirtschaft in Westfalen 1919-1969* (Paderborn: Ferdinand Schöningh, 1997).

10. Hans-Ulrich Wehler, *Deutsche Gesellschaftsgeschichte*, vol. 3. *1849-1914* (Munich: C. H. Beck, 1995), 652-61, 685-99.
11. Hans-Ulrich Wehler, *Deutsche Gesellschaftsgeschichte*, vol. 4. *1914-1945* (Munich: C. H. Beck, 2003), 57-64, 274-5, figures 58; Willi A. Boelcke, 'Wandlungen der deutschen Agrarwirtschaft in der Folge des Ersten Weltkrieges', *Francia*, 3 (1975), 498-532, here 501-7.
12. Max Rolfes, 'Landwirtschaft 1914-1970', in Hermann Aubin and Wolfgang Zorn (eds), *Handbuch der deutschen Wirtschafts- und Sozialgeschichte*, vol. 2 (Stuttgart: Ernst Klett, 1976), 741-5, here 766, 771. More detail in Berthold et al., *Produktivkräfte*, 239-241; Boelcke, 'Wandlungen', 507-10, 517-8.
13. Rolfes, 'Landwirtschaft 1914-1970', 757-8, 766; details in Berthold et al., *Produktivkräfte*, 243-54, 265-6. The figure for tractors in Wehler, *Gesellschaftsgeschichte*, vol. 4, 279-80.
14. Klaus Herrmann, 'Die Veränderung landwirtschaftlicher Arbeit durch Einführung neuer Technologien im 20. Jahrhundert', *Archiv für Sozialgeschichte*, 28 (1988), 203-37, here 224-5.
15. Petzina et al., *Sozialgeschichtliches Arbeitsbuch*, 82.
16. Robert G. Moeller, 'Winners as Losers in the German Inflation: Peasant Protest over the Controlled Economy, 1920-1923', in Gerald D. Feldman et al. (eds), *Die deutsche Inflation—eine Zwischenbilanz* (Berlin and New York: de Gruyter, 1982), 255-88; Jonathan Osmond, 'Peasant Farming in South and West Germany during War and Inflation 1914 to 1924: Stability or Stagnation?', in Feldman et al., *Die deutsche Inflation*, 289-307; Theine, *Westfälische Landwirtschaft*, 109-13; Eric D. Kohler, 'Inflation and Black Marketeering in the Rhenisch Agricultural Economy 1919-1922', *German Studies Review*, 8 (1985), 43-64. On the slow dismantling of controls Martin Schumacher, *Land und Politik: Eine Untersuchung über politische Parteien und agrarische Interessen 1914-1923* (Düsseldorf: Droste, 1978), 130-85; Becker, *Handlungsspielräume*, 100-7.
17. Benjamin Ziemann, *War Experiences in Rural Germany, 1914-1923* (Oxford and New York: Berg, 2007), 177-81, 198-200; Detlev J. K. Peukert, *The Weimar Republic: The Crisis of Classical Modernity*, tr. Richard Deveson (New York: Hill & Wang, 1993), quote 66.
18. Becker, *Handlungsspielräume*, 210-33; see Wolfram Pyta, *Dorfgemeinschaft und Parteipolitik 1918-1933: Die Verschränkung von Milieu und Parteien in den protestantischen Landgebieten Deutschlands in der Weimarer Republik* (Düsseldorf: Droste, 1996), 194-5.
19. Rolfes, 'Landwirtschaft', 772.
20. Becker, *Handlungsspielräume*, 133-56; Wehler, *Gesellschaftsgeschichte*, vol. 4, 279.
21. Rolfes, 'Landwirtschaft', 748; Wehler, *Gesellschaftsgeschichte*, vol. 4, 281.
22. Becker, *Handlungsspielräume*, 92-4.
23. Horst Gies, *Richard Walther Darré. Der "Reichsbauernführer", die nationalsozialistische "Blut und Boden"-Ideologie und Hitlers Machtergreifung* (Vienna. Cologne. Weimar: Böhlau, 2019), 555; see Dietrich Hertz-Eichenrode, *Politik und Landwirtschaft in Ostpreußen 1919-1930: Untersuchung eines Strukturproblems* (Cologne. Opladen: Westdeutscher Verlag, 1969), 145-57.
24. Figures: Petzina et al., *Sozialgeschichtliches Arbeitsbuch*, 57; Becker, *Handlungsspielräume*, 74, 76.
25. See the pertinent remarks in Gerhard A. Ritter and Klaus Tenfelde, *Arbeiter im Deutschen Kaiserreich 1871 bis 1914* (Bonn: J. H. W. Dietz Nachf., 1992), 223-5.

26. Günther Kapfhammer, 'Knechte und Mägde in Schwaben: Zur Lage lohnabhängiger Landarbeiter in einer bäuerlichen Region', in Konrad Köstlin (ed.), *Historische Methode und regionale Kultur: Karl S. Kramer zum 70. Geburtstag* (Berlin and Vilseck: Tesdorpf, 1987), 127–42, quote 135; Hannsjörg Bergmann, *Der Bayerische Bauernbund und der bayerische Christliche Bauernverein 1919-1928* (Munich: C. H. Beck, 1986), 245–9; Helma Meier-Kaienburg, *Frauenarbeit auf dem Land: Zur Situation abhängig beschäftigter Frauen im Raum Hannover 1919-1939* (Bielefeld: Verlag für Regionalgeschichte, 1992), 95. On Saxony, see Elizabeth Bright Jones, 'A New Stage of Life? Young Farm Women's Changing Expectations and Aspirations about Work in Weimar Germany', *German History*, 19 (2001), 549–70.
27. Petzina et al., *Sozialgeschichtliches Arbeitsbuch*, 57.
28. Bergmann, *Der Bayerische Bauernbund*, 248.
29. Alf Lüdtke, 'Hunger in der Großen Depression. Hungererfahrungen und Hungerpolitik am Ende der Weimarer Republik', *Archiv für Sozialgeschichte*, 27 (1987), 145–76.
30. Bernd Kölling, *Familienwirtschaft und Klassenbildung: Landarbeiter im Arbeitskonflikt. Das ostelbische Pommern und die norditalienische Lomellina 1901-1921* (Vierow: SH Verlag, 1996), 159–333; see Simon Constantine, *Social Relations in the Estate Villages of Mecklenburg, c. 1880-1924* (Aldershot: Ashgate, 2007), esp. 37–68. Figures: Becker, *Handlungsspielräume*, 76–8; Heinrich August Winkler, *Der Schein der Normalität: Arbeiter und Arbeiterbewegung in der Weimarer Republik 1924 bis 1930*, 2nd ed. (Berlin. Bonn: J. H. W. Dietz Nachf., 1988), 100.
31. Jens Flemming, 'Die Landarbeit in der Zeit der Industrialisierung: Der "preußische Weg"', in Helmuth Schneider (ed.), *Geschichte der Arbeit. Vom Alten Ägypten bis zur Gegenwart*, 2nd ed. (Frankfurt am Main. Berlin. Vienna: Ullstein, 1983), 243–302, quote 264; Becker, *Handlungsspielräume*, figure 79.
32. Jens Flemming, 'Landarbeiter zwischen Gewerkschaften und "Werksgemeinschaft": Zum Verhältnis von Agrarunternehmern und Landarbeiterbewegung im Übergang vom Kaiserreich zur Weimarer Republik', *Archiv für Sozialgeschichte*, 14 (1974), 351–418, figures 356, 373, 402; see Baranowski, *Sanctity*, 40–3; Schumacher, *Land und Politik*, 296–309.
33. Flemming, 'Landarbeiter', 405; see Flemming, 'Die Bewaffnung des "Landvolks": Ländliche Schutzwehren und agrarischer Konservatismus in der Anfangsphase der Weimarer Republik', *Militärgeschichtliche Mitteilungen*, 26 (1979), 7–36; on the TENO see Kölling, *Familienwirtschaft*, 291–2.
34. Baranowski, *Sanctity*, 45–50; Flemming, 'Landarbeiter', 391–418.
35. Kölling, *Familienwirtschaft*, 198–234, quote 225; see Constantine, *Social Relations*, 69–86; Rolf Schulte, 'Landarbeiter und Großgrundbesitz in der Weimarer Republik am Beispiel des Altkreises Eckernförde', *Demokratische Geschichte*, 1 (1986), 161–95, here 178–83. Propagating the benefits of payment in kind was more than just conservative ideology, as Flemming, 'Landarbeiter', 403–4, argues.
36. Christoph Nonn, *Verbraucherprotest und Parteiensystem im wilhelminischen Deutschland* (Düsseldorf: Droste, 1996).
37. Schumacher, *Land und Politik*, 105–16.
38. Kölling, *Familienwirtschaft*, 310–33; Baranowski, *Sanctity*, 79–80.
39. Winkler, *Schein der Normalität*, 103.
40. Helmut Lensing and Bernd Robben, *'Wenn der Bauer Pfeift, dann müssen die Heuerleute kommen!' Betrachtungen und Forschungen zum Heuerlingswesen in Nordwestdeutschland*,

9th ed. (Haselünne: Verlag der Studiengesellschaft für Emsländische Regionalgeschichte, 2019), 220–47.

41. Hans-Jürgen Puhle, *Agrarische Interessenpolitik und preußischer Konservatismus im wilhelminischen Reich (1893-1914): Ein Beitrag zur Analyse des Nationalismus in Deutschland am Beispiel des Bundes der Landwirte und der Deutsch-Konservativen Partei*, 2nd ed. (Bonn-Bad Godesberg: Verlag Neue Gesellschaft, 1975).

42. Bergmann, *Der Bayerische Bauernbund*, 32–5, 302–4; Ziemann, *War Experiences*, 182, 190. Figure: Lutz Fahlbusch and Edgar Hartwig, 'Vereinigung der deutschen Bauernvereine 1900–1934', in Dieter Fricke (ed.), *Lexikon zur Parteiengeschichte*, vol. 4 (Cologne: Pahl-Rugenstein, 1985), 344–57, here 344; see Schumacher, *Land und Politik*, 387–420.

43. Jens Flemming, *Landwirtschaftliche Interessen und Demokratie: Ländliche Gesellschaft, Agrarverbände und Staat 1890–1925* (Bonn: Verlag Neue Gesellschaft, 1978), 161–251, figures 168; Stephanie Merkenich, *Grüne Front gegen Weimar: Reichs-Landbund und agrarischer Lobbyismus 1918–1933* (Düsseldorf: Droste, 1998), 57–110; Schumacher, *Land und Politik*, 236–47, 467–90.

44. The membership figure in Jochen Černý and Lutz Fahlbusch, 'Reichs-Landbund (RLB) 1921–1933', in Fricke (ed.), *Lexikon*, vol. 3, 688–712, here 709. The service function is emphasized by Pyta, *Dorfgemeinschaft*, 95–6.

45. Merkenich, *Grüne Front*, 195–217, 287–319.

46. Jonathan Osmond, *Rural Protest in the Weimar Republic. The Free Peasantry in the Rhineland and Bavaria* (Basingstoke and London: Macmillan, 1993).

47. Fritz Blaich, 'Der "Winzersturm von Bernkastel": Ursachen und Auswirkungen eines Steuerstreiks in der Weimarer Republik', *Zeitschrift für Agrargeschichte und Agrarsoziologie*, 33 (1985), 2–36.

48. Jürgen Bergmann and Klaus Megerle, 'Protest und Aufruhr der Landwirtschaft in der Weimarer Republik (1924–1933): Formen und Typen der Agrarbewegung im regionalen Vergleich', in Jürgen Bergmann et al., *Regionen im historischen Vergleich: Studien zu Deutschland im 19. und 20. Jahrhundert* (Opladen: VS Verlag, 1989), pp. 200–87, here 284–5.

49. Bergmann and Megerle, 'Protest', 267–85; Robert G. Moeller, *German Peasants and Agrarian Politics, 1914–1924: The Rhineland and Westphalia* (Chapel Hill, NC, and London: University of North Carolina Press, 1986), 139–59.

50. Bergmann and Megerle, 'Protest', 285–6.

51. Gerhard Stoltenberg, *Politische Strömungen im schleswig-holsteinischen Landvolk 1928–1933* (Düsseldorf: Droste, 1962); Alexander Otto-Morris, *Rebellion in the Province: The Landvolkbewegung and the Rise of National Socialism in Schleswig-Holstein* (Frankfurt am Main: Lang, 2013). On the socio-economic context see the classic study by Rudolf Heberle, *Landbevölkerung und Nationalsozialismus: Eine soziologische Untersuchung der politischen Willensbildung in Schleswig-Holstein 1918 bis 1932* (Stuttgart: Deutsche Verlags-Anstalt, 1963).

52. Alexander Otto-Morris, '"Only United can we Escape Certain Ruin": Rural Protest at the Close of the Weimar Republic', *Rural History*, 20 (2009), 187–208; Klaus Wernecke, 'Landvolkbewegung und Öffentlichkeit im Raum Lüneburg 1928–1932', *Demokratische Geschichte*, 23 (2012), 51–91.

53. See the speech by Hamkens, cited in: Wernecke, 'Landvolkbewegung', 70–71; Otto-Morris, *Rebellion*, 130–38, 158–62.

54. Report by the Criminal Police Bureau Flensburg, 25 April 1929, in Stoltenberg, *Politische Strömungen*, 207–10, quotes 208, 210.

55. Ibid., 209. See Pyta, *Dorfgemeinschaft*, 198–9.
56. Werner Freitag, 'Landvolkbewegung und Terrorrüge (K.-S. Kramer): Annäherungen an den Eberborg-Konflikt 1929 in Sevelten', in Heimatbund für das Oldenburger Münsterland (ed.), *Nationalsozialismus im Oldenburger Münsterland: Beiträge zum 2. Studientag des Geschichtsausschusses im Heimatbund für das Oldenburger Münsterland* (Cloppenburg: Heimatbund für das Oldenburger Münsterland, 2000), 24–39, quote 24.
57. Jürgen Falter, Thomas Lindenberger, and Siegfried Schumann, *Wahlen und Abstimmungen in der Weimarer Republik: Materialien zum Wahlverhalten 1919–1933* (Munich: C. H. Beck, 1986), 67, 72–3.
58. Horst Gies, 'NSDAP und landwirtschaftliche Organisationen in der Endphase der Weimarer Republik', *Vierteljahrshefte für Zeitgeschichte*, 15 (1967), 341–76; idem, *Richard Walther Darré*, 551–620; Johnpeter H. Grill, 'The Nazi Party's Rural Propaganda before 1928', *Central European History*, 15 (1982), 149–85.
59. Pyta, *Dorfgemeinschaft*, 325–83.
60. Pyta, *Dorfgemeinschaft*, esp. 83–144, 433–71.
61. Jürgen W. Falter, *Hitlers Wähler* (Munich: C. H. Beck, 1991), esp. 162, 177–8, 256–66, 314–24, figures 262; Falter, 'Economic Debts and Political Gains: Electoral Support for the Nazi Party in Agrarian and Commercial Sectors, 1928–1933', *Historical Social Research*, 17 (1992), 3–21.
62. Eric J. Hobsbawm, 'Peasants and Politics', *Journal of Peasant Studies*, 1 (1973), 3–22, quote 20.
63. Falter, *Hitlers Wähler*, 364–371.
64. Karl Rohe, *Wahlen und Wählertraditionen in Deutschland: Kulturelle Grundlagen deutscher Parteien und Parteiensysteme im 19. und 20. Jahrhundert* (Frankfurt am Main: Suhrkamp, 1992), 146–7; see the data in Falter et al., *Wahlen*, 67–8, 72–4. Some examples for the resentment of traditional conservatives in Pomerania against the NSDAP in Baranowski, *Sanctity*, 162–3, whose argument, however, goes in a different direction.
65. Falter, *Hitlers Wähler*, 260–1; see Zdenek Zofka, 'Between Bauernbund and National Socialism: The Political Reorientation of the Peasants in the Final Phase of the Weimer Republic', in Thomas Childers (ed.), *The Formation of the Nazi Constituency* (London: Croom Helm, 1986), 37–63.
66. Hellmut von Gerlach, *Von Rechts nach Links* (Frankfurt am Main: Fischer, 1987; 1st ed. 1937), 226.
67. Hagen Schulze, *Otto Braun oder Preußens demokratische Sendung* (Frankfurt/Main: Propyläen, 1977), 267–77; see Schumacher, *Land und Politik*, 189–215.
68. Adolf Münzinger, *Der Arbeitsertrag der bäuerlichen Familienwirtschaft: Eine bäuerliche Betriebserhebung in Württemberg*, 2 vols. (Berlin: Paul Parey, 1929), vol. 2, 811–2.
69. Manfred Kittel, *Provinz zwischen Reich und Republik: Politische Mentalitäten in Deutschland und Frankreich 1918–1933/36* (Munich: Oldenbourg, 2000), 300–7. Kittel provides only normative sources, which do not reflect the perceptions of the peasants.

Bibliography

Baranowski, Shelley, *The Sanctity of Rural Life: Nobility, Protestantism and Nazism in Weimar Germany* (New York: Oxford University Press, 1995).
Heberle, Rudolf, *From Democracy to Nazism: A Regional Case Study on Political Parties in Germany* (New York: Fertig, 1970).

Kaschuba, Wolfgang, and Lipp, Carola, *Dörfliches Überleben: Zur Geschichte materieller und sozialer Reproduktion ländlicher Gesellschaft im 19. und frühen 20. Jahrhundert* (Tübingen: Tübinger Vereinigung für Volkskunde, 1982).

Kölling, Bernd, *Familienwirtschaft und Klassenbildung. Landarbeiter im Arbeitskonflikt: Das ostelbische Pommern und die norditalienische Lomellina 1901–1921* (Vierow: SH Verlag, 1996).

Moeller, Robert G., *German Peasants and Agrarian Politics, 1914–1924: The Rhineland and Westphalia* (Chapel Hill, NC. London: University of North Carolina Press, 1986).

Otto-Morris, Alexander, *Rebellion in the Province: The Landvolkbewegung and the Rise of National Socialism in Schleswig-Holstein* (Frankfurt/Main: Lang, 2013).

Pyta, Wolfram, *Dorfgemeinschaft und Parteipolitik 1918–1933: Die Verschränkung von Milieu und Parteien in den protestantischen Landgebieten Deutschlands in der Weimarer Republik* (Düsseldorf: Droste, 1996).

Ziemann, Benjamin, *War Experiences in Rural Germany 1914–1923* (Oxford. New York: Berg, 2007).

CHAPTER 23

WEIMAR BODIES

Gender, Sexuality, and Reproduction

UTE PLANERT

WHEN after four years of world war a wave of revolutions swept across Europe and the Weimar Republic became a laboratory of modernity, these fundamental changes also affected gender norms, body politics, and reproduction. With her short bob haircut and cigarette holder, the so-called 'New Woman' conquered the stage of the big cities and the Weimar constitution stipulated that 'in principle, men and women have the same rights'. Women's activists hoped that changes in gender relations would also result in 'a complete remodelling of the cultural, economic, social and political structures of our existence'.[1] While images of masculinity changed in the aftermath of the war and the public debated sexual reform(s) and companionate marriage, Berlin evolved into the Mecca of gay and lesbian subculture. Discussions on the rationalization of sexuality permeated both the media and the culture of everyday life. Authorities and politicians favoured regulations over bans. Cultivation of the body became a mass phenomenon, encompassing health imperatives of the welfare state, performance standards of the 'economy of human beings', and ideas of improvement within consumer society. Eugenic concepts were widespread, manifesting themselves in specific measures. During the last years of the Weimar Republic, liberalization of the gender order went on the defensive. The remasculinization of the public sphere and the significance of homosocial forms of bonding illustrate to what extent the demise of the Weimar Republic was facilitated by the wish to transfer ambiguous gender relations into the hegemony of a clear-cut masculinity.

THE CHANGING GENDER ORDER

The gender order that had been established in the transformation from feudal to bourgeois society broke down during the Weimar Republic. Around 1800, the estate order of the Ancien Régime had been superseded by a societal concept based on a biologically informed dualism of gender.[2] The reference to antiquity and its marble statues not only provided a political and educational ideal but also served as justification of hegemonic white masculinity and European superiority.[3] From this moment on, medicine and human sciences increasingly penetrated the interior of the human body, enshrining supposedly bodily differences such as 'normal' and 'deviant', 'healthy' and 'sick', 'savage' and 'civilized', 'male' and 'female', 'Jewish', 'insane', or 'homosexual'.[4] In the emerging bourgeois society, the body became both the basis and evidence for the classification of human differences, serving to legitimize power relations and social differences.

As early as in the 1820s, the naturalization of gender differences that was firmly cemented within the dualism of 'gender characters' had become a cultural matter of course.[5] This concept contrasted a weak female body, characterized by reproduction, with the male physique that, thanks to its strength and determination, predetermined men to represent women economically, politically, and socially. In contrast to the promise of equality during the revolutionary period, a citizenship concept evolved in the processes of nation-state formation during the 'long' nineteenth century that linked citizenship, military service, and political participation. Books on the physical training of male bodies that were first published during the revolutionary wars against France connected physical strength, fitness for military service, and voluntary subordination to the needs of the nation, which merged into the ideal of the German man. Barracks, but also gymnastic clubs, became schools of masculinity. Here, men assimilated the virtues of self-discipline, endurance, order, and obedience that proved vital in the emerging industrial society.[6] The male body was disciplined into a 'machine body' while the female 'genus body' secured the reproductive future of family, state, and nation, during the twentieth century also encompassing the increasingly racially interpreted 'people's body' (*Volkskörper*).[7]

In Imperial Germany's emerging industrial society, the German women's movement achieved several successes, ranging from the admission of girls and women to grammar schools (*Gymnasien*) and universities, to the opening of parties and associations, to suffrage protests marking international women's days initiated by female supporters of the Social Democratic Party. Critics hyped these efforts into a national danger that had become possible only through the 'degeneration of the male characteristic qualities'. In their view, this was due to the transition from the 'heroic to the technological era' during the long years of peace from 1871 onwards. Thus, *völkisch*-conservative and Protestant-national circles celebrated the First World War as the recurrence of a time of 'masters' and fathers' rights', when heroic warriors would put an end to the 'disgraceful feminization of our modern intellectual culture life'.[8] However, the reality of the war, with its slaughtering and mutilating of male bodies, was hardly suited to stabilizing male hegemony. Hopes and ideas of heroic masculinity were shattered by the reality of industrial warfare. In light of millions being left dead and disabled, many anti-feminists anxiously wondered whether men would be 'physically capable' of taking up their places at the home front that had been temporarily filled by female stand-ins.[9]

Of the men who were eligible for conscription 85 per cent served in the war until 1918. Historian Sabine Kienitz estimates that 2.7 million returned from the front physically or mentally damaged.[10] They learned the hard way that it was difficult for the young republic to honour its repeated promises of a grateful fatherland. All too often they found themselves having to fight for social recognition and meagre benefits; and many came away empty-handed. Given the productivity imperative of an increasingly efficiency-oriented economy, damaged bodies failed, despite advanced prosthesis technology, to keep up. This included doing basic jobs that were typically held by women, in which many disabled veterans found themselves.[11] The war had left the male body damaged. The 'heroes of the fatherland' returned as losers; although they had survived they were exhausted, worn down, and broken. Years of war had undermined male authority. The cultural and social identity of what was 'male' seemed to be more ambiguous than ever before. By no means did the First World War usher in an era of new male glory, on the contrary, it shattered the idea of masculinity. In terms of foreign policy, the war ended with defeat, and domestically with political gender equality.

Acceleration and change marked this epoch. Nothing, however, demonstrated change as palpably and strikingly as the image of the 'New Woman', which was disseminated by contemporary mass media. Clothes, lifestyle, and leisure activities as well as a 'rational' perspective on sexuality stood in sharp contrast to traditional ideas of femininity, showing that the values and norms of Imperial Germany had lost their formative power. By dealing with sexuality and physicality in a different way, the younger generation tried to distance themselves from pre-war society and display their own modernity.[12] The fast-paced radical transformation and social change manifested themselves most prominently and emblematically in the figure of the 'New Woman' and her appearance. Even liberal spirits were surprised by this speed of change. The 'historic woman from the day before yesterday with her lace-up corset, wrapped in shawls up to the neck, with several skirts and underskirts, has evolved into the woman of today in only one swift generation', noted author Stefan Zweig in amazement. His colleague, Robert Musil, stated biliously that the battle of women's liberation has finally been won 'by tailors rather than by activists of emancipation'.[13]

Indeed, the invention of zip fasteners and snap buttons, new methods of industrial production, and the rise of ready-to-wear clothing contributed significantly to the new appearance of women. As early as around the turn of the century, efforts were made to liberate women from crinolines and corsets, which were deemed increasingly harmful to health. However, enthusiasm for flowing 'reform dresses' remained limited to avant-garde followers of the life reform movement. Indeed, hems did not move up before the war. Then the design of dresses became plainer, not only due to shortages of material and fabric but also because millions of women needed clothes that allowed for easy movement and comfort on their way to ammunition plants and other factories.[14]

After 1918, the exhausted female worker from the wartime period became the 'new woman' of the Weimar Republic, who was featured and stage-managed by the press. Businesses in the emerging consumer society had discovered the growing number of young professional women, particularly in the sector of white-collar workers, as a new market. Furthermore, for the first time the eight-hour day enabled a broad spectrum of society to enjoy leisure time and visiting places of entertainment. The emancipated beauty was largely a creation of the film, advertising, and entertainment industries, who played with the desires of a new generation of women and their hope of becoming someone equally as 'shiny'. The Paris fashion designer Paul Poiret created straight-line dresses worn without a corset. The garçonne style celebrated masculinity and the Americanization of mass culture conquered the 'girl culture' of revue theatres of the capitals that was vilified as 'technocratic'.[15] Big-city mass media stage-managed all facets of the new slender femininity in shimmering colours, featuring both passion and cool dominance and playing with gender roles in a way that inclines to same-sex relations. The abolition of censorship and new forms of expression of the artistic avant-garde contributed to a change in the representation of femininity and permissiveness that would have been unimaginable in Imperial Germany.[16]

Articles in the contemporary press reflect how disturbing this new aesthetics of the female body was for male observers. Indeed, a deep shock was felt at the new look, as it was perceived as a break with traditional tastes, morals, and desires that had previously been taken for granted. 'The woman is no longer a romantic creature', lamented Otto Flake, whose essays were among the most widely read prose of the Weimar years.[17] Instead of worship of the eternal feminine and eroticism of the mysterious providing release from the hardships of male existence, uncertainty and sobriety ruled. As Stefan Zweig noted, never had there been 'such a turbulent and radical transformation of all ethical and sexual relations in favour of the woman'. He was convinced that 'a future cultural history would focus even more on this complete revaluation and transformation of the European woman … than on the World War'.[18]

The 'New Woman' prompted a comprehensive discourse on social modernization and the critique of civilization. In reality, however, the repercussions of emancipation efforts were more ambivalent than the contemporary discussion suggests.[19] The Weimar Constitution stipulated civic equality of the sexes. At the National Assembly elections, 17 million women were called to the ballot box for the first time. Overall, 83 per cent of eligible voters cast their vote while, according to local gender-specific counts, female turnout remained a few percentage points below this figure.[20] With forty-one female representatives in the National Assembly, women had a share of only 9.6 per cent, which, on average, dropped to 7 per cent during the following years. All parties established women's committees in response to the new group of voters. In doing so, they created a segregated internal party structure according to gender, accompanied by a content-focus specialization of female politicians that would continue to exist until the 1980s. It was a widely held belief—shared by many women's organizations—that forms of 'extended motherliness' were the domain of female engagement. Thus, the action scope of many female politicians, not only during the Weimar Republic but also until well into the time of the Federal Republic, remained within the borders of education, health, and social politics, while men still dominated so-called 'high politics'.[21]

Regarding the legal position of women, the principle of equality was contrary to family law regulations of Imperial Germany's civil code that were still valid in Weimar

Germany and beyond. Husbands continued to hold sole custody rights, power of disposition over their wives' assets, the right to determination in all family matters, and the right to revoke an employment contract concluded by the wife.[22] The contradiction between constitutional and family law was repeatedly criticized by the women's movement and discussed at legal conferences. There was general agreement on a much-needed reform to eliminate these inconsistencies. Differences over specifics brought these reform efforts to a standstill.[23] Some legal discriminations including the 'celibacy of female teachers'—the mandatory dismissal of female civil servants upon marriage—were abolished in 1919, but reinstated as early as October 1923 due to labour-market considerations.[24]

Within the labour market, women faced further discrimination. Immediately after the war, many women were forced out of their jobs to make way for returning soldiers.[25] They were also predominantly low-skilled workers who could be more easily replaced by rationalization. According to the normative model of the male breadwinner, female labour was only an additional income, which justified significantly lower pay. Collective labour agreements for female white-collar employees frequently deducted 10 to 25 per cent of the salary, based on the assumption that women could cook and sew for themselves, therefore having less needs than men, justifying them being paid less.[26] After a decline in the wake of demobilization, the female employment rate grew again during the Weimar period, however, changes were less significant than suggested by ubiquitous press coverage on the 'New Woman'. Indeed, the 1925 occupation census showed almost 2 million more gainfully employed women than the one from 1907. However, the female employment rate calculated had only marginally increased, from 34.9 to 35.6 per cent (68 per cent for men in 1925). The number of women employed in agriculture and domestic service had dropped by 20 per cent compared to 1907, but still accounted for more than half of the female workforce, while less than a fifth of all gainfully employed women worked in industrial enterprises.[27] The number of female students increased, while women working as teachers, doctors, and in other academic professions were numerically negligible. Only after 1922, in the face of fierce resistance from professional associations, were women admitted to professions involved in the administration of the law. As they were simply not appointed as prosecutors or judges, they had to find employment as legal professionals in business organizations and trade bodies. Despite having a doctoral degree, women were the exception at hospitals and universities; instead of gaining a professorship, libraries and laboratories were the end of the line. The expanding social administration of the new republic offered better career chances; it was widely accepted that women should be predominantly responsible for tasks in the context of 'social motherliness' as the bourgeois women's movement in Imperial Germany had campaigned for.[28]

Changes were particularly visible within the expanding service industries. Here, the number of female white-collar employees had tripled compared with the pre-war period and reached slightly less than 1.5 million, accounting for almost 13 per cent of all gainfully employed women. Higher skilled jobs were usually reserved for men, while women worked in low-skilled positions. Therefore, many female white-collar occupations typically were temporary jobs between leaving school and marriage. In 1925, more than 90 per cent of all female employees were unmarried and two-thirds of them were younger than 25.[29] It was, first and foremost, these young saleswomen, typists, and 'office girls' in the big cities who, at least to a certain degree, adopted the image of the 'New Woman' and its promising liberties. Yet the financial situation of the majority of these single women was so precarious that their much-lauded independence was often nothing more than a stopover on their way to marriage. The author Irmgard Keun has vividly portrayed the fate of these young women in her novels. Her heroines, such as the protagonist of the novel *Gilgi—One of Us* (1931), spend money on their appearance rather than on food, they bravely starve, freeze, sew, and mend against their poverty, relying on invitations of generous admirers to escape the tristesse of their tiny attic rooms for the duration of a restaurant visit. They fight off their superiors' harassment and fear losing their jobs, they walk a fine line between money shortages, a love of adventure, and clandestine prostitution, always threatened by the repercussions of their permissiveness. 'She almost translates life into literature', wrote Erika Mann about *Gilgi*, which was published in the Social Democratic newspaper *Vorwärts* in 1932 as a serialized novel.[30] The fate of the novel's protagonists reflected a life full of worries and uncertainty, completely at odds with the glamour of the 'New Women' that was featured in the press, whose sort of life was reserved for a small group of women with upper class backgrounds and bohemian circles.

BODY CULTURE AND PERFORMANCE: HOW SPORT INFLUENCED THE NEW MAN

Irmgard Keun's heroines made every effort to keep their bodies in shape through gymnastic exercises, which is indicative of a fundamental change in the awareness of one's own body that affected both men and women in different ways. Ever since, in 1811, Friedrich Ludwig Jahn opened the first open-air gymnasium at the Berlin Hasenheide, promoting physical exercise as the weapon of choice in the fight against French hegemony, physical exercise became a collective practice of male military training. In contrast, from the beginning of the twentieth century, followers of *Körperkultur* (literally, body culture) as part of the life reform movement were committed to defying processes of degeneration caused by the modern lifestyle through physical exercise. While naturism, yoga, bodybuilding, or rhythmic gymnastics found only a small group of followers during Imperial Germany, cultivation of one's own body became a mass movement in the Weimar Republic. In the emerging consumer society, the body was considered not only a means of national defence but also a product of individual commitment. Under the Weimar welfare state, concerns about economic performance and public health superseded the political objective of national power. Sport, increasingly featured by the media, served as the driving force behind practices of performance orientation and competition.[31]

This paradigm of performance began to flourish even before the First World War. Since the Enlightenment, discourses on hygiene had described the modern body as an 'irritable machine'. It had to be under the control of the self who was held responsible for the body's sickness or health. Industrial capitalism turned labour and performance into factors that could be physically measured and utilized. Initially, it was believed that performance could only be somewhat improved without damaging the body. In the age of Fordism and Taylorism, however, the human body was increasingly subjected to productivity norms of capitalist exploitability and technological efficiency. The concept of *Menschenökonomie* (the economy of human beings) determined the value of a human being by incorporating it into national economic calculations. Thus, the body became part of a capitalist cost-benefit calculation and self-optimization was imposed upon the individual for the benefit of society.[32]

In this sense, the Weimar welfare state aimed at restoring people's health, labour productivity, and performance after the losses and injuries of the Great War. More than in any other Western state, *Volksgesundheit* (the health of the people) was regarded as a cost factor of the welfare state that state authorities, health insurers, and economic associations wanted to improve.[33] Mass sports with the objectives of performance and improvement were deemed to be an appropriate means and a promising tool not only to keep the working population physically fit but also for their character development. In particular, reformers targeted young workers, recommending physical exercise by referring to better chances of social advancement through self-discipline and self-management.[34] The rise of sports icons such as the boxer Max Schmeling, featured by the media and new marketing strategies, confirmed and fostered these dreams.[35]

Consequently, the 1920s saw the comprehensive expansion of sport venues and the promotion of sports by municipal bodies, associations, and businesses. Cities competed for the construction of stadiums; commercialized sports competitions attracted millions of spectators. New methods of improvement in performance, both legal and illegal, pushed the limits of physical strength further and further. While in factories new methods of rationalization based on timekeeping subjected workers' bodies to optimized work processes, sportspeople were chasing record after record in front of large audiences. Be it at sports competitions or in work processes of the assembly line society, benchmarking, competition, and the expectation of improvement became matters of course.[36]

The world of sports became increasingly accessible to women. Before the turn of the century women's tennis had already become a popular leisure-time activity of the upper class. Cycling and rowing gradually gained social acceptance. In the context of the movement around *Körperkultur*, several schools of rhythmic gymnastics opened their doors around the turn of the century. They became so popular during the Weimar Republic that the word *mensendiecken*—after the American health reformist Bess Mensendiek—became part of German vocabulary.[37] In contrast to the body ideal of the pre-war period, which focused on grace and daintiness, during the Weimar Republic strength and performance gained in importance for women. Just like its male counterpart, the 'floppy' and 'untrained' female body had to get into shape through daily exercise to reach a 'normal prototype' (*Normalvorbild*).[38] Even beyond gymnastic exercises women discovered the new liberties that sports, from fencing to athletics, offered to them, bowing to the normative ideal of slender femininity. In the late Weimar Republic, 1.2 million women were actively involved in sports organizations. Depending on political views, this could be regarded as vehicle of emancipation, means of class struggle, or tool to improve work performance.[39]

The convergence of the two sexes in the context of sports did not mean the end of gender-specific differences, though. This became particularly obvious during fierce debates about women's aptitude for competitive sport. Many (male) physicians claimed competitions to be harmful for reproduction. Their female colleagues, in return, carried out mass examinations at gymnastics festivals to prove that competitive sports had no negative effects on female sexual functions.[40] In the era of mass sports, female reproduction was still linked to the 'people's body' (Volkskörper) defined either nationally or in racial hygiene terms, even gaining significance in light of the war losses.

For men, bodily training was still equated with military strength (*Wehrhaftigkeit*). Against the backdrop of Allied armament restrictions, physical exercise became a replacement for military service and sports festivals turned into shows of male performance and military strength. This was particularly true of the mass events of the nationalist German gymnasts and the 'German Combat Games' (*Deutsche Kampfspiele*). They were established when Germany was excluded from the Olympic Games and often held in newly built venues in Berlin and the occupied Rhineland. Therefore, they turned into a poorly concealed demonstration of political power and nationalist defiance.[41] In this way, even in a consumer and mass society, which was permeated by performance requirements and practices of self-optimization following targets of technological rationality, the male soldierly body ideal lived on. For some observers such as Siegfried Kracauer, during the Weimar Republic the 'culture of the body' appeared to have become the 'main form of existence' for men and women alike.[42] He saw perfectly choreographed bodies at numerous mass events and rationalized processes of synchronized movement in the large-scale shows of the revue theatres as reflections of the relations of production: an empty 'ornament of the mass', which found its way from the fragmented work processes in offices and factories into the entertainment culture of large cities.[43]

Industrialized modernity was reflected in the choreography of thoroughly staged mass scenes, in the ubiquitous presence of machines in artworks, or in the equation of male bodies with machines in contemporary literature. The New Objectivity (*Neue Sachlichkeit*) regarded technological modernity as irreversible and developed a view of emotionless disillusion. 'Cool Conduct' was a common reaction to the uncertainties of the time. Ernst Jünger has stylized this emotional coldness as 'heroic realism', embodied by the disciplined, hardened worker. This figure bore clear similarities to the image of the First World War warrior from Jünger's *Storms of Steel* (*In Stahlgewittern*), who, hard as steel, merged with modern technology into a human machine unable to feel pain.[44] Indeed, from the late 1920s, images of aggressive-heroic virility dominated the cover pages of magazines. Right- and left-wing outlets tried to outperform each other, conveying soldierly masculinity with almost identical gestures. The figure of the citizen civilian was, at best, featured by the liberal press.[45] The shift of political conflicts from being negotiated in parliament to being contested in the streets resulted in the cult of the masculine taking over the public domain, excluding women from an arena of the political that was gaining increasing importance. Uniformed men fighting for public space and the growing significance of combat leagues during the last years of the Weimar Republic contributed substantially to the remasculinization of political culture and to a renewed militarization of hegemonic masculinity.[46]

The paramilitary formations of the radical right were characterized outwardly by decisive toughness and inwardly by emotional societalization through comradeship and acts of violence. They shared the rejection of the present, denouncing it and its intellectual pioneers as 'Jewish' and 'feminized'. The high priests of the masculine countered the alleged degeneration through female cultural influences with theories of homosocial community-building propagated by all-male associations (*Männerbünde*) that were based on rituals, a hierarchical structure, and the exclusion of women. They vigorously rejected the bourgeois view of the family as the smallest cell of the state. For them, the state was a purely male act of creation. They intended to replace bourgeois society with a male-dominated community, led by a charismatic leader, a counter-society to the much-hated Weimar democracy ruled by 'female instincts'.[47] It is no coincidence that an emancipated mannish woman embodied liberalism and democracy in the visual propaganda of the NSDAP. The republic was also depicted as a woman in other publications of the right-wing camp, contrasted with an Aryanized worker type as the only one capable of bringing about the downfall of the 'feminized' society.[48] While for Hans Blüher, the intellectual creator of the *Männerbund*-concept, homoerotic foundations of all-male associations had been a key factor, National Socialists purged their ideas of male bonding from any homoerotic impact.[49] The ideology of all-male associations (i.e. a tightly knit group based on male bonding) resonated with large groups of the bourgeois milieu: even the liberal German Democratic Party, which had entered the 1919 election campaign as the 'women's party', regarded its all-male intellectual centre as a *Männerbund* in the late years of the Weimar Republic.[50]

Physical Desire and Eugenically Optimized Reproduction: Rationalization and Regulation of Sexuality

The difference between the Weimar Republic and Imperial Germany was nowhere more evident than in the context of romantic relationships, physicality, and sexuality. Particularly Berlin, but also other larger cities, attracted unconventional lifestyles during the 1920s. This also applied to homosexuality, which became visible in the Weimar period as never before. As a scientific concept, homosexuality did not come into being before the last third of the nineteenth century. The 'contrary sexuality' was deemed pathological and a matter for psychiatrists and lawyers. From the turn of the century, the Scientific Humanitarian Committee of the Jewish physician and sexual reformist, Magnus Hirschfeld, campaigned for the abolition of Article 175 of the Penal Code that made male homosexuality a punishable offence. Plans from the immediate pre-war period to expand the article to women were dropped.[51] Hirschfeld's theory of sexual intermediate types (*sexuelle Zwischenstufen*) assumed a variety of sexual orientations, liberating sexual identities beyond the heteronormative matrix from their image of sickness and deviation. Hirschfeld's Institute for Sexual Science incorporated homosexuality into a comprehensive concept of sexual reform, combining medical care, political activism, and scientific research. In 1919 Hirschfeld took part in the first movie worldwide featuring the precarious social situation of homosexual men. Its director, Richard Oswald, who had made several sex education films, was later involved in the production of film classics such as *M* and *The Testament of Dr Mabuse*.[52]

Oswald's film *Different from the Others* was produced during the short period in the first Weimar years when censorship was suspended. Art, magazines, and literature, as well as the homosexual press, all flourished. Several friendship circles and ladies clubs emerged in major German cities, centring around the journals *Freundschaft* (Friendship), *Garçonne* (The Bachelor Girl), *Die Freundin* (The Girlfriend), the newsletter of the German League for Human Rights, and the journal *Der Eigene* (The Unique) that had already been published in Imperial Germany. The variety of titles was not only due to different political views, but also to the fact that personal ads and supposedly indecent content repeatedly served as the pretext for censorship during the following years of the Weimar Republic, which the journals tried to circumvent by inventing new titles.

Owing to its liberal police authorities, Berlin was the undisputed centre of gay, lesbian, and transsexual life, with more night bars, pubs, and restaurants than anywhere else in Europe.[53] It was fashionable to be seen here, and not only for those involved in theatre, film, literature, and art who were more or less openly homo- or bisexual. Bars and clubs for 'girlfriends' and 'boyfriends' also opened in other large or medium-sized cities; about thirty existed in Hamburg and twenty in Cologne. The 1920s spirit of departure found expression in a liberalization of sexual morality, allowing for the portrayal of same-sex love in fine art. Jeanne Mammen's paintings depicting cafés and clubs of the milieu, transvestite venues, and lesbian dance clubs became visual testimonies of this time. Klaus Mann wrote *Der Fromme Tanz* (1926, *The Pious Dance*), the first gay novel of the Weimar Republic. With the director Gustav Gründgens and his sister Erika in the leading role, he brought the play *Anja and Esther* (1925), a lesbian love story, to the stage. In 1931, the screen adaption of Christa Winsloe's play *Mädchen in Uniform* (*Girls in Uniform*), with Erika Mann in a supporting role, showed the first lesbian kiss in the history of film. However, the public depiction of homosexuality in general remained contested, as Christian and conservative circles feared it might seduce minors and pose a risk as propaganda of non-normative sexual behaviour.[54]

In the meantime, the heterosexual public discussed 'companionate marriage', a concept from the American juvenile court judge Ben Lindsey that was swiftly translated into German. To the dismay of church representatives, he championed to make it legal for childless couples to practise birth control and get divorced without problems and spousal maintenance payments.[55] The German debate removed the concept companionate marriage from its legal context, interpreting it as a form of cohabitation on an equal footing of two individuals, with both having the right to a fulfilled sexuality and a love life before marriage.[56] Indeed, in contrast to, for instance, the United Kingdom, marriage in the Weimar Republic was no longer the only respectable lifestyle for women. While sex before marriage had always been common in the proletarian milieu, young women with a bourgeois background also began to arrogate sexual liberties for themselves, without reducing their chances of getting married later. The high war losses had, to some extent, mitigated the stigma of being an unmarried or single mother. Divorce figures tripled. After re-establishing 'teachers' celibacy' it was a matter of course that female civil servants and public employees could not get married if they wanted to keep their jobs.[57]

A wave of diverse publications tried to solve the frequently invoked 'marriage crisis'. The book *Die vollkommene Ehe* (*The Perfect Marriage*) by the Dutch gynaecologist Henrik van der Velde became a bestseller on this topic. It entailed detailed instructions on how to have more fun in bed, focusing, for the first time, on the female orgasm and the satisfaction of both partners. It was published in Germany in 1926, enjoyed its 42nd edition only six years later and reached millions of readers in both Europe and the USA.[58] Contrary to the criticism of his opponents, Van der Velde did not aim to weaken traditional relationships. The opposite was true: sexuality practised according to scientific advice and expert instructions was intended to achieve a fulfilled love life and thus counteract a high divorce rate. The 'scientization of the social' (Lutz Raphael) also affected the rationalization of sexuality. New liberties were accompanied by the regulation of behaviour according to scientific expertise.

Sexual education was deemed the need of the hour. Talks on sex education and family planning were overcrowded, and brochures and marriage advice literature boomed. In newly established clinics for sexual health, female and male doctors, who often came from the labour or sexual reform movement, gave out information on contraceptives and sexual hygiene.[59] In Imperial Germany, the bourgeois women's movement had refused membership to Helene Stöcker, a sexual reformist, owing to her demands for 'free love' and support for unmarried mothers. In the Weimar years, her German League for the Protection of Mothers and Sexual Reform—needed in light of the 150,000 illegitimate children born annually—opened a branch in the premises of the Hamburg local state health insurance.[60] In contrast to Imperial Germany's pronatalism and its population policy, which aimed at quantity and repression, the young republic chose welfare policy measures to increase its birth rate. Compared to other industrial countries, the Weimar Republic had high standards for the protection of mothers.[61] The republic adopted demands of the women's movement in other fields too. The Law for Combating Venereal Diseases, issued in 1927, decriminalized prostitution, favouring health checks and social welfare instead of vice squad surveillance. In doing so, the law abandoned double standards that only held prostitutes, and not their customers, accountable for the transmission of sexual diseases.[62] As recent research has emphasized, the consensus on liberal sexual policies of the Weimar Republic that favoured regulation over prohibition did have its limits. The everyday life of prostitutes and sex workers, for instance, did not change much. In public welfare, discrimination against deviant sexualities still played a major role, in particular for young women with frequent sexual contact and young homosexual men. Proposals to decriminalize male homosexuality made it into the committee of legal affairs in the Reichstag, but failed to be put to the vote in plenary.[63]

Abortions remained a punishable offence. Even before the Great Depression, medical experts reckoned that around 800,000 illegal abortions occurred annually, from which, at least according to some estimates, 10,000 women died and 50,000 suffered irreversible lifelong damage; these figures subsequently increased.[64] The 1926 amendment of §218 took 'mitigating circumstances' into consideration, and abortion was no longer punished with penal servitude but prison sentence. Having said that, abortion law still ignored the everyday reality of millions of women. Thus, during the late years of the Weimar Republic a mass movement emerged against abortion law, supported by a broad coalition of social democrats, communists, sexual reformists, artists, physicians, and intellectuals. Events with a view to public appeal, such as *Cyankali* (*Cyanide*), a theatre drama on abortion that was also turned into a movie in 1930, written by the communist physician and writer Friedrich Wolf, attracted international attention.[65] However, these protests amounted to nothing. Bourgeois parties and the Catholic Centre Party strongly objected against any amendment. Even Pope Pius XI joined the discussion in 1930 with an encyclical on Christian marriage that prohibited contraception and equated abortion to murder, while referring to the eugenic objective of a 'strong and healthy offspring' as reasonable.[66]

It is no surprise that the papal encyclical affirmed the patriarchal gender order. Its detailed discussion of eugenic efforts is, on the other hand, striking. As early as at the beginning of the twentieth century, the regulation of reproduction was a much-debated topic in around thirty countries. The form of these discussions differed depending on specific national circumstances, but they all aimed to resolve social and political problems of modernity through a biological programme.[67] Francis Galton's publications on the inheritance of human intelligence and the rediscovery of Mendel's genetics were substantial contributions to this. From the turn of the century, social Darwinism and a widespread fear of degeneration brought about intense debates on the possibility of influencing and improving human reproduction. A veritable 'international of racists', which aimed for the supremacy of an imagined Aryan race, and authors who suggested criminality and 'moral imbecility' would be inheritable, were not the only ones who championed eugenic objectives.[68] A broad social spectrum ranging from physicians and economists to the political left, church circles, the women's and the sexual reform movements shared ideas—albeit in different forms—of preventing sickness and suffering and improving society through eugenic measures. Helene Stöcker combined the demand for sexual self-determination with the criticism of patriarchy based on eugenics, and Magnus Hirschfeld expected happier human beings from eugenic measures.[69] In particular, the link between eugenics and social welfare policies proved to have serious effects. As early as 1911, the Social Democratic politician Henriette Fürth argued that social policy should 'if possible preserve everything that comes into life', and that consequently 'everything that comes into life and is to be preserved, must be worth preserving'.[70] Her party colleague Oda Olberg coined the expression: 'Not only must we ensure a life fit for human beings but also human beings worth living'.[71] Exhibitions on hygiene that focused on health, sport, and performance of men and women by considering generative aspects found large audiences.[72] Up until then women had been the main targets of pronatalist pleas, but the 'preservation of good biological genetic material' now also became the national duty of men.[73] The 'right to health' was increasingly linked with 'the duty to preserve it'.[74] The racial hygienist claim that social deviance, deviant sexual behaviour, and criminality were caused by genetics resonated with large parts of the population and even many liberal thinkers. The idea of 'criminality caused by biological contamination', as the Social Democratic Minister of Justice, Gustav Radbruch, expressed it, played a major role in the debates on the Weimar penal reform. Therefore, bourgeois and Social Democratic representatives voted in favour of the voluntary sterilization of 'habitual criminals' in return for being discharged from preventive detention. The discussion surrounding the decriminalization of homosexuality also showed that the respectability of the many was at the expense of the few, which were still regarded as deviant and degenerated.[75]

During the Weimar Republic, debates on eugenics that had already been held in Imperial Germany intensified, resulting in the establishment of institutions of qualitative population policy. In 1923, the first chair of racial hygiene was inaugurated; four years later the Kaiser Wilhelm Institute of Anthropology, Human Heredity, and Eugenics in Berlin opened its doors.[76] In 1920, the Reich Health Council (Reichsgesundheitsrat) had already recommended to 'keep individuals physically and mentally unfit for producing healthy children' from getting married, for the purpose of 'rebuilding the German people' and 'creating healthy offspring'. From then on, registrar's offices distributed eugenic flyers.[77] Subsequently, the Prussian state established several marriage guidance offices, although these institutions were mainly in demand because of the advice they offered on contraception rather than on eugenics. In 1923, pointing to financial and welfare reasons, representatives from SPD-led Thuringia advised the Reich government to establish a legal framework for the voluntary sterilization of individuals that had been declared incompetent with the consent of their legal guardian. Similar suggestions were made in Saxony, where the Zwickau medical officer of health, Gerhard Boeters, triggered fierce discussions and was partly met with criticism for his suggestions of forced sterilization in people exhibiting health disorders such as blindness or hearing impairment, low intellectual abilities, 'criminality' or motherhood out of marriage.[78]

In the context of the Great Depression, with the Weimar welfare state facing extreme challenges caused by increasing social costs and declining financial strength, more efforts were made to align the health system with eugenic principles and population policy.[79] The Protestant Inner Mission with its several institutions for physically and mentally disabled persons decided to rearrange its welfare work and base its 'differentiated relief work' on the health value of the individual.[80] Even the Centre Party gradually abandoned its reluctance towards eugenic measures.[81] In Prussia, where the Centre Party governed in coalition with the SPD, the State Council as the representative of the financially overstretched cities headed by the Cologne mayor Konrad Adenauer passed a resolution to reduce public expenditure for the 'mentally and physically inferior' to a level 'that a completely impoverished people can afford'.[82] The culmination of the debate was marked by an expert hearing on 'Eugenics at the Service of People's Welfare' in July 1932. Its results were reflected in a draft bill stipulating several measures for the production of healthy offspring that also included voluntary sterilization for certain genetic diseases. The draft bill was not yet put into law by the end of the Weimar Republic, yet the Nazis built upon it when they passed the much tougher 'Law for the Prevention of Genetically Diseased Offspring' on 14 July 1933.[83]

Rather than assuming the presence of straightforward continuities we must weigh up all the different factors to assess this development. Eugenic views were clearly widespread in many milieus of the Weimar Republic, and the scientific institutionalization of this theory was advancing. Indeed, looking at specific actors we can see continuities between late Imperial Germany and the Weimar Republic through to Nazi Germany. Having said that, how exactly eugenics was understood and which consequences were to be drawn from it differed substantially during the Weimar Republic, ranging from the promotion of a healthy environment for the education of children to state-controlled reproduction prevention. Under the circumstances of a democratic welfare state, far-reaching measures beyond the distribution of flyers were not able to command a majority, though this did not exclude that physicians or social welfare workers acted on their own authority. Only under the pressure of the Great Depression did the rationale of health economics translate into considerations about a reduced care for disabled people and measures of birth prevention. Whether or not the recommendations of experts or municipal initiatives would have been able to reach consensus and been put into practice must remain open, given the end of the Weimar Republic shortly afterwards.[84]

The Weimar Republic was a laboratory of modernity, particularly in respect to sexuality, bodies, and gender order. Between liberalization, individualism, and progressive departures, on the one hand, and regulations, collectives, and resistance, on the other, many developments continued from Imperial Germany into Weimar, whereas others also newly emerged. War and revolution accelerated the increasing presence of women in public and professional life; the constitution of the new republic declared that men and women had the same fundamental rights. Social changes, particularly in urban spaces, facilitated sexual libertinage, allowing for a transgression of the boundaries of heteronormativity. This sexual revolution was accompanied by a plethora of scientific discourses and institutions, which rebounded on lived sexuality. The rationalization of sexuality linked liberalization with regulation. While the Weimar Republic pursued a liberal sexual policy in international comparison, some areas were excluded from this. Despite mass protests the prohibition of abortion remained in force. The criminalization of male homosexuality and discrimination against deviant lifestyles also continued.

Not just sexuality and dealing with the body, but also the bodies themselves changed. Sport became the engine of performance improvement and competition in the Fordist industrial modernity of the inter-war period. The heroes of commercialized sport competitions and the media icons of consumer society were body role models that both men and women emulated in gender-specific ways. Businesses and municipalities fostered mass sports as a means of promoting public health. The Weimar welfare state considered 'people's health' as a cost factor in the context of a national economy of human beings that imposed on the individual the duty of self-optimizing for the benefit of the entire society.

The sought-for right to health stood alongside the duty to preserve it. Under the banner of rational reproduction, not only women but also men were, for the first time, considered as species-beings. Considerations of eugenic reproduction control resonated with a broad public, much like the view that social deviance, 'moral debility', and criminality were caused by undesirable hereditary factors. The eugenic consensus of the Weimar Republic propelled the establishment of scientific institutions and impacted curricula, exhibitions, and marriage counselling. Despite all these discussions, the implementation of regulatory measures did not gain a majority. Plans for voluntary sterilization and the eugenic alignment of health policies only took shape under the pressure of the Great Depression, but they would not be put into effect before the National Socialists seized power.

The change in gender relations during the Weimar Republic caused much concern and uncertainty, even among sympathetic intellectuals. The republic's liberal sexual policy was met with unease and resistance by the right fringe of the political spectrum. Parts of the *völkisch* camp denounced democracy for being 'feminized' and dreamed of a future state reigned by a *Männerbund*. Street fighters from right- and left-wing combat leagues gave rise to a remasculinization of public space in the late Weimar Republic, while during the Depression professional women increasingly faced criticism as alleged 'double earners'. Instead of elegant dandies, hypermasculine nature guys dominated the cover pages of journals and magazines, and in the media the androgynous 'New Woman' made way for a staid 'Gretchen' and the praise of motherhood.[85] Gender and body, sexuality and reproduction, were inherent elements of the political conflicts of modernity— and, at the end of the Weimar Republic, were more contested than ever before.[86]
Translated from German by Christine Brocks.

NOTES

1. Else Herrmann, *So ist die neue Frau* (Berlin: Avalun-Verlag, 1929), 11–12.
2. Claudia Honegger, *Die Ordnung der Geschlechter. Die Wissenschaften vom Menschen und das Weib, 1750–1850* (Frankfurt/Main: Suhrkamp, 1991).

3. Raewyn Connell, *Masculinities* (Berkeley, CA: University of California Press, 1995); Maren Möhring, *Marmorleiber: Körperbildung in der deutschen Nacktkultur (1890–1930)* (Cologne: Böhlau, 2004).
4. Katrin Schmersahl, *Medizin und Geschlecht: Zur Konstruktion der Kategorie Geschlecht im medizinischen Diskurs des 19. Jahrhunderts* (Opladen: Leske + Budrich, 1998); Sander L. Gilman, *The Jew's Body* (New York: Routledge, 1991).
5. See for further literature Ute Planert, *Antifeminismus im Kaiserreich: Diskurs, soziale Formation und politische Mentalität* (Göttingen: Vandenhoeck & Ruprecht, 1998).
6. Ute Frevert, *A Nation in Barracks: Modern Germany, Military Conscription and Civil Society* (Oxford, New York: Berghahn, 2004).
7. Ute Planert, 'Der dreifache Körper des Volkes: Sexualität, Biopolitik und die Wissenschaft vom Leben', *Geschichte und Gesellschaft*, 26 (2000), 539–76.
8. Friedrich Sigismund 1916, quoted in Planert, *Antifeminismus*, 282.
9. For instance, Max Glage 1915, quoted in Planert, *Antifeminismus*, 285.
10. Sabine Kienitz, 'Fürs Vaterland? Körperpolitik, Invalidität und Geschlechterordnung nach dem Ersten Weltkrieg', in Gabriele Metzler and Dirk Schumann (eds), *Geschlechter(un)ordnung und Politik in der Weimarer Republik* (Bonn: Dietz, 2016), 155–79, here 159.
11. Sabine Kienitz, *Beschädigte Helden. Kriegsinvalidität und Körperbilder 1914–1923* (Paderborn: Schöningh, 2008).
12. Eric D. Weitz, *Weimar Germany: Promise and Tragedy* (Princeton: Princeton University Press, 2007), 297–330.
13. Stefan Zweig, 'Zutrauen zur Zukunft', in Friedrich Markus Hübner (ed.), *Die Frau von morgen wie wir sie wünschen* (Leipzig: E.A. Seemann, 1929), 7–17, here 8; and Robert Musil, 'Die Frau von gestern und morgen', in Hübner, *Die Frau von morgen*, 91–102.
14. Gesa Kessemeier, *Sportlich, sachlich, männlich: Das Bild der 'Neuen Frau' in den Zwanziger Jahren. Zur Konstruktion geschlechtsspezfischer Körperbilder in der Mode der Jahre 1920 bis 1929* (Dortmund: Edition Ebersbach, 2000).
15. Katie Sutton, *The Masculine Woman in Weimar Germany* (New York: Berghahn Books, 2011); on the contemporary notion of 'girl culture' see Ute Planert, 'Kulturkritik und Geschlechterverhältnis: Zur Krise der Geschlechterordnung zwischen Jahrhundertwende und "Drittem Reich"', in Wolfgang Hardtwig (ed.), *Ordnungen in der Krise: Zur politischen Kulturgeschichte Deutschlands 1900–1933* (Munich: Oldenbourg, 2007), 193–214, here 207.
16. Katharina von Ankum (ed.), *Women in the Metropolis: Gender and Modernity in Weimar Culture* (Berkeley, CA: University of California Press, 1997).
17. Otto Flake, 'Die alte Aufgabe—die neue Form', in Hübner, *Die Frau von morgen*, 161–8.
18. Zweig, 'Zutrauen zur Zukunft', 7–8.
19. As an overview see Helen Boak, *Women in the Weimar Republic* (Manchester: Manchester University Press, 2013).
20. Jürgen Falter, Thomas Lichtenberger, and Siegfried Schumann, *Wahlen und Abstimmungen in der Weimarer Republik. Materialien zum Wahlverhalten 1919–1933* (Munich: C. H. Beck, 1986), 41.
21. Hedwig Richter and Kerstin Wolff (eds), *Frauenwahlrecht. Demokratisierung der Demokratie in Deutschland und Europa* (Hamburg: Hamburger Edition, 2018); Julia Sneeringer, *Winning Women's Votes: Propaganda and Politics in Weimar Germany* (Chapel Hill, NC: University of North Carolina Press, 2002).
22. Heide-Marie Lauterer, 'Grundrechte, staatsbürgerliche Gleichberechtigung und Familienrecht in der Weimarer Republik', in Frauen & Geschichte Baden-Württemberg

e.V. (ed.), *50 Jahre Grundgesetz: Menschen- und Bürgerrechte als Frauenrechte* (Königstein/Taunus: Helmer, 2000), 132–44.

23. Dieter Schwab, 'Gleichberechtigung und Familienrecht im 20. Jahrhundert', in Ute Gerhard (ed.), *Frauen in der Geschichte des Rechts: Von der Frühen Neuzeit bis zur Gegenwart* (Munich: C. H. Beck, 1997), 790–827.

24. 'Verordnung zur Herabminderung der Personalausgaben des Reiches vom 27. Oktober 1923', *Reichsgesetzblatt*, 108 (30 Oct. 1923).

25. Susanne Rouette, *Sozialpolitik als Geschlechterpolitik: Die Regulierung der Frauenarbeit nach dem Ersten Weltkrieg* (Frankfurt/Main: Campus, 1993).

26. Ute Frevert, *Women in German History: From Bourgeois Emancipation to Sexual Liberation*, tr. Stuart McKinnon-Evans (New York: Berg, 1989), 179.

27. Ibid., 176–7. Frevert gives a lower figure for the numerical increase in female employment.

28. Christoph Sachße, *Mütterlichkeit als Beruf: Sozialarbeit, Sozialreform und Frauenbewegung 1871–1929* (Frankfurt/Main: Suhrkamp, 1986).

29. Frevert, *Women in German History*, 179.

30. Quoted in Ingo Leiß and Hermann Stadler, *Deutsche Literaturgeschichte*, vol. 9. *Weimarer Republik 1918–1933* (Munich: dtv, 2003), 136.

31. Michael Hau, *The Cult of Health and Beauty in Germany: A Social History 1890–1930* (Chicago: University of Chicago Press, 2003); Bernd Wedemeyer-Kolwe, *'Der neue Mensch': Körperkultur im Kaiserreich und in der Weimarer Republik* (Würzburg: Königshausen & Neumann, 2004).

32. Philipp Sarasin, *Reizbare Maschinen: Eine Geschichte des Körpers 1765–1914* (Frankfurt/Main: Suhrkamp, 2001). The term *Menschenökonomie* had already been introduced before 1914 by racial hygienists such as Wilhelm Schallmayer and Rudolf Goldscheid. Planert, 'Der dreifache Körper des Volkes', 547.

33. Stefan Scholl, 'Biopolitik und Sport in historischer Perspektive', in Scholl (ed.), *Körperführung: Historische Perspektiven auf das Verhältnis von Körperführung und Sport* (Frankfurt/Main: Campus, 2018), 7–40.

34. Michael Hau, *Performance Anxiety: Sport and Work from the Empire to Nazism* (Toronto: University of Toronto Press, 2017).

35. Jon Hughes, *Max Schmeling and the Making of a National Hero in Twentieth-Century Germany* (Basingstoke: Palgrave Macmillan, 2018).

36. Frank Becker, 'Der Sportler als "moderner Menschentyp": Entwürfe für eine neue Körperlichkeit in der Weimarer Republik', in Clemens Wischermann and Stefan Haas (eds), *Körper mit Geschichte: Der menschliche Körper als Ort der Selbst- und Weltdeutung* (Stuttgart: Franz Steiner, 2000), 223–43.

37. Wedemeyer-Kolwe, 'Der neue Mensch', 37.

38. D. Knospe, *Funktionelles Frauenturnen* (1924), quoted in Planert, 'Der dreifache Körper', 57.

39. Eric N. Jensen, *Body by Weimar: Athletes, Gender, and German Modernity* (Oxford, New York: Oxford University Press, 2010).

40. Gertrud Pfister, 'Neue Frauen und weibliche Schwäche—Geschlechterarrangements und Sportdiskurse in der Weimarer Republik', in Michael Krüger (ed.), *Der deutsche Sport auf dem Weg in die Moderne: Carl Diem und seine Zeit* (Berlin, Münster: Lit.-Verlag, 2009), 285–310.

41. Noyan Dinçkal, *Sport, Raum und (Massen-)Kultur in Deutschland 1880–1930* (Göttingen: Vandenhoeck & Ruprecht, 2013).

42. Siegfried Kracauer, *Die Angestellten: Kulturkritischer Essay* (Frankfurt/Main: Suhrkamp, 1981), 96.
43. Siegfried Kracauer, *Das Ornament der Masse: Essays* (Frankfurt/Main: Suhrkamp, 1963).
44. Ernst Jünger, *Der Arbeiter: Herrschaft und Gestalt* (Stuttgart: Klett-Cotta, 1982); Helmut Lethen, *Cool Conduct: The Culture of Distance in Weimar Germany* (Berkeley, CA: University of California Press, 2002); Daniel Morat, 'Kalte Männlichkeit? Weimarer Verhaltenslehren im Spannungsfeld von Emotionen- und Geschlechtergeschichte', in Manuel Borutta and Nina Verheyen (eds), *Die Präsenz der Gefühle: Männlichkeit und Emotion in der Moderne* (Bielefeld: transcript Verlag, 2010), 153–77.
45. Wilhelm Marckwardt, *Die Illustrierten der Weimarer Zeit: Publizistische Funktion, ökonomische Entwicklung und inhaltliche Tendenzen* (Munich: Minerva-Publikationen, 1982).
46. With further references see Daniel Siemens, 'Erobern statt verführen: Die Kategorie Geschlecht in der Politik der Straße der Weimarer Republik', in Metzler and Schumann, *Geschlechter(un)ordnung*, 255–77.
47. Planert, 'Kulturkritik', here 212.
48. Schmersahl, *Medizin und Geschlecht*.
49. Claudia Bruns, *Politik des Eros: Der Männerbund in Wissenschaft, Politik und Jugendkultur (1880–1934)* (Cologne: Böhlau, 2008).
50. Angelika Schaser, *Helene Lange und Gertrud Bäumer: Eine politische Lebensgemeinschaft* (Cologne: Böhlau, 2000), 234, 247.
51. Susanne zur Nieden (ed.), *Homosexualität und Staatsräson: Männlichkeit, Homophobie und Politik in Deutschland, 1900–1945* (Frankfurt/Main: Campus, 2005).
52. James Steakley, *'Anders als die Andern': Ein Film und seine Geschichte* (Hamburg: Männerschwarm Verlag, 2007).
53. Curt Moreck, *Führer durch das lasterhafte Berlin* (Berlin: Verlag moderner Stadtführer, 1930); Ruth Roellig, *Berlins lesbische Frauen* (Leipzig: Gebauer, 1928).
54. Robert Beachy, *Gay Berlin: Birthplace of a Modern Identity* (New York: Berghahn, 2014); Marti Lybeck, *Desiring Emancipation: New Women and Homosexuality in Germany, 1890–1933* (Albany, NY: State University of New York Press, 2014).
55. Ben B. Lindsey and John Wainwright Evans, *The Companionate Marriage* (New York: Boni & Liveright, 1927).
56. Lola Landau, 'Kameradschaftsehe', *Die Tat* 20/2 (1929), 831–5.
57. Cornelie Usborne, 'Sex Reform and Moral Panic. Perceptions of Young Woman's Sexual Mores in the Weimar Republic', in Mark Roseman (ed.), *Generations in Conflict: Youth Revolt and Generation Formation in Germany 1770–1968* (Cambridge: Cambridge University Press, 1995), 137–63; Frevert, *Women in German History*, 193.
58. Henrik van der Velde, *Die vollkommene Ehe: Eine Studie über ihre Physiologie und Technik* (Leipzig, Stuttgart: Benno Konegen, 1926).
59. Kristine von Soden, *Sexualberatungsstellen in der Weimarer Republik, 1919–1933* (Berlin: Edition Hentrich, 1988).
60. Frevert, *Women in German History*, 189, 198.
61. Cornelie Usborne, *The Politics of the Body in Weimar Germany: Women's Reproductive Rights and Duties* (London: Palgrave Macmillan, 1992).
62. Julia Roos, *Weimar through the Lens of Gender: Prostitution Reform, Women's Emancipation and German Democracy, 1919–1933* (Ann Arbor: University of Michigan Press, 2010).

63. Detlev J. K. Peukert, *Grenzen der Sozialdisziplinierung: Aufstieg und Krise der deutschen Jugendfürsorge 1878 bis 1932* (Cologne: Bund, 1986); Martin Lücke, '"Die Bekämpfung des Lasters von der Quelle"—Zur Regulierung von devianter männlicher Sexualität im Fürsorgewesen der Weimarer Republik', in Metzler and Schumann (eds), *Geschlechter(un) ordnung*, 135–54.
64. Atina Grossman, 'Abortion and Economic Crisis: The 1931 Campaign Against §218 in Germany', *New German Critique*, 14 (1978), 119–37, here 121–2.
65. Atina Grossmann, *Reforming Sex. The German Movement for Birth Control and Abortion Reform, 1920–1950* (New York, Oxford: Oxford University Press, 1995).
66. Pius XI., 'Casti conubii', *Acta Apostolicae Sedis*, 22 (1930), 539–92.
67. Alison Bashford and Philippa Levine (eds), *The Oxford Handbook of the History of Eugenics* (Oxford: Oxford University Press, 2010).
68. Stefan Kühl, *Die Internationale der Rassisten: Aufstieg und Niedergang der internationalen Bewegung für Eugenik und Rassenhygiene im 20. Jahrhundert* (Frankfurt/Main: Campus, 1997).
69. Magnus Hirschfeld, *Weltreise eines Sexualforschers* (Frankfurt/Main: Eichborn Verlag, 2006), 25. On the controversial debate on eugenic views within the women's movement see Ann Taylor Allen, 'German Radical Feminism and Eugenics, 1900–1908', *German Studies Review*, 11 (1988), 31–56; Ulrike Manz, *Bürgerliche Frauenbewegung und Eugenik in der Weimarer Republik* (Königstein im Taunus: Ulrike Helmer Verlag, 2007).
70. Quoted in Michael Schwartz, *Sozialistische Eugenik: Eugenische Sozialtechnologien in Debatten und Politik der deutschen Sozialdemokratie 1890–1933* (Bonn: J. H. W. Dietz, 1995), 67.
71. Oda Olberg 1914, quoted in Schwarz, *Sozialistische Eugenik*, 57.
72. Sebastian Weinert, *Der Körper im Blick. Gesundheitsausstellungen vom späten Kaiserreich bis zum Nationalsozialismus* (Berlin: De Gruyter, 2017).
73. Carl von Behr-Pinnow 1928, quoted in Planert, 'Der dreifache Körper', 570.
74. Emil Abderhalden 1921, quoted in Planert, 'Der dreifache Körper', 564.
75. Gustav Radbruch, *Gesamtausgabe, 9. Strafrechtsreform* (Heidelberg: C. F. Müller 1992), 250; Laurie Marhoefer, *Sex and the Weimar Republic: German Homosexual Emancipation and the Rise of the Nazis* (Toronto: University of Toronto Press, 2015).
76. See, also on the following, Peter Weingart, Jürgen Kroll, and Kurt Bayertz, *Rasse, Blut und Gene. Geschichte der Eugenik und Rassenhygiene in Deutschland* (Frankfurt/Main: Suhrkamp, 1988), 230–300.
77. 'Leitsätze des Reichsgesundheitsrates' 26 Feb. 1920, printed in von Soden, *Sexualberatungsstellen*, 166.
78. Karl Boeters, 'Entwurf zu einem Gesetz für den Deutschen Reichstag über "Die Verhütung unwerten Lebens durch operative Maßnahmen"', *Zeitschrift für Sexualwissenschaft*, 13 (1926/7), 139–40.
79. Weingart, Kroll and Bayertz, *Rasse, Blut und Gene*, 262–7.
80. Sabine Schleiermacher, 'Die Innere Mission und ihr bevölkerungspolitisches Programm', in Heidrun Kaupen-Haas (ed.), *Der Griff nach der Bevölkerung: Aktualität und Kontinuität nazistischer Bevölkerungspolitik* (Nördlingen: Franz Gero Verlag, 1986), 73–89, here 77.
81. Richter and Wolff, *Frauenwahlrecht*.
82. Quoted in Johannes Vossen, *Gesundheitsämter im Nationalsozialismus: Rassenhygiene und offene Gesundheitsfürsorge in Westfalen, 1900–1950* (Essen: Klartext, 2001), 166.
83. Vossen, *Gesundheitsämter*, 166–7.

84. Young-Sun Hong, *Welfare, Modernity and the Weimar State* (Princeton: Princeton University Press, 2014); Edward Ross Dickinson, 'Biopolitics, Fascism, Democracy. Some Reflections on our Discourse about Modernity', *Central European History*, 37 (2004), 1–48.
85. Hung shows how young women tried to combine this changed image of women with their claim for emancipation; Jochen Hung, 'The Modernized Gretchen: Transformations of the 'New Woman' in the Late Weimar Republic', *German History*, 33 (2015), 52–79.
86. On the debate whether liberal sexual policies of the Weimar Republic facilitated the rise of the Nazis see recently Jochen Hung, 'A Backlash Against Liberalism? What the Weimar Republic can Teach us about Today's Politics', *International Journal for History, Culture and Modernity*, 5 (2018), 91–110.

Bibliography

Beachy, Robert, *Gay Berlin: Birthplace of a Modern Identity* (New York: Alfred A. Knopf, 2014).
Boak, Helen, *Women in the Weimar Republic* (Manchester: Manchester University Press, 2013).
Grossmann, Atina, *Reforming Sex: The German Movement for Birth Control and Abortion Reform, 1920–1950* (New York, Oxford: Oxford University Press, 1995).
Hong, Young-Sun, *Welfare, Modernity and the Weimar State* (Princeton: Princeton University Press, 2014).
Marhoefer, Laurie, *Sex and the Weimar Republic. German Homosexual Emancipation and the Rise of the Nazis* (Toronto: University of Toronto Press, 2015).
Metzler, Gabriele, and Dirk Schumann (eds), *Geschlechter(un)ordnung und Politik in der Weimarer Republik* (Bonn: J. H. W. Dietz, 2016).
Planert, Ute, 'Der dreifache Körper des Volkes: Sexualität, Biopolitik und die Wissenschaft vom Leben', *Geschichte und Gesellschaft*, 26 (2000), 539–76.
Roos, Julia, *Weimar through the Lens of Gender: Prostitution Reform, Women's Emancipation and German Democracy, 1919–1933* (Ann Arbor: University of Michigan Press, 2010).
Schwartz, Michael, *Sozialistische Eugenik. Eugenische Sozialtechnologien in Debatten und Politik der deutschen Sozialdemokratie 1890–1933* (Berlin: J. H. W. Dietz, 1995).
Sneeringer, Julia, *Winning Women's Votes. Propaganda and Politics in Weimar Germany* (Chapel Hill, NC: University of North Carolina Press, 2002).
Sutton, Katie, *The Masculine Woman in Weimar Germany* (New York: Berghahn, 2011).
Usborne, Cornelie, *The Politics of the Body in Weimar Germany. Women's Reproductive Rights and Duties* (London: Palgrave Macmillan, 1992).
Weingart, Peter, Jürgen Kroll, and Kurt Bayertz, *Rasse, Blut und Gene: Geschichte der Eugenik und Rassenhygiene in Deutschland* (Frankfurt/Main: Suhrkamp, 1988).

CHAPTER 24

TRANSNATIONAL VISIONS OF MODERNITY

America and the Soviet Union

MARY NOLAN

AMERICA and Russia 'are the two poles of the contemporary era' wrote the German novelist Arthur Holitscher after trips to both nations in the 1920s. Whether he and a multitude of other Weimar Germans admired or abhorred developments in these vast continental powers that flanked the heartland of Europe, they could not ignore the power, cultural innovations, and ideological appeal of states that seemed young and vigorous in comparison to 'old sinking Europe'.[1] While some Weimar Germans longed to restore the imperial political and military order and preserve cultural and social traditions in toto, others sought to defend endangered economic structures, political ideologies, and social institutions through their partial modernization. Still others searched for alternative futures that would be modern yet distinctively German in order to revive Germany's troubled economy, stabilize its fragile democracy, invigorate culture, and restore Germany's place in the global order.[2] Both the reluctant and the enthusiastic proponents of change looked abroad to 'the two most modern states in the world'—America and the Soviet Union.[3]

Germans had long been fascinated by America, as the United States was usually called.[4] Although it is only one part of North and South America, the threat and promise of the United States was always debated in terms of the perennially contested concepts of Americanism and Americanization. Before the First World War, Germans encountered America in journalism and fiction—as well as through travel, trade, and investment. They were intrigued by the tempo of New York, the grandeur of the Niagara Falls, and the exoticism of the Wild West. While recognizing America's impressive industrialization, they felt the German economy held its own and regarded America as militarily insignificant and culturally immature. However interesting, America was neither a threat nor a model.[5] Indeed, influence ran the other way, for American academics and social reformers came to Germany to learn about intellectual developments and progressive social policies.[6]

Germans were also attentive to developments in the Russian Empire. From the 1880s onward, economic opportunities and Russian hunger for foreign loans encouraged Imperial German banks and businesses to turn eastward and the two nations became major trading partners.[7] Many Germans admired Russian literature, ballet, and music but others regarded Slavs as primitive and Russia as non-European. All agreed that its overwhelmingly agrarian economy and pervasive poverty marked it as economically and socially backward, even as they disagreed on whether the autocratic state, Russian culture, or ostensible Slavic inferiority were to blame. Russia was expected to learn from Germany, which claimed to have a cultural mission in the east.[8]

After the First World War, Germans turned both west and east more intensively. They studied, wrote about, and travelled to these rising powers, each of which was also present in varied ways within Germany. America sent loans, goods, jazz, and movies as well as tourists and students. The Russian presence was denser and different; there were hundreds of thousands of Russian exiles from Bolshevism but also numerous Soviet state officials and cultural figures as well as representatives of the Comintern. Berlin was, in Karl Schlögel's words, 'a Russian city'.[9] The Weimar Republic came to have 'ever tighter actual and material ties to the West' but also displayed 'a most intensive but ambivalent intellectual-political 'east orientation'.[10]

Germans had many reasons to look to transnational models. Military defeat was followed by a divisive political revolution, social turmoil, and open armed conflict. The economy suffered from inflation, then hyperinflation, a loss of exports, and lack of technological innovation. Aspirations for *Weltpolitik* were in shambles. Germany was also without a template for reviving its economy, rethinking the relationship of high and low culture, restoring or revamping gender relations, or reassessing Germany's place in the new global order. Past discourses about America and Russia no longer spoke to postwar problems, but Weimar Germans could not but look outward, for Germany's disruptive changes were paralleled by dramatic transformations in Russia and America. Each claimed to represent the direction in which the future was heading, a vision of modernity which others could—indeed must—embrace.

Concepts and Commentators

The Bolshevik Revolution offered an alternative not only to Tsarist autocracy but also to liberal democracy and capitalism. It was an experiment in its early stages that promised a socialized economy and classless society, the liberation of women and transformation of the family. Reality proved far different, as Russia was wracked by civil war, deindustrialization, and famine. Lenin and the Communist Party, not workers' councils, controlled the state. After 1921, the New Economic Policy introduced a more stable mixed economy, and ambitious economic and social reforms were postponed. Yet however wide the gap between the promise of communism and its realization, Soviet Russia did offer a distinctive alternative to Weimar's democratic capitalism that was modern in theory and aspiration, if not in practice. War did not fundamentally alter the American political system, but it greatly aided its economy. Before becoming a belligerent in 1917, its banks and businesses sent loans, weapons, and supplies to Britain and France and its manufacturing sector and investments abroad expanded significantly. America dominated the post-war economic order, leaving Germany as well as victorious Britain and France far behind.[11] America offered an actual, robustly developed model rather than an aspirational one. Many Germans hoped America and Soviet Russia might offer solutions to the multiple crises—real and imagined—which afflicted Weimar. They believed that the material world could be designed and contingency managed. In varied combinations they drew on 'nostalgia for the imperial past, neoconservative notions of eternal return, fascination with technology, obsessions with the American future, and careful attention to the Bolshevik experiment' to do so.[12] Historian Rüdiger Graf insists that Weimar Germans viewed crisis optimistically as an opportunity; it signalled an open situation in a world that was malleable. Crisis was an impetus to choose between a problematic present and a dramatically reconfigured future.[13]

There was a widespread consensus that the future lay outside of Europe. America and the Soviet Union were seen as quintessentially modern, other Western European nations were not. Yet Germans disagreed about what modernity meant and which aspects were desirable or disturbing. Weimar debates about transnational visions of modernity, like the concept of modernity itself, were capacious, elastic, and elusive, referring now to actual conditions, now to projections and fabrications. They encompassed literary and artistic modernism, technology, industrialization, urban life, mass culture, and gender.[14] For some, modernity implied reason and predictability, for others experimentation and contingency. For some modernity and democratic mass politics went hand in hand, while others hoped political modernity would take left-wing or right-wing authoritarian forms. Few saw modernity as a unified totality that would develop in the teleological manner prescribed by modernization theory. Some scholars insist that modernity has been used in too many different ways to be analytically useful.[15] But in Weimar, the concepts of the modern and modernity informed discourse and guided policy.

Modernity was usually discussed not in abstract terms, but with reference to the specific attributes, attitudes, and institutions associated with America and to aspirations as well as actual conditions in the Soviet Union. The 'modern and America were synonymous', it has been argued.[16] True, but this equation raises as many questions as it answers. What characteristics of society, culture, identity, and behaviour distinguished America from Germany? Was Americanization desirable or possible? Did the Soviet Union offer a stark alternative to America or did its economy borrow heavily from America even as its political system and ideology diverged radically? Was Germany more like Russia or America? Although they disagreed about the substance and merits of American and Soviet modernity, most contemporary observers shared two assumptions. First, the USSR and the USA were not binary opposites but rather distinctive combinations of economic and cultural elements considered modern. Beneath different political systems and levels of development were elusive but important commonalities. Second, the Soviet Union and America offered models from whose elements Germans could pick and choose in an effort to produce a distinctively German version of modernity. Negotiation and selective appropriation rather than wholehearted embrace or total rejection characterized attitudes toward America. Reactions to the Soviet Union were by no means divided neatly into Communist uncritical admiration and total condemnation by all others. For many, fascination and admiration for the regime's ambitions coexisted with criticism of the results and their political and social costs.

Government officials and politicians of all political persuasions, capitalists and workers, engineers and housewives, journalists, academics, artists, and cultural critics all engaged with transnational models. Observers developed their views from newspapers, magazines, and travelogues; lectures on the Soviet economy or American culture; Hollywood and Soviet movies and American jazz. Some hoped to reach a broad popular audience; others aimed at cultural and political elites or technical experts and industrialists. Although most had at best a partial view of these distant and internally diverse countries, they held forth with confidence in parliamentary debates, the press, and hundreds of articles and books, public lectures and private reports. A few travelled to the USA or USSR. Most travellers to America came for business or professional reasons, were sponsored by their firm, their newspaper, or their trade union and could choose their own itinerary. The US government did not play a role but the German government did, eager to promote a positive image of Germany in America and encourage a revision of the Versailles Treaty. It sponsored student exchanges via the Academic Exchange Service, the Alexander von Humboldt Foundation, and the American Work Student Service. This new form of cultural diplomacy sent a few hundred German students across the Atlantic. They were well received and many became enthusiastic supporters of American economic practices, cultural products, and mores.[17] Visitors to Soviet Russia, whether travelling alone, as did Arthur Holitscher in 1921 and Walter Benjamin in 1926–7, or on group tours had to plan travel through official Soviet agencies.[18] Some travelled quite freely, others had more restrictive itineraries, but a few were exposed only to Potemkin villages by manipulative Soviet officials.[19] Travel reports became an extremely popular genre through which to describe and judge developments in America and the Soviet Union.[20]

Class and occupation, gender and generation, political party allegiance and place of residence, shaped Germans' views as did pre-war knowledge of or stereotypes about Russia and America, wartime experiences, and individual and collective aspirations for the post-war order.[21] Scholars like Peter Berg argue that 'the German picture of America really involved an explicitly German problematic … Such a picture is … the result of the most diverse interests. One's own presumptions, hope and fear shape it.'[22] This is only partially true. According to Alice Salomon, Germany's pioneer social worker, exposure to America would lead a German 'to think without the assumptions with which he was raised ... He grasps more sharply the past of his own nation ... he glimpses the future of humanity.'[23] Hans Siemsen, a Berlin-based left-wing journalist who travelled to the Soviet Union in 1931, insisted that it was important to learn from Russia's successes and failures, even if one did not want to imitate developments there.[24] America and the Soviet Union provided languages in which to debate new forms of production and consumption, mass culture and mass society, and definitions of masculinity and femininity, family and domesticity. When German issues were discussed through American or Soviet models, new understandings of German problems and possible solutions emerged.

From 1917 to 1924, debates about transnational models of modernity focused primarily on Soviet Russia, as Germans called it. America occupied centre stage from 1924 to 1929. When the Depression devastated the US and Stalin's Five-Year Plan was in full swing, Germans once again looked eastward.[25] The economies of both nations received the most attention, followed by new forms of mass culture. The gendered character of both the public and private sphere received extensive attention. Politics did not. Neither American democracy nor the Soviet self-described dictatorship of the proletariat provided appealing models for Weimar Germans seeking to modernize and stabilize Germany's fledgling republic. During the chaotic days of the November Revolution in 1918 and the subsequent often violent conflicts between the new state and radical workers, the Bolsheviks provided an abstract model of militancy to German workers, soldiers, and the new German Communist Party (KPD). Developments in the two states quickly diverged, however, and only Communists saw the Bolshevik's left-wing authoritarian one-party state as a possible model, even as they as well as non-communist leftists acknowledged its hierarchical, dictatorial, and repressive character.[26] Social democratic and liberal or Catholic observers were much more negative, while conservative nationalists saw Soviet authoritarianism and its anti-Western orientation as an acceptable alternative to Western liberalism, even as they rejected the ideology and economic model underlying both.

Nor was more attention paid to the American political system. Communists dismissed American democracy as bourgeois, hypocritical, and dominated by 'moneybags', while liberal intellectuals viewed it favourably and those on the right rejected liberalism completely.[27] Most commentators about *Amerikanismus*, however, ignored American politics, for the US did not speak to Weimar political problems and aspirations. Germany's democratic republic with its multiparty system and broad spectrum of political ideologies bore no resemblance to that in America. America still had no socialism or even social democracy; its legal system was different, its bureaucracy smaller and less interventionist, its welfare state underdeveloped. Weimar's fledgling democracy was fragile, but Germans were actively involved in developing structures and institutions, symbols and habits, that enhanced the legitimacy and stability of the republic. Weimar was a 'democracy in the making' of a sort similar to those in many European countries.[28] America was the exception. Thus economy, culture, and gender form the main foci of this chapter.

Alternative Economic Models

Any discussion of Weimar views of transnational visions of modernity must begin with economics, for it was multiple economic crises that propelled so many to look abroad. The First World War distorted German production, destabilized its currency, disrupted its foreign trade, and imposed harsh deprivations on its population. Peace brought the loss of 13 per cent of its territory and 10 per cent of its population, as well as its navy and merchant marine and much of its army. Once profitable investments in Russia vanished and, from being the world's third largest creditor, Germany became its biggest debtor.[29] Reparations contributed to Weimar's dismal economic prospects but so too did self-inflicted inflation, the loss of technological leadership, and the decline of global trade. By contrast, America emerged from the war with a growing economy and expanded foreign trade and investment. New methods of mass production, embodied in the concept of Fordism, came to fruition. From being a debtor nation, the US became the world's principal creditor. As the British pound weakened and the gold standard that anchored the global financial order was suspended during and after the war, the dollar became one of—if not the—pivotal world currency. Although the American government was reluctant to intervene in German economic affairs, private banks and the Federal Deposit Bank of New York renegotiated reparations with the 1924 Dawes Plan, and US loans flowed into German businesses and local and regional governments for the next five years.[30] Both American economic success and the presence of American money and firms made Weimar's engagement with America's model of economic modernity all but unavoidable.

Three questions dominated the discussions about economic Americanism. What was the secret of American economic success and were these enabling conditions unique to the US? Could and should Germany emulate modern American mass production? If so, what would be the implications for German quality work, labour relations, and consumption patterns? Business owners and leaders of industrial and trade organizations, engineers and factory managers, politicians, academics, journalists, and trade unionists eagerly jumped into the ensuing, very public debate. However contradictory their answers to these questions, most were confident that Germans could learn from America and reshape the German economy. While most only read about the US, many went to see what was most modern firsthand, namely the industrial heartland of Chicago, Pittsburgh, and above all Detroit.

While Germans admired America's enviable economic success and new forms of production and consumption, they disagreed about whether these were best explained by America's size and natural resources or its technological achievements and innovative products, by its entrepreneurial culture or its distinctive labour relations. Engineers, for example, expressed unqualified praise for the efficiency and simplicity of American technology and factory organization, insisting that, if only engineers were allowed to emulate these practices, many of Germany's problems could be solved. Carl Köttgen, the head of the giant Siemens electro-technical firm and acting head of the national productivity board charged with rationalizing the German economy (Reichskuratorium für Wirtschaftlichkeit, RKW), published the book *Economic America* after his 1925 trip across the Atlantic.[31] He insisted that America's economic achievements resulted in part from an abundance of natural resources and cheap food, in part from pervasive standardization, mechanization, and mass production, and in part from the more intensive work pace and longer work day. Because production had been modernized and productivity improved, higher wages and expanded consumption were possible. Social Democrats disagreed; some saw technology rather than more intensive work as key, while others argued that higher wages spurred technological modernization, organizational rationalization, and the mass production of consumer durables. They praised American capitalists for understanding the importance of the domestic market and possibilities of vastly expanded consumption and urged German industrialists to follow suit.[32]

Germans agreed that Fordism was 'the key to understanding economic relations in the USA'.[33] Much of the American economy was not as modern as Ford's automobile plants, yet, they insisted, these embodied the elusive essence of Americanism. Germans enthusiastically read Henry Ford's *My Life and Work*, first published in 1922, with a German translation appearing in 1923. The book was part autobiography, part company history, and part exposition of his approach to capitalism, labour relations, and consumption. Industrialists, engineers, trade unionists, and cultural critics praised and criticized different aspects of Ford's economic and political programme, with some embracing his blatant antisemitism and others ignoring it.[34] More than 200,000 copies were sold in Germany by decade's end and it was 'the canonical work of the period of stabilization'.[35] Those who could travelled to Detroit to see the vast River Rouge plant in person. The engineer Franz Westermann was captivated by the size, technical construction, and 'living spirit' of this automobile factory and regarded his visit as 'the most powerful experience of his life'.[36] Yet, there was no agreement about what Fordism meant, for both Ford's ideology and the system he developed could be read in multiple ways. Some saw Fordism as a quintessentially rationalized and integrated system of mass production, others as a new way of stimulating demand for mass-produced consumer durables, and still others as an ideology of entrepreneurial leadership and management that claimed to produce social peace on the shop floor and beyond.

Observers across the political and class spectrum described Fordism as a system of production in similar ways. They noted the size and speed of the Ford works and other modern factories, the integration of production from raw materials to the finished product, the introduction of flow production and the assembly line, the coexistence of advanced technology and a minute division of labour. Simplification, standardization, and constant innovation enhanced productivity. And Fordism did so not by extracting more labour from the individual worker, as Taylorism prescribed; rather, it optimized all factors of production. Fordism was 'the basic "ideal" of the rationalization of production, its exemplary embodiment'. Rationalization, the preferred German term for efficiency, was always linked to Americanization.[37] Admiration for the Fordist ethos of productivism was widespread. For engineers, it was an end in itself, as well as a means to improve the status and power of technocrats. For capitalists, American methods held out the promise of lower costs, greater competitiveness in export markets, and higher profits. Labour, whether social democratic or communist, shared the Fordist faith in expanding production through science, technology, and rationalization.

For all their enthusiasm about Fordist production methods, they disagreed which could be introduced in Germany and whether they required new forms of mass consumption. In addition to the assembly line, specialized machines and a minute division of labour, Ford had pioneered the $5 a day wage and the inexpensive model T car that more skilled workers and farmers could afford. He argued that supply needed to create its own demand through better wages, advertising, and credit buying. This approach to consumption proved particularly contentious in Weimar Germany. Capitalists argued that Germany was too poor and its domestic market too small to introduce full-scale Fordism; business lacked funds for massive technical modernization, let alone a high wage policy. Germany should focus on closing inefficient firms, integrating production, and intensifying work so as to restore the export of specialized, quality products.[38] Social Democrats disagreed, insisting that higher wages would pressure firms to rationalize and the resulting expansion of demand would generate money for further rationalization in a virtuous cycle.[39] They did share capital's belief that Germany was too poor to support mass-produced inexpensive cars or household consumer durables. Fritz Tarnow, a leading trade unionist, enthusiastic endorser of Fordism, and member of the 1925 social democratic trade union delegation to the USA, advised capital to produce 'not baking ovens but bread'. This slogan revealed the difficulty in grasping what was distinctively modern about the American economy, for it focused on the satisfaction of basic needs of a traditional sort, rather than the creation of new needs.[40]

Ford ran his automobile empire according to well-publicized ideas about service, firm leadership, and labour relations. Some Germans regarded Ford's ideology of service to the community as essential to Fordism and compatible with ideas of service to the nation. Others saw his insistence on centralizing firm leadership in a single person as the essence of his philosophy and a justification for eliminating trade unions as well as shareholders. The German Institute for Technical Work Schooling, DINTA, some industrialists, like Alfred Vögler, head of the steel manufacturer Vereinigte Stahlwerke, and the academic Friedrich von Gottl-Ottlilienfeld promoted Ford's call for a new authoritarian yet ostensibly benevolent firm leadership that would create an organic factory community. Fordism, they insisted, promised material prosperity, harmonious labour relations, and joy in work—a white socialism in place of the red alternative.[41]

Even those most enthusiastic about Fordism worried that it would spell the end of German quality work and the specialized products for which Germany was noted. It might eliminate the skilled worker and his—for the skilled were always male—joy in work. Employers, scientists of work, and right-wing politicians sought to preserve German quality work in order to protect markets at home and abroad and promote job satisfaction and a *Berufsethos*, or vocational ethic that, it was hoped, would weaken support for unions and left parties. They criticized American rationalized work as intense, monotonous, and deskilled. Social Democrats, Communists, and Christian trade unionists were divided about whether jobs at River Rouge were substantially more onerous than those in the average German factory. Some claimed rationalized work was less fatiguing and more satisfyingly rhythmic than work in factories without a minute division of labour and flow production. Others were willing to accept oppressive assembly line labour in return for higher wages and mass consumption. According to industrialists and the RKW, Germany needed to protect quality work by cutting taxes and social policy payments, lowering wages, and lengthening the workday. Trade unionists countered that better pay, expanded vocational training, and a greater worker voice in shaping production would best protect German quality work.[42]

Industrialists and trade unionists who visited American factories remarked on the informal interactions between workers and foremen, engineers, and managers, and the absence of trade unions. Capital applauded the latter, but had no desire to introduce less hierarchical practices in their factories. Trade unionists insisted that American owners and managers created a less autocratic shop floor because that paid off economically and politically, but they doubted that trust was very deep or fundamental conflicts eliminated. They did not want German firms to emulate American labour relations.[43]

Many visitors to America were dazzled by the array of consumer goods, from cars, radios, and refrigerators to the thousands of smaller products sold through Sears and Roebuck catalogues. Whereas puritan principles had once informed economic attitudes, the pleasures of mass consumption now defined American culture. The economist, prolific author, and America enthusiast Moritz J. Bonn praised the resulting 'democratization of need satisfaction', even as he noted that twice a year the Sears and Roebuck catalogues 'create the same form of life for a large part of the American population'.[44] The economic geographer Alfred Rühl complained bitterly about the oppressive homogeneity of American homes, that 'reveal nothing of the personality of the builder or owner'.[45] While walking through the streets of Chicago, Arthur Feiler, the business editor of the *Frankfurter Zeitung*, lamented 'the monstrous uniformity of all those passing individuals' dressed and coiffed alike.[46] America represented the antithesis of the class-specific, bourgeois mode of consumption prevalent in Germany as throughout Europe.[47] Social Democrats disagreed, citing their 1925 trade union delegation whose members carefully counted the different kinds of bedframes, alarm clocks, and cars to show that standardization and diversity could coexist.[48]

Throughout most of the 1920s, Soviet Russia did not feature prominently in German debates about economic modernity. The First World War, the Civil War, and centralization, collectivization, and chaos of war communism killed millions and resulted in deurbanization, deindustrialization, and deproletarianization, a decline in the number of industrial workers. From 1921 to 1928 the New Economic Policy reintroduced a mixed economy, which expanded rural and urban production and consumption, but failed to modernize them. The 1922 Treaty of Rapallo established diplomatic and economic relations between Germany and the Soviet Union, but the relationship was transactional on both sides, for neither saw the other as a model to emulate. Moreover, Russians, like Germans, regarded America as a source of concrete knowledge about everything from industrial technology and mechanized agriculture to electrification.

Ford's autobiography was a bestseller there as well. Leon Trotsky was confident that 'Americanized Bolshevism will triumph and smash imperialist Americanism.'[49] Soviet engineers and economists regarded American unskilled and semiskilled assembly line work as more suited to Russia's labour force, largely of peasant origin, than German capitalism's skilled labour force and export orientation.[50]

The Soviets were not able to adopt American methods and technologies until the decade's end. Nonetheless, they worked assiduously to persuade supportive, indifferent, and hostile Germans of the value of their vision and the possibility of its realization. It began with Karl Radek, a leading Bolshevik, who spent 1919 in Berlin's Moabit prison and under house arrest. He held 'a political salon', visited by journalists, politicians, and left intellectuals. Industrial leaders like Walther Rathenau came hoping to re-establish their pre-war business ties to Russia, while conservative figures were looking for an ally against the Versailles system. Radek maintained these many-sided contacts during subsequent visits to Berlin as a Comintern representative.[51] The Soviet All-Union Society for Cultural Ties Abroad (VOKS) worked to spread knowledge about Soviet culture and society in Germany and bring visitors to the Soviet Union. It helped establish the Society of Friends of the New Russia in 1923 to reach out to those ideologically sympathetic to the USSR. Albert Einstein, the sex reformer Helene Stöcker, the authors Thomas and Heinrich Mann, and the architect Bruno Taut were among its members, who numbered 1,300 by 1930.[52] The VOKS also cultivated influential, centrist intellectual and cultural figures. It established links with academics, especially in the German Society for the Study of Eastern Europe (DGSO), led by the most prominent German historian of modern Russia, Otto Hoetzsch.[53] Hoetzsch, who was a German National People's Party parliamentary deputy, saw Russia as a fellow pariah nation and potential ally; it was not an economic model to emulate, but was worthy of study. He made Berlin a world centre for research on contemporary Russia.[54] This research on Eastern Europe, dominant in Weimar, differed markedly from the research of institutes like the Leipzig Stiftung für Deutsche Volks-und Kulturbodenforschung, which focused only on Germans in Eastern Europe and used medieval history to claim ostensible German rights.[55] The Soviets courted other German nationalists, among them the National Bolshevik, Ernst Niekisch, who saw the Soviet Union as an alternative to Western capitalism; its state planning and autarky might offer Germany a means to escape from Western dominance and fulfil nationalist aspirations.[56]

Many Germans were receptive to learning about Soviet Russia and several thousand visited in the 1920s; some did so from political conviction; others from fascination mixed with ambivalence; and still others from enmity. Communists were the most numerous. Communist friendship societies and the Comintern publicized Soviet achievements and brought German comrades for visits, while Willi Münzenberg's *Arbeiter Illustrierte Zeitung* showcased the Soviet model or atypical elements thereof. German Communist Party leaders and lower level cadres came for meetings and training courses with the Bolsheviks, but relations were far from harmonious. The two parties had distinctive histories, operated in quite different societies, and developed incompatible models of party behaviour and political practice. KPD leaders bowed to Soviet wishes; those lower down did not regard the militant, militarized, and conspiratorial Soviet party officials as role models, while the latter regarded German communists as effeminate, 'chattering bureaucrats'.[57]

Nor were German communist assessments of Soviet economic and social developments uniformly positive. To be sure, KPD members were overall less critical than others; Alfons Goldschmidt in the early 1920s and the artist Heinrich Vogeler in the early 1930s painted rosy pictures of existing conditions.[58] Others focused primarily on Soviet ambitions and long-term prospects. After a visit there in 1923, Otto Corbach claimed to have seen 'the very first beginnings of a completely new world'. After his 1931 trip Franz Carl Weiskopf wrote an enthusiastic book about the new economy of the future and the new Soviet person in the making.[59] Others did report on present material deprivations, economic shortcomings, and authoritarian politics. Assessing the prospects of Americanized Bolshevism in his 1925 *Ford or Marx: The Practical Solution to the Social Question,* Jakob Walcher, a member of the KPD leadership, insisted that American technology and organizational innovations were compatible with socialism; indeed, only under communism would the benefits of these methods accrue to workers. But they did not yet exist in the Soviet Union.[60] Overall, KPD visitors spoke less about the economy during the NEP years than about politics, culture, and questions of equality.[61]

Non-communist leftists were more critical of what they saw but seldom totally negative. Arthur Holitscher who visited during war communism, admitted that the Bolsheviks 'had a great idea, perhaps the greatest that humans have ever had'. But it was being realized through an extraordinary centralization of production and administration. The state ruled through 'iron compulsion' and eliminated individual freedom. This was not the kind of socialism Holitscher desired.[62] Many described the pros and cons of the Soviet system fairly objectively and none claimed that it functioned better than capitalism, but most avoided passing an overall judgement or predicting the future.[63] Only German Social Democrats completely dismissed the Soviet project; its authoritarian politics, repression of socialists, and foolish violation of the conditions for creating socialism that Marxist theory prescribed produced a dystopian failure.[64] At decade's end, however, German views became more positive.

After 1928 Stalin began translating the promise of a non-capitalist modernity into the ambitious and disruptive policies of forced agricultural collectivization and industrialization. The First Five-Year Plan that proved so costly to peasants and workers was built in part by importing American machinery and factory blueprints and the hiring of American engineers and workers.[65] The goal was a 'Soviet Americanism', and the creation of 'Russian Americans' who would have the work ethic and skills of their American counterparts.[66] At the same time the American model was in crisis, as the US experienced mass unemployment, bank failures, and an unprecedented drop in production. Germany suffered even more and Germans turned eastward in search of an economic model.

Germans were among the many foreigners who studied and visited the Soviet Union. Some were captivated by 'the romance of economic development',[67] others were searching for a socialist alternative to their depression-ridden capitalist countries. Still others saw the Soviet Union as a challenge to Western modernity. Some came to work in the Soviet economy, others studied it under the auspices of Arplan (the Working Group for the Study of the Soviet Russian Planned Economy). Arplan brought together a diverse group of Weimar intellectuals and academics, ranging from the leftists Karl Wittvogel and Friedrich Pollock to right-wing nationalists such as Ernst Jünger and Hans Zehrer. Hoetzsch was involved, for he was fascinated by the potency of the Soviet Union, its 'will to life', even as he opposed standardization, collectivization, and Stalin's cultural revolution. Arplan held conferences and disseminated literature on Soviet planning and in 1932 organized a delegation to visit the highpoints of Soviet development. Like German travellers to America, those visiting the Soviet Union came away with different impressions. A few saw an admirable alternative to Weimar, others sadly unrealized ambitions or practices to avoid at all costs.[68]

Thousands of German technical experts and workers went to the Soviet Union for reasons ranging from ideological conviction and adventure to unemployment at home or orders from their employers. Like Americans, they hoped to introduce modern methods, but soon became disillusioned by the gap between Soviet ambitions and achievements and by the material conditions and cultural level of Soviet workers.[69] Siemsen toured a newly opened tractor factory in Stalingrad and the gigantic Dnieprostroi dam and found a confusing mixture of American capitalist methods, compulsion, and unreasonably ambitious plans. One German worker he interviewed had nothing but praise for his living conditions, but looked down on his Russian co-workers, saying 'They certainly aren't German.' Another said conditions in Rostov were fine for a single man but those with families were understandably not bringing them. A third German did not want to return to capitalist Europe.[70] Many left intellectual visitors admitted that Russian workers had a much lower standard of living than German ones, but felt they were more optimistic about the future.[71]

Most of those working in or studying the emerging communist economy did not see it as a model for Weimar. It was impossible to ignore the chaos and compromises, mistakes and retreats, the poorly functioning factories, shoddy goods, and housing shortages. Americanized elements were at best partially realized versions of the originals; and the distinctively communist elements fell far short of their promise. Yet, many commenters contextualized these failings, emphasizing the legacy of Tsarism and war and the need to see socialism as an experiment in process. Franz Carl Weiskopf, who visited the USSR six times between 1926 and 1932, stressed the positives, like no unemployment, rather than housing shortages, and focused on the future toward which communism was heading, even if its contours were unclear. He optimistically called one of his books *Transfer into the Twenty-First Century*.[72] Even Siemsen, who was more critical, concluded that Soviet Russia was neither hell nor paradise but rather 'a field of struggle and work for humanity which believed in the future'. For all its many failings and the fact that so many had suffered, the Soviet Union was 'one of the greatest accomplishments of world history'. Nonetheless, he insisted, it was not one that Germany could or should try to imitate.[73]

KULTUR, MASS CULTURE, AND GENDER

American and Soviet mass culture presented challenges to German national identity, culture and everyday life. Germany prided itself on being a *Kulturnation*, filled with great artists, musicians, and authors, opera houses, museums, and theatres. Intellectual and artistic elites and the broad middle classes identified with high culture, and Social Democrats wanted workers to have access to it. Many Germans claimed that America lacked a well-developed high culture and its citizens did not value European cultural achievements. Moreover, women controlled what cultural institutions there were.[74] Germans claimed to value the spiritual and intellectual, while Americans prioritized materialism; Germans sought to cultivate the inner development of the individual, while Americans pursued visible economic success. Americans were men of action and instrumental rationality, while Germans appreciated complexity and ambiguity. Germans had depth and history while Americans were superficial and looked only to the future.[75]

However simplistic, class-specific, and self-serving such binaries were, they provided a lens through which many assessed American and Soviet mass culture. As Susan Buck-Morss has argued, 'Not only cinema but mass culture generally had a positive meaning in the United States and the Soviet Union that it lacked in the ethnically constructed imaginaries of Western European nations, where 'masses,' a visual phenomenon, and 'culture', a literary one, tended to be viewed as antithetical extremes'.[76] According to Andreas Huyssen, 'political, psychological, and aesthetic discourse ... consistently and obsessively genders mass culture and the masses as feminine while high culture, whether traditional or modern, clearly remains the privileged realm of male activities'.[77] The much more commodified and prevalent American mass culture presented the greatest danger, especially to youth. According to the educator and Protestant cleric, Günther Dehn, 'it is not socialism but Americanism that will be the end of everything as we have known it'.[78]

Germans worried that American jazz, all-girl dance teams, and above all Hollywood films would undermine German high culture. According to one alarmed commentator, the millions of movie-going Germans 'are all co-opted by American taste, they are made equal, made uniform ... The American film is the new world militarism'.[79] Hollywood catered to popular desires for entertainment, escape, and the distracted feminine sensibilities of movie-going 'little shop girls'.[80] American movies drew audiences away from traditional theatres and competed with the more serious German films.

There was reason to worry. While the war eroded European dominance in the global movie industry and ushered in American hegemony, it also enabled the rapid growth of German cinema, led by Ufa (Universum Film AG). After 1921, however, American films re-entered the German market and the pre-war *Kino-Debatte* about the dangers cinema presented to theatre and literature resumed. According to many religious leaders, educators, conservative politicians, and Social Democrats, movies, especially

Hollywood ones, had deleterious effects on youth, offended religious, social, and sexual standards, and needed to be censored.[81] Cultural commentators focused on the conflict between art—books, plays, and serious films—and entertainment—popular movies, whether American or German. Critics and movie producers debated whether American success was due to its large market and wealth, to Hollywood's technical sophistication and skilled actors, or to film narratives which critics regarded as incoherent and childish while admitting their broad appeal. They were unsure whether there was a homogeneous transnational mass public that shared a desire for entertainment or whether there were nationally specific tastes that only a cinema rooted in a particular history and culture could satisfy. Intensified economic competition between Hollywood and Ufa led many to wonder whether Germans would have to imitate American film techniques, acting styles, management, and marketing practices in order to challenge America's cinematic hegemony—or simply to survive.[82]

Many German producers and directors argued that adopting American techniques, technology, and marketing practice was necessary but disagreed about imitating Hollywood content. The anxiety about American cinematic modernity was greater than that surrounding Fordism, the confidence about building a distinctly German model less robust, for Hollywood had a palpable presence in Germany that Fordism did not. Yet the generational and gender anxieties that religious leaders and cultural critics projected onto Hollywood films may have been exaggerated. Although the number of American feature and short films increased dramatically over the 1920s, they played primarily in big cities.[83] The number of movie theatres and patrons grew, yet roughly half of all Weimar Germans probably never went to the movies; in 1926 only seven out of a hundred Germans regularly saw a movie while sixty-seven out of a hundred Americans did. In smaller German towns, well attended theatres and opera houses played a traditional, often middle-brow repertoire.[84]

Soviet culture attracted less attention and aroused less anxiety. German intellectuals and artists who visited the Soviet Union were exposed to regime-sponsored culture. Some, like Walter Benjamin, saw many plays while in Moscow, giving mixed or negative reviews to most.[85] Most left intellectual visitors judged Soviet literature mediocre at best and Soviet popular films miserable. Many noted a vast gap between the cultural level and tastes of the avant-garde and the Russian population at large.[86] Holitscher viewed the Proletkult's efforts to create a new revolutionary aesthetic for the masses as utopian.[87] By decade's end, Soviet art and literature became quite conservative and visitors were preoccupied with the Five-Year Plan rather than culture. Soviet culture was visibly present in Germany; Meyerhold's Moscow Art theatre performed in Berlin, and films like Eisenstein's *Battleship Potemkin* played in big cities. The Malik Publishing house, run by Wieland and John Herzfelde and George Grosz, published Soviet literature.[88] In the late 1920s, Hoetzsch's DGSO was instrumental in bringing Soviet natural scientists and historians to meet with their German counterparts.[89] These initiatives drew more restricted audiences than Hollywood films and jazz did; if they created more openness to Soviet culture among educated circles, they did not threaten to seduce the masses as American popular culture did.

Germans reflected on the new American and Soviet norms and forms of femininity and masculinity, domesticity and sexuality, that they encountered or imagined. They projected their own deep anxieties about gender and generation, whose ostensibly natural order had been thrown into turmoil by war, inflation, and democratization. The figure of the American woman was central to these anxious musings, for she seemed to exemplify the opportunities, contradictions, and ambiguities of modernity. Germans drew her portrait from the real and imagined experiences of middle-class American women and families. She was ostensibly more equal and free in both public life and within the home and had more access to education, employment, and leisure time than her German counterpart. Young, stylish, and liberated, she might reject marriage altogether or combine work and motherhood. Variants of the modern woman existed around the world; Germany had a visible *Girlkultur* and rising female employment, but in Weimar the modern new woman was coded as American.[90]

American women were not central to Fordist production, but German observers accorded them prime responsibility for mass consumption which they claimed promoted material abundance but tasteless uniformity and an accessible but superficial popular culture. Women played a prominent role in education and the arts. Moritz Bonn claimed 'The man devoted himself to business; the woman to culture'.[91] According to Alice Salomon, this led to a 'feminization of culture', of which she approved.[92] Many men were deeply disturbed, blaming American women for that nation's lack of depth, subtlety, and creativity and criticizing the American man for abdicating cultural and intellectual leadership in his single-minded pursuit of the almighty dollar. Was this model of middle-class masculinity, they asked nervously, a prerequisite for economic modernity American style?

America did not present an alternative to marriage, motherhood, and the nuclear family, but it challenged German ideas about domesticity. Many middle-class German feminists and home economics specialists admired American homes for their functional kitchens, electrification, and abundant appliances and canned goods. Yet most commentators thought Germans were too poor to afford appliances or costly prepared foods. The German home could be modernized, however, if women purchased standardized dishes, pots and pans, and cutlery and went about their daily tasks in a rationally planned manner. Most important, however, the German woman should regard domestic labour as a *Beruf*, a profession or vocation, that was vital to both family happiness and national prosperity. She needed to imbue her home with the proper spirit, one said to be lacking in the mechanized, rationalized but cold modern American home. To many Germans the modern American woman abdicated her proper role in the private sphere of marriage, family, and domesticity. This was a price few Germans wanted to pay.[93] Nor were Americans a model for love and sexuality. Some observers admired the independent American women, who escaped 'the egotistical rule of the man'.[94] Others found America a confusing mixture of puritanism and repression; its women were flirtatious but unerotic, athletic but asexual. They approached love with rational calculation rather than passion. For Siegfried Kracauer and the psychotechnician Fritz Giese, the Tiller Girls, an all-woman precision dance team, were the consummate expression of these gender contradictions and of the American obsession with technology and rationalization in intimate and affective matters as well as in public and productivist ones.[95]

The Soviet Union also pioneered a new gender order and German reactions were equally mixed. The new man, a brawny, militant, and politically committed factory worker, was the iconic figure; he had his equivalent in the KPD, a decidedly male party in its membership and ideological valorization of the male proletariat. But the KPD figure was more a product of the pre-war socialist movement, wartime experiences, and the 1918/19 revolution than a borrowing from the Soviet Union. And many Communists found the Soviet version of the militant, revolutionary male too extreme and unsuited for the German context.[96] Germans working in the Soviet Union encountered some who embodied the desired enthusiasm for building socialism, but many others who lacked skill, discipline, and dedication. Outside communist circles, the Soviet new man seemed dangerously militant and ideological. Most leftists and radical feminists commented positively on rights accorded women in politics, the economy, and the family, for the Soviets were far ahead of the rest of Europe and the US. But observers were often better informed about laws and official policy than about actual conditions. Many were ambivalent or critical when some Bolsheviks advocated replacing romantic love with rationalized sexuality.[97] Weimar sex reformers, feminists, and social democratic doctors along with Communists praised the pioneering Soviet legalization of abortion and sought to emulate this in the unsuccessful campaign for the abolition of paragraph 218 of the German penal code.[98]

There was a Soviet new woman or rather several competing ones. The female tractor driver as the epitome of the new working woman and the committed Bolshevik who practised revolutionary asceticism garnered official approval. But other Soviet new women modelled themselves on their American or Western European sisters about whom they learned from Hollywood films and foreign visitors. They eschewed austere anti-materialism in favour of short hair and skirts, dancing, cosmetics, and sex. But with their homemade clothes and poverty, they were pale imitations of their Western counterparts.[99] Although some Soviet Communists like Alexandra Kollontai advocated both free love and the socialization of housework, German Communists propagated a rather traditional nuclear family with a working wife, who rationalized her home and supported her husband's political commitments.[100]

Conclusion

Looking to transnational models of modernity created more conflicts than consensus. Capital and labour advocated contradictory paths to a reformed and modernized but distinctively German organization of production. They differed about the possibility and desirability of mass consumption American style, and even those most open to it had great difficulty imaging what a German form might look like. Yet America did spur

Germans to define competing visions of the future they wanted. None of these entailed either slavish imitation or wholesale rejection; rather they reflected in varied and conflicting forms a desire to adopt some aspects of Americanism, adapt others and reject still others to create a negotiated, hybrid form of modernity. The minority on the left who looked toward the Soviet Union for alternatives to Weimar were equally selective about what they hoped to emulate economically and politically, reserving praise more for aspirations than for what had been realized. Those on the right were interested not in economic or cultural emulation but rather in instrumentalizing the Soviet Union in support of their anti-Western, anti-liberal views.

During the Weimar years, Germans adopted very little of the American model, and nothing of the Soviet one. Some firms adopted Taylorist time and motion studies but few built assembly lines, introduced new technologies or fully integrated production. If River Rouge was the future, German remained distinctly unmodern throughout the 1920s. Nor were workers able to secure significantly higher wages or expand consumption possibilities. Only the middle and upper classes could afford cars and household appliances; at most, workers might be able to buy a motorcycle.[101] Much as capital and right-wing politicians admired Ford's approach to management and trade unions, realizing his practices was impossible under Weimar's democratic order and strong labour laws. American mass culture was more influential and the movie industry became more Americanized than other sectors, for neither Ufa's cooperation with American studios in the short-lived Parufamet joint venture nor competition with them at home and abroad prevented Hollywood's hegemony.[102]

By 1933 the allure of America had diminished considerably. Views of the Soviet Union were more mixed but Germans were increasingly excluded from working there. Nonetheless, attention to transnational models by no means disappeared. National Socialism strove to build a distinctive fascist model that combined economic modernity with nationalism, militarism, illiberalism, antisemitism, and cultural and gender traditionalism. Hitler strongly criticized American politics and culture, but he was fascinated by Fordism, pressured American firms to help modernize the German economy in preparation for war, and allowed Hollywood films to be shown until the late 1930s.[103] The Nazis failed to build a fascist alternative to Americanism or crush the Soviet model, and defeat in 1945 opened the way for a much more extensive German engagement with transnational visions. Through force and persuasion, money and culture, public and private channels America and the Soviet Union sought to impose their models of production and consumption, culture and gender on their parts of a divided Germany, forcing Germans once again to negotiate with these contentious models of modernity.

NOTES

1. Arthur Holitscher, *Wiedersehen mit Amerika: Die Verwandlung der USA* (Berlin: S. Fischer, 1930), 11–3.

2. Rüdiger Graf, *Die Zukunft der Weimarer Republik: Krisen und Zukunftsaneignungen in Deutschland, 1918–1933* (Munich: R. Oldenbourg, 2008).
3. Paul Wengraf, *Amerika-Europa-Russland* (Vienna/Leipzig: Zahn & Diamant, 1927), 39.
4. Dan Diner, *America in the Eyes of the Germans: An Essay on Anti-Americanism* (Princeton: Marcus Weiner, 1996).
5. Mary Nolan, *The Transatlantic Century: Europe and America, 1890–2010* (Cambridge: Cambridge University Press, 2012), 33–6. Alexander Schmidt, *Reisen in die Moderne: Die Amerika-Diskurse des deutschen Bürgertums vor dem Ersten Weltkrieg im europäischen Vergleich* (Berlin: Akademie, 1997).
6. Daniel T. Rodgers, *Atlantic Crossings: Social Politics in a Progressive Age* (Cambridge, MA: Harvard University Press, 1998), 70–5.
7. Matthias Heeke, *Reisen zu den Sowjets: Der ausländische Tourismus in Russland 1921–1941* (Münster: Lit Verlag, 2003), 55.
8. Michael Burleigh, *Germany Turns Eastward: A Study of Ostforschung in the Third Reich* (Cambridge: Cambridge University Press, 1988), 5–6.
9. Karl Schlögel, *Berlin, Ostbahnhof Europas: Russen und Deutsche in ihrem Jahrhundert* (Berlin: Siedler, 1998), 8–13.
10. Gerd Koenen, *Der Russland-Komplex: Die Deutschen und der Osten 1900–1945* (Munich: C. H. Beck, 2005), 15.
11. Robert Zieger, *America's Great War: World War I and the American Experience* (Lanham, MD: Rowman & Littlefield, 2000), 16, 30–1. Paul Kennedy, *The Rise and Fall of the Great Powers* (New York: Vintage, 1987), 258–9, 266–71.
12. Peter Fritzsche, 'Landscape of Danger, Landscape of Design: Crisis and Modernism in Weimar Germany', in Thomas W. Kniesche and Stephen Brockmann (eds), *Dancing on the Volcano: Essays on the Culture of the Weimar Republic* (Columbia, SC: Camden House, 1994), 34–42, quote 41. Peter Fritzsche, 'Did Weimar Fail?', *Journal of Modern History*, 68 (1996), 633.
13. Rüdiger Graf, 'Either-Or: The Narrative of "Crisis" in Weimar Germany and in Historiography', *Central European History*, 43 (2010), 592–615, here 600–2; Moritz Föllmer, Rüdiger Graf, and Per Leo, 'Die Kultur der Krise in der Weimarer Republik', in Föllmer and Graf (eds), *Die 'Krise' der Weimarer Republik: Zur Kritik eines Deutungsmusters* (Frankfurt/Main: Campus, 2005), 23–33.
14. Fritzsche, 'Landscape', 34.
15. Frederick Cooper, *Colonialism in Question: Theory, Knowledge, History* (Berkeley, CA: University of California Press, 2005), 113–50.
16. Alf Lüdtke, Inge Marssolek, and Adelheid von Saldern (eds), *Amerikanisierung: Traum oder Albtraum im Deutschland des 20. Jahrhunderts* (Stuttgart: Franz Steiner, 1996), 9.
17. Elisabeth Pillar, *German Public Diplomacy and the United States, 1918–1933* (Stuttgart: Franz Steiner, 2020), ch. 5.
18. Arthur Holitscher, *Drei Monate in Sowjet Russland* (Berlin: S. Fischer, 1921). Walter Benjamin, *Moscow Diary* (Cambridge, MA: Harvard University Press, 1986).
19. Eva Oberloskamp, *Reisen deutscher und französischer Linksintellektueller in die Sowjetunion 1917–1939* (Berlin: De Gruyter, 2011), 201–3, 313–14. Heeke, *Reisen*, 473–94.
20. About 900 reports of travels to the Soviet Union were published in Germany between 1921 and 1941. Heeke, *Reisen*, 1.
21. Mary Nolan, *Visions of Modernity: American Business and the Modernization of Germany* (New York: Oxford University Press, 1994), 17–29.

22. Peter Berg, *Deutschland und Amerika, 1918-1929: Über das deutsche Amerikabild der zwanziger Jahre* (Lübeck and Hamburg: Matthiesen, 1963), 8.
23. Alice Salomon, *Kultur im Werden: Amerikanische Reiseeindrücke* (Berlin: Ullstein, 1924), 7-8.
24. Hans Siemsen, *Russland Ja und Nein* (Berlin: Rowohlt, 1931), unnumbered foreword.
25. Heeke, *Reisen*, 13-17.
26. Oberloskamp, *Reisen*, 228-44.
27. Ricardo Bavaj, 'Pluralizing Democracy in Weimar Germany', in Paul Nolte (ed.), *Transatlantic Democracy in the Twentieth Century: Transfer and Transformation* (Berlin and Boston: Walter de Gruyter, 2016), 63-8.
28. Kathleen Canning, 'Remembering and Forgetting Germany's First Democracy: Reflections on the Founding of the Weimar Republic in 2019', *Bulletin of the German Historical Institute*, 65 (2019), 33-6. Tim B. Müller, 'The Opportunities and Challenges of Democracy: Weimar and Beyond', *Bulletin of the German Historical Institute*, 65 (2019), 113-19.
29. Nolan, *Transatlantic Century*, 62-6.
30. For a detailed discussion of America's rise during and after the war see Adam Tooze, *The Deluge: The Great War and the Remaking of the Global Order, 1916-1931* (London: Penguin, 2015).
31. Carl Köttgen, *Das wirtschaftliche Amerika* (Berlin: VDI-Verlag, 1925).
32. ADGB, *Amerikareise deutscher Gewerkschaftsführer* (Berlin: Verlagsgeschäft des Allgemeinen deutschen Gewerkschaftsbundes, 1926), passim.
33. Friedrich Aereboe, *Wirtschaft und Kultur in den Vereinigten Staaten von Nord Amerika* (Berlin: Paul Parey, 1930), 10.
34. Christiane Eifert, 'Antisemit und Autokönig: Henry Fords Autobiographie und ihre deutsche Rezeption in den 1920er-Jahren', *Zeithistorische Forschungen/Studies in Contemporary History*, 6 (2009), 219-29.
35. Helmut Lethen, *Neue Sachlichkeit 1924-1932: Studien zur Literatur des 'Weissen Sozialismus'* (Stuttgart: Metzler, 1970), 20.
36. Franz Westermann, *Amerika, wie ich es sah. Reiseskizzen eines Ingenieurs* (Halberstadt: H. Meyer, 1926), 99.
37. Modest Rubinstein, 'Die kapitalistische Rationalisierung', *Unter dem Banner des Marxismus*, 3/4 (1929), 550.
38. Köttgen, *Das wirtschaftliche Amerika*, passim.
39. ADGB, *Amerikareise*, 31-63, 157-75.
40. Fritz Tarnow, *Warum arm sein?* (Berlin: Verlagsgeschäft des Allgemeinen deutschen Gewerkschaftsbundes, 1928), 42.
41. Friedrich von Gottl-Ottlilienfeld, *Fordismus? Paraphrasen über das Verhältnis von Wirtschaft und technischer Vernunft bei Henry Ford und Frederick W. Taylor* (Jena: G. Fischer, 1924). Philipp Gassert, '"Without Concessions to Marxist of Communist Thought": Fordism in Germany, 1923-1939', in David E. Barclay and Elisabeth Glaser-Schmidt (eds), *Transatlantic Images and Perceptions* (Cambridge: Cambridge University Press,1997), 222-30.
42. Nolan, *Visions*, 84-103.
43. Ibid., 103-7.
44. Moritz J. Bonn, *Die Kultur der Vereinigten Staaten von Amerika* (Berlin: Wegweiser Verlag, 1930), 286. Moritz J. Bonn, *'Prosperity': Wunderglaube und Wirklichkeit im amerikanischen*

Wirtschaftsleben (Berlin: Fischer, 1931), 46. Bonn, *Amerika und sein Problem* (Munich: Meyer & Jessen, 1925), 88.
45. Alfred Rühl, *Vom Wirtschaftsgeist in Amerika* (Leipzig: Quelle & Meyer, 1927), 2.
46. Arthur Feiler, *America Seen through German Eyes* (New York: New Republic, 1928), 122.
47. Victoria de Grazia, *Irresistible Empire: America's Advance through Twentieth-Century Europe* (Cambridge, MA: Belknap Press 2005), 1-14.
48. ADGB, *Amerikareise*, 56-64.
49. Hans Rogger, 'Amerikanizm and Economic Development in Russia', *Comparative Studies in Society and History*, 23/3 (1981), 385.
50. Rogger, 'Amerikanizm', passim. David Shearer, *Industry, State and Society in Stalin's Russia, 1926-1934* (Ithaca, NY: Cornell University Press, 1996), 139-40.
51. Schlögel, *Berlin, Ostbahnhof*, 200-11. Koenen, *Der Russland-Komplex*, 278-86.
52. Michael David-Fox, *Showcasing the Great Experiment: Cultural Diplomacy and Western Visitors to the Soviet Union, 1921-1941* (Oxford: Oxford University Press, 2012), 62-3, 72.
53. David-Fox, *Showcasing*, 38-9, 61, 72-3.
54. Burleigh, *Germany Turns Eastward*, 15-6, 33. Schlögel, *Berlin, Ostbahnhof*, 316-9. Christoph Mick, 'Kulturbeziehungen und außenpolitisches Interesse: Neue Materialien zur "Deutschen Gesellschaft zum Studium Osteuropas" in der Zeit der Weimarer Republik', *Osteuropa*, 43 (1993), 914-28.
55. Burleigh, *Germany Turns Eastward*, 25-32. Ingo Haar and Michael Fahlbusch (eds), *German Scholars and Ethnic Cleansing, 1919-1945* (Oxford: Berghahn Books, 2007).
56. Michael David-Fox, *Crossing Borders, Modernity, Ideology and Culture in Russia and the Soviet Union* (Pittsburgh, PA: University of Pittsburgh Press, 2015), 190-1.
57. Bert Hoppe and Mark Keck-Szajbel, 'Iron Revolutionaries and Salon Socialists: Bolsheviks and German Communist in the 1920s and 1930s', *Kritika*, 10 (2009), 499-526, quote 526.
58. Koenen, *Der Russland-Komplex*, 302. Heeke, *Reisen*, 628.
59. Graf, *Die Zukunft*, 252-8.
60. Jacob Walcher, *Ford oder Marx: Die praktische Lösung der sozialen Frage* (Berlin: Neuer Deutscher Verlag, 1925), passim.
61. Oberloskamp, *Reisen*, 227, 244.
62. Holitscher, *Drei Monate*, 17-8, 35, 37.
63. Oberloskamp, *Reisen*, 261-3. Koenen, *Der Russland-Komplex*, 533-8.
64. Oberloskamp, *Reisen*, 146.
65. Peter G. Filene, *Americans and the Soviet Experiment, 1917-1933* (Cambridge, MA: Harvard University Press, 1967), 236-7. Stephen Kotkin, *Magnetic Mountain: Stalinism as a Civilization* (Berkeley, CA: University of California Press, 1995), 142-50.
66. Alan M. Ball, *Imagining America: Influence and Images in Twentieth-Century Russia* (Lanham, MD: Rowman & Littlefield, 2003), 26.
67. David Engerman, *Modernization from the Other Shore: American Intellectuals and the Romance of Russian Development* (Cambridge, MA: Harvard University Press, 2003), 157.
68. David-Fox, *Crossing Borders*, 201-9. Schlögel, *Berlin, Ostbahnhof*, 314.
69. Hoppe and Keck-Szajbel, 'Iron Revolutionaries', 510-1.
70. Siemsen, *Russland*, 149, 152, 169, 260.
71. Oberloskamp, *Reisen*, 252-3.
72. Ibid., 253.
73. Siemsen, *Russland*, 261.

74. Moritz J. Bonn, *Geld und Geist: Vom Wesen und Werden der amerikanischen Welt* (Berlin: S. Fischer, 1927), 153. Arthur Holitscher, *Amerika heute und morgen: Reiseerlebnisse* (Berlin: S. Fischer, 1912), 386. Salomon, *Kultur*, 69–70.
75. Bonn, *Amerika*, 126. Feiler, *America*, 68, 262–7. Rühl, *Vom Wirtschaftsgeist*, 11–6. Wengraf, *Amerika-Europa-Russland*, 29.
76. Susan Buck-Morss, *Dreamworld and Catastrophe: The Passing of Mass Utopia in East and West* (Cambridge, MA: MIT, 2000), 148.
77. Andreas Huyssen, 'Mass Culture as Woman: Modernism's Other', in Huyssen *After the Great Divide: Modernism, Mass Culture, Postmodernism* (Bloomington, IN: Indiana University Press, 1987), 47.
78. Günther Dehn, *Proletarische Jugend: Lebensgestaltung und Gedankenwelt der großstädtischen Proletarierjugend* (Berlin: Furche, 1929), 39.
79. Anton Kaes, 'The Debate about Cinema: Charting a Controversy', *New German Critique*, 40 (1987), 21.
80. Sabine Hake, 'Girls and Crisis: The Other Side of Diversion', *New German Critique*, 40 (1987), 147–64.
81. Thomas J. Saunders, *Hollywood in Berlin: American Cinema and Weimar Germany* (Berkeley, CA: University of California Press, 1994), 26–30.
82. Saunders, *Hollywood*, 85, 148, 165–9.
83. Ibid., 54.
84. Karl Christian Führer, 'High Brow and Low Brow Culture', in Anthony McElligott (ed.), *Weimar Germany* (Oxford: Oxford University Press, 2009), 276–8.
85. Benjamin, *Moscow Diary*, passim.
86. Oberloskamp, *Reisen*, 272.
87. Holitscher, *Amerika*, 98.
88. Koenen, *Der Russland-Komplex*, 356–9.
89. Mick, 'Kulturbeziehungen', 916.
90. Nolan, *Visions*, 120–7. Patrice Petro, *Joyless Streets: Women and Melodramatic Representation in Weimar Germany* (Princeton: Princeton University Press, 1989), 90–110, 127–39.
91. Moritz J. Bonn, *Geld und Geist: Vom Wesen und Werden der amerikanischen Welt* (Berlin: S. Fischer, 1927), 153.
92. Salomon, *Kultur*, 24, 69–70.
93. Mary Nolan, 'Housework Made Easy: The Taylorized Housewife in Weimar Germany's Rationalized Economy', *Feminist Studies*, 16 (1990), 549–78. Nancy Reagin, *Sweeping the German Nation: Domesticity and National Identity in Germany, 1870–1945* (New York: Cambridge University Press, 2006).
94. Wengraf, *Amerika-Europa-Russland*, 37.
95. Fritz Giese, *Girlkultur: Vergleiche zwischen amerikanischen und europäischen Rhythmus und Lebensgefühl* (Munich: Delphin, 1925). Siegfried Kracauer, 'The Mass Ornament', *New German Critique*, 5 (1975), 67–70.
96. Hoppe and Keck-Szajbel, 'Iron Revolutionaries', 510–1.
97. Oberloskamp, *Reisen*, 281–2, 301–3.
98. Atina Grossmann, *Reforming Sex: The German Movement for Birth Control and Abortion Reform, 1920–1950* (Oxford: Oxford University Press, 1995), 78–106.
99. Anne E. Gorsuch, 'The Dance Class or the Working Class', in Alys Eve Weinbaum, Lynn M. Thomas, Priti Ramamurthy, Uta G. Poiger, Madeleine Yue Dong, and Tani E Barlow (eds),

The Modern Girl around the World: Consumption, Modernity, and Globalization (Durham, NC: Duke University Press, 2008), 174–93.
100. Eric D. Weitz, *Creating German Communism, 1890–1990: From Popular Protest to Socialist State* (Princeton: Princeton University Press, 1997), 205–24.
101. Nolan, *Visions*, 131–78.
102. Saunders, *Hollywood*, 146–70.
103. Philipp Gassert, *Amerika im Dritten Reich: Ideologie, Propaganda und Volksmeinung, 1933–1945* (Stuttgart: Franz Steiner, 1997).

Bibliography

Buck-Morss, Susan, *Dreamworld and Catastrophe: The Passing of Mass Utopia in East and West* (Cambridge, MA: MIT, 2000).
Diner, Dan, *America in the Eyes of the Germans: An Essay on Anti-Americanism* (Princeton: Marcus Weiner, 1996).
David-Fox, Michael, *Showcasing the Great Experiment Cultural Diplomacy and Western Visitors to the Soviet Union, 1921–1941* (Oxford: Oxford University Press, 2012).
Heeke, Matthias, *Reisen zu den Sowjets: Der ausländische Tourismus in Russland 1921–1941* (Münster: Lit Verlag, 2003).
Hoppe, Bert, and Mark Keck-Szajbel, 'Iron Revolutionaries and Salon Socialists: Bolsheviks and German Communist in the 1920s and 1930s', *Kritika*, 10 (2009), 499–526.
Koenen, Gerd, *Der Russland-Komplex: Die Deutschen und der Osten 1900–1945* (Munich: C. H. Beck, 2005).
Nolan, Mary, *Visions of Modernity: American Business and the Modernization of Germany* (New York: Oxford University Press, 1994).
Oberloskamp, Eva, *Reisen deutscher und französischer Linksintellektueller in die Sowjetunion 1917–1939* (Berlin: De Gruyter, 2011).
Pillar, Elisabeth, *German Public Diplomacy and the United States, 1918–1933* (Stuttgart: Steiner, 2020).
Saunders, Thomas J., *Hollywood in Berlin: American Cinema and Weimar Germany* (Berkeley, CA: University of California Press, 1994).
Schlögel, Karl, *Berlin, Ostbahnhof Europas: Russen und Deutsche in ihrem Jahrhundert* (Berlin: Siedler, 1998).

CHAPTER 25

GERMAN JEWS IN THE WEIMAR REPUBLIC

SHARON GILLERMAN (†)

COMMENTING in 1923 on the relationship between his Germanness and Jewishness, Franz Rosenzweig, the celebrated German-Jewish philosopher, noted that, 'If life were at one stage to torment me and tear me into [these] two pieces ... I would not be able to survive this operation ... I ... ask ... not to torment me with this truly life-threatening question, but to leave me whole.'[1] This sentiment of the inextricability of Germanness and Jewishness was typical for many highly acculturated German Jews during the Weimar Republic, however diverse their individual commitments. Far from their integration being delusional, as the scholar Gershom Scholem famously asserted, German Jews had indeed become part of the fabric of German society over the course of the nineteenth and early twentieth centuries.[2] Yet despite German Jews' deep attachment to German culture and German universal values, the notion that *Deutschtum* and *Judentum* represented opposing forces was an established antisemitic theme that gained much wider currency after the First World War. Opposition to the republic was symbolized by identifying its 'Jewish spirit', signifying through such an association Jews' 'natural' alienness to true Germans.[3]

The abstraction of 'the Jew', in the collective singular, as distinct from 'the German' became a significant category in Weimar political discourse, a negative means to delineate a new German national vision. Yet the Jewish population in the Weimar era was heterogeneous, with multiple and evolving engagements through which members identified themselves as both Jews and Germans. Some of their actions as political actors and culture shapers in the republic rendered them particularly visible. Yet the unity built into the category of 'the Jew' stood in stark contrast to the diversity among Jews living in Germany. Who were the Jews in post-war Germany and what shaped their identities and civic, social, cultural, and religious lives, as Jews and Germans simultaneously?

In order to answer these questions, this chapter addresses the relative lack of attention to Jews as a collectivity in Weimar histories. While historians have devoted attention to how 'the Jew' was symbolized in political discourse, and to individual Jews who helped shape politics and culture in the republic, there has been less focus on the agency, cultures, and identities of German Jews as a group, whose integration, interactions, exclusions, and self-assertions form an integral part of Weimar history. This chapter will thus provide a general profile of Jews in Germany, in religious, demographic, economic, and organizational terms. It will then examine the new possibilities and constraints for Jews in the Weimar Republic's political and social environments. Finally, it will look at how Jews participated in shaping broader aspects of Weimar cultural and intellectual life while also voicing, at times, Jews' unique experiences, tensions, and sensibilities. Both within and beyond specifically Jewish religious and cultural spheres, Jews continued to re-envision both Jewish and German belonging during the Weimar Republic in ways that had and still have profound implications.

Population, Demography, and Changing Communal Dynamics

The promise of emancipation for the Jews in Germany over the nineteenth century was predicated upon expectations that Jews transform themselves and their religious practice to conform to the customs and values of the larger society. Even the greatest champions of the Jews demanded their complete assimilation, or erasure of difference, in most areas except religion. Whereas traditional Jewish society had been built upon both a religious and national basis, nineteenth-century Jews sought to shed their national identity through acculturation and religious reform, and reconfigure Judaism into a confession parallel to that of Protestantism or Catholicism. Yet even as 'German citizens of the Jewish faith'—as their national communal organization, the Central-Association of German Citizens of the Jewish Faith (CV), dubbed them—Jews nevertheless persisted as a distinctive group, even as they conformed to expectations for acculturation. By the beginning of the First World War, the majority had already broken with orthodox Jewish tradition and entered the middle class. A segment had converted or simply left the community; others had created new forms of community within more secular and cultural frameworks, and maintained distinctive family cultures. Their hopes for a renewed national unity inclusive of Jews, articulated by the Kaiser's August 1914 call for a civil truce, were dashed by the 1916 government census, which, prompted by antisemitic agitation, sowed doubt on Jewish participation in the war effort.[4] Shaken by the discrepancy between their integration as Germans fighting for their nation and the view of them as harming the collective, Germany's Jews entered the republic aware of the dissonance between their sense of belonging as Germans and their depiction as outsiders.

On the eve of the Weimar Republic, the Jewish population in Germany numbered around 550,000, representing no more than 0.9 per cent of the German population. While Jews bore diverse social, economic, political, and religious commitments and affiliations, they nevertheless shared a set of distinctive demographic characteristics. First and foremost, German Jews had become, since the nineteenth century, 'town dwellers par excellence'.[5] Their concentration in Germany's large cities grew more pronounced during the Weimar era, with more than 50 per cent of the Jewish population living in ten cities with more than 100,000 residents.[6] By the 1920s, nearly one-third of all German Jews lived in Berlin, and nearly two-thirds lived in large cities. Despite their urban preponderance, Jews had also established a presence in the rural areas and small towns in Bavaria, Baden, Württemberg, and Hesse, where about one in five German Jews resided. Though dispersed across these rural communities, in some municipalities, such as the village Rhina near Kassel, 10–15 per cent of the population was Jewish.[7] Even in the large metropolises, the Jewish population retained a certain cohesion, usually concentrating in certain districts. In Berlin, for example, 80 per cent of all Jews lived in six of the city's twenty administrative districts.[8]

The occupational structure of the Jewish population also differed significantly from that of the population at large due in part to historical prohibitions against Jews practising certain trades. Given their historical experience in trade, commerce, and banking and regional familial networks, German Jews were highly concentrated in the field of commerce; about 60 per cent of Jews owned small and mid-sized businesses. Jews were similarly highly overrepresented in the free professions such as medicine, law, and journalism, making up 16 per cent of Germany's lawyers and 11 per cent of its doctors. In both business and the free professions, Jews were also self-employed at a far higher rate than non-Jewish Germans: 50 per cent of Jews in business and the professions were self-employed, in comparison to the average rate of about 16 per cent. With the growth of white-collar jobs during the Weimar Republic, the proportion of Jewish white-collar workers jumped from 10.8 in 1907 to 21 per cent of the Jewish working population in 1933, with much of the growth in this sector the result of increased women's employment.[9] While the majority of Jews had established themselves in the middle class by the late nineteenth century, a small but highly visible upper class existed as well. Such well-known figures as the industrialist Walther Rathenau, the owners of large retail concerns such as Schocken and Tietz, as well as the owners of publishing houses of Mosse and Ullstein were among many prominent Jews in economic life. There also existed a Jewish working class, much smaller than in the rest of the German population, comprised largely, though not entirely, of East European Jews who had settled in Germany after the First World War and did not hold German citizenship.

The 1923 hyperinflation hit middle-class Jews particularly hard. Shopkeepers lost their savings, and pensioners, also overrepresented among Jews, suffered as the value of fixed incomes dropped. A considerable segment of the middle classes became impoverished and dependent on the support of the state and the Jewish community. During the Great Depression, too, the self-employed were hit especially hard. Rising antisemitism led to boycotts against Jewish businesses, and Jewish white-collar workers suffered a higher and more rapid rate of job loss than non-Jewish workers overall.[10] Long before the economic crises, but even more so afterwards, Jewish community leaders had sought to direct young Jews into non-commercial professions, as both a practical solution to Jews' threatened economic situation and a means to defend against antisemitic conspiracy theories about alleged Jewish economic manipulation.

The unique demographic profile of the Jewish population as predominantly urban dwellers meant that Jews experienced many of the social changes associated with modernization earlier and with greater intensity. This is particularly evident in changing birthrates among Jews. Owing to traditional religious behaviours, Jews had higher birthrates than other Germans, but by 1880 Jews began to lead all other population subgroups in lowering their birthrates. In 1920, the annual Jewish birthrate in Germany had dropped to 15 live births per 1,000, in comparison with 24 per 1,000 generally. During the crisis period of 1930–2, the birthrate dropped even further, indicating that the demographic profile of German Jews was more sensitive to political and economic crises than that of non-Jewish Germans.[11] Changes in birthrates not only decreased the size of the Jewish minority in Germany and risked reducing the number of sustainable communities, but also raised a new set of questions about the long-term survival of a community that was historically focused on achieving civic equality and social integration. The organized Jewish community began to focus greater concern on its ability to reproduce itself, less motivated by earlier fears of persecution or expulsion but instead under conditions of comparable comfort and success.

Changing birthrates were also related to shifts in Jewish marriage patterns, with increases in mixed marriages, especially among urban Jews. While Jews historically emphasized in-marriage owing to religious dictates and communal cohesion, the nineteenth-century states did not permit interfaith marriages, requiring conversion of the Jewish partner when Jewish-Christian unions did take place. Once civil marriage was introduced in 1875, marriages between Jewish and Christian Germans began to gradually rise, from 4.6 per cent in Prussia in 1880, to 12.8 per cent in 1912.[12] During the Weimar Republic, the trend increased. While 17 per cent of all marriages among Jews in Germany in the 1920s were mixed unions, the frequency in Berlin was over 30 per cent.[13] Yet even with rising intermarriage, endogamy remained a stronger impulse among Jews than among Catholics and Protestants.[14] In general, more men than women entered into mixed marriages, making it harder for Jewish women to find Jewish spouses. Though less common than between different Christian denominations, intermarriage signified to many Jews an abandonment of the Jewish community that threatened community survival and triggered leadership to work toward Jewish communal re-engagement.

Predictions of Jewish demographic decline led Jewish policy-makers to promote the idea of national Jewish population policy aimed at increasing the birthrate. The female body thus came to be a subject of interest and concern to the larger Jewish public and social and medical experts who argued that Jews' successful assimilation was threatening the biological continuity and distinctiveness of Jews. Though divided over their vision for the Jewish community, many leaders supported a pronatalist stance to raise a new generation—reflecting contemporary values—that was 'strong in body and vigorous in mind'.[15] Warning against the rationalization of sexual life, Jewish leaders undertook propaganda campaigns, conferences, the creation of marriage bureaus, financial aid to promote early marriage, and expanded medical care for women and children. Yet here, as in other undertakings, German Jewry acted in the service of both broadly German and uniquely Jewish interests, implementing state policy initiatives for improving national health and for cultivating its own distinct population.

An important factor shaping the constitution of the Jewish community in its demographic development, occupational profile, class structure, welfare activities, and political and religious orientations was the growing presence of East European Jews. Arriving during the First World War either as forced or hired labourers, their already growing wartime numbers swelled immediately after the war as thousands more Jews fled eastern Europe in the wake of pogroms in Poland and the Ukraine. The 1910 census reported that 79,000 Jews from eastern Europe lived in Germany; by 1925, some 108,000 Jews were of foreign origin, coming overwhelmingly from eastern Europe, constituting 19.1 per cent of Germany's Jewish population. Recently arrived East European Jews formed a distinctive body within German Jewry and their difference from the westernized German Jews had a variety of implications for German Jewish self-understanding. Occupying the lowest social stratum, working often in manual labour and as artisans and petty traders, they spoke Yiddish, tended towards larger families, were less acculturated to German and German Jewish ways, sometimes wore distinctive religious garb, and practised a more traditional form of Judaism. As a result, native German Jewish attitudes towards this group were complex and ambivalent. At one level, the East European embodiment of a difference that German Jews had laboured over generations to erase made them uneasy and threatened to jeopardize their own standing in German society. At the same time, the very significant antisemitism targeting the eastern Jew, who became a useful symbol of Jewish difference in the hands of antisemites, led German Jews to rally in solidarity with their East European co-religionists. Finally, encounters with '*Ostjuden*' gave some German Jews, particularly Zionist-oriented intellectuals, a sense of connection to an authentic Jewish past, whose dense ethnic and religious culture was far removed from what they saw as colourless assimilated Jewry. As a group that tended to immigrate to large cities, the East European population also increased German Jewry's already disproportionately high urban concentration, especially in cities like Berlin and Munich.[16]

The legal and organizational framework governing Jewish communal life was the *Gemeinde*. An extension of the premodern autonomous Jewish community, yet parallel to Catholic and Protestant institutions, the Jewish communities in Germany during the Weimar Republic continued to exist as legal entities that incorporated all the Jews in any area of residence. As publicly constituted corporations, the *Gemeinden* were empowered to collect tax revenues to pay for the maintenance of their religious institutions and services. The *Gemeinde*, therefore, was a much more comprehensive body than the religious congregation. It organized the community's religious and ritual affairs and appointed rabbis, but also extended beyond the religious into social, educational, and welfare institutions. By the 1920s, large *Gemeinden*, such as Berlin's, with almost 200,000 members, were dense networks of social, economic, and welfare institutions. While some of the smaller *Gemeinden* had difficulty sustaining themselves owing to the economic crises and the outmigration of the rural population, the *Gemeinde* expanded its functions in large cities.

The fact that the *Gemeinde* represented nearly all Jews in religious matters should not be taken to suggest that Weimar Jews formed a particularly religiously observant collective. Strict religious observance of Judaism had already declined as Jews became increasingly secularized over the nineteenth century, and most adhered to Liberal Judaism which adapted Judaism to more modernized religious forms. While there remained significant Orthodox communities, even the more traditional Jews in rural communities in the 1920s were selective in their religious observance. The majority of Jews in cities such as Hamburg, Frankfurt, Breslau, and Berlin did not attend synagogue, and if they did, it was mainly on the High Holidays.[17] It is estimated that no more than 15 to 20 per cent of German Jews observed traditional Jewish dietary laws, called *kashrut*.

As a representative body, the *Gemeinde* was an arena for competing visions of Jewish life and, as such, a site of political struggle and sometimes fierce conflict. Conflicts generally centred around the different religious visions of Liberal and Orthodox Jews. By the time of the republic, a large part of *Gemeinde* politics encompassed opposition by Zionists and others against the Liberal establishment. A new challenge in the form of the Jewish People's Party (Jüdische Volkspartei), emerged in 1919. Those with Zionist sympathies, together with East European Jews, and the Orthodox, formed a party stressing a national-Jewish position, emphasizing the ethnic character of Judaism, and promoting greater emphasis on social and educational institutions.[18] These challenges were accompanied by increasingly vociferous demands for democratizing communal life by extending the vote to women and the foreign-born. Demands for equal representation sought to overturn a system assuring representatives of the wealthiest class an absolute majority on most *Gemeinde* boards.

Beyond the official *Gemeinde*, German Jews created numerous local and national organizations reflecting their ideological diversity and competing visions. Most important in shaping and articulating Jews' ideal of a German-Jewish synthesis was the Central Association of German Citizens of the Jewish Faith (CV), founded in 1893 as a defence organization against increased antisemitic agitation. Aligned with, and in many ways representative of, the liberal, religious, and political worldview of the majority of middle-class Jews, its mission was to emphasize Jews' German patriotism while defending Jewish honour through education, political engagement, and legal action. The CV championed the emancipationist formula that Jews were German by nationality, while Jews by faith. Four years after the CV's founding, the Zionist Organization of Germany emerged to challenge the Liberal stance. Responding to the same forces as the CV—a rise in antisemitism and the increasingly successful integration of German Jews—Zionists saw antisemitism as an unavoidable feature of diaspora life and assimilation as a failure that led Jews to forgo deeply held Jewish bonds. Insisting that Jews were united not by religion, but by nationality, most Zionists in Germany did not intend to move to Palestine but embraced Zionism as a new self-definition enabling the recovery of ethnicity and stronger bonds of community. Most still affirmed their *Deutschtum* alongside their Jewish national consciousness, a synthesis among acculturated Jews that Zionist leader Kurt Blumenfeld characterized as 'postassimilatory' Zionism.[19]

During the Weimar Republic, the CV remained the largest Jewish organization in Germany, encompassing 20 to 25 per cent of households.[20] Although Zionists denounced the CV as 'assimilationist', the CV and Zionists were, in retrospect, more alike than the era's fierce ideological disputes would suggest. Indeed, the CV can now be understood as marking the entry of Jews as a collectivity into the German public sphere. With its readiness to act collectively for Jewish interests and fighting antisemitism in public rather than behind the scenes, it paradoxically endorsed a separate identity even as it promoted the ideal of Jews being distinguished by faith alone. As historian Shulamit Volkov argues, Zionism and the CV both represented a new form of self-assertion and self-understanding of Jews as a minority group, and this tendency toward self-assertion only strengthened during the Weimar Republic.[21]

Jews in their Social and Political Environments

German Jews displayed a deep commitment to political liberalism throughout their modern history. As perhaps the most distinctive feature setting Jews apart from other Germans, their particular investment in liberalism became painfully apparent towards the end of the republic, as Jews stood quite alone in the face of liberalism's collapse. During the Enlightenment, liberalism had envisioned the removal of Jewish legal disabilities through emancipation of the Jews, even as many German liberals did not fully accept it. With all its shortcomings in Germany, liberalism promoted an ideal of civil tolerance and promised the subordination of church to state. Most Jews eagerly embraced the universalist vision it offered for an open society that offered equality of opportunity rather than a social order based on feudal privileges. And it was the liberal national state, as against the conservative Christian one, which promised to deliver Jews' hoped-for equality of opportunity. Even as the promise of liberalism failed to be entirely realized, Jews held deeply to a liberal vision not only in support of narrowly defined Jewish interests, but in the spirit of building the nation as a whole.[22]

While the overwhelming majority of Jews supported liberal politics throughout the period of the republic, the revolutionary period saw pronounced Jewish participation in leftist and radical politics. Individual Jews played a prominent role in the revolutionary activities of 1918/19. The socialist-dominated provisional government of the republic, led by the six-person Council of People's Representatives, had two Jewish members, Hugo Haase (USPD) and Otto Landsberg (SPD). Jews also held leading posts in the new Prussian cabinet, which had a Jewish Prime Minister, Paul Hirsch, and several Jewish ministers, including Kurt Rosenfeld as Minister of Justice and Hugo Simon as Finance Minister. And in Berlin, three of the four positions of the city's governing council were held by Jews.[23] Rosa Luxemburg, one of the dynamic leaders of the communist Spartacus League, supported the so-called Spartacus uprising in January 1919 in

Berlin. But in no city was participation in revolutionary events as shaped by Jews as in Munich. Kurt Eisner, the Bavarian leader of the Independent Socialist Party (USPD), led the November revolution in Bavaria that overthrew the Wittelsbach monarchy, serving briefly as prime minister of the revolutionary government. He also appointed the Jewish-born Edgar Jaffé as Minister of Finance, and Felix Fechenbach, who served as his private secretary in the State Chancellery, was Jewish. The two more radical soviet republics following Eisner's assassination in February 1919 were led by Jewish figures Gustav Landauer, Ernst Toller, and Erich Mühsam, followed by the second council republic, led by Russian-born Eugen Leviné.

Whether supporting the republic or working towards a more radical vision, Jewish political participation in these first two years represented an immensely expanded Jewish role on the political stage. Before November 1918, Jews had never achieved positions higher than parliamentary deputies or party functionaries in the German government.[24] Neither before nor after the revolutionary period were there so many Jewish figures playing a central role in German politics. Yet the prominence of Jews in revolutionary movements became fodder for nationalists and a central trope within the discourse of radical nationalist and even centrist politics, with profound implications for Jews and the republic. For many in the Jewish community, this highly visible association of Jews with revolution led to much unease. Many sought to distance themselves from the radical figures by referring to them as people of 'Jewish descent', while the writer Jakob Wassermann portrayed them as outsiders not part of the Jewish community.[25] Because the revolutionaries' Jewishness figured so prominently in false arguments equating Jews with communism, the revolutionaries' relationship to Judaism or Jewishness has gone largely unexplored. Yet Michael Brenner has shown that, while few maintained formal ties to the *Gemeinde*, some, particularly Eisner and Landauer, felt themselves connected in certain ways to the Jewish community. Eisner refused to disassociate himself from Judaism and was deeply influenced by the German Jewish philosopher Hermann Cohen's blend of Kantian ethics, socialism, and the biblical prophetic tradition, while Gustav Landauer's spiritual pursuits led him to maintain connections to the Jewish community.[26]

The fact that most German Jews were opposed to even moderate socialism, not to mention more radical revolution, is evident in Jewish voting patterns in the republic. Most Jews voted consistent with their liberal ideals, continuing their electoral behaviour from the later part of the Empire. Their political ideals did not change greatly with the upheavals of 1918. While Jews voted for all parties, Jewish support for the right was negligible. The majority voted for the DDP, the left-liberal party founded in 1919 that most closely embodied the republic's liberal principles. The DDP would be home to most Weimar Jews until the crisis years, and even after 1930, Jews abandoned the party more slowly than other members. The presence of such prominent figures as Albert Einstein and the liberal publishers Rudolf Mosse and Theodor Wolff among its founding members suggested to many its 'Jewish' make-up. Indeed, with its vision of liberalism, its stance against antisemitism, and the fact that Jews were prominent at all levels of the party, the DDP quickly became labelled a 'Judenpartei' by the right.

The SPD was the next largest party for which a substantial minority of Jews voted, with estimates of the proportion of Jews voting SPD reaching as high as 28 per cent. Its attitude toward antisemitism helped draw Jews, as did its standing as the largest party supporting the republic, and Jews were disproportionately active as SPD theoreticians, propagandists, and party activists. Jews also voted for the Centre and the DVP, particularly in the south of Germany, with possibly up to 4 per cent of the Jewish vote going to the KPD. After 1930, as many Germans moved to the DNVP and the Nazi party, the collapse of the moderate centre forced Jews to reassess their position. While some remained faithful to the DDP even until July 1932, many moved to the remaining parties supporting the republic: the SPD and Centre, with likely a much smaller portion going to the KPD.[27]

After the high exposure in the first two years of the republic, few Jews occupied high political office, either at the Reich or state level. There were notable exceptions to this rule: Walther Rathenau was appointed Foreign Minister in 1922, and the social democrat Rudolf Hilferding served as Finance Minister in 1923 and again in 1928–30. But Jewish public figures were mostly reluctant to accept such prominent positions because of the fierce wave of antisemitism unleashed during these early years. In 1920, Ludwig Haas was proposed as a Reichswehr Minister for the DDP but declined, just as Max Warburg refused the Finance Minister position.[28] Because of the political climate, Einstein and Warburg had tried to persuade Rathenau not to accept the position as Foreign Minister. After Rathenau's assassination by right-wing forces, only Rudolf Hilferding remained as a Jewish government minister and there was a gradual reduction of public political activity of Jews during the middle and end of the Weimar Republic. Despite not holding the highest public positions, Jews nevertheless remained fully engaged in public life, with the number of Jews in civil service increasing, a key area of exclusion in Imperial Germany. Jews finally reached high ranks including some judges and state prosecutors, while Jews had also become part of the state administration and city administrations and were active in organs defending civil liberties. In Frankfurt am Main, for example, a city with a higher Jewish population than average, many members of the City Council were Jewish. All in all, as with the republic as a whole, politics during the era reflected both inclusion and exclusion. Opportunities for Jewish political participation and public service were substantially broadened while significant constraints remained. Yet despite differences in how Jews aligned politically and defined their relationship with the Jewish community, and despite the fact that the republic did not fully realize its liberal promise, Jews remained uniquely committed to its survival.

The extent of Jewish integration in German society during the republic has sometimes been presented within opposing narrative frames: as a period of unprecedented integration or one of increasing antisemitism and exclusion. While historians continue to illuminate the nature of the period's antisemitism, it would be too simple to take the existence of antisemitism as an uncomplicated reflection of social relations between Jews and non-Jews as a whole. While the revolutionary period witnessed an explosion of antisemitic expression and violence, and racial thinking became more prevalent than during the Imperial period, determining how the multiplicity of Weimar Jews experienced the changing impact of antisemitism and what they made of it is far more difficult. There was no single force of antisemitism exerting its impact in a uniform manner, but rather manifold expressions in a variety of situations and intensities, from racial exclusion based on *völkisch* thinking to old attitudes and stereotypes generalizing the behaviour of one Jew to that of the group. In representing Jews' participation in social life, then, no single narrative can adequately encapsulate Jewish social realities. The most we can do is provide a picture of the 'coexistence of openness and closedness' in German society, as historian Till van Rahden has framed it, suggesting that the interplay of forces shaping Jewish/non-Jewish interactions in different social contexts were diverse, depending on geography, generation, class, gender, religion, and the specifics of interpersonal relationships.[29]

One of the most significant frameworks for Jews' participation in German social life was the association or *Verein*, which functioned as a central institution in German community life. More formalized and structured than friendships, associations were institutions that formalized connections between individuals, through the forging of new civic spaces, laying a foundation from which social relationships emerged. For urban bourgeois Jews in particular, participating in both specifically Jewish as well as general bourgeois forms of association was a crucial feature of their civic and social engagement. Jews frequently joined and sometimes led *Vereine* with a cultural, social, charitable, athletic, business, military, or political focus. Jewish professionals were active in affairs of their corresponding professional association, while businessmen and tradesmen frequently belonged to and led commercial and industrial associations.[30] Associational life remained widely open to Jews during the republic even into the final years. In areas where *völkisch* ideas had taken root quickly, however, such as in Breslau, Jews assumed leadership roles less frequently, even in the early 1920s.[31] Bourgeois Jewish women continued their active engagement from the Imperial period in both Jewish and general charitable societies, as well as in the feminist movement. Jewish, Catholic, and Protestant women volunteered jointly in social welfare work, and, increasingly worked side-by-side in paid employment as social workers. Some of the leading figures in social welfare and policy work, for example, Henriette Fürth and Siddy Wronsky, were active in both general German and specifically Jewish organizations. Many other Jewish women, like Alice Salomon, Frieda Wunderlich, and Helene Simon, worked on general German social work and social policy.[32]

The rapid expansion of social welfare institutions also reflects an important dynamic in the Jewish community's sense of its position in Germany. While the Jewish community, like other confessional organizations, had to navigate a range of post-war social problems and economic crises, their articulation of a sense of crisis inhered with prescriptions for communal renewal. Jewish communities faced an unprecedented scale of need among their members, owing to the fragile economic and social position of East European immigrants, an orphan population, a rising rate of 'endangered youth', war veterans and war widows, middle-class economic collapse, unemployment, and the precarious position of pensioners. The welfare expenditures of the *Gemeinde* in Berlin accounted for one-third of its total budget, and by 1930, this level of investment in welfare became typical for Jewish communities across the country.

To organize and increasingly regulate Jewish social life, Weimar Jews created a national system of youth welfare and youth guardianship offices, remade institutions for wayward youth, established occupational retraining programmes, worker welfare bureaus, and shelters for the homeless, unemployed, and transient. Redefining the nature of social need, Jewish social work—primarily a women's profession—transformed social crises into opportunities to strengthen the Jewish population. Thus, welfare as a realm of social engagement linked to the larger goal of strengthening the German and Jewish *Gemeinschaft*. In the process, an increasingly expansive and vibrant social domain that Jews created during the Weimar Republic came to resemble, in the words of one social worker, 'a little state within a larger one'.[33] Their view of social crisis led Weimar Jews to formulate expansive, bold visions for community that shared a similar spirit with that of the broader Jewish cultural renaissance.

In everyday life, as neighbours, parents of schoolchildren, members of associations, in politics, leisure, and in the workplace, Jewish men and women interacted extensively with other Germans. One of the most visible markers of these close contacts was the steady rate of mixed marriages, which were highest in cities which offered more opportunities for social contact and where social strictures governing Jewish communal life were less stringently followed. Interconfessional marriages took place more frequently among Jews in the lower classes, where mixing between Jews and non-Jews was greatest, owing to a greater openness to Jews in this milieu than within the mercantile middle class.[34] In the city of Cologne, historian Nicola Wenge found that women had more social contacts with non-Jewish Germans than men, yet men throughout Germany entered mixed marriages more frequently than women.[35]

On the whole, Jews, especially those in the middle classes, formed their most intimate social bonds with other Jews, but some maintained close non-Jewish friendships as well. Children probably mixed even more than many adults did, as the overwhelming majority of Jewish children attended public schools. Jewish children sometimes experienced exclusion at school, originating from other children more than from teachers, while Jewish teachers in some locations could be subjected to antisemitic abuse by students.[36] Universities were a site where young Jewish men might most typically encounter increased antisemitism and exclusion, particularly foreign and foreign-born Jewish students. Historically, German universities had been the standard-bearers of traditional conservative values, while student fraternities, catering to the social elites, had long been fertile ground for antisemitism. At the beginning of the republic, the overwhelming majority of student fraternities formed an organization espousing *völkisch* ideals and antisemitism and the Jewish fraternities were virtually excluded from student politics.[37] Yet alongside this reality, research on Jewish female university students makes clear how difficult it is to extrapolate individual experiences from the facts of organized antisemitism. Excepting foreign students, Harriet Pass Friedenreich finds that, until 1930, almost none of the 433 Jewish women at universities in Germany and Austria she studied reported experiencing antisemitism at the university.[38]

One strategy Jews used to navigate pockets of German society where antisemitism threatened was to avoid those areas of social life that might prove hostile. This can be seen in the ways bourgeois Jews engaged middle-class leisure activity. Along with other middle-class Germans, Jews made a practice of traveling for vacations to hotels and seaside resorts. While the majority of Jews continued to enjoy their vacations throughout the Weimar years, some reported encountering antisemitism from other guests or the occasional hotel owner, or they witnessed displays of Nazi activity. The CV responded by composing lists of antisemitic hotels and resorts that was published in the national Jewish weekly, *Israelitisches Familienblatt,* advising Jewish readers which accommodations and destinations to avoid. Jewish travellers, for example, were advised to avoid Munich entirely as the capital of antisemitism.[39] By 1932, a list no longer sufficed, leading the CV to establish a special service for Jews traveling in Germany. It was less possible to navigate anti-Jewish violence, which often targeted neighbourhoods where East European Jews lived. At the end of 1923, at the highpoint of the hyperinflation and rampant break-ins, looting, and violence, there was a spate of violent incidents in the Scheunenviertel in Berlin, and in Beuthen, Oldenburg, and Nuremberg. Even during the more stable period from 1924 to 1930, antisemitic disturbances erupted in the city of Kassel and the countryside in Hesse, where Jewish cattle dealers were singled out for abuse.[40]

Until the economic crisis, even with the growing prominence of the 'Jewish Question' in the political sphere and the scattered, episodic nature of antisemitism elsewhere, historians have yet to fully assess how widely the political antisemitism of the Weimar years and rise in racial thinking changed the substance of social relations during the so-called 'stable' years. In many ways, Jews flourished in their private and public lives, particularly in the upper-middle-class milieus where most Jews lived both among other Jews and non-Jews. They enjoyed a high degree of social integration in many areas, even as both social boundaries put up by non-Jews and cultural affinities among Jews led them to stay ethnically or religiously bonded to one another. Certainly, too, some of the less acculturated East European Jews and recent refugees were much less integrated.

Yet the sharp rise of antisemitism and the growing fortunes of the Nazi party towards the end of the Weimar Republic had a broader and more measurable impact on everyday life than in the earlier years of the republic, and there were signs of a growing exclusion of Jews in a variety of spheres, although this varied by city and region. Though most sports organizations continued to include Jews till the end of the Weimar Republic, a few clubs began to undermine Jews' continued participation by adopting Aryan paragraphs, and some cultural and business associations became less welcoming to Jews.[41] Max Liebermann, appointed president of the Prussian Academy of Arts in 1920, resigned his post under pressure in 1932. By the early 1930s, Catholic and Protestant groups that had once collaborated with Jewish groups withdrew from many of those relationships and antisemitism in some places rose to a new dimension of social exclusion.[42]

Under the impact of the economic crisis, some Jews suffered harassment, especially in small towns, where boycotts against doctors and shopkeepers damaged business and the bonds of sociability that had once obtained. Street violence and political terror were on the rise in general and violent attacks on Jews became more frequent. On the eve of Rosh Hashanah, the Jewish New Year celebration, in September 1931, nearly a thousand SA men converged on the commercial district surrounding Berlin's most fashionable street, the Kurfürstendamm, attacking Jews walking home from synagogue, and those mistaken for Jews.[43] Although this violence against upper-class Jews in Berlin was very unusual, these events signalled not only the penetration of Nazi influence into many areas of society previously untouched, but also the lack of support for Jews by the larger public.

So how did Jews respond to the rise in antisemitism and anti-democratic forces on the right? Approaches to this question were long mired in the politics of the period, with an implicit recurring accusation that Jews denied the danger facing them and that their responses to antisemitism were inadequate. This critique was articulated primarily by the Zionist opponents of the CV, for whom the existence of antisemitism was the key source and legitimation of their ideological opposition to life in the diaspora, and by extension, the liberal approach of the CV. Scholarship since then has illuminated the numerous ways in which both ordinary Jews and Jewish leaders interpreted and responded to antisemitism. One of the more conventional ways Jewish activists and leaders reacted to eruptions of antisemitism was to hew to past patterns of exercising self-restraint and waiting as inconspicuously as possible until the storm died down. A parallel approach emphasized Jewish public behaviour that did not reinforce antisemitic stereotypes. The *Rabbinerverband*, for example, reminded Jews at a time of high *völkisch* agitation in 1922, that the behaviour of every individual reflected on the group. Male writers and Jewish feminists alike called on women and mothers in particular to counteract the negative association of Jewish women with excessive consumption by returning to what Zionist rabbi Emil Bernhard Cohn, writing in the feminist *Jüdischer Frauenbund* newspaper in 1932, called 'the highest virtue of Jewish womanhood ... modesty'.[44]

Other approaches Jews took followed precisely the opposite line. Many Jews organized physical self-defence. During the anti-Jewish violence in the largely East European Jewish Scheunenviertel district of Berlin at the height of the hyperinflation in November 1923, some twenty members of the Reichsbund Jüdischer Frontsoldaten (Reich League of Jewish Front Line Soldiers, RJF) armed themselves with wooden clubs and pistols in order to protect the area's largely Orthodox Jews from assault. Realizing they could not rely solely on the state or others for protection, young people, students, and demobilized soldiers organized spontaneous responses to incidents across Germany during the Kapp putsch, and the Rosh Hashanah attacks in Berlin.[45] Similar responses took place spontaneously in the early 1930s. In the Berlin *Gemeinde*, a secret Jüdischer Abwehrdienst (Jewish Defence Service, JAD) was formed by RJF and representatives from Zionist athletic associations Makkabi and Bar-Kochba that had 250–300 members and maintained links to Berlin's police.[46]

The most far-reaching collective response to antisemitism came from the Centralverein. One focus of its defence activities during the Weimar Republic was what historian Stefanie Schüler-Springorum calls 'writing against antisemitism'.[47] The CV ran a campaign to combat antisemitism by creating a news service that produced communiques for the press.⁴⁸ They published journals distributed monthly to 30,000 public figures and politicians, wrote and distributed pamphlets and educational literature, and placed advertisements in Jewish newspapers before elections calling on Jewish voters to avoid voting for antisemitic parties. Writing as a response to antisemitism extended well beyond the CV: communal leaders, rabbis, intellectuals, and community activists persistently wrote about the subject and it featured prominently in the Jewish press. As in the Kaiserreich, the CV pressed legal actions addressing antisemitic speech and the honour of Jews. But it now more vigorously undertook legal actions against anti-Jewish boycotts, physical assaults, and cemetery desecration. It lodged protests with state parliaments and governments, and forged political alliances where possible, receiving additional support from the very small Abwehr Verein (League to Combat Antisemitism).⁴⁹

Beginning in 1929, their focus shifted to working more directly to build political support for parties loyal to the republic and opposing National Socialism. The CV set up an independent agency for propaganda against the NSDAP, with Jewish and non-Jewish journalists collaborating in attacking the movement. They furnished anti-Nazi parties, organizations, and publications with money and propaganda to influence republican politicians in the SPD, Centre, and BVP to defend Jews. Balancing its commitment to political neutrality while opposing the NSDAP, the CV even secretly collaborated with the Reichsbanner Schwarz Rot Gold, an organization founded to defend the republic, and largely led by SPD members.⁵⁰ Although little collaboration existed between the CV and the Zionists even after 1930, the Zionist Organization of Germany and the CV both tried unsuccessfully to get Chancellor Brüning and his successor von Papen to take a stand against antisemitism.

Jewish defence activities did not ultimately turn the tide against National Socialism, but neither did the actions of Communists, Social Democrats, or the Catholic Centre party with their millions of voters behind them. But like Jews in much of Europe and America, and like German Jews in preceding generations, they had no choice but to perservere. Responding increasingly aggressively during the final years of the republic, they did not close their eyes to looming danger. Indeed, it may have been their experience of antisemitism in the past that led them to think that they would weather the storm ahead. As Peter Pulzer concluded, 'it was not ignorance of antisemitism that gave Jews a false sense of security in 1932, but their relative success, up to then, in containing it'.⁵¹

German Culture, Jewish Culture, Weimar Culture

As Jews contended with a combination of openness and closedness in Weimar social life, they were active and deliberate participants in refashioning both German and Jewish cultural expression. Looking at forms of cultural participation and practices allows us to explore how Jews defined and redefined their notions of belongingness to German and Jewish culture and community. How did the dynamic of belonging and exclusion come to expression both in the general cultural sphere and the specifically Jewish one? Historically, Jewish engagement in German culture in the lead-up to emancipation had been an important arena for Jewish self-definition. Unable to fully belong to the Christian nation nor to find a place in *völkisch*-oriented notions of Germanness, Jews forged an essentially new form of Jewish identity and culture in which the ideals of German culture provided much of the substance. The middle-class ideal of *Bildung*, understood as self-cultivation, character formation, and aesthetic refinement, drove Jews' integration into German society through embracing the primacy of the cultural sphere.

Since the beginning of the republic, antisemites perceived a decadent modern culture as a product of the destructive revolutionary movement and part and parcel of the 'stab-in-the-back' myth. Much that was culturally innovative or controversial was deemed a Jewish invention that, like defeat in the First World War and the republic, was poisoning German culture and the national soul. Within antisemitic discourse, Jews' prominence in German culture in a democracy fully committed to their equality was one of many signs that the Weimar Republic was a 'Jewish republic'. Yet this view of Jewish predominance in culture was not limited to antisemites. After 1933, some Jews looked back upon the thriving culture of Weimar and pointed proudly to Jewish members of the avant-garde as symbols of German-Jewish success. In 1937, the writer Arnold Zweig asserted that the accomplishments of Weimar culture were inseparable from Jewish achievements, arguing that 'German Jews ... are the advanced guard and the representatives of Western Europe in the German mental composition'.[52] Long after the war, historian Walter Laqueur argued that without the Jews there would have been no 'Weimar culture', and historian George Mosse noted that Weimar's modernist culture had been sometimes called an 'internal Jewish dialogue'.[53]

There has long been an emphasis on Jews' conspicuous presence in German culture during the republic and it is certainly true that many Jews were crucial shapers of Weimar culture. Jews were highly overrepresented in modernist movements, perhaps more visibly and actively than in any other realm including politics, the press, and the economy. In literature, theatre, music, architecture, cinema, journalism, and criticism, the outsider, using Peter Gay's formulation, had become insider.[54] The most significant concentration of Jews was in literature, where almost a third of German expressionist authors and many of the most popular writers, including Alfred Döblin, Arnold Zweig, Jacob Wassermann, and Emil Ludwig were Jewish.[55] Theatre was also decisively shaped by Jewish directors, playwrights, set designers, and actors. Jews similarly played a disproportionate role in intellectual life, primarily in liberal and left circles, editing and contributing to the important newspapers of the moderate and left-wing press, including Mosse's *Berliner Tageblatt* and the rival Ullstein's *Berliner Illustrierte Zeitung*.[56] Nearly two-thirds of the cultural critics associated with the left-wing journal *Die Weltbühne* were Jewish, as were most of the scholars affiliated with the Marxist-influenced approach to 'critical theory' surrounding Frankfurt's Institute for Social Research.[57]

Yet interpretations of Jews' high profile in the realms of modernist and intellectual culture have created a somewhat distorted portrait of Weimar Jews. Influential scholars, such as Peter Gay, have insisted that Jews participating in 'Weimar culture' were 'wholly assimilated', downplaying the role that the Jewishness of the creator may have played in shaping cultural production.[58] More recent histories problematizing Jewish assimilation have reconsidered the complex set of forces shaping Jews and their cultural work, pointing to the multiple ways those with a range of Jewish identifications created new perspectives critiquing bourgeois culture, nationalism, and even emancipation, reflecting the creative tensions of German and Jewish identities.[59] Even if their art or thought bore no distinctively Jewish features, many scholars now consider more closely the background of shared culture, sensibilities, 'habitus', and a distinctive outsider position that led Jewish artists and intellectuals—from intellectuals and scientists like Sigmund Freud and his followers, philosophers from Ernst Bloch to Hannah Arendt, and artists, designers, and architects such as Erich Mendelsohn, Ernest Sohn, and Ruth Adler-Schnee, to name a few examples—to respond to their unique position in German society in multiple registers.

Newer research has also built on more recent understandings of culture to expand the portrait of Jewish participation in Weimar cultural life. For Jews were not only disproportionately represented in the dazzling high culture most associated with the Weimar Republic. In fact, Jewish creative presence as entertainers, entrepreneurs, and advertisers was even more extensive in the dynamic sphere of popular culture, which included circus, revue, variety, cabaret, and cinema. Popular urban entertainment styles challenged the narrative and aesthetic coherence of high culture by offering more heterogeneous and fragmented formats, juxtaposing satire, parody, experimental avant-garde, and physical performance as on the cabaret stage or in the films of Ernst Lubitsch. Modern popular culture, appealing to a much wider section of the population, allowed Jews to present their concerns and aspirations while also speaking to the non-Jewish lower-middle and middle classes.[60] In the budding film industry, the Jewish presence became visible in unprecedented ways, as many German Jewish filmmakers promoted 'the formation of a liberal, multicultural, transnational bourgeois society, in which "the Jew" could be different, but equal'.[61] German Jewish performers, directors, and producers of live entertainment and film also created new spheres of sociability, challenging the boundaries of insiders and outsiders, to convey visions of a more liberal society.

Cultural studies approaches have helped deepen our understanding of German Jewish cultures by turning to everyday practices such as fashion and style choices and consumer practices to explore how Jews negotiated, affirmed, or even sought to erase their appearance of Jewishness in certain contexts. What the range of Jewish cultural creations and strategies makes clear is that Jews did not participate in German culture as either Jews or Germans, but as German Jews with sensibilities rooted often in multiple cultures and different class backgrounds and gender identities, frequently without engaging explicitly Jewish themes, but sometimes with Jewish elements. Jews' participation in German culture contradicted the emancipation ideology that expected Jews to adapt to a static mainstream culture, until there remained no further perceived differences between Germans and Jews. Instead, in high culture as well as mass urban entertainment, Jews with varied but sometimes shared sensibilities were active agents in creating and co-constituting Weimar cultures in partnership with non-Jews as they shaped new values and visions for German life during the Weimar Republic. Jewish acculturation, or Peter Gay's notion of 'wholly assimilated' Jews, was not equivalent to the effacing of Jewish identity.

Sports offered an important way to work toward social integration, and Jews were active in nearly all types of sporting societies.[62] Yet there were different energies and motives shaping Weimar Jews' engagement with sports. An embrace of physical culture was also a feature of a newly energized German Jewish youth culture revolting against their parents' bourgeois world. During the republic, the Jewish youth movement expanded from the original Zionist Blau Weiss, founded in 1907, to a range of groups spanning a broader ideological spectrum, including Liberal, Orthodox, and even the liberal German Jewish Veterans' organization. From the twenty existing youth organizations in Frankfurt am Main in 1932, for example, sixteen were founded during the republic, and, by 1933, at least one in three young Jews in Weimar had been a member of a Jewish youth organization.[63]

Thus, alongside the integrative role of sports in promoting acculturation, sports also functioned as a means of Jewish cultural differentiation. While Zionists had first initiated sports clubs around the turn of the century, aiming to create a 'new Jew' through sport, nationalism, and the cultivation of the body, after the First World War, many more non-Zionist Jewish sports clubs emerged to promote Jewish socializing, connection, and physical development through gymnastics, soccer, track and field, boxing, and jujitsu.[64] Even as there was a significant growth in the number and type of specifically Jewish sporting associations during the Weimar Republic, the majority of Jews participated in general German clubs and teams, helped found and fund these organizations, and held offices within these *Vereine*.[65] Jewish women were highly overrepresented in athletic activities in Germany overall, with the highest ranking German tennis players being Jewish women.[66]

The impulse propelling the sweeping desire for renewal that touched nearly every aspect of Jewish cultural and community life was the urge to reimagine and reconstitute *Gemeinschaft*. For Jews, this drive to recover a distinctive Jewish *Gemeinschaft*—built on authentic bonds between its members—originated not solely from the exclusions of antisemitism, but also in the forces shaping the larger search for *Gemeinschaft* in German culture and politics. Yet the path to *Gemeinschaft* based on a renewed connection with Jewishness resulted also from what Shulamit Volkov describes as 'dissimilation', a process beginning in the 1890s whereby Jews who had successfully integrated became aware both of the limits of assimilation and an internal drive to recover something of the Jewish past that had been lost or watered down. Franz Kafka memorably conveyed this sense in his 1919 letter to his father, referring to an 'insignificant scrap of Judaism' which 'all dribbled away while you were passing it on'.[67]

Two of Weimar's leading visionaries of community who energized and envisioned a new relationship between both strands of the German and Jewish for a generation of Jews disconnected from Jewish life were the philosophers Martin Buber and Franz Rosenzweig. Buber furthered a stylized Hasidic heritage for modern Jews, translating and popularizing the magical tales of East European rabbis and offering a mystical view of the Jewish people, deeply infused in certain respects by *völkisch* ideas. Rosenzweig, who famously turned from considering conversion to Christianity to an embrace of Judaism, sought to lead German Jews in recovering *Judentum* as an equally vital and powerful force as their *Deutschtum*. As the leading figure of the Jewish renaissance, Rosenzweig believed only a new type of learning could help alienated Jews pivot toward a Jewish world. Opening the Frankfurt Free Jewish Lehrhaus in August 1920, Rosenzweig, later with Buber, helped reinvent Jewish tradition by making Jewish knowledge, texts, and traditions accessible through classes, study groups, and seminars. Activities at the Lehrhaus were attended by members of all social strata and age groups, and frequented by many young intellectuals, becoming a model that would be duplicated across Germany. Buber and Rosenzweig also collaborated in reconstituting Jewish tradition through a new scholarly translation of the Bible into a Hebraized German meant to reflect the original Hebrew text, imbuing the German-speaking Jewish reader, according to one Berlin Liberal rabbi, with a 'new healthy Romanticism that leads into the … depths of our souls'.[68]

Buber and Rosenzweig were part of a larger intellectual shift challenging liberal formulations of Judaism as a 'religion of reason', such as those articulated by the neo-Kantian philosopher Hermann Cohen. This new Jewish sensibility was anti-bourgeois, anti-liberal, and anti-establishment, leading intellectuals like Walter Benjamin, Gershom Scholem, Ernst Bloch, Franz Rosenzweig, and even Georg Lukács to create works, as Steven Aschheim has shown, that fused 'radical and Jewish thematics'.[69] Whether found in Benjamin's messianic communism, Scholem's recovery of mysticism, Bloch's utopian messianism, or Rosenzweig's notion of redemption, all shared a perspective that challenged Enlightenment notions of gradual historical progress and combined messianic, utopian, and modernist modes of thought.

Critical engagement with modernism and a new Jewish sensibility was neither limited to middle-class native-born Jews nor confined to the German language. The presence of East European Jews helped make Germany, and Berlin in particular, into sites of a flourishing modernist and popular Yiddish culture. With more than twenty journals and a plethora of publishing houses, Berlin was second only to Warsaw in Yiddish publishing.[70] Berlin also became the world's most important centre for modern Hebrew literature in the early 1920s, boasting an enclave of writers including the most celebrated poet, Chaim Nahman Bialik, and the writer Shmuel Yosef Agnon. East European intellectuals encountered one another and local German Jewish intellectuals in Berlin, most famously at the storied Romanisches Café. Both native German and East European intellectuals helped advance Jewish scholarship in a variety of fields, with a Jewish public ever more interested in consuming their work. When the Polish Jewish historian Simon Dubnow, who was living in Berlin, published the ten-volume German edition of his *World History of the Jewish People,* the press produced 100,000 copies.

Weimar Jewish life was thus energized and constantly redefined by the experiences and ideas of Jews coming from a wide variety of class backgrounds, geographic origins, and relationships with Judaism and religiosity. Without abandoning their active engagement with German culture, German Jews breathed new life into a reinvigorated Jewish public sphere. Just as German citizens were in conflict over what it meant to be German, German Jews continued to reconceptualize what it meant to be both German and Jewish. The forms these new meanings took during the Weimar Republic are evidenced in the astonishing expansion of Jewish cultural life, the largest expansion in size and range since the pre-1800 period.[71] Underlying the diversity of the new associations, institutions, organizations, attitudes, thought, forms of culture, scholarship, and religious experience was a growing recognition that the liberal binary of German by nation/Jew by confession was no longer a satisfactory self-definition for many Weimar Jews. 'I am a German of the Jewish tribe', wrote the industrialist and future Foreign Minister Walther Rathenau in 1918, a German Jew who maintained a connection neither to the official community nor to Judaism.[72] This active embrace of Jewishness as ethnicity, a *Schicksalsgemeinschaft* (community of fate), with a shared sense of history and fate became so widespread that, by the end of the republic, even Ludwig Holländer, the head of the CV which had often promoted that older, bifurcated ideal, argued the Jews were not a religious community, but one as proud of their 'tribal history' as 'any other German tribe'.[73]

Conclusion

Despite the dynamic complexity of Weimar Jewish experience, Jewish history writing about the Weimar Republic has been weighed down by German Jewry's catastrophic end. For several generations, scholars tended to view Weimar Jewish history through the lens of the Holocaust, identifying in Jews either an 'excessive assimilation' that illustrated their 'failure' to understand they were never truly accepted, or blaming them for being unaware of their vulnerability to a future that few Germans could imagine. But reading Weimar backwards, as more recent scholars have demonstrated, eclipses the many simultaneous vectors of development that were at play at the time. The vectors of Jewish life during the Weimar Republic were many and sometimes contradictory. None, however, pointed inexorably toward total destruction. As singular narratives of the republic have given way to more multi-faceted examinations, so too can narratives of Weimar Jewry that have focused heavily on antisemitism and the rise of the Nazis give way to those that shed light on the cultural richness and provocative tensions of these complex and contradictory fourteen years. Seen on its own terms, Weimar Jewish history represented both a continuation and intensification of the dynamics of German Jewish history more generally, in which the forces of inclusion and exclusion, as well as the tensions between universalism and particularism, became even more pronounced. As Weimar Jews redefined their notions of belonging, many reclaimed a particularism without renouncing the humanistic and liberally inflected notions of *Deutschtum*, continuing to work toward shaping a culture in which they could be at home. Yet during the final years of the republic, their notion of *Deutschtum* diverged ever more from that held by other Germans. By 1933, the delicate web weaving together German and German Jewish lives and cultures ceased being viable, and the challenges German Jews now faced were of an entirely different order.

Notes

1. Cited in Steven Aschheim, *In Times of Crisis: Essays on European Culture, Germans and Jews* (Madison, WI: University of Wisconsin Press, 2001), 92. The latest draft of this chapter was revised and finalized by Paul Lerner and Mark Quigley.
2. See Gershom Scholem, *On Jews and Judaism in Crisis: Selected Essays* (New York: Schocken, 1976). There is a vast scholarly literature on Scholem. Useful introductions to Scholem's place in and views of German Jewish history include Noam Zadoff, *Gershom Scholem: From Berlin to Jerusalem and Back* (Waltham, MA: Brandeis University Press, 2017) and Jay Howard Geller, 'From Berlin and Jerusalem: The Germanness of Gershom Scholem', *Journal of Religious History*, 35 (2011), 211–32.
3. Aschheim, *In Times of Crisis*, 88.
4. Werner Angress, 'Das deutsche Militär und die Juden im Ersten Weltkrieg', *Militärgeschichtliche Mitteilungen*, 19 (1976), 77–146; Tim Grady, *A Deadly Legacy: German Jews and the Great War* (New Haven: Yale University Press, 2017), 137–42.
5. The frequently quoted line comes from Werner Sombart, *Die Juden und das Wirtschaftsleben* (Leipzig: Duncker & Humblot, 1911), 414.
6. Jan Palmowski, 'Between Dependence and Influence: Jews and Liberalism in Frankfurt am Main, 1864–1933', in Henning Tewes and Jonathan Wright (eds), *Liberalism, Anti-Semitism, and Democracy: Essays in Honour of Peter Pulzer* (Oxford: Oxford University Press, 2001), 76–101, here 77.
7. Trude Maurer, 'Education and Vocational Training', in Marion A. Kaplan (ed.), *Jewish Daily Life in Germany, 1618–1945* (Oxford: Oxford University Press, 2005), 273.
8. Ibid.
9. Marion Kaplan, *The Making of the Jewish Middle Class: Women, Family, and Identity in Imperial Germany* (Oxford: Oxford University Press, 1994); Werner Mosse, *The German-Jewish Economic Elite, 1820–1935: A Social-Cultural Profile* (Oxford: Oxford University Press, 1989).
10. Trude Maurer, 'Career and Employment', in Kaplan, *Jewish Daily Life*, 307–9.
11. Steven Lowenstein, 'Population History of German Jewry 1815–1839: Based on the Collections and Preliminary Research of Professor Osiel Oscar Schmetz' (unpublished manuscript, 2020), 100.
12. Ibid., 78.
13. Avraham Barkai, *German Jewish History in Modern Times* (New York: Columbia University Press, 1996), 32.

14. Kerstin Meiring, *Die Christlich-Jüdische Mischehe in Deutschland 1840–1933* (Hamburg: Dölling & Galitz, 1998), 100.
15. Cited in Sharon Gillerman, *Germans into Jews: Remaking the Jewish Social Body in the Weimar Republic* (Stanford, CA: Stanford University Press, 2009), 71.
16. Jack Wertheimer, *Unwelcome Strangers: East European Jews in Imperial Germany* (Oxford: Oxford University Press, 1987), esp. ch. 4; Michael Brenner, *The Renaissance of Jewish Culture in Weimar Germany* (New Haven. London: Yale University Press, 2009), 33.
17. Michael Meyer, '*Gemeinschaft* within *Gemeinde*: Religious Ferment in Weimar Liberal Judaism', in Michael Brenner and Derek J. Penslar (eds), *In Search of Jewish Community: Jewish Identities in Germany and Austria, 1918–1933* (Bloomington, IN: Indiana University Press, 1998), 15–35, here 16.
18. Michael Brenner, 'The Jüdische Volkspartei: National-Jewish Communal Politics in Weimar Germany', *Year Book of the Leo Baeck Institute*, 35 (1990), 219–43, here 220.
19. Kurt Blumenfeld, *Erlebte Judenfrage: Ein Vierteljahrhundert deutscher Zionismus* (Stuttgart: Deutsche Verlags-Anstalt, 1962), 88.
20. Avraham Barkai, '*Wehr dich!*' *Der Centralverein deutscher Staatsbürger jüdischen Glaubens (C.V.) 1893–1938* (Munich: C. H. Beck, 2002), 370.
21. Shulamit Volkov, 'German Jews between Fulfillment and Disillusion: The Individual and the Community', in Brenner and Penslar, *In Search of Jewish Community*, 1–14; Shulamit Volkov, *Germans, Jews, and Antisemites: Trials in Emancipation* (Cambridge: Cambridge University Press, 2006), 276–86.
22. Peter Pulzer, *Jews and the German State: The Political History of a Minority, 1848–1933* (Detroit: Wayne State University Press, 2003), 34.
23. Ibid., 208.
24. Michael Brenner, *Der lange Schatten der Revolution: Juden und Antisemiten in Hitlers München, 1918-1923* (Frankfurt/Main: Suhrkamp, 2019), 23.
25. George Mosse, *German Jews Beyond Judaism* (Bloomington, Ind.: Indiana University Press, 1985), 69.
26. Brenner, *Der Lange Schatten der Revolution*.
27. Pulzer, *Jews and the German State*, 243.
28. Ibid., 213.
29. Till van Rahden, *Jews and Other Germans: Civil Society, Religious Diversity, and Urban Politics in Breslau, 1860–1925*, trans. Marcus Brainard (Madison, WI, London: University of Wisconsin Press, 2008), 241. See also Nicola Wenge, *Integration und Ausgrenzung in der städtischen Gesellschaft: Eine jüdisch-nichtjüdische Beziehungsgeschichte Kölns 1918–1933*. (Mainz: Philipp von Zabern, 2005), 20.
30. Till van Rahden, 'Jews and the Ambivalences of Civil Society in Germany, 1800–1933: Assessment and Reassessment', *Journal of Modern History*, 77 (2005), 1027–47, here 1037.
31. See van Rahden, *Jews and Other Germans*, 233.
32. Gillerman, *Germans into Jews*, 20, 98.
33. Gertrud Ehrmann, 'Die deutsche Frauenbewegung und die jüdischen Frauen', *Blätter des Jüdischen Frauenbundes*, 3/4 (1927), 4.
34. Wenge, *Integration*, 87–97.
35. On social contacts, see Wenge, *Integration*, 74–6. According to the *Statistisches Jahrbuch für das Deutsche Reich*, between 1918 and 1933, the rate was between 59 and 63% for men. Cited in Lowenstein, 'Population History', 259.

36. See van Rahden, *Jews and Other Germans*, 234. The numbers of Jewish university students decreased during the Weimar Republic, 4% among male students, 7% among female students.
37. Geoffrey Giles, *Students and National Socialism in Germany* (Princeton: Princeton University Press, 1985), 17.
38. Harriet Pass Freidenreich, 'Gender, Identity, and Community: Jewish University Women in Germany and Austria', in Brenner and Penslar, *In Search of Jewish Community*, 154–75, here 166.
39. Brenner, *Der lange Schatten der Revolution*, 183.
40. Avraham Barkai, 'Jewish Life in its German Milieu', in Avraham Barkai and Paul Mendes-Flohr (eds), *German Jewish History in Modern Times*, vol. 4. *Renewal and Destruction, 1918–1945* (New York: Columbia University Press, 1998), 50. On Berlin, see Molly J. Loberg, *The Struggle for the Streets of Berlin: Politics, Consumption, and Urban Space, 1914–1945* (Cambridge: Cambridge University Press, 2018), ch. 2.
41. Jacob Borut, 'Jews in German Sports during the Weimar Republic', in Gideon Reuveni and Michael Brenner (eds), *Emancipation through Muscles: Jews and Sports in Europe* (Lincoln, NE: University of Nebraska Press, 2006), 79.
42. Wenge, *Integration*, 127.
43. Loberg, *Struggle for the Streets*, 190.
44. Gillerman, *Germans into Jews*, 34.
45. Stefanie Schüler-Springorum, 'Fighting Back! How to Deal with Antisemitism: A Historical Perspective', *Leo Baeck Institute Year Book*, 62 (2017), 245–62, here 249.
46. Avraham Barkai, 'Political Orientations and Crisis Consciousness', in Barkai and Mendes-Flohr, *German Jewish History in Modern Times*, vol. 4, 121–4.
47. Schüler-Springorum, 'Fighting Back', 250.
48. Barkai, *Wehr Dich!*, 107.
49. Barkai, 'Political Orientations', 110–14.
50. Barkai, *Wehr Dich!*, 198.
51. Peter Pulzer, 'Between Hope and Fear: Jews and the Weimar Republic', in Wolfgang Benz, Arnold Paucker, and Peter Pulzer (eds), *Jews in the Weimar Republic* (Tübingen: Mohr Siebeck, 1998), 279.
52. Arnold Zweig, *Insulted and Exiled: The Truth about German Jews* (London: Miles, 1937), 83. Zweig makes an extended case for the contributions of Jews to German history and culture over the course of the book. See esp. 14, 83–5, 99.
53. See Zweig, *Insulted and Exiled*; Walter Laqueur, *Weimar: A Cultural History* (New Brunswick, NJ, London: Transaction, 2011), 73; Mosse, *German Jews beyond Judaism*, 22.
54. Peter Gay, *Weimar Culture: The Outsider as Insider* (New York: W. W. Norton, 2001).
55. Jost Hermand, 'Juden in der Kultur der Weimarer Republik', in Walter Grab and Julius H. Schoeps (eds), *Juden in der Weimarer Republik: Skizzen und Porträts* (Darmstadt: Primus Verlag, 1998), 9–37, here 28.
56. Ibid., 17.
57. Jack Jacobs, *The Frankfurt School, Jewish Lives, and Antisemitism* (Cambridge: Cambridge University Press, 2015).
58. Peter Gay, *Freud, Jews, and Other Germans: Masters and Victims in German Modernist Culture* (Oxford: Oxford University Press, 1979).
59. Among recent works in this vein, see Ofer Ashkenazi, *Weimar Film and Modern Jewish Identity* (Basingstoke: Palgrave, 2012); Lisa Silverman, *Becoming Austrians: Jews and*

Culture between the World Wars (Oxford: Oxford University Press, 2012); Kerry Wallach, *Passing Illusions: Jewish Visibility in Weimar Germany* (Ann Arbor: University of Michigan Press, 2017); Steven Aschheim, *Beyond the Border: The German Jewish Legacy Abroad* (Princeton: Princeton University Press, 2018); Jeanette R. Malkin and Freddie Rokem, *Jews and the Making of Modern Jewish Theater* (Iowa City: University of Iowa Press, 2010).

60. Peter Jelavich, 'Popular Entertainment and Mass Media: The Central Arenas of German-Jewish Cultural Engagement', in Steven Aschheim and Vivian Liska (eds), *The German-Jewish Experience Revisited* (Boston: De Gruyter, 2015), 106.
61. Ashkenazi, *Weimar Film and Modern Jewish Identity*, 15.
62. The *Alpenverein*, which promoted climbing and hiking in the Alps, was a key exception across much of Germany, as was horse riding. See Borut, 'Jews in German Sports', 79.
63. See Michael Brenner, 'Turning Inward: German-Jewish Youth in Weimar Germany', in Brenner and Penslar, *In Search of Jewish Community*, 56–73, here 59; Jacob Borut, '"Verjudung des Judentums": Was there a Zionist Subculture in Weimar Germany?', in Brenner and Penslar, *In Search of Jewish Community*, 92–114, here 97.
64. Borut, 'Verjudung des Judentums', 100.
65. Borut, 'Jews in German Sport', 78.
66. Gertrud Pfister and Toni Nieweth, 'Jewish Women in Gymnastics and Sport in Germany, 1898–1938', *Journal of Sports History*, 26 (1999), 287–325.
67. Franz Kafka, *Letter to his Father*, trans. Ernst Kaiser and Eithene Wilkins (New York: Schocken, 1966), 81.
68. Cited in Brenner, *Renaissance of Jewish Culture*, 107.
69. Steven Aschheim, *Culture and Catastrophe: German and German Jewish Confrontations with National Socialism and Other Crises* (Basingstoke. London: Macmillan Press, 1996), 36.
70. Gennady Estraikh, 'Introduction: Yiddish on the Spree', in Estraikh and Mikhail Krutikov (eds), *Yiddish in Weimar Berlin: At the Crossroads of Diaspora Politics and Culture* (London: Legenda, 2010), 8.
71. Borut, 'Verjudung des Judentums', 93.
72. Cited in Till van Rahden, 'Germans of the Jewish Stamm: Visions of Community between Nationalism and Particularism, 1850–1933', in Nils Roemer and Mark Roseman (eds), *German History from the Margins* (Bloomington, IN: Indiana University Press, 2006), 27–47, here 32.
73. Ibid., 33.

Bibliography

Ashkenazi, Ofer, *Weimar Film and Modern Jewish Identity* (Basingstoke: Palgrave, 2012).
Barkai, Avraham, *German Jewish History in Modern Times* (New York: Columbia University Press, 1996).
Barkai, Avraham, and Paul Mendes-Flohr (eds), *German Jewish History in Modern Times*, vol. 4. *Renewal and Destruction, 1918–1945* (New York: Columbia University Press, 1998).
Brenner, Michael, *The Renaissance of Jewish Culture in Weimar Germany* (New Haven: Yale University Press, 2009).
Brenner, Michael, and Derek J. Penslar (eds), *In Search of Jewish Community: Jewish Identities in Germany and Austria, 1918–1933* (Bloomington, IN: Indiana University Press, 1998).

Gillerman, Sharon, *Germans into Jews: Remaking the Jewish Social Body in the Weimar Republic* (Stanford, CA: Stanford University Press, 2009).
Kaplan, Marion A. (ed.), *Jewish Daily Life in Germany, 1618–1945* (Oxford: Oxford University Press, 2005).
Pulzer, Peter Pulzer, *Jews and the German State: The Political History of a Minority, 1848–1933* (Detroit: Wayne State University Press, 2003).
Rahden, Till van, *Jews and Other Germans: Civil Society, Religious Diversity, and Urban Politics in Breslau, 1860–1925*, trans. Marcus Brainard (Madison, WI, London: University of Wisconsin Press, 2008).
Wallach, Kerry, *Passing Illusions: Jewish Visibility in Weimar Germany* (Ann Arbor: University of Michigan Press, 2017).

CHAPTER 26

YOUTH AND YOUTH MOVEMENTS

Relations, Challenges, Developments

BARBARA STAMBOLIS

In the Weimar Republic, the view that forward-looking changes were to be expected from the younger generation was a widespread and hopeful vision. In many cases, youth and old age were portrayed as opposites, youth being seen as the epitome of new beginnings, dynamism, and progress, old age, on the other hand, as weakness, powerlessness, and decay. These conceptions were linked to ideas critical of contemporary culture around 1900, when 'youth' and 'youthfulness' had developed into deeply symbolic key words for social renewal.[1] Social and life reform endeavours were based on the realization that adolescence was not only a transitional stage between childhood and adulthood, but an independent life phase worthy of protection. The phase of youth was believed to be characterized by special challenges to be understood specifically as opportunities for personality development. Adolescence was characterized by a need for new beginnings, a longing to broaden horizons and a pronounced search for identity, for which keywords such as self-determination and freedom were central. This understanding of youth found its way into youth protection and youth welfare initiatives after 1918. At the same time, it was also necessary to define who was regarded as a youth from a legal point of view. Freedom for appropriate development was to be granted to adolescents from all social classes, regardless of the fact that most of them had completed their basic education and already begun gainful employment, that a smaller proportion attended school for longer, and that a minority did not finish higher education until their mid-twenties and so were by no means independent until then. The protection and care of young people in the Weimar Republic definitely formed a broad field of political and social intervention.

Another aspect of scientific and social youth discourse was the demographic development in Germany, which pointed to a juvenization. Statistics show that at the turn of the nineteenth to twentieth century the German population was younger than ever before.

The decline in infant mortality, due to a whole bundle of factors, played a considerable role in this development. As a result, the proportion of under 14-year-olds in Germany by 1900 was around 35 per cent, slightly higher than in the rest of Europe.[2] Against the background of the then widespread national striving for competitiveness and recognition, this led, on a political level, to the catchy formula that, as a young nation, Germany was demographically superior to its neighbours. Nevertheless, during and after the First World War concern grew that in the longer term a decline in population might be on the horizon. The large number of young war victims gave new impetus to such fears.

The idea of a society marked by differences between youth and old age, the resulting conflicts, and the vision of a youthful emergence are reflected typically in the book *Das Recht der jungen Völker* (The right of the young peoples) published in 1919. Its author, the *völkisch* critic of contemporary culture, Arthur Moeller van den Bruck, spoke explicitly of a struggle between 'old and young nations'. He declared Germany to be a 'young nation', destined for future greatness.[3] A central idea of the book was that the sacrifices that, in particular, young soldiers had made on the battlefield should be seen as an inheritance and a mandate to help Germany achieve new prestige and self-respect. Influential educators also took up such visionary ideas, which could be filled with political content in many different ways. For example, in his popular book *Psychologie des Jugendalters* (Psychology of adolescence) published in 1924, Eduard Spranger combined empirically founded insights into the phase of youth with speculative philosophical statements. He experimented with the idea of the 'young nation' being able to develop political power like a genie released from the lamp.[4] As early as 1927, such mental constructions were reflected in the slogan *Macht Platz ihr Alten* (Make room, old ones) coined by Gregor Strasser (born in 1892), at that time head of propaganda for the National Socialist German Worker's Party (NSDAP).[5] Fiction also resonated with such slogans. The writer Ernst Jünger, for instance, who as a front-line fighter was able to contribute his own experience and who glorified participation in the First World War, repeatedly conjured up the coming rule of tough, relentless, and battle-tested youth.[6] Especially in the last years of the republic, politically explosive slogans were derived from the construct of a 'youthful empire'. However, this 'youth empire' (*Jugendreich*) was by no means to be equated with the National Socialist 'Third Reich'.[7]

In 1928, the sociologist and philosopher Karl Mannheim analysed *Das Problem der Generationen* (The problem of the generations), i.e. time-specific questions of age groups and their experiences. In this essay, to which age-group research has since then repeatedly referred, he described age, birth, and embeddedness in time (*Zeitheimat*), i.e. experiences and influences whilst growing up, as constitutive for people feeling that they belong together as a generation and being able to distinguish themselves from older and younger people. He saw this as being the case in different ways for those born in the 1890s and those who followed. Thus, Mannheim attempted to describe the social transformation processes of the Weimar Republic and emerging critical developments. With the term 'generation', he offered an interpretation that was highly plausible at the time of publication.[8] Mannheim was by no means the only scientist to interpret historical change with the help of generations.[9] However, only Mannheim's concept of generations combined social crisis phenomena and subjective perceptions of them in a plausible way.[10]

Both from 1918 to 1933 and in retrospective interpretations by historians, two generations who had experienced war in different phases of their lives are at the centre of attention. Those born between 1900 and 1918 experienced the Weimar Republic as young people and are known—in a more narrowly defined age cohort of those born between 1900 and 1908—as the 'war youth generation' of the First World War.[11] They were directly and persistently confronted with the physical and psychological effects of the war. According to information from October 1924, there were around 962,000 fatherless or motherless children in Germany as a result of the war. In 1931, the number of orphans who had lost both father and mother during or after the war was estimated to be around 50,000.[12] Their experiences and influences differ from those of the generation who served at the front during the First World War and, as they were born between 1890 and 1899, they were already adults when the First World War ended.[13] The war youth generation experienced hunger, the absence of their fathers, excessive strain on their mothers, and deaths of relatives. They had, therefore, been forced to grow up early and often lived in precarious circumstances even after the end of the war.[14]

FOUNDATIONS OF SOCIAL REFORM POLICY IN EDUCATION AND YOUTH PROTECTION

The majority of the members of the constituent National Assembly agreed that sweeping efforts were needed to achieve societal and democratic change. Above all, bringing up the younger generation was a national political concern of great importance.[15] Lowering the voting age from 25 to 20, the basic right to education, and the introduction in the constitution of universal eight-year compulsory schooling and obligatory attendance at an institution of further education up to the age of 18 testify to the central role in constituting the republic that the young generation played. The focus was on the right to education, which education reformers and republican politicians understood as an opportunity for children and adolescents to develop their personality freely. A central idea of the education and school policy of the established Weimar parties was to provide young people with a republican upbringing in the spirit of enlightenment and humanitarian traditions. This goal was incorporated into Article 148 of the constitution as 'civic education'. It dealt in particular with moral virtues such as treating the different-minded respectfully.[16] However, serious party-political differences and clashes of opinion already emerged during the drafting of this article of the constitution.[17] At the Reichsschulkonferenz (Reich School Conference) in 1920, where more than 650 experts came together to reorganize the school system, there was broad agreement on the responsibility associated with accomplishing this task. However, no agreement could be reached on the construction of the school system. There were fundamental differences, for example, on the subject of confessional schools—in which the pupils were taught religion and all humanities subjects either from a Protestant or a Catholic perspective—between the Catholic Centre Party on the one hand and the Social Democratic Party (SPD) and left-liberal German Democratic Party (DDP) on the other. The latter two parties rejected these schools because they associated them with a strong political influence of the churches on large sections of the population, and were thus reminiscent of conditions before 1914. Above all, they stood to contradict the democratic principles of a standard state primary school, which was free of charge.

There was also no consensus on the form and content of civic education. The adoption of the Weimar Constitution on 11 August 1919 was celebrated every year, with a holiday from classes and a ceremony including a speech and musical performances.[18] However, it was difficult to arouse enthusiasm for these celebrations. On the tenth anniversary of the constitution in 1929, many grammar-school pupils demonstratively stayed away from the events, interrupted speakers, and removed republican flags.[19] While the German People's Party (DVP) gradually came closer to advocating civic education on the basis of the republic, anti-democratic resentment intensified in the Communist Party (KPD), the German National People's Party (DNVP), and the NSDAP. This tendency can be seen, for example, in the struggle of teachers' associations to define the contents of civic education and the forms in which they were to be conveyed. It was also almost impossible to reach consensus on the importance of international reconciliation, freedom, and responsibility for democratic systems of government that was to be emphasized in lessons. Furthermore, agreement could not be reached regarding the tasks and content of history lessons and both existing or newly developed textbooks which were used to teach them.

Landerziehungsheime (independent boarding schools) were among the pedagogical fields of experimentation that underwent expansion. They grew in number from around ten before 1914 to several dozen in the course of the 1920s and were mostly located in attractive countryside away from larger cities. Here adolescents lived in communities, learning and spending their free time together. Ideally, educators were to be trusted by their students and would have authority without being authoritarian. However, as these private institutions charged school fees, almost only children from middle-class families enjoyed the benefits of such an education. Over the course of the 1920s, a strong polarization of opinions can be observed, which inhibited the implementation of educational concepts just as much as economic factors. Although the urgency of democratic education was particularly pressing in the final phase of the republic, its realization was called into question by political and economic developments and reformist forces were marginalized, particularly in the SPD and the DDP. Until 1933, civic education as defined in Article 148 of the constitution was not included in any of the constitutions of the seventeen federal states and it was not a resounding success in practice.[20]

The fact that adolescents were to be given care and protection in the broadest sense was reflected in the Weimar Constitution in August 1919. Articles 120, 121, and 123 formulated this as a societal mandate. Hence, young people had a right to education, for which their parents were responsible, but in which state and municipal authorities could intervene if it appeared to be too great a responsibility for the families. Illegitimate and legitimate children were given the same rights. Not least, adolescents were to be protected against 'exploitation' and 'neglect'.[21] This constitutional mandate represented a challenge and a chance to reinforce youth welfare in practice, but at the same time offered opportunities for severe control and discipline. In the Reich Youth Welfare Law, which came into force in 1924, these principles of the constitution took on a more concrete form. The law stipulated that public welfare was to take over the education and upbringing of minors if the family did not fulfil its duties.[22] As a result, youth welfare offices at federal state and municipal levels were entrusted with essential youth welfare tasks. In contrast to before the First World War, it was now no longer the principles of care for the poor that were decisive, but pedagogical considerations of support and protection. The demands on the staff were immense.[23] They were responsible for infants, toddlers, school-age adolescents, and young people who had already left school.

Under the Juvenile Justice Act of 1923, minors were regarded differently to adults, in theory at least. The age of criminal responsibility was raised from 12 to 14; from a legal point of view, boys and girls between the ages of 14 and 18 were considered juveniles. From this time on, before sentencing the courts had to clarify whether juveniles could be held responsible for crimes committed on the basis of their intellectual development and living conditions. The investigations were conducted by the youth authorities, not by the police, and the court hearings were not public. The word 'punishment' was to be avoided and the term 'educational measure' was to be used instead. Moreover, many provisions of general criminal law, such as the death penalty or life imprisonment, did not apply in juvenile criminal law. Therefore, it seemed logical to speak of the juvenile court as an 'educational court'.[24] When juvenile criminal law came into force, it was celebrated as a groundbreaking innovation. Indeed, the juvenile penal system was in some places reformed in an exemplary fashion, such as the Hamburg juvenile prison.[25] Its director, Curt Bondy, expressly relied on preventive and, in the case of delinquency, pedagogical measures.

Alongside legislative measures, a professionalization of youth social work also took place. The professional ideal was the 'comrade and helper' who was to encourage young people to help themselves, motivate them to take personal responsibility and inspire them to act together.[26] He was therefore a person of trust, an older brother, and youth leader with authority, yet not authoritarian. The Soziale Arbeitsgemeinschaft Berlin-Ost (Social Working Group Berlin-East) or the Gilde Soziale Arbeit (Guild of Social Work)—both associations of those working in the social work sector—are examples of the commitment of people who wanted to help to overcome social differences. They worked in educational institutions for those that were considered morally at risk or in institutions for young people growing up in problematic family circumstances who were in need of relaxation and looking for companionship.[27] The theologian, pedagogue, and pacifist Friedrich Siegmund-Schultze, a leading member of the Soziale Arbeitsgemeinschaft Berlin-Ost, issued strong warnings about the long-term personal and social consequences of precarious living conditions for children and adolescents.[28]

Many of those active in youth welfare and social work after 1918 had come into contact with the youth movement before 1914, and their political opinions had then been influenced by war experiences.[29] The ideals of the youth movement led them to choose social professions in which they could take care of the needs of special 'problem' groups of adolescents.[30] The majority did not want to manage social problems of their time bureaucratically, but rather aimed to help and support.[31] When asked whether nature or nurture was the decisive factor for prospects and opportunities in life, almost all said the latter. To them, milieu factors did not seem fateful, rather they could be influenced by education. In social work, it was not least women who were able to follow professional training paths and combine their work with ideas of a 'lived youth movement', for example, as kindergarten teachers, children's nurses, youth and family welfare workers.[32] However, even in reform-oriented social work, the boundaries between helping people to help themselves, monitoring and coercion were fluid. In juvenile prisons and institutional care, discipline, order, and, above all, work as a pedagogical means to force conforming behaviour, continued to play a considerable role. Such measures were part of a tradition of drill and obedience education, which led to tension and, often, to the failure of reform-oriented projects.[33]

Between Self-Determination and Control: The Youth Movement

At the turn of the century, young people of both the working and middle classes were literally 'on the move'. Around 1900, middle-class adolescents, most of them grammar-school pupils, met in small groups, for which the term Wandervogel (literally: hiking birds) was soon coined. They undertook excursions into nature lasting several days and spent the nights in barns, or met regularly in huts where they made their 'nests'. In this way, they had access to a short-term escape from the demands of their parents and an education system based on obedience and rigour, gaining their own space free of adult interference or control. Male adolescents were granted this opportunity more often than females, but there were already several groups of young women and girls in the youth movement's founding years.[34] The ideal for interactions between the sexes was 'comradely', i.e. friendly, but ascetic, non-erotic, coexistence.[35] The Wandervogel had approximately 25,000 members prior to 1914. Around the same time, a proletarian youth movement developed in which separating the sexes played a lesser role. It also took up young people's demands for independence, but focused primarily on the right to leisure time that had yet to be achieved. Proletarian adolescents did not see themselves as new blood for the workers' movement. Nevertheless, the organized working-class youth was, in its early stages and even later, often not recognized as a youth movement.[36] Young Jewish Germans also organized themselves from the beginning of the twentieth century, the bourgeois youth movement holding a great attraction for many of them. However, experiences of antisemitic hostility led them to found their own organizations. The Jewish Wanderbund Blau-Weiß (Hiking Association Blue-White), founded in 1912, explicitly took its bearings from the Wandervogel, and in 1916 another group, Kameraden. Deutsch-jüdischer Wanderbund (Comrades. German-Jewish Hiking Association), came into being.[37]

In October 1913, with the 'First Freideutsche Youth Day' on the Meissner, a mountain ridge east of Kassel, the bourgeois youth movement created a foundation myth to which members were to refer from then on. On the eve of this event, initiators expressed the core of the youth movement's self-image, its striving for autonomy, in a formula. Their decisive sentence was that the Freideutsche Youth intended to 'shape their lives on their own terms, with their own responsibility, according to their inner concept of truthfulness'.[38] The Meissner Convention can be described as an alcohol- and nicotine-free open-air event, where participants sang and danced around the campfire, but also made speeches with very different socio-critical emphases. In addition to a number of adult agitators and supporters, 2,000 to 3,000 young people from groups inspired by the ideas of life reform and reform education took part. Many had backpacks with them, girls and young women wore long, full skirts, boys and young men open-collared shirts, velvet jackets, and knee breeches. They looked uncomplicated and modern but at the same time old-fashioned, with their braids and clothing reminiscent of traditional national costumes. A festive character dominated this key event of the youth movement. Alongside pacifist tones, there were also some sharp nationalist ones.[39] Members of working-class youth associations and the scouting movement were not represented at this event.[40] The latter, following the British model, had established themselves before the outbreak of the First World War as a hierarchically structured educational movement with military influences and soon had around 80,000 members.

Before 1914, many young people tried to distance themselves from the social mainstream of an increasingly aggressive nationalism. Nevertheless, many members of the youth movement volunteered as soldiers, about a quarter of whom did not return from the war. To honour the memory of the fallen, in 1920 the Wandervogel movement acquired Ludwigstein, a castle ruin on the river Werra east of Kassel, which suited their preference for medieval romanticism. They turned it into a memorial and in 1923 youth movements held a Meissner event there, aiming to tie it in with the one in 1913. An anniversary celebration, however, was not considered; it seemed unthinkable. Rather, a discussion about the sustainability of the core terms of the Meissner formula of 1913 under the fundamentally changed social conditions seemed to suggest itself. This debate revealed that national *völkisch*, bourgeois left-liberal, and socialist-communist positions stood irreconcilably alongside each other and that there was no agreement on the orientation to be provided for young people.[41]

The youth movement landscape of the Weimar Republic was a colourful one. It encompassed an immense number of groups, spin-offs, and new foundations.[42] Some groups were oriented towards self-determination while others were less so, instead having a distinct hierarchical structure. The field was also complex from an ideological point of view, and it was not uncommon for political changes of direction to make it difficult to undertake a classification in terms of 'left' and 'right'. The model of small groups, in which young people organized their free time in a self-determined way and without adult interference, remained attractive. This is evidenced, for example, by the scouts ordaining in 1919 that they were to become a youth movement, renouncing strict military organizational models and hierarchical structures.[43] In 1920, the Bund Deutscher Neupfadfinder (League of German New Scouts) was founded based on this self-concept, however it existed only until 1924. In the Deutsche Freischar, founded in 1926, Wandervogel and scout traditions had their place, but this group also only existed for a short time. It is clear that the post-war youth movement differed greatly from its beginnings before 1914 in terms of experiences, models, community-building symbols, and rituals. The emphasis on 'maleness' and *männerbündisches* (male bonding) is regarded as one of the decisive characteristics of the youth movements in the Weimar Republic. Cossacks and samurai, the knightly order, heroic soldierly virtues, the appearance in 'uniform', i.e. standardized clothing, as well as the waving of flags and military roll-call rituals were all signs of a change in style.

This can be seen, for example, in the deutsche jungenschaft vom 1.11., dj.1.11 for short, founded in 1929. Although insignificant in terms of membership numbers, in the youth movement scene it was a well-noticed elitist *Bund* for boys. It had a charismatic leader, Eberhard Koebel, born in 1907, who went under the pseudonym *tusk* (the German). The hallmark of this group was the *Kohte*, a tent common in Lapland in which a fire could be lit, as well as a dark blue jacket and a flag on which a falcon above three waves was depicted.[44] From the point of view of youth aesthetics these new creative means of expression undoubtedly corresponded to the front generation that left its mark on the youth movement after 1918. In total the bündische Jugend (bündische Youth) had around 70,000 to a maximum of 90,000 members. Their appearance and not least their songs are a reflection of youth cultural changes that distinguish the pre- and post-war periods. The guitar and lute were increasingly replaced by drums and trumpets, and with them the rhythms to which the young people marched changed.

A number of young Jewish Germans were members of bündische Youth groups. However, they were increasingly excluded and therefore turned to Jewish youth groups in their search for an intellectual and spiritual home. Their discussions of the value of coeducational groups took a similar course to the bündische Youth as a whole. Some girls preferred female groups, seeing them as an opportunity to broaden their horizons and spend some carefree time together with female friends. Others found the comradely interaction between the sexes particularly appealing. A special challenge for young German Jews of both sexes was to find a balance between cultural German and Jewish identity. Thus, whilst still using well-known youth movement songbooks such as the *Zupfgeigenhansl*, they also published their own, which included traditional Jewish songs and new Hebrew ones. Especially members of the Wanderbund Blau-Weiß and the German-Jewish Scout Association Kadima, which emerged from the former in 1926, were influenced by Zionist tendencies and convinced of the idea of an independent Jewish state. The Kameraden, founded in 1916, on the other hand, rejected this orientation. In 1932, some 1,600 young people were active in this group, but it lost a lot of members to the Zionist Werkleute that split off from it. Specific preparation for the emigration to Palestine was to be served by special training centres for the trades and agriculture, in which forms of youthful community life were practised. In the 1930s, these *Hachshara* centres, places where emigrants were made fit for emigration, literally became safe havens.[45]

Cooperation between youth *Bünde* of different persuasions took place within the framework of a few cross-border pacifist initiatives, which began in Freiburg in 1923 under the leadership of German Catholics involved in the peace movement. They climaxed in a European youth meeting near Paris in 1926, where scouts from countries including England and France, members of denominational German youth groups, and socialist youths from various European countries met.[46] However, this remained an exception; only a few adolescents travelled long distances or planned cross-border encounters between young people.[47] More widespread were *Grenzlandfahrten* (borderland trips), where *völkisch* nationalist groups demonstrated for a revision of the German borders. These were based on the Treaty of Versailles.[48]

However, an incomplete picture emerges if, after this overview of communities within the youth movement, the following aspect is not emphasized: very many adolescents belonged to neither *Bünde* nor youth associations, but were nevertheless 'on the move'. The youth hostels, of which in 1925 there were already 2,000, were not frequented primarily by youth groups, but above all by young nature tourists. They arrived by bus and motorbike, used this accommodation as a cheap alternative to hotels and often—contrary to what the founders of the youth hostel association had imagined—consumed tobacco and alcohol. Around 1930, roughly a third of all guests in youth hostels were girls and young women who wanted to do sports and spend their leisure time in an uncomplicated and convivial way.[49] In a broad sense, in the 1920s young people 'on the move' also included loose groups of adolescents belonging to subcultural milieus in the large cities that were looking for opportunities to spend their leisure time with other young people away from organized youth associations. These allowed them to withdraw from parental control and disciplining influences. They met on the streets or at fairgrounds, went to cinemas and dances if they had enough money, and smoked and drank alcohol. They were modern, i.e. open to sports such as football, boxing, canoeing, and cycling; they were attracted to jazz and swing. But they also went on trips to the countryside. Hats with feathers, sturdy shoes, and imaginative names revealed the influence of the youth movement. Yet the way they presented themselves encompassed a broader spectrum of opportunities for creative expression; for example, they also wore cowboy shirts or leather trousers with braces, thus signalling their understanding of autonomy. One example is the Edelweißpiraten (Edelweiss Pirates) who did not conform to any cliché. They provoked and were considered 'wild' and dangerous in the sense of being a threat to security and order.[50]

Around a third of the young people who were organized in 1926 were members of youth associations that belonged to the umbrella organization Reichsausschuss Deutscher Jugendverbände (Reich Committee of German Youth Associations). Youth sport associations were most strongly represented, having around two million members, followed by Catholic youth associations which had around one million members, Protestant youth associations with around 600,000, trade union youth with around 400,000, the working-class youth with around 90,000, and the communist youth association with around 55,000 members. Male adolescents were organized to a greater extent than female ones. However, many girls and young women were active in sports clubs.

The Katholische Jungmännerverband Deutschlands (Catholic Young Men's Association of Germany) had some 365,000 members in 1933 and the Deutsche Jugendkraft. Reichsverband für Leibesübungen in katholischen Vereinen (German Youth Strength. Reich Committee for Physical Exercises in Catholic Associations) around 690,000 members.[51] They were part of a world determined by church officials, religious morals, and traditional Catholicism. Catholic reformers, younger priests, for example, and many Catholic youths, expressed their criticism and demanded that religious events such as church services and pilgrimages be turned into an attractive community experience for young people more fitting for the times and take elements of the youth *Bünde* into account. These ideas were echoed above all in the Bund Neudeutschland (League New Germany), founded in 1919 for male secondary schools pupils, and in Quickborn which with its centre at Rothenfels Castle on the river Main developed into an innovative experimental space for modern young Catholic life. Here there was also room for arguments about the opportunities and limitations of self-determination and the necessary leadership of young people.[52] A clear yes to tight leadership was then applied in Sturmschar, which split off from the Katholischen Jungmännerverband in 1930. It was popular not least because of its youth *Bund* character and soon boasted 25,000 members.[53]

The Protestant youth associations were faced with the dilemma that sport, music, travel, and camping was far more appealing to young people than any religious offers. The strongest in terms of numbers were the Reichsverband der evangelischen Jungmännerbünde (Reich Committee of Protestant Young Men's Bünde) with around 265,000 members and the Evangelische Reichsverband weiblicher Jugend (Protestant Reich Committee of Female Youth) with around 226,000 in 1932. Even in rural regions with few leisure opportunities they fell sharply in popularity.[54] In the public space, the Protestant associations had a much less defined profile than their Catholic counterparts, which at mass events such as the *Katholikentage*—an annual gathering of Catholic lay associations—presented an impressive image of unity and youthfulness in the final years of the republic. The Christian Scouts were increasingly popular, but also positioned themselves politically in clear proximity to the NSDAP.[55]

The party youth organisation of the Social Democrats was the Sozialistische Arbeiterjugend (Socialist Working Class Youth), which emerged from predecessor institutions in 1922 and still had some 100,000 members around 1923, yet had shrunk to approximately 56,000, i.e. almost half, by 1929. It served—so was the official party view—the upbringing and education of adolescents between 14 and initially 18, then 20, years of age, as well as their preparation for political party work. Nevertheless, it cannot be denied that it was part of the youth movement. Although the regularly held Youth Days were socialist mass events with the character of a public demonstration, the way that young people perceived themselves differed markedly from the officially intended view. In private photographs serving as a reminder of activities undertaken together, the focus was not on the speakers and crowds of listeners or the camp character of the events. The young people did not present themselves in an orderly manner 'in rank and file', but often in small groups, at a lake while bathing or on bicycles, for example.[56] The question of political control by the party was repeatedly addressed by the SPD, but so was the question of the decreasing attractiveness of the Sozialistische Arbeiterjugend. Similar developments can be observed in the youth organizations of other parties. The fact that socialist education was to begin in childhood as opposed to adolescence played a significant role in social democracy. The Kinderfreundebewegung (Friends of the Children Movement), a social democratic working group dating back to 1923, dedicated itself to this aim. From 1927 onwards, it organized camps which 2,000 and more minors attended at the same time, with significant participation from socialist youth organisations. The camps bore the programmatic name *Kinderrepubliken* (Children's Republics)[57] and are deserving of some attention as they were one of many reform initiatives explicitly devoted to democratic goals. While attending these camps, children were required to organize and manage themselves, settle disputes, and respect majority decisions. Yet they were no more than islands of reform and experimentation, playing only a marginal role in the party work of the SPD. Criticism of the SPD came particularly from Jungsozialisten (Young Socialists). With only 3,000 to 4,000 members between the ages of 20 and 30, this group often belonged to the front generation and reproached the Social Democrats for being outdated and failing to adequately woo the post-war youth. In this respect they agreed with younger members of other parties, who also complained of deficits in youth policy. This is true for the Demokratische Jugend (Democratic Youth) of the DDP, to around 10,000 young adults of the Centre Party united in the Windthorstbund from 1928 onwards, and to those who, from 1920 onwards, spoke for the young generation in the centre-right DVP in the Hindenburgjugend (Hindenburg Youth).[58]

It is not possible to unequivocally determine the relationship between the youth associations mentioned above and the Hitler Youth, which had a membership of some 40,000 before 1933 and did not belong to the Reichsausschuss Deutscher Jugendverbände. The Hitler Youth, founded in 1926, was mostly only perceived more strongly in connection with the rise of National Socialism from 1930 onwards. The same applies to the Nationalsozialistischer Schülerbund (National Socialist League of Pupils) and even more so to the Nationalsozialistischer Deutscher Studentenbund (National Socialist German Student's League), whose beginnings lie in 1929 and were accompanied by immediate successes among the academic youth.[59]

Disappointed Youth and Political Developments since the Late 1920s

From the second half of the 1920s, there were thorough studies conducted from the perspectives of various social science disciplines, which painted a gloomy picture of the conditions in which post-war adolescents were growing up and the future they faced.[60] These studies emphasized the long-term consequences of the war in the sense of the general physical and psychological impairment of entire age groups. In 1927, for example, it was stated that employees of educational and welfare institutions as well as political decision-makers were confronted with massive challenges. The question was also raised as to how young people could develop perspectives if they lacked economic and social foundations, and how they would position themselves politically. In 1927, an exhibition on the living conditions of young people in Berlin not only provided information about their precarious circumstances, but also unmistakably revealed a situation which was already politically explosive and becoming even more so.[61] Some socio-political achievements, such as the law to introduce a state unemployment insurance scheme, which was passed with broad approval by the Reichstag in 1927, had hardly any positive effect on young unemployed people. Apprentices were not subject to compulsory insurance under the 1927 law on labour exchange and unemployment insurance. For young people under 21 years of age, benefit payments could depend on serving compulsory hours or attending courses for the unemployed. Thus, young people primarily depended on support from their families or welfare services. They did not benefit from social policy measures, but rather experienced an increasingly helpless welfare state and overburdened politicians who were in an unconvincing parliamentary system and incapable of taking action.

By the time of the Reichstag election in May 1928 at the latest, the parties had turned their attention to young voters in particular. Since 1924, around 4.6 million young and first-time voters of the post-war youth, who were born in the high-birthrate years between 1904 and 1908, had joined the electoral roll. Lower voter turnout and the loss of votes by the bourgeois parties in comparison with 1924 aroused concerns. Contemporary analyses attributed this to a declining electorate among the younger generation. It is true that the Social Democrats achieved an exceptionally good result in these elections and that the National Socialists did not have any significant successes. But fear grew, not least among the Bismarck Jugend (Bismarck Youth) of the Deutschnationale Volkspartei, but also among the Jungdemokraten (Young Democrats) in the DDP or among the ranks of the DVP, that in future even larger groups of young voters would rather go to the sports field than the ballot box, i.e. that they would become disinterested in politics or give their vote to the radical right or left.[62] The results of the Reichstag elections in September 1930, resulting in the huge success of the NSDAP in which young voters also had their share, were extremely alarming. Further first-time voters had joined them. Overall, around a quarter of all voters now belonged to the front-line and post-war generations, while the parties, with few exceptions, were represented by politicians who had been socialized in Imperial Germany.[63] Only social democrats and communists had been able to keep their voter shares in the younger generation, the latter clearly winning the larger share of young voters.

According to a popular assessment at the time, the ageing of the Reichstag was a manifestation of the incompetence of the entire political system, which had no support among young people. Weimar was seen as a 'republic of the old'.[64] In the SPD, the generation question became a central issue.[65] And the SPD tried to gain influence through non-parliamentary party organizations, for instance through the founding of the Eiserne Front (Iron Front) in 1931, a coalition of various associations to defend the republic with significant participation from the Reichsbanner Schwarz Rot Gold (Reich Banner Black Red Gold). Its youth department, the Jungbanner, had a mobilizing influence because it offered young people the opportunity to make themselves publicly heard in uniform. To a limited extent, the Eiserne Front managed to convey the impression that extra-parliamentary space did not belong exclusively to anti-republican forces.[66]

The ageing leadership and lack of representation of young people in the higher echelons led, for example, to intensive efforts in the Catholic Centre Party to increase its attractiveness for younger voters. At the same time, efforts to give the *Katholikentage* a fighting face and to take a stand for a 'militant' democracy were intensified with visible success. Church youth events that included both singing and marching stood under the banner of 'loyalty', 'sacrifice', and 'Christian heroism'. Saints, bishops, and leading politicians were stylized as 'leaders' to whom 'allegiance' was to be pledged. A 'heroic cult of Christ', the depiction of Catholic saints as youthfully male, and the increased importance of the archangel Michael as a fighter, were expressions of a profound change of style in Catholic youth work.[67]

It was characteristic of the overall situation around 1930 that adolescents and young adults from all social classes were faced with uncertain prospects for the future and fierce competition in the training and labour market. They described their circumstances in drastic words. Even years after the end of the war, their situation was still highly stressful due to having war-traumatized or missing fathers, cramped living conditions, restricted financial circumstances, and a high level of responsibility for relatives. A 1930 survey of more than 2,000 15- to 17-year-old vocational school students included numerous female trainees from craft and social occupations. The results illustrate the seriousness with which those who had had to grow up early took responsibility for their families. They viewed their limited freedom realistically.[68] Explicit attention was paid to the views of life and the world held by female adolescents, a group that was mostly regarded as being objective, sceptical, and capable. At the same time, however, fears and serious uncertainties about the future could also be observed. The occupational independence they longed for, as a typist, telephone operator, hairdresser, or clothes shop assistant, for example, often moved completely beyond their reach.

University graduates and young, unskilled industrial workers of both sexes were equally affected. Young girls of all classes were at a disadvantage compared to male applicants for both apprenticeships and jobs that required no training. They were forced to restrict themselves to domestic work and were deprived of their financial independence, leading them to perceive themselves as being immensely belittled.[69] Vocational guidance centres reported that more and more pupils from secondary schools were seeking information because traditional career patterns and paths proved to be no longer viable. Rising matriculation figures at the end of the 1920s and beginning of the 1930s were also an indication of this great uncertainty. These numbers were by no means primarily due to the fact that girls were also interested in academic studies, but rather indicated the withdrawal of young people from the middle classes into an extended 'educational moratorium'. An 'academic proletariat' was being formed, critical observers warned, not least in view of the fact that during Easter 1932, i.e. under highly crisis-ridden economic conditions, one of the years with the highest birthrates left secondary school.[70] The many working students who had to finance their own studies in the years after 1918 reappeared on the dark horizon. When, towards the end of the 1920s, the war youth generation of the First World War spoke up for themselves, their balance sheet was bitter. They claimed to lack courage and *joie de vivre* and saw callousness, scepticism, and distrust as being their core qualities.

After the end of the war, adolescents (and adult women) had to make way for soldiers returning from the war. In the years that followed, structural economic changes, not least in connection with rationalization processes, led to new problems, and the economic crisis from 1929 onwards again exacerbated the situation. Youth welfare workers spoke of the war continuing for the next generation even after it had ended, not least because of the depressing situation on the labour market. Statistics show that in 1926 some 17 per cent of 14- to 21-year-olds were unemployed, in 1929 the unemployment rate among 14- to 25-year-olds was around 19 per cent. However, the group of 20- to 25-year-olds was much more greatly affected: 23.5 per cent were registered as unemployed in June 1933.[71] Since the end of the 1920s, the youth welfare departments and the Reichsanstalt für Arbeitsvermittlung und Arbeitslosenversicherung (Reich Agency for Labour Exchange and Unemployment Insurance) had pointed out the alarming situation to ministries and youth associations. At the same time, they complained about the limited resources available to youth welfare and an increasing inability to act as a result of general austerity measures. The Reichsausschuss der deutschen Jugendverbände drew up an emergency programme aiming to do justice to the provision of advisory and support services for young people despite the limited financial resources available.[72]

In particular, the establishment of 'labour camps' sparked controversial debates about values, concepts of humankind, and the political implications of disciplinary measures. In 1931, an emergency decree issued by the Brüning government introduced the 'voluntary labour service' to take care of young unemployed people from an educational and social welfare point of view, but also to counter fears that unemployment among young people could lead to increased juvenile delinquency. Among the proponents were paramilitary associations such as Stahlhelm with its large membership or the Jungdeutsche Orden, an elitist group dedicated to overcoming the party state. But also groups belonging to the youth movement such as Wandervogel or Freischar organized camps in which physical work, education, and vocational training were combined. In June 1931, the Reichanstalt für Arbeitsvermittlung und Arbeitslosenunterstützung was entrusted with financing and promoting the 'voluntary labour service'. This went hand in hand with the dismantling of welfare state services as the concrete measures were mainly the responsibility of denominational groups, trade unions, sports, and military associations.[73]

Meeting the challenges and hardships of the time in a 'heroic' way was an ideal to which youth associations of both the political right and the left were committed. 'Iron discipline' and 'strength of will' were principles followed by young people who, for example, underwent endurance tests, either individually or, preferably, in groups.[74] Developmental psychological studies found evidence in diary entries that girls also approved of these 'virtues'.[75] Around 1930, a heroic narrative of the world war prevailed, which at the same time aided the goal of 'toughening up' adolescents to gain acceptance. This is not least reflected in Nazi propagandist ideas of tough, soldierly young people forced to endure hunger, thirst, and cold under extreme conditions and thus conformed to the idealized image of the front soldier.[76] In the last years of the republic, the NSDAP was able to present itself as a 'youthful' party. For young male adults with a tendency towards activism it certainly provided options in their search for fields of activity.[77]

Conclusion

The Weimar Republic has often been analysed with regard to the rise of National Socialism and the failure of the Republic. For some time now, however, there have been clear shifts in what the research emphasizes. The years between 1918 and 1933 are considered to have a quality of their own. Even today, not interpreting the Weimar Republic as 'the anteroom to the Third Reich' poses a particular challenge with regard to the topic of youth and youth movements from 1918 to 1933.[78] This chapter emphasizes the contradictory, ambivalent aspects of these years. There were optimistic beginnings and crisis-ridden developments that hindered them. A consideration of youth and youth movements is, on the one hand, particularly suited to describing socio-political and legislative innovations, initiatives, and opportunities. Crucial initiatives in the field of youth welfare gave rise to the justified hope that the conditions under which adolescents grew up could improve. In the 1920s, legal regulations and social initiatives intertwined to advance reform processes. A broad consensus on these values indicated a solid foundation on which youth welfare and support services could build. This was supported by some social democrats, the Centre Party, and social and educational reformers who saw Weimar as a promising, forward-looking social and cultural project.[79] An excitement about the future and reform optimism with which life reformers and members of the youth movements had claimed autonomy for adolescents before the outbreak of the First World War continued in the 1920s. In addition, multifaceted types of youth communities developed, which were expressions of the changed needs and expectations of young people during the inter-war period. On the other hand, it cannot be denied that excessive demands contributed to a crisis of legitimacy of the democratic political system. Its representatives ultimately failed to secure broad support among the younger generation. The answers to social and societal youth issues thus proved to be a seismographic indicator of the stability or instability of the Weimar Republic.

From 1918 to 1933, the complex crisis phenomena were dominated by generational conflicts. They took into account the fact that a democratically constituted society only stands on firm foundations if it finds convincing answers to the questions of its youth about the future. Nevertheless, young people had considerable freedom to shape their own lives. There were also significant political and educational efforts to redesign the conditions for growing up. Focusing on 1933 alone certainly narrows the wide spectrum of experiences of those age groups for which, as children and adolescents, the First World War was a formative experience.

Translated from German by Nicola Bartlett.

Notes

1. Thomas Koebner, Rolf-Peter Janz, and Frank Trommler (eds), *'Mit uns zieht die neue Zeit': Der Mythos Jugend* (Frankfurt/Main: Suhrkamp, 1985); Chad Ross, *Naked Germany. Health, Race and the Nation* (Oxford: Berg, 2005), 1–14; Michael Hau, *The Cult of Health and Beauty in Germany: A Social History 1890–1930* (Chicago: University of Chicago Press, 2003).
2. Detlev J. K. Peukert, *Jugend zwischen Krieg und Krise: Lebenswelten von Arbeiterjungen in der Weimarer Republik* (Cologne: Bund-Verlag, 1987), 36.
3. Arthur Moeller van den Bruck, *Das Recht der jungen Völker* (Munich: Piper, 1919).
4. Eduard Spranger, *Psychologie des Jugendalters* (Leipzig: Quelle & Meyer, 1924, 9th edn. 1927); see Barbara Stambolis, *Mythos Jugend: Leitbild und Krisensymptom. Ein Aspekt der politischen Kultur im 20. Jahrhundert* (Schwalbach, Taunus: Wochenschau Verlag, 2003), 36–9.
5. Georg Strasser, 'Macht Platz, ihr Alten!' in Strasser, *Kampf um Deutschland: Reden und Aufsätze eines Nationalsozialisten* (Munich: Zentralverlag der NSDAP, 1932), 171–4, here 171–2.
6. Matthias Schöning (ed.), *Ernst Jünger-Handbuch: Leben-Werk-Wirkung* (Stuttgart: J. B. Metzler, 2014).
7. Irmtraud Götz von Olenhusen, *Jugendreich, Gottesreich, Deutsches Reich: Junge Generation, Religion und Politik, 1928–1933* (Cologne: Verlag Wissenschaft und Politik, 1987).
8. Karl Mannheim, 'Das Problem der Generationen', *Kölner Vierteljahresschrift für Soziologie*, 7 (1928), 157–85; Jürgen Zinnecker, '"Das Problem der Generationen": Überlegungen zu Karl Mannheims kanonischem Text', in Jürgen Reulecke (ed.), *Generationalität und Lebensgeschichte im 20. Jahrhundert* (Munich: Oldenbourg, 2003), 33–58.
9. Stambolis, *Mythos Jugend*, 75–8.
10. Richard Bessel, 'The "Front Generation" and the Politics of Weimar Germany', in Mark Roseman (ed.), *Generations in Conflict: Youth Revolt and Generation Formation in Germany 1770–1968* (Cambridge: Cambridge University Press, 1995), 121–36; Ulrike Jureit, 'Ein Rhythmus der Geschichte? Generationengeschichtliche Deutungsmuster zum 20. Jahrhundert', in Rüdiger Hachtmann and Sven Reichardt (eds), *Detlev Peukert und die NS-Forschung* (Göttingen: Wallstein, 2015), 85–101.
11. Andrew Donson, *Youth in the Fatherless Land: War Pedagogy, Nationalism, and Authority in Germany, 1914–1918* (Cambridge, MA: Harvard University Press, 2010); Barbara Stambolis, *Aufgewachsen in 'eiserner Zeit': Kriegskinder zwischen Erstem Weltkrieg und Weltwirtschaftskrise* (Göttingen: Haland & Wirth, 2014).

12. Robert Weldon Whalen, *Bitter Wounds. German Victims of the Great War 1914-1939* (Ithaca, NY: Cornell University Press, 1984), 47.
13. Robert Wohl, *The Generation of 1914* (Cambridge, MA: Harvard University Press, 1980).
14. Mark Roseman, 'Generationen als "Imagined Communities": Mythen, generationelle Identitäten und Generationenkonflikte in Deutschland vom 18. bis zum 20. Jahrhundert', in Ulrike Jureit and Michael Wildt (eds), *Generationen: Zur Relevanz eines wissenschaftlichen Grundbegriffs* (Hamburg: Hamburger Edition, 2005), 180–99.
15. Wolfgang Keim and Ulrich Schwerdt (eds), *Handbuch der Reformpädagogik in Deutschland (1890-1933)*, 2 vols (Frankfurt: Peter Lang, 2013).
16. Christoph Führ, *Zur Schulpolitik der Weimarer Republik: Die Zusammenarbeit von Reich und Ländern im Reichsschulausschuss (1919-1923) und im Ausschuss für das Unterrichtswesen (1924-1933). Darstellung und Quellen*, 2nd ed. (Weinheim: Beltz, 1972), 160.
17. Reinhard Vent, 'Stellungnahmen der politischen Parteien zur Staatsbürgerkunde im Preußischen Landtag (1919-1931)', in Ulrich Heinemann (ed.), *Sozialisation und Bildungswesen in der Weimarer Republik* (Stuttgart: Klett, 1976), 231–49.
18. Nadine Rossol, 'Repräsentationskultur und Verfassungsfeiern der Weimarer Republik', in Detlef Lehnert (ed.), *Demokratiekultur in Europa: Politische Repräsentation im 19. und 20. Jahrhundert* (Cologne: Böhlau, 2011), 261–79; Tobias Rülcker, 'Feste und Feiern', in Keim and Schwerdt, *Handbuch der Reformpädagogik*, 1189–204.
19. Barbara Stambolis, *Der Mythos der jungen Generation: Ein Beitrag zur politischen Kultur der Weimarer Republik* (Bochum Ph.D. diss. 1982), 190–2.
20. Kurt Sontheimer, 'Politische Bildung zwischen Utopie und Verfassungswirklichkeit', *Zeitschrift für Pädagogik*, 9 (1963), 167–80, 172.
21. Elisabeth Harvey, *Youth and the Welfare State in Weimar Germany* (Oxford: Clarendon Press, 1993), 169.
22. Edward Ross Dickinson, *The Politics of German Child Welfare from the Empire to the Federal Republic* (Cambridge, MA: Harvard University Press, 1996), 129–68.
23. C. Wolfgang Müller, *JugendAmt: Geschichte und Aufgabe einer reformpädagogischen Einrichtung* (Weinheim: Beltz, 1994), 37.
24. Walter Friedländer, *Jugendrecht und Jugendpflege. Handbuch des deutschen Jugendrechts* (Berlin: Arbeiterjugend-Verlag, 1930), 101.
25. Harvey, *Youth and Welfare State*, 21–2.
26. Peter Dudek, *Leitbild: Kamerad und Helfer. Sozialpädagogische Bewegung in der Weimarer Republik am Beispiel der 'Gilde Soziale Arbeit'* (Frankfurt/Main: Dipa, 1988).
27. Jens Wietschorke, *Arbeiterfreunde: Soziale Mission im dunklen Berlin 1911-1933* (Frankfurt/Main: Campus, 2013); Barbara Stambolis, 'Die Gilde Soziale Arbeit: Jugendfürsorge vor dem Hintergrund der Erfahrungen zweier Weltkriege', in Barbara Stambolis (ed.), *Die Jugendbewegung und ihre Wirkungen. Prägungen, Vernetzungen, gesellschaftliche Einflussnahmen* (Göttingen: V&R unipress, 2015), 355–74.
28. Stambolis, *Eiserne Zeit*, 76.
29. Juliane Jacobi, 'Jugendbewegung als Erziehungsbewegung. Exkurs: Martin Buber, Lehrer und "geistiger" Führer', in Ulrike Pilarczyk et al., *Gemeinschaft in Bildern: Jüdische Jugendbewegung und zionistische Erziehungspraxis in Deutschland und Palästina/Israel* (Göttingen: Wallstein, 2009), 28–41, 29.
30. Harvey, *Youth and Welfare State*, 155.

31. Norbert Schwarte, 'Sozialpädagogische Bewegung', in Diethart Kerbs and Jürgen Reulecke (eds), *Handbuch der deutschen Reformbewegungen* (Wuppertal: Peter Hammer, 1998), 331–42, 332; Harvey, *Youth and Welfare State*, 156.
32. Elisabeth Meyer-Renschhausen, 'Frauenbewegung', in Kerbs and Reulecke (eds), *Handbuch der deutschen Reformbewegungen*, 167–79, 177.
33. Christoph Hamann, 'Jungen in Not? Zur Visualisierung der Fürsorgeerziehung vor 1933. Das Beispiel Struveshof', in Barbara Stambolis and Markus Köster (eds), *Jugend im Fokus von Film und Fotografie: Zur visuellen Geschichte von Jugendkulturen im 20. Jahrhundert* (Göttingen: V&R unipress, 2016), 115–40, 119.
34. G. Ulrich Großmann, Claudia Selheim, and Barbara Stambolis (eds), *Aufbruch der Jugend: Deutsche Jugendbewegung zwischen Selbstbestimmung und Verführung* (Nuremberg: Verlag des Germanischen Nationalmuseums, 2013).
35. Meike Sophia Baader, 'Geschlechterverhältnisse, Sexualität und Erotik in der bürgerlichen Jugendbewegung', in Großmann et al., *Aufbruch der Jugend*, 58–66.
36. Alexander A. Schwitanski, 'Statische Bilder als Bilder von Bewegung: Beobachtungen zu Ambiguitäten der Arbeiterjugend und ihrer Bildpraktiken', in Stambolis and Köster, *Jugend im Fokus*, 59–80, here 59–63.
37. Moshe Zimmermann, 'Juden jugendbewegt', in Großmann et al., *Aufbruch der Jugend*, 105–12.
38. Translation by Walter Laqueur, *Young Germany: A History of the German Youth Movement* (London: Routledge & Kegan Paul, 1962), 31.
39. Jürgen Reulecke and Barbara Stambolis (eds), *100 Jahre Jugendherbergen 1909–2009: Anfänge—Wandlungen—Rück- und Ausblicke* (Essen: Klartext, 2009), 17–22.
40. Eckart Conze and Matthias D. Witte (eds), *Pfadfinden: Eine globale Erziehungs- und Bildungsidee aus interdisziplinärer Sicht* (Wiesbaden: Springer, 2012).
41. Barbara Stambolis and Jürgen Reulecke (eds), *100 Jahre Hoher Meißner (1913–2013): Quellen zur Geschichte der Jugendbewegung* (Göttingen: V&R unipress, 2015), 117–9, 159–63.
42. Laqueur, *Young Germany*.
43. Ulrich Herrmann, '"Fahrt" oder "Camp": Wandervogel und Scout. Distanz und Nähe zweier Jugendkulturen vor dem Ersten Weltkrieg', in Jürgen Reulecke and Hannes Moyzes (eds), *Hundert Jahre Pfadfinden in Deutschland* (Schwalbach, Taunus: Wochenschau Verlag, 2010), 13–27.
44. Jürgen Reulecke, 'Die Jungenschaft seit Ende der 1920er Jahre: der Start in eine dritte jugendbewegte Phase', in Großmann et al., *Aufbruch der Jugend*, 100–4.
45. Ilka von Cossart and Ulrike Pilarczyk, 'Hachschara: Der Weg in ein neues Leben', in Irmgard Klönne and Ilana Michaeli (eds), *Gut Winkel, die schützende Insel. Hachschara 1933–1941* (Münster: LIT-Verlag, 2007), 223–48.
46. Barbara Stambolis, *Jugendbewegung, Europäische Geschichte online: Transnationale Bewegungen und Organisationen*, http://ieg-ego.eu/de/threads/transnationale-bewegungen-und-organisationen/internationale-soziale-bewegungen/barbara-stambolis-jugendbewegung (2011).
47. Hans Manfred Bock, 'Der DAAD in den deutsch-französischen Beziehungen', in Peter Alter (ed.), *Der DAAD in der Zeit: Geschichte, Gegenwart und zukünftige Aufgaben—vierzehn Essays* (Cologne: DAAD, 2000), 197–217.
48. Reulecke and Stambolis, *100 Jahre Jugendherbergen*, 57–68, 159–74.

49. Dirk Schumann, 'Youth Culture, Consumption, and Generational Dispositions in Twentieth-Century Germany', in Hartmut Berghoff, Uffa Jensen, Christina Lubinski, and Bernd Weisbrod (eds), *History by Generations: Generational Dynamics in Modern History* (Göttingen: Wallstein, 2013), 125–45.
50. Alfons Kenkmann, *Wilde Jugend: Lebenswelt großstädtischer Jugendlicher zwischen Weltwirtschaftskrise, Nationalsozialismus und Währungsreform* (Essen: Klartext, 1996), 49–54.
51. Götz von Olenhusen, *Jugendreich*, 53; Detlev J. K. Peukert, *The Weimar Republic. The Crisis of Classical Modernity*, trans. Richard Deveson (New York: Hill and Wang, 1992), 90.
52. Stambolis and Reulecke, *100 Jahre Hoher Meißner*, 13.
53. Götz von Olenhusen, *Jugendreich*, 89–93.
54. Markus Köster: *Jugend, Wohlfahrtsstaat und Gesellschaft im Wandel: Westfalen zwischen Kaiserreich und Bundesrepublik* (Paderborn: Ferdinand Schöningh, 1999), 94–100.
55. Götz von Olenhusen, *Jugendreich*, 215–20.
56. Schwitanski, *Arbeiterjugend und ihre Bildpraktiken*.
57. Roland Gröschel (ed.), *Auf dem Weg zu einer sozialistischen Erziehung: Beiträge zur Vor- und Frühgeschichte der sozialdemokratischen 'Kinderfreunde' in der Weimarer Republik* (Essen: Klartext, 2006).
58. Wolfgang R. Krabbe (ed.), *Politische Jugend in der Weimarer Republik* (Bochum: Universitätsverlag Brockmeyer, 1993), 38–72.
59. Eberhard Kolb and Dirk Schumann, *Die Weimarer Republik*, 8th, rev. ed. (Munich: Oldenbourg, 2013), 119.
60. Wilhelm Flitner, 'Der Krieg und die Jugend', in Otto Baumgarten, Erich Foerster, Arnold Rademacher, and Wilhelm Flitner (eds), *Geistige und sittliche Wirkungen des Krieges in Deutschland* (Stuttgart: Deutsche Verlags-Anstalt, 1927), 217–356.
61. Reichsausschuss der deutschen Jugendverbände (ed.), *Junges Deutschland: Ausstellung der deutschen Jugend. Ausstellungskatalog Schloss Bellevue* (Berlin: Reichsdruckerei, 1927).
62. Stambolis, *Mythos Jugend*, 165, 166.
63. Dirk Lau, *Wahlkämpfe der Weimarer Republik: Propaganda und Programme der politischen Parteien bei den Wahlen zum Deutschen Reichstag von 1924 bis 1930* (Baden-Baden: Tectum, 2008), 266–7.
64. Krabbe, *Politische Jugend*.
65. Theodor Haubach, 'Die Generationenfrage und der Sozialismus' (1930), in Wolfgang Luthardt (ed.), *Sozialdemokratische Arbeiterbewegung und Weimarer Republik*, vol. 2 (Frankfurt/Main: Suhrkamp, 1978), 81–93.
66. Marcel Böhles, *Im Gleichschritt für die Republik: Das Reichsbanner Schwarz-Rot-Gold in Baden und Württemberg 1924 bis 1933* (Essen: Klartext, 2016), 72–80, 112–21.
67. Götz von Olenhusen, *Jugendreich*, 143.
68. Günter Krolzig, *Der Jugendliche in der Großstadtfamilie: Auf Grund von Niederschriften Berliner Berufsschüler und -schülerinnen* (Berlin: F. A. Herbig, 1930), 77–106.
69. Christina Benninghaus, *Die anderen Jugendlichen: Arbeitermädchen in der Weimarer Republik* (Frankfurt/Main and New York: Campus, 1999), 138–54.
70. Hans Zehrer, 'Akademisches Proletariat', *Die Tat*, 22 (1931), 816–23, 816.
71. Harvey, *Youth and Welfare State*, 108–9.
72. Ibid., 131–6.
73. Ursula Büttner, *Weimar: Die überforderte Republik 1918–1933. Leistung und Versagen in Staat, Gesellschaft, Wirtschaft und Kultur* (Stuttgart: Klett-Cotta, 2008), 477.

74. Arndt Weinrich, *Der Weltkrieg als Erzieher: Jugend zwischen Weimarer Republik und Nationalsozialismus* (Essen: Klartext, 2013), 209.
75. Charlotte Bühler (ed.), *Jugendtagebuch und Lebenslauf* (Jena: Gustav Fischer, 1931); Büttner, *Weimar: Die überforderte Republik*, 1, 5.
76. Weinrich, *Weltkrieg als Erzieher*, 209.
77. Dirk Schumann, *Political Violence in the Weimar Republic 1918–1933: Fight for the Streets and Fear of Civil War* (New York: Berghahn, 2009).
78. Anthony McElligott, 'In Search of a Führer: Bourgeois Youth and Weimar Politics', in Rüdiger Hachtmann and Sven Reichardt (eds), *Detlev Peukert und die NS-Forschung* (Göttingen: Wallstein, 2015), 69–84, 69; John Alexander Williams, *Turning to Nature in Germany. Hiking, Nudism, and Conservation, 1900–1940* (Stanford, CA: Stanford University Press, 2007), 206–7.
79. Peter D. Stachura, *Weimar Republic and the Younger Proletariat: An Economic and Social Analysis* (New York: St Martin's Press, 1989), 3–4.

Bibliography

Dickinson, Edward Ross, *The Politics of German Child Welfare from the Empire to the Federal Republic* (Cambridge, MA: Harvard University Press, 1996).
Großmann, G. Ulrich, Claudia Selheim, and Barbara Stambolis (eds), *Deutsche Jugend zwischen Selbstbestimmung und Verführung* (Nuremberg: Verlag des Germanischen Nationalmuseums, 2013).
Harvey, Elisabeth, *Youth and the Welfare State in Weimar Germany* (Oxford: Clarendon Press, 1993).
Laqueur, Walter, *Young Germany. A History of the German Youth Movement* (London: Routledge & Kegan Paul, 1962).
Peukert, Detlev J. K., *Jugend zwischen Krieg und Krise: Lebenswelten von Arbeiterjungen in der Weimarer Republik* (Cologne: Bund-Verlag, 1987).
Roseman, Mark (ed.), *Generations in Conflict: Youth Revolt and Generation Formation in Germany 1770–1968* (Cambridge: Cambridge University Press, 1995).
Stachura, Peter D., *Weimar Republic and the Younger Proletariat: An Economic and Social Analysis* (New York: St Martin's Press, 1989).
Stambolis, Barbara (ed.), *Jugendbewegt geprägt: Essays zu autobiographischen Texten von Werner Heisenberg, Robert Jungk und vielen anderen* (Göttingen: V&R unipress, 2013).
Stambolis, Barbara, *Aufgewachsen in 'eiserner Zeit': Kriegskinder zwischen Erstem Weltkrieg und Weltwirtschaftskrise* (Giessen: Haland & Wirth, 2014).
Williams, John Alexander, *Turning to Nature in Germany. Hiking, Nudism, and Conservation, 1900–1940* (Stanford, CA: Stanford University Press, 2007).

PART V
CULTURE

CHAPTER 27

MASS CULTURE

JOCHEN HUNG

In 1926, the publisher Samuel Fischer complained about the way ordinary Germans spent their leisure time: 'People practice sports, dance, spend their evening hours by the radio, in the cinema, and, outside working hours, everyone is so busy that nobody has time to read ... '[1] What Fischer addressed here was the booming mass-cultural landscape of the Weimar Republic, ranging from modern spectator sports to the 'new' mass media, such as film and radio. For representatives of German high culture, this new mass culture was a dangerous threat to traditional bourgeois values of culturedness and *Bildung*. The problem, as they saw it, was less that this was 'low' culture, which had always been popular among the uneducated strata of German society, but that it was now produced on an industrial scale, disseminated through the most modern means of communication, and sold aggressively, like a common commodity.

However, Fischer's motivation to raise the alarm about the way people spent their free time was not only the state of German culture. As a publisher, he was also worried about declining sales and a loss of his audience. In this sense, 'mass culture' has always been a construct, drawing together separate phenomena such as the cinema, pulp fiction, and football matches. It was used by representatives of the middle class in order to both address and criticize the general nature of modernity and defend their cultural influence.[2] And it was constructed in opposition to 'high culture', a term used to designate a canon seen as educational, uplifting, intellectually stimulating, sometimes elitist. and representative of the most noble aspects of civilization. However, despite its ideological nature, the concept of 'mass culture' is still useful, as it highlights several important processes in modern societies that shaped the development of modern Western culture. With industrialization, a new stratum of waged labourers, often labelled 'the masses', developed in urban centres, who for the first time commanded a modest disposable income that could be spent on entertainment and diversion and who had a particular need for physical and mental relaxation. Thus, 'mass culture' is closely intertwined with industrial capitalism: it developed as a function in industrial society—to contribute to the recovery of the labour force—and was itself produced with industrial means and for profit. At the same time, the development of 'mass culture' coincided with a growing emancipation of its main audience, who won political rights and generally claimed a voice in the public sphere. The weakening of the traditional cultural canon, dominated by the middle class, and the wider appreciation of 'mass culture' went hand in hand with this process of emancipation. Finally, the rise of 'mass culture' gave its audience the opportunity to construct identities beyond their milieu, class, religion, or location, and addressed a growing individualization that was also part of modernity. This has led some scholars to claim that 'mass culture' is inherently emancipatory, democratizing, and egalitarian.[3] Others have interpreted it as a tool of homogenization and oppression. Research on the behaviour of mass media audiences has shown that they are far too heterogeneous to make such generalizations. Thus, for the sake of clarity and focus, in this chapter 'mass culture' will be used in the sense of 'popular commercialized cultures'.[4] Culture is used in the plural here in order to avoid the image of one homogeneous 'mass culture'. Instead, this chapter puts a focus on the various audiences and their modes of reception, addressing both the opportunities of individualization and the fact that the experience of consuming mass culture was often still shaped by gender, class, ethnicity, and location.

In Germany, mass cultures developed during the late nineteenth century as part of a broader transnational trend and were closely intertwined with the country's rapid industrialization and *Gründerzeit* capitalism.[5] In the Weimar Republic, these existing mass cultures expanded and changed through technological innovations (such as the introduction of radio and sound film and innovations in printing), the growth of new and existing audiences owing to social transformations (such as the growing number of white-collar workers and the emancipation of women) and new regulatory frameworks based on political changes (such as the abolition of censorship in the Weimar Constitution). The most significant change, however, was the expansion of leisure time through social improvements such as shorter working hours and regulated holidays.[6] People in the Weimar Republic had more free time than before and most turned to mediated and 'physical' mass cultures, from the cinema to football and popular theatre, to fill it. These achievements were small and contentious—the eight-hour day, introduced in 1918, was effectively abolished again in the early 1920s—but the horizon of expectations had changed irreversibly: many people of all walks of life increasingly saw leisure time as a right, rather than a privilege for a select few. It was in the Weimar Republic that the idea of free time changed into the idea of 'leisure time' (*Freizeit*) that was to be organized and structured.[7] In 1929, the term *Freizeit* entered the German dictionary—a sign that the idea of leisure had become widely accepted. Because of these transformations, historian Eberhard Kolb has argued that 'it was only after 1918 that a "modern mass culture", in the true sense, arose in Germany'.[8]

One of the most important characteristics of Weimar-era mass cultures was the central role of the modern mass media in their dissemination: the 1920s saw the development of a tightly integrated media ensemble comprising sound film, radio, popular recorded music, the mass press and book clubs, which remained stable until the proliferation of television in the 1960s.[9] This not only meant that contemporary mass cultures reached more people, but that these cultures were shaped by diverse cross-media influences, such as the increasingly visual content of popular newspapers as a reaction to the rise of cinema. This went hand in hand with an early form of 'media convergence', i.e. the merging of old and new media on the technological, economic and cultural level.[10] The development of this media ensemble interacted with 'physical' mass cultures, such as funfairs, popular theatre, and spectator sports: for example, the popularity of football and boxing led to the establishing of specialized publications and dedicated sections in newspapers and on the radio, while the heightened media attention turned popular athletes into veritable 'stars'.

As important was the change in the way mass cultures were perceived after 1918. Many Weimar-era intellectuals, artists, politicians and even some representatives of 'high culture', such as Nobel-prize winning novelist Thomas Mann, embraced the idea of 'the popular' and welcomed a cultural democratization.[11] However, there was also a large group rejecting 'mass culture', with Samuel Fischer only one voice amongst many. As a consequence, the term acquired a highly politicized symbolic meaning as the cultural expression of a new, democratized society and the foreign influences it was supposedly subjected to.

MEDIATED MASS CULTURES: READING, CINEMA, AND RADIO

While cinema and, from 1923, radio grew in popularity during the 1920s, the predominant way Germans consumed culture in the Weimar Republic was still by reading. By the beginning of the First World War, Germany had attained full literacy and reading had become firmly established as one of the nation's most important forms of entertainment and self-improvement. A flourishing market of popular literature had developed around the turn of the century, with the introduction of novels that were serialized in periodicals and series of novels and non-fiction books in cheap paperback format, such as Reclam's 'Universal-Bibliothek' (1867), Langewiesche's 'blue books' (1909), and Ullstein's 'red books' (1910). In consequence, the reading public changed from a traditionally bourgeois, middle-class audience towards a broad and diverse readership, a process that intensified after 1918.[12] Germans read more than ever before in the Weimar Republic, even if German reading culture changed: readers increasingly opted for periodicals and newspapers, rather than the book, as their preferred medium. It is indeed viable to speak of a general cultural adjustment to the key medium of the newspaper during the Weimar Republic. For example, 70 per cent of households in late 1920s Hamburg held a subscription to one of six different local newspapers.[13] The periodical press occupied a central place in the cultural consumption of many Germans in the Weimar Republic: it supplied its millions of readers not only with news and information but also entertainment and distraction. Most newspapers and magazines carried serialized novels, which played an important part in their circulation and popularity.[14]

The coverage of mass spectator sports—most importantly football—also became an integral part of press content in the Weimar Republic.[15] Newspapers were particularly important for people who only commanded a small entertainment budget. In 1928, a female textile worker from Dresden listed reading the newspaper as her only leisure-time pursuit, even at the weekend.[16] In 1932, the American journalist Hubert R. Knickerbocker reported about a poor working-class family in Berlin that would rather go hungry than give up their daily papers.[17]

The rising popularity of newspapers and periodicals seemed indicative of 'the transition of German society from a book-reading bourgeois society to a newspaper-reading mass society'.[18] This sparked contemporary fears of a 'book crisis', the feeling that the German book trade, and intellectual life in general, was in terminal decline.[19] However, these fears were largely unfounded. In the 1920s, the establishing of many popular book clubs, such as the Volksverband der Bücherfreunde (1919), Büchergilde Gutenberg (1924), Der Bücherkreis (1924) and the Deutsche Buchgemeinschaft (1924), opened up new mass audiences of book readers: the Volksverband alone counted 750,000 paying members by 1931.[20] The popularity of the book clubs was rooted primarily in their affordability: due to bulk-buying and guaranteed sales, they were able to sell their books for up to 50 per cent below the average market price. This made their reading material affordable to large sections of the population, even during the multiple economic crises that haunted the Weimar Republic. Despite this growth of readership, people in the book trade still worried about what kind of books were consumed. The publisher Friedrich Oldenbourg argued in 1925 that 'war and revolution have created a completely new class of readers', who were in danger of falling under the spell of cheap entertainment and 'the kitsch of the day'.[21] The sociologist and cultural critic Siegfried Kracauer shared this feeling and explained the supposed deteriorating quality of popular literature by the fact that the social situation of the German reading audience, which was dominated by the middle class, had changed profoundly. The increasing 'proletarianization' of the bourgeoisie, he argued, led them to look for books like Richard Voss' *Zwei Menschen*, a melodramatic love story set in South Tyrol, 'brimming with the kind of sentimentality (devoid of any literary form) that appeals to the anonymous masses'.[22] However, the fears of the middle class abandoning traditional bourgeois culture seem to be overstated, at least in case of the book clubs. Their programme was in fact dominated by classics and challenging works, from Goethe's *Faust* to Thomas Mann's Nobel-prize winning novel *Buddenbrooks* and Friedrich Wolf's expressionistic *Kreatur*. Also, rather than creating a homogeneous mass readership, the book clubs seem to have strengthened class differences, each one addressing a specific readership with a tailored programme. For example, the Bücherkreis, founded with support from the SPD, published Eduard Bernstein's *Sozialdemokratische Lehrjahre* ('A Social Democratic Apprenticeship') and Chancellor Hermann Müller's memoirs, while the Volksverband addressed a mainly middle-class audience with canonical works like Dante's *Divine Comedy* and an introduction to German painting by art historian Franz Dülberg.

The popularity of the cinema generated even more extreme fears about a cultural degeneration and 'massification' than the supposed decline of the book. Cinema had been part of popular leisure culture in Germany since the end of the nineteenth century, but mostly in the context of established recreational locations, for example, as an attraction at the funfair or in irregular showings at a public house.[23] At the beginning of the twentieth century, the first permanent film houses were established and their popularity exploded, turning cinema into an established mass medium. This growth continued in the 1920s: between 1919 and 1928, the number of cinemas in Germany expanded from 2,836 with 980,000 seats to 5,267 with a total of 1,876,600 seats.[24] At the end of the decade, the film scholar Alexander Jason estimated that Germans went to the cinema six million times per week.[25] However, these numbers only tell half the story. In the Weimar Republic, cinema as an institution, medium, and art form not only expanded, but diversified: for example, in the large towns, a new type of 'film palace'—opulently designed cinemas with a capacity between 1,000 and over 2,000 seats—were introduced alongside the traditional neighbourhood cinemas. Whereas cinema had been a decidedly working-class medium before, it had now become a respectable leisure pursuit among the middle class.[26]

The fact that the medium transcended class barriers has often been seen as a sign of a homogeneous, standardizing 'mass culture'.[27] However, the experience of the majority of German cinemagoers was often very different. While the medium theoretically appealed to all strata of society, white-collar workers were particularly attracted to the cinema, spending a much higher proportion of their entertainment budgets on it than other groups. People's social background also determined which films they consumed: different types of theatres—premier 'movie palaces', middling film houses, and 'workers' theatres'—showed quite different types of films. For example, in the cinemas frequented by the middle class, foreign films were unpopular, while working-class audiences preferred both American and Soviet films. The deeply entrenched regional identities in Germany also shaped the way cinema was consumed: the tastes and moral sensibilities of the audience varied considerably between Munich and Hamburg or Berlin and Stuttgart. The German film industry addressed these differences with specialized productions that were tailored to a regional, rather than a national, audience: films like *German Hearts at the German Rhine* or *I will Stay Faithful to you, my Palatinate* strengthened regional identities rather than undermining them. Even when people saw the same film, the experience varied considerably, depending on their location. A silent movie like Charlie Chaplin's *The Gold Rush*, for example, could be screened at a bourgeois cinema palace with a full orchestra playing, while the musical accompaniment in the small working-class cinemas often consisted only of an amateur musician. Often, small establishments would also show films at a much faster speed than more up-market cinemas in order to be able to cram two movies into one screening. The modes of reception varied accordingly, with middle-class audiences adapting bourgeois conventions of silent consumption common to the theatre and the opera, while screenings in working-class cinemas were a raucous affair that often involved drinking and eating and a constant commentary of the action shown on the screen. The introduction of sound film at the end of the 1920s narrowed the space for such an active reception and standardized the experience to some extent. However, by that time, the importance of the cinema already declined. With the Great Depression, the number of cinema visits decreased sharply, partly because of the shrinking entertainment budgets of the population and partly because of downsides of the new technology: the quality of early sound films was often inadequate and there was only a small number of German-language films available. Also, for a large part of the population, the cinema was not part of their leisure activities at all. In the 1920s, almost half of the German population still lived in rural areas far from Germany's larger towns, where most of the country's cinemas were located. These people could only very rarely take part in the 'mass culture' offered in the cinema—film remained 'an overwhelmingly urban phenomenon'.[28] Others, like many single women or young people, simply could not afford to watch films on a regular basis, even if they lived in the urban centres.

Just like cinema, the popularity of recorded music reached a peak during the Weimar Republic.[29] At the industry's high point in 1929, 427,200 gramophones and thirty million records were sold in Germany. The ability to mass-produce sound recordings gave rise to the phenomenon of the 'hit' (*Schlager*)—popular records produced for quick consumption and often superseded by the next 'hit' after a couple of months or even weeks. At the beginning of the decade, recorded music was primarily consumed communally in pubs and inns, but soon the gramophone became a staple of home life for millions of Germans. This was reflected in its appearance: the design gradually hid the technical innards and resembled a piece of furniture that could easily be accommodated in the home.[30] In contrast to the cinema, however, the gramophone was a decidedly middle-class medium, owing to its relatively high cost. The rise of recorded music in the Weimar Republic reconfigured German musical traditions, undermining the role of both live performances by professional musicians and the long-standing *Hausmusik* tradition of lay musicians in a private setting. In other ways, however, it reaffirmed existing structures and tastes. For example, despite boosting the introduction of jazz and other international music styles, the gramophone strengthened Germans' predilection for folk songs and waltzes. At the same time, the creation of popular 'hits' boosted the demand to hear them played live by orchestras.[31]

Radio was the only genuinely new medium of the Weimar era. On 29 October 1923, the first regular entertainment broadcast (*Unterhaltungsfunk*) went on the air in Germany.[32] Just like the gramophone, its early use was often communal, in pubs or the house of a neighbour affluent enough to be able to buy a receiver. However, ownership expanded quickly, and one year after the first broadcast, already 550,000 radio receivers were registered in Germany. By the end of 1929, this number had risen to more than three million. Despite its rising popularity and the attempts of the labour movement to establish a dedicated 'workers' broadcasting' (*Arbeiterfunk*), radio remained a dominantly middle-class medium in the Weimar Republic. This was not only because of the generally high cost of the receiver and the necessary licence fee, but also because of its content: the new medium developed under the tight control of state authorities that aimed to use its 'educational mission' to counter the waning cultural influence of the middle class. This was reflected in radio programming, as peak listening times during the evening were dominated by content that was deemed 'educational', such as lectures, literary features, or classical music, while light entertainment was often relegated to niche slots around midnight. High costs and restrictive programming were not the only reasons why the radio, despite its growing popularity, generally remained a rather exclusive medium: the most common radio sets were only able to receive broadcasts in a short radius around the transmitters, which were located in or close to bigger conurbations. This meant that the radio audience was overwhelmingly urban: in 1927, 1.4 million of the 1.7 million registered radio receivers in Germany were located in the urban centres. There were attempts to bring the new medium to rural areas in so-called 'radio buses', but the quality of sound and reception of these mobile receivers seems to have been so miserable that they in fact drove away potential consumers. However, even in urban centres like Berlin the spread of the radio was uneven. While the overall ownership rate among the city's households was 40 per cent in 1933, there were huge differences between districts. In affluent Dahlem, in the south-west of Berlin, over 82 per cent of households owned a radio; in the working-class districts in the east of the city, the rate was considerably lower. With the growth of its mainly urban, middle-class audience, private listening became the dominant form of radio consumption. During the late 1920s, the radio set developed its typical form: headphones were replaced by loudspeakers integrated into the radio set, which changed its status from a technical apparatus to a piece of furniture. At the same time, consumption practices changed from modes of reception modelled on concerts or lectures, with people even dressing up to listen to a broadcast, to the medium accompanying and structuring daily life. Many housewives, for example, welcomed the home entertainment provided by the radio and would schedule chores to coincide with particular programmes. With its rising popularity, radio programming expanded, from only a few hours a day in the early 1920s to around ten hours during the week and up to eighteen hours on Sundays at the end of the decade.

Characteristic of the mass cultures of the Weimar Republic are the various cross-media influences boosted by the convergence of the media ensemble of the 1920s. For example, the introduction of electrical recording in 1926 not only improved sound quality, but also made recorded music compatible with the new medium of radio. New gramophone/radio set combinations were introduced to the market, making both technologies more accessible to common consumers.[33] The introduction of sound film in the late 1920s paved the way for a close relationship between the cinema and recorded music, with 'hits' from popular movies being released as records.[34] The popularity of cinema catered to 'the ever-increasing demand for visual experience and instruction' in Weimar Germany, which reinforced the growth of visual content in the print media.[35] Illustrated magazines and tabloid newspapers became the characteristic press publications of the era, after the abolishing of censorship had gotten rid of the last constraints on design and layout.[36] Film influenced the press not only in terms of production and layout, but also in terms of content: the developing 'star' system with its cult of the celebrity actor relied on a growing number of publications, from dedicated film journals and mass-market newspapers, catering to their audience's interest in the cinema.[37] The same happened when radio appeared: rather than displacing older media, the new mass medium was embraced by them, with new magazines for radio enthusiasts and new formats in existing publications that reported on broadcasting times, programming trends, and practical advice on the servicing of the radio set.[38] The radio, on the other hand, was seen as a 'spoken newspaper' rather than a medium in its own right during the first few years of its popularization.[39] Already in 1925, publisher Friedrich Oldenbourg underlined the profound influence film and radio had on the book. Not only did it lead to an increased visualization and a changed writing style that was influenced by the spoken word, he argued, the book itself had lost its status as an autonomous medium, as it now often served as the raw material for films and radio plays.[40] The book trade adapted to these challenges by publishing novels based on popular movies and offering illustrated film books with scene stills.[41] Some publishers went even further in embracing all the new media that challenged their old business model during the 1920s. Popular novels like *All Quiet on the Western Front* and *Berlin Alexanderplatz*, for example, were first published in serialized form in newspapers, then as books, then (in the latter case) as a radio play and were then turned into films.[42] Ullstein, the publisher of *All Quiet on the Western Front*, was exemplary for these cross-media tendencies of Weimar mass culture. The company aggressively used its many magazines and newspapers as a distribution channel for its book publications and embraced the growth of the cinema as another revenue stream for its content production.[43]

'Das Weekend': Physical Mass Culture

According to Siegfried Kracauer, the new mass media not only influenced each other but also interacted with physical space: the panoramas of the themed restaurants in Berlin's new type of 'pleasure palaces', such as Haus Vaterland or Moka Efti, were 'born of the popular *Schlager*', which had shaped the expectations of customers with romanticized descriptions of far-away places.[44] For Kracauer and many of his contemporaries, such nightlife establishments, together with cinema palaces, football stadiums, funfairs, and popular theatre, were the physical embodiment of a growing 'mass culture'. Kracauer saw these locations as part of a 'process that creates the *homogeneous cosmopolitan audience* in which everyone has the *same* responses, from the bank director to the sales clerk, from the diva to the stenographer'.[45]

In Weimar Germany, these physical mass cultures were closely linked to the free weekend, which became a social institution for broad swathes of the population. The idea of a mass leisure culture combined several important currents in German culture: the pre-war Wandervogel and reform movements had stressed the importance of physical and mental recuperation in a modern, industrialized society—ideally, through a turn to 'untouched' nature. The war and, after 1918, a growing popular interest in competitive sports heightened the awareness of the body and the significance of physical fitness. At the same time, the growth of efficient public transport turned spectator sports and day excursions into mass activities.[46] Finally, the increasing standardization and rationalization of work in Weimar Germany, even in white-collar professions, made a clear differentiation between everyday life and free time, filled with extraordinary experiences and diversion, a pressing concern. A Weimar-era guide explaining how to spend the free weekend emphasized the recent democratization of leisure time: 'The weekend has—almost overnight—become a powerful concept that nobody can ignore. Countless interests, that until now were entertained only by a small and exclusive group, have suddenly become *a necessity for the great masses*.'⁴⁷ In 1927, at the opening of an exhibition in Berlin about the new *Wochenende* phenomenon, speakers such as the politician Marie Elisabeth Lüders and the city's mayor Arthur Scholtz stressed its 'importance in relation to health and demographic policy', representing 'a social issue of extensive significance'.⁴⁸ The modern mass media played a central role in the exhibition: portable gramophones and radio sets were presented as an important part of the recreational activities that should fill people's free time, which underlines the degree to which physical and mediated mass cultures were intertwined in Weimar Germany.⁴⁹ The Ullstein publishing house capitalized on this close integration: not only did the company's programme include popular guides for weekend tours and maps for outings with the automobile, its customers could even directly book tours and holidays in its many shops all over Germany.⁵⁰ Its literary products were marketed as the material necessary to fill leisure time. A well-known advertisement depicted a Berliner inconsolable about forgetting his *Ullsteinbuch* on the train: 'What am I supposed to do now at the lake?'⁵¹

In Weimar Germany, the *Wochenende* was clearly differentiated from conventional leisure-time activities, such as the traditional Sunday outing, as a very modern phenomenon. As an import from Anglo-American culture, it had an inherently modern allure, but it was also seen as fitting the demands of a highly industrialized and urbanized society. While the retreat into nature still played an important role, Weimar-era weekenders encountered it in structured, consumerist activities that involved modern sports equipment, such as rowing, sailing, and camping. In 1929, the journalist Marie Leitner drew a kaleidoscopic picture of a whole nation beyond class boundaries—golf-playing managers, proletarian women working out with their sports union, hiking young couples, and playing children—taking part in mass recreation during a weekend, only to return to their daily drudgery in the evening: 'And with colourful lights, with a noisy roar, the city welcomes its slaves again.'⁵²

Despite the fact that thousands pursued these activities, great importance was attached to their individualist character. The popular hit 'Weekend and Sunshine' ('Wochenend und Sonnenschein'), released in 1930, captured this feeling: 'Weekend and sunshine / And then alone with you in the woods / I don't need anything else to be happy.'⁵³ A vivid image of the leisure-time pursuits of ordinary Germans is painted by the film *People on a Sunday* from the same year.⁵⁴ The film includes semi-documentary shots of crowds enjoying themselves in funfairs, parks, and sport stadiums, but the main plot revolves around the weekend plans of a group of young Berliners, which include going to the cinema and reading newspapers. On Sunday, they join thousands of others spending the day on one of the many lakes in the city's green belt. Their open-air leisure time on the shore is often structured by media consumption, such as reading tabloid newspapers and listening to their mobile gramophone.

A way to escape working life for a short while without leaving the city boundaries was at funfairs, which 'became increasingly popular after the Great War'.[55] In contrast to today's amusement parks, which are mostly located outside urban centres, the funfairs of the early twentieth century were a decidedly urban phenomenon. Most funfairs in Germany were modelled on the famous Luna Park at Coney Island: there were 'Luna-Parks' in Berlin, Hamburg, Leipzig, and Dortmund, offering a similar formula of rides, shooting galleries, concert halls, beer gardens, and restaurants.[56] Electrified amusements that delivered modern experiences of speed, disorientation, entertainment, and exotic thrills, such as scenic railway roller coasters (*Gebirgsszeneriebahn*), were the main attractions of these parks. Siegfried Kracauer reported on such a ride in Berlin's Luna-Park, which took its passengers through a New York-inspired urban landscape of skyscrapers, noting the absurdity of escaping the city for a 'metropolitan illusion'.[57] Still, he acknowledged the sublime nature of these escapist experiences for the roller-coaster passengers that made them forget working life for a fleeting moment: 'These people ... are no longer workers, common people, and employees. They are people who exist in the moment, who, like flying lines, extend from one pole to another. From the mountain to the valley, from the heights to the depths and once again back up to the heights.'[58] The modern mass media were also integrated into the physical spaces of funfairs: in 1924, one of the new attractions of Berlin's Luna-Park was a 'radio house', a dance hall that played 'wireless' music for its visitors, with individual headphones for the more expensive seats in the booths surrounding the dance floor.[59] Because of their size—the Luna-Park in Berlin had room for over 60,000 visitors—and varied attractions that catered to a broad range of audiences, funfairs were seen as spaces of 'mass culture', where people from all social strata rubbed shoulders with each other.[60] However, the core audience was recruited from the petite bourgeoisie and, while some of the visitors were tourists and out-of-towners, most lived in close vicinity to the funfair. Inside the fair itself, class differences were also enforced by measures like the *Weinzwang*, the rule that more expensive wine had to be ordered on the more desirable tables, and higher entrance fees on so-called 'elite days'.

The urban recreational culture of the funfairs, characterized by exotic escapism and sensory thrills, also spread beyond their confines. The Haus Vaterland complex, for example, offered a variety of exotic locations under one roof, from a 'Wild-West-Bar' to a Spanish *bodega*, and the Moka Efti café boasted an escalator that took its guests from street level up to its orientalist interior. While the size and design of these establishments were unique to Weimar-era Berlin, dance halls, bars, theatres, and other night-life establishments had long tried to create a space of the extraordinary to lure in their audience. For example, the architecture of the Metropol-Theater in Berlin, built in 1898 but still an important location of popular entertainment in the Weimar Republic, recreated the flair of famous Parisian theatres. Since its rise at the end of the nineteenth century, popular musical theatre has been interpreted as an aspect of 'mass culture' and representative of modernity itself.[61] By the mid-1920s, Berlin alone boasted over fifty theatres with a total of around 43,000 seats.[62] However, the theatres did little to create the homogeneous cosmopolitan audience

Kracauer envisioned. While there were spaces, such as the restaurant or the gallery of the theatre, where the audience often mixed, the spatial separation of cheap and expensive seats made class differences all the more tangible.[63]

One of the central aspects of Weimar leisure culture was modern spectator sports. Football and boxing matches, a popular pastime before the war, became mass events all over Germany: after 1918, most cities in the Ruhr area, Germany's industrial centre, built football stadiums that held between 25,000 and 50,000 spectators.[64] In 1923, 64,000 people watched the Hamburger Sportverein win the German football championship in Berlin's Deutsches Stadion. Much more significant, however, were the numbers of people who went to see the multitude of matches on a local level: in 1929, over 523,000 matches were registered with the German Football Association, with a total audience that numbered in the millions.[65] The mass media played a central role in the popularization of competitive sports. New illustrated magazines, such as *Kicker* and *Boxsport*, both founded in 1920, helped to turn athletes like Hans Breitensträter and Max Schmeling into celebrities similar to film stars. In April 1924, regular sports reports became a fixture on the new medium of radio, which had only been introduced to the German public the year before. When Breitensträter challenged Paul Samson-Körner for the German heavyweight championship in 1925, even serious broadsheet newspapers, such as the *Vossische Zeitung* and the *Berliner Tageblatt*, reported prominently on the sold-out fight.[66] The close partnership of popular sports and popular culture is most evident in Schmeling's role as the lead character in the film *Liebe im Ring* (1930), one of the first German sound films, which included the musical number 'The Heart of a Boxer'.[67] Contemporary observers even argued that the prominent place of boxing in the media contributed more to the sport's popularity than the actual fights.[68] Mass sports events seemed to break down class barriers and mould one homogeneous audience feverishly following the action on the lawn, the court, or in the ring. The journalist Georg Schwarz, for example, described how during the six-day-race in Dortmund's Westfalenhalle, which had opened in 1925 with 16,000 seats, businessmen mingled with miners.[69] However, spectator sports in fact remained a fairly bourgeois affair, even in the case of football.[70] Watching sports was often also a male activity: mass spectator sports such as football and boxing were only popular among men, while women preferred hiking and swimming.[71]

'Americanization', 'Cultural Bolshevism', and 'Imploitation': Fears of Mass Culture

The popularity of mediated and physical mass cultures caused alarm among middle-class observers. In 1926, the pedagogue Heinrich Kautz crestfallenly reported on the allure of light entertainment among workers in Ruhr area:

> One has to see it to believe how the industrial people (*Industrievolk*) crowd first before the advertising hoarding and then the hall doors. Whether it's hot or cold, soaking wet or stormy, the people patiently endure their polonaise, more patiently than they did in front of the grocery store during war rationing, and wait in all humility until the hall empties again and they can laugh and shout a bit for their hard-earned money.[72]

Particularly when it came to young or female audiences, the consumption of mass culture was often medicalized in terms such as 'cinema addiction', 'radiotism', or 'radiotitis'.[73] Not only did this industrially produced culture make the 'lower' classes less susceptible to the positive, educational influences of 'high art', but it seemed to even change the very nature of art itself. For Oldenbourg, the book became a mere link in a capitalist supply chain, while works of art, the philosopher Walter Benjamin famously argued, lost their 'aura' among mechanically produced films and photographs. These discourses about 'mass culture' were part of a broader engagement with the nature of modernity itself. Most often, this took the form of a defensive reaction intended to shore up traditional bourgeois cultural dominance. These fears were reflected in the regulation of mass culture that existed in the Weimar Republic despite the official abolition of censorship after 1918. Already in 1920, concerns about the harmful influence of the cinema led to the adoption of the Motion Picture Law, which was overseen by film assessment boards in Berlin and Munich. According to the text of the law, the boards could stop the release of a film if it was 'capable of endangering public order and safety, injuring religious feelings, having a morally brutalizing or immoral effect, endangering the image of Germany or Germany's relationships to foreign countries'. In 1926, after a vicious public campaign and a contentious debate in parliament, the Law for the Protection of Youth from Dirty and Trashy Writings was introduced, designed to protect young people from the harmful influence of worthless or pornographic literature.

These regulations were promoted aggressively by conservative and right-wing circles, including the German National People's Party (DNVP) and the churches.[74] Their rejection of 'mass culture' was often cloaked in anti-Americanism: the USA stood for an alien cultural influence threatening a supposedly pure German *Kultur* with its soulless modernism and profane primitivism.[75] This image of American culture as both excessively rationalized and inherently uncivilized was most vividly expressed in the German reception of jazz, which was often characterized by references to assembly-line production and industrial division of labour as well as racist notions of black primitiveness.[76] In a similar fashion, the Soviet Union stood for the home of an alien 'mass culture'. Particularly during the final years of the Weimar Republic, the political catchphrase of 'cultural bolshevism' was used to designate and denigrate modern popular culture.[77] Finally, the spread of 'mass culture' was also linked to a Jewish influence.[78] For example, the publishing house Ullstein, whose owners had Jewish roots, was described as 'the department store of German intellectual life', appealing to the basest instincts of its audience.[79]

While conservatives were most outspoken in their rejection, there was a critical engagement with the phenomenon of 'mass culture' all over Weimar's political spectrum, including many liberals and leftist intellectuals. For the labour movement, from social democrats to communists, 'mass culture' depoliticized its consumers and stood in the way of the development of socialist education and class consciousness.[80] In 1931, the playwright Bertolt Brecht, who often experimented with new media in his work, called the mass leisure culture of the Weimar Republic an 'imploitation' (*Einbeutung*) of the working masses—an industrialized, profit-oriented system and the companion piece of their exploitation at work.[81] Observers like Kracauer, Benjamin, and Adorno often argued along similar lines. What differentiated many leftist critics of 'mass culture' from their conservative counterparts was the fact that they believed in the possibility of an emancipatory mass culture and did not reject outright 'the mass' as a bearer of culture. Both Benjamin and Kracauer saw the cinema as a 'training ground' for the masses to develop a revolutionary consciousness or at least a more resilient mindset attuned to modernity. Sports arenas also appeared as spaces of a new, active engagement with culture that seemed more fitting for a modern society than the staid forms of appreciation in the opera house. For example, to the critic Herbert Ihering '[t]he mass in the sports palaces' was preferable to the polite theatre audience.[82] Their emotional involvement and passionate participation with the action on the field or in the ring seemed to promise a rejuvenation of the bourgeois engagement with 'high culture'. In 1932, the high-brow intellectual magazine *Der Querschnitt* argued that the ideals of fair play in competitive sport—respecting the opponent, accepting defeat, playing by the rules—taught the audience how to behave as responsible citizens in a modern mass society.[83] In the same year, the film *Kuhle Wampe*, based on a script co-written by Brecht that was originally called 'Weekend Kuhle Wampe', contrasted petit-bourgeois leisure culture with socialist team sports.[84] While the tabloid newspapers and day excursions of the petite bourgeoisie only provide escapist entertainment to keep their minds from their ever more precarious situation, the sports events organized by the workers mould the participants into a strong collective mentally and physically ready to change the world.

Conclusion

For both enemies and proponents of 'mass culture', it seemed to be an essential aspect of modernity and characteristic of a fundamentally transformed society. However, large parts of the population did not have access to most forms of modern entertainment, either because of tight household budgets or because of their location far from urban centres. Even among the ones who could afford to visit the cinema and buy a gramophone or a radio, the number of people who chose to watch modernist masterpieces like Fritz Lang's *Metropolis* or to listen to the latest jazz record was small. The most popular films of the era were often schmaltzy romances or historical dramas.[85] One of the most popular songs of the Weimar era was the sentimental *Schlager* 'Das gibt's nur einmal', a musical number from the historical comedy *Der Kongress tanzt*, set during the Congress of Vienna in 1814–15.[86] More than a triumph of modernism, Weimar mass cultures were often a blend of high technology and conventional cultural forms.

The history of Universum Film AG (Ufa), Germany's biggest film production company, is representative in this respect.[87] Today, Ufa is mostly know for some of the most acclaimed masterpieces of modern German cinema, such as Robert Wiene's *The Cabinet of Dr Caligari*, Fritz Lang's *Dr Mabuse the Gambler*, and F. W. Murnau's *Faust*. However, these films were overshadowed by the number of pedestrian potboilers, comedies, and costume dramas the company produced, which often proved much more popular than Ufa's high-brow productions. The company's arguably most ambitious film, *Metropolis*, was a commercial failure and contributed to its financial woes that led to its take-over by arch-conservative media magnate Alfred Hugenberg in 1927. Hugenberg was the leader of the DNVP, a party that railed against 'cultural liberalism' and the 'discharge of the democratic spirit that is the obedience before the masses'.[88] The DNVP had also led the charge in introducing censorship of mass culture. Hugenberg himself, however, had no such qualms: next to Ufa, he also controlled one of the most successful tabloids in Berlin, the *Nachtausgabe*, and the illustrated magazine *Scherl's Magazin*, both mass-market publications with a modern design but following a clearly conservative political line.

This dynamic mixture of romantic, conservative, or reactionary politics and modern appearance was also reflected in the cultural programme of the Nazis. Despite officially rejecting Weimar's 'decadent' culture, the movement was in fact deeply rooted in it. Already in the Weimar Republic, the Nazis used modern technology and aesthetics to spread their message, from the illustrated tabloid *Der Angriff* to recorded speeches by Hitler, Nazi sports events, and the 'aesthetics of violence' of the SA.[89] Once in power, they moved to 'purify' German culture and purge it of 'Jewish-Bolshevik' influences. However, despite the official narrative of a 'cultural rebirth', this meant a narrowing of existing Weimar-era cultures rather than the creation of a genuine Nazi culture. While mass cultures were generally subjected to less draconian censorship measures than 'high art', many cultural producers who did not fit the regime's political or racist rules lost their livelihood or were forced to leave the country. Others, however, thrived: Ufa, for example, still churned out its popular musical comedies and costume dramas, and many Weimar-era film stars, such as Lilian Harvey and Heinz Rühmann, continued to play a central role in German movie productions. These continuities with Weimar mass cultures sometimes led to tensions with the regime's official ideology. For example, most female stars of Nazi cinema did not conform to the National Socialist ideal of femininity at all.[90] A similar image emerges when we focus on physical mass cultures: there was an attempt to boost and at the same time control and centralize leisure activities, for example, through the 'Strength through Joy' organization. All sports organizations were *gleichgeschaltet* after 1933 and Jewish athletes were forced to retire. Still, boxing, an individualist and intensely competitive sport without a long tradition in Germany, was embraced by the regime. Max Schmeling's fight against the German boxing star Walter Neusel in 1934 that drew more than 80,000 spectators was organized in collaboration with 'Strength through Joy'.[91]

After 1945, Adorno railed against the attempts to rehabilitate the culture of the Weimar era as an early victim of the Nazis. For him, there had never been much difference between Weimar culture and Nazi culture: '[A]t the latest with the stabilization of the German currency, … German culture stabilized itself in the spirit of the Berlin illustrated magazines, which yielded little to that of the Nazis' "Strength through Joy", Reich autobahns, and jaunty exhibition-hall Classicism.'[92] We do not necessarily have to subscribe to Adorno's implication that Weimar-era mass cultures paved the way for Hitler. But his focus on the continuities beyond 1933 provides a helpful perspective on their history. The mass cultures of Weimar Germany, despite their image as part of a cutting-edge 'Weimar culture', were neither automatically modernist nor all inherently progressive.

NOTES

1. Cited in Gideon Reuveni, 'Reading, Advertising and Consumer Culture in the Weimar Period', in Karl Christian Führer and Corey Ross (eds), *Mass Media, Culture and Society in Twentieth-Century Germany* (Basingstoke: Palgrave Macmillan, 2006), 204–16, here 204.
2. The following draws on Antje Dietze and Maren Möhring, 'Einleitung. Produktionswelten der Massenkultur', *Geschichte und Gesellschaft*, 46 (2020), 5–24; Kaspar Maase, *Grenzenloses Vergnügen: Der Aufstieg der Massenkultur 1850–1970* (Frankfurt: Fischer, 1997), 16–37.
3. Maase, *Genzenloses Vergnügen*, 24.
4. I am following the definitions by Adelheid von Saldern, 'The Hidden History of Mass Culture', *International Labor and Working-Class History*, 37 (1990), 32–40; Corey Ross, 'Mass Culture and Divided Audiences: Cinema and Social Change in Inter-War Germany', *Past and Present*, 193 (2006), 157–95. See Dietze and Möhring, 'Einleitung', 8–12 for a detailed discussion of the concept of 'mass culture'.
5. For early mass culture in Germany, see Maase, *Grenzenloses Vergnügen*; Lynn Abrams, *Workers' Culture in Imperial Germany. Leisure and Recreation in the Rhineland and Westphalia* (London: Routledge, 1992).
6. Christine Keitz, 'Die Anfänge des modernen Massentourismus in der Weimarer Republik', *Archiv für Sozialgeschichte*, 33 (1993), 179–209, here 184; Abrams, *Workers' Culture*; Reinhard Schmitz-Scherzer, *Freizeit* (Stuttgart: Teubner, 1985), 35.
7. Adelheid von Saldern, 'Die Zeit fährt Auto … Zeit- und Raumveränderungen im Zeichen der Moderne', in Adelheid von Saldern and Sid Auffarth (eds), *Wochenend und schöner Schein. Freizeit und modernes Leben in den Zwanziger Jahren* (Berlin: Elephanten Press, 1991), 7–13.
8. Eberhard Kolb, *The Weimar Republic* (Abingdon: Routledge, 2005), 95.
9. Axel Schildt, 'Das Jahrhundert der Massenmedien. Ansichten zu einer künftigen Geschichte der Öffentlichkeit', *Geschichte und Gesellschaft*, 27 (2001), 177–206.
10. For the concept of media convergence, see Henry Jenkins, *Convergence Culture: Where Old and New Media Collide* (New York: NYU Press, 2006).
11. Sabina Becker, *Experiment Weimar: Eine Kulturgeschichte Deutschlands 1918–1933* (Darmstadt: WBG, 2018), 254–68.
12. Lynda J. King, *Best-Sellers by Design: Vicki Baum and the House of Ullstein* (Detroit: Wayne State University Press, 1988), 19–44.

13. Karl Christian Führer, 'Politische Kultur und Journalismus. Tageszeitungen als politische Akteure in der Krise der Weimarer Republik 1929–1933', *Jahrbuch für Kommunikationsgeschichte*, 10 (2008), 26–51.
14. Bernhard Fulda, *Press and Politics in the Weimar Republic* (Oxford: Oxford University Press, 2009), 29–34.
15. Bernhard Fulda, 'Industries of Sensationalism: German Tabloids in Weimar Germany', in Karl Christian Führer and Corey Ross (eds), *Mass Media, Culture and Society in Twentieth-Century Germany* (Basingstoke: Palgrave Macmillan, 2006), 183–203, here 186–8.
16. Alf Lüdtke (ed.), *'Mein Arbeitstag, mein Wochenende': Arbeiterinnen berichten von ihrem Alltag 1928* (Hamburg: Ergebnisse, 1991), 48.
17. Hubert R. Knickerbocker, *Germany—Fascist or Soviet?* (London: John Lane, 1932), 14.
18. Reuveni, 'Reading, Advertising and Consumer', 205.
19. Gideon Reuveni, *Reading Germany. Literature and Consumer Culture in Germany before 1933* (New York: Berghahn, 2006), 18–55.
20. Urban van Melis, 'Buchgemeinschaften', in *Geschichte des deutschen Buchhandels im 19. und 20. Jahrhundert*, vol. 2. *Die Weimarer Republik 1918–1933* (Berlin: de Gruyter, 2008), 553–88, here 556; King, *Best-Sellers by Design*, 39.
21. Friedrich Oldenbourg, 'Über die Zukunft des Buches', cited in Berthold Brohm, 'Das Buch in der Krise. Studien zur Buchhandelsgeschichte der Weimarer Republik', *Archiv für Geschichte des Buchwesens*, 51 (1999), 189–331, here 199.
22. Siegfried Kracauer, *The Mass Ornament: Weimar Essays*, tr. Thomas Levin (Cambridge, MA: Harvard University Press, 1995), 96.
23. Abrams, *Workers' Culture*, 172–3.
24. Corey Ross, *Media and the Making of Modern Germany: Mass Communications, Society, and Politics from the Empire to the Third Reich* (Oxford: Oxford University Press, 2008), 122.
25. Alexander Jason (i.e. Alexander Abchasi), *Handbuch der Filmwirtschaft* (Berlin: Verlag für Presse, Wirtschaft und Politik, 1930), cited ibid.
26. Karl Christian Führer, 'Auf dem Weg zur "Massenkultur"? Kino und Rundfunk in der Weimarer Republik', *Historische Zeitschrift*, 262 (1996), 739–81.
27. The following is mostly based on Ross, 'Mass Culture and Divided Audiences'; Führer, 'Massenkultur'.
28. Ross, 'Mass Culture and Divided Audiences', 161.
29. For the following, see Ross, *Media and the Making of Modern Germany*, 128–40; Corey Ross, 'Entertainment, Technology and Tradition: The Rise of Recorded Music from the Empire to the Third Reich', in Karl Christian Führer and Corey Ross (eds), *Mass Media, Culture and Society in Twentieth-Century Germany* (Basingstoke: Palgrave Macmillan, 2006), 25–43; Brian Currid, *A National Acoustics. Music and Mass Publicity in Weimar and Nazi Germany* (Minneapolis: University of Minnesota Press, 2006).
30. Ross, 'Entertainment', 27.
31. Ross, 34–7; Currid, *A National Acoustics*, 65–118.
32. The following is based on Ross, *Media and the Making of Modern Germany*, 128–40, 150–62; Inge Marßolek, 'Radio in Deutschland 1923–1960: Zur Sozialgeschichte eines Mediums', *Geschichte und Gesellschaft*, 27 (2001), 207–39; Carsten Lenk, *Die Erscheinung des Rundfunks: Einführung und Nutzung eines neuen Mediums 1923–1932* (Opladen: Westdeutscher Verlag, 1997); Karl Christian Führer, 'A Medium of Modernity? Broadcasting in Weimar Germany, 1923–1932', *Journal of Modern History*, 69 (1997),

722–53; Führer, 'Massenkultur'; Kate Lacey, *Feminine Frequencies. Gender, German Radio, and the Public Sphere, 1923-1945* (Ann Arbor: University of Michigan Press, 1996).
33. Ross, 'Entertainment', 27.
34. Currid, *A National Acoustics*, 65–118.
35. Kolb, *Weimar Republic*, 96.
36. Fulda, 'Industries'.
37. Joseph Garncarz, 'The Star System in Weimar Cinema', in Christian Rogowski (ed.), *The Many Faces of Weimar Cinema. Rediscovering Germany's Filmic Legacy* (New York: Camden House, 2010), 116–33.
38. Lenk, *Erscheinung*, 35–7.
39. See e.g. Ludwig Kapeller, 'Nicht "gesprochene Zeitung" – sondern "Rundfunk" (1924)', in Albert Kümmel and Petra Löffler (eds), *Medientheorie 1888-1933* (Frankfurt: Suhrkamp, 2002), 156–7.
40. Oldenbourg, 'Über die Zukunft des Buches', 273.
41. Jasmin Lange, *Der deutsche Buchhandel und der Siegeszug der Kinematographie 1895-1933: Reaktionen und strategische Konsequenzen* (Wiesbaden: Harrassowitz, 2010), 253–4.
42. Peter Jelavich, *Berlin Alexanderplatz: Radio, Film, and the Death of Weimar Culture* (Berkeley, CA: University of California Press, 2006).
43. Lange, *Der deutsche Buchhandel*, 253–4.
44. Siegfried Kracauer, *The Salaried Masses. Duty and Distraction in Weimar Germany*, tr. Quintin Hoare (London: Verso, 1998), 93.
45. Kracauer, *The Mass Ornament*, 325. Emphasis in the original.
46. Erik Norman Jensen, *Body by Weimar: Athletes, Gender, and German Modernity* (Oxford: Oxford University Press, 2013); Abrams, *Workers' Culture*, 170; Angela Schwarz, 'Die Erfindung des Wochenendes in der Presse der Weimarer Republik', in Katja Leiskau, Patrick Rössler, and Susann Trabert (eds), *Deutsche illustrierte Presse: Journalismus und visuelle Kultur in der Weimarer Republik* (Baden-Baden: Nomos, 2016), 275–304; Anthony McElligott, *The German Urban Experience: Modernity and Crisis, 1900-1945* (London: Routledge, 2001), 97–128.
47. Edmund Heilpern, 'Kaufmännische Reklame und Wochenende', in Karl Tramm and Karl Vetter (eds), *Das Wochenende: Anregungen zur praktischen Durchführung* (Berlin: Mosse, 1928), 197–201, here 199. Emphasis in the original.
48. Cited in Schwarz, 'Die Erfindung des Wochenendes', 284.
49. Lenk, *Erscheinung*, 193–4.
50. For Ullstein, see Jochen Hung, 'The "Ullstein Spirit": The Ullstein Publishing House, the End of the Weimar Republic and the Making of Cold War German Identity, 1925–77', *Journal of Contemporary History*, 53 (2018), 158–84.
51. Lange, *Der deutsche Buchhandel*, 159.
52. Maria Leitner, 'Eine ganze Stadt erholt sich. Sommer-Sonntag in Berlin', *Tempo*, 1 July 1929, 5.
53. Peter Sloterdijk, *Critique of Cynical Reason*, tr. Michael Eldred (Minneapolis: University of Minnesota Press, 1987), 502.
54. Matthias Uecker, '"Das Leben [...] So ist es und nicht anders." Constructions of Normality in *Menschen am Sonntag*', in Jochen Hung, Godela Weiss-Sussex, and Geoff Wilkes (eds), *Beyond Glitter and Doom. The Contingency of the Weimar Republic* (Munich: iudicium, 2012), 162–75.
55. Abrams, *Workers' Culture*, 170.

56. Claudia Puttkammer and Sacha Szabo, *Gruss aus dem Luna-Park: Eine Archäologie des Vergnügens. Freizeit- und Vergnügungsparks Anfang des zwanzigsten Jahrhunderts* (Berlin: WVB, 2007).
57. Siegfried Kracauer, 'Roller Coaster', tr. Thomas Levin, *Qui Parle: Literature, Philosophy, Visual Arts, History*, 5 (1992), 58–60.
58. Ibid.
59. Lenk, *Erscheinung*, 76.
60. For the following, see Johanna Niedbalski, *Die ganze Welt des Vergnügens: Berliner Vergnügungsparks der 1880er bis 1930er Jahre* (Berlin: be.bra, 2018).
61. Len Platt, Tobias Becker, and David Linton, 'Introduction', in Len Platt, Tobias Becker, and David Linton (eds), *Popular Musical Theatre in London and Berlin* (Cambridge: Cambridge University Press, 2014), 1–22.
62. Tobias Becker, *Inszenierte Moderne, Populäres Theater in Berlin und London, 1880–1930* (Berlin: De Gruyter Oldenbourg, 2014), 417–20.
63. Ibid., 109–20.
64. Matthias Uecker, *Zwischen Industrieprovinz und Großstadthoffnung: Kulturpolitik im Ruhrgebiet der zwanziger Jahre* (Wiesbaden: Springer, 1994), 310.
65. Christiane Eisenberg, 'Massensport in der Weimarer Republik: Ein statistischer Überblick', *Archiv für Sozialgeschichte*, 33 (1993), 137–77, here 148.
66. Jon Hughes, *Max Schmeling and the Making of a National Hero in Twentieth-Century Germany* (London: Palgrave Macmillan, 2018), 34–5.
67. Ibid., 52.
68. Eisenberg, 'Massensport', 139.
69. Uecker, *Industrieprovinz*, 318.
70. Eisenberg, 'Massensport', 171–3.
71. Detlev J. K. Peukert, *Jugend zwischen Krieg und Krise: Lebenswelten von Arbeiterjungen in der Weimarer Republik* (Cologne: Bund, 1987), 170.
72. Heinrich Kautz, *Im Schatten der Schlote: Versuche zur Seelenkunde der Industriejugend* (Einsiedeln: Benzinger, 1926), cited in Uecker, *Industrieprovinz*, 318.
73. Eve Rosenhaft, 'Lesewut, Kinosucht, Radiotismus: Zur (geschlechter-)politischen Relevanz neuer Massenmedien in den 1920er Jahren', in Alf Lüdtke, Inge Marszolek, and Adelheid von Saldern (eds), *Amerikanisierung: Traum und Alptraum im Deutschland des 20. Jahrhunderts* (Stuttgart: Franz Steiner, 1996), 119–43.
74. Luke Springman, 'Poisoned Hearts, Diseased Minds, and American Pimps: The Language of Censorship in the Schund Und Schmutz Debates', *German Quarterly*, 68 (1995), 408–29; Margaret F. Stieg, 'The 1926 German Law to Protect Youth Against Trash and Dirt: Moral Protectionism in a Democracy', *Central European History*, 23 (1990), 22–56.
75. For mass culture and anti-Americanism, see Egbert Klautke, *Unbegrenzte Möglichkeiten: 'Amerikanisierung' in Deutschland und Frankreich, 1900–1933* (Stuttgart: Steiner, 2003), 239–68; Adelheid von Saldern, 'Überfremdungsängste. Gegen die Amerikanisierung der deutschen Kultur in den zwanziger Jahren', in Lüdtke et al., *Amerikanisierung*, 213–44.
76. Theodore F. Rippey, 'Rationalisation, Race, and the Weimar Response to Jazz', *German Life and Letters*, 60 (2007), 75–97.
77. Björn Laser, *Kulturbolschewismus! Zur Diskurssemantik der 'totalen Krise' 1929–1933* (Frankfurt: Peter Lang, 2010), 326–33.
78. Saldern, 'Überfremdungsängste', 217–22.

79. Lynkeus, *Der deutsche Buchhandel und das Judentum: Ein Menetekel* (Leipzig: Hammer, 1925), 17–9.
80. Dieter Langewiesche, 'Das neue Massenmedium Film und die deutsche Arbeiterbewegung in der Weimarer Republik', in Jürgen Kocka, Hans-Jürgen Puhle, and Klaus Tenfelde (eds), *Von der Arbeiterbewegung zum modernen Sozialstaat: Festschrift für Gerhard A. Ritter zum 65. Geburtstag* (Munich: K. G. Saur, 1994), 114–30; Adelheid von Saldern, 'Massenfreizeitkultur im Visier: ein Beitrag zu den Deutungs- und Entwicklungsversuchen während der Weimarer Republik', *Archiv für Sozialgeschichte*, 33 (1993), 21–58, here 44–54.
81. Bertolt Brecht, 'Der Dreigroschenprozess. Ein soziologisches Experiment', in *Versuche*, vol. 3 (Berlin: Kiepenheuer, 1931). For Brecht's concept of 'imploitation', see Roswitha Mueller, 'Learning for a New Society: The *Lehrstück*', in *The Cambridge Companion to Brecht* (Cambridge: Cambridge University Press, 1994), 79–95.
82. Herbert Ihering, 'Publikum und Bühnenwirkung', cited in Uecker, *Industrieprovinz*, 315.
83. André Maurois, 'Sittlicher Wert des Sports', *Der Querschnitt*, June 1932, 390.
84. Theodore F. Rippey, '*Kuhle Wampe* and the Problem of Corporal Culture', *Cinema Journal*, 47 (2007), 3–25.
85. Karl Christian Führer, 'High Brow and Low Brow Culture', in Anthony McElligott (ed.), *Weimar Germany* (Oxford: Oxford University Press, 2009), 260–81, here 274; Katherine Roper, 'Fridericus Films in Weimar Society: Potsdamismus in a Democracy', *German Studies Review*, 26 (2003), 493–514.
86. Currid, *A National Acoustics*, 94.
87. For the following, see Klaus Kreimeier, *The Ufa Story: A History of Germany's Greatest Film Company, 1918–1945* (Berkeley, CA: University of California Press, 1999).
88. Wilhelm Kähler, 'Deutschnationale Kulturpolitik', in Max Weiss (ed.), *Der Nationale Wille. Werden und Wirken der Deutschnationalen Volkspartei* (Leipzig: Vaterländischer Buchvertrieb, 1928), 188.
89. Moritz Föllmer, *'Ein Leben wie im Traum': Kultur im Dritten Reich* (Munich: C. H. Beck, 2016), 13–58.
90. Antje Ascheid, *Hitler's Heroines: Stardom and Womanhood in Nazi Germany* (Philadelphia: Temple University Press, 2003).
91. Hughes, *Max Schmeling*, 123–78.
92. Theodor Wiesengrund Adorno, *Minima Moralia: Reflections from a Damaged Life*, tr. E. F. N. Jephcott (London 1974), 57.

Bibliography

Abrams, Lynn, *Workers' Culture in Imperial Germany. Leisure and Recreation in the Rhineland and Westphalia* (London: Routledge, 1992).

Becker, Tobias, *Inszenierte Moderne: Populäres Theater in Berlin und London, 1880–1930* (Berlin: de Gruyter, 2014).

Currid, Brian, *A National Acoustics: Music and Mass Publicity in Weimar and Nazi Germany* (Minneapolis: University of Minnesota Press, 2006).

Fulda, Bernhard, *Press and Politics in the Weimar Republic* (Oxford: Oxford University Press, 2008).

Hughes, Jon, *Max Schmeling and the Making of a National Hero in Twentieth-Century Germany* (London: Palgrave Macmillan, 2018).

Jelavich, Peter, *Berlin Alexanderplatz: Radio, Film, and the Death of Weimar Culture* (Berkeley, CA: University of California Press, 2006).

Jensen, Erik N., *Body by Weimar: Athletes, Gender, and German Modernity* (Oxford: Oxford University Press, 2013).

King, Lynda J., *Best-Sellers by Design: Vicki Baum and the House of Ullstein* (Detroit: Wayne State University Press, 1988).

Kreimeier, Klaus, *The Ufa Story: A History of Germany's Greatest Film Company, 1918–1945* (Berkeley, CA: University of California Press, 1999).

Lacey, Kate, *Feminine Frequencies: Gender, German Radio, and the Public Sphere, 1923–1945* (Ann Arbor: University of Michigan Press, 1996).

Lange, Jasmin, *Der deutsche Buchhandel und der Siegeszug der Kinematographie 1895–1933: Reaktionen und strategische Konsequenzen* (Wiesbaden: Harrassowitz, 2010).

Lenk, Carsten, *Die Erscheinung des Rundfunks: Einführung und Nutzung eines neuen Mediums 1923–1932* (Opladen: Westdeutscher Verlag, 1997).

Maase, Kaspar, *Grenzenloses Vergnügen. Der Aufstieg der Massenkultur 1850–1970* (Frankfurt: Fischer, 1997).

Niedbalski, Johanna, *Die ganze Welt des Vergnügens: Berliner Vergnügungsparks der 1880er bis 1930er Jahre* (Berlin: be.bra, 2018).

Peukert, Detlev J. K., *Jugend zwischen Krieg und Krise. Lebenswelten von Arbeiterjungen in der Weimarer Republik* (Cologne: Bund, 1987).

Reuveni, Gideon, *Reading Germany. Literature and Consumer Culture in Germany before 1933* (New York: Berghahn, 2006).

Ross, Corey, *Media and the Making of Modern Germany. Mass Communications, Society, and Politics from the Empire to the Third Reich* (Oxford: Oxford University Press, 2008).

Uecker, Matthias, *Zwischen Industrieprovinz und Großstadthoffnung: Kulturpolitik im Ruhrgebiet der zwanziger Jahre* (Wiesbaden: Springer, 1994).

Wipplinger, Jonathan, *The Jazz Republic: Music, Race, and American Culture in Weimar Germany* (Ann Arbor: University of Michigan Press, 2017).

CHAPTER 28

GERMAN LITERATURE, 1918–1933

HELMUTH KIESEL

THE Weimar Republic was the heyday of German literature. Around 1930, outstanding achievements were made in all literary fields, which shaped the image of classical or reflective modernity and proved exemplary for the subsequent development of modernity after the disruption during the 'Third Reich'. Some lyrical examples are Gottfried Benn's montage-technique and the introduction of foreign words into poetry, for instance in his poem *Chaos* (1923); in drama Bertolt Brecht's *Saint Joan of the Stockyards* (*Die Heilige Johanna der Schlachthöfe*, 1930-2), a play in 'epic' and 'grand' style; and in epics Alfred Döblin's *Berlin Alexanderplatz* (1929), a montage novel of the modern metropolis. In addition, there were late works of already established authors such as Rainer Maria Rilke's *Duino Elegies* (1923) and Stefan George's last book of poems *The New Realm* (*Das neue Reich*, 1928), as well as great works by successful writers in more conventional but nonetheless modernistic style such as Thomas Mann's novel *The Magic Mountain* (*Der Zauberberg*, 1924) or Hugo von Hofmannsthal's play *The Tower* (*Der Turm*, 1925–7). There was also a vast plethora of poems, plays, novels, novellas, and reportages and essays in a literary style on all fields and topics of life—the world of work, youth, women, sport, sexuality—and particularly on political and social developments. This *Zeitliteratur* (literature of that time) was not only diagnostic but also wanted to intervene and be active in its involvement: examples include 'political theatre' (Erwin Piscator, 1921), the 'journalistic novel' (Joseph Roth, 1925) and 'utility poetry' (Kurt Tucholsky, 1928).[1]

Many of these works were very much a reflection of the time and thus are historically significant rather than of literary importance. However, they were part of the epoch and, therefore, contribute to a better understanding of it. Some products of this literature and also some works of literary ambition, such as Hans Grimm's novel *People without Space* (*Volk ohne Raum*, 1926) and Erwin Guido Kolbenheyer's trilogy of novel *Paracelsus* (1917–26), are frowned upon today and largely excluded from literary reception because they were, to some extent, committed to nationalist or *völkisch* thoughts that became paramount under National Socialism or even directly supported the emerging National Socialism. However, it is not justified to discredit all of these works for this reason. The criminal Nazi regime acts like a magnifying glass that disproportionally emphasizes particular aspects of a literary work.

Having said that, we should also not attempt to downplay this aspect. The literature of the Weimar Republic was, on occasion, in many ways very closely connected with precarious ideological currents of the decades around the First World War and contributed to their development and political implementation. However, it is unfair and misleading to judge this literature according to our present historical knowledge and insights. Rather, historical knowledge and historical justice require a dual and complementary perspective that understands the literary works of this period from the point of their origin, which was open to the future, as well as in the context of a catastrophic later history. Their fatal repercussions must be not omitted, nor a wrong teleology be suggested; the authors of the 1920s cannot be expected to know about later historical developments.

The literature of the Weimar Republic has been intensively researched so that an overview can be given in the following sections. However, it should be noted that this overview is necessarily selective. Some figures may illustrate this a little better: around 1926, 37,000 people in Germany worked in journalism and the publishing industry. Of these 7,000 declared themselves to be literary writers, and around 1,000 were women. The largest recent literary reference work, the *Literatur-Lexikon* (2011), edited by Walther Killy, which only lists authors that are significant in literary historical terms, has articles on 1,450 (or 20 per cent of) Weimar writers, 215 of them women. The larger part, about 80 per cent, is more or less forgotten. These roughly 7,000 authors produced approximately 4,000 fictional works annually, that is 56,000 publications during the Weimar Republic. Even contemporary media could only list a proportion of these publications.[2] This discrepancy between the overall production and the number of noticed works and authors results in an inevitable lack of clarity that must be borne in mind when examining 1920s literature. This is aggravated by the fact that research after 1945 has prioritized politically progressive and artistically modernistic literature rather than treating all literary fields equally. However, contemporary reception and statistics on book trade are a corrective that can flag authors and works that have been ignored by research.

ZEITLITERATUR: LITERATURE AS A MEDIUM OF REFLECTION AND MOBILIZATION

It has, for good reason, become common to regard the Weimar Republic as a specific historical epoch. The revolutionary foundation of the first German republic clearly separated it from the prior period and the demolition of the republican constitution by the Nazis marked its end politically. However, this is not true in cultural—particularly in literary cultural—terms. Dominant authors of the Weimar Republic experienced their socialization as writers well before 1918. Two examples demonstrate this: Thomas Mann inherited realism from Theodor Fontane, but added motifs of decadence and modernized it in his *Magic Mountain* (Der Zauberberg, 1924) by implementing a narrator who, in a metafictional fashion, reflected the construction principle and narrative style according to the then virulent debate on the 'crisis of the novel' or the 'narrative crisis'. Alfred Döblin, who studied medicine between 1900 and 1905, was highly influenced by recent psychiatric insights as well as by the emerging trends of expressionism and futurism. However, he was also harking back to naturalism and combined these diverse approaches to create a kaleidoscopic poetics of modernity during the second half of the 1920s. This found expression in his montage and hybrid novel *Berlin Alexanderplatz* (1929), which found massive attention among his contemporaries and is still deemed decisively characteristic for the Weimar era. It is, at the same time, a prime example of the reflective modernity that emerged during the 1920s: the combination of traditionalist and avant-garde narrative techniques, employed in a poetically reflective and graduated fashion.

The historian Eberhard Kolb has rightly noted that the culture of the Weimar Republic—deeply and in manifold ways divided—was a culture *during the period* rather than *of* the republic.[3] This is also true of its literature. There was, on the one hand, an avant-garde or modernistic type of literature linked to the sphere of the metropolis and thus sometimes disparaged as 'asphalt literature'. On the other, there was a traditionalist or anti-modern literature that worshipped the slower, cosier, and more comfortable lifestyle of the provinces and often indulged in the German past. Occasionally, mixtures occurred, for instance in the last volume of the trilogy of novels *Bauernadel* (1929–30) by Hermann Eris Busse, which describes the mechanization of the rural realm and the transformation of the peasant into an engineer. Mediations like this did not change the power and significance of the confrontation between modernity and anti-modernity.[4] Indeed, it was reflected not only in literary works but also in a kaleidoscope of programmatic and critical debates. In short, the literature of the Weimar Republic did not unanimously follow the path towards the international style of modernity; a large number of writers clung to anti-modernistic literary views. Cultural and literary history accounts of the last decades have often underestimated this divide, ignoring conservative parts of the literature, in particular because of their affiliation to nationalism or National Socialism, but also due to a present favouring modernity. This must be kept in mind in order to avoid the fallacy that assumes culture and literature in the Weimar Republic was predominantly, and in an enthusiastic and programmatic fashion, modernistic. This is only partly true. However, it must also be mentioned that Weimar's modernistic literature was more progressive than the traditionalist kind, addressing the problems of the time in a more differentiated fashion and having much more influence and importance for the further development of literature.

The First World War, the collapse of Imperial Germany, and the revolutionary foundation of the first German republic as the new form of the 'German Reich' (Germany's political name continued to be the same) created a set of new conditions for literary production, which will be briefly outlined. With the revolution of November 1918, censorship effectively came to an end, and Article 118 of the new constitution from 11 August 1919 formally abolished it. ('No censorship will take place.') However, this article also allowed for 'legal measures ... for the suppression of indecent and obscene literature', that is, investigations by public prosecutors and police confiscations. These were expanded and stipulated in law in 1926, triggering fierce protests from artists and writers. In addition, the Law for the Protection of the Republic, issued in July 1922 after the assassination of Foreign Minister, Walther Rathenau, and renewed and tightened in 1929, penalized the distribution of publications against the 'constitutional republican form of government'. Both laws were applied, resulting in the confiscation of publications and even the charge and detention of authors.[5] For example, the communist writer Johannes R. Becher was arrested in August 1925 for writing a smear poem on the newly elected President Paul von Hindenburg, albeit released in amnesty after a few days. The nationalist publicist Friedrich Georg Jünger was charged in 1928 with high treason for his mobilization pamphlet *The Rise of National Socialism* (*Aufmarsch des Nationalsozialismus*, 1926), but the prosecution's investigation came to nothing. Legal obstructions, particularly for left-wing authors, should not be underestimated, but they did not result in severe punishment and thus did not substantially restrict freedom of speech nor impede publication chances. The publishing market was, in contrast to the 'Third Reich', too large and the existing controlling authorities too small.

The abolition of censorship fostered the politicization of literature. This process had started as early as 1910. During the war, literature's move towards politics intensified, and received additional impetus with the November revolution when politics became an imperative—and even an obligation—for authors. They realized that they could no longer indulge in 'inwardness protected by power' (Thomas Mann[6]), but had to commit themselves to politics. Prime examples of this process of politicization are the works of Thomas Mann and Alfred Döblin. Both wrote their first political articles during the war years and continued to do so after 1918. The share of political and literary essays in both authors' works reached a similar proportion and significance during the Weimar Republic. During this time, the question of the right political direction started to permeate the works of both authors: Mann's *Magic Mountain* (*Der Zauberberg*, 1924)[7] and Döblin's *Berlin Alexanderplatz* (1929).[8] The director Erwin Piscator, to name another example, launched a decisively 'proletarian' theatre in Berlin in 1920 that performed his plays in the usual meeting halls of the working class. Piscator described this approach and the following developments in his 1929 book, *The Political Theatre* (*Das politische Theater*).

Ideologically, the Weimar years were dominated by polarization.[9] From the outset, terms such as 'adversary', 'enemy', and 'front' played a major role in both political journalism and programmatic literary works. In 1922, Arthur Moeller van den Bruck published the first anthology of a 'new conservatism' under the title *The New Front*. Wieland Herzfelde's publishing house Malik-Verlag printed the journal *The Adversary* (*Der Gegner*) between 1919 and 1924. In 1924, the Red Front Fighters' League (Roter Frontkämpferbund) was founded, which soon afterwards began publishing the magazine *The Red Front* (*Die Rote Front*). Johannes R. Becher described the situation in his 1926 novel *Levisite* as follows:

> Front against front
>   It tore through—
>   And it tore through, until even the connection by language was severed, even the same opportunities of experience.
>   Front against front, that is language against language, expression of emotion against expression of emotion, that is way of thinking against way of thinking, that is form of perception against form of perception, that is worldview against worldview.[10]

Thinking in frontlines also impacted the organization of authors. In 1925, renowned Berlin writers founded Group 1925, a cross-party 'companionate association', to assert the voice of 'intellect' in topical questions. The meetings were discontinued in 1927, not only because interest waned but also owing to irreconcilable political views. It was the time of party-political rather than cross-party thinking. In 1928, Becher founded the Association of Proletarian-Revolutionary Authors (Bund Proletarisch-Revolutionärer Schriftsteller, BPRS), and introduced its journal *Linkskurve* (*Left Turn*) with a programmatic piece, titled 'Our Front' ('Unsere Front'). In the same year, leading National Socialists founded the Combat League for German Culture (Kampfbund für deutsche Kultur, KfdK), which, unlike the BPRS, was not exclusively concerned with literature, but also intended to foster National Socialist literature. The BPRS was able to attract around 500 authors as members, developed a motivational programme for the support of proletarian-revolutionary literature, and published some decent 'Red-One-Mark-Novels' on topics from the world of industrial production and political activities for the preparation of the revolution. Willi Bredel's novels *Machine Factory N&K* (*Maschinenfabrik N&K*, 1930) and *Rosenhof Street* (*Rosenhofstraße*) were successful titles.[11] The KfdK failed to achieve similar success. Both political camps were critical of liberal or 'left bourgeois' authors such as Thomas Mann and Alfred Döblin, denouncing them as political failures or traitors.

The politicization of literature and the formation of political fronts among authors changed the views of many, albeit not of all, writers on literature. In March 1929, Alfred Döblin gave a speech in the national Berlin Academy of Poets under the slogan: 'Art is Not Free But Effective: Ars Militans'. Two years prior, in 1927, the communist physician and writer Friedrich Wolf published an extensive article on literary history, with the title 'Art is a Weapon!', that was 'on the rise of the great social movement', particularly in the current 'fight between different political worldviews'. Walter Benjamin transferred this view on literature to literary criticism, stating in his 1928 *One Way Street* (*Einbahnstraße*) under the header 'The Critic's Technique in Thirteen Theses': 'I. The critic is the strategist in the literary battle.—II. He who cannot take sides should keep silent.— ... V. "Objectivity" must always be sacrificed to partisanship, if the cause fought for merits this.— ... XI. Artistic enthusiasm is alien to the critic. In his hand the art-work is the shining sword in the battle of minds.'[12] Benjamin's 1931 essay *Left-Wing Melancholia* (*Linke Melancholie*) is a definitive realization of this principle.[13]

The politicization of writers led to the abundance of *Zeitliteratur*, literature of the time, which was written in close temporal proximity to political events and social processes, aiming to influence or reflect them from a certain perspective. The revolution was accompanied by numerous poems, manifestos, and essays, even larger literary works such as Ernst Toller's play *Masse-Mensch* (1921) and Bertolt Brecht's *Drums in the Night* (1922) or Bernhard Kellermann's novel *The 9 November* (1920). One of the first novels that described the events of war, collapse, revolution, and foundation of the republic, putting them into context, was Gustav Frenssen's *The Pastor of Poggsee* (*Der Pastor von Poggsee*, 1921). This novel is particularly remarkable insofar as it was—though written by a conservative author who later leaned towards National Socialism—decisively in favour of democracy, constitution, and the mental transformation of the time, almost in anticipation of the concept of 'constitutional patriotism' that was discussed by the political scientist and publicist Dolf Sternberger in 1970.[14] The following events and incidents of the critical early phase of the Weimar Republic—the Kapp-Lüttwitz putsch, battle of the Ruhr, borderland fighting, inflation, occupation of the Ruhr, Rhenish separatism, political murders, March Battles in Central Germany, 'Red October' in Hamburg, and the Hitler putsch—found their way into literary productions. German feuilletons repeatedly called for *Zeitromane* and *Zeitstücke*, novels and plays concerned with the analysis of the present and committed to topical problems, asked for 'novels of now' and 'plays of the present moment'. The notion *Zeitstück* is closely linked to the Weimar Republic.

The amount of this *Zeitliteratur* is immense. Joseph Roth alone wrote half a dozen novels on contemporary issues and a great number of articles between 1923 and 1929. *Zeitstücke* were published in large numbers, some of them by renowned authors such as Georg Kaiser, Ernst Toller, Carl Zuckmayer, and Hanns Johst. Others included revues on current topics such as *Red Revue* (*Roter Rummel*, 1924) by Erwin Piscator and satirical cabaret shows like *European Nights* (*Europäische Nächte*, 1924) by Walter Mehring, both shows with a topical focus that offered a critical perspective on society. A vast number of poems were critically concerned with political events and social conditions. Kurt Tucholsky published almost 600 poems between 1919 and 1932, sometimes two or three per week. Erich Weinert wrote more than 1,000 poems between 1919 and 1933, most of them in a critical, often satirical, and inflammatory tone. He recited many of them at political meetings or protest events. And these two authors are only the most prominent political poets of the Weimar Republic.

Some examples of the *Zeitliteratur* were markedly inflammatory. That is, they did not aim at critical reflection but incited downright partisanship, visible protest, and active intervention. It is hard to assess how successful this type of literature was in achieving these goals. The mobilizing effect of at least two plays is well documented: Peter Martin Lampel's *Revolt in the Reformatory* (*Revolte im Erziehungshaus*), which premiered in December 1928 in the Berlin Thalia Theatre and was performed every night for months on end, stimulated an intensive debate on houses of correction that led to a number of reforms. Friedrich Wolf's *Cyanide. §218* (*Cyankali. §218*), premiered in the Berlin Lessing Theatre in early September 1929, was performed on stages throughout the whole of Germany. It caused fierce debates, protest actions, and a motion from the KPD parliamentary group to scrap the anti-abortion paragraph 218 of the penal code. The extremist parties that wanted another—if need be violent—revolution and, to this end, accepted civil war, placed great faith in the mobilizing effect of literature. Both communist and National Socialist leadership supported and fostered the production of marching and battle songs, novels that advertised membership of the respective parties and their organizations, described propaganda campaigns and agitation work, and gave blatant instructions in the event of civil war. The most prominent examples for the communist camp were Willi Bredel's *Rosenhof Street* (*Rosenhofstraße*, 1931) and Walter Schönstedt's *Fighting Youth* (*Kämpfende Jugend*, 1931), and for the National Socialist camp Karl Aloys Schenzinger's *Hitler Youth Quex* (*Hitlerjunge Quex*, 1932).

Alongside this largely conventionally written literature, which focused on topical problems and aimed for immediate practical effect, there were also literary works concerned with topical issues that reflected the epochal situation in a more powerful and innovative fashion. They followed two motives: first, the wish for a new better, more just, and long-term peaceful society. Typical of this kind of literature is Brecht's statement from his 1928 essay *Über eine neue Dramatik* (*On a New Dramatic Art*): 'The cry for a new theatre is the cry for a new social order.' It was not only Brecht's plays *The Decision* (*Die Maßnahme*, 1930) and *Saint Joan of the Stockyards* (*Die Heilige Johanna der Schlachthöfe*, 1932) but even Georg Kaiser's earlier expressionist plays *Gas* (1918) and *Gas II* (1920) that showed an artistically innovative realization of this cry. The second motive is the desire to 'overcome historicism' and 'nihilism', that is, the attempt to replace the unsettling relativism of values that was the result of recognizing their historical development through a new way of defining supratemporal values.[15] This intellectual issue, its genesis, and its possible resolutions are topics addressed not only in major epoch-making novels such as Thomas Mann's *The Magic Mountain* (*Der Zauberberg*, 1924), Robert Musil's *The Man without Qualities* (*Der Mann ohne Eigenschaften*, 1930-3), and particularly Hermann Broch's *The Sleepwalkers* trilogy (*Die Schlafwandler*, 1930-2). Indeed, they are also subjects of historical novels, such as Erwin Guido Kolbenheyer's *Paracelsus* trilogy (1917-26) that transferred the topic of a revolutionary transition into the time of the Renaissance and the Reformation, as well as the mushrooming 'worldview literature'.[16] Here, writers verbosely laid bare their understanding of God and the world, humans and history, in a seemingly scientific, but often highly speculative fashion.

Phases and Styles

The political and social orientation of literature shaped its development from the beginning to the end of the Weimar Republic. At the same time, a specific emphasis on certain topics and in formal terms emerged in correlation with political and social developments, which are commonly divided into three phases: first, the crisis-prone period of foundation and consolidation of the republic (1918–23); second, the period of relative political and economic stabilization (1923/4–9); third, economic crisis and political decline (1929–33). Political and social changes that became clearly visible around 1923/4 and again around 1929/30 had significant influences on artistic work so that, despite all continuities, three phases can also be distinguished here.

The Expressionist and Dadaist Phase (1918–1923)

The period of foundation and consolidation of the republic, accompanied by deep and often violent conflicts, corresponds with—in terms of literary style and programmaticism—the heyday of expressionism and the virulence of political Dadaism. Initially, it brought about an apotheosis of expressionist lyric. The November revolution seemed to provide the chance to realize the hopes of salvation and renewal that expressionist authors had pursued. It took some time for the joy of the successful revolution to give way to disillusion about the republic that had failed to fulfil utopian hopes. In 1919, there was still talk of the 'elevation of the heart' and a 'revolution of morality'. Until 1923, several journals spread the spirit of expressionism. A torrent of poems, manifestos, and essays declared the coming of a new human being and the emergence of a new world in ecstatic language. The production of expressionist plays reached its peak only after 1918 and dominated the theatre world until 1922/3. Typical of this trend were the idealistic plays by Georg Kaiser, some of them written during the war—*The Coral* (*Die Koralle*, 1918), *Gas* (1918), *Hell Way Earth* (*Hölle Weg Erde*, 1919), *Gas II* (1920). They represent the continuous demand to leave the system of competitive industrial capitalism with its ruthless exploitation of people, its excess production of poor-quality goods, and the provisioning of weapons of destruction. This is realized in plays characterized by abstracting symbolization that depict types instead of individuals, and exemplary situations in the language of formulaic precision and do not shy away from slogans. Ernst Toller's oratorio-like revolutionary play *Mass Human Being* (*Masse Mensch*) that premiered, strictly choreographed, in Berlin in September 1921 and was directed by Jürgen Fehling on a sparsely furnished stage ('Andeutungsbühne', 'a stage of allusions', as the literary critic Alfred Kerr called it), was the paragon of expressionist stylized theatre.

Different to this tradition of idealistic 'proclamation drama' were the revolutionary plays by Reinhard Sorge, Walter Hasenclever, Hanns Johst, Hans Henny Jahnn, and Arnold Bronnen, which criticized repression in families and society in an anarchic fashion. They were examples of black expressionism with gross images of violence and grim endings. Bertolt Brecht's *Baal* (1918–22) can also be seen in this context but, as Hugo von Hofmannsthal stated, it went far beyond stylized expressionism due to its free composition. Another step away from expressionism was Georg Kaiser's play *Side by Side* (*Nebeneinander*, 1923), which presents three attitudes in three intertwined plots that competed against each other in 1923: ecstatic humanism of the expressionist phase that proved helpless and self-destructive; simultaneously emerging objectivity, presented as an attitude of responsible humanity; and a business-minded unscrupulousness that emerged during the inflation years and did not bode well for the future.

In autumn 1919, Kurt Pinthus wrote the preface to the later famous collection of poems *Dawn of Humanity* (*Menschheitsdämmerung*). He by no means considered this anthology of expressionist lyrics as a documentation of a past or a fading literary movement, but rather as a renewing 'symphony' of voices that were still worth being heard and for which Pinthus, in typical expressionist fashion, wanted to attract attention and successors: 'As one of those who stood right among them, I come forward and shout: ... Do not let it be enough! Instead, help, all of you, anticipating the will of humanity, create a more basic, clearer, purer being.' Apart from new productions that were shaped by expressionism and vitalizing evocations of the expressionist spirit, there were also farewells and rejections, declarations of death and eulogies. Kasimir Edschmid, who helped to form and poetologically promoted expressionism, stated in his opening speech of the 'first German expressionism exhibition' in Darmstadt in June 1920: 'What ten years ago began to intensely confuse the bourgeois, has not even the touching effect of sensation in the less god- blessed present of the year nineteenhundredandtwenty.... What back then was seen as an audacious gesture, is common today. The advance of the day before yesterday has become the affectation of yesterday and the yawn of today.'[17]

In spring 1921, Paul Hatvani conceded that expressionism, by discovering the metropolis and developing the 'simultaneous' style that corresponds with it, had achieved something that would last. However, he also stated that there was a general 'departure' from expressionism. In early 1922, Pinthus similarly noted in the preface to a new edition of *Dawn of Human Kind*—with the telling title *Nachklang* (*Echo*; literally 'aftersound')—that this anthology was 'not only a cohesive but also a concluded and conclusive testament of this era' because 'after the completion of this lyrical symphony nothing has been written that imperatively needs to be added'. The belief of the expressionist decade 'that paradise will immediately blossom from rubble through the will of all', Pinthus continued, had been 'blown away by the torments of the post-war time'.[18]

Berlin Dadaism artistically emphasized these 'torments' of the political and social reality and played them off against expressionism. In their scornful manifestos and aggressive collages the anarchist and socialist Dadaists ridiculed the attempt to establish a 'bourgeois' republic in Germany and give it the appearance of the realization of Weimar classicism's humanity ideals—a goal that they deemed to be reactionary. Indeed, many of their manifestos also mocked expressionist idealism as the latest form of a quixotic and self-betraying 'intellectuality'. With its often abstruse manifestos and burlesque posters and book illustrations, Berlin Dadaism was a strong and permanent attack on the expressionist spirit and, at the same time, a strong disillusionment that paved the way for New Objectivity. However, expressionism had not been entirely written off. Its utopianism remained virulent. Many authors drew on its narrative and expressive forms, its typecasting and densification of narrative. In Alfred Döblin's novel *Berlin Alexanderplatz* (1929) we can see on many occasions a mixture of expressionist, Dadaist, and naturalistic forms of expression.

The Phase of New Objectivity (1923–1929)

The endorsement of objectivity in both practical, everyday life and artistic questions of the world, that is, addressing its natural and social conditions, was not limited to the years between 1923 and 1929. Even in 1918, there was a call for more objectivity and a new orientation to nature. By 1923, however, this perspective became dominant and acquired a programmatic form.[19] In spring 1923, the director of the Mannheim Kunsthalle, Gustav Friedrich Hartlaub, invited fifty-two artists to take part in an exhibition under the title 'The New Objectivity' that was intended to showcase 'a compilation of post-expressionist art'. Over the following year, the commitment to a 'new' objectivity, or to a 'new' naturalism, grew. The aesthetics of New Objectivity were developed and promoted. Its main conceptual terms were: realism, concreteness, everydayness, applied art, objectivity over subjectivity, rationality over emotionalism and romanticism, clarity over glorification. Several works devoted to objectivity were published, even though only very few products were characterized by 'pure' or 'consequent' objectivity or neutrality. Very often, objectivity was artistically and stylistically refracted according to a certain conceptual or ideological orientation. In general, between the principle of objectivity that many authors wanted to satisfy and the claim of 'literary-ness' or 'poetic-ness' that they did not want to surrender, there was an unresolvable discrepancy; the more a text is recognizable as a poetic text, the more its objectivity is affected. Nonetheless, around the mid-1920s there was a great willingness to address the modern, mechanized, and mobilized world from an objective, not uncritical but largely constructive perspective. The rise of New Objectivity shows the willingness of progressive artists and authors to align artistic and cultural developments with social ones and those of civilization, that is, with the emergence of a modern, pluralistic, and culturally levelling mass society and the advancing mechanization of the lifeworld.

A prime example of literature that leans towards New Objectivity rather than expressionism is Ernst Toller's play *Hoppla, we are Alive* (*Hoppla, wir leben*, 1927): eight years after the revolution, a communist worker, Karl Thomas, is released from prison and taken in by Eva Berg, a comrade. During his time in prison, Karl has kept his revolutionary enthusiasm, while Eva now champions an evolutionary course and has committed to socially reformist party and trade union activities. When Eva asks Karl to leave after a night spent together because she wants to live on her own again, the gulf between the two positions widens:

> EVA BERG: As I speak to you I notice that the last eight years when you've been 'buried' have changed us more than a century would have changed us in normal times.
> KARL THOMAS: Yes, I think sometimes that I belong to a generation that has disappeared.
> EVA BERG: What the world has gone through since that episode.
> KARL THOMAS: You talk like that about the Revolution!
> EVA BERG: That Revolution was only an episode. It is past.

KARL THOMAS: What is left?
EVA BERG: We are. With our will to Honesty. With our strength to work anew.
KARL THOMAS: And suppose during one of these nights you started a child?
EVA BERG: I wouldn't give it birth.
KARL THOMAS: Because you don't love me?
EVA BERG: How you miss the point. Because it would be an accident. Because I shouldn't deem it necessary.[20]

Eva Berg's position towards society can be described as realistic, critical, and reform-oriented. Some novellas and novels from the second half of the 1920s present a similar position, for instance the novellas written by the young Joseph Breitbach from 1925 onwards and published in 1929 under the title *Red Against Red* (*Rot gegen Rot*), as well as Irmgard Keun's novel *Gilgi—One of Us* (*Gilgi—eine von uns*, 1931), which describes the difficult path of a young women living an emancipated life. Some books of photographs that became popular at the time were also characterized by an orientation towards objectivity, such as Heinrich Hauser's *Black District* (*Schwarzes Revier*, 1930) and Georg Schwarz's *Ruhr Coal Pit* (*Kohlenpott*, 1931), two major reportages illustrated with photographs about the Ruhr area. The reportage is the main genre of New Objectivity, however, its most famous representative, the 'raging reporter' Egon Erwin Kisch, shows that objectivity was often closely linked with critique and a political bias. The same is true of Erik Reger's major industrial novel *Union of the Firm Hand* (*Union der festen Hand*, 1931) and his social novel on local politics *The Vigilant Cockerel* (*Das wachsame Hähnchen*, 1932). While satirically exaggerating and criticizing, Reger provides a broad and informative portrayal of social conditions and events in both books. In a similar vein, Rudolf Brunngraber in his *Karl and the Twentieth Century* (*Karl und das zwanzigste Jahrhundert*, 1932) surrounded his protagonist Karl with detailed historical and statistical material, which gives the novel the character of an economics and technical historical non-fiction book. The sad fate Karl suffers up until 1931 makes the novel a biting indictment of a time that was characterized 'by an unprecedented objectivity'—or, in other words, ruthlessness—of economic life. In short, the trend towards objectivity and realism, which, as David Midgley and Sabina Becker have correctly argued, were main traits of 1920s literature, was closely linked to a tendency towards social and economic critique with an anti-capitalist thrust.[21]

The easing of tension from 1923–4 onwards, after the expressionist and revolutionary (or putschist) foundation years, is reflected particularly clearly in the success of Carl Zuckmayer's comedy *The Merry Vineyard* (*Der fröhliche Weinberg*, December 1924) and Erich Kästner's newspaper and utility lyrics. Zuckmayer's comedy is set in 'wine autumn 1921' and is centred around the sale of a vineyard, closely linked to matters of marriage and inheritance. Time and again, social tensions surface, but thanks to the confident humanity and liberality of patron Gunderloch, the play ends with a big reconciliation feast and three engagements. *The Merry Vineyard* corresponded with the conciliatory and optimistic mood of the prosperous mid-1920s and filled theatres for a long period of time. Around 1929, however, nationalist student groups who felt ridiculed by the character

Knuzius, a vain and pathetic junior lawyer, frequently disrupted performances. Erich Kästner's poems, which were published from 1926 in daily newspapers and in 1928 in an anthology, address the more or less existential needs and hardships of the people. However, they largely do so in a resigned fashion that is combined with hope, a capacity for suffering and optimism, rather than in a gesture of indictment and rebellion. This resonated with the audience. Their success suggests that many people must have felt addressed and understood by these 'mentally utilizable' lyrics. Walter Benjamin, however, denounced Kästner's poems in his essay *Left-Wing Melancholia* (*Linke Melancholie*, 1931) as a bad sedative of the people who should rather have been called to revolt against the capitalist system. Benjamin instead recommended Brecht's class-struggle-tinted poems from the *Reading Book for City Dwellers* (*Lesebuch für Städtebewohner*, 1930).[22] This is typical of the accelerating formation of frontlines during the time of the Great Depression, for the increasing impoverishment of urban masses, and newly surfacing hopes of a socialist revolution.

The Phases of Fragmentation/Radicalization and of 'Restoration' (1929–1933)

Around 1929–30, New Objectivity lost its position as the leading cultural concept for the intellectual and artistic elite. The reasons for this become obvious from the criticism that objectivity faced from 1929 onwards. These objections were partly political, partly aesthetic: politically active authors from both the right and the left accused the literature of New Objectivity of just accepting political and social grievances, of indulging in resignation and avoiding taking the stand which they deemed necessary for the sake of political and social progress. Other authors who argued in literary rather than political terms reproached New Objectivity for having 'demeaned the poet to a reporter' (Martin Raschke), abandoned the beautiful forms of previous literature, and betrayed traditional ideas of poetry as a visionary, creative, and meaningful activity based on intuition. While Joseph Roth's commitment to mere observation (instead of writing poetry) in the brief preface to his novel *Flight without End* (*Flucht ohne Ende*, 1927) was understood as a manifesto of New Objectivity, Roth published an apologia of decidedly poetic literature (*Long Live the Poet! Es lebe der Dichter!*) in 1929 and a comprehensive critique of reducing literature to a mere documentary form (*Enough with New Objectivity! Schluß mit der Neuen Sachlichkeit!*) in 1930.

This critique corresponded with two literary movements that started in 1929 and diverted from New Objectivity. First, there was the politically topical, markedly partisan, pugnacious, even fomenting literature of mobilization that was intended to decide the battle between socialist revolution and capitalist reaction or nationalist renewal. Second, there was an apolitical and timeless poetry that, in light of an unmistakable loss of quality, again followed bourgeois literary concepts, drew on ambitious literary forms, and intended to develop timeless concepts of meaning and values instead of tangible socio-political perspectives. Both the radicalized political literature and the 'restoration' of bourgeois concepts only to some extent resulted from the crisis starting in 1929. They had been in the making for a long time, but derived impetus through the processes of political, economic, and social destabilization. Both reflect the desire to get out of the crisis and establish a new order, be it through profound socio-political changes or a new intellectual basis of existence. In addition, it must be stated that the years between 1929 and 1933 were characterized by an exceptional heterogeneity in terms of literary programmatic concepts and styles. Indeed, the literature of the Weimar Republic was extremely polyphonous in general. During the last years, however, there was almost a 'turmoil of styles'. Everything was possible; different styles did not only coexist but were also mixed. As the works of Martin Raschke and Peter Huchel show, it was possible to develop a new interest in nature and, at the same time, seek to develop modern forms of expression.

Important topic fields and Formal-Poetic Innovations

The literature of the Weimar Republic covered a vast range of topics, including all existentially important fields such as love and death, childhood and youth, marriage and betrayal, the bourgeois way of life and the artistic world, work and leisure time, prostitution and homosexuality, sickness and adventure, proletarian existence and vagrancy, village life and urbanity, women's emancipation and criticism of the judiciary, Jews and Germans, the loss of religion and the seek for redemption, historical times and utopian worlds, the Great Depression and everyday problems. However, apart from current political affairs and classic topical fields—personal development, life crises, love affairs, social life, etc.—there are four areas in which Weimar authors were particularly interested.

War, Revolution, and the Post-War Period

It goes without saying that the war was the subject of several literary accounts.[23] The best existing estimate mentions 2,390 titles between 1919 and 1932. Many of them were, however, non-fiction books. The largest fiction group, with more than 670 publications, were war novels and novel-like war memoirs. It is significant that the appearance of these novels was not evenly spread throughout this time period: the number dropped from forty-seven annually in 1919–22 to at best thirty a year in the mid-1920s. Inflation and the book trading crisis certainly contributed to this decrease, but it seems that both audiences and literary producers gradually lost interest in the war as a topic. At any rate, the literary exploration of the war had two phases, marked by a caesura around the mid-1920s. From 1929, the production of war novels skyrocketed to eighty-two, reached its peak with 115 in 1930 and halved afterwards, another result of the loss of purchasing power owing to the Great Depression. In both phases pro-war, bellicist, and apologetic accounts as well as novels that were critical of the war, pacifist, and accusatory existed in parallel and against one another. It is striking that the great novelists (from Thomas Mann and Alfred Döblin to Robert Musil and Hermann Broch) refrained from writing about the war and yielded the floor to younger authors such as Ernst Jünger and Erich Maria Remarque. For them, war experiences were a 'capital', as Jünger explained in 1930, with which they could work.

The main pro-war works of the first phase were, first, Franz Schauwecker's book *In the Jaw of Death* (*Im Todesrachen*, 1919) with the subtitle *The German Soul in the Great War* (*Die deutsche Seele im Weltkriege*), which offered some sort of systematic phenomenology of external and internal war experiences. Second, Ernst Jünger's autobiographical memoir *Storm of Steel* (*In Stahlgewittern*, 1920), based on his war diary from 1914 to 1918, describes the trench war and the battles of material in a precise, matter-of-fact, yet also aesthetically enhanced and heroizing way, and with harrowing intensity. Third, Werner Beumelburg's *Douaumont* (1923), a semi-fictional account of the battle over the fort of the same name near Verdun that was very successful with the audience, became the model for many other volumes in the series Battles of the Great War (*Schlachten des Weltkrieges*). To name five examples of early pacifist literature: the anthologies *Man is Good* (*Der Mensch ist gut*) by Leonhard Frank and *Women Awaken* (*Die Frauen erwachen*) by Claire Studer (later Goll), both published in Switzerland in 1918, focus on the suffering of the people rather than on military events; Andreas Latzko's accusatory anthologies *Men in War* (*Menschen im Krieg*, first published in Zurich in 1917) and *Court of Peace* (*Friedengericht*, 1918); Bruno Vogel's book of literary sketches *Long Live the War* (*Es lebe der Krieg*, 1924–5) with shockingly realistic, partly surreal scenarios of horror, which caused the author to be charged with distributing indecent literature and blasphemy; and last but not least Ernst Friedrich's photobook *War Against War* (*Krieg dem Kriege*, 1924) that showed the gruesome truth of the war in photographs rather than words. Finally, two pacifist plays should be mentioned: Karl Kraus's documentary and accusatory-satirical large drama *The Last Days of Mankind* (*Die letzten Tage der Menschheit*, 1919–22) and Alfred Döblin's *Lusitania* (1920), a surrealist play and lament for the dead that describes the torpedoing of the eponymous British passenger steamer in May 1915.

The second phase of literary reflection of the war was introduced with pacifist books such as Arnold Zweig's *The Case of Sergeant Grischa* (*Der Streit um den Sergeanten Grischa*, 1927), Georg von der Vring's *Private Suhren* (*Soldat Suhren*, 1927) and Ludwig Renn's *War* (*Krieg*, 1928). All three of them were completed years before publication, but struggled to find a publishing house. The big success following the serialization of Zweig's *Grischa* in the *Frankfurter Zeitung* showed a new interest of readers and made publishers rethink. Moreover, in the wake of the upcoming year of remembrance 1928 there was a 'return of the Great War in literature', as Ernst Jirgal noted in a thoughtful study from 1931. It should be added that the revolution and the immediate post-war period with Free Corps activities, putsch attempts, and political murders were also topics of remembrance. The 'return' of war, revolution, and post-war battles caused fierce debates over their interpretation. It also propelled the resurfacing of confrontations between pro-war accounts with clear nationalist, revanchist inclinations and pacifist publications. The first group of books is represented by Franz Schauwecker's *Awakening of the Nation* (*Aufbruch der Nation*, 1930), Werner Beumelburg's *The Bosemüller Group* (*Die Gruppe Bosemüller*, 1930), and Hans Zöberlein's *Faith in Germany* (*Der Glaube an Deutschland*, 1931). The pacifist group includes the mentioned books by Zweig, Vring, and Renn, also Adrienne Thomas's novel on military hospitals *Katrin Becomes a Soldier* (*Die Katrin wird Soldat*, 1930) and Edlef Köppen's documentary montage novel *Higher Command* (*Heeresbericht*, 1930). The main work, however, was Erich Maria Remarque's novel *All Quiet at the Western Front* (*Im Westen nichts Neues*) that was serialized in the *Vossische Zeitung* from 10 November 1928 and published as a book in February 1929. It became an immediate and continuous success that contributed to driving the 'return of the Great War in literature'. Remarque describes the fate of a group of infantrymen, most of whom get killed on the Western front and who represent a 'lost' generation, depleted or thrown off course by the war. The further fate of this generation is the subject of Remarque's novel *The Road Back* (*Der Weg zurück*, 1931), as well as Ernst Glaeser's novels *Born in 1902* (*Jahrgang 1902*, 1928) and *Peace* (*Frieden*, 1930). Theodor Plievier addresses the revolution in his documentary novel *The Kaiser Goes, the Generals Remain* (*Der Kaiser ging, die Generäle blieben*, 1932); Ernst von Salomon writes about post-war battles and Free Corps activities including political murders in his autobiographical novel *The Outlaws* (*Die Geächteten*, 1930).

Academic studies usually stress the political, ethical, and aesthetic differences between pro-war literature and literature that criticizes the war. Yet it has become clear that their forms of expression show great similarities, which has caused paradoxes and unintended consequences. Only a few weeks after the publication of the book *All Quiet at the Western Front*, an article titled 'Pacifist War Propaganda' appeared in the left-leaning *Weltbühne* accusing Remarque and other pacifist authors of painting the war as an attractive adventure rather than deterring it. Conversely, Remarque confirmed that Jünger's war books had a strong 'pacifist' impact. In a similar vein, the SPD member of the Reichstag, Paul Levi, stated that there was 'hardly a fiercer indictment of war' than Jünger's *Storm of Steel*.

Loss of Territory, Borderland Battles, and Germanness Abroad

Immediately after the armistice on 11 November 1918, Germany had to vacate and give back to France the 'Imperial Territory' (Reichsland) Alsace Lorraine, which had been occupied in 1871.[24] In the wake of the Versailles peace treaty, further cessions of territory were imposed on Germany in 1920: Eupen-Malmedy to Belgium, North Schleswig to Denmark, West Prussia, Poznan, and east Upper Silesia to Poland, as well as the Hlučin region to Czechoslovakia. Germany lost about one-eighth of its territory and a tenth of its population. In addition, the loss of the Austrian 'land of the sun', South Tyrol, to Italy was a bitter experience for Germans too. Overall, about 10 million German-speaking people lived in old and newly founded neighbouring nation-states and were exposed to measures of political and cultural foreign rule. By 1925, about 770,000 Germans (according to some sources up to a million) left their—now foreign—homes and relocated to Germany. Just like the war, these developments—cessions, integration, and relocation that often went hand in hand with harassment and sometimes, as in Upper Silesia, with violence—became subjects of literature. A 1929 bibliography mentioned 250 publications on the topic of 'borderland Germans and Germanness abroad in narrative literature', devoted to borderland fights, measures of incorporation, deportation threats, but also peaceful cohabitation in the new state. We can roughly distinguish two tendencies. First, there are the works that told stories about fighting and borders in nostalgic remembrance of the lost way of life, lamenting the current discord, including August Scholtis's novel on Upper Silesia *Wind from the East* (*Ostwind*, 1932) and Otto Flake's novellas on South Tyrol *The Divorce* (*Die Scheidung*, 1926) and *Summer Novel* (*Sommerroman*, 1927). René Schickele's outstanding trilogy *The Inheritance on the Rhine* (*Das Erbe am Rhein*, 1925–31) describes the painful history of Alsace during the war and the post-war period. Other works present struggles over borders and subsequent measures of incorporation as historical injustice that demanded revision. Robbery, injury, suppression, and strangulation were frequently used as imagery; some authors depicted Germany as a mutilated body with bleeding flanks. An example of this is Arnolt Bronnen's novel on Upper Silesia *O.S.* (1929) that describes the bloody battles over the affiliation of the Annaberg in 1921. While the contested territory is finally lost, a prophecy at the end of this violence-obsessed Free Corps novel promises that 'the victims of those battles will not be in vain, even though betrayal deprived us of external success', but will be 'the seed of future victory'. Left-leaning authors considered it scandalous and the sign of a new ideological confusion that *O.S.* was published by the left-wing Rowohlt publishing house.

World of Labour

Building upon former achievements, during the 1920s the literature on the world of industrial labour experienced a strong quantitative increase, an aesthetic improvement, and topical and political differentiation.[25] The SPD and KPD in particular programmatically discussed and fostered this type of literature, through reading and writing groups, publication opportunities, and financial support. In the early 1920s, 'worker poets', that is, trained artisans or skilled workers who started writing during the war, dominated this scene, for instance Alfons Petzold, Karl Bröger, Heinrich Lersch, Paul Zech, and others. With confidence and feeling and aesthetically oriented towards bourgeois literature, they described their leading role in industrial production mostly in poems, but also in narrative and autobiographical fictional texts. While not omitting the exhausting conditions of industrial labour, they focused on an optimistic and constructive perspective. Bourgeois literary criticism perceived them with condescending benevolence.

An outstanding and widely received work was Heinrich Lersch's *Man in Iron* (*Mensch in Eisen*, 1925), with the subtitle *Songs of the People and Songs of Labour* (*Gesänge von Volk und Werk*). On more than 200 large-size pages with passages in free but nonetheless dithyrambic verse, he evoked the manifold experiences of a trained boiler maker like Lersch during the conditions of the war and the economic upheaval and restructuring in the postwar period. The poet becomes the herald, ushering in an era of enhanced production and social justice to be achieved through peaceful work as opposed to revolution. In contrast to this was the 'proletarian revolutionary' literature endorsed by the KPD: it championed the Marxian class-struggle doctrine—exemplary in Gustav von Wangenheim's play *The Mouse Trap* (*Die Mausefalle*, 1930)—commemorated the uprisings of the immediate post-war period—for instance in Karl Grünberg's novel *Burning Ruhr* (*Brennende Ruhr*, 1928–9)—emphasized and illustrated the exploitation of the proletariat—such as in Kurt Kläber's novel *Third Class Passengers* (*Passagiere der III. Klasse*, 1927–8) and in B. Traven's terrific novel *The Death Ship* (*Das Totenschiff*, 1926)—and gave instructions for the fight for better working conditions and dominating works councils—including Willi Bredel's novel *Machine Factory N&K* (*Maschinenfabrik N&K*, 1930).

In the second half of the 1920s, a new genre—the 'white-collar novel' or *Angestelltenroman*—emerged, gaining literary reputation with Martin Kessel's novel on office work, *Mr Brecher's Fiasco* (*Herrn Brechers Fiasko*, 1932), and success with audiences with Hans Fallada's novel *Little Man, What Now?* (*Kleiner Mann—Was nun?*, 1932) on the life of a salesman. These novels describe the seemingly upscale lifestyle of office workers and salespersons, which was, however, always under threat with extreme competition and performance pressure. This was particularly true for female employees, who were exposed to sexual assaults by their bosses in addition to the risk, which applied to both sexes, of losing their job in the event of economic changes. For this reason, 'white-collar novels' were also often about unemployment. In general, unemployment was an often addressed topic, including Bruno Nelissen Haken's novel *The Case of Bundhund* (*Der Fall Bundhund*, 1930) on employment offices, Ödön von Horváth's popular play *Kasimir and Karoline* (*Kasimir und Karoline*, 1932), Bertolt Brecht's play *Saint Joan of the Stockyards* (*Die Heilige Johanna der Schlachthöfe*, 1930–2) and the film *Kuhle Wampe or Who Owns the World?* (*Kuhle Wampe oder Wem gehört die Welt?*, 1932), written by Brecht and Slatan Dudow. In his comprehensive novel *Union of the Firm Hand* (*Union der festen Hand*, 1931), Erik Reger depicts the complete modern world of labour, from the management floor of a major corporation (Krupp), to the noisy machine halls, to the crowded working-class quarters.

Americanism, Urbanity, and Modern Womanhood

In 1926, Walther von Hollander's novel *The Feverish House* (*Das fiebernde Haus*) appeared, written in the context of inflation and social unrest, in which the story of a large Berlin block of flats serves as an example for a hopelessly disunited community representing German society sliding into a social and political abyss. At the same time, thanks to the currency reform and incoming American credits, the social mood, to some degree, lightened. The Golden Twenties brought about 'Americanism', which entered the professional and leisure life of metropolitan white-collar workers.[26] Berlin, an important industrial location with large working-class quarters, became a media metropolis and city of light where modern culture industries and a libertine lifestyle spread. This particularly benefited those young women who enjoyed an emancipated, independent lifestyle without traditional familial ties, be it as administrative civil servants or saleswomen in a major department store, as teachers or journalists, as doctors or solicitors. Several novels appeared around 1930, many written by women, which focused on modern urban life and the new chances for women. The way was paved by Wilhelm Speyer's *Charlotte Somewhat Crazy* (*Charlott etwas verrückt*, 1927) which created a great stir, as well as his novel *I Go Out and You Stay Here* (*Ich geh aus und du bleibst da*, 1931), but most of all Vicki Baum's novels *Helene* (*stud. chem. Helene Willfüer*) and *Grand Hotel* (*Menschen im Hotel*), both from 1929, Christa Anita Brück's *Destinies behind Typewriters* (*Schicksale hinter Schreibmaschinen*, 1930), Irmgard Keun's *Gilgi—One of Us* (*Gilgi—Eine von uns*, 1931), Gabriele Tergit's *Käsebier Conquers the Kurfürstendamm* (*Käsebier erobert den Kurfürstendamm*, 1931), and Marieluise Fleißer's *Frieda Geier: Travelling Flour Seller* (*Mehlreisende Frieda Geier*, 1931). In addition, Mascha Kaléko's first collection of poems *The Lyrical Shorthand Pad* (*Das lyrische Stenogrammheft*, 1933) should also be mentioned in this context.

The list of all female authors and publications is in fact much longer. But even these selected titles show that, at the latest, in the second half of the 1920s women started to play a larger role in literary production. Apart from well-known, older female authors, including Clara Viebig (b. 1860), Gabriele Reuter (b. 1859), Ricarda Huch (b. 1864), Else Lasker-Schüler (b. 1869), and Ina Seidel (b. 1885), younger women born around 1900 and who grew up during the years of social modernization and cultural flexibility started to make their mark as authors, featuring modern, often decidedly female topics, some with new forms of writing: Marieluise Fleißer introduced regional idioms and idiomatic expressions into literary language, which revealed the entrapment of people in linguistic patterns; Irmgard Keun's elaborated tone of naïve lust for life made her second novel *The Artificial Silk Girl* (*Das kunstseidene Mädchen*, 1932) a sensation; Elisabeth Langgässer used surrealist superimposition of reality, myths, and dreams in some of her novellas, particularly in *Proserpina: A Childhood Myth* (*Proserpina: Eine Kindheitsmythe*, 1933).

These female authors described life in all of its variety and with all of its problems. Gabriele Tergit's *Käsebier* novel presents a panorama of the urban bourgeoisie, whose wealth depended on the economic situation and whose lifestyle was influenced by a steady stream of new fashions. The women in this society enjoyed some emancipation, but also experienced dependency on fashions and the market. Fleißer's novel is situated in Ingolstadt, a small provincial town in the south of Germany, where the atmosphere was still narrow-minded and a freer and more modern lifestyle, seemingly possible to achieve through sport and professional activities, was ultimately impeded by economic hardship and a reactionary mindset. Other contemporaries portray life as more gloomy.

Erich Kästner's novel *Fabian* (1931) and Felix Riemkasten's novel *The Idol* (*Der Götze*, 1932-3) depict the media metropolis Berlin as the capital of a morally corrupt and ideologically disunited society that is heading towards the abyss. Strikingly, Josef Maria Frank's novel *Fever Heat* (*Volk im Fieber*, 1932), which addressed the dubious September 1930 Reichstag election, again employed the crisis metaphors of the early Weimar years.

Our earlier focus on the social dimension of Weimar literature should not let us forget the extensive and sustainable formal changes within the three main genres during the 1920s: lyric, epic, and drama. Particularly inspiring was the concept of montage cultivated by Dadaism. By breaking down material or intellectual coherence—and thus, for instance, the syntax and semantics of a text—and by isolating certain elements and piecing them together in a different way, montage was destructive and constructive at the same time, allowing for great flexibility of texts, often seeming both disconcerting and inspiring. Some of Gottfried Benn's pieces of prose, including *The Garden of Arles* (*Der Garten von Arles*, 1920), and many of his poems use montage as a technique. The same applies to Bertolt Brecht's *Three Penny Opera* (*Dreigroschenoper*, 1928) with its intermittent montage of episodes and songs and, in particular, to Alfred Döblin's fragmented urban novel *Berlin Alexanderplatz* (1929).

Other sources of conceptual and formal inspiration were the emerging new media film, radio, and gramophone. Many authors—including Kafka, Schnitzler, Döblin, and Thomas Mann—were frequent cinema-goers and keen, even enthusiastic, about the markedly demonstrative form of presentation that it entailed. It has often been said that cinema gave literature a specific cinematographic gaze, adding a filmic way of writing that manifested itself—in the works of Kafka, Schnitzler, Döblin, Feuchtwanger, Keun, and others—in filmic sequencing, the perspective of the camera, or in a filmic visiual language.[27] Some authors directly engaged with film: in 1919, Walter Hasenclever wrote a series of 138 filmic 'images', published under the title *The Plague* in 1920, the 'first film text printed in book form', according to its publisher. Arnold Bronnen visited the Babelsberg film studios, observed shooting, and learned to handle camera and the editing table. In Frank Thieß's novel *The Centaur* (*Der Zentaur*, 1931) a group of youths shoots a silent movie with exemplary scenes from Germany. The screening of the movie constitutes the end of the novel, which reports the film's content in a log-style fashion. Else Lasker-Schüler wrote a 'dream' for the seventh scene of her play *Arthur Aronymus and his Fathers* (*Arthur Aronymus und seine Väter*, 1932) that was intended to be shot as a talking film and shown during the theatre performance. Without overestimating the influence of film and cinema on novels and plays, it is more than fair to say that the former have served as important impulses for the latter.

In the 1920s, all three genres were characterized by traditional form and, more or less, strong modernizing elements, which existed alongside each other. In this chapter, we can only refer to a few main works of the period to substantiate this assumption without discussing other equally remarkable documents.

In the field of lyrics,[28] the particularly pronounced voices of the old greats Rainer Maria Rilke and Stefan George can be heard through the polyphony of old and new. The vocabulary and formal structure of their poetry is traditional, though not epigonal;

rather—particularly when considering Rilke's *Duino Elegies* (*Duineser Elegien*) and *Sonnets to Orpheus* (*Sonette an Orpheus*, both 1923)—a dedicated, albeit not pointedly avant-garde, modernity can be observed. As already noted by Kurt Tucholsky, Gottfried Benn and Bertolt Brecht defined the appearance of two new masters of lyricism, who of course pursued very different paths: Benn developed a decidedly artistic manner of speaking, which, through associative techniques of montage, striking connections from across many areas of knowledge and exquisite vocabulary, is fascinating though often also enigmatic. Döblin, who prompted Benn's admission into the Berlin Academy of Poets, said in his opening speech in April 1932 that in Benn's poetry 'knowledge' did not lie in a 'sentence alone', but in the 'atmosphere', 'in which the sentence appears', which must be comprehended through precise observation. Common methods of analysis and interpretation were, however, not yet sufficient to do this. The second verse of the poem *Chaos* can serve as an example here, which with nihilistic ecstasy creates a negative philosophy of history and anthropology. It applies to mankind:

> Infernal copy
> Malacia parasite;
> Undulating forms
> Ludicrous and sodomite:
> Adulations -: brains cut back
> A break in the sursum hinge,
> The gentleman -: their brains sprawl
> Corpse wax, adipocira.[29]

On the other hand, there prevails in Brecht's lyric—with even larger formal richness than Benn—a strong tendency for simplicity and forceful language, which are both achieved through extreme precision. He also explores the idea of popularity, which does not, however, act as an affirmation of entrenched patterns of thought but rather aims to disrupt them. In his poetological essay *On Non-Rhyming Lyric with Irregular Rhythms* (*Über reimlose Lyrik mit unregelmäßigen Rhythmen*, 1939), Brecht described a number of design and rhythmic techniques that he had already cultivated in the 1920s. No less than Benn did Brecht arrive at an anti-idealist reflection and interpretation of the modern condition of existence; though the latter was more preoccupied with the utility of his poems. The fact that Brecht gave his first big collection of poetry (1926/7) the title *Bertolt Brecht's Manual of Piety* (*Bertolt Brechts Hauspostille*), thus both parodically and with sincere nihilistic clarification placing it in the literary tradition of devotional and spiritual exercise books, is characteristic of its claim to have an impact, which is described in the prefixed *Introduction to the Use of Individual Lessons* (*Anleitung zum Gebrauch der einzelnen Lektionen*). Its quintessence is defined by the only poem in the 'Final Chapter', titled 'Against Temptation'. The first two verses are as follows:

> Don't let yourselves be tempted!
> There's no coming back.

> Day is in the doorway, leaving;
> Already you feel the night wind:
> Tomorrow will not come.
> Don't let yourselves be cheated!
> Life doesn't amount to much.
> Gulp it down in great helpings!
> It won't be enough for you
> When you have to leave it behind![30]

Brecht, at this point barely 30, is also appreciated for his innovations in the realm of drama, which outshine all of his other modifications: namely, the conception of 'epic' theatre.[31] This was, nonetheless, inspired by Georg Kaiser's reserved dramatic art based on theses and thought as well as Alfred Döblin's 'epicization' of the novel. The epicization of the theatre was first and foremost concerned with the expansion of the plot and dramatic dialogue through narrative framing, which shifted the action into a specific perspective. Narrative interjections were furthermore used, taking the shape of text plates or songs that aimed to disrupt illusion and create distance to disturb the instinctive and unreflective empathy of the audience. This forced them to think critically and assess rationally. In his 1930 essay *Notes on Opera: Rise and Fall of the City of Mahagonny*, Brecht distinguished, through a schematic comparison, between the traditional 'dramatic' and new 'epic' forms of theatre. At the same time, with the plays *Saint Joan of the Stockyards* and *The Decision*, both written between 1929 and 1932, Brecht presented two exemplary, if very different, works. *Saint Joan* is a 'spectacle' with 'great style', which has a politically and humanistically demanding plot and a linguistic design that is as impressive as it is differentiated. Indeed, its register ranges from the language of the German Classics to the blunt realism of the mercilessly exploited workers of the Chicago meat factories. Brecht portrayed an unavoidable, yet falsely exacerbated, crisis of the capitalist economy and a failed attempt at a workers' rebellion. This forces the hero of the work, who for religious reasons attempts to alleviate the misery of the workers, to understand that revolutionary action is only helpful when it is determined and steadfast in the face of violence. In the didactic work *The Decision*, featuring the music of Hanns Eisler, this recognition is elaborated in eight sequences, which depict a revolutionary operation with grave ideological consequences, namely the liquidation of a fellow comrade by Soviet agents in China. These sequences are set in a linguistic and musical form that aims at maximum indoctrination. On this aesthetic, Alfred Polgar wrote that it 'indirectly conveys knowledge and recognition to the audience, not least by firing them up through use of the piano, trumpet, trombone and drumkit'.[32]

Innovation in the realm of the novel has much to do with what Georg Lukács, in his 1916 *Theory of the Novel*, called 'transcendent homelessness'.[33] That is, the loss of a closed worldview, in whose 'totality' mankind's existence had a place and a meaning no matter what. The representation of this 'totality' was the objective of the great epic, according to Lukács, who followed Hegel on this point. The successor of the epic, the novel, could, on the grounds of the modern fragmentation of this worldview, no longer achieve wholeness. Indeed, modernity renders the 'totality' of the world and of being unascertainable and unrepresentable. From this realization emerged the 'narrative crisis' or the 'crisis of the novel', which was extensively debated throughout the 1920s.[34] In short, this debate concerned itself with the delegitimization and replacement of traditional narrative structures that characterized novels such as Theodor Fontane's *The Stechlin* (1899) and Thomas Mann's *Buddenbrooks* (1901). In them, an epoch-defining section of the world is described by an anonymous and authoritative third-person narrator—a 'ghost of narrative' (Thomas Mann[35]), so to speak—that brings to mind an enlightened consciousness, striving for objectivity and avoiding irrational and subjective judgements. The realistic novel attempts to hide its subjectivity and artistic construction, suggesting there is no real difference between the real world and the fictional world of narrative. In this way, the world and our existence within it are thought of as objective, tangible, and representable. On the other hand, following the questioning of the closed-world assumption by epistemology and science, it was demanded that cognitive condition, subjective perspective, and artistic construction be emphasized. Thomas Mann's reaction to this was delivered in his novel *The Magic Mountain* (1924), whose first-person narrator consistently pipes up to name the sources of his knowledge or their manner of representation. In his novel *The Steppenwolf* (1927), Herman Hesse uses large-scale montage in order to destroy the impression of a world that can only be perceived in one way and no other and to show one and the same thing, the Steppenwolf, from various different perspectives. Alfred Döblin took the commentating 'epicization' of the novel furthest, with his hybrid-novel *Berlin Alexanderplatz* (1929). In it, he introduces a narrator who, rather like a minstrel, begins by telling the reader the 'story of Franz Biberkopf' (the subtitle of the book). Furthermore, through the use of headers for each book or chapter, written like instructive preliminary and incidental remarks, the narrator continues to lead the reader through the novel: 'Here in the beginning, Franz Biberkopf leaves Tegel Prison into which a former foolish life had led him.... Here Franz Biberkopf who is a respectable, good-natured man, suffers his first blow.... Death sings his slow, slow song.'[36] Incidentally, Döblin uses montage excessively to emphasize the turbulent and colourful cosmopolitan life of the hero and, simultaneously, to put the entire action into the context of numerous mythological, religious, and philosophical allusions, presented as possibilities as opposed to unquestionable truths. Other authors chose different methods to capture the totality of existence. In his novel *The Man without Qualities* (*Der Mann ohne Eigenschaften*, 1930–3), Robert Musil used a technique called narrating 'from hundreds to thousands', in which the plot is narrated 'across a breadth' as opposed to along the 'thread' of biography, making it possible to discuss the epochal conditions and tendencies of existence in great breadth. Hermann Broch, in his *Sleepwalker* trilogy (1930–2), used the 'interdiscursive' or 'polyhistorical' novel, in which different narratives and philosophical treaties enlighteningly permeate and are superimposed upon one another.

Conclusion

In May 1929, an essay titled 'German Literature Shows its Face' was published in the magazine *Die Weltbühne*, claiming that literature had fulfilled the 'politicization postulate' (*Politisierungspostulat*) that expressionism and activism had established around 1910.[37] The cleft between politics and literature, which existed until the onset of expressionism, had been bridged. Societal problems moved to centre stage of literary creativity and were thus addressed. The everyday had gained a 'right to life on stages and in books'; 'business literature and utility-writing' had become important genres. Research has often confirmed this assessment that was made in 1929, despite the fact that, naturally, a large amount of non-political literature was being produced, including classic themes such as love, marriage, childhood, death, education, art, religion, and nature. It is difficult to determine how the politicization of literature affected the political and social development of the Weimar Republic because of the lack of empirical reader interest research. The politicized literature undoubtedly influenced the reading public's opinion of the republic; however, to what degree and in which direction remains an open question. Even pro-republican literature was often incredibly critical of it.

Next to the politicization of literature, literary innovations in all three genres should not be forgotten, and not only those that happened in influential works, but also the work that contributed to poetological foundations: with his academy lecture *Construction of the Epic Work* (*Der Bau des epischen Werks*, 1929), Döblin created a new concept for the epic that surpassed the narrative crisis. For a poetics of modern lyricism, there are approaches by Benn, and in modern dramaturgy Brecht. However, in both cases, further development was hindered by political circumstances. The 'Third Reich' and the Second World War had to be overcome before Brecht could consolidate his ideas for theatre in the modern and scientific age with his work *Small Organon for Theatre* (*Kleines Organon für das Theater*, 1949). Benn went on to outline his ideas for decisively modern lyrics in his lecture at the University of Marburg titled *Problems of Lyric Poetry* (*Probleme der Lyrik*, 1951). These texts were both of fundamental importance for the unfolding of the second wave of modernism in the 1950s.

Translated from German by Christine Brocks.

Notes

1. All quotations and details that are not specifically referenced are from Helmuth Kiesel, *Geschichte der deutschsprachigen Literatur 1918 bis 1933* (Munich: Beck, 2017).
2. Ibid., 152–62.
3. Eberhard Kolb, *Die Weimarer Republik*, 2nd ed. (Munich: Oldenbourg, 1988), 92.
4. David Midgley, *Writing Weimar: Critical Realism in German Literature, 1918–1933* (Oxford: Oxford University Press, 2000), 260–304; Kiesel, *Geschichte*, 130–52; Sabina Becker,

Experiment Weimar: Eine Kulturgeschichte Deutschlands 1918–1933 (Darmstadt: WBG Academic, 2018), 25–35.
5. Klaus Petersen, *Literatur und Justiz in der Weimarer Republik* (Stuttgart: J. B. Metzler, 1988).
6. Thomas Mann, *Essays*, vol. 4. *Achtung, Europa! Essays 1933–1938*, ed. Hermann Kurzke and Stephan Stachorski (Frankfurt/Main: Fischer, 1996), 65.
7. Thomas Mann, *Magic Mountain*, tr. H. T. Lowe-Porter (London: Vintage, 1999). Compare the conversations between the republican and humanist Lodovico Settembrini and the 'conservative revolutionary' Naphta in the second volume—the book was originally published in 2 vols.—chs 6 and 7.
8. Alfred Döblin, *Berlin Alexanderplatz: The Story of Franz Biberkopf*, tr. Eugene Jolas (Harmondsworth: Penguin, 1978), see esp. the sixth book, the chapter 'Defensive War against the Bourgeois', 277–86.
9. Kiesel, *Geschichte*, 840–50, 904–11.
10. Cited ibid., 841.
11. Ibid., 846–51, 906–11.
12. Walter Benjamin, *One-Way Street and Other Writings*, tr. Edmund Jephcott and Kingsley Shorter (London: NLB, 1979), 66–7.
13. Walter Benjamin, 'Left-Wing Melancholy', in Benjamin, *Selected Writings*, vol. 2/2. *1931–1934*, ed. Howard Eiland and Michael W. Jennings (Cambridge, MA. London: Belknap Press, 2005), 423–7.
14. Dolf Sternberger, *Verfassungspatriotismus* (Hanover: Landeszentrale für politische Bildung, 1982).
15. Lothar Köhn, *Überwindung des Historismus: Zu Problemen einer Geschichte der deutschen Literatur zwischen 1918 und 1933* (Berlin and Münster: Lit, 2018; originally publ. 1974).
16. Horst Thomé, 'Weltanschauungsliteratur: Vorüberlegungen zu Funktion und Texttyp', in Lutz Danneberg and Friedrich Vollhardt (eds), *Wissen in Literatur im 19. Jahrhundert* (Tübingen: Niemeyer, 2002), 338–80.
17. Cited in Kiesel, *Geschichte*, 64.
18. Both cited ibid., 64.
19. Sabina Becker, *Neue Sachlichkeit*, 2 vols. (Cologne and Weimar. Vienna: Böhlau, 2000), passim; Midgley, *Writing Weimar*, 14–56, 141–225; Becker, *Experiment*, 125–370.
20. Ernst Toller, *Hoppla*, tr. Hermon Ould (London: Ernest Benn, 1928), 59–60.
21. Midgley, *Writing Weimar*; Becker, *Neue Sachlichkeit*.
22. Benjamin, 'Left-Wing Melancholy'.
23. Midgley, *Writing Weimar*, 226–59; Kiesel, *Geschichte*, 495–537, 770–840.
24. Kiesel, *Geschichte*, 651–769; Walter Fähnders and Martin Rector, *Linksradikalismus und Literatur: Untersuchungen zur Geschichte der sozialistischen Literatur in der Weimarer Republik*, 2 vols. (Reinbek: Rowohlt, 1974).
25. Kiesel, *Geschichte*, 651–769; Fähnders and Rector, *Linksradikalismus*.
26. Becker, *Experiment*, 77–123, 185–313; Kiesel, *Geschichte*, 596–650.
27. Becker, *Experiment*, 371–417.
28. Kiesel, *Geschichte*, 1003–68.
29. Gottfried Benn, *Sämtliche Werke: Stuttgarter Ausgabe*, vol. 1. *Gedichte 1*, ed. Gerhard Schuster (Stuttgart: Klett-Cotta, 1986), 78. Tr. Martin Travers, <https://gottfriedbennpoems.com/the-poems/>.
30. Bertolt Brecht, *Werke: Große kommentierte Berliner und Frankfurter Ausgabe*, vol. 11. *Gedichte 1. Sammlungen 1938–1939*, ed. Jan Knopf and Gabriele Knopf (Berlin: Aufbau

Verlag and Suhrkamp, 1988), 116. Translation taken from Walter Benjamin, *Selected Writings*, vol. 4. *1938–1940*, ed. Howard Eiland and Michael W. Jennings (Cambridge, MA, and London: Belknap Press, 2003), 223.
31. Midgley, *Writing Weimar*, 117–40.
32. Cited in Kiesel, *Geschichte*, 1134.
33. Georg Lukács, *The Theory of the Novel: A Historico-Philosophical Essay on the Forms of Great Epic Literature*, tr. Anna Bostock (London: Merlin Press, 1971), 41.
34. Dietrich Scheunemann, *Romankrise: Die Entstehungsgeschichte der modernen Romanpoetik in Deutschland* (Heidelberg: Quelle & Meyer, 1978); Christian Schärf, *Der Roman im 20. Jahrhundert* (Stuttgart and Weimar: J. B. Metzler, 2001); Kiesel, *Geschichte*, 1169–201.
35. Thomas Mann, *Essays*, vol. 5. *Deutschland und die Deutschen. Essays 1938–1945*, ed. Hermann Kurzke and Stephan Stachorski (Frankfurt/Main: Fischer, 1996), 1–9.
36. Döblin, *Berlin Alexanderplatz*, 9, 452.
37. Hermann Kesser, 'Die deutsche Literatur zeigt ihr Gesicht', *Die Weltbühne*, 25/1 (1929), 789–93.

Bibliography

Becker, Sabina, *Experiment Weimar: Eine Kulturgeschichte Deutschlands 1918–1933* (Darmstadt: WBG Academic, 2018).
Becker, Sabina, *Neue Sachlichkeit*, 2 vols. (Cologne and Weimar. Vienna: Böhlau, 2000).
Fähnders, Walter, and Martin Rector, *Linksradikalismus und Literatur: Untersuchungen zur Geschichte der sozialistischen Literatur in der Weimarer Republik*, 2 vols. (Reinbek: Rowohlt, 1974).
Haß, Ulrike, *Militante Pastorale: Zur Literatur der antimodernen Bewegungen im frühen 20. Jahrhundert* (Munich: Fink, 1993).
Kaes, Anton (ed.), *Weimarer Republik: Manifeste und Dokumente zur deutschen Literatur 1918–1933* (Stuttgart: Metzler, 1983).
Kiesel, Helmuth, *Geschichte der deutschsprachigen Literatur 1918 bis 1933* (Munich: Beck, 2017).
Köhn, Lothar, *Überwindung des Historismus: Zu Problemen einer Geschichte der deutschen Literatur zwischen 1918 und 1933* (Berlin and Münster: Lit, 2018; originally publ. 1974).
Leydecker, Karl (ed.), *German Novelists of the Weimar Republic: Intersections of Literature and Politics* (Rochester, NY, and Woodbridge: Camden House, 2006).
Midgley, David, *Writing Weimar: Critical Realism in German Literature, 1918–1933* (Oxford: Oxford University Press, 2000).
Schärf, Christian, *Der Roman im 20. Jahrhundert* (Stuttgart and Weimar: Metzler, 2001).
Scheunemann, Dietrich, *Romankrise: Die Entstehungsgeschichte der modernen Romanpoetik in Deutschland* (Heidelberg: Quelle & Meyer, 1978).

CHAPTER 29

ARCHITECTURE, TOWN PLANNING, AND LARGE-SCALE HOUSING ESTATES

Challenges, Visions, and Proposed Solutions

BEATE STÖRTKUHL

The Bauhaus and the Berlin metropolis are two slogans characteristically associated with the architecture of the Weimar Republic, although Berlin was not the only 'hotspot' for modern architecture at the time, and the Bauhaus was not unique within the avant-garde movements.[1] Both buzzwords evoke the cuboid forms and the programmatic denial of ornament by the so-called Neues Bauen, or Modernism, which introduced a fundamentally new approach to architecture and town planning. Neues Bauen represented a relatively small proportion of the construction work undertaken, but it gained a high media presence and thus became a symbol of the social and technical modernization processes of the Weimar Republic. Urban development and the construction of housing and new settlements were key social policy challenges at the time, so architecture was a matter of great interest. There were intense and hotly argued discussions on the proposed solutions, especially since there were almost always financial limitations. Possibilities ranged from visions of metropolis to 'minimum dwellings', and from avant-garde notions of collective living for the 'new man' to housing patterns in the vernacular style, the so-called *Heimatstil*, inspired by regional architectural idioms.

Visions for a New Architecture After 1918: From Garden City to Large-Scale Housing Estates

The influence of the political turmoil of the months following the war reached into the fields of art and architecture. In Berlin, alongside the workers' and soldiers' councils, the 'November group' (Novembergruppe) and the 'Work Council for Art' (Arbeitsrat für Kunst) were established. They demanded that art should be democratized and made accessible to all layers of society: 'Art and the people must form an entity. Art shall no longer be a luxury for the few, but should be enjoyed and experienced by the broad masses. The aim is an alliance of the arts under the wing of architecture,' proclaimed the headnote of the flyer published on 1 March 1919 by the Work Council for Art, drawing on the formulation of the architect Bruno Taut.[2] The list of the founders and supporters of these closely intertwined groups reads like a who's who of the 1920s avant-garde, and included the architects Walter Gropius, Erich Mendelsohn, and Otto Bartning. It also hints at their roots in the early German Modernism of the pre-war years, as represented by the architects Hans Poelzig and Max Berg, and the expressionist artists Emil Nolde and Max Pechstein.[3] Many of the ideas in the announcements during the winter of 1918/19 were subsequently repeated in the Bauhaus manifesto published by Walter Gropius after the establishment of the experimental art school in Weimar in April 1919.[4] Significantly, the manifesto posited the leading role of architecture, a role it did indeed play in the construction of settlements and housing in the Weimar Republic, though not so prominently at the Bauhaus itself.[5]

Initially, the debates on architecture aimed high, taking little account of the weakness of the post-war economy and the paucity of suitable contractors. Bruno Taut elaborated visionary manifestos and expressive schemes for new towns and communities free of social demarcations.[6] Centres designated *Stadtkrone* (city crown) reminiscent of a medieval cathedral would serve as a social, cultural, and urban focus in generously laid-out garden cities; like the meeting halls (*Volkshäuser*) and union headquarters of the workers' movement, they would all be open to the public. Taut's inspiration came from pre-war reform ideas: the festival theatre built by Heinrich Tessenow in the garden city of Hellerau near Dresden in 1910–12 prefigured the *Stadtkrone* concept, as did the Centennial Hall inaugurated in 1913 in Breslau (Wrocław), the former capital of the Prussian province of Silesia. Max Berg, the Breslau city architect, had designed a monumental space on simple and egalitarian lines, without theatrical boxes, that would bring all those who attended events together on an equal footing for a fully shared experience.

In November 1918, the architect described his concept as a 'cathedral of democracy' to the workers' and soldiers' councils gathered in the Centennial Hall.[7]

The brilliantly lit, crystalline effect of the glazing and the gothic inspiration of the Wrocław Centennial Hall propelled Taut and his architect correspondents in the Crystal Chain—among them the brothers Hans and Wassili Luckhardt, and Hans Scharoun—into the realms of utopia, with all the connotations of expressionist glass architecture, oscillating between mysticism and Enlightenment.[8] It inspired the glass frontage of the now famous design submitted by Mies van der Rohe for the competition, announced in November 1921, to build a high-rise building at the Friedrichstrasse station in the centre of Berlin.[9] It was not only the younger generation of architects who dreamed of 'big buildings' and a new urban dominance. The 'high-rise craze' of the early post-war years gave expression to visionary artistic enthusiasm as well as to the desire to establish a cultural marker following defeat in war.[10] Both the daily press and specialist journals carried lively debates on the subject. It was no coincidence that the first post-war architecture competition to build a high-rise building was declared in spring 1920 in Danzig (today the Polish city of Gdańsk). Even while the peace negotiations were still raging over whether the town should remain within the German Reich, some of the schemes submitted explicitly took inspiration from the 'German' building traditions of the Hanse city.[11] The concept of the American city, an 'indictment in stone of the tyranny of capitalism', served as a negative foil for alternative blueprints, in which social concerns and urban challenges were given equal consideration:[12] Single high-rise buildings in suitable locations were to include both office and retail spaces, establishing shorter routes between the working areas. Furthermore, they would release flats hitherto inappropriately used as working spaces, and thus also contribute to solving the housing problem. A development funded by the public authorities or housing associations would avoid speculation in land prices, and major building projects would create work opportunities to train up construction apprentices. Only 'a nation with good social order' such as the Germans, it was claimed, could rise to such a challenge and 'produce an appropriately artistic result'.[13] In this context, the 'national' interpretation of the architectural style chosen became particularly significant. Vertical supports in the style of buttresses and scattered crown pins on the roofs conveyed a flavour of the gothic style. Typical of this specific 'gothic revival' was the competition already mentioned to build a high-rise building at the Berlin Friedrichstrasse station, which attracted 144 submissions.[14]

The few commercial high-rise buildings which had been built were not especially tall in comparison with their American forerunners, or with the designs created for the architectural competitions. According to building regulations, buildings were described as 'high-rise' if they had more than nine storeys, and those with more than twelve rarely gained planning permission. Nevertheless, reinforced concrete concealed behind clinker bricks created monumental, well-fortified façades—the complete opposite of the transparent and crystalline creations of the Crystal Chain. The Chilehaus built between 1922 and 1924 in Hamburg points its sharp nose towards the east, evoking the prow of a ship (Figure 29.1).[15] The theory of the architect, Fritz Höger, was that brick was a northern and Germanic building material. He was evoking the medieval Hanseatic League, which, he suggested, in its heyday had introduced the specific forms of 'German Gothic' (*deutsche Sondergotik*) as far afield as the Baltic States.[16] The Chilehaus was the subject of much media coverage; it came to be seen as the symbol of German recovery after the war and as the flagship of a national style termed Brick Expressionism.[17] Further high-rises were built in brick in French-occupied Rhineland—a region where bricks were not habitually used—and in the capital Berlin, up until the middle of the 1920s. Neighbouring states were puzzled by the nationalistic attitudes exhibited in the German sky-scraper debate.[18] Eventually, only a modest number of 'tower buildings' were actually built. There were few private investors willing to take on such major projects in the economic depression that followed the war, and public funds were focused on the need to address the serious housing crisis.

In a few cases, however, the revolutionary spirit of the times was realized in architectural projects: in the sculptural expressionist shapes of the Einsteinturm in Potsdam (1920–2) by Erich Mendelsohn, for example, and in Otto Bartning's works in the early

FIGURE 29.1 Fritz Höger: Chilehaus in Hamburg, 1922–4.
(photo: Adolf und Carl Dransfeld; Museum für Kunst und Gewerbe, Hamburg, Inv. Nr. P1998.87).

1920s, such as the Haus Wylerberg near Kleve. The visions of Expressionism came to fruition in Art Deco: the jagged crystalline forms of a 'modernized gothic' style were popular decorative elements until the late 1920s, especially as internal features. The former protagonists of the Work Council for Art and the November group, meanwhile, had already been heading in quite different artistic directions.

Housing provision had been stretched before the war, and shortages became dramatic after 1918. During the war, construction had stagnated; then during the immediate post-war years there was not only an economic crisis but also a boom in new households, and the state was forced to take the initiative. The constitution of the Weimar Republic, drawn up in August 1919, included the promise that every German should have a sanitary home and that all German families, especially those with numerous children, should have an appropriate home and opportunities for work.[19] Building social housing, both in urban and rural settings, became a core task of the new state. Many housing associations were set up as non-profit organizations immediately after the end of the war. They were financed proportionally by state institutions, municipalities, trade unions, and companies. In order to discourage speculation in land prices and to facilitate the availability of suitable land, municipalities retained the right to buy up land offered for sale, and even expropriation rights. As early as 1919, and in spite of the appalling economic situation, construction activity was already in full swing. Building even continued during the severe inflation in 1923 in the German part of Upper Silesia, where the demand for housing was especially strong owing to the partitioning of the land between Germany and Poland in 1922 and the consequent influx of German refugees.[20] From 1924, the state taxed earnings from property rental—the so-called *Hauszinssteuer*—and this yielded funds to enable further social housing. Between 1919 and 1926 around 1.1 million new homes were built across Germany, but this was only half of the number needed. Between 1926 and 1932 a further 1.7 million homes were built. This was a significant success in housing policy terms. And yet the growth in the population and the economic crisis meant that there was still a lack of cheap housing of a sufficiently good standard.[21]

In the Reich and in the Länder—for example, in the March 1918 Prussian housing law—legal specifications and planning practice in the housing sector were based on the reforms initiated before the war and the lessons learned from those experiences. A key element of the reforms had been the concept elaborated by the urban planner Rudolf Eberstadt: 'radial urban development'.[22] In contrast to the chaotic 'concentric' style of expansion characteristic of the industrial revolution, which threatened to choke the ancient city centre, Eberstadt's principle aimed to open up the urban area with green 'wedges'. The 'city' itself, in the centre, was to be reshaped to focus on commercial and cultural activity. New homes were only to be built in exceptional circumstances, mainly when existing domestic buildings were being refurbished or modernized. Furthermore, the high population density in the old cities was to be reduced, and insanitary older buildings were to be pulled down and replaced by new shops and offices—as had happened in the business quarter (*Kontorviertel*) in Hamburg, where the construction of the Chilehaus had initiated the process.[23] New settlements with open spaces were to be located at the edge of the cities, following the English concept of the garden city, designed to relieve pressure on the existing metropolis.[24] In order to extend the city's territory and gain space available for building, city municipalities worked towards incorporating neighbouring boroughs into their territory. The concept was dependent for its viability on the extension of public transport networks in order to link the new housing developments to the city centre and the industrial areas.

The Prussian state, via the so-called Provincial Housing Settlement Societies, ordered the 'planning and construction of small dwellings in small and medium-sized buildings', in order to 'provide the less well off members of society with sanitary and appropriate homes at an affordable price'.[25] The societies were to prepare standard designs for houses, flats, furniture, and gardens that would enable self-sufficiency, all to be published and disseminated by the societies themselves.

The pattern of this type of tiny dwellings, either detached or in a small block of up to four homes, with kitchen gardens, had been advocated since the 1910s by housing reform protagonists such as Theodor Fischer and Heinrich Tessenow as an alternative to tightly packed inner-city tenement houses with narrow and poorly lit and ventilated courtyards.[26] They counted among their disciples some of the leading housing development architects of the Weimar Republic: Bruno Taut, Ernst May, and Grete Schütte-Lihotzky, one of the few women in the profession.[27] The social housing developments in the immediate post-war years were uniformly simple in design, between 45 and 80 square metres, with a kitchen/living room and several bedrooms. The toilet and laundry were initially in the outhouse. The staidly shaped buildings boasted an ample roofline, coloured shutters, and trellises, and emanated a cosiness and vernacular feel that belied the economical building costs (Figure 29.2).

From a purely pragmatic point of view, an individual house with its own kitchen garden and accommodation for small animals enabled many to be largely self-sufficient during the economically difficult years that followed the war. There were also deeper emotional connotations to having your own small section of the homeland: the ties to one's own patch of land were to assure social peace within the Reich, and they also served to reinforce and make a public statement about the sense of national belonging, especially in the disputed border regions such as Silesia and East Prussia.[28] This mental freight vested in the building of housing estates and in their national idiom cast a long shadow: it was deployed during the 1920s in opposition to the development of large settlement blocks and to the Neues Bauen, and subsequently as a guiding principle in propaganda for Nazi cultural policies.[29] Albeit in some cases extensively altered, the inter-war small-scale housing developments are still a characteristic feature of the German landscape, many of them very similar in design and not markedly differentiated by region. Any small variations between the styles of early 1920s houses in Westphalia, Silesia, or even the Vienna region were not usually due to adaptation to local building idioms. They were far more likely to be due to the styles of the architects involved.

In large cities, however, the concept of low-rise housing projects in the garden city style—the so-called *Flachbauweise*, limited to two storeys—soon came up against economic realities. There was a need to make more efficient use of expensive building land

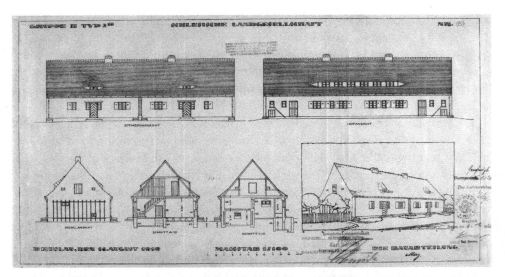

FIGURE 29.2 Ernst May: Standard tiny house design for the Goldschmieden development near Breslau, 1919.

(Muzeum Architektury we Wrocławiu, Inv. Nr. MAt-AB-31081; reproduced with permission of Muzeum Architektury we Wrocławiu).

if any realistic progress was to be made in addressing the housing crisis. Limiting urban sprawl would also enable the construction of the necessary infrastructure to reach all the newly built-up areas. The solution, in order to provide the volume of housing needed, was to build complexes composed of multi-storey blocks grouped around generous green areas with space for play and relaxation. This construction model for city dwellings had previously been used in the first housing cooperative projects, built in Berlin, Munich, and Hamburg before the First World War. It was in the Weimar Republic, however, that the development of larger housing projects was more widely adopted. Often they housed several thousand people, each project having its own services: laundry facilities, heating systems, shops, and pubs, and social provisions such as nurseries, schools, and churches. The individual character of each development was often underlined by a gate-like structure or an entrance building to mark the boundary with the neighbouring urban area.

It was after the inflation year of 1923 and the introduction of the tax on income from property rental in 1924 that the building boom began in the large cities. The specialist press was filled with discussions of the best floorplan for apartments where limited space was available.[30] Standard provision even for a small flat, it was argued, should include an indoor toilet or a small bathroom, central heating, and, where possible, a balcony. There was limited scope for variety: the floorplans for the Borstei estate (1924–9) in Munich, built in the 'homeland' style with a pitched roof, lattice windows, and shutters, were very similar to those in the flat-roofed brick buildings in the Hamburg Barmbek-Nord quarter (1926–30) with their horizontal window bars and concrete balcony parapets.

The Neues Bauen housing quarters in Hamburg and Cologne (Wilhelm Riphahn), 'New Frankfurt' (Ernst May), and the large Berlin estates are to this day seen as characteristic of the Weimar Republic. In reality, however, they represented only about a tenth of the housing built at the time. Most homes, whether in housing complexes or residential estates, were constructed in the style of so-called conservative Modernism, and Borstei in Munich is a good example: functional, typecast, providing the 'light, air and sun' that was required at the time for domestic architecture, and yet still faithful to traditional external appearances.[31] Most occupants favoured cosiness both in the style of a building and in their furnishing choices. The didactic tendency of the 'new way of living'—banish soft furnishings and decorative items in favour of tubular steel furniture and light materials—met with resistance, and incidentally proved a rich seam for cabarets and satire.[32] Showy items in the Modernist style were naturally commented and debated upon widely, both favourably and critically. The protagonists of Neues Bauen themselves energetically promoted their own theories, and they came over time to occupy an increasing number of key positions in the architectural and cultural world of the Weimar Republic.[33]

'THE LATEST IN ARCHITECTURE'—NEUES BAUEN HUBS IN THE WEIMAR REPUBLIC

Dutch architecture made a key contribution to the evolution towards Neues Bauen from the 'homeland' style of the garden city movement and the expressionist aspirations of the early post-war years.[34] One of those who served as a link between the architectural cultures of the two countries was the critic Adolf Behne, who acted as a seismograph for new artistic developments.[35] In 1915 he had been one of the first to mention Expressionism in architecture, and when he travelled to the Netherlands in the late summer of 1920 one of his main aims was to see the expressionist housing developments of Michel de Klerk in Amsterdam. Eventually, he was more fascinated by the abstract geometric idiom of the artistic group De Stijl, founded in 1917 around Piet Mondrian, Theo van Doesburg, and Jacobus Johannes Pieter Oud, and his specific interest was in the flat-roofed blocks of workers' accommodation completed in 1920 in Rotterdam-Spangen, which were organized in horizontal sections. On his return, Behne confronted the 'utopians' in the Work Council of Art and at the Weimar Bauhaus, exposing to them the 'objectivity' (*Sachlichkeit*) of the new Dutch architecture and the mechanical construction methods used.[36]

An intense programme of exchange began—or, more accurately, was reactivated after the interruption of the war: Adolf Meyer had after all studied architecture with the Dutch architect Johannes Ludovicus Mathieu Lauweriks. In 1911 he and his partner Walter Gropius designed the Fagus factory in Alfeld an der Leine—the prototype Bauhaus glass façade.[37] Oud, meanwhile, had for several months of 1911 worked as an assistant to Theodor Fischer in Munich; this not only developed his appreciation of a new style of domestic architecture, but no doubt also fostered collegiality with the kindred spirits among his fellow students, such as Bruno Taut and Erich Mendelsohn. Taut and Mendelsohn took several study and conference trips to Holland in the early 1920s.[38] Mendelsohn drew on the dynamism of the Amsterdam School and the functional forms favoured by De Stijl to create his own distinctive signature: flowing lines, horizontal bands of windows, and projecting sculptural profiles that interact with the 'liveliness of the street'.[39] His buildings, with their simple elegance and night-time lighting served as an advertisement in the cityscape, and led to his becoming the leading Weimar Republic architect for department stores and office buildings (Figure 29.3).[40]

In the summer of 1923 the Bauhaus put on its first exhibition in Weimar, setting the achievements of the Bauhaus School in the context of the international avant-garde. Oud spoke on 'The Development of Modern Architecture in the Netherlands', and he and the Bauhaus director Gropius selected the Dutch works shown in a presentation of 'International Architecture'.[41] According to Gropius, their aim was to show 'only the best and, in our opinion, the most modern of architecture: a dynamic architectural style, stripped of mouldings and ornaments'.[42] This was not a general survey of contemporary construction, but a demonstration of the new direction architecture was taking. Alongside the Dutch architects the exhibition also showed works by Le Corbusier, Karel Teige and other architects in the Czech artistic group Devětsil, Ludwig Mies van der Rohe, Erich Mendelsohn, and the brothers Bruno and Max Taut; the 'ancestors' of Modernism, much revered by the European avant-garde, were also featured: Peter Behrens, Hans Poelzig, and Frank Lloyd Wright. Gropius wrote this up as the start of a canon—frequently expanded by the Bauhaus in the following years—in the first volume of 'Bauhaus books', which appeared in 1925.[43]

The years 1921 to 1924 were key in development 'Towards a New Architecture', as Le Corbusier's influential manifesto was titled when it was published in book form in 1923.[44] The Russian Constructivists in the sphere of the state art academy WChUTEMAS in Moscow, including El Lissitzky and Wladimir Tatlin, also took part in the exchanges among a group that saw itself as an explicitly international group of avant-garde architects. A truly modern architecture was seen as characterized by pure forms and colours and a lack of ornamentation, key markers of its dedication to functionality. However, this Modernist style was certainly not as 'devoid of profile' as Gropius had asserted: linear mouldings and cantilever plates give rhythm to the interlaced shapes of the cuboid architecture. The German-speaking architects attached the label Neues Bauen ('New Building') to this new architectural idiom, and coined the analogous Neues Wohnen ('New Living Style') and Neues Frankfurt ('New Frankfurt').[45] The ideological foundation was the ambition to create a thoroughly modernized society, a 'new man'. In this project, Bauhaus was only one contributing actor among many. The right-wing nationalist government of Thuringia decided to discontinue funding for the allegedly 'socialist' institution, so for political reasons the Bauhaus decided to relocate to Dessau, in the Free State of Anhalt. The state and the city between them took on the financing of the institution. Its product design has ensured that the Bauhaus's fame has lasted into

FIGURE 29.3 Erich Mendelsohn, the Schocken department store in Stuttgart, 1926–8, photographed at night.

(unknown photographer; Stadtarchiv Stuttgart, Schenkung Nowak—Nachlass Arthur Ohler, Inv. Nr. 2679-FA 151/1/40; reproduced with permission of Stadtarchiv Stuttgart).

the twenty-first century, yet it was not able to sustain itself financially, since most of the objects it produced were not suitable for industrial fabrication.[46]

The new Dessau home of the Bauhaus, designed by Gropius, opened in December 1926 (Figure 29.4).[47] It was a manifesto for the developments in architectural and pedagogical thought. Studios and workshops, display areas and canteen, and even the

FIGURE 29.4 Walter Gropius: The Bauhaus in Dessau, 1925–6, from the southwest.
(photo: Beate Störtkuhl, 2016).

student accommodation, were all integrated into one complex—the first higher education campus of its kind in Germany. The homes for the staff and the director, however, were set somewhat apart in a small pine forest: the hierarchies were preserved, despite the liberal image of the institution. There was no formal teaching of architecture at the Bauhaus until the Swiss Hannes Meyer took over as director in 1928, though a number of students worked in Walter Gropius's private architectural practice.[48] This had been different at the Berlin United State School for Fine and Applied Art, led by Bruno Paul[49] and at the Breslau Academy for Art and Design, which under the directorship of Hans Poelzig (1903–16) had already enjoyed a reputation as one of the progressive art academies that provided apprentice workshops. Two architects belonging to the same Neues Bauen network, Adolf Rading and, from 1925, Hans Scharoun, built on the reputation of the Breslau institution.[50]

The building departments of municipalities and housing associations played a key part in establishing the new building style. In many cases, the initiative came from municipalities under social democratic leadership (and not only in large cities) or from housing associations closely linked to trade unions. The congenial cooperation between Martin Wagner and Bruno Taut in Berlin provides a good illustration of how much the individual contribution and style of the architects involved could bring to a project team. In 1924, they both started to work at the Berlin building department of DEWOG, the

German Housing Company for State Officials and Workers, Ltd. that had been founded by the General German Trade Union Federation. In 1926 Wagner took over from Ludwig Hoffmann, who clung to historic traditions, as head of the municipal building department in Berlin. Wagner was the intellectual mastermind of the Berlin Modernist housing estates, which since 2008 have featured on the list of UNESCO World Heritage sites.[51] Until 1933, Bruno Taut served as chief architect for some of the most significant of these housing projects. They include 'Onkel Toms Hütte', the 'Wohnstadt Carl Legien', and the particularly remarkable urban 'Hufeisensiedlung' ('Horseshoe estate'), built in Berlin Britz between 1925 and 1933 and providing some 2,000 dwellings. It derives its name from the horseshoe-shaped green space it is built around. The Hufeisensiedlung is a good example of diverse provision making a sensible compromise in terms of the usage of expensive inner-city land: around the blocks of flats, streets of terraced houses radiate out, offering the dream of an affordable home of one's own in a standardized style.

Taut used strong colours to add interest to the austere simplicity of the shapes and arrangement of the flats. On a long row of buildings, for example, to create contrast he left the balconies white and beige against the dark red render—the ensemble was soon dubbed the 'Red Front'. He used vivid colours for internal décor, too. Ernst May, who from 1925 was head of the municipal building department and mastermind of Neues Frankfurt, also liked to work with strong colour contrasts.[52] The term 'white modernity' was a buzzword, but it did not really correspond to reality. 'Building with colours'(farbiges Bauen) was a central feature not only for the avant-garde but also for so-called conservative Modernism, and both drew their original inspiration from pre-war reformed architectural thinking. The building departments of the housing associations served to offer training for the upcoming generations of architects. The 'Frankfurt courses in Neues Bauen' attracted architects and students from all over Europe and the USA, and the journal *Das neue Frankfurt* carried a discussion forum on Modernist housing estates.[53]

The 1927 exhibition 'Die neue Wohnung' ('The new home'), held in Stuttgart, offered a first opportunity to assess and discuss the current state of construction of flats and housing developments, and included a model estate funded by the city from its housing construction budget. It aimed to explore solutions for large housing estates and to experiment with new building materials and prefabricated standard components. Taking inspiration from the Ford concept of the industrial production line, the building sector was hoping to introduce standardization and also to reduce costs.[54] The exhibition was put on by the Deutscher Werkbund, an association of progressive architects, artisans, art critics, industrialists, and politicians established in 1907. The Werkbund wanted to shape a holistic living environment 'from sofa cushion to urban development' that would educate the tastes of consumers and—last but not least—raise the profile of German products across world markets.[55] In the mid-1920s a younger generation took on the leadership of the association; with Mies van der Rohe as the second chairman, and Hugo Häring, Ludwig Hilberseimer, Adolf Rading, and Hans Scharoun all on the committee, the organization was now led by representatives of the avant-garde.[56] In contrast to the national position taken up by the Werkbund during the First World War, the new leadership team was keen to emphasize its integration into an international network of thinkers.

And indeed the Stuttgart exhibition, under the leadership of Mies van der Rohe, showed clearly that it was reaching out across borders in intellectual terms.[57] The fifteen dwellings in the Weißenhof model development had been designed by a group of German architects (again including the 'ancestors of Modernism' Peter Behrens and Hans Poelzig), the Dutch Mart Stam and Jacobus Johannes Pieter Oud, the Swiss Le Corbusier (who lived in Paris), and the Austrian Josef Frank. The associated 'International exhibition of plans and models' in the Stuttgart conference hall showcased, among others, 'Praesens', the Polish avant-garde group. The presence of these distinguished participants was intended to underscore the claim of the 1923 Bauhaus exhibition that the concepts of the avant-garde now exerted a worldwide influence. This was confirmed with the establishment in 1928 of the International Congresses of Modern Architecture (Congrès Internationaux d'Architecture Moderne, CIAM),[58] in which Walter Gropius and Ernst May were the most prominent figures from Germany. May invited the 1929 congress to Frankfurt in order to debate 'The Minimum Dwelling'.[59] The first presentation of avant-garde architecture in the New World—it was principally a European phenomenon—took place in 1932 in the newly established New York Museum of Modern Art, where it was dubbed in English 'the International Style'.[60]

The terraced houses built by Oud and Stam in Stuttgart were the only ones to meet the challenge of providing the best possible budget small home that was well equipped in terms of contemporary expectations. The remaining buildings presented more individual solutions, especially the two detached houses by Le Corbusier, which were open-plan and internally equipped with built-in concrete furniture and strong colour schemes. Supporters of Modernism celebrated the exhibition as a 'victory for the new building style', and it inspired applied arts associations in neighbouring countries that were following the German example. Dwelling exhibitions that included model developments were held in the Czechoslovakian city of Brno in 1928, in Vienna in 1930, and in Prague and Zürich in 1932, though these were not attended by international architects.[61] In 1929 the Silesian branch of the German Werkbund and the Breslau Academy for Art and Design organized an exhibition on 'Living and Working Space' (Figure 29.5). They were not able to invite foreign architects to take part in designing the model estate because the city, which was funding the exhibition, advertised itself as the 'Metropolis of the German East' and wanted to highlight the potential of the Silesian border region.[62]

Leading cultural and political decision-makers were aware by the late 1920s that Neues Bauen had become a flagship for a new, progressive Germany. This was further confirmed when Mies van der Rohe was asked to be the artistic lead for the German section at the 1929 Barcelona World's Fair Exposition, and given the contract to build the German Pavilion. At the time he was still in private practice as an architect—it was not until 1930 that he took over as Director at the Bauhaus in Dessau.[63] For the first time since the First World War Germany featured on an international stage and, through the medium of architecture, plainly demonstrated the clean break with the pomp of the

FIGURE 29.5 Article by William Gaunt in the English journal *The Studio*, 1929, on the 'New architecture' in Germany, with an impression of the 1929 Breslau Werkbund exhibition 'Living and Working Space'. The photo shows the view from the roof-deck of the Lauterbach house onto the 'Ledigenheim' by Hans Scharoun.

(photo: Heinrich Klette, 1929).

Wilhelmine German Empire: Mies's minimalist flat-roofed building was built of steel, glass, and costly stone materials. There were plenty of examples in Barcelona evoking monumental and historical forms, especially in the Palau Nacional, the main hall of the Fair, which still stands; in this setting, the German Pavilion presented a radically modern contrast (Figure 29.6).

Private investors were quick to spot the advertising potential of the new architectural language. Department stores, film theatres, and other consumer buildings became symbols of modern city living. Many publishers produced opulent illustrated books to popularize the new 'Latest Style of Architecture'.[64] Clients drawn from the middle classes, academics, and industrialists all appreciated the simple elegance of light steel-framed furniture set in open spaces flooded with light. Neues Wohnen became a lifestyle, and had come a long way from the constraints of large-scale economical housing projects. Mies van der Rohe and his partner, the interior designer Lilly Reich, gained a reputation for creating luxurious homes and interiors, such as the villa for the Tugendhats, an entrepreneur couple, in Brno, Czechoslovakia (1928–30): its dividing walls were of marble and onyx, plate glass windows opened by an electrical motor that lowered them into the floor, and it featured the famous 'Barcelona Chair', still in production in the second decade of the twenty-first century.[65] In 1929/30 Adolf Rading designed a *Gesamtkunstwerk* building—both the structure and the interior, including the colour scheme—in the Neues Bauen style for Dr Rabe and his family in Zwenkau, near Leipzig (Figure 29.7). It provided both their home and the doctor's consulting

FIGURE 29.6 Mies van der Rohe: The German Pavilion at the Barcelona 1929 World Exposition, reconstructed in the 1980s. In the background, one of the neobaroque exhibition pavilions of 1929 is visible.

(photo: Beate Störtkuhl, 2004).

FIGURE 29.7 Adolf Rading and Oskar Schlemmer: Living room in Dr Rabe's house in Zwenkau near Leipzig, 1930–1.

(photo: Vladimír Šlapeta, Praha-Brno, 2015; reproduced with the permission of the photographer).

room. Rading commissioned his colleague Oskar Schlemmer, who had recently moved from the Bauhaus to the Breslau Academy, to provide the sculptural elements and the murals.[66]

'Conservative Modernism' and the Debate about the 'German' Roof

Neues Bauen, with its experimental approach, its rupture with traditional views on lifestyle and visual appearance, its 'left-wing' reputation, and its international outlook, had gained a high public profile and was provoking strong opposition in some quarters.[67] One dispute flared up at the 1927 Stuttgart Werkbund exhibition. Opposition came from the architecture professors at the Stuttgart Technical Academy, Paul Bonatz and Paul Schmitthenner, who protested that only the avant-garde were represented in the Weißenhof model estate, and maintained that social housing funds were being wasted.[68] They accused the buildings and furnishings presented of being 'soulless', 'cold', and 'un-German'; very soon a postcard began to circulate that caricatured the cuboid flat-roofed houses of the Weißenhof as an 'Arab village'. The opponents of the avant-garde were further buoyed up by faults that appeared in experimental materials used in some of the houses.

As early as 1927 Schmitthenner set up a competing project, a model development at Stuttgart Kochenhof; after some delays, he completed it in the autumn of 1933—after the National Socialist seizure of power—in the context of the 'German Wood for Housebuilding and Living' exhibition.[69] The specification at the exhibition was for all buildings to have a gabled roof. Other specifications—lattice windows, shutters—and internal design all placed the model village firmly in the 'homeland' vernacular style as it had been developed before the First World War. The leading personalities in architecture during the Weimar Republic had been trained in the pre-war reform movement, but they had parted ways in the early 1920s. One group viewed the new architectural shapes and industrial construction methods as well suited to modernizing both the social and the technical idiom, whereas the other strongly favoured traditional shapes and materials that offered feigned security within a world of seemingly growing confusion. This development was not unique to Germany; similar debates were being conducted in Poland, for example, though they were less acrimonious. In Germany, the concepts of 'international' and 'cosmopolitan' gained negative connotations tinged with racism and especially antisemitism. Publications such as *Kunst und Rasse* ('Art and Race', 1928) by Paul Schultze-Naumburg, one of the central figures of the reform movement around 1900, and *Das Deutsche Wohnhaus* ('The German Home', 1932) by Schmitthenner, contrasted Neues Bauen with a nationalistic interpretation of form, and laid the foundations for Nazi propaganda and cultural policies (Figure 29.8).[70]

There was frequent movement, however, between the two extremes: most architects were undogmatic in practice. Bruno Taut's 'horseshoe' development also included terraced housing with gabled roofs; Heinrich Tessenow, a pioneer of reform architecture often misrepresented as a traditionalist, joined the 'Ring', an association of advocates of Neues Bauen, set up in 1925 by Mies van der Rohe.[71] In 1928 Schmitthenner and others had established a competing association, the 'Block', but Tessenow did not become involved. Dominikus Böhm, a busy church architect in Cologne, made use of motifs inspired by the monuments of antiquity—columns, arches, clinker bricks—but the lack of ornamentation and moulding on his creations makes them far more evocative of modern industrial buildings (dubbed the 'cathedrals of work' by contemporaries) than of historical sacred buildings.[72] Paul Wolf, for many years head of the municipal building department in Dresden, pushed through a programme to modernize urban infrastructure: schools, care homes, sports amenities, covered swimming pools. He was no defender of Neues Bauen, but he tolerated the projects in the latest styles carried out by his colleagues.[73]

It was not until the 1990s that historians began to apply the term 'Modernism' more widely; it had previously been used specifically only in relation to the Weimar Republic avant-garde and to the aesthetic forms characteristic of the movement.[74] The concept of 'multiple modernisms', drawn from the social sciences, was eventually adopted in order

FIGURE 29.8 Comparison between one of Le Corbusier's houses in the Weißenhof estate, 1927 (left), and Paul Schmitthenner's 'House with a walled garden', 1930 (right). Both houses are situated in Stuttgart.

(from Paul Schmitthenner, *Die Baukunst im neuen Reich* (Munich, 1934), figures 12, 13).

to capture the different facets of the development of Modernism and to embrace any asynchronies and particular regional features.[75] This term is more inclusive and open than the previous circumlocutions referring to a 'different' or, even more judgemental, 'conservative Modernism'.

For most architects, issues of form had become of secondary importance by the year 1930. The financial crash of 1929 had catastrophic consequences for the construction industry; both private investors and public authorities were affected, and many housing projects came to a halt. Unemployment increased, erratically, and in the private housing market this often led to homelessness for those who were unable to pay their rent. Slatan Dudow's 1930 film *How the Berlin Worker Lives*, from the communist-sympathizing producers Prometheus Films, gave a vivid portrayal of the problem. In the face of this existential threat, the Reich government passed some emergency legislation at the start of October 1931 (the third Brüning emergency decree) to initiate a programme of so-called settlements for the unemployed (*Erwerbslosensiedlung*), to be constructed on low-cost land at the city's periphery and to provide kitchen gardens and animal stalls to promote self-sufficiency. In order to keep costs down, the future occupants were to take part in the construction work.[76]

The programme took inspiration from the small building settlements of the early post-war years. Standards were once again distinctly lower for the city-edge settlements, whereas they had gradually improved over the years of building large housing estates. Average homes were about 70 square metres in 1927, and these small houses were only 40 to 50 square metres.[77] Most had no bath or toilet, since the peripheral sites were not yet linked up to the main water and drainage services. The toilet and washing facilities were either in an outhouse or, where there was one, in the cellar. Paths and roads were unmetalled and the public transport links left much to be desired—a major disadvantage for those seeking work.

Architects and specialist publications devoted much attention to the urban and economic questions raised by the 'settlements for the unemployed'. In October 1931 Martin Wagner, the Berlin head of the municipal building department, led on announcing an architectural competition euphemistically entitled 'The Growing House': it proposed the construction of tiny houses that would lend themselves to extension when conditions became favourable. The submissions were principally in the Neues Bauen idiom.[78] When two months later a government decree ordered that standard designs be produced for detached and semi-detached houses with pitched roofs, this became the almost universal norm.[79] A high roofline offered the opportunity to add an extra habitable room in the roofspace at a later date. The return to the tiny house settlement blueprints of the early 1920s also meant a revival of the earlier patterns of houses. As a result, it is not always easy to tell whether a group of houses dates from 1919, 1932, or the Nazi era. The National Socialist housing policies followed seamlessly on from the design principles that emerged during the economic crash; and Nazi propaganda took the opportunity to draw a clear line under the large Neues Bauen housing estates of the Weimar Republic, which they derogatorily branded a symbol of the so-called 'System era'.

Against the background of the severe economic crisis in Germany, an explicit invitation arrived in 1930 to work with the Soviet government to construct more than a million housing units in new towns and settlements. Ernst May accepted, together with over twenty colleagues from Frankfurt. Hannes Meyer, the only true Socialist among the directors of the Bauhaus, also responded to the invitation from Moscow, with a number of his architecture graduates.[80] Meyer had been alleged to promote a one-sided political orientation at the school, and was therefore dismissed in August 1930. Any high-flying expectations, however, were brought to naught by Stalin's abrupt change in cultural policy, but for the supposedly left-wing architects a return to Germany in the wake of the National Socialist seizure of power was not an option. The Swiss Meyer was able to return to his home country, whereas May went into exile in Kenya.[81] The exodus from Germany had begun. The marginalization of all those of Jewish origin as well as the outlawing of Neues Bauen were both good reasons to leave the country. Some exiles, such as Erich Mendelsohn and Hugo Leipziger, were affected by both these factors. Most moved to Turkey, North and South America, and to the British Mandate territory of Palestine.[82] Yet even the advocates of 'German architecture', such as Schmitthenner and Schultze-Naumburg, did not find themselves carrying out the architectural work they might have hoped for during the Nazi era. They were left in the cold by Albert Speer and his circle, who introduced a competing set of younger colleagues, among them students and former colleagues of Neues Bauen architects, such as Ernst Neufert and Egon Eiermann.[83]

Looking back, what remains now? The National Socialist seizure of power in 1933 triggered biographical disruptions and formal caesuras, yet the major realignments in architecture and urban development during the Weimar Republic were significant in the long term. In terms of residential development, pressures on crowded inner cities were relieved so that they could become 'shopping cities', residential areas in the suburbs became more open and green, and the construction of infrastructure developed. This was made possible thanks to policies that for the first time enabled housing associations and municipalities to control the construction of social housing and to set new sanitary standards; in the light of the spectacular rent rises of the early twenty-first century these developments look exemplary. It did not prove possible, given the financial constraints of the 1920s, fully to solve the housing crisis, especially since the world financial crisis stirred up a new wave of unemployment and deprivation, but the balance sheet of housing construction during the Weimar Republic is on the whole positive. There were 2.8 million new homes built, and whereas the average household had comprised five people in 1918, by 1933 it was down to four.[84]

Only a small proportion of the homes constructed were in the 'new' architectural style, and yet its influence is what is best remembered. The leading personalities of Neues Bauen were members of a transnational European avant-garde network, but it was initially due to German exiles that the ideas circulated more globally. After 1945 the Modernism ostracized by the National Socialists acquired a new symbolic significance. Some champions of Neues Bauen were able to build on their success during the Weimar era: Hans Scharoun was commissioned to plan the reconstruction of Greater Berlin until the city was fully divided in 1948 and the Stalinist culture doctrine took over. During the following Cold War years, Otto Bartning, Walter Gropius, Le Corbusier, and other 'star architects' of international Modernism showcased the 1957 International Architecture Exhibition in the West Berlin Hansa quarter; their housing solutions were presented as a contrast to the Socialist Realism of the Stalin-Allee in East Berlin. Then at the 1958 World's Fair in Brussels the Federal Republic staged a pavilion group designed by Sep Ruf and Egon Eiermann in glass and steel that consciously echoed the self-representation of the Weimar Republic in the Barcelona Pavilion by Mies van der Rohe.[85]

Translated from German by Sarah Patey.

Notes

1. See e.g. the focus in two recent American publications on the Weimar Republic: Eric Weitz, *Weimar Germany: Promise and Tragedy* (Princeton: Princeton University Press, 2007), 41–79; John V. Maciuika, 'The Politics of Art and Architecture at the Bauhaus, 1919–1933', in Peter E. Gordon and John P. McCormick (eds), *Weimar Thought* (Princeton: Princeton University Press, 2013), 291–315.

2. Bruno Taut, 'Ein Architektur-Programm: Flugblatt des Arbeitsrats für Kunst', Christmas 1918, cited in Ulrich Conrads (ed.), *Programme und Manifeste zur Architektur des 20. Jahrhunderts* (Gütersloh: De Gruyter, 1975), 38–43.
3. The Work Council of Art had a stronger representation of architects, while the November group was stronger in the fine arts. On the former, see Manfred Schlösser, *Arbeitsrat für Kunst: Berlin 1918-1921* (Berlin: Akademie der Künste, 1980); on the latter see Thomas Köhler, Ralf Burmeister, and Janina Nentwig (eds), *Freiheit: Die Kunst der Novembergruppe 1918-1935* (Munich: Prestel, 2018).
4. Peter Hahn, 'Black Box Bauhaus: Ideen und Utopien der frühen Jahre', in Rolf Bothe (ed.), *Das frühe Bauhaus und Johannes Itten* (Ostfildern: Hatje, 1995), 13–35, here 17–18. On the Bauhaus more generally see Magdalena Droste, *Bauhaus 1919-1933*, rev. ed. (Cologne: Taschen, 2019); Philipp Oswalt, *Marke Bauhaus 1919-2019: Der Sieg der ikonischen Form über den Gebrauch* (Zurich: Scheidegger & Spiess, 2019).
5. Oswalt, *Marke Bauhaus*, 35–42.
6. Bruno Taut, *Die Stadtkrone* (Jena: Eugen Diederichs, 1919). On Taut, see Winfried Nerdinger and Kristina Hartmann (eds), *Bruno Taut 1880-1938: Architekt zwischen Tradition und Avantgarde* (Stuttgart and Munich: Deutsche Verlags Anstalt, 2001).
7. Paul Löbe, *Erinnerungen eines Reichstagspräsidenten* (Berlin: Arani, 1949), 49. On the Centennial Hall, see Jerzy Ilkosz, *Max Berg's Centennial Hall and Exhibition Grounds in Wrocław* (Wrocław: Muzeum Architektury, 2006).
8. For specialist terms, see Wolfgang Pehnt, *Die Architektur des Expressionismus*, 2nd rev. ed. (Stuttgart: G. Hatje, 1998). On the Crystal Chain correspondence, see Iain Boyd Whyte and Romana Schneider (eds), *The Cristal Chain Letters: Architectural Fantasies by Bruno Taut and his Circle* (Cambridge, MA: MIT Press, 1985).
9. Florian Zimmermann (ed.), *Der Schrei nach dem Turmhaus: Der Ideenwettbewerb am Bahnhof Friedrichstraße Berlin 1921/22* (Berlin: Argon, 1988).
10. Rainer Stommer, '"Germanisierung des Wolkenkratzers": Die Hochhausdebatte in Deutschland bis 1921', *Kritische Berichte*, 10 (1982), 36–54; Zimmermann, *Der Schrei*, 187–90.
11. Zimmermann, *Der Schrei*, 188; Dietrich Neumann, *Die Wolkenkratzer kommen! Deutsche Hochhäuser der zwanziger Jahre. Debatte. Projekte. Bauten* (Braunschweig and Wiesbaden: Vieweg, 1995), 169. In Aug. 1920 the Free City of Danzig was placed under the supervision of the League of Nations, not attached either to Germany or to Poland.
12. Max Berg, 'Hochhäuser im Stadtbild', *Wasmuths Monatshefte für Baukunst*, 6 (1921–2), 102. The head of the municipal building department in Breslau, Max Berg, was an important contributor to the debate; see Jerzy Ilkosz and Beate Störtkuhl (eds), *Hochhäuser für Breslau 1919-1932* (Delmenhorst: Aschenbeck & Holstein, 1997).
13. Berg, *Hochhäuser*, 102.
14. Zimmermann, *Der Schrei*.
15. Manfred F. Fischer, *Das Chilehaus in Hamburg. Architektur und Vision* (Berlin: Gebr. Mann, 1999).
16. Fritz Höger, 'Der neue deutsche Baustil', *Deutsche Bauzeitung*, 63 (1929), 575.
17. Fischer, *Das Chilehaus*, 57–67, quote 59.
18. L. C-S [Pseudonym for Le Cobusier], 'Curiosité? Non: anomalie!', *L'Esprit Nouveau: Revue Internationale d'Esthétique*, 2/9 (1921), 1017: 'L'emploi systématique de la verticale, en Allemagne, est un mysticisme …'.

19. See Art. 155 of the Weimar Constitution. A contemporary assessment of developments between 1918 and 1928 and the measures taken is Albert Gut (ed.), *Der Wohnungsbau in Deutschland nach dem Weltkriege* (Munich: Bruckmann, 1928). See Axel Schildt and Arnold Sywottek (eds), *Massenwohnung und Eigenheim: Wohnungsbau und Wohnen in der Großstadt seit dem Ersten Weltkrieg* (Frankfurt/Main and New York: Campus, 1988); Gert Kähler (ed.), *Geschichte des Wohnens. 1918-1945: Reform—Reaktion—Zerstörung* (Stuttgart: Deutsche Verlags-Anstalt, 1996).
20. Beate Störtkuhl, *Moderne Architektur in Schlesien 1900 bis 1939: Baukultur und Politik* (Munich: Oldenbourg, 2013), 156-63.
21. Statistical data are in Rolf Kornemann, 'Gesetze, Gesetze ... Die amtliche Wohnungspolitik in der Zeit von 1918 bis 1945 in Gesetzen, Verordnungen und Erlassen', in Kähler, *Geschichte des Wohnens*, 599-723, here 704-21.
22. Rudolf Eberstadt, *Handbuch des Wohnungswesens und der Wohnungsfrage*, 2nd rev. ed. (Jena: Fischer, 1910).
23. Gert Kähler, 'Nicht nur Neues Bauen. Stadtbau, Wohnung, Architektur', in Kähler, *Geschichte des Wohnens*, 303-401.
24. Kristina Hartmann, *Deutsche Gartenstadtbewegung: Kulturpolitik und Gesellschaftsform* (Munich: Heinz Moos, 1976).
25. Archiwum Państowe we Wrocławiu [State Archive in Wrocław], Rejencja Wrocławska, Sign. 16482: 'Bericht über die geschäftliche Lage der Schlesischen Heimstätte Breslau, Geschäftsjahr 1922', 117.
26. Heinrich Tessenow, *Hausbau und dergleichen* (Berlin: B. Cassirer, 1916).
27. On Schütte-Lihotzky see Marcel Bois and Bernadette Reinhold (eds), *Margarete Schütte-Lihotzky—Architektur—Politik—Geschlecht: Neue Perspektiven auf Leben und Werk* (Basel: Birkhäuser, 2019). On the part played by women architects in the 1920s see Mary Pepchinski, Christina Budde, Wolfgang Voigt, and Peter Cachola Schmal (eds), *Frau Architekt: Seit mehr als 100 Jahren: Frauen im Architektenberuf—Over 100 Years of Women as Professional Architects* (Tübingen: Berlin Wasmuth, 2017).
28. Ernst May, 'Oberschlesien!', *Schlesisches Heim* (1921), 299; Michael Prinz, *Der Sozialstaat hinter dem Haus: Wirtschaftliche Zukunftserwartungen, Selbstversorgung und regionale Vorbilder: Westfalen und Südwestdeutschland 1920-1960* (Paderborn: Schöningh, 2012).
29. Overview in Kähler, *Geschichte des Wohnens*; see also Maiken Umbach, 'The Deutscher Werkbund, Globalization and the Invention of Modern Vernacular' in Umbach and Bernd Hüppauf (eds), *Vernacular Modernism: Heimat, Globalization and the Built Environment* (Stanford, CA: Stanford University Press, 2005), 114-40.
30. Gut, *Der Wohnungsbau*.
31. See the illustrations in Gut, *Der Wohnungsbau*, and Kähler, *Geschichte des Wohnens*, 353-60.
32. Examples in Kähler, *Geschichte des Wohnens*, 357-8.
33. See Vittorio Magnago Lampugnani and Romana Schneider (eds), *Moderne Architektur in Deutschland 1900 bis 1950*, vol. 1. *Reform und Tradition* (Stuttgart: G. Hatje, 1992); vol. 2. *Expressionismus und Neue Sachlichkeit* (Stuttgart: G Hatje, 1994); Annemarie Jaeggi, 'Wanderprediger der Moderne', in Nina Wiedemeyer (ed.), *Original Bauhaus* (Munich: Prestel, 2019), 79-83.
34. The phrase quoted in the subheading comes from Gustav Adolf Platz, *Die Baukunst der neuesten Zeit*, 2nd rev ed. (Berlin: Propyläen, 1930).

35. On the Dutch impetus, see Antonia Gruhn-Zimmermann, 'Das Bezwingen der Wirklichkeit: Adolf Behne und die moderne holländische Architektur', in Magdalena Bushart (ed.), *Adolf Behne: Essays zu seiner Kunst- und Architekturkritik* (Berlin: Gebr. Mann, 2000), 117–45.
36. See Adolf Behne, 'Holländische Baukunst in der Gegenwart', *Wasmuths Monatshefte für Baukunst*, 6 (1921–2), 1–32.
37. Annemarie Jaeggi, *Fagus: Industriekultur zwischen Werkbund und Bauhaus* (Berlin: Jovis, 1998); Oswalt, *Marke Bauhaus*, 14–16.
38. Herman van Bergeijk, '"Ein großer Vorsprung gegenüber Deutschland": Die niederländischen Architekten auf der Bauhausausstellung von 1923 in Weimar', *RIHA Journal*, 64 (2013), online at: <https://www.riha-journal.org/articles/2013/2013-jan-mar/van-bergeijk-bauhausausstellung-1923 >; Ita Heinze-Greenberg, '"Gegen Mittag Land in Sicht": Reisen nach Holland, Palästina, in die USA und nach Rußland', in Regina Stephan (ed.), *Erich Mendelsohn, Architekt 1887–1953: Gebaute Welten* (Ostfildern: Hatje, 1998), 72–91, 75.
39. Heinze-Greenberg, 'Gegen Mittag Land in Sicht'. Quotes from Erich Mendelsohn, 'Die internationale Übereinstimmung des neuen Baugedankens oder Dynamik und Funktion (1923)', in Mendelsohn, *Das Gesamtschaffen des Architekten. Skizzen—Entwürfe—Bauten* (Berlin: Rudolf Mosse, 1930), 22–34, 27–8.
40. Stephan, *Erich Mendelsohn*.
41. See van Bergeijk, 'Ein großer Vorsprung'; Klaus-Jürgen Winkler, 'In der Wiege lag noch kein weißer Würfel. Zur Architektur am frühen Bauhaus', in Bothe, *Das frühe Bauhaus*, 283–319, here 298–308.
42. Letter from Gropius to Behne, 12 May 1923, quoted in van Bergeijk, 'Ein großer Vorsprung', n. 5.
43. Walter Gropius, *Internationale Architektur* (Munich: A. Langen, 1925); Ludwig Hilberseimer, *Internationale Neue Baukunst* (Stuttgart: Hoffmann, 1927); Platz, *Die Baukunst*. On the publicity impact of the 1923 Bauhaus Exhibition see Oswalt, *Marke Bauhaus*, 18–25.
44. Le Corbusier, *Vers une architecture* (Paris: G. Crès et Cie, 1923).
45. The modern orthography of the 1920s also allowed the lower case: 'neues bauen'. The term has become established in German historiography; see Norbert Huse, *'Neues Bauen' 1918 bis 1933: Moderne Architektur in der Weimarer Republik*, 2nd ed. (Berlin and Munich: Moos, 1985), 10–11.
46. Oswalt, *Marke Bauhaus 1919–2019*, 34, 43–5.
47. Monika Markgraf, *Die Dessauer Bauhausbauten* (Leipzig: Seeman, 2016); Oswalt, *Marke Bauhaus 1919–2019*, 35–42.
48. Droste, *Bauhaus*, 237–44, 404–12.
49. William Owen Harrod, 'The Vereinigte Staatsschulen für freie und angewandte Kunst and the Mainstream of German Modernism', *Architectural History: Journal of the Society of Architectural Historians of Great Britain*, 52 (2009), 233–69.
50. Vladimir Šlapeta, 'Adolf Rading: Der Lehrer und seine Schüler', in Jerzy Ilkosz and Beate Störtkuhl (eds), *Adolf Rading in Breslau: Neues Bauen in der Weimarer Republik* (Berlin and Boston: De Gruyter Oldenbourg, 2019), 139–65.
51. Jörg Haspel and Annemarie Jaeggi, *Siedlungen der Berliner Moderne* (Munich: Deutscher Kunstverlag, 2007); see <http://www.stadtentwicklung.berlin.de/denkmal/denkmale_in_berlin/de/weltkulturerbe/siedlungen/index.shtml> (accessed 31 Jan. 2020).

52. Christoph Mohr and Michael Müller, *Funktionalität und Moderne: Das Neue Frankfurt und seine Bauten 1925–1933* (Cologne: Fricke, 1984); Claudia Quiring, Wolfgang Voigt, Peter Cachola Schmal, and Eckhard Herrel (eds), *Ernst May (1886–1970)* (Munich. London and New York: Prestel, 2011).
53. Piotr M. Lubiński, 'Nowy Frankfurt [New Frankfurt]', *Architektura i Budownictwo*, 6 (1930), 467–77.
54. Karin Kirsch, *Die Weißenhofsiedlung: Werkbund-Ausstellung 'Die Wohnung'—Stuttgart 1927* (Stuttgart: Deutsche Verlags-Anstalt, 1987); on mechanization, see Eckart J. Gillen and Ulrike Lorenz (eds), *Konstruktion der Welt: Kunst und Ökonomie* (Bielefeld and Berlin: Kerber, 2018).
55. Joan Campbell, *Der Deutsche Werkbund 1907–1934* (Stuttgart: Klett-Cotta, 1981); Winfried Nerdinger (ed.), *100 Jahre Deutscher Werkbund, 1907/2007* (Munich: Prestel, 2007).
56. Campbell, *Der Deutsche Werkbund*, 232–6.
57. Hilberseimer, *Internationale Neue Baukunst*.
58. Helen Barr (ed.), *Neues Wohnen 1929/2009: Frankfurt und the Second Congrès International d'Architecture Moderne* (Berlin: Jovis, 2011).
59. Ibid.
60. Henry Russel Hitchcock and Philipp Johnson, *The International Style: Architecture since 1922* (New York: W. W. Norton, 1932). The history and some images from the exposition are online at <https://www.moma.org/calendar/exhibitions/2044> (accessed 15 Feb. 2020).
61. Jadwiga Urbanik (ed.), *A Way to Modernity: The Werkbund Estates 1927–1932* (Wrocław: Museum of Architecture in Wroclaw, 2016); Matthias Schirren (ed.), *Bauen und Wohnen: Die Geschichte der Werkbundsiedlungen* (Tübingen: Wasmuth, 2016).
62. Störtkuhl, *Moderne Architektur*, 246–52.
63. Paul Sigel, *Exponiert: Deutsche Pavillons auf Weltausstellungen* (Berlin: Bauwesen, 2000), 101–32.
64. Platz, *Die Baukunst*; Walter Müller-Wulckow, *Deutsche Baukunst der Gegenwart* (Königstein im Taunus and Leipzig: Langwiesche, 1929); see also Claudia Quiring, Andreas Rothaus, and Rainer Stamm (eds), *Neue Baukunst: Architektur der Moderne in Bild und Buch. Der Bestand Neue Baukunst aus dem Nachlass Müller-Wulckow im Landesmuseum Oldenburg* (Bielefeld-Berlin: Kerber, 2013).
65. Daniela Hammer-Tugendhat, Ivo Hammer, and Wolf Tegethoff, *Das Haus Tugendhat: Ludwig Mies van der Rohe* (Basel: Birkhäuser, 2015); Robin Schuldenfrei, *Luxury and Modernism: Architecture and the Object in Germany 1900–1933* (Princeton: Princeton University Press, 2018).
66. Vladimír Šlapeta, 'Adolf Rading and Oskar Schlemmer: Haus Dr. Rabe—Mensch und Raum', in Ilkosz and Störtkuhl, *Adolf Rading*, 109–35.
67. Barbara Miller Lane, *Architecture and Politics in Germany, 1918– 1945*, 2nd ed. (Cambridge, MA: Harvard University Press, 1985), 125–68.
68. Wolfgang Voigt and Hartmut Frank (eds), *Paul Schmitthenner, 1884–1963* (Tübingen: E. Wasmuth, 2003); Wolfgang Voigt and Roland May (eds), *Paul Bonatz, 1877–1956* (Tübingen: Wasmuth, 2011).
69. Stefanie Plarre, *Die Kochenhofsiedlung—das Gegenmodell zur Weißenhofsiedlung: Paul Schmitthenners Siedlungsprojekt in Stuttgart von 1927 bis 1933* (Stuttgart: Hohenheim, 2001); Umbach, 'Deutscher Werkbund', 135–9.
70. Paul Schultze-Naumburg, *Kunst und Rasse* (Munich: Lehmann, 1928); Paul Schmitthenner, *Baugestaltung, Folge 1: Das deutsche Wohnhaus* (Stuttgart: Deutsche Verlags-Anstalt, 1932).

See Anke Blümm, 'Entartete Baukunst'? Zum Umgang mit dem Neuen Bauen 1933–1945 (Munich: Wilhelm Fink, 2013).
71. Carsten Liesenberg, 'Heinrich Tessenow und die "andere Moderne"', in Beate Störtkuhl and Rafał Makała (eds), Nicht nur Bauhaus: Netzwerke der Moderne in Mitteleuropa (Berlin and Boston: De Gruyter Oldenbourg, 2020), 62–81.
72. Wolfgang Voigt and Ingeborg Flagge (eds), Dominikus Böhm 1880–1955 (Tübingen: Wasmuth, 2005).
73. Claudia Quiring and Hans-Georg Lippert (eds), Dresdner Moderne 1919–1933: Neue Ideen für Stadt, Architektur und Menschen (Dresden: Sandstein, 2019).
74. Lampugnani and Schneider, Moderne Architektur; Romana Schneider and Winfried Wang (eds), Moderne Architektur in Deutschland 1900 bis 2000, vol. 3. Macht und Monument (Stuttgart: Hatje, 1998).
75. Quiring and Lippert, Dresdner Moderne, 12.
76. Tilman Harlander, Karin Hater, and Franz Meiers, Siedeln in der Not: Umbruch von Wohnungspolitik und Siedlungsbau am Ende der Weimarer Republik (Hamburg: Christians, 1988).
77. Archiwum Państowe we Wrocławiu [State Archive in Wrocław], Akta miasta Wrocławia [Records of the city of Breslau], Sign. (2409), 12948: 'Reden und Material für Reden Oberbürgermeister Dr. Wagner', 1924–32, 8–14.
78. Martin Wagner, Das wachsende Haus: Ein Beitrag zur Lösung der städtischen Wohnungsfrage (Berlin and Leipzig: Deutsches Verlagshaus Bong, 1932).
79. Harlander et al., Siedeln in der Not, 82–100.
80. Thomas Flierl (ed.), Ernst May in der Sowjetunion 1930–1933: Texte und Dokumente (Berlin: Suhrkamp, 2012); Oswalt, Hannes Meyers, 366–82, 426–65.
81. Quiring et al., Ernst May.
82. Bernd Nicolai and Charlotte Benton (eds), Architektur und Exil: Kulturtransfer und architektonische Emigration 1930 bis 1950 (Trier: Porta Alba, 2003); Myra Warhaftig, Deutsche jüdische Architekten vor und nach 1933—das Lexikon. 500 Biographien (Berlin: Reimer, 2005); Jörg Stabenow and Ronny Schüler (eds), Vermittlungswege der Moderne— Neues Bauen in Palästina (1923–1948) (Berlin: Gebr. Mann, 2019); Artur Tanikowski, Gdynia–Tel Awiw, Warszawa: Muzeum Historii Żydów Polskich POLIN (Warsaw: Muzeum Miasta Gdyni, 2019).
83. Winfried Nerdinger, 'Bauhaus-Architekten im "Dritten Reich"', in Nerdinger (ed.), Bauhaus-Moderne im Nationalsozialismus: Zwischen Anbiederung und Verfolgung (Munich: Prestel, 1993), 153–78; Werner Durth, Deutsche Architekten: Biographische Verflechtungen 1900–1970 (Munich: dtv, 1992).
84. Statistics in Kornemann, 'Gesetze, Gesetze', in Kähler, Geschichte des Wohnens, 718.
85. Jörg Haspel and Thomas Flierl (eds), Stalinallee und Interbau 1957: Konfrontation, Konkurrenz und Koevolution der Moderne in Berlin (Berlin: Hendrick Bässler, 2017); Paul Sigel, Exponiert: Deutsche Pavillons auf Weltausstellungen (Berlin: Bauwesen, 2000), 179–205.

Bibliography

Cambell, Joan, *The German Werkbund: The Politics of Reform in the Applied Arts* (Princeton: Princeton University Press, 1978).

Huse, Norbert, *'Neues Bauen' 1918 bis 1933: Moderne Architektur in der Weimarer Republik*, 2nd ed. (Berlin and Munich: Moos, 1985).

Kähler, Gert (ed.), *Geschichte des Wohnens: 1918–1945. Reform—Reaktion—Zerstörung* (Stuttgart: Deutsche Verlags-Anstalt, 1996).

Lampugnani, Vittorio Magnago, and Romana Schneider (eds), *Moderne Architektur in Deutschland 1900 bis 1950*, 2 vols (Stuttgart: G. Hatje, 1994).

Miller Lane, Barbara, *Architecture and Politics in Germany, 1918–1945*, 2nd ed. (Cambridge, MA: Harvard University Press, 1985).

Neumann, Dietrich, *Die Wolkenkratzer kommen! Deutsche Hochhäuser der zwanziger Jahre. Debatte. Projekte. Bauten* (Braunschweig and Wiesbaden: Vieweg, 1995).

Nicolai, Bernd, and Charlotte Benton (eds), *Architektur und Exil: Kulturtransfer und architektonische Emigration 1930 bis 1950* (Trier: Porta Alba, 2003).

Oswalt, Philipp, *Marke Bauhaus 1919–2019: Der Sieg der ikonischen Form über den Gebrauch* (Zurich: Scheidegger & Spiess, 2019).

Pehnt, Wolfgang, *Die Architektur des Expressionismus*, 2nd ed. (Stuttgart: G. Hatje, 1998).

Quiring, Claudia, Wolfgang Voigt, Peter Cachola Schmal, and Eckhard Herrel (eds), *Ernst May (1886–1970)* (Munich: Prestel, 2011).

Stephan, Regina (ed.), *Erich Mendelsohn, Architekt 1887–1953: Gebaute Welten* (Ostfildern: Hatje, 1998).

CHAPTER 30

RELIGIOUS CULTURES AND CONFESSIONAL POLITICS

TODD H. WEIR AND UDI GREENBERG

For a long time, religion was a marginal theme in the study of the Weimar Republic. While scholars of the Imperial era often noted how deeply it shaped Germany's social, intellectual, and political life, the most influential synthetic accounts on Weimar, which were written in the 1980s, 1990s, and 2000s, made only passing reference to religion, leaving the topic mostly to specialized church historians.[1] Over the last few decades, however, scholars have increasingly recognized that debates about religion's place in the public sphere were central to Weimar's politics. Politicians regularly clashed over religion's proper role in education and public morality, and for many Germans, religion or the lack thereof was the anchor point of an entire social-cultural milieu, and often determined their choice of membership in unions, social organizations, and political parties.[2]

In this chapter, we set out the religious structures and dynamics that underpinned Weimar's political landscape. In particular, we focus on two axes, or two sets of relationships, that were established in the nineteenth century and which continued to dominate religious thought and politics: the rivalry between Protestants and Catholics, and the antagonism between Christians and secularists (other elements of religious conflict, especially over the status of Judaism and antisemitism, are discussed elsewhere in this handbook). We proceed in three parts. First, after a brief overview of the two axes' development in the imperial period, we explore their place in the republic's formation. We argue that the revolution of 1918/19 altered but did not fundamentally change the faultlines of religious politics and social tensions. Second, this chapter examines the religious cultures that evolved within the confessional camps. It surveys the main developments and debates that defined the Protestant, Catholic, and secularist milieus during the 1920s, and charts the relationships between them. Third, this chapter focuses on Weimar's final years from 1928 to 1933, when religious politics reached heightened intensity. We trace how anticlerical campaigns on the left helped spark intense anti-secularist mobilization among Christians, and how that, in turn, fostered authoritarian projects based on a hoped–for Catholic–Protestant cooperation (of which National Socialism represented one variant). Finally, we briefly reflect in the conclusion on the ways in which these confessional dynamics continued to shape German life after the republic's demise. We note how the interconfessional alliance between Catholics and Protestants was resurrected after the Second World War to provide a basis for Christian Democracy, the alliance that presided over West Germany's reconstruction. Confessional divides, then, were more than matters of church history. They had far-reaching impacts on cultural life and political stability both during and after the Weimar Republic.

THE TWO CONFESSIONAL AXES FROM THE IMPERIAL ERA TO THE REVOLUTION OF 1918/19

The term confession (*Konfession*) came from ecclesiastical language, and was initially used to refer to Lutheran adherents of the *Confessio Augustana* (1530).[3] However, after 1800, it came to be applied more generally to the Catholic and the Protestant churches and the social milieus that they organized, and it is in this sense that modern historians generally use it. Confessionalism is the rivalry and conflict between the three Christian churches (Lutheran, Reformed Protestant, and Catholic) produced in the course of the Reformation and Counter-Reformation. In Germany's nineteenth-century transition into modern nationhood, confessionalism played a significant role. The hostility between the Protestant majority (62 per cent of the population), which was strongest in northern and central Germany, and the Catholic minority (36 per cent), which was concentrated in the southern and western regions, was among the defining cultural and political dynamics of the Imperial era. With the forging of the new German state in the 1860s and 1870s new life was breathed into old tensions, as an avalanche of books and pamphlets on both sides tirelessly attributed to the other political subversion, social deviance, and sexual promiscuity. Confessional animosities shaped political life, most notoriously when the Protestant-led national authorities unleashed in the 1870s a harsh campaign to suppress Catholic autonomy and institutions, which contemporaries called the *Kulturkampf* (cultural struggle). But even after most restrictions on Catholic life were lifted in 1886/87, confessionalism continued to shape many Germans' participation in modern society. Church-going Catholics and Protestants often maintained separate sports clubs, reading groups, and labour unions; even party affiliation was strongly confessional, with the Centre Party being largely Catholic and the conservative and liberal parties largely Protestant. Indeed, even though believers sometimes defied these tensions through intermarriage and friendships, what one historian called Germany's 'second confessional age' lasted into the mid-twentieth century. Anti-Catholic and anti-Protestant organizations proliferated, while efforts to repeal legal discrimination against

Catholics, especially regarding public funding, faltered in 1903 and 1905, to be fully removed only after the First World War.[4]

Just as important for the empire's religious politics—and with crucial consequences for Weimar later—was the rise of a second confessional antagonism, the one between Christians of both churches and their secular opponents. Beginning in the 1840s, Germany witnessed the emergence of a broad cultural movement that advocated for secularism. What its proponents called for was not merely state neutrality in religious matters (the meaning most scholars today associate with the term 'secularism'), but rather the cultural transformation of society based on an immanent worldview that would largely replace established religions. While secularism's organizational roots were found in rationalist Christian sects, by the Imperial era, the movement became increasingly identified with socialism. Although the Social Democratic Party of Germany (SPD) endorsed state religious neutrality and private freedom of conscience, its press and organizations gave leeway to those who promoted radical calls for anti-religious culture. Socialist education associations, for example, encouraged workers to read anticlerical, popular scientific works such as Ludwig Büchner's *Force and Matter* (1855) or Ernst Haeckel's *Riddle of the Universe* (1899), which were materialist (arguing that only mechanical explanations of life were possible) as well as monistic (claiming that all phenomena of life—from biology to consciousness and culture—were ultimately expressions of the same universal and evolving substance). Many socialists had first 'converted' to this worldview before moving on to Marx (if they ever did). And they became susceptible to the campaigns of freethinkers calling for church leaving. By the outbreak of the First World War, many high-ranking socialists had formally renounced their church membership, and become confessionless 'dissidents', thus reinforcing the link between secularism and socialism in public perception. Protestant and Catholic leaders viewed these developments with deep alarm. Secularism, they argued, would lead to anarchy, replace family bonds with sexual promiscuity, and destroy Germany's school system (a field in which the churches had long been deeply involved). This threat led to a reorientation of Protestant and Catholic apologetics from defence of the specific truth of their confession to a general defence of Christianity. As one of the era's leading Protestant apologists stated in 1897: 'The Christian worldview currently faces a non-Christian one, and more and more there threatens a division of the whole line of thought in the modern world.'[5]

With confessional temperatures around both axes running high, many Germans greeted the announcement of war in August 1914 with relief. For they hoped that the joint war effort would bring an end to religious polarization, an optimism best captured by the Kaiser's famous speech just prior to the declaration of war, in which he stated 'I no longer recognize any parties or any confessions; today we are all German brothers and only German brothers.'[6] Some tentative steps were taken by the government to dismantle aspects of confessional discrimination. In 1917, for example, the government lifted the ban on the Jesuit order enacted during the *Kulturkampf*.[7] Yet, as the war dragged on, political divisions re-emerged and by the final year of the war three political camps had appeared, each with implications for the confessional landscape. On the left, a revolutionary socialist wing emerged that gathered most of the SPD's secularists. On the right, the Vaterlandspartei formed which combined national Lutheranism and a growing antisemitic *völkisch* wing, cheered by the Kaiser's talk of a 'Prussian-German-Germanic worldview' rising to win the war. In the middle, an interfactional dialogue took place between moderate socialists, members of the Centre Party, and liberal Democrats.[8]

When the revolution broke in November 1918, hastening the end of the war and establishing a new republic, its course and its consequences were informed by the dynamics of both confessional axes. At first, when the socialists emerged as the country's leaders, it appeared as though the revolution might bring about the triumph of secularism. The radical freethinker, Adolph Hoffmann, who from November 1918 to early January 1919 served as the Co-Minister of Education and Culture in Prussia, sought to secularize the German state by revolutionary fiat. He decreed the strict separation of church and state, the cutting of state subsidies for churches, the equality of dissident children, and the end of school prayer.[9] These policies, if implemented, would have removed the legal framework of the confessional system in Germany's largest state. Both Protestants and Catholics, however, mobilized against these measures. Parents across Prussia poured into the streets in mass demonstrations, and clerics and teachers issued proclamations decrying their destructive impact. Worried about the impact this would have on the electorate, moderate socialists rescinded most of Hoffmann's orders and postponed further action on religious matters until after elections to the National Assembly, which took place in January 1919.[10]

Despite assurances made by the moderate socialists, the Christian confessional parties ran their electoral campaigns for the National Assembly as a defence of Christianity. Following this logic, some Catholic and Protestant theologians, like Protestant minister from Nuremberg, J. Schiller, called for a joint Christian 'holy alliance' against the socialist 'materialism' and a few prominent politicians floated plans to create a single Christian party. However, existential anxiety led Christians to seek the safety of their traditional confessional structures, and proposals to unite the Centre Party with Protestant-dominated parties were nixed. When it came to forming a Reich government in February 1919, the Centre Party, led by Matthias Erzberger, chose to work with the SPD and liberal German Democratic Party (DDP). While its leaders were hardly enchanted with socialism or liberalism, they viewed cooperation as the best way to defend Catholic autonomy and end anti-Catholic discrimination, goals forged through the prolonged tensions with Protestants.[11] Crucial to this coalition, which formed the bedrock of Weimar democracy, was the flexibility of the socialist leadership in the policies of greatest concern to the Centre Party, namely those relating to its confessional prerogatives. This resulted in a number of compromises in the religious paragraphs of the Weimar Constitution, which modified rather than eliminated the confessional system. It has been called a 'limping' separation between state and church that satisfied no one, but produced a liveable solution for most. The constitution, which was ratified in August 1919, gave prominence to the SPD's promise of religious neutrality by declaring 'there is no state church', yet it left many of the churches' privileges intact.

State authorities continued to collect church taxes and clergy continued to maintain oversight over many publicly funded schools. In a further compromise, the constitution declared in principle that associations that 'dedicate themselves to the common cultivation of a worldview' could apply to become 'corporations of public law', meaning secularist associations could receive the same status given to churches. However, when such applications were later filed by socialist freethinkers they were largely rejected. In short, the outcome of revolution and state formation was a de facto preservation of the confessional system, despite de jure secularization.[12]

Because the republic was the product of a socialist–Catholic cooperation and had ended Protestantism's privileged position achieved by its close connection to the monarchy, it enjoyed little legitimacy among leading Protestants. A few prominent figures, like theologian Ernst Troeltsch, joined the liberals, and many urban and educated Protestants initially voted for the DDP. Protestantism's conservative wing, however, which included most members of the clergy, remained hostile to both secularists and Catholics, and to the new democratic regime. The revolution had ended Protestantism's unique ties to state institutions: since the Reformation, the monarchs of each German state also served as *summus episcopus* (supreme governor) of the local Protestant churches (the Prussian king, for example, was the head of the Protestant Church of the Old Union of Prussia), an arrangement made impossible by the abdication of the monarchs in 1918. Indeed, the loss of privileges—especially in political appointments—was conceived by many Protestant elites as a dreadful persecution. Conservative Protestants gathered in the German National People's Party (DNVP), which was founded in 1918 from a union of smaller conservative parties and which rejected the republic's legitimacy. In congresses and publications, many Protestants lambasted the republic as an importation of France's 'foreign' secularist and anticlerical model, and the Lutheran theologian Emanuel Hirsch proclaimed that 'Christian love ... must resist a democratic regime'.[13]

The party-political landscape that emerged from the revolution had a clear confessional arrangement, as shown by statistical information on the confessions of Weimar era parliamentarians (Table 30.1). Both the liberal and conservative parties were dominated by Protestants. The Centre Party retained its strictly Catholic identity, and continued to use a fortress as its main symbol, a sign of its defensive position in a hostile confessional landscape.[14] Secularists, whether freethinkers, free religious, or monists, were registered as confessionless dissidents and concentrated in the Marxist parties. The Communist party (KPD), formally founded in early 1919, profiled itself as the party of atheism and made church exit all but mandatory for its leadership. The SPD faction, although overwhelmingly comprised of dissidents, did have a significant number of Christian and Jewish identified members of the Reichstag. Still, most parties only gathered about 10 per cent of their members from another confession. The one exception was the National Socialist Workers Party (NSDAP), whose membership was largely Protestant but whose Reichstag delegates were about 20 per cent Catholic, making it Weimar's most interconfessional party. We return to National Socialist religious politics later in the chapter.

Table 30.1. The confessional identification of Reichstag deputies 1918–1933.

	Communist (KPD)	Socialist (SPD)	Liberal parties	Centre	Conservative parties (DNVP)	Other	Völkisch parties	NSDAP
Total number of deputies	213	341	195	214	212	43	27	347
Protestant	2	43	165	19	182	31	24	262
Catholic	0	14	17	194	28	9	2	64
Jewish	0	5	4	0	0	0	0	0
Dissidents	199	217	2	0	0	0	0	3
Not specified	12	62	7	1	2	3	1	18

Sources: Martin Schumacher (ed.), *M.d.R. Die Reichstagsabgeordneten der Weimarer Republik in der Zeit des Nationalsozialismus: Politische Verfolgung, Emigration und Ausbürgerung 1933–1945* (Düsseldorf: Droste, 1994), 29. Figures for the confessional orientation of NSDAP parliamentarians are taken from Max Schwarz (ed.), *M.d.R. Biographisches Handbuch der Reichstage* (Hanover: Verlag für Literatur und Zeitgeschehen, 1965).

CONFESSIONAL CULTURES AND RELATIONS DURING THE 1920S

On balance, the revolution and the compromises it facilitated ultimately maintained rather than upset the two axes of Germany's confessional system. Protestants and Catholics retained their mutual suspicion, while secularists continued to mobilize against both. Before turning to the interactions between the confessions, we look at their internal diversity, for when we use the term 'confession', like the terms 'milieu' or 'camp', we remain aware that these are concepts that help us make sense of a past religious and political landscape. They do not designate monolithic entities. Within each confessional milieu there were multiple divergent responses to events that followed the founding of the republic. These responses both reinforced confessional divisions and created limited room for interconfessional cooperation.

Protestantism was the most internally diverse religious culture in Germany. Alongside numerous small denominations, such as Mennonites, Seventh-Day Adventists, and Baptists, it was dominated by twenty-eight territorial churches (*Landeskirchen*), each of which drew either upon the Lutheran or the Reformed (following Ulrich Zwingli's and John Calvin's interpretation of the Reformation) heritages of their regions, except for those cases, as in Prussia, in which an administrative union between the two strands had been formed in the early nineteenth century. These churches tolerated a greater degree of theological variation than the more hierarchical Catholic Church. Two recognizable theological camps had emerged in the Wilhelmine period, each representing a different tradition of Protestant piety. Church liberals took inspiration from Friedrich Schleiermacher and conceived of Protestantism as a motor of progress, compatible and indeed supportive of scientific rationality. They saw Christianity as a historically evolving expression of religious truth, in which earlier dogmatic understandings of revelation were giving way to and finding expression in modern culture. Many so-called *Kulturprotestanten* (culture Protestants) were educated urbanites, who supported paths of social and political reform, including religious freedom in education. They were opposed by conservative or 'confessional' Protestants, who adhered to a 'positive' understanding of the truth of revelation and the traditional dogmas of the faith. Whereas many university theologians were liberal, most prominently Adolf von Harnack and Martin Rade, pastors in Germany's villages and small towns tended to be more conservative upholders of the patriarchal social order and fierce defenders of the monarchy.[15]

In response to the republic's new political realities, the Protestant churches embarked on internal restructuring. In 1922, the territorial churches founded the German Evangelical Church Federation, the first national organ to coordinate their work. Its complex structure, which blended clerical authority with elected lay representatives, organized national Protestant congresses (in 1924 in Bethel, in 1927 in Königsberg, and in 1930 in Nuremberg), at which theologians, journalists, and politicians sought to articulate a national Protestant agenda. Although many conservatives and liberals alike wanted to bring the church closer to the faithful in a 'people's church', the form of this *Volkskirche* was much debated. Church attendance among Protestants slightly declined throughout the 1920s, continuing a trend that began in the nineteenth century (mostly a result of many migrants from rural areas to the cities dropping from the church's orbit). However, the Protestant organizational universe remained vibrant. The largest organizations were dominated by conservative clergy, such as the Inner Mission, which was founded in 1848 to evangelize among the poor, particularly amongst the disaffected working classes in the growing cities. With its archipelago of charity services, educational endeavours, youth clubs, and publication apparatus, it comprised one of Germany's largest civil associations with close ties to state and politics. Similarly, the lay-led Evangelical Federation (*Evangelischer Bund*), which was founded in 1886 to mobilize against Catholicism, continued to boast a membership of over 300,000 during the 1920s, and its leaders engaged in vocal public advocacy, such as in defence of religious teachings in public schools. Between 1924 and 1930, the number of church papers climbed by 600 and reached a circulation of seventeen million, and the number of theology students jumped from 1,900 to 5,000.[16]

The collapse of monarchy and the revolution were deeply traumatic for both conservative and liberal wings of the Protestant Church, but their responses varied. Whereas Wilhelmine conservatives had been amongst the greatest supporters of the status quo, they now became political and theological revanchists. Berlin court pastor Bruno Doehring described the revolution as a 'stab in the back' of the fighting nation and decried the republic as a 'rebelling against God', while the DNVP politician and theologian Reinhard Mumm continued to express a hope for the monarchy's return. Only an authoritarian system, he claimed in works like *Christianity, Fatherland, National Community, Monarchy* (1928), could enjoy divine legitimacy, a sentiment that was echoed from the pulpits of many churches. Educator and politician Magdalene von Tiling, who led the German Protestant Women's Federation (Deutsch-Evangelischer Frauenbund), extended this logic to gender relations. Because women's essence was profoundly different than men's, she argued in fiercely anti-feminist publications, their social function had to be restricted to motherhood and family life, a belief that the Federation sought to popularize with manuals and public campaigns. These conservative circles, which tied confessional loyalties to nationalism and militarism, also railed against modern industrialism and urbanism, which they depicted as centres of decadence and social chaos. Under their influence, in 1929 the Protestant Church Federation founded a special settlement service, which helped encourage, train, and fund Protestants to migrate to agrarian regions, with the goal of restoring 'pure' and pious communities. Some conservatives offered theological innovations, such as nationalist Lutheran Paul Althaus, who sought common ground with *völkisch* thinkers. Together they promoted a theology of creation, which claimed that the German people had been entrusted by God with a divine mission that it could only fulfil through a return to military greatness and a purging of internal enemies from the national community.[17]

While nationalist conservatism was the dominant force among church leaders and lay organizations, many liberal leaders offered a different response to the new conditions of the Weimar Republic and sought to reconcile Protestant tradition with the bourgeois ethos of religious and political pluralism. Theologian Martin Rade, for example, whose weekly *Christliche Welt* was an important liberal mouthpiece, joined the DDP, welcomed the republic, and accepted separation of church and state as irreversible. He also called on the churches to go through a process of 'internal democratization', for example by subjecting the hierarchies to be elected by the laity. Jurist and politician Walter Simons, who briefly served as the country's foreign minister and was the head of the republic's highest court, similarly challenged his conservative counterparts' intense paternalism and nationalism. As the president of the Protestant Social Congress (Evangelisch-sozialer Kongress), a long-standing association of Protestant academics and politicians, he advocated for cooperation with workers and social reformers, and supported German diplomatic engagement with France and Britain.[18] The period also brought theological innovations. For some students of Harnack and Rade, the experiences of war and revolution had challenged the liberal faith in progress and thrust them into a position 'between the times' (Friedrich Gogarten). They rejected the liberal tradition in which 'all theology appears to dissolve into the discipline of history' (Rudolf Bultmann) and, in the place of earlier certitude, developed 'theologies of crisis', in which the radical break in time through the experience of God became central. As Karl Barth proposed in his epochal *Epistle to the Romans* (1919, revised in 1922), the divine is an unknown domain that cuts through human experience 'vertically from above'.[19] Another innovation was found in the movement of religious socialism, promoted by theologians Günther Dehn and Emil Fuchs, who argued that Protestantism was compatible with socialism's economic egalitarianism, a highly provocative claim even for moderates. In 1926 the Mannheim pastor Erwin Eckert founded the Federation of Religious Socialists in Germany (Bund religiöser Sozialisten in Deutschland), which aimed to provide a door for pious Christians and Jews to enter the SPD. Such voices, however, remained a minority in the Protestant universe. As the 1920s progressed, the vote share of the liberal DDP progressively declined as many churchgoing Protestants migrated to the right, and Christian socialism never gained traction beyond some small circles.[20]

The Catholic camp, too, witnessed a flurry of activity and intellectual ferment. Alongside stable, and in some regions even rising church attendance, social associations thrived. These included the People's Association for Catholic Germany (Volksverein für das katholische Deutschland), which was founded in 1890 to advocate for Catholic causes, and which boasted membership of over half a million members during the 1920s, and the charity Caritas, which was founded in 1897 to give relief to the poor. These well-established organizations were joined by new ones, such as the Mothers' Association for the Promotion of Christian Education (Mütterverein zur Förderung christlicher Kindererziehung), federations of Catholic employers, groups for the promotion of Catholic arts and music, and many others. Romano Guardini, one of Germany's most famous theologians and the leader of the youth movement Quickborn, promoted the laity as the heart of Catholic life. The church, he wrote in books like *The Opposite* (1925), had to be organized less on obedience to clerics and more on a lay community (a transition he sought to symbolize by changes to liturgy). The episcopal hierarchy, in part in an effort to control and tame these developments, inaugurated in 1928 a national programme of Catholic Action, which was an international campaign of lay activism spearheaded by Pope Pius XI to respond to the threat of secularism and secularization.[21]

Although the Catholic milieu maintained greater internal coherence than its Protestant counterparts, Catholics were also divided in their approach to modern politics, economics, and society. Conservatives subscribed to a paternalist vision of social relations, and vehemently rejected liberalism, church–state separation, and pluralism. Michael Faulhaber, the cardinal of Munich, condemned the Weimar Republic in 1922 as 'branded with the mark of Cain', a sentiment that was shared by the Bavarian People's Party (BVP), the Centre's Bavarian branch, which in November 1918 broke off from the national party to pursue a more authoritarian agenda. Reactionaries also railed against the modern economy and its class antagonism, which they hoped to heal by resurrecting the medieval guild spirit of paternal charity. 'In the strong and pious soil of the Middle Ages,' wrote Georg Moenius, the influential editor of the Munich-based journal *Allgemeine Rundschau*, 'saints and heroes were allowed to emerge as representative powers; in our time businessmen have taken their place.'[22] Such nostalgic opposition to an allegedly corrupt modernity was bolstered by the resurgence of popular piety. Mystics such as Therese Neumann, who claimed in the 1920s to see visions of saints and experience miraculous healing, generated enormous fascination, and helped their followers to articulate a desire for a 'pure' and homogeneously Catholic environment.[23]

Other Catholics, in contrast, especially in the industrialized and confessionally mixed Rhineland, claimed that Catholics must embrace and operate within modern society. Even if they formally rejected liberal views of the economy and politics, they insisted that these would not be replaced by medieval fantasies, but reformed and infused with Catholic values. Cologne mayor Konrad Adenauer, for example, in a widely covered speech in 1922, called on Catholics to embrace the republic, which he claimed was necessary for Catholic renewal. He was supported by networks of activists, urban reformers, and Christian union leaders. Some similarly sought to challenge the church's long-held hostility to capitalism. Jesuit economist Oswald von Nell-Breuning, for example, argued in *Basic Principles of Stock Exchange Morality* (1928) that the stock exchange, which had been long condemned by Catholic preachers, was in fact compatible with Catholic morality, a claim that was endorsed by Cologne's archbishop, Karl Joseph Schulte. In the pages of newspapers such as *Kölnische Volkszeitung* and magazines like *Hochland*, proponents of reform Catholicism envisioned a church that was not engaged in a rearguard struggle for tradition, but one that was open to change. As writer Paul-Ludwig Landsberg explained in *The World of the Middle Ages and us* (1922), the medieval church was 'dead', and a Catholic future was destined to build upon new principles.[24]

Even though secularists lost out in their effort to restructure German confessional laws during the revolution, they made significant inroads into the associations of the working-class milieus that reached their apogee in the late 1920s.[25] Several liberal intellectuals of the pre-war monist movement now reappeared as leading lights in the effort to build a 'collective culture' (*Gemeinschaftskultur*). Reality disappointed hopes that they would form a 'third pillar' of socialism alongside the parties and unions, but freethinkers substantially grew in number throughout the 1920s, reaching over half a million members by 1928. This growth was fuelled, in part, by an attractive cremation insurance policy offered by the main socialist freethought association.[26] Because cremation contravened church injunctions against destruction of the physical body, it proved an ideal means to challenge the church monopoly over burial. This was not the only area in which the socialist freethinkers sought to replicate the milieu-building functions of the churches. They offered an alternative confirmation ceremony called the *Jugendweihe*, backed the formation of secular (*weltliche*) schools, and promoted sexual reform and revision of the restrictive laws on abortion.[27]

These activities by secularists open a window on to the confessional dimensions of the upsurge of visionary cultural movements within the USPD and later the left-wing of the SPD. Marxist activists sought to achieve revolutionary ends through cultural experimentation and artistic innovation, which were known at the time as 'culture socialism' (*Kultursozialismus*). West German social historians writing in the 1980s, such as Dieter Langewiesche, argued that the 'utopia of the socialist society of the future [in which] the "New Man" would create the "New Society"' held little attraction for the educational institutions of the SPD and the unions, which remained characterized by 'connection to reality and pragmatism'.[28] Langewiesche interpreted *Kultursozialismus* as a 'cultural compensation', a 'consolation' for lack of real power.[29] Yet, the confessional history of the socialist movement suggests another reading, namely that cultural socialism was an expression of the secularist contribution to the wider socialist culture. The precise strength of this subculture of socialist secularism needs to be examined regionally. In rural areas and in some towns, it was nearly non-existent. In cities such as Berlin, however, the tradition of secularism meant that the churches had a hard time missionizing in working-class neighbourhoods. The Protestant minister and religious socialist Paul Piechowski complained to his consistory in 1926 that freethinkers were 'gaining ground among the workers' and that the local social democratic deputies in Berlin 'are nearly all Freethinkers themselves'.[30]

Alongside such internal debates and changes within the various confessional milieus, the 1920s also witnessed contradictory impulses in relationships between them. On the one hand, Weimar's pillarized public sphere preserved many of the animosities that defined confessional relations in the Imperial era. Anti-Catholic and anti-Protestant tropes circulated widely: the bestselling Catholic journalist Waldemar Gurian, for example, routinely blamed Protestants for their alleged lack of any transcendent values, making them responsible for modernity's decadence, nihilism, and violence, while scholar Joseph Bernhart claimed that Luther's 'monstrous error' of abolishing priestly celibacy had led to the denigration of marriage and ultimately to modern sexual hedonism. Protestant writers were just as prone to recycle confessional stereotypes. One of the most vocal was Lutheran Gerhard Ohlemüller, who led the International League for the Defence and Furtherance of Protestantism (Internationaler Verband zur Verteidigung und Förderung des Protestantismus) to fight Catholic 'infiltration'.[31] Such sentiments made efforts to break down the confessional boundary difficult. When a few conservative Catholic politicians broke from the Centre and sought to make the DNVP an interconfessional party, their efforts met with electoral apathy, and ultimately fizzled out. Clerical authorities expressed hostility to a growing interest in ecumenism, and in the encyclical *Mortalius animos* (1928) Pope Pius XI formally banned Catholics from joining interconfessional organizations. In the face of the growing strength of proletarian freethought, as well as the emergence of new spiritualist and pagan-*völkisch* sects, both Catholic and Protestant churches beefed up their apologetics organizations. The Protestant Church created, via the Inner Mission, in 1921 the Central Office for Apologetics (Apologetische Centralstelle), which engaged in research and training to fight growing threats from competing worldviews, and was a counterpart to the existing Apologetics Department of the Catholic Volksverein.[32]

Against the backdrop of persistent interconfessional suspicion, however, the 1920s also witnessed some pragmatic efforts of cooperation between the confessions. This was especially the case between Catholics and Protestants, who, despite pervasive mutual suspicion, occasionally found common ground over matters of gender and sexuality. Members of both Christian milieus, for example, mobilized to bolster traditional family structures, especially against efforts of feminists, socialists, and others to establish equality between married and unmarried mothers. It would be the end of marriage's sanctity, Christian clergy and politicians warned, if illegitimate children and their mothers could make financial or inheritance demands on the fathers. Joseph Mausbach, a prolific Catholic writer and politician, warned in his *Moral Theology* (1922) that equal rights for unwed mothers would lead to mass 'fornication'. The prominent Protestant activist Paula Müller-Otfried agreed, and predicted that 'if the status of unmarried mothers is improved many more women will imitate them' by engaging in extra-marital sex. Such arguments were echoed in parliamentary debates, when socialists and liberals in the Reichstag submitted proposals for equal rights of all mothers. In 1922, Catholics and Protestants successfully joined hands to block the proposed reform, which would not be implemented until decades later.[33] A similar cooperation forged around censoring what Christian writers and politicians called 'trash and filth' (*Schund and Schmutz*) literature, mostly erotic publications. In 1926, and against the socialists' and liberals' opposition, the Centre Party and the DNVP passed a law which empowered censorship panels to ban the sales of 'indecent' movies, advertisements and journals to the young.[34]

Socialists and Christians also found possibilities for collaboration. The divide persisted between socialist moderates, who were open to cooperation with liberal and Christian parties, and radicals, who supported more thoroughgoing transformation of society towards a secularist socialist culture. When the radicals briefly splintered into their own parties (USPD and KPD) in the republic's first years, the moderates moved towards a rejection of materialist and Marxist worldviews. In 1921, at its congress at Görlitz, the SPD adopted a new platform, which retreated from language of class struggle, and which, according to historian Heinrich August Winkler, was a short-lived attempt to replace dogmatic Marxism with a pragmatic and pluralist approach to politics that would have allowed socialists to leave their 'worldview and social ghetto' and forge instead a cross-class big-tent party, an aspiration only realized in the Bad Godesberg Programme of 1959.[35] The effort to forge a more pluralistic party culture also opened the way for the religious socialists, who found support in the party hierarchy but struggled against the hostility of the many freethinkers in the party base. However, when many of the radical Independents rejoined the SPD in 1921 and 1922, the party returned to early positions on matters of religion and worldview. And, to reunite its temporarily fractured milieu, the party adopted a platform at its 1925 Heidelberg Congress that reaffirmed the Marxist truisms of the pre-war era.[36] In short, although there were significant efforts by some milieu leaders to overcome confessional hostilities, often motivated by pragmatic calculations, most Germans in the Weimar Republic continued to live in confessionally segregated social worlds. What one leading historian has called German Catholics' 'incapacity for dialogue' applies to Protestants and secularists as well.[37]

Culture War and the Collapse of the Weimar Republic

In the late 1920s and early 1930s, Germany witnessed a renewed flaring of confessional conflict, one so intense that scholars have recently compared it to the *Kulturkampf* of the nineteenth century.[38] But unlike its nineteenth-century precursor, this culture war was marked less by animosities between Protestants and Catholics, than by intensified conflict between secularists and Christians. This was an international conflict, which deepened in 1928, when authorities in the Soviet Union launched a wide campaign of anti-religious agitation, hoping to eliminate the Christian clergy as a source of potential opposition. For Joseph Stalin and others, the campaign against religious organizations was integral to the party's project of collectivization and 'cultural revolution', which was to remake the Soviet economy and society.[39] The German Communist Party, which over the 1920s came increasingly under Soviet influence, was directed to increase its anti-religious propaganda and promote church-leaving as a weapon of 'class struggle'. Anticlericalism was also meant to extend communist influence in the socialist milieu. To win supporters away from the SPD, the KPD attacked the socialists for being soft on the religious front. For example, when the SPD-governed Prussian State agreed to a concordat with the Vatican in 1929 at the behest of its coalition partner the Centre Party, the communists accused the socialists of coming under the sway of Pope Pius XI. The treaty, they claimed, was similar to the recently signed agreement between the Vatican and fascist Italy (the Lateran Accords), and thus exposed the SPD as the party of 'social fascism'.[40] Although the KPD's efforts to usurp control of the 600,000-strong membership of the 'proletarian' freethought movement failed, socialist secularists also became more militant.[41]

The surge of Communist belligerency abroad and at home sent shock waves through the German Christian world. Catholics and Protestants alike were deeply alarmed by the prospects of potential Communist revolution—fears that were exacerbated by the deep effects of the Great Depression in 1929—and responded with anti-secularist mobilization of an unprecedented scale. The institutions of the Catholic milieu were receptive to the warning issued by Germany's bishops in February 1930, of the need to combat the 'storm waves of godlessness' that were threatening to wash over Germany.[42] Catholic newspapers such as *Germania* reported in detail about the horrors of anti-Christian violence in the Soviet Union, while Catholic associations organized local marches to protest against Communist brutality. Anti-secularism—which some conflated with Communism, while others associated with the entire left—in fact proved to be a useful integrative force for the diverse Catholic milieu. In the annual Catholic congresses (*Katholikentage*) of 1930 and 1931, in which Catholic activists and leaders gathered, speakers could agree that the defeat of secularism and Communism was the moment's most urgent task, and founded the Committee for the Struggle against Bolshevism, an organization to coordinate anti-Communist research, publications, and exhibitions.[43] Similar agitation swept the Protestant milieu. With the church leaders' support, the Inner Mission churned out hysterical anti-Communist articles for Germany's leading conservative newspapers and printed numerous anti-godless brochures and books. Some Protestant clergy made the struggle against freethought a core field of action. When Communists announced an 'anti-Easter march' through Brandenburg in 1930, General Superintendent Otto Dibelius called on his pastors to hold competing church services, adorn their churches with flags, and ring their bells.[44]

This *Kulturkampf* atmosphere had far-reaching political consequences for both the Catholic and Protestant milieus. Even before German politics plunged into crisis in 1930, it strengthened the voices of hardliners, who argued that the parliamentary democracy should be replaced with an authoritarian alternative. It was the republic's principle of religious neutrality, some argued, that facilitated spiritual indifference, which in turn led to militant secularism; only a strong leadership could thus suppress anti-Christian militant Marxism. In December 1928, following the collapse of the Centre-led coalition under Wilhelm Marx, conflicts erupted over the cooperation between Christian and non-believers in labour unions and over the Centre's commitment to republican government. After an intense internal debate, the party elected as its leader the conservative prelate Ludwig Kaas—the first priest at the helm of the party, founded in 1870—who openly called for 'leadership on a grand scale' and claimed that authoritarian state may be better positioned to protect the church. This shift to the right was mirrored among conservative Protestants, whose tolerance for democratic politics had long been lower than that of the Catholics. In 1928, the DNVP elected as its leader the media baron Alfred Hugenberg, who called for the Reichstag's dissolution and its replacement with an all-powerful executive. While some continued to believe in democratic politics, authoritarianism was clearly gaining ground in Christian politics. Eugen Bolz, a prominent Catholic leader and minister-president of Württemberg, spoke for many when he said in 1930, 'I have long been of the opinion that the parliament cannot solve severe domestic political problems. If a dictator for ten years were a possibility—I would want it.'[45]

It did not take long for some Catholics and Protestant conservatives to recognize how joint action against secularism might serve their shared desire for a return to authoritarian government. Weimar's final years thus witnessed several efforts to form an interconfessional front against liberalism and Marxism. The first undertaking began in 1930, when the conservative Protestant President Paul von Hindenburg appointed as chancellor the Catholic Heinrich Brüning, who was former leader of the Centre's delegation to the Reichstag and was known for his friendly relations with Protestants. With a goal of excluding the SPD from power and crafting a 'Christian' response to the mounting economic calamity, the two gathered Catholic and Protestant experts in a Commission for the Study of the Unemployment Question (Kommission zum Studium der Arbeitslosenfrage), and then sought to implement those with emergency decrees and without the parliament support.[46] The failure of these efforts—by 1932, unemployment almost doubled—opened the door to an even more reactionary interconfessional alliance. It was led by the devout Catholic aristocrat Franz von Papen, who in June 1932 replaced Brüning as chancellor. A long-time opponent of the republic, Papen had long argued that political sovereignty stemmed not from the people, but from God, and advocated for an aggressive suppression of liberalism, Marxism, and secularism. This mission, he concluded in 1930, would be best carried through cooperation with Protestants, which led him to join hands with the Protestant power broker and businessman Werner von Alvensleben and form the German Association for the Protection of Western Culture.[47] After his appointment as chancellor, and the formation of a largely aristocratic and nonpartisan cabinet opposed to 'cultural Bolshevism', von Papen sought to realize this interconfessional and anti-secularist vision, especially through education. The new Minister of Interior, Protestant lawyer Wilhelm von Gayl, drafted new plans to 'protect the free development of Christian schools and the Christian foundation of all education', which included the barring of confessionless teachers and closing secular schools that 'have no relationship to German national character (*Volkstum*)'.[48]

While those political constellations were confined to a small circle of powerful elites, another experiment at a Catholic–Protestant cooperation emerged under the wings of the National Socialist Party (NSDAP). As historians have increasingly noted, the National Socialists routinely presented themselves as the churches' natural allies in their struggle against secularism. While many of its leaders, such as philosopher Alfred Rosenberg, were widely acknowledged at the time to be anti-Christian, Adolf Hitler and others insisted that the party's fierce anti-Marxism aligned with Christian morality and traditions. Hitler maintained in October 1930 that Christians should embrace the swastika as a 'political sign that will unite the people who stand on the foundation of a non-Marxist, non-materialist, … deeply idealistic worldview'.[49] Crucially, the National Socialists insisted on their dedication to 'positive Christianity', a term which appeared on the party's founding manifesto and which signified a national unity that transcended the division between the confessions. In 1932, Hitler declared, 'in the struggle against the abuse of religion, I'm not a Catholic and not a Protestant, but a German Christian, who does not want our people to receive a new religious conflict on top of its other struggles'.[50] Thus the National Socialists positioned themselves squarely within Germany's existing confessional axes, by linking anti-Marxism, antisemitism, and anti-secularism, and by calling for Catholic–Protestant unity to restore national unity. As Hitler explained in a speech in 1928, the Christian confessions could not overcome their differences by 'beating, degrading or insulting each other', but only by coming together under the banner of National Socialism.[51]

Such statements were reinforced by the composition of the party's leadership, which, alone among the reactionary parties, included nominal Catholics, such as Hitler and Joseph Goebbels. Together these factors opened the NSDAP to nationalist Catholics.[52] Some of Catholicism's most enthusiastic interconfessional thinkers, such as theologian Robert Grosche and historian Joseph Lortz, welcomed cooperation between the church and the NSDAP.[53] In practice, however, the interconfessional rhetoric of 'positive Christianity' carried an anti-Catholic barb that exacerbated confessional tensions. National Socialist leaders lambasted the Centre Party as the main obstacle to anti-secularist unity (attacks they did not level against the DNVP). As early as 1925, Hitler claimed that 'no movement has waged the struggle against the Centre Party and the groups associated with it more energetically than our old party', not for religious reasons, 'but solely because a party which allies itself with atheistic Marxism for the oppression of its own people is neither Christian nor Catholic'.[54] Thus, National Socialist interconfessionalism appealed largely to Protestants. While Catholic voters mostly remained loyal to the Centre Party, their Protestant counterparts flocked to the NSDAP and in the elections in 1932 made it the largest party in the country. A number of leading Protestant clergy, such as Bishop Heinrich Rendtorff of Mecklenburg, spoke warmly of the party, and newspapers reported that some pastors had begun to identify Hitler as the saviour of German Christianity.[55]

Ultimately, the strands of anti-secularist interconfessionalism came together in January 1933, when the NSDAP and other nationalist parties formed a coalition, with Hitler as chancellor and von Papen as his deputy. Once in power, the National Socialists swiftly sought to end the confessional dynamics that defined Germany's religious politics throughout the Imperial and Weimar era, by eliminating secularism and suppressing the Catholic–Protestant tensions. First, the government implemented its anti-secularist promise. In February, it violently crushed the Communist party, and in March, it shut down the socialist freethought organizations (followed in a few months by the abolition of all socialist unions and parties).[56] Then, having already declared an end to 'the *Kulturkampf*' upon taking power, the National Socialists moved in early summer of 1933 to eliminate what they saw as the last vestiges of inter-Christian disunity.[57] Hitler forced the DNVP to disband in June. The following month, after concluding a concordat that brought with it the dissolution of the Centre Party, he boasted that he had succeeded in 'driving the last nail in the coffin' of the political parties and stopped priestly meddling in politics.[58] The NSDAP was not satisfied with the elimination of the confessional parties, and began to increase pressure on the churches to actively support the regime's mission. Hitler stated in a radio address on 22 July 1933 that 'Churches which fail to render to the State any positive support … [are] worthless.'[59] Within a short time of taking power, then, it became clear that the National Socialists were introducing new realities to all confessional milieus, whether Protestant, Catholic, or socialist-secular. For the next few years, each camp's politicians, thinkers, and members would be consumed by debates on how to respond to the new regime's brutal demands.

The conclusions to be drawn about the place of church milieus, secularism, and religious politics in the wider history of the Weimar Republic depend on what one seeks to explain. The question at the centre of much contemporary historical scholarship has been: what role did confessional antagonisms play in the republic's weaknesses and in the ascension of the National Socialist Party to power in January 1933?[60] Viewed from this perspective, the dynamics engendered by animosities along the two confessional axes explored in this chapter contributed to the instability of the political system. The long traditions of hostility between Germany's main social-cultural milieus, which were inherited from the Imperial era, made lasting coalitions difficult. Even as Catholics and socialists cooperated with each other during the republic's foundation and in governing coalitions throughout the 1920s, their deep differences over religion added fragility to any alliance. Similar conclusions can be reached about relations between confessional Catholics and liberals of various backgrounds, as well as between Protestant liberals and Protestant conservatives. During the republic's final years, the intensification of anti-secularist sentiments sent many Christians into the hands of the authoritarian and radical right. Perhaps most consequentially, the National Socialist Party skilfully mobilized the conceptual arsenal forged by church apologists and Christian conservatives. Under the banner of the term 'positive Christianity', it utilized Weimar's culture wars to argue that it alone could destroy secularism and modern Judaism (always linked in antisemitic rhetoric) and bring together both Catholics and Protestants into a nationalist unity. Weimar's *Kulturkampf* dynamics provided Hitler the opportunity to portray his party as Christianity's defender, not in religious terms, but in confessional ones. Just as the violent deeds of the brownshirts gave the NSDAP prominence in the low-grade civil war fought between the right and the Communists, so its call for extreme measures against freethought allowed it to appear as the standard-bearer of the Christian West on the religious front of that war.

If we look beyond the republic's collapse, however, the era's confessional dynamics acquire additional legacies. Here we may borrow a metaphor employed by historian Helmut Walser Smith, who likened the central event that historians seek to explain to a painting's 'vanishing point' around which all objects are aligned.[61] Alongside 1933, a second vanishing point in the story of Germany's religious politics could be 1946, the year in which Catholics and Protestants joined hands to form the Christian Democratic Union (CDU), an interconfessional alliance that would become West Germany's ruling party for most of the time from the founding of the Federal Republic in 1949. Drawing on the experiments of Weimar's last years as well as on the complex experiences under Hitler's rule, leaders of both Christian milieus concluded that only a robust cooperation could return organized religion to the centre of the nation's life. Nazism, they claimed, was a secular twin of Marxism, and it was up to the churches to provide the social, political, and ethical bulwark against their return. Under the leadership of Konrad Adenauer, who served as West Germany's chancellor for fourteen years from 1949 to 1963, the CDU would thus continue the anti-secular campaign in a decisively democratic key. As the leading force in the country's reconstruction, its agenda echoed much of the Catholic and Protestant demands in the 1920s, whether in education, family law, or anti-Communism.[62] Weimar's confessional axes, then, did not disappear with Nazism and war. With some alterations, they continued to shape West Germany's democratic politics for many years.

NOTES

1. See e.g. Detlev Peukert, *The Weimar Republic: The Crisis of Classical Modernity*, tr. Richard Deveson (London: Allen Lane, 1991); Eric Weitz, *Weimar Germany: Promise and Tragedy* (Princeton: Princeton University Press, 2007); Andreas Wirsching, *Die Weimarer Republik: Politik und Gesellschaft* (Munich: R. Oldenbourg, 2008). Important studies by church historians include Jonathan Wright, *Above Parties: The Political Attitudes of the German Protestant Church Leadership 1918–1933* (London: Oxford University Press, 1974); Klaus Scholder, *The Churches and the Third Reich*, vol 1. *Preliminary History and the Time of Illusions, 1918–1934*, tr. John Bowden (London: SCM, 1987); Jochen-Christoph Kaiser, *Arbeiterbewegung und organisierte Religionskritik: Proletarische Freidenkerverbände in Kaiserreich und Weimarer Republik* (Stuttgart: Klett Cotta, 1981); Kurt Nowak, *Evangelische Kirche und Weimarer Republik: Zum politischen Weg des deutschen Protestantismus zwischen 1918 und 1932* (Weimar: Hermann Böhlaus Nachfolger, 1981).

2. Major studies of the inter-war milieus include: Siegfried Weichlein, *Sozialmilieus und politische Kultur in der Weimarer Republik: Lebenswelt, Vereinskultur, Politik in Hessen* (Göttingen: Vandenhoeck & Ruprecht, 1996); Frank Bösch, *Das konservative Milieu: Vereinskultur und lokale Sammlungspolitik in ost- und westdeutschen Regionen: 1900–1960* (Göttingen: Wallstein, 2002); Heinz Hürten, *Deutsche Katholiken 1918–1945* (Paderborn: Schöningh, 1992).
3. Lucian Hölscher, 'Konfessionspolitik in Deutschland zwischen Glaubensstreit und Koexistenz', in Hölscher (ed.), *Baupläne der sichtbaren Kirche: Sprachliche Konzepte religiöser Vergemeinschaftung in Europa* (Göttingen: Wallstein, 2007), 11–52.
4. Olaf Blaschke, 'Das 19. Jahrhundert: Ein Zweites Konfessionelles Zeitalter?', *Geschichte und Gesellschaft*, 26 (2000), 38–75. See also Helmuth Walser Smith, *German Nationalism and Religious Conflict* (Princeton: Princeton University Press, 1995); Manuel Borutta, *Antikatholizismus: Deutschland und Italien im Zeitalter der europäischen Kulturkämpfe* (Göttingen: Vandenhoeck & Ruprecht, 2010).
5. Todd Weir, *Secularism and Religion in Nineteenth Century Germany* (Cambridge: Cambridge University Press, 2014), 158–161; Sebastian Prüfer, *Sozialismus statt Religion: Die deutsche Sozialdemokratie vor der religiösen Frage 1863–1890* (Göttingen: Vandenhoeck & Ruprecht, 2002). Quote is from Christoph Ernst Luthardt, *Die modernen Weltanschauungen und ihre praktischen Konsequenzen* (Leipzig: Dörffling & Franke, 1897 [1880]), 1.
6. Quotation of Kaiser's speech is from 'Zweite Balkonrede des Kaisers, August 1, 1914', in Ulrich Cartarius (ed.), *Deutschland im Ersten Weltkrieg: Texte und Dokumente* (Munich: dtv, 1982), 15.
7. Patrick J. Houlihan, *Catholicism and the Great War: Religion and Everyday Life in Germany and Austria-Hungary, 1914–1922* (New York: Cambridge University Press, 2015).
8. Quotation of Kaiser's speech is from 'Der Kampf der Weltanschauungen', *Mitteilungen aus dem Verein zum Abwehr des Antisemitismus*, 28/12–13 (10 July 1918), 57–9.
9. Ludwig Richter, *Kirche und Schule in den Beratungen der Weimarer Nationalversammlung* (Düsseldorf: Droste, 1996), 241. On 28 November Hoffmann issued a decree ordering the consistories to eliminate prayers for the King and the royal house from their services. On Adolph Hoffmann and the Protestant Church, see Gottfried Mehnert, *Evangelische Kirche und Politik* (Düsseldorf: Droste, 1959), 106–15.
10. Horst Groschopp (ed.), *Los von der Kirche: Adolph Hoffmann und die Staat-Kirche-Trennung in Deutschland* (Aschaffenburg: Alibri Verlag, 2009); Frank Gordon, 'Protestantism and Socialism in the Weimar Republic', *German Studies Review*, 11 (1988), 423–46.
11. Josef Selbst, 'Zeitlage und kirchliches Leben im Jahre 1918/19', in *Kirchliches Handbuch für das katholische Deutschland, 8. 1918–1919* (Freiburg i. B.: Herdersche, 1919), 80–147, here 141; Reinhard Richter, *Nationales Denken im Katholizismus der Weimarer Republik* (Münster: Lit, 2000).
12. Siegfried Weichlein, 'Von der Staatskirche zur religiösen Kultur: Die Entstehung des Begriffs der "Körperschaft öffentlichen Rechts" mit Blick auf die Kirchenartikel der Weimarer Reichsverfassung', in Hölscher, *Baupläne der sichtbaren Kirche*, 90–116.
13. Nowak, *Evangelische Kirche*; Bösch, *Das konservative Milieu*; Helge Matthiesen, *Greifswald in Vorpommern: Konservatives Milieu im Kaiserreich* (Düsseldorf: Droste 2000). Hirsch is cited in Klaus Tanner, 'Protestant Revolt against Modernity', in Rudy Koshar (ed.), *The*

Weimar Moment: Liberalism, Political Theology, and Law (New York: Lexington, 2012), 3–16, here 8.
14. Larry Eugene Jones, *The German Right, 1918–1930* (Cambridge: Cambridge University Press, 2020), esp. 67–8.
15. Lucian Hölscher, 'The Religious Divide: Piety in Nineteenth-Century Germany', in Helmut Walser Smith (ed.), *Protestants, Catholics, and Jews in Germany, 1800–1914* (Oxford, New York: Berg, 2001), 33–48.
16. Harry Oelke and Siegfried Hermle (eds), *Kirchliche Zeitgeschichte: Protestantismus und Weimarer Republik* (Leipzig: Evangelische Verlagsanstalt, 2020); Walter Fleischmann-Bisten, *Der Evangelische Bund in der Weimarer Republik und im sogenannten Dritten Reich* (Frankfurt/Main: Lang, 1989); the figures are mentioned in Scholder, *The Churches and the Third Reich*, vol. 1, 35.
17. Shelley Baranowski, *The Sanctity of Rural Life: Nobility, Protestantism, and Nazism in Weimar Prussia* (New York, Oxford: Oxford University Press, 1995); Gury Schneider-Ludorff, *Magdalene von Tiling: Ordnungstheologie und Geschlechterbeziehungen* (Göttingen: Vandenhoeck & Ruprecht, 2001), esp. 145–207; Norbert Friedrich, *Die christlich-soziale Fahne empor! Reinhard Mumm und die christlich-soziale Bewegung* (Stuttgart: Kohlhammer, 1997); Wolfgang Tilgner, *Volksnomostheologie und Schöpfungsglaube: Ein Beitrag zur Geschichte des Kirchenkampfes* (Göttingen: Vandenhoeck & Ruprecht, 1966), 181–7.
18. Jochen-Christoph Kaiser, *Sozialer Protestantismus im 20. Jahrhundert. Beiträge zur Geschichte der Inneren Mission 1914 bis 1945* (Munich: Oldenbourg, 1989).
19. Karl Barth, *Der Römerbrief (Zweite Fassung) 1922*, ed. Cornelis van der Kooi and Katja Tolstaja, in *Karl Barth Gesamtausgabe*, vol. 47 (Zurich: Theologischer Verlag. 2010), 51. On theologies of crisis, see Friedrich Wilhelm Graf, *Der Heilige Zeitgeist: Studien zur Ideengeschichte der protestantischen Theologie der Weimarer Republik* (Tübingen: Mohr Siebeck, 2010).
20. Siegfried Heimann and Franz Walter, *Religiöse Sozialisten und Freidenker in der Weimarer Republik* (Bonn: J. H. W. Dietz, 1993); Karlheinz Lipp, *Religiöser Sozialismus und Pazifismus: Der Friedenskampf des Bundes der Religiösen Sozialisten Deutschlands in der Weimarer Republik* (Pfaffenweiler: Centaurus, 1995).
21. Klaus Grosse Kracht, *Die Stunde der Laien? Katholische Aktion in Deutschland im europäischen Kontext 1920–1960* (Paderborn: Schöningh, 2016).
22. The quotes are from James Chappel, *The Challenge of Totalitarianism and the Remaking of the Church* (Cambridge, MA: Harvard University Press, 2018), 30. See also Christoph Hübner, *Die Rechtskatholiken, die Zentrumspartei, und die katholische Kirche in Deutschland bis zum Reichskonkordat von 1933* (Berlin: Lit, 2014); Gregory Munro, *Hitler's Bavarian Antagonist: Georg Moenius and the Allgemeine Rundschau of Munich* (New York: Mellen Press, 2006).
23. Michael E. O'Sullivan, *Disruptive Power: Catholic Women, Miracles, and Politics in Modern Germany* (Toronto: University of Toronto Press, 2018), esp. 53–76.
24. Stefan Gerber, *Pragmatismus und Kulturkritik: Politikbegründung und politische Kommunikation im Katholizismus der Weimarer Republik* (Paderborn: Schöningh, 2006); William Patch, *Christian Trade Unions in the Weimar Republic, 1918–1933* (New Haven: Yale University Press, 1985), 34–156; Noel D. Cary, *The Path to Christian Democracy: German Catholics and the Party System from Windthorst to Adenauer* (Cambridge, MA: Harvard University Press, 1996), 45–124; Paul-Ludwig Landsberg, *Die Welt des Mittelalters und Wir* (Bonn: F. Cohen, 1922), 103.

25. Peter Lösche and Franz Walter, 'Zur Organisationskultur der sozialdemokratischen Arbeiterbewegung in der Weimarer Republik. Niedergang der Klassenkultur oder solidargemeinschaftlicher Höhepunkt?', *Geschichte und Gesellschaft*, 15 (1989), 511–36.
26. Kaiser, *Arbeiterbewegung*, 180.
27. Weir, *Secularism and Religion*, 271.
28. Dieter Langewiesche, 'Erwachsenenbildung', in Dieter Langewiesche and Heinz-Elmar Tenorth (eds), *Handbuch der deutschen Bildungsgeschichte*, vol. 5. *1918-1945* (Munich: C. H. Beck, 1989), 348.
29. Dieter Langewiesche, 'Die Arbeitswelt in den Zukunftsentwürfen des Weimarer Kultursozialismus', in Albrecht Lehmann (ed.), *Studien zur Arbeiterkultur: Beiträge der 2. Arbeitstagung der Kommission "Arbeiterkultur" in der Deutschen Gesellschaft für Volkskunde in Hamburg vom 8. bis 12. Mai 1983* (Münster: Coppenrath, 1984), 51.
30. Piechowski to the Consistorial Council, 2 April 1926, Evangelisches Zentralarchiv Berlin, 14/2519, unpag.
31. Waldemar Gurian, *Die deutsche Jugendbewegung*, 3rd ed. (Habelschwerdt: Frankes Buchhandlung, 1924); Joseph Bernhart, 'Marriage as a Sacrament', in Hermann Keyserling (ed.), *The Book of Marriage* (New York: Harcourt, Brace & Co., 1926), 472–507, here 487; Gerhard Ohlemüller, *Beitrag zu den Konkordatsverhandlungen zwischen Deutschland und dem Vatikan* (Berlin: Säemann-Verlag, 1922), here 17.
32. On efforts of interconfessional cooperation on the right, see Larry Eugene Jones, 'Catholics on the Right: The Reich Catholic Committee of the German National People's Party, 1920–33', *Historisches Jahrbuch*, 126 (2006), 221–67.
33. Both Mausbach and Müller-Otfried are cited in Cornelie Usborne, *The Politics of the Body in Weimar Germany: Women's Reproductive Rights and Duties* (London: Palgrave Macmillan, 1992), 82.
34. Gideon Reuveni, *Reading Germany: Literature and Consumer Culture in Germany Before 1933* (New York: Berghahn, 2006), 221–73.
35. Heinrich August Winkler, 'Klassenbewegung oder Volkspartei? Zur Programmdiskussion in der Weimarer Sozialdemokratie 1920–1925', *Geschichte und Gesellschaft*, 8 (1982), 9–54, 33.
36. Ibid., 45.
37. The quote is from Thomas Ruster, *Die verlorene Nützlichkeit der Religion* (Paderborn: F. Schöningh, 1997), 173–9.
38. See e.g. the articles gathered in the special issue edited by Todd Weir, 'Europe's Interwar Kulturkampf', *Journal of Contemporary History* 53/3 (2018).
39. Victoria Smolkin, *A Sacred Space is Never Empty: A History of Soviet Atheism* (Princeton: Princeton University Press, 2018).
40. Stewart A. Stehlin, *Weimar and the Vatican* (Princeton: Princeton University Press, 1983).
41. Kaiser, *Arbeiterbewegung*, 164–72.
42. Quoted in Ulrich Kaiser, *Realpolitik oder antibolschewistischer Kreuzzug? Zum Zusammenhang von Rußlandbild und Rußlandpolitik der deutschen Zentrumspartei 1917–1933* (Frankfurt/Main: Lang, 2005), 190–1.
43. The information on the Committee is taken from Stadtarchiv Mönchengladbach, Algermissen papers, no. 15/7/5. More broadly, see Hürten, *Deutsche Katholiken*; Stefan Ummenhofer, *Wie Feuer und Wasser? Katholizismus und Sozialdemokratie in der Weimarer Republik* (Berlin: wvb, 2003); Horstwalter Heitzer, 'Deutscher Katholizismus und "Bolschewismusgefahr" bis 1933', *Historisches Jahrbuch*, 113 (1993), 355–87.

44. Mirjam Loos, *Gefährliche Metaphern: Auseinandersetzungen deutscher Protestanten mit Kommunismus und Bolschewismus* (Göttingen: Vandenhoeck & Ruprecht, 2020); Walter Fleischmann-Bisten and Heiner Grote, *Protestanten auf dem Wege: Geschichte des Evangelischen Bundes* (Göttingen: Vandenhoeck & Ruprecht, 1986); Nowak, *Evangelische Kirche*, 205–339. The information on Dibelius is from 'Protokoll über den Ephorenkonvent der Kurmark am 1. und 2. Mai 1930', Evangelisches Zentralarchiv Berlin, 7/3568, fo. 114.
45. Patch, *Christian Trade Unions in the Weimar Republic*, 125–156. Kaas is cited in Hans Mommsen, *The Rise and Fall of Weimar Democracy* (Chapel Hill, NC: University of North Carolina Press, 1996), 262. Bolz is cited in Richard Evans, *The Coming of the Third Reich* (New York: Penguin, 2006), 93.
46. On the efforts to forge an interconfessional cooperation under Brüning, see Noah B. Strote, *Lions and Lambs: Conflict in Weimar and the Ceation of Post-Nazi Germany* (New Haven: Yale University Press, 2017), 46–68.
47. Todd H. Weir, 'The Christian Front Against Godlessness: Anti-Secularism and the Demise of the Weimar Republic, 1928–1933', *Past and Present* 229 (2015), 201–38.
48. Lary Eugene Jones, 'Franz von Papen, Catholic Conservatives, and the Establishment of the Third Reich', *Journal of Modern History*, 83 (2011), 272–318; Rainer Bölling, *Volksschullehrer und Politik: Der Deutsche Lehrerverein 1918–1933* (Göttingen: Vandenhoeck & Ruprecht, 1978), 217.
49. Speech in Munich, 25 Oct. 1930, *Adolf Hitler: Reden, Schriften, Anordnungen*, vol. 4/1, ed. Constantin Goschler (Munich: Saur, 1996), 33. For a discussion of National Socialist confessional politics, see Todd H. Weir, 'Hitler's Worldview and the Interwar Kulturkampf', *Journal of Contemporary History*, 53 (2018), 597–621.
50. *Der Angriff*, 8 Apr. 1932. On the National Socialists' rhetoric of Catholic-Protestant reconciliation, see Doris L. Bergen, *Twisted Cross: The German Christian Movement in the Third Reich* (Chapel Hill, NC: University of North Carolina Press, 1996), esp. 101–11.
51. Adolf Hitler, *Hitler. Reden, Schriften, Anordnungen*, vol. 2/2. *Vom Weimarer Parteitag bis zur Reichstagswahl, August 1927–Mai 1928*, ed. Bärbel Dusik (Munich: Saur, 1992), doc. 237. On Nazism and confessionalism, see e.g. Richard Steigmann-Gall, *Holy Reich: Nazi Conceptions of Christianity, 1919–1945* (New York: Cambridge University Press, 2003), esp. 13–50.
52. Derek Hastings, *Catholicism and the Roots of Nazism* (New York: Oxford University Press, 2010).
53. Udi Greenberg, 'Catholics, Protestants, and the Violent Birth of European Religious Pluralism', *American Historical Review*, 124 (2019), 511–38. A useful collection of documents on German Catholicism and ecumenism in the 1930s is Jörg Ernesti (ed.), *Die Entdeckung der Ökumene: Zur Beteiligung der katholischen Kirche an der ökumenischen Bewegung* (Frankfurt/Main: Bonifatius, 2008).
54. *Völkischer Beobachter*, 26 Feb. 1925, reprinted in: Adolf Hitler, *Reden, Schriften, Anordnungen*, vol. 1. *Die Wiedergründung der NSDAP, Februar 1925–Juni 1926*, ed. Clemens Vollnhals (Munich: Saur, 1992), doc. 1.
55. A survey of clerical statements in favour of National Socialism is found in *Die Welt am Montag*, 20 (8 June 1931). More broadly, see Scholder, *Churches and Third Reich*, vol. 1, 127–45.
56. Weir, *Secularism and Religion*, 274.
57. *Völkischer Beobachter*, 8 Feb. 1933.

58. For two contrasting interpretations of the concordat with the Vatican, see Gerhard Besier and Francesca Piombo, *The Holy See and Hitler's Germany* (London: Palgrave Macmillan, 2007); Hubert Wolf, *Pope and Devil: The Vatican's Archives and the Third Reich*, tr. Kenneth Kronenberg (Cambridge, MA: Harvard University Press, 2010). Hitler's quote is from a speech to the SA on 21 July 1933; an English translation of parts of the speech is available in Norman H. Baynes (ed.), *The Speeches of Adolf Hitler: April 1922–August 1939* (London: Oxford University Press, 1942), vol. 1, 373–4.
59. Baynes, *Speeches*, vol. 1, 376.
60. See e.g. Manfred Kittel, 'Konfessioneller Konflikt und politische Kultur in der Weimarer Republik', in Olaf Blaschke (ed.), *Konfessionen im Konflikt: Deutschland zwischen 1800 und 1970: Ein zweites konfessionelles Zeitalter* (Göttingen: Vandenhoeck & Ruprecht, 2002), Steigmann-Gall, *Holy Reich*; Bergen, *Twisted Cross*.
61. Helmut Walser Smith, 'The Vanishing Point of German History: An Essay on Perspective', *History and Memory*, 17 (2005), 267–95.
62. Maria Mitchell, *The Origins of Christian Democracy: Politics and Confession in Modern Germany* (Ann Arbor: University of Michigan Press, 2012).

Bibliography

Fleischmann-Bisten, Walter, and Heiner Grote, *Protestanten auf dem Wege: Geschichte des Evangelischen Bundes* (Göttingen: Vandenhoeck & Ruprecht, 1986).
Hübner, Christoph, *Die Rechtskatholiken, die Zentrumspartei und die katholische Kirche in Deutschland bis zum Reichskonkordat von 1933* (Berlin: Lit, 2014).
Hürten, Heinz, *Deutsche Katholiken 1918–1945* (Paderborn: Schöningh, 1992).
Nowak, Kurt, *Evangelische Kirche und Weimarer Republik*, 2nd ed. (Weimar: Hermann Böhlaus Nachfolger, 1988).
Oelke, Harry, and Siegfried Hermle (eds), *Kirchliche Zeitgeschichte: Protestantismus und Weimarer Republik* (Leipzig: Evangelische Verlagsanstalt, 2020).
Patch, William, *The Christian Trade Unions in the Weimar Republic, 1918–1933* (New Haven: Yale University Press, 1985).
Richter, Reinhard, *Nationales Denken im Katholizismus der Weimarer Republik* (Münster: Lit, 2000).
Ruster, Thomas, *Die verlorene Nützlichkeit der Religion* (Paderborn: F. Schöningh, 1997).
Scholder, Klaus, *The Churches and the Third Reich*, vol 1. *Preliminary History and the Time of Illusions, 1918–1934*, tr. John Bowden (London: SCM, 1987).
Usborne, Cornelie, *The Politics of the Body in Weimar Germany: Women's Reproductive Rights and Duties* (Basingstoke: Palgrave Macmillan, 1992).
Weichlein, Siegfried, *Sozialmilieus und politische Kultur in der Weimarer Republik: Lebenswelt, Vereinskultur, Politik in Hessen* (Göttingen: Vandenhoeck & Ruprecht, 1996).
Weir, Todd, *Secularism and Religion in Nineteenth Century Germany: The Rise of the Fourth Confession* (Cambridge: Cambridge University Press, 2014).

CHAPTER 31

THE HUMANITIES AND SOCIAL SCIENCES

LUTZ RAPHAEL

THE situation of the humanities and social sciences in the Weimar Republic can be viewed from two angles. The first perspective emphasizes the political functionalization and self-mobilization of the humanities for *völkisch* and racist purposes, which after 1933 proved advantageous for Nazi power politics. After 1945, many argued that German scholars of the humanities, who were largely nationalist conservative, and their subject-specific thought patterns maintained a fundamental distance from Nazi racism and antisemitism. Intensive research has now disproved this.[1] The second perspective highlights the mass exodus of humanities scholars and social scientists who, either as victims of 'racial' persecution from 1933 or for political reasons, went into exile.[2] Focusing on this group of exiles provides insight into the Weimar Republic as an important phase of experimentation and methodological innovation within the humanities. According to this interpretation, those academics, historians, philologists, and social scientists who committed themselves to the ideology of the *völkisch* renewal, and thus led to narrowing of methodological approaches, only gained the upper hand from 1930, and across the board from 1933 onwards.[3] At any rate, the diversity of manifold positions, trends, and methodological experiments within the academic landscape of Weimar Germany is unmistakable. The extent to which emphasis is placed on its ambiguity and Janus-faced character, that is the mixture of methodological innovation and *völkisch* regression, largely depends on which of these two perspectives is highlighted.

Humanities Scholars as Mandarins: Fear of the Future, Discourses on Crisis, and Distance from Democracy

Intellectual trends and methodological programmes in the humanities do not evolve in a vacuum, rather, the social positions of university lecturers and professors shape their worldviews and future expectations. This is particularly true of the humanities scholars that existed in Imperial Germany from the turn of the century; an academic sector that was 'entirely furnished with male connotations', where its research and teaching was still represented exclusively by men even during the Weimar Republic.[4] Describing the elite group consciousness and social exclusion of humanities scholars working at universities, the sociologist Fritz K. Ringer has coined the term 'German mandarins', which refers to the civil servants of Imperial China.[5] Despite their privileged position, from as early as 1900 the German mandarins suffered from fears of declining social status and experiences of loss. In the wake of inflation, beginning in 1914, the German defeat, and the revolution of 1918/19 they felt the pressure upon them increasing. After a huge drop in income for civil servants during the war and post-war inflation, university professors' average salaries stabilized, not least owing to the generous adjustment to remunerations. Until 1930, university lecturers were exposed to a loss of purchasing power, which, compared to 1910, amounted to between 20 and 25 per cent. However, they still belonged to the 1 per cent of top earners in Germany.[6] Observing their students with either concern or scepticism reinforced their pessimism and mood of crisis, for the situation of the latter was by far more difficult after 1918 than it had been before the war. At the same time, increasing numbers of social climbers from white-collar and lower middle-class families—who were, in the eyes of the professors, unwelcome—joined the university student body, which had previously been predominantly bourgeois. The number of students enrolled in history and cultural studies courses at the twenty-three universities in Germany varied considerably. After reaching a low in the inflation year of 1923, the number of enrolled students doubled to about 20,000 in 1930. In 1930, the humanities (without law and theology) were the most popular subjects at the universities of Berlin (more than 3,000 students), Munich (1,800), Cologne (1,400), Hamburg (1,700), Bonn (1,200), and Jena (1,000).[7] The mandarins felt particularly uneasy about this rise in student numbers because the proportion of women grew significantly, reaching 20 per cent in the 1920s. Until 1908, German universities had successfully resisted the admittance of women.[8]

As a collective response to these developments, mandarins in the humanities and social sciences cultivated fears of the future, political and social resentments, as well as ideas of cultural pessimism. Educational politicians of the Weimar state were fully aware of this status group's material shortages and hardships. This is shown, for instance, by the Prussian Salary Law from 17 December 1927, which initiated *Verbeamtung*—the granting of a particular legal status by which individuals became civil servants with guaranteed tenure—of non-full professors (*Privatdozenten*, *Extraordinarien*, and honorary professors), that is, academic staff without a chair, who accounted for up to three-quarters of all teaching staff at some universities.[9] This measure provided basic security for these types of university teachers. At the same time, Weimar science policy fostered the increase of research and the expansion of universities. Thus, there was a touch of denial of reality and ingratitude in the mandarins' critical and elitist distance towards the republic.[10]

Even so, the (relative) material losses of university professors after 1918 were only one part of a 'triple dispossession'.[11] The second was the decline of a public appreciation for professors, particularly in the humanities, which, before 1914, had been a matter of course in Imperial Germany. But the privileges of this educated middle-class elite, their appreciation as a quasi-estate separated by *Bildung* (refined education) did not survive the demise of the Hohenzollern and other princes of Imperial Germany. The public of the Weimar Republic was more egalitarian and, despite frequent demonstrations of appreciation for great German minds by representatives of the republic, other social groups and their representatives soon caught up—in particular, organized workers. Third, most scholars of the humanities experienced the end of the monarchy and the democratic revolution of 1918/19 as the end of 'their' nation-state, meaning that the vast majority of German professors remained alienated from the democratic republic. In addition, educational politicians of the Weimar state enforced the access of Jewish academics to university chairs, against the persistent resistance of professors and, in many places, organized students. In doing so, they strengthened the diversity of the academic social milieu in confessional, religious, and ideological terms. Again, this incurred displeasure from the majority of the professoriate, who had been shaped by the spirit of cultural Protestantism (*Kulturprotestantismus*)—the symbiosis of Protestantism and modern culture based on science.

Two additional factors deepened the crisis mood among humanities scholars and social scientists after the revolutionary events of 1918/19. The first was the rise of a new kind of journalist and writer who, detached or even alienated from the world of academia, took up topics from the field of the humanities. In as early as late Imperial Germany, various associations with a scholarly-intellectual claim to knowledge, an ideological-religious message, and a sectarian and life-reformist drive for change had become increasingly popular and gained attention among educated people. The best-known and most successful example is the authors and programmes of the publishing house Eugen Diederichs-Verlag.[12] Others include anthroposophy, theosophy, the Monist League, the tightly knit circle of friends and admirers around the poet Stefan George, and many more. This form of writing for a popular audience, marked by a discussion of contemporary issues and arguing from an ideological point of view, attracted even more readers and supporters during the Weimar Republic. It became increasingly activist and radical, combining its critique of established academic sciences and humanities with far-reaching claims to provide a superior explanation of the world. Particularly, *völkisch*-nationalist ideologies resonated with a growing number of authors and publicists who were ambitious in discussing humanities-related topics but were denied access to an academic career path. Well-known right-wing authors of the Weimar period such as Arthur Moeller van den Bruck, Oswalt Spengler, Hans F. K. Günther, the brothers Ernst und Friedrich Georg Jünger, as well as the liberal Emil Ludwig and the left-wing Walter Benjamin, are among those who challenged the mandarins of the humanities.[13] The second factor is the generational difference. Different experiences of age cohorts during the First World War created similarities between peers within the educated classes.[14] In particular the returning front generation emphasized the differences between themselves and the older generation of university professors, finding enthusiastic followers among those students who had been teenagers during the war. The 'voice' of the young now carried considerably more weight than before 1914, demanding a new start and new orientations within their academic disciplines and the entire world of academia.[15]

Both factors changed the communication structures of German humanities scholars. They, more than ever, sought for their topics, terms, and controversies to be compatible with the reviews section of the newspapers, and to regain their threatened role as intellectual pioneers of the nation, conveying meaning through their willingness to debate, their loud rhetoric, and prophethood. Ultimately, they wanted their philosophical, historical, or philological publications to be discussed by a wider public. At the same time, key terms of controversies within the humanities became flag-words in public debates and political polemics.[16] Most of these words, such as *Volk* (people), *Gemeinschaft* (community), *Geist* (spirit), *Schicksal* (fate), were nationalistically charged and, in particular, marked by a distinct anti-international focus, to which almost all German humanities scholars committed themselves after their experiences of war propaganda and the persistent ostracism of German-speaking scientists and scholars in international scientific and scholarly organizations after 1914.[17] These shifts explain the close connection between debates within the humanities and social sciences and public political and ideological controversies of their time. This is particularly true of the cultural code of antisemitism. Already widespread among German mandarins during Imperial Germany, it evolved to include interpretations that determined action and had practical application in specialist discourses and policy advice.[18]

Following Fritz Ringer, two groups of university professors can be distinguished who had differing political and cultural orientations: the reformist 'modernists' and the authoritarian and conservative 'orthodox' majority, who were, in contrast, sceptical towards modernity.[19] Due to the impact of the 'triple dispossession', the latter, being the majority, took an even stronger political stance marked by national conservatism and cultural pessimism. As a result, the radical nationalist opposition to Weimar democracy was able to recruit many followers. In many universities' philosophy and law departments these ideological convergences and early political affiliations paved the way for a wave of National Socialist self-mobilization that swept across German universities between 1933 and 1934. After 1918, the relatively small camp of modernists grew, owing to the appointment of democratic professors who had been denied access to university posts in Imperial Germany. At the same time, the political spectrum of these modernists opened up to the left, also voicing social democratic and Marxian views and arguments at German universities. The orthodox majority saw them as a political danger and symptom of a cultural crisis, and sought to combat them aggressively. Political and cultural statements and debates became increasingly sharp and irreconcilable. Consequently, many appointments to a chair in the relevant disciplines were conflict-ridden. Their resentments towards the new democratic order and its ministries of education and cultural affairs rendered the national-conservative majority susceptible when democrats, Jews, or inconvenient outsiders were supported or even appointed as professors against majority will. State interference in university matters, which had been accepted in Imperial Germany, was now regarded as a political restriction of the freedom of science.[20]

Concepts and patterns of arguments that were circulating in public debates on art, literature, and politics became more important in almost all disciplines. In the bourgeois newspapers, Weimar academics voiced diagnoses of crisis that stimulated and provided justifications for the vague uneasiness of the educated middle classes. Of course, not all disciplines shared the same proximity to public debate and controversies. History, classics and modern languages (mostly English, Romance, and Russian literature), philosophy and theology, all of which were taught in German secondary schools (*Gymnasien*), as well as policy-oriented subjects such as constitutional theory and national economics, particularly resonated with public opinion. Some examples will serve to demonstrate this. After 1914, there was a vivid exchange of ideas about the concept of space. Karl Haushofer's geopolitical concept of space triggered broad debates and was met with great approval, while German newspapers' literary pages and science policy welcomed and endorsed a spatial history of cultural and social life. At the same time, Josef Nadler developed a regional 'Literary History of the German Tribes', which attracted growing attention and recognition. Cultural politics even supported efforts of historians to compile a survey of a supposedly Germanic cultural region. This was the political sting in the tail as the space being examined clearly exceeded the current borders of the German Reich and the Republic of Austria. *Lebensraum* (living space) became a key concept among the entire nationalist camp. The critique of metropolises and modernity stirred up the issue of which spatial designs and spatial relationships were politically desirable and socially necessary.

German professors were more than eager to act on this idea of resonating with the public. Martin Heidegger's 1927 *Being and Time* is another prominent example, not only for its broader reception and impact but also for the discursive strategy of the young philosopher, translating the political semantics of his time into an elaborated, philosophical language.[21] In this and other cases, specialist or philosophical concepts became adapted as politically and culturally applicable opinions.[22] Debates among Protestants inside and outside academia on the 'theology of crisis' are another prominent example of the constant transgression of key terms from the theological sphere to political, cultural, and social contexts.[23] The initial perception of a 'crisis' of liberal theology of the nineteenth century that had successfully adopted the methods of its neighbouring disciplines, philology and history, first developed into a critical debate on the disorientation of the liberal and pluralistic culture of modernity and then, after 1918, moved on to the unsettling of traditional orders of state and society. This resulted in a 'permanent struggle about core concepts'[24] in Protestant theology, including *Volk* (people) and *Volkskirche* (people's Church), *Ordnung* (order) and *Gemeinschaft* (community), that simultaneously concerned theological, political, and social issues. We will return to this idea when discussing the development of academic disciplines. Scholars of Germanic studies expanded their claim to educate the German nation and regarded their subject as the *allumfassende Erzieherin zum Volkstum* ('all-encompassing educator of national values'), redefining it as *Deutschkunde* (study of German culture).[25] Within linguistics, 'mother tongue' evolved into a key concept that Leo Weisgerber and his school used to incorporate their research into the wider political frame of *Volkwerdung* (becoming a people) and *Volksgemeinschaft* (people's community) in order to live up to the spirit of national renewal in times of crisis.[26]

Even some of its prophets were surprised by the positive response to the semantics of *Geist* (spirit) in political and cultural debates. Conjuring up the educational content of the humanities and their subjects, such as high-brow literature and art, state and constitution, ethics and law, evoked undivided support among the educated. Despite the material crisis, the official culture and education policy of the new republic drew on educated middle-class traditions. As a result, the conflict with representatives of avant-garde trends, denounced as 'materialistic' and lacking the qualities of the 'German spirit', became even more entrenched.[27] The 'materialist' camp ranged from Karl Mannheim's sociology of knowledge to Georg Lukács's, Ernst Bloch's, or Walter Benjamin's revisions of Marxian philosophy of history. The overwhelming majority of the humanities and social sciences eagerly contributed to cultural political polemics and daily debates that the republic experienced in abundance. Only very few academics gained a positive understanding of the so-called mass culture or contemporary literary and artistic avant-gardes. In this vein, 'spirit' became a concept that marked the staunch critique of contemporary society and modernity. At the same time, rationally unjustifiable claims to privileges and the truth could easily be hidden behind this notion. The so-called 'aesthetic fundamentalism' that had already existed in Imperial Germany had widespread impact.[28] Clearly, the humanities and social sciences enjoyed much attention, which does not correspond with the 'crisis' that was talked about with a lot of consternation. The discussions met the ideological needs of many educated people and those enthusiastic about education, but, at the same time, it resulted in a plethora of divergent views. The irritated tone of the debates illustrates that there was a low tolerance for ambiguity, a tolerance which continued to decrease.

Conditions at Universities and Subject Profiles

Scholars of the humanities and social sciences in the Weimar Republic worked under generally similar institutional conditions as those in Imperial Germany. The academic structure of most universities comprised the typical four faculties (theology, medicine, law, philosophy). Only at the newly founded universities in Cologne (1919, refounded after the closure under French occupation in 1798) and Frankfurt (1914) were separate economic and social science faculties established.[29] For this reason, the subjects that are today defined as humanities and social sciences were usually allocated to three faculties: theology, law, and philosophy. Only the medical faculty was—institutionally and often also spatially—distinct. However, at smaller universities, natural sciences were also part of the philosophical faculties, which were the home of most humanities. From the 1880s onwards, German humanities scholars increasingly distanced themselves from their colleagues in the natural sciences. Theology remained an essential element of the German nineteenth-century knowledge system, and Protestant theology in particular saw itself as a critical-hermeneutic discipline and thus maintained close relations to history. In a similar vein, connections between theology and its neighbouring disciplines such as philosophy, Germanic studies, law, classical philology, and archaeology were close.[30] Faculties of law and political science were further important places of research in the humanities and social sciences because they also hosted subjects such as philosophy of law, sociology of law, public and international law, and economic sciences.

The most important institutional novelty in the Weimar Republic concerned public funding of scientific and scholarly research. In 1920, the still existing German Research Foundation (Deutsche Forschungsgemeinschaft, DFG) was founded as an 'emergency foundation of German research' in order to resolve the financial problems that humanities and natural science research projects faced due to inflation during the postwar period.[31] Humanities research projects amounted to a significant share of DFG applications. Even in 1931, '47 per cent of research grants were given to the humanities and social sciences'.[32] These subsidies allowed for the founding of specialist journals, the continuation of ongoing large-scale projects such as source editions and editions of classical authors, and, first and foremost, the start of new 'community projects' based on collaboration such as the *Atlas der Deutschen Volkskunde* (Atlas of German Folklore). The DFG placed special emphasis on supporting projects in the humanities and social sciences that were politically visible and popular with the public. With this it followed a wider tendency of public funding to foster politically desirable projects that could help fight the Versailles Treaty. The fashionable so-called *Volksforschung* (ethnic folk research) and archaeology received generous public funding, as historians worked on the publicly funded edition of documents *Die große Politik der europäischen Kabinette* with more than forty volumes, which was intended to refute the claim of the

German war guilt.[33] American foundations also supported the social sciences, albeit on a smaller scale, with subsidies for book purchases and bursaries.[34]

Before 1914, the humanities had already reached a level of differentiation that lasted until the 1950s. During the Weimar period, the humanities developed and specialized further only through the foundation of new or expansion of existing chairs. This is particularly true of new subjects such as sociology and psychology. Based on their own specialist journals, they were able to establish themselves as specialized discourse communities, failing, however, to establish distinct academic courses and degrees.[35] Political economics (*Volkswirtschaftslehre*) was the only subject that introduced its own diploma in 1923 after its three-year Ph.D. course was oversubscribed (as it was the shortest way to a doctoral degree in the humanities and social sciences).[36] Sociology benefited from the new political and social power balance, since the inclusion of social, cultural, and political contexts was now deemed to be indispensable for a deeper understanding of 'spiritual connections' and 'values'. Sociologists largely regarded their discipline as a form of theoretical synthesizing, a theory of society, or as a social philosophy. At many universities, the subject was integrated accordingly and taught together with history, linguistic sciences, economics, and political science as a tool to widen perspectives.[37]

It was arguably during the Weimar period that *Geisteswissenschaften*—the German term for 'the humanities'—became the firmly established concept that it still is today in the German-speaking world, despite various epistemological frictions. Coined by Wilhelm Dilthey in the 1880s and linked with an ambitious project of philological hermeneutics, the notion *Geisteswissenschaften* began to spread in all disciplines after the turn of the century.[38] Subsequently, a plethora of disparate interpretations have been ascribed to the 'method of the humanities' between 1910 and 1945. In 1883, Dilthey proposed to refer to 'all the disciplines that have socio-historical reality as their subject matter' as 'human sciences'.[39] For him, it was a characteristic of these subjects that they 'not only want to explain this intellectuality (*Geistigkeit*) as real but also understand and interpret their meaning'.[40] The formula 'explaining versus understanding', which was flexible and open to different interpretations, prevailed and still dominates the superficial everyday knowledge (*doxa*, in Pierre Bourdieu's terminology) of most German-speaking humanities scholars. During the inter-war period, this approach became more distinct for most humanities scholars in that it distanced them from solely rational explanations based on external circumstances as well as from 'merely' comprehending historical interpretations and institutions of 'human life'. In 1927, the philosopher Erich Rothacker wrote:

> I have attempted to address what the humanities mean when they talk about understanding. If a work is conceived, no understanding in the strict sense is involved. Is it explained, there is likewise no understanding. But where we find ourselves compelled to seek for something that is individually vital in a work, something that is not completely lost in concepts nor completely explicable, we believe to encounter attempts at true understanding, at understanding in the incisive sense.[41]

Rothacker used the formula 'objective idealism' to define the epistemological foundations of the humanities that he described in this fashion.[42] References to German nineteenth-century humanities played an important role in this respect: in addition to the philosophy of German idealism, Romanticism and nineteenth-century German historiography were constructed as normative points of reference for an independent 'German' science and humanities culture.

The newly defined unity among the humanities gained cohesion predominantly thanks to joint enemy stereotypes. Positivism was one of them, although this notion had different meanings.[43] It referred primarily to the alien 'western' academic current founded by Auguste Comte that was informed by methods and theories from the natural sciences and based on the laws of nature and causal connections. This enemy had already been identified and defined during Imperial Germany, together with its materialist ally, Marxism. Both academic concepts were deemed politically dangerous. During the Weimar years, many other approaches were lumped together with positivism, even those that did not regard themselves 'positivistic', including philological specialist research that was not geared towards synthesis. Even historical relativism, which emphasized the narrow limits of scientific objectivity within the field of historical knowledge, was now associated with 'positivism'. Most proponents of the new methods of the humanities during the Weimar years aspired to commit their research to objectively valid and ultimate values. They were thus tapping into debates on the universality and rationality of cultural values from around the turn of the century that had been critical of modern culture. Many scholars of jurisprudence, political sciences, and Germanic studies used the phenomenological study of essences and ambitious variations of an 'objective idealism' informed by Hegelian philosophy. These realignments not only opened up new horizons for fresh topics and interpretations, but also blurred the boundaries between scholarly verifiable matters and merely subjective impressions or, rather, ideological hopes. 'Idealism' became the commonly accepted cipher of an epistemological justification of scientific and scholarly work that was deemed the only legitimate one.

It is no surprise that, in opposition to these romantically embellished, idealistic positions a counter approach under the sign of rationalism emerged. It sharply and clearly criticized the new tendencies to transgress limits. Max Weber's famous 1917 lecture on 'Science as Profession', published in 1919, was only the beginning. Sociologists of knowledge such as Karl Mannheim, neo-positivists like Rudolf Carnap, or the Viennese school of law around Hans Kelsen voiced harsh criticisms of the new mainstream among the humanities.[44] In 1934, the German scholar Julius Kraft, a member of the department of theoretical economics and sociology at the university of Frankfurt until he was forced to leave Germany in 1933, published a rationalist critique with the telling title *Die Unmöglichkeit der Geisteswissenschaft (The Impossibility of the Human Sciences)*.[45] Counter positions like this one, however, were rather rare at German universities. The majority of humanities scholars regarded them as part of a much larger scientistic-materialistic threat, emanating from the natural sciences and the technology of modern civilization that already dominated society both in the West and the Soviet Union.

The spectrum of disciplines that saw themselves as being part of the humanities ranged from law to psychology, from philosophy to the philologies, from archaeology to contemporary history.[46] Theology and philosophy, with their all-encompassing offers to interpret culture and their claims to provide higher meaning, sat enthroned above the other individual disciplines. Cultural debates of the Weimar years were fraught with open and covert references to theological concepts and lines of argument.[47] Academic philosophy remained the most important producer of justifications and ideas based on the theory of science. However, sociology with its plethora of large-scale theories emerged as a competitor to this claim. In retrospect, it becomes clear that, in the majority of disciplines, the unspecified and ritualized invocation of a methodological crisis was increasingly linked to a rhetoric of an epistemic 'break', which suggested innovation and revival while traditional methods and research topics were in fact continued.

The historical school of economics, for instance, hardly survived the end of the First World War.[48] Controversies over methods before 1914 had shaken up the key epistemological positions of this approach. The critique concluded that the inductive description of changing institutions and different forms of economic activities—the core of the approach taken by the Historische Schule—could not be seen as the basis for the ethical evaluation of the current structure of state and economy. The historical school, the critique continued, also failed in pointing out regularities for the prognosis and control of contemporary economic crises. Its promise to be beneficial for politics and economy was considered exhausted and empty. Resistance mounted within the discipline against its empiricist approach, which was informed by economic history. This resistance united reform-oriented minds within the historical school who were inspired by sociology and the humanities such as Othmar Spann, Friedrich von Gottl-Ottilienfeld, the later Werner Sombart, and Alfred Weber with proponents of neo-classical economics, or rather the Austrian school and its theory of marginal utility.[49] Typically, the mostly younger challengers tried to get the majority of their colleagues behind them via a debate on theoretical and methodological key questions. However, this attempt failed due to internal subject-specific, but even more so due to economic and socio-political differences. As a result of this conflict, 'neo-liberal' market theorists, proponents of a seminal approach that proved to have a promising future, began to emerge. They ranged from social liberal theorists such as Emil Lederer to subsequent ordo-liberals like Wilhelm Röpke, Alexander Rüstow, or Walter Eucken, to Friedrich von Hayek, a representative of the Austrian school of economics.[50] They were in close contact with international debates in economics. These currents were of great importance, particularly at the beginnings of a political-economic theory of neoliberalism.

Proponents of a new dialectic theology within Protestant theory, such as Karl Barth, Friedrich Gogarten, or Rudolf Bultmann, also belonged to a younger generation. They firmly regarded their new approach as a 'theology of crisis'. In doing so, they claimed to adequately respond to the unsettling of religious and political-cultural certainties caused by the First World War and the revolution. In particular, this theology critically addressed the amalgamation of Protestant theology with specifically bourgeois cultural values and with liberal-conservative concepts of politics and society. Its inner theological critique focused on 'the theological teachers' historical-hermeneutic understanding' of the discipline.[51] After a short initial phase of cooperation (1919–22), different projects of 'dialectic theology' grew rapidly apart from each other. Four aspects can be identified that illustrate how the new theology influenced both neighbouring disciplines as well as contemporary political and cultural debates. First, the younger theologians criticized the loss of orientation of modern culture in light of the ideological pluralism at the time. This critique strongly resonated with neighbouring disciplines. Second, they demanded a 'post-critical' scriptural interpretation that should be the basis of ultimate justifications of norms and authority beyond historical change. To this end, the spokesmen of 'dialectic theology' and their pupils developed a concept of God that carried the difference between God and man to the extreme, combining the concept of a distant God with the general principle of an 'intransigently strong subject with agency'.[52] The proponents of the new approach considered it a theology of 'crisis' also because, fourth, they intended to revive the eschatological qualities of Christian teaching, believing that the idea of 'the end' of history was relevant for the present day. Dialectic theology attracted much attention and resonated with both the Protestant academic milieu of the Weimar Republic and Catholic and Jewish intellectual circles, displaying several overlaps with the contemporary existential philosophy of Martin Heidegger. Both approaches were compatible with political fantasies of redemption from the right and the left.[53] They provided problem analyses and concepts for the current cultural crisis, for a situation of political and social decision-making, and for the option of a radical and revolutionary break with history and tradition. Multi-voiced and heated theological discourses showed overlaps with and references to political and moral debates on democracy, nation, people's community, and the concept of leadership. The national-*völkisch* effervescence that existed within the traditionally national-conservative and national-liberal cultural Protestantism created a welcoming environment for these sharp controversies within the Protestant theological camp.

The escalating confrontations among Protestant theologians were similar to the situation within philosophy. There, neo-Kantianism was declared the common enemy. Neo-Hegelians, phenomenologists, existential philosophers, and philosophers of life (*Lebensphilosophen*) mobilized against the neo-Kantian Marburg school around Paul Natorp and Hermann Cohen and criticized their epistemology.[54] Opening philosophy up to issues beyond the scientific-theoretical justification of the humanities and the natural sciences was an objective that united this multifaceted group of critics. Metaphysics, ontology, or rather the phenomenological study of essences were discovered as research fields for new creations of systems and critical reflection, just as the philologies and cultural sciences were reoriented along the lines of the new concept of the humanities as *Geisteswissenschaften*.

In Germanic studies and other modern languages disciplines, established standards and routines were easy targets for criticism after 1918.[55] Meanwhile, the accusation of positivism was—as already mentioned—charged with anti-Western resentments. Specialist philological studies, as well as rather sober and restrained syntheses and overviews of different epochs, were disparagingly rejected as being obsessed with facts and details. During the 1920s and 1930s, the 'method of the humanities' (*geisteswissenschaftliche Methode*) opened up enormous interpretative scope to the scholars of literature and linguistics.[56] They discovered and described literary characteristics of different epochs and epoch-spanning constants in terms of the history of ideas.[57] Wide-ranging, complete interpretations of the Gothic and the Romantic period led to large-scale accounts of different subjects and topics.[58] This inclination to interpret tradition, classics, and deep meaning through the lens of the 'new' humanities was countered by a renewed interest in questions of the history of reception and sociology of literature.[59] Both Marxian materialists and *völkisch* racial theorists could get behind this approach, as they aimed to explain the production of art, literature, and science from social, demographical, and economic conditions, or the forms of social structure that were arising from such material circumstances. The extent to which these works were based on empirical and philological verification differed hugely. However, the opening up of literature and linguistics to a study of collective (social) entities or, rather, contexts in terms of the history of ideas, first and foremost in philosophy and theology, developed into a common way of thinking during these decades.[60]

Historical scholarship also had its own share of bubbly experimentation, even though the national-conservative majority adhered to its traditional methods and topics. Friedrich Meinecke's turn to a history of political ideas remained the exception; most historians still favoured a person-centred history of political and military events.[61] However, the proponents of a dominant political history had to strike their colours in light of the *Kulturraumforschung* (research into cultural regions) that had been eyed with suspicion until 1914 and that now started its triumph as an 'ethnic history of the people' (*Volksgeschichte*).[62] This academic current examined long-term processes such as settlement patterns, development of agricultural methods, and the form of dwellings as elementary for the shaping of geographic spaces. Its predominant interpretive pattern was ethnogenesis, either in a *völkisch*-culturalistic or in a socio-biological sense. By including different methods, such as cartography, onomatology, human geography, and research of place names, the *Volksgeschichte* hugely expanded the methodological canon of historical regional studies and history.[63] The proponents of this approach tapped into the construed notion of a community of front-line fighters, which helped them to gain academic recognition among historians and establish institutional clusters.[64] As already mentioned, interdisciplinary research groups of historical regional studies and the *völkisch* research into cultural regions were among the most widely funded research projects of the humanities during the 1920s and 1930s. Borderland struggle (*Grenzlandkampf*) and homeland protection (*Heimatschutz*) rested on a broad nationalist political consensus, and their activists could rely on the benevolent support of the methodologically conservative, but staunchly nationalist, majority of the discipline. The small number of liberal and social democratic historians around Friedrich Meinecke and the Protestant theologian Ernst Troeltsch in Berlin faced greater difficulties. Other than a few early works by Hedwig Hintze, Eckart Kehr, or Hans Baron, their new approaches to creating a critical national history and a political social history of the modern era would only gain a higher profile in exile after 1933.

Constitutional doctrine (*Staatsrechtslehre*) in jurisprudence also saw a programmatic realignment—once again at odds with 'positivism'. Here, the term referred to the school of so-called legal positivism that was dominant during Imperial Germany. It rejected the theory of natural law and other external references, instead championing a historical-critical construction of laws that were predetermined and connected to each other by their common origin as the basic norm.[65] Critics of legal positivism regarded this self-restraint as a weakness. Natural law theories, or rather fundamental principles of the discipline based on the sociology and the philosophy of law, increasingly superseded and replaced a pure legal positivism.[66] In addition, the democratic revolution and the republican constitution created new political circumstances and contexts of reasoning for constitutional theorists. Notions such as 'people's sovereignty' and 'basic rights' required legal interpretations, formulations, and implementations. Law was thus involved in the political conflicts of the Weimar Republic much more directly than other disciplines. Proponents of the democratic and constitutional state such as Hans Kelsen, Gerhard Anschütz, Hugo Preuß, Heinrich Triepel, and Hermann Heller felt compelled to defend the constitution that they had helped to draft against anti-liberal and national-conservative critics like Carl Schmitt, Erich Kaufmann, and Rudolf Smend.[67] Unsurprisingly, foundational works on constitutional theory that were published in the Weimar Republic by democratic theorists defending the new order caused heated controversies. In terms of academic methodology and theory, the new jurisprudence based on 'the methods of the humanities' on the one hand and the school of legal positivism on the other found followers in both political camps, the proponents and opponents of democracy. Only Hans Kelsen and the Austrian school with its theory of the democratic constitutional state, inspired by neo-Kantianism, went a separate way—defending the ideological pluralism of multiple political interests of the new democratic order.[68] As a result, this approach received criticism from all sides. The frontlines in jurisprudence were thus similar to those in economics and sociology: advocates of values that transcended time and normative orientations were confronted by proponents of a concept of science limited to methodology and logic, who insisted on a difference between value judgements and scientific statements.[69] In contrast to this, academic trends inspired by 'the method of the humanities' favoured a 'formation of concepts that overcome opposition' (*gegensatzaufhebende Begriffsbildung*). This was in order to widen the field of legal interpretation into a systematic reconstruction of overarching social 'orders' (*Ordnungen*), where the law only had to regulate things that corresponded with the 'essence' of the matter or the wider social configurations.[70] This approach hugely expanded the potential for criticism from the vantage point of jurisprudence, and its claim to offer meaningful interpretations. Both opportunities were frequently used in the struggle over Weimar's democracy and the interpretation of its constitution, with the national-conservative and radical nationalist camps within the discipline leading the way.

Beyond Disciplinary Boundaries: The Humanities as Field of Struggle and Experimentation for the Interpretation of Modernity

Despite the differences between disciplines and subject groups, it is remarkable that the humanities and social sciences during the Weimar era were in their majority committed to certain overarching, trans-disciplinary topics and concepts, including the slogans that dominated contemporary debates such as *Geist* (spirit), *Ganzheit* (the whole), *Raum* (space), and *Volk* (people). These concepts gained the status of ultimate justifications or 'historical ideas'.[71] From 1918 onwards, many humanities scholars had recourse to them. These concepts determined which phenomena attracted academic attention and which figures of argumentation were used within the different disciplines, while the concepts themselves (*Volk*, *Raum*, *Geist*) inevitably remained undefined.

The shared feature of these concepts was the epistemic, and very soon also the ethical and political, priority that was given to the whole over its parts. After 1918, this precedence of 'the whole' evolved into the most intensely defended basic principle within the humanities. Holistic theories were the basis of most research approaches. Unsurprisingly, 'idealistic' concepts dominated, however, it is striking that materialist counter-concepts chose very similar constructions and arguments. For instance, Georg Lukács's 1923 essay collection titled *Geschichte und Klassenbewusstsein* (*History and Class Consciousness*), which swiftly became a classic of a new Marxist philosophy of history and social philosophy, focused on the concept of 'totality'.[72] It is no coincidence that Lukács emphasized the traces of Hegelianism in Marx's work. Young representatives of the Frankfurt school of 'critical' social theory followed him in this respect, developing his insights on the structure of capitalism as a closed system into the foundation of their radical critique and theory of society.[73] Reference to this position, which clearly remained marginal during the Weimar Republic, illustrates that the idea of 'the whole' was not only utilized by the political right, even though after 1933 most proponents of holistic concepts were part of the scholarly and scientific landscape of the Third Reich controlled by the Nazis.

The holistic programme forced the humanities to describe in greater detail the overall structure, its elements and internal relations, which they gave theoretical precedence over the analysis of singular phenomena. This need to analyse overarching structures proved a widespread challenge, as the complexity of these formations was the crux for all disciplines. It is a common characteristic of the German humanities that they attempted to resolve this problem by referring to philosophical concepts developed during the nineteenth century. After more than seventy years, Hegel's dialectic was rediscovered and the 'formation of concepts that overcome opposition' began not only to be used in law departments. Neighbouring disciplines also used this approach to dissolve conceptual antinomies such as what is and what ought to be, idea and matter, individual and community, in new syntheses. The concept of essences was revaluated and applied by contemporary phenomenological philosophy. Here, the 'intuitive perception of essences' (*Wesensschau*) was considered as a way out of the pitfalls that historical cultural research entailed, as it necessarily produced colourful yet ultimately diverse and arbitrary results. Thus, *Wesensschau* was meant to counter the random results of culturalistic approaches. Yet in many of these debates, resulting antagonistic opposites could only be reconciled by mere play on words, without actually resolving the logical problems.

Clearly, the reason for this is that the concept of 'spirit' was a theoretical obstacle in developing new formats of description and explanatory models. 'Spirit', used as conceptual and explanatory tool, constantly forced scholars to choose the internal perspective of empathic interpretation, or rather to intuitively relate ideas, thoughts, and emotions, when examining links between literary works, networks of persons, ideas of space, and geographic-social environments. It was the great advantage of the established concept of 'spirit' and its related category of 'becoming' that it considered the dynamics of changes in symbolic systems, and even their temporal and factual priority to changes in material, economic, and institutional structures. The humanities used this privileging of the symbolic dimension to create a bulwark against any form of causal 'explanation' based on external causes. At the same time, the concept of 'spirit' was highly charged with theological and philosophical underpinnings: for many mandarins, upholding the concept of 'spirit' meant to express their Protestant or Catholic belief in an intelligible world order that was deducible by reason. The semantic of *Geist* (spirit) allowed these ideological needs to be articulated in a way that seemed appropriate with the autonomy of scientific reason. This becomes apparent in the malicious polemics against Karl Mannheim's sociology of knowledge. While Mannheim emphasized social conditions of the process of knowledge production, his critics in the *Geisteswissenschaften* were convinced that the notion of the 'spirit' was irreducible to any social conditions.

The external critique by materialist approaches was adopted in the humanities by translating two key terms from the political language of the time into the terminology of the relevant disciplines: *Volk* and *Gemeinschaft* (community) evolved into constructs that encompassed the inexplicable causal interrelations of elements within a structural context. However, in doing so, *völkisch*-nationalist scholars came dangerously close to the much-maligned materialism, here in form of a racial theory based on biology and racial hygiene, which increasingly claimed the concept of *Volk* exclusively for itself. Helped by the political and ideological debates of the 1920s and 1930s, the language of this new biological racism penetrated the semantics of 'spirit' in the humanities ever further. Scholarly texts increasingly referred to categories such as *Verwurzelung* (rootedness) and *Entwurzelung* (rootlessness), *Minderwertigkeit* (inferiority), or racial-*völkisch* 'homogeneity'. This created a common terminology that was, before 1933, already shared by both the new humanities and by biological racism, together with its spin-offs racial antisemitism and racial hygiene. Again, right-wing journalism paved the way for racial semantics permeating academic production. The mutual penetration of racial semantics and rhetoric of 'spirit' created political and ideological common ground between the largely NSDAP-leaning students and their mostly right-wing professors. At the same time, it gave leeway for materialist research that had been rejected and frowned upon until then. These overlaps are particularly striking in the research into cultural regions, a subject that evolved into *the* interdisciplinary research field par excellence. Philologists and sociologists such as Gunter Ipsen and Hans Freyer combined different perspectives, adapted Karl Marx and Max Weber, and expanded the field of common terminology for the humanities and racial research.[74] In particular notions such as 'mother tongue' were successful because they presupposed the *völkisch* foundation of a homogeneous community as a constitutional characteristic of a research subject that was then defined as being exclusively a matter of the humanities.[75] The concept of 'spirit' had already been charged with nationalist meaning from 1914 onwards. During the 1920s, it increasingly gained *völkisch* connotations, and thus prepared its close connection with sociobiological, racial concepts after 1933.[76]

Even today, the humanities in Germany have difficulties taking stock of the intellectual achievements of their disciplines between 1918 and 1933. Most of their academics remained in office after 1933 and continued working under the Nazi dictatorship. Many displayed an utter lack of intellectual distance and moral judgement vis-à-vis the Nazi regime. As a result, we find a long, dark shadow falling over the ideas, methods, and research projects that enabled such a self-mobilization for the 'Third Reich'. For a long time, the academic minority that was forced into exile and their research achievements shone all the brighter. The list of these scholars is long: Aby Warburg, Ernst Cassirer, Theodor W. Adorno, Walter Benjamin, Siegfried Kracauer, Hans Rosenberg, or Hans Baron, to name but a few. Recent research has adopted a more nuanced view of the intellectual legacy of the exiled scholars, revealing its time- and place-specific similarities with the mandarins' way of thinking. The emerging picture is neither clear nor homogeneous. Often, the exiled scholars amended their position under the impact of the Nazi dynamics. Indeed, only very few cases show a direct transplantation of Weimar approaches into new academic research contexts, though they nonetheless existed. Particularly contested was, and still is, the legacy of contemporary intellectuals such as Carl Schmitt and Martin Heidegger. The antisemitic foundation of their theories that recent studies have unveiled is an obstacle to their unbiased rediscovery or further use. Dialectic theology as the most important innovation of the Weimar period is no easy legacy for today's Protestant theology either. If anything, Weimar's democratic constitutional theory is arguably the discipline that has successfully restored its reputation.[77]

Conclusion

To sum up, four overall trends can be identified. First, the humanities reacted highly sensitively to the shifts in the relationships between science, politics, and public after the upheavals in 1918. The common desire for a comprehensive worldview can be seen as an indicator of the increasingly tighter link between internal academic and public debates. The demand grew for scientific and scholarly legitimization and expertise to evaluate different ways of life and political programmes. At the same time, the mandarins' willingness to meet these needs and expectations of the public increased. Accordingly, communication between the humanities, culture, and politics was very intense—with ambivalent results. On the one hand, the attention to contemporary politics and cultural phenomena inspired new research questions and theories, clearly increasing the willingness to innovate within the humanities and social sciences. On the other hand, it blurred the boundaries between worldview, opinion, and specialist scientific and scholarly knowledge—in many cases beyond recognition.

Second, the ideologically motivated search to find ultimate justifications for research in the humanities and social sciences spawned a plethora of proposals. The most popular contemporary variety, namely the return to ultimate values of a cultural context that was considered to transcend time, is the least acceptable and most incompatible with modern concepts of science. Contemporary critics, on the other hand, played an important role in further developing methodological concepts and premises in the humanities and social sciences, either as neo-positivism or critical rationalism and philosophy of language (Rudolf Carnap, Karl Popper, Ludwig Wittgenstein, and others), or as critical theory and other variations of Western Marxism, or, finally, as different forms of rationalist historicism following Weber, Ernst Cassirer, and others.

Third, particular attention was placed in all disciplines on the integration of research subjects on cultural matters into wider collective contexts. Diachronic and synchronic perspectives created many interdisciplinary links between relevant humanities and social sciences subjects. Assumptions about the configuration of cultural phenomena remained largely speculative.

Fourth, the political and social situation in Germany after its defeat, the revolution, and the foundation of a democratic state radicalized the status anxieties of German professors, producing what can be described as a 'moral panic'. The loss of political and moral judgement, the susceptibility to nationalist radicalism, and the development of antisemitic resentments were the most striking peculiarities of this moral panic. It was not just a character trait that remained outside the mandarins' academic work. Rather, it influenced research in the humanities and social sciences profoundly. This was a crucial precondition for the broad cooperation and mobilization of most humanities scholars and social scientists in favour of the Nazi regime and its ideological goals. They welcomed the new national scientific field that was politically controlled after 1933 as a way out of the 'crisis' and as an authoritarian stabilization of their own vested interests.

Translated from German by Christine Brocks.

Notes

1. Peter Schöttler (ed.), *Geschichtsschreibung als Legitimationswissenschaft, 1918–1945* (Frankfurt/Main: Suhrkamp, 1999); Frank-Rutger Hausmann (ed.), *Die Rolle der*

Geisteswissenschaften im Dritten Reich 1933–1945 (Munich: Oldenbourg, 2002); Hartmut Lehmann and Otto G. Oexle (eds), *Nationalsozialismus in den Kulturwissenschaften*, vol. 1. *Fächer, Milieus, Karrieren* (Göttingen: Vandenhoeck & Ruprecht 2004); Holger Dainat and Lutz Danneberg, *Literaturwissenschaft und Nationalsozialismus* (Tübingen: Max Niemeyer Verlag, 2003).

2. Claus-Dieter Krohn, *Wissenschaft im Exil: Deutsche Sozial- und Wirtschaftswissenschaftler in den USA und die New School for Social Research* (Frankfurt/Main and New York: Campus, 1987); Marianne Hassler and Jürgen Wertheimer, *Der Exodus aus Nazideutschland und die Folgen: Jüdische Wissenschaftler im Exil* (Tübingen: Attempto-Verlag, 1997); Karin Orth, *Die NS-Vertreibung der jüdischen Gelehrten: Die Politik der Deutschen Forschungsgemeinschaft und die Reaktionen der Betroffenen* (Göttingen: Wallstein, 2016); Michael Grüttner and Sven Kinas, 'Die Vertreibung von Wissenschaftlern aus den deutschen Universitäten 1933–1945', *Vierteljahrshefte für Zeitgeschichte*, 55 (2007), 123–86.

3. Kathrin Groh, *Demokratische Staatsrechtslehrer in der Weimarer Republik: Von der konstitutionellen Staatslehre zur Theorie des modernen demokratischen Verfassungsstaats* (Tübingen: Mohr Siebeck, 2010); Friedrich Wilhelm Graf, *Der heilige Zeitgeist: Studien zur Ideengeschichte der protestantischen Theologie in der Weimarer Republik* (Tübingen: Mohr Siebeck, 2011).

4. Falko Schnicke, *Die männliche Disziplin: Zur Vergeschlechtlichung der deutschen Geschichtswissenschaft 1780–1900* (Göttingen: Wallstein, 2015), 455.

5. Fritz K. Ringer, *The Decline of the German Mandarins: The German Academic Community, 1890–1933* (Cambridge, MA: Harvard University Press, 1969).

6. Hartwin Spenkuch 'Republikanische Wissenschaftspolitik im Freistaat Preußen: Problemlagen, Professorenberufungen, Leistungen', in Berlin-Brandenburgische Akademie der Wissenschaften (ed.), *Wissenschaftspolitik in der Weimarer Republik: Dokumente zur Hochschulentwicklung im Freistaat Preußen und zu ausgewählten Professorenberufungen in sechs Disziplinen (1918 bis 1933)*, 2nd ed. (Berlin: De Gruyter, 2018), 1–188, here 18.

7. Hartmut Titze, *Wachstum und Differenzierung der deutschen Universitäten 1830–1945* (Göttingen: Vandenhoeck & Ruprecht, 1995), 83, 104, 291, 334, 375.

8. Ibid., 43.

9. Spenkuch 'Republikanische Wissenschaftspolitik', 21–2.

10. Ibid., 2–79; Michael Grüttner (ed.), *Die Berliner Universität zwischen den Weltkriegen: 1918–1945* (Berlin and Boston: De Gruyter, 2012), 83–113.

11. Dieter Langewiesche, 'Die Eberhard-Karls-Universität Tübingen in der Weimarer Republik: Krisenerfahrung und Distanz zur Demokratie an deutschen Universitäten', *Zeitschrift für Württembergische Landesgeschichte*, 51 (1992), 345–81, here 365.

12. Gangolf Hübinger (ed.), *Versammlungsort moderner Geister: Der Eugen Diederichs Verlag—Aufbruch ins Jahrhundert der Extreme* (Munich: Eugen-Diederichs-Verlag, 1996).

13. Georg Bollenbeck and Clemens Knobloch (eds), *Resonanzkonstellationen: Die illusionäre Autonomie der Kulturwissenschaften* (Heidelberg: Synchron, 2004); Pierre Bourdieu, *The Political Ontology of Martin Heidegger* (Stanford, CA: Stanford University Press, 1991); Clemens Knobloch,'Volkhafte Sprachforschung': Studien zum Umbau der Sprachwissenschaft in Deutschland zwischen 1918 und 1945* (Tübingen: Niemeyer, 2005).

14. Ernst Schulin, 'Weltkriegserfahrung und Historikerreaktion', in Wolfgang Küttler, Jörn Rüsen, and Ernst Schulin (eds), *Krisenbewußtsein, Katastrophenerfahrungen und

Innovationen 1880–1945 (Frankfurt/Main: Fischer Taschenbuch-Verlag, 1997), 165–88; Graf, *Der heilige Zeitgeist*.
15. Jan Eckel, *Hans Rothfels: Eine intellektuelle Biographie im 20. Jahrhundert* (Göttingen: Wallstein, 2005); Schulin, 'Weltkriegserfahrung'.
16. Bollenbeck and Knobloch, *Resonanzkonstellationen*.
17. Gabriele Metzler, 'Deutschland in den internationalen Wissenschaftsbeziehungen', in Michael Grüttner et al. (eds), *Gebrochene Wissenschaftskulturen: Universität und Politik im 20. Jahrhundert* (Göttingen: Vandenhoeck & Ruprecht, 2010), 55–82.
18. Wiebke Wiede, *Rasse im Buch: Antisemitische und rassistische Publikationen in Verlagsprogrammen der Weimarer Republik* (Berlin and Boston: De Gruyter, 2011); Per Leo, *Der Wille zum Wesen: Weltanschauungskultur, charakterologisches Denken und Judenfeindschaft in Deutschland 1890–1940* (Berlin: Matthes & Seitz, 2013).
19. Ringer, *Decline*, 128–42.
20. Christian Tilitzki, *Die deutsche Universitätsphilosophie in der Weimarer Republik und im Dritten Reich*. 2 vols (Berlin: Akademie Verlag, 2002); Spenkuch, 'Republikanische Wissenschaftspolitik', 1–188.
21. Martin Heidegger, *Sein und Zeit* [1927], in *Martin Heidegger Gesamtausgabe*, vol. 2 (Frankfurt/Main: Vittorio Klostermann, 2018 [1st ed. 1927]; Johannes Fritsche, *Geschichtlichkeit und Nationalsozialismus in Heideggers Sein und Zeit* (Baden-Baden: Nomos, 2014).
22. Bourdieu, *Political Ontology*.
23. Graf, *Der heilige Zeitgeist*, 12–28, 111–38.
24. Ibid., 77.
25. Jost Hermand, *Geschichte der Germanistik* (Reinbek bei Hamburg: Rowohlt, 2017), 86.
26. Knobloch, *Volkhafte Sprachforschung*, 87–110.
27. Dirk Hoeges, *Kontroverse am Abgrund: Ernst Robert Curtius und Karl Mannheim. Intellektuelle und 'freischwebende Intelligenz' in der Weimarer Republik* (Frankfurt/Main: Fischer Taschenbuch Verlag, 1994).
28. Stefan Breuer, *Ästhetischer Fundamentalismus: Stefan George und der deutsche Antimodernismus* (Darmstadt: Wissenschaftliche Buchgesellschaft, 1995).
29. Roman Köster, *Die Wissenschaft der Außenseiter: Die Krise der Nationalökonomie in der Weimarer Republik* (Göttingen: Vandenhoeck & Ruprecht, 2011), 71.
30. Graf, *Der heilige Zeitgeist*.
31. Karin Orth and Willy Oberkrome (eds), *Die Deutsche Forschungsgemeinschaft 1920–1970: Forschungsförderung im Spannungsfeld von Wissenschaft und Politik* (Stuttgart: Steiner Verlag, 2010).
32. Patrick Wagner, 'Grenzwächter und Grenzgänger der Wissenschaft: Die Deutsche Forschungsgemeinschaft und die Geistes- und Sozialwissenschaften 1920–1970', in Orth and Oberkrome (eds), *Die Deutsche Forschungsgemeinschaft*, 347–62, here 349.
33. Wagner, 'Grenzwächter und Grenzgänger', 358; Willy Oberkrome, 'Geschichte, Volk und Theorie: Das "Handbuch des Grenz- und Auslandsdeutschtums"', in Schöttler, *Geschichtsschreibung als Legitimationswissenschaft*, 104–127; Michael Fahlbusch, *Die Volksdeutschen Forschungsgemeinschaften in Deutschland 1931–1935* (Baden-Baden: Nomos Verlag, 1999); Johannes Lepsius and Albrecht Mendelssohn-Bartholdy (eds), *Die große Politik der europäischen Kabinette 1871–1914: Sammlung der diplomatischen Akten des Auswärtigen Amtes*, 40 vols (Berlin: Deutsche Verlags-Gesellschaft für Politik und Geschichte, 1922–1927).

34. Judith Syga-Dubois, *Wissenschaftliche Philanthropie und transatlantischer Austausch in der Zwischenkriegszeit: Die sozialwissenschaftlichen Förderprogramme der Rockefeller-Stiftungen in Deutschland* (Cologne: Böhlau, 2019).
35. Erhard Stölting, *Akademische Soziologie in der Weimarer Republik* (Berlin: Duncker & Humblot, 1986).
36. Köster, *Wissenschaft der Außenseiter*, 73.
37. Stölting, *Akademische Soziologie*; Köster, *Wissenschaft der Außenseiter*, 169–80.
38. Christoph König and Eberhard Lämmert (eds), *Literaturwissenschaft und Geistesgeschichte 1910 bis 1925* (Frankfurt/Main: Fischer-Taschenbuch-Verlag, 1993).
39. Wilhelm Dilthey, *Selected Works*, vol 1. *Introduction to the Human Sciences* (Princeton: Princeton University Press, 1989), 56. Translator's note: In English translations of Dilthey's works, *Geisteswissenschaften* is usually translated as 'human sciences', a term that today encompasses a wider range of disciplines including history, philosophy, genetics, sociology, psychology, evolutionary biology, biochemistry, neurosciences, ethnology, and anthropology.
40. Erich Rothacker, *Logik und Systematik der Geisteswissenschaften* (Munich and Berlin: Oldenbourg, 1927), 13.
41. Ibid., 124.
42. Ibid., 59.
43. Friedrich Wilhelm Graf, Gangolf Hübinger, and Rita Aldenhoff-Hübinger (eds), *Kultur und Kulturwissenschaften um 1900*, vol. 2. *Idealismus und Positivismus* (Stuttgart: Steiner, 1997).
44. Ringer, *Decline*, 200–26.
45. Julius Kraft, *Die Unmöglichkeit der Geisteswissenschaft*, 3rd ed. (Hamburg: Meiner 1977).
46. Heinz-Elmar Tenorth, Volker Hess, and Dieter Hoffmann (eds), *Transformation der Wissensordnung*, vol. 5. *Geschichte der Universität Unter den Linden Praxis ihrer Disziplinen, 1810–2010* (Berlin: Akademie, 2010).
47. Graf, *Der heilige Zeitgeist*, 64–5.
48. Köster, *Die Wissenschaft der Außenseiter*, 31–60.
49. Köster, *Die Wissenschaft der Außenseiter*, 89–120; Hauke Janssen, *Nationalökonomie und Nationalsozialismus: Die deutsche Volkswirtschaftslehre in den dreißiger Jahren* (Marburg: Metropolis-Verlag, 1998), 20–120; Friedrich Lenger, *Werner Sombart 1863–1941: Eine Biographie*, 2nd ed. (Munich: Beck, 1995), 306–31.
50. Janssen, *Nationalökonomie und Nationalsozialismus*; Köster, *Wissenschaft der Außenseiter*; Marc Lüdders, *Die Suche nach einem Dritten Weg: Beiträge der deutschen Nationalökonomie in der Zeit der Weimarer Republik.* (Frankfurt/Main: Lang, 2004).
51. Graf, *Der heilige Zeitgeist*, 115.
52. Ibid., 127.
53. Ibid., 111–61, 205–368, 425–59.
54. Ulrich Sieg, *Geist und Gewalt: Deutsche Philosophen zwischen Kaiserreich und Nationalsozialismus* (Munich: Carl Hanser, 2013), 151–192; Christian Tilitzki, *Die deutsche Universitätsphilosophie in der Weimarer Republik und im Dritten Reich*, 2 vols (Berlin: Akademie, 2002).
55. Hermand, *Geschichte der Germanistik*; König and Lämmert, *Literaturwissenschaft und Geistesgeschichte*.

56. König and Lämmert, *Literaturwissenschaft und Geistesgeschichte*; Holger Dainat, 'Klassische und Germanische Philologien', in Tenorth et al., *Transformation der Wissensordnung*, 461–94
57. Hermand, *Geschichte der Germanistik*, 83–97.
58. Hans Much, *Vom Sinn der Gotik* (Dresden: Reissner, 1923); Julius Petersen, *Die Wesensbestimmung der deutschen Romantik* (Leipzig: Quelle & Meyer, 1926), Walther Rehm, *Der Todesgedanke in der deutschen Dichtung vom Mittelalter bis zur Romantik* (Halle/Saale: Niemeyer, 1928).
59. Levin L. Schücking, *Soziologie der literarischen Geschmacksbildung* (Munich: Rösl, 1923).
60. Graf, *Der heilige Zeitgeist*; D. Timothy Goering, *Friedrich Gogarten (1887–1967): Religionsrebell im Jahrhundert der Weltkriege* (Berlin: De Gruyter Oldenbourg, 2017).
61. Bernd Faulenbach, 'Nach der Niederlage: Zeitgeschichtliche Fragen und apologetische Tendenzen in der Historiographie der Weimarer Republik', in Schöttler, *Geschichtsschreibung als Legitimationswissenschaft*, 31–51.
62. Willy Oberkrome, *Volksgeschichte: Methodische Innovation und völkische Ideologisierung in der deutschen Geschichtswissenschaft 1918–1945* (Göttingen: Vandenhoeck & Ruprecht, 1993); Matthias Middell, *Weltgeschichtsschreibung im Zeitalter der Verfachlichung und Professionalisierung: Das Leipziger Institut für Kultur- und Universalgeschichte 1890–1990*, vol. 2 (Leipzig: Akademische Verlagsanstalt, 2005).
63. Oberkrome, *Volksgeschichte*.
64. Ingo Haar, '"Revisionistische" Historiker und Jugendbewegung: Das Königsberger Beispiel', in Schöttler, *Geschichtsschreibung als Legitimationswissenschaft*, 52–103; Oberkrome, *Volksgeschichte*; Middell *Weltgeschichtsschreibung*.
65. Michael Stolleis, *Geschichte des öffentlichen Rechts in Deutschland*, vol. 3 (Munich: Beck, 2017), 159–63.
66. Ibid., 171–86.
67. Kathrin Groh, *Demokratische Staatsrechtslehrer in der Weimarer Republik: Von der konstitutionellen Staatslehre zur Theorie des modernen demokratischen Verfassungsstaats* (Tübingen: Mohr Siebeck, 2010); Christoph Gusy (ed.), *Demokratisches Denken in der Weimarer Republik* (Baden-Baden: Nomos, 2000).
68. Hans Kelsen, *Verteidigung der Demokratie: Abhandlungen zur Demokratietheorie*, ed. Matthias Jestaedt (Tübingen: Mohr Siebeck, 2006).
69. Stolleis, *Geschichte des öffentlichen Rechts*, 163–71; Groh, *Demokratische Staatsrechtslehrer*.
70. Oliver Lepsius, *Die gegensatzaufhebende Begriffsbildung: Methodenentwicklungen in der Weimarer Republik und ihr Verhältnis zur Ideologisierung der Rechtswissenschaft im Nationalsozialismus* (Munich: C. H. Beck, 1994).
71. Siegfried Kracauer, *Geschichte—vor den letzten Dingen* (Frankfurt am Main: Suhrkamp, 2009), 110.
72. Georg Lukàcs, *Geschichte und Klassenbewusstsein: Studien über marxistische Dialektik* (Berlin: Malik-Verlag, 1923).
73. Jörg Später, *Siegfried Kracauer: Eine Biographie.* (Berlin: Suhrkamp 2016); Rolf Wiggershaus, *Die Frankfurter Schule: Geschichte, theoretische Entwicklung, politische Bedeutung*, 4th ed. (Munich: Dt. Taschenbuch-Verlag, 1980).
74. Jerry Z. Muller, *The Other God that Failed: Hans Freyer and the Deradicalization of German Conservatism* (Princeton: Princeton University Press, 1987); Haar, '"Revisionistische" Historiker'.
75. Knobloch, *Volkhafte Sprachforschung*, 87–110.

76. Ibid., 287–310; Wiede, *Rasse im Buch*.
77. Groh, *Demokratische Staatsrechtslehrer*.

Bibliography

Breuer, Stefan, *Ästhetischer Fundamentalismus: Stefan George und der deutsche Antimodernismus* (Darmstadt: Primus Verlag, 1995).

Eckel, Jan, *Geist der Zeit: Deutsche Geisteswissenschaften seit 1870* (Göttingen: Vandenhoeck & Ruprecht, 2008).

Graf, Friedrich Wilhelm, *Der heilige Zeitgeist: Studien zur Ideengeschichte der protestantischen Theologie in der Weimarer Republik* (Tübingen: Mohr Siebeck, 2011).

Groh, Kathrin, *Demokratische Staatsrechtslehrer in der Weimarer Republik: Von der konstitutionellen Staatslehre zur Theorie des modernen demokratischen Verfassungsstaats* (Tübingen: Mohr Siebeck, 2010).

Grüttner, Michael (ed.), *Die Berliner Universität zwischen den Weltkriegen: 1918–1945* (Berlin and Boston: de Gruyter, 2012).

Hübinger, Gangolf (ed.), *Versammlungsort moderner Geister: Der Eugen Diederichs Verlag. Aufbruch ins Jahrhundert der Extreme* (Munich: Diederichs, 1996).

König, Christoph, and Eberhard Lämmert (eds), *Literaturwissenschaft und Geistesgeschichte 1910 bis 1925* (Frankfurt/Main: Fischer Taschenbuch Verlag, 1993).

Ringer, Fritz K., *The Decline of the German Mandarins: The German Academic Community, 1890–1933* (Cambridge, MA: Harvard University Press, 1969).

Schöttler, Peter (ed.), *Geschichtsschreibung als Legitimationswissenschaft: 1918–1945* (Frankfurt/Main: Suhrkamp, 1999).

Stölting, Erhard, *Akademische Soziologie in der Weimarer Republik* (Berlin: Duncker & Humblot, 1986).

CHAPTER 32

VISUAL WEIMAR

The Iconography of Social and Political Identities

KERRY WALLACH

Weimar culture was flooded with symbolic images, and a wide range of social and political types emerged within its visual landscape. It is difficult to imagine Weimar without the New Woman, the shop girl, the jazz musician, the athlete, the worker, the disillusioned veteran, the unemployed, the revolutionary, or even the budding Nazi. The shorthand established by widely disseminated images of these and other types—particularly in photographs, advertisements, and films, but also as literary and cultural figures—provided an iconographic framework for the construction of identities. Whereas some chose to emulate or pursue membership in a social group based on these types and their collective appeal, others disavowed or otherwise negatively responded to such archetypes and the collectives they represented. Key to understanding the iconography (a term which here refers to visual content including symbolic forms and motifs) of Weimar's social and political identities is the notion of how these images reinforced and also challenged depictions of visible difference.[1]

The mass media in which images appeared likewise played a crucial role in facilitating the visibility of iconic types. Widespread use of Leica and Ermanox cameras starting in the mid-1920s helped make photography more accessible, and photojournalism became increasingly popular. With around four thousand newspapers and magazines published for Weimar readers, including over thirty dailies in Berlin alone, images featured in periodicals could reach the masses very quickly.[2] Photojournalists, artists, and graphic designers were commissioned to create the images and advertisements that filled these pages. Major illustrated weeklies from the *Berliner Illustrirte Zeitung* (*BIZ*) to the *Arbeiter Illustrierte Zeitung* (*AIZ*) enjoyed large circulations of nearly two million and 450,000, respectively, and were responsible for sharing some of the most widely known images.[3] Standard newspapers stayed competitive by using outside publishing houses to produce attractive weekly illustrated supplements.[4] Cinemas, too, gained prominence as Germans sought out innovative forms of entertainment. The German film industry responded to the growing interest in moving images by producing over 3,500 full-length feature films from 1919 to 1933.[5] Most were genre films, suggesting filmgoers became accustomed to seeing certain types and plotlines repeated on screen.

To analyse Weimar's images and the major trends among them, visual cultural studies offers a number of methods and theories, including some that originated in the Weimar years. Theorists of visual culture today commonly consider the literal and symbolic messages of images, the historical contexts of meanings and subjects, the role of accompanying text, as well as the role of the viewer in deciphering meaning.[6] This interpretive model draws from the reception of Weimar photography and photobooks, which has much to teach about visual analysis.[7] For example, artist Johannes Molzahn's aptly titled essay, 'Stop Reading! Look!' (1928), was symptomatic of the growing importance of images in newspapers and photobooks and their educational value. Bauhaus professor László Moholy-Nagy similarly emphasized the need to become visually literate given the growing ubiquity of photographs.[8] And in his 1931 essay, 'A Short History of Photography', cultural theorist Walter Benjamin pointed out the significance of photographer August Sander's portraits in the photo series *Antlitz der Zeit* ('Face of our Time', 1929). According to Benjamin, Sander's series of faces provided an 'atlas of instruction' in 'physiognomic awareness', which Benjamin anticipated would become increasingly meaningful with shifts in political power. In this essay Benjamin also famously inquired, 'Won't inscription become the most important part of the photograph?'[9] Text cannot be ignored in the analysis of images. Sander's photographs used captions to transform anonymous subjects into types, often based on their professions. The types became iconic in and of themselves, eclipsing the relevance of individuals. Some scholars interpret Sander's series as subtly questioning narratives of progress within modernity.[10] These early theories of image analysis suggest that Weimar visual culture successfully constructed original constellations of images and introduced new ways of viewing and interpreting them. Images took on symbolic potential in light of how they were represented, used, and perceived. The symbolic or iconographic potential of images was thus closely tied to their reception.

Finally, with Weimar culture's imperative to look also came subtle instructions on how to see—including warnings about deception. Even as some texts contained captions or guidelines for interpreting visual images, others challenged the stability or reliability of common categories of difference (gender, race, class) and instead taught viewers to look twice. Art historian Maria Makela has suggested that the blurring of identity in Weimar culture related to the widespread perception 'that one could no longer trust vision as a means of gauging class, ethnicity, or … gender, sexuality, and age'.[11] Blurred and changeable identities were typical for Weimar. Viewers were insecure about misreading these identities and the ensuing 'feeling of being duped', which was exacerbated by such phenomena as doctored April Fools' photomontages in illustrated papers and the many imposter characters in early Weimar cinema.[12] Whether accurate or misleading, visual attributes were paramount in conveying information about identities. The complexity of this visually encoded information prompted viewers to stare at, scrutinize, and attempt to decipher the messages about their subjects contained in each image. In the following, this chapter explores how visual representations of gendered, racialized, and political and class differences called attention to these categories in both divisive and unifying ways.

Gendered Figures: Disabled Veterans to Fashionable Façades

Otto Dix's *Großstadt* ('Metropolis') triptych painting from 1928 introduces viewers to a Weimar nightclub's interior and exterior spaces. The triptych form recalls medieval altarpieces and their ability to harness the power of familiar symbols.[13] Inside the nightclub, in the centre panel, jazz musicians entertain decadent and fashionably dressed clientele, some dancing. On the street outside, we see a fallen soldier, a crippled veteran, a begging amputee, as well as numerous scantily clad streetwalkers. As with many other works associated with *Neue Sachlichkeit* or New Objectivity, Dix's painting opens up a discussion of several key gendered types that recurred in Weimar culture. The disfigured men's bodies reflect on war's destruction. Women's bodies are on display, contested sites of decorative ornament and pleasure. Here, too, at least one person challenges the gender binary and confronts viewers with hard-to-place androgyny. Dix's painting is one of many images that helped to codify, uphold, and subvert common and idealized notions of belonging and difference that played out along gender lines.

The category of gender—and related notions of sexuality—provided Weimar culture with the means to construct new iconic figures and dismantle traditional ones. Many of the gendered figures now associated with the 1920s and early 1930s were not new, but rather updated versions of modern women and men that began to emerge around the turn of the century: the soldier injured in the Great War; the criminal or ex-con down on his luck in a rough economy; the masculine-inspired New Woman with short, bobbed hair, ready to work as a stenographer or shopgirl; the hypersexualized female dancer; and the femme fatale, now wearing furs and reading fashion magazines such as *Die Dame*. Sexually transgressive practices from prostitution and pornography to cross-dressing, androgyny, and homosexuality (or non-heterosexuality) were a constant source of fascination for Weimar society.[14] Visual representations of transgressive practices can be found in countless films and works of art that draw the viewer's attention to the roles gender and sexual difference played. Again, the possible blurring of gender and sexual identities complicated these texts' reception. In each instance, the available visual evidence and clues may or may not have sufficed to help viewers determine who or what exactly was depicted.

Masculinity and male identity were often bound up with representations of the First World War. Artists, photographers, and filmmakers all attempted to harness the great potential of visual images to reflect critically on the treatment of soldiers who returned with scars, wounds, trauma, or other signs of battle. For example, Otto Dix's *Die Skatspieler* ('Skat Players', 1920) foregrounds disfigured and amputated veterans with a hearing aid and prosthetic jaws.[15] George Grosz's drawing of a Berlin street scene featuring an amputee beggar with an Iron Cross was a widely known image of disabled veterans.[16] Some images served as political caricatures or as part of political pamphlets or campaigns. Grosz illustrated a different 1921 pamphlet with the slogan 'Der Dank des Vaterlandes' ('The Thanks of the Fatherland'). In the cover illustration, an arm reaches through a crutch to hold out a military-style cap; the Communist Party of Germany also used this image on election posters in 1924.[17] Although these images reflected a common urban sight, official investigations determined that many street beggars were in fact peacetime disabled men who could earn more from begging in a military uniform.[18] In this case, popular images heightened the visibility of disabled men and veterans and associated them with economic problems. Disability and disabled male bodies came to symbolize weakness, defeat, and vagrancy even when they were not actually what they seemed.

Photographs and documentary film footage of wounded soldiers and soldiers in battle were regularly used for political purposes, including as evidence against fighting wars that demoralized a generation of men. Notably, Ernst Friedrich's photobook, *Krieg dem Kriege!—War Against War!* (1924), embedded close-up graphic photos of the faces of wounded and mutilated soldiers—among other horrific and shocking images—within a pacifist narrative of victimization to protest war and military action.[19] Some of these photographs were also exhibited in the Anti-War Museum in Berlin, which Friedrich founded in 1925. Susan Sontag suggested that these photographs were 'superior to any painting' in terms of how they affected viewers; however, the photographs originated in a medical publication about the achievements of reconstructive surgery, not the effects of war.[20] Plastic surgery became increasingly popular throughout the Weimar period; it was difficult for many people to come to terms with the fact that faces could change and render someone unrecognizable from his or her former self.[21] Friedrich's use of these particular images of the war-disabled thus reflects both male vulnerability and change-ability, which hints at the disruption caused by both wounds and surgical procedures.

It was not only veterans with visible physical damage who featured prominently in iconic images of men's post-war suffering. One historian has suggested that the 'male hysteric ... haunted the German imagination' in the Weimar Republic.[22] Post-war psychological trauma, shell shock, and memory loss—which were more difficult to depict in still images—were common themes of Weimar films.[23] Many of these films are set not on the battlefield, but as encounters with those psychologically damaged by war. The early Expressionist film *Nerven* ('Nerves', 1919) addressed madness, hallucination, and suicide among revolutionaries and other characters.[24] Known widely for its formal Expressionist innovations and surprise ending, *Das Cabinet des Dr Caligari* ('The Cabinet of Dr Caligari', 1920) used the genre of horror to project wartime anxieties onto residents of an insane asylum. In *Caligari*, it remains unclear who is the insane patient, and who the director of the asylum. Profound unease about confused identities is also the theme of many Weimar films about soldiers returning from war. In *Mensch ohne Namen* ('The Man without a Name', 1932), a protagonist who suffered from amnesia for sixteen years must verify his identity after being declared dead. This film implies somewhat alarmingly that there may be no way to confirm someone's alleged identity in the absence of visible scars.[25] Whether implicitly or explicitly, images of those physically and psychologically damaged in the war offer a reflection on the unstable status of men within German society.

Weimar's focus on athleticism and sports also put gendered bodies on display, which emphasized physical differences between men and women (women's bodies are discussed further below). Athletes became celebrities as images of their muscular physiques were put on display and circulated. For example, well-known boxer Hans Breitensträter was immediately invited to work with gallery owner Alfred Flechtheim upon arriving in Berlin, and Galerie Flechtheim published artist Rudolf Großmann's lithographs of Breitensträter in 1921.[26] Similarly, boxer Max Schmeling was featured repeatedly as his winnings continued to grow (see figure. 32.1). Satirical magazines including *Simplicissimus* and *Ulk* depicted Schmeling as someone who had ascended to greater heights than Goethe or Bismarck, and whose earnings had surpassed Thomas Mann's.[27] At least three artists made formal portraits of Schmeling; George Grosz's appeared in the magazine *Der Querschnitt*.[28] In contrast, less athletic bodies were subjected to criticism and were believed to reflect a nation in crisis, as discussed below in the section on political figures.

Weimar's constant state of crisis—whether real or perceived—catalysed both corruption and criminality, particularly as objects of scandal or obsession. Crime rates rose with

FIGURE 32.1 Boxer Max Schmeling with his manager and trainer, 1930.

Photograph by Georg Pahl.

inflation in the early 1920s but decreased sharply after 1924. Still, the fantasy of lawlessness persisted, and murderers and underworld figures loomed large in Weimar culture.[29] Visual culture helped popularize criminal figures, mostly men—though women criminals also featured prominently on occasion. Many of Weimar's most infamous murderers became iconic through media representations. London's Jack the Ripper (active circa 1888) had inspired a series of copycat *Lustmord* or 'lust murder' attacks on prostitutes and others that conflated sex and violence, and these persisted in different forms. Broadly conceived, such violence reflected a crisis of gender anxiety, masculinity, and sexuality. In many instances, criminal motivation was related to the fascination with the 'other', and 'abnormal' forms of sexuality also entered the fray.[30] Such killers simultaneously shocked the public and held its attention: Carl Grossmann, who dismembered women; homosexual serial killer Fritz Haarmann; child murderer Peter Kürten, who terrorized Düsseldorf.[31] Grossmann's case provided a set of visual themes for such artists as George Grosz and Otto Dix, including mutilated and violated female bodies.[32] The remarkable visuals of Fritz Lang's film *M* (1931), which was criticized for exploiting the real case of Peter Kürten, bring together 'mass murder, mass culture, and mass public' by allowing viewers to reflect on how the masses might contribute to criminal investigations. The shot of the murderer examining himself in a mirror to see the identifying chalk 'M' on his back offers insight into how outsiders could be physically marked as other, as Todd Herzog has argued.[33] Terrifying individuals and threatening situations created a culture obsessed with both criminal and sexual deviance and their consequences.

Thus unsurprisingly, many quintessential Weimar stories and films centre on criminal protagonists who have become representative of Weimar culture. They represent the continuation of a long-time fascination with crime stories, while also adding modern, new dimensions. Bertolt Brecht's hit crime drama, *Die Dreigroschenoper* ('The Threepenny Opera', 1928), which G. W. Pabst made into a musical film in 1931, introduced an underworld in which beggars threaten to pretend to be disabled to deceive the public and disrupt the queen's coronation.[34] Rudolf Forster's performance as gangster boss and antihero Mackie Messer (Mack the Knife) in the film version made a particularly strong impression; his razor-sharp moustache hinted at the cruel and sinister deeds of an apparently dashing, elegant gentleman. In contrast, Franz Biberkopf, the seemingly hapless protagonist of Alfred Döblin's *Berlin Alexanderplatz* (1929 novel; 1930 radio play; 1931 film), attempted to rehabilitate himself into an upstanding citizen after a four-year prison sentence for involuntary manslaughter. Despite his brutal treatment of women, Biberkopf was for many a sympathetic character broken in part by the system.[35] Heinrich George's portrayal of Biberkopf recalled the actor's previous roles, many consisting of similar 'good-natured brutality'.[36] Mackie Messer and Franz Biberkopf represent different types of male criminals who mistreated women and at times managed to evade the law through duplicity.

Women criminals, too, were the subjects of many media scandals; the femme fatale became a common fixture in films. Criminality and violence were often entangled with sexual transgression or difference here as well. In 1923, the sensational five-day trial of two women rocked the German press. Ella Klein and Margarete Nebbe, who became lovers while both were married to men, slowly poisoned Ella's husband and plotted to kill Margarete's husband. Their case was immortalized in Alfred Döblin's work *Die beiden Freundinnen und ihr Giftmord* ('The Two Girlfriends and their Murder by Poisoning', 1924), which included Döblin's illustrations of phases of their case to chart alleged sexual pathology.[37] This story associates criminal lesbians with 'a female masculinity that is characterized by excessive sexuality'.[38] The perversion mapped onto women who transgressed sexual boundaries is also on full display in *Die Büchse der Pandora* ('Pandora's Box', 1929), the breakout German film for actress Louise Brooks, who starred as Lulu. This Lulu figure updated playwright Frank Wedekind's femme fatale and exemplified the New Woman on screen in many ways.[39] Brooks's spellbinding Lulu exemplified the iconic women who challenged laws and conventions with their appearance, behaviour, and emancipated sexuality.[40]

The *Neue Frau* or New Woman, one of the Weimar period's most iconic figures, was known for her self-determination in defying the status quo, and especially for challenging gender boundaries. After 1924, ubiquitous visual representations of slim, masculinized modern women with short *Bubikopf* (pageboy bob) hairstyles helped create and popularize this symbol of feminist liberation. In addition to Louise Brooks, such actresses as Asta Nielsen, Pola Negri, and Tilla Durieux wore and were associated with the *Bubikopf* and its symbolism.[41] The New Woman was often depicted as sporty or athletic, as in Lotte Laserstein's painting, *Tennisspielerin* ('Tennis Player', 1929). The fashionable New Woman wore makeup and short skirts or pants, smoked cigarettes, drove automobiles, frequented cinemas and dance halls, and—in contrast to her American counterpart, the flapper—went to work.[42] White-collar working women were represented as stenographers, journalists, designers, and shop girls. Paintings such as Käthe Münzer-Neumann's *Die Berufstätige* ('The Working Woman', 1929), which was featured in an exhibition on *Die Frau von heute* ('The Woman of Today'), simply showed a woman wearing a tie seated at a table, with her exact profession left somewhat ambiguous (see figure. 32.2).[43] Newly empowered with disposable incomes and the right to vote, women began to be seen as sought-after consumers, moviegoers, and voters.[44]

Images of the New Woman unquestionably impacted the way people thought about the roles of women and gender during the Weimar period. Much has been written about mass media representations of the New Woman in advertisements, fashion magazines, newspaper supplements, photography, and film.[45] The New Woman was an especially effective mode of visual address 'because she was both desirable and recognizable'.[46] She appeared in countless product logos (e.g. Bahlsen cookies, designed by Bauhaus artist Martel Schwichtenberg) and advertisements for such products as cosmetics, household items (especially Persil detergent), stockings, shoes, furs, and clothing.[47] She enticed potential consumers in advertisements for department stores including KaDeWe and Hermann Tietz in Berlin. While some scholars have argued that the New Woman was more of a myth or fictional type, others have pointed to the real ways in which women modelled their tastes after the New Woman, for example by using makeup and dress to experiment with gender presentation.[48] And the New Woman was a formidable role model, particularly for such Bauhaus photographers as Marianne Brandt who used

FIGURE 32.2 *Die Frau von heute* (The Woman of Today) Exhibition organized by the Verein der Künstlerinnen zu Berlin, 1929. The painting *Die Berufstätige* (The Working Woman) by Käthe Münzer-Neumann can be seen in the top row on the left.

self-portraits as an intervention into what images of women and new forms of femininity could accomplish.[49]

Female bodies had special symbolic potential; women's legs in particular represented both rationalized and sexualized aspects of gender difference. On display everywhere thanks to the shortest hemlines in history, legs appeared as a new sex symbol, often clad in either silk or artificial silk (rayon) stockings. Illustrated magazines including *Das Magazin* boldly called for women to reveal their legs.[50] Of course, legs also featured prominently in a range of dance performances. In his essay, 'Das Ornament der Masse' ('The Mass Ornament', 1927), Siegfried Kracauer suggested that the legs of the dancers in the Tiller Girls revue moved in such a mechanized way that they corresponded to hands in a factory.[51] Actress Marlene Dietrich's character Lola Lola famously caught the eye of Professor Unrat in the film *Der blaue Engel* ('The Blue Angel', 1930) by exposing her legs, including her inner thighs. For her part, Dietrich gained notoriety for singing a popular song about how all of Berlin was crazy about her legs. One of the many artistic images titled *Beine* ('Legs', c. 1927–9) by the photographer Yva (Else Neuländer-Simon), whose work included many photographs of objects for product advertisements, was included alongside still-lifes in the 1929 Film und Foto exhibition.[52] Such legs simultaneously symbolized sexual availability and the objectification of women's bodies. Legs-as-art also begged the question as to whether life was masquerading as art, or vice versa.

Perhaps the most arresting visual affronts to traditional notions of gender were ambiguously gendered representations of bodies. Androgyny in paintings, photographs, and films helped disrupt the ways gender and sexuality were perceived and understood. Scientists such as Magnus Hirschfeld developed models for assessing sexuality that were contingent on gender and gender expression, and Hirschfeld further argued for the existence of sexual intermediaries.[53] Artist Oskar Schlemmer explored gender-neutral bodies in paintings and other art installations.[54] Such paintings as Willy Jaeckel's *Dame mit Zigarette* ('Woman with Cigarette', 1925), Otto Dix's *Bildnis der Journalistin Sylvia von Harden* ('Portrait of the Journalist Sylvia von Harden', 1926), and Christian Schad's *Sonja* (1928), as well as August Sander's photograph *Sekretärin* ('Secretary', 1931), portrayed androgynous seated women with bobbed hair and cigarettes.[55] For all of these images, the title alerts the viewer that the subject is female, but the images themselves disavow typical forms of femininity, resulting in a disconnect. The same could be said for some works by Jeanne Mammen, whose watercolours regularly paired two androgynous-looking female figures.[56] Films starring such actresses as Ossi Oswalda and Elisabeth Bergner featured stories of cross-dressing and gender confusion. Several actresses became known for playing *Hosenrollen*, or pants-roles.[57] In other cases, androgyny and cross-dressing symbolized alternate sexualities. Photographer Lotte Jacobi's double portrait of Erika and Klaus Mann famously depicted the sister and brother both wearing white shirts and neckties, and with similar hairstyles, suggesting a trend toward sameness that transcended gender difference (see figure. 32.3).[58] Some representations of non-traditional

FIGURE 32.3 Klaus and Erika Mann, 1930, Munich.
Photograph by Lotte Jacobi. University of New Hampshire. Used with permission.

FIGURE 32.4 Transvestites in the Eldorado Bar, Berlin, circa 1929.
Photograph by Herbert Hoffmann. Original title: 'Which lady is real? Don't give yourself a headache: only the one in the middle.'

gendered figures were designed to confound, as in one image of transvestites in the Eldorado Bar (see figure. 32.4). With the decline of Weimar culture in the early 1930s came a greater emphasis on traditional gender roles, especially mothers.[59]

RACIALIZED OTHERS: JEWS, BLACKS, AND OTHER MINORITIES

Nazi propaganda relied heavily on visual constructions of racial difference that were already widespread long before 1933. With the emergence of new scientific and pseudo-scientific biomedical fields in the late nineteenth century, visual evidence played an increasingly central role in establishing physiological, hereditary, and pathological norms.[60] Images in circulation during the Weimar period reflect developments in the burgeoning field of nationalistic race theory that coincided with the growing popularity of photography. Indeed, it is difficult to imagine modern race theory without its photographic visualizations of what supposedly constituted racial difference and above all set 'other' racialized identities—especially Jews, Blacks, and so-called gypsies—against white 'German' or 'Aryan' appearance. This section examines how visual representations and coding constructed notions of racial otherness, as well as the ways images were used and manipulated to create racial groups. Important here, too, are instances when racialized difference was allegedly invisible or difficult to see. In these cases, appearances were thought to be misleading or deceptive.

Photography played a critical role in documenting alleged physical differences between Germans and others designated racially non-white or non-German, though photography was not considered to be entirely reliable. Although scientific writings since the 1870s had described certain visually perceptible racial types (including two 'pure' types: the 'blonde' and the 'brunette'), publications of the 1920s depended even more on photographs and illustrations.[61] Scientist Eugen Fischer, whose work on African populations of mixed descent (1913) led to a career in genetics that extended to the Nazi regime, laid the groundwork for using photographs in studies about race. But by prioritizing actual bloodlines over appearance, Fischer concluded that photographs could deceive—they could not show recessive genes—and thus were not fully trustworthy.[62] Race theorist Hans F. K. Günther's work, *Rassenkunde des deutschen Volkes* ('Racial Science of the German People', 1922), which was reprinted numerous times and heavily influenced racist Nazi ideologies, contained dozens of photographic examples of racial types. Amos Morris-Reich has argued that Günther's own suspicions impacted his photographic series because Günther believed racial characteristics had become more camouflaged and thus were more difficult to see. Careful observation of numerous images was necessary to detect what he understood to be racial essence.[63] The notion that it was at times difficult to see difference often led to caricatures or exaggerations designed to render difference conspicuously visible.

The differences postulated by race scientists impacted visual culture well beyond the academic realm. Like Günther, race theorist Ludwig Ferdinand Clauß clustered photographs to show different racial types, and also to show movement and facial expressions.[64] He juxtaposed and contrasted photos of Jews and others with images of 'Nordic' types. Interestingly, Clauß's work was perceived as less biased, and excerpts and images from his *Seele und Antlitz der Rassen und Völker* ('On the Soul and Face of Races and Peoples', 1929) were reprinted in the illustrated *Israelitisches Familienblatt*, a Jewish newspaper whose editors sought to arm readers with a scientific basis for challenging allegations of racial inferiority. Here and elsewhere, systems of differentiating German racial types from others were not seen as harmful as long as the 'other' was seen as different but not inferior.[65] Yet growing right-wing nationalism continued to privilege so-called 'Aryan' colouring and appearance. By the Weimar Republic's final years, advertisements and other images in illustrated magazines no longer featured dark-haired women or others who could have been interpreted as Jewish.[66] Blond became the dominant hair colour in German magazines by the early 1930s.[67]

The process of visually excluding Jewishness from Germanness involved racializing Jews as a population, or attributing distinctive stereotypical traits to Jews. As Sander Gilman and other scholars have shown, the Western tradition has long considered the Jewish body inherently different.[68] Visual constructions of Jewish otherness appeared in countless antisemitic cartoons in both mainstream and right-wing periodicals beginning in the nineteenth century. Popular satirical magazines including the Vienna-based *Kikeriki* regularly published cartoons that reproduced Jewish-coded figures with despicable physical features.[69] Nazi Party member Julius Streicher's virulently antisemitic newspaper *Der Stürmer* sold 25,000 copies weekly even before Hitler took power. The paper began including cartoons in 1925 and photographs in 1930; many of its cartoons were repulsive anti-Jewish caricatures by cartoonist Philippe Rupprecht, penname 'Fips'. In Fips's hand, 'the Jew' was 'short, fat, ugly, unshaven, drooling, sexually perverted, bent-nosed, with piglike eyes'.[70] These unflattering stereotypes also recurred in photographs in works like Günther's *Rassenkunde des jüdischen Volkes* ('Racial Characteristics of the Jewish People', 1930), which attempted to relate Jewish features physiognomically to those of peoples of Near Eastern and Oriental racial origin. Günther's work also repeated age-old stereotypes of Jews as people who limped, were flatfooted, and had a distinctive accent and manner of speaking (*Mauscheln*).[71] Because many of these and other distinctive traits could be concealed, Jews were also widely suspected of trying to 'pass' for non-Jews.

As a precaution against growing antisemitism, some Weimar Jews found ways to encode and display Jewishness to make it more ambiguous but still visible to those with a trained eye. In contrast to the stereotypical hair and eye colour and exaggerated features found in Nazi caricatures, Jews emphasized their connections to Jewish organizations. Photographs of members of student fraternal organizations that were part of the Kartell-Convent deutscher Studenten jüdischen Glaubens (Association of German Students of the Jewish Faith) demonstrate that these students proudly wore the distinctive colour (*Couleur*) yellow—which had long been associated with Jewishness—on caps, sashes or bands, and pins. Zionist student groups sometimes paired yellow with the colours blue and white or with a Star of David. Similarly, members of the Reichsbund jüdischer Frontsoldaten (Reich League of Jewish Front Line Soldiers, RjF) advocated for members to wear their 'RjF' lapel pins, which made them easily recognizable to one another in public.[72] Jewish periodicals, such as Martin Buber's journal *Der Jude* and the *Israelitisches Familienblatt*, famously displayed variations on the word 'Jew' or 'Israelite' in their titles and mastheads, and some—for example, *Die jüdische Frau* (1925–7)—boldly included such symbols as a menorah on their covers. Jewish visual artists including Hermann Struck, Ludwig Meidner, Jakob Steinhardt, and Rahel Szalit-Marcus used subtle characteristics to depict Jewish or biblical subjects in etchings, woodcuts, lithographs, paintings, and illustrations.

Aside from Jews, Blacks constituted the racialized minority group most often depicted in visual culture, yet images of Blacks signified quite differently. Before the Weimar period, caricatures of Black figures were widespread in advertisements produced by most colonial powers. The rise of modern advertising culture was intertwined with the subjugation of colonized peoples.[73] In the 1920s, several phenomena affected depictions of Black people. On the one hand, grotesque and racist images were central to the Rhineland's *schwarze Schmach* or 'Black Shame' campaign, and such imagery and scare tactics persisted for decades. On the other hand, Black jazz musicians and other performers symbolized American culture's influence, though these were sometimes overshadowed by more overtly racist images.

When the Allied Forces sent Black troops from French colonies in Africa to occupy important areas of Germany following the Treaty of Versailles, a new fear emerged of non-white violent 'beasts' who could commit sexual crimes against white German women. Newspapers, novels, pamphlets, caricatures, posters, postcards, photographs, films, and other propaganda materials promoted the 'Black Horror' stereotype. They targeted the 'Negro pest' on the Rhine and warned against their allegedly primitive forms of sexuality.[74] The satirical magazine *Kladderadatsch*, for example, featured caricatures depicting Black men as gorillas attacking or ravaging white women.[75] Stamps and flyers with disturbing images of large, militaristic black men further fuelled the campaign against the African French soldiers.[76] Many of these images exploited fears of racial mixing stoked by Eugen Fischer and others who studied German colonial populations. Such fears led to debates about mixed marriages and the *Mulattisierung* or 'mulattoization' of white Europe.[77] Underlying this discourse was the idea that racial difference in the form of Blackness would become less visible—and therefore more dangerous—with the mixing of populations. Racial difference was considered all the more dangerous when it could not easily be seen.

Taken symbolically, images of Black American performers often stood for American culture or jazz culture. Such images were generally coded as other or exotic, and although jazz itself was highly contested, images of Black jazz did not offer a simple criticism of their subjects. Rather, jazz was sometimes depicted as a means to liberate the body. As Jonathan Wipplinger has shown, 'jazz bands' began performing in Berlin in 1921, and with them came a number of highly visible Black performers.[78] Otto Dix responded with representations of Black jazz musicians in paintings like *An die Schönheit* ('To Beauty', 1922).[79] Josephine Baker's performances with La Revue nègre in 1925 and 1926—many in her famous banana skirt—played on nostalgia for the lost colonial past and profoundly influenced German perceptions of jazz as sexualized and even primitive (see figure. 32.5).[80] The cabaret sequence in Walter Ruttmann's avant-garde film *Berlin, Die Sinfonie der Großstadt* (1927) includes glimpses of both a quartet of Black singers and a female dancer in a skirt reminiscent of Baker's bananas (in addition to endless rows of dancers' legs). But it was the images of Black saxophone musicians that appeared time and again in visual culture. Photographs such as Yva's *Charleston* (1927), a multiple exposure photograph of women dancing around a Black saxophone player, were splashed across the covers of magazines including the *BIZ*.[81] For those who rejected American and Jewish culture, the film *The Jazz Singer*, starring Al Jolson, which first played in German theatres as a silent version in 1928 and a sound version in 1929, supported perceptions of jazz as created by Blacks and marketed by Jews. The Nazis famously changed the Weimar-era trope of a Black saxophone player—further known for its association with Ernst Krenek's 1927 jazz opera *Jonny spielt auf* ('Jonny Strikes Up')—by marking the saxophonist with a Star of David, which became the face of the *Entartete Musik* (Degenerate Music) exhibition in 1938.[82] This grotesque image again dehumanized both Blacks and Jews by emphasizing physical difference using derogatory imagery that couldn't be unseen.

FIGURE 32.5 Josephine Baker in the role of a modern schoolgirl in La Revue nègre, Paris, 1925.

Visual constructions of racialized difference also brought other minorities to the fore. Sinti and Roma peoples were among those categorized as *Zigeuner* (gypsies) and were depicted as particularly visible outliers. In fact, the term 'gypsy' extended beyond a strictly racialized group to include others who embraced the fantasy of a Bohemian lifestyle. The category also included vagabonds, beggars, prostitutes, and even artists. Gypsies were often characterized negatively as childlike, asocial, homeless, unruly, or criminal.[83] Images of gypsies in the Weimar period ranged from drawings and lithographs by Expressionist artist Otto Pankok, who had lived with many Sinti near Düsseldorf, as well as paintings by Jewish artist Julo Levin and his students, to far less sympathetic portrayals of stereotypical gypsy characters.[84] In addition, numerous films from the 1910s and Weimar period were considered part of the *Zigeunerdrama* genre, including some that dealt with artists or 'foreign' customs.[85] Many representations of gypsies did not attempt a realistic portrayal and instead defaulted to traits that invoked an objectionable lifestyle.

Countless images in Weimar culture reinforced notions of racialized difference, but even photographs were not fully trusted to convey information about race. Many who believed in the importance of visible racial difference were also apt to believe that it was sometimes difficult or impossible to see, which subsequently elevated the significance of factors like heredity and ancestry. Visual culture nevertheless contains key examples of how images were used to convey information about physiognomy, race, and the alleged racial inferiority of minorities.

Class and Political Power Struggles

Weimar's visual culture was inextricably intertwined with its swift political changes. Photographs in illustrated periodicals and photomontages, along with films, posters, and pamphlets, had the potential to garner political support and at times even wielded their own political power. Iconic images of key politicians became ubiquitous symbols of particular political events or movements. Imagery emphasizing the working class fuelled political parties across the spectrum, from the Communists to the National Socialists. In fact, some of these images relied on common symbols or slogans—for example, 'work and bread'—that made it difficult to discern which party they represented. Politicized images targeting such nebulous groups as 'the workers', 'the masses', and 'the Germans' indicate that visual language was but one part of a larger affective appeal. Still, the ways political parties and members of other movements visualized leaders, heroes, and adherents reveals much about their platforms and ideologies with respect to gender, race, and class difference.

In the 1920s and early 1930s, the likenesses of key political figures circulated among mass readerships as never before due to *Illustrierten*. Both the people depicted and the ways they were portrayed reflect the Weimar Republic's dance with democracy. Photographs provided enduring evidence of a political moment that had occurred, and some moments were restaged so that they could be captured on film. Certain political images, such as photographs of SPD politician and future Chancellor Philipp Scheidemann's call for a democratic republic from the window of the Reich Chancellery on 9 November 1918, were at once iconographic and iconic. With arms outstretched, Scheidemann called upon a sea of workers and soldiers to reject the old monarchy and embrace the new democracy. Photographs of Karl Liebnecht, who had declared a free socialist republic on 9 November, showed him amidst similar political fervour at a rally.

In contrast, other iconic images reflected a nation in crisis. The infamous, unflattering photograph of President Friedrich Ebert and Defence Minister Gustav Noske in swimming trunks that appeared on the *BIZ*'s cover on 21 August 1919, the day Ebert took the oath of office, demonstrates how images of men's bodies were used to defamatory political ends. This cover image provided 'a vivid corporeal metaphor for the state of the postwar republic at its very inception', as well as an impetus to heal the national body.[86] If the men leading the country lacked dignity and were seen as weak and soft, then the republic itself had reason to fixate on physical self-improvement. Other images, such as Erich Salomon's supposedly candid snapshots of political figures including Foreign Minister Gustav Stresemann and President Paul von Hindenburg, likewise showed Weimar leadership in all of its precariousness.[87] However, Salomon's choice of photographs in the final version of his photobook also advocated for the ailing republic by favourably depicting certain scenes and by omitting prominent German politicians from the far right or far left, as Daniel Magilow has pointed out.[88]

Many images of political figures—especially those who became more iconic when they were murdered—indeed supported the notion that Weimar was struggling under the weight of revolutions and political transformations. Avant-garde artists responded to the violent deaths of Spartacists Rosa Luxemburg and Karl Liebknecht in January 1919, and of the prime minister of the Bavarian Republic, Kurt Eisner, in February 1919, with a 'visual iconography of martyrdom, redemption, and resurrection', especially in a portfolio of woodcuts titled *Lebendige* ('The Living').[89] Artist Käthe Kollwitz commemorated Liebknecht's death using traditional Christian iconography: a mother and her baby, among other mourners, bent in deference to the deceased (see figure. 32.6).[90] Foreign Minister Walther Rathenau, the first German Jew to hold such a high governmental position, became a warning of the dangers of antisemitism when he was assassinated by right-wing extremists in 1922. Rathenau's image came to symbolize both progress and doom for Jewish acculturation. He was beloved in the Jewish press; one of his self-portraits appeared on the cover of the first issue of *Das jüdische Magazin* in July 1929. He further served as a martyr of the republic in general.[91]

Any study of political figures in Weimar must also mention the prevalence of photographs of Adolf Hitler, beginning in 1925 with the frontispieces in different editions of *Mein Kampf*. Hitler's 'personal photographer' Heinrich Hoffmann took

FIGURE 32.6 Woodcut by Käthe Kollwitz, Commemoration of Karl Liebknecht's death, 1919.

many of the photos of Hitler in circulation and for celebratory volumes like *Das Antlitz des Führers* (The Führer's Countenance, 1939). Earlier photographs of Hitler enable the beholder to feel greater proximity to the subject, whereas later photographs depict him in statesman's poses.[92] The ways political figures were depicted is of great significance for how iconic images made an impact.

Photography in art, especially in avant-garde photomontage, served as a potent political tool in the Weimar period. Many montages compiled images and text in a sophisticated way that required several levels of interpretation; others offered more overt political commentary. In many instances, the positioning of a photographic image within an unexpected or unlikely context prompted viewers to reconsider its meaning. Deborah Ascher Barnstone and Elizabeth Otto have proposed that artistic resistance alters dominant worldviews through commentary and functions as political resistance through critique of accepted cultural symbols and meanings.[93] For example, Dadaist photomonteur John Heartfield was the master of modifying photographs for political ends, and his montages demonstrate both complex critiques of bourgeois capitalism and shameless caricatures of nationalism and Adolf Hitler. Together with satirist Kurt Tucholsky, Heartfield created the photobook *Deutschland, Deutschland über alles* (1929), which excoriated Germany for its capitalist cultural practices, militarism, and political leadership past and present.[94] Many of Heartfield's most political montages also appeared on the cover of the Communist *AIZ*, including *Der Sinn des Hitlergrusses* ('The Meaning of the Hitler Salute'), which circulated in October 1932, two weeks before national elections. In this montage, a capitalist behind Hitler deposits a handful of cash into Hitler's saluting hand.[95] Its power lies in how it modifies actual photographs; viewers know that some of this image is genuine, although the overall product is fabricated. The act of looking behind the scenes to separate the 'real' photograph from the art leads to an understanding of its critique. Then as today, such modified images—which we now sometimes refer to as 'photoshopped' or a 'deepfake', in the case of videos—were delightfully deceptive and considered dangerous.

Workers and the unemployed were the subject of countless photographs of Weimar's periods of economic instability. The concept of a collective 'Arbeiter-Fotografie' (Workers' Photography) was promoted through anonymity in *Arbeiter-Fotograf*, which included only photographers' initials, and the *AIZ*, which generally eschewed photo credits.[96] Yet there were still established leftist photographers who became known as individuals. Walter Ballhause, for example, photographed the effects of the world economic crisis from 1930 to 1933, including queues in front of employment agencies, the unemployed sitting on park benches, and housewives searching for edible scraps in the waste from weekly markets.[97] Taken from the up-close perspective by a member of the social class depicted, Ballhause's images differ from those of such press photographers as Willy Römer. Some of Römer's images seem posed or composed, and he did not go unnoticed by many of his subjects. Römer's images of the inflation period in 1922 and 1923 show old beggar women, women waiting in line for meat, children bringing home scraps from the market, and mountains of worthless banknotes. One photo of unemployed men and women from 1931 captures a sea of faces turned upward toward the camera, some smiling.[98] Whereas Römer did photograph some workers, he also documented the ascent of Hitler and the Nazi Party in 1932 and 1933, including masses of people giving the Hitler salute. All of these photos challenge viewers to determine and question possible political messages.

Propaganda images of workers were used to mobilize people across the political spectrum. They appeared on political posters, in pamphlets and periodicals, and in theatre and film. The worker stood in for the average person; the worker became the 'face of the masses', a powerful if nebulous symbol in and of itself.[99] All parties included images of women workers, though parties varied in their support for married women as workers. The Communist Party appealed to women to join the revolutionary struggle while simultaneously depicting them as too downtrodden to fight; in contrast, the National Socialist party promised women 'emancipation from emancipation' and a return to marriage and the family.[100] Early Nazi propaganda, taking a cue from advertising theory, relied heavily on the memorable visuals created by pairing symbols with a political 'brand'.[101] Like several political campaigns used by the Communist Party, many National Socialist posters from the early 1930s also appealed to workers with basic promises of work and bread. One Nazi poster campaign for the 1932 Reichstag elections paired the slogan 'Arbeit und Brot' with images of factory smokestacks or outstretched hands receiving tools (see figure. 32.7). The swastika is secondary to the symbols of work in these posters.[102] The worker himself—or herself—needs the context of additional images or words to be fully politicized.

In the early 1930s, a number of films mobilized images of workers for Communist purposes. Filmmaker Slatan Dudow, who would later make films in East Germany, directed several notable films during the late Weimar period including *Zeitprobleme: Wie der Arbeiter wohnt* ('How the Berliner Worker Lives', 1930) and *Kuhle Wampe oder: Wem gehört die Welt?* ('Kuhle Wampe or Who Owns the World?', 1932). A short documentary-style film, *Zeitprobleme* included close-ups of individual workers' faces that placed the viewer in much greater proximity than the portraits of someone like photographer August Sander. With an early focus on an employment office (*Arbeitsamt*), the word 'Arbeit' appears on signs and documents in the film's first few minutes with great frequency. In *Kuhle Wampe*, a feature film with a script and song lyrics by Bertolt Brecht, young workers unite to participate in a sports day that culminates in everyone singing 'The Solidarity Song'. In keeping with the song's lyrics that emphasize the word 'forward', many sequences in *Kuhle Wampe* are rapid montages that show forward motion. The film's final scene in the S-Bahn conveys that only those unsatisfied with the world will use their power to change it. This appeal to collective power suggests that radical change is still possible, though great challenges stand in its way. This underlying tension between political messages and the supposedly authentic portrayals of workers characterizes many such images.

FIGURE 32.7 'Arbeit und Brot' (Work and Bread), Nazi Party Poster for the Reichstag elections in November 1932.

Conclusion

Because of the rapid changes in technology and the broad reach of illustrated periodicals, photography, films, and advertisements, the sheer volume of images created and disseminated in Weimar Germany suggests that Weimar visual culture is worth studying on its own terms. Acts of looking, seeing, and gazing took place in new venues and in innovative ways. Yet viewers were also mistrustful of images that had the potential to be unreliable. Ambivalence prevailed with respect to the representation of social groups, from veterans and criminals to New Women and Jews; the contours and differences of these groups were not always clearly defined. Such ambiguities made room for both fluidity and volatility among and between members of social groups. In many representations of political groups, however, strong collective symbols hint at attempts toward unambiguous identification. But here, too, political ideologies were not always immediately clear, and some slogans and images were deliberately vague.

With the rise of National Socialism in 1933, Weimar visual culture was rapidly extinguished. Still, there are some noteworthy continuities between the periods: images remained central, and such themes as athletic bodies persisted well into the 1930s. Traditional gender roles were prevalent, including a renewed emphasis on motherhood, fatherhood, and family, which played out visually in both overt and subtle ways. Swastikas appeared in the foreground and background of countless Nazi-era photographs taken in urban areas. Already by the summer of 1933, *Die Dame* featured an image of Magda Goebbels with her baby daughter: blond women and their 'Aryan' babies were the best that German fashion had to offer.[103] In stark contrast, many people associated with various forms of difference—visible and invisible—became the subjects of propaganda campaigns and were persecuted on new levels from eugenics to genocide. Much of what characterized Weimar culture was obscured, erased, or exiled. In its place, new propaganda mills offered a dramatically different way of seeing that left little room for subtlety or nuance.

Notes

1. On the evolution and use of the terms 'iconography' and 'iconology' in the Weimar period, see Emily J. Levine, *Dreamland of Humanists: Warburg, Cassirer, Panofsky, and the Hamburg School* (Chicago: University of Chicago Press, 2013).
2. Corey Ross, *Media and the Making of Modern Germany: Mass Communications, Society, and Politics from the Empire to the Third Reich* (New York: Oxford University Press, 2008), 147.
3. Anton Kaes, Martin Jay, and Edward Dimendberg (eds), *The Weimar Republic Sourcebook* (Berkeley, CA: University of California Press, 1994), 641, 643; and Peter de Mendelssohn,

Zeitungsstadt Berlin: Menschen und Mächte in der Geschichte der deutschen Presse (Berlin: Ullstein, 1959).
4. Konrad Dussel, *Pressebilder in der Weimarer Republik: Entgrenzung der Information* (Berlin: LIT Verlag, 2012), 43.
5. Christian Rogowski, 'Preface', in Rogowski (ed.), *The Many Faces of Weimar Cinema: Rediscovering Germany's Filmic Legacy* (Rochester, NY: Camden House, 2010), xii.
6. See n. 1 to this chapter. Cf. Jessica Evans and Stuart Hall, 'What is Visual Culture?', in Evans and Hall (eds), *Visual Culture: The Reader* (London: SAGE Publications, 1999), 1–7. Cited here, among others, are Roland Barthes, W. J. T. Mitchell, and Walter Benjamin.
7. Cf. Anton Holzer, 'Picture Stories: The Rise of the Photoessay in the Weimar Republic', *International Journal for History, Culture and Modernity*, 6/1 (2018), 1–39.
8. Cf. Pepper Stetler, *Stop Reading! Look! Modern Vision and the Weimar Photographic Book* (Ann Arbor: University of Michigan Press, 2015).
9. Walter Benjamin, 'Little History of Photography', in *Walter Benjamin: Selected Writings*, vol. 2. *1927–1934*, ed. Michael W. Jennings, Howard Eiland, and Gary Smith (Cambridge, MA: Belknap Press, 1999), 507–30, 527.
10. Daniel H. Magilow, *The Photography of Crisis: The Photo Essays of Weimar Germany* (University Park: Pennsylvania State University Press, 2012), 97.
11. Maria Makela, 'Rejuvenation and Regen(d)eration: *Der Steinachfilm*, Sex Glands, and Weimar-Era Visual and Literary Culture', *German Studies Review*, 38/1 (2015), 35–62; here 56; and Maria Makela, 'Mistaken Identity in Fritz Lang's *Metropolis*', in Elizabeth Otto and Vanessa Rocco (eds), *The New Woman International: Representations in Photography and Film from the 1870s through the 1960s* (Ann Arbor: University of Michigan Press, 2011), 175–93.
12. Cf. Daniel H. Magilow, 'April Fools' in Weimar: Photography and Crisis in the *Illustrierten*', *Monatshefte*, 109/2 (2017), 255–69; and Noah Isenberg, introduction to Isenberg (ed.), *Weimar Cinema: An Essential Guide to the Classic Films of the Era* (New York: Columbia University Press, 2009), 1-12, here 5–6. Isenberg references Peter Sloterdijk's term for the Weimar Republic, namely the 'German Republic of Imposters'.
13. Cf. Sabine Rewald, Ian Buruma, and Matthias Eberle, *Glitter and Doom: German Portraits from the 1920s* (New Haven: Yale University Press, 2006), 212–13.
14. Cf. Mary Ann Doane, *Femmes Fatales: Feminism, Film Theory, Psychoanalysis* (New York: Routledge, 1991), 142.
15. Cf. Dorothy Price, 'A "Prosthetic Economy": Representing the "Kriegskrüppel" in the Weimar Republic', *Art History*, 42/4 (2019), 750–79; and Maria Tatar, 'Entstellung im Vollzug: Das Gesicht des Krieges in der Malerei', in Claudia Schmölders and Sander L. Gilman (eds), *Gesichter der Weimarer Republik: Eine physiognomische Kulturgeschichte* (Cologne: DuMont, 2000), 113–30.
16. Deborah Cohen, *The War Come Home: Veterans in Britain and Germany, 1914–1939* (Berkeley, CA: University of California Press, 2001), 149–50.
17. Carol Poore, *Disability in Twentieth-Century German Culture* (Ann Arbor: University of Michigan Press, 2007), 23–4.
18. Cohen, *War Come Home*, 151.
19. Cf. Astrid Wenger-Deilmann, '1924: Die "Kriegszermalmten": Die visuelle Schockrhetorik des Antikriegsdiskurses', in Gerhard Paul (ed.), *Das Jahrhundert der Bilder*, vol. 1 (Göttingen: Vandenhoeck & Ruprecht, 2009), 308–15.

20. Susan Sontag's *Regarding the Pain of Others* (2003), 24, cited in Annelie Ramsbrock, 'The "Face of War" in Weimar Visual Culture', in Jennifer Evans, Paul Betts, and Stefan-Ludwig Hoffmann (eds), *The Ethics of Seeing: Photography and Twentieth-Century Germany* (New York: Berghahn Books, 2018), 57–78, here 57. Cf. Annelie Ramsbrock, *The Science of Beauty: Culture and Cosmetics in Modern Germany, 1750–1930*, tr. David Burnett (New York: Palgrave Macmillan, 2015), 87.
21. Cf. Sander L. Gilman, *Making the Body Beautiful: A Cultural History of Aesthetic Surgery* (Princeton: Princeton University Press, 1999).
22. Paul Lerner, *Hysterical Men: War, Psychiatry, and the Politics of Trauma in Germany, 1890–1930* (Ithaca, NY: Cornell University Press, 2003), 250.
23. Anton Kaes, *Shell Shock Cinema: Weimar Culture and the Wounds of War* (Princeton: Princeton University Press, 2009).
24. Barbara Hales, 'Unsettling Nerves: Investigating War Trauma in Robert Reinert's *Nerven* (1919)', in Rogowski, *Many Faces*, 31–47.
25. Cf. Kerry Wallach, *Passing Illusions: Jewish Visibility in Weimar Germany* (Ann Arbor: University of Michigan Press, 2017), 148–58.
26. Marion Beckers and Elisabeth Moortgat, *Die Riess: Fotografisches Atelier und Salon in Berlin 1918–1932* (Berlin: Das Verborgene Museum e.V., 2008), 102.
27. Th. Th. Heine, 'Deutschlands Aufstieg', *Simplicissimus*, 35/15 (7 July 1930); and Walter Herzberg, 'Zwei Machthaber', *Ulk*, 58/48 (29 Nov. 1929). Cf. Erik N. Jensen, *Body by Weimar: Athletes, Gender, and German Modernity* (New York: Oxford University Press, 2010), 60–1, 76.
28. Jon Hughes, *Max Schmeling and the Making of a National Hero in Twentieth-Century Germany* (Cham: Palgrave Macmillan, 2018), 42.
29. Todd Herzog, *Crime Stories: Criminalistic Fantasy and the Culture of Crisis in Weimar Germany* (New York: Berghahn Books, 2009), 2.
30. Scott Spector, *Violent Sensations: Sex, Crime, and Utopia in Vienna and Berlin, 1860–1914* (Chicago: University of Chicago Press, 2016), 166–71.
31. Maria Tatar, *Lustmord: Sexual Murder in Weimar Germany* (Princeton: Princeton University Press, 1995), 41–52.
32. Sace Elder, 'Prostitutes, Respectable Women, and Women from "Outside": The Carl Grossmann Sexual Murder Case in Postwar Berlin', in Richard F. Wetzell (ed.), *Crime and Criminal Justice in Modern Germany* (New York: Berghahn Books, 2014), 185–206, here 185.
33. Herzog, *Crime Stories*, 110–33, here 112. Herzog further points to the visual similarities between this shot in *M* and Felix Nussbaum's 1943 painting *Self-Portrait with Jewish Identity Card*, which highlights the Nazi obsession with being able to identify the Jew as other. Cf. Todd Herzog, '"Den Verbrecher erkennen": Zur Geschichte der Kriminalistik', in Schmölders and Gilman, *Gesichter der Weimarer Republik*, 51–77.
34. Cf. Poore, *Disability in Twentieth-Century German Culture*, 27–8.
35. Cf. Tatar, *Lustmord*, 135–47.
36. Peter Jelavich, *Berlin Alexanderplatz: Radio, Film, and the Death of Weimar Culture* (Berkeley, CA: University of California Press, 2006), 222.
37. Cf. Veronika Fuechtner, *Berlin Psychoanalytic: Psychoanalysis and Culture in Weimar Republic Germany* (Berkeley, CA: University of California Press, 2011), 53–5.
38. Katie Sutton, 'Bridging the Rural/Urban Divide: Representations of Queer Female Experience in 1920s Germany', in Florence Feiereisen and Kyle Frackman (eds), *From

Weimar to Christiania: German and Scandinavian Studies in Context (Newcastle, UK: Cambridge Scholars Publishing, 2007), 37–53, here 45.
39. Margaret McCarthy, 'Surface Sheen and Charged Bodies: Louise Brooks as Lulu in *Pandora's Box* (1929)', in Isenberg, *Weimar Cinema*, 217–36.
40. Doane, *Femmes Fatales*, 143, 152.
41. Sabine Hake, 'In the Mirror of Fashion', in Katharina von Ankum (ed.), *Women in the Metropolis: Gender and Modernity in Weimar Culture* (Berkeley, CA: University of California Press, 1997), 185–201, here 189.
42. Janet Ward, *Weimar Surfaces: Urban Visual Culture in 1920s Germany* (Berkeley, CA: University of California Press, 2001), 11, 82–90.
43. Käthe Münzer-Neumann, 'Die Berufstätige', *Die Dame*, 57/9 (Jan. 1930), 38. In the exhibition catalogue, Münzer-Neumann's painting had the full title '*Die Berufstätige (Kinoschauspielerin Aga v. Rosen)*'. Verein der Künstlerinnen zu Berlin, *Die Frau von heute Ausstellung. Gemälde, Graphik, Plastik*, exhibition catalogue, Nov. 1929, Staatsbibliothek zu Berlin, Stiftung Preußischer Kulturbesitz.
44. Cf. Julia Sneeringer, *Winning Women's Votes: Propaganda and Politics in Weimar Germany* (Chapel Hill, NC: University of North Carolina Press, 2002).
45. Cf. Mila Ganeva, *Women in Weimar Fashion: Discourses and Displays in German Culture, 1918–1933* (Rochester, NY: Camden House, 2008).
46. Darcy Buerkle, 'Gendered Spectatorship, Jewish Women and Psychological Advertising in Weimar Germany', *Women's History Review*, 15/4 (2006), 625–36, here 631.
47. On the marketing of Persil, cf. Martina Heßler, '1922: Die "weiße Dame": Eine Frauenfigur der Werbung im Wandel der Zeit', in Paul, *Das Jahrhundert der Bilder*, vol. 1, 284–91.
48. Ward, *Weimar Surfaces*, 86; and Jill Suzanne Smith, *Berlin Coquette: Prostitution and the New German Woman, 1890–1933* (Ithaca, NY: Cornell University Press, 2013), 140, 149.
49. Elizabeth Otto, *Haunted Bauhaus: Occult Spirituality, Gender Fluidity, Queer Identities, and Radical Politics* (Cambridge, MA: MIT Press, 2019), 110–21; and Elizabeth Otto and Patrick Rössler, *Bauhaus Women: A Global Perspective* (London: Herbert Press, 2019), 80–5.
50. Barbara Kosta, *Willing Seduction: The Blue Angel, Marlene Dietrich, and Mass Culture* (New York: Berghahn Books, 2009), 108 n. 17.
51. Siegfried Kracauer, 'The Mass Ornament', in Thomas Y. Levin (tr. and ed.), *The Mass Ornament: Weimar Essays* (Cambridge, MA: Harvard University Press, 1995), 75–88, here 79. Cf. Kate Elswit, *Watching Weimar Dance* (New York: Oxford University Press, 2014), 48–58.
52. Mila Ganeva, 'Fashion Photography and Women's Modernity in Weimar Germany: The Case of Yva', *NWSA Journal*, 15/3 (2003), 1–25, here 13.
53. Cf. Elena Mancini, *Magnus Hirschfeld and the Quest for Sexual Freedom: A History of the First International Sexual Freedom Movement* (New York: Palgrave Macmillan, 2010).
54. Cf. Deborah Ascher Barnstone, 'Androgyny in Oskar Schlemmer's Figural Art', in Elizabeth Otto and Patrick Rössler (eds), *Bauhaus Bodies: Gender, Sexuality, and Body Culture in Modernism's Legendary Art School* (New York: Bloomsbury Visual Arts, 2019), 217–39.
55. Cf. Rewald, *Glitter and Doom*, 146–8; and Hake, 'In the Mirror of Fashion', 189.
56. Cf. Thomas Köhler and Annelie Lütgens (eds), *Jeanne Mammen: The Observer, Retrospective 1910–1975* (Munich: Hirmer Verlag, 2017).
57. Cf. Katie Sutton, *The Masculine Women in Weimar Germany* (New York: Berghahn Books, 2011), 126–50.

58. Marion Beckers and Elisabeth Moortgat, *Atelier Lotte Jacobi: Berlin–New York* (Berlin: Das Verborgene Museum e.V., 1998), 75.
59. Cf. Sneeringer, *Winning Women's Votes*, 274.
60. Cf. Kevin S. Amidon, 'Intersexes and Mixed Races: Visuality, Narrative, and "Bastard" Identity in Early Twentieth-Century Germany', in Deborah Ascher Barnstone and Thomas O. Haakenson (eds), *Representations of German Identity: German Visual Culture*, vol. 1 (New York: Peter Lang, 2013), 103–27. On the term pseudoscience, cf. Amos Morris-Reich, *Race and Photography: Racial Photography as Scientific Evidence, 1876–1980* (Chicago: University of Chicago Press, 2016), 17–21.
61. Andrew Zimmerman, 'Anti-Semitism as Skill: Rudolf Virchow's "Schulstatistik" and the Racial Composition of Germany', *Central European History*, 32/4 (1999), 409–29, here 413.
62. Morris-Reich, *Race and Photography*, 71–5.
63. Ibid., 117–55, here 122–4.
64. Ibid., 156–86, here 159.
65. Wallach, *Passing Illusions*, 39–40.
66. Buerkle, 'Gendered Spectatorship', 631.
67. Irene Guenther, *Nazi Chic? Fashioning Women in the Third Reich* (Oxford: Berg, 2004), 91–2, 98–109.
68. Cf. Sander Gilman, *The Jew's Body* (New York: Routledge, 1991); and Jay Geller, *The Other Jewish Question: Identifying the Jew and Making Sense of Modernity* (New York: Fordham University Press, 2011).
69. Julia Schäfer, *Vermessen, gezeichnet, verlacht: Judenbilder in populären Zeitschriften 1918–1933* (Frankfurt am Main: Campus Verlag, 2005).
70. Randall L. Bytwerk, *Julius Streicher: Nazi Editor of the Notorious Anti-Semitic Newspaper Der Stürmer* (New York: Cooper Square Press, 2001), 56–7.
71. Alan E. Steinweis, *Studying the Jew: Scholarly Antisemitism in Nazi Germany* (Cambridge, MA: Harvard University Press, 2006), 28, 33.
72. Wallach, *Passing Illusions*, 52–5.
73. David Ciarlo, *Advertising Empire: Race and Visual Culture in Imperial Germany* (Cambridge, MA: Harvard University Press, 2011), 3.
74. Cf. Iris Wigger, *The 'Black Horror on the Rhine': Intersections of Race, Nation, Gender and Class in 1920s Germany* (London: Palgrave Macmillan, 2017).
75. Cf. 'Der schwarze Terror in deutschen Landen', *Kladderadatsch*, 73/22 (30 May 1920).
76. Cf. Julia Roos, 'Nationalism, Racism and Propaganda in Early Weimar Germany: Contradictions in the Campaign Against the "Black Horror on the Rhine"', *German History*, 30/1 (2012), 45–74.
77. Tina Campt, *Other Germans: Black Germans and the Politics of Race, Gender, and Memory in the Third Reich* (Ann Arbor: University of Michigan Press, 2004), 37–61.
78. Jonathan O. Wipplinger, *The Jazz Republic: Music, Race, and American Culture in Weimar Germany* (Ann Arbor: University of Michigan Press, 2017), 37, 46.
79. This painting includes a tin drum bearing the name 'Tom Boston', the pseudonym of an African American jazz artist who performed in Germany in the 1920s. Wipplinger, *The Jazz Republic*, 47–8.
80. Dorothy Price and Camilla Smith, 'Weimar's Others: Art History, Alterity and Regionalism in Inter-War Germany', *Art History*, 42/4 (2019), 628–51, here 639.
81. Marion Beckers and Elisabeth Moortgat (eds), *Yva: Photographien 1925–1938* (Berlin: Das Verborgene Museum, 2001), 44–6.

82. Cf. Wallach, *Passing Illusions*, 82–4, and Wipplinger, *Jazz Republic*, 226–37.
83. Anna-Lena Sälzer, 'Arme, Asoziale, Außenseiter. Künstler- und Zigeuner-Diskurse von 1900 bis zum Nationalsozialismus', in Herbert Uerlings and Iulia-Karin Patrut (eds), *'Zigeuner' und Nation: Repräsentation—Inklusion—Exklusion* (Frankfurt am Main: Peter Lang, 2008), 203–30.
84. Susan Tebbutt, 'Disproportional Representation: Romanies and European Art', in Nicholas Saul and Susan Tebbutt (eds), *The Role of the Romanies: Images and Counter-Images of 'Gypsies'/Romanies in European Cultures* (Liverpool: Liverpool University Press, 2004), 159–77, here 167–8.
85. Anjeana Hans, 'The *Zigeunerdrama* Reloaded: Leni Riefenstahl's Fantasy Gypsies and Sacrificial Others', in Barbara Hales, Mihaela Petrescu, and Valerie Weinstein (eds), *Continuity and Crisis in German Cinema, 1928–1936* (Rochester, NY: Camden House, 2016), 151–66, here 154.
86. Jensen, *Body by Weimar*, 3–4. Cf. Walter Mühlhausen, '1919: Die Weimarer Republik entblößt Das Badehosen-Foto von Friedrich Ebert und Gustav Noske', in Paul, *Das Jahrhundert der Bilder*, vol. 1, 236–43.
87. Erich Salomon, *Berühmte Zeitgenossen in unbewachten Augenblicken* (Munich: Schirmer/Mosel, 1931).
88. Magilow, *Photography of Crisis*, 137–40.
89. Debbie Lewer, 'Revolution and the Weimar Avant-Garde: Contesting the Politics of Art, 1919–1924', in John Alexander Williams (ed.), *Weimar Culture Revisited* (New York: Palgrave Macmillan, 2011), 1–21, here 3–4.
90. Neil MacGregor, *Germany: Memories of a Nation* (New York: Vintage Books, 2017), 409–10.
91. Shulamit Volkov, *Walther Rathenau: Weimar's Fallen Statesman* (New Haven: Yale University Press 2012), 26, 209.
92. Claudia Schmölders, *Hitler's Face: The Biography of an Image*, tr. Adrian Daub (Philadelphia: University of Pennsylvania Press, 2006), 77.
93. Deborah Ascher Barnstone and Elizabeth Otto, 'How Art Resists', in Ascher Barnstone and Otto (eds), *Art and Resistance in Germany* (New York: Bloomsbury Visual Arts, 2019), 1–20, here 7.
94. This book is available online <https://archive.org/details/DeutschlandDeutschlandUeberAlles>. Cf. Andrés Mario Zervigón, *John Heartfield and the Agitated Image: Photography, Persuasion, and the Rise of Avant-Garde Photomontage* (Chicago: University of Chicago Press, 2012); and Sabine T. Kriebel, *Revolutionary Beauty: The Radical Photomontages of John Heartfield* (Berkeley: University of California Press, 2014).
95. Sabine Kriebel, 'Montage as Meme: Learning from the Radical Avant-Gardes', in Ascher Barnstone and Otto, *Art and Resistance*, 135–49, here 143.
96. Rudolf Stumberger, *Klassen-Bilder: Sozialdokumentarische Fotografie 1900–1945* (Konstanz: UVK Verlagsgesellschaft, 2007), 146–7.
97. Stumberger, *Klassen-Bilder*, 147.
98. Willy Römer, *Berlin in den Weltstadtjahren. Fotografien von Willy Römer, 1919–1933*, ed. and with a text by Enno Kaufhold (Berlin: Braus Berlin, 2012), 64–81, 161.
99. Karen J. Kenkel, 'Das Gesicht der Masse: Soziologische Visionen', in Schmölders and Gilman, *Gesichter der Weimarer* Republik, 206–27.
100. Sneeringer, *Winning Women's Votes*, 282, 272–3.

101. Gerhard Paul, *Aufstand der Bilder: Die NS-Propaganda vor 1933* (Bonn: Verlag J. H. W. Dietz Nachf., 1990), 33.
102. Paul, *Aufstand der Bilder*, 247–84; cf. image plates between pages 240 and 241: 72, 73, 75.
103. Curt Meyer, 'Frau Dr. Goebbels', *Die Dame*, 60/19 (June 1933), 1.

Bibliography

Ankum, Katharina von (ed.), *Women in the Metropolis: Gender and Modernity in Weimar Culture* (Berkeley, CA: University of California Press, 1997).

Ciarlo, David, *Advertising Empire: Race and Visual Culture in Imperial Germany* (Cambridge, MA: Harvard University Press, 2011).

Ganeva, Mila, *Women in Weimar Fashion: Discourses and Displays in German Culture, 1918–1933* (Rochester, NY: Camden House, 2008).

Magilow, Daniel H., *The Photography of Crisis: The Photo Essays of Weimar Germany* (University Park, PA: Pennsylvania State University Press, 2012).

Meskimmon, Marsha, *We Weren't Modern Enough: Women Artists and the Limits of German Modernism* (Berkeley, CA: University of California Press, 1999).

Morris-Reich, Amos, *Race and Photography: Racial Photography as Scientific Evidence, 1876–1980* (Chicago, IL: University of Chicago Press, 2016).

Otto, Elizabeth, *Haunted Bauhaus: Occult Spirituality, Gender Fluidity, Queer Identities, and Radical Politics* (Cambridge, MA: MIT Press, 2019).

Schönfeld, Christiane (ed.), *Practicing Modernity: Female Creativity in the Weimar Republic* (Würzberg: Königshausen & Neumann, 2006).

Sneeringer, Julia, *Winning Women's Votes: Propaganda and Politics in Weimar Germany* (Chapel Hill, NC: University of North Carolina Press, 2002).

Wallach, Kerry. *Passing Illusions: Jewish Visibility in Weimar Germany* (Ann Arbor, MI: University of Michigan Press, 2017).

Ward, Janet, *Weimar Surfaces: Urban Visual Culture in 1920s Germany* (Berkeley, CA: University of California Press, 2001).

CHAPTER 33

THE PRESENCE OF THE FIRST WORLD WAR IN WEIMAR CULTURE

CLAUDIA SIEBRECHT

OPENING her war diary on 7 January 1921 for the first time in one and a half years, Agnes Zenker decided to write an ending to the journal that she had started after the outbreak of war as a 14-year-old schoolgirl. She explained that, although she found no joy in writing about the current circumstances, she still wanted to note all the important things for her future grand- and greatgrandchildren before putting it away for good.

> Wickedness, lowliness, materialism, brutality, nastiness, theft, murder: all of this is now commonplace among people. There is nothing they shy away from. Church, God, religion is nonsense. This is what things look like among the people. In addition, there is inflation, illness and strike. Who would have thought that our proud, victorious campaign would end like this? Since we have signed the Versailles peace terms, we are completely in the hands of the enemy. They can demand everything, everything.[1]

Zenker evoked a society of shady, deceitful individuals in which social relations had changed for the worse and where a soaring crime rate, rejection of order, and values exposed the bad behaviour and character of people, a situation that, to her, was compounded by restrictions to national sovereignty resulting from the peace treaty. The account, based on Zenker's observations in a village in the Ore Mountains south of Dresden, is impressionistic, but also fed off national press coverage and echoed a more widely perceived situation as contemporary commentators deplored a decline in moral standards and traditional values. For many this went hand in hand with an idealization of the pre-war world.[2] But Zenker's account of post-war decline was less about ascertaining social change, for her it was a tangible way to express disorientation, uncertainty, and shock caused by the conflict and its end. The post-war status quo was a disappointment that diverged from her expectations for the nation's future which, we learn from her diary, she was still invested in, trusting that 'Germany would heal'. But for Zenker and her contemporaries, the process of recovery entailed looking for answers that could explain the breakdown of the old order and outcome of the war and give meaning to the sacrifices delivered for the national cause. The answers found by Germans in the 1920s and early 1930s were fiercely disputed, changed over time, and were multifaceted and often ambiguous.

Responses to the 'outbreak of peace', as phrased in eager anticipation by one soldier in October 1918, were predominantly positive.[3] The end of war seemed overdue and was welcomed by most soldiers, sailors, and workers, and the population at large also longed for an end of the fighting and dying.[4] At the end of November 1918, awaiting his return from the front, a mother from Stralsund in northern Germany wrote to her son that she was glad that 'the murder' was over.[5] Although many Germans had wanted war to end, confusion and ignorance of the realities of the military situation in 1918 prevailed and the population was unprepared for the impending defeat and its consequences. The public largely scorned at peace at any price, rejected responsibility for the war's outbreak, and expected a 'peace of law and justice' and favourable terms they saw as honourable commensurate with Germany's position.[6] Few understood that these notions constituted nothing but—as so aptly put by the Protestant theologian Ernst Troeltsch—the 'dreamland of the armistice period'.[7] For large parts of the public, army, and old elites, Germany had not been defeated, but had agreed to an armistice. It was therefore expected that peace would be a dialogue, even though this position conveniently disregarded the *Diktatfrieden* (dictated peace) imposed by Germany on the Soviet Union just one year earlier.[8] The Versailles Treaty was considered as undeserved and coerced by the former enemies. It was critiqued and almost uniformly rejected by the German National Assembly, an act that can be seen as constitutive for embedding the legacy of the war in the political culture of the republic.[9] Men, women, children had been drawn into and self-mobilized for a conflict whose scale, nature, and extent had been unimaginable for contemporaries and whose outcome was fundamentally different from what they had imagined. Expectations diverged for contemporaries who thought the war to be about territorial expansion, political standing, cultural renewal, personal adventure, but also for those who believed they were defending their homes and families, and men who thought they would return able-bodied and did not. The strain of sustaining war, supporting families, and coping with losses was also far from how many mothers or wives thought war would be like. Ten million soldiers lost their lives between 1914 and 1918.[10] Historians have estimated that every family in the main belligerent countries mourned a male relation who died in the war. Thus, distinct cultures of remembrance emerged in European post-war societies.[11] How these sacrifices and losses could be endowed with meaning was the central question that motivated memories and remembrances of the war in Weimar Germany.

This chapter begins by considering Weimar Germany as a post-war society and by addressing the key historiographical strands that interpret the political and cultural significance of the lost war. It demonstrates the importance of the war's legacy for Weimar political culture by looking at commemorative practices on a national, local, and individual level and by reflecting on some examples of the memory of the war in art, literature, photography, and film. It has often been argued that commemorative practices and cultural representations of the war in Germany were dominated by the nationalist right, or that a strict binary divide between the commemorative politics of the left and the right shaped this field.[12] This was, of course, a very important constellation for the memory of the war in the Weimar Republic, but the political differences were not always that clear cut on the ground and the republican or nationalist interpretations of the war did not necessarily offer the answers people were looking for. This chapter suggests that it is precisely the plurality and ambivalence of war memories in Weimar Germany that needs to be accounted for. How and why people remembered the way they did is best understood not only at the level of the nation, but by looking at local communities, families, and individuals.

Peace, Defeat, and the Legacy of Wartime Sacrifice

The immediate circumstances in which people lived in the aftermath of war shaped how they remembered. The logistical challenges of demobilization had been efficiently dealt with as returning soldiers were integrated into the reorganized labour market. Yet the war had produced not only material hardship, but had also added a sense of unjustness to widening economic inequality and social conflicts over housing shortages and declining public health, employment practices, and insufficient state support.[13] The widespread support of the war effort had raised the expectation that sacrifices would be acknowledged by the government, an attitude that was indicative of a changed relationship between individuals and the state.[14] The accelerating inflation threatened the livelihoods of sections of the population. Amongst those hit hard were disabled veterans and their families and war dependents such as widows and orphans. They amounted to nearly 10 per cent of the German population.[15] By the early 1920s, no less than seven war victims' organizations with different political affiliations and with approximately 1.4 million members campaigned for their interests. Of these, the SPD (Social Democratic Party) affiliated Reichsbund der Kriegsbeschädigten, Kriegsteilnehmer und Kriegshinterbliebenen (Reich League of Disabled War Veterans, Ex-Servicemen, and War Dependants), founded in Berlin in 1917, was the largest pressure group with over 800,000 members in the early 1920s.[16] Political solutions were found to care for disabled veterans, widows, and orphans. They culminated in the 1920 Reich Pension Law, which many saw as the heart of the Weimar welfare state and which incurred high expenses for the state, but nonetheless provided inadequately for many in need.[17] Many families who had lost the father as breadwinner in the war struggled to survive on state support.[18] The war pensions system was unable to cope with the scale of applications on both an administrative and financial level and available funds were severely restricted from the late 1920s. Looking back in 1931, a war widow from Berlin who underwent professional re-training to make a living and bring up her child wrote:

> Us war widows have often bitterly asked ourselves that if moral and humane obligations were insufficient reasons to make a difference, would it not have made more sense to grant reasonably sufficient pensions so that the orphans, whose fathers had already been taken from them, could fully retain the care of their mothers?[19]

Many war widows commented on the discrepancy between the valorization of the war dead in public rhetoric and the lack of actual support during the years of the hyperinflation.[20] For Gertrud Bäumer, one of the most influential members of the German women's movement, a Reichstag delegate, and vice chair of the left-liberal German Democratic Party (DDP), the widows were 'heroes' and their struggles were evidence that 'the war has not yet been fought or suffered to an end.'[21]

Historians posit that a 'culture of defeat' manifested itself in Germany after the shock of military defeat, which seeks to explain developments in the post-war era when the lost war became a national trauma, led to myth building, revenge fantasies, and a denial of the political realities.[22] The German population at large is understood to have suffered a psychological breakdown caused by the strongly felt humiliation of defeat which was linked to national self-elevation at the beginning of war.[23] The denial was fed, arguably, by a continued belief in military prowess and by a sense of moral and cultural superiority. It served not only as a rejection of the political circumstances that were externally enforced through the Versailles Treaty, but also meant that blame for the defeat was allocated domestically. The so-called 'stab in the back' legend held the home front, including Jews, women, and Social Democrats, responsible for the disastrous outcome of the war as it was their alleged lack of support that undermined the efforts of German soldiers.[24] When this illusionary belief in an alternate political future persisted in some sections of German society, despite a radically changed political situation, it is easy to see why one might reason that Weimar Germany never became a 'peace-time society'.[25]

The Foreign Ministry funded a very concrete attempt to rectify the position of Germany after the war that denied German war guilt and responsibility for atrocities through the 'innocentist campaign' through the publication of the journal *Die Kriegsschuldfrage* ('The Question of War Guilt') from 1923 to 1928.[26] Writing in the first issue of 1923, the military historian Hans Delbrück challenged firmly the idea that 'Germany had frivolously ignited the war and that she was rightfully punished as harshly as possible.' He emphasized instead the extent of the Russian military mobilization in 1914, posited that Germany was actually the last of the great powers to mobilize, and offered a reading of the pre-war diplomatic policies of the German and Austrian Emperors as peaceful and appeasing.[27] This effort could be seen to exemplify a process of failed 'cultural demobilization'.[28] Enduring commitment to the national cause and persistent images of external and internal enemies demonstrate how war cultures remained relevant in the aftermath of the conflict in Germany. Fuelled by emotions of hate, loyalty, suffering, and revenge, the failed cultural demobilization goes some way towards explaining the ideological politicization of the war's legacy including paramilitary violence in the aftermath of the war. The violent actions of paramilitary groups, for example the Freikorps, have informed the argument that the soldiers' experiences during the First World War brutalized men to such a degree that integration into a regular civilian life was impossible as their lives centred around continued armed conflict and remobilization.[29] The violent actions of this paramilitary organization have dominated the historical perception of veterans and are seen as especially pertinent in Germany. The 'brutalization theory' seems to point to a continuity from the First World War, over the rise of the nationalist right and to the Nazi seizure of power.[30] But this idea should not be overstated. It is important to remember that the Freikorps never had more than 400,000 members and not all of them were veterans.[31] Nevertheless, for the right, a mythical version of frontline service, that centred on a notion of brotherhood formed in the trenches and celebrated the military prowess of the individual in service of the nation, came to stand for the war experience between 1914 and 1918. Although an idealized account of what war was like, it was a powerful narrative that attracted Germans of a new generation who had been too young to serve at the front. In the last years of the republic, members of this new generation, who had never experienced war at the front, rather than the war veterans, radicalized in pursuit of redeeming the nation's sacrifices.[32]

Approximately six million men returned from the front in November 1918.[33] While over half of those cut ties with their military lives, many others embraced membership of a veterans' association, which were established largely according to political allegiance. The largest one was the republican Reichsbanner black-red-gold founded in 1924 and with a peak membership of 900,000–1,000,000 in 1925/6. The nationalist Stahlhelm, founded in 1918, was significantly smaller, with a peak membership of approximately 350,000 members in 1932. The communist Rote Frontkämpferbund (Red Front Fighter's League) founded in 1924 saw its peak membership of 127, 000 in 1927.[34] While representing the social and economic interests of veterans, these organizations also were communities that accumulated and focused the emotional and psychological legacies of those who had served in the war. The friendship found amongst fellow veterans was, for many, a replacement of comradeship forged in the trenches. The connections and coping mechanisms that had aided men in enduring war remained relevant in its aftermath as men mourned their comrades, their mutilated bodies, and some also the outcome of the war. The question what meaning could be given to a war that had been lost and cost so much was therefore one the veterans were deeply invested in. The activities of their leagues dominated Weimar commemorative culture nationally but were particularly prevalent on a local level and included proposals for war memorials, public marches, and social events as well as the commemoration of specific battles and remembrance ceremonies. It is here that veterans' associations grappled with and clashed over ways how to remember the fallen. For many on the left it was a difficult balance to mourn the dead without questioning their sacrifice by rejecting the war and thereby the cause their comrades had died for, while those on the right broadly favoured overt heroization and glorification of the war dead. A clear anti-war stance was taken by the Friedensbund der Kriegsteilnehmer (Peace League of Ex-Servicemen), a pacifist veterans' organization founded in 1919 and with approximately 30,000 members in 1922. This group's intention was to keep alive the memory of the war's suffering, 'the blood and pain', imploring veterans as those who 'knew what war was like' to fight for peace in international unity.[35] The commemorative activities of the two largest associations representing veterans and war victims, the Reichsbund and the Reichsbanner, were framed as decidedly republican events. The 'patriotic pacifism' of the veterans organized in the Reichsbanner, while also based on a mythologized version of the war experience, meant that their mythology of the war was used to highlight the legitimacy of the republic.[36] The nationalist right was therefore not the only or prevailing actor of remembrance as a diverse republican war memory represented a central part of Weimar political culture.

Contemporary attempts to understand the legacy of war for the German people already pointed to the importance of myths and illusions. In 1927, an academic study concluded that the 'tragic extent' to which the population's sense of reality had been disturbed was one of the most important moral consequences of the war.[37] Sustaining four years of war had only been possible, the author Otto Baumgarten, a Protestant theologian who had been a member of the 1919 peace delegation, contended, because of an 'idealized, ideological and illusionary adjustment of the political possibilities, realities, and probabilities' that left deep tracks in the national psyche.[38] The impact of the defeat on German society is perhaps more inclusively captured by the notion of 'cultural trauma' as the military defeat uprooted the deep emotional investment in the war and the regime.[39] For many, the war had been an existential conflict that was fought in defence of culture and country, as contemporaries saw their own national identity at stake. Some also believed that Germany had a 'cultural mission' to fulfil. But the trauma also related to the scale of human and material destruction and a disregard for cultural and legal norms in the waging of war. In Germany as well as in most European countries this informed an anti-war discourse.

While the defeat is certainly central to how Germans gauged their wartime losses, it would be misleading to think that victory would have redeemed all sacrifices. In both France and Britain, notions of the futility of war and senseless slaughter of the common soldier are key to how the war was and still is remembered. As tempting as it is to adapt the 'culture of defeat' as a meta-narrative for the history of Weimar Germany, it seems better suited to explain the trajectory of the success of nationalist war memory than its varied nature on the ground. Largely leapfrogging over the 'contested commemorations' of the 1920s turns the vantage point of 1933 into a self-fulfilling prophecy, linking the unfulfilled promises of national unity in 1914 directly to the attraction of Nazism and its political takeover.[40] The First World War was undoubtedly politically and culturally relevant for the Nazi regime.[41] Yet the 'mental horizon' of Weimar Germans, so deeply shaped by the war's legacies and losses, had been variable as private memory and local remembrance practices show.[42] Commemorative rituals and cultural representations offer insights into how the needs of the living to remember, to grieve, and to communicate their hopes and disappointments were met.[43] At stake for all, not only the left and right, was both a version of the past that would determine the political direction for the nation's future, and a present that made the nature of the war experience worthwhile and validated its profound impact on individuals and their sense of self.

Remembering the War Dead in Weimar Germany

'War Celebration in Berlin' is how the British *Times* entitled a report of Germany's first national war remembrance ceremony on 3 August 1924.[44] The 'celebration' actually resembled much more a funeral and was a complex event at which tensions regarding the war and its legacy came to the fore. The rituals performed at the event appeared solemn and devout as government officials arrived while a requiem was played by the Reichswehr bands in front of the parliament building.[45] It was followed by a wreath-laying ceremony and speeches by religious representatives of the Reichswehr, a Protestant minister and a Catholic chaplain. A Jewish rabbi was prevented from participating.[46] Whereas Germany's European neighbours remembered the fallen of the war on 11 November, the day of the armistice, the event in Berlin took place on the anniversary of the German declaration of war on France. The Weimar officials thus avoided associating the war dead with defeat. In his address, Reich President Friedrich Ebert, who himself had lost two sons in the war, called on all Germans to observe this day of 'memory and mourning':

> With deep sorrow we mourn Germany's sons who died the soldiers' death so that Germany would live; with compassion we remember the wounds of those damaged by the war and the pain of the bereaved, in awe we bow to the heroic deeds of our nation in arms and to the enduring staunchness of the home front, to the unparalleled spirit of sacrifice, the extraordinary endurance of our nation in war.[47]

Ebert's message was inclusive in the sense that the cost of the war for all Germans was honoured as he addressed a population putatively unified by their wartime experiences. All speeches at the event framed the war losses as a valiant sacrifice for the nation. As Ebert reaffirmed the trope of the defensive war and pledged to continue the fight for 'Germany's rightful place among the nations on earth', the event shows that valorization of the war dead was not incompatible with republican political culture (Figure 33.1).

For some contemporary observers such as the radical left-wing author Kurt Tucholsky who reviewed the event, the 'kitschy memorial day' was driven by a 'genuine fatherland spirit' and he wondered how:

> Today, after these ten years, adult Germans gather together and speak of the poor, pointlessly fallen victims of the slaughter without the burning desire; 'How can we avoid the next one? How? How?' Not one, without exception, not one of these

FIGURE 33.1 Friedrich Ebert speaking at the national ceremony for the war dead. Berlin, 3 August 1924.

Photograph by Georg Pahl.

influential German men musters the moral courage to turn his back on these advertisements for war. Not a single person can speak about war other than to proclaim, in a more or less skilfully veiled way, a cry of vengeance for a new massacre. That all this is possible should suffice to justify my calling it a disgrace.[48]

Tucholsky, a veteran himself, was one of the key pacifist voices in Weimar who maintained the conviction that war was futile and who was wary of militaristic memorialization of the dead. Opposing war on ethical grounds, he spearheaded organizations and pacifist initiatives, such as the international 'Anti-War-Year' campaign of 1924, that was supported by many renowned artists and writers. What Tucholsky criticized here, were precisely the symbolic gestures, the ritual, and rhetoric that, to him, failed to condemn the meaninglessness of wartime sacrifices.

While an audience for the official ceremony had gathered outside the Reichstag, the ceremony did not draw in the general public. The planned two-minute silence was almost generally ignored as thousands of Berliners in the nearby park, unaware and uninformed of the reasons behind the flags, salutes, circling airplanes, and military parades, were picnicking in a holiday spirit.[49] This shows that top-down commemorative actions at state level did not necessarily speak to the masses. The event was nonetheless seen as important by actors of the political left who attempted to subvert the proceedings.

Communists disrupted the silence by shouting 'No more war', distributing leaflets and singing 'The International', after which about fifty members of the group were arrested, and a violent street fight developed that caused a panic among the spectators. While the event was choreographed by state officials, those who acted on the ground were important agents of remembrance, a dynamic that is also evident in the protracted search for a national war memorial.[50]

When Reich President Ebert launched the plan for the creation of a national war memorial (Reichsehrenmal) during the August 1924 remembrance ceremony, he put the project into the hands of the people as it was to be financed by donations and suggestions for the design were encouraged.[51] This resulted in an overwhelming response from local communities across Germany who were keen to accommodate the planned national memorial. In the end, the eventual use of the Neue Wache (New Guard House) in Berlin, redesigned as a war memorial, as the national site of remembrance was more due to pragmatic than any other considerations. As funding was granted by the Reich government, the unveiled site was dedicated to not just the Prussian but all German war dead in 1931. But the Neue Wache was a contested memorial site. The veterans' associations objected the dedication of the site and, moreover, in a unified effort, they had already developed their own idea for a national war memorial which was to take the form of a 'Holy Grove' in Bad Berka (near Weimar). Although the memorial was never built, this joint campaign for the 'Holy Grove' was extraordinary considering the tense and generally antagonist relations between the veterans' organizations. It also points to the common ground that could be found in the need to commemorate the dead. For some veterans, remembrance at the national site had been envisaged as unfolding a transformative force for the nation's future. In 1931, the vice chairman of the nationalist Stahlhelm stressed that 'the collective honouring of the dead would lead to a new rise of Germany's unity'.[52] For August Diehl, a veteran who had served on the Western Front in the First World War, the 'Holy Grove' would have dissolved all differences within the population and created a genuine national army.[53]

The practice of reburying unknown soldiers that was central to national war remembrance in Britain and France and in twelve further former belligerents—including defeated nations like Austria and Bulgaria—also resonated across a broad political spectrum in Germany.[54] While on one level the tombs of the unknown soldiers captured universal and unprecedented aspects of the violence of the conflict that had caused unprecedented numbers of war dead and men missing in action, it also meant that different political readings of the war were projected onto it. Members of the Reichsbanner saw an egalitarian notion of wartime sacrifice represented by the unknown soldier, which appealed to their political principles and was reflected in their remembrance rituals. In 1929, at the Constitution Day celebrations on 11 August, Reichsbanner members marched past a temporary national memorial erected in front of the Brandenburg Gate in Berlin that resembled the high plinths of the cenotaphs in London and Paris. The French capital had a temporary cenotaph erected in 1919. At the Reichsbanner memorial in Berlin 'all war dead' were honoured alongside the dead of the Reichsbanner and those who had died for the republic. For the nationalist right, by contrast, the unknown soldier came to represent the sacrifice of the individual for the fatherland as destiny.[55] At the Tannenberg war memorial in East Prussia, built from 1924 to 1927, the interned bodies of twenty unknown soldiers formed part of the site's design. Tannenberg became a central memorial for the nationalist right.

The search for appropriate and meaningful ways to remember the dead is reflected in the broad variety of local war memorials in the 1920s, ranging from simple plaques with iron crosses, laurel branches over trophies, and warrior figures to entire compounds with gardens, groves, and porticos. Many also included Christian iconography such as angels, saints, and variations of the pietà—traditional motifs with the power to mediate grief.[56] The omnipresent newly built war memorials in the 1920s are material examples of the degree to which European emotional cultures had been transformed by the experience of wartime death and bereavement.[57] War memorials and commemorative rituals offer insights into whether and how the needs of the living to grieve and have their loss validated were met.[58] But some contemporaries also came to realize that there was no redemption.[59] Amongst local stakeholders, memorial designs were often the subject of deep-seated disagreement and involved municipal committees, fundraisers, church officials, congregations, veterans' organizations, women's, and youth groups who were all committed to see wartime death represented in a way that they saw artistically appropriate, politically acceptable, or personally meaningful. Form, content, and rituals mattered immensely in local communities.

In the central German city of Kassel, for example, the planned inaugural festivities for the city's war memorial in 1926 caused a bitter controversy between veterans and municipal officials.[60] The Kurhessische Kriegerbund, the veterans' organization which had proposed and acted as a patron for the memorial, had planned a closed event for the day and invited local veterans who were also members of the national umbrella organization, the Reichskriegerbund Kyffhäuser. The city magistrate had also been invited but made its attendance conditional on the inclusion of other veterans' organizations to preserve the impartial character of the memorial. Members of the Kurhessische Kriegerbund pointed out that the Kyffhäuser was an impartial organization that saw itself as serving the nation and the fatherland but not a political party. Although it is true that the Kyffhäuser had abandoned its aggressively anti-social democratic stance and had acquired a broad spectrum of members, it nonetheless stood for conservative and national values.[61] The festive mayoral inauguration of the site did not take place until two years later and then, in 1928, included the republican veterans' organization Reichsbanner as well as local politicians and representatives of the city administration. This time, the nationalist veterans' organizations Stahlhelm and the communist Rote Frontkämpferbund refused to attend. In his address, the mayor included an appeal for peace which, although embedded in an emphasis of worthy sacrifice for the nation, nonetheless represented a critical addition to his message.[62] Interesting here is that the conflict arose over the participation at the event and the importance attached to the ownership of and presence at the site, but not over the memorial itself. Indeed, all factions had embraced the memorial design plans from the start. Furthermore, the plans for the rededication of the Prinzengarten in the city centre into a war memorial terraced garden with a sculpture at its heart were greeted as 'uniquely beautiful'. The Social Democratic politician Philipp Scheidemann, then the mayor of Kassel, expressed his appreciation of the artistic design in November 1920 and granted financial support of 50,000 marks.[63] Ultimately, however, it was precisely the design of the memorial that would bring out tensions over the connection between artistic representation and the meaning of war experiences over the next years, coming to a height in 1933.

At the heart of the conflict was the sculpture titled *Der Gefallene* (The Fallen) in the centre of the memorial site. The naked figure wrapped in cloth without uniform or weapons was designed by the art professor Hans Sautter who was director of the school of arts and crafts and SPD delegate in the municipal parliament. Importantly, no military insignia were included in the design, avoiding the martial glorification of death in war and potentially also including the non-military war dead (Figure 33.2).

Sautter's sculpture resembled a range of common inter-war memorial designs of the 'sleeping dead', but elsewhere the sleeping dead were represented in a more militarized manner. Portraying battlefield death as a deep and joyous sleep meant that death could be denied and that the war could be seen to be not yet fully over.[64] As a concept, it did not envision transcendence but rather fed the notion that the dead could return to save the fatherland when needed. But revenge, as much as transcendence, can be seen as integral to a search for meaning and consolation in a traumatized society.[65] How evocative these

FIGURE 33.2 *Der tote Krieger im Ehrenmal am Auehang*, date unknown.

Stadtarchiv Kassel.

messages remained is visible in the treatment of memorials after 1933, when the 'peacefully sleeping' Kassel soldier was defamed and covered up first with wood and then with a stone slab and the artist Sautter was arrested. The newspaper *Kasseler Post* reported in December 1933 that the sculpture had long been seen as unworthy by wide circles. A veteran wrote in the newspaper to explain that the sculpture represented only death, but not the meaning of that death. He continued that it showed only the suffering of the individual but was not a testimony to the suffering of two million German brothers and it did not capture, he stated, what bound them forever to those who returned and to the fatherland.[66] The actual design of the sculpture that veterans had supported in the early 1920s had thus become a matter of contention in the early 1930s as the framing of wartime sacrifice had shifted profoundly. The memorial was reinstalled after the Second World War.

The reception of the commemorative sculptures and planned memorials by Ernst Barlach, who had become one of the most prolific memorial artists in the 1920s, exemplifies not only the degree to which memorial designs divided communities but also the support that his work generated. Barlach, like many other artists, had initially supported the war effort. He trained as a reserve soldier but received an early exemption and his views of the war changed. His memorial designs and sculptures were still, sublime pieces, aiming to achieve a deep reflection on death in war. In his hometown Güstrow, there were mixed feelings over his design plans to install a floating figure known as *Der Schwebende* or *Der schwebende Engel* (floating angel) in the church. Both the parish and local community were concerned about the design's suitability as a war memorial and its accessibility for common Mecklenburgians. Yet the project also had committed support and was eventually inaugurated in 1927.

Conversely, in 1928, in the town of Malchin the local Königin-Luise Bund (the women's branch of the nationalist veterans' organization Stahlhelm) who had been the chief fundraiser for the planned municipal war memorial, were able to prevent the realization of the chosen design which was Barlach's motif of a falling rider.[67] The piece was not considered to be an honourable and worthy memorial to the town's fallen. But then, in the same year, his war memorial *Der Geisteskämpfer* (Spiritual Warrior) was inaugurated in Kiel, although nationalist circles began massive smear campaigns in reaction to his memorials erected in both Güstrow and Kiel. In Magdeburg, Barlach's memorial design for the cathedral, a wooden panel of soldiers and grieving figures, was set up on a trial basis in 1929. The Prussia state had co-funded the project and insisted on its permanent installation, despite the opposition from the cathedral priest, a Stahlhelm member, and the church council. The sculpture was removed from the Dome in 1934, denounced as 'un-German, un-Christian and pacifist'.[68] It returned to the Dome in 1955. Barlach's memorial art elsewhere was received and treated in much the same pattern. The responses show the degree to which the symbolic language of war memorials mattered. For people in the various communities, it was not just a question of establishing a commemorative site, but the meaning imbued in the memorial design was crucial. Similar examples of contested local commemorations existed throughout the country and were often most visible between republican and nationalist groups.[69] But these conflicts point to additional layers of meaning beyond a left–right political dichotomy. People responded to the representation of sacrifice also on a deeply personal and emotional level. Tangible manifestations include, for example, war memorials that explicitly address the pain of bereaved mothers, such as the life-sized pietà design by the artist Ruth Schaumann in Frankfurt's Frauenfriedenskirche.[70]

Local memorial sites were important for contemporaries, as were formalized remembrance ceremonies and the representation of the war in art and literature. Yet in private, at home, in the family, and in the local community, individuals had already found ways to grieve and remember and some had developed such rituals during the war years. Testimonies from diaries and memoirs show ways in which experiences of the First World War had become part of family history and tradition and formed an emotional archive of war often crossing generations.[71] Here, in these private accounts, a more vernacular war memory is visible as well as remembrance practices that were part of everyday life and often centred on lasting bereavement. Historian Jay Winter emphasizes the importance of compassion as a response to the death toll of the war.[72] One such example is the 16-year-old trainee nurse Piete Kuhr from Scheidemühl in the province of Posen, who, at the end of November 1918, bound a wreath with her friend Gretel for the cemetery of the town's prisoner-of-war camp. In her diary, she recalled Gretel asking whether they should not place it at 'our heroes' cemetery' and noted her reply: 'No. The others have no one who brings them a wreath.'[73] When they arrived at the site, both marvelled at how much the cemetery had grown and what had caused the deaths of these men. This remarkable gesture of sympathy highlights the importance of the agency of individuals in shaping the post-war remembrance culture. Familiar rituals offered a frame in which the 'enemy' dead could be considered part of a joint experience of tragedy. The war dead were also remembered in people's homes. The artist Käthe Kollwitz, whose son Peter died in Belgium in 1914, used his bedroom as a memorial site, sat there to grieve and read—in the Bible or Peter's favourite books for example—and regularly placed flowers on his bed to mark particular days and dates.[74] In other families, photographs of the fallen became shrines or retained a special meaning. Hulda G., for example, lost her boyfriend, a submarine officer, during the First World War and kept a picture of him in her bedroom throughout her married life with a new husband.[75] In her memoirs, Eva Sternheim-Peters wrote about her aunt who had donated her golden wedding band in 1914 to support the war effort and wore the iron bracelet she received in return for the rest of her life, even though she emigrated with her Jewish husband in 1933.[76] There are also examples of actual memorial sites being erected in private gardens, as the one built for Heinrich Westermann by his brother in the family home.[77]

War memories were constructed, moreover, as they were being told and retold at family gatherings, a process that was shaped as much by remembering as forgetting.[78] We learn from Anita Lasker-Wallfisch's memoirs that her father regularly entertained the family with his war stories, while the family was having coffee and cake on Saturday afternoons.[79] The recollections of Eva Sternheim-Peters also convey the importance of the retelling of her brothers' experiences from the battle of Langemarck within the family as well as the omnipresence of wartime keepsakes around the house.[80] Re-reading preserved letters and holding on to photographs of sons, brothers, fathers, or husbands who had been at the front were important parts of familial remembrance rituals. The wartime service of family members could also challenge an entire family's identity.[81] Here the examples of Jewish families are particularly striking as the records of those who had served at the front were preserved by families not only throughout the 1920s, but brought into exile by those who left Germany in the 1930s. Wartime service features prominently in the family archives of Jewish émigrés in the UK, for example, and contain remarkable photo albums such as the one of Victor Ehrenberg's service at the Western Front.[82] Indeed, the war record was of such relevance that Jewish veterans and families held on to war letters and photographs throughout their deportations and some even brought these mementos into concentration camps. The acknowledgement and remembrance of wartime loss also occurred without broad ideological descriptors as the dead were mourned as familial tragedies.

Weimar Artists Depict the First World War

The war experience and conflicts over its representation and meaning left deep traces in the cultural world of the 1920s. If we understand the relationship between art, literature, film, and war as constituent, then it was manifested as a fundamental subconscious transformation in Weimar culture.[83] The impact of the war went deeper than a thematic strand in literature or art of the 1920s and is commensurate with the existential nature of the war experience that deeply affected people's sense of self and their sense of their place in the world. There were very concrete ways in which artists confronted and dealt with the war and war experiences in their work. In addition, the war was embodied and tangibly represented in cultural objects. Art, photographs, and artefacts from the war years were vectors of memory, whose meaning was mediated over time by contemporaries. The war and its impact were also a subject matter in art, literature, and film, conveying different tensions that emerged from the very specific character of the respective medium. The aim here is not to present an overview of artistic or thematic developments, as Weimar's artistic representation of war is not easily separated into genres, styles, or schools. Instead, this chapter addresses some examples of how war experiences were mediated and the manner in which meaning was constructed in art and by artists. What stand out as overarching themes are the tensions between the emotional legacy of wartime death and the interpretation of the soldiers' sacrifice.

Literature was dominated by writing veterans as it was widely held that the truth about war was embedded in experience and could only be conveyed by those who had been at the front. In the immediate aftermath of the war, personal war writing played a key role in addressing the contemporary need to preserve an account of the event and document the 'true' nature of the conflict. Diaries, memoirs, and letters by those who had fought at the front were published widely. A similar function was fulfilled by regimental accounts and documentary histories such as the multivolume official military history of the First World War that was compiled by the national archive.[84] War writing was also produced by women and represented no less of an existential experience, but their works were published in much lower numbers if at all. Claire Goll, for example, produced a stark short story, *Die Frauen erwachen*, in which a woman finds it unbearable to live with someone who has killed another human being in war. Unable to escape the harrowing visions of her husband at war and/or the marriage, she ultimately kills herself.[85] A moral impasse created by the war, in which actions and decisions of women reveal their true character, is one way in which female writers addressed the war's impact beyond the front. While Goll ultimately conveys a pacifist message, other female writers of the 1920s, such as Ricarda Huch, presented alternative visions.[86]

The writings of hundreds of veterans did not generate a widely accepted uniform narrative of the conflict. Through writing, veterans dealt with and interpreted retrospectively their war experiences, which varied greatly on an individual level despite generic similarities of combat and comradeship. These accounts presented versions of individual 'truths' about the war's legacy. In some accounts, including the memoirs of officers such as Ludendorff or Hindenburg, the war remained a heroic endeavour only lost because the army was betrayed by the home front. Others, such as Ernst Jünger, presented the war experience as a hardening and ultimately worthwhile experience.[87] But yet other texts graphically addressed the misery, suffering, and violence of the war. For such writers as Andreas Latzko, Leonhard Frank, Bruno Vogel, and Fritz von Unruh telling about the war's violence and destruction also meant holding to account those whom they considered to be responsible for it.[88]

The various editions of the popular collection of war letters by fallen German students published throughout the 1920s by the Freiburg professor Philipp Witkop, demonstrate how his changing forewords and exclusion of particular letters in later editions constructed a war narrative of patriotic commitment and heroic sacrifice for the nation.[89] The precise nature of what the war experience meant remained a relevant question throughout the Weimar period. For Carl Zuckmayer, the one book that offered truth on the subject and revealed 'what went on in these people, what happened inside, in the mines and sap of the soul, in the blood, in the tissue' was Erich Maria Remarque's 1929 *All Quiet on the Western Front*:

> For it is concerned with the fundamental fact of our life and future being, with the primal stratum, and with the cellular core of centuries. This is the war as we experienced it at the front, we, a very defined generation formed in only a few years, who had had no life before the war, no form, and no content, who were born of the war and crushed by it, and who—along with its dead—live on beyond the war as a singular new beginning.[90]

The book was widely perceived as an anti-war book, centring on a young protagonist, his friends, and their deadly fate in the war. For contemporaries, the protagonist of *All Quiet on the Western Front* was either the relatable suffering soldier or the anti-hero. The public controversy and responses to the book largely mapped onto the politicized memory tropes of the left and the right in Weimar. But the conflict reached a new dimension when Lewis Milestones's film adaptation arrived in German cinemas in 1930. The sabotage of screenings, intimidations of audiences by the nationalist right, and the release of mice by the Nazis during a screening in Berlin are well known. The film was censored, viewed as defeatist and untrue, and while an ensuing legal battle was won and the film reopened in cinemas, the case shows the escalating ends used to prevent the circulation of a particular version of the war. The new medium of film, especially sound film, was increasingly relevant for shaping an image of war that fed into the sharpening conflict over what the political legacy of the war experience should be. In *Westfront 1918* by Georg Pabst, the carnage of the front presented with sound, created an account of war that was embraced by the anti-war movement, but rejected by those who felt it negated the worthiness of wartime sacrifices.[91] Both films have sparked a particular visual language of war in which content and form created additional layers of meaning. A fundamental critique of late Weimar anti-war film, voiced by recent scholarship, is the limitation of its critical message. It cast the soldier as victim but did not uncover the structural dynamics of the violence of modern war.[92] But perhaps it is crucial to reappraise that ambivalence and contradictions were inherently part of contemporary 'anti-war' film, literature, and art.

A similar challenge of representation and the meaning of war was embodied in photography. Here, the framing of wartime photographs added meaning to their role as vectors of memory. Thousands of photographs from the war years were in circulation and most were taken by soldiers themselves, who sent photos home or created photo albums of their time at war. Conflict arose here over the documentary character of photographic images and the associated 'true' reality they seemingly captured. The degree to which photographs were politicized and how they were put to use is well illustrated by Ernst Friedrich's book *War Against War*—first published in 1924 and quickly published in many other European countries. It was a multilingual anti-war treatise with graphic portrayals of the disfiguring impact of modern weaponry that sought to shock its audience.[93] The graphic photographs of facial wounds and mutilations reprinted in the book seemed to present an unequivocal anti-war message that the pacifist Friedrich was keen to disseminate. But by capturing disfigurement, the cameras captured also the 'impossibility to regain a human face'.[94] The photographs were a record of the gap between initial expectations of the war and its realities that could not be bridged. Ernst Friedrich had been a conscientious objector during the First World War. He was an anarchist who opposed militarism, who championed education as a tool to prevent another war, and who was repeatedly subjected to police harassment, sued, and frequently arrested for his activism in the 1920s. Right-wingers repeatedly vandalized his anti-war museum in Berlin.[95] But just as Friedrich had hoped to support anti-war education with visual evidence of its cost, photographs were also employed for very different pedagogical purposes. In 1919, a teacher from Landau in Hesse, for example, ordered a montage of photographs that he had collected of the city's 'brave and loyal fallen heroes' for the classroom of year one pupils so they would be a 'shining example for all times'. Names of the fallen were deliberately not included, he explained, as the children were not to absent-mindedly read the names but to 'deeply impress the faces in their hearts'. Families of the dead were also presented with a printed copy of the montage at a commemorative event held at the local school on Totensonntag (Sunday of the Dead) in 1919.[96]

The search for appropriate ways to express the war experience was a matter of deep reflection by artists including Ernst-Ludwig Kirchner, Otto Dix, George Grosz, Max Beckmann, Oskar Schlemmer, and Käthe Kollwitz, many of whom experimented with different techniques and changed how they made art.[97] For Käthe Kollwitz, finding an artistic form that conveyed the depth of her emotional pain from losing her son in the war took years.[98] The work produced by artists in the 1920s was part of a journey in which the self-mobilization for war in August 1914 represented a key moment. Many artists were veterans who had seen frontline service, such as Otto Dix, George Grosz, and Gert Wollheim, or had worked as paramedics or ambulance drivers like Erich Heckel and Max Beckmann. Others were auxiliary workers, volunteered over-aged, or supported the war from home.[99] Female artists, too, had supported the war effort by, for example, producing posters, working as nurses, or supporting the service of sons and husbands. Most of these artists went through a process of disillusionment in face of the realities of the war and the mounting death toll.[100] The artists struggled to align the war that unfolded with the one they had imagined. In addition, among those who had seen frontline service, a high proportion of artists suffered from shell-shock, some were personally injured, and most had lost close friends or relatives in the war. The decidedly anti-war stance that much of the war art of the 1920s projects, the stark turns in technique, thematic choices, or notions of ambiguity are impossible to understand without acknowledging the artists' initial mobilization for war and their subsequent disillusionment, emotional trauma, and dislocation. Some artists produced graphic and violent work to shock and express their disgust over the nature of the war. For others, the representation of the cost of the war was not necessarily connected to a wider anti-war message or pacifist statement, but a deeply personal expression of trauma, physical and emotional pain, or anger. Artists, too, faced the difficulty of how to represent the war experience in a way that could convey trauma and sacrifice while not making it meaningless, although for some this may have been the ultimate conclusion.

Much of the Weimar war art, indeed, explicitly shows the wounds of war. Some artists did so by returning visually to the trenches, while others showed the wounded and disabled in their new lives. A large number of artists actually depicted themselves, painted their transformed selves, mutilated in mind or body after having gone to war, thereby exposing the gulf between the initial expectations and realties of war in particularly stark terms. But displaying art in public that explicitly showed the impact of war and modern weaponry could be difficult. Gert Wollheim's 1919 painting *Verwundeter* (Wounded), which was bought by the Düsseldorf Art Gallery and exhibited as a new acquisition, was removed from the display after visitors complained.[101] It showed a man suffering from an abdominal wound and holding on to his spilling intestines, and was an autobiographical piece that relived Wollheim's own injury during the war.

Confronting society with the nature of the war and its shared consequences was the subject matter of a number of the graphic art portfolios that were published in the 1920s. Max Beckmann's portfolio *Die Hölle* (Hell), explicitly invited the spectators on a tour of contemporary society, promising on the title-page that visitors 'will not be disappointed' and presenting apocalyptic impressions of contemporary life inside. Käthe Kollwitz's *Folge Krieg* (War Series) produced between 1918 and 1923 confronted the emotional legacy of sacrifice. The works of Otto Dix and George Grosz of the 1920s, also represented an assessment of the cost of the war and the impossibility of returning to the world that existed before. The individual war experience or war trauma was central to the art produced in the 1920s. The complexities of the ways in which war experience was given or defied meaning points to the importance of nuance and ambivalence in the cultural representations of war that have eluded easy answers and categorization since the 1920s.

Conclusion

Weimar Germany's political, commemorative, and artistic cultures were profoundly shaped by the variety of ways in which contemporaries remembered the war, reconfigured their war experiences, and grieved their losses. Retracing the rituals, forms, and content of how Germans remembered the war and its dead in the 1920s is to acknowledge their importance and relevance for what it was at the time. Weimar war memory was about the memory of the war in the Weimar Republic. It was not a straight path towards nationalist radicalization and it also went deeper than a polarized political division of left versus right. The attraction to understand Weimar war memory as a moment of politicized binary opposition and ultimate nationalist dominance after 1933 is clear, but it simply ignores the lived realities of the 1920s.

Remembrance in Weimar Germany was not only a top-down process but also driven from below as a large variety of groups, organizations, and also individuals in German society were engaged in commemorative activities. At the heart of these activities was the memory of the war dead. The commemorative actions of groups and individuals demonstrate, moreover, that the nature of the rituals and forms contemporaries found to remember the dead and express lasting bereavement mattered deeply. Cultural representations of war in art, literature, photography, and film also show that the meaning given to wartime sacrifice was pluralistic and indicate the experiential imperative behind their production. Conflicts regarding artistic representations, disputed memorial designs, and 'contested commemorations' were all part of how Weimar Germans remembered the war. They show just how difficult it was for many to acknowledge the war losses and live with the consequences of wartime sacrifice. But just as these conflicts allow us to understand the enduring quest for meaning, shared communal rituals and simple personal gestures provide some insights into the ways in which the emotional legacy of the war was mediated in post-war society.

Acknowledgement

I would like to thank Robert Cook, Daniel Steinbach, and Gerhard Wolf for reading drafts of this chapter.

Notes

1. Diary entry Agnes Zenker, 7 January 1921. Gerold Kiendl (ed.), *Kriegstagebuch Agnes Zenker*, Bergen <https://www.zenker.se/History/nessi_tagebuch.shtml#Oktober_1918>.
2. Richard Bessel, *Germany After the First World War* (Oxford: Clarendon Press, 1993), 221–2.
3. Soldier's letter, 15 Oct. 1918, in Bernd Ulrich and Benjamin Ziemann (eds), *Krieg im Frieden: Die umkämpfte Erinnerung an den Ersten Weltkrieg* (Frankfurt/Main: Fischer, 1997), 31; Bernd Ulrich, *Die Augenzeugen: Deutsche Feldpostbriefe in Kriegs- und Nachkriegszeit 1914 – 1933* (Essen: Klartext, 1997).
4. Roger Chickering, *Imperial Germany and the Great War*, 3rd ed. (Cambridge: Cambridge University Press, 2014), 215–16.
5. Letter Emma Schiel to her son 'Otting', 27 Nov. 1918, in Eberhard Schiel (ed.), *Mein lieber Sohn und Kamerad: Stralsunder Briefe aus dem Ersten Weltkrieg* (Kückenshagen: Scheunen-Verlag, 1996), 313.
6. Jost Dülffer, 'Frieden schließen nach einem Weltkrieg? Die mentale Verlängerung der Kriegssituation in den Friedenschluss', in Jost Dülffer and Gerd Krumeich (eds), *Der verlorene Frieden: Politik und Kriegskultur nach 1918* (Essen: Klartext, 2002), 30.
7. Chickering, *Imperial Germany*, 216; Wolfgang Schivelbusch, *The Culture of Defeat: On National Trauma, Mourning and Recovery*, 2nd ed. (New York: Picador, 2004), 17.
8. John Horne, 'Kulturelle Demobilmachung 1919–1939: Ein sinnvoller historischer Begriff?', in Wolfgang Hardtwig (ed.), *Politische Kulturgeschichte der Zwischenkriegszeit 1918–1939* (Göttingen: Vandenhoeck & Ruprecht, 2005), 136–7.
9. Dülffer, 'Frieden', 33.
10. Antoine Prost, 'The Dead', in Jay Winter (ed.), *The Cambridge History of the First World War*, vol. 3 (Cambridge: Cambridge University Press, 2014), 587–91.
11. Stéphane Audoin-Rouzeau and Annette Becker, *14–18: Understanding the Great War* (New York: Hill & Wang, 2002), 203–12; Jay Winter, *Sites of Memory, Sites of Mourning: The Great War in European Cultural History* (Cambridge: Cambridge University Press, 1995).
12. George L. Mosse, *Fallen Soldiers: Reshaping the Memory of the World Wars* (Oxford and New York: Oxford University Press, 1990); Schivelbusch, *Culture of Defeat*; Peter Fritzsche, *Germans into Nazis* (Cambridge, MA, and London: Harvard University Press, 1999); Sabine Behrenbeck, *Der Kult um die toten Helden: nationalsozialistische Mythen, Riten und Symbole 1923 bis 1945*, 2nd ed. (Cologne: SH-Verlag, 2011).
13. Bessel, *Germany*, 169–94; Hans-Ulrich Wehler, *Deutsche Gesellschaftsgeschichte*, vol. 4. *Vom Beginn des Ersten Weltkriegs bis zur Gründung der beiden deutschen Staaten 1914–1949* (Munich: C. H. Beck, 2003), 223; Wolfgang J. Mommsen, 'The Social Consequences of World War I: The Case of Germany', in Arthur Marwick (ed.), *Total War and Social Change* (London: Macmillan, 1988), 26.
14. Hans Mommsen, 'Einleitung', in Mommsen (ed.), *Der Erste Weltkrieg und die europäische Nachkriegsordnung: Sozialer Wandel und Formveränderung der Politik* (Cologne: Böhlau, 2000), 8.

15. Robert W. Whalen, *Bitter Wounds: German Victims of the Great War, 1914–1939* (Ithaca, NY: Cornell University Press, 1984), 16.
16. Ibid., 128; Christian Weiß, '"Soldaten des Friedens": Die pazifistischen Veteranen und Kriegsopfer des "Reichsbundes" und ihre Kontakte zu den französischen anciens combattants, 1919–1933', in Wolfgang Hardtwig (ed.), *Politische Kulturgeschichte der Zwischenkriegszeit 1918–1939* (Göttingen: Vandenhoeck & Ruprecht, 2005), 184.
17. Whalen, *Bitter Wounds*, 131–9.
18. Karin Hausen, 'The German Nation's Obligations to the Heroes' Widows of World War 1', in Margaret Randolph Higonnet, Jane Jenson, Sonya Michel, and Margaret Collins White (eds), *Behind the Lines: Gender and the Two World Wars* (New Haven and London: Yale University Press, 1987), 126–40.
19. Helene Hurwitz-Stranz (ed.), *Kriegerwitwen gestalten ihr Schicksal: Lebenskämpfe deutscher Kriegswitwen nach eigenen Darstellungen* (Berlin: Heymanns Verlag, 1931), 32–3.
20. Ibid.
21. Gertrud Bäumer, 'Vorwort', in Hurwitz-Stranz, *Kriegerwitwen*, 9.
22. Schivelbusch, *Culture of Defeat*.
23. Ibid., 166–87.
24. Ibid., 173–5; Boris Barth, *Dolchstoßlegenden und politische Desintegration: Das Trauma der deutschen Niederlage im Ersten Weltkrieg 1914–1933* (Düsseldorf: Droste, 2003).
25. Bessel, *Germany*, 283–4.
26. Alan Kramer, 'The First World War and German Memory', in Heather Jones, Jennifer O'Brien, and Christoph Schmidt-Supprian (eds), *Untold War: New Perspectives in First World War Studies* (Leiden and Boston: Brill, 2008), 387.
27. Hans Delbrück, 'Die Behandlung der Kriegsschuldfrage', in Zentralstelle für Erforschung der Kriegsursachen (ed.), *Die Kriegsschuldfrage, Monatsschrift für internationale Aufklärung*, 1 (July 1923), 1–3.
28. Horne, 'Kulturelle Demobilmachung', 132–7.
29. Klaus Theweleit, *Male Fantasies: Women, Floods, Bodies, History*, vol. 1 (Cambridge: Polity, 1987) and for a recent take on the brutalization theory see Robert Gerwarth and John Horne, 'Paramilitarism in Europe After the Great War: An Introduction', in Gerwarth and Horne (eds), *War in Peace: Paramilitary Violence in Europe after the Great War* (Oxford: Oxford University Press, 2012), 1–21.
30. Mosse, *Fallen Soldiers*, 159–81.
31. Bessel, *Germany*, 258.
32. Michael Wildt, *Generation of the Unbound: The Leadership Corps of the Reich Security Main Office* (Jerusalem: Yad Vashem, 2002); Kurt Sontheimer, *Antidemokratisches Denken in der Weimarer Republik* (Munich: Nymphenburger Verlagshandlung, 1962), 110; Bessel, *Germany*, 256–9; Arndt Weinrich, *Der Weltkrieg als Erzieher: Jugend zwischen Weimarer Republik und Nationalsozialismus* (Essen: Klartext, 2013), 17.
33. Bessel, *Germany*, 69.
34. Benjamin Ziemann, *Contested Commemorations: Republican War Veterans and Weimar Political Culture* (Cambridge: Cambridge University Press, 2013), 15.
35. 'Der Weltkrieg als Weltversöhner: Ein Aufruf des Friedensbundes der Kriegsteilnehmer', *Berliner Volkszeitung*, 19 Oct. 1919.
36. Ziemann, *Contested Commemorations*.
37. Otto Baumgarten, *Geistige und sittliche Wirkungen des Krieges in Deutschland* (Stuttgart: Deutsche Verlags-Anstalt, 1927), 13–14.

38. Ibid.
39. Alan Kramer, 'The First World War as Cultural Trauma', in Richard Bosworth (ed.), *The Oxford Handbook of Fascism* (Oxford: Oxford University Press, 2009), 48–9.
40. Schivelbusch, *Culture of Defeat*, 200ff.; Fritzsche, *Germans*, 6–7.
41. Gerd Krumeich (ed.), *Nationalsozialismus und Erster Weltkrieg* (Essen: Klartext, 2010).
42. On the 'mental horizon' see Alon Confino, 'Collective Memory and Cultural History: Problems of Method', *American Historical Review*, 102 (1997), 1403.
43. Reinhart Koselleck, 'War Memorials. Identity Formations of the Survivors', in Koselleck, *The Practice of Conceptual History: Timing History, Spacing Concepts* (Stanford, CA: Stanford University Press, 2002), 285–326.
44. 'War Celebration in Berlin', *The Times*, 4 Aug. 1924, 7.
45. Sabine Behrenbeck, 'The Nation Honours the Dead: Remembrance Days for the Fallen in the Weimar Republic and the Third Reich', in Karin Friedrich (ed.), *Festive Culture in Germany and Europe from the 16th Century to the 20th Century* (Lewiston, NY: Edwin Mellen Press, 2000), 306–12.
46. Walter Mühlhausen (ed.), *Friedrich Ebert—Reden als Reichspräsident, 1919–1925* (Bonn: J. H. W. Dietz Nachf., 2017), 356 note 3.
47. Friedrich Ebert, 'Ansprache bei der Gedenkfeier für die Opfer des Weltkrieges, 3 August 1924', in Mühlhausen, *Friedrich Ebert*, 355–8, here 356.
48. Kurt Tucholsky, 'The Spirit of 1914' (7 August 1924), in Anton Kaes, Martin Jay, and Edward Dimendberg (eds), *The Weimar Republic Sourcebook* (Berkeley, CA: University of California Press, 1995), 20–2.
49. 'War Celebration in Berlin', *The Times*, 4 Aug. 1924, 7.
50. Jay Winter and Emmanuel Sivan, 'Introduction', in Winter and Sivan (eds), *War and Remembrance in the Twentieth Century* (Cambridge: Cambridge University Press, 1999), 10.
51. *Berliner Tageblatt*, 3 Aug. 1924.
52. Cited in August Diehl, *Das Reichsehrenmal: Ein Prüfstein und Wahrzeichen deutscher Kultur im Dritten Reich* (Halle: Vaterländischer Verlag, 1933), 9.
53. Ibid., 29.
54. Ken Inglis, 'Entombing Unknown Soldiers: From London and Paris to Baghdad', *History and Memory*, 5 (1993), 7; Jay Winter, *War Beyond Words. Languages of Remembrance from the Great War to the Present* (Cambridge: Cambridge University Press, 2017), 145; Nadine Rossol, *Performing the Nation in Interwar Germany: Sport, Spectacle and Political Symbolism, 1926–1936* (Basingstoke: Palgrave Macmillan, 2010), 84; Benjamin Ziemann, 'Die deutsche Nation und ihr zentraler Erinnerungsort: Das "Nationaldenkmal für die Gefallenen im Weltkriege" und die Idee des "Unbekannten Soldaten", 1914–1935', in Helmut Berding, Klaus Heller, and Winfried Speitkamp (eds), *Krieg und Erinnerung: Fallstudien zum 19. und 20. Jahrhundert* (Göttingen: Vandenhoeck & Ruprecht 2000), 80.
55. Inglis, 'Entombing Unknown Soldiers', 19; Ziemann, 'Die deutsche Nation', 87.
56. Volker Probst, *Bilder vom Tode: Eine Studie zum deutschen Kriegerdenkmal in der Weimarer Republik am Beispiel des Pietà-Motives und seiner profanierten Varianten* (Hamburg: Wayasbah, 1986), 4–6; Meinhold Lurz, *Kriegerdenkmäler in Deutschland. 1. Weltkrieg*. vol. 3 (Heidelberg: Esprint 1985), 92–6; Jay Winter, 'The Great War and the Persistence of Tradition: Languages of Grief, Bereavement, and Mourning', in Bernd Hüppauf (ed.), *War, Violence and the Modern Condition* (Berlin and New York: de Gruyter, 1997), 33–45.

57. Winter, *Sites of Memory*.
58. Koselleck, 'War Memorials', 285–326.
59. Winter, *War Beyond Words*.
60. Stadtarchiv Kassel, S 5 A, 244, *Kasseler Post*, 12 Apr. 1926.
61. Benjamin Schulte, *Veteranen des Ersten Weltkrieges: Der Kyffhäuserbund von 1918 bis 1933* (Bielefeld: transcript, 2020).
62. Stadtarchiv Kassel, S 5 A, 244.
63. Stadtarchiv Kassel, S 5 A, 244, *Hessische Post Kassel*, 24 Nov. 1920.
64. Stefan Goebel, 'Re-membered and Re-mobilised: The "Sleeping Dead" in Interwar Germany and Britain', *Journal of Contemporary History*, 39 (2004), 487–501.
65. Goebel, 'Re-membered', 501.
66. Stadtarchiv Kassel, S 5 A, 244, *Kasseler Post*, 4 Dec. 1933.
67. Ilona Laudan, 'Ein Engel für den Güstrower Dom: Zur Entstehungsgeschichte des Güstrower Ehrenmals', in Volker Probst (ed.), *Ernst Barlach: Das Güstrower Ehrenmal* (Leipzig: Seemann, 1998), 32.
68. Ibid., 32.
69. Nadine Rossol, 'Commemoration, Cult of the Fallen (Germany)', in *1914-1918-online. International Encyclopedia of the First World War* (Berlin: Freie Universität Berlin, 10 Aug. 2014), DOI: 10.15463/ie1418.10442.
70. Probst, *Bilder vom Tode*, 158.
71. Claudia Siebrecht, 'The Tears of 1939: German Women and the Emotional Archive of the First World War', in Claire Langhamer, Lucy Noakes, and Claudia Siebrecht (eds), *Total War: An Emotional History* (Oxford: Oxford University Press/The British Academy, 2020), 78–97.
72. Winter, *Sites of Memory*, 6.
73. Diary entry by Piete Kuhr, 28 Nov. 1918, publ. as Jo Mihaly, *… da gibt's ein Wiedersehn! Kriegstagebuch eines Mädchens 1914–1918* (Freiburg: Kerle, 1982), 376.
74. Diary entries by Käthe Kollwitz, 24 Dec. 1915 and 8 Jan. 1916, in Jutta Bohnke-Kollwitz (ed.), *Käthe Kollwitz: Die Tagebücher, 1908–1943* (Berlin: Siedler, 1999), 205, 211.
75. Margarete Dörr, *Wer die Zeit nicht miterlebt hat … Frauenerfahrungen im Zweiten Weltkrieg und in den Jahren danach*, vol. 3. *Das Verhältnis zum Nationalsozialismus und zum Krieg* (Frankfurt/Main: Campus, 1998), 428.
76. Eva Sternheim-Peters, *Die Zeit der großen Täuschungen: Mädchenleben im Faschismus* (Bielefeld: AJZ-Verlag, 1989), 18.
77. *Heinrich Westermann, gefallen am 17. Januar 1915 bei Pont à Mousson: Ein Gedenkblatt zu seinem 10 jährigen Todestage von seinem Onkel Ernst Reinstorf in Wilhelmsburg* (Wilhelmsburg: Schüthe, 1925).
78. Aleida Assmann, *Cultural Memory and Western Civilization* (Cambridge: Cambridge University Press, 2012), 19–20.
79. Anita Lasker-Wallfisch, *Inherit the Truth, 1939–1945: The Documented Experiences of a Survivor of Auschwitz and Belsen* (London: Giles de la Mare, 1996), 29.
80. Sternheim-Peters, *Die Zeit*, 15–22.
81. On memory and identity see Koselleck, 'War Memorials', 285–326; Assmann, *Cultural Memory*, 119ff.
82. The Keep Archive, Sussex, SxMs96/12/33/1, Victor Ehrenberg Photoalbum Western Front.
83. Bernd Hüppauf, 'Experiences of Modern Warfare and the Crisis of Representation', *New German Critique*. 59 (1993), 41–76.

84. Markus Pöhlmann, *Kriegsgeschichte und Geschichtspolitik: Der Erste Weltkrieg. Die amtliche deutsche Militärgeschichtsschreibung, 1914–1956* (Paderborn: Schöningh, 2002), 163–93.
85. Claire Studer (Goll), *Die Frauen erwachen* (Frauenfeld: Huber, 1918).
86. Angelika Döpper-Henrich, '*.. Es war eine trügerische Zwischenzeit': Schriftstellerinnen der Weimarer Republik und ihr Verhältnis zu den gesellschaftlich-politischen Umgestaltungen ihrer Zeit* (Kassel: Kassel University Press, 2004), 152–71.
87. Ernst Jünger, *In Stahlgewittern: Aus dem Tagebuch eines Stoßtruppführers* (Hanover: Self-published, 1920).
88. Vanessa Ther, '"Humans are Cheap and the Bread is Dear": Republican Portrayals of the War Experience in Weimar Germany', in Jones et al., *Untold War*, 357–84.
89. Manfred Hettling and Michael Jeismann, 'Der Weltkrieg als Epos: Philipp Witkops Kriegsbriefe gefallener Studenten', in Gerhard Hirschfeld, Gerd Krumeich, and Irina Renz (eds), *Keiner fühlt sich hier mehr als Mensch.. Erlebnis und Wirkung des Ersten Weltkriegs* (Essen: Klartext, 1993), 178–83.
90. Carl Zuckmayer, 'Review of Erich Maria Remarque's All Quiet on the Western Front' (Jan. 1929) in Kaes et al., *Weimar Republic Sourcebook*, 23–4.
91. Bernadette Kester, *Film Front Weimar: Representations of the First World War in German Films of the Weimar Period, 1919–1933* (Amsterdam: Amsterdam University Press, 2003), 127–36.
92. Hüppauf, 'Crisis of Representation', 62–3.
93. Ernst Friedrich, *Krieg dem Kriege* (Berlin: Verlag Freie Jugend, 1924).
94. Hüppauf, 'Crisis of Representation', 62.
95. Gerd Krumeich, 'Ein einzigartiges Werk', in Ernst Friedrich, *Krieg dem Kriege*, new ed. (Berlin: Ch. Links Verlag, 2015), xxii–xxiv.
96. Heinrich Höhle, 'Kriegstagebuch eines Lehrers aus Landau, 1914–1919', in *Hessische Quellen zum Ersten Weltkrieg* <https://www.lagis-hessen.de/de/purl/resolve/subject/qhg/id/15-9> (accessed 14 Sept. 2020), 20.
97. Matthias Eberle, *World War I and the Weimar Artists: Dix, Grosz, Beckmann, Schlemmer* (New Haven and London: Yale University Press, 1985).
98. Regina Schulte, 'Käthe Kollwitz's Sacrifice', *History Workshop Journal*, 41 (1996), 193–221.
99. Wolfgang J. Mommsen, 'German Writers, Artists and Intellectuals and the Meaning of War 1914–1918', in John Horne (ed.), *State, Society and Mobilisation during the First World War* (Cambridge: Cambridge University Press, 1997), 21–38.
100. Claudia Siebrecht, *The Aesthetics of Loss: German Women's Art of the First World War* (Oxford: Oxford University Press, 2013).
101. Richard Cork, 'Das Elend des Krieges: Die Kunst der Avantgarde und der Erste Weltkrieg', in Rainer Rother (ed.), *Die letzten Tage der Menschheit: Bilder des Ersten Weltkrieges* (Berlin: Ars Nicolai, 1994), 376.

Bibliography

Bessel, Richard, *Germany After the First World War* (Oxford: Clarendon Press, 1993).
Dülffer, Jost, and Gerd Krumeich (eds), *Der verlorene Frieden: Politik und Kriegskultur nach 1918* (Essen: Klartext, 2002)

Eberle, Matthias, *World War I and the Weimar Artists: Dix, Grosz, Beckmann, Schlemmer* (New Haven and London: Yale University Press, 1985).

Mosse, George L., *Fallen Soldiers: Reshaping the Memory of the World Wars* (Oxford and New York: Oxford University Press, 1990).

Probst, Volker, *Bilder vom Tode. Eine Studie zum deutschen Kriegerdenkmal in der Weimarer Republik am Beispiel des Pietà-Motives und seiner profanierten Varianten* (Hamburg: Wayasbah, 1986).

Schivelbusch, Wolfgang, *The Culture of Defeat: On National Trauma, Mourning and Recovery* (New York: Metropolitan Books, 2003).

Ulrich, Bernd, and Benjamin Ziemann (eds), *Krieg im Frieden: Die umkämpfte Erinnerung an den Ersten Weltkrieg* (Frankfurt/Main: Fischer, 1997).

Whalen, Robert W., *Bitter Wounds: German Victims of the Great War, 1914–1939* (Ithaca, NY: Cornell University Press, 1984).

Winter, Jay, *Sites of Memory, Sites of Mourning: The Great War in European Cultural History* (Cambridge: Cambridge University Press, 1995).

Ziemann, Benjamin, *Contested Commemorations. Republican War Veterans and Weimar Political Culture* (Cambridge: Cambridge University Press, 2013).

Index

A

abdication 30, 364, 684
abortion 13, 484, 532, 535, 556, 635, 689
absolutism, parliamentary 133
abuse, sexual 479
Academic Exchange Service 544
acculturation 564, 579, 739
Addison, Joseph 81
Adenauer, Konrad 260, 466, 534, 689, 696
Adler-Schnee, Ruth 578
Adorno, Theodor W. 621, 623, 717
Adversary, The 632
advertisement 9, 155–6, 175–6, 299, 438, 490, 576, 617, 662, 691, 724, 730–1, 734–5, 742, 757
Africa 9–11, 123, 131, 153, 458, 734, 736
Agfa 437
Agnon, Samuel Joseph 580
agriculture 16, 203, 369, 376, 446, 476–7, 499–501, 503–6, 512–14, 525, 549, 595
   agrarians 377
   agrarian crisis 186, 375, 508, 510, 514–15
   large landed 99, 379n13
   organized 108
   agricultural sector 10, 235, 501, 506
Albersdorf 511
alcohol 175, 483–4, 487, 593, 595
Alexander von Humboldt Foundation 544
Alfeld 661
Alighieri, Dante 612
All-Union Society for Cultural Ties Abroad 550
Allemann, Fritz René 3
Allgemeine Rundschau 688
Allies 34, 55, 63, 76, 145, 204, 221–3, 228, 230–1, 235, 243, 245–6, 251–2, 257, 319, 344, 375, 407, 432, 443–4, 458

Alps 410, 585n62
Alsace-Lorraine 34, 149, 198, 211, 245, 252, 431
Althaus, Paul 687
Altona 198
Alvensleben, Werner von 693
America 414, 541–6, 549, 552–3, 555–7, 576, 672
American Work Student Service 544
Americanism 546–7, 550–1, 553, 557, 645–6
Americanization 9, 524, 541, 543, 547, 619
amnesty 632
Amsterdam 433, 661
Amsterdam School 662
Ancien Régime 522
androgyny 726, 732
Angriff, Der 622
Anhalt 79, 193, 196, 269, 662
Annaberg 644
annexations 28, 143, 341
Anschluss 141–2, 147, 151–3, 155–7, 228, 257
Anschütz, Gerhard 133, 714
anthroposophy 704
anti-Americanism 620, 626n75
anti-Bolshevism 228, 383, 395
anti-capitalism 66
anti-communism 195, 462, 692, 696
anti-liberalism 208, 337n52, 371, 461, 557, 580, 714
anti-Marxism 694
anti-materialism 556
anti-modernism 205, 631
anti-parliamentarianism 126–7, 172, 377, 387
anti-republicanism 49, 75, 77, 81, 98, 129, 144–5, 148–9, 153, 155, 172, 174, 176, 181, 196, 242, 251, 269, 272, 282–3, 345–6, 364–7, 369, 372–3, 405, 415, 419, 463, 599
anti-secularism 692, 694
anti-socialism 79, 371, 462

Anti-War Museum 727, 765
anticlericalism 456, 462, 692
antiquity 522, 670
antisemitism 150–1, 154–6, 272, 367, 383, 394–6, 404–9, 411–19, 547, 557, 565, 567–76, 579, 581, 670, 694, 702, 705, 735, 739
   conspiracy 417
   as a cultural code 404
   racial 14, 65–6, 156, 374, 404, 417, 716
   rampant 1, 61, 65
   secondary 404
Appens, Wilhelm 8
Applegate, Celia 205
apprenticeships/apprentices 306, 479, 482, 486, 598–9, 656, 664
Arbeiter Illustrierte Zeitung 351, 489, 550, 724, 740
Arbeiter Turn- und Sportbund 349
Arbeiter-Fotograf 740
Arbeiterbauer 500
Arbeiterwohlfahrt 347
arbitration, binding 252, 307
archaeology 708, 711
architecture 1, 8, 194, 205, 207–8, 577, 618, 654–6, 661–2, 664, 666–70, 672–3
Arendt, Hannah 578
Argentina 153, 501, 503
aristocracy 326, 350, 364, 372, 380n33, 508
armament 219, 222, 230, 234, 308, 430, 457, 528
   First Armament Programme 229, 234
   Second Armament Programme 229
armistice 27–9, 34, 41, 50, 146, 219, 221, 242, 643, 751, 756
arms race 317
Army Supreme Command 28, 31, 40, 42, 145, 219–20, 222, 250, 430
Arplan 552
Art Deco 658
artillery 222, 231, 235
artisans 300, 321, 365, 367, 454, 456, 458, 460–1, 499, 514, 567, 644, 665
Aryan: paragraph 154, 574
   'race' 146, 154, 406, 532
Aschheim, Steven 580
Asia 433, 447
Aspirin 434

assassinations 40, 50, 54, 73, 129, 146, 268, 270, 272, 277, 280, 323, 369, 411, 511, 570–1, 632
assimilation 564, 566, 568–9, 578–9, 581
Association for Fighting for Red Sporting Unity (Kampfgemeinschaft für Rote Sporteinheit) 488
Association for Germandom Abroad (Verein für das Deutschtum im Ausland) 149
Association of German Students of the Jewish Faith (Kartell-Convent deutscher Studenten jüdischen Glaubens) 735
Association of Proletarian-Revolutionary Authors (Bund Proletarisch-Revolutionärer Schriftsteller) 633
associational life 11, 349, 455, 461–4, 468, 471n33, 572
atheism 684
athleticism 728
Aubin, Hermann 205–6
Augspurg, Anita 35
austerity 53, 64, 66, 88–9, 202, 234, 296, 300, 376, 600
Australia 501
Austria 28, 33, 141, 143, 147–8, 151–2, 155, 157, 171, 204, 246, 255, 257, 259, 274, 430, 446, 573, 706, 758
Austria-Hungary 151
Austrian school of economics 711
Austro-German People's League 152, 155
Austro-Prussian War 147
authoritarianism 30, 85, 102, 127, 374, 545, 693
autocracy 31, 242, 341, 542
autonomy 202, 367, 439, 593, 595, 601, 716
   bargaining 293–5, 307–8
   Catholic 681, 683
   tariff 368
   trade policy 432–3
avant-garde 8, 60, 155, 349, 389, 438, 524, 554, 577–8, 631, 648, 654–5, 662, 665–6, 669–70, 673, 707, 736, 739–40

B

Babelsberg film studios 647
Bad Berka 758
Bad Godesberg 691
Baden 79, 196, 199, 268–9, 271, 500, 508, 565
Baden, Max von 29–30, 41, 164

Baechler, Christian 259
Baker, Josephine 736–7
Balkan 28
Ballhause, Walter 740
Baltic Sea 30, 219, 410
Baltic States 231, 657
Bamberg 209
banking crisis 100, 257, 485
bankruptcies 53, 64, 202, 511
Baptists 685
Bar-Kochba 575
Barcelona 666, 668, 673
Barlach, Ernst 761
Barmat, Henry 412–13
Barmat, Julius 412–13
Barnstone, Deborah Ascher 740
Baron, Hans 713, 717
Barth, Emil 182
Barth, Karl 687, 711
Bartning, Otto 655, 657, 673
Basque Country 208
battle cruiser A (Panzerkreuzer A) 78, 86, 88, 130, 322
Bauer, Gustav 49–50, 182–3
Bauhaus 1, 8–9, 207–8, 467, 654–5, 661–4, 666, 669, 672–3, 725, 730
Baum, Marie 324
Baum, Vicki 646
Bäumer, Gertrud 317, 324–5, 327, 753
Baumgarten, Otto 755
Bavaria 1, 30, 33, 35, 38–41, 51, 54, 61–3, 73, 79–82, 99, 101, 128–9, 168, 193, 196–200, 202–3, 206, 222, 231–2, 249–50, 365, 372, 384, 390, 504, 508–9, 565, 570
  Upper 500, 502
Bavarian Palatinate 61, 205
Bavarian People's Party (Bayerische Volkspartei, BVP) 51, 61, 75–6, 80–2, 106–7, 168, 173, 179, 183–5, 199, 202, 366, 371–2, 416, 478, 488, 576, 688
Bavarian Swabia 500
Bayer company 434
Bebel, August 155
Becher, Johannes R. 632–3
Beck, Ludwig 236
Becker, Johann 183
Becker, Sabina 639

Beckmann, Max 766–7
Beer Hall Putsch 125, 198 *see also* Hitler putsch
Behne, Adolf 661
Behrens, Peter 662, 666
Beiersdorf company 433–4
Belgium 9, 56, 149, 192n76, 219, 233, 242, 249, 252, 255, 368, 643, 762
benefits 77, 99, 132, 291–3, 296–9, 306, 308, 523, 598
  cuts 305
  retirement 105, 300, 302, 376
  unemployment 78, 105, 258, 301–2, 304
Benjamin, Walther 544, 554, 580, 620–1, 633, 640, 705, 707, 717, 725
Benn, Gottfried 629, 647–8, 651
Berg, Eva 638–9
Berg, Max 655
Berg, Peter 544
Bergner, Elisabeth 732
Bergsträsser, Ludwig 85
Berlin Academy of Poets 633, 648
Berliner Illustrirte Zeitung (*BIZ*) 724, 736, 738
Berliner Tageblatt 27, 37, 39, 41, 79, 155, 268, 271, 283, 577, 619
Berliner Volks-Zeitung 268, 271
Berman, Sheri 464
Bernays, Marie 325
Berndt, Emil 283
Bernhard, Georg 268
Bernhart, Joseph 690
Bernkastel 510
Bernstein, Eduard 345, 612
Berthelot, Philippe 257
Bessel, Richard 483
Best, Werner 385
Bethel 686
Beumelburg, Werner 642–3
Beuthen 574
Beyerle, Konrad 132–3
big business 323, 349, 445, 458–60, 462
Bildung 455–8, 460–1, 467–8, 577, 609, 704
biology 395, 682, 716
birthrate 481, 566, 598, 600
bishops 374–5, 489, 599, 692
Bismarck Youth (Bismarck Jugend) 598

Bismarck, Otto von 28, 54, 72, 79, 143–5, 147, 202, 371, 488, 501, 728
'Black Shame' ('Schwarze Schmach') 735
Bloch, Ernst 578, 580, 707
blockade, British naval 39, 51, 430, 501–2, 514
'blood and soil' 149, 157, 515
Blüher, Hans 529
Blumenfeld, Kurt 568
Board of Aldermen 34
Bodin, Jean 60
Böhm, Dominikus 670
Bolshevism 34, 150, 254, 344, 542, 550–1, 619, 692–3
Bolz, Eugen 693
Bonatz, Paul 669
Bondy, Curt 591
Bonn 3, 165, 206, 703
Bonn, Moritz J. 59, 549, 555
Borchardt, Knut 429, 436
Border Defence East (Grenzschutz Ost) 221, 226, 231–2, 234, 235–6
borderland Germans (*Grenzlanddeutsche*) 148, 644
Borstei estate 660–1
Bosch company 434
Bosch, Robert 440
Böss, Gustav 268
bourgeoisie 4, 48, 51, 58–9, 65, 172, 177, 299–300, 408, 455, 488, 499, 612, 646
  petty 386, 393, 456, 618, 621 see also *Bürgertum*
boxing 466, 490, 579, 595, 611, 619, 622
Boxsport 619
boycotts 130, 253, 282, 408, 419, 565, 574, 576
Bracher, Karl Dietrich 3, 6, 95
Brandenburg 203, 499, 503, 510, 692
Brandenburg Gate 51, 283, 758
Brandler, Heinrich 61
Brandt, Marianne 730
Brandt, Willy 260
Braun, Otto 80, 85, 103, 195, 198, 235–6, 269, 280, 346, 514
Brauns, Heinrich 76, 79, 182–4, 234
Braunschweig 35, 38, 79, 196, 199, 437
Brazil 153
Brecht, Arnold 269, 273

Brecht, Bertolt 1, 621, 629, 634–6, 640, 645, 647–9, 651, 729, 741
Bredel, Willi 633, 635, 645
Breitbach, Joseph 639
Breitensträter, Hans 619, 728
Bremen 30, 38–9, 196, 199
Brenner, Michael 570
Breslau 206, 390, 498, 568, 572, 655, 660, 667, 674n12
Breslau Academy for Art and Design 664, 666, 669
Briand, Aristide 255–7
Brick Expressionism 657
Brigade Ehrhardt 50–1, 223, 406
Britain 7, 29, 88, 123, 244, 246, 248–50, 252, 254–5, 258, 317, 432, 447, 464, 543, 687, 755, 758
British Foreign Office 80
Brittany 208
Britz 665
Brno 666, 668
Broch, Hermann 635, 642, 650
Brockdorff-Rantzau, Ulrich von 182, 245, 253
Bröger, Karl 265, 278, 644
Bronnen, Arnolt 636, 644, 647
Brooks, Louise 730
brownshirts see SA Stormtroopers
Brück, Christa Anita 646
Brüning, Heinrich 75, 86, 88–9, 97–103, 111, 126, 185, 202, 234–5, 243, 245, 257–9, 324, 354, 364, 373, 375–7, 387, 393, 442, 446, 485, 510, 576, 600, 671, 693
Brunner, Otto 206
Brunngraber, Rudolf 639
Brunswick see Braunschweig
Brussels 673
'brutalization theory' 392, 754, 769n29
Buber, Martin 580, 735
Buchenwald 317
Büchergilde Gutenberg 612
Bücherkreis, Der 612
Büchner, Ludwig 682
Buchrucker, Bruno 232
Buck-Morss, Susan 553
Buisson, Ferdinand 10
Bulgaria 153, 758

Bülow, Bernhard von 244–5, 256–7, 259, 433, 501, 503
Bultmann, Rudolf 687, 711
Bürgerblock 75, 79, 83
Bürgerbräukeller 63
Bürgertum 4, 319, 455–7, 461–2, 467–8
business owners 14, 295, 546
Business Party (Wirtschaftspartei) 178, 323, 367, 369, 425n86, 460
Busse, Hermann Eris 631
Büttner, Ursula 268

C

C&A Brenninkmeijer 438
cabarets 465, 578, 634, 661, 736
'cabinet of barons' 376–7
Calvin, Jean 685
Canada 171, 501, 503
Canetti, Elias 59, 66
capital: British 251
  domestic 431
  flight 433, 446
  foreign 367, 432, 444–5
  imports 446
  markets 367–8, 418, 431, 436, 444
  nominal 58
  owners 343, 436, 445
capitalism 65, 202, 329, 333, 342, 346, 352–4, 356, 372, 386, 388, 405–6, 414, 417–18, 438, 542–3, 547, 550–1, 610, 656, 689, 715, 740
  'crisis of' 6
  industrial 454, 527, 609, 636
  modern 59
Caritas 688
Carl Zeiss company 433
Carnap, Rudolf 710, 718
cartelization 317, 435, 440, 447
cartels 255, 262n36, 329, 440–1, 443
Cassirer, Ernst 717–18
Catalonia 208
Catholic Action 688
Catholic Church 686
Catholic People's Association 690
Catholic Workers' Associations 268, 488–9
Catholic Young Men's Association of Germany (Katholische Jungmännerverband Deutschlands) 596

Catholicism 48, 168, 199, 373, 468, 564, 596, 686, 689, 694
Catholics 17, 143, 156, 169, 186, 365, 371–5, 416, 456, 458, 466, 566, 595, 680–5, 688–96
celibacy 525, 531, 690
Cell of Law and Order (Ordnungszelle) 51, 54, 62
cemetery 408, 576, 762
censorship 85, 224, 405, 467, 524, 530, 610, 615, 620, 622, 632, 691
Centennial Hall 655–6
Central Administration of German Employers' Associations (Hauptstelle Deutscher Arbeitgeberverbände) 439
Central Association of Employers and Employees (Zentralarbeitsgemeinschaft) 343, 439
Central Association of German Citizens of the Jewish Faith (Centralverein deutscher Staatsbürger jüdischen Glaubens) 147, 272, 395–6, 407–8, 410, 418–19, 564, 568–9, 574–6, 581
Central Association of German Conservatives 366, 370
Central Association of German Industrialists (Centralverband Deutscher Industrieller, CDI) 439
Central Commission for Workers' Sport and Hygiene (Zentralkommission für Arbeitersport und Körperpflege) 488
Central Office for Apologetics (Apologetische Centralstelle) 690
Central Powers 28–9
centralization 127–8, 200, 212, 224, 391, 549, 551
Centre Party (Zentrum) 13, 48, 122, 166, 168, 173–4, 179, 193, 199, 202, 251, 267–71, 278, 280, 291, 323–4, 348, 363, 371, 387, 415–17, 460, 478, 488–9, 508, 510, 532, 534, 576, 590, 597, 599, 601, 681, 684, 691, 694–5
  chairman 100, 103, 126, 250, 683
  chancellor 172, 257, 387
  coalition with 55, 57, 80, 122, 144, 156, 164, 177, 222, 242, 692
  left wing of 142, 146, 234
  members of 152, 157, 371, 683
  politicians 50, 74, 97, 102, 169, 200, 234, 245, 277, 281, 412

Chamber of Deputies (France) 330
Chamberlain, Austen 82, 256
Chambers of Crafts 169
Chaplin, Charlie 465, 490, 613
charity 35, 302, 347, 486, 686, 688
checks and balances 125, 135
Chemnitz 61
Chicago 546, 549, 649
Chicago Daily News 31
Chicherin, Georgy Vasilyevich 253
Children's Republics (*Kinderrepubliken*) 597
Chilehaus 656-8
China 153, 228, 649, 703
Christaller, Walter 203
Christian Democracy 681
Christian Democratic Union, CDU 17, 696
Christian Liberal Association for the Defence against Antisemitism (Verein zur Abwehr von Antisemitismus) 418
Christian National Peasants' and Farmers' Party (Christlich-Nationale Bauern- und Landvolkpartei, CNBLP) 98, 178, 369-70
Christian People's Party (Christliche Volkspartei) 97, 372
Christian-Social People's Service (Christlich-sozialer Volksdienst) 98, 179, 370
Christianity 5, 154, 367, 371, 416, 456, 478, 580, 682-3, 686-7, 696
  positive 383, 694-5
Christlich-Soziale Partei 364
Christliche Welt 687
church(es) 175, 201, 243, 349, 366, 371-2, 393, 590, 599, 689-90, 694-6, 750
  attendance 489, 688
  Christian 40, 303, 371, 476, 620, 660, 681-2
  circles 532
  council 761
  historians 680-1
  institutions 303
  Landeskirchen 685-6
  leaders 687, 692
  leaving 682, 684, 692
  members 383, 682
  representatives 531, 596, 687, 692, 759
  seperation of state and 41, 569, 683, 687-8
  services 596, 692

state 41, 683
taxes 684
cinema 8, 17, 57, 60, 175, 233, 409, 438, 454, 464-5, 467, 553-4, 577-8, 595, 609-17, 620-2, 647, 724-5, 730, 765
citizenship 13, 148, 156, 164-6, 187, 276, 383, 464, 522, 565
civic truce (*Burgfrieden*) 28-30, 33, 39, 405
civil code 524
civil service 50, 52, 99, 131-2, 321, 347, 363, 368, 409-10, 571
civil war 10, 13, 42, 61, 88, 106, 119, 125, 131, 197, 207, 221, 231, 249, 341, 354, 392, 408, 542, 549, 635, 696
class: antagonism 167, 688
  consciousness 478-8, 621, 715
  society 65, 356, 397, 454
  struggle 166, 277, 346, 454, 528, 640, 645, 691-2 *see also* middle class
  working class
classicism 122, 623, 637
classics 530, 612, 649, 706, 713
Clauß, Ludwig Ferdinand 734
clergy 134, 208, 371-3, 684, 686, 690, 692, 694
clerics 683, 688
clothing 438, 484, 523, 593-4, 730
clubs and societies 349, 464, 468, 461, 484, 490, 574
  athletics 488
  book 610, 612
  Catholic social 489
  gymnastics 488, 522
  hiking 205
  jazz 454
  ladies 530
  local 463
  sports 579, 596, 681
  swimming 462
  workers' 488
  youth 686
coalition-building 73-6, 78-9, 81, 87, 89
coalitions 49, 53, 75, 79, 169-70, 177, 198, 212, 267, 322, 346, 348, 373, 695
Coburg 196
Cohen, Hermann 570, 580, 712
Cohn, Emil Bernhard 575
Cohn, Oscar 421n15

Collective Agreement Ordinance 293
collective bargaining 203, 293–5, 306–8, 343, 366, 376, 506
collectivization 549, 551–2, 692
Colloque Walter Lippmann 329
Cologne 109, 152, 377, 466, 530, 573, 661, 670, 689, 703, 708
colonies 9–11, 149, 156, 246, 255, 259, 364, 383, 431, 736
Combat League for German Culture (Kampfbund für deutsche Kultur, KfdK) 633
combat leagues 61–2, 235, 324, 462, 529, 535
Comintern 34, 54, 61, 344, 351–2, 542, 550
commemorations 12, 352, 462, 739, 754–5, 761, 767
Commission for the Study of the Unemployment Question (Kommission zum Studium der Arbeitslosenfrage) 693
Committee for the Struggle against Bolshevism 692
Commonwealth 447
communication, mass 80, 175, 407
Communism 351, 356, 543, 549, 551–2, 570, 580, 692
Communist Party (USSR) 542
Communist Party-Opposition (KPD-O) 74
community of fate 581
compulsory arbitration 375
Comrades. German-Jewish Hiking Association (Kameraden. Deutschjüdischer Wanderbund) 593
comradeship 529, 754, 764
Comte, Auguste 710
concentration camps 317, 763
concerts 465, 487, 615, 618
concordat 373, 692, 695, 701n58
Coney Island 618
confession 16–17, 143, 169, 283, 365, 513, 564, 581, 681–2, 684–5, 690, 694
  confessional camps 680
  confessional conflict 5, 691
  confessional divisions 685
  confessionalism 386, 681, 694–5
  interconfessional alliance 681, 693, 696
confiscations 83, 87, 246, 432, 632
Congress (USA) 123

Congress of Councils 37–8, 121, 222
Congress of Vienna 622
conscription 218, 222, 229, 233, 237, 498, 504, 523
conservatism 101, 365, 462, 468
  'moderate' 85
  national 687, 705
  'new' 632
  reactionary 168
Conservative People's Party (Konservative Volkspartei) 98, 370
Constitution, Imperial 30, 120
Constitution, Russian 131
Constitutional Committee 131
Constitutional Court for the Protection of the Republic 410
constitutionalism 131, 365
Constructivism 662
consumer: choices 282, 464, 467
  co-operatives 349, 458
  goods 51, 437–8, 466, 549
  society 436–8, 521, 523, 526, 535
  urban 230, 499, 502, 507
consumption 218, 368, 436–7, 455–6, 464, 467–8, 491, 502, 545–9, 557, 575, 613–14
  alcohol 484, 487
  cultural 611, 615, 620
  food 484
  habits 485
  mass 438, 548–9, 555–6
  media 465, 618
contraception 484, 532–3
Copenhagen 210
Corbach, Otto 551
corporatist state 144
corruption 8, 50, 65, 412–13, 728
Council of People's Representatives 27, 30, 32, 34, 37–8, 121, 182, 219–21, 230, 292–4, 505, 569
council system 164–5
counter-mobilization 31
Counter-Reformation 681
counter-revolution 36–40, 51, 231, 384
craftsmen 186, 407, 480
Credit-Anstalt für Handel und Gewerbe 445
crime rate 7, 728, 750
critical theory 577, 718

culture struggle (*Kulturkampf*) 371, 416, 682, 691, 693, 695–6
culture wars 41, 81, 681, 691, 695
culture: bourgeois 578, 612
   commemorative 754
   'cultural Bolshevism' 619–20, 693
   'of defeat' 753, 755, 768
   high 465, 553, 578–9, 609, 611, 621
   'low' 609
   mainstream 579
   mass 4, 9, 15, 17, 464, 476, 490–1, 524, 543, 545, 553, 557, 609–23, 707, 729
   middle-class 464
   physical 579
   popular 8, 475, 490, 554–5, 578, 619–20
   pro-republican 348
   religious 5, 16, 567, 680–2, 685
   remembrance 762
   republican 285, 340, 348
   'culture socialism' 688–9
culturedness 455, 609
Cuno, Wilhelm 56–7, 183
currency: devaluation 52, 55, 57–9, 296, 444
   foreign 51, 56, 59, 247, 431, 503
   reform 57–9, 64, 66, 300–1, 303, 307, 323, 646
   revaluation 65, 73, 87
   stabilization 248, 300–1, 447, 503, 510
Curtius, Julius 76, 184–5, 256–7
Cuxhaven 30, 38
Czechoslovakia 151, 171, 232, 252, 257, 331, 644, 666, 668

D

D'Abernon, Edgar Vincent Lord 252
Dadaism 636–7, 647
Dahlem 615
Dame, Die 726, 743
Danube 199
Danzig 149, 211, 245, 253, 656 *see also* Gdansk
Darmstadt 441, 637
Darmstädter- und Nationalbank 445
Darré, Walther 512–13
Däumig, Ernst 41
Dawes Plan 65, 75–6, 250–5, 367–8, 414, 431, 444–5, 481, 546
De Stijl 9, 661–2

de-globalization 9, 435
debts, national 429, 431, 443, 447
decadence 631, 687, 690
decentralization 193–5, 201, 207, 212, 370, 430
decriminalization 533
defeat, military 40, 50, 132, 172, 187, 205, 292, 364–5, 397, 419, 542, 753, 755
deflation 257
degeneration 49, 150, 395, 465, 522, 526, 529, 532, 612
Dehn, Günther 553, 687
deindustrialization 542, 549
Delbrück, Hans 244, 753
demilitarization 252
demobilization 32–3, 36–7, 39, 48, 51–2, 220, 230, 292–5, 480, 525, 752–4
democracy: American 545
   'authoritarian' 387
   Christian 681
   destruction of 4, 6, 120, 136, 383
   direct 33, 127, 130, 135, 172–3
   economic 39
   enemies of 134, 149, 386, 535, 714
   experiment in 121, 142
   liberal 119, 266, 371, 382, 542
   'mass' 329
   militant 134, 599
   parliamentary 1, 3, 5, 11, 17, 27, 41, 79, 98–9, 105, 110, 121–2, 144–5, 164–5, 187, 234, 285, 317, 327, 333, 342, 349, 356, 365–6, 375, 377, 397, 405, 418, 441, 460, 463, 693
   participatory 17
   representative 133
   'rock of' 80
   supporters of 151, 156, 634
   visions of 88
Democratic Alliance (Alliance démocratique) 332
Democratic Youth (Demokratische Jugend) 597
democratization 32, 187, 193, 219, 274, 276, 326, 344, 436, 458, 461, 468, 491, 549, 555, 611, 617, 687
demonstrations 38, 353–4, 377, 467, 503, 510–11, 683, 704
Denmark 143, 149, 210, 643

department stores 408, 456, 458, 465, 620, 646, 662–3, 668, 730
deportations 763
depression 111, 245, 255–6, 258–9, 447, 503, 552
  agrarian 368
  economic 14, 460, 463, 465, 501, 657
Deputy Reich Protector of Bohemia and Moravia 385
Dernburg, Bernhard 182
desecration 408, 417, 576
Dessau 662–4, 666
Detœuf, Auguste 330
Detroit 546–7
Deutsch-Lux 444
Deutsche Allgemeine Zeitung 174
Deutsche Buchgemeinschaft 612
Deutsche Freischar 594
Deutsche Gaue 208
deutsche jungenschaft vom 1.11. 594
Deutsche Lufthansa AG 203
Deutsche Rentenbank 57, 444
Deutsche Republik 268, 271, 284
Deutsche Zeitung 29
Deutscher Bund Heimatschutz 209
Deutscher Landarbeiter-Verband (DLV) 505–7, 509
Deutscher Werkbund 8, 205, 207–8, 665–7, 669
Deutsches Stadion 619
Deutschvölkische Partei 364
Devětsil 662
diaspora 153, 568, 575
Dibelius, Otto 692
dictatorship 60, 62–4, 85, 128, 144, 177, 187, 545
  class 32
  military 134, 234, 236, 457
  'national' 61
  Nazi 1, 18, 141, 236, 266, 394, 397, 492, 717
  party 106, 195
  proletarian 344
  right-wing 17, 198, 384
Diederichs, Eugen 704
Diehl, August 758
Dietrich, Hermann 69n51, 185, 257
Dietrich, Marlene 731
Dilthey, Wilhelm 709
disability 298–300, 569, 727

disarmament 228, 248, 256, 258–9
discrimination 408, 419, 456, 525, 532, 535, 681–3
disenfranchisement 123
dissimilation 579
Dißmann, Robert 343
division of labour 415, 547–9, 620
divorce rate 531
Dix, Otto 298, 726, 729, 732, 736, 766–7
Dnieprostroi dam 552
Döblin, Alfred 577, 629, 631–3, 637, 642, 647–51, 729–30
doctors 58–9, 298, 389, 455–7, 459, 461, 525, 531, 556, 565, 574, 646
Doeberl, Michael 206
Doehring, Bruno 686
Doesburg, Theo van 9, 661
domesticity 545–5
donors 321–3
Dopsch, Alfons 206
Dortmund 618–19
Dresden 59, 197, 208, 440, 465, 612, 655, 670, 750
Dubnow, Simon 581
Dudow, Slatan 645, 671, 741
Duesterberg, Theodor 101, 109, 375–6
Duisberg, Carl 99
Duisburg 55, 82, 443
Dülberg, Franz 612
Durieux, Tilla 730
Düsseldorf 55, 729, 737
Düsseldorf Art Gallery 766
Dymow, Ossip 408

E

East Asia 9–10
East Prussia 34, 50, 203, 211, 228, 245, 271, 499, 514, 659, 759
East-Elbian provinces 17, 99, 203, 415, 505–6, 509–10
Eastern Aid programme (Ostpreußenhilfe) 442
Eberstadt, Rudolf 658
Ebert-Groener 'pact' 219
Ebert, Friedrich 29–30, 32–8, 42, 50, 61–3, 73–4, 80, 121, 125, 129, 135, 172, 182, 219–24, 248, 265, 267, 277, 281–2, 326, 342, 344–5, 350, 371, 738, 756–8

Eckert, Erwin 688
economization of the body 298
economy: agrarian 369, 501–3, 509, 542
   American 547–8
   British 447
   capitalist 1, 454, 649
   centralized 195
   controlled 52, 502, 507–8, 515
   French 447
   global 430, 433–4, 446
   'of human beings' 521, 527
   industrial 5, 27, 218
   international 250
   market 329, 439, 498
   peacetime 48, 296, 328
   planned 351
   socialized 366, 542
   Soviet 544, 552, 692
   war 52, 195, 326, 328, 431, 655
ecumenism 690
Edelweiss Pirates 595
Edschmid, Kasimir 637
education 16, 65, 80, 131, 150, 208, 277, 285, 320, 396, 418, 437–8, 484, 487, 534, 568, 591–2, 596, 600, 651, 680, 686, 694, 696, 704, 706–7, 765
   access to 303, 589
   adult 210
   civic 269, 589–90
   co- 17
   higher 455, 458, 587, 664
   physical 233
   political 35, 174–5, 346
   professional 513
   reform 593
   right to 303, 589
   sex 530–1
   socialist 597, 621, 682 *see also Bildung*
egalitarianism 688
Ehrenberg, Victor 763
Ehrhardt, Hermann 223, 236
Eichhorn, Emil 38, 344
Eichsfeld 209
Eiermann, Egon 673
Eigene, Der 530
eight-hour workday 31, 57–8, 64, 121, 343–4, 366–8, 458, 480–1, 507, 524, 610

Einert, Fritz 276–7
Einstein, Albert 550, 570–1
Einsteinturm 657
Eisenstein, Sergei 554
Eisler, Hanns 649
Eisner, Kurt 30, 33, 35, 39–41, 54, 195, 406, 570, 739
El-Tayeb, Fatima 156
Eldorado Bar 733
election: campaign 165, 173–6, 270, 281, 321, 348, 393, 413, 415, 418–19, 507–8, 529
   competitive 326
   direct 74, 81–2, 85, 87, 89, 172
   Landtag 323–4
   local 271, 350
   national 97, 121, 165, 243, 317, 321, 344, 350, 366–9, 372, 477, 740
   National Assembly 13, 35, 37–8, 41, 180, 269, 324, 512, 524
   presidential 74, 101–2, 107, 109, 130, 145, 172–3, 176, 354
   regional 369
   snap 50, 64
   state 80, 101, 181, 199–200, 350 *see also* Reichstag elections
electorate 35, 105, 165–6, 170–1, 173, 180–1, 194, 276, 319, 364, 392, 598, 683
   Catholic 106
   Centre Party's 371–3
   conservative 460
   DNVP's 366–7, 369–70
   female 366
   middle-class 463
   Protestant 514
electrification 437, 549, 555
elites: agrarian 366, 376
   bourgeois 4, 120, 174
   business 366
   conservative 100, 102, 104, 106, 110–11, 144, 256, 364, 366, 370–1, 374–8
   economic 105, 108
   industrial 375
   liberal 174, 186
   local 34
   municipal 34
   Nationalist 367
   Old Prussian 168

old 340, 343, 751
  social 320, 389–90, 573
  traditional 317
elitism 364, 366, 386, 389
emancipation 13, 29, 35, 351, 404–5, 415, 504,
  523–4, 528, 564, 568–9, 577–8, 610, 641,
  646, 741
emergency decrees 64, 125, 128–9, 172, 202, 250,
  258, 300, 306, 324, 375–6, 387, 600, 671, 693
emergency farm programme 99
emergency powers 63, 95, 97–8, 105, 110, 125, 135
emigrants 148, 595
employees 77, 203, 294–6, 300, 304, 320, 323,
  347, 387, 432, 439, 441, 448, 459, 477, 480,
  531, 598, 618
  administrative 298, 409
  clerical 454, 456, 458, 461, 465
  and employers 169, 301–2, 307
  female 526, 645
  rights 295, 308
  white-collar 165, 321, 365, 454, 468, 525
  and workers 49, 52, 64–5, 293
employers' associations 293–5, 304, 306,
  439–40, 480
employment 211, 247, 307, 478–81, 483, 491,
  572, 752
  agricultural 500, 504–5, 513–14
  casual 487
  female 525, 555, 565
  full 53
  gainful 477, 514, 587
  offices 203, 294, 304, 645, 740–1
  public-sector 459
  rate 296
enabling laws 64, 326, 336n39 *see also* laws:
  Enabling Act
encyclical 532, 690
endogamy 566
enfranchisement 13, 35, 366
Engels, Friedrich 155, 421n15
engineers 460, 544, 546–7, 549–51
England 175, 207, 317, 483, 595
Enlightenment 405, 527, 569, 580, 589, 656
Entente 39–40, 253, 413
entertainment 437–8, 524, 528, 553–4, 578–9,
  609, 611–14, 618, 621, 724
  light 465, 490, 615, 619

  mass 475
  popular 618
epicization 649–50
episcopacy 374
equality of opportunity 569
equity capital ratio 444
Erlangen 389
Ermanox 724
eroticism 524
Erzberger, Matthias 50, 52, 54, 146, 182, 200,
  245, 268, 280–1, 369, 371, 407, 683
Erzgebirgsverein 209
escapism 618
Escherich, Georg 231
Essen 97, 483
Essen Program 97
estate owners/ownership 365–6, 375, 386, 499,
  502, 505–9, 513–14
etchings 735
ethnic Germans' (*Volksdeutsche*) 141, 331
ethnicity 151, 568, 581, 610, 725
Eucken, Walter 329, 711
Eugen Diederichs-Verlag 704
Eugenic at the Service of People's Welfare 534
eugenics 533–4, 743
Eupen-Malmedy 149, 643
Europe 150, 157, 172, 206, 243, 254–5, 257, 280,
  291, 305, 328, 330, 382, 394, 430, 446, 503,
  521, 530–1, 541, 543, 549, 552, 556, 576, 588,
  665, 736
  Central 143–4, 148, 245, 258
  Eastern 27, 42, 151–2, 395, 406, 408, 412, 433,
  550, 567
  Northern 166
  South-eastern 259
  Western 75, 208, 258, 260, 577
Evangelical Federation 686
evictions 354, 485
exchange: economic 56
  foreign 445–6
  global 430
  gold 444
  labour 77, 598
  rate 52, 57
  stock 405, 414, 689
  student 544
  transnational 9–10

exclusion 5, 14, 18, 62, 82, 121, 134, 147, 154–6, 372, 394, 396, 406–7, 409, 414–15, 419, 529, 571–4, 577, 581, 703, 764
Executive Council 36, 324
executive powers 63, 73, 224
exhibition 205, 533, 535, 598, 617, 623, 637–8, 662, 665–70, 673, 692, 730–1, 736
exile 12, 329, 333, 393, 409, 458, 514, 542, 672–3, 702, 714, 717, 743, 763
expansionism 151
export: and import 9, 222
  industry 432, 446
  markets 9, 58, 548
  rate 434
  sector 432
  volume 9, 434–5
Express Service of the Foreign Office 433
Expressionism 466, 631, 636–8, 651, 658, 661
expropriation 59, 343, 383, 512, 658
  of the former princes 84, 130, 132, 174, 281, 413
expulsion 62, 143, 415, 566
extremism 17, 186, 353, 463

F

Facta, Luigi 384
Fagus factory 661
Fallada, Hans 199, 645
Falter, Jürgen 186, 393, 513–14
family: farms 321, 478, 500, 505, 508, 513
  income 483
  labour 500, 504, 513
  law 133, 524–5, 696
  life 687
  nuclear 555–6
  planning 484, 531
  size 479
  structures 504, 690
  working-class 483, 612
farmers 65, 88, 98–9, 321, 323, 346, 369, 386, 405, 407, 442, 456, 459, 480, 500–2, 508, 511–12, 548
Fascism 152, 209, 355, 382, 384, 397
Faßhauer, Minna 35
Fatherland Party (Deutsche Vaterlandspartei) 50, 364, 683
Faulhaber, Michael von 41, 688

Fechenbach, Felix 570
Federal Constitutional Court 133
Federal Council (Bundesrat) 120–1
Federal Deposit Bank of New York 546
Federal Republic of Germany 1, 3, 17, 72–3, 165, 171, 194, 196, 201, 211–12, 259, 268, 301, 325, 466, 468, 524, 673, 696
federalism 11, 127, 129, 195–6, 199, 201–2, 210, 212
Federation of German Employers' Associations (Vereinigung Deutscher Arbeitgeberverbände) 439
Federation of Religious Socialists in Germany (Bund religiöser Sozialisten in Deutschland) 688, 691
Federation of the Christian German Peasants' Associations 508, 510
Fehling, Jürgen 636
Fehrenbach, Constantin 55, 182, 268, 373
Feiler, Arthur 549
Feldman, Gerald D. 6, 53
femininity 523–4, 528, 545, 555, 622, 731–2
feminists 458, 522, 555–6, 575, 690
feminization 522, 555
fertilizer 441, 498, 501
Feuchtwanger, Ludwig 60, 647
film: anti-war 765
  documentary 727
  feature 725, 741
  filmmaker 176, 741
  genre 725
  industry 578, 613, 724
  musical 729
  production 7, 490, 622
  sound 8, 610, 613–15, 619, 765
  stars 619, 622
Finland 222
First World War: after 144, 146, 148, 150–1, 153, 157, 205, 207–9, 218, 260, 383, 412, 433, 438, 440, 443, 542, 563, 565, 579, 588, 582, 711
  before 105, 165–6, 320, 330, 371, 432–4, 437, 441, 447, 455, 527, 541, 591, 593, 601, 660, 670
  consequences 96, 274, 318, 430–1, 457, 477
  during 157, 227, 229, 293, 341, 354, 433, 441, 501, 564, 567, 589, 611, 665, 705, 754, 765
  experiences/lessons 164, 211, 602, 612, 762
  loss of 145, 211, 242, 577
  victims of 298

victors 119
violence of 208
Fischer, Eugen 734, 736
Fischer, Samuel 609, 611
Fischer, Theodor 659, 662
Five-Year Plan 545, 551, 554
flag controversy 280
Flag Decree 77, 280–1
Flake, Otto 524, 644
Flechtheim, Alfred 728
Fleißer, Marieluise 646
Fletcher, Alfred 145
Flick, Friedrich 442
Föllmer, Moritz 396, 398n1
Fontane, Theodor 631, 650
food 59, 207, 297, 483, 498–500, 505, 526, 547, 555
  crisis 430
  distribution 33
  exports 434
  foodstuffs 296, 437, 481
  prices 436
  products 51–2, 61, 435
  provision 52, 342, 457, 502, 507, 514
  shortages 29, 430
  supply 430, 484
football 488, 490, 595, 609–12, 616, 619
Ford company 437, 444, 547–8
Ford, Henry 547–8, 550, 557
Fordism 527, 546–8, 554, 557, 665
Foreign Organization of the NSDAP 153
Foreign Trade Bureau at the Foreign Office 433
Forster, Rudolf 729
Fraenkel, Ernst 135, 345
France 10, 41, 55–6, 61, 63, 123, 143, 149, 171, 205, 207, 226, 233, 242, 244, 245–50, 252, 254–5, 257–58, 277, 330, 332, 368, 431, 434, 446, 462, 483, 514, 522, 543, 595, 643, 684, 687, 755–6, 758
Franco-German reconciliation 79, 257
François-Poncet, André
Franconia 384–5, 389, 509
Frank, Christian 208
Frank, Josef 666
Frank, Leonhard 642, 764
Frankfurt Parliament 143, 147
Frankfurt school 715

Frankfurt/Main 30–1, 34–5, 88, 246, 273–5, 319, 332, 466, 490, 568, 571, 579, 661–2, 665–6, 672, 708, 710, 762
Frankfurter Zeitung 164, 271, 549, 642
Franz-Eher-Verlag 442
Frau, Die 36
Frauenfriedenskirche 762
Free Conservatives (Freikonservative Partei) 364
Free Corps (Freikorps) 37–40, 42, 49–51, 56, 73, 144, 146, 220–3, 230–1, 246, 344–5, 406, 411, 461, 506, 642–4, 754
Free Jewish Lehrhaus 580
Free Peasantry 509–10
Free Thinkers 489
Free Trade Unions 4, 39, 78, 88, 294, 308, 477
freedom: of assembly 15, 32, 131
  of association 41, 49
  of conscience 165, 682
  of opinion 54, 456
  of property 131
  of scholarship 131
  of speech 121, 632
  of the press 54, 131
  personal 30, 131, 504
  religious 131, 686
freemasonry 372
freethinkers 682, 684, 689–91
Freiburg 595, 764
Freideutscher Youth Day 593
Freiligrath, Ferdinand 273–4
Freizeit 610
Frenssen, Gustav 634
Freyer, Hans 717
Frick, Wilhelm 196, 202
Friedländer, Saul 406
Friedrich, Ernst 642, 727, 765
Friedrichstrasse 656
Friends of the Children Movement (Kinderfreundebewegung) 597
Fritzsche, Peter 6, 391
Fromm, Erich 482
front generation 594, 597, 705
Fuchs, Emil 687
Führer 141, 146, 176
Fürth, Henriette 533, 572
futurism 631

G

Galton, Francis 532
garden cities 205, 208, 655, 659, 661
Gatzke, Hans 259
Gaunt, William 667
Gaus, Friedrich 252
Gay, Peter 8, 577–9
Gayl, Wilhelm Freiherr von 105, 185, 694
Gdansk 210, 656
Geiger, Theodor 186, 386, 454–5, 460, 464, 466–7
Gelsenberg affair 442
Gelsenkirchener Bergwerks-AG 442
gender 5, 27, 365, 476, 486, 543–5, 554–7, 572, 578, 610, 690, 729–32, 738
   inequality 325, 393, 523
   differences 371, 522, 528, 725–6, 731
   norms 490, 521
   order 521, 532, 534, 556
   relations 521, 535, 542, 687
   research 393
   roles 1, 524, 726, 733, 743
General Commission of the German Trade Unions 294
General German Trade Union Federation (Allgemeiner Deutscher Gewerkschaftsbund, ADGB) 108, 477, 481, 665 see also Free Trade Unions
General Motors 437, 445
General Staff 120, 227, 236
genetics 532–3, 721n39, 734
Geneva 228, 258, 331–2
Geneva Disarmament Conference 228, 234
Genoa 55, 248
George, Heinrich 729
George, Stefan 629, 647, 704
Gereke, Günther 108
Gerlach, Hellmut von 514
German Association for the Protection of Western Culture 693
German Association of Agricultural Workers (Deutscher Landarbeiter-Verband, DLV) 505–7, 509
German Association of Chambers of Commerce and Industry 331
German Colonial Society (Deutsche Kolonialgesellschaft, DKG) 10
German Combat Games 528
German Communist Party (Kommunistische Partei Deutschlands, KPD) 14, 37–8, 49, 51, 54, 61–2, 73–4, 82–8, 126, 129–30, 174, 177, 179, 181, 197–8, 224, 234, 279, 308, 341, 344–5, 347–56, 386, 391, 393, 412–13, 417, 477–8, 486, 488–9, 491, 545, 550–1, 556, 571, 590, 635, 644–5, 684, 691–2, 695, 727, 741
German Communist Workers' Party (Kommunistische Arbeiterpartei Deutschlands, KAPD) 54
German Conservative Party (Deutsch-Konservative Partei) 364
German Democratic Party (Deutsche Demokratische Partei, DDP) 12, 14, 16, 48–9, 54–5, 57, 62, 74–6, 79–85, 122–3, 130, 142, 144, 147, 152, 156–7, 164, 166, 168, 170–1, 175, 177, 179–85, 198, 222, 245, 251, 253, 267–70, 274, 278, 280–1, 319, 321–5, 331, 365, 369, 371, 393, 412, 416–17, 419, 461, 511, 514, 529, 570–1, 590, 597–8, 683–4, 687–8, 753
German Democratic Republic (GDR) 260
German Emergency Association against the Black Shame (Deutscher Notbund gegen die Schwarze Schmach) 150
German Evangelical Church Federation 686
German Football Association 619
German Gentlemen's Club (Deutscher Herrenklub) 109
German Housing Company for State Officials and Workers (Deutsche Wohnungsfürsorge AG, DEWOG) 664–5
German Institute for Technical Work Schooling (Deutsches Institut für technische Arbeitsschulung, DINTA) 548
German League for Human Rights (Deutsche Liga für Menschenrechte) 83, 530
German League for the Protection of Mothers and Sexual Reform 531
German Modernism 8, 655
German National Association of Commercial Employees (Deutschnationaler Handlungsgehilfenverband) 405
German National People's Party (Deutschnationale Volkspartei,

DNVP) 13, 48–9, 63, 65, 74–81, 83, 85–6,
  88, 97–8, 100–1, 104, 106, 109–10, 144–5,
  154, 166–8, 174–8, 181, 184–5, 199, 209, 224,
  234, 251, 253, 256, 283, 303, 324, 363–76, 386,
  411–12, 414–17, 442, 460, 462–3, 509–10,
  514, 550, 571, 590, 620, 622, 684, 686, 690–1,
  693–5
German People's Party (Deutsche Volkspartei,
  DVP) 48–9, 53, 55–7, 63, 74–7, 79–82, 96–7,
  106, 146, 151, 154, 168, 179–85, 197, 199, 247,
  250–1, 253, 269, 317, 319, 321–5, 332, 366–7,
  369, 374, 386, 412, 416, 442, 462–3, 509,
  571, 590, 597–8
German Potash Syndicate (Deutsches
  Kalisyndikat) 440
German Protestant Church Federation 686–7
German Protestant Women's Federation
  (Deutsch-Evangelischer
  Frauenbund) 687
German Question 142–4, 153
German Research Foundation (Deutsche
  Forschungsgemeinschaft, DFG) 708
German Social Democratic Party
  (Sozialdemokratische Partei
  Deutschlands, SPD): abstentions 85
  and DDP 14, 55–7, 144, 268, 270, 274, 280,
    417, 590, 683
  executive committee 80
  and grand coalition 75, 79–81, 164, 177, 222,
    267–9, 278, 369
  and KPD 61, 74, 79, 83–4, 88, 174, 197, 341,
    344, 350–1, 386, 391, 477–8, 488–9, 491,
    644, 692
  leadership of 29–30, 83, 103
  members 142, 147, 155, 157, 259, 347, 488, 513,
    576, 643
  parliamentary group 77, 97, 195, 684
  and USPD 13, 16, 28, 53–4, 417, 419, 689, 691
  votes 166, 170, 180, 346–7, 350, 571
German Society for the Study of Eastern
  Europe (Deutsche Gesellschaft zum
  Studium Osteuropas, DGSO) 550, 554
German State Party (Deutsche Staatspartei,
  DStP) 179, 185, 324–5, 416, 512
German Student Union 390
German Workers' Party (Deutsche Arbeiter
  Partei, DAP) 98, 383

German Youth Strength. Reich Committee
  for Physical Exercises in Catholic
  Associations (Deutsche Jugendkraft.
  Reichsverband für Leibesübungen in
  katholischen Vereinen) 596
German-Hanoverian Party (Deutsch-
  Hannoversche Partei) 171, 178
German-Jewish Scout Association
  Kadima 594
German-Völkisch Freedom Party
  (Deutschvölkische Freiheitspartei) 412
German-Völkisch Protection and Defiance
  Federation (Deutschvölkischer Schutz-
  und Trutzbund, DVSTB) 384, 402, 406
Germania 692
Germanness 143, 145, 150, 154, 156–7, 563, 577,
  644, 734
Germans abroad (*Auslandsdeutsche*) 148, 153, 156
Gesellschaft für Soziale Reform 326
Gesinde 500, 504–5
Geßler, Otto 62–3, 182–4, 224, 232, 268, 326
Geyer, Curt 54
Geyer, Michael 218
ghetto 406, 691
Giese, Fritz 555
Gilman, Sander 734
Glaeser, Ernst 643
Glanzstoff 445
Gleichheit, Die 35
Goebbels, Joseph 101, 105, 209, 212, 385, 391,
  415, 467, 694
Goebbels, Magda 743
Goethe, Johann Wolfgang von 612, 728
Gogarten, Friedrich 687, 711
gold standard 53, 60, 330, 444, 447, 546
Goldschmidt, Alfons 551
Goll, Claire 642, 764
Göll, Franz 656
Göring, Hermann 104, 106, 385
Görlitz 691
Görlitz programme 53
Gotha 196–7, 231
gothic style 656, 658
Göttingen 390, 465–7
Gottl-Ottlilienfeld, Friedrich von 711
government of 'national concentration' 110, 377
Graf, Oskar Maria 41

Graf, Rüdiger 7, 543
gramophones 437, 614, 617
Grand Coalition 56–7, 62, 75, 77–9, 86, 88, 126, 181, 183, 185, 197, 305, 369, 374, 387
greater German solution 143, 147, 152, 156
Greifswald 390
Grimm, Dieter 120
Grimm, Hans 629
Grisar, Erich 204
Groener, Wilhelm 37, 103, 111, 184–5, 219–20, 222, 225, 235–6
Gropius, Walter 8, 655, 661–4, 666, 673
Grosche, Robert 694
Grossmann, Carl 729
Großmann, Rudolf 728
Grosz, George 60, 298, 554, 727–9, 766–7
Grünberg, Karl 645
Gründerzeit 610
Gründgens, Gustav 530
Grzesinski, Albert 281, 346
Guardini, Romano 688
Guild of Social Work (Gilde Soziale Arbeit) 591
Gumbel, Emil Julius 54, 232
Günther, Hans F.K. 705, 734–5
Güstrow 761
Gutehoffnungshütte 433–4, 441, 444
Guttentag 498
gymnastics 208, 348–9, 461–2, 488, 526–8, 579

H

Haarmann, Fritz 729
Haas, Ludwig 147–8, 268, 271, 571
Haase, Hugo 29–30, 182, 569
habitus 65, 578
Habsburg Empire 143, 148, 222
Hachshara centres 595
Haeckel, Ernst 682
Haenisch, Konrad 156, 231
Hague Conference 255
Hamburg 30, 34, 61–2, 73, 79, 81, 196, 199–200, 203, 319, 322, 344, 347, 385, 488, 530–1, 568, 591, 611, 613, 618, 634, 657–8, 660–1, 703
Hamburg Barmbek-Nord 660
Hamburg Points 37, 39, 222, 656
Hamburger Sportverein 619
Hamkens, Wilhelm 511
Hamm, Eduard 183, 234, 331

Händel, Georg Friedrich 465–6
Haniel family 441
Hanover 83, 199, 209, 500, 511
Hanseatic League 656
HAPAG shipping company 56
Harden, Silvia von 732
Häring, Hugo 665
Harnack, Adolf von 686–7
Hartlaub, Gustav Friedrich 638
Harvey, Lilian 622
Harzburg 100–1, 109, 377
'Harzburg Front' 278
Hasenclever, Walter 636, 647
Hasenheide 526
Hasidism 580
Hatvani, Paul 637
Haus Vaterland 438, 616, 618
Haus Wylerberg 658
Hauser, Heinrich 204, 639
Haushofer, Karl 706
Hauszinssteuer 658
Hayek, Friedrich von 711
health: insurance 58, 291, 306, 531
    public 58, 209, 526, 535, 752
    sexual 531
Heartfield, John 740
heavy industry 4, 108–9, 233, 246, 262n36, 307, 317, 365, 375, 387, 415, 434, 439–40, 442–3
Heberle, Rudolf 199
Hecht, Ben 31
Heckel, Erich 766
Heckscher-Ohlin model 435
hedonism 690
Hegel, Georg Wilhelm Friedrich 649, 710, 715
Heidegger, Martin 706, 712, 717
Heidelberg 31, 33, 54, 255, 691
Heidelberg programme 346
Heim, Claus 511
Heim, Georg 508
Heimat 11, 149, 205, 207–10
Heimat League (Heimatbund) 208–9
Heinze, Karl Rudolf 182
Held, Heinrich 80–2
Helfferich, Karl 251, 411
Heller, Hermann 126–7, 345, 714
Hellerau 208, 655
Hergt, Oskar 75, 184, 366
Hermann Tietz 730

Hermes 433
Hermes, Andreas 183
Herzfelde, John 554
Herzfelde, Wieland 554, 632
Herzog, Todd 729
Hesse 79, 88, 196, 200, 269, 500, 508–9, 565, 574, 765
Hesse-Kassel 199, 209
Hesse, Hermann 650
Hesse, Konrad 212
Heuerlinge 507–8
Heuss, Theodor 268, 317, 325, 327
Heydrich, Reinhard 385
Heye, Wilhelm 229
Heymann, Lida Gustava 35–6
High Sea Fleet 29, 222
Hiking Association Blue-White (Wanderbund Blau-Weiß) 579, 593–4
Hilberseimer, Ludwig 665
Hilferding, Rudolf 78, 183, 185, 571
Himmler, Heinrich 385
Hindenburg Programme 430
Hindenburg Youth (Hindenburgjugend) 597
Hindenburg, Paul von 72, 74, 81–3, 85–7, 95, 97, 100–2, 104, 106–7, 109–11, 119–21, 124–6, 129, 134–5, 145, 172–3, 199, 219, 253, 256, 258, 280–1, 354, 371, 374–8, 632, 693, 738, 764
Hintze, Hedwig 713
Hirsch, Emanuel 684
Hirsch, Paul 569
Hirschfeld, Magnus 530, 533, 732
Hirtsiefer, Heinrich 291
Historische Schule 711
history, regional (Landesgeschichte) 205–6, 210
Hitler party 443, 463
Hitler putsch 73, 224, 250, 270, 408, 634
Hitler Youth 389, 393, 597
Hitler, Adolf 1, 6, 16, 54, 61, 63, 86, 98–101, 103–9, 124, 129, 134–5, 141, 145–6, 150–1, 154, 173, 177, 198, 201, 209–11, 233, 235, 256, 258–9, 317, 375–7, 383–5, 390, 393–4, 397
  appointment as chancellor 95–6, 106, 110–11, 245, 354–5, 419, 735
  dictatorship 266, 492
  rise to power 109, 200, 204, 308
Hlučín region 643

hoarding 33, 620
Hobbes, Thomas 60
Hobsbawm, Eric 330, 514
Höch, Hannah 1
Hochland 689
Hoesch, Leopold von 257
Hoetzsch, Otto 550, 552, 554
Hoffmann, Adolph 683
Hoffmann, Heinrich 739
Hoffmann, Johannes 40
Hoffmann, Ludwig 665
Hoffmann, Paul 347
Hofmannsthal, Hugo von 629, 636
Höger, Fritz 656–7
Hohenzollern dynasty 27, 30, 84–6, 143, 280–1, 704
holidays, paid 483
Holitscher, Arthur 541, 544, 551, 554
Holländer, Ludwig 581
Hollander, Walther von 645
Hollywood 409, 490, 544, 553–4, 556–7
Holocaust 18, 404, 419, 581
Holtfrerich, Carl-Ludwig 53
Holy Grove 758
Holy See 373 *see also* Vatican
Hölz, Max 54
home guards (Einwohnerwehren) 220, 223, 230–2, 239n58
homeland defence 219–20, 230–1, 233–6
homeless people 57, 306, 386, 485, 573, 649, 671, 737
homeowners 323, 460
homeworkers (*Heimarbeiter*) 479, 482
Hoover, Herbert 258
Höpker-Aschoff, Hermann 198, 201
Horváth, Ödön von 645
House of Commons 330
houses of correction 303, 634
housework 487, 556
housing 201, 208, 267, 308, 483–5, 654–6, 661, 668, 670–2
  associations 656, 658, 664–5, 673
  conditions 484
  crisis 33, 657, 660, 673
  emergency 485
  market 52
  shortages 412, 485, 552, 752
  social 658–9, 669, 673

Huch, Ricarda 646, 764
Huchel, Peter 641
Hufeisensiedlung 665
Hugenberg, Alfred 75, 97–8, 100–1, 106, 109–11, 174, 181, 256, 364, 366, 369–70, 373–4, 377, 412, 415, 433, 438–9, 441–2, 509, 622, 693
Hughes, Charles Evans 249
humanism 636
Humboldt, Alexander von 544
Hungary 112n4, 222, 257, 446
hunger 99, 430, 484, 505, 542, 589, 601
Huyssen, Andreas 553
hygiene 485, 527, 533
   racial 150, 396, 528, 533, 716
   sexual 5, 531
hyperinflation 4, 48, 53, 55–9, 61, 66, 133, 224, 296, 300, 323, 367, 385, 408, 414, 432–3, 436–7, 443–4, 459, 476, 480–1, 502–3, 506, 542, 565, 574–5, 753

I

iconography 176, 298, 347, 724, 739, 759
IG Farbenindustrie 434, 440–1
Ihering, Herbert 621
illiberalism 318, 557
Illustrierte Reichsbanner Zeitung 271
immigrants 156–7, 412, 572
immigration 10, 150, 383, 412, 505
Imperial Chemical Industries 441
Imperial Germany 2, 9–10, 36, 49, 53, 128, 143, 145, 151, 153, 165, 167–8, 170–1, 174–5, 177, 180, 193–6, 198, 200, 208, 283, 285, 291, 293–7, 299, 307, 326, 348, 373, 382, 385, 392, 396–7, 404, 407–9, 416, 419, 430, 436, 438–41, 455–7, 490, 505, 522–6, 529–31, 533–4, 571, 598, 631, 703–10, 714
Imperial Navy 219
Imperial Territory (Reichsland) 198, 643
imperialism 152, 251, 331, 477
imposters 725
inclusivity 157
Independent Social Democratic Party of Germany (Unabhängige Sozialdemokratische Partei Deutschlands, USPD) 13, 16, 28–30, 33–4, 37–8, 41, 49, 51, 53–4, 121–2, 124, 166, 177, 179, 182, 195, 221, 234, 280, 341–5, 350–1, 411, 417, 419, 569–70, 689, 691

individualism 328, 396, 466, 534
industrialism 687
industrialists 9, 31, 63, 247, 295, 307, 321, 343, 365–6, 368, 371, 376–7, 433, 438–40, 442, 446, 448, 455–8, 460–1, 544, 547–9, 665, 668
industrialization 475–6, 486, 541–3, 549, 551, 609–10
industry: chemical 58, 432, 434–5, 437, 440–1, 477, 482
   coal 39
   construction 671
   electro-technologies 477
   electronic 295
   export 432, 446
   film 578, 613, 724
   heavy 4, 108–9, 233, 246, 262n36, 307, 317, 343, 365, 375, 387, 415, 434, 439–40, 442–3
   iron and steel 58, 295, 434, 440
   machinery 9, 435, 477–8, 551
   metal 479
   mining 58, 186, 247, 438–9
   pharmaceutical 441
   publishing 630
   service 525
   textiles 459, 477, 480–1
   wood crafts 480
inequality 65, 133, 167, 203–4, 292, 393, 395, 446, 482, 504, 752
inflation 52–3, 55–61, 64–6, 95, 98, 227, 247–8, 296–301, 323, 350, 413, 429, 431, 433, 438, 443–6, 457, 459–60, 480–1, 502–3, 505, 542, 546, 555, 634, 637, 641, 645, 658, 660, 703, 708, 729, 740, 750, 752
infrastructure 51–2, 226, 234, 430, 432, 660, 670, 673
Ingolstadt 646
Inner Mission 534, 686, 690, 692
insolvencies 446
Institute for Austrian Historical Research 207
Institute for Sexual Science 530
Institute for Social Research 577
integration: economic 435
   national 132, 168, 173
   political 171
   vertical 441
intellectuals 119, 226, 277, 329, 365, 436, 532, 535, 552, 554, 611, 717
   Jewish 567, 576, 578, 580

left-wing 266, 322, 550, 621
liberal 545, 689
republican 268, 277
right-wing 266, 372
interconfessionalism 694–5
intergenerational contract 301
intermarriage 566, 681
International Chamber of Commerce 330–2
International Congresses of Modern Architecture 666
International Court at The Hague 157
International League for the Defence and Furtherance of Protestantism (Internationaler Verband zur Verteidigung und Förderung des Protestantismus) 690
internationalism 142, 330–2, 352, 356, 466
invalidity 296, 301–2, 306, 308
Ipsen, Gunter 717
Iron Cross 727, 759
Iron Front (Eiserne Front) 103, 278, 599
isolation 250, 331, 479, 488
Israel 171
Israelite Welfare Office 409
Israelitisches Familienblatt 574, 734–5
Italy 108, 152–3, 171, 192n76, 198, 209, 252, 257, 644, 692

J

Jacob, Heinrich Eduard 155
Jacobi, Lotte 732
Jaeckel, Willy 732
Jaffé, Edgar 570
Jahnn, Hans Henry 636
James, Harold 95
January uprising 38
Japan 447
Jarres, Karl 82–3, 183, 268
Jason, Alexander 613
jazz 7, 467, 490, 542, 544, 553–4, 595, 614, 620–1, 736
club 454
live 465
musician 724, 726, 735
Jena 703
Jesuit order 682, 689
Jewish Defence Service (Jüdischer Abwehrdienst) 575

Jewish People's Party 568
Jewishness 563, 570, 578–9, 581, 734–5
Jewry 414, 567, 581
Jews: 'Jewish census' 405, 564
Jewish community 565–7, 570–2
East European Jews (*Ostjuden*) 565, 567–8, 575, 580
'Eastern Jewish question' 412
exclusion of 14, 155, 372, 409, 419, 574
Jewish *Gemeinde* 567–8, 570, 572, 575
integration of 571, 577
Orthodox 466, 564, 568, 575, 579
Jewish participation 564, 569, 572, 578
Jewish population 60, 141, 408–9, 418, 563–7, 571, 573
Jewish public 566, 571, 575, 580–1
Jirgal, Ernst 642
job creation 105, 108
Johannsen, Otto 511
Johst, Hanns 634, 636
Jolson, Al 736
Jones, Larry Eugene 6, 180
Joos, Joseph 268
journalism 541, 565, 577, 630, 632, 716
journeymen 480, 482, 486
Judaism 389, 416, 564, 567–8, 570, 579–81, 680, 695
Jude, Der 735
judges 65, 129, 133–4, 272, 410, 458, 525, 571
judiciary 40, 385, 392, 410, 641
jüdische Frau, Die 735
jüdische Magazin, Das 739
Jüdischer Frauenbund 575
Jung, Edgar Julius 388
Jung, Ottmar 87
Jünger, Ernst 8, 528, 552, 588, 642–3, 764
Jünger, Friedrich Georg 632, 705
Junker 227, 415
jurisprudence 710, 714
juvenization 587

K

Kaas, Ludwig 100, 103, 106, 262n39, 373–6, 693
KaDeWe 730
Kaffee HAG 438
Kafka, Franz 579, 647
Kahr, Gustav Ritter von 51, 61–3, 197, 224

Kaiser Wilhelm Institute of Anthropology,
    Human Heredity, and Eugenics 533
Kaiser, Georg 634, 636
Kaiserreich 34, 80, 279, 319, 322, 456, 468, 576
    see also Imperial Germany
Kaléko, Mascha 646
Kampfkabinett 106
Kant, Immanuel 570, 580
Kanzlerdemokratie 72
Kapp-Lüttwitz putsch 50–1, 54, 173, 177, 197,
    204, 225, 231, 277, 280, 346, 365, 443, 461,
    509, 575, 634
Kapp, Wolfgang 50, 223
Kardorff, Siegfried von 365
kashrut 569
Kashubs 211
Kassel 565, 574, 593, 759–61
Kasseler Post 761
Kästner, Erich 639–40, 647
Katholikentage 596, 599, 692
Kaufmann, Erich 714
Kautz, Heinrich 619
Kazan 229
Keaton, Buster 490
Kehr, Eckart 713
Kellermann, Bernhard 634
Kellogg-Briand pact 256
Kellogg, Frank B. 256
Kelsen, Hans 127, 710, 714
Kempf, Rosa 36
Kenya 672
Kerr, Alfred 636
Kessel, Martin 645
Kessler, Harry Graf 42, 244, 268
Keun, Irmgard 526, 639, 646–7
Keynes, John Maynard 55, 247, 431
Kicker 619
Kiebingen 500
Kiel 29–30, 37, 219, 342, 761
Kienitz, Sabine 523
Kierkegaard, Søren 6
Kikeriki 735
Killy, Walther 630
Kirchheimer, Otto 132
Kirchner, Ernst-Ludwig 766
Kisch, Egon Erwin 639
Kläber, Kurt 645

Kladderadatsch 736
Klein, Ella 729
Kleinbürgertum 456 see also bourgeoisie, petty
Klemperer, Victor 31, 59–60, 465
Klerk, Michel de 661
Kleve 658
Knickerbocker, Hubert R. 612
Knorr & Hirth 441
Koch, Erich 182, 268
Kochenhof 670
Kocka, Jürgen 2
Koebel, Eberthard 594
Kolb, Eberhard 610, 631
Kolb, Walter 152
Kolbenheyer, Erwin Guido 629, 635
Kollontai, Alexandra 556
Kollwitz, Käthe 279, 739, 762, 766–7
Kollwitz, Peter 762
Kölnische Volkszeitung 79, 689
Königsberg 203, 271, 686
Kontorviertel 658
Köppen, Edlef 643
Körle 500
Körperkultur 526–7
Köster, Adolf 54, 182–3, 268
Köttgen, Carl 546
Kötzschke, Richard 205–6
Kracauer, Siegfried 386, 438, 454–5, 466, 528,
    555, 612, 616, 618–19, 621, 717, 731
Kraft, Julius 710
Kraus, Karl 642
Krenek, Ernst 736
Kreuz-Zeitung 145
Kriegsschuldfrage, Die 753
Kroener, Bernhard 237
Krüger, Peter 259
Krupp von Bohlen und Halbach,
    Gustav 99–100
Kuhr, Piete 762
Kulturnation 143, 553
Kulturprotestanten 686
Külz, Wilhelm 184, 268
Kunsthalle 638
Künstler, Franz 175
Kurfürstendamm 575
Kurhessischer Kriegerbund 759
Kürten, Peter 729

Küster, Willy 265
Kyffhäuser League 227, 285, 759

L

La Revue nègre 736–7
labour movement 29, 31–5, 39, 48, 50–1, 168,
    419, 443, 592, 614, 621, 655
  Catholic 372, 375, 460
  Christian 97, 99, 365, 367, 371–2, 375, 460
  socialist 103, 108, 283, 285, 417, 506–7, 509
labour: agricultural 16, 478, 482, 499, 504,
    507, 512
  blue-collar 478
  collective agreements 212, 293–4, 307,
    328, 480
  camps 600
  costs 295, 485
  emigration 412
  family 500
  immigration 10
  industrial 477–9, 481–2, 644–5
  market 78, 294–5, 307, 436, 466, 504, 525,
    599–600, 752
  organized 4, 106, 108, 375–6, 509
  protections 120
  relations 546–9
  rights 120
  waged 484, 609
labourers: day 505–7, 509, 514
  farm 372
  female 482
  waged 609
Laemmle, Carl 409
laity 687–8
Lampel, Peter Maria 634
Lamprecht, Karl 205
Landau 765
Landauer, Gustav 570
Landbünde (Rural Leagues) 506, 509
Landmann, Ludwig 268
landowners, large 2, 99, 367, 375
Landsberg-Steinfurt, Alfred von 372
Landsberg-Velen, Engelbert von 372
Landsberg, Otto 182, 372, 569
Landsberg, Paul Ludwig 689
Landvolkbewegung 88
Lang, Fritz 8, 621–2, 729

Lange, Helene 324
Langemarck 762
Langewiesche publishing house 611
Langewiesche, Dieter 689
Langgässer, Elisabeth 646
Langnam Association 440
Lanz company 501
Lanz, Heinrich 501
Lapland 594
Laqueur, Walter 577
Laserstein, Lotte 730
Lasker-Schüler, Else 646–7
Lasker-Wallfisch, Anita 762
Lateran Accords 692
Latin America 430, 433, 447, 541, 672
Latzko, Andreas 642, 764
Lau, Matthias 81
Lausanne 258
Lausanne Conference 446
Lauwerik, Johannes Ludovicus
    Mathieu 661
law: constitutional 72, 133, 336n39
  equality before the 131, 133
  family 133, 524–5, 696
  international 206, 243, 246, 331, 447, 708
  juvenile criminal 591
  labour 132, 557
  lawmakers 132, 134
  national 125, 128
  natural 714
  and order 51, 63–4, 355, 364
  police 132
  rule of 88, 132–3, 419, 456
  school of 710
  as a subject 458, 565, 703, 706–8, 711,
    714–15
  tax 201
laws: Anti-Socialist Laws 348, 487
  Auxiliary Service Law 121
  Basic Law 3, 17, 72, 204
  Law for Combating Venereal Diseases 532
  Defence Law 223
  Enabling Act 74, 110, 317, 327
  Law against the 'Enslavement of the
    German People' 370
  'Freedom Law' 370
  Juvenile Justice Act 591

laws: Anti-Socialist Laws (*cont.*)
  Law on Labour Exchanges and
    Unemployment Insurance (Gesetz
    über Arbeitsvermittlung und
    Arbeitslosenversicherung, AVAVG) 77–8
  Motion Picture Law 620
  Law for the Prevention of Genetically
    Diseased Offspring 534
  Law for the Protection of the Republic 54,
    272, 369, 410, 632
  Law for the Protection of Youth from Dirty
    and Trashy Writings 85, 620
  Provisional Agricultural Labour Act 507
  Prussian Salary Law 704
  Reich Pension Law
    (Reichsversorgungsgesetz, RVG) 202,
    298–9
  Reich Youth Welfare Law 303, 591
  Representation of the People Act 13, 123
  Servants' Laws 505
  Trading with the Enemy Act 432
  Unemployment Law 308
  Works Councils Act 296
lawyers 4, 85, 125, 127, 133, 326, 455–6, 459–61,
  530, 565
lay organizations 687
Le Corbusier 662, 666, 671, 673
League New Germany (Bund
  Neudeutschland) 596
League of Farmers (Bund der Landwirte,
  BdL) 35, 63, 251, 366, 405, 508–9
League of Industrialists (Bund der
  Industriellen, BdI) 439
League of Nations 10, 76, 144, 149, 151–2, 228,
  242–3, 245–6, 252–3, 255, 330–3, 368,
  674n11
League to Combat Antisemitism (Abwehr
  Verein) 576
left, radical 12, 14, 29, 35, 39, 88, 128, 166, 169,
  221, 230, 266, 271, 277, 326, 349, 461–2,
  466, 756
Legien, Carl 294, 343
Lehnert, Detlef 166
Leibholz, Gerhard 133–4
Leica 437, 724
Leipzig 65, 85, 205–6, 235, 319, 341, 347, 353,
  361n70, 410, 479, 550, 618, 668–9

Leipzig Stiftung für Deutsche Volks- und
  Kulturbodenforschung 211, 550
Leipziger, Hugo 672
leisure society 455
Leitner, Marie 617
Leitz company 437
Leitz, Ernst 437
Lemmer, Ernst 85
Lenin, Wladimir Iljitsch 120, 352, 542
Lepman, Jella 393
Lepsius, Mario Rainer 167
Lequis, Arnold 220
Lersch, Heinrich 644–5
Lessing Theatre 634
Levi, Paul 643
Levin, Julo 737
Leviné, Eugen 40, 570
Liberal Party (UK) 330
liberalism: communal 319
  economic 318, 327–30, 332
  laissez-faire 329
  left 461
  neo- 329, 711
  ordo- 329
  political 317–20, 322–4, 327, 330, 333, 456, 569
  right-wing 168, 327
  Western 187, 545
liberties, civil 28, 30, 571
Liebermann, Max 574
Liebknecht, Karl 31, 36–8, 54, 341, 344, 739
Liebknecht, Wilhelm 155
life expectancy 436
Lindsey, Ben 531
Linkskurve 633
Lipetsk 229
Lippe 193, 196, 200
Lippmann, Walter 329
Lipset, Seymour 186
Lissitzky, El 662
literary criticism 633, 645
literature 57, 59, 74, 86, 194, 291, 465, 526, 528,
  530–1, 552–3, 576–7, 580, 629–35, 638–44,
  647, 691, 707, 713, 752, 762–3, 765, 767
  anti-modern 631
  antisemitic 407
  bourgeois 644
  Hebrew 580

pacifist 642
political 641, 651
politicization of 632-3, 651
popular 611-12
pornographic 620
'revolutionary' 633, 645
Russian 542, 544, 706
war 8, 642-3
Zeitliteratur 629, 634
lithographs 728, 735, 737
Lithuania 222
Litten, Hans 466
living costs 296, 481
living space (*Lebensraum*) 151, 209, 257, 395, 436, 706
living standards 436, 438, 446, 455, 485
Lloyd George, David 31, 246, 248, 330
Löbe, Paul 77, 147, 268, 271, 288n40
Loë, Clemens Freiherr von 510
Lohse, Hinrich 385
London 729, 758
London Conference 250-51
London Schedule of Payments 431, 443
London Ultimatum 55, 231-2, 431
Loos, Adolf 207
looting 54, 60-1, 408, 480, 493n24, 574
Lortz, Joseph 694
Lossow, Otto von 197-8, 224
Loucheur, Louis 247, 332
loudspeakers 176, 212, 615
Lower Franconia 509
Lübeck 30, 196, 199-200
Lubitsch, Ernst 578
Luckhardt, Hans 656
Luckhardt, Wassili 656
Ludendorff, Erich 28-9, 37, 41, 50, 61, 120-1, 127, 219, 384, 764
Lüders, Marie-Elisabeth 325, 617
Ludwig, Emil 577, 705
Ludwigstein 593
Lukács, Georg 580, 649, 707, 715
Luna Park 618
Lüninck, Ferdinand von 372, 510
Luppe, Hermann 268
Lusatia 211
Luther, Hans 72, 75-7, 83, 85, 183-4, 252-3, 280-1, 368

Luther, Martin 690
Lutheran Church 373, 681, 685
Lutheranism 683
Lüttwitz, Walther von 50, 223, 236, 238n27
Luxembourg 255, 510
Luxemburg, Rosa 35-8, 54, 341, 344, 406, 569, 739
lyricism 648, 651

M

M.A.N. company 433
Machiavelli, Niccolò 60
Maercker, Georg 220
Magazin, Das 731
magazines 465, 489, 528, 530, 535, 544, 611, 616, 621, 633, 651, 689, 724
  fashion 726, 730
  Heimat 209
  illustrated 615, 619, 622-3, 731, 734
  market for 438
  satirical 728, 735-6
  sport 491
  women's 35
Magdeburg 199, 270, 761
Magilow, Daniel 739
Maier, Charles S. 221
Majority Social Democratic Party of Germany (Mehrheitssozialdemokratische Partei Deutschlands, MSPD) 29-32, 37-40, 42, 48, 50-1
Majority Socialists 323, 366, 371
Makela, Maria 725
Makkabi 575
Malchin 761
Malik Publishing house 554, 632
Malmedy 149, 643
malnourishment 300
Maltzan, Adolf Georg von 244, 248, 253
Mammen, Jeanne 530, 732
Manchester Guardian 229
Mann, Erika 526, 530, 732
Mann, Heinrich 550
Mann, Klaus 530, 732
Mann, Thomas 40, 267, 611-12, 629, 631-3, 635, 642, 647, 650, 728
Männerbünde (all-male associations) 529
Mannheim 38, 268, 638, 688

Mannheim, Karl 588, 707, 710, 716
Marburg 14, 331, 651
Marburg school 712
Marburg Student Corps 231
March Action 54
March on Rome 198, 384
Marienthal 485
market: black 33, 52, 61, 394, 502
 capital 367–8, 418, 431, 436, 444
 credit 58
 export 9, 58, 548
 free 329, 433
 housing 52, 671
 labour 78, 294–5, 307, 436, 466, 504, 525, 599–600, 752
 global/international/world 99, 367–8, 418, 430–5, 446–8, 501, 665
 stock 445, 485
Marr, Wilhelm 154, 404
marriage 132–3, 485, 525–6, 532–3, 555, 639, 641, 651, 690, 741, 764
 'companionate' 521, 532
 counselling 535
 interfaith 566, 573, 681
 'mixed' 156, 566, 573, 736
 patterns 566
Marseillaise 41
Marx, Karl 155, 417, 682, 715, 717
Marx, Wilhelm 74–6, 82–5, 98, 102, 172–3, 183–4, 199, 250, 268, 367–8, 371, 373, 693
Marxism 63, 154, 405–6, 416, 476, 691, 693, 696, 710, 718
Marxists 145, 157, 355, 405
masculinity 13, 220, 521–4, 529, 545, 555, 726, 729–30
masculinization 36
Masuria 211
materialism 365, 371, 385, 553, 683, 716, 750
May, Ernst 659, 660–1, 665–6, 672
McElligott, Anthony 88
mechanization 5, 482, 499, 501–2, 547, 631, 638
Mechterstädt 231
Mecklenburg 200, 694
Mecklenburg-Schwerin 79, 196, 199–200, 499
Mecklenburg-Strelitz 79, 196, 199–200, 499
Mecklenburg, Luise Herzogin zu 154, 761
media: consumption 465, 618

corporations 438, 441–3
cross-media 610, 616
magnat 367, 377, 622
mass 9, 413, 523–4, 609–10, 616–19, 724, 730
 new 175–6, 611, 616, 621, 647
 print 175, 409, 615
medical care 436, 530, 566
medicine 522, 565, 631, 708
Mehring, Walter 634
Meidner, Ludwig 735
Mein Kampf 145–6, 739
Meinecke, Friedrich 713
Meissner 593
Memel Territory 54
Mende, Clara 325
Mendelsohn, Erich 578, 655, 657, 662–3, 672
Mendelssohn, Franz von 331
Mennonites 685
Menschenökonomie 527
Mensendieck, Bess 527
merchant navy 279–80, 546
Merck company 441
Mergel, Thomas 74, 78, 285
Merseburg 39
Mertens, Carl 232
Merton, Richard 317, 332–3
Metropol-Theater 618
Metternich, Klemens Wenzel Lothar von 79
Mexico 153
Meyer, Adolf 661
Meyer, Hannes 664, 672
middle class: associational life 349, 488, 574
 cohesion 458, 462, 464
 councils *(Bürgerräte)* 35
 educated 4, 59, 365, 455, 467, 577, 704, 706–7
 dissolution/fragmentation of 320, 322–3
 families 57, 590, 703
 Jews 456, 565, 568, 580
 lower 144, 186, 386, 394, 454, 456–7, 461, 578
 mercantile 573
 nationalist 82, 86, 233, 370, 456
 parties 74
 'old' 365, 480
 and SPD 347
 upper 299, 455, 574
 values 460, 466
 voters 81, 106, 373, 460, 463

Midgley, David 639
migrants 166, 686
Milestone, Lewis 467, 765
milieus 169, 175, 210, 534, 680
  antisemitic 418
  concept of 180, 186
  confessional 690, 693, 695–6
  middle-class 574
  social 396, 681
  social-moral 167, 180
  socio-political 406, 417
  subcultural 595
  working-class 349, 355, 689
militarism 2, 31, 37, 122, 151, 553, 557, 687, 740, 765
militarization 51, 230, 285, 529
Military Inter-Allied Commission of Control (Interalliierte Militär-Kontrollkommission, IMKK) 227
military: action 39, 253–4, 727
  defeat 40, 50, 132, 172, 187, 205, 292, 364–5, 397, 419, 542, 753, 755
  leadership 477
  operations 40, 226
  personnell 226, 229
  service 233, 292, 522, 528
  'strike' 219, 230
Mining Association (Zechenverband) 439
Mining Society (Bergbauverein) 439
minority/ies: Catholic 371, 374, 416, 681
  ethnic 131, 331, 735, 737–8
  Danish 199
  German 141, 151–2, 210, 244, 253–4
  government 55, 72, 75, 79–80, 83, 85, 89, 253, 257–8, 324
  Jewish 407, 417–19, 566, 569, 571
  national 148, 199
  Polish 199
  rights 330–1
Misch, Carl 285
missionary societies 9
Mittelstand 59, 65, 186, 386, 393, 454, 456, 458–60, 468, 514
Moabit 550
mobility: horizontal 10
  spatial 211
  upward 482

mobilization: counter- 31
  nationalist 88
  political 11, 13, 31, 390
  popular 30
  mass 266, 392
  revolutionary 12, 32, 54
  republican 54, 278, 280
  self- 230, 462, 702, 706, 717, 766
  social 231
  for war 501, 766
model, input 319–20
model, output 320
modernity: ambivalence of 5
  beacon of 9
  classical 4, 629
  economic 546, 549, 551, 555, 557
  fascist 382
  'heroic' 226
  industrialized 528, 535
  laboratory of 521, 534
  liberal 131
  'organic' 397
  political 205, 543
  'white' 665
modernization 4, 208, 503, 524, 541, 547–8, 566, 646, 654
  theory 543
Moeller van den Bruck, Arthur 588, 632, 705
Moenius, Georg 688
Moholy-Nagy, László 725
Moka Efti 616, 618
Molkenbuhr, Hermann 279
Moltke, Helmuth von 227
Molzahn, Johannes 725
Mommsen, Hans 3–5, 461, 464
monarchy 105, 128, 144, 164, 265, 276–7, 279–82, 320, 322, 342, 364, 366, 372, 463, 475, 570, 684, 686–7, 704, 738
Mondrian, Piet 661
monists 684, 704
Morris-Reich, Amos 734
mortgages 368, 459, 502–3
Moscow 61, 351–2, 554, 662, 672
Moscow Art theatre 554
Moses, Julius 411
Mosse publishing house 441, 565, 577
Mosse, George 577

Mosse, Rudolf 570
Mössingen 355
most-favoured-nation clause 248, 332, 433, 503
motherhood 466, 533, 535, 555, 687, 743
Mothers' Association for the Promotion of Christian Education (Mütterverein zur Förderung christlicher Kindererziehung) 688
motion of no-confidence 101, 104, 135
motorization 437
movement: Arts and Crafts 205
    bündisch youth 389
    Catholic labour 372, 375, 460
    Christian labour 97, 99, 365, 367, 375
    council 30–6, 39, 221, 342, 461
    extreme-right 467
    feminist 572
    freethought 692
    Heimat 194, 205, 208–9, 212
    Heimatschutz 209–10
    Hitler 176, 370, 377–8, 391
    Jewish youth 579
    life reform 205, 207–8, 484, 489, 523, 526, 587, 593, 601, 704
    literary 637, 640
    modernist 577
    national 63, 82, 147
    Nazi 100, 110, 176, 234–6, 277, 374–5, 385, 389, 392, 396, 407, 415, 419
    pacifist 35
    peace 9, 34, 595
    proletarian youth 592
    reform 207, 616, 670
    revolutionary 31, 53, 164, 340, 570, 577
    right-wing 333, 384, 468
    sexual reform 531–2
    strike 354
    social protest 32
    socialist 556, 689
    teetotalist 484
    völkisch 210, 395, 404, 408, 415
    workers' movement 35, 592, 655
    youth 1, 324, 592–6, 600–1, 688
Mühsam, Erich 570
Müller-Otfried, Paula 691
Müller, Hermann 51, 75–6, 78–80, 97, 111, 155, 182, 185, 305, 346, 387

Müller, Richard 35
multi-party system 169–71, 244
Mumm, Reinhard 687
Münchener Neueste Nachrichten 441–2
Munich 30, 33, 35–6, 40, 63, 73, 173, 198, 207, 209, 221, 224, 235, 246, 367, 382–3, 385, 390, 408, 441, 463, 567, 570, 574, 613, 620, 660–2, 671, 688, 703, 732
Munich Council Republic 207, 221
Münzenberg, Willi 360n51, 489, 550
Münzer-Neumann, Käthe 730–1
Murnau, F. W. 622
Museum of Modern Art 666
music: Afro-American 465
    classical 283, 465, 615
    jazz 7, 724, 726, 735–6
    popular 9, 490, 618, 622
    recorded 610, 614–15
Musil, Robert 523, 635, 642, 650
Mussolini, Benito 198, 384
Muthesius, Hermann 207
mysticism 580, 656

N

N. V. Nederlandse Kunstzijdefabriek 445
Nadler, Josef 706
Nahman Bialik, Chaim 580
Namibia 153
National Assembly 12–13, 16, 31–2, 35–9, 41, 48, 121–4, 166, 170, 172–3, 177–8, 180, 193–5, 222, 245, 269, 275, 279–80, 319, 323–4, 342–4, 350, 364, 371, 412, 508, 512, 524, 589, 683, 751
national community (*Volksgemeinschaft*) 14, 131, 143, 153–7, 199, 332, 363, 382, 388, 392, 462, 687 *see also* people's community
national comrades (*Volksgenossen*) 142, 157
National Council (Reichsrat) 30, 36, 105, 128–30, 194, 196
National Federation of German Industry (Reichsverband der Deutschen Industrie, RDI) 99–100, 108, 328, 367, 429, 438–40
National Liberal Party 250, 319, 366
'national opposition' 86, 369–70, 374, 377
National Socialism 132, 176, 186, 277, 317, 325, 327, 332, 353, 363, 382–3, 388, 391–2, 394–7, 446, 491–2, 557, 576, 597, 601, 630–2, 634, 681, 694, 743

National Socialist Association of
  Legal Professionals (Bund
  Nationalsozialistischer Deutscher
  Juristen, BNSDJ) 389–90
National Socialist Factory Cell
  Organizations 391
National Socialist Freedom Party
  (Nationalsozialistische Freiheitspartei,
  NSFP) 385
National Socialist German Students' League
  (Nationalsozialistischer Deutscher
  Studentenbund, NSDStB) 389–90, 597
National Socialist German Worker's Party
  (Nationalsozialistische Deutsche
  Arbeiterpartei, NSDAP) 13–14, 54, 56,
  79, 86, 98–101, 103–4, 106–11, 141, 167, 173,
  177–8, 181, 186, 196, 199–200, 209, 235–6,
  303, 308, 346, 370, 382–94, 397, 407, 409,
  414–19, 442, 510–15, 529, 576, 588, 590,
  596, 598, 601, 684–5, 694–6, 717
National Socialist League of Physicians
  (Nationalsozialistischer Deutscher
  Ärztebund, NS-DÄB) 389–90
National Socialist League of Pupils
  (Nationalsozialistischer Schülerbund) 597
National Socialist Pastors' League
  (Nationalsozialistischer Evangelischer
  Pfarrerbund, NSEP) 389, 577
National Socialist Teachers' League
  (Nationalsozialistischer Lehrerbund,
  NSLB) 389
National Socialist: ideology 154, 233, 390
  leadership 107, 154, 325
  movement 100, 110, 176, 234–6, 277, 374–5,
    385, 389, 392, 396, 407, 415, 419
  rhetoric 396, 460
  seizure of power 2, 106, 181, 295, 308, 350,
    390, 408, 415, 436, 670, 672–3, 754
  victory 104
  voters 513
national spirit 141–2, 325, 327
national war memorial (Reichsehrenmal) 758
National Women's Committee of the
  DNVP 366
nationalism 40, 79, 142, 144, 149, 153, 186, 188,
  205, 209, 245, 318, 386, 404, 456–7, 466,
  477, 557, 578–9, 631, 687, 740

anti-republican 155, 364–5
authoritarian 141
conservative 147
ethno- 207
racist 151, 375
radical 101, 146, 374, 593
republican 147–8, 151, 156–7, 274
right-wing 734
nationalization 39, 121, 168, 207
Nationalsozialer Verein 326
Natorp, Paul 712
naturalism 631, 638
naturism 526
Naumann, Friedrich 131, 170, 326
Naumburg Rifle Battalion 30
Nawiasky, Hans 129
Nazification 23n91, 512, 514
Nazism 101, 107, 363, 374, 468, 491, 696, 755
Nebbe, Margarete 729
Negri, Pola 730
Nelissen-Haken, Bruno 645
Nell-Breuning, Oswald von 685
neo-Kantianism 712, 714
Netherlands 153, 171, 433, 661, 662
neue Frankfurt, Das 665
Neues Bauen 208, 654, 659, 661–2, 664–6,
  668–70, 672–3
Neues Frankfurt 662, 665
Neufert, Ernst 673
Neukölln 84, 88, 175
Neuländer-Simon, Else 731
Neumann, Paul 347
Neumann, Therese 688
Neurath, Konstantin Freiherr von 185, 258–9
Neusel, Walter 622
New Economic Policy 542, 549
New Guard House (Neue Wache) 758
New Objectivity (*Neue Sachlichkeit*) 5, 226,
  466, 528, 637–40, 726
New Woman 16, 467, 504, 521, 523–6, 535, 555–6,
  724, 726, 730
New York 541, 546, 618, 666
Niagara Falls 541
Niekisch, Ernst 550
Nielsen, Asta 730
Nobel Peace Prize 10, 256
nobility 17, 227, 371, 386, 499

Nolde, Emil 655
Norddeutsche Wollkämmerei 445
North Schleswig 643
North Sea 281
North Western Group 440
North-West German Association of Hirelings (Nordwestdeutsche Heuerleute-Verband) 508
Northern Confederation 198
Noske, Gustav 29, 37–40, 50, 182, 221, 223, 231, 738
novellas 629, 639, 644, 646
novels 204, 526, 611, 616, 629, 631, 633–5, 639, 641–3, 645–7, 650, 736
'November criminals' 54, 392, 405
November group (Novembergruppe) 655, 658, 674n3
Nowack, Wilhelm 152
nudism 489
Nuremberg 268, 574, 683, 686
Nuschke, Otto 268
nutrition 487

O

Oberfohren, Ernst 109
occupations 633, 636, 638–40, 650, 661, 710
October Reforms 29, 32, 41, 164
Oeser, Rudolf 183, 268
Offenbach 88
Office of Alien Property Custodian 432
Office of Ministerial Affairs 235, 374
Ohlemüller, Gerhard 690
Olberg, Oda 533
Oldenbourg, Friedrich 612, 616, 620
Oldenburg 196, 200, 500, 511–12, 574
opera 465–6, 553–4, 613, 621, 647, 649, 729, 736
opposition, fundamental 223, 384, 390
Ordinance on the Arbitration System 203
Ore Mountains 750
Organization Consul 146, 406
Orgesch (Organization Escherich) 231
orphans 5, 296, 299, 477, 589, 752–3
Ossietzky, Carl von 266, 277–8, 284
Österreichisch-Deutscher Volksbund 152
Oswald, Richard 530
Oswalda, Ossi 732
Otto, Elizabeth 740

Ottoman Empire 42, 219
Oud, Jacobus Johannes Pieter 661–2, 666
Overy, Richard 7

P

Pabst, Georg Wilhelm 729, 765
Pacelli, Eugenio 373
pacifism 225, 755
Palestine 568, 595, 672
Pan-German League 63, 86, 144, 149, 365, 405–6
Pankok, Otto 737
Papen, Franz von 102–11, 129, 185, 198, 236, 258–9, 355, 364, 372–3, 376–8, 442, 576, 693, 695
paragraph 218 13, 532, 556, 634–5
paramilitary organizations 84–5, 96, 103, 144, 146–8, 198, 220, 222, 231, 235, 365, 383–5, 406, 462, 529, 599–600, 754
Paris 205, 329, 524, 595, 666, 737, 758
Paris Peace Conference 195, 222, 244, 383
parliamentarianism 49, 386, 390, 393
parliamentarism 33, 85, 105, 326, 329, 378, 460
parliamentarization 29, 75, 193, 377
parliamentary: culture 78, 87, 89
  democracy 1, 3, 5, 11, 17, 27, 41, 79, 98–9, 105, 110, 121–2, 144–5, 164–5, 187, 234, 285, 317, 327, 333, 342, 349, 356, 365–6, 375, 377, 397, 405, 418, 441, 460, 463, 693
  party 85, 387, 412, 599
  representation 164, 166, 172–3
  rule 3, 457
  system 1, 17, 73, 97, 123, 125, 147, 170, 225, 234, 249, 340, 414, 468, 598
participation, political 165–6, 172, 267, 276–7, 285, 442, 458, 461, 522, 570–1
particularism 81, 582
parties: anti-republican 129, 174, 242, 365, 419
  antisemitic 405, 418, 576
  bourgeois 16, 48, 53, 63, 75, 84–5, 103, 170, 183, 257, 299, 305, 321, 366, 369, 371, 376, 442, 532, 598
  catch-all 320, 514
  communist 351, 360n50
  conservative 166, 168, 180, 348, 363–4, 370, 372, 631, 634
  liberal 65, 135, 177, 271, 318–24, 327, 332–3, 367, 369, 371, 417, 460, 570, 681

mass 319–20, 344, 350, 386, 388
people's 97, 168, 186, 347, 386
republican 16, 80, 156, 181, 243, 247, 270–1, 276–8, 280–2, 375
socialist 13, 98, 414, 419
splinter 170, 321, 324, 327, 364, 367, 369, 460
worldview 373
Party for Revaluation and Reconstruction (Aufwertungs- und Wiederaufbaupartei) 460
party: rallies 271
　system 77, 97, 134, 145, 168–71, 199, 244, 317, 460, 545
　whip 327
Parufamet 557
Pass Friedenreich, Harriet 573
pastors 4, 14, 34, 386, 389, 455, 457, 686, 692, 695
patents 432, 434, 441, 444
paternalism 483, 687
patriotism 142, 568
　'constitutional' 634
Paul, Bruno 664
Paulskirche 35, 273–5, 280
pauperization 298
Peace League of Ex-Servicemen (Friedensbund der Kriegsteilnehmer) 755
peace: compromise 242
　dictated 751
　economy 48
　movement 9, 34, 595
　negotiated 364
　negotiation 195, 656
　resolution 48, 50, 371
　settlement 9, 149, 328, 365, 368
　treaty 28, 39, 49, 51, 222, 248, 430, 643, 750
peasant associations (*Bauernvereine*) 373, 508, 510
peasant councils (*Bauernräte*) 35
Pechstein, Max 655
pension 133, 296–9, 301–2, 306, 308, 368, 376
　'psychosis' 299
　scheme 58, 291
　state 220, 296, 299
　war 297, 752
　widow's 299

pensioners 164, 296–7, 299, 321, 459, 565, 572
　small capital (*Kleinkapitalrentner*) 300, 302–3, 308
people of colour 143, 154
People's Association for Catholic Germany (Volksverein für das katholische Deutschland) 688
People's Bloc (*Volksblock*) 82, 172
people's body (*Volkskörper*) 395, 522, 528
People's Church 686, 707
People's Commissar for Education 35
people's community (*Volksgemeinschaft*) 13–14, 143–5, 149, 154–5, 169–70, 187, 277, 321, 325, 363, 377, 388, 393, 396–7, 407, 409, 419, 462, 511, 707, 712
people's health 292, 527, 535
People's Justice Party (Volksrechtspartei, VRP) 324
people's militia (*Volkswehr*) 220, 230
People's Naval Division (Volksmarinedivision) 37, 220
people's state (*Volksstaat*) 53, 276–7, 284, 291
people's welfare 292, 534
Permanent Court of International Justice 331–3
persecution 18, 253, 348, 396, 566, 684, 702
Petri, Franz 206
Petzold, Alfons 644
Peukert, Detlev 4–6, 74, 89, 486–7
Pfeffer von Salomon, Franz 235, 392
philosophy 548, 648, 706–16, 718
photographs 31, 109, 175, 283, 352, 597, 620, 639, 642, 724–5, 727, 731–41, 743, 762–3, 765
photography 5, 176, 437, 724–5, 730, 733–4, 740, 742, 752, 765, 767
photojournalism 204, 724
photomontage 1, 208, 725, 738, 740
physical exercise 526–8
physicians 4, 297, 460, 528, 530, 532, 534, 633
Piechowski, Paul 690
Pinthus, Kurt 637
Piscator, Erwin 629, 632, 634
Pittsburgh 546
Pius XI 532, 688, 690, 692
plebiscites 124, 149, 169, 173–4, 188, 210, 231, 245–6, 253, 256 *see also* referendums
Plievier, Theodor 643

pluralism 120–1, 123–4, 126–7, 285, 687–8, 712, 714
Poelzig, Hans 655, 662, 664, 666
poems 265, 273, 278, 629, 632, 634, 636–7, 640, 644, 646–8
pogrom 60, 406–8, 417–18, 567
Pohl, Karl Heinrich 259, 262n36
Poincaré, Raymond 55, 248–51, 255
Poiret, Paul 524
Poland 10, 149, 151, 171, 221–2, 231, 245–6, 248, 252–5, 257–8, 260, 331, 458, 505, 567, 643, 658, 670
Polgar, Alfred 649
police 17, 32, 35, 54, 129, 132, 201, 270, 279, 282, 340, 352, 384, 408–10, 412, 419, 479, 502, 510, 530, 591, 632, 765
   Bavarian 224
   Berlin 38, 344, 575
   force 62–3, 129, 271, 340, 346, 355, 392
   local 281
   military 29
   Munich 40
   Prussian 84, 88, 269, 271, 346
   report 384, 511–12
   state 62, 198
policy: 'of abstention' 78
   cultural 209, 659, 670, 672, 706–7
   education 80, 707
   foreign 55, 76–7, 79, 81, 85, 111, 151, 222, 228, 234–5, 242–5, 248–52, 254, 256, 258–60, 321, 331, 351, 523
   'of fulfillment' 151
   'of gathering' 374, 442
   population 531, 533–4, 566
   racial 395
   rapprochement 55, 488
   school 39, 589
   social 77–8, 89, 202–3, 291–2, 298–9, 302–3, 306, 308, 348, 475, 533, 542, 549, 572, 598, 654
   trade 432–3
Polish corridor 228
Polish-Soviet War 228
political economics (*Volkswirtschaftslehre*) 709
politicization 81, 169, 307, 477, 510–11, 632–4, 651, 754

politics: body 147, 209, 521
   performative 166, 279, 282, 285
   populist 392
   power 11, 243, 250, 702
   religious 680, 682, 684, 695–6
Pollock, Friedrich 552
Pomerania 203, 211, 265, 499–500, 506–7, 514, 519n64
Poncet, André François 108
poor relief 297
Popitz, Johannes 201
Popper, Karl 718
populism 17, 35, 366, 377
Portugal 153
Posen 149, 203, 211, 221, 231, 500, 762
positivism 710, 712, 714, 718
posters 14, 40, 82, 145, 176, 273, 352, 394, 410, 637, 727, 736, 738, 741–2, 766
Potsdam 147, 657
poverty 57, 202, 479, 526, 542, 556
POWs 10, 498
Prague 666
Preparatory Disarmament Conference 228
presidential: cabinet 123, 126, 185, 202, 305
   decree 75, 96, 99, 126, 129, 202, 256
   emergency powers 98, 135
   elections 74, 101–2, 107, 109, 130, 145, 172–3, 176, 354
   powers 89, 125, 134–5
pressure groups 10–11, 13, 83, 328, 503, 506, 508–12, 752
Preuß, Hugo 16, 122, 124, 126–9, 131, 182, 193–4, 198, 267, 280, 326, 405, 714
price: controls 52, 61, 366, 481
   fixing 440
   erosion of 434, 444
   increase 52, 297, 443
   market 502, 612
priests 34, 375, 489, 529, 596
production, mass 328, 437–8, 546–7
productivity 5, 482, 500–2, 514, 523, 527, 547
professionalization 226, 303, 391, 591
professors 389, 409, 455, 457–9, 461–2, 525, 669, 703–6, 717–18
Progressive People's Party 319
Proletarian Hundreds (Proletarische Hundertschaften) 61–2, 198

proletarianization 59, 549, 612
proletariat 40, 88, 156, 347, 352, 417, 545, 556, 600, 645
Prometheus Films 671
propaganda 33, 149, 233, 266, 441, 508, 531, 692, 736
  antisemitic 406–7, 414–15, 417–18
  campaigns 566, 635, 743
  communist 176, 350–2, 417
  Nazi 14, 101, 103, 383, 390–1, 394, 409, 529, 588, 659, 670, 672, 733, 741
  against the Nazis 576
  republican 273
  right-wing 150–1, 270, 413
  visual 176, 529, 741
  völkisch 418
  war 195, 643, 705
property, private 132, 364, 456, 464
proportional representation 123, 168, 170–1, 176, 327, 330
prostheses 523, 727
prostitution 57, 479, 526, 532, 641, 726, 729, 737
protectionism 245, 328, 368, 433, 435, 447
protective custody (*Schutzhaft*) 62, 64, 224
Protestant Church 41, 371–2, 462, 681, 686, 690
Protestant Church Federation 687
Protestant Church of the Old Union of Prussia 684
Protestant Reich Committee of Female Youth (Evangelische Reichsverband weiblicher Jugend) 596
Protestant Social Congress 687
Protestantism 167, 456, 564, 684–7
  cultural 704, 712
Protocols of the Elders of Zion 405
Provincial Housing Settlement Societies 659
Provisional National Council 36
Prussia 17, 34, 51, 62, 79, 80–1, 99, 101, 103, 108, 120, 127–9, 140, 143, 149, 193–8, 200–1, 203, 211, 222, 225, 231–2, 235, 245, 269, 271, 342, 346, 352, 355, 370, 375, 387, 415, 503, 506, 508–9, 534, 566, 683, 685, 761
  Old 168
Prussian Academy of Arts 574
Prussian Ministry for Culture 269
Prussian Ministry of Education and Culture 683

Prussian Ministry of the Interior 232
Prussian state government 102–3, 376
Prussian state parliament 28, 37 85, 102, 508–9
psychology 588, 709, 711, 721n39
public: debt 52
  health 58, 209, 526, 535, 752
  morality 680
  works programme 102, 108
publishing houses 38, 441–2, 554, 565, 580, 617, 620, 632, 643, 644, 704, 724
pulp fiction 8, 609
Pulzer, Peter 576
putsch attempts 51, 119, 392, 414, 642
Pyrmont 196

Q
Queen Luise League (Bund Königin Luise) 154
Querfront 107
Querschnitt, Der 621, 728
Quickborn 596, 688
Quidde, Ludwig 10

R
Rabbinerverband 575
Rabe, Erich 668–9
race: 'Aryan' 154, 406, 532
  concept of 146, 154
  Germanic 150–1, 395
  hatred 155
  Jews as a 394–5, 406, 410, 415
  racial hygiene 150, 396, 528, 533, 716
  racism 143, 146, 150–1, 154, 155–7, 352, 405–6, 670, 702, 705, 716
  theory 410, 733–4, 737–8
Radbruch, Gustav 127, 141–2, 148, 156, 276, 345, 533
Rade, Martin 686–7
Radek, Karl 54, 61, 550
radicalism 34, 38–9, 100, 104, 169, 350, 372, 377–8, 387, 392, 718
Rading, Adolf 664–5, 668–9
radio 8–9, 83, 108, 175, 203, 209, 212, 437, 464, 490, 609–11, 614–19, 621, 647, 695, 729
Rahden, Till van 572
Raphael, Lutz 531
Raschke, Martin 640–1

Rathenau, Walther 29, 48, 54, 73, 129, 146, 183, 247–8, 268, 272, 277, 280–2, 323, 369, 384, 407, 410–11, 429–30, 511, 550, 565, 571, 581, 632, 739
rationalization 5, 203, 212, 460, 476, 482, 485, 521, 525, 527, 529, 531, 534, 547, 548, 556, 566, 600, 616
realism 5, 226, 249–50, 528, 631, 638–9, 649, 673
rearmament 54, 218, 227–30, 234–7, 251, 256, 258–60
Reclam publishing house 611
reconciliation 10, 79, 142, 181, 257, 366, 590, 639
recovery, economic 98, 105, 247, 354, 432, 459
Red Army 40, 228
Red Front Fighter's League (Roter Frontkämpferbund, RFB) 84, 392, 632, 754
Red Front, The 633
Red October 634
Red Ruhr Army (Rote Ruhrarmee) 51, 204
Redlich, Oswald 206
Redslob, Edwin 269, 273–4, 283–4
referendum 74, 81, 86, 89, 125–6, 130, 152, 173–4, 211, 364, 374
　on the expropriation of the princes 82–7, 130, 132, 135, 174, 281, 413
　in support of leaving the League of Nations 332
　against the Young Plan 130, 174, 370
reform: constitutional 28–9, 242, 250
　currency 57–9, 64, 66, 300–1, 303, 307, 323, 646
　educational 16, 267, 601
　electoral 342
　penal 533
　political 28, 49, 308, 491, 686
　religious 564
　sexual 521, 530–2, 689
　social 320, 542
Reformation 635, 681, 684–5
Reformed Protestant Church 681, 685
refugees 10, 52, 166, 574, 658
Reger, Erik 204, 639, 645
regionalization 194, 210
Reich Agency for Labour Exchange and Unemployment Insurance (Reichsanstalt für Arbeitsvermittlung und Arbeitslosenversicherung) 600

Reich Art Custodian (Reichskunstwart) 12, 268, 273–4, 283–4
Reich Association of German Industry (Reichsverband der Deutschen Industrie, RDI) 99–100, 328–9, 367, 429, 438–40
Reich Association of the German Heavy Industry (Reichsverband der deutschen Schwerindustrie) 440
Reich Audit Office 229
Reich Banner Black-Red-Gold (Reichsbanner Schwarz-Rot-Gold) 12, 16, 85, 103, 147–8, 152–3, 155, 265, 271–8, 280–5, 348, 354, 392, 418, 576, 599, 754–5, 758
Reich Catholic Committee 365, 372
Reich Chancellery 78, 234, 738
Reich commissioners 62, 197
Reich Committee of German Youth Associations (Reichsausschuss Deutscher Jugendverbände) 595, 597
Reich Committee of Protestant Young Men's Bünde (Reichsverband der evangelischen Jungmännerbünde) 596
Reich Congress of Workers and Soldiers' Councils 36
Reich Court 65, 235
Reich Finance Reform 200–3
Reich Health Council 533
Reich League of Disabled War Veterans, Ex-Servicemen and War Dependants (Reichsbund der Kriegsbeschädigten, Kriegsteilnehmer und Kriegerhinterbliebenen) 267, 274, 752, 755
Reich League of Jewish Front Line Soldiers (Reichsbund Jüdischer Frontsoldaten, RJF) 575, 735
Reich Main Security Office (Reichssicherheitshauptamt, RSHA) 385
Reich Ministry of Agriculture 76, 97, 110, 369, 375
Reich Ministry of Defence 50, 76, 107, 268, 738
Reich Ministry of Economic Affairs 76, 110, 331
Reich Ministry of Finance 50, 52, 75–6, 78, 182–5, 198, 200, 234, 257, 332, 368, 407, 569–71
Reich Ministry of Foreign Affairs 182–5
Reich Ministry of the Interior 54, 62, 78, 82, 97, 103, 105, 175, 182–5, 268–9, 271, 325, 385, 506, 694

Reich Ministry of Labour 76–9, 110, 182–5, 234, 291, 293, 297, 302, 306–7, 506
Reich Ministry of the Occupied Territories 97
Reich Ministry of Reconstruction 247
Reich Ministry of the Reichswehr 62–3, 221, 224–5, 228–9, 232–6, 571
Reich Office for Statistics 437, 481–2
Reich Organization Leadership (Reichs-Organisations-Leitung der NSDAP) 107
Reich Party for Civil Rights and Deflation (Reichspartei für Volksrecht und Aufwertung) 171
Reich Party for People's Justice and Revaluation 369
Reich Party of the German *Mittelstand* (Reichspartei des deutschen Mittelstandes) 460
Reich Productivity Board (Reichskuratorium für Wirtschaftlickeit, RKW) 547, 549
Reich Rural League (Reichslandbund, RLB) 86, 88, 99, 108 251, 366–7, 372, 509–10, 513
Reich School Conference 589
Reich Treasury Administration 200
Reich War Ministry 37
Reich, Lilly 668
Reichsbahn 64, 226
Reichsbank 444–5
Reichsbanner, Das 270, 276
Reichsblock 82, 172–3
Reichsexekution 62, 197, 326
Reichsknappschaft 58
Reichsnotopfer 50
Reichsorganisation der demokratischen Jugend 85
Reichspost 64
Reichstag elections: 6 June 1920 48, 178, 243, 247, 344, 407, 419
  4 May 1924 65, 75, 79, 178, 251, 323, 350, 386, 413, 415
  20 May 1928 75, 79–80, 178, 346, 387, 463, 598
  14 September 1930 80, 86, 88, 99, 126, 178, 257, 324, 346, 372, 387–8, 445, 454, 464, 512–14, 598, 647
  31 July 1932 84, 103, 177–8, 346–7, 512–13, 571
  6 November 1932 105, 110, 177–8, 180–1, 235, 332, 346, 350, 353, 742

Reichswehr 49–52, 61–3, 73, 97, 106–7, 197–8, 204, 218–19, 221–37, 279, 383, 408, 506, 756
Reinhardt, Walther 223, 236
religion 15, 166–7, 209, 371–2, 408, 417, 466, 564, 568, 572, 580, 590, 610, 641, 651, 680, 682, 691, 694–6, 750
  religious cultures 5, 16, 567, 680, 682, 685
  freedom of 131, 416, 686
  religious morality 502
  religious neutrality 682–3, 693
  religious paragraphs 683
  political 394
  religious teachings 686
Remarque, Erich Maria 8, 409, 467, 643–4, 764
remasculinization 521, 529, 535
Remscheid 384
Renn, Ludwig 642–3
reparations 48–9, 53, 55–7, 65, 97, 102, 130, 149, 151, 174, 200, 202, 204, 244–51, 255, 257–9, 325, 328, 344, 365, 370, 375, 406, 429, 431–2, 443–8, 458, 462, 481, 510, 546
  campaign against 387
  debates on 413–14
  staggered 367
Reparations Commission 56, 248, 443
representation: parliamentary 164, 166, 172–3
  political 167, 170, 462, 499, 507, 513
  proportional 123, 168, 170–1, 176, 327, 330
reproduction 150, 175, 521–22, 528, 532, 534–5
republic without republicans 12, 148, 157, 177, 266
Republican Complaint Agency (Republikanische Beschwerdestelle) 272
Republican Leader's League (Republikanischer Führerbund) 270
Republican Reich League (Republikanischer Reichsbund) 270
Republican Student Cartel (Republikanisches Studentenkartell) 152
Republican Union (Republikanische Union) 268, 270
republicanism 82, 85, 181, 267, 276–7, 340, 346
republicans from reason (*Vernunftrepublikaner*) 250, 317
Republikanischer Schutzbund 148
Reusch, Paul 100, 108, 440–2
Reuß 195–6
Reuter, Gabriele 646

revisionism 10–11, 151–2, 228, 331
revolution of 1848–49 35, 131, 143, 246, 273–5
Revolution, French 27, 41, 372
Revolution, Russian 341–2, 349
revolution, sexual 18, 534
Revolutionary Shop Stewards *(Revolutionäre Obleute)* 30, 341
Revolutionary Workers' Choral Club 488
Rhenish Palatinate 268, 509
Rhenish-Westphalian Coal Syndicate 440
Rhina 565
Rhine province 235
Rhineland 61, 75, 154, 168, 193, 199, 246–9, 252–6, 259, 268, 368, 372, 385, 489, 508–9, 689
 'bastards' 150
 occupied 34, 76, 88, 102, 151–2, 228, 235, 244–5, 253–5, 367, 370, 528, 657
Riemerschmid, Richard 207
Riemkasten, Felix 647
Rilke, Rainer Maria 629, 647–8
Ringer, Fritz K. 73, 703, 705
Riphahn, Wilhelm 661
Ritschl, Albrecht 431
River Elbe 99, 108, 499
River Main 596
River Moselle 510
River Rhine 36, 119, 149–50, 232, 247, 249, 368, 477, 509, 736
River Rouge 547, 549, 557
River Werra 593
Rödinghausen 500
Rohe, Karl 167–8, 180–1
Rohe, Mies van der 8, 208, 656, 662, 665–6, 668, 670, 673
Röhm, Ernst 383, 385, 392
Rollei 437
Romanisches Café 580
Römer, Willy 740–1
Röpke, Wilhelm 329, 711
Roselius, Ludwig 438
Rosenberg, Alfred 385, 416, 694
Rosenberg, Arthur 28–9
Rosenberg, Frederic von 183
Rosenberg, Hans 2, 717
Rosenfeld, Kurt 569
Rosenzweig, Franz 563, 580

Rosh Hashanah 575
Ross, Corey 490
Rostov 552
Rote Fahne, Die 84
Roth, Joseph 506, 629, 634, 640
Rothacker, Erich 709–10
Rothenfels Castle 596
Rotterdam 661
Rowohlt publishing house 644
Royal Navy 29
Royal Palace 31
Rühl, Alfred 549
Rühmann, Heinz 622
Ruhr area 39, 51, 55–6, 119, 199, 204, 268, 345, 443, 477, 619, 639
Ruhr campaign (Ruhrkampf) 56, 209
 passive resistance 56–7, 61, 63, 232, 249, 413
 sabotage 56, 232, 765
Ruhr Iron Strike 440
Ruhr, occupation of the 48, 56, 63, 125, 149, 224, 245, 249, 251, 634
Ruhrort 55, 443
rule of law 88, 132–3, 419, 456
Rupprecht, Philipp 735
Rural League (Landbund) 171, 178, 199, 506, 509–10
Russia 31, 35, 40–1, 151, 166, 222, 242, 248, 295, 343, 352, 366, 501, 541–6, 549–50, 552
 Bolshevik 28, 30
 Soviet 225, 228
Rüstow, Alexander 329
Ruttmann, Walter 736

S

SA Stormtroopers (Sturmabteilung) 13, 103, 129, 134, 235–6, 256, 355, 383, 385, 388–9, 391–3, 407–9, 415, 575, 622, 696, 701n58
Saar region 149
Saemisch, Friedrich 202
saleswomen 526, 646
Salomon, Alice 324, 544, 555, 572
Salomon, Bruno von 511
Salomon, Erich 738–9
Salomon, Ernst von 643
Salomon, Franz Pfeffer von 235, 392
Sammartino, Annemarie 150
Samson-Körner, Paul 619

Sander, August 725, 732, 734, 741
Sauckel, Fritz 385
Sautter, Hans 760–1
savings 59–60, 87, 293, 368, 431, 459, 480, 485, 565
Saxony 62, 79, 85, 125, 193, 203, 222, 324, 344, 346, 350, 365, 369, 387, 391, 504, 533
  and Thuringia 61, 73, 129, 197–8, 210, 249, 326
Saxony-Altenburg 196
Saxony-Gotha 196
Saxony-Meiningen 196
Saxony-Weimar-Eisenach 196
Schad, Christian 732
Schäffer, Hans 185, 234
Scharoun, Hans 656, 664–5, 667, 673
Schätzel, Georg 76
Schaumann, Ruth 762
Schaumburg-Lippe 196
Schauwecker, Franz 642–3
Scheidemann, Philipp 31–2, 49–50, 182, 229, 342, 738, 760
Scheidemühl 762
Schemm, Hans 389
Schenzinger, Karl Aloys 635
Scherl-Verlag 441
Scherl's Magazin 622
Scheunenviertel 60, 408, 417–18, 574–5
Schickele, René 644
Schiele, Martin 97, 99, 184, 268, 369, 375
Schiller, J. 683
Schirach, Baldur von 389
Schlageter, Albert Leo 56
Schleicher, Kurt von 97, 100–4, 106–11, 185, 233–6, 374–7
Schlemmer, Oskar 669, 732, 766
Schlenker, Max 440
Schleswig 149, 210, 643
Schleswig-Holstein 88, 186, 199, 210, 385, 500, 511–14
Schleswig-Holstein Association 210
Schleswig-Holsteiner, Der 210
Schlögel, Karl 542
Schmalkalden 276
Schmeling, Max 527, 619, 622, 728
Schmidt-Hannover, Otto 109
Schmidt-Wodder, Johannes 210

Schmitt, Carl 60, 129, 132, 188, 714, 717
Schmitthenner, Paul 208, 669–72
Schnitzler, Arthur 647
Scholem, Gershom 563, 580
Scholtis, August 644
Scholtz, Arthur 617
schools 41, 201, 207, 233, 283, 371, 390, 409, 527, 573, 660, 670, 684, 686, 689, 694, 763
  confessional 590
  and education 16, 131
  elementary 458, 504, 513
  grammar 455, 458–9, 522, 590
  policies 39, 589
  primary 269, 389, 484, 590
  secondary 4, 411, 596, 599–600, 706
Schotte, Walther 105
Schrader, Ernst 270
Schröder, Kurt von 109
Schubert, Carl von 244, 252–4, 257
Schücking, Walther 331–2
Schüler-Springorum, Stefanie 575
Schulte, Karl Joseph 689
Schulze-Naumburg, Paul 208, 670, 672
Schumacher, Fritz 207
Schütte-Lihotzky, Grete 659
Schwäbischer Alpenverein 209
Schwarz, Georg 619
Schwarzburg-Rudolstadt 196
Schwarzburg-Sondershausen 196
Schweitzer, Hans Herbert 394
Schwichtenberg, Martel 730
sciences: academic 705
  defence (*Wehrwissenschaften*) 233
  human 522, 709–10
  natural 708, 710, 712
  political 60, 708–10
  social 597, 670, 702, 704–5, 707–9, 715, 718
Scientific Humanitarian Committee 530
seaside resorts 281, 409, 574
Second World War 329, 437, 651, 681, 761
Section for Women's Rights 35
secularism 16, 371, 476, 682–3, 688, 690, 692–5
secularization 489, 684, 688
Seeckt, Hans von 51, 62–3, 73, 80, 222–6, 228–9, 248, 250, 253
Seeler, Erwin 488
Seeler, Uwe 488

Seidel, Ina 646
Seißer, Hans von 198
Seldte, Franz 82, 109–10
self-determination 119, 121, 127, 144, 151–2, 157, 242, 500, 533, 587, 592–3, 596, 730
Sender, Toni 31, 34
Senger, Alexander von 208
separatism: Polish 119
　Rhenish 634
servants: domestic 133, 478–9, 482, 512
　female 479, 504
　Gesinde 500, 504–5
　male 478
Settlement Association of the Ruhr Coal Mining District (Siedlungsverband Ruhrkohlenbezirk) 204
Seventh-Day Adventists 685
Severing, Carl 51, 80, 185, 232, 234, 268, 271, 346
Sevesten 512
sexuality 5, 13, 16, 523, 529–31, 535, 555–6, 629, 690, 725–6, 729–30, 732, 736
　homosexuality 530, 532–3, 535, 641, 726
　sexual hygiene 5, 531
　sexual life 566
　rationalization of 521, 531, 534
　sex work 479, 532
　transsexuality 530
Seydoux, Jacques 247
shopkeepers 454, 456, 458, 460–1, 480, 499, 565, 574
Siegmund-Schultze, Friedrich 591
Siemens company 547
Siemsen, Hans 545, 552
Silesia 168, 199, 203, 499, 655, 659
　Upper 35, 54, 149, 152, 210, 231, 246–7, 268, 364, 371, 431, 440, 498, 643–4, 658
Silverberg, Paul 440
Simon, Helene 572
Simon, Hugo 569
Simons, Walter 182, 248, 687
Simplicissimus 728
Simson, Eduard 194
single lists (Einheitslisten) 199–200
Sinti and Roma 737
Sklarek, Leo 413
Sklarek, Max 413
Sklarek, Willi 413

smaller German solution 143–4, 147, 155
Smend, Rudolf 132, 714
Smith, Helmut W. 17, 696
social Darwinism 151, 532
Social Democratic Party of Austria 148
social engineering 5, 394–5
social fascism 692
social insurance system 297, 301
Social Working Group Berlin-East (Soziale Arbeitsgemeinschaft Berlin-Ost) 591
socialism 154, 199, 202, 277, 346–7, 349–50, 356, 365, 370, 372, 385, 389, 417, 545, 548, 551–3, 556, 570, 682–3, 689
　council 40
　cultural 689
　municipal 430
　religious 687–8
Socialist International, Second 351
Socialist Realism 673
Socialist Working Class Youth (Sozialistische Arbeiterjugend) 596–7
socialization 30, 39, 49, 132, 172, 340, 342–3, 386, 440, 446, 504, 514, 556, 631
Society of Friends of the New Russia 550
society: bourgeois 521–2, 529, 578, 612
　capitalist 386, 397
　of citizens 167
　civil 218, 234, 464
　class 65, 356, 397, 454
　consumer 436–8, 521, 523, 526, 535
　industrial 4, 522, 609
　modern 1, 4, 60, 609, 621, 681, 689
　socialist 344, 689
sociology 708–11, 714, 721n39
　of knowledge 707, 716
　of literature 713
Sohn, Ernest 578
soldier, unknown 758–9
soldiers' councils 33, 121, 165, 230
Sollmann, Wilhelm 183, 268, 277, 283–4
Sombart, Werner 59, 711
Sonderweg 2
Sontag, Susan 727
Sontheimer, Kurt 3
Sorge, Reinhard 636
South Tyrol 152, 209, 644
South West Africa 153

sovereignty 127–8, 150, 209, 218, 260, 330–1, 368, 750
  democratic 32
  fiscal 105, 201
  parliamentary 73
  political 206, 210, 693
  popular 32, 34, 42, 120, 372, 714
  of the states 196–7, 200–1
  territorial 152
Soviet Declaration of the Rights of Labouring and Exploited People 131
Soviet Union 9, 55, 228, 244–5, 248, 252–4, 258–9, 343, 351–2, 356, 433, 541, 543–5, 549–57, 620, 692, 710, 751
Spa 55
Spahn, Martin 372–3
Spain 205, 207
Spann, Othmar 711
Spartacists 36–8, 41, 344, 366, 569, 739
Speer, Albert 672
Spengler, Oswalt 225, 705
Speyer, Wilhelm 646
sports 57, 390, 465–6, 600, 609, 617, 621, 728, 74
  associations/clubs 278, 579, 681
  competitions 527
  competitive 616, 619
  events 283, 621–2
  mass 527, 535
  organizations 528, 574
  spectator 8, 490, 609, 611–12, 616, 619
  women and 595–6
  workers' 278, 349
Spranger, Eduard 588
SS Schutzstaffel 385
stab-in-the-back 40, 50, 61, 145, 405, 577
stabilization 48, 53, 60, 95, 248, 300–1, 350, 367–8, 387, 447, 459–60, 481, 503, 506, 510, 547, 623, 636, 641, 718
Stalin, Josef 352, 545, 551–2, 672, 692
Stalingrad 552
Stam, Mart 666
standardization 328, 547, 549, 552, 616, 665
Star of David 735–6
State Court (Staatsgerichtshof) 124, 128, 410
State Electoral Association 199
state of emergency 50–1, 60–2, 64, 66, 73–4, 80, 106, 125, 224, 384, 506

Steel Helmet (Stahlhelm) 82, 85, 101, 109, 144, 151, 153–4, 227, 235, 256, 365, 372, 374–6, 392, 462–3, 600, 754, 758–9, 761
Stegerwald, Adam 97, 185, 373, 375
Steinbach, Franz 206
Steinhardt, Jakob 735
Stenbock-Fermor, Alexander Graf 479
Stennes, Walther 388
stereotypes 393, 404–6, 412, 544, 572, 575, 690, 710, 735–6
sterilization 533–4
Stern-Rubarth, Edgar 79
Stern, Fritz 318
Sternberger, Dolf 634
Sternheim-Peters, Eva 762
Stettin 229, 506
Stingl, Karl 76
Stinnes-Legien agreement 4, 31, 39, 294–5, 343, 432, 480–1
Stinnes, Hugo 58, 63, 151, 294, 343
Stöcker, Helene 531, 533, 550
Storm, Eric 205
Stralsund 751
Strasser, Gregor 104, 107–10, 415, 588
Streicher, Julius 385, 735
Strength through Joy 622–3
Stresemann, Gustav 57, 61–2, 76–7, 79, 81, 85, 97, 124, 146, 151, 168, 181, 183–5, 197, 199, 243–4, 247, 249–58, 267, 282, 323, 326, 331, 367–8, 370, 374, 416, 463, 466, 738
strike: agricultural 506
  breakers 506
  delivery 509
  general 38–9, 50–1, 53, 61, 225, 344, 354, 355
  'military' 219, 230
  movement 354
  munitions 30
  political 49
  tax 511
Struck, Hermann 735
student fraternities 405, 408–9, 461, 463, 573
Stülpnagel, Joachim von 225–6, 228, 232–3, 236
Stürmer, Der 735
Stürmer, Michael 6, 73, 78
Sturmschar 596
Stuttgart 50, 208, 409, 415, 613, 663, 665–6, 669–71

Stuttgart School 208
Stuttgart State Theatre 408
Stuttgart Technical Academy 669
subsidies 254, 304, 459, 466, 683, 708–9
Süddeutsche Verlagsgesellschaft 441
Sudetenland 210
suffrage: female 3, 13, 166, 171, 180, 276, 324, 458
   proportional 170
   plutocratic 458, 461
   protests 522
   restricted 120, 320
   universal 1, 15, 31, 41, 123, 143, 164–5, 172, 461, 475
swastika 50, 354, 410, 511, 694, 741, 743
Switzerland 203, 433, 642
Sylt 281
symbolism 34, 82, 89, 148, 227, 730
symbols, political 16, 176, 266, 279–82
synagogue 408, 568, 575
Szalit-Marcus, Rahel 735

T

tabloids 351, 412, 466, 615, 618, 621–2
Tag, Der 169
Tage-Buch, Das 271
taming strategy 102–3, 107, 377
tariff 108, 251, 328, 332, 368–9, 433, 439, 501, 503
   Bülow 433, 501, 503
   law 254
Tarnow, Fritz 353, 548
Tatlin, Wladimir 662
Taut, Bruno 483, 550, 655–6, 659, 664–5, 670
Taut, Max 662,
tax: credits 105
   church 684
   direct 200–1
   incentives 105
   income 52, 201, 203, 376
   increases 52, 64, 201, 387, 431, 444
   indirect 200–1
   rate 200–1
   relief 368
   strikes 511
   system 52, 201, 306
   taxpayer 52, 202, 305, 413
Taylorism 5, 527, 547

teachers 4, 14, 35, 165, 231, 269, 352, 386, 389–90, 409, 455, 458–60, 499, 525, 531, 573, 590, 592, 646, 683, 694, 704, 712
Technische Nothilfe (TENO) 506
Teige, Karel 662
telegraphy 203, 441
telephone 203, 599
television 18, 610
Temporary Volunteers (Zeitfreiwillige) 220, 231
tenants 65, 458, 483–4
Tergit, Gabriele 646
Territorial Defence (Landesschutz) 232–3
Tessenow, Heinrich 655, 659, 670
Thalia Theatre 634
Thälmann, Ernst 83, 88
theatre 1, 33, 57, 465, 487, 530, 532, 553, 577, 613, 618–19, 621, 635–6, 639, 651, 655, 668, 741
   'epic' 649
   movie 489, 554, 736
   performances 408, 438, 554, 647
   political 32, 490, 629
   popular 610–11, 616
   'proletarian' 632
   revue 524, 528
theology 686–7, 690, 703, 706–8, 711–13, 717
theosophy 704
Theresienwiese 30
Thieß, Frank 647
Thimme, Annelise 259
Third Reich 1–2, 5, 96, 207, 224, 233, 259, 264, 363, 372, 376, 385, 396–7, 465, 492, 588, 601, 629, 632, 651, 715, 717
Third Republic, French 123
Thoiry 255
Thoma, Richard 132
Thomas, Adrienne 643
Thomas, Karl 638–9
Thomas, Katherine [d.i. Jella Lepman] 393
Three Arrows 354
Thuringia 61–2, 73, 79–80, 129, 181, 196–8, 200, 210, 231, 249, 326, 344, 365, 385–5, 387, 503, 533, 662
Thyssen company 444
Thyssen, Fritz 442
Tiling, Magdalene von 687
Tiller Girls 555, 731
Times 756

Tocqueville, Alexis de 29
Toller, Ernst 570, 634, 636, 638
Tory party 181, 365
tourism 207
trade unions 35, 49, 51, 53, 56, 58, 175, 243, 267,
    271, 300, 341, 343, 345, 347, 354, 366, 376,
    436, 475, 600, 658, 664
  abolishing 224, 548
  Christian 308, 478, 489
  and employers 4, 31, 293–5, 304, 306–7, 557,
    439, 480, 557
  Hirsch-Duncker 478
  members 480–2, 488
  Social Democratic 267, 376, 505, 548
  socialist 695
  'yellow' 478
trade: book 612, 616, 630
  balance 431–2
  deficit 447
  foreign 245, 433, 435, 546
  free 81, 242, 328, 435–6, 439
  international 245, 258, 503
  policy autonomy 432–3
  relations 332, 430, 433
  restrictions 330
transfer protection clause 431, 445
transnationalism 9
transportation 203, 212, 432, 479
trauma 13, 96, 187, 298, 726–7, 753, 755, 766–7
travelogues 194, 544
Traven, B. 645, 689
treason 41, 51, 54, 62, 86, 145, 227, 235–6, 272,
    385, 392, 632
Treaties of Paris 383
Treaty of Brest-Litovsk 28
Treaty of Locarno 10, 75–6, 81, 83, 181, 226,
    228, 252–6, 260, 368
Treaty of Rapallo 55, 229, 244, 248, 253, 549
Treaty of Riga 248
Treaty of Versailles 4, 9–10, 40, 50–1, 53–4, 58,
    119, 144–5, 148–9, 151, 177, 210, 218, 222–3,
    225–9, 231–2, 234–5, 237, 243–8, 251–5,
    257–60, 319, 323, 328, 330–1, 364–5, 368–9,
    371, 405, 430–2, 443, 458, 503, 510, 544,
    550, 595, 643, 708, 736, 750–1, 753
Trendelenburg, Ernst 331
Treviranus, Gottfried Reinhold 97

Triepel, Heinrich 714
Troeltsch, Ernst 266, 684, 713, 751
Troop Office (Truppenamt) 225–7
Trotsky, Leon 550
Tsar 341
Tsarism 552
Tucholsky, Kurt 266, 273, 629, 634, 648, 740,
    756–7
Tugendhat, Fritz 668
Tugendthat, Grete 668
Turkey 672

U

Ufa 8, 553–4, 622
Ukraine 222, 567
Ulk 728
Ullstein publishing house 441, 565, 577,
    616–17, 620
Ulm 235
Unemployment Insurance
    (Arbeitslosenversicherung ALV) 203
unemployment: benefits 78, 301–2, 304
  insurance 89, 96, 105, 126, 201, 302, 304–5,
    368, 485, 598, 600
  long-term 485–6
  mass 353, 387, 551
unification 141, 147, 152, 201, 210, 260, 317, 370,
    476
Union of German Employers'
    Associations (Verein Deutscher
    Arbeitgeberverbände) 439
unitarianism 193, 196
United Patriotic Associations of Germany
    (Vereinigte Vaterländische Verbände) 365
United State School for Fine and Applied
    Art 664
universities 40, 206, 233, 243, 272, 389–90,
    409, 455, 458, 462, 522, 525, 573, 703–4,
    706, 708–10
Unruh, Fritz von 764
Unser Eichsfeld 209
urbanization 475–6, 549, 687
USA 9, 53, 123, 126, 131, 153, 204, 243–4, 246,
    248–9, 252, 258, 305, 328, 352, 395, 432–5,
    447, 464, 501, 503, 531, 541, 544, 547–8, 553,
    557, 620, 665
Usborne, Cornelie 6

V

Vatican 692
Velde, Theodor Hendrik van de 531
Vereinigte Stahlwerke 440–2, 444
Viebig, Clara 646
Vienna 147, 152, 155, 207, 622, 659, 666, 735
Viktor Emanuel III 384
village community 14, 498, 512–13, 515
violence: against Jews 141, 407–8, 575
  paramilitary 222, 754
  political 82, 87, 96, 149, 353–4
  street 81, 89, 409, 416, 574
Vogel, Bruno 642, 764
Vogeler, Heinrich 551
Vögler, Alfred 548
Voigtländer 437
Völkisch National Committee of the German National People's Party (Völkischer Reichsausschuß der Deutschnationalen Volkspartei) 154
Völkischer Beobachter 384–5, 442
Volkov, Shulamit 404, 417, 569, 579
Volksbegehren 84
Volksforschung 708
Volksgeschichte 713
Volksgesundheit 209, 292, 527
Volksmarinedivision 37, 220
Volksverband der Bücherfreunde 612
Voluntary Labour Service (Freiwilliger Arbeitsdienst) 105, 229, 600
Vorwärts 38–9, 79, 229, 271, 277, 417, 526
Vorwerk, Heinrich 512
Voss, Richard 612
Vossische Zeitung 79, 268, 271, 387, 489, 619, 643
voters: agrarian 512–14
  behaviour of 98, 180, 570
  Catholic 82, 694
  dissatisfied 181, 321
  female 13, 324, 366, 371, 393
  first-time 166, 180, 598
  Jewish 416, 576
  left-wing 85
  male 324, 393
  middle-class 106, 373, 460
  non-voters 174, 186
  protest 126

voting system 124, 135, 168, 170–1, 327
Vring, Georg von der 642

W

Wagenfeld, Karl 208
wages: binding minimum standards of 294, 307
  cuts of 354
  piece-rate 482
Wagner, Martin 664–5, 672
Walcher, Jakob 551
Waldeck 140, 196
Wandervogel 205, 592–4, 600, 616
Wandt, Heinrich 8
Wangenheim, Gustav von 645
War Raw Materials Department (Kriegsrohstoffabteilung) 430
war veterans 155, 166, 231, 271, 298, 321, 348, 572, 754
  associations 270, 274, 285
  disabled 299
  Jewish 579, 763
  nationalist 365
  organizations 276, 759
  republican 270, 759
war: aims 34, 144, 242
  atrocities 9, 256, 753
  bonds 28, 431, 443, 457
  credits 341
  'cripples' 57, 298–9
  dead 83, 271, 281, 753, 755–8, 760, 762, 767
  defensive 341, 756
  diary 642, 750
  effort 34, 40, 120, 366, 564, 682, 752, 761–2, 766
  experience 274, 419, 506, 592, 642, 754–6, 760, 763–7
  guerrilla 226
  guilt 243–5, 256, 368, 709, 753
  invalids 52
  letters 763–4
  memorials 283–4, 593, 754, 758–62
  memory of the 83, 752, 755, 767
  nurses 35, 766
  propaganda 195, 643, 705
  remembrance 756, 758, 762
  -weariness 28

INDEX 815

writing 763–4
Warburg, Aby 717
Warburg, Max 57, 571
Warmia 211
Washington 253
Wassermann, Jakob 570, 577
WChUTEMAS 662
Weapons and Ammunition Procurement Office (Waffen- und Munitions-Beschaffungsamt, Wumba) 430
Weber, Alfred 60, 322, 711
Weber, Max 5, 31, 33, 122, 124, 172, 177, 244, 710, 717–18
Wedding 88, 762
Wedekind, Frank 730
Wehler, Hans-Ulrich 2, 6
Wehrmacht 229, 236
Wehrverband Reichsflagge 385
Weimar 16, 121, 195–6, 323
Weimar Coalition 48–9, 80, 122, 156, 164, 172, 177, 182–3, 222, 267, 271, 365, 371–5, 419
Weimar Constitution 3, 11–13, 15, 106, 119–20, 122, 127, 129–33, 141, 146, 164, 196, 232, 243, 246, 269, 277, 323, 326, 364–6, 409, 440, 521, 524, 610, 683
  Article 24 104
  Article 48 49, 61–2, 64, 89, 95, 97–9, 102, 105, 111, 125–6, 128–9, 134–5, 172, 224, 375, 387
  Article 118 632
  Articles 120, 121, and 123 590
  Article 137 41
  Article 148 589–90
  Article 175 530
  Constitution Day 12, 148, 265, 273, 275–6, 282–4, 758
  'failure' of the 88, 134, 136
  preamble 156, 291
Weinert, Erich 634
Weisgerber, Leo 707
Weiskopf, Franz Carl 551–2
Weißenhof 208, 666, 669–71
welfare: family 592
  local 340, 347–8
  municipal 297, 302, 305
  progressive 1
  social 35, 301, 340, 347, 353, 355–6, 532–4, 572, 600

  state 1, 4–5, 49, 169, 194, 202–4, 291–2, 340, 347, 349, 353–6, 385, 429, 459, 521, 526–7, 533–5, 545, 598, 600, 752
  unemployment 292–4, 300–1, 304
  youth 303, 308, 573, 587, 591–2, 600–1
Wels, Otto 37
Weltbühne, Die 271, 577, 643, 651
Weltpolitik 542
Wenge, Nicola 573
West Germany 134, 168, 204
West Prussia 149, 203, 231, 500, 643
West, Franklin C. 77
Westarp, Kuno von 366, 368–9, 374
Westermann, Franz 547
Westermann, Heinrich 762
Westfalenhalle 619
Westphalia 102, 168, 199, 205, 208–10, 372, 500, 507–8, 659
Wetzlar 437
widows 296
  war 5, 274, 298–9, 477, 572, 752–3
Wiene, Robert 622
wild settlements 306
Wilhelm I 194
Wilhelm II 27, 30, 120, 143, 227, 282, 364, 369, 458, 477
Wilhelmshaven 29
Willikens, Werner 513
Wilson, Woodrow 28, 242–3
Winckler, Johann Friedrich 366
Windthorstbund 597
Winkler, Heinrich August 4, 6, 478–9, 481, 507, 691
Winsloe, Christa 530
Winter, Jay 762
Wipplinger, Jonathan 736
Wirth, Joseph 55, 97, 152, 182–3, 185, 234, 243, 247–8, 268, 271, 277, 288n40, 373, 375, 411
Wirtschaftsgemeinschaft 199
Wissell, Rudolf 77–9, 182, 185, 231
Wistrich, Robert S. 404
Witkop, Philipp 764
Wittelsbach 30, 570
Wittgenstein, Ludwig 718
Wittvogel, Karl 552
Wohnstadt Carl Legien 665
Wolf, Friedrich 532, 612, 633, 634

Wolf, Paul 670
Wolff, Theodor 27, 33, 37, 39, 41, 79, 268, 322, 570
Wolffs Telegraphisches Büro 203
Wollheim, Gert 766
Women's Suffrage Society 35
women's: associations 150
  bodies 726, 728, 731
  citizenship 13
  emancipation 351, 641
  liberation 523
  movement 324–5, 522, 525, 531–2, 753
  organizations 524
  suffrage 166, 171, 180, 324–5
  votes 325
woodcuts 735, 739
Work Council for Art (Arbeitsrat für Kunst) 655, 658
Workers and Soldiers Councils 30, 33, 36, 340, 366, 655–6
workers: agricultural 235, 499, 505–7, 513–15
  factory 500, 504, 556
  female 180, 476, 478, 490, 523
  industrial 186, 230, 351, 456, 459, 475–6, 478, 482, 489–91, 499, 507, 515, 549, 599
  radical 340, 343, 356, 545
  revolutionary 204, 454
  rural 30, 186, 491, 505, 507
  seasonal 505
  skilled 347, 351, 412, 482–3, 489, 548, 644
  unemployed 292–3, 304, 353–4, 376–7, 393
  unskilled 306, 351, 476, 483, 525
  white-collar 58–60, 347, 367, 376, 391, 489, 523, 565, 610, 613, 646
Workers' Gymnastics and Sports League (Arbeiter Turn- und Sportbund) 349
Workers' Olympics 490
Workers' Radio Association 490
workers': associations and clubs 488, 490
  broadcasting 614
  councils (*Arbeiterräte*) 28, 33, 35, 39, 542
  self-protection units 51
workforce 292, 294, 478, 482
  agricultural 504
  civilian 477
  female 525

unskilled 302
waged 505
working class: daily life 475
  families 300, 483–4, 612
  identity 475–6, 490
  industrial 475–7, 480, 482, 487, 492
  international 143, 154, 457
  Jewish 565
  men 121
  milieu 168, 233, 349, 355, 689
  movement 340–5, 347, 350–1, 353–6
  quarters 464, 488, 615, 645–6, 690
  republicans 277
  press 442
  socialist 167, 462
  veterans 274
  women 13
  youth 592–3, 596
working conditions 293–4, 307, 477–80, 482, 507, 645
workplace accident insurance 291
works councils (*Betriebsräte*) 296, 308, 323, 480, 645
World Economic Conference 331–2
world economic crisis 95–6, 100, 332, 740
World's Fair Exposition 666
Worpswede 205
Wright, Frank Lloyd 662
Wright, Jonathan 259
Wronsky, Siddy 572
Wunderlich, Frieda 572
Württemberg 79, 101, 196, 200, 222, 365, 384, 500, 514, 565, 693
Württembergische Bürgerpartei 415

X

xenophobia 412

Y

Yiddish 567, 580
Young Democrats (Jungdemokraten) 598
Young German Order (Jungdeutscher Orden) 324–5, 365, 416, 462
Young Plan 74, 76, 86–8, 109, 174, 255–6, 370, 377, 387, 415, 445
Young Socialists (Jungsozialisten) 597

Young, Owen D. 414
youth: associations 593, 595–7, 600–1
  centres 303
  clubs 686
  'endangered' 572
  hostels 595
  organizations 349, 579, 597
Youth Days 596

Z

Zahn-Harnack, Agnes von 325
Zech, Paul 644
Zehrer, Hans 552
Zeigner, Erich 62, 197
Zeiss, Carl 433
Zenker, Agnes 35

Zentralkommission für Arbeitersport und
  Körperpflege 488
Zetkin, Clara 35
Ziemann, Benjamin 77
Zionism 466, 568–9
Zionist Organization of Germany 568, 576
Zöberlein, Hans 643
Zollitsch, Wolfgang 482
Zossen 37
Zuckmayer, Carl 634, 639, 764
Zurich 433, 642, 666
Zweig, Arnold 577, 642–3
Zweig, Stefan 59, 523–4
Zwenkau 668–9
Zwickau 533
Zwingli, Ulrich 685